OXFORD EU LAW LIBRARY

General Editors

ROBERT SCHÜTZE
Professor of European and Global Law, Durham Law School and
Co-Director, Global Policy Institute, Durham Law School

PIET EECKHOUT
Professor of EU Law and Dean of the Faculty of Laws, UCL;
Academic Director of the European Institute

EU Citizenship Law

OXFORD EU LAW LIBRARY

The aim of the series is to publish important and original studies of the various branches of EU law. Each work provides a clear, concise, and critical exposition of the law in its social, economic, and political context, at a level which will interest the advanced student, the practitioner, the academic, and government officials.

OTHER TITLES IN THE LIBRARY

European Migration Law
Daniel Thym

EU Securities and Financial Markets Regulation
Fourth Edition
Niamh Moloney

EU Diplomatic Law
Sanderijn Duquet

EU Constitutional Law
Koen Lenaerts, Piet Van Nuffel, Tim Corthaut

EU Customs Law
Third Edition
Timothy Lyons

Principles and Practice in EU Sports Law
Stephen Weatherill

EU Justice and Home Affairs Law
Fourth Edition
Steve Peers

EU Procedural Law
Koen Lenaerts, Ignace Maselis, Kathleen Gutman, Janek Tomasz Nowak

EU Anti-Discrimination Law
Second Edition
Evelyn Ellis and Philippa Watson

EU Securities and Financial Markets Regulation
Third Edition
Niamh Moloney

The EU Common Security and Defence Policy
Panos Koutrakos

EU External Relations Law
Second Edition
Piet Eeckhout

EU Employment Law
Fourth Edition
Catherine Barnard

EU Citizenship Law

NIAMH NIC SHUIBHNE
Professor of EU Law at the University of Edinburgh

OXFORD
UNIVERSITY PRESS

OXFORD
UNIVERSITY PRESS

Great Clarendon Street, Oxford, OX2 6DP,
United Kingdom

Oxford University Press is a department of the University of Oxford.
It furthers the University's objective of excellence in research, scholarship,
and education by publishing worldwide. Oxford is a registered trade mark of
Oxford University Press in the UK and in certain other countries

© Niamh Nic Shuibhne 2023

The moral rights of the author have been asserted

First Edition published in 2023

All rights reserved. No part of this publication may be reproduced, stored in
a retrieval system, or transmitted, in any form or by any means, without the
prior permission in writing of Oxford University Press, or as expressly permitted
by law, by licence or under terms agreed with the appropriate reprographics
rights organization. Enquiries concerning reproduction outside the scope of the
above should be sent to the Rights Department, Oxford University Press, at the
address above

You must not circulate this work in any other form
and you must impose this same condition on any acquirer

Public sector information reproduced under Open Government Licence v3.0
(http://www.nationalarchives.gov.uk/doc/open-government-licence/open-government-licence.htm)

Published in the United States of America by Oxford University Press
198 Madison Avenue, New York, NY 10016, United States of America

British Library Cataloguing in Publication Data

Data available

Library of Congress Control Number: 2023942258

ISBN 978-0-19-879531-5

DOI: 10.1093/oso/9780198795315.001.0001

Printed and bound by
CPI Group (UK) Ltd, Croydon, CR0 4YY

Links to third party websites are provided by Oxford in good faith and
for information only. Oxford disclaims any responsibility for the materials
contained in any third party website referenced in this work.

Foreword

I feel proud and privileged to have been asked to contribute a Foreword to this remarkable book in which Professor Nic Shuibhne traces the evolution of EU citizenship law from its ambitious beginnings to the sounds of uncertain trumpets from Brussels and Luxembourg.

European citizenship is a rather special, and indeed emotional, topic for me, for two reasons: first, because I was Judge Rapporteur in *Martínez Sala*[1] and *Grzelczyk*,[2] which added citizenship to the legal inheritance promised in *Van Gend en Loos*,[3] and second, because, having been a proud European citizen, I have been summarily deprived of that status and the rights that go with it.

In 1990, soon after the fall of the Berlin Wall, Antonio La Pergola, President of the Venice Commission[4] and later Advocate General, evoked the idea of 'a Europe, not so much as a system of States as, rather, a common home fit for man'.

> Let us think of Europe as we would think of a single citizenship, which is the measure of a common heritage, and which serves in assessing the essential problems of man – the relationship between the individual and power, political freedoms and social rights, the transition from single-party State to party-pluralism, developments of the of the revolution for democracy and after which must follow the development of the system then established, which grows and matures one step at a time, through patience and experience in the light of events past.[5]

It was in the same aspirational vein that, in the Maastricht Treaty (1992), the Heads of State announced that they were 'resolved to establish a citizenship common to the nationals of their countries' which would 'strengthen the protection of [their] rights and interests'.[6] The legal consequences of these ideas were considered by the Court of Justice five years later in *Martínez Sala*.

The circumstances of the case were that Mrs Martínez Sala, a Spanish national who had lived in Germany for some 25 years, was refused a child-rearing allowance to which she was entitled only if she was in possession of a residence permit. While such a permit had been issued to her almost continuously in the past, the German authorities refused or failed to issue a new one, so stymying her right to the child-bearing allowance. As so often, the Court was called upon to remedy a manifest injustice.

---

[1] Case C-85/96 *Martínez Sala*, EU:C:1998:217.

[2] Case C-184/99 *Grzelczyk*, EU:C:2001:458.

[3] Case 26/62 *Van Gend en Loos*, EU:C:1963:1.

[4] The European Commission for Democracy through Law, an advisory body of the Council of Europe. It was conceived by La Pergola, then Minister for Community Policies of Italy, and first met in Venice from 31 March–1 April 1989.

[5] Speech by Antonio La Pergola at the second Venice Conference, 19 January 1990, reprinted in *Liber Amicorum Antonio La Pergola* (Pieter van Dijk and Simona Granata-Menghini, eds), Juristförlaget i Lund, republished 2008, at p 44, and available at <https://www.venice.coe.int/files/articles/LiberAmicoriumLaPergola.pdf> (accessed 23 May 2023).

[6] Preamble and Article B of the Treaty on European Union.

In his Opinion, Antonio La Pergola, the Advocate General in the case, brought out the concept of citizenship as:

> a new right, common to all citizens of the Member States without distinction ... the fundamental legal status guaranteed to the citizen of every Member State by the legal order of the Community and now of the Union ... [T]he status of citizen of the Union derives once and for all from the Treaty.[7]

The Court followed the Advocate General, holding that:

> [A] citizen of the European Union lawfully resident in the territory of the host Member State, can rely on Article 6 of the Treaty in all situations which fall within the scope ratione materiae of Community law.[8]

In *Gzelcyzk*, the Member States, with the honourable exception of Portugal, sought to row back on *Martinez Sala*. At the hearing, the representative of one Member State asserted that it was never intended that Article 8a[9] should have any legal effect at all. The Court did not oblige, stating that:

> Union citizenship is destined to be the fundamental status of nationals of the Member States, enabling those who find themselves in the same situation to enjoy the same treatment in law irrespective of their nationality, subject to such exceptions as are expressly provided for.[10]

It is important to recognise that the aspirational implications of this statement of the law are balanced by two qualifications: first that non-discrimination applies where the situation is the same, and second, that it may subject to limitations where these are *expressly* provided for.

Professor Nic Shuibhne traces the origins of these ideas in earlier case law and the current development towards a more literalist approach stressing the ultimate authority of the Member States. This has become apparent in the treatment of Union nationals in the Brexit negotiations and now in the bleak acceptance by the Court of Justice[11] that the EU does not, after all, measure up to Antonio la Pergola's dream of '*a Europe, not so much as a system of States as, rather, a common home fit for man*'.

Those of us who have lost our rights as citizens include *thousands of British people who live and work in the countries of the Union, musicians and scientists who can no longer pursue their calling with their fellows in Europe as they used to do, and especially the many young people who have been deprived of the privileges and opportunities that their European contemporaries enjoy. The high priests of European integration can take little credit for the needless bureaucracy that torments and excludes their erstwhile citizens and their families.*

Nor is the loss one way only. Difficult as UK/EU relations have sometimes been, the EU has now been deprived of the contribution that the British have made, and would have continued

---

[7] AG La Pergola in *Martínez Sala* (EU:C:1997:335), para 18 of the Opinion.
[8] *Martínez Sala*, para 63
[9] Article 8a EC, see now Article 20 TFEU.
[10] *Grzelczyk*, para. 31.
[11] See Case C-673/20 *Préfet du Gers*, EU:C:2022:449.

to make, to the evolution of the Union and its legal framework. As the crisis in Ukraine has demonstrated, the interdependence of the UK and the countries of Europe is too close to be disentangled on the simplistic hypotheses of textual analysis. We can surely do better than that.[12]

David Edward
Edinburgh
February 2023

---

[12] As Professor Nic Shuibhne further explores in two recent essays: 'Protecting the legal heritage of former Union citizens: *EP v. Préfet du Gers*' (2023) 60 Common Market Law Review 475; and '"What" are former citizens of the European Union? Articulating the implications of a new legal status' in A Bouveresse, A Iliopoulou-Penot, and J Rondu (eds), *European Citizenship: What Added Value?/La citoyenneté européenne: quelle valeur ajoutée?* (Bruylant-Larcier 2023).

Preface

The objective of this book is to articulate, explain, and analyse the legal framework and the legal developments that have shaped the status of Union citizenship and the rights that it confers on Member State nationals. The scale of that task on its own terms—of trying, in essence, to say what EU citizenship law actually 'is'—meant that little justice could be done to the wider perspectives that have been and can be taken on Union citizenship, both within and beyond the discipline of EU law. Instead, this work aims to provide a comprehensive legal reference point for the progression of those debates and for the continuing study and practice of EU citizenship law.

Witnessing closely the reactions of those who lost their Union citizenship after 31 January 2020, while living in Scotland yet personally retaining the privilege of Member State nationality myself, reversed any misconceptions I might have had about the thinness of citizenship as a social, political, and even emotional connection to the European Union. But I still tend to express some caution about what we can expect of Union citizenship. Yes, we can do EU citizenship law better. At the same time, citizenship will not provide all the answers to all the questions or doubts that we have about the Union, or its Member States, in increasingly challenging times. Nevertheless, in my view, Union citizenship is extraordinary. Its legal evolution is imperfect, its legal framework is complicated, and its full legal potential is as yet unrealised. Even so, Union citizenship is still extraordinary. It provides a place for us to be our best legal selves, to consider the worth and deepen the protection of the person, and to defend a European Union where principles and values really do matter.

On reaching this stage, so many thanks are owed, starting with the OUP team for suggesting the idea for this book in the first place and for waiting with remarkable patience for its completion over the unforeseen events of Brexit and the Covid-19 pandemic. Much of the research was undertaken with the support of a Leverhulme Trust Major Research Fellowship (2016–2019). Thanks also to Franca Feisel for her research assistance in summer 2019. I deeply appreciate the critical friends, in all senses of those words, that I have made and continue to make in the EU legal academic community. Whether working on Union citizenship or not, so many of you have made a difference to this work, but I must mention Professor Sir David Edward, who has done more than most to make EU citizenship law better; and the researchers whose citizenship-focused PhDs I have been lucky enough to examine—I name them here as a representative group to illustrate just how much remarkable and diverse ideas, policy work, and legal practice can push a field in new directions: so, keep going, Stephen Coutts, Joske Graat, Maria Haag, Cherry James, Katerina Kalailzaki, Hester Kroeze, Charlotte O'Brien, Roderic O'Gorman, Pauline Phoa, Stephanie Reynolds, Fulvia Ristuccia, Martijn van den Brink, Alice Welsh, and Adrienne Yong. Finally, thanks yet again to my three families: as someone who left where she came from, thank you to the family members who have become friends; to the friends who have become family; and to the family from which I came.

NNS
Edinburgh/Kerry
August 2022

Contents

Table of Cases	xvii
EU Legislation	xlix

1. Introducing EU Citizenship Law ... 1
   1. Chapter Overview ... 1
   2. Defining EU Citizenship Law: The Legal Framework ... 2
   3. Distinguishing EU Citizenship Law: Personal and Material Scope ... 7
      - 3.1 Personal Scope: Who is a Union Citizen? ... 8
      - 3.2 Material Scope: 'Specific Expression' of Rights ... 12
   4. Progressing EU Citizenship Law: The Principal Actors ... 15
      - 4.1 Implementing EU Citizenship Law: The Role of the EU Legislator ... 16
      - 4.2 Interpreting EU Citizenship Law: The Role of the Court of Justice ... 19
   5. Organising EU Citizenship Law: Overview of Chapters ... 23

2. Union Citizenship: Introducing the Legal Framework ... 27
   1. Chapter Overview ... 27
   2. Origins of a Legal Framework: From EU Free Movement Law to EU Citizenship Law ... 28
      - 2.1 Predating EU Citizenship Law: Economic Free Movement Rights ... 30
      - 2.2 Presaging EU Citizenship Law: General Free Movement Rights ... 33
   3. Legal Framework I: Articles 20 and 21 TFEU ... 38
      - 3.1 Article 20 TFEU ... 39
      - 3.2 Article 21 TFEU ... 44
      - 3.3 Restricting the Right to Move and Reside: Derogation and Justification ... 46
        - 3.3.1 Defining a restriction of rights ... 46
        - 3.3.2 Defending a restriction of rights: derogation and justification ... 49
      - 3.4 Restricting the Right to Move and Reside: Proportionality ... 51
        - 3.4.1 Conditions 'too general and exclusive' ... 52
        - 3.4.2 Proportionality and the protection of national public finances ... 54
        - 3.4.3 Evidencing proportionality ... 60
      - 3.5 Asymmetric Movement ... 63
   4. Legal Framework II: Directive 2004/38 ... 67
      - 4.1 Aims and Objectives of the Directive ... 69
      - 4.2 The Scope of the Directive ... 72
      - 4.3 Balancing Rights with Conditions and Limits ... 75
   5. Legal Framework III: Significant Themes in EU Citizenship Law ... 78
      - 5.1 Establishing a Connection with EU Law ... 78
        - 5.1.1 Causal connection between rights exercised and impact of restrictions ... 78
        - 5.1.2 Connecting factors and internal situations ... 81
      - 5.2 Ensuring the Effectiveness of Union Citizenship Rights ... 84
      - 5.3 Union Citizenship and the EU Charter of Fundamental Rights ... 85
        - 5.3.1 Citizenship rights as fundamental rights ... 86
        - 5.3.2 Union citizenship and fundamental rights ... 88
      - 5.4 The Dual Function of Integration Requirements ... 89

	5.5	Union Citizenship and Matters Reserved to Member State Competence	93
6.	The Territory of the Union: Integrating Law, Place, and Values		94
7.	Concluding Remarks		106
	Further Reading		107

3. **Who is Protected? Part I: Union Citizenship and Member State Nationality**   109
   1. Chapter Overview   109
   2. Determining Member State Nationality: The Role of EU Law   110
      2.1 EU Law and Member State Decisions to Withdraw Nationality: *Rottmann*   110
      2.2 Applying *Rottmann*   113
         2.2.1 Member State decisions withdrawing nationality   114
         2.2.2 Acquiring Member State nationality   118
         2.2.3 After nationality: citizenship and withdrawal from the European Union   124
   3. The Legal Implications of Dual Nationality   129
   4. Concluding Remarks   136
   Further Reading   137

4. **Who is Protected? Part II: Defining the Family Members of Union Citizens**   139
   1. Chapter Overview   139
   2. Protecting Family Members in EU Citizenship Law: Guiding Principles   140
   3. Scope of Protection and Key Definitions   144
      3.1 Directive 2004/38: Scope of Application   144
      3.2 Family Members: Who is Protected and to What Extent?   146
         3.2.1 Article 2(2)(a): spouses   150
            3.2.1.1 Same-sex spouses   151
            3.2.1.2 What does 'in the host State' mean?   155
            3.2.1.3 The status of third-country national family members under host State immigration rules   159
         3.2.2 Partners other than spouses   162
            3.2.2.1 Article 2(2)(b): registered partners   163
            3.2.2.2 Article 3(2)(b): unmarried partners   164
         3.2.3 Article 2(2)(c): 'direct descendants who are under the age of 21'   171
   4. Dependent Relatives   174
      4.1 Article 2(2): Direct Relatives in the Descending and Ascending Lines   175
      4.2 Article 3(2)(a): 'Other Family Members'   179
   5. Concluding Remarks   185
   Further Reading   186

5. **Union Citizenship and the Home Member State**   187
   1. Chapter Overview   187
   2. Rights Facilitating a Political Connection to the Union   189
      2.1 Voting Rights from the Home Member State Perspective   190
         2.1.1 Defining the national electorate   193
         2.1.2 Voting rights (and the right to vote) in the context of imprisonment   197
         2.1.3 Voting rights in the context of free movement   200
      2.2 Mechanisms Facilitating Participation   204
         2.2.1 The European Citizens' Initiative   205
            2.2.1.1 ECI procedures and conditions   206
            2.2.1.2 An emerging jurisprudence   210
         2.2.2 Petitioning the European Parliament   217
         2.2.3 Applying to the European Ombudsman   219

    2.3 Surrogate Home States: Diplomatic and Consular Protection in
Third Countries   220
- 3. Residence Rights for Family Members in the Union Citizen's Home State: Article 20 TEU   226
  - 3.1 The Game-Changer: *Ruiz Zambrano*   229
  - 3.2 First Responses: Explaining—and Containing—*Ruiz Zambrano*   233
    - 3.2.1 The nature of *Ruiz Zambrano* rights   236
    - 3.2.2 Being 'obliged' to leave the territory of the Union   236
    - 3.2.3 Beneficiaries of *Ruiz Zambrano* rights: the requirement of dependency   239
    - 3.2.4 The Charter of Fundamental Rights   241
  - 3.3 Progressing Residence Rights Based on Article 20 TFEU   243
    - 3.3.1 Refining the assessment of eligibility for Article 20 TFEU residence rights   243
    - 3.3.2 Embedding the Charter of Fundamental Rights   248
      - 3.3.2.1 From *Dereci* to *Chavez-Vilchez*   248
      - 3.3.2.2 And beyond?   251
    - 3.3.3 The limits of residence rights based on Article 20 TFEU   252
- 4. Concluding Remarks   259
- Further Reading   260

6. Union Citizenship and the Host State Part I: Rights to Enter, Reside, and Remain—Directive 2004/38   261
   1. Chapter Overview   261
   2. Articles 4 and 5: Rights of Exit and Entry   263
   3. Article 6: The Right to Reside for up to Three Months   269
   4. The Right to Reside for More than Three Months   274
      - 4.1 Article 7(1)(a): Workers and Self-Employed Persons   275
      - 4.2 Article 7(1)(b): General Right to Reside   279
        - 4.2.1 'Sufficient resources'   280
        - 4.2.2 'Comprehensive sickness insurance'   283
      - 4.3 Article 7(1)(c): Students   287
      - 4.4 Jobseekers   290
   5. Administrative Formalities   296
      - 5.1 Article 8: Union Citizens   301
        - 5.1.1 Registration requirements: Union citizens   302
        - 5.1.2 Registration requirements: Union citizens who are family members   304
        - 5.1.3 Article 8(4): 'sufficient resources'   306
      - 5.2 Articles 5–6 and 9–11: Family Members who are not Union Citizens   309
        - 5.2.1 Right of entry   309
        - 5.2.2 Right of residence   311
   6. Retaining the Right to Reside   317
      - 6.1 Article 14: Retaining the Right to Reside   318
      - 6.2 Article 7(3): Retaining the Status of Worker or Self-Employed Person   321
      - 6.3 Articles 12 and 13: Family Members   329
        - 6.3.1 Article 12: death or departure of the Union citizen   330
        - 6.3.2 Article 13: divorce, annulment of marriage, or termination of registered partnership   332
        - 6.3.3 Interpreting Articles 12 and 13   334
   7. Directive 2004/38 and Abuse of Rights   340
      - 7.1 Locating Article 35: Abuse of Rights and EU Free Movement Law   341

	7.2 Clarifying Article 35: Commission Guidance	344
	7.3 Interpreting Article 35: *McCarthy II*	348
8.	Concluding Remarks	351
	Further Reading	352

7. **Union Citizenship and the Host State Part II: Equal Treatment and the Concept of Lawful Residence** — 353
   1. Chapter Overview — 353
   2. Foundations: The Concept of Lawful Residence and Its Relationship to Equal Treatment in EU Citizenship Law — 356
      - 2.1 Before Directive 2004/38: Lawful Residence, Equal Treatment, and the Case Law of the Court of Justice — 358
         - 2.1.1 Union citizenship, equal treatment, and lawful residence: case law foundations — 358
         - 2.1.2 Union citizenship, equal treatment, and lawful residence: jobseekers — 365
      - 2.2 Directive 2004/38, Equal Treatment, and the Host State: Article 24 — 370
         - 2.2.1 Article 24: drafting history — 372
         - 2.2.2 Article 24(2): express derogations from equal treatment — 374
         - 2.2.3 Article 24(1): an implicit derogation from equal treatment? — 380
   3. Union Citizenship, Lawful Residence, Equal Treatment, and Directive 2004/38: The Revised Framework — 381
      - 3.1 No Right to Reside: *Dano, Alimanovic*, and *Commission v UK* — 382
         - 3.1.1 Directive 2004/38 and lawful residence: early case law — 383
         - 3.1.2 *Dano* — 390
         - 3.1.3 *Alimanovic* — 395
         - 3.1.4 *Commission v UK* — 399
      - 3.2 Residing on the Basis of Directive 2004/38 — 405
         - 3.2.1 Article 6: lawful residence within the first three months — 405
         - 3.2.2 Article 7(1)(a): lawful residence and the economically active — 407
         - 3.2.3 Article 7(1)(b): lawful residence and the economically autonomous — 410
         - 3.2.4 Article 7(1)(c): students — 413
         - 3.2.5 Articles 7(1)(d), 12, and 13: family members — 414
         - 3.2.6 Article 14(4)(b): jobseekers — 415
      - 3.3 Residence Based on (Other) EU Legislation: Article 10 of Regulation 492/2011 — 416
      - 3.4 Residence Based on EU Primary Law — 418
         - 3.4.1 Articles 45 and 49 TFEU — 418
         - 3.4.2 Article 21 TFEU — 419
      - 3.5 Residence Based on or Authorised by National Law — 419
   4. Lawful Residence and Equal Treatment: Implications — 425
      - 4.1 The Consequences of Unlawful and/ or Unsupported Residence in a Host State — 426
      - 4.2 The Charter of Fundamental Rights — 431
   5. Concluding Remarks — 437
   - Further Reading — 439

8. **Union Citizenship and the Host State Part III: The Right of Permanent Residence** — 441
   1. Chapter Overview — 441
   2. Conceiving a Right of Permanent Residence: Directive 2004/38 — 443
   3. Permanent Residence: The Legal Framework — 446
      - 3.1 Who is Eligible and in What Circumstances? — 446

3.1.1 Family members	447
3.1.2 Absence from the host State	452
3.1.3 Exemptions from Article 16	454
3.2 The Requirements of Legal and Continuous Residence	457
3.2.1 Continuous residence	458
3.2.2 Legal residence	458
3.3 Administrative Formalities	467
4. Concluding Remarks	469
Further Reading	470
9. The Right to Move and Reside: Beyond the Directive	**471**
1. Chapter Overview	471
2. EU Citizenship Law and Multi-State Life: Living Across Different Places	473
2.1 Coordinating Social Security for Multi-State Life: Basic Principles	473
2.2 The Intersection of the Economic Freedoms and Union Citizenship: Reinforcing or Undermining Legal Constructs of Integration?	475
2.3 Multi-State Life and Family Member Residence Rights	479
3. EU Citizenship Law and Multi-State Past Life: Protecting Leavers and Returners	482
3.1 The Origins of EU Legal Protection for the Leaver/Returner: Articles 45 and 49 TFEU	483
3.2 Progressing Protection for the Leaver/Returner: Article 21 TFEU	487
3.3 Refining the Scope of Protection	490
4. Concluding Remarks	498
Further Reading	498
10. Excluding Union Citizens: Public Policy, Public Security, and Public Health	**499**
1. Chapter Overview	499
2. Before Directive 2004/38: Foundational Principles	501
3. Directive 2004/38: The Revised Legal Framework	508
3.1 Public Policy, Public Security, and Public Health: General Principles	510
3.1.1 Defining public health	511
3.1.2 Defining public policy and public security	512
3.1.3 Restricting free movement on grounds of public policy or public security: principles of assessment	516
3.2 Articles 28(2) and 28(3): Enhanced Protection Against Expulsion	526
4. Directive 2004/38: Administrative Formalities and Procedural Safeguards	539
4.1 Article 30: Notification of Decisions	540
4.2 Article 31: Procedural Safeguards	545
4.3 Article 32: Duration of Exclusion Orders	547
4.4 Article 33: Expulsion as a Penalty or Legal Consequence	551
5. Concluding Remarks	552
Further Reading	553
Index	555

Table of Cases

CASE LAW OF THE COURT OF JUSTICE: ALPHABETICAL

Case C-243/19 *A v Veselības ministrija*, EU:C:2020:872 .... 54n.176
Case C-679/16 *A (Aide pour une personne handicapée)*, EU:C:2018:601 .... 78n.316, 85n.362, 94n.430, 94n.431, 287n.143, 464n.138, 487–88n.103
Case C-35/20 *A (Franchissement de frontières en navire de plaisance)*, EU:C:2021:813 .... 11n.52, 265n.15, 266n.24, 482n.69
Case C-535/19 *A (Soins de santé publics)*, EU:C:2021:595 .... 284–85, 285n.127, 285n.128, 286n.134, 353–54n.4, 392n.226, 410n.335, 427n.415
Joined Cases 115 and 116/81 *Adoui and Cornuaille*, EU:C:1982:183 .... 501–2n.15, 504n.35, 505n.38, 517n.102, 541n.252, 541n.257, 547n.296, 548n.304, 548n.306, 551n.322
Case C-93/12 *Agrokonsulting-04*, EU:C:2013:432 .... 550n.316
Case C-617/10 *Åkerberg Fransson*, EU:C:2013:105 .... 88n.381, 250n.353, 432, 432n.440, 433n.449, 433n.451
Case C-109/01 *Akrich*, EU:C:2003:491 .... 89n.388, 96n.444, 96n.446, 159n.106, 159n.108, 160, 161–62, 342n.448, 357n.15, 393n.237, 496n.148, 496n.149, 497
Case C-434/10 *Aladzhov*, EU:C:2011:750 .... 51n.158, 55n.183, 265n.18, 509n.69, 513n.88, 514n.90, 520n.122, 521n.126
Case C-529/11 *Alarape and Tijani*, EU:C:2013:290 .... 22n.132, 75n.290, 135n.184, 156n.94, 259n.400, 331n.386, 332n.392, 385–86, 386n.183, 397n.253, 442n.8, 450n.51, 461n.118, 462n.120, 463, 490n.119, 490n.121, 490n.122
Case C-423/98 *Albore*, EU:C:2000:401 .... 514n.92, 515n.95, 515n.96
Case C-67/14 *Alimanovic*, EU:C:2015:597 .... 56n.191, 59n.208, 59n.209, 59–60n.210, 60n.216, 62n.228, 74n.285, 283n.120, 295n.187, 296n.194, 353–54n.4, 366n.72, 370, 396n.246, 396n.247, 396n.248, 396n.251, 397n.256, 398n.257, 398n.258, 399n.260, 403–4, 408–9, 411–13, 415n.357, 417n.364, 418, 419, 427n.412, 438
Case C-86/12 *Alokpa and Moudoulou*, EU:C:2013:645 ...... 42n.101, 171n.181, 176n.210, 233n.254, 235n.264, 239n.283, 239n.285, 243–44, 245, 249, 255n.378, 281n.111, 481n.60
Case C-589/15 P *Anagnostakis*, EU:C:2017:663 .... 212n.145, 213n.148, 213n.149
Case C-281/98 *Angonese*, EU:C:2000:296 .... 46n.120, 291n.167
Case C-309/96 *Annibaldi*, EU:C:1997:631 .... 432n.439
Case C-292/89 *Antonissen*, EU:C:1991:80 .... 29n.11, 130n.148, 291–94, 292n.170, 292n.172, 293–94n.180, 294n.186, 295, 296n.196, 366–67
Joined Cases C-404/15 and C-659/15 PPU *Aranyosi and Căldăraru*, EU:C:2016:198 .... 98n.453
Case C-107/94 *Asscher*, EU:C:1996:251 .... 275n.77
Case C-64/16 *Associação Sindical dos Juízes Portugueses*, EU:C:2018:117 .... 198n.63
Case C-410/18 *Aubriet*, EU:C:2019:582 .... 276n.81, 476–77
Joined Cases C-57/09 and C-101/09 *B and D*, EU:C:2010:661 .... 522n.135

Joined Cases C-316/16 and C-424/16 *B and Vomero*, EU:C:2018:256 . . . . 53n.168, 75n.295,
91n.398, 92n.411, 104n.501, 262n.5, 296n.195, 355n.8, 357n.16,
371n.100, 429n.426, 441n.3, 460n.106, 464n.134, 467,
499n.1, 509n.68, 527n.165, 534n.209, 534n.210,
535, 536n.219, 536n.221, 537n.228
Case C-93/18 *Bajratari*, EU:C:2019:809 . . . . .171n.181, 255n.378, 267n.32, 282–83, 282n.112,
282n.113, 427n.415
Case C-89/17 *Banger*, EU:C:2018:570 . . . . 70n.264, 84n.357, 166n.146, 166n.149, 168n.159,
168n.161, 183n.247, 183n.248, 185n.255, 495n.143
Case C-472/11 *Banif Plus Bank*, 2013:88 . . . . 543n.272
Case C-413/99 *Baumbast and R*, EU:C:2002:493 . . . . . 7n.26, 45n.116, 58, 58n.198, 60n.216, 76n.300,
76n.302, 155n.89, 156, 156n.92, 183, 231n.245, 235, 239, 261n.3, 280n.106,
283, 283n.122, 284, 329n.382, 332n.389, 353–54n.4, 358,
364n.53, 364n.55, 364n.58, 381–82, 387n.193,
397–98, 419, 421, 438, 484–85,
484n.74, 484n.76, 485n.82
Case C-20/16 *Bechtel*, EU:C:2017:488 . . . . 14n.75
Case C-161/15 *Bensada Benallal*, EU:C:2016:175 . . . . 550n.315, 550n.317
Case C-274/96 *Bickel and Franz*, EU:C:1988:563 . . . . 35n.49, 35n.50
Case C-209/03 *Bidar*, EU:C:2005:169 . . . . 38n.78, 56n.189, 61n.221, 92n.404, 92n.405,
280n.106, 288n.149, 360n.29, 361n.33, 362n.37, 363, 363n.48,
364n.49, 364n.51, 364n.52, 373, 373n.106, 376–77nn.130–31,
387n.189, 393n.230, 401n.275, 413, 421n.389, 438–39
Case 24/86 *Blaizot*, EU:C:1988:43 . . . . 35n.56, 287n.139
Case C-438/14 *Bogendorff von Wolffersdorff*, EU:C:2016:401 . . . . . . 38n.82, 38n.83, 51n.158, 79n.322,
341n.445, 464n.138, 512n.81, 513n.85
Case 67/74 *Bonsignore*, EU:C:1975:34 . . . . 499n.2, 503n.27
Case C-415/93 *Bosman*, EU:C:1995:463 . . . . 13n.59, 46n.119
Case 30/77 *Bouchereau*, EU:C:1977:172 . . . . . . 503n.24, 504–5, 504n.31, 504n.33, 504n.34, 517n.102,
523n.138, 530n.178
Case C-303/08, *Bozkurt*, EU:C:2010:800 . . . . 538n.232, 539n.243
Case C-238/15 *Bragança Linares Verruga and Others*, EU:C:2016:949 . . . . 475–76n.26
Case C-73/08 *Bressol and Others*, EU:C:2010:181 . . .50n.148, 61n.222, 63, 66n.245, 66n.247, 359n.21
Case C-140/12 *Brey*, EU:C:2013:565 . . . . 53, 54n.173, 55n.187, 56n.190, 280n.105, 280n.106,
283n.119, 308n.259, 308n.262, 353–54n.4, 386, 386n.185, 387n.190,
388n.194, 388n.197, 389n.206, 393, 394, 395, 395n.242,
397n.256, 400, 400n.271, 401n.273, 401n.274, 401n.276,
403–4, 405n.296, 411–13, 411n.343,
427n.412, 430, 438n.479
Case 197/86 *Brown*, EU:C:1988:323 . . . . 323n.345, 363n.48, 367n.79
Case C-20/03 *Burmanjer and Others*, EU:C:2005:307 . . . . 33n.40
Case C-168/20 *BJ and OV*, EU:C:2021:907 . . . . 74n.286, 171n.177, 273n.63, 276n.85, 277n.90,
408n.323, 474n.14
Case C-398/19 *BY*, EU:C:2020:1032 . . . . 101n.480
Case C-249/11 *Byankov*, EU:C:2012:608 . . . . 84n.359, 521n.126, 549n.308, 549n.310,
549n.311, 549n.312
Case C-308/93 *Cabanis-Issarte*, EU:C:1996:169 . . . . 140n.11
Case 802/18 *Caisse pour l'avenir des enfants*, EU:C:2020:269 . . . . 169n.167, 276n.81
Case C-442/02 *CaixaBank France*, EU:C:2004:586 . . . . 34n.42
Case C-348/96 *Calfa*, EU:C:1999:6 . . . . .504n.32, 506n.52, 516n.100, 548n.304
Case 72/83 *Campus Oil*, EU:C:1984:256 . . . . 514n.92, 515n.96
Case C-390/99 *Canal Satélite Digital*, EU:C:2002:34 . . . . 33n.39
Case C-60/00 *Carpenter*, EU:C:2002:434 . . . . 81n.334, 141n.13, 297n.201, 479n.51,
480, 480n.57, 481

Case 9/74 *Casagrande*, EU:C:1974:74 .... 33n.38
Case C-379/09 *Casteels*, EU:C:2011:131 .... 46n.120
Case C-212/97 *Centros*, EUC:1999:126 .... 340–41n.441, 341n.445, 343n.452, 343n.456,
344n.461, 497n.153
Case C-709/20 *CG*, EU:C:2021:602 .... 14n.69, 18n.103, 78n.316, 88n.386, 258n.397, 339n.433,
353–54n.4, 419, 420n.379, 420n.380, 420n.382, 421, 422–23,
423–24n.400, 425, 425n.402, 425n.404, 427n.416, 428,
435n.463, 436n.468, 438n.478, 459n.96, 461–62, 478n.48
Case C-578/08 *Chakroun*, EU:C:2010:117 .... 388n.196
Case C-578/08 *Chakroun*, EU:C:2009:776 .... 280n.105
Case C-133/15 *Chavez-Vilchez*, EU:C:2017:354 .... 8n.35, 18n.98, 85n.365, 85n.366, 88n.385,
116n.45, 139n.1, 139n.3, 143n.26, 172n.187, 233n.252, 236n.269, 244n.317,
245, 245n.322, 247, 250, 250n.354, 251n.356, 256, 274–75n.76,
385n.180, 414n.353, 437n.473, 460n.107
Case C-94/18 *Chenchooliah*, EU:C:2019:693 ..... 144n.33, 159n.105, 298n.203, 298n.205, 298n.209,
299n.212, 427n.413, 540n.250
Case C-459/14 *Cocaj*, EU:C:2015:546 .... 163–64n.134
Case C-405/01 *Colegio de Oficiales de la Marina Mercante Española*, EU:C:2003:515 .... 501n.11
Case C-138/02 *Collins*, EU:C:2004:172 .... 7n.29, 14n.73, 57n.194, 78n.316, 91n.399, 91n.401,
130n.147, 130n.148, 362n.37, 368n.82, 368n.86, 369n.89,
370, 370n.96, 374–75, 396, 397–98, 438–39, 445n.27
Case C-673/16 *Coman*, EU:C:2018:385 .... 7n.29, 22n.132, 38n.82, 49n.140, 70n.264,
84n.358, 88n.380, 94n.429, 96–97, 97n.448, 139n.6, 141n.17,
145n.37, 148n.47, 152n.67, 152n.68, 153n.71, 153n.75,
153n.77, 154n.78, 154n.82, 154n.83, 255n.382, 267n.32,
268n.39, 464n.136, 491n.127, 495n.141, 502n.23, 513n.85
Case C-147/03 *Commission v Austria*, EU:C:2005:427 .... 50n.145, 61, 61n.218, 61n.225, 63,
64n.236, 65n.243
Case C-75/11 *Commission v Austria*, EU:C:2012:605 .... 14n.77, 20n.113, 77n.312, 92n.412,
94n.428, 359n.21, 359n.22, 379n.148,
381n.159, 431, 431n.435, 432
Case C-328/20 *Commission v Austria*, EU:C:2022:468 .... 277n.92, 278n.94, 379n.143, 407,
410n.333, 478n.43, 478n.45
Case 321/87 *Commission v Belgium*, EU:C:1989:176 .... 301n.229
Case C-47/93 *Commission v Belgium*, EU:C:1994:181 .... 35n.56, 287n.139
Case C-278/94 *Commission v Belgium*, EU:C:1996:321 .... 293n.178, 293n.179, 367n.80, 368n.84,
369n.91
Case C-344/95 *Commission v Belgium*, EU:C:1997:81 .... 294n.182, 303n.234
Case C-323/97 *Commission v Belgium*, EU:C:1998:347 .... 202n.92
Case C-408/03 *Commission v Belgium*, EU:C:2006:192 .... 20n.113, 53n.169, 282n.114, 297n.198,
387n.193, 459n.98, 502n.16
Case C-515/14 *Commission v Cyprus*, EU:C:2016:30 .... 13n.59, 60n.217
Case C-808/21 *Commission v Czech Republic*, pending 200n.79
Case 249/86 *Commission v Germany*, EU:C:1989:204 .... 141n.13
Case C-441/02 *Commission v Germany*, EU:C:2006:253 .... 501n.12, 503n.27
Case C-141/07 *Commission v Germany*, EU:C:2008:492 .... 54n.175
Case C-269/07 *Commission v Germany*, EU:C:2009:527 .... 474n.12
Case C-185/96 *Commission v Greece*, EU:C:1997:425 .... 18n.100
Case C-398/98 *Commission v Greece*, EU:C:2001:565 .... 515n.96
Case C-61/08 *Commission v Greece*, EU:C:2011:340 .... 501n.11
Case C-180/14 *Commission v Greece*, EU:C:2015:840 .... 403n.284
Case C-89/08 P *Commission v Ireland and Others*, EU:C:2009:742 .... 543n.272
Case 63/86 *Commission v Italy*, EU:C:1988:9 .... 277n.90
Case C-424/98 *Commission v Italy*, EU:C:2000:287 .... 37n.73, 84n.356, 303n.234, 308n.264

xx   TABLE OF CASES

Case C-388/01 *Commission v Italy*, EU:C:2003:30 .... 65n.244
Case C-111/91 *Commission v Luxembourg*, EU:C:1993:92 .... 32n.31, 277n.88, 474n.17
Case C-299/01 *Commission v Luxembourg*, EU:C:2002:394 .... 171n.177, 277n.90, 406n.298, 474n.14
Case C-68/89 *Commission v Netherlands*, EU:C:1991:226 .... 297n.199
Case C-50/06 *Commission v Netherlands*, EU:C:2007:325 ...... 84n.358, 356n.14, 365n.60, 365n.62,
  365n.63, 502n.19, 505n.44, 506n.53, 540n.247
Case C-542/09 *Commission v Netherlands*, EU:C:2012:346 .... 60n.217, 91n.402, 379n.142,
  428n.419, 445n.26, 463n.128, 474n.18,
  477n.34, 478n.44, 490n.117
Case C-233/14 *Commission v Netherlands*, EU:C:2016:396 .... 20n.113, 70n.263, 379n.149,
  381n.159, 403n.287, 403n.289, 413n.350
Case C-814/21 *Commission v Poland*, pending... 200n.79
Case C-367/98 *Commission v Portugal*, EU:C:2002:326 .... 34n.45
Case C-157/03 *Commission v Spain*, EU:C:2005:225.................................. 160n.115
Case C-287/02 *Commission v Spain*, EU:C:2005:368.................................. 550n.318
Case C-503/03 *Commission v Spain*, EU:C:2006:74 .... 309n.268, 309n.269, 503n.26
Case C-104/06 *Commission v Sweden*, EU:C:2007:40 .... 325n.351
Case C-308/14 *Commission v UK*, EU:C:2016:436............. 48n.133, 50n.147, 62n.229, 75n.292,
  319n.324, 350n.505, 353–54n.4, 380n.157, 381–82, 399n.262,
  399n.264, 399n.265, 400n.266, 400n.271, 400n.272, 401n.273,
  401n.274, 401n.276, 402n.278, 402n.279, 402n.282, 403–4,
  403n.285, 407, 410–13, 411n.343, 423–24n.400
Case C-247/20 *Commissioners for Her Majesty's Revenue and Customs
  (Assurance maladie complète)*, EU:C:2022:177 .... 77n.314, 136n.185, 258n.399, 283n.121,
  284–85, 286, 286n.136, 353–54n.4,
  384n.175, 410n.336, 441n.1, 449n.41
Case 186/87 *Cowan*, EU:C:1989:47 .... 34, 35n.49, 552n.326
Case 32/75 *Cristini*, EU:C:1975:120 .... 32n.32, 277n.88, 367n.77, 474n.15
Case C-304/14 *CS*, EU:C:2016:674....... 53n.168, 85n.364, 88n.385, 172n.185, 248n.343, 254n.372,
  255, 526n.153
Joined Cases C-147/11 and C-148/11 *Czop and Punakova*, EU:C:2012:538....... 84n.361, 172n.184,
  459n.103, 490n.116
Joined Cases C-122/99 and C-125/99 *D and Sweden v Council*, EU:C:2001:304 .... 151n.61
Case C-224/98 *D'Hoop*, EU:C:2002:432............. 6n.19, 46n.118, 50n.143, 52, 52n.160, 78n.317,
  85n.362, 94n.430, 369n.90, 369n.92, 370, 416n.358,
  434n.454, 476n.29, 488n.107, 489n.109
Joined Cases 28–30/62 *Da Costa*, EU:C:1963:6...................................... 23n.133
Case C-336/94 *Dafeki*, EU:C:1997:579... 350n.503
Case C-544/18 *Dakneviciute*, EU:C:2019:761 .... 328n.373, 328n.374, 408n.320, 409n.327,
  418n.375, 471n.4
Case C-333/13 *Dano*, EU:C:2014:2358 .... 15n.78, 22n.125, 56n.191, 57n.195, 59, 59n.204,
  59n.206, 60n.216, 62n.228, 75n.292, 76n.297, 77n.313, 88n.384,
  286n.132, 318n.319, 318n.321, 350n.505, 353–54n.4,
  361–62, 390–95, 390n.208, 390n.210, 391n.218, 392n.225,
  392n.228, 393n.235, 394n.239, 394n.240, 395n.244, 396n.247,
  400, 400n.271, 401n.273, 401n.274, 401n.276, 403–4, 408n.316,
  411–12, 411n.342, 411n.343, 412n.344, 414, 416, 417n.363, 418,
  419, 421, 422–23, 427, 430n.430, 431, 433–37, 433n.447,
  433n.448, 433n.450, 438n.477
Case C-546/11 *Dansk Jurist—og Økonomforbund*, EU:C:2013:603 .... 393n.230
Case 8/74, *Dassonville*, EU:C:1974:82 .... 30n.21
Case C-406/04 *De Cuyper*, EU:C:2006:491 .... 75n.291, 487–88n.103
Case C-230/17 *Deha Altiner and Ravn*, EU:C:2018:497....... 81n.335, 142n.22, 159n.104, 492n.130,
  494n.138
Case C-650/13 *Delvigne*, EU:C:2015:648 .... 22n.129, 94n.429, 188n.4, 191–92n.19, 195, 196–98,
  198n.59, 198n.62, 198n.64, 198–99n.66,
  199–201, 199n.68, 200n.73, 213–14

Case 12/86 *Demirel*, EU:C:1987:400. .... 538n.236
Case C-221/11 *Demirkan*, EU:C:2013:583 .... 538n.236
Joined Cases C-401/15 to C-403/15 *Depesme and Kerrou*, EU:C:2016:955. .... 150n.54, 169–70,
169n.167, 169n.168
Case C-256/11 *Dereci and Others*, EU:C:2011:734. .... 75n.293, 81n.337, 85n.364, 88n.385, 89n.388,
188n.5, 235n.265, 236–37n.271, 237n.275, 238–39, 239–40n.288,
240–41, 241n.297, 244, 245, 247n.338, 248n.341, 249
Case C-246/17 *Diallo*, EU:C:2018:499 ..... 60n.213, 84n.356, 148n.46, 312n.283, 312n.287, 313n.292
Case C-325/09 *Dias*, EU:C:2011:498 .... 92n.408, 104n.503, 303n.240, 384, 385–86, 385n.178,
445n.23, 454n.72, 459n.97, 459n.99, 459n.100,
460–62, 463n.129, 464n.134, 533n.197
Case 267/83 *Diatta*, EU:C:1985:67 .... 155, 155n.84, 155n.85, 156n.90, 158, 345n.464, 451n.57
Case C-9/08 *Donnici*, EU:C:2009:44 .... 200n.79
Case C-186/01 *Dory*, EU:C:2003:146. .... 515n.95
Case C-451/11 *Dülger*, EU:C:2012:504 .... 73n.280
Case C-244/06 *Dynamic Medien*, EU:C:2008:85 .... 141n.14
Joined Cases C-297/88 and C-197/89 *Dzodzi*, EU:C:1990:360 .... 546n.289
Case C-193/16 *E*, EU:C:2017:542 .... 518n.105, 532n.188, 552n.329
Case 389/87 *Echternach and Moritz*, EU:C:1989:130. .... 483n.72, 484n.75, 484n.77
Case C-54/99 *Église de scientology*, EU:C:2000:124 .... 515n.93
Case C-291/05 *Eind*, EU:C:2007:771 ...... 14n.71, 141n.13, 313n.291, 486n.96, 487, 490–91, 495–96
Case C-173/09 *Elchinov*, EU:C:2010:581. .... 54n.176
Case C-17/16 *El Dakkak and Intercontinental*, EU:C:2017:341. .... 95n.436
Case C-275/12 *Elrick*, EU:C:2013:684 .... 78n.316, 94n.431
Case C-300/04 *Eman and Sevinger*, EU:C:2006:545. .... 110n.5, 195, 195n.38, 195n.42, 195n.44,
196, 197, 201n.82, 258n.396, 258n.398
Case C-110/99 *Emsland-Stärke*, EU:C:2000:695, paras 52–53 .... 341n.443, 344n.461
Case C-380/18 *EP (Menace pour l'ordre public)*, EU:C:2019:1071. .... 503n.26
Case C-260/89 *ERT*, EU:C:1991:254 .... 432n.439
Case C-135/99 *Elsen*, EU:C:2000:647. .... 475n.20
Case C-544/15 *Fahimian*, EU:C:2017:255 .... 515n.97, 520–21, 521n.123, 521n.124
Case C-411/20 *Familienkasse Niedersachsen-Bremen*, EU:C:2022:602 .... 273n.64, 353–54n.4,
406n.299, 406n.300, 406n.304, 411,
411n.339, 428n.418, 464n.138
Case C-411/98 *Ferlini*, EU:C:2000:530. .... 46n.119
Case C-234/97 *Fernández de Bobadilla*, EU:C:1999:367 .... 356n.10
Case C-452/04 *Fidium Finanz*, EU:C:2006:631. .... 33n.40
Case C-158/07 *Förster*, EU:C:2008:630 .... 60n.211, 326n.362, 362n.38, 377n.135, 387n.189,
393n.230, 401n.275, 403–4
Case C-541/15 *Freitag*, EU:C:2017:432 .... 18n.99, 131n.154, 195n.43, 434n.458
Case C-343/17 *Fremoluc*, EU:C:2018:754 .... 82n.343
Case 1/72 *Frilli*, EU:C:1972:56 .... 396n.245
Case C-719/19 *FS*, EU:C:2021:506 .... 269n.43, 271n.53, 272n.57, 273n.68, 295–96, 298n.204,
299n.215, 348n.494, 353–54n.4, 379n.146,
426n.411, 427n.414, 458n.92, 548n.301
Case C-7/94 *Gaal*, EU:C:1995:118 .... 484n.78
Joined Cases C-381/18 and C-382/18 *GS and VG (Menace pour l'ordre public)*,
EU:C:2019:1072 .... 503n.26
Case C-175/94 *Gallagher*, EU:C:1995:415. .... 546n.290
Case C-148/02 *Garcia Avello*, EU:C:2003:539. .... 48n.132, 78n.316, 79n.320, 94n.423, 131n.154,
131n.155, 131n.158, 132, 132n.161, 133–34, 196n.47, 229n.233,
235n.268, 258n.398, 343n.455, 362n.38, 464n.138
Case C-299/14 *García-Nieto*, EU:C:2016:114 .... 59n.208, 273n.62, 318n.320, 353–54n.4,
380n.155, 396n.246, 397n.256, 398n.257, 398n.258,
398n.259, 399n.260, 405n.293, 438
Case C-233/12 *Gardella*, EU:C:2013:449. .... 87n.377
Case C-467/04 *Gasparini and Others*, EU:C:2006:610. .... 80n.324

Joined Cases C-502/01 and C-31/02 *Gaumain-Cerri and Barth*, EU:C:2004:413 . . . . 275n.78
Case C-430/10 *Gaydarov*, EU:C:2011:749 . . . . 51n.157, 266n.22, 509n.69, 510n.72, 515n.93,
    543n.269, 545n.286, 545n.287, 545n.288
Case C-55/94 *Gebhard*, EU:C:1995:411 . . . . .33n.40, 34n.46, 87n.375
Case C-213/05 *Geven*, EU:C:2007:438 . . . . 475n.24
Case C-376/89 *Giagounidis*, EU:C:1991:99 . . . . 265n.19
Case C-20/12 *Giersch*, EU:C:2013:411 . . . . 54n.180, 475n.23, 475n.25, 476–77
Case C-336/96 *Gilly*, EU:C:1998:221 . . . . 14n.74, 131, 131n.151
Case C-257/99 *Givane and Others*, EU:C:2003:8 . . . . 322n.335, 322n.337, 326n.362
Case C-63/99 *Gloszczuk*, EU:C:2001:488. . . . . 344n.460
Case C-710/19 *GMA (Demandeur d'emploi)*, EU:C:2020:1037 . . . . . . 71n.271, 294, 295–96, 295n.187,
    295n.188, 300n.223, 353–54n.4, 366n.71,
    366n.72, 415–16, 460n.108
Case C-103/08 *Gottwald*, EU:C:2009:597 . . . . .13n.61, 52n.165, 92n.412
Case C-190/98, *Graf*, EU:C:2000:49 . . . . 34n.41
Case 293/83 *Gravier*, EU:C:1985:69 . . . . .35n.55, 65n.243, 287n.138, 367n.79
Case C-62/91 *Gray*, EU:C:1992:177 . . . . 51n.152
Case C-159/90 *Grogan*, EU:C:1991:378. . . . . 80n.325
Case C-353/06 *Grunkin and Paul*, EU:C:2008:559 . . . . 13n.61, 51n.151, 79n.322, 93n.420,
    131n.157, 196n.47, 235n.268, 267n.33, 422n.395
Case C-184/99 *Grzelczyk*, EU:C:2001:458 . . . . .7n.29, 14n.76, 22n.128, 38n.79, 55n.186, 56n.188,
    57–58, 59n.205, 76n.301, 83n.346, 106n.516, 112n.16, 228n.231, 262n.6,
    274n.72, 280n.106, 281n.109, 288n.146, 288n.148, 288n.151,
    289, 319n.327, 353n.1, 353n.2, 353–54n.4, 358, 359, 359n.24, 360,
    360n.26, 361, 362n.37, 362n.38, 363n.45, 363n.46, 364n.56, 368,
    368–69n.88, 373–74, 377, 380, 380–82, 386–87, 388n.198,
    390, 394n.240, 401n.275, 407, 413n.349, 414,
    419, 426, 434n.454, 437n.476, 464n.138
Case C-442/16 *Gusa*, EU:C:2017:1004. . . . . 69n.259, 70n.262, 86n.373, 276n.86, 325n.352, 326,
    326n.356, 326n.358, 366n.66, 409n.331, 474n.14
Case C-488/21 *GV v Chief Appeals Officer and Others*, pending. 178n.224
Joined Cases C-396/05, C-419/05 and C-450/05 *Habelt, Möser and Wachter*,
    EU:C:2007:810 . . . . 54n.178
Case C-45/12 *Hadj Ahmed*, EU:C:2013:390 . . . . 432n.442
Case C-212/05 *Hartmann*, EU:C:2007:437 . . . . .475n.21, 476–77
Case 137/84 *Heinrich*, EU:C:1985:335 . . . . 356n.11
Case C-287/05 *Hendrix*, EU:C:2007:494 . . . . 486n.93
Joined Cases C-393/99 and C-394/99 *Hervein and Hervillie*, EU:C:2002:182. . . . . . . 90n.393, 473n.11
Case 222/86 *Heylens and Others*, EU:C:1987:442 . . . . 543n.270, 545n.286
Case C-632/13 *Hirvonen*, EU:C:2015:765 . . . . 13n.67, 22n.126
Case 249/83 *Hoeckx*, EU:C:1985:139 . . . . 277n.88, 417n.367, 474n.16
Joined Cases C-245/94 and C-312/94 *Hoever and Zachow*, EU:C:1996:379 . . . . 399n.263, 474n.13
Case C-524/06 *Huber*, EU:C:2008:724 . . . . 7n.29, 77n.305, 305n.247, 306n.250, 306n.254, 437–38,
    464n.138
Case 263/86 *Humbel and Edel*, EU:C:1988:451 . . . . .35n.54, 287n.141, 483n.71
Case C-156/21 *Hungary v Parliament and Council*, EU:C:2022:97 . . . . 106–7n.518
Case C-364/10 *Hungary v Slovakia*, EU:C:2012:630. . . . . 21n.122
Joined Cases C-392/04 and C-422/04 *i-21 Germany and Arcor*, EU:C:2006:586 . . . . 549n.310
Case C-289/20 *IB (Habitual residence of a spouse—Divorce)*, EU:C:2021:955 . . . . 399n.264
Case C-310/08 *Ibrahim*, EU:C:2010:89 . . . . 75n.288, 75n.289, 294n.183, 329n.381, 331n.388,
    397n.254, 416n.360, 489n.111
Case C-40/11 *Iida*, EU:C:2012:691 . . . . 41n.98, 80n.329, 81, 81n.332, 84n.354, 85n.364,
    116n.45, 148n.49, 153n.70, 155n.87, 156n.91, 157, 158,
    176n.210, 189n.9, 189n.11, 226n.215, 228n.226,
    235n.264, 236n.269, 236n.270, 240n.290,
    334n.401, 433n.451, 451n.57, 481n.60
Case C-897/19 PPU *IN*, EU:C:2020:262 . . . . .11n.51, 11n.53, 72n.275, 106, 106n.512, 129n.141

Case C-251/06 *ING. AUER*, EU:C:2007:658 .... 20–21n.117
Case 66/80 *International Chemical Corporation (ICI)*, EU:C:1981:102 .... 23n.133
Case C-258/04 *Ioannidis*, EU:C:2005:559 .... 13n.66
Case C-420/16 P *Izsák and Dabis*, EU:C:2019:177 .... 214n.157, 215n.158, 215n.160
Case 13/63 *Italian Government v Commission*, EU:C:1963:20 .... 64n.238
Case C-163/17 *Jawo*, EU:C:2019:218 .... 434–35n.459, 435n.460
Case C-268/99 *Jany*, EU:C:2001:616 .... 531n.185
Case C-1/05 *Jia*, EU:C:2007:1 .... 160n.109, 176n.213, 177–78, 177n.216, 177n.218,
    177n.219, 177n.220
Case C-33/07 *Jipa*, EU:C:2008:396 .... 263n.10, 505n.41, 509n.69, 515n.93, 520n.122, 521n.126
Case C-601/15 PPU *JN*, EU:C:2016:84 .... 515n.97
Case C-181/19 *Jobcenter Krefeld*, EU:C:2020:794 .... 14n.69, 15n.80, 75n.287, 75n.289, 170,
    170n.169, 170n.174, 273n.63, 353–54n.4, 417n.365, 417n.368,
    418n.374, 419, 423n.396, 424n.401, 428, 429–30,
    461n.117, 478n.48, 489n.110
Case 222/84 *Johnston*, EU:C:1986:206 .... 545n.286
Case C-198/13 *Julian Hernández*, EU:C:2014:2055 .... 432n.444, 433n.451
Case C-502/19 *Junqueras*, EU:C:2019:1115 .... 189n.15, 192n.21, 200n.79
Case C-370/17 *K and B*, EU:C:2018:877 .... 142n.19
Joined Cases C-331/16 and C-366/16 *K and HF*, EU:C:2018:296 .... 17n.91, 460n.106, 515n.93,
    521n.129, 522n.130, 522n.135, 523n.136, 523n.137,
    523n.139, 523n.140, 523n.141, 524–25, 537n.227
Case C-82/16 *KA and Others*, EU:C:2018:308 ...... 41n.97, 85n.365, 136n.186, 172n.186, 172n.188,
    230–31n.242, 237n.274, 246n.331, 247n.334, 247n.335,
    247n.336, 247n.339, 250n.354, 251n.359, 252n.360,
    253n.365, 253n.366, 255, 255n.381, 257n.391
Joined Cases C-402/05 P and C-415/05 P *Kadi and Al Barakaat International
    Foundation*, EU:C:2008:461 .... 543n.270, 543n.271
Case C-391/95 *Kadiman*, EU:C:1997:205 .... 156n.93
Case C-571/10 *Kamberaj*, EU:C:2012:233 .... 433n.451, 434–35, 435n.461
Case C-192/99 *Kaur*, EU:C:2001:106 .... 110n.5, 122n.92, 194n.33, 343n.453
Case C-558/14 *Khachab*, EU:C:2016:285 .... 280n.105
Joined Cases C-267/91 and C-268/91 *Keck and Mithouard*, EU:C:1993:905 .... 439n.484
Case 139/85 *Kempf*, EU:C:1986:223 .... 277n.89, 293–94n.180
Case C-158/96 *Kohll*, EU:C:1998:171 .... 54n.176, 393n.230
Case C-300/15 *Kohll and Kohll-Schlesser*, EU:C:2016:361 .... 13n.68
Case 115/78 *Knoors*, EU:C:1979:31 .... 356n.10, 497n.150
Case C-285/95 *Kol*, EU:C:1997:280 .... 344n.460, 533n.198
Case C-19/92 *Kraus*, EU:C:1993:125 .... 34n.46, 356n.10
Case C-285/98 *Kreil*, EU:C:2000:2 .... 515n.95
Case C-299/95 *Kremzow*, EU:C:1997:254 .... 79n.318, 80–81, 228n.226
Case C-555/07 *Kücükdeveci*, EU:C:2010:21 .... 433n.452
Case C-398/09 *Lady & Kid and Others*, EU:C:2011:540 .... 514n.90
Case 39/86 *Lair*, EU:C:1988:322 .... 32n.34, 36n.58, 287n.142, 323n.345, 363n.48, 367n.79
Case C-234/02 P *Lamberts*, EU:C:2004:174 .... 220n.191
Case C-162/09 *Lassal*, EU:C:2010:592 ...... 22n.132, 46n.118, 68n.257, 84n.358, 87n.374, 383n.167,
    384n.169, 441n.4, 445n.23, 453n.69, 456n.80,
    458n.94, 462–63, 464n.136
Case 66/85 *Lawrie-Blum*, EU:C:1986:284 .... 32n.29, 275n.77, 478n.47
Case 316/85 *Lebon*, EU:C:1987:302 .... 175n.206, 176n.209, 293n.177, 367n.78, 368n.85
Case C-43/99 *Leclere and Deaconescu*, EU:C:2001:303 .... 324n.346, 368n.81
Case 53/81 *Levin*, EU:C:1982:105 .... 275n.77, 408n.317
Joined Cases C-197/11 and C-203/11 *Libert*, EU:C:2013:288 .... 22n.132
Case C-591/10 *Littlewoods Retail and Others*, EU:C:2012:478 .... 549n.311
Case C-216/18 PPU *LM*, EU:C:2018:586 .... 97n.450
Case C-46/12 *LN*, EU:C:2013:97 .... 15n.79, 77n.312, 290n.162, 290n.164, 341–42, 342n.449,
    379n.144, 381n.159, 393n.237, 408n.317

Case C-165/16 *Lounes*, EU:C:2017:862 . . . . 20–21n.117, 86n.371, 90n.391, 93n.416, 119n.65,
133n.167, 133n.168, 133n.171, 133n.173, 134n.174, 134n.176, 134Rzn.178,
134n.180, 135–36, 135n.182, 139n.4, 141n.17, 145n.38, 146n.40,
152–53, 202n.89, 255n.379, 434n.458, 479n.50, 482n.69
Joined Cases 286/82 and 26/83 *Luisi and Carbone*, EU:C:1984:35 . . . . 29n.10, 34
Case C-169/18 *Mahmood and Others*, EU:C:2019:5. . . . . 348n.494
Case C-359/13 *Martens*, EU:C:2015:118 . . . . 49n.137, 53n.166, 85n.363, 94n.430, 94n.431,
122–23n.95, 487–88n.103
Case C-85/96 *Martínez Sala*, EU:C:1998:217 . . . . 18n.103, 19n.109, 22n.127, 47n.124, 59n.207,
79, 128n.133, 150n.54, 288n.147, 296n.196, 297n.200, 323n.345,
353n.2, 353–54n.4, 358–59, 358n.18, 358n.20, 359n.24, 360–61,
361n.34, 362–63, 362n.37, 363n.46, 368–69n.88, 372n.105,
380–82, 383, 384–85, 386–87, 390, 401n.275, 402n.278,
419, 421, 422–23, 425, 467n.155
Case C-10/05 *Mattern and Cikotic*, EU:C:2006:220 . . . . 149n.53
Case 235/87 *Matteuci*, EU:C:1988:460. . . . . 32n.35
Case C-434/09 *McCarthy*, EU:C:2011:277 . . . . 20n.116, 21, 42n.103, 70n.263, 79n.323, 82n.340,
84n.355, 87n.374, 131n.156, 132n.163, 132n.165, 133, 133n.167,
136n.186, 145n.38, 146n.39, 152–53, 233, 233n.257,
234n.261, 234n.263, 235n.266, 235n.268, 236,
238–40, 241, 245, 255n.378
Case C-202/13 *McCarthy II*, EU:C:2014:2450. . . . . 96n.444, 96n.445, 140n.10, 315, 315n.307,
316n.311, 316n.312, 341, 341n.444, 348–50, 349n.495, 349n.499,
350n.506, 393n.237, 394n.238, 394n.239, 464n.136, 509n.70, 520n.122
Case C-127/08 *Metock and Others*, EU:C:2008:449 . . . . 8n.36, 22, 48n.135, 70n.262, 70n.263,
77n.307, 84n.358, 86n.371, 86n.372, 96n.444, 127n.127, 139n.2, 141n.13,
142n.18, 142n.20, 144n.29, 154n.81, 160n.110, 160n.111, 160n.112,
160n.113, 160n.115, 160n.116, 161n.121, 161n.122, 162n.124,
162n.126, 230–31n.242, 316n.311, 340–41n.441, 341n.442,
357n.15, 394n.238, 438n.483, 448n.35, 448n.38,
464n.136, 509n.70, 509n.71, 520n.122
Case C-400/12 *MG*, EU:C:2014:9 . . . . 92n.409, 142n.20, 467n.151, 529, 534n.208, 534n.210,
534n.211, 535n.213, 535n.216
Case C-369/90 *Micheletti*, EU:C:1992:295. . . . . . . 93n.422, 110–13, 110n.5, 110n.6, 117n.50, 118n.59,
121n.86, 122–23n.95, 129–30, 131n.155, 343n.453, 343n.455
Case C-142/05 *Mickelsson and Roos*, EU:C:2009:336. . . . . 34n.43
Joined Cases C-11/06 and 12/06 *Morgan and Bucher*, EU:C:2007:626 . . . . 52n.161, 54n.177,
78n.316, 79n.319, 80n.327, 92n.412,
94n.431, 487–88n.103
Joined Cases 35/82 and 36/82 *Morson and Jhanjan*, EU:C:1982:368 . . . . 226n.217
Case 180/83 *Moser*, EU:C:1984:233 . . . . 227n.221
Case 7/75 *Mr and Mrs F*, EU:C:1975:80. . . . . .8n.34, 33n.37
Case C-459/99 *MRAX*, EU:C:2002:461 . . . . 141n.13, 160n.114, 297n.201, 300n.225, 311n.277,
311n.280, 356n.13, 356n.14, 365n.62, 502n.22, 507n.58
Case C-293/03 *My*, EU:C:2004:821 . . . . 41, 42
Case C-115/15 *NA*, EU:C:2016:487 . . . . 19n.110, 22n.132, 68n.257, 69n.258, 85n.364, 143n.27,
172n.183, 235n.264, 331–32, 332n.390, 336n.410, 336n.413,
337n.418, 338, 338n.426, 339, 339n.433, 490n.118
Case C-354/95 *National Farmers' Union*, EU:C:1997:379 . . . . 132n.159
Case C-340/97 *Nazli*, EU:C:2000:77. . . . . 539n.243
Case C-499/06 *Nerkowska*, EU:C:2008:300. . . . . 85n.362, 93n.413
Case 92/63 *Nonnenmacher*, EU:C:1964:40 . . . . 30n.20, 30n.23
Case C-128/22 *NORDIC INFO*, pending. 512n.80
Joined Cases C-368/20 and C-369/20 *NW*, EU:C:2022:298 . . . . 11n.52
Case C-456/12 *O and B*, EU:C:2014:135 . . . . 17n.90, 70n.263, 142n.21, 273n.66, 313n.291, 341n.444,
348n.494, 482, 482n.65, 491n.123, 491n.128, 492n.130,
492n.131, 493, 493n.135, 494, 495–96, 497, 535n.218

Joined Cases C-356/11 and C-357/11 *O and S*, EU:C:2012:776 .... 84n.355, 85n.364, 85n.365,
            117n.51, 148n.46, 172n.187, 183n.245, 238–39,
            238n.281, 240n.289, 240n.292, 241n.296,
            243, 243n.310, 245
Case C-244/13 *Ogieriakhi*, EU:C:2014:2068 ...... 84n.358, 157–58, 157n.98, 159, 334n.400, 451n.55,
            452n.58
Case C-36/02 *Omega*, EU:C:2004:614 .... 33n.40
Case C-378/12 *Onuekwere*, EU:C:2014:13. .... 77n.311, 92n.408, 104n.504, 156–59, 156n.94,
            157n.95, 450n.51, 451–52, 451n.52, 463, 463n.131, 464,
            464n.134, 464n.135, 464n.139, 466–67,
            534n.212, 535n.214
Opinion 2/13, EU:C:2014:2454 .... 67n.251
Case C-718/19 *Ordre des barreaux francophones and germanophone and Others
    (Mesures préventives en vue d'éloignement)*, EU:C:2021:505 .... 10n.43, 269n.42, 518n.107,
            518–19n.109, 519n.110
Joined Cases C-482/01 and C-493/01 *Orfanopoulos and Oliveri*,
    EU:C:2004:262 .... 49n.142, 74n.284, 328n.369, 499n.2, 499n.3,
            501–2n.15, 504n.34, 506n.51, 507n.56, 507n.60,
            516n.100, 530n.178, 537n.230
Case C-100/01 *Oteiza Olazabal*, EU:C:2002:712 .... 13n.62, 500n.5, 504n.37, 506n.50
Case C-215/03 *Oulane*, EU:C:2005:95 .... 177n.219, 266n.24, 271n.51
Case C-206/94 *Paletta*, EU:C:1996:182 .... 497n.152
Case C-218/15 *Paoletti*, EU:C:2016:748. .... 46n.118, 85n.367, 86n.368
Case C-295/90 *Parliament v Council*, EU:C:1992:294 .... 36n.61
Case 98/79 *Pecastaing*, EU:C:1980:69. .... 546n.289, 546n.290, 547n.297
Joined Cases C-372/09 and C-373/09 *Peñarroja Fa*, EU:C:2011:156 .... 543n.269, 545n.288
Case C-32/19 *Pensionsversicherungsanstalt (Cessation d'activité après l'âge du
    départ à la retraite)*, EU:C:2020:25 .... 456n.82
Case C-312/93 *Peterbroeck*, EU:C:1995:437 .... 549n.310
Case C-184/16 *Petrea*, EU:C:2017:684 .... 304, 304n.242, 500n.9, 541n.254, 542n.258, 550n.319,
            550n.320, 551n.323
Case 24/75 *Petroni*, EU:C:1971:129 .... 51n.154
Case C-182/15 *Petruhhin*, EU:C:2016:630. .... 13n.61, 14n.76, 17n.91, 22n.125, 50n.149, 88n.383,
            98n.454, 98n.459, 98n.462, 99–100, 99n.467, 100n.473,
            101n.479, 102–3, 104, 104n.499, 105n.509, 359n.22,
            422, 422n.391, 428n.423, 431n.437, 434n.455
Case C-348/09 *PI*, EU:C:2012:300 ...... 515n.93, 517, 530, 531n.179, 531n.183, 531n.184, 531n.185,
            531n.186, 532n.188, 532n.189, 533n.204
Case 157/79 *Pieck*, EU:C:1980:179 .... 297n.198
Case 41/84 *Pinna*, EU:C:1986:1 .... 473n.9, 478n.42
Case C-191/16 *Pisciotti*, EU:C:2018:222 .... 50n.149, 51n.156, 100n.469,
            100n.474, 428n.423
Case C-157/21 *Poland v Parliament and Council*, EU:C:2022:98 .... 106–7n.518
Case C-349/06 *Polat*, EU:C:2007:581 .... 73n.279, 521n.124
Case 63/08 *Pontin*, EU:C:2009:666 .... 549n.311
Case C-206/21 *Préfet de Saône-et-Loire*, removed from the register 47n.123
Case C-673/20 *Préfet du Gers*, EU:C:2022:449 .... 8n.31, 11n.47, 40n.87, 48n.132, 109n.3,
            122n.88, 124n.104, 125n.107, 125n.110, 125n.113, 126–27n.124,
            187n.2, 196n.49, 197, 197n.52, 197n.55, 200n.78, 353n.1
Case C-618/16 *Prefeta*, EU:C:2018:719 .... 75n.291, 328n.375, 329, 366n.67, 408n.321
Case C-367/11 *Prete*, EU:C:2012:668 .... 13n.66, 53n.166, 92n.407, 359n.22, 375n.122
Joined Cases C-523/11 and C-585/11 *Prinz and Seeberger*, EU:C:2013:524 .... 93n.414, 94n.431,
            411n.338
Case C-418/18 P *Puppinck*, EU:C:2019:1113 ...... 69n.259, 189n.15, 205n.109, 211n.134, 216n.165,
            219n.185
Case C-224/02 *Pusa*, EU:C:2004:273 .... 20n.115, 48n.136, 60n.212, 78n.317, 85n.362, 94n.424
Case C-94/07 *Raccanelli*, EU:C:2008:425. .... 291n.167

xxvi TABLE OF CASES

Case C-83/11 *Rahman*, EU:C:2012:519 . . . . 84n.357, 166, 166n.146, 166n.149, 166n.150, 167, 167n.152, 168, 180n.230, 180n.232, 181, 181n.237, 182, 182n.240, 183n.246, 183n.247, 183n.248, 183n.249, 305n.244, 314n.297, 314n.301
Case C-247/17 *Raugevicius*, EU:C:2018:898 . . . . 103n.491, 104, 104n.499, 105n.509, 117n.50, 359n.22, 422n.392
Case C-152/03 *Ritter-Coulais*, EU:C:2006:123 . . . . 275n.78
Case C-363/89 *Roux*, EU:C:1991:41, para. 23 . . . . 266n.23, 325n.350, 328n.373
Case C-357/89 *Raulin*, EU:C:1992:87 . . . . 36n.57, 287n.140
Case 59/85 *Reed*, EU:C:1986:157 . . . . 162n.127, 163–66, 164n.138, 169n.165, 170–71, 276n.80, 495n.143
Case C-522/10 *Reichel-Albert*, EU:C:2012:475 . . . . 14n.70
Case 65/81 *Reina*, EU:C:1982:6 . . . . 32n.33, 474n.15
Case C-165/14 *Rendón Marín*, EU:C:2016:675 . . . . 42n.102, 42n.104, 43n.106, 53n.168, 60n.216, 84n.354, 84n.355, 85n.364, 85n.365, 113n.26, 120n.74, 143n.25, 171n.182, 172n.187, 176n.210, 236n.269, 237n.274, 243n.312, 253n.368, 255, 281n.111, 299n.211, 449n.44, 503n.27, 506n.53, 524n.146, 525n.152
Case C-896/19 *Repubblika v Il-Prim Ministru*, EU:C:2021:311 . . . . 198n.63
Case C-423/12 *Reyes*, EU:C:2014:16 . . . . 76n.303, 176n.211, 176n.213, 176n.214, 177–78, 177n.218, 177n.220, 177n.221, 181n.237, 305n.243, 314n.296
Case C-327/18 PPU *RO*, EU:C:2018:733 . . . . 105n.505
Case C-227/89 *Rönfeldt*, EU:C:1991:52 . . . . 362n.41
Case C-135/08 *Rottmann*, EU:C:2010:104 . . . . 7n.29, 8n.32, 40n.92, 41n.96, 42, 83n.347, 93n.415, 94n.432, 109n.2, 111n.7, 111n.10, 111n.13, 112, 112n.15, 112n.16, 112n.17, 112n.18, 112n.20, 113–15, 113n.24, 116n.49, 118–19, 119n.71, 120n.72, 122, 122n.87, 123n.99, 125, 129–30, 188–89, 188n.7, 199n.67, 229n.233, 230n.239, 232–33, 232n.248, 232n.250
Case C-363/89 *Roux*, EU:C:1991:41 . . . . 266n.23, 325n.350, 328n.373
Case 20/85 *Roviello*, EU:C:1988:283 . . . . 65n.244
Case 48/75 *Royer*, EU:C:1976:57 . . . . 128n.133, 262n.8, 278n.95, 297n.198, 501–2n.15, 502n.16, 502n.17, 546n.291
Joined Cases 117/76 and 16/77 *Ruckdeschel*, EU:C:1977:160 . . . . 391n.217
Case C-544/07 *Rüffler*, EU:C:2009:258 . . . . 22n.130, 434n.454
Case C-34/09 *Ruiz Zambrano*, EU:C:2011:124 . . . . 6n.17, 22n.125, 24n.138, 41n.95, 42, 53, 79, 82–84, 83n.346, 83n.347, 83n.348, 83–84n.353, 89, 94–95, 96–97, 99, 112n.15, 118–19, 132n.162, 140n.9, 145n.37, 187–88n.3, 188n.8, 196, 230n.234, 230n.235, 230n.240, 231, 232, 232n.247, 233, 234, 235, 236–37, 238–40, 241–42, 243, 244, 247, 248, 249, 254n.376, 255n.378, 256n.384, 258–59, 431n.436, 437n.472, 471–72n.5
Case C-391/09 *Runevič-Vardyn and Wardyn*, EU:C:2011:291 . . . . 38n.80, 48n.131, 51n.150, 78n.316, 79n.322, 464n.138
Case C-113/89 *Rush Portuguesa*, EU:C:1990:142 . . . . 279n.101
Case 36/75 *Rutili*, EU:C:1975:137 . . . . 503n.25, 542n.261
Case C-754/18 *Ryanair Designated Activity Company*, EU:C:2020:131 . . . . 11n.52
Case C-2/21 *Rzecznik Praw Obywatelskich*, EU:C:2022:502 . . . . 268n.40
Case C-457/12 *S and G*, EU:C:2014:36 . . . . 81n.333, 150n.57, 276n.82, 480n.59, 481n.61, 482, 493
Case C-76/90 *Säger*, EU:C:1991:331 . . . . 34n.44
Case 8/77 *Sagulo and Others*, EU:C:1977:131 . . . . 301n.229
Case C-551/07 *Sahin*, EU:C:2008:75 . . . . 160n.111, 509n.71
Case C-507/12 *Saint Prix*, EU:C:2014:2007 . . . . 22n.130, 74n.283, 171n.176, 256n.385, 294n.184, 296n.196, 327n.363, 327n.365, 328, 328n.369, 328n.370, 339, 408n.319, 409n.329, 409n.330, 418n.375, 453n.66, 471n.3
Case C-69/10 *Samba Diouf*, EU:C:2011:524, ... 545n.287

Case 175/78 *Saunders*, EU:C:1979:88. . . . . .31n.27, 81n.336, 228n.227, 266n.23
Case C-208/09 *Sayn-Wittgenstein*, EU:C:2010:806 . . . . . . 13n.61, 13n.65, 48n.134, 51n.151, 79n.322,
94n.427, 502n.23, 513n.84, 513n.85
Case C-403/03 *Schempp*, EU:C:2005:446. . .48n.132, 82, 82n.342, 94n.425, 110n.4, 150n.56, 234n.262
Case C-419/92 *Scholz*, EU:C:1994:62. . . . . 134n.176
Case C-261/13 P *Schönberger*, EU:C:2014:2423 . . . . 15n.82, 210n.132, 218n.179, 219
Case C-473/15 *Schotthöfer and Steiner*, EU:C:2017:633 . . . . 434n.455
Case C-279/93 *Schumacker*, EU:C:1995:31. . . . . 93n.421
Case C-76/05 *Schwarz and Gootjes-Schwarz*, EU:C:2007:492. . . . . 13n.64, 171n.180
Case 76/72 *Scutari*, EU:C:1973:46 . . . . 33n.38
Joined Cases C-65/95 and C-111/95 *Shingara and Radiom*, EU:C:1997:300 . . . . . . 504n.37, 546n.289
Case 44/65 *Singer*, EU:C:1965:212 . . . . 31n.26
Case C-370/90 *Singh*, EU:C:1992:296 . . . . .141n.13, 155n.86, 340–41n.441, 471–72n.5, 485,
485n.86, 486–88, 486n.94, 490–91, 495–96, 497n.150
Case C-218/14 *Singh II*, EU:C:2015:476. . . . . 22n.132, 143n.24, 143n.28, 159, 159n.103,
274–75n.76, 283n.117, 332, 334n.398, 334n.401, 335n.402,
335n.404, 336–37, 336n.409, 338,
338n.426, 339, 339n.433
Case C-206/13 *Siragusa*, EU:C:2014:126 . . . . 432, 432n.446
Case C-273/97 *Sirdar*, EU:C:1999:523 . . . . 515n.95
Case C-193/94 *Skanavi and Chryssanthakopoulos*, EU:C:1996:70 . . . . 13n.63
Case C-129/18 *SM*, EU:C:2019:248 . . . . .173n.194, 173n.195, 183n.246, 183n.247, 184–85,
184n.250, 184n.254
Case C-15/11 *Sommer*, EU:C:2012:731 . . . . 46n.118
Case C-145/04 *Spain v United Kingdom*, EU:C:2006:543 . . . . 21n.122, 76n.299, 193n.25, 193n.26,
194n.30, 194n.33, 194n.34, 194n.35, 195,
196, 197, 197n.54, 197n.56, 199–200
Case 143/87 *Stanton*, EU:C:1988:378. . . . . 30n.22
Case C-503/09 *Stewart*, EU:C:2011:500. . . . . 52n.164, 55n.182, 85n.362, 90n.397, 431n.435,
434n.454, 487–88n.103
Case C-836/18 *Subdelegación del Gobierno en Ciudad Real (Conjoint d'un citoyen
de l'Union)*, EU:C:2020:119. . . . . 226n.216, 235n.264, 247n.332, 247n.335, 252, 252n.363,
253n.365, 253n.367, 255n.380, 256, 256n.387,
257n.392, 258, 258n.395
Joined Cases C-451/19 and C-532/19 *Subdelegación del Gobierno en Toledo
(Séjour d'un membre de la famille—Ressources insuffisantes)*,
EU:C:2022:354 . . . . 247n.339, 251n.355, 254n.371, 257n.394
Case C-484/93 *Svensson and Gustavsson*, EU:C:1995:379. . . . . 50n.145
Case C-90/97 *Swaddling*, EU:C:1999:96 . . . . 399n.264
Case C-483/17 *Tarola*, EU:C:2019:309. . . . . 68n.257, 70n.265, 71n.267, 326n.360, 329n.377,
366n.68, 366n.69, 407n.314, 408n.318,
408n.324, 408n.326, 474n.14, 477n.37
Case C-69/14 *Târşia*, EU:C:2015:662. . . . . 550n.316
Case C-192/05 *Tas-Hagen and Tas*, EU:C:2006:676 . . . . 92n.406, 94n.426, 227n.225, 487–88n.103
Case C-480/08 *Teixeira*, EU:C:2010:83 . . . . 75n.287, 75n.289, 172n.184, 397n.254,
489n.111, 490n.120
Case C-418/11 *Texdata Software*, EU:C:2013:588 . . . . 432n.443
Case C-411/22 *Thermalhotel Fontana*, pending 512n.80
Case C-475/93 *Thévenon*, EU:C:1995:371. . . . . 362n.41
Case C-220/12 *Thiele Meneses*, EU:C:2013:683. . . . . 7n.29, 49n.141, 52n.163, 55n.181, 94n.431,
464n.138, 513n.86
Case C-221/17 *Tjebbes*, EU:C:2019:189 . . . . 40n.92, 114n.29, 115n.32, 115n.40, 115n.41, 116n.44,
116n.46, 117, 118, 119–20, 122n.87, 122n.92, 123–24n.101,
125, 130n.145, 226n.214, 233n.252
Case C-254/98 *TK-Heimdienst*, EU:C:2000:12. . . . . 80n.326
Case C-22/18 *TopFit and Biffi*, EU:C:2019:497 . . . . .46n.119, 50n.144, 89n.390
Joined Cases C-58/13 and C-59/13 *Torresi*, EU:C:2014:2088 . . . . 418n.373

Case C-456/02 *Trojani*, EU:C:2004:488 . . . . .55n.186, 280n.106, 353–54n.4, 358, 360n.30, 361, 361n.36, 362–63, 363n.46, 364n.49, 368, 381–82, 384–85, 386n.188, 390, 401n.275, 419, 421n.389, 423n.397, 423–24n.400, 425, 425n.405, 426n.408
Case C-145/09 *Tsakouridis*, EU:C:2010:708 . . . . 21n.118, 88n.379, 90n.394, 514, 515n.95, 515n.96, 515n.98, 516n.100, 528n.167, 529n.173, 530–31, 530n.178, 531n.182, 531n.183, 532, 533, 534n.209
Case C-520/04 *Turpeinen*, EU:C:2006:703 . . . . 13n.66, 487–88n.103
Case C-420/15 *U*, EU:C:2017:408. .13n.60, 13n.65, 42n.100, 49n.139, 479n.50
Joined Cases C-64/96 and C-65/96 *Uecker and Jacquet*, EU:C:1997:285 . . . . 82n.339, 227n.223
Case 15/69 *Ugliola*, EU:C:1969:46 . . . . 50n.145
Case 75/63 *Unger*, EU:C:1964:19 . . . . 30n.23, 366n.65
Case C-50/00 P *Unión de Pequeños Agricultores*, EU:C:2002:462 . . . . 545n.286
Case C-378/10 *VALE építési*, EU:C:2012:440 . . . . 549n.310
Case 33/74 *Van Binsbergen*, EU:C:1974:131 . . . . 30n.21, 340–41n.441
Case C-368/98 *Vanbraekel*, EU:C:2001:400. . . . . 54n.176
Case 100/63 *van der Veen*, EU:C:1964:65 . . . . 433n.453
Case 33/64 *van Dijk*, EU:C:1965:19 . . . . 31n.25
Case 41/74 *Van Duyn*, EU:C:1973:133. . . . . 502, 502n.23, 505n.40
Case 26/62 *Van Gend en Loos*, EU:C:1963:1 . . . . 1n.2, 129n.143
Case C-450/06 *Varec*, EU:C:2008:91 . . . . 543n.272
Joined Cases C-22/08 and C-23/08 *Vatsouras and Koupatantze*,
    EU:C:2009:344 . . . . 11n.47, 22n.128, 22n.129, 77n.304, 91n.400, 353–54n.4, 364n.55, 375nn.118–19, 379n.148, 390, 395, 397–98, 405n.296
Case C-35/98 *Verkooijen*, EU:C:2000:294 . . . . 54n.174
Case C-490/20 *VMA v Stolichna obshtina, rayon 'Pancharevo'*,
    EU:C:2021:1008 . . . . .7n.29, 11n.47, 47n.123, 48n.132, 90n.397, 141n.17, 153n.70, 163n.131, 172n.190, 201n.84, 267n.29, 267n.33, 267n.34, 353n.1, 353n.3
Case C-208/07 *Von Chamier-Glisczinski*, EU:C:2009:455 . . . . 14n.70, 51n.153
Case 5/88 *Wachauf*, EU:C:1989:321 . . . . 432n.439
Case C-91/08 *Wall*, EU:C:2010:182 . . . . 549n.310
Case 36/74 *Walrave and Koch*, EU:C:1974:140 . . . . 46n.119
Case 118/75 *Watson and Belmann*, EU:C:1976:106 . . . . 265–66n.21, 276n.83, 310n.275, 506n.46
Case C-372/04 *Watts*, EU:C:2006:325 . . . . 54n.176
Case C-32/93 *Webb*, EU:C:1994:300 . . . . 327n.364
Case C-70/94 *Werner*, EU:C:1995:328 . . . . 515n.96
Case C-118/20 *Wiener Landesregierung (Révocation d'une assurance de naturalisation)*,
    EU:C:2022:34 . . . . 38n.80, 40n.91, 84n.359, 114, 117, 117n.54, 117n.57, 118n.60, 119n.67, 119n.71, 120n.72, 120n.73, 120n.75, 122n.87, 122n.92, 125, 129–30
Case C-621/18 *Wightman*, EU:C:2018:999 . . . . 125n.107, 128, 128n.135
Case C-378/97 *Wijsenbeek*, EU:C:1999:439 . . . . 45, 46n.117, 266n.24, 301n.229
Case 221/81 *Wolf*, EU:C:1982:363 . . . . 515n.99
Case C-123/08 *Wolzenburg*, EU:C:2009:616 . . . . 52n.159, 97n.449, 103n.498, 297n.200, 446–47n.30, 467–68, 467n.155
Case C-505/19 *WS*, EU:C:2021:376 . . . . 80n.324
Case C-302/18 *X v Belgische Staat*, EU:C:2019:830 . . . . 282n.112
Case C-930/19 *X v Belgian State*, EU:C:2021:657 . . . . 11n.48, 48n.132, 143n.28, 338n.429, 339n.430, 340n.435, 436n.471
Case C-357/98 *Yiadom*, EU:C:2000:604 . . . . .360n.29, 499n.2, 546n.292
Case C-87/12 *Ymeraga*, EU:C:2013:291 . . . . 24n.139, 88n.385, 236n.269, 242n.305, 242n.307, 296–97n.197, 481n.60
Case C-221/07 *Zablocka-Weyhermüller*, EU:C:2008:681 . . . . 487–88n.103
Case C-543/12 *Zeman*, EU:C:2014:2143 . . . . 51n.155
Case C-554/13 *Zh and O*, EU:C:2015:377 . . . . 523n.139
Case C-200/02 *Zhu and Chen*, EU:C:2004:639 . . . . 35–36, 35n.52, 56n.192, 77n.306, 77n.308, 82, 82n.341, 117n.50, 123n.97, 131n.156, 171n.179, 172n.183, 175n.207, 176n.209, 229n.233, 231n.245, 232–33, 235,

236, 239n.284, 243, 255n.378, 267n.32, 274n.72, 281n.110,
282–83, 342–43n.450, 343n.451, 343n.453, 343n.454,
364n.55, 387n.193, 449n.44, 450n.49,
457n.89, 492n.133, 496n.148
Case C-371/08 *Ziebell*, EU:C:2011:809 .... 11n.50, 74n.281, 537n.230, 538n.231, 538n.233,
538n.238, 538n.241, 539n.244
Joined Cases C-424/10 and C-425/10 *Ziolkowski and Szeja*, EU:C:2011:866 .... 18n.101, 20n.112,
46n.118, 68n.257, 385–86, 385n.179, 414n.352, 416n.361,
425, 459n.103, 460–63, 460n.104, 460n.106,
460n.109, 461n.113, 490n.122
Case C-454/19 *ZW*, EU:C:2020:947... 141n.14
Case C-300/11 *ZZ*, EU:C:2013:363............ 22n.130, 84n.360, 142n.20, 434n.456, 542, 542n.265,
543n.268, 543n.270, 543n.271, 543n.272,
544n.273, 544n.274, 547n.299

CASE LAW OF THE COURT OF JUSTICE: NUMERICAL

Case 26/62 *Van Gend en Loos*, EU:C:1963:1 .... 1n.2, 129n.143
Joined Cases 28–30/62 *Da Costa*, EU:C:1963:6.. 23n.133
Case 13/63 *Italian Government v Commission*, EU:C:1963:20 .... 64n.238
Case 75/63 *Unger*, EU:C:1964:19 .... 30n.23, 366n.65
Case 92/63 *Nonnenmacher*, EU:C:1964:40 .... 30n.20, 30n.23
Case 100/63 *van der Veen*, EU:C:1964:65 .... 433n.453
Case 33/64 *van Dijk*, EU:C:1965:19 .... 31n.25
Case 44/65 *Singer*, EU:C:1965:212 .... 31n.26
Case 15/69 *Ugliola*, EU:C:1969:46 .... 50n.145
Case 1/72 *Frilli*, EU:C:1972:56 .... 396n.245
Case 76/72 *Scutari*, EU:C:1973:46 .... 33n.38
Case 8/74, *Dassonville*, EU:C:1974:82 .... 30n.21
Case 9/74 *Casagrande*, EU:C:1974:74 .... 33n.38
Case 33/74 *Van Binsbergen*, EU:C:1974:131 .... 30n.21, 340–41n.441
Case 36/74 *Walrave and Koch*, EU:C:1974:140.. 46n.119
Case 41/74 *Van Duyn*, EU:C:1973:133..................................... 502, 502n.23, 505n.40
Case 67/74 *Bonsignore*, EU:C:1975:34 .... 499n.2, 503n.27
Case 7/75 *Mr and Mrs F*, EU:C:1975:80..8n.34, 33n.37
Case 24/75 *Petroni*, EU:C:1971:129 .... 51n.154
Case 32/75 *Cristini*, EU:C:1975:120 .... 32n.32, 277n.88, 367n.77, 474n.15
Case 36/75 *Rutili*, EU:C:1975:137... 503n.25, 542n.261
Case 48/75 *Royer*, EU:C:1976:57......... 128n.133, 262n.8, 278n.95, 297n.198, 501–2n.15, 502n.16,
502n.17, 546n.291
Case 118/75 *Watson and Belmann*, EU:C:1976:106 .... 265–66n.21, 276n.83, 310n.275, 506n.46
Joined Cases 117/76 and 16/77 *Ruckdeschel*, EU:C:1977:160 .... 391n.217
Case 8/77 *Sagulo and Others*, EU:C:1977:131 .... 301n.229
Case 30/77 *Bouchereau*, EU:C:1977:172 .... 503n.24, 504n.31, 504n.33, 504n.34, 517n.102,
523n.138, 530n.178
Case 115/78 *Knoors*, EU:C:1979:31 .... 356n.10, 497n.150
Case 175/78 *Saunders*, EU:C:1979:88.........................31n.27, 81n.336, 228n.227, 266n.23
Case 98/79 *Pecastaing*, EU:C:1980:69.......................... 546n.289, 546n.290, 547n.297
Case 157/79 *Pieck*, EU:C:1980:179 .... 297n.198
Case 66/80 *International Chemical Corporation (ICI)*, EU:C:1981:102 .... 23n.133
Case 53/81 *Levin*, EU:C:1982:105... 275n.77, 408n.317
Case 65/81 *Reina*, EU:C:1982:6... 32n.33, 474n.15
Joined Cases 115 and 116/81 *Adoui and Cornuaille*, EU:C:1982:183............501–2n.15, 504n.35,
505n.38, 517n.102, 541n.252, 541n.257,
547n.296, 548n.304, 548n.306, 551n.322
Case 221/81 *Wolf*, EU:C:1982:363 .... 515n.99
Joined Cases 35/82 and 36/82 *Morson and Jhanjan*, EU:C:1982:368 .... 226n.217

Joined Cases 286/82 and 26/83 *Luisi and Carbone*, EU:C:1984:35 .... 29n.10, 34
Case 72/83 *Campus Oil*, EU:C:1984:256 .... 514n.92, 515n.96
Case 180/83 *Moser*, EU:C:1984:233 .... 227n.221
Case 249/83 *Hoeckx*, EU:C:1985:139 .... 277n.88, 417n.367, 474n.16
Case 267/83 *Diatta*, EU:C:1985:67 .... 155, 155n.84, 155n.85, 156n.90, 158, 345n.464, 451n.57
Case 293/83 *Gravier*, EU:C:1985:69 .... 35n.55, 65n.243, 287n.138, 367n.79
Case 41/84 *Pinna*, EU:C:1986:1 .... 473n.9, 478n.42
Case 137/84 *Heinrich*, EU:C:1985:335 .... 356n.11
Case 222/84 *Johnston*, EU:C:1986:206 .... 545n.286
Case 20/85 *Roviello*, EU:C:1988:283 .... 65n.244
Case 59/85 *Reed*, EU:C:1986:157 .... 162n.127, 163–66, 164n.138, 169n.165, 170–71,
                                                                      276n.80, 495n.143
Case 66/85 *Lawrie-Blum*, EU:C:1986:284 .... 32n.29, 275n.77, 478n.47
Case 139/85 *Kempf*, EU:C:1986:223 .... 277n.89, 293–94n.180
Case 316/85 *Lebon*, EU:C:1987:302 .... 175n.206, 176n.209, 293n.177, 367n.78, 368n.85
Case 12/86 *Demirel*, EU:C:1987:400 .... 538n.236
Case 24/86 *Blaizot*, EU:C:1988:43 .... 35n.56, 287n.139
Case 39/86 *Lair*, EU:C:1988:322 .... 32n.34, 36n.58, 287n.142, 323n.345, 363n.48, 367n.79
Case 63/86 *Commission v Italy*, EU:C:1988:9 .... 277n.90
Case 197/86 *Brown*, EU:C:1988:323 .... 323n.345, 363n.48, 367n.79
Case 222/86 *Heylens and Others*, EU:C:1987:442 .... 543n.270, 545n.286
Case 249/86 *Commission v Germany*, EU:C:1989:204 .... 141n.13
Case 263/86 *Humbel and Edel*, EU:C:1988:451 .... 35n.54, 287n.141, 483n.71
Case 143/87 *Stanton*, EU:C:1988:378 .... 30n.22
Case 186/87 *Cowan*, EU:C:1989:47 .... 34, 35n.49, 552n.326
Case 235/87 *Matteuci*, EU:C:1988:460 .... 32n.35
Case 321/87 *Commission v Belgium*, EU:C:1989:176 .... 301n.229
Case 389/87 *Echternach and Moritz*, EU:C:1989:130 .... 483n.72, 484n.75, 484n.77
Case 5/88 *Wachauf*, EU:C:1989:321 .... 432n.439
Joined Cases C-297/88 and C-197/89 *Dzodzi*, EU:C:1990:360 .... 546n.289
Case C-68/89 *Commission v Netherlands*, EU:C:1991:226 .... 297n.199
Case C-113/89 *Rush Portuguesa*, EU:C:1990:142 .... 279n.101
Case C-260/89 *ERT*, EU:C:1991:254 .... 432n.439
Case C-227/89 *Rönfeldt*, EU:C:1991:52 .... 362n.41
Case C-292/89 *Antonissen*, EU:C:1991:80 .... 29n.11, 130n.148, 291–94, 292n.170, 292n.172,
                                                        293–94n.180, 294n.186, 295, 296n.196, 366–67
Case C-357/89 *Raulin*, EU:C:1992:87 .... 36n.57, 287n.140
Case C-363/89 *Roux*, EU:C:1991:41 .... 266n.23, 325n.350, 328n.373
Case C-376/89 *Giagounidis*, EU:C:1991:99 .... 265n.19
Case C-76/90 *Säger*, EU:C:1991:331 .... 34n.44
Case C-159/90 *Grogan*, EU:C:1991:378 .... 80n.325
Case C-295/90 *Parliament v Council*, EU:C:1992:294 .... 36n.61
Case C-369/90 *Micheletti*, EU:C:1992:295 .... 93n.422, 110–13, 110n.5, 110n.6, 117n.50, 118n.59,
                                                            121n.86, 122–23n.95, 129–30, 343n.453, 343n.455
Case C-370/90 *Singh*, EU:C:1992:296 .... 141n.13, 155n.86, 340–41n.441, 471–72n.5, 485,
                                                            485n.86, 486–88, 486n.94, 490–91, 495–96, 497n.150
Case C-62/91 *Gray*, EU:C:1992:177 .... 51n.152
Case C-111/91 *Commission v Luxembourg*, EU:C:1993:92 .... 32n.31, 277n.88, 474n.17
Joined Cases C-267/91 and C-268/91 *Keck and Mithouard*, EU:C:1993:905 .... 439n.484
Case C-19/92 *Kraus*, EU:C:1993:125 .... 34n.46, 356n.10
Case C-419/92 *Scholz*, EU:C:1994:62 .... 134n.176
Case C-32/93 *Webb*, EU:C:1994:300 .... 327n.364
Case C-47/93 *Commission v Belgium*, EU:C:1994:181 .... 35n.56, 287n.139, 459n.99
Case C-279/93 *Schumacker*, EU:C:1995:31 .... 93n.421
Case C-308/93 *Cabanis-Issarte*, EU:C:1996:169 .... 140n.11
Case C-312/93 *Peterbroeck*, EU:C:1995:437 .... 549n.310
Case C-415/93 *Bosman*, EU:C:1995:463 .... 13n.59, 46n.119

Case C-475/93 *Thévenon*, EU:C:1995:371 . . . . 362n.41
Case C-484/93 *Svensson and Gustavsson*, EU:C:1995:379 . . . . 50n.145
Case C-7/94 *Gaal*, EU:C:1995:118 . . . . 484n.78
Case C-55/94 *Gebhard*, EU:C:1995:411 . . . . 33n.40, 34n.46, 87n.375
Case C-70/94 *Werner*, EU:C:1995:328 . . . . 515n.96
Case C-107/94 *Asscher*, EU:C:1996:251 . . . . 275n.77
Case C-175/94 *Gallagher*, EU:C:1995:415 . . . . 546n.290
Case C-193/94 *Skanavi and Chryssanthakopoulos*, EU:C:1996:70 . . . . 13n.63
Case C-206/94 *Paletta*, EU:C:1996:182 . . . . 497n.152
Joined Cases C-245/94 and C-312/94 *Hoever and Zachow*, EU:C:1996:379 . . . . 399n.263, 474n.13
Case C-278/94 *Commission v Belgium*, EU:C:1996:321 . . . . 293n.178, 293n.179, 367n.80, 368n.84,
369n.91, 459n.99
Case C-336/94 *Dafeki*, EU:C:1997:579 . . . . 350n.503
Joined Cases C-65/95 and C-111/95 *Shingara and Radiom*, EU:C:1997:300 . . . . . . 504n.37, 546n.289
Case C-285/95 *Kol*, EU:C:1997:280 . . . . 344n.460, 533n.198
Case C-299/95 *Kremzow*, EU:C:1997:254 . . . . 79n.318, 80–81, 228n.226
Case C-344/95 *Commission v Belgium*, EU:C:1997:81 . . . . 294n.182, 303n.234
Case C-354/95 *National Farmers' Union*, EU:C:1997:379 . . . . 132n.159
Case C-391/95 *Kadiman*, EU:C:1997:205 . . . . 156n.93
Joined Cases C-64/96 and C-65/96 *Uecker and Jacquet*, EU:C:1997:285 . . . . 82n.339, 227n.223
Case C-85/96 *Martínez Sala*, EU:C:1998:217 . . . . 18n.103, 19n.109, 22n.127, 47n.124, 59n.207,
79, 128n.133, 150n.54, 288n.147, 296n.196, 297n.200, 323n.345, 353n.2,
353–54n.4, 358–59, 358n.18, 358n.20, 359n.24, 360–61, 361n.34, 362–63,
362n.37, 363n.46, 368–69n.88, 372n.105, 380–82, 383, 384–85,
386–87, 390, 401n.275, 402n.278, 419, 421, 422–23, 425, 467n.155
Case C-158/96 *Kohll*, EU:C:1998:171 . . . . 54n.176, 393n.230
Case C-185/96 *Commission v Greece*, EU:C:1997:425 . . . . 18n.100
Case C-274/96 *Bickel and Franz*, EU:C:1988:563 . . . . 35n.49, 35n.50
Case C-309/96 *Annibaldi*, EU:C:1997:631 . . . . 432n.439
Case C-336/96 *Gilly*, EU:C:1998:221 . . . . 14n.74, 131, 131n.151
Case C-348/96 *Calfa*, EU:C:1999:6 . . . . 504n.32, 506n.52, 516n.100, 548n.304
Case C-90/97 *Swaddling*, EU:C:1999:96 . . . . 399n.264
Case C-212/97 *Centros*, EUC:1999:126 . . . . . . 340–41n.441, 341n.445, 343n.452, 343n.456, 344n.461,
497n.153
Case C-234/97 *Fernández de Bobadilla*, EU:C:1999:367 . . . . 356n.10
Case C-273/97 *Sirdar*, EU:C:1999:523 . . . . 515n.95
Case C-323/97 *Commission v Belgium*, EU:C:1998:347 . . . . 202n.92
Case C-340/97 *Nazli*, EU:C:2000:77 . . . . 539n.243
Case C-378/97 *Wijsenbeek*, EU:C:1999:439 . . . . 45, 46n.117, 266n.24, 301n.229
Case C-35/98 *Verkooijen*, EU:C:2000:294 . . . . 54n.174
Case C-190/98, *Graf*, EU:C:2000:49 . . . . 34n.41
Case C-224/98 *D'Hoop*, EU:C:2002:432 . . . . 6n.19, 46n.118, 50n.143, 52, 52n.160, 78n.317,
85n.362, 94n.430, 369n.90, 369n.92, 370, 416n.358,
434n.454, 476n.29, 488n.107, 489n.109
Case C-254/98 *TK-Heimdienst*, EU:C:2000:12 . . . . 80n.326
Case C-281/98 *Angonese*, EU:C:2000:296 . . . . 46n.120, 291n.167
Case C-285/98 *Kreil*, EU:C:2000:2 . . . . 515n.95
Case C-357/98 *Yiadom*, EU:C:2000:604 . . . . 360n.29, 499n.2, 546n.292
Case C-367/98 *Commission v Portugal*, EU:C:2002:326 . . . . 34n.45
Case C-368/98 *Vanbraekel*, EU:C:2001:400 . . . . 54n.176
Case C-398/98 *Commission v Greece*, EU:C:2001:565 . . . . 515n.96
Case C-411/98 *Ferlini*, EU:C:2000:530 . . . . 46n.119
Case C-423/98 *Albore*, EU:C:2000:401 . . . . 514n.92, 515n.95, 515n.96
Case C-424/98 *Commission v Italy*, EU:C:2000:287 . . . . 37n.73, 84n.356, 303n.234, 308n.264
Case C-43/99 *Leclere and Deaconescu*, EU:C:2001:303 . . . . 324n.346, 368n.81
Case C-54/99 *Église de scientology*, EU:C:2000:124 . . . . 515n.93
Case C-63/99 *Gloszczuk*, EU:C:2001:488 . . . . 344n.460

Case C-110/99 *Emsland-Stärke*, EU:C:2000:695, paras 52–53 .... 341n.443, 344n.461
Joined Cases C-122/99 and C-125/99 *D and Sweden v Council*, EU:C:2001:304 .... 151n.61
Case C-135/99 *Elsen*, EU:C:2000:647 .... 475n.20
Case C-184/99 *Grzelczyk*, EU:C:2001:458 .... 7n.29, 14n.76, 22n.128, 38n.79, 55n.186, 56n.188,
    57–58, 59n.205, 76n.301, 83n.346, 106n.516, 112n.16, 228n.231, 262n.6, 274n.72,
    280n.106, 281n.109, 288n.146, 288n.148, 288n.151, 289, 319n.327, 353n.1,
    353n.2, 353–54n.4, 358, 359, 359n.24, 360, 360n.26, 361, 362n.37,
    362n.38, 363n.45, 363n.46, 364n.56, 368, 368–69n.88, 373–74,
    377, 380–81, 381–82, 386–87, 388n.198, 390, 394n.240,
    401n.275, 407, 413n.349, 414, 419, 426,
    434n.454, 437n.476, 464n.138
Case C-192/99 *Kaur*, EU:C:2001:106 .... 110n.5, 122n.92, 194n.33, 343n.453
Case C-257/99 *Givane and Others*, EU:C:2003:8 .... 322n.335, 322n.337, 326n.362
Case C-268/99 *Jany*, EU:C:2001:616 .... 531n.185
Case C-390/99 *Canal Satélite Digital*, EU:C:2002:34 .... 33n.39
Joined Cases C-393/99 and C-394/99 *Hervein and Hervillie*, EU:C:2002:182 .... 90n.393, 473n.11
Case C-413/99 *Baumbast and R*, EU:C:2002:493 ..... 7n.26, 45n.116, 58, 58n.198, 60n.216, 76n.300,
    76n.302, 155n.89, 156, 156n.92, 157, 231n.245, 235, 239, 261n.3, 280n.106,
    283, 283n.122, 284, 329n.382, 332n.389, 353–54n.4, 358, 364n.53,
    364n.55, 364n.58, 381–82, 387n.193, 397–98, 419, 421, 438,
    484–85, 484n.74, 484n.76, 485n.82
Case C-459/99 *MRAX*, EU:C:2002:461 .... 141n.13, 160n.114, 297n.201, 300n.225, 311n.277,
    311n.280, 356n.13, 356n.14, 365n.62,
    502n.22, 507n.58
Case C-50/00 P *Unión de Pequeños Agricultores*, EU:C:2002:462 .... 545n.286
Case C-60/00 *Carpenter*, EU:C:2002:434 ..... 81n.334, 141n.13, 297n.201, 479n.51, 480, 480n.57, 481
Joined Cases C-482/01 and C-493/01 *Orfanopoulos and Oliveri*, EU:C:2004:262 .... 49n.142,
    74n.284, 328n.369, 499n.2, 499n.3, 501–2n.15, 504n.34,
    506n.51, 507n.56, 507n.60, 516n.100, 530n.178, 537n.230
Case C-100/01 *Oteiza Olazabal*, EU:C:2002:712 .... 13n.62, 500n.5, 504n.37, 506n.50
Case C-109/01 *Akrich*, EU:C:2003:491 .... 89n.388, 96n.444, 96n.446, 159n.106, 159n.108, 160,
    161–62, 342n.448, 357n.15, 393n.237,
    496n.148, 496n.149, 497
Case C-186/01 *Dory*, EU:C:2003:146 .... 515n.95
Case C-299/01 *Commission v Luxembourg*, EU:C:2002:394 .... 171n.177, 277n.90, 406n.298, 474n.14
Case C-388/01 *Commission v Italy*, EU:C:2003:30 .... 65n.244
Case C-405/01 *Colegio de Oficiales de la Marina Mercante Española*, EU:C:2003:515 .... 501n.11
Joined Cases C-502/01 and C-31/02 *Gaumain-Cerri and Barth*, EU:C:2004:413 .... 275n.78
Case C-36/02 *Omega*, EU:C:2004:614 .... 33n.40
Case C-138/02 *Collins*, EU:C:2004:172 .... 7n.29, 14n.73, 57n.194, 78n.316, 91n.399, 91n.401,
    130n.147, 130n.148, 362n.37, 368n.82, 368n.86, 369n.89, 370,
    370n.96, 374–75, 396, 397–98, 438–39, 445n.27
Case C-148/02 *Garcia Avello*, EU:C:2003:539 .... 48n.132, 78n.316, 79n.320, 94n.423, 131n.154,
    131n.155, 131n.158, 132, 132n.161, 133–34, 196n.47, 229n.233,
    235n.268, 258n.398, 343n.455, 362n.38, 464n.138
Case C-200/02 *Zhu and Chen*, EU:C:2004:639 .... 35–36, 35n.52, 56n.192, 77n.306, 77n.308, 82,
    82n.341, 117n.50, 123n.97, 131n.156, 171n.179, 172n.183, 175n.207, 176n.209,
    229n.233, 231n.245, 232–33, 235, 236, 239n.284, 243, 255n.378, 267n.32,
    274n.72, 281n.110, 282–83, 342–43n.450, 343n.451, 343n.453,
    343n.454, 364n.55, 387n.193, 449n.44, 450n.49,
    457n.89, 492n.133, 496n.148
Case C-224/02 *Pusa*, EU:C:2004:273 .... 20n.115, 48n.136, 60n.212, 78n.317, 85n.362, 94n.424
Case C-234/02 P *Lamberts*, EU:C:2004:174 .... 220n.191
Case C-287/02 *Commission v Spain*, EU:C:2005:368 .... 550n.318
Case C-441/02 *Commission v Germany*, EU:C:2006:253 .... 501n.12, 503n.27
Case C-442/02 *CaixaBank France*, EU:C:2004:586 .... 34n.42

Case C-456/02 *Trojani*, EU:C:2004:488 .... 55n.186, 280n.106, 353–54n.4, 358, 360n.30, 361, 361n.36, 362–63, 363n.46, 364n.49, 368, 381–82, 384–85, 386n.188, 390, 401n.275, 419, 421n.389, 423n.397, 423–24n.400, 425, 425n.405, 426n.408
Case C-20/03 *Burmanjer and Others*, EU:C:2005:307 .... 33n.40
Case C-147/03 *Commission v Austria*, EU:C:2005:427 .... 50n.145, 61, 61n.218, 61n.225, 63, 64n.236, 65n.243
Case C-152/03 *Ritter-Coulais*, EU:C:2006:123 .... 275n.78
Case C-157/03 *Commission v Spain*, EU:C:2005:225 .... 160n.115
Case C-209/03 *Bidar*, EU:C:2005:169 .... 38n.78, 56n.189, 61n.221, 92n.404, 92n.405, 280n.106, 288n.149, 360n.29, 361n.33, 362n.37, 363, 363n.48, 364n.49, 364n.51, 364n.52, 373, 373n.106, 376–77nn.130–31, 387n.189, 393n.230, 401n.275, 413, 421n.389, 438–39
Case C-215/03 *Oulane*, EU:C:2005:95 .... 177n.219, 266n.24, 271n.51
Case C-293/03 *My*, EU:C:2004:821 .... 41, 42
Case C-403/03 *Schempp*, EU:C:2005:446...48n.132, 82, 82n.342, 94n.425, 110n.4, 150n.56, 234n.262
Case C-408/03 *Commission v Belgium*, EU:C:2006:192........ 20n.113, 53n.169, 56n.192, 282n.114, 297n.198, 387n.193, 459n.98, 502n.16
Case C-503/03 *Commission v Spain*, EU:C:2006:74 .... 309n.268, 309n.269, 503n.26
Case C-145/04 *Spain v United Kingdom*, EU:C:2006:543 .... 21n.122, 76n.299, 193n.25, 193n.26, 194n.30, 194n.33, 194n.34, 194n.35, 195, 196, 197, 197n.54, 197n.56, 199–200
Case C-258/04 *Ioannidis*, EU:C:2005:559 .... 13n.66
Case C-300/04 *Eman and Sevinger*, EU:C:2006:545......... 110n.5, 195, 195n.38, 195n.42, 195n.44, 196, 197, 201n.82, 258n.396, 258n.398
Case C-372/04 *Watts*, EU:C:2006:325 .... 54n.176
Joined Cases C-392/04 and C-422/04 *i-21 Germany and Arcor*, EU:C:2006:586 .... 549n.310
Case C-406/04 *De Cuyper*, EU:C:2006:491 .... 75n.291, 487–88n.103
Case C-452/04 *Fidium Finanz*, EU:C:2006:631... 33n.40
Case C-467/04 *Gasparini and Others*, EU:C:2006:610 .... 80n.324
Case C-520/04 *Turpeinen*, EU:C:2006:703 .... 13n.66, 487–88n.103
Case C-1/05 *Jia*, EU:C:2007:1 .... 160n.109, 176n.213, 177–78, 177n.216, 177n.218, 177n.219, 177n.220
Case C-10/05 *Mattern and Cikotic*, EU:C:2006:220 .... 149n.53
Case C-76/05 *Schwarz and Gootjes-Schwarz*, EU:C:2007:492.................... 13n.64, 171n.180
Case C-142/05 *Mickelsson and Roos*, EU:C:2009:336.................................... 34n.43
Case C-192/05 *Tas-Hagen and Tas*, EU:C:2006:676 .... 92n.406, 94n.426, 227n.225, 487–88n.103
Case C-212/05 *Hartmann*, EU:C:2007:437 .... 475n.21, 476–77
Case C-213/05 *Geven*, EU:C:2007:438.. 475n.24
Case C-287/05 *Hendrix*, EU:C:2007:494 .... 486n.93
Case C-291/05 *Eind*, EU:C:2007:771 ...... 14n.71, 141n.13, 313n.291, 486n.96, 487, 490–91, 495–96
Joined Cases C-396/05, C-419/05 and C-450/05 *Habelt, Möser and Wachter*, EU:C:2007:810 .... 54n.178
Joined Cases C-402/05 P and C-415/05 P *Kadi and Al Barakaat International Foundation*, EU:C:2008:461 .... 543n.270, 543n.271
Joined Cases C-11/06 and 12/06 *Morgan and Bucher*, EU:C:2007:626 .... 52n.161, 54n.177, 78n.316, 79n.319, 80n.327, 92n.412, 94n.431, 487–88n.103
Case C-50/06 *Commission v Netherlands*, EU:C:2007:325 ...... 84n.358, 356n.14, 365n.60, 365n.62, 365n.63, 502n.19, 505n.44, 506n.53, 540n.247
Case C-104/06 *Commission v Sweden*, EU:C:2007:40 .... 325n.351
Case C-244/06 *Dynamic Medien*, EU:C:2008:85 .... 141n.14
Case C-251/06 *ING. AUER*, EU:C:2007:658 .... 20–21n.117
Case C-349/06 *Polat*, EU:C:2007:581.. 73n.279, 521n.124
Case C-353/06 *Grunkin and Paul*, EU:C:2008:559.............. 13n.61, 51n.151, 79n.322, 93n.420, 131n.157, 196n.47, 235n.268, 267n.33, 422n.395
Case C-450/06 *Varec*, EU:C:2008:91 .... 543n.272

Case C-499/06 *Nerkowska*, EU:C:2008:300 .... 85n.362, 93n.413
Case C-524/06 *Huber*, EU:C:2008:724 .... 7n.29, 77n.305, 305n.247, 306n.250, 306n.254, 437–38,
                                                                                              464n.138
Case C-33/07 *Jipa*, EU:C:2008:396 .... 263n.10, 505n.41, 509n.69, 515n.93, 520n.122, 521n.126
Case C-94/07 *Raccanelli*, EU:C:2008:425 .... 291n.167
Case C-141/07 *Commission v Germany*, EU:C:2008:492 .... 54n.175
Case C-158/07 *Förster*, EU:C:2008:630 .... 60n.211, 326n.362, 362n.38, 377n.135, 387n.189,
                                                                        393n.230, 401n.275, 403–4
Case C-208/07 *Von Chamier-Glisczinski*, EU:C:2009:455 .... 14n.70, 51n.153
Case C-221/07 *Zablocka-Weyhermüller*, EU:C:2008:681 .... 487–88n.103
Case C-269/07 *Commission v Germany*, EU:C:2009:527 .... 474n.12
Case C-544/07 *Rüffler*, EU:C:2009:258 .... 22n.130, 434n.454
Case C-551/07 *Sahin*, EU:C:2008:75 .... 160n.111, 509n.71
Case C-555/07 *Kücükdeveci*, EU:C:2010:21 .... 433n.452
Case C-9/08 *Donnici*, EU:C:2009:44 .... 200n.79
Joined Cases C-22/08 and C-23/08 *Vatsouras and Koupatantze*,
    EU:C:2009:344 .... 11n.47, 22n.128, 22n.129, 77n.304, 91n.400, 353–54n.4, 364n.55,
                                             375nn.118–19, 379n.148, 390, 395, 397–98, 405n.296
Case C-61/08 *Commission v Greece*, EU:C:2011:340 .... 501n.11
Case 63/08 *Pontin*, EU:C:2009:666 .... 549n.311
Case C-73/08 *Bressol and Others*, EU:C:2010:181 ...50n.148, 61n.222, 63, 66n.245, 66n.247, 359n.21
Case C-89/08 P *Commission v Ireland and Others*, EU:C:2009:742 .... 543n.272
Case C-91/08 *Wall*, EU:C:2010:182 .... 549n.310
Case C-103/08 *Gottwald*, EU:C:2009:597 .... 13n.61, 52n.165, 92n.412
Case C-123/08 *Wolzenburg*, EU:C:2009:616 .... 52n.159, 97n.449, 103n.498, 297n.200,
                                                                  446–47n.30, 467–68, 467n.155
Case C-127/08 *Metock and Others*, EU:C:2008:449 .... 8n.36, 22, 48n.135, 70n.262, 70n.263,
               77n.307, 84n.358, 86n.371, 86n.372, 96n.444, 127n.127, 139n.2, 141n.13, 142n.18,
                 142n.20, 144n.29, 154n.81, 160n.110, 160n.111, 160n.112, 160n.113, 160n.115,
                  160n.116, 161n.121, 161n.122, 162n.124, 162n.126, 230–31n.242, 316n.311,
                       340–41n.441, 341n.442, 357n.15, 438n.483, 448n.35, 448n.38,
                                                        464n.136, 509n.70, 509n.71, 520n.122
Case C-135/08 *Rottmann*, EU:C:2010:104 .... 7n.29, 8n.32, 40n.92, 41n.96, 42, 83n.347, 93n.415,
                   94n.432, 109n.2, 111n.7, 111n.10, 111n.13, 112, 112n.15, 112n.16, 112n.17,
                   112n.18, 112n.20, 113–15, 113n.24, 116n.49, 118–19, 119n.71, 120n.72, 122,
                              122n.87, 123n.99, 125, 129–30, 188–89, 188n.7, 199n.67,
                                             229n.233, 230n.239, 232–33, 232n.248, 232n.250
Case C-303/08, *Bozkurt*, EU:C:2010:800 .... 538n.232, 539n.243
Case C-310/08 *Ibrahim*, EU:C:2010:89 .... 75n.288, 75n.289, 294n.183, 329n.381, 331n.388,
                                                                        397n.254, 416n.360, 489n.111
Case C-371/08 *Ziebell*, EU:C:2011:809 .... 11n.50, 74n.281, 537n.230, 538n.231, 538n.233,
                                                                        538n.238, 538n.241, 539n.244
Case C-480/08 *Teixeira*, EU:C:2010:83 ...75n.287, 75n.289, 172n.184, 397n.254, 489n.111, 490n.120
Case C-578/08 *Chakroun*, EU:C:2010:117 .... 388n.196
Case C-578/08 *Chakroun*, EU:C:2009:776 .... 280n.105
Case C-34/09 *Ruiz Zambrano*, EU:C:2011:124 .... 6n.17, 22n.125, 24n.138, 41n.95, 42, 53, 79,
                 82–84, 83n.346, 83n.347, 83n.348, 83–84n.353, 89, 94–95, 96–97, 99, 112n.15,
                   118–19, 132n.162, 140n.9, 145n.37, 187–88n.3, 188n.8, 196, 230n.234, 230n.235,
                       230n.240, 231, 232, 232n.247, 233, 234, 235, 236–37, 238–40, 241–42,
                             243, 244, 247, 248, 249, 254n.376, 255n.378, 256n.384, 258–59,
                                                                431n.436, 437n.472, 471–72n.5
Joined Cases C-57/09 and C-101/09 *B and D*, EU:C:2010:661 .... 522n.135
Case C-145/09 *Tsakouridis*, EU:C:2010:708 .... 21n.118, 88n.379, 90n.394, 514, 515n.95,
                                        515n.96, 515n.98, 516n.100, 528n.167, 529n.173, 530–31,
                                            530n.178, 531n.182, 531n.183, 532, 533, 534n.209
Case C-162/09 *Lassal*, EU:C:2010:592 ...... 22n.132, 46n.118, 68n.257, 84n.358, 87n.374, 104n.503,
                 383n.167, 384n.169, 441n.4, 445n.23, 453n.69, 456n.80, 458n.94, 462–63, 464n.136

Case C-173/09 *Elchinov*, EU:C:2010:581 .... 54n.176
Case C-208/09 *Sayn-Wittgenstein*, EU:C:2010:806 ...... 13n.61, 13n.65, 48n.134, 51n.151, 79n.322,
94n.427, 502n.23, 513n.84, 513n.85
Case C-325/09 *Dias*, EU:C:2011:498 ....92n.408, 303n.240, 384, 385–86, 385n.178, 445n.23,
454n.72, 459n.97, 459n.99, 459n.100, 460–62, 463n.129, 464n.134, 533n.197
Case C-348/09 *PI*, EU:C:2012:300 ...... 515n.93, 517, 530, 531n.179, 531n.183, 531n.184, 531n.185,
531n.186, 532n.188, 532n.189, 533n.204
Joined Cases C-372/09 and C-373/09 *Peñarroja Fa*, EU:C:2011:156............ 543n.269, 545n.288
Case C-379/09 *Casteels*, EU:C:2011:131 .... 46n.120
Case C-391/09 *Runevič-Vardyn and Wardyn*, EU:C:2011:291 .... 38n.80, 48n.131, 51n.150,
78n.316, 79n.322, 464n.138
Case C-398/09 *Lady & Kid and Others*, EU:C:2011:540 .... 514n.90
Case C-434/09 *McCarthy*, EU:C:2011:277 .... 20n.116, 21, 42n.103, 70n.263, 79n.323, 82n.340,
84n.355, 87n.374, 131n.156, 132n.163, 132n.165, 133, 133n.167, 136n.186,
145n.38, 146n.39, 152–53, 233, 233n.257, 234n.261, 234n.263,
235n.266, 235n.268, 236, 238–40, 241, 245, 255n.378
Case C-503/09 *Stewart*, EU:C:2011:500............. 52n.164, 55n.182, 85n.362, 90n.397, 431n.435,
434n.454, 487–88n.103
Case C-542/09 *Commission v Netherlands*, EU:C:2012:346 .... 60n.217, 91n.402, 379n.142,
428n.419, 445n.26, 463n.128, 474n.18, 477n.34, 478n.44, 490n.117
Case C-69/10 *Samba Diouf*, EU:C:2011:524... 545n.287
Case C-378/10 *VALE építési*, EU:C:2012:440 .... 549n.310
Case C-571/10 *Kamberaj*, EU:C:2012:233......................... 433n.451, 434–35, 435n.461
Case C-591/10 *Littlewoods Retail and Others*, EU:C:2012:478 .... 549n.311
Case C-364/10 *Hungary v Slovakia*, EU:C:2012:630.................................... 21n.122
Case C-430/10 *Gaydarov*, EU:C:2011:749............. 51n.157, 266n.22, 509n.69, 510n.72, 515n.93,
543n.269, 545n.286, 545n.287, 545n.288
Joined Cases C-424/10 and C-425/10 *Ziolkowski and Szeja*, EU:C:2011:866 .... 18n.101, 20n.112,
46n.118, 68n.257, 385–86, 385n.179, 414n.352, 416n.361,
425, 459n.103, 460–63, 460n.104, 460n.106,
460n.109, 461n.113, 490n.122
Case C-434/10 *Aladzhov*, EU:C:2011:750 .... 51n.158, 55n.183, 265n.18, 509n.69, 513n.88,
514n.90, 520n.122, 521n.126
Case C-522/10 *Reichel-Albert*, EU:C:2012:475... 14n.70
Case C-617/10 *Åkerberg Fransson*, EU:C:2013:105 .... 88n.381, 250n.353, 432, 432n.440,
433n.449, 433n.451
Case C-15/11 *Sommer*, EU:C:2012:731 .... 46n.118
Case C-40/11 *Iida*, EU:C:2012:691........ 41n.98, 80n.329, 81, 81n.332, 84n.354, 85n.364, 116n.45,
148n.49, 153n.70, 155n.87, 156n.91, 157, 158, 176n.210, 189n.9, 189n.11, 226n.215,
228n.226, 235n.264, 236n.269, 236n.270, 240n.290, 334n.401, 433n.451, 451n.57, 481n.60
Case C-75/11 *Commission v Austria*, EU:C:2012:605 .... 14n.77, 20n.113, 77n.312, 92n.412,
94n.428, 359n.21, 359n.22, 379n.148, 381n.159, 431, 431n.435, 432
Case C-83/11 *Rahman*, EU:C:2012:519............... 84n.357, 166, 166n.146, 166n.149, 166n.150,
167, 167n.152, 168, 180n.230, 180n.232, 181, 181n.237,
182, 182n.240, 183n.246, 183n.247, 183n.248, 183n.249,
305n.244, 314n.297, 314n.301
Joined Cases C-147/11 and C-148/11 *Czop and Punakova*,
EU:C:2012:538 .... 84n.361, 172n.184, 459n.103, 490n.116
Joined Cases C-197/11 and C-203/11 *Libert*, EU:C:2013:288........................... 22n.132
Case C-221/11 *Demirkan*, EU:C:2013:583 .... 538n.236
Case C-249/11 *Byankov*, EU:C:2012:608................. 84n.359, 521n.126, 549n.308, 549n.310,
549n.311, 549n.312
Case C-256/11 *Dereci and Others*, EU:C:2011:734..... 75n.293, 81n.337, 85n.364, 88n.385, 89n.388,
188n.5, 235n.265, 236–37n.271, 237n.275, 238–39, 239–40n.288,
240–41, 241n.297, 244, 245, 247n.338, 248n.341, 249
Case C-300/11 *ZZ*, EU:C:2013:363............ 22n.130, 84n.360, 142n.20, 434n.456, 542, 542n.265,
543n.268, 543n.270, 543n.271, 543n.272, 544n.273, 544n.274, 547n.299

Joined Cases C-356/11 and C-357/11 *O and S*, EU:C:2012:776 . . . . 84n.355, 85n.364, 85n.365,
  117n.51, 148n.46, 172n.187, 183n.245, 238–39,
  238n.281, 240n.289, 240n.292, 241n.296, 243, 243n.310, 245
Case C-367/11 *Prete*, EU:C:2012:668 . . . . 13n.66, 53n.166, 92n.407, 359n.22, 375n.122
Case C-418/11 *Texdata Software*, EU:C:2013:588 . . . . 432n.443
Case C-451/11 *Dülger*, EU:C:2012:504 . . . . 73n.280
Case C-472/11 *Banif Plus Bank*, 2013:88 . . . . 543n.272
Joined Cases C-523/11 and C-585/11 *Prinz and Seeberger*, EU:C:2013:524 . . . . 93n.414, 94n.431,
  411n.338
Case C-529/11 *Alarape and Tijani*, EU:C:2013:290 . . . . 22n.132, 75n.290, 135n.184,
  156n.94, 259n.400, 331n.386, 332n.392, 385–86, 386n.183,
  397n.253, 450n.51, 461n.118, 462n.120, 463,
  490n.119, 490n.121, 490n.122
Case C-546/11 *Dansk Jurist—og Økonomforbund*, EU:C:2013:603 . . . . 393n.230
Case C-20/12 *Giersch*, EU:C:2013:411 . . . . 54n.180, 475n.23, 475n.25, 476–77
Case C-45/12 *Hadj Ahmed*, EU:C:2013:390 . . . . 432n.442
Case C-46/12 *LN*, EU:C:2013:97 . . . . 15n.79, 77n.312, 290n.162, 290n.164, 341–42, 342n.449,
  379n.144, 381n.159, 393n.237, 408n.317
Case C-86/12 *Alokpa and Moudoulou*, EU:C:2013:645 . . . . . . 42n.101, 171n.181, 176n.210, 233n.254,
  235n.264, 239n.283, 239n.285, 243–44, 245, 249,
  255n.378, 281n.111, 481n.60
Case C-87/12 *Ymeraga*, EU:C:2013:291 . . . . 24n.139, 88n.385, 236n.269, 242n.305, 242n.307,
  296–97n.197, 481n.60
Case C-93/12 *Agrokonsulting-04*, EU:C:2013:432 . . . . 550n.316
Case C-140/12 *Brey*, EU:C:2013:565 . . . . 53, 54n.173, 55n.187, 56n.190, 280n.105, 280n.106,
  283n.119, 308n.259, 308n.262, 353–54n.4, 386, 386n.185, 387n.190, 388n.194,
  388n.197, 389n.206, 393, 394, 395, 395n.242, 397n.256, 400, 400n.271, 401n.273,
  401n.274, 401n.276, 403–4, 405n.296, 411–13, 411n.343, 427n.412, 430, 438n.479
Case C-220/12 *Thiele Meneses*, EU:C:2013:683 . . . . 7n.29, 49n.141, 52n.163, 55n.181, 94n.431,
  464n.138, 513n.86
Case C-233/12 *Gardella*, EU:C:2013:449 . . . . 87n.377
Case C-275/12 *Elrick*, EU:C:2013:684 . . . . 78n.316, 94n.431
Case C-378/12 *Onuekwere*, EU:C:2014:13 . . . . 77n.311, 92n.408, 104n.504, 156–59, 156n.94, 157n.95,
  450n.51, 451–52, 451n.52, 463, 463n.131, 464, 464n.134,
  464n.135, 464n.139, 466–67, 534n.212, 535n.214
Case C-400/12 *MG*, EU:C:2014:9 . . . . 92n.409, 142n.20, 467n.151, 529, 534n.208, 534n.210,
  534n.211, 535n.213, 535n.216
Case C-423/12 *Reyes*, EU:C:2014:16 . . . . 76n.303, 176n.211, 176n.213, 176n.214, 177–78,
  177n.218, 177n.220, 177n.221, 181n.237, 305n.243, 314n.296
Case C-456/12 *O and B*, EU:C:2014:135 . . . . 17n.90, 70n.263, 142n.21, 273n.66, 313n.291,
  341n.444, 348n.494, 482, 482n.65, 491n.123, 491n.128, 492n.130,
  492n.131, 493, 493n.135, 494, 495–96, 497, 535n.218
Case C-457/12 *S and G*, EU:C:2014:36 . . . . 81n.333, 150n.57, 276n.82, 480n.59, 481n.61, 482, 493
Case C-507/12 *Saint Prix*, EU:C:2014:2007 . . . . 22n.130, 74n.283, 171n.176, 256n.385, 294n.184,
  296n.196, 327n.363, 327n.365, 328, 328n.369, 328n.370, 339, 408n.319,
  409n.329, 409n.330, 418n.375, 453n.66, 471n.3
Case C-543/12 *Zeman*, EU:C:2014:2143 . . . . 51n.155
  Opinion 2/13, EU:C:2014:2454 . . . . 67n.251
Joined Cases C-58/13 and C-59/13 *Torresi*, EU:C:2014:2088 . . . . 418n.373
Case C-198/13 *Julian Hernández*, EU:C:2014:2055 . . . . 432n.444, 433n.451
Case C-202/13 *McCarthy II*, EU:C:2014:2450 . . . . 96n.444, 96n.445, 140n.10, 315, 315n.307,
  316n.311, 316n.312, 341, 341n.444, 348–50, 349n.495, 349n.499, 350n.506,
  393n.237, 394n.238, 394n.239, 464n.136, 509n.70, 520n.122
Case C-206/13 *Siragusa*, EU:C:2014:126 . . . . 432, 432n.446
Case C-244/13 *Ogieriakhi*, EU:C:2014:2068 . . . . . . 84n.358, 157–58, 157n.98, 159, 334n.400, 451n.55,
  452n.58
Case C-261/13 P *Schönberger*, EU:C:2014:2423 . . . . 15n.82, 210n.132, 218n.179, 219

Case C-333/13 *Dano*, EU:C:2014:2358 .... 15n.78, 22n.125, 56n.191, 57n.195, 59, 59n.204, 59n.206, 60n.216, 62n.228, 75n.292, 76n.297, 77n.313, 88n.384, 286n.132, 318n.319, 318n.321, 350n.505, 353–54n.4, 361–62, 390–95, 390n.208, 390n.210, 391n.218, 392n.225, 392n.228, 393n.235, 394n.239, 394n.240, 395n.244, 396n.247, 400, 400n.271, 401n.273, 401n.274, 401n.276, 403–4, 408n.316, 411–12, 411n.342, 411n.343, 412n.344, 414, 416, 417n.363, 418, 419, 421, 422–23, 427, 430n.430, 431, 433–37, 433n.447, 433n.448, 433n.450, 438n.477
Case C-359/13 *Martens*, EU:C:2015:118 .... 49n.137, 53n.166, 85n.363, 94n.430, 94n.431, 487–88n.103
Case C-554/13 *Zh and O*, EU:C:2015:377 .... 523n.139
Case C-632/13 *Hirvonen*, EU:C:2015:765 .... 13n.67, 22n.126
Case C-650/13 *Delvigne*, EU:C:2015:648 ....22n.129, 94n.429, 188n.4, 191–92n.19, 195, 196–98, 198n.59, 198n.62, 198n.64, 198–99n.66, 199–201, 199n.68, 200n.73, 213–14
Case C-67/14 *Alimanovic*, EU:C:2015:597 .... 56n.191, 59n.208, 59n.209, 59–60n.210, 60n.216, 62n.228, 74n.285, 283n.120, 295n.187, 296n.194, 353–54n.4, 366n.72, 370, 396n.246, 396n.247, 396n.248, 396n.251, 397n.256, 398n.257, 398n.258, 399n.260, 403–4, 408–9, 411–13, 415n.357, 417n.364, 418, 419, 427n.412, 438
Case C-69/14 *Târşia*, EU:C:2015:662 .... 550n.316
Case C-165/14 *Rendón Marín*, EU:C:2016:675 .... 42n.102, 42n.104, 43n.106, 53n.168, 60n.216, 84n.354, 84n.355, 85n.364, 85n.365, 113n.26, 120n.74, 143n.25, 171n.182, 172n.187, 176n.210, 236n.269, 237n.274, 243n.312, 253n.368, 255, 281n.111, 299n.211, 449n.44, 503n.27, 506n.53, 524n.146, 525n.152
Case C-180/14 *Commission v Greece*, EU:C:2015:840 .... 403n.284
Case C-218/14 *Singh II*, EU:C:2015:476................. 22n.132, 143n.24, 143n.28, 159, 159n.103, 274–75n.76, 283n.117, 332, 334n.398, 334n.401, 335n.402, 335n.404, 336–37, 336n.409, 338, 338n.426, 339, 339n.433
Case C-233/14 *Commission v Netherlands*, EU:C:2016:396 .... 20n.113, 70n.263, 379n.149, 381n.159, 403n.287, 403n.289, 413n.350
Case C-299/14 *García-Nieto*, EU:C:2016:114 .... 59n.208, 273n.62, 318n.320, 353–54n.4, 380n.155, 396n.246, 397n.256, 398n.257, 398n.258, 398n.259, 399n.260, 405n.293, 438
Case C-304/14 *CS*, EU:C:2016:674 .... 53n.168, 85n.364, 88n.385, 172n.185, 248n.343, 254n.372, 255, 526n.153
Case C-308/14 *Commission v UK*, EU:C:2016:436.... 48n.133, 50n.147, 62n.229, 75n.292, 319n.324, 350n.505, 353–54n.4, 380n.157, 381–82, 399n.262, 399n.264, 399n.265, 400n.266, 400n.271, 400n.272, 401n.273, 401n.274, 401n.276, 402n.278, 402n.279, 402n.282, 403–4, 403n.285, 407, 410–13, 411n.343, 423–24n.400
Case C-438/14 *Bogendorff von Wolffersdorff*, EU:C:2016:401 ...... 38n.82, 38n.83, 51n.158, 79n.322, 341n.445, 464n.138, 512n.81, 513n.85
Case C-459/14 *Cocaj*, EU:C:2015:546 .... 163–64n.134
Case C-515/14 *Commission v Cyprus*, EU:C:2016:30 .... 13n.59, 60n.217
Case C-558/14 *Khachab*, EU:C:2016:285.. 280n.105
Case C-115/15 *NA*, EU:C:2016:487 .... 19n.110, 22n.132, 68n.257, 69n.258, 85n.364, 143n.27, 172n.183, 235n.264, 331–32, 332n.390, 336n.410, 336n.413, 337n.418, 338, 338n.426, 339, 339n.433, 490n.118
Case C-133/15 *Chavez-Vilchez*, EU:C:2017:354 .... 8n.35, 18n.98, 85n.365, 85n.366, 88n.385, 116n.45, 139n.1, 139n.3, 143n.26, 172n.187, 233n.252, 236n.269, 244n.317, 245, 245n.322, 247, 250, 250n.354, 251n.356, 256, 274–75n.76, 385n.180, 414n.353, 437n.473, 460n.107
Case C-161/15 *Bensada Benallal*, EU:C:2016:175 .... 550n.315, 550n.317
Case C-182/15 *Petruhhin*, EU:C:2016:630. ....13n.61, 14n.76, 17n.91, 22n.125, 50n.149, 88n.383, 98n.454, 98n.459, 98n.462, 99–100, 99n.467, 100n.473, 101n.479, 102–3, 104, 104n.499, 105n.509, 359n.22, 422, 422n.391, 428n.423, 431n.437, 434n.455

Case C-218/15 *Paoletti*, EU:C:2016:748. . . . . .46n.118, 85n.367, 86n.368
Case C-238/15 *Bragança Linares Verruga and Others*, EU:C:2016:949 . . . . 475–76n.26
Case C-300/15 *Kohll and Kohll-Schlesser*, EU:C:2016:361. . . . . 13n.68
Joined Cases C-401/15 to C-403/15 *Depesme and Kerrou*, EU:C:2016:955. . . . . 150n.54, 169–70,
169n.167, 169n.168
Joined Cases C-404/15 and C-659/15 PPU *Aranyosi and Căldăraru*, EU:C:2016:198. . . . . 98n.453
Case C-420/15 *U*, EU:C:2017:408. . . . . 13n.60, 13n.65, 42n.100, 49n.139, 479n.50
Case C-473/15 *Schotthöfer and Steiner*, EU:C:2017:633 . . . . 434n.455
Case C-541/15 *Freitag*, EU:C:2017:432 . . . . .18n.99, 131n.154, 195n.43, 434n.458
Case C-544/15 *Fahimian*, EU:C:2017:255. . . . . 515n.97, 520–21, 521n.123, 521n.124
Case C-589/15 P *Anagnostakis*, EU:C:2017:663 . . . . 212n.145, 213n.148, 213n.149
Case C-601/15 PPU *JN*, EU:C:2016:84 . . . . 515n.97
Case C-17/16 *El Dakkak and Intercontinental*, EU:C:2017:341. . . . . 95n.436
Case C-20/16 *Bechtel*, EU:C:2017:488 . . . . 14n.75
Case C-64/16 *Associação Sindical dos Juízes Portugueses*, EU:C:2018:117. . . . . 198n.63
Case C-82/16 *KA and Others*, EU:C:2018:308 . . . . . . 41n.97, 85n.365, 136n.186, 172n.186, 172n.188,
230–31n.242, 237n.274, 246n.331, 247n.334, 247n.335, 247n.336, 247n.339,
250n.354, 251n.359, 252n.360, 253n.365, 253n.366, 255, 255n.381, 257n.391
Case C-184/16 *Petrea*, EU:C:2017:684. . . . . 304, 304n.242, 500n.9, 541n.254, 542n.258, 550n.319,
550n.320, 551n.323
Case C-165/16 *Lounes*, EU:C:2017:862 . . . . 20–21n.117, 86n.371, 90n.391, 93n.416, 119n.65,
122–23n.95, 133n.167, 133n.168, 133n.171, 133n.173, 134n.174, 134n.176,
134n.178, 134n.180, 135–36, 135n.182, 139n.4, 141n.17, 145n.38, 146n.40,
152–53, 202n.89, 255n.379, 434n.458, 479n.50, 482n.69
Case C-191/16 *Pisciotti*, EU:C:2018:222 . . . . .50n.149, 51n.156, 100n.469, 100n.474, 428n.423
Case C-193/16 *E*, EU:C:2017:542, ... 518n.105, 532n.188, 552n.329
Joined Cases C-316/16 and C-424/16 *B and Vomero*, EU:C:2018:256. . . . . 53n.168, 75n.295,
91n.398, 92n.411, 104n.501, 262n.5, 296n.195, 355n.8, 357n.16, 371n.100,
429n.426, 441n.3, 460n.106, 464n.134, 467, 467n.152, 499n.1, 509n.68,
527n.165, 534n.209, 534n.210, 535, 536n.219, 536n.221, 537n.228
Joined Cases C-331/16 and C-366/16 *K and HF*, EU:C:2018:296. . . . . 17n.91, 460n.106, 515n.93,
521n.129, 522n.130, 522n.135, 523n.136, 523n.137, 523n.139,
523n.140, 523n.141, 524–25, 537n.227
Case C-420/16 P *Izsák and Dabis*, EU:C:2019:177 . . . . 214n.157, 215n.158, 215n.160
Case C-442/16 *Gusa*, EU:C:2017:1004. . . . . 69n.259, 70n.262, 86n.373, 276n.86, 325n.352, 326,
326n.356, 326n.358, 366n.66, 409n.331, 474n.14
Case C-618/16 *Prefeta*, EU:C:2018:719 . . . . 75n.291, 328n.375, 329, 366n.67, 408n.321
Case C-673/16 *Coman*, EU:C:2018:385. . . . . .7n.29, 22n.132, 38n.82, 49n.140, 70n.264, 84n.358,
88n.380, 94n.429, 96–97, 97n.448, 139n.6, 141n.17, 145n.37, 148n.47,
152n.67, 152n.68, 153n.71, 153n.75, 153n.77, 154n.78, 154n.82,
154n.83, 255n.382, 267n.32, 268n.39, 464n.136,
491n.127, 494–95, 502n.23, 513n.85
Case C-679/16 *A (Aide pour une personne handicapée)*, EU:C:2018:601. . . . . .78n.316, 85n.362,
94n.430, 94n.431, 287n.143, 464n.138, 487–88n.103
Case C-89/17 *Banger*, EU:C:2018:570 . . . . 70n.264, 84n.357, 166n.146, 166n.149, 168n.159,
168n.161, 183n.247, 183n.248, 185n.255, 495n.143
Case C-163/17 *Jawo*, EU:C:2019:218 . . . . 434–35n.459, 435n.460
Case C-221/17 *Tjebbes*, EU:C:2019:189. . . . . . . 40n.92, 114n.29, 115n.32, 115n.40, 115n.41, 116n.44,
116n.46, 117, 118, 119–20, 122n.87, 122n.92, 123–24n.101,
125, 130n.145, 226n.214, 233n.252
Case C-230/17 *Deha Altiner and Ravn*, EU:C:2018:497. . . . . . . 81n.335, 142n.22, 159n.104, 492n.130,
494n.138
Case C-246/17 *Diallo*, EU:C:2018:499 . . . . .60n.213, 84n.356, 148n.46, 312n.283, 312n.287, 313n.292
Case C-247/17 *Raugevicius*, EU:C:2018:898 . . . . 103n.491, 104, 104n.499, 105n.509, 117n.50,
359n.22, 422n.392
Case C-343/17 *Fremoluc*, EU:C:2018:754 . . . . 82n.343
Case C-370/17 *K and B*, EU:C:2018:877 . . . . 142n.19

Case C-483/17 *Tarola*, EU:C:2019:309............ 68n.257, 70n.265, 71n.267, 326n.360, 329n.377,
    366n.68, 366n.69, 407n.314, 408n.318, 408n.324, 408n.326, 474n.14, 477n.37
Case C-22/18 *TopFit and Biffi*, EU:C:2019:497 ....46n.119, 50n.144, 89n.390
Case C-93/18 *Bajratari*, EU:C:2019:809 ....171n.181, 255n.378, 267n.32, 282–83, 282n.112,
    282n.113, 427n.415
Case C-94/18 *Chenchooliah*, EU:C:2019:693 ..... 144n.33, 159n.105, 298n.203, 298n.205, 298n.209,
    299n.212, 427n.413, 540n.250
Case C-129/18 *SM*, EU:C:2019:248 ....173n.194, 173n.195, 183n.246, 183n.247, 184–85,
    184n.250, 184n.254
Case C-169/18 *Mahmood and Others*, EU:C:2019:5................................. 348n.494
Case C-216/18 PPU *LM*, EU:C:2018:586... 97n.450
Case C-302/18 *X v Belgische Staat*, EU:C:2019:830 .... 282n.112
Case C-327/18 PPU *RO*, EU:C:2018:733.. 105n.505
Case C-380/18 *EP (Menace pour l'ordre public)*, EU:C:2019:1071...................... 503n.26
Joined Cases C-381/18 and C-382/18 *GS and VG (Menace pour l'ordre public)*,
    EU:C:2019:1072 .... 503n.26
Case C-410/18 *Aubriet*, EU:C:2019:582............................. 276n.81, 476–77, 476n.27
Case C-418/18 P *Puppinck*, EU:C:2019:1113 .... 69n.259, 189n.15, 205n.109, 211n.134,
    216n.165, 219n.185
Case C-544/18 *Dakneviciute*, EU:C:2019:761............. 328n.373, 328n.374, 408n.320, 409n.327,
    418n.375, 471n.4
Case C-621/18 *Wightman*, EU:C:2018:999 .... 125n.107, 128, 128n.135
Case C-754/18 *Ryanair Designated Activity Company*, EU:C:2020:131.................... 11n.52
Case 802/18 *Caisse pour l'avenir des enfants*, EU:C:2020:269 .... 169n.167, 276n.81
Case C-836/18 *Subdelegación del Gobierno en Ciudad Real (Conjoint d'un citoyen de l'Union)*,
    EU:C:2020:119 .... 226n.216, 235n.264, 247n.332, 247n.335, 252, 252n.363, 253n.365,
    253n.367, 255n.380, 256, 256n.387, 257n.392, 258, 258n.395
Case C-32/19 *Pensionsversicherungsanstalt (Cessation d'activité après l'âge du départ à la
    retraite)*, EU:C:2020:25 .... 456n.82
Case C-181/19 *Jobcenter Krefeld*, EU:C:2020:794............ 14n.69, 15n.80, 75n.287, 75n.289, 170,
    170n.169, 170n.174, 273n.63, 353–54n.4, 417n.365, 417n.368,
    418n.374, 419, 423n.396, 424n.401, 428, 429–30,
    461n.117, 478n.48, 489n.110
Case C-243/19 *A v Veselības ministrija*, EU:C:2020:872 .... 54n.176
Case C-398/19 *BY*, EU:C:2020:1032 .... 101n.480
Joined Cases C-451/19 and C-532/19 *Subdelegación del Gobierno en Toledo
    (Séjour d'un membre de la famille—Ressources insuffisantes)*, EU:C:2022:354 ....247n.339,
    251n.355, 254n.371, 257n.394
Case C-454/19 *ZW*, EU:C:2020:947... 141n.14
Case C-502/19 *Junqueras*, EU:C:2019:1115...........................189n.15, 192n.21, 200n.79
Case C-505/19 *WS*, EU:C:2021:376.. 80n.324
Case C-535/19 *A (Soins de santé publics)*, EU:C:2021:595............. 284–85, 285n.127, 285n.128,
    286n.134, 353–54n.4, 392n.226, 410n.335, 427n.415
Case C-710/19 *GMA (Demandeur d'emploi)*, EU:C:2020:1037...... 71n.271, 294, 295–96, 295n.187,
    295n.188, 300n.223, 353–54n.4, 366n.71, 366n.72, 415–16, 460n.108
Case C-718/19 *Ordre des barreaux francophones and germanophone and Others
    (Mesures préventives en vue d'éloignement)*, EU:C:2021:505 .... 10n.43, 269n.42, 518n.107,
    518–19n.109, 519n.110
Case C-719/19 *FS*, EU:C:2021:506 .... 269n.43, 271n.53, 272n.57, 273n.68, 295–96, 298n.204,
    299n.215, 348n.494, 353–54n.4, 379n.146,
    426n.411, 427n.414, 458n.92, 548n.301
Case C-896/19 *Repubblika v Il-Prim Ministru*, EU:C:2021:311 .... 198n.63
Case C-897/19 PPU *IN*, EU:C:2020:262 ....11n.51, 11n.53, 72n.275, 106, 106n.512, 129n.141
Case C-930/19 *X v Belgian State*, EU:C:2021:657 .... 11n.48, 48n.132, 143n.28, 338n.429,
    339n.430, 340n.435, 436n.471
Case C-35/20 *A (Franchissement de frontières en navire de plaisance)*,
    EU:C:2021:813 ....11n.52, 265n.15, 266n.24, 482n.69

Case C-118/20 *Wiener Landesregierung (Révocation d'une assurance de naturalisation)*,
  EU:C:2022:34 . . . . 38n.80, 40n.91, 84n.359, 114, 117, 117n.54, 117n.57, 118n.60, 119n.67,
    119n.71, 120n.72, 120n.73, 120n.75, 122n.87, 122n.92, 125, 129–30
Case C-168/20 *BJ and OV*, EU:C:2021:907 . . . . 74n.286, 171n.177, 273n.63, 276n.85, 277n.90,
    408n.323, 474n.14
Case C-247/20 *Commissioners for Her Majesty's Revenue and Customs
  (Assurance maladie complète)*, EU:C:2022:177 . . . . 77n.314, 136n.185, 258n.399, 283n.121,
    284–85, 286, 286n.136, 353–54n.4, 384n.175,
    410n.336, 441n.1, 449n.41
Case C-289/20 *IB (Habitual residence of a spouse—Divorce)*, EU:C:2021:955 . . . . 399n.264
Case C-328/20 *Commission v Austria*, EU:C:2022:468 . . . . 277n.92, 278n.94, 379n.143, 407,
    410n.333, 478n.43, 478n.45
Joined Cases C-368/20 and C-369/20 *NW*, EU:C:2022:298 . . . . 11n.52
Case C-411/20 *Familienkasse Niedersachsen-Bremen*, EU:C:2022:602 . . . . 273n.64, 353–54n.4,
    406n.299, 406n.300, 406n.304, 411,
    411n.339, 428n.418, 464n.138
Case C-490/20 *VMA v Stolichna obshtina, rayon 'Pancharevo'*, EU:C:2021:1008 . . . . 7n.29, 11n.47,
    47n.123, 48n.132, 90n.397, 141n.17, 153n.70,
    163n.131, 172n.190, 201n.84, 267n.29, 267n.33,
    267n.34, 353n.1, 353n.3
Case C-673/20 *Préfet du Gers*, EU:C:2022:449 . . . . .8n.31, 11n.47, 40n.87, 48n.132, 109n.3,
    122n.88, 124n.104, 125n.107, 125n.110, 125n.113,
    126–27n.124, 187n.2, 196n.49, 197, 197n.52, 197n.55, 200n.78, 353n.1
Case C-709/20 *CG*, EU:C:2021:602 . . . . 14n.69, 18n.103, 78n.316, 88n.386, 258n.397,
    339n.433, 353–54n.4, 419, 420n.379, 420n.380, 420n.382,
    421, 422–23, 423–24n.400, 425, 425n.402, 425n.404, 427n.416,
    428, 435n.463, 436n.468, 438n.478, 459n.96, 461–62, 478n.48
Case C-2/21 *Rzecznik Praw Obywatelskich*, EU:C:2022:502 . . . . 268n.40
Case C-156/21 *Hungary v Parliament and Council*, EU:C:2022:97 . . . . 106–7n.518
Case C-157/21 *Poland v Parliament and Council*, EU:C:2021:978 . . . . 198n.63
Case C-157/21 *Poland v Parliament and Council*, EU:C:2022:98 . . . . 106–7n.518
Case C-206/21 *Préfet de Saône-et-Loire*, removed from the register 47n.123
Case C-488/21 *GV v Chief Appeals Officer and Others*, pending. 178n.224
Case C-808/21 *Commission v Czech Republic*, pending. 200n.79
Case C-814/21 *Commission v Poland*, pending. 200n.79
Case C-128/22 *NORDIC INFO*, pending. 512n.80
Case C-411/22 *Thermalhotel Fontana*, pending 512n.80

AG OPINIONS: ALPHABETICAL

AG Szpunar in Case C-35/20 *A (Franchissement de frontières en navire
  de plaisance)*, EU:C:2021:456 . . . . .266n.25, 266n.26, 266n.27
AG Saugmandsgaard Øe Case C-535/19 *A (Soins de santé publics)*,
  EU:C:2021:114 . . . . 285n.131, 410n.334
AG Mengozzi in Case C-434/10 *Aladzhov*, EU:C:2011:547 . . . . 55n.183, 521n.125
AG Bot in Case C-529/11 *Alarape and Tijani*, EU:C:2013:9 . . . . 398n.258, 416n.361, 442n.8,
    456n.79, 462n.125
AG Wathelet in Case C-67/14 *Alimanovic*, EU:C:2015:210. . . . . . . .6n.15, 21n.118, 374n.115, 375–76,
    377–78, 381–82, 383n.162, 395n.242,
    395n.243, 397n.253, 397n.254, 397n.255,
    416n.359, 428–29, 428–29n.424
AG Mengozzi in Case C-86/12 *Alokpa and Moudoulou*, EU:C:2013:197 . . . . 239n.284, 434n.456
AG Sharpston in Case C-436/15 *Alytaus regiono atliekų tvarkymo centras*, EU:C:2017:33. . . . 95n.439
AG Darmon in Case C-292/89 *Antonissen*, EU:C:1990:387 . . . . 292n.171, 293n.175
AG Szpunar in Joined Cases C-316/16 and C-424/16 *B and Vomero*, EU:C:2017:797. . . . . . .534n.207,
    535n.215, 536n.220
AG Szpunar in Case C-93/18 *Bajratari*, EU:C:2019:512 . . . . 255n.378, 282n.113

AG Bobek in Case C-89/17 *Banger*, EU:C:2018:225. . . . . 20n.111, 141n.16, 168n.157, 168n.163,
  178n.226, 495n.144
AG Geelhoed in Case C-413/99 *Baumbast and R*, EU:C:2001:385. . . . . 77n.309, 377, 472n.7
AG Geelhoed in Case C-209/03 *Bidar*, EU:C:2004:175 . . . . 58n.197, 77n.310, 363n.48, 364n.50,
  376n.130, 377n.133, 378
AG Wathelet in Case C-438/14 *Bogendorff von Wolffersdorff*, EU:C:2016:11 . . . . . . 341n.445, 513n.84
AG Mayras in Case 67/74 *Bonsignore*, EU:C:1975:22. . . . . 503n.28
AG Léger in Case C-214/94 *Boukhalfa*, EU:C:1995:381 . . . . 96n.440
AG Wathelet in Case C-238/15 *Bragança Linares Verruga and Others*,
  EU:ECLI:2016:389 . . . . .14n.72, 378, 378n.141, 476n.28, 476n.30
AG Sharpston in Case C-73/08 *Bressol and Others*, EU:C:2009:396. . . . . . . 50n.148, 54n.179, 57n.196,
  66n.246, 66n.248, 399n.265
AG Wahl in Case C-140/12 *Brey*, EU:C:2013:337. . . . . 56n.193, 57n.195, 58n.202, 279n.104,
  308n.261, 321n.331, 381–82, 382n.160,
  388n.196, 389n.205, 389n.207, 394–95
AG Bobek in Case C-129/19 *BV*, EU:C:2020:375 . . . . 95n.434
AG Hogan in Case C-398/19 *BY*, EU:C:2020:748. . . . . 101n.479
AG Mengozzi in Case C-429/11 *Byankov*, EU:C:2012:380 . . . . 549n.309
AG Stix-Hackl in Case C-60/00 *Carpenter*, EU:C:2001:447 . . . . 480n.53
AG Richard de la Tour in Case C-709/20 *CG*, EU:C:2021:515 . . . . .411n.342, 419n.378,
  423–24n.400, 425n.403, 437n.472,
  437n.473, 461n.116
AG Szpunar in Case C-133/15 *Chavez-Vilchez*, EU:C:2016:659. . . . . . . 171n.178, 231n.246, 246n.330,
  251n.358, 419n.378
AG Szpunar in Case C-94/18 *Chenchooliah*, EU:C:2019:433 . . . . 134n.176
AG Ruiz-Jarabo Colomer in Case C-138/02 *Collins*, EU:C:2003:409. . . . . 57n.194, 130n.149,
  368–69n.88
AG Wathelet in Case C-673/16 *Coman*, EU:C:2018:2 . . . . . . 20n.112, 151–52n.65, 157n.97, 163n.132,
  164n.135, 164n.137, 451n.54, 481n.63
AG Kokott in Case C-75/11 *Commission v Austria*, EU:C:2012:536 . . . . 380n.154, 419n.377
AG Richard de la Tour in Case C-328/20 *Commission v Austria*, EU:C:2022:45 . . . . 478n.40, 478n.47
AG Slynn in Case 293/85 *Commission v Belgium*, EU:C:1987:367 . . . . 65n.243
AG Ruiz-Jarabo Colomer in Case C-408/03 *Commission v Belgium*,
  EU:C:2005:638 . . . . 45n.113
AG Sharpston in Case C-542/09 *Commission v Netherlands*, EU:C:2012:79. . . . . 410n.332
AG Sharpston in Case C-233/14 *Commission v Netherlands*, EU:C:2016:50. . . . . .290n.160,
  403n.286, 403n.288, 413n.351
AG Cruz Villalón in Case C-308/14 *Commission v UK*, EU:C:2015:666 . . . . .303, 304n.241,
  318n.322, 319, 321, 321n.332, 400n.269,
  401n.277, 429n.427, 430n.432
AG Hogan in Case C-247/20 *Commissioners for Her Majesty's Revenue and
  Customs (Assurance maladie complète)*, EU:C:2021:778 . . . . 286n.133, 450n.47
AG Lagrange in Case 6/64 *Costa v ENEL*, EU:C:1964:51. . . . . 17n.93
AG Geelhoed in Case C-224/98 *D'Hoop*, EU:C:2002:103 . . . . 370n.99, 439n.485, 482n.69
AG Wathelet in Case C-333/13 *Dano*, EU:C:2014:341. . . . . 59n.205, 61n.226, 320n.328, 375n.123,
  381–82, 383n.162, 392n.225, 392n.227, 393n.230,
  393n.231, 393n.232, 395, 397–98
AG Cruz Villalón in Case C-650/13 *Delvigne*, EU:C:2015:363 . . . . .192n.20, 193n.29, 198n.61
AG Cruz Villalón in Case C-222/11 *Demirkan*, EU:C:2013:237. . . . . 70n.263, 84n.356, 538n.237,
  538n.240
AG Mengozzi in Case C-256/11 *Dereci*, EU:C:2011:626 . . . . . . 20n.111, 42n.105, 238n.276, 240n.291,
  241n.302
AG Trstenjak in Case C-325/09 *Dias*, EU:C:2011:86 . . . . 18n.101, 76n.297, 328n.369, 384n.170,
  384n.176, 385n.177, 454n.76, 459n.98,
  459n.102, 460n.105, 463n.130
AG Bot in Case C-451/11 *Dülger*, EU:C:2012:331 . . . . 74n.282
AG Darmon in Case 389/87 *Echternach and Moritz*, EU:C:1989:35 . . . . 484n.79, 485n.84

AG Tizzano in Case C-145/04 *Spain v United Kingdom* and Case C-300/04
   Eman and Sevinger, EU:C:2006:231 . . . . 191–92n.19, 193, 194n.34, 194n.36, 195, 198
AG Szpunar in Case C-411/20 *Familienkasse Niedersachsen-Bremen*,
   EU:C:2021:1017 . . . . 350n.509, 407n.313, 410n.334
AG Mazák in Case C-158/07 *Förster*, EU:C:2008:399 . . . . 52n.162, 378–79, 378n.138, 381
AG Rantos in Case C-719/19 *FS*, EU:C:2021:104 . . . . 272n.56, 273n.67, 274n.71, 348n.494,
   426n.410, 427
AG Jacobs in Case C-148/02 *Garcia Avello*, EU:C:2003:311 . . . . .89n.389, 132n.160, 472n.6
AG Wathelet in Case C-299/14 *García-Nieto*, EU:C:2015:366 . . . . .383n.162, 391n.216,
   399n.261, 428n.420
AG Geelhoed in Case C-213/05 *Geven*, EU:C:2006:616 . . . . 361n.35
AG Mengozzi in Case C-20/12 *Giersch*, EU:C:2013:70 . . . . 476n.32
AG Alber in Case C-257/99 *Givane and Others*, EU:C:2002:297 . . . . 323n.341, 323n.344
AG Sharpston in Case C-212/06 *Government of the French Community and Walloon
   Government*, EU:C:2007:398 . . . . .43n.109, 83, 83n.350, 227n.222, 228n.228, 228n.229
AG Sharpston in Case C-353/06 *Grunkin and Paul*, EU:C:2008:246 . . . . 19n.106
AG Alber in Case C-184/99 *Grzelczyk*, EU:C:2000:518 . . . . 277n.87, 360n.29
AG Wathelet in Case C-442/16 *Gusa*, EU:C:2017:607 . . . . .69n.259, 69–70n.260, 296n.194,
   325n.351, 326n.357, 383n.162, 396n.250, 457n.89
AG Geelhoed in Case C-212/05 *Hartmann*, EU:C:2006:615 . . . . 275n.78, 475–76
AG Kokott in Case C-287/05 *Hendrix*, EU:C:2007:196 . . . . 477n.33
AG Poiares Maduro in Case C-524/06 *Huber*, EU:C:2008:194 . . . . 48n.130, 306n.253, 437n.475
AG Mazák in Case C-310/08 *Ibrahim*, EU:C:2009:641 . . . . 417n.362
AG Trstenjak in Case C-40/11 *Iida*, EU:C:2012:296 . . . . 236n.270, 241n.301, 329n.379
AG Tanchev in Case C-897/19 PPU *IN*, EU:C:2020:128 . . . . 106n.511
AG Ruiz-Jarabo Colomer in Case C-258/04 *Ioannidis*, EU:C:2005:375. 13n.66
AG Lagrange in Case 13/63 *Italian Government v Commission*, EU:C:1963:9 . . . . . . 65n.240, 65n.242
AG Wathelet in Case C-163/17 *Jawo*, EU:C:2018:613 . . . . 435n.460
AG Pitruzzella in Case C-181/19 *Jobcenter Krefeld*, EU:C:2020:377 . . . . . 56n.193, 170n.173, 382n.160
AG Saugmandsgaard Øe in Case C-331/16 *K and HF*, EU:C:2017:973 . 425n.406, 523n.136, 524n.147
AG Sharpston in Case C-82/16 *KA and Others*, EU:C:2017:821 . . . . . . .230–31n.242, 246n.331,
   247n.335, 252n.361, 256n.383, 347n.481
AG Campos Sánchez-Bordona in Case C-300/15 *Kohll and Kohll-Schlesser*,
   EU:C:2016:86 . . . . 328n.372, 456n.78
AG Jacobs in Case C-168/91 *Konstantinidis*, EU:C:1992:504 . . . . 32, 32n.36
AG La Pergola in Case C-299/95 *Kremzow*, EU:C:1997:58 . . . . 227n.220
AG Jacobs in Case C-412/93 *Leclerc-Siplec*, EU:C:1994:393 . . . . 65n.241
\AG Trstenjak in Case C-162/09 *Lassal*, EU:C:2010:266 . . . . 383n.164, 446, 446n.29
AG Mengozzi in Case C-42/11 *Lopes Da Silva Jorge*, EU:C:2012:151 . . . . 446–47n.30
AG Bot in Case C-165/16 *Lounes*, EU:C:2017:407 . . . . 90n.392, 133n.172, 235n.265, 492n.130
AG Sharpston in Case C-359/13 *Martens*, EU:C:2004:2240 . . . . 49n.137
AG La Pergola in Case C-85/96 *Martínez Sala*, EU:C:1997:335 . . . . 76n.299, 196n.46, 262n.6,
   358n.19, 359n.23, 359n.25, 362n.39, 364n.54
AG Kokott in Case C-434/09 *McCarthy*, EU:C:2010:718 . . . . 233n.256, 234n.260, 384n.169,
   384n.176, 385n.182, 461n.114
AG Szpunar in Case C-202/13 *McCarthy II*, EU:C:2014:345 . . . . 6n.16, 75n.294, 317n.316,
   345n.463, 349n.498, 350n.504,
   479n.50, 496n.146
AG Cosmas in Case C-160/96 *Molenaar*, EU:C:1997:599 . . . . 277n.91
AG Ruiz-Jarabo Colomer in Joined Cases C-11/06 and C-12/06 *Morgan and Bucher*,
   EU:C:2007:174 . . . . 6n.16
AG Trabucchi in Case 7/75 *Mr and Mrs F*, EU:C:1975:75 . . . . 33n.38
AG Wathelet in Case C-115/15 *NA*, EU:C:2016:259 . . . . 19n.108, 68n.257, 90n.396, 233n.255,
   247n.333, 248n.344, 250n.350, 250n.351,
   337n.420, 338n.424, 338n.427, 457n.90
AG Geelhoed in Case C-413/01 *Ninni-Orasche*, EU:C:2003:117 . . . . 363n.47
AG Sharpston in Case C-456/12 *O and B*, EU:C:2013:837 . . . . .6n.18, 249n.347, 493n.134

AG Bot in Joined Cases C-356/11 and C-357/11 *O and S*, EU:C:2012:595 . . . . 239n.286, 240n.295
AG Lenz in Case C-237/94 *O'Flynn*, EU:C:1996:206 . . . . 65n.244
AG Bot in Case C-244/13 *Ogieriakhi*, EU:C:2014:323 . . . . 158n.101, 452n.59, 481n.63
AG Bot in Case C-378/12 *Onuekwere*, EU:C:2013:640 . . . . 60n.214, 157n.96, 451n.53, 464n.133,
464n.136, 465n.142, 466n.147, 535n.217
AG Stix-Hackl in Joined Cases C-482/01 and C-493/01 *Orfanopoulos and
Oliveri*, EU:C:2003:455 . . . . 500n.8
AG La Pergola in Case C-171/96 *Pereira Roque*, EU:C:1997:425 . . . . 359n.23
AG Szpunar in Case C-184/16 *Petrea*, EU:C:2017:324. . . . . . 541n.257, 542n.259, 550n.319, 551n.322
AG Bot in Case C-182/15 *Petruhhin*, EU:C:2016:330 . . . . 98n.453
AG Bot in Case C-348/09 *PI*, EU:C:2012:123 . . . . 532n.192, 533n.199, 533n.202
AG Bot in Case C-191/16 *Pisciotti*, EU:C:2017:878 . . . . 101n.477
AG Collins in Case C-673/20 *Préfet du Gers*, EU:C:2022:129 . . . . 40n.89, 109n.2, 122n.90,
124n.106, 125n.108, 126–27n.124,
129n.139, 129n.140, 197n.51
AG Wathelet in Case C-618/16 *Prefeta*, EU:C:2018:125 . . . . 324n.349
AG Cruz Villalón in Case C-367/11 *Prete*, EU:C:2012:501 . . . . 14n.73
AG Sharpston in Joined Cases C-523/11 and C-585/11 *Prinz and Seeberger*,
EU:C:2013:90 . . . . .53n.167, 53n.172, 60n.215, 93n.415, 398n.258, 404n.292
AG Bobek in Case C-418/18 P *Puppinck*, EU:C:2019:640 . . . . 189n.14, 205n.107, 205n.110,
211n.137, 211n.138, 216n.167, 217n.170
AG Bot in Case C-83/11 *Rahman*, EU:C:2012:174. . . . . 166n.148, 167n.153, 167n.155, 248n.342
AG Bot in Case C-247/17 *Raugevicius*, EU:C:2018:616 . . . . 92n.411, 104n.500, 446–47n.30
AG Jääskinen in Case C-522/10 *Reichel-Albert*, EU:C:2012:114 . . . . 14n.70
AG Szpunar in Case C-165/14 *Rendón Marín* and Case C-304/14 *CS*,
EU:C:2016:75 . . . . 19n.104, 93n.417, 250n.350, 499n.4,
500n.6, 525n.150
AG Mengozzi in Case C-423/12 *Reyes*, EU:C:2013:719 . . . . . . 143n.24, 176n.212, 178n.224, 178n.225
AG Poiares Maduro in Case C-135/08 *Rottmann*, EU:C:2009:588. . . . . 93n.419, 111n.14, 113n.23,
120n.78, 122n.94, 123n.100, 124n.103, 189n.12, 196,
197n.51, 204n.102, 232n.249, 431n.434
AG Sharpston in Case C-34/09 *Ruiz Zambrano*, EU:C:2010:560 . . . . 19n.105, 82n.344,
83, 83n.352, 123n.97, 141, 141n.15, 179n.228, 228–9,
229n.232, 231n.246, 233n.251, 233n.253, 234n.260,
343–44n.459, 434n.457
AG Sharpston in Case C-457/12 *S and G*, EU:C:2013:837. . . . . .81n.334, 481n.63, 482n.66
AG Wahl in Case C-507/12 *Saint Prix*, EU:C:2013:841 . . . . 327n.364
AG Geelhoed in Case C-403/03 *Schempp*, EU:C:2005:62 . . . . 80n.328, 82n.344
AG Ruiz-Jarabo-Colomer in Joined Cases C-65/95 and C-111/95
Shingara and Radiom, EU:C:1996:451. . . . . 37n.76
AG Tesauro in Case C-370/90 *Singh*, EU:C:1992:229 . . . . 486n.91
AG Kokott in Case C-218/14 *Singh II*, EU:C:2015:306 . . . . . . 334n.397, 335n.407, 428n.422, 481n.63
AG Campos Sánchez-Bordona in Case C-129/18 *SM*, EU:C:2019:140 . . . . 173n.194
AG Pitruzella in Case C-22/21 *SRS and AA*, EU:C:2022:183 . . . . .163n.130, 181n.238,
182n.241, 184n.253
AG La Pergola in in Joined Cases C-4/95 and C-5/95 *Stöber and Pereira*, EU:C:1996:225 . . . . . 37n.75
AG Kokott in Case C-192/05 *Tas-Hagen and Tas*, EU:C:2006:150 . . . . 422n.393
AG Kokott in Case C-480/08 *Teixeira*, EU:C:2009:642 . . . . 294n.185, 417n.362, 419n.377
AG Mengozzi in Case C-221/17 *Tjebbes and Others*, EU:C:2018:572 . . . . .43n.108, 114n.28, 120,
120n.77, 123–24n.101
AG Tanchev in Case C-22/18 *TopFit and Biffi*, EU:C:2019:181 . . . . 46n.119, 46n.121, 129n.139
AG Geelhoed in Case C-456/02 *Trojani*, EU:C:2004:112 . . . . 57n.194, 284n.123, 361n.35
AG Bot in Case C-145/09 *Tsakouridis*, EU:C:2010:322 . . . . 515n.94, 530n.177, 532
AG Darmon in Case C-171/91 *Tsiotras*, EU:C:1992:486 . . . . 322n.334
AG Gand in Case 61/65 *Vaassen-Göbbels*, EU:C:1966:25 . . . . 31, 31n.28
AG Ruiz-Jarabo Colomer in Joined Cases C-22/08 and C-23/08 *Vatsouras
and Koupatantze*, EU:C:2009:150. . . . . 358n.17, 376n.129, 397n.255

AG Kokott in Case C-490/20 *VMA v Stolichna obshtina, rayon 'Pancharevo'*,
    EU:C:2021:296 .... 201n.84, 268n.40
AG Mengozzi in Case C-208/07 *von Chamier-Glisczinski*, EU:C:2008:493.................. 14n.70
AG Trabucchi in Case 118/75 *Watson and Belmann*, EU:C:1976:79 .... 34n.47
AG Szpunar in Case C-118/20 *Wiener Landesregierung (Révocation d'une
    assurance de naturalisation)*, EU:C:2021:530 ....113n.27, 117n.53, 117n.55, 119n.66, 120
AG Cosmas in Case C-378/97 *Wijsenbeek*, EU:C:1999:144 .... 7n.27, 46n.117, 76n.299, 86n.370,
                                                                                    423n.398
AG Bot in Case C-123/08 *Wolzenburg*, EU:C:2009:183......... 52n.159, 422, 422n.394, 446–47n.30
AG Bobek in Case C-505/19 *WS*, EU:C:2020:939 .... 82n.345
AG Kokott in Case C-318/13 *X*, EU:C:2014:333...................................... 38n.81
AG Szpunar in Case C-930/19 *X v Belgian State*, EU:C:2021:225............... 339n.433, 339n.434
AG Léger in Case C-357/98 *Yiadom*, EU:C:2000:174................................. 540n.250
AG Tizzano in Case C-200/02 *Zhu and Chen*, EU:C:2004:307 ......86n.370, 175n.208, 342–43n.450,
                                                                            343n.456, 343n.457
AG Bot in Case C-371/08 *Ziebell*, EU:C:2011:244 .... 74n.282
AG Bot in Joined Cases C-424/10 and C-425/10 *Ziolkowski and Szeja*,
    EU:C:2011:575 ....18n.101, 385n.181, 385n.182, 461n.113, 461n.114, 461n.115
AG Mengozzi in Case C-300/11 *ZZ*, EU:C:2012:563 .... 542n.266

AG OPINIONS: NUMERICAL

AG Lagrange in Case 13/63 *Italian Government v Commission*, EU:C:1963:9 ...... 65n.240, 65n.242
AG Lagrange in Case 6/64 *Costa v ENEL*, EU:C:1964:51................................. 17n.93
AG Gand in Case 61/65 *Vaassen-Göbbels*, EU:C:1966:25 .... 31, 31n.28
AG Mayras in Case 67/74 *Bonsignore*, EU:C:1975:22................................. 503n.28
AG Trabucchi in Case 7/75 *Mr and Mrs F*, EU:C:1975:75 .... 33n.38
AG Trabucchi in Case 118/75 *Watson and Belmann*, EU:C:1976:79 .... 34n.47
AG Slynn in Case 293/85 *Commission v Belgium*, EU:C:1987:367 .... 65n.243
AG Darmon in Case 389/87 *Echternach and Moritz*, EU:C:1989:35 .... 484n.79, 485n.84
AG Darmon in Case C-292/89 *Antonissen*, EU:C:1990:387 .... 292n.171, 293n.175
AG Tesauro in Case C-370/90 *Singh*, EU:C:1992:229 .... 486n.91
AG Jacobs in Case C-168/91 *Konstantinidis*, EU:C:1992:504 .... 32, 32n.36
AG Darmon in Case C-171/91 *Tsiotras*, EU:C:1992:486 .... 322n.334
AG Jacobs in Case C-412/93 *Leclerc-Siplec*, EU:C:1994:393 .... 65n.241
AG Léger in Case C-214/94 *Boukhalfa*, EU:C:1995:381 .... 96n.440
AG Lenz in Case C-237/94 *O'Flynn*, EU:C:1996:206 .... 65n.244
AG La Pergola in in Joined Cases C-4/95 and C-5/95 *Stöber and Pereira*,
    EU:C:1996:225 .... 37n.75
AG Ruiz-Jarabo-Colomer in Joined Cases C-65/95 and C-111/95
    Shingara and Radiom, EU:C:1996:451... 37n.76
AG La Pergola in Case C-299/95 *Kremzow*, EU:C:1997:58 .... 227n.220
AG La Pergola in Case C-85/96 *Martínez Sala*, EU:C:1997:335 .... 76n.299, 196n.46, 262n.6,
                                                               358n.19, 359n.23, 359n.25, 362n.39, 364n.54
AG Cosmas in Case C-160/96 *Molenaar*, EU:C:1997:599............................. 277n.91
AG La Pergola in Case C-171/96 *Pereira Roque*, EU:C:1997:425 .... 359n.23
AG Cosmas in Case C-378/97 *Wijsenbeek*, EU:C:1999:144 .... 7n.27, 46n.117, 76n.299, 86n.370,
                                                                                    423n.398
AG Geelhoed in Case C-224/98 *D'Hoop*, EU:C:2002:103 .... 370n.99, 439n.485, 482n.69
AG Léger in Case C-357/98 *Yiadom*, EU:C:2000:174................................. 540n.250
AG Alber in Case C-184/99 *Grzelczyk*, EU:C:2000:518................... 277n.87, 360n.29
AG Alber in Case C-257/99 *Givane and Others*, EU:C:2002:297 .... 323n.341, 323n.344
AG Geelhoed in Case C-413/99 *Baumbast and R*, EU:C:2001:385............. 77n.309, 377, 472n.7
AG Stix-Hackl in Case C-60/00 *Carpenter*, EU:C:2001:447 .... 480n.53
AG Geelhoed in Case C-413/01 *Ninni-Orasche*, EU:C:2003:117 .... 363n.47
AG Stix-Hackl in Joined Cases C-482/01 and C-493/01 *Orfanopoulos
    and Oliveri*, EU:C:2003:455... 500n.8

AG Ruiz-Jarabo Colomer in Case C-138/02 *Collins*, EU:C:2003:409............57n.194, 130n.149,
                                                                                                   368–69n.88
AG Jacobs in Case C-148/02 *Garcia Avello*, EU:C:2003:311..............89n.389, 132n.160, 472n.6
AG Tizzano in Case C-200/02 *Zhu and Chen*, EU:C:2004:307......86n.370, 175n.208, 342–43n.450,
                                                                                                  343n.456, 343n.457
AG Geelhoed in Case C-456/02 *Trojani*, EU:C:2004:112 ....57n.194, 284n.123, 361n.35
AG Geelhoed in Case C-209/03 *Bidar*, EU:C:2004:175..........58n.197, 77n.310, 363n.48, 364n.50,
                                                                                               376n.130, 377n.133, 378
AG Geelhoed in Case C-403/03 *Schempp*, EU:C:2005:62.......................80n.328, 82n.344
AG Ruiz-Jarabo Colomer in Case C-408/03 *Commission v Belgium*, EU:C:2005:638........45n.113
AG Tizzano in Case C-145/04 *Spain v United Kingdom* and Case C-300/04 *Eman
   and Sevinger*, EU:C:2006:231....................191–92n.19, 193, 194n.34, 194n.36, 195, 198
AG Ruiz-Jarabo Colomer in Case C-258/04 *Ioannidis*, EU:C:2005:375....................13n.66
AG Kokott in Case C-192/05 *Tas-Hagen and Tas*, EU:C:2006:150......................422n.393
AG Geelhoed in Case C-212/05 *Hartmann*, EU:C:2006:615......................275n.78, 475–76
AG Geelhoed in Case C-213/05 *Geven*, EU:C:2006:616...............................361n.35
AG Kokott in Case C-287/05 *Hendrix*, EU:C:2007:196.................................477n.33
AG Ruiz-Jarabo Colomer in Joined Cases C-11/06 and C-12/06 *Morgan
   and Bucher*, EU:C:2007:174..6n.16
AG Sharpston in Case C-212/06 *Government of the French Community and Walloon
   Government*, EU:C:2007:398..............43n.109, 83, 83n.350, 227n.222, 228n.228, 228n.229
AG Sharpston in Case C-353/06 *Grunkin and Paul*, EU:C:2008:246......................19n.106
AG Poiares Maduro in Case C-524/06 *Huber*, EU:C:2008:194.........48n.130, 306n.253, 437n.475
AG Mazák in Case C-158/07 *Förster*, EU:C:2008:399..............52n.162, 378–79, 378n.138, 381
AG Mengozzi in Case C-208/07 *von Chamier-Glisczinski*, EU:C:2008:493..................14n.70
AG Ruiz-Jarabo Colomer in Joined Cases C-22/08 and C-23/08 *Vatsouras
   and Koupatantze*, EU:C:2009:150..............................358n.17, 376n.129, 397n.255
AG Sharpston in Case C-73/08 *Bressol and Others*, EU:C:2009:396........50n.148, 54n.179, 57n.196,
                                                                                             66n.246, 66n.248, 399n.265
AG Bot in Case C-123/08 *Wolzenburg*, EU:C:2009:183.........52n.159, 422, 422n.394, 446–47n.30
AG Poiares Maduro in Case C-135/08 *Rottmann*, EU:C:2009:588........93n.419, 111n.14, 113n.23,
                                                                     120n.78, 122n.94, 123n.100, 124n.103, 189n.12, 196,
                                                                     197n.51, 204n.102, 232n.249, 431n.434
AG Mazák in Case C-310/08 *Ibrahim*, EU:C:2009:641................................417n.362
AG Bot in Case C-371/08 *Ziebell*, EU:C:2011:244....................................74n.282
AG Kokott in Case C-480/08 *Teixeira*, EU:C:2009:642..............294n.185, 417n.362, 419n.377
AG Sharpston in Case C-34/09 *Ruiz Zambrano*, EU:C:2010:560................19n.105, 82n.344,
                                                           83, 83n.352, 123n.97, 141, 141n.15, 179n.228, 228–29,
                                                           229n.232, 231n.246, 233n.251, 233n.253, 234n.260,
                                                                                                  343–44n.459, 344n.457
AG Bot in Case C-145/09 *Tsakouridis*, EU:C:2010:322....................515n.94, 530n.177, 532
AG Trstenjak in Case C-162/09 *Lassal*, EU:C:2010:266....................383n.164, 446, 446n.29
AG Trstenjak in Case C-325/09 *Dias*, EU:C:2011:86.........18n.101, 76n.297, 328n.369, 384n.170,
                                                                       384n.176, 385n.177, 454n.76, 459n.98,
                                                                       459n.102, 460n.105, 463n.130
AG Bot in Case C-348/09 *PI*, EU:C:2012:123......................532n.192, 533n.199, 533n.202
AG Kokott in Case C-434/09 *McCarthy*, EU:C:2010:718.............233n.256, 234n.260, 384n.169,
                                                                                            384n.176, 385n.182, 461n.114
AG Sharpston in Case C-542/09 *Commission v Netherlands*, EU:C:2012:79..............410n.332
AG Bot in Joined Cases C-424/10 and C-425/10 *Ziolkowski and Szeja*,
   EU:C:2011:575..................18n.101, 385n.181, 385n.182, 461n.113, 461n.114, 461n.115
AG Mengozzi in Case C-434/10 *Aladzhov*, EU:C:2011:547......................55n.183, 521n.125
AG Jäskinen in Case C-522/10 *Reichel-Albert*, EU:C:2012:114..........................14n.70
AG Trstenjak in Case C-40/11 *Iida*, EU:C:2012:296................236n.270, 241n.301, 329n.379
AG Mengozzi in Case C-42/11 *Lopes Da Silva Jorge*, EU:C:2012:151...................446–47n.30
AG Kokott in Case C-75/11 *Commission v Austria*, EU:C:2012:536............380n.154, 419n.377
AG Bot in Case C-83/11 *Rahman*, EU:C:2012:174.........166n.148, 167n.153, 167n.155, 248n.342

AG Cruz Villalón in Case C-222/11 *Demirkan*, EU:C:2013:237 .... 70n.263, 84n.356,
    538n.237, 538n.240
AG Mengozzi in Case C-256/11 *Dereci*, EU:C:2011:626 .... 20n.111, 42n.105, 238n.276,
    240n.291, 241n.302
AG Mengozzi in Case C-300/11 *ZZ*, EU:C:2012:563 .... 542n.266
AG Bot in Joined Cases C-356/11 and C-357/11 *O and S*, EU:C:2012:595 .... 239n.286, 240n.295
AG Cruz Villalón in Case C-367/11 *Prete*, EU:C:2012:501 .... 14n.73
AG Mengozzi in Case C-429/11 *Byankov*, EU:C:2012:380 .... 549n.309
AG Bot in Case C-451/11 *Dülger*, EU:C:2012:331 .... 74n.282
AG Sharpston in Joined Cases C-523/11 and C-585/11 *Prinz and Seeberger*,
    EU:C:2013:90 .... 53n.167, 53n.172, 60n.215, 93n.415, 398n.258, 404n.292
AG Bot in Case C-529/11 *Alarape and Tijani*, EU:C:2013:9 .... 398n.258, 416n.361, 442n.8,
    456n.79, 462n.125
AG Mengozzi in Case C-20/12 *Giersch*, EU:C:2013:70 .... 476n.32
AG Mengozzi in Case C-86/12 *Alokpa and Moudoulou*, EU:C:2013:197 .... 239n.284, 434n.456
AG Wahl in Case C-140/12 *Brey*, EU:C:2013:337 .... 56n.193, 57n.195, 58n.202, 279n.104,
    308n.261, 321n.331, 381–82, 382n.160, 388n.196,
    389n.205, 389n.207, 394–95
AG Bot in Case C-378/12 *Onuekwere*, EU:C:2013:640 .... 60n.214, 157n.96, 451n.53, 464n.133,
    464n.136, 465n.142, 466n.147, 535n.217
AG Mengozzi in Case C-423/12 *Reyes*, EU:C:2013:719 ...... 143n.24, 176n.212, 178n.224, 178n.225
AG Sharpston in Case C-456/12 *O and B*, EU:C:2013:837 .... 6n.18, 249n.347, 493n.134
AG Sharpston in Case C-457/12 *S and G*, EU:C:2013:837 .... 81n.334, 481n.63, 482n.66
AG Wahl in Case C-507/12 *Saint Prix*, EU:C:2013:841 .... 327n.364
AG Szpunar in Case C-202/13 *McCarthy II*, EU:C:2014:345 .... 6n.16, 75n.294, 317n.316,
    345n.463, 349n.498, 350n.504, 479n.50, 496n.146
AG Bot in Case C-244/13 *Ogieriakhi*, EU:C:2014:323 .... 158n.101, 452n.59, 481n.63
AG Kokott in Case C-318/13 *X*, EU:C:2014:333 .... 38n.81
AG Wathelet in Case C-333/13 *Dano*, EU:C:2014:341 .... 59n.205, 61n.226, 320n.328, 375n.123,
    381–82, 383n.162, 392n.225, 392n.227, 393n.230,
    393n.231, 393n.232, 395, 397–98
AG Sharpston in Case C-359/13 *Martens*, EU:C:2004:2240 .... 49n.137
AG Cruz Villalón in Case C-650/13 *Delvigne*, EU:C:2015:363 .... 192n.20, 193n.29, 198n.61
AG Wathelet in Case C-67/14 *Alimanovic*, EU:C:2015:210 .... 6n.15, 21n.118, 374n.115, 375–76,
    377–78, 381–82, 383n.162, 395n.242, 395n.243, 397n.253,
    397n.254, 397n.255, 416n.359, 428–29, 428–29n.424
AG Szpunar in Case C-165/14 *Rendón Marín* and Case C-304/14 *CS*,
    EU:C:2016:75 .... 19n.104, 93n.417, 250n.350, 499n.4, 500n.6, 525n.150
AG Kokott in Case C-218/14 *Singh II*, EU:C:2015:306 ...... 334n.397, 335n.407, 428n.422, 481n.63
AG Sharpston in Case C-233/14 *Commission v Netherlands*,
    EU:C:2016:50 .... 290n.160, 403n.286, 403n.288, 413n.351
AG Wathelet in Case C-299/14 *García-Nieto*, EU:C:2015:366383n.162, 391n.216, 399n.261, 428n.420
AG Cruz Villalón in Case C-308/14 *Commission v UK*, EU:C:2015:666 .... 303, 304n.241,
    318n.322, 319, 321, 321n.332, 400n.269,
    401n.277, 429n.427, 430n.432
AG Wathelet in Case C-438/14 *Bogendorff von Wolffersdorff*, EU:C:2016:11 ...... 341n.445, 513n.84
AG Wathelet in Case C-115/15 *NA*, EU:C:2016:259 .... 19n.108, 68n.257, 90n.396, 233n.255,
    247n.333, 248n.344, 250n.350, 250n.351, 337n.420,
    338n.424, 338n.427, 457n.90
AG Szpunar in Case C-133/15 *Chavez-Vilchez*, EU:C:2016:659 .... 171n.178, 231n.246, 246n.330,
    251n.358
AG Bot in Case C-182/15 *Petruhhin*, EU:C:2016:330 .... 98n.453
AG Wathelet in Case C-238/15 *Bragança Linares Verruga and Others*,
    EU:ECLI:2016:389 ....14n.72, 378, 378n.141, 476n.28, 476n.30
AG Campos Sánchez-Bordona in Case C-300/15 *Kohll and Kohll-Schlesser*,
    EU:C:2016:86 .... 328n.372, 456n.78

AG Sharpston in Case C-436/15 *Alytaus regiono atliekų tvarkymo centras*,
    EU:C:2017:33 .... 95n.439
AG Sharpston in Case C-82/16 *KA and Others*, EU:C:2017:821 .... 230–31n.242, 246n.331,
    247n.335, 252n.361, 256n.383, 347n.481
AG Bot in Case C-165/16 *Lounes*, EU:C:2017:407 .... 90n.392, 133n.172, 235n.265, 492n.130
AG Szpunar in Case C-184/16 *Petrea*, EU:C:2017:324...... 541n.257, 542n.259, 550n.319, 551n.322
AG Bot in Case C-191/16 *Pisciotti*, EU:C:2017:878 .... 101n.477
AG Szpunar in Joined Cases C-316/16 and C-424/16 *B and Vomero*,
    EU:C:2017:797 .... 534n.207, 535n.215, 536n.220
AG Saugmandsgaard Øe in Case C-331/16 *K and HF*,
    EU:C:2017:973 .... 425n.406, 523n.136, 524n.147
AG Wathelet in Case C-442/16 *Gusa*, EU:C:2017:607 .... 69n.259, 69–70n.260, 296n.194,
    325n.351, 326n.357, 383n.162, 396n.250, 457n.89
AG Wathelet in Case C-618/16 *Prefeta*, EU:C:2018:125 .... 324n.349
AG Wathelet in Case C-673/16 *Coman*, EU:C:2018:2 ...... 20n.112, 151–52n.65, 157n.97, 163n.132,
    164n.135, 164n.137, 451n.54
AG Bobek in Case C-89/17 *Banger*, EU:C:2018:225.......... 20n.111, 141n.16, 168n.157, 168n.163,
    178n.226, 495n.144
AG Wathelet in Case C-163/17 *Jawo*, EU:C:2018:613 .... 435n.460
AG Mengozzi in Case C-221/17 *Tjebbes and Others*, EU:C:2018:572 .... 43n.108, 114n.28, 120,
    120n.77, 123–24n.101
AG Bot in Case C-247/17 *Raugevicius*, EU:C:2018:616.............. 92n.411, 104n.500, 446–47n.30
AG Tanchev in Case C-22/18 *TopFit and Biffi*, EU:C:2019:181.......... 46n.119, 46n.121, 129n.139
AG Szpunar in Case C-93/18 *Bajratari*, EU:C:2019:512 .... 255n.378, 282n.113
AG Szpunar in Case C-94/18 *Chenchooliah*, EU:C:2019:433 .... 134n.176
AG Campos Sánchez-Bordona in Case C-129/18 *SM*, EU:C:2019:140 .... 173n.194
AG Bobek in Case C-418/18 P *Puppinck*, EU:C:2019:640 .... 189n.14, 205n.107, 205n.110,
    211n.137, 211n.138, 216n.167, 217n.170
AG Bobek in Case C-129/19 *BV*, EU:C:2020:375 .... 95n.434
AG Pitruzella in Case C-181/19 *Jobcenter Krefeld*, EU:C:2020:377 ..... 56n.193, 170n.173, 382n.160
AG Hogan in Case C-398/19 *BY*, EU:C:2020:748............................ .... 101n.479
AG Bobek in Case C-505/19 *WS*, EU:C:2020:939 .... 82n.345
AG Saugmandsgaard Øe Case C-535/19 *A (Soins de santé publics)*,
    EU:C:2021:114 .... 285n.131, 410n.334
AG Richard de la Tour in Case C-709/20 *CG*, EU:C:2021:515 ..... 411n.342, 419n.378, 423–24n.400,
    425n.403, 437n.472, 437n.473, 461n.116
AG Rantos in Case C-719/19 *FS*, EU:C:2021:104...................... 272n.56, 273n.67, 274n.71,
    348n.494, 426n.410, 427
AG Tanchev in Case C-897/19 PPU *IN*, EU:C:2020:128 .... 106n.511
AG Szpunar in Case C-930/19 *X v Belgian State*, EU:C:2021:225............... 339n.433, 339n.434
AG Szpunar in Case C-35/20 *A (Franchissement de frontières en navire
    de plaisance)*, EU:C:2021:456 .... 266n.25, 266n.26, 266n.27
AG Szpunar in Case C-118/20 *Wiener Landesregierung (Révocation d'une
    assurance de naturalisation)*, EU:C:2021:530 .... 113n.27, 117n.53, 117n.55, 119n.66, 120
AG Hogan in Case C-247/20 *Commissioners for Her Majesty's Revenue and
    Customs (Assurance maladie complète)*, EU:C:2021:778 .... 286n.133, 450n.47
AG Richard de la Tour in Case C-328/20 *Commission v Austria*, EU:C:2022:45 .... 478n.40, 478n.47
AG Szpunar in Case C-411/20 *Familienkasse Niedersachsen-Bremen*,
    EU:C:2021:1017 .... 350n.509, 407n.313, 410n.334
AG Kokott in Case C-490/20 *VMA v Stolichna obshtina, rayon 'Pancharevo'*,
    EU:C:2021:296 .... 201n.84, 268n.40
AG Collins in Case C-673/20 *Préfet du Gers*, EU:C:2022:129.............. 40n.89, 109n.2, 122n.90,
    124n.106, 125n.108, 126–27n.124,
    129n.139, 129n.140, 197n.51
AG Pitruzella in Case C-22/21 *SRS and AA*, EU:C:2022:183 .... 163n.130, 181n.238,
    182n.241, 184n.253

CASE LAW OF THE GENERAL COURT

Case T-450/12 *Anagnostakis*, EU:T:2015:739 .... 212n.141
Case T-58/08 P *Commission v Roodhuijzen*, EU:T:2009:385 .... 163–64n.134
Case T-44/14 *Costantini*, EU:T:2016/223, para. 65 .... 212n.140, 214n.152
Case T-754/14 *Effler*, EU:T:2017:323 .... 215n.162, 216n.166
Case T-529/13 *Izsák and Dabis*, EU:T:2016:282 .... 214n.157, 215n.160, 215n.161
Case T-209/00 *Lamberts*, EU:T:2002:94 .... 220n.189
Case T-646/13 *Minority SafePack*, EU:T:2017:59 .... 209n.126, 213–14, 213n.146, 213n.148,
213n.149, 213n.150
Case T-789/19 *Moerenhout v Commission*, EU:T:2021:260 .... 208n.125, 214n.153
Case T-561/14 *One of Us and Others*, EU:T:2018:210 .... 208n.124, 209n.129, 210n.132, 211n.133,
211n.135, 211n.138, 214n.155, 219n.182, 219n.183, 219n.185
Case T-228/02 *Organisation des Modjahedines du peuple d'Iran v Council*, EU:T:2006:384 ..... 540n.249
Case T-47/03 *Sison v Council*, EU:T:2007:207 .... 540n.249

EUROPEAN COURT OF HUMAN RIGHTS

Alilouch El Abasse v Netherlands, App No 14501/89, 6 January 1992 .... 150–51n.58
Aoulmi v France, No 50278/99 .... 515n.99
Gochev v Bulgaria, App No 34383/03, 26 November 2009 .... 521n.126
Ignatov v Bulgaria, Application No 50/02, 2 July 2009 .... 521n.126
MSS v Belgium and Greece, App No 30696/09, 21 January 2011 .... 434–35n.459, 435n.460
Oliari and Others v Italy, App No 18766/11, 21 July 2015 .... 157n.97, 164n.136
Orlandi and Others v Italy, App No 26431/12, 14 December 2017 .... 153n.75
Pajić v Croatia, App No 68453/13, 23 February 2016 .... 157n.97
Riener v Bulgaria, App No 46343/99, 23 May 2006 .... 514n.89
Ruiz-Mateos v Spain, Series A no. 262, 23 June 1993 .... 543n.272
Vallianatos and Others v Greece, App No 29381/09, 7 November 2013 .... 153n.75, 157n.97

EUROPEAN FREE TRADE ASSOCIATION COURT (EFTA COURT)

Case E-4/11 *Clauder*, [2011] EFTA Ct. Rep. 216 .... 73n.278, 441n.4, 441n.6, 447–48, 447n.31,
448n.36, 449n.39, 456
Case E-15/12 *Wahl*, 22 July 2013 .... 73n.278
Case E-26/13 *Gunnarsson*, 15 November 2013 .... 73n.278
Case E-28/15 *Jabbi*, 21 September 2016 .... 73n.278
Case E-4/19 *Campbell*, 13 May 2020 .... 73n.278

EUROPEAN HUMAN RIGHTS REPORTS (EHRR)

Ahmut v The Netherlands (1996) 24 EHRR 62 .... 248n.342
Gül v Switzerland (1996) 22 EHRR 93 .... 248n.342
Hirst v United Kingdom (No 2) (2006) 42 EHRR 41 .... 198n.58, 199n.72
Jeunesse v The Netherlands (2015) 60 EHRR 17 .... 248, 249n.346, 252n.361, 347n.482
Matthews v United Kingdom (1999) 28 EHRR 361 .... 193n.25, 197
Scoppola v Italy (2013) 56 EHRR 19 .... 199n.72
Shindler v United Kingdom (2013) 58 EHRR 9 .... 193n.24

INTERNATIONAL COURT OF JUSTICE (ICJ)

Nottebohm, ICJ Reports 1955, 6 April 1955 .... 122n.94, 123n.96

UNITED KINGDOM

HC v SSWP [2017] UKSC 73 .... 256n.384, 437n.472
R (on the application of Sanneh) v Secretary of State for Work and Pensions,
    [2013] EWHC 793 (Admin) 248n.345
Shirley McCarthy v Secretary of State for the Home Department [2008] EWCA Civ 641 ... 235n.267

EU Legislation

1. DIRECTIVES

Directive 64/221/EEC on the coordination of special measures concerning the movement and residence of foreignnationals which are justified on grounds of public policy, public security or public health, OJ 1963–1964 Sp Ed P117............29n.10, 34, 49–50, 291–92, 309, 311, 356–57, 365,501n.13, 502, 503n.26, 504, 505–6, 508–9, 510–11, 517, 526, 537, 539n.243, 548
  Art 1......................147t, 291–92
  Art 2............................503n.26
  Art 2(2).....................501, 509–10
  Art 3(1)................501, 503, 517n.102
  Art 3(2)................501, 503, 517n.102
  Art 3(4)............................501
  Art 4..........................501, 511
  Art 4(1)............................501
  Art 4(2)............................501
  Art 4(3)............................501
  Arts 5–9............................501
  Art 5(2)............................517
  Art 6..........................542n.260
  Art 7..........................540n.251
  Art 8......................501n.14, 545
  Art 9..............................502
  Annex 1..........501n.14, 501–2n.15, 511
Council Directive 68/360/EEC of 15 October 1968 on the abolition of restrictions on movement and residence within the Community for workers of Member States and their families, 1968 OJ L257/13..........8n.33, 16, 28n.8, 71n.268, 177n.217, 265n.19, 292–93, 297n.199, 302n.233, 303n.240, 321, 324, 385, 454, 459
  Art 1.............................147t
  Art 2..........................263n.12
  Art 3..........................263n.12
  Art 4(3)........................176–77
  Art 8..........................269–70
  Art 21.........................265n.19

Directive 73/148/EEC on the abolition of restrictions on movement and residence within the Community for nationals of Member States with regard to establishment and the provision of services, 1973 OJ L172/14.........7n.23, 16, 29n.10, 34, 71n.269, 297n.199, 479–80, 479n.52, 492
  Art 1.............................147t
  Art 1(1)........................479–80
  Art 1(2).......................179n.229
  Art 2..........................263n.12
  Art 3..........................263n.12
  Art 4..........................269–70
  Art 4(2).......................265n.19
Directive 75/34/EEC concerning the right of nationals of a Member State to remain in the territory of another Member State after having pursued therein an activity in a self-employed capacity, 1975 OJ L14/10............452
  Art 4.......................452nn.62–63
Directive 90/364/EEC on the right of residence, 1990 OJ L180/26.........7n.25, 16, 36, 58, 175–76, 269–70, 280, 282–84, 288–89, 302n.233, 308–9, 342, 357n.15, 358n.19, 359–60, 362, 363, 364–65, 370–71, 380–81, 403–4, 443–44
  Art 1......147t, 284n.123, 287, 306, 308, 448
  Art 1(1)................37n.70, 37n.72
  Art 2(2)........................49–50
  Art 5..........................272n.56
  Art 6..........................271–72
Directive 90/365/EEC on the right of residence for employees and self-employed 2004/occupational activity, 1990 OJ L180/28.........7n.25, 16, 36, 49–50, 269–70, 280, 287, 288–89, 302n.233, 306, 308–9, 359–60, 363, 370–71, 443–44, 448
  Art 1.....................147t, 357n.15
  Art 1(1)...........................286
Directive 90/366 on the right of residence for students..........36, 49–50

Art 1 287
Art 2 287
Art 3 287–88
Art 4 287
Council Directive 91/477/EEC on control
   of the acquisition and possession
   of weapons, 1991 OJ L256/51, as
   amended by Directive 2008/51/
   EC, 2008 OJ L 179/5 .... 51n.155
Council Directive 92/85/EEC on the
   introduction of measures to encourage
   improvements in the safety and health
   at work of pregnant workers and
   workers who have recently given
   birth or are breastfeeding,
   1992 OJ L348/1.
Art 8 .... 328n.369
Directive 93/96/EEC on the right of
   residence for students, 1
   993 OJ L317/59 .... 7n.25, 16, 36,
      55–56, 57–58, 146, 148–49, 269–70, 287,
      288–89, 302n.233, 303n.234, 307, 357n.15,
      359–60, 361, 363, 370–71, 376, 380–81,
      403–4, 413, 426, 443–44
Art 1 ...... 37n.70, 37n.72, 147t, 288, 357n.15
Art 3 .... 362–63, 377–78
Art 4 288–89
Council Directive 93/109/EC laying down
   detailed arrangements for the exercise
   of the right to vote and stand as a
   candidate in elections to the European
   Parliament for citizens of the Union
   residing in a Member State of which
   they are not nationals, 1993 OJ
   L329/34 ...... 191n.18, 192, 202–3, 258–59
Art 3 .... 203n.96
Art 5 .... 203n.96
Art 6 .... 202n.91
Art 6(1) 203
Art 8(2) 203n.94
Art 10 .... 202n.91
Council Directive 94/80/EC laying down
   detailed arrangements for the exercise
   of the right to vote and to stand as a
   candidate in municipal elections by
   citizens of the Union residing in a
   Member State of which they are not
   nationals, 1994 OJ L368/38 .... 191n.18,
      192, 202–3
Art 2(1) 203n.93
Art 2(1)(b) 202–3
Art 4 .... 203n.95
Art 4(1) 203n.96
Art 5(1) 203
Art 5(3) 203n.93
Art 7 .... 203n.94
Art 12 .... 203n.93
Art 14 .... 203n.93
Directive 95/46/EC of the European
   Parliament and of the Council on the
   protection of individuals with regard
   to the processing of personal data and
   on the free movement of such data,
   1995 OJ L281/31 .... 305n.249
Council Directive 2003/86/EC on the right
   to family reunification, 2003
   OJ L251/12 .... 9–10, 81n.331,
      142n.19, 162n.125, 172n.187,
      242–43, 339–40, 346n.473,
      388n.196, 503n.26
Recital 8 .... 142n.19
Recital 9 10
Recital 10 10
Art 4(1)(b) 174n.200
Art 4(1)(c) 174n.200
Art 4(1)(d) 174n.200
Art 4(2) 174n.203
Art 7(2) 310n.273
Art 15(3) 338–39
Art 15(4) 340n.438
Directive 2003/109 concerning the
   status of third-country nationals
   who are long-term residents, 2003 OJ
   L16/44 .... 9–10, 81n.331, 143n.23, 236,
      434–35, 539n.245
Art 5(1)(a) 282n.112
Art 5(2) 310n.273
Art 11(1)(d) 435n.461
Directive 2004/28 483
Directive 2004/31 .... 420n.382
Directive 2004/38/EC on the right of
   citizens of the Union and their family
   members to move and reside freely
   within the territory of the Member
   States, 2004 OJ L158/77 ...... 6n.20, 7n.23,
      7n.25, 8, 10n.44, 11–12, 14–15, 16–17,
      19–21, 22, 23–25, 23n.137, 27, 36,
      43–44, 49–50, 51, 56, 67–78, 84n.356, 90,
      98n.458, 115n.40, 127–28, 133, 134–35,
      139–40, 143, 144, 146, 150, 150–51n.58,
      153, 155, 156, 160, 161–63, 171–72,
      172n.187, 174–75, 177, 178, 185, 188–89,
      226, 235, 236, 240n.290, 242, 253, 254,
      255–56, 257, 258–59, 261, 286, 307, 323,
      347–48, 350, 351, 354–55, 358–70,
      381–425, 441, 442, 448, 469, 471–72,
      471n.1, 472n.8, 474n.14, 477, 479n.50,
      482, 484n.80, 486n.95, 487–88, 489,
      490–91, 492–93, 492n.130, 495n.141,
      495n.143, 499n.1, 500, 501–7, 496, 498,
      501–2n.15, 504n.34, 505–6, 505n.40, 507,
      508–52, 509n.70, 514n.91, 518n.104,
      521n.127, 525n.151, 529n.172, 539n.245,
      542n.262, 545n.284, 553

Preamble 86, 323–24
Recitals 1–4 70
Recital 1 . . . . 69, 86, 143n.24, 261, 273
Recital 2 273
Recital 3 . . . . . 6–7, 16, 69–70, 71–72, 86n.373,
          160, 273, 326n.357, 357, 471
Recital 4 . . . . 6–7, 16, 69, 86n.373, 261,
          326n.357, 357, 471
Recital 5 . . . . 140–41, 143n.24, 261, 316
Recital 6 . . . . 166, 180, 495
Recital 8 6–7
Recital 9 . . . . 290–91, 293–94
Recital 10 . . . . . . .56n.191, 69, 76, 91, 262, 279,
          280, 387, 396n.247, 423–24n.400
Recital 11 . . . . 69, 86, 262, 297, 304
Recital 14 . . . . 305n.246, 314
Recital 15 . . . . 158, 329–30, 338, 451–52
Recital 16 . . . . . 54n.173, 69, 263n.9, 279n.104,
          290–91, 293–94, 320, 388, 426
Recitals 17–19 69
Recital 17 . . . . 383–84, 385, 441, 442,
          458–60, 463–64
Recital 18 . . . . 91, 442
Recital 19 . . . . 372n.104, 445n.19, 452, 456
Recital 20 . . . . 69, 261, 371, 372n.102
Recital 21 . . . . 69, 371, 372n.102, 404, 405
Recital 22 .50, 69, 508–9
Recitals 23–24 69
Recital 23 . . . . .301, 500, 508–9, 524
Recital 24 . . . . .526–27, 527n.166, 529, 531
Recital 25 . . . . .539–40, 542
Recital 26 539–40
Recital 27 548
Recital 28 . . . . .69, 262–63, 340, 344
Recital 31 . . . . 69, 153n.76, 183–84, 261
Recital 38 . . . . 309n.267
Recital 39 . . . . 309n.267
Ch I–VII 68
Ch III .269, 446, 448–49
Ch IV 271, 443, 447
Ch VI 161, 298, 301, 319, 510, 510n.73,
          539n.246, 540, 550
Art 1 . . . . 72, 140
Art 1(a) 69–70
Art 1(c) 50
Art 2 . . . . 140, 145n.35, 169–70, 471–72
Art 2(2) 143, 146, 147–50, 160, 161, 166,
          167–68, 169, 175–79, 180–81, 182–83,
          238–39, 240–41, 274n.75, 309, 311,
          314–15, 365, 420, 447, 449, 486n.95, 495
Art 2(2)(a) 150–62, 163, 267n.31,
          336–37, 495n.142
Art 2(2)(b) 148–49, 151, 152–54, 162–64,
          165–66, 172–73, 332–33, 455
Art 2(2)(c) 145n.35, 148,
          171–74, 172–73n.191, 175, 176–77, 178,
          178n.224, 181n.237, 183, 240–41,
          267n.31, 304–5, 314

Art 2(2)(d) 148, 175–77, 240–41, 304–5,
          314, 482n.66
Art 2(3) 335
Art 3 . . . . .165n.145, 471–72
Art 3(1) 16–17, 20–21n.117, 72, 75,
          132, 144, 145–46, 148, 153–54, 156–57,
          158–59, 230, 233, 261, 275–76, 334–35,
          420, 421, 447, 450, 452, 471–72, 481n.64
Art 3(2) 146n.44, 148–49, 150,
          165–66, 167–68, 172n.183,
          179–80, 181, 182–84,
          289–90, 316, 494–95
Art 3(2)(a) 165n.142, 166n.146,
          167n.154, 173, 174, 175–77, 175n.208,
          179–85, 179n.229, 240–41, 305, 314, 315
Art 3(2)(b) 150, 151, 162–63, 164–71,
          165n.142, 179–85, 264, 314, 495
Art 4 . . . . .262, 263–69
Art 4(1) 264–65n.14, 265–66, 267n.28,
          268–69, 519n.113
Art 4(3) 267–68
Art 5 . . . . . 96–97, 160n.113, 262, 263–69, 271,
          300, 309–17, 460
Art 5(1) 264–65n.14, 301
Art 5(2)–(5). 265n.17
Art 5(2) 309, 310, 311–12, 313n.290,
          315, 349
Art 5(3) 310
Art 5(4) 301, 310, 311
Art 5(5) 265–66, 301, 302, 310, 516
Art 6 . . . . 59, 71–72, 76, 91, 139n.6, 142,
          144, 145–46, 254, 262, 263n.11,
          269–71, 271–73, 274–75, 278–79,
          290–91, 293, 294, 295–96, 299, 300,
          309–17, 318, 320, 354–55, 365, 371n.101,
          373, 374, 380, 384, 385, 405, 407, 426,
          446n.28, 455, 460, 491–92, 493, 494, 511
Art 6(1) 262n.7, 269, 271–72, 273, 302,
          311, 398n.257, 405, 406–7,
          416, 458, 491–92
Art 6(2) 148n.49, 185n.256, 261–62,
          262n.7, 311
Art 7 . . . . .14–15, 55, 58–59, 60, 71–72,
          74–75, 94n.430, 144, 145–46, 255, 262,
          269–70, 271–72, 274–75, 278–79, 293,
          294, 295–96, 300, 303–4, 318, 319, 321,
          324n.347, 327, 354–55, 365–66, 375–76,
          380, 384, 385, 386, 401–2, 403–4, 408–9,
          410–11, 412, 416–17, 419, 424, 426, 438,
          446n.28, 455, 460, 491–92, 493, 494
Art 7(1) . . . 47n.123, 76, 91, 142, 153–54, 239,
          254, 255–56, 276, 281n.108, 293–94,
          299–300, 325, 328, 331n.386, 333–34,
          335n.405, 337, 365, 385–86, 409n.331,
          411–12, 415, 416, 447–48, 459–60,
          461–63, 493, 494, 537
Art 7(1)(a) 7–8n.30, 55, 59–60n.210,
          71–72, 262, 262n.7, 274–79, 293, 302,

   318, 324, 326, 330, 331, 333, 334–35, 365–66, 378–79, 386n.184, 392, 405, 407–10, 414–15, 418–19, 447, 462
Art 7(1)(b) 7–8n.30, 54, 55, 56–59, 61–62, 135–36, 171, 262, 262n.7, 274–75, 277, 278–86, 289n.157, 294, 302, 303n.234, 304, 308, 318, 319, 320, 325, 330, 331, 333, 334–35, 358–59, 375–76, 386n.184, 387, 387n.191, 388–89, 391–92, 393, 399, 403–4, 405, 408–9, 410–13, 414–15, 419, 421, 434n.456, 447, 448n.34, 449, 450, 457
Art 7(1)(c) 148–49, 175–76, 262, 262n.7, 274–75, 277, 287–90, 289n.156, 289n.157, 302–3, 304, 308, 318, 320, 330, 331, 333, 334–35, 359n.22, 365, 379, 380, 386n.184, 403–4, 403n.287, 405, 408–9, 412–15, 419, 447
Art 7(1)(d) 262, 274–75, 330, 333, 365, 408–9, 414–15, 447, 448n.34
Art 7(2) 142, 148n.49, 159, 160n.113, 255–56, 262n.7, 274–75, 334–35, 336–37, 385–86, 414–15, 447, 461–62, 463–64, 493
Art 7(3) 74, 262n.7, 290n.165, 317–18, 321–29, 365–66, 397–98, 407–8, 456, 471, 518–19n.109
Art 7(3)(a) 324n.349, 327, 328–29, 408–9
Art 7(3)(b) . . . 325, 326, 328–29, 365–66, 408–9
Art 7(3)(c) 59, 59–60n.210, 328–29, 365–66, 395, 396, 398, 408–9, 415n.357
Art 7(3)(d) 328–29, 408–9
Art 7(4) 148–49, 175–76, 289–90
Art 8 . . . . 283, 296, 302, 303–4, 428, 438, 446n.28, 501–2n.15, 511n.76
Art 8(1) 302, 303
Art 8(2) 180n.231, 302, 304, 550
Art 8(3) 302, 303, 303n.234
Art 8(4) 54, 271n.52, 279n.104, 280n.105, 306–9, 330, 331, 333, 388–89, 403–4, 410, 411
Art 8(5) 180n.231, 304, 313n.294, 314n.295
Art 8(5)(d) 176–77
Art 8(5)(f) 166–67
Arts 9–11 . . . . 296, 309–17, 309, 310
Art 9 . . . . 446n.28
Art 9(1) 160n.113
Art 9(2) 311
Art 9(3) 311
Art 10 . . . . 96–97, 181n.237, 264, 275–76, 311, 313, 314, 315, 316–17, 348–50, 446n.28
Art 10(1) . . . 160n.113, 311–12, 311n.276, 313
Art 10(2) 313, 313n.290, 314
Art 10(2)(c) 148n.49
Art 10(2)(d) 176–77

Art 10(2)(e) 180
Art 10(2)(f) 166–67
Art 11 . . . . 275–76, 315, 446n.28
Art 11(1) 315
Art 11(2) 311–12, 315
Art 12 . . . . 143, 145n.35, 155, 159, 317–18, 319, 320, 329–32, 334–40, 354–55, 385, 401–2, 405, 410–11, 414–15, 426, 446n.28, 456, 460, 481n.64, 482–83, 489, 494
Art 12(1) 262n.7, 331, 333–34
Art 12(2) 262n.7, 298n.205, 329, 331, 333–34, 386n.184, 429n.425, 447, 461n.119
Art 12(3) 262n.7, 331–32, 415, 428–29
Art 13 . . . . 143, 145n.35, 155, 159, 317–18, 319, 320, 329–30, 332–40, 354–55, 385, 401–2, 405, 410–11, 414–15, 426, 446n.28, 456, 460, 481n.64, 482–83, 494
Art 13(1) 262n.7, 333–34
Art 13(2) 143, 262n.7, 298n.205, 329, 333–34, 336–37, 338–40, 386n.184, 429n.425, 436–37, 447, 461n.119
Art 13(2)(a) 333–35, 336
Art 13(2)(b) 333–34
Art 13(2)(c) 332, 333–34, 336–37, 338, 339–40
Art 13(2)(d) 333–34
Art 14 . . . . 55, 262, 262n.7, 271n.52, 277–78, 295–96, 298, 308–9, 317–21, 320n.328, 354–55, 407, 428, 438, 446n.28
Art 14(1) 59, 76, 91, 264–65n.14, 295–96, 318–21, 398–99, 405, 406–7
Art 14(2) 76, 91, 279n.104, 295–96, 307, 318, 319, 321, 334–35, 401–2, 410–11, 412–13
Art 14(3) 55, 279n.104, 319, 410–11, 426
Art 14(4) 295–96, 319
Art 14(4)(a) 320, 409n.331
Art 14(4)(b) 58n.203, 290–91, 293–94, 295, 295n.191, 296n.194, 298, 320, 366–67, 371–72, 371n.101, 373, 374–76, 385, 396, 397–98, 402n.281, 403–4, 405, 405n.297, 408–9, 415–16, 417–18, 419n.376, 422–23, 426, 460, 494
Art 15 . . . . . 55, 262, 271–72, 271n.52, 297–98, 301, 355n.9, 428, 438, 446n.28, 499n.1, 513, 539n.246
Art 15(1) 55, 273, 297–300, 308–9, 318n.318, 320, 321, 341, 355, 411–12, 413, 426, 458, 540n.250
Art 15(2) 300
Art 15(3) 298–99, 318n.318, 321n.331, 339–40, 341, 547n.300
Art 16–18 371
Art 16 . . . . 20–21n.117, 104, 135, 145–46, 156–57, 171, 235n.265, 286, 303,

EU LEGISLATION   liii

Art 16(1) 327–28, 383–84, 386, 425, 442, 442n.7, 443, 448–49, 453, 454–55, 458–60, 463, 469, 475–76, 494, 536–37
Art 16(1) 74–75, 76, 91, 92, 135–36, 142, 156–57, 262n.7, 382n.161, 383–85, 414, 416, 446, 447–49, 450, 454, 455, 457n.89, 458–61, 462, 463–64, 493
Art 16(2) 104, 145n.35, 156–58, 262n.7, 385–86, 447, 449, 450, 451–52, 461–62, 463, 463–65, 493, 535n.214
Art 16(3) 315, 327–28, 445n.21, 452, 453, 454, 458, 466
Art 16(4) 77–78, 445, 452, 453, 454, 457, 464, 466, 528
Art 17 . . . . 145n.35, 323–24, 327–28, 442, 442n.7, 443, 447, 454–55, 456
Art 17(1)(a) 456–57
Art 17(1)(d) 262n.7
Art 17(3) 262n.7, 456
Art 17(4) 262n.7, 445n.22
Art 18 . . . . 145n.35, 264–65n.14, 330, 330n.384, 333n.394, 429n.425, 442n.7, 447
Art 19 . . . . 442n.7, 467–69
Art 19(1) 467–68
Art 19(2) 467–68
Art 20 . . . . 442n.7, 467–68, 518–19
Art 20(1) 351, 468–69
Art 21 . . . . 458, 467–68, 518–19
Art 21(1) 351
Art 22 . . . . 72, 145–46, 266n.23
Art 23 . . . . 149–50, 178, 272–73
Art 23(3) 73
Art 24 . . . . 14–15, 58n.203, 74–75, 76, 279n.104, 286, 290n.161, 354–55, 357, 370–81, 384, 390–91, 403, 405, 416–18, 424, 425–26, 461–62, 490n.121
Art 24(1) 149–50, 170, 254, 258, 372, 373–74, 380–82, 389, 391–92, 393, 395, 396, 400–1, 403, 408–9, 412, 413, 414–15, 416–17, 419, 419n.377, 420, 421, 422–23, 424–25, 428–29
Art 24(2) 14–15, 38n.78, 58, 59, 74–75, 77–78, 91, 92n.404, 170, 272–73, 277, 289, 290, 318–21, 372, 374–80, 381–82, 388–89, 390, 391–92, 395, 396, 397–98, 400–1, 403, 404, 405, 406–7, 408–9, 411, 413, 414–16, 417–18, 424, 427–29, 445n.19
Art 25 469
Art 25(1) 469
Art 25(2) 469, 517n.102
Art 26 . . . . 264–65n.14, 469
Art 26(2) 527n.158
Art 27 . . . . 55, 271, 298–99, 304, 349–50, 426n.410, 509n.69, 509n.70, 515–16, 518, 543–44, 551, 552
Art 27(1) 50–51, 54–55, 265–66, 499n.1, 509–10, 513, 519n.114, 521, 522, 528, 539n.245, 540, 541, 550
Art 27(2) 503n.26, 510–11, 512, 517, 517n.102, 520–23, 524, 529, 531–32, 539n.245, 550
Art 27(3) 128n.134, 510n.73
Art 27(4) 510–11
Art 28 . . . . 298–99, 347–48, 425n.406, 466–67, 517, 520, 526, 530, 534, 535, 536–37, 538, 547, 551
Art 28(1) 298–99, 510–11, 515–16, 517, 524–26, 524n.146, 531–32, 533, 550
Art 28(2) 76n.298, 499n.1, 514, 515–16, 526–39, 539n.245
Art 28(3) 76n.298, 92, 298n.207, 467, 499n.1, 514, 515–16, 526–39, 539n.245, 547
Art 28(3)(a) 73–74, 499n.1, 528, 529, 534–37
Art 28(3) (b) 171n.182
Art 29 . . . . 253n.364, 510–11, 512, 551
Art 29(2) 511n.76
Art 29(3) 511
Art 30 . . . . 55, 271n.52, 297–98, 316n.310, 318n.318, 321, 340, 341, 349n.502, 426, 428, 429–30, 438, 504n.30, 539–45
Art 30(1) 540, 541
Art 30(2) 298, 540n.249, 542
Art 30(3) 299, 545
Arts 30–34 540
Art 31 . . . . . . 55, 168n.160, 185n.255, 271n.52, 297–98, 316n.310, 318n.318, 321, 340, 341, 349n.502, 426, 428, 429–30, 438, 539–40, 545–47
Art 31(1) 168, 184–85, 495n.143, 540n.249, 547n.294
Art 31(2) 298, 547, 552
Art 31(3) 298–99, 524, 547
Art 31(4) 547
Art 32 . . . . 304, 539–40, 547–51
Art 32(1) 548, 549, 551
Art 32(2) 551
Art 33 551–52
Art 33(1) 552
Art 33(2) 531–32, 537n.229, 548
Art 33(4) 518
Art 34 539–40
Art 35 . . . . 161, 262–63, 316, 340, 341–43, 344–50, 509n.70, 539n.246
Art 36 . . . . 266–67, 267n.28
Art 37 . . . . 18, 360, 383n.164, 384, 385, 424–25, 460–61

Art 39 269–70
Council Directive 2004/114/EC on
the conditions of admission of
third-country nationals for the
purposes of studies, pupil
exchange, unremunerated
training or voluntary service,
2004 OJ L375/12 . . . . 515n.97, 521n.123
Council Directive 2006/112/EC on the
common system of value added tax
2006 OJ L347/1 . . . . 433n.451
Directive 2008/115 on common
standards and procedures in Member
States for returning illegally staying
third-country nationals, 2008 OJ
L348/98 . . . . 237n.274, 500n.9, 518–20,
518–19n.109, 542n.258
Art 7(3) 518–19n.109, 519–20
Art 12(2) 541
Arts. 15–18 . . . . 518–19n.109
Directive 2009/50/EC on the conditions of
entry and residence of third-country
nationals for the purposes of highly
qualified employment, 2009
OJ L155/17 . . . . 10n.45
Directive 2011/36/EU on preventing and
combating trafficking in human beings
and protecting its victims,
2011 OJ L101/1 . . . . 347n.485
Directive 2011/93/EU on combating the
sexual abuse and sexual exploitation of
children and child pornography,
2011 OJ L335/1 . . . . 531n.187
Directive 2011/95/EU on standards for
the qualification of third-country
nationals or stateless persons
as beneficiaries of international
protection, for a uniform status for
refugees or for persons eligible for
subsidiary protection, and for the
content of the protection granted,
2011 OJ L337/9 . . . . 521n.129
Art 12(2) 521–23, 522n.134
Directive 2011/98/EU on a single
application procedure for a single
permit for third-country nationals to
reside and work in the territory of a
Member State and on a common set
of rights for third-country workers
legally residing in a Member State,
2011 OJ L343 9–10
Council Directive 2013/1/EU amending
Directive 93/109/EC as regards certain
detailed arrangements for the exercise
of the right to stand as a candidate in
elections to the European Parliament
for citizens of the Union residing in a
Member State of which they
are not nationals,
2013 OJ, L26/27 . . . . 202n.91
Directive 2013/33/EU laying down
standards for the reception of
applicants for international
protection, 2013 OJ L180/96 . . . . . . 515n.97
Directive 2014/36/EU on the conditions
of entry and stay of third- country
nationals for the purpose of
employment as seasonal workers,
2014 OJ L94/375 . . . . 10n.41
Directive 2014/54/EU on measures
facilitating the exercise of rights
conferred on workers in the context of
freedom of movement for
workers, 2014 OJ L128/8
Recital 1 169
Art 2 . . . . 169n.168
Directive 2014/66/EU on the
conditions of entry and residence
of third- country nationals in the
framework of an intra- corporate
transfer, 2014 OJ L157/1 . . . . 10n.42
Council Directive 2015/637/EU on
the coordination and cooperation
measures to facilitate consular
protection for unrepresented citizens
of the Union in third countries and
repealing Decision 95/553/EC,
2015 OJ L106/1 . . . . . 96n.441, 190, 222–23,
225n.207
Recital 3 223
Recital 4 223–24
Recital 7 224
Recital 13 225–26
Recital 14 225–26
Recital 23 224–25
Art 2(1) 224
Art 2(2) 224
Art 4 224
Art 5 . . . . .224, 225–26
Art 6 224
Art 7(1) 224–25
Art 7(2) 224–25
Art 7(3) 224–25
Art 8 225–26
Art 8(3) 225–26
Art 9 225–26
Art 10–13 224–25
Art 13 224–25
Art 13(3)–(4) 224–25
Arts 14–15 225–26
Arts 14(3) 225–26
Art 15 225–26
Annex I 225–26
Annex II 225–26

Directive 2016/801/EU on the conditions
   of entry and residence of third-
   country nationals for the purposes of
   research, studies, training, voluntary
   service, pupil exchange schemes or
   educational projects and au pairing,
   2016 OJ L132/21 . . . . 9n.38
Directive 2018/957/EU amending
   Directive 96/71/EC concerning the
   posting of workers in the framework
   of the provision of services,
   2018 OJ L173/16 . . . . 279n.101
Directive 2019/997/EU establishing an EU
   Emergency Travel Document
   and repealing Decision
   96/409/CFSP, 2019 OJ L163/1 225–26
   Recital 3 . . . . 225n.211
   Art 1 225–26
   Art 3 225–26
   Art 4 . . . . 225–26n.212
   Art 5 . . . . 225–26n.212
   Art 6 . . . . 225–26n.212
   Art 7 . . . . 225–26n.212
   Arts 8–13 . . . . 225–26n.212
   Art 14 . . . . 225–26n.212
   Art 15 . . . . 225–26n.212
   Art 16 . . . . 225–26n.212
   Art 17 . . . . 225–26n.212
Directive 2020/2184/EU on the quality
   of water intended for human
   consumption (recast),
   2020 OJ L 435/1 . . . . 217n.171
Directive 2009/50/EC on the conditions of
   entry and residence of third-country
   nationals for the purposes of highly
   qualified employment, 2009
   OJ L155/17 (the 'Blue Card'
   Directive) 10n.40
   Art 2 . . . . 10n.40
   Art 5 . . . . 10n.40

2. REGULATIONS

Regulation 1612/68/EEC on freedom of
   movement for workers within the
   Community, 1968 OJ L257/13 16,
      96n.446, 146, 155, 158, 162, 168–69,
      170–71, 275–76, 281n.109, 289,
      291n.169, 292–93, 323–24, 367–69,
      472n.7, 484–85, 484n.74, 487, 488
   Preamble 140–41
   Recital 3 489
   Recital 5 33
   Art 2 . . . . 368n.85
   Art 3(1) 293
   Art 5 . . . . 29n.11, 47n.128, 368n.85
   Art 7 489
   Art 7(2) 32, 149–50, 168–69, 358n.20,
      368n.83, 368n.85, 488
   Art 10 . . . . 8n.33, 28n.8, 147t, 155–56,
      155n.84, 157, 159–60, 175n.206,
      226–27, 383–84n.168, 486–87, 489
   Art 10(1) 73n.280
   Art 10(1)(a) 487
   Art 10(2) 179n.229
   Art 10(3) 155–56, 156n.90
   Art 11 . . . . 149n.53, 489
   Art 12 . . . . . 135n.184, 156, 157, 383–84n.168,
      483–85, 483n.70, 484n.76, 489, 490
Commission Regulation 1251/70/EEC
   on the right of workers to remain in
   the territory of a Member State after
   having been employed in that State,
   1970 OJ L142/24, ... 321, 322, 323–24
   Art 1 . . . . 147t
   Art 2 326
   Art 2(1)(a) 445n.19
   Art 3(2) 322–23
   Art 4(1) 452
   Art 4(2) 452
   Art 7 323–24
Regulation 1408/71 on the application of
   social security schemes to employed
   persons and their families moving
   within the Community, OJ 1971
   L149/2 . . . . 291n.169
   Art 4(1)(h) 47n.128, 358n.20
   Art 69(1) 29n.11
Regulation 539/2001 listing the third
   countries whose nationals must be
   in possession of visas when crossing
   the external borders and those whose
   nationals are exempt from that
   requirement, 2018 OJ L303/39, 2001
   OJ L81/1 . . . . 264, 264n.13, 309
Council Regulation 1030/2002/EC laying
   down a uniform format for residence
   permits for third-country nationals,
   2002 OJ L157/1 . . . . 9n.38
   Art 5 . . . . 312n.282
Regulation 883/2004 on the coordination
   of social security systems, 2011 OJ
   L166/1 . . . . 74–75, 169n.167, 277n.88,
      284–85, 291–92, 319, 401–2, 433–34,
      433n.452, 436–37, 473n.10, 474–75
   Recital 8 473–74
   Art 1(j) 387–88, 399
   Art 1(z) 401n.273
   Art 3(1)(a) 285n.127
   Art 3(1)(j) 401n.273, 406–7
   Art 3(3) 387
   Art 4 . . . . 380–81, 387–88, 390–91,
      399–400, 401n.277
   Art 7 473–74

Art 11(3)(e).... 285n.129, 399, 400, 410n.335
Art 64........................... 273n.62
Art 64(1) 291
Art 64(1)(c)........................... 291
Art 67...........................473–74
Art 70............................401–2
Art 70(2) 390–91, 400–1
Art 70(4) 387–88, 401n.276
Council Regulation 2252/2004/EC on
  standards for security features and
  biometrics in passports and travel
  documents issued by the Member
  States, 2004 OJ L141/1 ...... 7n.22, 31n.24,
                                63–64, 265n.18
  Art 18...........................63–64
  Art 28...........................63–64
  Art 62(3) 63–64
  Annex III........................63–64
  Annex IV........................63–64
Regulation 562/2006 establishing a
  Community Code on the rules
  governing the movement of persons
  across borders (Schengen Borders
  Code), 2006 OJL105/1 .... 266n.26
  Art 6(1)(e)...................... 503n.26
  Art 21...........................265–66
Commission Regulation 635/2006/EC
  repealing Regulation (EEC) No 1251/
  70 on the right of workers to remain
  in the territory of a Member State after
  having been employed in that State,
  2006 OJ L112/9..................323–24
Regulation 810/2009/EC establishing a
  Community Code on Visas
  (Visa Code), 2009 OJ L243/1
  Art 23...........................309–10
Regulation 211/2011/EU on the citizens'
  initiative, 2011 OJ L65/1 206–7,
                                217n.170, 219–20
  Recital 2.......................211, 214
  Art 4(2) 212
  Art 4(2)(b)..............214–15, 214n.156
  Art 4(3) 212, 213
  Art 6(3)(b)......................214–15
  Art 10(1)(c).................. 209n.129, 211
  Art 15.............................. 211
  Annex II...........................215
Regulation 492/2011 on freedom of
  movement for workers within the
  Union, 2011 OJ L141/1 ....6n.21,
    16n.84, 74–75, 148n.48, 149–50, 169,
    171–72, 259n.400, 273n.63, 275–76,
    291–92, 294, 328–29, 336n.412, 405,
    417–18, 419, 422–23, 442, 471n.2,
                        472, 474, 475, 490
  Arts 1–6............. 291, 292n.171, 328–29
  Art 7(1) 417

Art 7(2) 74–75, 169–71, 275–76,
                277, 367–68, 370–71, 408n.323,
                417–18, 474, 475–76, 476n.32
Art 10......... 74–75, 156, 169–70, 263n.10,
                329n.380, 331–32, 383–84, 396, 403,
                415n.355, 416–18, 416n.361, 426,
                428–29, 430n.428, 450n.47, 461–63,
                469, 471, 478–79, 483n.70, 490n.121
Commission Implementing Regulation
  1179/2011/EU laying down technical
  specifications for individual online
  collection systems pursuant to
  pursuant to Regulation (EU) No
  211/2011 on the European citizens'
  initiative, 2011 OJ L301/3 .... 206n.116
Regulation 604/2013/EU establishing
  the criteria and mechanisms for
  determining the Member State
  responsible for examining an
  application for international
  protection lodged in one of the
  Member States by a third-country
  national or a stateless person,
  2013 OJ L180/31............434–35n.459
Regulation 1141/2014 on the statute
  and funding of European political
  parties, 2014 OJ L371/1 .... 192n.23
Regulation 2016/399/EU on a Union Code
  on the rules governing the movement
  of persons across borders (Schengen
  Borders Code), 2016 OJ L77/1 .... 503n.26
Regulation 2016/679/EU on the protection
  of natural persons with regard to the
  processing of personal data and on
  the free movement of such data, and
  repealing Directive 95/46/EC
  (General Data Protection Regulation),
  2016 OJ L119/1................ 305n.249
Regulation 2018/1806/EU listing the
  third countries whose nationals
  must be in possession of visas when
  crossing the external borders and
  those whose nationals are exempt
  from that requirement, 2018
  OJ L303/39 .... 264n.13, 309
Regulation 2019/788/EU on the
  European citizens' initiative,
  2019 OJ L 130/55 .... 96n.443, 206–7,
                                213n.147
  Recital 6............................ 207
  Recital 9......................... 96n.443
  Art 1.............................215–16
  Art 2(1) 207
  Art 3....................... 96n.443, 207
  Art 3(2) 207
  Art 4.............................207–8
  Art 4(1) 207–8

Art 4(2) 207–8
Art 4(3) 207–8
Art 4(4) 207–8
Art 4(5) 207–8
Art 4(6) 207–8
Art 5......................................208–9
Art 5(1) 208–9
Art 5(2) 208–9
Art 5(7) 207–9
Art 6(1) 208–9
Art 6(3) 208–9, 212
Art 6(4) 208–9, 219n.184
Art 6(7) 208–9, 219n.184
Arts 8–14................................. 209
Art 8...................................... 209
Art 8(1) 209
Art 9...................................... 209
Art 9(3) 209
Art 9(6) 209
Art 10..................................... 209
Art 11................................ 209n.128
Art 11(4) 209n.128
Art 12..................................... 209
Art 12(1) 209
Art 13..................................... 209
Art 14..................................... 209
Art 14(1) 209
Art 14(2) 209
Art 15.......................209–11, 219n.184
Art 15(2) 210
Art 16..................................... 210
Art 17..................................... 210
Art 17(1) 210
Art 18..................................... 210
Art 18(2) 210
Art 18(3) 210
Art 19..................................... 210
Art 20..................................... 210
Art 25..................................... 210
Annex I 206–7
Annex II.................................207–9
Annex III................................. 209
Regulation 2019/1157/EU on
    strengthening the security of
    identity cards of Union citizens and
    of residence documents issued to
    Union citizens and their family
    members exercising their right of free
    movement, 2019 OJ L188/67...... 265n.18
Commission Delegated Regulation
    2019/1673/EU replacing Annex I
    to Regulation (EU) 2019/788 of the
    European Parliament and of the
    Council on the European citizens'
    initiative, 2019 OJ L257/1 206–7
Commission Implementing Regulation
    2019/1799/EU laying down technical
    specifications for individual online
    collection systems pursuant to
    Regulation (EU) 2019/788 of the
    European Parliament and of the
    Council on the European citizens'
    initiative, 2019 OJ L274/3 .... 206n.116
Regulation 2019/1381/EU on the
    transparency and sustainability of the
    EU risk assessment in the food chain,
    2019 OJ L 231/1................ 217n.171
Regulation 2020/1042/EU laying down
    temporary measures concerning the
    time limits for the collection, the
    verification and the examination
    stages provided for in Regulation (EU)
    2019/788 on the European citizens'
    initiative in view of the COVID-19
    outbreak, 2020 OJ L231/7 206–7

3. DECISIONS

Decision no 1/80 ....73, 156n.93, 537,
                                538, 539n.243
    Art 7....................... 73n.280, 537
    Art 14(1) 537, 538–39
Decision 94/262/EC on the regulations
    and general conditions governing the
    performance of the Ombudsman's
    duties, 1994 OJ L113/15............. 220
Council Decision 96/409/CFSP on the
    establishment of an emergency travel
    document, 1996 OJ L168/4 225–26
Council Decision 95/553/EC regarding
    protection for citizens of the European
    Union by diplomatic and consular
    representations, 1995 OJ L314/73 222
    Art 1..................................... 222
    Art 2..................................... 222
    Art 3..................................... 222
    Art 4..................................... 222
    Art 5(1) 222
    Art 5(2) 222
    Art 6(1) 222
    Art 7...................................222–23
    Art 8...................................222–23
Decision 647/96/EC of the European
    Parliament and of the Council
    adopting a programme of Community
    action on the prevention of AIDS and
    certain oiher communicable diseases
    within the framework for action in the
    field of public health (1996 to 2000),
    1996 OJ L95/16................. 508n.66
Council Decision 2002/192/EC concerning
    Ireland's request to take part in some
    of the provisions of the Schengen
    acquis, 2002 OJ L64/20........... 265n.18

Council Framework Decision 2002/584/
JHA on the European arrest warrant
and the surrender procedures between
Member States—Statements made by
certain Member States on the adoption
of the Framework Decision, 2002 OJ
L190/1 . . . . 97n.449, 356n.14
Council Framework Decision 2004/
757/JHA laying down minimum
provisions on the constituent elements
of criminal acts and penalties in the
field of illicit drug trafficking, 2004 OJ
L335/8 . . . . 515n.99
Decision no 1/2020 of the Joint Committee
established under the Agreement
between the European Community
and its Member States, of the one
part, and the Swiss Confederation,
of the other, on the free movement
of persons of 15 December 2020
amending Annex II to that Agreement
on the coordination of social security
schemes [2021/137] PUB/2021/4,
2021 OJ L42/15 . . . . 72–73n.276
Council Decision 2002/772/EC,
Euratom, 2002 OJ L283/1 . . . . 192n.22
Commission Decision 2017/652/EU on the
proposed citizens' initiative entitled
'Minority SafePack — one million
signatures for diversity in Europe',
2017 OJ L92/100 213

4. OTHER

1976 Act concerning the election of the
members of the European Parliament
by direct universal suffrage 193–94
Act 1 . . . . 192, 194
Art 1(3) 198
Act 2 192
Act 3 192
Act 8 192
Agreement between the European Union
and the Republic of Iceland and the
Kingdom of Norway on the surrender
procedure between the Member States
of the European Union and Iceland
and Norway, OJ 2006 L292/2 . . . .72–73n.276
Agreement between the European Union
and the Republic of Iceland and the
Kingdom of Norway on the surrender
procedure between the Member States
of the European Union and Iceland
and Norway, OJ 2006 L292/2 105–6
Agreement establishing an Association
between the European Economic
Community and Turkey (signed at
Ankara, 12 September 1963)
1977 OJ L361/28 . . . 11n.49, 63n.234, 73–74
Agreement on the European Economic
Area, OJ 1994 L1/3 . . . . 106n.511
Agreement on the gradual abolition of
checks at their common borders ('the
Schengen Agreement'), 2000
OJ L239/1313
Art 21 . . . . 312n.282
Art 54 . . . . 80n.324
Agreement on the withdrawal of the
United Kingdom of Great Britain and
Northern Ireland from the European
Union and the European Atomic
Energy Community, OJ 2019 CI
384/01 . . . . 12, 125n.112, 126, 127, 139–40,
262n.7, 264–65n.14,
442n.7, 471–72n.5
Title III 473n.10
Pt II 11n.52, 126n.118, 127–28, 144–45,
187n.2, 262–63, 420n.381,
473n.10, 500n.10
Ch 3 12
Ch 4 . . . . 12, 126n.118
Ch 6 . . . . 12, 126n.118
Ch 8 . . . . 126n.118
Ch 10 . . . . 12, 126n.118
Art 2(b) 471–72n.5
Art 3(1) 471–72n.5
Art 6 . . . . 127n.130
Art 9(a)(i) 148n.45
Art 9(a)(ii) 172n.183
Art 9(b) 471–72n.5
Art 9(c) 144–45, 471–72n.5
Art 9(d) 275–76n.79
Art 10 . . . . 127–28, 127n.126, 144–45,
165n.142, 187n.2, 264–65n.14,
539n.246
Art 10(1) 145n.35
Art 10(1)(a)–(d) 145n.35, 165n.142,
172–73n.191, 275–76n.79
Art 10(1)(c) 275–76n.79
Art 10(1)(d) 275–76n.79
Art 10(1)(e)(ii) 144–45, 148n.45
Art 10(1)(e)(iii) 172–73n.191
Art 10(2) 165n.142
Art 10(3) 165n.142, 187n.1
Art 10(4) 165n.142
Art 10(5) 165n.142
Art 11 . . . . 371n.101, 453n.67
Art 13 . . . . 262n.7
Art 13(2) 275–76n.79, 329n.378
Art 13(3) 275–76n.79, 329n.378
Art 13(4) 329n.378
Art 14 . . . . 264–65n.14
Art 15 . . . . 264–65n.14, 371n.101
Art 15(1) 442n.7, 446n.28

Art 15(2)	453n.64
Art 15(3)	453n.67
Art 17	275–76n.79, 290n.163
Art 17(1)	275–76n.79
Art 18(1)	127–28, 297n.198, 420n.381
Art 18(1)(h)	442n.7
Art 18(1)(k)	303n.234, 306n.255
Art 18(1)(l)	306n.255, 309n.265
Art 18(1)(m)	309n.265
Art 18(1)(p)	128n.134, 442n.7, 510n.73
Art 18(1)(r)	510n.73
Art 20	128n.134, 340n.439, 510n.73
Art 20(1)	510n.73
Art. 21	510n.73, 539n.246
Art 22	272n.61
Art 23	371n.101
Art 23(3)	340n.439
Art 24	264–65n.14, 275–76n.79
Art 24(3)	471–72n.5
Art 25	264–65n.14, 275–76n.79
Art 25(1)	471–72n.5
Art 25(3)	471–72n.5
Art 26	275–76n.79, 471–72n.5
Art 30	473n.10
Art 36	127n.130, 473n.10
Art 39	127n.126
Art 89(1)	284–85n.126
Art 126	420
Art 127(1)(b)	196–97
Art 158(1)	127n.128
Art 165(1)	127n.129
Amsterdam Treaty	40–41, 109
Charter of Fundamental Rights of the European Union (CFR)	2, 6n.14, 84n.360, 85–89, 105n.509, 114, 120, 136, 179, 198–99n.66, 219–20, 233n.252, 261, 351, 355, 382, 412–13, 425–26, 531n.187, 553
Preamble	216n.165
Title II	198–99n.66
Title V	5, 86
Art 1	5, 88–89, 104, 153, 185, 258, 339n.433, 395, 431–32, 433, 436–37
Art 4	434–35
Art 7	5, 47n.123, 88–89, 114–16, 139, 140–41, 153, 157, 158–59, 163–64, 172n.187, 183–84, 185, 224, 241–43, 245–46, 248, 249–50, 251, 252, 253, 257, 258, 267–68n.35, 335–36, 339n.434, 345, 431–32, 434n.456, 436, 449n.40, 450, 452, 481n.64, 525–26
Art 9	345
Art 14	5, 431–32
Art 15(2)	5, 7n.24, 87n.377, 292n.171
Art 19	103–4, 105n.509
Art 20	5, 38, 243–59, 338–40, 395, 431–32, 433, 512
Art 21	5, 153, 155, 185, 230n.234, 338–39, 431–32
Art 21(1)	47n.123, 69, 251, 339–40, 541
Art 21(2)	10–11, 46–47, 437n.472
Art 24	5, 47n.123, 88–89, 116, 140–41, 172n.187, 184n.253, 185, 230n.234, 250, 251, 253, 267–68n.35, 431–32, 434n.456, 436
Art 24(2)	114–16, 140–41, 184, 242–43, 245–46, 250, 253, 267–68n.35, 436
Art 24(3)	172, 241n.301, 242–43
Art 25	5, 431–32
Art 26	5, 251, 431–32
Art 33	5, 431–32, 434n.456
Art 34	5, 230n.234, 431–32, 435n.461
Art 34(2)	437n.472
Art 34(3)	434–35, 435nn.461–62
Art 35	5, 431–32
Art 39	5, 86, 187n.2, 191, 191n.17, 192, 196–97
Art 39(1)	191, 192, 198, 200
Art 39(2)	188, 191, 198, 199–200, 200n.76
Art 40	5, 187n.2, 191, 191n.17, 200
Art 41	5, 86, 204–5
Art 41(1)	205n.106
Art 41(4)	205n.106
Art 42	5, 15n.81
Art 43	5, 15n.81, 219–20
Art 44	5, 86, 217–18, 219n.182
Art 45	5, 86, 87, 273
Art 45(1)	6n.14, 86
Art 45(2)	6n.14
Art 46	223
Art 47	5, 184–85, 198n.63, 298–99, 431–32, 540n.248, 542, 543–45
Art 48	221
Art 49(1)	86n.368, 199
Art 49(3)	266–67, 267n.28
Art 51	251, 395, 433
Art 51(1)	88, 198, 198n.63, 199–200, 241, 242, 250, 298–99, 395, 425, 432, 433–34
Art 51(2)	88, 241–42, 433, 434n.456
Art 52(1)	87, 199, 252, 542
Art 52(2)	87, 249–50, 327n.368
Art 52(3)	85n.367, 163–64
Art 52(7)	198–99n.66
Art 53(1)	183–84
Convention implementing the Schengen Agreement of 14 June 1985 between the Governments of the States of the Benelux Economic Union, the Federal Republic of Germany and the French Republic on the gradual abolition of checks at their common borders, signed in Schengen on 19 June 1990 and which entered into force on	

26 March 1995, 2000
  OJ L239/19 . . . . 80n.324, 503n.26
  Art 96 . . . . 503n.26
  Art 96(2)(a) 503n.26
  Art 96(3) 503n.26
Convention on Protection of Children
  and Co- operation in Respect of
  Intercountry Adoption, signed at
  The Hague on 29 May 1993 . . . . . . 173n.197
Convention on the Reduction
  of Statelessness
  Art 7(1) 112n.19
  Art 7(3) 112n.19
  Art 8(2) 112n.19
Convention on the Transfer of Sentenced
  Persons 1983 103
  Art 2 103
Convention to Eliminate All Forms of
  Discrimination Against Women
  Art 16(1)(b). 150–51n.58
Court's Rules of Procedure
  Art 94 82
Declarationno 2 onnationality of a Member
  State, annexed by the Member States
  to the TEU 111
Declaration of the European Commission
  on issues related to the abuse of the
  right of free movement of persons
  Annex VII 348n.491
EC Treaty 139, 322–23, 501
  Art 5a 40–41n.93
  Art 8(2) 42–43
  Art 8a vi
  Art 8a(2) 44n.112
  Art 18(2) 44n.112
  Art 18(3) 43–44
  Art 189 192
  Art 190(1) 194
EEC Treaty 28–30, 304, 501
  Art 2 64–65
  Art 10 312–13
  Art 48(2) 28n.6
  Art 49 . . . . 28n.6
  Art 226 64–65
EU–USA Agreement
  Art 17 99–100
European Convention for the Protection
  of Human Rights and Fundamental
  Freedoms (ECHR) 85–86, 105
  Art 3 . . . . 435n.460
  Art 8 . . . . 88, 140–41, 156n.92, 161–62,
        163–64, 168n.164, 183–84, 241,
        248, 252, 338, 485, 507
  Art 8(1) 241–42, 449n.40
  Protocol No 1, Art 3 . . . . 193, 195n.41, 197–98
European Convention onnationality
  Art 4(c) 112n.19
  Art 7(2) 114n.28

Geneva Convention
  Art 1F. 521–23, 522n.134
Lisbon Treaty. . . . 40–41, 42–43, 44n.111, 85–86,
        88–89, 105–6, 192, 197–98,
        201n.85, 204–5
Nice Treaty 44
Rules of Procedure of the European Parliament
  r 226 218
  r 227 218
Second Protocol amending the (European)
  Convention on the Reduction of Cases
  of Multiple Nationality and Military
  Obligations in Cases of Multiple
  Nationality, signed at Strasbourg on 2
  February 1993 . . . . 114n.28
Trade and Cooperation Agreement
  between the European Union
  and the European Atomic Energy
  Community, of the one part, and the
  United Kingdom of Great Britain and
  Northern Ireland, of the other part,
  OJ 2020 L444/14 . . . . 128n.137
Treaty of Rome 7
Treaty on European Union (Maastricht
  Treaty, TEU) (1992) . . . . v, 1, 19, 44, 71, 363
  Preamble vn.6, 2, 45n.114, 216n.165
  Art B vn.6
  Art 1 . . . . 2, 45n.114
  Art 2 . . . . . 17n.91, 27n.3, 97, 106, 106–7n.518,
        189n.15, 205, 208–9, 216n.165,
        268n.40, 522n.134, 523
  Art 3 . . . . 17n.91, 66, 522n.134, 523
  Art 3(2) 2, 45, 94–95
  Art 3(3) 107n.519
  Art 3(4) 23n.134, 439
  Art 3(5) 2, 25n.140, 45, 98–99, 106,
        220–21, 268–69
  Art 4(2) 38, 49, 64n.235, 123–24n.101,
        153, 200–1, 268–69,513n.85, 543n.267
  Art 4(3) 66, 98–99, 101–2, 107n.521, 121,
        122–23n.95, 153n.74, 312–13, 549
  Art 6 . . . . vi, 85–86
  Art 6(1) 85–86, 87, 198–99n.66,
        241–42, 432
  Art 6(3) 85–86, 113n.23, 211–12
  Art 8(1) 106
  Art 9 . . . . . 8n.31, 39–40, 39n.84, 109, 124–25,
        129, 268–69
  Art10 . . . . 45, 189–90, 192, 199–200
  Art 10(1) 189n.15, 192, 216n.165, 312–13
  Art 10(2) 5
  Art 10(3) 5, 24, 45, 188, 190–91, 200, 205,
        207, 213–14
  Art 10(4) 192n.23
  Art 11 . . . . 4, 24, 45, 96, 188, 189,
        190, 205
  Art 11(4) 96n.442, 187n.2, 205, 206,
        209n.129, 211, 215–16, 219n.182

Art 13 . . . . 4, 204–5
Art 13(3) 188
Art 14 . . . . 192, 199–200
Art 14(2) 192
Art 14(3) 5, 94n.429, 190–91, 198, 199–200
Art 19(1) 198n.63
Art 35 . . . . 222n.197
Art 50 . . . . 5, 12, 39–40, 104–5, 124, 129
Art 50(1) 121–22, 125
Art 50(2) 124
Art 50(3) 124
Art 52 95–96
Art 52(1) 95–96
Art 55(1) 4, 204–5
Treaty on the Functioning of the
 European Union (TFEU). 2, 480
 Title V 9–10, 11–12, 122–23n.95
 Pt II. 2, 4
 Art 4(2) 9
 Art 6(e) 287
 Arts 8–13. . . . . 5n.12
 Art 8 . . . . 5n.12
 Art 11 . . . . 5n.12
 Art 18 . . . . 2, 6n.19, 10–11, 13n.66, 14–15,
   28, 35–36, 38, 42, 46–47, 48n.132,
   77–78, 79, 83, 97–98, 100, 102–4, 125,
   197, 226–27, 230n.234, 287–88, 289,
   306n.253, 339–40, 353nn.1–2, 356–57,
   358–59, 360–64, 368–69, 373–75, 378,
   380–81, 383, 384–85, 390–91, 403,
   411n.342, 416–17, 419, 420, 421,
   422–23, 424, 425–26, 433–34,
   435–36, 461–62, 474, 490n.121
 Art 18(1) 363, 377–78, 390–91
 Art 19 2
 Arts 20–24. . . . . 2, 5–6, 13, 21n.119
 Arts 20–25 . . . . 5, 200n.73
 Art 20 . . . . vin.9, 3, 6n.17, 8, 8n.31, 13n.66,
   15nn.81–82, 19–21, 23–24, 27, 38,
   39–40, 41–42, 43, 46–47, 51, 53, 55n.181,
   75, 78–79, 81n.331, 82–85, 88, 90, 99,
   109, 111–12, 113–15, 116–19, 120,
   121, 122, 124–25, 127, 129–30, 131,
   132, 135–36, 139, 140, 143, 145–46,
   148n.48, 162n.125, 171–72, 172n.187,
   175n.208, 176n.210, 183n.245, 187n.2,
   188–89, 199–200, 220–21, 228, 229, 230,
   230n.234, 231, 232, 234–35, 236–37,
   238, 239–41, 242–43, 244, 244n.321,
   245, 246–47, 248, 249–50, 251,
   252–59, 268–69, 279n.101, 336n.412,
   338n.428, 358, 359, 359n.23, 360–61,
   362, 368, 381, 384–85, 400, 425, 427–28,
   430–32, 433–34, 436–37, 437n.472,
   487–88n.103, 498, 525–26, 525n.150
 Art 20(1) 8, 24, 27, 39–41, 42, 43–44,
   43n.108, 109, 111, 124, 194n.34,
   195, 261n.2, 271–72, 281, 299

Art 20(2) 4, 5, 6, 16, 39, 42–44, 51, 69,
   76–77, 96, 193–94, 194n.34, 201–2,
   201n.81, 238, 261, 390–91,
   405, 420, 464,519, 553
Art 20(2)(a) 39, 87, 390
Art 20(2)(b)–(d) 39, 241–42
Art 20(2)(b) 124–25, 187n.2, 190–91,
   198, 200
Art 20(2)(c) 116, 220–21, 222, 226
Art 20(2)(d). 217–18, 219n.186
Arts 21–24. 39
Art 21 . . . . 3, 6–7, 8, 13–15, 17–18, 19–21,
   23–24, 27, 38, 39, 41–42, 43, 44, 45,
   46–47, 48–51, 51n.158, 55n.181, 58,
   75, 76–77, 77n.314, 78–81, 82, 84–85,
   87, 88, 98–99, 100, 102–4, 114–15,
   116n.43, 120, 127, 129–30, 131, 132,
   133–36, 139, 139n.6, 141–42, 143,
   145–46, 148, 148n.48, 152–53, 159n.104,
   168, 170, 171–72, 176n.210, 187–88,
   189n.10, 200–2, 226, 230n.234, 232,
   234–35, 236, 239, 241n.301, 243,
   244n.318, 249, 252–53, 254, 255, 256,
   257, 258–59, 262n.7, 265, 267–68,
   275–76, 277n.87, 279n.101, 281, 289,
   295–96, 336n.412, 338n.428, 342,
   358–59, 359n.23, 360, 360n.29, 361–62,
   363–64, 365n.59, 370–71, 374–75,
   379–81, 383, 384–85, 396, 397–98, 400,
   405, 412–13,415–16, 417, 419, 421,
   422–23, 424, 425–26, 427–28, 430–31,
   433–34, 436–37, 438, 446, 449, 450,
   454n.76, 469,471, 472, 474–75, 480, 483,
   487–91, 487–88n.103, 493,, 494–95, 498,
   503n.26, 505–6, 508n.62, 513
Art 21(1) 6, 7, 12–13, 16, 27, 35–36, 39,
   41, 42, 45, 50, 51, 67–68, 69, 70,
   76–77, 78, 80n.324, 87, 89–90,
   96–97, 102–3, 119n.65, 133n.171,
   133n.173, 134–35, 142, 154n.79, 200,
   234n.260, 235n.265, 261, 267–68,
   271–72, 281, 283–84, 299, 313n.290,
   364–65, 381, 387,390–91, 405, 420, 422,
   435–36, 464, 491–92, 494–95, 519, 549, 553
Art 21(2) 44–46, 48n.132, 96
Art 21(3) 44
Arts 22–24. 27, 39, 127
Art 22 . . . . .3–4, 16, 187n.2, 188,
   190–91, 200n.79
Art 22(2) 86, 194, 195
Art 23 . . . . 4, 16, 24, 96, 188, 190, 220–21,
   222–24, 222n.197, 225–26
Art 24 . . . . . 4, 15, 16, 24, 96, 96n.442,188, 190,
   204–5, 212, 217–18, 219n.186
Art 24(1) 135, 187n.2
Art 25 . . . . .4, 43–44, 201–2
Art 26 . . . . 316n.310
Art 34 . . . . 80n.326, 438–39

Art 36 . . . . 514n.92
Arts 45–47 73
Arts 45–48 . . . . 30, 30n.20
Art 45 . . . 7, 8, 12–13, 14nn.71–72, 14n.74, 32,
   34, 41–42, 42n.100, 46, 47–48, 51, 74, 81,
   87n.377, 130–31, 130n.148, 140n.11,
   148n.48, 170–71, 227, 254, 262n.7,
   266n.23, 269–70, 272–73,273n.63,
   275–76, 278–79, 290, 292, 293,294,
   295–96, 300n.223, 322–24, 322n.334,
   325, 327–28, 329, 342, 356, 358,
   366–69, 374–75, 379, 383–84,
   384n.175, 393n.237, 396, 397–98,
   405, 408n.317, 409, 415–16, 418–19,
   422–23, 427–28, 463, 471, 472, 474–75,
   477, 479n.50, 480, 481, 483–88,
   489, 493, 498
Art 45(1) 31–32, 291
Art 45(2) 170n.171, 291, 368–69, 374–75,
   375n.118, 375n.120, 417–18, 501
Art 45(3) 107n.521, 275–76, 295–96, 537, 538
Art 45(3)(c) 321
Art 45(3)(d) 321
Art 45(4) 501n.11
Art 48 . . . . 30–31, 87n.377, 473n.10,
   474–75, 486n.93
Art 49 . . . . 7, 8, 13, 32, 34, 42, 46, 74n.286,
   160n.114, 254, 262n.7, 272–73, 273n.63,
   275–76, 277, 278–79, 325, 328, 356,
   406n.298, 408n.317, 409, 418–19,
   427–28, 471, 474–75, 483–88,
   493, 498
Art 51 . . . . 501n.11
Art 52 . . . . 107n.521
Art 52(1) 501
Art 52(2) 95n.435
Art 56 . . . . . 7, 8, 13, 32, 34, 35, 42, 46, 80n.325,
   272–73, 278–79, 472, 479–80
Art 62 . . . . 107n.521, 501, 501n.11
Art 63(2) 95–96
Art 67(1) 95n.438
Art 67(2) 9, 95n.438
Art 67(3) 95n.438
Art 77 . . . . 9, 316n.310
Art 77(2)(c) 9
Art 79 9
Art 79(1) 9
Art 79(2) 9
Art 79(2)(a) 9
Art 79(2)(b) 9, 129n.142
Art 79(4) 9
Art 79(5) 9
Art 83(1) 531–32
Arts 119–144 212
Art 127(1)(b) 187n.2
Art 157 228
Art 165(2) 287
Art 166 . . . . 35–36, 287

Arts 198–204 195
Art 207(3) 215–16
Art 207(4) 215–16
Art 218 215–16
Art 223(1) 4, 191, 193–94
Art 225 211
Art 227 . . . . 4, 15, 24, 188, 217–19
Art 228 . . . . 4, 15n.81, 24, 188
Art 228(1) 219–20
Art 241 211
Art 258 21
Art 259 . . . . 21, 193
Art 263 210–11
Art 267 . . . . 13, 21–22, 23n.133, 51, 79–80
Art 288 215–16
Art 294 . . . . 4n.5, 44n.112
Art 296 . . . . 212, 213, 214
Art 326 . . . . 107n.521
Art 346(1)(a) 543n.267
Art 352 . . . . 36n.61
Art 355 95–96
Protocol No 19 . . . . 95n.437
Protocol No 20, Art 1 . . . 316, 317n.314, 348–49
Protocol No. 21 . . . . 9n.37, 9n.38, 95n.437
Protocol No. 22 . . . . 9n.37, 9n.38, 95n.437
Annex 195, 508
United Nations Convention on the
   Rights of the Child, of 20
   November 1989 . . . . 527n.166, 528, 531n.187

5. NATIONAL INSTRUMENTS

Bulgaria

Constitution
   Art 25(1) 267

Germany

Weimar Constitution
   Art 109 512

Ireland

Constitution
   Art 9.2.1 . . . . 343–44n.459
Nationality and Citizenship
   Act 2004 . . . . 343–44n.459

Netherlands

Law on Nationality 114, 116

Romania

Civil Code 152

United Kingdom

European Parliament (Representation)
   Act 2003 193
Immigration Act 1971 193–94

1
Introducing EU Citizenship Law

1. Chapter Overview

The aim of this book is to try to say what EU citizenship law 'is'.[1] It articulates, explains, and analyses the legal framework and legal developments that have shaped the status of Union citizenship and the rights conferred on Member State nationals. This chapter establishes how 'EU citizenship law' is understood for that purpose. It examines how the rights, and obligations, associated with Union citizenship relate to other rights conferred by EU law and other objectives pursued by the Union, which in turn uncovers the distinctive meaning and scope—the added legal value—of Union citizenship.

Union citizenship is a novel and complex legal status: conferred by and aiming to foster attachment to the European Union as a supranational polity, but only through holding the nationality of one of the Member States; concerned mainly, but not exclusively, with the transnational dimensions of the citizen's life; implemented and enforced (or hindered) primarily through the actions and decisions of national authorities, within parameters set and supervised by Union institutions. As a legal status, Union citizenship evolves in more concrete legal form the statement in *Van Gend en Loos* that:

> [T]he Community constitutes a new legal order of international law for the benefit of which the states have limited their sovereign rights, albeit within limited fields, and the subjects of which comprise not only Member States *but also their nationals*. Independently of the legislation of Member States, Community law therefore not only imposes obligations on individuals but is also intended to confer upon them *rights which become part of their legal heritage*.[2]

Since its formal conception through the Maastricht Treaty, Union citizenship has catalysed an extraordinary, and ongoing, legal experiment, the processes and implications of which are traced throughout this book. But the legal story examined here sits in deeper and wider economic, political, social, and even emotional contexts. Because Union citizenship is also an idea: a vector of European integration, collective personhood, and multi-layered identities that reflects the paradoxically inclusive and exclusive qualities of citizenship more generally.

The chapter is organised around *defining*, *distinguishing*, and *progressing* EU citizenship law. Following a brief overview of relevant Treaty provisions and secondary legislation (Section 2), the relationship between Union citizenship and other sources of EU rights is outlined (Section 3), examining in particular the 'specific expression' method normally used

---

[1] Borrowing from K Lenaerts and JA Gutierrez-Fons, 'To say what the law of the EU is: methods of interpretation and the European Court of Justice' (2014) 20 Columbia Journal of European Law 3.
[2] Case 26/62 *Van Gend en Loos*, EU:C:1963:1 (emphasis added). On the significance of this judgment for 'embryonic forms of Union citizenship', see FG Jacobs, 'Citizenship of the Union: a legal analysis' (2007) 31 European Law Journal 591 at 592–93.

to determine which legal provisions apply in particular situations, which in turn defines the scope of this book. The respective contributions of the main institutional actors involved in the construction and progression of EU citizenship law—the EU legislator and the Court of Justice as well as national authorities and national courts—are then introduced (Section 4), and an overview of the chapters that follow is provided (Section 5).

2. Defining EU Citizenship Law: The Legal Framework

Union citizenship is central to the purpose, identity, and ambitions of the European Union as well as to the policies and objectives that it pursues. Building on the preambles to the Treaty on European Union (TEU) and Treaty on the Functioning of the European Union (TFEU), which frame Union objectives around perceived benefits for the 'peoples' of the Member States, Article 1 TEU asserts that '[t]his Treaty marks a new stage in the process of creating an ever closer union among the peoples of Europe, in which decisions are taken as openly as possible and as closely as possible to the citizen'. Article 3(2) TEU establishes that the Union 'shall offer its citizens an area of freedom, security and justice without internal frontiers, in which the free movement of persons is ensured in conjunction with appropriate measures with respect to external border controls, asylum, immigration and the prevention and combating of crime'. And Article 3(5) TEU requires that '[i]n its relations with the wider world, the Union shall uphold and promote its values and interests and contribute to the protection of its citizens'. Similarly, the preamble to the Charter of Fundamental Rights of the European Union (CFR) signals that the Union 'places the individual at the heart of its activities, by establishing the citizenship of the Union and by creating an area of freedom, security and justice'. In realising these objectives, what EU law then produces in terms of substantive rights and obligations concerns Union citizens across multiple fields of activity, with consumer protection, criminal law and surrender procedures, data protection, action on climate and the environment, and policies on social protection and inclusion providing just some key examples.

Part Two of the TFEU addresses 'Non-Discrimination and Citizenship of the Union'. Article 18 TFEU establishes that '[w]ithin the scope of application of the Treaties, and without prejudice to any special provisions contained therein, any discrimination on grounds of nationality shall be prohibited'.[3] Article 19 TFEU creates legislative competence for the taking of 'appropriate action to combat discrimination based on sex, racial or ethnic origin, religion or belief, disability, age or sexual orientation'.[4] Articles 20–24 TFEU then 'establish' the status of Union citizenship and outline a basic framework of related rights and obligations:

---

[3] Article 18 TFEU also provides that '[t]he European Parliament and the Council, acting in accordance with the ordinary legislative procedure, may adopt rules designed to prohibit such discrimination'.

[4] Article 19 TFEU provides: '1. Without prejudice to the other provisions of the Treaties and within the limits of the powers conferred by them upon the Union, the Council, acting unanimously in accordance with a special legislative procedure and after obtaining the consent of the European Parliament, may take appropriate action to combat discrimination based on sex, racial or ethnic origin, religion or belief, disability, age or sexual orientation. 2. By way of derogation from paragraph 1, the European Parliament and the Council, acting in accordance with the ordinary legislative procedure, may adopt the basic principles of Union incentive measures, excluding any harmonisation of the laws and regulations of the Member States, to support action taken by the Member States in order to contribute to the achievement of the objectives referred to in paragraph 1'.

Article 20

1. Citizenship of the Union is hereby established. Every person holding the nationality of a Member State shall be a citizen of the Union. Citizenship of the Union shall be additional to and not replace national citizenship.
2. Citizens of the Union shall enjoy the rights and be subject to the duties provided for in the Treaties. They shall have, inter alia:
   (a) the right to move and reside freely within the territory of the Member States;
   (b) the right to vote and to stand as candidates in elections to the European Parliament and in municipal elections in their Member State of residence, under the same conditions as nationals of that State;
   (c) the right to enjoy, in the territory of a third country in which the Member State of which they are nationals is not represented, the protection of the diplomatic and consular authorities of any Member State on the same conditions as the nationals of that State;
   (d) the right to petition the European Parliament, to apply to the European Ombudsman, and to address the institutions and advisory bodies of the Union in any of the Treaty languages and to obtain a reply in the same language.

These rights shall be exercised in accordance with the conditions and limits defined by the Treaties and by the measures adopted thereunder.

Article 21

1. Every citizen of the Union shall have the right to move and reside freely within the territory of the Member States, subject to the limitations and conditions laid down in the Treaties and by the measures adopted to give them effect.
2. If action by the Union should prove necessary to attain this objective and the Treaties have not provided the necessary powers, the European Parliament and the Council, acting in accordance with the ordinary legislative procedure, may adopt provisions with a view to facilitating the exercise of the rights referred to in paragraph 1.
3. For the same purposes as those referred to in paragraph 1 and if the Treaties have not provided the necessary powers, the Council, acting in accordance with a special legislative procedure, may adopt measures concerning social security or social protection. The Council shall act unanimously after consulting the European Parliament.

Article 22

1. Every citizen of the Union residing in a Member State of which he is not a national shall have the right to vote and to stand as a candidate at municipal elections in the Member State in which he resides, under the same conditions as nationals of that State. This right shall be exercised subject to detailed arrangements adopted by the Council, acting unanimously in accordance with a special legislative procedure and after consulting the European Parliament; these arrangements may provide for derogations where warranted by problems specific to a Member State.

2. Without prejudice to Article 223(1) and to the provisions adopted for its implementation, every citizen of the Union residing in a Member State of which he is not a national shall have the right to vote and to stand as a candidate in elections to the European Parliament in the Member State in which he resides, under the same conditions as nationals of that State. This right shall be exercised subject to detailed arrangements adopted by the Council, acting unanimously in accordance with a special legislative procedure and after consulting the European Parliament; these arrangements may provide for derogations where warranted by problems specific to a Member State.

Article 23

Every citizen of the Union shall, in the territory of a third country in which the Member State of which he is a national is not represented, be entitled to protection by the diplomatic or consular authorities of any Member State, on the same conditions as the nationals of that State. Member States shall adopt the necessary provisions and start the international negotiations required to secure this protection.

The Council, acting in accordance with a special legislative procedure and after consulting the European Parliament, may adopt directives establishing the coordination and cooperation measures necessary to facilitate such protection.

Article 24

The European Parliament and the Council, acting by means of regulations in accordance with the ordinary legislative procedure, shall adopt the provisions for the procedures and conditions required for a citizens' initiative within the meaning of Article 11 of the Treaty on European Union, including the minimum number of Member States from which such citizens must come.

Every citizen of the Union shall have the right to petition the European Parliament in accordance with Article 227.

Every citizen of the Union may apply to the Ombudsman established in accordance with Article 228.

Every citizen of the Union may write to any of the institutions or bodies referred to in this Article or in Article 13 of the Treaty on European Union in one of the languages mentioned in Article 55(1) of the Treaty on European Union and have an answer in the same language.

Article 25 TFEU requires the Commission to report (to the European Parliament, the Council, and the Economic and Social Committee) every three years on the application of Part Two of the Treaty, taking into account 'the development of the Union'. It also establishes legislative competence for the Council, acting unanimously and under a special legislative procedure, to 'strengthen or add to the rights listed in Article 20(2)' on the basis of these reports.[5] At the time of writing, the Commission had published nine reports,[6] but no legislative measures have yet been adopted on the basis of Article 25 TFEU.

---

[5] The ordinary legislative procedure is outlined in Article 294 TFEU. Following the special legislative procedure, Article 25 TFEU requires that the consent of the European Parliament must be obtained and that any provisions adopted must be approved by the Member States 'in accordance with their respective constitutional requirements'.

[6] Linked to its latest (at the time of writing) Article 25 TFEU Report (On progress towards effective EU citizenship 2016–2020, COM(2020) 731 final), see also EU Citizenship Report 2020: Empowering Citizens and

The TFEU provisions outlined above must also be read alongside other provisions of the TEU and CFR, notably Articles 10(2),[7] 10(3),[8] and 14(3)[9] TEU, and Title V ('Citizens' Rights) CFR, which affirms the rights to vote and stand as a candidate in both European Parliament (Article 39 CFR) and municipal elections (Article 40 CFR), good administration (Article 41 CFR), access to documents (Article 42 CFR), refer cases of maladministration to the European Ombudsman (Article 43 CFR), petition the European Parliament (Article 44 CFR), freedom of movement and residence (Article 45 CFR), and diplomatic and consular protection (Article 46 CFR). Most other provisions of the Charter address 'everyone' but Article 15(2) CFR, reflecting the economic freedoms conferred by the TFEU, addresses Union citizens only.[10] More generally, other Charter provisions have wider resonance for EU citizenship law, especially Articles 1 (human dignity), 7 (respect for private and family life), 14 (right to education), 20 (equality before the law), 21 (non-discrimination), 24 (rights of the child), 25 (rights of the elderly), 26 (integration of persons with disabilities), 33 (family and professional life), 34 (social security and social assistance), 35 (health care), and 47 (right to an effective remedy) CFR.

The extent to which Union citizenship rights are ring-fenced within Articles 20–25 TFEU is an open question.[11] Article 20(2) TFEU declares that Union citizens enjoy 'the rights provided for in the Treaties'—not just in *that* part of the Treaties—and, since the Lisbon Treaty, that the rights listed expressly in that provision are rights that citizens have 'inter alia'. However, Union citizenship is not included in any of the mainstreaming clauses that require the Union to take account of certain interests or policies 'in defining and implementing its policies and activities',[12] and protection of Union citizens in the event of the withdrawal of a Member State from the Union is not mentioned at all in Article 50 TEU.

While fully recognising the extent to which Union citizenship connects to much of what the Union is and much of what the Union does, the scope of EU citizenship law is necessarily more narrowly drawn for present purposes.[13] Drawing from the frame of Union citizenship

---

Protecting their Rights, 15 December 2020, COM(2020) 730 final, which refers to the Commission's six headline ambitions for Europe to set out 'a number of concrete actions and priorities around the four main themes: strengthening democratic participation, citizens' empowerment and fostering inclusion of citizens in the EU; facilitating the exercise of free movement and simplifying daily life; protecting and promoting EU citizenship; and protecting EU citizens in Europe and abroad, including in times of crisis/emergency' (para 1).

[7] ie 'Citizens are directly represented at Union level in the European Parliament. Member States are represented in the European Council by their Heads of State or Government and in the Council by their governments, themselves democratically accountable either to their national Parliaments, or to their citizens.'

[8] ie 'Every citizen shall have the right to participate in the democratic life of the Union. Decisions shall be taken as openly and as closely as possible to the citizen.'

[9] ie 'The members of the European Parliament shall be elected for a term of five years by direct universal suffrage in a free and secret ballot.'

[10] ie 'Every citizen of the Union has the freedom to seek employment, to work, to exercise the right of establishment and to provide services in any Member State'.

[11] For example, Shaw has characterised 'the gradual accretion of policy competences and the step-by-step policy-making work of the Court and the other institutions in the fields of social policy, free movement of persons, education and vocational training, and cultural policy as expressions of European citizenship and associated rights' (J Shaw, 'Citizenship of the Union: towards post-national membership?', Jean Monnet Working Paper no. 6/97, <https://jeanmonnetprogram.org/archive/papers/97/97-06-.html> (accessed 24 May 2023), Part III, 4). Exploring Union citizenship as a 'global principle of interpretation' post-Lisbon, see N Nic Shuibhne, 'EU citizenship after Lisbon' in D Ashiagbor, N Countouris, and I Lianos (eds), *The European Union after the Treaty of Lisbon* (CUP 2012) 136 at 142–51.

[12] See esp Articles 8–13 TFEU, which require, for example, the elimination of inequalities between men and women (Article 8) and the integration of environmental protection (Article 11).

[13] For an example of how the legal qualities of citizenship are shaping wider Union policies, see A Iliopoulou-Penot, 'The construction of a European digital citizenship in the case law of the Court of Justice of the EU' (2022) Common Market Law Review 969.

constructed by EU primary law, as outlined above, EU citizenship law is therefore defined for the purposes of this book as *situations that engage Articles 20–24 TFEU directly*. The chapters that follow aim to articulate, explain, and analyse EU citizenship law on that basis; alert to the wider economic, political, and social influences that shape its development but assessing through legal analysis how EU citizenship law has evolved; what its different elements entail; how these elements combine to produce the wider system of EU citizenship law; and, to the extent possible, how that system might evolve further into the future.

The legal history and legal framework of Union citizenship are presented in more detail in Chapter 2. The electoral and other political rights outlined in Articles 22–24 TFEU (examined in Chapter 5) are the most distinctive legal elements of Union citizenship, significantly enriched by the principles and mechanisms of representative and participatory democracy conceived by the Lisbon Treaty. But it is undeniable that the right to move and reside freely within the territory of the Member States, conferred by Articles 20(2) and 21(1) TFEU,[14] is the most developed dimension of EU citizenship law to date. Freedom of movement and residence is typically depicted as 'a founding principle on which the Union is built'[15] and Union citizenship has been described as 'virtually synonymous with freedom of movement'.[16] Freedom of movement is such a defining feature of Union citizenship that even its *potential* exercise must be protected into the future in the absence of any cross-border movement (or other cross-border connection) yet realised.[17] Its legal protection is characterised more generally by the facilitation of citizen choice[18] and underpinned by a guarantee of equal treatment,[19] promises that are assessed across the chapters that follow.

The right to move and reside is 'facilitated' by Directive 2004/38 (recitals 4 and 8), which aims to 'simplify and strengthen' (recital 3) the right and to establish the limitations and conditions (Article 21 TFEU) under which it is exercised.[20] The Directive is returned to in Section 4. However, other legislative measures continue to apply in specific circumstances, especially in connection with freedom of movement for workers[21] and the coordination

---

[14] The Court refers almost exclusively to Art 21(1) TFEU in connection with the right to move and reside. The right to move and reside freely is also protected by Article 45(1) CFR. Article 45(2) CFR further provides that '[f]reedom of movement and residence may be granted, in accordance with the Treaties, to nationals of third countries legally resident in the territory of a Member State'. On the relationship between citizenship rights in the Treaties and in the Charter of Fundamental Rights respectively, see Chapter 2.

[15] AG Wathelet in Case C-67/14 *Alimanovic*, EU:C:2015:210, para 2 of the Opinion; for Hyltén-Cavallius, its 'creationist bone' (K Hyltén-Cavallius, *EU Citizenship at the Edges of Freedom of Movement* (Hart Publishing 2020) 10).

[16] AG Szpunar in Case C-202/13 *McCarthy II*, EU:C:2014:345, fn23 of the Opinion, citing European Commission, Proposal of 11 August 2011 for a Decision of the European Parliament and of the Council on the European Year of Citizens (2013) (COM(2011) 489 final, 1. Similarly, AG Ruiz-Jarabo Colomer described freedom of movement and residence as the 'central right' of Union citizenship, citing European Council, 'The Hague programme: strengthening freedom, security and justice in the European Union', 2005 OJ C53/1, para 1.1 (Joined Cases C-11/06 and C-12/06 *Morgan and Bucher*, EU:C:2007:174, para 67 of the Opinion).

[17] See esp the line of case law based on Article 20 TFEU in connection with securing residence for third-country national family members in a Union citizen's home State, beginning with Case C-34/09 *Ruiz Zambrano*, EU:C:2011:124. See further, Chapter 5.

[18] eg AG Sharpston in Case C-456/12 *O and B*, EU:C:2013:837, para 45 of the Opinion: '[t]he essence of that right is the freedom to choose whether or not to move to another Member State and/or to reside there'.

[19] eg Case C-224/98 *D'Hoop*, EU:C:2002:432, para 35, referring to 'the principles which underpin the status of citizen of the Union, that is, the guarantee of the same treatment in law in the exercise of the citizen's freedom to move'. Most developments in EU citizenship law concern the prohibition on nationality discrimination in Article 18 TFEU, though some engagement with wider understandings of equal treatment is also emerging; see further, Section 4 and Chapters 2 and 6 in particular.

[20] Directive 2004/38/EC on the right of citizens of the Union and their family members to move and reside freely within the territory of the Member States, 2004 OJ L158/77.

[21] Regulation 492/2011 on freedom of movement for workers within the Union, 2011 OJ L141/1. On the relationship between the Regulation and Directive 2004/38, see esp Chapters 6, 7, and 9.

of social security.²² Complexities produced by the interaction of different sources of EU rights are introduced in the next section and examined in more detail in several chapters of the book.

3. Distinguishing EU Citizenship Law: Personal and Material Scope

As will be seen in Chapter 2, the right to move and reside within the territory of the Member States has a long pre-citizenship history in EU law through the foundational rights conferred by the Treaty of Rome in the context of economic activity, for the purposes of work (now Article 45 TFEU), establishment (now Article 49 TFEU), and services (now Article 56 TFEU²³).²⁴ EU legislation adopted in the early 1990s extended the right to move and reside to certain categories of persons not covered by those Treaty provisions,²⁵ but Article 21(1) TFEU conferred the first 'general' right to move and reside in EU primary law.

In one sense, this citizenship-based right, which is directly effective,²⁶ produces autonomous constitutional significance, that is, significance for freedom of movement and residence beyond the objective of achieving the EU internal market through rights attached to work, establishment, and services.²⁷ For the Commission, the creation of Union citizenship established a 'new legal and political environment'.²⁸ The deeply evocative idea of Union citizenship as the 'fundamental status of nationals of the Member States' was first articulated by the Court of Justice in 2001 and has been repeated in almost every citizenship-relevant judgment ever since.²⁹ At the same time, however, the rights conferred by Articles 45, 49, and 56 TFEU remain virtually unaltered since they were first drafted for the Treaty of Rome and, especially when attention is focused on the extent to which the right to move and reside can be limited or restricted, the exercise of economic activity in a host Member State can still make a critical legal difference.³⁰

---

²² Regulation 883/2004 on the coordination of social security systems, 2011 OJ L166/1. On the relationship between this Regulation and Directive 2004/38, see esp Chapters 6, 7, and 9.

²³ Article 56 TFEU addresses the provision of services only; free movement rights to receive services were extended by legislation, notably Directive 73/148/EEC on the abolition of restrictions on movement and residence within the Community for nationals of Member States with regard to establishment and the provision of services, 1973 OJ L172/14, now repealed and replaced by Directive 2004/38.

²⁴ As noted in Section 2, these rights are also now protected by Article 15(2) CFR, which provides that '[e]very citizen of the Union has the freedom to seek employment, to work, to exercise the right of establishment and to provide services in any Member State'.

²⁵ Directive 90/364/EEC on the right of residence, 1990 OJ L180/26; Directive 90/365/EEC on the right of residence for employees and self-employed persons who have ceased their occupational activity, 1990 OJ L180/28; and Directive 93/96/EEC on the right of residence for students, 1993 OJ L317/59. All three measures required beneficiaries to be covered by comprehensive sickness insurance and to have sufficient resources to avoid becoming a burden on the social assistance system of the host Member State, and all three were repealed and replaced by Directive 2004/38. See further, Chapter 2.

²⁶ Case C-413/99 *Baumbast and R*, EU:C:2002:493, para 84.

²⁷ eg AG Cosmas in Case C-378/97 *Wijsenbeek*, EU:C:1999:144, paras 85–86 of the Opinion (suggesting at para 86 that 'freedom of movement constitutes a goal in itself and is inherent in the fact of being a citizen of the Union, and is not merely a parameter of the common market').

²⁸ COM(2001) 257 final, para 1.3.

²⁹ Case C-184/99 *Grzelczyk*, EU:C:2001:458, para 31. See subsequently eg Case C-138/02 *Collins*, EU:C:2004:172, para 61; Case C-524/06 *Huber*, EU:C:2008:724, para 69; Case C-135/08 *Rottmann*, EU:C:2010:104, para 43; Case C-220/12 *Thiele Meneses*, EU:C:2013:683, para 19; Case C-673/16 *Coman*, EU:C:2018:385, para 30; and Case C-490/20 *VMA v Stolichna obshtina, rayon 'Pancharevo'*, EU:C:2021:1008, para 41.

³⁰ For example, the right to reside in a host Member State for more than three months is not subject to requirements concerning sickness insurance or sufficiency of financial resources when an EU citizen is either working or

In terms of defining the scope of EU citizenship law more specifically, can Article 21 TFEU and Articles 45/49/56 TFEU apply concurrently or are they mutually exclusive? This question concerns the *material scope* of EU citizenship law, and it is returned to in Section 3.2. First, in Section 3.1, the *personal scope* of EU citizenship law is outlined, asking *who* citizens of the Union are in legal terms.

3.1 Personal Scope: Who is a Union Citizen?

At one level, the personal scope of EU citizenship law is straightforward: according to Article 20(1) TFEU, Member State nationals are Union citizens, and, conversely, third-country nationals are not.[31] Determining Member State nationality remains an exclusive national competence. However, 'the fact that a matter falls within the competence of the Member States does not alter the fact that, in situations covered by European Union law, the national rules concerned must have due regard to the latter'.[32] In light of the significance of holding Member State nationality, it will be seen in Chapter 3 that the Court of Justice has established a role for EU law with respect to reviewing national processes on the acquisition and loss of nationality in circumstances (to date) where loss of Union citizenship could result.

However, the relationship between EU citizenship law and third-country nationals is more complex than Article 20 TFEU suggests. Two points examined in more detail across the chapters that follow can be briefly noted here. First, certain family members of Member State nationals are protected by EU citizenship law irrespective of their own nationality, building on principles established in foundational economic free movement law.[33] That protection is not conferred on family members in their own right but is instead *derived* from the Member State national who moves. In other words, family reunification rights were created not, primarily, as fundamental rights per se but to facilitate a Member State national's capacity to move;[34] they are 'not autonomous rights of [third-country] nationals but rights derived from those enjoyed by a Union citizen'.[35] As the Court observed in *Metock*, '[e]ven before the adoption of Directive 2004/38, the Community legislature recognised the importance of ensuring the protection of the family life of nationals of the Member States in order to eliminate obstacles to the exercise of the fundamental freedoms guaranteed by the EC Treaty'.[36] Certain rights in Directive 2004/38 do come close to escaping the boundaries of derived rights by being extended to family members 'exclusively on a personal basis', as examined in Chapter 6. More generally, how family members are defined for the purposes of EU citizenship law is addressed in Chapters 4 (host State) and 5 (home State).

---

self-employed there within the meaning of EU law: compare Articles 7(1)(a) and 7(1)(b) of Directive 2004/38; see further, Chapters 6 and 7.

[31] As the Court has established, '[b]y Article 9 TEU and Article 20 TFEU, the authors of the Treaties ... established an *inseparable and exclusive link* between possession of the nationality of a Member State and not only the acquisition, but also the retention, of the status of citizen of the Union' (Case C-673/20 *Préfet du Gers*, EU:C:2022:449, para 48, emphasis added).

[32] Case C-135/08 *Rottmann*, EU:C:2010:104, para 41.

[33] See esp Article 10 of Regulation 1612/68/EEC on freedom of movement for workers within the Community, OJ 1968 Sp Ed L257/2, p 475 (building on Regulation No 15, 1961 OJ 57/1073). See also, Directive 68/360/EEC on the abolition of restrictions on movement and residence within the Community for workers of Member States and their families, OJ 1968 Sp Ed L257/13, p 485. See further, Chapter 2.

[34] eg Case 7/75 *Mr and Mrs F*, EU:C:1975:80, paras 19–20.

[35] Case C-133/15 *Chavez-Vilchez*, EU:C:2017:354, para 62.

[36] Case C-127/08 *Metock and Others*, EU:C:2008:449, para 56.

Second, the legal inclusion reflected and entrenched by Union citizenship necessarily raises questions about the *degree* of legal exclusion of third-country nationals. These are not legal questions only; they are cultural, moral, social, and political questions too. The incremental expansion of Union competence for its external borders is one of the most significant legal developments post-Maastricht. That Treaty's construction of a three-pillar Union architecture—the third limb of which addressed 'Justice and Home Affairs'—evolved post-Lisbon to the Area of Freedom, Security and Justice (AFSJ), a field of shared Union/Member State competence according to Article 4(2) TFEU. Title V TFEU now sets out relevant Union competences.[37] According to Article 67(2) TFEU, the purpose of the AFSJ is to 'ensure the absence of internal border controls for persons and … a common policy on asylum, immigration and external border control, based on solidarity between Member States, which is fair towards third-country nationals'. A detailed list of objectives in Article 77 TFEU (for which the Union is required 'to develop a policy') includes 'the conditions under which nationals of third countries shall have the *freedom to travel* within the Union for a short period' (Article 77(2)(c)). Article 79 TFEU then establishes competence with respect to freedom of movement and residence. Article 79(1) references 'fair treatment of third-country nationals residing legally in Member States' as one of the aims of the Union's common immigration policy. Article 79(2) empowers the European Parliament and Council, using the ordinary legislative procedure, to adopt measures in several areas, including 'the conditions of entry and residence, and standards on the issue by Member States of long-term visas and residence permits, including those for the purpose of family reunification' (Article 79(2)(a)) and the definition of the rights of third-country nationals residing legally in a Member State, including the conditions governing freedom of movement and of residence in other Member States' (Article 79(2)(b)). Reflecting the sensitive balance between Union and national competence on these questions, Article 79(4) empowers the Union to 'establish measures to provide incentives and support for the action of Member States with a view to promoting the integration of third-country nationals residing legally in their territories, excluding any harmonisation of the laws and regulations of the Member States' while Article 79(5) establishes that Article 79 'shall not affect the right of Member States to determine volumes of admission of third-country nationals coming from third countries to their territory in order to seek work, whether employed or self-employed'.

Measures adopted under Title V TFEU that concern freedom of movement and residence for third-country nationals within the Union fall into two broad categories. First, infrastructure measures aim to put a comprehensive regulatory framework in place, the most significant examples being Directive 2003/86 on the right to family reunification, Directive 2003/109 on third-country nationals who are long-term residents, and Directive 2011/98 on a single application procedure for a single permit for third-country nationals to reside and work in the territory of a Member State.[38] Second, sectoral legislation addresses areas of specific activity, advancing a Union framework for legal migration more incrementally and connecting to wider Union policy objectives. Key examples include directives establishing

---

[37] Note, however, Protocol No 21 on the opt-in framework developed for Ireland and (at the time) the UK, and Protocol No 22 on the opt-out position of Denmark.

[38] Council Directive 2003/86/EC on the right to family reunification, 2003 OJ L251/12 and Directive 2003/109/EC concerning the status of third-country nationals who are long-term residents, 2003 OJ L16/44. See also, Regulation 1030/2002/EC laying down a uniform format for residence permits for third-country nationals, 2002 OJ L157/1 and Directive 2011/98/EU on a single application procedure for a single permit for third-country nationals to reside and work in the territory of a Member State and on a common set of rights for third-country workers legally residing in a Member State, 2011 OJ L343/1. None of these measures applies in/to either Denmark or Ireland in accordance with (respectively) Protocols No 22 and 21.

uniform procedures for third-country national researchers and students,[39] highly qualified workers,[40] seasonal workers,[41] and intra-corporate transfer.[42] Title V measures have in common the aim of systematising, for immigration into and residence within EU Member States, applicable conditions and administrative procedures, as well as ensuring adequate procedural safeguards and pathways for review of decisions taken by competent national authorities. They seek to balance the setting of common criteria in EU law with preserving appropriate space for Member State discretion, but with significantly more weight given to the latter than in EU free movement law as it concerns Union citizens. These distinctions are justified on the basis that that the underpinning objectives are different.[43]

An example can be seen in the Family Reunification Directive (2003/86): while recital 9 references protection for 'members of the nuclear family' (i.e. spouses and minor children), recital 10 assures that '[i]t is for the Member States to decide whether they wish to authorise family reunification for relatives in the direct ascending line, adult unmarried children, unmarried or registered partners as well as, in the event of a polygamous marriage, minor children of a further spouse and the sponsor'.[44] This approach means that different levels of protection can apply in different Member States. The fragmentation of the Union system into discrete Member State regulatory spaces is particularly problematic with respect to the Long-Term Residents Directive (2003/109): five years of legal and continuous residence *in one Member State* must be achieved to gain *Union* long-term resident status. In other words, periods of residence in other Member States—even those based on EU law[45]—require a reset of the entitlement clock. In essence, Member State nationals have a right to move to other Member States and third-country nationals do not, with limited exceptions. Recognising cumulative periods of legal residence in the Union per se, even if split across different Member States, would fundamentally transform the extent to which third-country nationals could be said to enjoy *freedom* of movement under EU law.[46]

Additionally, the Court of Justice considers that 'Article 18 TFEU concerns situations coming within the scope of EU law in which a national of one Member State suffers

---

[39] Directive 2016/801/EU on the conditions of entry and residence of third-country nationals for the purposes of research, studies, training, voluntary service, pupil exchange schemes or educational projects and au pairing, 2016 OJ L132/21. This measure does not apply in/to Denmark or Ireland.

[40] Directive 2009/50/EC on the conditions of entry and residence of third-country nationals for the purposes of highly qualified employment, 2009 OJ L155/17 (the 'Blue Card' Directive). This measure does not apply in/to Denmark or Ireland. 'Highly qualified employment' is defined in Article 2 of the Directive; for further conditions, see Article 5.

[41] Directive 2014/36/EU on the conditions of entry and stay of third-country nationals for the purpose of employment as seasonal workers, 2014 OJ L94/375. This measure does not apply in/to Denmark or Ireland.

[42] Directive 2014/66/EU on the conditions of entry and residence of third-country nationals in the framework of an intra-corporate transfer, 2014 OJ L157/1. This measure does not apply in/to Denmark or Ireland.

[43] See eg in the context of expulsion from a Member State, Case C-718/19 *Ordre des barreaux francophones and germanophone and Others (Mesures préventives en vue d'éloignement)*, EU:C:2021:505; see further, Chapter 10.

[44] Moreover, recital 10 continues: '[w]here a Member State authorises family reunification of these persons, this is without prejudice of the possibility, for Member States which do not recognise the existence of family ties in the cases covered by this provision, of not granting to the said persons the treatment of family members with regard to the right to reside in another Member State, as defined by the relevant [EU] legislation'. See in contrast, the uniform approach required by Directive 2004/38, examined in Chapter 4.

[45] Except for periods of residence within the scope of the Blue Card Directive (2009/50).

[46] In its 2021 work programme ('A Union of vitality in a world of fragility'), the Commission announced that 'it will propose a number of measures on legal migration, which will include … a revision of the long-term residents Directive' (COM(2020) 690 final). In April 2022, as part of a package of measures, the Commission published its proposal for a revised directive concerning the status of third-country nationals who are long-term residents (recast), COM(2022) 650 final. See generally, K Hamenstädt, 'Expulsion and "legal otherness" in times of growing nationalism' (2020) 45 European Law Review 452; and D Kochenov and M van den Brink, 'Pretending there is no Union: non-derivative quasi-citizenship rights of third-country nationals in the EU' in D Thym and

discriminatory treatment in relation to nationals of another Member State solely on the basis of his or her nationality and *is not intended to apply* to cases of a possible difference in treatment between nationals of Member States and nationals of third countries'.[47] It has also confirmed that Article 21(2) CFR (which 'corresponds to' Article 18 TFEU) 'is not intended to apply to cases of a possible difference in treatment between nationals of Member States and nationals of third countries'.[48]

However, it is also the case that not all third-country nationals are excluded equally. As outlined above, different circumstances are regulated by EU legislation, establishing different levels of protection across the framework of measures adopted under Title V TFEU. That gradation of legal rights also extends to agreements that the Union has entered into with third parties. Historically, for example, the EU–Turkey Association Agreement extended significant protection to Turkish nationals lawfully resident in an EU Member State,[49] entailing, in some circumstances, the application of principles of EU free movement law by analogy—though that protection reaches its limits with respect to aspects of Directive 2004/38 connected more centrally to the concept of Union citizenship.[50] More recently, and most remarkably, the Court referred to the criteria of proximity, longstanding common values, and European identity in the European Economic Area (EEA) Agreement's preamble to underline 'the special relationship between the European Union, its Member States and the EFTA States'.[51] For the 'special relationship' between Iceland and the Union specifically, which 'goes beyond economic and commercial cooperation', the Court observed that Iceland is a party to the EEA Agreement, applies the Schengen *acquis*, participates in the common European asylum system, and is a party to the Agreement on surrender with the Union.[52] In that light, the Court found that the position of an Icelandic national is '*objectively comparable with* that of an EU citizen'.[53] Moreover, since 'the provisions of the Agreement on the surrender procedure are very similar to the corresponding provisions' of the Framework Decision on the European arrest warrant, relevant Union citizenship case law must be applied to Icelandic nationals 'by analogy'.[54] That ruling and its implications are returned to in Chapter 2 in considering the legal and conceptual scope of the 'territory of the Union'. More generally, since Directive 2004/38 is a text with EEA relevance yet the concept of Union citizenship that underpins the Directive has no equivalent in the EEA, this aspect of the scope

---

M Zoeteweij-Turhan (eds), *Rights of Third-Country Nationals under EU Association Agreements: Degrees of Free Movement and Citizenship* (Brill 2015) 65.

[47] Joined Cases C-22/08 and C-23/08 *Vatsouras and Koupatantze*, EU:C:2009:344, para 52 (emphasis added); confirmed in eg Case C-673/20 *Préfet du Gers*, EU:C:2022:449 (Chapter 3); and Case C-490/20 *VMA v Stolichna obshtina, rayon 'Pancharevo'*, EU:C:2021:1008 (Chapter 6).

[48] Case C-930/19 *X v Belgian State*, EU:C:2021:657, paras 50–51.

[49] Agreement establishing an Association between the European Economic Community and Turkey (signed at Ankara, 12 September 1963) 1977 OJ L361/28.

[50] See eg in the context of enhanced protection against expulsion from a Member State, Case C-371/08 *Ziebell*, EU:C:2011:809; see further, Chapter 10.

[51] Case C-897/19 PPU *IN*, EU:C:2020:262, para 50.

[52] ibid para 44. In some respects, the Schengen *acquis* is deeply connected to and even emblematic of EU free movement law; however, given its distinct history and the fact that it both includes third countries and excludes some Member States, it remains a parallel framework. On the intersection of free movement law and border control under Schengen, see eg Joined Cases C-368/20 and C-369/20 *NW*, EU:C:2022:298, esp paras 87–90; and Case C-754/18 *Ryanair Designated Activity Company*, EU:C:2020:131, esp para 40. See further, Case C-35/20 *A (Franchissement de frontières en navire de plaisance)*, EU:C:2021:813, considered in Chapter 6.

[53] Case C-897/19 PPU *IN*, EU:C:2020:262, para 58 (emphasis added).

[54] ibid paras 74–75.

of EU citizenship law is returned to in Section 4 and the specific example of the right of permanent residence is discussed in more detail in Chapter 8.

Finally, reflecting on EU citizenship law and third-country nationals through the theme of exclusion necessarily raises the United Kingdom's withdrawal from the Union and its deliberate, large-scale loss of Union citizenship.[55] Reflecting both the Union-focused approach of this book and the wide range of consequences and challenges produced, Brexit is addressed across different chapters of the book where its implications are relevant rather than considered in one separate chapter. The protection of Union citizens impacted most acutely by Brexit was established as a political priority early in the withdrawal negotiations,[56] even though, as noted above, Article 50 TEU, which outlines the process for withdrawing from the Union, is silent on the implications for and protection of citizens: both for those who remain Union citizens but reside in the withdrawing State and for nationals of the withdrawing State who lose Union citizenship at the point of withdrawal from the Union. Relevant provisions of the EU–UK Withdrawal Agreement[57] are therefore considered in Chapters 3 (Member State nationality), 4 (rights of family members), 6 (right to reside), and 10 (expulsion from a Member State) in particular. While the Agreement aims for continuity of residence security overall, it will be seen that significant exclusions from EU citizenship law are applied in a range of situations. Managing the implications, and the fallout, for both continuing and former Union citizens in the Brexit context will thus challenge the adaptability, ethics, and responsiveness of Union and national institutions for some time yet to come.[58]

3.2 Material Scope: 'Specific Expression' of Rights

As introduced above and illustrated in more detail in Chapter 2, both the origins and continuing development of EU citizenship law are inherently tied to the free movement of

---

[55] See eg C Closa, 'Citizenship of the Union and nationality of the Member States' (1995) 32 Common Market Law Review 487; S Coutts, 'Citizens of elsewhere, everywhere and… nowhere? Rethinking Union citizenship in light of Brexit' (2018) 69 Northern Ireland Legal Quarterly 231; O Garner, 'The existential crisis of citizenship of the European Union: the argument for an autonomous status' (2018) 20 Cambridge Yearbook of European Legal Studies 116; D Kostakopoulou, 'Scala civium: citizenship templates post-Brexit and the European Union's duty to protect EU citizens' (2018) 56 Journal of Common Market Studies 854; C O'Brien, 'Between the devil and the deep blue sea: vulnerable EU citizens cast adrift in the UK Post-Brexit' (2021) 58 Common Market Law Review 431; D O'Keeffe, 'Union citizenship' in D O'Keeffe and P Twomey (eds), *Legal Issues of the Maastricht Treaty* (Wiley 1994) 87; V Roeben, P Minnerop, J Snell, and P Telles, 'Revisiting Union citizenship from a fundamental rights perspective in the time of Brexit' (2018) 5 European Human Rights Law Review 450; E Spaventa, 'Mice or horses? British citizens in the EU 27 after Brexit as "former EU citizens"' (2019) 44 European Law Review 589; and AP van der Mei, 'Member State nationality, EU citizenship and associate EU citizenship' in N Cambien, D Kochenov, and E Muir (eds), *European Citizenship under Stress: Social Justice, Brexit and Other Challenges* (Brill 2020) 441.

[56] See esp European Council (Art 50) guidelines for Brexit negotiations, 29 April 2017, para 8: '[t]he right for every EU citizen, and of his or her family members, to live, to work or to study in any EU Member State is a fundamental aspect of the European Union. Along with other rights provided under EU law, it has shaped the lives and choices of millions of people. Agreeing reciprocal guarantees to safeguard the status and rights derived from EU law at the date of withdrawal of EU and UK citizens, and their families, affected by the United Kingdom's withdrawal from the Union will be the first priority for the negotiations. Such guarantees must be effective, enforceable, non-discriminatory and comprehensive, including the right to acquire permanent residence after a continuous period of five years of legal residence. Citizens should be able to exercise their rights through smooth and simple administrative procedures'.

[57] Agreement on the withdrawal of the United Kingdom of Great Britain and Northern Ireland from the European Union and the European Atomic Energy Community, OJ 2019 CI 384/01.

[58] Further information on the implementation of Part Two of the Agreement on Citizens' Rights to date is available at <https://ec.europa.eu/info/strategy/relations-non-eu-countries/relations-united-kingdom/eu-uk-withdrawal-agreement/citizens-rights_en#joint-reports-on-the-implementation-of-residence-rights> (accessed 24 May 2023).

persons in EU law more generally. For example, restrictions on workers that are directly or indirectly discriminatory on the grounds of nationality breach Article 45 TFEU in principle, but so do non-discriminatory restrictions that might prevent or deter a worker from exercising freedom of movement.[59] On that basis, measures 'liable to hinder or render less attractive the exercise by EU nationals of the fundamental freedoms guaranteed by the Treaty'[60] are precluded by Article 45 TFEU and similar thresholds for non-compliance with EU free movement law apply when determining restrictions of the rights conferred by Article 21(1) TFEU too.[61]

The inter-connected nature of different rights to move and reside protected by the Treaty is reflected in this book where relevant. Conversely, important differences between the general right to move and reside conferred by Union citizenship, on the one hand, and rights to move and reside connected with economic activity, on the other, are also highlighted. However, as explained in Section 2, the scope of EU citizenship law is defined for present purposes as situations that engage Articles 20–24 TFEU directly. In that light, it can first be noted that Article 21 TFEU is normally applied only as a *residual* source of rights within the wider Treaty framework of free movement law. The right to move and reside conferred by Article 21(1) is, in other words, considered to find 'specific expression' in Articles 45,[62] 49,[63] and 56[64] TFEU. A Member State national who resides in another Member State might be present and active there on several parallel bases: for example, someone might be working while studying, and also a family member of another Union citizen residing there; and almost everyone present in another Member State will receive services there. As a general rule, is not necessary to consider Article 21 TFEU where the facts of the situation fall within the scope of one of the economic free movement Treaty provisions.[65] Moreover, the relevance of the economic freedoms should be ascertained *first*.[66] In preliminary reference proceedings under Article 267 TFEU—which, as will be seen in Section 4, account for the majority of EU citizenship rulings—the Court of Justice will recast the referring court's question(s) to frame the dispute around the correct Treaty provision where necessary.[67]

Inevitably, though, a neat separation between Articles 21 TFEU and the economic freedoms is not always evident—or possible. Where it is not clear in a preliminary reference case which Treaty provision might be applicable, the Court will consider both Article 21 TFEU and potentially relevant economic freedoms, leaving it to the referring court to make the final determination based on the circumstances of the case,[68] the fact that the same

---

[59] eg Case C-415/93 *Bosman*, EU:C:1995:463, paras 99–100; and Case C-515/14 *Commission v Cyprus*, EU:C:2016:30, para 47.
[60] Case C-420/15 *U*, EU:C:2017:408, para 20.
[61] On the prohibition of direct and indirect nationality discrimination, eg Case C-103/08 *Gottwald*, EU:C:2009:597, para 27; and Case C-182/15 *Petruhhin*, EU:C:2016:630, paras 31–33. On non-discriminatory restrictions, eg Case C-353/06 *Grunkin and Paul*, EU:C:2008:559, para 21; and Case C-208/09 *Sayn-Wittgenstein*, EU:C:2010:806, para 70. See further, Chapter 2.
[62] eg Case C-100/01 *Oteiza Olazabal*, EU:C:2002:712, para 26.
[63] eg Case C-193/94 *Skanavi and Chryssanthakopoulos*, EU:C:1996:70, para 22.
[64] eg Case C-76/05 *Schwarz and Gootjes-Schwarz*, EU:C:2007:492, para 34.
[65] eg Case C-420/15 *U*, EU:C:2017:408, paras 13–19. For a rare exception, analysing Article 21 TFEU 'irrespective of whether the person concerned engaged in an economic activity' (in this case, provision of services under Article 56 TFEU), see Case C-208/09 *Sayn-Wittgenstein*, EU:C:2010:806, paras 39–42.
[66] eg Case C-520/04 *Turpeinen*, EU:C:2006:703, para 13; and Case C-367/11 *Prete*, EU:C:2012:668, para 20. Occasionally, the judgment of the Court and the Opinion of the Advocate General present an analysis of different legal provisions in the same case, eg in Case C-258/04 *Ioannidis*, the judgment (EU:C:2005:559) was based on Article 45 TFEU but the Opinion of AG Ruiz-Jarabo Colomer (EU:C:2005:375) had focused on Articles 18 and 20 TFEU.
[67] eg Case C-632/13 *Hirvonen*, EU:C:2015:765, paras 20–22.
[68] eg Case C-300/15 *Kohll and Kohll-Schlesser*, EU:C:2016:361, paras 20–35.

logic underpins restrictions of all free movement rights making an indeterminate analysis possible in that sense. However, as will be seen in several chapters of the book, placing a situation within the scope of the economic freedoms can make a material legal difference for the person in question. An important example concerns a Union citizen's entitlement to equal treatment as regards social assistance in a host Member State, examined in detail in Chapter 7.[69] Holding the status of Union citizen does not mean that privileges attached to economic free movement will be extended—or that limitations permitted within the economic freedoms can be overcome.[70] However, EU citizenship law does influence interpretation of the economic freedoms,[71] and that influence is usually positive with respect to the level of substantive protection extended.[72] It will also be seen merging economic Treaty freedoms and Union citizenship creates 'hybrid' protection in novel ways, especially for jobseekers.[73]

In cases involving nationality discrimination, Article 18 TFEU is also applied as a source of residual rights. On that basis, noting that Article 18 applies 'without prejudice to any special provisions' in the Treaties, prohibitions on nationality discrimination found in the economic freedom provisions will prevail.[74] In other words, Article 18 TFEU 'applies *independently* only to situations governed by EU law for which the TFEU lays down no specific rules of non-discrimination'.[75] Article 21 TFEU does not explicitly prohibit nationality discrimination and it therefore tends to be read 'in conjunction with' Article 18 TFEU.[76] The standard phrasing applied is as follows: '[e]very citizen of the Union may ... rely on Article 18 TFEU, which prohibits any discrimination on grounds of nationality, in all situations falling within the scope *ratione materiae* of EU law, and those situations include the exercise of the freedom conferred by Article 21 TFEU to move and reside within the territory of the Member States'.[77] However, there is a further 'specific expression' complication because Article 24(1) of Directive 2004/38 provides that 'all Union citizens residing on the basis of this Directive in the territory of the host Member State shall enjoy equal treatment with the nationals of that Member State within the scope of the Treaty'. That guarantee of equal treatment with host State nationals is also '[s]ubject to such specific provisions as are expressly

---

[69] eg Compare the reasoning and outcomes in Case C-181/19 *Jobcenter Krefeld*, EU:C:2020:794 and Case C-709/20 *CG*, EU:C:2021:602. See further, Chapter 7.

[70] eg Compare the judgment of the Court in Case C-208/07 *von Chamier-Glisczinski* (EU:C:2009:455, para 85, confirming that EU social security coordination linked to the free movement of workers permits disparities across national schemes and legislation) with the Opinion of AG Mengozzi (EU:C:2008:493, paras 72–73 of the Opinion, reasoning that national legislation could place Union citizens who exercised free movement rights at a comparative disadvantage). In contrast, the Court took a more expansive approach in Case C-522/10 *Reichel-Albert* (EU:C:2012:475), by engaging Article 21 TFEU; but compare the Opinion of AG Jääskinen (EU:C:2012:114), who looked at applicable secondary legislation only.

[71] eg Case C-291/05 *Eind*, EU:C:2007:771, para 32, where the Court stated that its interpretation of Article 45 TFEU and related legislation was 'substantiated by the introduction of the status of citizen of the Union'. See further, Chapter 9.

[72] Though that is not always the case: for example, AG Wathelet has criticised transposition of the 'genuine link' reasoning applied in citizenship law to the free movement of workers; see Case C- 238/15 *Bragança Linares Verruga and Others*, EU:ECLI:2016:389, paras 34ff of the Opinion. On 'genuine link' reasoning, see Chapter 2; on the relationship between Articles 21 and 45 TFEU more generally, see Chapter 9.

[73] eg Case C-138/02 *Collins*, EU:C:2004:172, paras 63–64. In *Prete*, AG Cruz Villalón explained that the right in question was 'based directly on Article [45 TFEU], interpreted in the light of the provisions on citizenship of the Union' (Case C-367/11, EU:C:2012:501, para 29 of the Opinion). See further, Chapters 6 and 7.

[74] eg For Article 45 TFEU, Case C-336/96 *Gilly*, EU:C:1998:221, para 38.

[75] Case C-20/16 *Bechtel*, EU:C:2017:488, para 30 (emphasis added).

[76] Case C-184/99 *Grzelczyk*, EU:C:2001:458, para 30; confirmed in eg Case C-182/15 *Petruhhin*, EU:C:2016:630, para 30.

[77] Case C-75/11 *Commission v Austria*, EU:C:2012:605, para 39.

provided for in the Treaty and secondary law', which produces a complex legal chain from Article 18 TFEU, which is 'without prejudice to any special provision in the Treaties'; to Article 21 TFEU, a 'special provision' in that respect, which states that citizenship rights 'shall be exercised in accordance with the conditions and limits defined by the Treaties *and by the measures adopted thereunder*'; and to Directive 2004/38, which establishes general conditions and limits on the right to move and reside (especially in Article 7) as well as specific derogations from equal treatment in Article 24(2).[78] The implications of this 'specific expression' construct are examined in more detail in Chapters 2, 6, and 7, where it will be seen that contrasting approaches have been applied in different circumstances. A positive outcome (from the perspective of the citizen) is likely if the Court refers to Article 24 of the Directive as 'merely' a specific expression of Article 18 TFEU,[79] especially if some connection to economic activity can also be demonstrated.[80]

4. Progressing EU Citizenship Law: The Principal Actors

EU citizenship law was created, through the Treaties, by the Union's Member States and has since been fleshed out through a dynamic partnership between the EU legislator and the EU judiciary. Behind that statement, however, lies a dense network of connections between and contributions made by a whole range of EU and national actors—not least Union citizens themselves, who are vital contributors to the development of EU citizenship law through the fact that their experiences generate the questions that national authorities must resolve, including national courts, which might then refer questions to the Court of Justice for guidance on the interpretation and application of EU citizenship law. In Chapter 5, the mechanism of the European Citizens' Initiative (Article 24 TFEU) shows how Union citizens can contribute directly to the shaping of Union governance. Additionally, several Union actors engage in the governance of Union citizenship as part of their wider roles, including the European Ombudsman,[81] the Petitions Committee of the European Parliament (PETI),[82] and the Committee of the Regions.[83] However, the brief context-setting discussion that follows focuses more specifically on the EU legislator and EU judiciary, introducing key features of 'who' tends to do 'what' in the making, implementation, and enforcement of EU citizenship law, and thereby identifying some of the questions pursued through more detailed discussions and examples across the chapters that follow.

---

[78] eg Case C-333/13 *Dano*, EU:C:2014:2358, paras 59–61.
[79] eg Case C-46/12 *LN*, EU:C:2013:97, para 33.
[80] eg Case C-181/19 *Jobcenter Krefeld*, EU:C:2020:794, paras 67–71.
[81] See Articles 20, 24, and 228 TFEU and Articles 42 (right to good administration) and 43 (European Ombudsman) CFR. See generally, N Vogiatzis, *The European Ombudsman and Good Administration in the European Union* (Palgrave Macmillan 2018); and G Tridimas and T Tridimas, 'Public awareness of EU rights and the functions of the European Ombudsman: some unpleasant findings' in HCH Hofmann and J Ziller (eds), *Accountability in the EU: The Role of the European Ombudsman* (Edward Elgar Publishing 2017) 74. See further, Chapter 5.
[82] Articles 20, 24, and 227 TFEU; on the discretion enjoyed by PETI in dealing with petitions submitted to it, see Case C-261/13 P *Schönberger*, EU:C:2014:2423. See further, Chapter 5.
[83] eg 'From local to European: Putting citizens at the centre of the EU agenda', <https://cor.europa.eu/en/engage/brochures/Documents/From%20local%20to%20European/4082_Citizens%20Consult_brochure_N_FINAL.pdf> (accessed 24 May 2023). Note especially the work of the Committee's Commission for Citizenship, Governance, Institutional and External Affairs (CIVEX), the remit of which includes the AFSJ, the Charter of Fundamental Rights, and 'active citizenship' (<https://cor.europa.eu/en/our-work/Pages/civex.aspx> (accessed 24 May 2023)).

4.1 Implementing EU Citizenship Law: The Role of the EU Legislator

By embedding the significance of legislative conditions and limits in primary law, Articles 20(2) and 21(1) TFEU convey the central importance of the EU legislator to EU citizenship law. In Chapter 5, it will be seen that legislation to support the rights conferred by Articles 22 (electoral rights), 23 (protection in the territory of a third country), and 24 (citizens' initiatives) TFEU has proven patchier and slower to put in place than legislation on the right to move and reside. This is not so surprising when it is remembered that, as noted in Section 2 of this chapter and explained in more detail in Chapter 2, Directive 2004/38 replaces two strands of EU legislation that preceded it: first, several longstanding measures that regulated different aspects of movement and residence for the purposes of economic activity; and second, 1990s legislation that created a general (though more conditioned) right to move and reside for certain categories of persons. This field-capturing rationale is expressed in recitals 3 and 4 of the Directive's preamble:

> (3) Union citizenship should be the fundamental status of nationals of the Member States when they exercise their right of free movement and residence. It is therefore necessary to codify and review the existing Community instruments dealing separately with workers, self-employed persons, as well as students and other inactive persons in order to simplify and strengthen the right of free movement and residence of all Union citizens.
>
> (4) With a view to remedying this sector-by-sector, piecemeal approach to the right of free movement and residence and facilitating the exercise of this right, there needs to be a single legislative act to amend Council Regulation (EEC) No 1612/68 of 15 October 1968 on freedom of movement for workers within the Community,[84] and to repeal the following acts: Council Directive 68/360/EEC of 15 October 1968 on the abolition of restrictions on movement and residence within the Community for workers of Member States and their families,[85] Council Directive 73/148/EEC of 21 May 1973 on the abolition of restrictions on movement and residence within the Community for nationals of Member States with regard to establishment and the provision of services,[86] Council Directive 90/364/EEC of 28 June 1990 on the right of residence,[87] Council Directive 90/365/EEC of 28 June 1990 on the right of residence for employees and self-employed persons who have ceased their occupational activity[88] and Council Directive 93/96/EEC of 29 October 1993 on the right of residence for students.[89]

Where the provisions of Directive 2004/38 are examined in detail—mainly, in Chapters 4, 6, 7, 8, 9, and 10—both advantages and limitations of comprehensive framework legislation of this kind will be highlighted. The intersection of the Directive and other elements of EU citizenship law will also be assessed. For example, in Chapter 9, it will be seen that the Court increasingly applies the Directive's conditions 'by analogy' in cases where the Directive does not actually apply—usually because the Union citizen is in his/her home State rather than in

---

[84] 1968 OJ L257/2, now repealed and replaced by Regulation 492/2011 on freedom of movement for workers within the Union, 2011 OJ L141/1.
[85] 1968 OJ L257/13.
[86] 1973 OJ L172/14.
[87] 1990 OJ L180/26.
[88] 1990 OJ L180/28.
[89] 1993 OJ L317/59.

a host Member State and is not therefore a 'beneficiary' of the Directive within the meaning of Article 3(1).[90] It will also be seen that free movement rights for Union citizens intersect with Union measures and policies more widely.[91]

In terms of shaping the content of the Directive, the contributions of the different institutions that comprise the EU legislator are striking when the measure's legislative history is traced. The Commission published two proposals for the Directive,[92] and amendments secured to the adopted text by both the European Parliament and the Council will be flagged where relevant. Especially through reflecting on the limiting amendments secured by the Council, there are glimmers of how the reality of 'sharing' competence for Union citizenship plays out. In that light, the words of Advocate General Lagrange in *Costa v ENEL* remain powerfully relevant:

> The system of the common market is based upon the creation of a legal system separate from that of the Member States, but nevertheless intimately and even organically tied to it in such a way that the mutual and constant respect for the respective jurisdictions of the Community and national bodies is one of the fundamental conditions of a proper functioning of the system instituted by the Treaty and, consequently, of the realization of the aims of the Community.[93]

The structure, aims, and scope of Directive 2004/38 are introduced in more detail in Chapter 2 but as a general point, it can be emphasised that the Directive represents in many respects (its aim of comprehensiveness notwithstanding) a legal skeleton. The rights provided for in the Directive also comprise—drilling inwards and at each level becoming more difficult to examine for very practical reasons connected to language, scale, and sources—their interpretation by the Court of Justice, the legislative acts and other measures that implement the Directive into national laws, interpretations by national courts and tribunals, interpretations in non-binding yet influential measures such as administrative guidance notes, and application through countless human decisions taken every day across all of the EU Member States.[94]

In that light, it is impossible to gather a complete or even properly comprehensive understanding of EU citizenship law through one study. As EU legal researchers, we get to see—and must always remember that we are only seeing—just the tip of the iceberg of EU citizenship law: the (minority) of decisions or outcomes that do not go unchallenged, and even more precisely, challenges pursued through several stages of legal redress. Alongside

---

[90] eg Case C-456/12 *O and B*, EU:C:2014:135. See further, Chapter 9. However, there are limitations on the extent to which the Directive can apply by analogy: see further, Chapter 2. Article 3(1) of Directive 2004/38 establishes that '[t]his Directive shall apply to all Union citizens *who move to or reside in a Member State* other than that of which they are a national, and to their family members as defined in point 2 of Article 2 who accompany or join them'.

[91] eg Note the Court's reference to conduct demonstrating 'a disposition hostile to the fundamental values enshrined in Articles 2 and 3 TEU, such as human dignity and human rights' in Joined Cases C-331/16 and C-366/16 *K; HF*, EU:C:2018:296, para 60. Note also, the references to Article 3(5) TEU and to the objectives of EU criminal law in Case C-182/15 *Petruhhin*, EU:C:2016:630, paras 44 and 47. On the values on which the Union is founded, as expressed in Article 2 TEU, see Chapter 2.

[92] COM(2001) 257 final; COM(2003) 199 final.

[93] AG Lagrange in Case 6/64 *Costa v ENEL*, EU:C:1964:51, pp 605–606.

[94] Chapter VII of the Report of the High Level Panel on the free movement of persons chaired by Mrs Simone Veil, and presented to the Commission on 18 March 1997, provided an early sketch of the complexity of actors and processes involved in the implementation and enforcement of citizenship rights. See further, Chapter 2.

field-spanning reports from the European Commission[95] and the European Parliament,[96] work that aims to interrogate the practice of citizenship across the Member States therefore provides particularly crucial insights—and continues to suggest the need for practical change and further research.[97] For example, administrative practice at national level profoundly shapes how EU citizenship law is applied and experienced in reality.[98] While the Court of Justice has emphasised that 'discretion enjoyed by the competent [national] authorities ... must be exercised ... in such a way as to give full effect to Article 21 TFEU',[99] administrative practice that does not reach this standard can, in and of itself, infringe EU law.[100]

A final point on the intersection of EU legislation and national law in the context of Union citizenship: Article 37 of Directive 2004/38 provides that '[t]he provisions of this Directive shall not affect any laws, regulations or administrative provisions laid down by a Member State which would be more favourable to the persons covered by this Directive'. However, Article 37 has limited reach in legal terms. In *Ziolkowski and Szeja*, the Court ruled that the legal consequences of any system that a Member State chooses to introduce that is more favourable than that required by the Directive are material under national law only: in other words, 'it is for each Member State to decide not only whether it will adopt such a system but also the conditions and effects of that system, in particular as regards the legal consequences of a right of residence granted on the basis of national law alone'.[101] In the context of residence rights in a host Member State, for example, more favourable systems than the three-stage system set out in Directive 2004/38—constructed around time periods of up to three months, between three months and five years, and more than five years[102]—do not displace the conditions set out in the Directive for the purpose of accessing the rights protected by EU law.[103]

---

[95] See generally, <https://ec.europa.eu/info/policies/justice-and-fundamental-rights/eu-citizenship/eu-citizenship_en> (accessed 24 May 2023).

[96] eg 'Obstacles to the right of free movement and residence for EU citizens and their families: comparative analysis', study commissioned by the European Parliament's Policy Department for Citizens' Rights and Constitutional Affairs at the request of the LIBE and PETI Committees, 2016, <http://www.europarl.europa.eu/RegData/etudes/STUD/2016/571375/IPOL_STU(2016)571375_EN.pdf> (accessed 24 May 2023).

[97] eg A Valcke, 'EU citizens' rights in practice: exploring the implementation gap in free movement law' (2019) 21 0289; N Nic Shuibhne and J Shaw, General Report in *Union Citizenship: Development, Impact and Challenges*, XXVI FIDE Congress 2014, Vol 2, available at <http://fide2014.eu/pdf/FINAL-Topic-2-on-Union-Citizenship.pdf> (accessed 24 May 2023); outputs from the bEUcitizen project, available at <http://beucitizen.eu> (accessed 24 May 2023); work from the European Union Agency for Fundamental Rights, especially 'Making EU citizens' rights a reality: national courts enforcing freedom of movement and related rights', August 2018, available at <http://fra.europa.eu/en/publication/2018/free-movement> (accessed 24 May 2023); and the 'EU Rights and Brexit Hub' project based at the University of York, <https://www.eurightshub.york.ac.uk> (accessed 24 May 2023).

[98] See eg Case C-133/15 *Chavez-Vilchez*, EU:C:2017:354, paras 36–37, where the referring court outlines how restrictive administrative guidelines shaped the disputes at issue.

[99] Case C-541/15 *Freitag*, EU:C:2017:432, paras 44–45.

[100] eg Case C-185/96 *Commission v Greece*, EU:C:1997:425, paras 22–24. The 1997 Report of the High Level Panel on the free movement of persons—ie prior to the adoption of Directive 2004/38 and the processes that it has put in place—indicated two areas of concern with respect to 'a lack of administrative flexibility' (p 78): first, that 'the officials concerned are unaware of the [Union] dimension of their duties and apply the rules over-enthusiastically (especially the restrictions on the free movement of persons, which protect the interests of their own Member State), sometimes to the extent of distorting the [Union] rules they are supposed to be applying'; and second, that national officials, 'by failing to cooperate with their opposite numbers in other Member States, often through lack of mutual trust, unnecessarily complicate matters for individuals who, in their movements, fall within the jurisdiction of two or more Member States'.

[101] Joined Cases C-424/10 and C-425/10 *Ziolkowski and Szeja*, EU:C:2011:866, para 50. This interpretation was advanced by AG Trstenjak in Case C-325/09 *Dias*, EU:C:2011:86, paras 81–83 of the Opinion. See in contrast, AG Bot in *Ziolkowski and Szeja* (EU:C:2011:575), paras 35–38. These positions are discussed in Chapter 7.

[102] See further, Chapter 6.

[103] See further, Chapter 7; and compare, in particular, Case C-85/96 *Martínez Sala*, EU:C:1998:217 and Case C-709/20 *CG*, EU:C:2021:602.

4.2 Interpreting EU Citizenship Law: The Role of the Court of Justice

In his joint Opinion for *Rendón Marín* and *CS*, Advocate General Szpunar stated that the 'vast jurisprudential endeavour, by means of which the Court has made citizenship of the Union an effective reality, has been, and continues to be, carried out progressively and in close cooperation with national courts in the context of references for a preliminary ruling'.[104] That observation sums up both the incremental construction of EU citizenship case law, returned to below, and the crucial role of national courts and tribunals in feeding its evolution. In that light, a defining feature of EU citizenship case law and of its analysis concerns whether the 'right' balance is achieved between sometimes competing interests, whether that concerns legislative 'versus' judicial construction of EU citizenship law, rights relative to conditions/limits, or Union and Member State competences or perspectives respectively.

Fundamentally, the legal development of Union citizenship is a shared competence—and also a shared responsibility—of the Union and its Member States.[105] Capturing the complexity of the challenges and choices faced by the Court of Justice as a result, Advocate General Sharpston remarked—with respect to areas 'in which it behoves the Court to tread softly, and with care'—that 'just because it must tread softly, that does not mean that it must fear to tread at all'.[106] She further observed that '[t]he discussions which precede the adoption of [Union] legislation or multilateral agreements are necessarily longer, more thorough and wider-ranging than can ever be achieved in the context of a preliminary reference procedure before the Court'.[107] When the situation in question is not covered by EU legislation, the Court should therefore 'beware of encroaching to any unnecessary extent on Member States' competence' while, '[a]t the same time, it must not dilute or weaken the concept of citizenship of the Union—the "fundamental status of nationals of the Member States"—or deprive the rights flowing from that status of real meaning'.[108]

As an institutional actor navigating these concerns, the pivotal part played by the Court of Justice in animating the distinctive legal potential of Union citizenship in the first place,[109] and determining the parameters of its implications ever since then, is undeniable. Its role in the crafting of Union citizenship can also be controversial. As noted already in this chapter, for example, the Court has drawn Union citizenship rights for Union citizens who reside in their home Member States from both Article 20 (Chapter 5) and Article 21 (Chapter 9) TFEU. With respect to interpreting the provisions of Directive 2004/38, which concerns rights in a host State, the Court normally applies its standard method of legislative interpretation, considering the 'wording, context and objectives'[110] of the relevant provision.

---

[104] AG Szpunar in Case C-165/14 *Rendón Marín* and Case C-304/14 *CS*, EU:C:2016:75, para 110 of the Joint Opinion.

[105] eg '[B]y ratifying the Maastricht Treaty and the subsequent amending Treaties, the Member States accepted that – because their nationals are also EU citizens – the task of dealing with tensions or difficulties arising from those citizens' exercise of free movement rights is a shared one' (AG Sharpston in Case C-34/09 *Ruiz Zambrano*, EU:C:2010:560, para 130 of the Opinion).

[106] AG Sharpston in Case C-353/06 *Grunkin and Paul*, EU:C:2008:246, para 41 of the Opinion.

[107] ibid para 45 of the Opinion.

[108] ibid para 46 of the Opinion; see similarly, AG Wathelet in Case C-115/15 *NA*, EU:C:2016:259, also referencing the fundamental status of Union citizenship to suggest that it 'cannot therefore be an empty shell' (para 111 of the Opinion).

[109] Case C-85/96 *Martínez Sala*, EU:C:1998:217.

[110] eg Case C-115/15 *NA*, EU:C:2016:487, para 39.

It is also clear, though, that the Court takes account too of wider developments since the Directive was adopted; for example, societal change, which is often already reflected in the case law of the European Court of Human Rights (ECtHR).[111] As a general rule, and as 'required by both the uniform application of EU law and the principle of equality', the Court will emphasise that a provision of the Directive that 'makes no express reference to the law of the Member States for the purpose of determining its meaning and scope must normally be given an autonomous and uniform interpretation throughout the European Union'.[112] More substantively, prominent themes that emerge from reading across the Court's extensive body of EU citizenship case law—such as proportionality, effectiveness of rights, and degrees of integration—will be introduced in Chapter 2.

With respect to enforcing EU citizenship law, there are relatively few examples of the Commission pursuing infringement proceedings against a Member State.[113] For the preliminary rulings procedure,[114] it remains the case in EU citizenship law (as in EU law more generally) that 'it is not for the Court to rule on the interpretation of provisions of national law and that it must generally take account, under the division of jurisdiction between the [Union] courts and the national courts, of the factual and legislative context, as described in the order for reference, in which the question put to it is set'.[115] Nevertheless, the Court almost always finds that decisions taken at national level should be evaluated for compliance with EU citizenship law. However, either narrower or wider margins of discretion can be extended to Member States when justifying restrictions of rights. It is not always obvious what might be left for the referring court to 'decide'—especially when determining the proportionality of Member State decisions. In other words, the degree of detail provided by the Court of Justice's rulings can constrain the degree of discretion retained by referring courts and tribunals.

Additionally, the Court sometimes reframes the question(s) referred to it so that the legal reach of the case is significantly stretched. For example, in *McCarthy*, the referring court focused its questions solely on Directive 2004/38,[116] but the Court of Justice broadened the scope of the case also to consider whether the claimant could rely directly on Articles 20 or 21 TFEU.[117] In her Opinion, Advocate General Kokott had examined the questions referred

---

[111] On this point, see eg AG Bobek in Case C-89/17 *Banger*, EU:C:2018:225, para 37 of the Opinion. See more generally, on the 'complementary' protection of fundamental rights offered by national law, Union law and ECHR law, AG Mengozzi in Case C-256/11 *Dereci*, EU:C:2011:626, paras 39–42 of the View.

[112] AG Wathelet in Case C-673/16 *Coman*, EU:C:2018:2, para 34 of the Opinion; referring to eg Joined Cases C-424/10 and C-425/10 *Ziolkowski and Szeja*, EU:C:2011:866, paras 31–34.

[113] eg Case C-75/11 *Commission v Austria*, EU:C:2012:605 (reduced fares on public transport for students); Case C-408/03 *Commission v Belgium*, EU:C:2006:192 (national implementation of Directive 2004/38); Case C-233/14 *Commission v Netherlands*, EU:C:2016:396 (maintenance aid for studies).

[114] At the level of national proceedings, the 1997 Report of the High Level Panel on the free movement of persons also emphasised the 'key role' played by legal professionals in the 'effective application' of Union law, underlining that 'if individuals are to be able to ensure that their rights are upheld, the judiciary in question, responsible for applying [Union] law as a matter of course, must be sufficiently trained and informed in order to discharge this duty properly. The same applies to lawyers and, more generally, to all legal professionals, who are responsible for advising and defending the interests of their clients'; expressing some concern, however, that while there are 'undoubtedly good specialists in [Union] law in the Union, ... practitioners as a whole have unfortunately not yet developed a systematic "[Union] reflex", that is, a natural tendency to look for the implications of [Union] law in the cases they have to deal with' (pp 77–78).

[115] Case C-224/02 *Pusa*, EU:C:2004:273, para 37.

[116] Case C-434/09 *McCarthy*, EU:C:2011:277, para 21.

[117] ibid paras 24–26, noting that 'even though, formally, the national court has limited its questions to the interpretation of Articles 3(1) and 16 of Directive 2004/38, such a situation does not prevent the Court from providing the national court with all the elements of interpretation of European Union law which may be of assistance in adjudicating on the case before it, whether or not that court has specifically referred to them in the questions'

solely on the basis of the Directive and suggested that it would be appropriate to reopen the oral procedure if the Court was minded 'to consider further developing the status of Union citizen' on the basis that '[t]he parties involved in the present proceedings have hitherto been given occasion to set out their arguments on this issue entirely in passing only, towards the end of the hearing' and that '[t]hey should in my view still have the opportunity to deal with it in greater depth. Also, further Member States would then in all probability be prompted to present oral argument before the Court'.[118]

Advocate General Kokott's suggestion (not followed in *McCarthy*) also raises the question of actors with the capacity to influence litigation and reflecting on it across the evolution of EU citizenship case law over time reveals some interesting trends. As might be expected for an area of law innately connected to individual rights, over 90 per cent of citizenship judgments delivered by the time of writing were issued in preliminary ruling proceedings— notably higher than the 60–70 per cent average of preliminary ruling judgments from the Court of Justice more generally.[119] The percentage of cases ruled on by the Grand Chamber (close to half[120] compared to 7–12 per cent generally) and cases in which there was an Advocate General's Opinion (over 80 per cent compared to 55–68 per cent generally) demonstrably exceed the average, underscoring the constitutional significance and the political as much as practical salience of EU citizenship law.[121] As noted earlier, there have been relatively few infringement proceedings: at the time of writing, nine cases initiated by the Commission under Article 258 TFEU proceeded to the judicial stage (in seven of which the Commission was successful or partly successful), and two cases were initiated by a Member State against another Member State under Article 259 TFEU.[122]

In terms of Member States sending the greatest volume of preliminary references, Germany leads the table, with its national courts and tribunals referring nearly one-quarter of all Article 267 TFEU citizenship cases. Prior to Brexit, the United Kingdom followed closely behind at almost one-fifth.[123] Both Germany and the UK have also sent submissions, whether written and/or oral, for more citizenship cases than any other Member States, each getting involved in over 40 per cent of all citizenship cases respectively. At one level, that is to be expected, noting that these are also the States most frequently involved directly in the

---

(para 24, citing Case C-251/06 *ING. AUER*, EU:C:2007:658, para 38). See similarly eg Case C-165/16 *Lounes*, EU:C:2017:862, paras 28–30. See generally, U Šadl and A Wallerman Ghavanini, '"The referring court asks, in essence": is reformulation of preliminary questions by the Court of Justice a decision writing fixture or a decision-making approach?' (2019) 25 *European Law Journal* 416.

[118] AG Kokott in Case C-439/09 *McCarthy*, EU:C:2010:708, para 46 of the Opinion. However, in other cases, the Court has ruled only on the Directive and did not consider whether rights drawn directly from the Treaty might apply: eg compare the judgment of the Court (EU:C:2015:210) and the Opinion of AG Wathelet (EU:C:2015:210, esp paras 112 ff.) in Case C-67/14 *Alimanovic*; see further Chapter 7.
[119] EU citizenship law was defined for this purpose on the basis of cases that engaged Articles 21–24 TFEU directly; more general statistics and trends on the Court's activity are drawn from the Judicial Activity part of its Annual Reports, available at <https://curia.europa.eu/jcms/jcms/Jo2_7000/en/> (accessed 24 May 2023).
[120] This figure includes the Full Court formation for citizenship cases before the Grand Chamber formation was introduced in 2004.
[121] Thus 'revealing of the manner and degree to which constitutional orders interact' (L Besselink, '*Spain v UK, Eman and Sevinger, Sevinger and Eman v Netherlands*' (case comment) (2008) 45 Common Market Law Review 787 at 799.
[122] Case C-145/04 *Spain v United Kingdom*, EU:C:2006:543 (on the right to vote in European Parliament elections); Case C-364/10 *Hungary v Slovakia*, EU:C:2012:630 (on restricting freedom of movement).
[123] It is interesting that Germany sends the greatest volume of preliminary references to the Court compared to the other Member States in any event, whereas the UK's figure for citizenship law references was significantly higher than its level of references generally. Conversely, France is a comparative outlier, sending far more references to the Court in general than it has done in the specific field of EU citizenship law.

proceedings. That qualification makes the next set of Member States—that is, those that send written and/or oral submissions but are not directly involved in the proceedings—interesting to note: a second cluster of 'most engaged' States includes Denmark, the Netherlands, Poland, and Belgium, followed by a third cluster of Austria, Greece, France, Ireland, the Czech Republic, and Italy.

Metock remains the case that attracted the highest number of Member State submissions (11) to date. Perhaps it was not so surprising, then, that political agreement was reached to overturn key aspects of that ruling as part of the EU's pre-Brexit political negotiations with the UK in February 2016.[124] It is also evident that lines of case law generally regarded as significant or controversial duly attracted multiple Member State submissions: for example, eight submissions in *Ruiz Zambrano*; six in *Dano*; and eight in *Petruhhin*.[125] But eight Member States also made submissions in *Hirvonen*—a case heard by the Sixth Chamber, with no Advocate General's Opinion, and the subject matter of which even committed citizenship scholars might struggle to recall.[126] However, considering the decision no longer to publish reports for the hearing, it has become difficult to appreciate in any depth whether or how Member State (or other) submissions are influencing the case law. In that light, the gradual opening of the Historical Archives of the Court of Justice will provide a fruitful new avenue for research when the timeline of the Archives joins the timeline of EU citizenship case law.[127]

Except for the Commission, which engages in all cases before the Court, it is somewhat surprising that other EU institutions rarely get involved in EU citizenship cases at all. Both the Council[128] and the European Parliament[129] have sent submissions in just a handful of cases each—fewer than the EFTA Surveillance Authority[130]—and one of those cases, *Vatsouras and Koupatantze*, required both institutions to intervene since it concerned the validity of a provision of Directive 2004/38.[131] Non-state actors such as NGOs have also made perhaps surprisingly few appearances thus far, though these do appear to be growing.[132]

Reflecting, finally, on the Court of Justice's responsibility for and beyond each specific case before it, the analysis in this book aims both to explain the individual elements of EU citizenship law and to organise and reflect on them more systemically. This difficult balancing act is

---

[124] See Declaration of the European Commission on issues related to the abuse of the right of free movement of persons, Annex VII of *A New Settlement for the United Kingdom within the European Union*, extract of the conclusions of the European Council of 18–19 February 2016, 2016 OJ C691/1. See further, Chapters 4 and 6.

[125] Case C-34/09 *Ruiz Zambrano*, EU:C:2011:124, see Chapter 5; Case C-333/13 *Dano*, EU:C:2014:2358, see Chapters 6 and 7; Case C-182/15 *Petruhhin*, EU:C:2016:630, see Chapters 2 and 10.

[126] Case C-632/13 *Hirvonen*, EU:C:2015:13; the case concerned the applicable income tax regime for a Swedish national residing in Finland and receiving a Swedish pension. On questions raised by lives 'split' across two or more Member States, see Chapter 9.

[127] The Historical Archives of the Court of Justice are based at the European University Institute in Florence, 'compris[ing] documents produced or received by the institutions in the accomplishment of their task, provided that they have been selected to be permanently retained and date from more than 30 years ago' (<https://curia.europa.eu/jcms/jcms/P_184874/en/> (accessed 24 May 2023)). See further, Editorial Comments 'The Court of Justice in the Archives' (2019) 56 Common Market Law Review 899. Not too long, then, until the case file for *Martínez Sala* can be accessed.

[128] eg Case C-184/99 *Grzelczyk*, EU:C:2001:458; Joined Cases C-22/08 and C-23/08 *Vatsouras and Koupatantze*, EU:C:2009:344.

[129] eg Joined Cases C-22/08 and C-23/08 *Vatsouras and Koupatantze*, EU:C:2009:344; Case C-650/13 *Delvigne*, EU:C:2015:648, on the right to vote in European Parliament elections (see Chapter 5).

[130] eg Case C-544/07 *Rüffler*, EU:C:2009:258; Case C-300/11 *ZZ*, EU:C:2013:363; Case C-507/12 *Saint Prix*, EU:C:2014:2007.

[131] See further, Chapters 6 and 7.

[132] eg Case C-162/09 *Lassal*, EU:C:2010:592; Joined Cases C-197/11 and C-203/11 *Libert*, EU:C:2013:288; Case C-529/11 *Alarape and Tijani*, EU:C:2013:290; Case C-218/14 *Singh II*, EU:C:2015:476; Case C-115/15 *NA*, EU:C:2016; and Case C-673/16 *Coman*, EU:C:2018:385.

reflected in the preliminary reference procedure itself through the fact that the Court must offer in each case guidance that is specific to the questions referred to it by the national court or tribunal, on the one hand; yet at a level of abstraction that it is comprehensible and can be applied to sufficiently similar situations across all of the Member States, on the other.[133] The Court is therefore acting simultaneously as a first instance and a constitutional court. On the first point, however, only a national court or tribunal can actually resolve the case before it and thus, even when acting in 'first instance mode', the Court of Justice cannot determine questions of fact or the outcome of the proceedings even though its guidance on relevant questions of EU law is binding on the referring institution. And even under constitutional court mode, on the second point, the Court of Justice does not have capacity to render national rules invalid or void. The main obligation in terms of the primacy of EU law entails only the disapplication of conflicting national rules.[134] Additionally, some findings seem so directly and deeply tied to the particular facts of a case that extracting the principles of wider significance from the Court's judgments becomes a difficult task.

It must be acknowledged that progressing EU citizenship law is a necessarily incremental and iterative process, requiring adaptive and sometimes even corrective steps when the implications of particular judicial—or indeed legislative—choices only become clear(er) over time.[135] Nevertheless, it is the responsibility of the Court of Justice to be alert to and fulfil the demands its complicatedly fused first instance and constitutional functions: to practise the highest standards of jurisprudence in both resolving specific disputes and stewarding a coherent wider system of EU citizenship law. The role of national courts in providing a constructive 'feedback loop'[136] can be emphasised again in that light. The EU legislator must also remain actively engaged with assessing the fitness for purpose of relevant EU legislation, and of the guidance that steers the application and interpretation of that legislation.[137] And, ultimately, the Member States must accept responsibility for the fundamental status that they themselves created, and thus for the Union citizens created in consequence.

5. Organising EU Citizenship Law: Overview of Chapters

Key features of EU citizenship law have been briefly introduced in this chapter and that task continues and expands into Chapter 2, which has two main objectives. First, Chapter 2 traces the *origins and legal history* of EU citizenship law, focusing mainly on Articles 20 and 21 TFEU to illustrate the formative influence of EU economic free movement law on the construction of EU citizenship law but equally, then, to show how more citizenship-specific

---

[133] On the *erga omnes* effect of rulings under Article 267 TFEU, see Joined Cases 28–30/62 *Da Costa*, EU:C:1963:6, and Case 66/80 *International Chemical Corporation (ICI)*, EU:C:1981:102, para 13.

[134] See generally, M Dougan, 'Primacy and the remedy of disapplication' (2019) 56 Common Market Law Review 1459. Member State responsibility for addressing resulting non-compliance with EU law in a more systemic way connects, however, to the principle of sincere cooperation expressed in Article 4(3) TEU.

[135] As depicted by K Lenaerts, 'EU citizenship and the Court's "stone-by-stone" approach' (2015) 1 International Comparative Jurisprudence 1.

[136] T Horsley, *The Court of Justice of the European Union as an Institutional Actor: Judicial Lawmaking and its Limits* (CUP 2018) Chapter 6.

[137] See esp Communication from the Commission to the European Parliament and the Council on guidance for better transposition and application of Directive 2004/38/EC on the right of citizens of the Union and their family members to move and reside freely within the territory of the Member States, COM(2009) 313 final. The Commission has now indicated that it intends to update this critical guidance for the first time: see EU Citizenship Report 2020: Empowering Citizens and Protecting their Rights, 15 December 2020, COM(2020) 730 final, para 3.1, Action 7. See also, Communication on Free movement of EU citizens and their families: five actions to make a difference, COM(2013) 837 final.

advances were conceived and advanced over time. Second, Chapter 2 provides a summary account of EU citizenship law's constitutive legal framework: presenting Articles 20 and 21 TFEU and Directive 2004/38 in more detail; drawing out core functional principles; and examining the interplay between the primary rights conferred by the Treaties and the regulation of their exercise by secondary law. Themes that recur across EU citizenship law—including the effectiveness of the rights conferred by EU law, the significance of the Charter of Fundamental Rights, and requirements of host State integration—are also introduced, and the intersection of Union citizenship and other Union objectives is further examined through the legal and wider conception of the territory of the European Union.

Chapters 3 and 4 address the *personal scope* of EU citizenship law—'who' it applies to—in two senses. First, Chapter 3 discusses the 'direct' personal scope of EU citizenship law by examining the constitutive link between Union citizenship and Member State nationality, reflecting the statement in Article 20(1) TFEU that '[e]very person holding the nationality of a Member State shall be a citizen of the Union'. Second, Chapter 4 introduces how EU citizenship law indirectly affects the rights of certain family members of Union citizens. In most respects, the rights that family members, irrespective of their own nationality, derive from Union citizens are set out in Directive 2004/38 as interpreted by the Court of Justice, though further sources of family reunification rights are considered in other chapters of the book where relevant.

Chapter 5 explores the extent to which EU citizenship law confers rights on Union citizens within their *home Member States*. It covers two main areas in this respect. First, reflecting the guarantee in Article 10(3) TEU that '[e]very citizen shall have the right *to participate in the democratic life of the Union*', Chapter 5 outlines the intersection of EU citizenship law and electoral rights exercised in the home State and it also examines the four procedures for citizen engagement provided for in Article 24 TFEU: the citizens' initiative, building on Article 11 TEU; the right to petition the European Parliament in accordance with Article 227 TFEU; applying to the European Ombudsman under Article 228 TFEU; and guarantees when writing to certain Union institutions or bodies. The protection by diplomatic or consular authorities of any Member State to which Union citizens present in the territory of a third country are entitled where the Member State of which they are nationals is not represented (Article 23 TFEU) is also considered here on the premise of another Member State acting as the home State 'surrogate' for Union citizens in these circumstances. Electoral rights guaranteed on a basis of equal treatment with host State nationals are also considered in this chapter, from the perspective that it is the role of the home State that has raised most legal questions in this respect to date. Second, Chapter 5 also examines the body of rights built around precluding 'national measures which have the effect of depriving citizens of the Union of the genuine enjoyment of the substance of the rights conferred by virtue of their status as citizens of the Union'.[138] These situations include, to date, losing the status of Union citizenship (Chapter 3) and, for the purposes of Chapter 5, *preventing (continuing) residence within the territory of the Union*. Relevant rights are based on Article 20 TFEU, characterised as 'exceptional' by the Court and rationalised ultimately as securing conditions that facilitate the capacity of Union citizens to exercise free movement rights in the future.[139]

The most developed part of EU citizenship law to date—the *right to move to and reside in another Member State* (the 'host State')—is examined across Chapters 6 to 10. Chapters 6, 7, 8, and 10 address questions that fall within the scope of Directive 2004/38, looking at

---

[138] Case C-34/09 *Ruiz Zambrano*, EU:C:2011:124, para 42.
[139] Case C-87/12 *Ymeraga*, EU:C:2013:291, paras 34–37.

the rights to move to, reside in, and remain in a host State (Chapter 6); the significance of residing lawfully in the host State as a precondition for equal treatment with host State nationals (Chapter 7); achieving a right of permanent residence in a host State (Chapter 8); and the legal parameters placed by Union law around national decisions that restrict the right to move and reside freely, notably through expulsion from a host State and framed around reasons of public health, public policy, and public security (Chapter 10). In contrast, Chapter 9 considers situations in which there has been cross-border movement (thus distinguishing them from what is covered in Chapter 5), yet the Directive does not apply. The main examples concern lives 'split' across more than one Member State where the application of the Directive is ruled out because the exercise of free movement rights occurred in the past; or because free movement continues in the present, but the relevant claim concerns the Union citizen's home rather than the host State.

Overall, and across all the chapters, the legal analysis presented in this book aims to reflect broader perspectives on the construction, application, and progression of EU citizenship law and it asks us to anticipate what futures Union citizenship might yet have. It is also important to consider how Union citizenship both reflects and itself progresses the functioning, nature, and values of the European Union. As so vividly expressed by the Commission, 'Union policies and actions ... form a *unique ecosystem* underpinned by instruments and structures that cannot be separated from each other'.[140] Union citizenship both embodies and advances this understanding of the European Union and of the wider objective of European integration that the Union serves and pursues as well as the values to which it is committed. At the time of writing, these interests are consistently and seriously challenged. The Union's citizens have a vital part indeed to play in determining the future of the polity that created them.

---

[140] Internal EU27 preparatory discussions on the framework for the future relationship: 'Regulatory issues', TF50 (2018) 32—Commission to EU 27, 21 February 2018, <https://ec.europa.eu/info/sites/info/files/slides_regulatory_issues.pdf> (accessed 24 May 2023), emphasis added.

2
Union Citizenship
Introducing the Legal Framework

1. Chapter Overview

This chapter provides an overview of the main legal features of Union citizenship, principally in relation to Articles 20 and 21 TFEU.[1] It presents the provisions and principles that define and advance the applicable legal framework. It also introduces significant themes within EU citizenship law that recur and are considered in more detail across later chapters of the book.

EU citizenship law has deep foundations in the free movement of persons more generally (Section 2). It will be seen that approaches, objectives, and tensions that predated the creation of Union citizenship strongly shaped—and in many respects continue to inform—its legal framework. Examination of the rights conferred by Articles 20 and 21 TFEU (Section 3) introduces the most critical balancing task that the Treaty requires: between the rights conferred by Union citizenship, on the one hand, and the conditions and limits that may legitimately restrict them, on the other. In legislative terms, that task is progressed principally through Directive 2004/38, which regulates the right to move and reside provided for in both Articles 20(1) and 21(1) TFEU (Section 4).[2]

Important themes that have emerged from the case law of the Court of Justice are then considered in Section 5, which addresses how a connecting factor to EU citizenship law is established, the emphasis placed on ensuring the effectiveness of Union citizenship rights, the significance of the Charter of Fundamental Rights, the role of integration requirements with respect to host States, and the intersection of Union citizenship and fields that remain within Member State competence. Finally, the territory of the European Union as the 'place' within which Union citizenship is experienced is explored (Section 6). Both the internal and external borders of that territory are considered through the example of case law on the extradition of Union citizens to third states. That discussion and the chapter more generally also encourage reflection on the connection between the territory of the Union and the values that construct and sustain it.[3]

---

[1] Articles 22–24 TFEU and related legislation are addressed in Chapter 5.
[2] Directive 2004/38/EC on the right of citizens of the Union and their family members to move and reside freely within the territory of the Member States, 2004 OJ L158/77.
[3] Article 2 TEU establishes that '[t]he Union is founded on the values of respect for human dignity, freedom, democracy, equality, the rule of law and respect for human rights, including the rights of persons belonging to minorities. These values are common to the Member States in a society in which pluralism, non-discrimination, tolerance, justice, solidarity and equality between women and men prevail'.

2. Origins of a Legal Framework: From EU Free Movement Law to EU Citizenship Law

This section does not seek to provide a comprehensive history of Union citizenship.[4] Instead, it identifies how EU law on the free movement of persons, based on the Treaty's economic freedoms, imprinted on EU citizenship law. For present purposes, that occurred in three important ways.

First, an impulse towards 'humanising' the person can be seen from the earliest developments in free movement law, even though it was neither suggested by the Community's founding documents—beyond a general sense that the new polity was about something more than coal, steel, or capital per se[5]—nor expressed in the adopted EEC Treaty.[6] Rather, it was a deliberate regulatory and interpretative choice, mainly to facilitate integration in a host State following the exercise of free movement and connected in many respects to what is now Article 18 TFEU and non-discrimination on the grounds of nationality.[7] Innovations such as rights for the family members of Member State nationals who came within the personal scope of the economic freedoms,[8] irrespective of the nationality of the family members themselves, were undoubtedly linked to the practical consideration that 'few persons are likely to want to immigrate to another country for any length of time unless their families can accompany them'.[9] But the relevant legislation was framed around fundamentally human concerns too, returned to in Section 2.1.

At the same time, the family reunification framework developed for free movement law also illustrates that rights extended to the nationals of other Member States would in some respects produce something beyond *equal* treatment with host State nationals: that rights based on EU law could be more favourable than rights conferred by national immigration law. In that sense, how people should be treated in a community envisaged and built around freedom of movement exceeded non-discrimination objectives and reflected wider ambitions of promoting, not just facilitating, cross-border mobility. Providing other examples of

---

[4] For an extensive account, see S O'Leary, *The Evolving Concept of Community Citizenship: From the Free Movement of Persons to Union Citizenship* (Kluwer Law International 1996).

[5] eg The Spaak Report considers regional balance and equality of treatment where it deals with the free movement of workers (*Rapport des Chefs de Délégations aux Ministres des Affaires Etrangères* (Secretariat of the Intergovernmental Conference, Brussels, 21 April 1956, 88–89), but there was no indication of particular importance being attached to persons in the proposed common market. Later, the Commission White Paper on Completing the Internal Market was written primarily in language of 'hard practical fact' (COM(85) 310 final, 6): it does invoke the 'people of Europe' (eg paras 219 and 220) but more in the context of the Community overall than the specific importance of persons within it.

[6] eg Article 48(2) EEC referred to the abolition of discrimination with respect to 'employment, remuneration and other conditions of work and employment' only, while Article 49 EEC enabled the Council to 'issue directives or make regulations setting out the measures required to bring about, by progressive stages, freedom of movement for workers' followed by a list of specific areas for action concerning workers, such as cooperation between national employment services and reforming administrative procedures and practices (eg qualifying periods for eligibility for employment 'the maintenance of which would form an obstacle to liberalisation of the movement of workers').

[7] The Report of the High Level Panel on the free movement of persons chaired by Mrs Simone Veil, and presented to the Commission on 18 March 1997, commented that Article 18 TFEU, 'as a result in particular of the decisions of the Court, quickly became understood as the expression not merely of non-discrimination but of the recognition of the equality, in rights and in dignity, of all Community citizens in all fields covered by the Treaty' (available at <http://aei.pitt.edu/39963/1/A4409.pdf> (accessed 24 May 2023), 15).

[8] See esp Article 10 of Regulation 1612/68/EEC on freedom of movement for workers within the Community, OJ 1968 Sp Ed L257/2, p 475 (building on Regulation No 15, 1961 OJ 57/1073). See also, Directive 68/360/EEC on the abolition of restrictions on movement and residence within the Community for workers of Member States and their families, OJ 1968 Sp Ed L257/13, p 485.

[9] TC Hartley, *EEC Immigration Law* (North-Holland 1978) 130.

this point, the EU legislator expanded the scope of the EEC Treaty provisions on services to include protection for receiving as well as providing them,[10] and envisioned rights for persons looking for work—for jobseekers—long before the judicial fleshing out of that figure in *Antonissen*.[11] That pioneering work meant that 'even the *original* Treaty could be seen, as indeed may have been the ultimate intention of its authors, as creating fundamental rights for individuals'.[12]

Second, the humanising impulse evident in free movement law produced both an idea and a language of European 'citizenship', invoked by academic commentators[13] and the Community's own institutions. As early as 1961, for example, the Commission characterised freedom of movement as an expansion of personal and not just economic freedom: as '*le premier aspect d'une citoyenneté européene*'.[14] Through a process of repeated institutional reference to and reflection on the notion of a European citizenship, its cultural, political, and social dimensions were further developed.[15]

Third, while some sense of the citizen as a political actor was envisaged,[16] the emerging *legal* content of Union citizenship was predominantly anchored to freedom of movement— to rights already conferred by the EEC Treaty for purposes of work, establishment, and services. At one level, a correlative understanding of Union citizenship and freedom of movement reflects the fact that the sphere of transnational mobility is where functional support from the Community was most relevant: Member State nationals did not need a replication of rights they already held as citizens of their own respective States, but they did need rights and legal protections that transcended the capacity of any one State. However, the intensity of the correlation with free movement raised concerns about the capacity of Union citizenship to mature as a legal status, concerns that coalesce now around the limitations of market citizenship as a sub-optimal citizenship form,[17] the reservation of Union citizenship

---

[10] Directive 64/221/EEC on the coordination of special measures concerning the movement and residence of foreign nationals which are justified on grounds of public policy, public security, or public health, OJ 1963– 1964 Sp Ed P117; Directive 73/148/EEC on the abolition of restrictions on movement and residence within the Community for nationals of Member States with regard to establishment and the provision of services, 1973 OJ L172/14. The right to receive services is returned to in Section 2.2, but it can be noted that legislative protection in situations of service receipt predated the Court's ruling on this question in Joined Cases 286/82 and 26/83 *Luisi and Carbone*, EU:C:1984:35.

[11] See Regulation 1612/68, Article 5; Regulation 1408/71 on the application of social security schemes to employed persons and their families moving within the Community, 1971 OJ L149/2, Article 69(1); and Case C-292/89 *Antonissen*, EU:C:1991:80. The intersection of EU citizenship law and the rights of jobseekers is examined in Chapters 6 and 7.

[12] FG Jacobs, 'Foreword' in RCA White, *Workers, Establishment and Services in the European Union* (OUP 2004) v (emphasis in original).

[13] eg AC Evans 'European citizenship' (1982) 45 Modern Law Review 497. Similarly, Hartley refers to 'Community citizens' to indicate 'those persons within the personal scope of the Community provisions' (TC Hartley, *EEC Immigration Law* (North-Holland 1978) 87).

[14] Evans (ibid) 499, referring to P.E. Deb., No. 48, 135, 22 November 1961. Commission Vice-President Sandri referred to freedom of movement as 'an incipient form of European citizenship' in 1968 (Bull. EC 11–1968, 5–9).

[15] See esp the Tindemans Report in 1975 (Bull. EC Suppl. 1–76); the 1984 Draft Treaty on European Union (1984 OJ C77/53); and the work of the Adoninno Committee (Bull. EC Supp. 7/85 and 'A People's Europe', Bull. EC Supp. 2/88).

[16] See J Shaw, *The Transformation of Citizenship in the European Union: Electoral Rights and the Restructuring of Political Space* (CUP 2007) Chapter 4.

[17] eg M Everson, 'The legacy of the market citizen' in J Shaw and G More (eds), *New Legal Dynamics of European Union* (Clarendon Press 1995) 73; PJ Neuvonen, *Equal Citizenship and Its Limits in EU Law: We The Burden?* (Hart Publishing 2016); N Nic Shuibhne, 'The resilience of EU market citizenship' (2010) 47 Common Market Law Review 1597; C O'Brien, 'I trade, therefore I am: legal personhood in the European Union' (2013) 50 Common Market Law Review 1643; S Reynolds, 'Union citizenship: placing limitations on a human-centred approach?' in N Feirreira and D Kostakopoulou (eds), *The Human Face of the European Union: Are EU Law and Policy Humane Enough?* (CUP 2016) 155; M van den Brink, 'The problem with market citizenship and the beauty of free movement' in F Amtenbrink, G Davies, D Kochenov, and J Lindeboom (eds), *The Internal Market and the Future of European Integration: Essays in Honour of Laurence W. Gormley* (CUP 2019) 246; and F Wollenschläger, 'A new

as a mobility-triggered status and for Member State nationals only,[18] and the stunted appreciation ad furthering of personhood in EU law that results from all of these concerns.[19]

Against that background, the main characteristics of two different types of pre-citizenship free movement rights will now be considered in more detail: first, economic free movement rights (Section 2.1), and second, the general free movement rights created by EU legislation (Section 2.2).

2.1 Predating EU Citizenship Law: Economic Free Movement Rights

For present purposes, three things are striking about the earliest judgments that the Court of Justice delivered on the free movement of workers. First, the reasoning of the Court extended beyond discrimination and into protection against disadvantage or deterrence sooner than is often appreciated. Especially for the coordination of social security entitlement, the Court's early concern for 'the elimination of legislative obstacles' that might hinder the free movement of workers[20] was essentially predictive of the liberal approach to restrictions of goods and services in *Van Binsbergen* and *Dassonville*, which came a decade later.[21] The Court also indicated (before the adoption of the Maastricht Treaty) that the free movement of persons was 'intended to facilitate the pursuit by *Community citizens* of occupational activities of all kinds throughout the Community' and 'national legislation which might place Community citizens at a disadvantage when they wish to extend their activities beyond the territory of a single Member State' was therefore precluded.[22]

Second, facilitating the personal liberty of the worker was paramount. In that light, the Court considered that '[t]he establishment of as complete a freedom of movement for workers as possible' was the principal objective of Articles 45–48 TFEU.[23]

Third, many of these cases were not actually about situations connected to work at all. An early cluster of judgments concerned the reach of Regulation No 3, the first measure

---

fundamental freedom beyond market integration: Union citizenship and its dynamics for shifting the economic paradigm of European integration' (2011) 17 European Law Journal 1.

[18] Most obviously, in the context of Brexit: eg S Coutts, 'Citizens of elsewhere, everywhere and... nowhere? Rethinking Union citizenship in light of Brexit' (2018) Northern Ireland Legal Quarterly 231; A Łazowski, 'When *Cives Europae* became bargaining chips: free movement of persons in the Brexit negotiations' (2018) 18 ERA Forum 469; C O'Brien, 'Between the devil and the deep blue sea: vulnerable EU citizens cast adrift in the UK post-Brexit' (2021) 58 Common Market Law Review 431; V Roeben, P Minnerop, P Telles, and J Snell 'Revisiting Union citizenship from a fundamental rights perspective in the time of Brexit' (2018) 5 European Human Rights Law Review 450; and E Spaventa, 'Mice or horses? British citizens in the EU27 after Brexit as "former EU citizens"' (2019) 44 European Law Review 589 and 'Brexit and the free movement of persons: what is EU citizenship really about?' in N Nic Shuibhne (ed), *Revisiting the Fundamentals of EU Law on the Free Movement of Persons* (OUP 2023) forthcoming.

[19] C O'Brien, 'I trade therefore I am' (n 17); L Azoulai, S Barbou des Places, and E Pataut (eds), *Constructing the Person in EU Law: Rights, Roles, Identities* (Hart Publishing 2016); and D Kramer, 'From worker to self-entrepreneur: The transformation of *homo economicus* and the freedom of movement in the European Union' (2017) 23 European Law Journal 172.

[20] Case 92/63 *Nonnenmacher*, EU:C:1964:40, para 1. The judgment continued: '[i]n case of doubt [Articles 45-48 TFEU] and the measures taken in implementation of them must therefore be construed so as to avoid placing migrant workers in an unfavourable legal position, particularly with regard to social security'.

[21] Case 33/74 *Van Binsbergen*, EU:C:1974:131; Case 8/74, *Dassonville*, EU:C:1974:82.

[22] Case 143/87 *Stanton*, EU:C:1988:378, para 13 (emphasis added).

[23] Case 75/63 *Unger*, EU:C:1964:19, para 1. In *Nonnenmacher*, the Court observed similarly that the Treaty provisions 'are designed to establish the greatest possible freedom of movement for workers'.

adopted to coordinate national social security systems.[24] For example, in *Unger*, the applicant worked in the Netherlands and sought reimbursement of medical expenses there that were incurred while she was visiting her parents in Germany, a State with no connection to her occupational activity. In *van Dijk*, the facts concerned social security benefits following a traffic accident involving a frontier worker who resided in the Netherlands but worked in Germany; the accident occurred in the Netherlands on a day off and was unconnected with work.[25] In *Singer*, considering the applicability of Regulation No 3 to the payment of benefits in Germany following the death of a German national while on holiday in France, the Court restated the objective of ensuring the 'greatest possible freedom for workers' and reasoned that '[i]t would not be in conformity with that spirit to limit the concept of "worker" solely to migrant workers *stricto sensu* or solely to workers required to move for the purpose of their employment. Nothing in Article [48 TFEU] imposes such distinctions, which would in any case tend to make the application of the rules in question impracticable'.[26] These cases demonstrate something that continues to shape EU free movement law today: that *what* the claimant was doing was less important than *where* the facts played out. In other words, the critical significance of movement—of the cross-border connection—was born. In *Saunders*, the Court confirmed that '[t]he provisions of the Treaty on freedom of movement for workers cannot ... be applied to situations which are *wholly internal to a Member State*, in other words, where there is *no factor connecting them* to any of the situations envisaged by [Union] law'.[27]

The circumstances of *Vaassen-Göbbels*, which concerned the payment of benefits to the widow of a deceased worker who had transferred her own place of residence from the Netherlands to Germany following the death of her husband, illustrated both the wide scope of free movement law and its concern for family members in a more human sense. Bringing her circumstances within the framework of Regulation No 3, Advocate General Gand observed:

> [I]n this case the result which is reached is to apply Regulation No 3 concerning migrant workers to a worker's widow, who has never worked herself and who, after having obtained her widow's pension, transfers her residence to another Member State for reasons other than to take up gainful employment. The *Beambtenfonds* asks whether that is a reasonable result. One may reply that Article 4 provides that the provisions of the Regulation apply to the survivors of wage-earners or persons treated as such. The intention behind this very sweeping proposition is to eliminate anything which could, even as a mere possibility, restrict the free movement of workers.[28]

As noted earlier, the Court later justified such a wide interpretation of the Treaty provisions on free movement of persons through the language of 'Community citizens', reflecting the

---

[24] Article 48 TFEU now provides that '[t[he European Parliament and the Council shall, acting in accordance with the ordinary legislative procedure, adopt such measures in the field of social security as are necessary to provide freedom of movement for workers; to this end, they shall make arrangements to secure for employed and self-employed migrant workers and their dependants: (a) aggregation, for the purpose of acquiring and retaining the right to benefit and of calculating the amount of benefit, of all periods taken into account under the laws of the several countries; (b) payment of benefits to persons resident in the territories of Member States'. See also, Regulation 883/2004 on the coordination of social security systems, 2011 OJ L166/1.
[25] Case 33/64 *van Dijk*, EU:C:1965:19.
[26] Case 44/65 *Singer*, EU:C:1965:212, p 971.
[27] Case 175/78 *Saunders*, ECLI: EU:C:1979:88, para 11 (emphasis added).
[28] AG Gand in Case 61/65 *Vaassen-Göbbels*, EU:C:1966:25, p 285.

submission of the claimant in *Lawrie-Blum*, for example, that '[a] restrictive interpretation of Article [45(1) TFEU] would reduce freedom of movement to a mere instrument of economic integration, would be contrary to its broader objective of creating an area in which Community citizens enjoy freedom of movement'.[29]

The Court's case law on Article 7(2) of Regulation 1612/68 is of particular importance for the construction of EU citizenship law. Article 7(2)[30] established that workers who are nationals of other Member States 'shall enjoy the same social and tax advantages as national workers'. Specific restrictions on the payment of benefits permitted by other EU legislation could be overcome if the benefit could also be classified as a social and tax advantage.[31] The Court also detached 'social and tax advantages' from the context of work, finding that 'in view of the equality of treatment which the provision seeks to achieve, the substantive area of application must be delineated so as to include all social and tax advantages, *whether or not attached to the contract of employment*'.[32] As the Court later clarified, 'the advantages which [Article 7(2)] extends to workers who are nationals of other Member States are all those which, whether or not linked to a contract of employment, are generally granted to national workers primarily because of their objective status as workers *or by virtue of the mere fact of their residence on the national territory* and the extension of which to workers who are nationals of other Member States therefore seems suitable to facilitate their mobility within the Community'.[33] Drawing from the preamble to the Regulation, the Court considered that social and tax advantages connect to 'promoting [the] social advancement' of EU workers in a host State.[34] That idea establishes a link between the worker and the *society*—not just the labour market—of the host State. The Court also suggested that Article 7(2) 'imposes *responsibility* in the social sphere on each Member State with regard to every worker who is a national of another Member State'.[35]

In *Konstantinidis*, Advocate General Jacobs merged strands of the Court's case law that touched on free movement rights, fundamental rights, and a conception of European citizenship, asserting that:

> [A] Community national who goes to another Member State as a worker or self-employed person under Articles [45, 49 or 56] of the Treaty is entitled not just to pursue his trade or profession and to enjoy the same living and working conditions as nationals of the host State; he is in addition entitled to assume that, wherever he goes to earn his living in the European Community, he will be treated in accordance with a common code of fundamental values, in particular those laid down in the European Convention on Human Rights. In other words, he is entitled to say '*civis europeus sum*' and to invoke that status in order to oppose any violation of his fundamental rights.[36]

---

[29] Case 66/85 *Lawrie-Blum*, EU:C:1986:284, para 12.
[30] Now replaced by Article 7(2) of Regulation 492/2011 on freedom of movement for workers within the Union, 2011 OJ L141/1.
[31] Case C-111/91 *Commission v Luxembourg*, EU:C:1993:92, para 21: 'since Regulation No 1612/68 is of general application regarding the free movement of workers, Article 7(2) thereof may apply to social advantages which, at the same time, fall specifically within the scope of Regulation No 1408/71'.
[32] Case 32/75 *Cristini*, EU:C:1975:120, para 13 (emphasis added).
[33] Case 65/81 *Reina*, EU:C:1982:6, para 12 (emphasis added).
[34] Case 39/86 *Lair*, EU:C:1988:322, para 22.
[35] Case 235/87 *Matteuci*, EU:C:1988:460, para 16 (emphasis added).
[36] AG Jacobs in *Konstantinidis*, EU:C:1993:115, para 24 of the Opinion.

As a point of contrast, Chapter 1 introduced the fact that rights for the family members of Member State nationals are not, in structural terms, conferred on family members as persons in their own right but rather *derived* from the Member State national who moves: in other words, family reunification rights were created not, primarily, as fundamental rights but to facilitate the Member State national's capacity to move and to institute more security of residence for them in the host State thereafter.[37] That construction reflects a paradox still evident in EU citizenship law: that the functional and instrumental dimensions of respect for private and family life are acknowledged as openly as any deeper appreciation of the qualities of dignity and respect that underpin them. Both dimensions were reflected in the fifth recital of Regulation 1612/68, which stated that 'the right of freedom of movement demands for its exercise, conditions which are objectively those of liberty and dignity, the elimination of obstacles which impede the mobility of workers, especially as regards the right of the worker to be reunited with his family, and the conditions of integration of such family in the environment of the host country'.[38]

Taken together, the foundational principles that constructed economic free movement law as summarised above thus begin to suggest a legal framework (1) where what is pursued in another Member State is less important than where it is pursued, that is, than the existence of a cross-border connection; (2) ensuring the greatest possible freedom of movement is the acknowledged underpinning objective; (3) which requires a wide interpretation of EU rights so that Member State nationals who move are not placed at a disadvantage for having done so. As a result, EU free movement rights were built upon a merged understanding of the functional and the normative, of the economic and the social: of the rights of the individual, on the one hand, and the contribution of freedom of movement to European integration more systemically, on the other.

2.2 Presaging EU Citizenship Law: General Free Movement Rights

The idea of a 'general' right to move and reside can be understood in two ways. In one meaning, it might question the relevance of formal categories such as 'work' or 'establishment' that are not always legally significant or do not always function well either conceptually or in practice (the latter point being of particular relevance at present as the nature of work and of the workplace radically transforms). In some instances, the Court has suggested that whichever Treaty freedom is applied is not a material concern.[39] But more generally, the applicable Treaty freedom(s) will be identified and EU law entails mechanisms for working that out.[40] Either way, distinctions across the freedoms are in many respects smoothed over

---

[37] eg Case 7/75 *Mr and Mrs F*, EU:C:1975:80, paras 19–20.
[38] This recital was generally used by the Court to support a broad reading of the Regulation in the context of family member rights; eg Case 76/72 *Scutari*, EU:C:1973:46, paras 13–16; Case 9/74 *Casagrande*, EU:C:1974:74, paras 6–8. See in particular, AG Trabucchi in *Mr and Mrs F*, EU:C:1975:75, esp p 696: '[t]he migrant worker is not regarded by Community law — nor is he by the internal legal systems — as a mere source of labour but is viewed as a human being'; the Advocate General therefore envisaged 'a legal system corresponding to the concept of social justice and to the requirements of European integration, not only of the economy but of the people'.
[39] eg Case C-390/99 *Canal Satélite Digital*, EU:C:2002:34 para 31: '[w]here a national measure restricts both the free movement of goods and the freedom to provide services, the Court will in principle examine it in relation to one only of those two fundamental freedoms where it is shown that, in the circumstances of the case, one of them is entirely secondary in relation to the other *and may be considered together with it*' (emphasis added).
[40] eg Distinguishing work and establishment, Case C-55/94 *Gebhard*, EU:C:1995:411, paras 23–27. More generally, the Court will focus on which freedom 'prevails' and which is 'secondary', eg Case C-36/02 *Omega*, EU:C:2004:614, para 26; Case C-20/03 *Burmanjer and Others*, EU:C:2005:307, para 34; and Case C-452/04 *Fidium Finanz*, EU:C:2006:631, para 34.

by the application of broadly the same principles irrespective of the Treaty provision at issue. For example, the fact that a measure does not have to discriminate directly against workers,[41] companies,[42] products,[43] services,[44] or capital[45] to constitute a restriction of free movement[46] suggests that determining the Treaty right(s) actually triggered in a given situation is less important—that freedom of movement is instead protected *generally*.

However, the idea of a general free movement right also means a right to move to and reside in another Member State without the requirement to pursue or engage in economic activity there. In that light, two developments can be considered: first, the generalising of rights that do still fall in one of the economic free movement categories, and second, free movement rights that are decoupled from Articles 45, 49, and 56 TFEU, that is, from work, establishment, and services, altogether.

On the generalising of rights that do fall formally within Articles 45, 49, or 56 TFEU, the Court's generous interpretative approach in case law on the free movement of workers was highlighted in Section 2.1 to demonstrate a looseness of connectivity between the *personal scope*—who the individual is (for present purposes, a worker, self-employed person, or provider/recipient of services)—and the *material scope*—what that individual is claiming (for example, social and tax advantages in the host State)—of free movement law. The evolution of the case law on services illustrates the same point. In *Watson and Belmann*, Advocate General Trabucchi argued against recognising freedom to receive services on the basis of Article 56 TFEU. In his view, that development would be 'inconsistent with the very structure of the Treaty, which provides for freedom of movement in respect of specific categories of professional or trade activities' and therefore 'the most that can be done is to recognize freedom of movement for recipients of services also but only in so far as it appears to be indissolubly linked with the right to movement of those who have to provide those services'.[47] Critically, he preferred 'to avoid the fiction of using the actual wording of the Treaty to justify *the extension to all citizens of the Community of a right to freedom of movement* which the Treaty intended to apply only to *clearly defined categories* of persons'.[48] Here, the Advocate General touched on the essence of a general right to move and suggested that recognising freedom to receive services independently of Treaty-mandated protection of their provision constituted, in effect, such a general right: few who cross a border into another Member State will receive no services there at all, irrespective of why they went there in the first place.

Advocate General Trabucchi's view thus called into question the protection extended legislatively to service recipients by Directives 64/221 and 73/148. However, in *Luisi and Carbone*, the Court confirmed the legitimacy of that step. The restrictions limiting transfers of foreign currency challenged in those proceedings could indeed be connected directly to payments for medical and tourism services received in other Member States. Subsequent case law dissolved the directness of that link. In *Cowan*, the claimant's entitlement to compensation for injury resulting from an assault sustained when he was a tourist in France was not connected to any particular services that he received there. Presaging Advocate General Jacobs' *civis europeus sum* idea, the Court reasoned:

---

[41] eg Case C-190/98, *Graf*, EU:C:2000:49, para 18.
[42] eg Case C-442/02 *CaixaBank France*, EU:C:2004:586, para 11.
[43] eg Case C-142/05 *Mickelsson and Roos*, EU:C:2009:336, para 26
[44] eg Case C-76/90 *Säger*, EU:C:1991:331, para 12.
[45] eg Case C-367/98 *Commission v Portugal*, EU:C:2002:326, para 44.
[46] eg Case C-19/92 *Kraus*, EU:C:1993:125, para 29; Case C-55/94 *Gebhard*, EU:C:1995:411, para 37.
[47] AG Trabucchi in Case 118/75 *Watson and Belmann*, EU:C:1976:79; (1976) ECR 1185 at 1204.
[48] ibid 1205 (emphasis added).

When Community law guarantees a natural person the freedom to go to another Member State *the protection of that person from harm in the Member State in question*, on the same basis as that of nationals and persons residing there, is a corollary of that freedom of movement. It follows that the prohibition of discrimination is applicable to recipients of services within the meaning of the Treaty as regards protection against the risk of assault and the right to obtain financial compensation provided for by national law when that risk materializes.[49]

Similarly, in *Bickel and Franz*, a case that post-dates the Maastricht Treaty but was resolved on the basis of freedom to receive services rather than Union citizenship, the Court observed that Article 56 TFEU 'covers all nationals of Member States who, independently of other freedoms guaranteed by the Treaty, visit another Member State *where they intend or are likely to receive services*'.[50] On that basis, equal treatment extended to the language in which criminal proceedings against Mr Bickel and Mr Franz would be conducted, even though such proceedings concerned prosecutions incidental to being present in the host State rather than to the provision or receipt of services there more concretely.[51]

An impression thus emerges of services as a useful pretext: as a hook for manifesting the protection of the Treaty in situations that materialised through the experience of free movement in a general sense rather than through service provision or service receipt more concretely. However, extrapolating a general right to move from services in this way has its limits. The defining characteristic of services is that the exercise of that freedom, whether for provision or receipt, is inherently *temporary* in nature. In *Zhu and Chen*, for example, the Court confirmed that 'the provisions on freedom to provide services do not cover the situation of a national of a Member State who establishes his principal residence in the territory of another Member State with a view to receiving services there for an indefinite period'.[52] It therefore ruled out the possibility that Directive 73/148 could be used 'as a basis for a right of residence of indefinite duration'.[53]

Turning to rights both formally and actually disconnected from the economic freedoms, the Court could, by the time of *Zhu and Chen*, engage the general right to move and reside conferred by Article 21(1) TFEU as a dimension of Union citizenship. The Treaty provisions on citizenship were not, however, the first general free movement rights *deliberately* decoupled from economic activity in EU free movement law. First, in the Court's case law, while publicly funded education was considered not to fall within the scope of the Treaty provisions on services,[54] Member State nationals who moved to another State for the purposes of study were protected through combining what is now Article 166 TFEU on vocational training and Article 18 TFEU on nationality discrimination, especially as regards the conditions of access to education such as the payment of tuition fees.[55] The significance of mobility in the field of education was thereby promoted and, as a category of persons not tied to any of the economic free movement provisions, students were, in legal terms, profoundly special. The scope of vocational training was held to cover university studies,[56] and a right

---

[49] Case 186/87 *Cowan*, EU:C:1989:47, para 17 (emphasis added). Explicitly using the language of 'Community citizens', see AG Lenz (EU:C:1988:563), para 1 of the Opinion; and for discussion of the right to receive services in both abstract and concrete senses, see paras 22 ff.
[50] Case C-274/96 *Bickel and Franz*, EU:C:1988:563, para 15 (emphasis added).
[51] ibid para 16.
[52] Case C-200/02 *Zhu and Chen*, EU:C:2004:639, para 22.
[53] ibid para 23.
[54] Case 263/86 *Humbel and Edel*, EU:C:1988:451, paras 15–19.
[55] Case 293/83 *Gravier*, EU:C:1985:69.
[56] Case 24/86 *Blaizot*, EU:C:1988:43; Case C-47/93 *Commission v Belgium*, EU:C:1994:181.

to reside in the host State for the duration of the relevant course of studies was implied.[57] However, the protective reach of the Treaty was not, at the time, extended to host State obligations for the payment of maintenance grants.[58]

Second, general free movement rights were created in three directives adopted (initially) in 1990: Directive 90/364 on the right of residence,[59] Directive 90/365 on the right of residence for employees and self-employed persons who have ceased their occupational activity,[60] and Directive 90/366 on the right of residence for students, replaced by Directive 93/96 following a successful legal basis challenge by the European Parliament.[61] The idea of general movement and residence rights, linked conceptually and in legal basis terms to the furthering of the common market, had been envisaged for some time. In a 1975 report presented to the Council by the Commission, responding to a political initiative of the Heads of State or Government,[62] the prospect of such 'special rights' was examined.[63] The report expressly questioned whether these rights overlapped with or were distinct from 'the idea of European citizenship'.[64] In 1979, the Commission proposed a directive to establish a right of residence for the nationals of Member States in the territory of another State.[65] Its beneficiaries were defined by exclusion, that is, those who did not come within the scope of existing legislation on the free movement of persons. Family members, as defined in the directive, would also be covered. But two points attract particular attention for present purposes. First, the proposed directive introduced a right of 'permanent residence' that was realised later through the adoption of Directive 2004/38.[66] Second, Article 4(1) of the draft directive indicated that 'Member States *may* require those citizens to provide proof of sufficient resources to provide for their own needs and the dependent members of their family' (emphasis added).

The Commission's 1979 proposal was not adopted,[67] owing to prolonged disagreement about questions of legal basis.[68] The progression of general movement and residence rights was absorbed more generally into planning for the Single European Act, with proposals for three separate directives introduced in 1989[69] and all three measures initially adopted, as noted above, in 1990. Specific provisions of the 1990s Directives are considered in more detail in later chapters (where the successor provisions included now in Directive 2004/38 are examined), but three preliminary points can be noted here. First, the *opportunity* for Member States to require sufficient resources in the 1979 proposal became a *condition* of the right of residence in the 1990s Directives, alongside the possession of comprehensive

---

[57] Case C-357/89 *Raulin*, EU:C:1992:87, para 34.
[58] Case 39/86 *Lair*, EU:C:1988:322.
[59] 1990 OJ L180/26.
[60] 1990 OJ L180/28.
[61] 1990 OJ L180/30 and 1993 OJ L317/59 respectively. See also, Case C-295/90 *Parliament v Council*, EU:C:1992:294, which resulted in the reference to what is now Article 352 TFEU being removed.
[62] Final communiqué issued at the European Summit, Paris, 9–10 December 1974, Bulletin of the European Communities December 1974, No 12, point 11.
[63] COM(75) 321 final, *Towards European Citizenship—the granting of special rights*.
[64] ibid Annex 2.
[65] 1979 OJ C207/14.
[66] On the right of permanent residence under Directive 2004/38, see Chapter 8.
[67] However, the European Parliament noted that the proposal 'introduces a new dimension to previous legislation on freedom of movement and the right of establishment since it extends these rights to all citizens of the Community, independently of the pursuit of an economic activity' and thus described it as the 'first step towards the creation of a European citizenship' (1980 OJ C117/48).
[68] S O'Leary, 'The free movement of persons and services' in P Craig and G de Búrca (eds), *The Evolution of EU Law* (1st edn OUP 1999) 377 at 381.
[69] See 1989 OJ C191/2 (students), 1989 OJ C191/3 (retired persons), and 1989 OJ C191/5 (general rights); for the amended proposals, see 1990 OJ C26/15 (students), 1990 OJ C26/19 (retired persons), 1990 OJ C26/22 (general rights).

sickness insurance cover.[70] The general right to move and reside was therefore decoupled from economic activity in terms of opening up the personal scope of free movement to all Member State nationals in principle; but it was not decoupled from interests of an economic nature—effecting a transition from economic *activity* to economic *autonomy* that still characterises EU citizenship law today. Member State nationals who exercised the general right to move and reside put in place by the Directives were thus described as 'peripheral market actors'.[71]

However, second, reflecting their particular history as a special category of persons in free movement law, less onerous requirements were signalled for students: they had to *declare* that they had sufficient resources rather than *have* them.[72] Third, as confirmed by successful infringement proceedings against Italy, Member States were not permitted to add further conditions to those provided for in the Directives.[73]

The creation of Union citizenship by the Maastricht Treaty elevated general rights to move and reside from secondary to primary law, and Advocates General at the Court of Justice began to speculate about the implications of that development. In *Boukhalfa*, Advocate General Léger acknowledged that Union citizenship 'embraces aspects which have already largely been established in the development of Community law and in this respect it represents a consolidation of existing Community law'.[74] At the same time, he called on the Court 'to ensure that its full scope is attained', which required ultimately, in his view, 'citizens of the Union being treated absolutely equally, irrespective of their nationality'.[75] In *Shingara and Radiom*, Advocate General Ruiz-Jarabo Colomer described Union citizenship as a 'considerable qualitative step forward in that ... it separates that freedom from its functional or instrumental elements (the link with an economic activity or attainment of the internal market) and raises it to the level of a genuinely independent right inherent in the political status of the citizens of the Union'.[76]

However, an observation in the 1997 Report of the High Level Panel on the free movement of persons is also worth recalling: 'in the minds of European citizens free movement conjures up an idea which goes well beyond the rights actually conferred by the Treaty. For

---

[70] See Articles 1(1) of Directives 90/364 and 90/365, and Article 1 of Directive 93/96.

[71] G More, 'The principle of equal treatment: from market unifier to fundamental right?' in P Craig and G de Búrca (eds), *The Evolution of EU Law* (1st edn, OUP 1999) 517 at 540.

[72] Article 1 of Directive 93/96 establishes that 'the Member States shall recognize the right of residence for any student who is a national of a Member State and who does not enjoy that right under other provisions of Community law, and for the student's spouse and their dependent children, *where the student assures the relevant national authority, by means of a declaration or by such alternative means as the student may choose that are at least equivalent, that he has sufficient resources* to avoid becoming a burden on the social assistance system of the host Member State during their period of residence, provided that the student is enrolled in a recognized educational establishment for the principal purpose of following a vocational training course there and that he is covered by sickness insurance in respect of all risks in the host Member State'. Compare eg Article 1(1) of Directive 90/364: 'Member States shall grant the right of residence to nationals of Member States who do not enjoy this right under other provisions of Community law and to members of their families as defined in paragraph 2, provided that they themselves and the members of their families *are covered by sickness insurance* in respect of all risks in the host Member State *and have sufficient resources* to avoid becoming a burden on the social assistance system of the host Member State during their period of residence'. All emphasis added. These distinctions are returned to in Chapters 6 and 7.

[73] Case C-424/98 *Commission v Italy*, EU:C:2000:287; the Commission's case was upheld with respect to both the substance of the resources condition and the means that could be used to demonstrate that it was met.

[74] AG Léger in Case C-214/94 *Boukhalfa*, EU:C:1996:174, para 63 of the Opinion.

[75] ibid. See similarly, AG La Pergola in in Joined Cases C-4/95 and C-5/95 *Stöber and Pereira*, EU:C:1996:225, para 50 of the Opinion; observing also that the Treaty provisions on citizenship represented 'progress of major significance in the construction of Europe'.

[76] AG Ruiz-Jarabo-Colomer in Joined Cases C-65/95 and C-111/95 *Shingara and Radiom*, EU:C:1996:451, para 34 of the Opinion.

many people, it suggests a right to move to and live in the countries of the Union without having to comply with any particular formalities, *which is not in fact the case*'.[77]

3. Legal Framework I: Articles 20 and 21 TFEU

It was explained in Chapter 1 that, in principle, the right of Union citizens to move and reside freely within the territory of the Member States, expressed in both Articles 20 and 21 TFEU, is a residual right, invoked only when the situation in question does not fall within the scope of the Treaty's economic freedoms. In that sense, the general right to move and reside conferred by Union citizenship adds a new band of *personal scope* to EU primary law. Union citizenship has also expanded the *material scope* of EU law. For example, it was noted in Section 2.2 that conditions for access to education in another Member State were brought within the scope of the Treaty's provisions on vocational training but that equal treatment did not extend to eligibility for student maintenance grants. However, in *Bidar*, the Court reversed that position, finding that precisely because of the introduction of Union citizenship, 'the situation of a citizen of the Union who is lawfully resident in another Member State falls within the scope of application of the Treaty within the meaning of the first paragraph of [Article 18 TFEU] for the purposes of obtaining assistance for students, whether in the form of a subsidised loan or a grant, intended to cover his maintenance costs'.[78]

The Court of Justice has directly linked the statement that Union citizenship is 'destined to be the fundamental status of nationals of the Member State'[79] to 'the importance *attached by primary law* to the status of citizen of the Union'.[80] In a general sense, EU primary law establishes the 'normative parameters'[81] within which Union and national rules and practices will be assessed. On that basis, EU legislation must comply with the provisions of the Treaty as interpreted by the Court of Justice. However, the prominence granted by both Articles 20 and 21 TFEU to secondary law—for the laying down of the 'conditions and limitations' in accordance with which citizenship rights must be exercised—adds further complexity. Additionally, as introduced in Chapter 1, the Treaties also attach importance to different interests at the same time. For example, in *Bogendorff von Wolffersdorff*, considering national rules on name registration, the Court acknowledged that the relevant provision of the national constitution could be taken into account for the purpose of justifying restrictions on free movement 'as an element of the national identity of a Member State, referred to in Article 4(2) TEU'.[82] However, the Court also invoked the multi-dimensional nature of EU law, observing that 'the EU legal system undeniably seeks to ensure the observance of the principle of equal treatment as a general principle of law [which is] also enshrined in Article 20 of the Charter'.[83] As will be seen here and in later chapters, the challenge of balancing competing interests and conflicting objectives runs through much of EU citizenship law.

---

[77] Report of the High Level Panel on the free movement of persons chaired by Mrs Simone Veil, and presented to the Commission on 18 March 1997, 85 (emphasis added).

[78] Case C-209/03 *Bidar*, EU:C:2005:169, para 42. The limitations since placed on equal access to student maintenance grants by Article 24(2) of Directive 2004/38 are addressed in Chapter 7.

[79] Case C-184/99 *Grzelczyk*, EU:C:2001:458, para 31.

[80] Case C-391/09 *Runevič-Vardyn and Wardyn*, EU:C:2011:291, para 60 (emphasis added); see also eg Case C-118/20 *Wiener Landesregierung (Révocation d'une assurance de naturalisation)*, EU:C:2022:34, para 58.

[81] AG Kokott in Case C-318/13 *X*, EU:C:2014:333, para 49 of the Opinion.

[82] Case C-438/14 *Bogendorff von Wolffersdorff*, EU:C:2016:401, para 64. See similarly, Case C-673/16 *Coman*, EU:C:2018:385, para 43.

[83] Case C-438/14 *Bogendorff von Wolffersdorff*, para 70.

In this part of the chapter, Articles 20 and 21 TFEU are first outlined in more detail. After a brief overview of each provision (Sections 3.1 and 3.2 respectively), the fundamental building blocks of EU free movement law—restriction and justification (Section 3.3) and proportionality (Section 3.4)—are discussed in the specific context of the right to move and reside conferred by Union citizenship. The question of whether asymmetric movement can be accommodated in EU citizenship law is also introduced (Section 3.5).

3.1 Article 20 TFEU

In one sense, Article 20 TFEU is an 'umbrella' provision: it offers a concise overview of the rights that Union citizenship confers, which are then fleshed out in more detail in Articles 21–24.

Article 20 TFEU

1. Citizenship of the Union is hereby established. Every person holding the nationality of a Member State shall be a citizen of the Union. Citizenship of the Union shall be additional to and not replace national citizenship.[84]
2. Citizens of the Union shall enjoy the rights and be subject to the duties provided for in the Treaties. They shall have, *inter alia*:
   (a) the right to move and reside freely within the territory of the Member States;
   (b) the right to vote and to stand as candidates in elections to the European Parliament and in municipal elections in their Member State of residence, under the same conditions as nationals of that State;
   (c) the right to enjoy, in the territory of a third country in which the Member State of which they are nationals is not represented, the protection of the diplomatic and consular authorities of any Member State on the same conditions as the nationals of that State;
   (d) the right to petition the European Parliament, to apply to the European Ombudsman, and to address the institutions and advisory bodies of the Union in any of the Treaty languages and to obtain a reply in the same language.

These rights shall be exercised in accordance with the conditions and limits defined by the Treaties and by the measures adopted thereunder.

The right to move and reside freely in Article 20(2)(a) is normally addressed in practice under Article 21(1) (Section 3.2) and Articles 22–24 further develop the political rights outlined in paragraphs (b) to (d) of Article 20(2) (Chapter 5). Additionally, the final sentence of Article 20(2), on the placing of conditions and limits on the exercise of citizenship rights, is essentially repeated in Article 21(1) and is returned to in Sections 3.3, 3.4, and 4.

However, Article 20(1) TFEU makes three distinct contributions that function independently of the other provisions in this part of the TFEU. First, most fundamentally, it determines

---

[84] These statements are also found in Article 9 TEU.

who Union citizens are: every person holding the nationality of a Member State. More direct citizenship pathways—for persons holding any nationality who can demonstrate sufficient connection to the Union, especially through long-term residence within its territory—have long been considered;[85] a discussion focused more recently on the loss of Union citizenship of British nationals following Brexit.[86] However, in *Préfet du Gers*, the Court ruled that '[b]y Article 9 TEU and Article 20 TFEU, the authors of the Treaties ... established an *inseparable and exclusive link* between possession of the nationality of a Member State and not only the acquisition, but also the retention, of the status of citizen of the Union'.[87] Since holding Member State nationality is 'an essential condition for a person to be able to acquire and retain the status of citizen of the Union and to benefit fully from the rights attaching to that status', losing it 'therefore entails, for the person concerned, the *automatic* loss of his or her status as a citizen of the Union'.[88] For British nationals, that occurred on 1 February 2020 and it is 'irrelevant' that they might previously have exercised free movement.[89] Member State nationality is therefore the only route to Union citizenship for now and, in consequence, all Member State nationals *are* Union citizens, whether they like it or not.[90] Conversely, only the loss of Member State nationality for an individual—voluntarily (ie choosing to give up Member State nationality[91]) or involuntarily (ie having Member State nationality withdrawn[92])—or a defined group of individuals following their Member State's withdrawal from the Union under the Article 50 TEU procedure can bring about the loss of Union citizenship. Member State nationality and Union citizenship are otherwise symbiotically tied, a constitutive bond examined in more detail in Chapter 5.

Second, Article 20(1) TFEU characterises Union citizenship as an 'additional' citizenship, stating further that it does not 'replace' national citizenship. This qualifier was introduced by the Amsterdam Treaty,[93] and originally provided that Union citizenship 'shall complement

---

[85] eg C Closa, 'Citizenship of the Union and nationality of the Member States' (1995) 32 Common Market Law Review 487; and D O'Keeffe, 'Union citizenship' in D O'Keeffe and P Twomey (eds), *Legal Issues of the Maastricht Treaty* (Wiley 1994) 87.

[86] eg Coutts, 'Citizens of elsewhere, everywhere and... nowhere?' (n 18); D Kostakopoulou, '*Scala civium*: citizenship templates post-Brexit and the European Union's duty to protect EU citizens' (2018) 56 Journal of Common Market Studies 854; O'Brien, 'Between the devil and the deep blue sea' (n 18); Roeben, Minnerop, Snell, and Telles, 'Revisiting Union citizenship from a fundamental rights perspective in the time of Brexit' (n 18); Spaventa, 'Mice or horses?' (n 18); and AP van der Mei, 'Member State nationality, EU citizenship and associate EU citizenship' in N Cambien, D Kochenov, and E Muir (eds), *European Citizenship under Stress: Social Justice, Brexit and Other Challenges* (Brill 2020) 441.

[87] Case C-673/20 *Préfet du Gers*, EU:C:2022:449, para 48 (emphasis added).

[88] ibid para 57 (emphasis added).

[89] ibid para 58. AG Collins agreed that '[t]he exercise of rights conferred by Union law does not furnish any legal basis upon which an individual's *status* as a Union citizen falls to be determined' (AG Collins in Case C-673/20 *Préfet du Gers*, EU:C:2022:129, para 61 of the Opinion, emphasis added).

[90] The automaticity of acquiring Union citizenship as a result of acquiring Member State nationality raises particular challenges around the commodification of nationality: see Report from the Commission to the European Parliament, the Council, the European Economic and Social Committee and the Committee of the Regions on Investor Citizenship and Residence Schemes in the European Union, COM(2019) 12 final, identifying risks 'in terms of security, money laundering, corruption, circumvention of EU rules and tax evasion' as well as 'shortcomings in the transparency and governance of such schemes' (24). See also, the accompanying Staff Working Document (SWD(2019) 5 final). See generally, S Carrera, 'The price of EU citizenship: the Maltese citizenship-for-sale affair and the principle of sincere cooperation in nationality matters' (2014) 21 Maastricht Journal of European and Comparative Law 406; O Parker, 'Commercializing citizenship in crisis EU: the case of immigrant investor programmes' (2016) 55 Journal of Common Market Studies 234; and J Shaw, 'Citizenship for sale: could and should the EU intervene?' in R Bauböck (ed), *Debating Transformations of National Citizenship* (Springer 2018) 61. See further, Chapter 5.

[91] eg Case C-118/20 *Wiener Landesregierung (Révocation d'une assurance de naturalisation)*, EU:C:2022:34; see further, Chapter 5.

[92] eg Case C-135/08 *Rottmann*, EU:C:2010:104 and Case C-221/17 *Tjebbes*, EU:C:2019:189. See further, Chapter 5.

[93] The Amsterdam Treaty also introduced a framework for enhanced cooperation, with Article 5a EC providing that closer cooperation may be authorised provided that it 'does not concern citizenship of the Union or

and not replace national citizenship'. The current wording was settled by the Lisbon Treaty. The language of 'additional' citizenship can certainly be read as a limiting expression. But it can also be understood in an empowering way since, as noted in Section 2, Union citizenship has particular practical importance because it expands the available legal protection in situations where one State acting alone could not achieve the same result. In that light, Union citizenship contributes—'adds'—a layer of *supranational* protection beyond *national* regulatory reach for specific needs that manifest (primarily but, as will be seen below, not exclusively) because of *transnational* life. As many of the chapters in this book show, the complex interplay of these national, supranational, and transnational dimensions of Union citizenship is one of its defining features—sustaining, in turn, one of the defining challenges of EU citizenship law.[94]

Third, Article 20 TFEU protects Member State nationals within their home States when measures taken by the latter 'have the effect of depriving [them] of the genuine enjoyment of the substance of the rights conferred by virtue of their status as citizens of the Union'.[95] Two sets of circumstances have fallen within the scope of Article 20 TFEU on that basis thus far: first, national measures concerning the acquisition or loss of Member State nationality that provoke the loss of Union citizenship in consequence,[96] and second, residence rights in the home State for third-country national family members on whom a Union citizen is dependent.[97] This case law is addressed in Chapter 5, but a preliminary question can be considered here: which aspect of Article 20 TFEU, more precisely, actually generates these rights?

The case law is ambiguous on this point since it calls for three potentially contradictory assertions to be reconciled: first, the statement in some judgments that Article 20 TFEU cannot be applied independently; second, the 'intrinsic connection'[98] between rights protected under Article 20 TFEU and the right to move and reside freely within the territory of the Member States, which is normally addressed under Article 21(1) TFEU; third, the careful separation of rights falling under Articles 20 and 21 TFEU respectively that is usually emphasised in the case law. On the first point, consider this statement in *My*:

> Article [20 TFEU], whilst establishing citizenship of the Union, merely provides that citizens of the Union enjoy the rights conferred by the Treaty and are subject to the duties imposed thereby. *It cannot therefore be applied independently of the specific provisions of the Treaty which govern the rights and duties of the citizens of the Union.* Article [21 TFEU],

discriminate between nationals of Member States'. Article 326 TFEU now absorbs that requirement as part of more general commitments to compliance with the Treaties ('[a]ny enhanced cooperation shall comply with the Treaties and Union law. Such cooperation shall not undermine the internal market or economic, social and territorial cohesion. It shall not constitute a barrier to or discrimination in trade between Member States, nor shall it distort competition between them').

[94] See further, S Coutts, 'The shifting geometry of Union citizenship: a supranational status from transnational rights' (2019) 21 Cambridge Yearbook of European Legal Studies 318; S Iglesias Sanchez, 'A citizenship right to stay? The right not to move in a Union based on free movement' in D Kochenov (ed), *EU Citizenship and Federalism: The Role of Rights* (CUP 2017) 371; and F Strumia, 'Supranational citizenship enablers: free movement from the perspective of home Member States' (2020) 45 European Law Review 507.
[95] Case C-34/09 *Ruiz Zambrano*, EU:C:2011:124, para 42.
[96] eg Case C-135/08 *Rottmann*, EU:C:2010:104.
[97] eg Case C-82/16 *KA and Others*, EU:C:2018:308. Exploring the further potential of Article 20 TFEU beyond the situations recognised to date, see K Kalaitzaki, 'The application of EU fundamental rights during the financial crisis: EU citizenship to the rescue?' (2021) 27 European Public Law 331; for a contrasting perspective, see M van den Brink, 'Is it time to abolish the substance of EU citizenship rights test?' (2021) 23 European Journal of Migration and Law 13.
[98] Case C-40/11 *Iida*, EU:C:2012:691, para 72.

which sets out generally the right of every citizen of the Union to move and reside freely within the territory of the Member States, finds specific expression in Article [45 TFEU] in relation to the freedom of movement for workers.[99]

At first glance, that would appear to rule out any possibility that Article 20 TFEU could have autonomous legal effect, signalling it more as the type of 'umbrella' provision noted above: summarising the rights that follow but not constituting any rights on its own terms. However, a closer look at the text, and at the differently expressed version of the same idea in *U*,[100] suggests instead that the reasoning in *My* concerns the 'specific expression' concept discussed in Chapter 1, determining *which* provision of the Treaty should be applied to the relevant facts. In other words, in both *My* and *U*, the Court was not ruling out any independent effect for Article 20 TFEU, merely ruling out the application of Article 20 TFEU in the circumstances of the cases at hand. The case law built subsequently upon *Rottmann* and *Ruiz Zambrano* would not make any sense otherwise.

The second and third points are more difficult to unpick. On the one hand, the Court has emphasised not only the exceptional character of rights conferred by Article 20 TFEU,[101] but also their 'intrinsic' connection to freedom of movement and residence.[102] While the right to move and reside is independently protected by, and normally attributed to, Article 21(1) TFEU, it is also one of the rights listed in Article 20(2) TFEU. However, when national measures are assessed against the test of depriving Member State nationals of the genuine enjoyment of the substance of their Union citizenship rights, this always occurs with reference to Article 20 TFEU only.[103] As a result, Article 20 rights are considered when rights based on Article 21 have already been ruled out or, at least, as an *alternative* source of rights that the referring court should consider when it is not clear from the reference whether Article 20 or Article 21 might apply.[104] In the most developed line of the case law in this context—concerning residence permits for third-country national family members upon whom Union citizens are dependent in the latter's home State—the Court refers simply to 'Article 20 TFEU' without being more specific. It could then be argued that the very existence of the status of Union citizenship, enunciated in the opening line of Article 20(1) TFEU, itself generates (independent) rights. In *Ruiz Zambrano*, for example, the Court referred in a general way to the conferring of Union citizenship on all Member State nationals by Article 20 TFEU (para 40) and its understanding of Union citizenship as their 'fundamental status' (para 41), before determining Article 20 TFEU's preclusion of national measures depriving Union citizens of their rights '[i]n those circumstances' (para 42).

On the other hand, Article 20(2) states that Union citizens 'have, *inter alia*' the rights listed there. This phrase was added by the Lisbon Treaty and potentially suggests that unenumerated rights are also protected.[105] Furthermore, the open-ended quality of the current '*inter alia*' phrasing could be contrasted with the original (ie Maastricht, until Lisbon)

---

[99] Case C-293/03 *My*, EU:C:2004:821, paras 32–33. The case was resolved by reading Article 4(3) TEU in conjunction with the Staff Regulations of Officials of the European Communities.
[100] Case C-420/15 *U*, EU:C:2017:408, paras 13–19. The case was resolved on the basis of Article 45 TFEU, with the Court having ruled out the application of Articles 18, 20, 49, and 56 TFEU.
[101] eg Case C-86/12 *Alokpa and Moudoulou*, EU:C:2013:645, para 32.
[102] eg Case C-165/14 *Rendón Marín*, EU:C:2016:675, para 75.
[103] Articles 20 and 21 TFEU as alternative legal bases for Union citizenship rights was first emphasised in Case C-434/09 *McCarthy*, EU:C:2011:277, paras 48–56.
[104] eg *Rendón Marín*, paras 33–37, 49, and 68.
[105] In *Dereci*, AG Mengozzi remarked that 'the list of rights enjoyed by Union citizens' in Article 20(2) TFEU is 'clearly not exhaustive' (Case C-256/11 *Dereci*, EU:C:2011:626, para 38 of the View).

wording of Article 8(2) EC, which stopped at the statement that '[c]itizens of the Union of the Union shall enjoy the rights conferred by this Treaty and shall be subject to the duties imposed thereby'.

In *Rendón Marín*, the Court partly adopted the first perspective—in suggesting that Article 20 TFEU rights stem from the *conferral* of citizenship on Member State nationals and the fundamental nature of that *status*—but also considered that they stem from the character of *the right to move and reside* as a 'primary and individual right'.[106] On the latter point, and following a brief overview of case law in which Article 20 rights were found to apply, the Court stated:

> [T]he above situations have the common feature that, although they are governed by legislation which falls, *a priori*, within the competence of the Member States, namely legislation on the right of entry and residence of third-country nationals outside the scope of provisions of secondary legislation which provide for the grant of such a right under certain conditions, they nonetheless have an intrinsic connection with the freedom of movement and residence of a Union citizen, which prevents the right of entry and residence being refused to those nationals in the Member State of residence of that citizen, in order not to interfere with that freedom.[107]

Article 20 TFEU is thus applied independently of Article 21 TFEU[108] yet also 'intrinsically' connected to it, which suggests that Article 21 is applied in situations where the right to move and reside has been exercised while Article 20 protects the more abstract possibility of exercising it in principle. That construction crosses into questions about actual or potential exercise of rights, on the one hand, and hypothetical exercise of rights, on the other,[109] and it could therefore be suggested that Article 20 rights entail an exception to the idea that the hypothetical exercise of rights is not protected by EU law. This point is returned to in Section 5.1.

Finally, Article 20(1) TFEU refers not only to rights that Union citizens enjoy but also to the fact that Union citizens are 'subject to the duties provided for in the Treaties'. It has never been clear what these duties actually are, where they are 'provided for', or how being subject to them differs from fulfilling conditions attached to the exercise of Union citizenship rights by either the Treaties or secondary legislation. Additionally, while Article 25 TFEU confers competence on the EU legislator in the field of citizenship, it is only to 'strengthen or to add to *the rights* listed in Article 20(2)'. Thus, while there is some consensus that they are an important dimension of citizenship generally,[110] duties remain an under-specified feature of Union citizenship specifically. In this book, aspects of EU citizenship law that might edge towards a conception of *duty*—such as the requirement to comply with the conditions for

---

[106] *Rendón Marín*, paras 69–70.
[107] ibid para 75.
[108] In *Tjebbes*, AG Mengozzi observed that Article 20(1) TFEU has been applied where 'the only connection with EU law was citizenship of the Union' (Case C-221/17 *Tjebbes and Others*, EU:C:2018:572, para 32 of the Opinion).
[109] eg AG Sharpston in Case C-212/06 *Government of the French Community and Walloon Government*, EU:C:2007:398, para 65 of the Opinion: 'for a measure to constitute an obstacle, it is sufficient that it should be reasonably likely to have that effect on migrant workers'. See generally, N Nic Shuibhne, *The Coherence of EU Free Movement Law: Constitutional Responsibility and the Court of Justice* (OUP 2013) Chapter 5.
[110] eg R Davis, 'Citizenship of the Union... rights for all?' (2002) 27 European Law Review 121; D Kochenov, 'EU citizenship without duties' (2014) 20 European Law Journal 482 (cf R Bellamy, 'A duty free Europe? What's wrong with Kochenov's account of EU citizenship rights' (2015) 21 European Law Journal 558); and D Kostakopoulou, *EU Citizenship Law and Policy: Beyond Brexit* (Edward Elgar 2020) Chapter 3.

lawful residence in a host State set out in Directive 2004/38 (Chapters 6 and 7); or not to become a risk to public policy or public security while residing there (Chapter 10)—are framed instead around the idea of *responsibility*. In that understanding, responsibility engages the Member States and Union institutions as well as Union citizen themselves.

3.2 Article 21 TFEU

The text of Article 21 TFEU is largely unchanged since the Maastricht Treaty, though the limitation concerning legislative competence in Article 21(3) was not added until the adoption of the Nice Treaty.[111] Additionally, the legislative competence in Article 21(2) was previously subject to a requirement of unanimity in the Council.[112]

Article 21 TFEU

1. Every citizen of the Union shall have the right to move and reside freely within the territory of the Member States, subject to the limitations and conditions laid down in the Treaties and by the measures adopted to give them effect.
2. If action by the Union should prove necessary to attain this objective and the Treaties have not provided the necessary powers, the European Parliament and the Council, acting in accordance with the ordinary legislative procedure, may adopt provisions with a view to facilitating the exercise of the rights referred to in paragraph 1.
3. For the same purposes as those referred to in paragraph 1 and if the Treaties have not provided the necessary powers, the Council, acting in accordance with a special legislative procedure, may adopt measures concerning social security or social protection. The Council shall act unanimously after consulting the European Parliament.

In *Commission v Belgium*, Advocate General Ruiz-Jarabo Colomer suggested that Article 21 TFEU:

[C]reates a privileged legal status with four characteristic features. First, it is a *personal guarantee*, which forms the bedrock of the Union's system of coexistence. Furthermore, as it is structured, it has *direct effect*, and is therefore immediately applicable and can be relied upon by its beneficiaries. Thirdly, it is *not unconditional*, since there is no such thing as an unfettered right. Article [21(1) TFEU] itself contains the qualification that its exercise is subject to the limitations and conditions laid down in the Treaty itself and by the measures adopted to give it effect, a point which the case-law has made repeatedly. Lastly, *as a fundamental right, it merits a broad interpretation*, which entails a highly restrictive interpretation of any conditions to be attached, confining such conditions, in the name of the principle of proportionality, to the aspects strictly indispensable in order to safeguard

---

[111] The Nice Treaty text of Article 18(3) EC provided that '[p]aragraph 2 shall not apply to provisions on passports, identity cards, residence permits or any other such document or to provisions on social security or social protection'. The current wording of Article 21(3) TFEU was enacted by the Lisbon Treaty.

[112] As Article 8a(2) EC; however, following Nice, Article 18(2) EC altered the legislative process to what is now the ordinary legislative procedure (see further, Article 294 TFEU).

any collective values which might limit freedom, whilst not undermining the scope of that freedom.[113]

The third and fourth 'characteristic features' suggested above—that Union citizenship rights are not unconditional, and that they should be interpreted broadly while conditions and limits placed on them should be construed narrowly—are addressed in more detail in Sections 3.3, 3.4, and 4. The first two points will be looked at briefly here.

First, Advocate General Ruiz-Jarabo Colomer perfectly captured the significance of Union citizenship in both individual and systemic terms (already established for free movement rights historically, as shown in Section 2) by depicting it as both a 'personal guarantee' and a status that 'forms the bedrock of the Union's existence'. The nature of Union citizenship rights as personal rights—raising the question of citizenship rights *as* fundamental rights—is considered further in Section 5.3. On the systemic dimension, much is demanded of Union citizenship as a status that both guides and rationalises the very purposes of the Union, its credentials of good governance and legitimacy, and the objectives and actions that it pursues. The Treaties clearly acknowledge that the Union—and more particularly, its policies and substantive achievements—are *for* its citizens. For example, looking inwards, Article 3(2) TEU establishes that the Union 'shall offer its citizens an area of freedom, security, and justice without internal frontiers, in which the free movement of persons is ensured in conjunction with appropriate measures with respect to external border controls, asylum, immigration and the prevention and combating of crime'. Looking outwards, Article 3(5) TEU states that '[i]n its relations with the wider world, the Union shall uphold and promote its values and interests and contribute to the protection of its citizens'. A system of Union governance rooted in subsidiarity in which 'decisions are taken as closely as possible to the citizen' is affirmed.[114] And through Articles 10 and 11 TEU, the Lisbon Treaty better articulated and further progressed the role of the citizen in legitimising the Union through mechanisms that facilitate both representative and participatory democracy, which include the European Citizens' Initiative and are examined in Chapter 5. That discussion essentially assesses Article 10(3) TEU's promise that '[e]very citizen shall *have the right to participate* in the democratic life of the Union', underlining that the Union has advanced significantly as a citizenship-*capable* polity over time.[115] In Section 6 of this chapter, the significance of the values on which the Union is founded are also further considered.

Second, the Court confirmed in *Baumbast* that the rights conferred by Article 21 TFEU are directly effective because it meets the necessary criteria of clarity and precision.[116] Powering the vibrancy of EU citizenship case law, the significance of the fact Union citizens can raise arguments based on Article 21 directly in their national courts and tribunals cannot be overstated. Before the ruling in *Baumbast* in 2002, the Commission had argued in *Wijsenbeek* that the direct effect of Article 21(1) was 'incontestable':

> The right to move and reside freely within the territory of the Member States is recognised directly in that provision, without any reservation and without the slightest scope for the exercise of discretion, to every citizen of the Union. The fact that this right is subject to the

---

[113] AG Ruiz-Jarabo Colomer in Case C-408/03 *Commission v Belgium*, EU:C:2005:638, para 33 of the Opinion (emphasis added).

[114] See the preamble to and Article 1 of the TEU.

[115] See further, N Nic Shuibhne, 'The outer limits of EU citizenship: displacing economic free movement rights?' in C Barnard and O Odudu (eds), *The Outer Limits of European Union Law* (Hart Publishing 2009) 167.

[116] Case C-413/99 *Baumbast and R*, EU:C:2002:493, para 84.

'limitations and conditions laid down in this Treaty and by the measures adopted to give it effect' does not affect this conclusion in any way ... The implementing measures which the Council may take under Article [21(2) TFEU] are to facilitate the exercise of the rights referred to in paragraph (1) and they confirm the direct effect of that latter provision.[117]

Article 21 TFEU 'must be applied to the *present* effects of situations arising *previously*'.[118] Additionally, in *TopFit and Biffi*, case law on the horizontal scope of the Treaty's economic freedoms was transposed to EU citizenship law, with the Court finding that 'the rules of a national sports association ... which govern the access of EU citizens to sports competitions, are subject to the rules of the Treaty, in particular Articles 18 and 21 TFEU'.[119] However, while Article 45 TFEU can apply to one private employer individually,[120] the Commission's understanding that 'Articles 18 and 21 TFEU apply to a national federation ... governed by private law, so that the actions of a private, and in this case monopolistic entity, do not undermine abolition by the State of barriers to free movement'[121] is likely to confine the reach of Article 21 TFEU more narrowly. It would thus align instead with the capture of rules having *collective* impact on establishment and services by Articles 49 and 56 TFEU respectively, rather than with case law on the free movement of workers.

3.3 Restricting the Right to Move and Reside: Derogation and Justification

Legal assessments of restrictions of the right to move and reside conferred by Union citizenship follow the same three-step inquiry applied in free movement law generally. First, is there a restriction of the right? Second, if there is, is the restriction justifiable in principle? Third, even if it is justifiable in principle, is the restriction proportionate? Proportionality is addressed separately in Section 3.4; here, the first two steps are outlined in more detail.

3.3.1 Defining a restriction of rights

Both discriminatory and non-discriminatory restrictions of the right to move and reside fall within the scope of the Treaty. The right to equal treatment on nationality grounds is not mentioned explicitly in Article 20 or 21 TFEU but, as seen in Chapter 1, Article 18 TFEU

---

[117] Case C-378/97 *Wijsenbeek*, EU:C:1999:439, para 35. The Governments of the Netherlands, Finland, and the United Kingdom argued, in contrast, that Article 21 TFEU 'does not create a right to move and reside freely which goes beyond the existing provisions of the Treaty and the measures adopted to give it effect' (para 37). See further, AG Cosmas (EU:C:1999:144), paras 88–96 of the Opinion.

[118] Case C-224/98 *D'Hoop*, EU:C:2002:432, para 25 (emphasis added). An example is provided by the specific context of EU accession: see esp Joined Cases C-424/10 and C-425/10 *Ziolkowski and Szeja*, EU:C:2011:866, para 58; Case C-162/09 *Lassal*, EU:C:2010:592, para 39; and Case C-218/15 *Paoletti*, EU:C:2016:748, para 41. On the extent of the preference that should be extended to the nationals of accession States, as Union citizens, during transition periods, see Case C-15/11 *Sommer*, EU:C:2012:731.

[119] Case C-22/18 *TopFit and Biffi*, EU:C:2019:497, para 40. See generally, paras 28–41, citing, inter alia, Case 36/74 *Walrave and Koch*, EU:C:1974:140; Case C-415/93 *Bosman*, EU:C:1995:463; and Case C-411/98 *Ferlini*, EU:C:2000:530. See, in contrast, AG Tanchev (EU:C:2019:181): having found that the situation fell within the scope of Article 49 TFEU, he argued that 'the main proceedings do not present an occasion on which to consider taking the *significant constitutional step* of expanding its case-law on Article 21 TFEU and the component elements of European citizenship to the horizontal context of a dispute between private parties, which would thereby oblige non-State actors to comply with them' (para 56 of the Opinion, emphasis added); see further, paras 99–110 of the Opinion.

[120] Case C-281/98 *Angonese*, EU:C:2000:296; Case C-379/09 *Casteels*, EU:C:2011:131.

[121] AG Tanchev in *TopFit and Biffi*, para 39 of the Opinion; he also points out that 'Article 21 TFEU disputes classically concern relations between the citizen and the State' (para 101 of the Opinion).

applies to any situations falling 'within the scope of application of the Treaties'.[122] Article 21(2) CFR further confirms that '[w]ithin the scope of application of the Treaties and without prejudice to any of their specific provisions, any discrimination on grounds of nationality shall be prohibited'.[123]

In its path-breaking judgment in *Martínez Sala*, the Court of Justice established that the right not to be discriminated against on nationality grounds, in any situations falling within the material scope of the Treaty, 'attaches' to the status of Union citizenship through Article 20 TFEU.[124] The appellant was a Spanish national residing in Germany. Her application for a child-raising allowance in Germany was rejected, in accordance with applicable national rules, because she was neither a German national nor in possession of a residence permit. She had previously exercised economic activity in Germany and determining whether she remained within the scope of Article 45 TFEU for the purposes of entitlement to the benefit as a social and tax advantage was left to the referring court. More generally, though, the Court also found that 'for a Member State to require a national of another Member State who wishes to receive a benefit such as the allowance in question to produce a document which is constitutive of the right to the benefit and which is issued by its own authorities, when its own nationals are not required to produce any document of that kind, amounts to unequal treatment'.[125] Moreover, 'such unequal treatment constitutes discrimination prohibited by Article [18 TFEU]' in situations within 'the sphere of application of the Treaty'.[126]

The Court then took the first step in a legal revolution: should the referring court find that Mrs Martínez Sala was not a worker within the meaning of Article 45 TFEU, she would still fall within the personal scope of the Treaty's provisions on Union citizenship as 'a national of a Member State lawfully residing in the territory of another Member State'.[127] As regards material scope, the Court just observed that 'reference should be made to the replies given to the first, second and third questions, according to which the child-raising allowance in question in the main proceedings indisputably falls within the scope *ratione materiae* of Community law', that is, to the paragraphs of the judgment characterising the child-raising allowance as a social and tax advantage for which workers were eligible on a basis of equal treatment with host State workers.[128] In other words, no direct link between how the appellant fell within

[122] See further Chapter 7, which considers the full text of Article 18 in more detail ('[w]ithin the scope of application of the Treaties, *and without prejudice to any special provisions contained therein*, any discrimination on grounds of nationality shall be prohibited').
[123] Article 21(1) CFR prohibits discrimination 'on any ground such as sex, race, colour, ethnic or social origin, genetic features, language, religion or belief, political or any other opinion, membership of a national minority, property, birth, disability, age or sexual orientation' yet this wider (than nationality) span of discrimination has gained surprisingly little traction in free movement law as yet. Questions referred by the national court in (Case C-206/21 *Préfet de Saône-et-Loire*, later removed from the register) would have offered the opportunity to consider discrimination on the grounds of disability in connection with 'sufficient resources' under Article 7(1) of Directive 2004/38. In *VMA*, 'discrimination on the basis of the sexual orientation of the child's parents' was recognised, but linked to Articles 7 (respect for private and family life) and 24 (best interests of the child) CFR rather than to Article 21(1) CFR. See further, Section 5.3. See generally, Editorial comments 'Charting deeper and wider dimensions of (free) movement in EU law' (2021) 58 Common Market Law Review 969; and from a policy perspective, eg Communication from the Commission, Union of Equality: LGBTIQ Equality Strategy 2020–2025, COM(2020) 698 final, esp Section 3.
[124] Case C-85/96 *Martínez Sala*, EU:C:1998:217, para 62.
[125] ibid para 54.
[126] ibid para 55.
[127] ibid para 61. The basis for Mrs Martínez Sala's lawful residence in Germany and the significance of lawful residence in EU citizenship law more generally are examined in Chapter 7.
[128] On that point, the Court held that 'a benefit such as the child-raising allowance . . which is automatically granted to persons fulfilling certain objective criteria, without any individual and discretionary assessment of personal needs, and which is intended to meet family expenses, falls within the scope *ratione materiae* of Community law as a family benefit within the meaning of Article 4(1)(h) of Regulation No 1408/71 and as a social advantage within the meaning of Article 7(2) of Regulation No 1612/68' (ibid para 28; see generally, paras 22–28).

the personal scope of the Treaty (as a lawfully resident Union citizen) and the nature of the benefit in question (linked to legislation on social and tax advantages for workers) was either established or required.[129]

The Court's emphasis on equal treatment with host State nationals was soon entrenched as a fundamental component of Union citizenship,[130] and it now tends to be expressed in four steps. First, Union citizenship is the 'fundamental status' of the nationals of the Member States; second, that status enables 'such nationals who find themselves in the same situation to enjoy, within the scope *ratione materiae* of the Treaty, the same treatment in law irrespective of their nationality'; third, situations falling within the scope of the Treaty 'include those which involve the exercise of the fundamental freedoms guaranteed by the Treaty, in particular those involving the freedom to move and reside within the territory of the Member States, as conferred by Article 21 TFEU'; and therefore, fourth, 'Article 21 TFEU contains not only the right to move and reside freely in the territory of the Member States but also ... a prohibition of any discrimination on grounds of nationality'.[131] To determine whether unequal treatment is demonstrated, the Court applies its standard discrimination test: citizens in comparable situations must not be treated differently and, conversely, citizens who are not in comparable situations must not be treated in the same way.[132]

Article 21 TFEU precludes restrictions that are directly discriminatory (rules that discriminate both in law and in fact) and rules that are indirectly discriminatory ('a provision of national law must be regarded as indirectly discriminatory if it is intrinsically liable to affect nationals of other Member States more than nationals of the host State and there is a consequent risk that it will place the former at a particular disadvantage'[133]). However, discrimination is not *required* to establish a restriction of Article 21 TFEU and, following free movement law generally, non-discriminatory rules or practices that hinder[134] or obstruct[135] the right to move and reside—or that are liable to do so—will suffice. Arguments based on Article 21 can also be raised by a Union citizen against their home State where free movement rights have been exercised previously,[136] and it is 'irrelevant that considerable time has

---

[129] However, there is now evidence of stronger concern to link the rights conferred by citizenship more directly to the claims asserted in more recent case law: this point it returned to in Section 5.1.

[130] Several Advocates General have underlined the significance of non-discrimination for Union citizenship: see eg AG Poiares Maduro in Case C-524/06 *Huber*, EU:C:2008:194, para 18 of the Opinion, reflecting the centrality of equal treatment to Union citizenship emphasised in earlier case law (eg by AG Léger in Case C-214/94 *Boukhalfa*, EU:C:1996:174, para 63 of the Opinion): '[t]he prohibition of discrimination on the basis of nationality is no longer merely an instrument at the service of freedom of movement; it is at the heart of the concept of European citizenship and of the extent to which the latter imposes on Member States the obligation to treat Union citizens as national citizens. Though the Union does not aim to substitute a "European people" for the national peoples, it does require its Member States no longer to think and act only in terms of the best interests of their nationals but also, in so far as possible, in terms of the interests of all EU citizens'.

[131] Case C-391/09 *Runevič-Vardyn and Wardyn*, EU:C:2011:291, paras 61–62 and 65.

[132] For a rare example of a finding that discriminatory treatment was not at issue by applying that approach, see Case C-403/03 *Schempp*, EU:C:2005:446, para 28. See further, the discussion on Case C-148/02 *Garcia Avello*, EU:C:2003:539 in Section 5.1 and in Chapter 3. As introduced in Chapter 1, the Court considers that the prohibition of discrimination on the grounds of nationality in Article 18 TFEU applies only to situations involving Member State nationals and cannot be invoked to assess differences in treatment between Union citizens and third-country nationals: see eg Case C-673/20 *Préfet du Gers*, EU:C:2022:449; and Case C-490/20 *VMA v Stolichna obshtina, rayon 'Pancharevo'*, EU:C:2021:1008. The Court has also confirmed that Article 21(2) CFR, which 'corresponds to' Article 18 TFEU, 'is not intended to apply to cases of a possible difference in treatment between nationals of Member States and nationals of third countries' (Case C-930/19 *X v Belgian State*, EU:C:2021:657, paras 50–51).

[133] Case C-308/14 *Commission v UK*, EU:C:2016:436, para 77.

[134] eg Case C-208/09 *Sayn-Wittgenstein*, EU:C:2010:806, para 70.

[135] eg Case C-127/08 *Metock and Others*, EU:C:2008:449, paras 56 and 62.

[136] eg Case C-224/02 *Pusa*, EU:C:2004:273, para 20. See further, Chapter 9.

elapsed' since then.[137] The right to move and reside conferred by Article 21 TFEU thus extends widely in its protective reach.

3.3.2 Defending a restriction of rights: derogation and justification

In free movement law generally, directly discriminatory breaches of Treaty rights should be derogated from only on grounds explicitly provided for in the Treaty. For work, establishment, and services, that means reasons based on public policy, public security, or public health.[138] However, according to the case law, restrictions that are either indirectly discriminatory or non-discriminatory may, additionally, be justified on the more general, open-ended basis of 'overriding reasons relating to the public interest'.[139] The opportunity to submit derogation and justification arguments means that courts engage in a balancing exercise, assessing whether the restriction placed on freedom of movement should be accepted, in principle, for good public interest reasons. In some instances, the argument put forward by a Member State to defend a restriction of free movement rights will overlap with objectives protected by the EU Treaties, but national and Union interests can also be in tension. For example, in *Coman*, the Court had to consider whether the term 'spouse' in Directive 2004/38 obliged a Member State to recognise a same-sex marriage lawfully concluded in another Member State. The substance of this case is discussed in Chapter 4. For present purposes, the Court acknowledged that Article 4(2) TEU does require the Union to respect the national identities of the Member States. But it also considered that 'the right to respect for private and family life guaranteed by the Charter is a fundamental right' and that a 'national measure that is liable to obstruct the exercise of freedom of movement for persons may be justified only where such a measure is consistent with the fundamental rights guaranteed by the Charter'.[140]

The approach applied to derogation and justification in free movement law generally also applies in EU citizenship law: a derogation can be based on protection of public policy, public security, or public health, while indirectly discriminatory and non-discriminatory restrictions may be defended by 'an overriding reason in the public interest'.[141] Derogations based on public policy, public security, or public health first entered EU citizenship law in the same way as the requirement to be economically autonomous if not economically active in a host State, that is, through the 1990s Residence Directives. Articles 2(2) of Directive 90/364, Directive 90/365, and Directive 93/96 identically established that 'Member States shall not derogate from the provisions of this Directive save on grounds of public policy, public security or public health. In that event, Directive 64/221/EEC shall apply'. The Court later stated in *Orfanopoulos and Oliveri* that Union citizenship requires 'a *particularly restrictive* interpretation of the derogations' from the right to move and reside.[142] Measures based on public policy, public security, or public health must now comply with relevant provisions of Directive 2004/38, examined in detail in Chapter 10. With respect to justification more broadly, the Court often refers to public interest grounds as 'objective considerations

---

[137] Case C-359/13 *Martens*, EU:C::2015:118, para 32. The Court cited AG Sharpston in support of this point but did not repeat a proviso in her analysis: 'in circumstances where there has been a *continuing* exercise of the right to reside in another Member State' (EU:C:2004:2240, para 106 of the Opinion, emphasis added; see also, para 107).
[138] Articles 45(3), 52, and 62 TFEU.
[139] Case C-420/15 *U*, EU:C:2017:408, para 29.
[140] Case C-673/16 *Coman*, EU:C:2018:385, paras 43–48.
[141] Case C-220/12 *Thiele Meneses*, EU:C:2013:683, para 49.
[142] Joined Cases C-482/01 and C-493/01 *Orfanopoulos and Oliveri*, EU:C:2004:262, para 65 (emphasis added); see also para 64.

independent of the nationality of the persons concerned'.[143] For the horizontal application of Article 21 TFEU, extended to date in a case concerning a sporting association only, the Court adjusted its language to find that 'a restriction on the freedom of movement of EU citizens can be justified only where it is based on objective considerations and is proportionate to the legitimate objective pursued by the rules at issue'.[144]

Not all restrictions based on public policy, public security, or public health will be discriminatory but, in principle, discriminatory restrictions should *only* be accepted for these reasons.[145] However, there is some ambiguity on this point,[146] and so we must ask: can directly discriminatory restrictions on the right to move and reside conferred by Article 21 TFEU be defended only on grounds of public policy, public security, or public health, or can a general defence of overriding reasons in the public interest be more widely invoked? Recital 22 of Directive 2004/38 states that '[t]he Treaty allows restrictions to be placed on the right of free movement and residence on grounds of public policy, public security or public health'. Article 1(c) establishes that the Directive lays down 'the limits placed on the rights [of free movement and residence, and of permanent residence] on grounds of public policy, public security or public health'. Article 27(1) then states that 'Member States may restrict the freedom of movement and residence of Union citizens and their family members, irrespective of nationality, on grounds of public policy, public security or public health' with the qualifier that '[t]hese grounds shall not be invoked to serve economic ends'.

Article 27(1) opens Chapter IV of the Directive, which details the framework within which all decisions based on public policy, public security, or public health must be taken. The fact that decisions to expel a Union citizen from a host State necessarily concern only the nationals of other States would suggest, on one view, that only the express derogation grounds can apply in situations of direct discrimination. Further supporting that view, it seemed previously that the Court either did not examine the nature of the contested restriction very deeply,[147] or opted in any event for one of those three grounds when the nature of the discrimination at issue was not entirely clear-cut.[148] However, in case law on the extradition of Union citizens to a third state, which raises questions about differential treatment between a Member State's own nationals and other Union citizens and is discussed further in Section 6, the Court stated very generally that 'measures which restrict a fundamental freedom, such as that laid down in Article 21 TFEU, may be justified by objective considerations'.[149] The Court

---

[143] Case C-224/98 *D'Hoop*, EU:C:2002:432, para 36.

[144] Case C-22/18 *TopFit and Biffi*, EU:C:2019:497, para 48. See further, para 52: 'the freedom of private associations to adopt sporting rules cannot authorise them to limit the exercise of rights conferred on individuals by the Treaty'.

[145] As the Commission has argued, by analogy with the free movement of workers: 'it follows from the case-law of the Court, in particular from Case 15/69 *Ugliola* [EU:C:1969:46] and Case C-484/93 *Svensson and Gustavsson* [EU:C:1995:379], that a discriminatory measure may be justified only on the exceptional grounds expressly provided for in the Treaty, namely public policy, public security and public health' (Case C-147/03 *Commission v Austria*, EU:C:2005:427, para 51). In its ruling, the Court characterised the contested restriction as indirectly discriminatory and therefore considered a wider range of public interest arguments.

[146] Mirroring ambiguity in free movement law more generally on this question too, especially for justification arguments based on environmental protection; see further, N Nic Shuibhne, 'Exceptions to the free movement rules' in C Barnard and S Peers (eds), *EU Law* (4th edn OUP 2023), forthcoming, Section 3.2.

[147] eg Case C-308/14 *Commission v UK*, EU:C:2016:436, esp paras 33–35 (discussed in Chapters 6 and 7). See further, C O'Brien, 'The ECJ sacrifices EU citizenship in vain: *Commission v UK*' (2017) 54 Common Market Law Review 209 at 224–27.

[148] eg Case C-73/08 *Bressol and Others*, EU:C:2010:181, paras 40–54; compare AG Sharpston (EU:C:2009:396, paras 41 ff of the Opinion).

[149] Case C-182/15 *Petruhhin*, EU:C:2016:630, para 38; confirmed in eg Case C-191/16 *Pisciotti*, EU:C:2018:222, para 46. See further, Section 6.

referred to its judgment in *Runevič-Vardyn and Wardyn* on this point,[150] but in that case—as well as in the case law referred to there[151]—the factual circumstances did not involve discrimination on the grounds of nationality. Whether the case law's recent turn has wider implications for defending discriminatory restrictions or is confined to the particular context of extradition remains to be seen.

Finally, the capacity of the EU legislator to restrict Treaty freedoms is similarly constrained in free movement law generally. For example, while Article 45 TFEU 'does not prohibit the [Union] legislature from attaching conditions to the rights and advantages which it accords in order to ensure freedom of movement for workers or from determining the limits thereto',[152] and while it has 'wide discretion' in that respect,[153] these powers must be exercised 'in conformity with the provisions of the Treaty'.[154] However, the Treaty provisions on citizenship differ from the economic freedoms in one vital respect: Articles 20 and 21 TFEU expressly empower the EU legislator to place limitations and conditions on the exercise of the rights conferred. After listing these rights, Article 20(2) TFEU establishes that they 'shall be exercised in accordance with the conditions and limits defined by the Treaties *and by the measures adopted thereunder*'. For the right to move and reside specifically, Article 21(1) TFEU reinforces the role of the legislator by making the right 'subject to the limitations and conditions laid down in the Treaties *and by the measures adopted to give them effect*'. While Directive 2004/38 is key in this respect, any EU legislation that intersects with free movement can constitute a measure adopted pursuant to the Treaties that defines the conditions and limits under which the right to move and reside is exercised.[155] The implications of the legislative power built into Articles 20 and 21 TFEU are returned to in Section 4.2.

3.4 Restricting the Right to Move and Reside: Proportionality

Even if a restriction of free movement rights is justifiable in principle, it must also be 'proportionate to the legitimate objective pursued'.[156] More specifically, the contested measure must, first, be 'appropriate to ensure the achievement of the objective it pursues'; and second, 'not go beyond what is necessary to attain it'.[157] These criteria are consistently reaffirmed across different strands of EU citizenship law. It could even be said that most disputes are resolved, in reality, at this final stage of the Court's analysis of restrictions on citizenship rights (although, in principle, the determination of proportionality is left to the referring court or tribunal in preliminary reference proceedings under Article 267 TFEU[158]).

---

[150] Case C-391/09 *Runevič-Vardyn and Wardyn*, EU:C:2011:291, para 83.
[151] ie Case C-353/06 *Grunkin and Paul*, EU:C:2008:559, para 29; and Case C-208/09 *Sayn-Wittgenstein*, EU:C:2010:806, para 81.
[152] Case C-62/91 *Gray*, EU:C:1992:177, para 11.
[153] Case C-208/07 *Von Chamier-Glisczinski*, EU:C:2009:455, para 40.
[154] Case 24/75 *Petroni*, EU:C:1971:129, para 20.
[155] eg Case C-543/12 *Zeman*, EU:C:2014:2143, characterising Directive 91/47 as such a measure (with reference to Article 20(2) TFEU) to the extent that it 'concerns the free movement of the holders of firearms, in particular hunters and sport shooters' (para 39). Council Directive 91/477/EEC on control of the acquisition and possession of weapons, 1991 OJ L256/51 (amended by Directive 2008/51/EC, 2008 OJ L 179/5).
[156] *Pisciotti*, para 46.
[157] Case C-430/10 *Gaydarov*, EU:C:2011:749, para 40.
[158] For guidance on the questions that a referring court or tribunal should examine, see eg Case C-434/10 *Aladzhov*, EU:C:2011:750, para 47; and Case C-438/14 *Bogendorff von Wolffersdorff*, EU:C:2016:401, paras 72-83 (where, at para 80, the Court referred to the required 'weighing up [of] the right to freedom of movement conferred on citizens of the Union under Article 21 TFEU and the legitimate interests pursued by the restrictions placed by the [national] legislature').

Importantly, there are two different ways in which proportionality analysis might be undertaken: first, assessing the appropriateness and necessity of a contested restriction in a general sense (for example, considering national legislation's compliance with EU law more abstractly); or second, assessing the appropriateness and necessity of its application in the circumstances of an individual Union citizen's situation more concretely.[159] Related questions can be explored further by considering proportionality vis-à-vis conditions that are 'too general and exclusive' (Section 3.4.1), the protection of national public finances (Section 3.4.2), and the significance of evidence and proof (Section 3.4.3).

3.4.1 Conditions 'too general and exclusive'

In *D'Hoop*, a Belgian national who had completed her secondary education in France challenged Belgian rules that made the grant of a 'tideover' allowance—which 'aims to facilitate for young people the transition from education to the employment market'[160]—conditional on having completed secondary education in Belgium. The Court developed a 'real link' test to measure the degree to which the applicant was connected to the Belgian employment market, as explained further in Section 5.4. But for present purposes, the Court rejected the application of 'a single condition concerning the place where the diploma of completion of secondary education was obtained' because it was 'too general and exclusive in nature': '[i]t unduly favours an element which is not necessarily representative of the real and effective degree of connection between the applicant for the tideover allowance and the geographic employment market, to the exclusion of all other representative elements. It therefore goes beyond what is necessary to attain the objective pursued'.[161]

The wider principle drawn from *D'Hoop* is that a condition restricting citizenship rights 'may not be so general in scope that it systematically excludes ... regardless of [the] actual degree of integration into society'.[162] Most cases triggering this dimension of proportionality review concern conditions governing the payment of benefits to Union citizens, whether by a home or host State. The Court has acknowledged that, '[i]n relation to the extent to which the recipient of a benefit is connected with the society of the Member State concerned [and] with regard to benefits that are not governed by EU law ... Member States enjoy a broad discretion in deciding which criteria are to be used when assessing the extent of that connection'.[163] However, the fact that the applicable rules 'do not, in themselves, appear to be unreasonable' will not save them if the relevant condition 'unduly favours an element which is not necessarily representative of the real and effective degree of connection between the claimant and [the] Member State, to the exclusion of all other representative elements'.[164] Conversely, conditions imposed by national rules will be 'all the more valid' where they are 'interpreted widely, so that other connecting factors allow a sufficiently close connection to [Member State] society to be established'.[165]

---

[159] Similarly, while judicial review of secondary legislation against directly effective Treaty provisions, fundamental rights and/or general principles is a standard feature of EU law, whether proportionality analysis, as part of that review, focuses on the application of the rule in general or on its application in an individual case can have significant bearing on the outcome: eg compare the judgment of the Court in Case C-123/08 *Wolzenburg*, EU:C:2009:616 with the Opinion of AG Bot (EU:C:2009:183), esp paras 67–74 of the judgment and paras 63–68 of the Opinion. These points are picked up in Section 5.2 and in Chapter 8 on the right of permanent residence.
[160] Case C-224/98 *D'Hoop*, EU:C:2002:432, para 38.
[161] ibid para 39. Applied in the context of education grants in eg Joined Cases C-11/06 and C-12/06 *Morgan and Bucher*, EU:C:2007:626, para 46.
[162] AG Mazák in Case C-158/07 *Förster*, EU:C:2008:399, para 129 of the Opinion.
[163] Case C-220/12 *Thiele Meneses*, EU:C:2013:683, para 37.
[164] Case C-503/09 *Stewart*, EU:C:2011:500, para 95.
[165] Case C-103/08 *Gottwald*, EU:C:2009:597, para 38.

Factors that national authorities should consider—characterised in Section 5.4 as factors that demonstrate the *degree of integration* of the Union citizen in the relevant State—include duration of residence, family circumstances such as marriage to a national of the State or dependency on family members working there, actively seeking work in the State, or the nationality of the applicant for claims made in their home Member States in situations having cross-border dimensions.[166] The underlying objective is to extend to Union citizens an opportunity to demonstrate links of sufficient connection to a State that are not captured when national rules entail little or no flexibility. Advocate General Sharpston has suggested that even where such flexibility is extended, it 'appears possible to reconcile a careful assessment of individual circumstances with the need to ensure legal certainty, transparency and administrative efficiency'.[167] However, the potential for tension between these interests is returned to in Section 3.4.2.

A concern closely related to conditions that are 'too general and exclusive' attaches to rules that produce 'automatic' consequences.[168] In *Commission v Belgium*, for example, the second plea in the infringement proceedings challenged Belgian legislation under which 'failure by the national of a Member State to produce, within a specified period, the supporting documents necessary for the grant of a residence permit automatically entails the service of an order for deportation'.[169] Three points from the judgment can be highlighted. First, presaging language used later in *Ruiz Zambrano* for rights conferred by Article 20 TFEU, deportation as an automatic—as distinct from a possible—consequence of a Union citizen's failure to produce the documents required 'impairs the very substance of the right of residence directly conferred by [Union] law'.[170] This is because, second, the underpinning legislation 'does not allow account to be taken of the reasons why the person concerned did not take the necessary administrative measures or of whether he was able to establish that he fulfilled the conditions which [Union] law attached to his right of residence'.[171] Third, the Court dismissed as 'of no relevance' the argument that 'there is in practice no immediate enforcement of orders for deportation' and emphasised that 'the fact that the deportation orders are allegedly qualified does not alter the fact that those measures are disproportionate to the seriousness of the infringement and are liable to deter citizens of the Union from exercising their right to freedom of movement'.[172]

The judgment in *Brey* brought these lines of case law together by considering national rules that determine outcomes through conditions that are too general and exclusive, which generate, in turn, automatic consequences:

---

[166] eg Case C-367/11 *Prete*, EU:C:2012:668, paras 40 and 44–51; Case C-359/13 *Martens*, EU:C:2015:118, paras 40–43 (in para 41 of which the Court refers also to 'language skills or the existence of other social and economic factors').

[167] AG Sharpston in Joined Cases C-523/11 and C-585/11 *Prinz and Seeberger*, EU:C:2013:90, para 107 of the Opinion.

[168] eg Addressing the limits of Member State discretion regarding the expulsion of Union citizens, see eg Case C-165/14 *Rendón Marín*, EU:C:2016:675, paras 59–64; and Case C-304/14 *CS*, EU:C:2016:674, paras 43–49. Expulsion is considered in Chapter 10; judgments such as that in Joined Cases C-316/16 and C-424/16 *B and Vomero*, EU:C:2018:256, illustrate the 'overall assessment' that national authorities are generally required to make in individual cases.

[169] Case C-408/03 *Commission v Belgium*, EU:C:2006:192, para 67.

[170] ibid para 68.

[171] ibid para 69.

[172] ibid para 70; the arguments submitted by Belgium in this context are outlined in para 59. See similarly, AG Sharpston in Joined Cases C-523/11 and C-585/11 *Prinz and Seeberger*, EU:C:2013:90, para 112 of the Opinion: 'the fact that ministerial discretion can be exercised so as not to apply an unjustified restriction of EU citizenship rights in certain circumstances does not alter the analysis. What is precluded by EU law is precluded'.

[A] mechanism, whereby nationals of other Member States who are not economically active are *automatically barred* by the host Member State from receiving a particular social security benefit ... does not enable the competent authorities of the host Member State, where the resources of the person concerned fall short of the reference amount for the grant of that benefit, to carry out – in accordance with the requirements under, inter alia, Articles 7(1)(b) and 8(4) of that directive *and the principle of proportionality* – an overall assessment of the specific burden which granting that benefit would place on the social assistance system as a whole *by reference to the personal circumstances characterising the individual situation* of the person concerned.[173]

However, when a Member State seeks to defend restrictions in national rules on the basis of protecting its public finances, the function of proportionality can alter.

3.4.2 Proportionality and the protection of national public finances

In free movement law generally, 'aims of a purely economic nature cannot constitute an overriding reason in the general interest justifying a restriction of a fundamental freedom guaranteed by the Treaty'.[174] The logic here is counter-protectionist, since the EU's internal market aims precisely to subdue national barriers. At the same time, however, it is accepted that 'interests *of an economic nature*'[175] can provide a legitimate defence for free movement restrictions. That reasoning was first developed in case law on access to medical services,[176] and later applied to other public spending sectors including education[177] and social security.[178] In many of these cases, the public interest defence is arguably not of a *purely* economic nature. But public money will always be spent on something,[179] and it can therefore be difficult to draw a precise line between acceptable 'of an economic nature' defence and unacceptable 'purely economic nature' justification.[180]

EU citizenship law both maps and departs from the approach taken for the economic freedoms. As noted in Section 3.3.2, Article 27(1) of Directive 2004/38 establishes that public policy, public security, or public health 'shall not be invoked to serve economic ends',

---

[173] Case C-140/12 *Brey*, EU:C:2013:237, para 77 (emphasis added). See also, recital 16 of Directive 2004/38: 'As long as the beneficiaries of the right of residence do not become an unreasonable burden on the social assistance system of the host Member State they should not be expelled. Therefore, an expulsion measure should not be the automatic consequence of recourse to the social assistance system. The host Member State should examine whether it is a case of temporary difficulties and take into account the duration of residence, the personal circumstances and the amount of aid granted in order to consider whether the beneficiary has become an unreasonable burden on its social assistance system and to proceed to his expulsion. In no case should an expulsion measure be adopted against workers, self-employed persons or job-seekers as defined by the Court of Justice save on grounds of public policy or public security'. See further, Chapters 6, 7, and 10.

[174] Case C-35/98 *Verkooijen*, EU:C:2000:294, para 48.

[175] Case C-141/07 *Commission v Germany*, EU:C:2008:492, para 60 (emphasis added).

[176] Case C-158/96 *Kohll*, EU:C:1998:171, para 50; Case C-368/98 *Vanbraekel*, EU:C:2001:400, para 47; Case C-372/04 *Watts*, EU:C:2006:325, paras 103–104; and Case C-173/09 *Elchinov*, EU:C:2010:581, para 42. Confirmed more recently in eg Case C-243/19 *A v Veselības ministrija*, EU:C:2020:872, para 47.

[177] eg Joined Cases C-11/06 and 12/06 *Morgan and Bucher*, EU:C:2007:626, para 36.

[178] eg Joined Cases C-396/05, C-419/05 and C-450/05 *Habelt, Möser and Wachter*, EU:C:2007:810, para 83.

[179] In *Bressol*, AG Sharpston referred to the 'inescapable fact that every public service provided by our welfare states is dependent on there being sufficient budgetary means to finance it' (Case C-73/08, EU:C:2009:396, para 91 of the Opinion).

[180] eg Case C-20/12 *Giersch*, EU:C:2013:411, paras 47–56. See further, S Arrowsmith, 'Rethinking the approach to economic justifications under the EU's free movement rules' (2015) 68 Current Legal Problems 307; J Snell, 'Economic justifications and the role of the state' in P Koutrakos, N Nic Shuibhne, and P Syrpis (eds), *Exceptions from EU Free Movement Law: Derogation, Justification and Proportionality* (Hart Publishing 2016) 12; and P Oliver, 'When, if ever, can restrictions on free movement be justified on economic grounds?' (2016) 41 European Law Review 147.

reflecting the case law on aims of a purely economic nature vis-à-vis the economic freedoms. For example, the Court ruled in *Thiele Meneses* that 'while budgetary considerations may underlie a Member State's choice of social policy and influence the nature or scope of the social protection measures which it wishes to adopt, they do not in themselves constitute an aim pursued by that policy' since '[r]easons of a purely economic nature cannot constitute overriding reasons in the public interest justifying a restriction of a fundamental freedom guaranteed by the Treaty'.[181] However, and continuing to map the economic freedom case law, that does not rule out a defence of restrictions on citizenship rights on the basis of interests of an economic nature. Thus in *Stewart*, the Court confirmed that 'it is legitimate for the national legislature ... to guarantee the financial balance of a national social security system'.[182] Similarly, it considered in *Aladzhov* that 'since the purpose of recovery of debts owed to a public authority, in particular the recovery of taxes, is to ensure the funding of actions of the Member State concerned on the basis of the choices which are the expression of, *inter alia*, its general policy in economic and social matters', this meant that 'the measures adopted by the public authorities in order to ensure that recovery also cannot be considered, as a matter of principle, to have been adopted exclusively to serve economic ends, within the meaning of Article 27(1) of Directive 2004/38'.[183]

However, Article 15(1) of the Directive states that the procedural safeguards in Articles 30 and 31[184] 'shall apply by analogy to all decisions restricting free movement of Union citizens and their family members on grounds *other than* public policy, public security or public health'. That statement signals that restrictions may therefore concern grounds 'other than' those provided for in Article 27. For present purposes, the key provision is Article 14. It establishes the conditions under which Union citizens and their family members retain a right of residence in the host State,[185] linking to the conditions in Article 7 in particular, that is, being a worker or self-employed (Article 7(1)(a)); or otherwise, reflecting the conditions first introduced in the 1990s Residence Directives, having comprehensive sickness insurance and sufficient financial resources not to become a burden on the social assistance of the host State (Article 7(1)(b)). Article 14(3) then states that '[an] expulsion measure shall not be the *automatic* consequence of a Union citizen's or his or her family member's recourse to the social assistance system of the host Member State'—confirming inversely that expulsion on such grounds *may* be legitimate so long as relevant decisions of national authorities comply with the framework outlined in Articles 14, 15, 30, and 31 of the Directive.[186] In that light, the Court therefore openly accepts that 'the exercise of the right of residence for citizens of the Union can be subordinated to the legitimate interests of the Member States' and that such interests include 'the protection of their public finances'.[187]

In early citizenship case law, concern for protecting national public finances was acknowledged but balanced against the broader requirements of Union citizenship. Thus in

---

[181] Case C-220/12 *Thiele Meneses*, EU:C:2013:683, para 43. In the context of national conditions for the award of an education grant, Germany had argued that 'preventing an unreasonable burden and maintaining the national framework of exportable education and training grants are objectives of public interest, capable of justifying a restriction of the fundamental freedoms conferred by Articles 20 TFEU and 21 TFEU' (para 42).
[182] Case C-503/09 *Stewart*, EU:C:2011:500, para 89.
[183] Case C-434/10 *Aladzhov*, EU:C:2011:750, para 38. See further, AG Mengozzi (EU:C:2011:547), paras 33–38 of the Opinion and especially the statement in para 34 that 'the idea that the function of tax is to procure resources for the State with a view to redistribution in order to ensure a minimum degree of social cohesion seems to me very far from purely economic reasoning'.
[184] See further, Chapter 10.
[185] See further, Chapter 6.
[186] eg Case C-184/99 *Grzelczyk*, EU:C:2001:458, para 42; Case C-456/02 *Trojani*, EU:C:2004:488, para 45.
[187] Case C-140/12 *Brey*, EU:C:2013:565, para 55.

Grzelczyk, drawing from language in the preambles to the 1990s Directives, the Court determined that 'beneficiaries of the right of residence must not become an *unreasonable* burden on the public finances of the host Member State', which meant that 'Directive 93/96 ... accepts *a certain degree of financial solidarity* between nationals of a host Member State and nationals of other Member States, particularly if the difficulties which a beneficiary of the right of residence encounters are temporary'.[188] However, the language of the Court later changed to reflect greater accommodation of the interests of the State. For example, in *Bidar*, it held that 'although the Member States must, in the organisation and application of their social assistance systems, show a certain degree of financial solidarity with nationals of other Member States', it is nevertheless 'permissible for a Member State to ensure that the grant of assistance to cover the maintenance costs of students from other Member States does not become an unreasonable burden which could have consequences for the overall level of assistance which may be granted by that State'.[189]

In EU citizenship law, the public finance defence directly informs the Court's definition of social assistance for the purposes of Directive 2004/38: 'all assistance schemes established by the public authorities, whether at national, regional or local level, to which recourse may be had by an individual who does not have resources sufficient to meet his own basic needs and those of his family and who by reason of that fact may, during his period of residence, become a burden on the public finances of the host Member State which could have consequences for the overall level of assistance which may be granted by that State'.[190] The Court recognises that it is an objective of the Directive to '[prevent] Union citizens who are nationals of other Member States from becoming an unreasonable burden on the social assistance system of the host Member State'.[191] Thus the requirement of lawful residence in a host State—essentially, that Union citizens must be either economically active or economically autonomous—depends mainly, for the latter, on having sufficient financial resources, which is explicitly tied to the objective of protecting the public finances of the Member States.[192]

Two broad themes underpin the altered balance in case law between promoting a certain degree of financial solidarity with nationals of other Member States, on the one hand, and protecting national public finances, on the other. First, as indicated above, there is the question of what constitutes *lawful residence* in a host State and, relatedly, of where responsibility for supporting Union citizens who do move to another State actually lies. These questions are addressed in Chapter 7, and Advocate General Wahl summarised the essential dilemma at the heart of them in *Brey*: '[t]he idea that a Union citizen could say "*civis europeus sum*" and invoke that status against hardships encountered in other Member States was famously pioneered 20 years ago. The present case raises the question whether that status can be relied upon today, against the economic difficulties of modern life'.[193] Second, there is also more explicit discussion of abuse of free movement rights. In *Collins*, a case assessing the lawfulness

---

[188] *Grzelczyk*, para 44 (emphasis added).
[189] Case C-209/03 *Bidar*, EU:C:2005:169, para 56.
[190] *Brey*, para 61.
[191] Case C-67/14 *Alimanovic*, EU:C:2015:597, para 50; referring to Case C-333/13 *Dano*, EU:C:2014:2358, para 74. See further, recital 10 of Directive 2004/38.
[192] eg Case C-200/02 *Zhu and Chen*, EU:C:2004:639, para 33; and Case C-408/03 *Commission v Belgium*, EU:C:2006:192, para 41.
[193] AG Wahl in Case C-140/12 *Brey*, EU:C:2013:337, para 1 of the Opinion. See similarly, AG Pitruzella in Case C-181/19 *Jobcenter Krefeld*, EU:C:2020:377, para 1 of the Opinion: '[a]s I prepare this Opinion, the European Union is going through an unprecedented public health crisis, to which the Member States have responded by demonstrating equally unprecedented solidarity as regards health-related matters. In the present case, it is the limits of social solidarity which the Court is called upon to clarify'.

of national conditions curtailing entitlement to jobseeker's allowance, the Commission suggested that a residence requirement 'may be justified on objective grounds necessarily intended to avoid "benefit tourism" and thus the possibility of abuse by work-seekers who are not genuine'.[194] That argument connects to the assertion that Article 7(1)(b) of Directive 2004/38 'seeks to prevent economically inactive Union citizens from using the welfare system of the host Member State to finance their livelihood'.[195]

But there is an unresolved tension in free movement law with respect to where *use* of free movement rights ends and *abuse* of free movement rights begins. Consider the following passage from Advocate General Sharpston in *Bressol*:

> [T]he French Community legislator appears to be relying on the familiar 'free rider' argument: students moving abroad to study reap the benefits from publicly funded education in the host Member State but do not contribute to financing it through (their parents') national taxes, nor do they necessarily themselves 'pay back' by staying to work in the host Member State and becoming taxpayers there. The implicit argument is that the non-Belgian students concerned are committing some form of abuse. That is plainly not the case. Students moving to another Member State in order to pursue their education there are exercising their right to freedom of movement – a right which, as citizens of the Union, they are entitled to enjoy without any discrimination based on nationality. Their supposed intentions, invoked by the legislator of the French Community, are quite irrelevant.[196]

The concept of abuse of free movement rights is returned to in Chapter 6. For present purposes, what becomes critical is the link between the justification of protecting national public finances, on the one hand, and assessing the proportionality of a Union citizen's claim, on the other.

More specifically, for citizens falling within the scope of Article 7(1)(b) of the Directive—that is, citizens who are neither working nor self-employed in the host State and are therefore required to have comprehensive sickness insurance and sufficient financial resources—the Court now considers not just the claim of the individual citizen in a given case, but also the implications of further (potential) claims on public spending in a more aggregate sense. This adapted approach to proportionality review—from the individual/specific to the general/systemic—is one of the most notable shifts in EU citizenship case law in recent years. It was noted above that, in *Grzelczyk*, the Court tempered the Directive 93/96's requirement of sufficient resources by pointing to the temporary nature of the difficulties experienced by a French student residing in Belgium in its analysis of proportionality: he applied for a minimum subsistence allowance in Belgium only in his final year of university, having previously supported himself through loans and part-time work. The Court agreed that Union citizens should not become an *unreasonable* burden on the social assistance system of the host State, but reasoned that this implied that becoming a *reasonable* burden was legitimate. In other

---

[194] Case C-138/02 *Collins*, EU:C:2004:172, para 50. See similarly, AG Ruiz-Jarabo Colomer (EU:C:2003:409, para 75 of the Opinion). In *Trojani*, AG Geelhoed defined 'social tourism' as 'moving to a Member State with a more congenial social security environment' (Case C-456/02, EU:C:2004:112, para 13 of the Opinion).

[195] AG Wahl in Case C-140/12 *Brey*, EU:C:2013:337, para 38 of the Opinion. See similarly, the Court's reference in *Dano* to Union citizens 'who exercise their right to freedom of movement *solely in order to obtain another Member State's social assistance* although they do not have sufficient resources to claim a right of residence' (*Dano*, para 78 (emphasis added)).

[196] AG Sharpston in Case C-73/08 *Bressol*, EU:C:2009:396, para 95 of the Opinion.

words, the Court acknowledged the conditions set by EU legislation 'as such, but attenuated their severity in the light of the circumstances of the case at hand'.[197]

That approach was extended further in *Baumbast*. The Court first confirmed that the right to reside within the territory of another Member State is conferred by Article 21 TFEU subject to the limitations and conditions laid down by the Treaty and by the measures adopted to give it effect.[198] However, it then ruled that 'the *application* of the limitations and conditions acknowledged in Article [21 TFEU] ... is subject to judicial review'.[199] More specifically, 'those limitations and conditions *must be applied* in compliance with the limits imposed by [Union] law and in accordance with the general principles of that law, *in particular the principle of proportionality*'.[200] The Court thus concluded that 'to refuse to allow Mr Baumbast to exercise the right of residence which is conferred on him by Article [21 TFEU] by virtue of the application of the provisions of Directive 90/364 on the ground that his sickness insurance does not cover the emergency treatment given in the host Member State would amount to a disproportionate interference with the exercise of that right'.[201]

However, that case concerned Mr Baumbast's right to reside per se. For claims to equal treatment more specifically, the Court has endorsed generalised proportionality assessment in its case law on Article 7(1)(b) of Directive 2004/38, assessing the purpose and objectives of the national rule rather than on its application in individual cases. This shift in perspective is examined in more detail in Chapter 7. In summary, notwithstanding the fact that detailed guidance for national authorities on what should be taken into account in the assessment of proportionality in individual cases was provided in *Brey*—albeit with reference to 'the specific burden which granting that benefit would place on the national social assistance system as a whole'[202]—the Court adjusted its approach from requiring a demonstration of proportionality in the application of national rules in each individual case (*Grzelczyk*, *Baumbast*) to presuming the proportionality of national rules that give effect to the conditions in Article 7 of the Directive without requiring an assessment of their application in an individual case where, to date at least, either (i) the claimant is not lawfully resident in the host State within the meaning of EU law, and/or (ii) the restrictions in national rules mirror the derogations from equal treatment provided for in Article 24(2) of the Directive.[203]

As regards the first situation, the Court emphasised in *Dano* that in order to protect its public finances, a Member State must 'have the possibility, pursuant to Article 7 of Directive

---

[197] AG Geelhoed in Case C-209/03 *Bidar*, EU:C:2004:175, para 41 of the Opinion.
[198] Case C-413/99 *Baumbast and R*, EU:C:2002:493, para 85.
[199] ibid para 86 (emphasis added).
[200] ibid para 91 (emphasis added).
[201] ibid para 93. See generally, K Hailbronner, 'Union citizenship and access to social benefits' (2005) 42 Common Market Law Review 1245; and M Dougan, 'The constitutional dimension to the case law on Union citizenship' (2006) 31 European Law Review 613; and 'The bubble that burst: exploring the legitimacy of the case law on the free movement of Union citizens' in M Adams, H de Waele, J Meeusen, and G Straetmans (eds), *Judging Europe's Judges: The Legitimacy of the Case Law of the European Court of Justice* (Hart Publishing 2013) 127.
[202] Case C-140/12 *Brey*, EU:C:2013:237, para 64; see further, paras 75–79.
[203] Article 24 of the Directive provides: '1. Subject to such specific provisions as are expressly provided for in the Treaty and secondary law, all Union citizens residing on the basis of this Directive in the territory of the host Member State shall enjoy equal treatment with the nationals of that Member State within the scope of the Treaty. The benefit of this right shall be extended to family members who are not nationals of a Member State and who have the right of residence or permanent residence. 2. By way of derogation from paragraph 1, the host Member State shall not be obliged to confer entitlement to social assistance during the first three months of residence or, where appropriate, the longer period provided for in Article 14(4)(b), nor shall it be obliged, prior to acquisition of the right of permanent residence, to grant maintenance aid for studies, including vocational training, consisting in student grants or student loans to persons other than workers, self-employed persons, persons who retain such status and members of their families'. The 'longer period provided for in Article 14(4)(b)' concerns jobseekers. See further, Chapters 6 and 7.

2004/38, of refusing to grant social benefits to economically inactive Union citizens'.[204] In distinction from essentially every other judgment across the span of EU citizenship law, the word 'proportionality' was not mentioned at all.[205] Where it featured in limited form and by inference, it related to assessing whether or not the claimant resided lawfully in the host State—'the financial situation *of each person* concerned should be examined specifically, without taking account of the social benefits claimed, in order to determine whether he meets the condition of having sufficient resources to qualify for a right of residence under Article 7(1)(b) of Directive 2004/38'[206]—and not with respect to considering entitlement to the benefit applied for per se. As explained further in Chapter 7, lawful residence was always a precondition for equal treatment claims in EU citizenship law;[207] what has changed is *how* lawful residence is now determined.

Shortly after its ruling in *Dano*, the Court developed in *Alimanovic* the second situation in which 'no such individual assessment is necessary in circumstances such as those at issue in the main proceedings':[208] where national rules reflected a derogation already provided for in the contested national rules—for example, as in *Alimanovic* itself, the fact that Article 24(2) excludes jobseekers from entitlement to social assistance in the host State. Further developing its reasoning on the systemic impact of social assistance claims, the Court observed:

> [A]s regards the individual assessment for the purposes of making an overall appraisal of the burden which the grant of a specific benefit would place on the national system of social assistance at issue in the main proceedings as a whole, it must be observed that the assistance awarded to a single applicant can scarcely be described as an 'unreasonable burden' for a Member State, within the meaning of Article 14(1) of Directive 2004/38. However, while an individual claim might not place the Member State concerned under an unreasonable burden, the accumulation of all the individual claims which would be submitted to it would be bound to do so.[209]

To rationalise its position, the Court emphasised the principle of legal certainty: '[b]y enabling those concerned to know, without any ambiguity, what their rights and obligations are, the criterion referred to both in [national law], and in Article 7(3)(c) of Directive 2004/38, namely a period of six months after the cessation of employment during which the right to social assistance is retained, is consequently such as to guarantee a significant level of legal certainty and transparency in the context of the award of social assistance by way of basic provision, while complying with the principle of proportionality'.[210]

---

[204] Case C-333/13 *Dano*, EU:C:2014:2358, para 78.
[205] An (implicit) analysis of proportionality can be found in the Opinion of AG Wathelet, who observed that 'in circumstances such as those in the main proceedings, recourse to the social assistance system will not be temporary but will be prolonged indefinitely in the absence of any attempt at all to seek employment', thus contrasting with the temporary duration of the assistance sought in eg *Grzelczyk* (AG Wathelet in *Dano*, EU:C:2014:341, para 134 of the Opinion).
[206] Case C-333/13 *Dano*, EU:C:2014:2358, para 80 (emphasis added).
[207] See Case C-85/96 *Martínez Sala*, EU:C:1998:217, para 61: '[a]s a national of a Member State *lawfully residing* in the territory of another Member State, the appellant in the main proceedings comes within the scope *ratione personae* of the provisions of the Treaty on European citizenship'.
[208] Case C-67/14 *Alimanovic*, EU:C:2015:597, paras 56–59. A similar conclusion was reached with respect to Article 6 of the Directive in Case C-299/14 *García-Nieto*, EU:C:2016:114; see further, Chapter 7.
[209] *Alimanovic*, para 62.
[210] Case C-67/14 *Alimanovic*, EU:C:2015:597, para 61. Article 7(3)(c) of the Directive was the basis for the applicants' lawful residence in the host State in *Alimanovic*, *contra* the legal position of Ms Dano. That provision establishes that a Union citizen who is no longer a worker or self-employed in the host State may retain that status (and thus continue to reside there lawfully under Article 7(1)(a) of the Directive) where 'he/she is in duly recorded

Legal certainty and transparency are not new elements in the framing of proportionality assessment. For example, in *Förster*, the Court confirmed that 'in order to be proportionate, a residence requirement must be applied by the national authorities on the basis of clear criteria known in advance'.[211] Relatedly, national rules that compel a Union citizen to demonstrate or prove what is required must not 'make it impossible in practice or excessively difficult' to do so.[212] Legal certainty and transparency requirements are not, therefore, controversial even though they can displace a requirement to consider how the application of a measure or rule plays out in a given case. EU law provides guidance that sets parameters around the discretion of national authorities and enables their decisions to be reviewed, providing an administrative and/or judicial safety net, as appropriate. These parameters are also explicitly linked to ensuring the effectiveness of rights[213] and to the proper division of functions between the EU legislature and the EU judiciary.[214]

However, 'the most transparent and efficient measure is not necessarily a proportionate measure. Whether it is depends on other elements such as the design and structure of the scheme, the overall coherence of the scheme and the objective being considered'.[215] That observation brings us back to the critical question of balance: how best can different interests and principles, all of which are relevant within the system of EU law, be accommodated in terms of both appropriately resolving an individual case and constructing a coherent (and workable) system of EU citizenship law? Case law coherence is vital in achieving both objectives, but it is not yet clear whether approaches applied in previous case law have been reversed in general, or temporarily displaced in general, or reversed or displaced only in the specific context of social assistance claims when Union citizens do not meet the conditions in Article 7 of the Directive.[216] These questions have particular resonance for the concept of lawful residence in a host State and the contingent scope of equal treatment that results. They are examined in detail in Chapter 7.

3.4.3 Evidencing proportionality

In free movement law, the Court consistently requires that the proportionality of a restriction must be *demonstrated*. For example, in case law on the free movement of workers, assertions about protecting the balance of the social security system must be accompanied by 'specific evidence substantiating [the] arguments. Such an objective, detailed analysis, supported by figures, must be capable of demonstrating, with solid and consistent data, that there are genuine risks'.[217] In other words, Member States must do more than assert a risk to the relevant public interest(s) at stake: they must *prove* it.

---

involuntary unemployment after completing a fixed-term employment contract of less than a year or after having become involuntarily unemployed during the first twelve months and has registered as a job-seeker with the relevant employment office. In this case, the status of worker shall be retained for no less than six months'. See further, Chapter 6.

[211] Case C-158/07 *Förster*, EU:C:2008:630, para 56.
[212] Case C-224/02 *Pusa*, EU:C:2004:273, para 44. See further, Section 3.4.3.
[213] eg Case C-246/17 *Diallo*, EU:C:2018:499, paras 61–68.
[214] eg AG Bot in Case C-378/12 *Onuekwere*, EU:C:2013:640, paras 70–73 of the Opinion.
[215] AG Sharpston in Joined Cases C-523/11 and C-585/11 *Prinz and Seeberger*, EU:C:2013:90, para 105 of the Opinion.
[216] The Court has revived the *Baumbast* finding, post-*Dano/Alimanovic*, that 'limitations and conditions must be applied in compliance with the limits imposed by EU law and in accordance with the general principles of EU law, in particular the principle of proportionality' in considering residence rights rather than social assistance claims (Case C-165/14 *Rendón Marín*, EU:C:2016:675, para 45).
[217] Case C-515/14 *Commission v Cyprus*, EU:C:2016:30, para 54; see also, Case C-542/09 *Commission v Netherlands*, EU:C:2012:346, para 82. See generally, N Nic Shuibhne and M Maci, 'Proving public interest: the growing impact of evidence in free movement case law' (2013) 50 Common Market Law Review 965.

As a general rule, the same approach applies in EU citizenship law, with judgments in the field of university education providing a useful illustration. In *Commission v Austria*, national rules applied different criteria for access to further studies depending on whether students obtained a secondary education diploma in Austria or elsewhere, constituting indirect discrimination on the grounds of nationality. Responding to an argument about protecting 'the existence of the Austrian education system in general and the safeguarding of the homogeneity of higher education in particular', the Court emphasised that 'it is for the national authorities which invoke a derogation from the fundamental principle of freedom of movement for persons to show in each individual case that their rules are necessary and proportionate to attain the aim pursued' and that '[t]he reasons which may be invoked by a Member State by way of justification must be accompanied by an analysis of the appropriateness and proportionality of the restrictive measure adopted by that State and specific evidence substantiating its arguments'.[218] The Court criticised the facts that 'Austria simply maintained at the hearing that the number of students registering for courses in medicine could be five times the number of available places, which would pose a risk to the financial equilibrium of the Austrian higher education system and, consequently, to its very existence',[219] that 'no estimates relating to other courses have been submitted to the Court and that the Republic of Austria has conceded that it does not have any figures in that connection',[220] and that 'the Austrian authorities have accepted that the national legislation in question is essentially preventive in nature'.[221]

If the judgment in *Commission v Austria* can be framed as *negative guidance*—that is, guidance to Member States about what not to do—the Court subsequently provided *positive guidance* in *Bressol*. More specifically, it outlined the considerations to be addressed by the referring court when determining whether restrictions placed on access to certain medical and paramedical university courses in Belgium were proportionate to the objective of protecting public health. The Court confirmed that the Belgium's demonstration of the appropriateness and necessity of the measures adopted must entail 'objective, detailed analysis, supported by figures, [and] must be capable of demonstrating, with solid and consistent data, that there are genuine risks to public health'.[222] It then provided a series of detailed questions for the referring court to consider.[223] On the necessity criterion in particular, the referring court was required to assess whether protection of public health 'could be attained by less restrictive measures'.[224]

Once again, however, there has been an evident shift towards a more presumptive approach in cases concerning access to social assistance. In *Dano*, the 'essentially preventive' nature of the contested German legislation (an approach rejected in *Commission v Austria*[225]) was acknowledged by Advocate General Wathelet.[226] However, he suggested that '[a]lthough the referring court provides no precise information about the existence of such a risk, it none

---

[218] Case C-147/03 *Commission v Austria*, EU:C:2005:427, paras 66 and 63.
[219] ibid para 64.
[220] ibid para 65.
[221] ibid para 65. In *Bidar*, the Court similarly dismissed arguments about limiting the temporal effects of its judgment on access to maintenance grants on the grounds of lack of evidence (Case C-209/03 *Bidar*, EU:C:2005:169, para 70).
[222] Case C-73/08 *Bressol and Others*, EU:C:2010:181, para 71.
[223] ibid paras 72–81.
[224] ibid para 77.
[225] *Commission v Austria*, para 65.
[226] AG Wathelet in Case C-333/13 *Dano*, EU:C:2014:341, para 131 of the Opinion, including the statement that the legislation 'serves to prevent abuse and a certain form of "benefit tourism"'.

the less refers to the limits of basic provision systems financed from taxation in the light of the amounts involved, amounts which might encourage immigration of Union citizens whose average income is considerably lower'.[227] In the Court's judgment, the preventive objective was attributed to the Directive itself in the statement that 'Article 7(1)(b) of Directive 2004/38 seeks to prevent economically inactive Union citizens from using the host Member State's welfare system to fund their means of subsistence'.[228] Subsequently, in *Commission v UK*, the Court reversed the standard approach to burden of proof in free movement law by concluding that 'the Commission, which has the task of proving the existence of the alleged infringement and of providing the Court with the evidence necessary for it to determine whether the infringement is made out' had not 'provided evidence or arguments showing that such checking does not satisfy the conditions of proportionality, that it is not appropriate for securing the attainment of the objective of protecting public finances or that it goes beyond what is necessary to attain that objective'.[229] It is certainly true that the Commission must establish that an infringement is 'made out' but the task of defending the proportionality of national rules is normally attributed to the defendant Member State.

It will be seen in Chapter 10 that, in the context of expulsion of Union citizens from a host State, established principles on the *demonstration* of proportionality—especially with respect to rejecting preventive measures and requiring instead an examination of individual circumstances—still hold firm. This point further suggests that case law on access to social assistance and other social benefits has become a specific offshoot with distinctively limiting features. However, even if limited in scope, the social assistance case law raises a challenge to the virtue of evidence over speculation that must be confronted. In particular, re-reading the 1997 report of the High Level Panel on the free movement of persons suggests that some of the concerns highlighted then are even more raw over two decades later:

> [I]t is both surprising and regrettable that population movements within the European Union are not the subject of more extensive study, whether quantitative or qualitative. Before reaching a decision on the desirability or the scope of a measure concerning the free movement of persons, it is not unimportant to know roughly the number or people affected by the proposal or what the consequences would be. Confronted by economic and social difficulties much greater than in the past, Europe's citizens are anxious about their future. Accordingly, they will not accept further steps in the construction of Europe or its enlargement unless they feel that their own concerns are being taken into account in a practical way.[230]

The significance of another caution expressed in the report is similarly striking: '[o]f all the rules of [Union] law, it is precisely the provisions relating to migration which are most closely linked to the historical complexities and multicultural nature of European society. Hitherto, this perspective has not received enough consideration in [Union] practice. A certain degree of attention has therefore been paid in this report to the cultural aspects of migration, despite the difficulty of adequately circumscribing phenomena which cannot be quantified

---

[227] ibid para 133 of the Opinion.
[228] Case C-333/13 *Dano*, EU:C:2014:2358, para 76; confirmed in Case C-67/14 *Alimanovic*, EU:C:2015:597, para 50.
[229] Case C-308/14 *Commission v UK*, EU:C:2016:436, para 85.
[230] Report of the High Level Panel on the free movement of persons chaired by Mrs Simone Veil, and presented to the Commission on 18 March 1997, 85–86.

using economic and social data'.²³¹ The relevance and importance of these factors for the evolution—and ethics—of EU citizenship law are returned to at several points in the chapters that follow.

3.5 Asymmetric Movement

A final question relating to how restrictions of rights are justified concerns the fact that freedom of movement is not practised at the same level or in the same ways across the Union's Member States. Resulting asymmetric movement patterns might connect to geographical location—for example, to more intensive mobility levels necessarily experienced in frontier areas—or to other factors such as employment opportunities or languages. Examples were seen in Section 3.4.3 regarding conditions for access to university education, where national rules aimed to protect access for home State students and thus to disincentivise German students seeking to attend Austrian universities (*Commission v Austria*) and French students seeking to attend Belgian universities (*Bressol*).

Arrangements for specific instances of asymmetric movement are already embedded in EU free movement law: for example, in the provisions of Regulation 883/2004 that address the special position of frontier workers.²³² But more generally, how, if at all, should clusters of mobility be managed within EU citizenship law, balancing the right of Union citizens to move and reside freely on a basis of choice and equal treatment, on the one hand, with the reality that challenges faced by Member States through the realisation of free movement— and by home as well as host States²³³—are not going to be equally distributed, on the other? For example, where specific challenges can be evidenced, meeting the standards advocated in Section 3.4.3, should EU citizenship law accommodate instances of *partial* discrimination, that is, differential treatment for the nationals of *some* Member States (beyond the specific context of transitional arrangements put in place for the accession of new Member States to the Union²³⁴) to mitigate effects produced by unevenness in the exercise of free

---

[231] ibid 16. Tracing these ideas in both historical and contemporary perspective, see S Barbou des Places, 'Is free movement (law) fully emancipated from migration (law)?' in N Nic Shuibhne (ed), *Revisiting the Fundamentals of EU Law on the Free Movement of Persons* (OUP 2023) forthcoming.

[232] See esp Articles 18, 28, and 62(3), and Annexes III and V, of Regulation 883/2004.

[233] See eg S Currie, 'Scapegoats and guinea pigs: free movement as a pathway to confined labour market citizenship for European Union accession migrants in the UK' (2022) 51 Industrial Law Journal 277; and I Goldner Lang and M Lang, 'The dark side of free movement: when individual and social interests clash' in S Mantu, P Minderhoud, and E Guild (eds), *EU Citizenship and Free Movement: Taking Supranational Citizenship Seriously* (Brill 2020) 382.

[234] Accession to the Union entails 'conversion' to Member State nationality for third-country nationals. No significant arrangements for freedom of movement and residence were adopted for the 1973 enlargement. However, for both the 1981 and 1986 enlargements, transitional mechanisms were put in place for the free movement of workers. Additionally, the EU–Turkey Association Agreement, which came into force in 1964, was conceived as an interim step towards accession. Post-Maastricht enlargement of the Union accelerated in scale, with accessions in 1995 (Austria, Finland, and Sweden), 2004 (Cyprus, Czech Republic, Estonia, Hungary, Latvia, Lithuania, Malta, Poland, Slovakia, and Slovenia), 2007 (Romania and Bulgaria), and 2013 (Croatia). Across these accession processes, transition arrangements were put in place to delay freedom of movement in some respects for new Member State nationals. The 1995 accession of Austria, Finland, and Sweden should also be considered in conjunction with two significant external frameworks that stem from processes resulting in non-accession of the four European Free Trade Area (EFTA) countries: the EEA Agreement concluded with Iceland, Liechtenstein (returned to in Section 4), and the bilateral agreements concluded with Switzerland. See generally, I Goldner Lang, 'Transitional arrangements in the enlarged European Union: how free is the free movement of workers?' (2008) 3 Croatian Yearbook of European Law and Policy 241; and M Dougan, 'A spectre is haunting Europe... free movement of persons and the Eastern enlargement' in C Hillion (ed), *EU Enlargement: A Legal Approach* (Hart Publishing 2004) 113.

movement? This is a difficult question in both conceptual and practical terms, challenging a fundamental association between equality and uniformity in EU free movement law, with reference to both Union citizens and to the Member States.[235] The danger is that the fragile fabric of EU equal treatment commitments is inadvertently unravelled. However, as Brexit has arguably demonstrated, there is also some risk in not confronting the question and, as noted in Section 3.3.1, EU equal treatment principles also ask that situations that are different should not be treated in the same way.

We saw in Section 3.4 that the justification arguments submitted by Austria in *Commission v Austria*—concerning 'safeguarding of the homogeneity of the Austrian education system' and the suggestion that by extending more lenient conditions of access to university beyond its own nationals, 'it can expect a large number of holders of diplomas awarded in other Member States to try to attend university and higher education courses in Austria and [that] situation would cause structural, staffing and financial problems'[236]—were sharply dismissed by the Court of Justice, but mainly because of the absence of any evidence to demonstrate the claimed impacts. Reflecting further on the substance of a possible justification in such circumstances, the reasoning of the Court in *Italian Government v Commission* provides an interesting starting point. Article 226 EEC was a transitional provision in the Treaty of Rome, establishing a mechanism for 'strictly necessary' protective measures that derogated in certain circumstances from the EEC Treaty's rules on the functioning of the common market.[237] In dismissing a complaint against a Commission decision authorising protective measures in France for imports from Italy only, the Court underlined that '[t]he different treatment of non-comparable situations does not lead *automatically* to the conclusion that there is discrimination'.[238] It ruled that the Commission 'must take into account that in cases of doubt the "common" nature of the market will suffer less if derogation from the rules of the Treaty is made only *within the framework of the relations between two Member States*' and that the Commission was 'entitled to make a distinction between countries rather than between undertakings in the Common Market when there are reasonable grounds for such a distinction' and that '[t]his is so when it is possible to find, within a given country, a price level which is clearly different from the price level in the other countries'.[239]

That reasoning does offer a way to think about partial discrimination through the lens of dissimilar situations: to conceptualise situations of asymmetric movement as situations that non-discrimination would *require* to be treated differently. In the same case, however,

---

[235] Article 4(2) TEU requires, *inter alia*, that '[t]he Union shall respect *the equality of Member States before the Treaties* as well as their national identities, inherent in their fundamental structures, political and constitutional, inclusive of regional and local self-government'.

[236] Case C-147/03 *Commission v Austria*, EU:C:2005:427, para 50.

[237] Article 226 EEC provided: '[i]f, during the transitional period, difficulties arise which are serious and liable to persist in any sector of the economy or which could bring about serious deterioration in the economic situation of a given area, a Member State may apply for authorisation to take protective measures in order to rectify the situation and adjust the sector concerned to the economy of the common market. On application by the State concerned, the Commission shall, by emergency procedure, determine without delay the protective measures which it considers necessary, specifying the circumstances and the manner in which they are to be put into effect. The measures authorised under paragraph 2 may involve derogations from the rules of this Treaty, to such an extent and for such periods as are strictly necessary in order to attain the objectives referred to in paragraph 1. Priority shall be given to such measures as will least disturb the functioning of the common market'. That mechanism has much in common with restrictions on the free movement of workers agreed between the UK and EU27 in February 2016; see Section D of the Decision of the Heads of State or Government, meeting within the European Council, concerning a new settlement for the United Kingdom within the European Union, 18–19 February 2016, 2016 OJ C691/1. See further, N Nic Shuibhne, 'Reconnecting free movement of workers and equal treatment in an unequal Europe' (2018) 43 European Law Review 477.

[238] Case 13/63 *Italian Government v Commission*, EU:C:1963:20, part (b) of the judgment (emphasis added).

[239] ibid (emphasis added).

Advocate General Lagrange emphasised the *transitional* nature of Article 226 EEC: it enabled 'those exceptions considered as *necessary departures from* the rules of the Common Market' and was intended 'to cope, in the two very precise cases for which it provides, with the possible insufficiency of the normal provisions provided in the Treaty, so that the Common Market should operate under the conditions described in Article 2 [EEC]'.[240] In other words, specific arrangements that might, exceptionally, be put in place for one or a limited number of Member States were envisaged for the transitional period only. A 'common' market that could be fragmented in this way was impermanent by definition and the freedoms conferred by the EEC Treaty would not tolerate differences with respect to some Member States (or their nationals) because they aimed to diminish the significance of all intra-EU borders as much as possible[241]—a position that also aligns with the objective of ensuring the 'greatest possible freedom of movement' guiding case law on the free movement of workers at the same time, outlined in Section 2.1. Moreover, for Advocate General Lagrange, 'there is in the Treaty a declaration, or a reminder, of certain principles, which it would not be permissible to ignore. Thus it is with non-discrimination, a general principle of law, and of economic law in particular, *which goes beyond the mere framework of the establishment of a Common Market*: such a principle must be respected'.[242]

Thus the more standard correlation between equal treatment and *uniformity* in EU free movement law was reflected in *Gravier*, for example, in the statement that a finding of inequality of treatment based on nationality is 'not affected by the mere fact that there are certain exceptions to the distinction made between Belgian and foreign students, some based on nationality, such as the special situation of Luxembourg students, and some on other criteria such as the residence in Belgium of parents who pay taxes in that country'.[243] Similarly, in his Opinion for *O'Flynn*, Advocate General Lenz underlined that 'whether the condition at issue here, established by the law of the United Kingdom, disadvantages only the nationals of a single other Member State or whether it disadvantages the nationals of all other Member States' was 'irrelevant' since '[i]t follows from the Court's case-law that there is discrimination on grounds of nationality even if the provision in question of one Member State disadvantages only some nationals of other Member States'.[244]

There have, in contrast, been few reflections on the legitimacy of differential treatment in situations of asymmetric movement, with Advocate General Sharpston's Opinion in *Bressol*

---

[240] AG Lagrange in Case 13/63 *Italian Government v Commission*, EU:C:1963:9 (1963) ECR 181 at 182, emphasis added). Article 2 EEC provided that '[i]t shall be the aim of the Community, by establishing a Common Market and progressively approximating the economic policies of Member States, to promote throughout the Community a harmonious development of economic activities, a continuous and balanced expansion, an increased stability, an accelerated raising of the standard of living and closer relations between its Member States'.

[241] This objective was the basis for extending free movement law beyond discrimination through 'market access'—see eg AG Jacobs in Case C-412/93 *Leclerc-Siplec*, EU:C:1994:393. See generally, J Snell, 'The notion of market access: a concept or a slogan?' (2010) 47 Common Market Law Review 437.

[242] AG Lagrange in *Italian Government v Commission*, 182–83 (emphasis added).

[243] Case 293/83 *Gravier*, EU:C:1985:69, para 14. In his subsequent Opinion for related infringement proceedings, however, it is not entirely clear if AG Slynn objected to the (still in force) Belgian rules at the level of principle or because of the absence, as also seen later in *Commission v Austria*, of sufficient evidence of detrimental impact (AG Slynn in Case 293/85 *Commission v Belgium*, EU:C:1987:367 (pp 340–42)).

[244] AG Lenz in Case C-237/94 *O'Flynn*, EU:C:1996:206, para 29 of the Opinion; citing Case 20/85 *Roviello*, EU:C:1988:283, para 16. On seeking to justify restrictive measures because discriminatory effects are also felt by some groups within a Member State, see eg Case C-388/01 *Commission v Italy*, EU:C: 2003:30, para 14: 'it is immaterial whether the contested measure affects, in some circumstances, nationals of the State in question resident in other parts of the national territory as well as nationals of other Member States. In order for a measure to be treated as being discriminatory, it is not necessary for it to have the effect of putting at an advantage all the nationals of the State in question or of putting at a disadvantage only nationals of other Member States, but not nationals of the State in question'.

still providing the main exception. For the Court, conditions that restricted access to certain university courses in Belgium were found to '[create] a difference in treatment between resident and non-resident students' and therefore to constitute indirect discrimination.[245] At the level of principle, she stated that '[t]he prohibition on discrimination should indeed be seen as the cornerstone of the Treaty precisely because it leaves Member States' regulatory autonomy intact—provided that their laws apply equally to nationals and non-nationals'; in that light, '[t]he key underlying principle is that all citizens of the Union must be treated as individuals, without regard to their nationality. "Free and equal access to education for all" therefore means exactly what it says. It may not mean "free and equal access to education for all my nationals".'[246] However, while she agreed that problems faced in trying to ensure sufficient access to medical and paramedical courses for Belgian nationals 'must be resolved in a way that is not a variant of "equality for those inside the magic circle" … but that respects the "fundamental status" of EU citizenship by ensuring equal access to education for all EU citizens regardless of nationality', she did characterise such problems as 'not insignificant'.[247] Thus she accepted the complexity of asymmetric movement situations, 'emphasis[ing] the importance, for the development of the Union, of freedom of movement for students based on equality' yet recognising that '[e]qually, however, the EU must not ignore the very real problems that may arise for Member States that host many students from other Member States'.[248] In her view, the EU legislator and the Member States should seek solutions that comply with Protocol No 30 on the application of the principles of subsidiarity and proportionality, which:

> … provides that action at Union level is justified where, 'the objectives of the proposed action cannot be sufficiently achieved by Member States' action in the framework of their national constitutional system and can therefore be better achieved by action on the part of the [Union]'. It also provides for the following guidelines to be used in examining whether that condition is fulfilled: (i) the issue under consideration has transnational aspects which cannot be satisfactorily regulated by action by Member States; (ii) actions by Member States alone or lack of [Union] action would conflict with the requirements of the Treaty or would otherwise significantly damage Member States' interests; (iii) action at [Union] level would produce clear benefits by reason of its scale or effects compared with action at the level of the Member States.… [O]ne of the objectives of the [Union] listed in Article [3 TEU] is to promote solidarity among the Member States, and that the Member States have a mutual duty of loyal cooperation on the basis of Article [4(3) TEU]. It seems to me that those provisions are very pertinent here. Where linguistic patterns and differing national policies on access to higher education encourage particularly high volumes of student mobility that cause real difficulties for the host Member State, it is surely incumbent on both the host Member State and the home Member State actively to seek a negotiated solution that complies with the Treaty.[249]

---

[245] Case C-73/08 *Bressol and Others*, EU:C:2010:181, para 44.
[246] AG Sharpston in Case C-73/08 *Bressol and Others*, EU:C:2009:396, para 142 of the Opinion.
[247] ibid para 143 of the Opinion. The Belgian Government's justification arguments concerned both sustaining the quality of medical and paramedical education in Belgium and risks to the protection of public health; see Case C-73/08 *Bressol and Others*, EU:C:2010:181, paras 49–61.
[248] AG Sharpston in *Bressol and Others*, para 151 of the Opinion.
[249] ibid paras 152 and 154 of the Opinion.

A case for action at EU level is clearly made out in the passage extracted above with respect to the requirements of proportionality and subsidiarity for the exercise of Union competence. There is also the suggestion that bilateral arrangements between certain Member States, within parameters set by EU law, might be feasible. However, what is less clear is how, under either approach, 'a negotiated solution' producing corridors operating differential conditions for freedom of movement—on a basis of partial nationality discrimination, in other words—'complies with the Treaty'. Are such solutions an acknowledged restriction of Union citizenship rights but one that can be defended as justifiable and proportionate? In what circumstances, beyond the specific example of education, might they be considered? What form would they take in practice: for example, would compensatory mechanisms coordinated by the Union, which might also entail some responsibility for home Member States,[250] be appropriate? Would these draw from the Union's established approach to regional or structural funds, for example, or its framework for navigation of differing national social security systems?

There is undoubted scope for deeper investigation of these questions. EU equal treatment law presupposes comprehensive inclusion or exclusion when Member States develop policies that intersect with freedom of movement but, at the same time, asymmetric movement challenges aspects of that approach. However, even if Treaty-compliant mechanisms can be conceived[251]—and even if they can be found to conform with the conceptual starting point of equal treatment, which enatails not treating different situations in the same way—drawing from an approach based on exceptional measures designed for the circumstances of transition to rework the trajectory of EU citizenship law more fundamentally and more permanently should be contemplated with caution, remembering from Chapter 1 that 'Union policies and actions ... form a unique ecosystem underpinned by instruments and structures that cannot be separated from each other'.[252]

4. Legal Framework II: Directive 2004/38

Directive 2004/38 regulates exercise of the rights to enter, reside, and remain in the territory of another Member State, rights that constitute 'an integral part of the legal heritage of every citizen of the European Union'.[253] In developing its first proposal for the Directive,[254] the Commission had to navigate the basic tension written into Article 21(1) TFEU and introduced in Section 3.2: that '[e]very citizen of the Union shall have the right to move and reside freely within the territory of the Member States', on the one hand; but that it is

---

[250] See eg M Haag, *A Sense of Responsibility: The Shifting Roles of the Member States for the Union Citizen* (Florence: European University Institute 2019, EUI PhD theses, Department of Law); and Strumia, 'Supranational citizenship enablers' (n 94).

[251] A basic precondition of Union membership itself, in light of the 'structured network of principles, rules and mutually interdependent legal relations linking the EU and its Member States, and its Member States with each other' designed to further 'the process of integration that is the *raison d'être* of the EU itself' (Opinion 2/13, EU:C:2014:2454, paras 167 and 172). See further, M Cremona and N Nic Shuibhne, 'Integration, membership and the EU neighbourhood) (2022) 59 Common Market Law Review 155.

[252] Internal EU27 preparatory discussions on the framework for the future relationship: 'Regulatory issues', TF50 (2018) 32—Commission to EU 27, 21 February 2018, <https://ec.europa.eu/info/sites/info/files/slides_regulatory_issues.pdf> (accessed 24 May 2023).

[253] Communication from the Commission to the European Parliament and to the Council on the follow-up to the recommendations of the High-Level Panel on the Free Movement of Persons, COM(1998) 403 final, 2.

[254] COM(2001) 257 final.

conferred 'subject to the limitations and conditions laid down in the Treaties and by the measures adopted to give them effect', on the other. It was necessary that the Directive would reflect the 'fundamental status' attributed to Union citizenship by then in the case law and also confront the magnitude of challenges faced by Union citizens actually exercising their rights. Simplification of the disjointed legislative framework introduced in Section 2 was a central objective,[255] and adapting free movement law to the changing nature and practices of mobility itself was another tangible concern.[256] At the same time, and again reflecting case law, appropriate exceptions had to be provided for, both with respect to public policy, public security, and public health, and to the fact that burdens on host States should be reasonable.

The seven chapters of the Directive convey its structure: 'general provisions', including key definitions such as 'beneficiary' and 'family member' (Chapter I); the right of entry and exit (Chapter II); the right of residence (Chapter III); the right of permanent residence (Chapter IV); provisions common to the right of residence and the right of permanent residence and covering, for example, territorial scope and equal treatment (Chapter V); restrictions on entry and residence on grounds of public policy, public security, or public health, and relevant procedural safeguards (Chapter VI); and 'final provisions', which address, for example, abuse of rights and the Commission's reporting obligations on the application of the Directive (Chapter VII).

As introduced in Chapter 1, Directive 2004/38 produces much of the substance of EU citizenship law—in terms of the content of its provisions, their application in practice, and their interpretation in the case law. Insights from the Directive's drafting history are included where specific provisions of the Directive are analysed in the chapters that follow, reflecting the fact that '[t]he origins of a provision of EU law may also contain information relevant to its interpretation'.[257] A disaggregation of the actors that constitute the EU legislator emerges from that discussion: to summarise very generally, the Commission and European Parliament were more typically aiming to progress the right to move and reside through the prism of Union citizenship, while the Council was more likely to insert conditions and limits upholding Member State interests.

To frame the book's more detailed analysis of the Directive in later chapters, three preliminary questions are introduced here, addressing the aims and objectives of the Directive (Section 4.1), its scope (Section 4.2), and how it negotiates the rights, conditions, and limits equation in Articles 20(2) and 21(1) of the Treaty (Section 4.3).

---

[255] eg Communication from the Commission to the European Parliament and to the Council on the follow-up to the recommendations of the High-Level Panel on the Free Movement of Persons, COM(1998) 403 final, 1: 'beneficiaries have been compartmentalised in a way that is no longer in keeping with modem forms of mobility or with the establishment of citizenship of the Union'.

[256] eg The Opinion of the Economic and Social Committee on the Commission's original proposal for the Directive (COM(2001) 257 final) noted that '[t]he current rules, designed primarily to deal with the situation of worker moving with their families to reside for a long period of time in another Member State, are ill-suited to the kind of mobility that has become commonplace over recent years' (2002 OJ C149/46, para 1.7).

[257] Case C-483/17 *Tarola*, EU:C:2019:309, para 37. Examples of engagement with the Directive's *travaux préparatoires* include Case C-162/09 *Lassal*, EU:C:2010:592I, para 55; and Joined Cases C-424/10 and C-425/10 *Ziolkowski and Szeja*, EU:C:2011:866, para 43. However, neither recourse to the drafting history nor application of the standard legislative interpretative method—ie examining the Directive's wording, scheme, and objectives—guarantees consistency of outcome: compare eg the judgment in Case C-115/15 *NA*, EU:C:2016:487 with the Opinion of AG Wathelet (EU:C:2016:259). This case, on retention of residence rights in the context of divorce from a Union citizen, is discussed in Chapters 4 and 6.

4.1 Aims and Objectives of the Directive

The aims and objectives of Directive 2004/38 are articulated in its preamble, emphasising that the conception of Union citizenship as the fundamental status of Member State nationals made it necessary 'to codify and review' existing EU measures 'dealing separately' with workers, self-employed persons, students, 'and other inactive persons' in order both 'to simplify and strengthen' the right to move and reside for all Union citizens' (recital 3). The Directive thus repeals and replaces several measures in order to remedy the previous 'sector-by-sector, piecemeal approach' (recital 4). It underlines that the 'fundamental and personal right of residence in another Member State is conferred directly on Union citizens by the Treaty' (recital 11), and that all Union citizens (and their family members) residing in a Member State 'on the basis of' the Directive should enjoy 'equal treatment with nationals in areas covered by the Treaty, subject to such specific provisions as are expressly provided for in the Treaty and secondary law' (recital 20). The Directive establishes a 'tighter definition of the circumstances and procedural safeguards subject to which Union citizens and their family members may be denied leave to enter or may be expelled' (recital 22). It also 'respects the fundamental right and freedoms and observes the principles recognised in particular by the Charter of Fundamental Rights', which requires Member States to implement the Directive 'without discrimination between [its] beneficiaries' on grounds 'such as' those listed in Article 21(1) of the Charter' (recital 31).

However, the preamble references too the statements on limitations and conditions in Articles 20(2) and 21(1) TFEU (recital 1), the requirement that Union citizens should not 'become an unreasonable burden on the social assistance system of the host Member State during an initial period of residence' (recital 10) or during longer periods of residence (recital 16), the significance of integration in the host State (recitals 17–19 and 23–24), the requirement to reside in a host State 'on the basis of this Directive' in order to enjoy equal treatment with host State nationals (recital 20), the discretion retained by Member States with respect to entitlement to social assistance in certain circumstances (recital 21), and the objective of 'guard[ing] against abuse of rights or fraud, notably marriages of convenience or any other form of relationships contracted for the sole purpose of enjoying the right of free movement and residence' (recital 28).

As introduced in Chapter 1, the Court applies its standard method of legislative interpretation to Directive 2004/38 in considering the 'wording, context and objectives'[258] of the relevant provision(s). To determine context and objectives, the Court frequently refers to the aims of the Directive to support its interpretations[259]—with pliable effects. Advocate General Wathelet has suggested that a 'hierarchy' of objectives can be drawn from the Directive's preamble: that the measure 'is intended, first and foremost' to facilitate and strengthen the primary right to move and reside freely within the territory of the Member States.[260] Much

---

[258] eg Case C-115/15 *NA*, EU:C:2016:487, para 39.

[259] See generally, Case C-418/18 P *Puppinck*, EU:C:2019:1113, paras 75–76: 'the recitals of an EU act constitute important elements for the purposes of interpretation, which may clarify the intentions of the author of that act. However, the preamble to an EU act has no binding legal force and cannot be relied on as a ground either for derogating from the actual provisions of the act in question or for interpreting those provisions in a manner that is clearly contrary to their wording'. It is relatively rare for the Court to compare different language versions of the Directive but see eg Case C-442/16 *Gusa*, EU:C:2017:1004, paras 32–34; see similarly, AG Wathelet (EU:C:2017:607), paras 47–50 of the Opinion.

[260] AG Wathelet in *Gusa*, para 52 of the Opinion (see generally, paras 51–53 of the Opinion). Similarly, in its Communication to the European Parliament on the common position adopted by the Council on the draft directive (Common Position (EC) No 6/2004 of 5 December 2003, 2004 OJ C54 E/12), the Commission indicated that '[t]he main objective of the proposal is to facilitate exercise of the right of freedom of movement and residence

of the case law does indeed reflect that understanding. However, different aims expressed in the preamble can also be offset against each other. In case law that advances the protection of the citizen, the Court tends to refer mainly to recital 3;[261] deriving from it in *Metock*, for example, that the Directive 'aims *in particular* to "strengthen the right of free movement and residence of all Union citizens"'.[262] In contrast, where a more rights-limiting outcome is reached, the Court frames the purpose of the Directive quite differently. Thus in *McCarthy*, discussed in Chapter 5, the Court first recalled the *Metock* approach but then stated: 'whilst it is true that ... Directive 2004/38 aims to facilitate and strengthen the exercise of the primary and individual right to move and reside freely within the territory of the Member States that is conferred directly on each citizen of the Union, the fact remains that *the subject of the directive concerns*, as is apparent from Article 1(a), *the conditions governing the exercise of that right*'.[263]

Perhaps the formulation used in *Coman*—that strengthening the right to move and reside is 'one of' of the Directive's objectives[264]—better captures the balancing of different interests that the Court must undertake when its case law is considered as a whole. Similarly, in *Tarola*, the Court observed that '*the purpose of* Directive 2004/38, as may be seen from recitals 1 to 4 thereof, is to facilitate the exercise of the primary and individual right to move and reside freely within the territory of the Member States, which is conferred directly on citizens of the Union by Article 21(1) TFEU, and that *one of the objectives of that directive* is to strengthen that right'.[265] It is interesting that even the Council—the institution that ensured a more conservative measure than that originally proposed by the Commission and supported by the European Parliament—did not overtly emphasise the more limiting objectives in the Directive's preamble that have been drawn from by the Court more often in recent years. In its common position, the Council considered that the proposed Directive served 'several purposes':

[T]o bring together the complex corpus of existing legislation into a single legislative instrument establishing a single system applicable to all categories of person (workers, students, non-active persons);

by reducing administrative formalities to the absolute minimum, by defining as clearly as possible the status of family members, by creating a right of permanent residence to be given after a number of years of continuous legal residence in a Member State and by restricting the possibility for Member States to refuse or terminate right of residence on public policy grounds' (SEC/2003/1293 final, para 2).

[261] ie 'Union citizenship should be the *fundamental status* of nationals of the Member States when they exercise their right of free movement and residence. It is therefore necessary to codify and review the existing Community instruments dealing separately with workers, self-employed persons, as well as students and other inactive persons in order *to simplify and strengthen* the right of free movement and residence of all Union citizens' (emphasis added).
[262] eg Case C-127/08 *Metock and Others*, EU:C:2008:449, para 59 (emphasis added). See similarly, paras 82–83, referring to recitals 1, 4, 5, and 11. Also referring to the aim of 'strengthening' the right to move and reside, see eg *Gusa*, para 40.
[263] Case C-434/09 *McCarthy*, EU:C:2011:277, para 33 (emphasis added); having cited (para 59 of) *Metock* in para 31. See similarly eg Case C-456/12 *O and B*, EU:C:2014:135, paras 35 and 41; and Case C-233/14 *Commission v Netherlands*, EU:C:2016:396, para 81. Interestingly, the reverse can be seen in Case C-140/12 *Brey*, EU:C:2013:237 ie the Court first cited the more limiting idea (para 53) but later referred to the 'strengthening' aim (para 71).
[264] Case C-673/16 *Coman*, EU:C:2018:385, para 18; repeated in Case C-89/17 *Banger*, EU:C:2018:570, para 21.
[265] Case C-483/17 *Tarola*, EU:C:2019:309, para 23 (emphasis added).

to streamline the current legislation, taking into consideration the case law of the ECJ and the provisions of the Charter of Fundamental Rights regarding family unity and the protection of family life;

to simplify the conditions and administrative formalities associated with the right of free movement and residence in the Member States;

to facilitate the right of free movement and residence of family members of a Union citizen, irrespective of nationality.[266]

At the same time, as illustrated in particular by the discussion on lawful residence in Chapter 7, the Council did secure amendments in the adopted version of the Directive that give greater weight to national interests by restricting certain rights. Nevertheless, when interpreting these limits, the Court normally asserts that 'in view of the context of Directive 2004/38 and the objectives that it pursues, its provisions cannot be interpreted restrictively and must not in any event be deprived of their practical effect'.[267] These points are picked up in Section 4.3.

A final reflection on the aims and objectives of the Directive concerns the advantages but also the weaknesses of comprehensive or framework EU measures. The objective of 'remedying' the 'piecemeal approach' to free movement rights, which saw similar provisions spread across several legislative instruments—divided sometimes by objective,[268] sometimes by sector[269]—is undoubtedly sensible. For example, locating the objective of legislative cohesion in Maastricht's significant primary law change, the 1997 High Level Panel Report recommended 'that a review or, at least, a consolidation of the provisions of secondary legislation take place with a view to ensuring compatibility with Treaty requirements in the wake of the process of clarification and amendment spanning from the Single European Act to the Maastricht Treaty'.[270]

But it would be misleading to infer that Directive 2004/38 therefore does—or could—regulate every conceivable domain and question of free movement, and gaps in its provision are highlighted where relevant in the chapters that follow. For example, the impulse to consolidate legislative measures collapsed together certain legal categories or removed them from the Directive's vocabulary, if not its reach, altogether. Thus, while the residence rights of workers and self-employed persons are provided for in Article 7(1)(a) of the Directive, residence rights for jobseekers and for persons providing or receiving services are more complicated; assembled for jobseekers by reading across several provisions of the Directive,[271] and absorbed into the more general framework of Articles 6 and 7 on duration of residence in the host State for service providers and recipients.[272] Conversely, the organisation of residence

---

[266] Common Position (EC) No 6/2004 of 5 December 2003, 2004 OJ C54 E/12, 25.

[267] *Tarola*, para 38.

[268] eg Council Directive 68/360/EEC of 15 October 1968 on the abolition of restrictions on movement and residence within the Community for workers of Member States and their families, 1968 OJ L257/13, alongside Regulation 1612/68/EEC.

[269] eg Directive 73/148/EEC on the abolition of restrictions on movement and residence within the Community for nationals of Member States with regard to establishment and the provision of services, 1973 OJ L172/14; or the three separate though largely identical measures extending general free movement rights in the 1990s (Section 2.2).

[270] Report of the High Level Panel on the free movement of persons chaired by Mrs Simone Veil, and presented to the Commission on 18 March 1997, 28.

[271] See esp Case C-710/19 *GMA (Demandeur d'emploi)*, EU:C:2020:1037, discussed in Chapter 6.

[272] The European Parliament Report on the Commission's original proposal for the Directive (COM(2001) 257 final) proposed adding *recipients* of services to Article 7(a) (European Parliament Report of 23 January 2003 on Commission proposal (COM(2001) 257), A5-0009/2003, Amendment 27). This amendment was accepted by the Commission in its revised proposal (COM(2003) 199 final) but ultimately rejected before the measure's adoption. See further, Chapter 6.

rights around three distinct temporal stages—returned to in Section 4.3—hardens other category distinctions more sharply, especially as between working and self-employed citizens, on the one hand, and 'other inactive persons' (recital 3), on the other. This division becomes especially significant when it is mapped onto related equal treatment claims.[273]

4.2 The Scope of the Directive

In three key respects, Directive 2004/38 communicates its own scope. First, establishing the *personal scope* of the Directive, Article 3(1) defines the Directive's 'beneficiaries': it applies 'to all Union citizens who move to or reside in a Member State other than that of which they are a national, and to their family members as defined in point 2 of Article 2 who accompany or join them'. Thus the Directive can only ever apply[274] when there is a clear—physical—and *continuing* cross-border connection. Second, the *material scope* of the Directive is articulated in Article 1:

This Directive lays down:
(a) the conditions governing the exercise of the right of free movement and residence within the territory of the Member States by Union citizens and their family members;
(b) the right of permanent residence in the territory of the Member States for Union citizens and their family members;
(c) the limits placed on the rights set out in (a) and (b) on grounds of public policy, public security or public health.

Third, regarding *territorial scope*, Article 22 of the Directive confirms that the rights of residence and permanent residence 'shall cover the whole territory of the host Member State and that 'Member States may impose territorial restrictions on the right of residence and the right of permanent residence only where the same restrictions apply to their own nationals'. More generally, the Directive is addressed to the Union's Member States and thus spans the territory of the Union, understood as the collective territories of the Member States and returned to in Section 6.

As introduced in Chapter 1, the Directive is also a 'Text with EEA Relevance', which extends its territorial scope to the three European Economic Area States: Iceland, Liechtenstein, and Norway. As discussed further in Section 5.4.2, 'the special relationship between the European Union, its Member States and the EFTA States' has been acknowledged by the Court of Justice.[275] Catalysed by the criteria of proximity, long-standing common values, and European identity in the EEA Agreement's preamble, '[i]t is in the light of that special relationship that one of the principal objectives of the EEA Agreement must be understood, namely to provide for *the fullest possible realisation* of the free movement of goods, persons, services and capital within the whole EEA, so that the internal market established within the European Union *is extended to* the EFTA States'.[276] However, the concept of Union

---
[273] See further, Chapter 7.
[274] Directly at least; on application of the Directive 'by analogy', see Chapters 5 and 9.
[275] Case C-897/19 PPU *IN*, EU:C:2020:262, para 50.
[276] ibid (emphasis added). Switzerland is an EFTA State but not a party to the EEA Agreement; bilateral arrangements on the free movement of persons are provided for in the Agreement between the European Community and its Member States, of the one part, and the Swiss Confederation, of the other, on the free movement of persons, 2002 OJ L114/6, as amended (see eg following the withdrawal of the United Kingdom from the European Union, Decision No 1/2020 of the Joint Committee established under the Agreement between the European Community

citizenship that underpins the Directive has no equivalent in the EEA, presenting a challenge for EEA States to ensure appropriate implementation of the Directive, on the one hand, while unpicking citizenship-specific dimensions of its interpretation where relevant, on the other.

The most significant challenges that have arisen to date for the EFTA Court have mainly concerned the free movement and residence rights that are based directly on the Treaty on the part of the Union.[277] From the perspective of EU law, the extent to which citizenship-rooted elements of Directive 2004/38 can—or should—be translated to the EEA has been less extensively considered.[278] However, how Directive 2004/38 interacts with or influences the interpretation of agreements concluded with third states has arisen in connection with applying the Directive (by analogy) beyond the context of the EEA. For example, for the EU–Turkey Association Agreement, it is established case law that 'the principles laid down in Articles [45–47 TFEU] must be extended, *so far as possible*, to Turkish nationals who enjoy the rights conferred by Decision No 1/80'.[279] It is recognised that Directive 2004/38 now regulates some aspects of these principles, especially in connection with the rights of family members.[280] But certain provisions of the Directive are tied more innately to the status of Union citizenship. In *Ziebell*, distinguishing the general concepts of public policy, public security, and public health in EU free movement law, on the one hand, from the enhanced protection against expulsion provided for in Article 23(3) of the Directive, on the other, the Court ruled:

> [U]nlike European Union law as it results from Directive 2004/38, the EEC–Turkey Association pursues solely a purely economic objective and is restricted to the gradual achievement of the free movement of workers. By contrast, *the very concept of citizenship*, as it results from the mere fact that a person holds the nationality of a Member State and not from the fact that that person has the status of a worker, and which, according to the Court's settled case-law, is intended to be the fundamental status of nationals of the Member States ... [It] is a feature of European Union law at its current stage of development

and its Member States, of the one part, and the Swiss Confederation, of the other, on the free movement of persons of 15 December 2020 amending Annex II to that Agreement on the coordination of social security schemes [2021/137] PUB/2021/4, 2021 OJ L42/15). See further, C Tobler, 'The EU-Swiss sectoral approach under pressure: not Least Because of Brexit' in S Lorenzmeier, R Petrov, and C Vedder (eds), *EU External Relations Law. Shared Competences and Shared Values in Agreements Between the EU and Its Eastern Neighbourhood* (Springer 2021) 107.

[277] See further, CNK Franklin and HH Fredriksen, 'Differentiated citizenship in the European Economic Area' in D Kostakopoulou and D Thym (eds), *Research Handbook on European Union Citizenship Law and Policy* (Edward Elgar 2022) 297.

[278] eg C Burke and Ó Ísberg Hannesson 'Citizenship by the back door? *Gunnarsson*' (2015) 52 Common Market Law Review 1111; T Burri and B Pirker, 'Constitutionalization by association? The doubtful case of the European Economic Area' (2013) 32 Yearbook of European Law 207; CNK Franklin, 'Square pegs and round holes: the free movement of persons under EEA law' (2017) 19 Cambridge Yearbook of European Legal Studies 165; and HH Fredriksen and CNK Franklin, 'Of pragmatism and principles: the EEA Agreement 20 years on' (2015) 52 Common Market Law Review 629. These contributions assess the decisions of the EFTA Court in Case E-4/11 *Clauder*, 8 April 2013; Case E-15/12 *Wahl*, 22 July 2013; Case C-26/13 *Gunnarsson*, 15 November 2013; Case E-28/15 *Jabbi*, 21 September 2016; and Case E-4/19 *Campbell*, 13 May 2020 (available at <https://eftacourt.int/cases/> (accessed 24 May 2023)).

[279] Case C-349/06 *Polat*, EU:C:2007:581, para 29 (emphasis added).

[280] eg Case C-451/11 *Dülger*, EU:C:2012:504, para 49: 'in the determination of the scope of "member of the family" for the purposes of the first paragraph of Article 7 of Decision No 1/80, reference should be made to the interpretation given to that concept in the field of freedom of movement for workers who are nationals of the Member States of the European Union and, more specifically, to the scope given to Article 10(1) of Regulation No 1612/68' but with the repeal and replacement of that provision by Directive 2004/38 then noted in para 51. On the definition of 'family member' under Directive 2004/38, see Chapter 4.

and justifies the recognition, for Union citizens alone, of guarantees which are considerably strengthened in respect of expulsion, such as those provided for in Article 28(3)(a) of Directive 2004/38.[281]

Thus the Court does not preclude the application by analogy of all provisions of Directive 2004/38 in the context of relevant external agreements, only those connected with 'the very concept of citizenship'.[282] Where the EFTA Court—and/or the Court of Justice—might yet draw that boundary in the context of the EEA remains to be seen.

Three final (related) points can be noted regarding the material scope of Directive 2004/38. First, it is acknowledged that the Directive is not exhaustive in its regulation of free movement rights. Second, consideration must therefore be given to how it interacts with other—still applicable—EU legislative measures. Third, where a situation does not fall within the scope of either the Directive or other EU legislation, the primary rights conferred directly by the Treaty must still be considered.

The judgment in *Saint-Prix* illustrates the first point. Article 7(3) of the Directive provides that a Union citizen who is no longer a worker or self-employed person retains that status in certain circumstances, which include being temporarily unable to work because of illness or vocational training linked to previous employment. Pregnancy and childbirth are therefore not included, but the Court ruled that Article 7(3) does not '[list] exhaustively the circumstances in which a migrant worker who is no longer in an employment relationship may nevertheless continue to benefit from that status'.[283] The Court drew retained worker status from Article 45 TFEU directly, though making it conditional on the person concerned returning to work or finding another job 'within a reasonable period'—a test developed 'by analogy' with retention of worker status during a term in prison.[284] Questions that then arise, considered where relevant in later chapters, include whether other 'circumstances' might be added to the provisions of the Directive in appropriate cases—as well as why, in other cases, they might not.[285]

On the second point, Directive 2004/38 repealed and replaced almost all legislative measures that had previously regulated the exercise of free movement and residence rights but with one significant exception: it *amended* certain provisions of what is now Regulation 492/2011—concerning the definition family members and discussed in Chapter 4—but the Regulation otherwise remains in force and therefore independently regulates certain aspects of freedom of movement for workers. In particular, while Article 24 of the Directive concerns equal treatment for Union citizens who reside in a host State on the basis of the Directive at a general level, with derogations specified in Article 24(2), Article 7(2) of the Regulation continues to require that Member State nationals who work in the host State are treated equally with host State workers as regards social and tax advantages.[286] Additionally,

---

[281] Case C-371/08 *Ziebell*, EU:C:2011:809, paras 72–73 (emphasis added). This case is considered further in Chapter 10.
[282] Reflecting further on this distinction, see AG Bot in Case C-451/11 *Dülger*, EU:C:2012:331, paras 40–59 of the Opinion. In his Opinion for Ziebell, AG Bot distinguished, in particular, the right of permanent residence and the extended protection against expulsion conferred by Directive 2004/38 on Union citizens (EU:C:2011:244, para 53 of the Opinion).
[283] Case C-507/12 *Saint Prix*, EU:C:2014:2007, para 38. See further, Chapter 6.
[284] ibid para 41, referring to Joined Cases C-482/01 and C-493/01 *Orfanopoulos and Oliveri*, EU:C:2004:262, para 50.
[285] See eg the discussion on Case C-67/14 *Alimanovic*, EU:C:2015:597 in Chapter 7.
[286] The same principles have been extended to self-employed workers on the basis of Article 49 TFEU; see eg Case C-168/20 *BJ and OV*, EU:C:2021:907 and see further, Chapter 6.

rights of residence can still be based on what is now Article 10 of Regulation 492/2011, which enables the children of migrant workers to complete their education in a host Member State under circumstances of equal treatment with host State nationals.[287] Derived residence rights have been extended on this basis to third-country nationals who are the child(ren)'s 'primary carers'.[288] Residence rights based on the Regulation have also been decoupled from the conditions for lawful residence in Article 7 of the Directive.[289] However, rights conferred by the Regulation and the Directive respectively do not then intersect in more protective respects. For example, failure to comply with the conditions for the right to reside in a host State in Article 7 of the Directive can later rule out a right of permanent residence there even though the relevant period of residence was based on the Regulation, that is, legal residence in a general sense but not within the meaning of Article 16(1) of the Directive.[290] Instances of crossover between the Directive and Regulation 883/2004 on the coordination of social security systems also arise,[291] and related case law regarding entitlement to both social assistance and social security benefits has been controversial, as discussed in Chapter 7.[292]

On the third point, where the Directive (or other EU legislation) does not apply in a particular situation, 'it is necessary to consider whether the Union citizens concerned by those disputes may rely on the provisions of the Treaty'.[293] The case law considered in Chapters 5 and 9, which involves claims made against a Union citizen's home State—either in the absence or following the exercise of freedom of movement respectively—provides important examples of how recourse to primary law rights can expand the scope of EU citizenship law. However, the influence of the Directive can still be felt: its provisions can be applied 'by analogy' where they do not apply directly (normally, because the claimant is not 'in' a host State and is therefore not a beneficiary of the Directive under Article 3(1)). Through the method of applying the Directive by analogy, a more concrete framework is superimposed on the brief and general statements of rights expressed in the Treaties, aiding legal certainty. However, reservations about this approach have also been advanced in light of 'the principle of the hierarchy of primary law and secondary legislation. [I]t is secondary legislation that ought to be interpreted in the light of the Treaties, and not vice versa'.[294] That interpretative dilemma introduces another fundamental question, to which we now turn: to what extent is meaningful judicial review of EU secondary law constrained by the wording of Articles 20 and 21 TFEU?

4.3 Balancing Rights with Conditions and Limits

Perhaps the most significant structural function of the Directive is its mapping of 'a gradual system as regards the right of residence in the host Member State, which reproduces, in essence, the stages and conditions set out in the various instruments of European Union law and case-law preceding that directive and culminates in the right of permanent residence':[295]

---

[287] Case C-480/08 *Teixeira*, EU:C:2010:83; Case C-181/19 *Jobcenter Krefeld*, EU:C:2020:794. See further, Chapters 6, 7, and 9.
[288] Case C-310/08 *Ibrahim*, EU:C:2010:89.
[289] *Teixeira*, para 70; *Ibrahim*, para 56; *Jobcenter Krefeld*, para 38. See further, Chapter 7.
[290] Case C-529/11 *Alarape and Tijani*, EU:C:2013:290, para 35. See further, Chapters 7 and 8.
[291] eg Case C-406/04 *De Cuyper*, EU:C:2006:491; Case C-618/16 *Prefeta*, EU:C:2018:719.
[292] eg Case C-333/13 *Dano*, EU:C:2014:2358 (social assistance) and Case C-308/14 *Commission v UK*, EU:C:2016:436 (social security benefits).
[293] Case C-256/11 *Dereci and Others*, EU:C:2011:734, para 59.
[294] AG Szpunar in Case C-202/13 *McCarthy II*, EU:C:2014:345, para 82 of the Opinion.
[295] Joined Cases C-316/16 and C-424/16 *B and Vomero*, EU:C:2018:256, para 51.

First, for periods of residence of up to three months, Article 6 of Directive 2004/38 limits the conditions and formalities of the right of residence to the requirement to hold a valid identity card or passport and, under Article 14(1) of the directive, that right is retained as long as the Union citizen and his family members do not become an unreasonable burden on the social assistance system of the host Member State ... Secondly, for periods of residence longer than three months, the right of residence is subject to the conditions set out in Article 7(1) of Directive 2004/38 and, under Article 14(2) thereof, that right is retained only if the Union citizen and his family members satisfy those conditions. It is apparent from recital 10 in the preamble to the directive in particular that those conditions are intended, inter alia, to prevent such persons from becoming an unreasonable burden on the social assistance system of the host Member State ... Thirdly, it follows from Article 16(1) of Directive 2004/38 that Union citizens acquire the right of permanent residence after residing legally for a continuous period of five years in the host Member State and that that right is not subject to the conditions referred to in the preceding paragraph. As stated in recital 18 in the preamble to the directive, once obtained, the right of permanent residence should not be subject to any further conditions, with the aim of it being a genuine vehicle for integration into the society of that State [.][296]

A Union citizen's incremental entitlement to equal treatment with nationals of the host State, guaranteed by Article 24 of the Directive, connects to the three residence stages outlined above.[297] However, the Directive structures protection against expulsion around three different periods: residence in the host State for up to five years, for between five and ten years, and after ten years.[298]

The setting and implications of these temporal frameworks relate to one of the central questions of EU citizenship law: the extent to which conditions and limits established in secondary law can legitimately constrain the primary law rights conferred by the Treaties. In the first phase of EU citizenship case law, the Court emphasised the importance and facilitated judicial review of the conditions and limits attached to citizenship rights by EU legislation. As introduced in Section 3.4.2, that approach was initially based on two key principles: first, that conditions and limits placed on a right protected by primary EU law may limit its *exercise* but not its *existence*,[299] and second, that such conditions and limits are subject to judicial review.[300] Further case law confirmed but also advanced that understanding: conceiving Union citizenship as the fundamental status of Member State nationals,[301] and attributing direct effect to the right to move and reside conferred by Article 21 TFEU.[302] The Court emphasised that restrictions of rights must be interpreted narrowly because the free movement of Union citizens constitutes 'one of the foundations of the European Union',[303] invoking proportionality to displace or depreciate the application of conditions and limits in

---

[296] ibid paras 52–54.
[297] eg Case C-333/13 *Dano*, EU:C:2014:2358, paras 69–72; anticipated by AG Trstenjak in Case C-325/09 *Dias*, EU:C:2011:86, paras 76–79 of the Opinion. This point is elaborated in Chapters 7 and 8.
[298] See further, Article 28(2) and 28(3) of the Directive, discussed in Chapter 10.
[299] The distinction between the existence and the exercise of a right was introduced to EU citizenship law by AG La Pergola in Case C-85/96 *Martínez-Sala*, EU:C:1997:335, para 18 of the Opinion; see similarly, AG Cosmas in Case C-378/97 *Wijsenbeek*, EU:C:1999:144, paras 90–96 of the Opinion. It mirrors the prohibition on impairing 'the very essence' of fundamental rights and thereby depriving them of their effectiveness; see eg Case C-145/04 *Spain v United Kingdom*, EU:C:2006:543, para 94, referencing ECtHR case law.
[300] Case C-413/99 *Baumbast and R*, EU:C:2002:493, para 86.
[301] Case C-184/99 *Grzelczyk*, EU:C:2001:458, para 31.
[302] *Baumbast and R*, para 84.
[303] Case C-423/12 *Reyes*, EU:C:2014:16, para 23.

individual cases (without calling into question the proportionality of the limits and conditions per se).[304] It also required, in line with Articles 20(2) and 21(1) TFEU, that exceptions from equal treatment should be 'expressly provided for',[305] ensuring that processes of application and interpretation did not 'add to' the limits and conditions in EU legislation,[306] and reviewing restrictions of free movement rights for compliance with EU fundamental rights.[307]

The case law summarised above was unified by a sense that introducing the status of Union citizenship to the Treaties—to primary EU law—meant *something*. The fact that the conditions and limits enabled by Articles 20(2) and 21(1) TFEU 'are based on the idea that the exercise of the right of residence of citizens of the Union can be subordinated to the legitimate interests of the Member States' was acknowledged.[308] But fundamentally, there was recognition that Article 21 TFEU 'imposes an obligation on the [Union] legislature to ensure that a citizen of the European Union can actually enjoy the rights conferred' on them.[309] In that light, assessing the application of legislative conditions in individual cases was not necessarily perceived as 'undermining' the EU legislator, but instead as necessary for ensuring that what was politically agreed was 'applied in conformity with the fundamental provisions of the [EU] Treaty'.[310]

Over time, however, fissures in this legal framework materialised in the case law. For example, linking to the discussion on integration requirements in Section 5.4, the Court ruled in *Onuekwere* that 'undermining of the link of integration between the person concerned and the host Member State justifies the loss of the right of permanent residence *even outside the circumstances mentioned* in Article 16(4) of Directive 2004/38',[311] at odds with the principle that limits and conditions in secondary legislation should not be 'added to' extra-legislatively. Similarly, the conception of Article 24(2) of the Directive as a 'specific expression' of Article 18 TFEU has been differently presented as either qualifying Article 24(2) as 'merely' such a specific expression, which must therefore be interpreted narrowly as a derogation from the principle of equal treatment,[312] or as absorbing the requirements of Article 18 TFEU so that *only* Article 24(2) should be considered, and without further evaluating the circumstances of a case in light of Article 18 TFEU or the general principle of equal treatment.[313] At the same time, and notwithstanding case law narrowing in some respects, Treaty rights continue to be engaged also to extend the *protections* and not just the conditions and limits of Directive 2004/38.[314] The relative weight attributed to rights and to conditions and

---

[304] eg Joined Cases C-22/08 and C-23/08 *Vatsouras and Koupatantze*, EU:C:2009:344.
[305] eg Case C-524/06 *Huber*, EU:C:2008:724, para 69.
[306] eg Case C-200/02 *Zhu and Chen*, EU:C:2004:639, para 33.
[307] eg Case C-127/08 *Metock*, EU:C:2008:449, para 56.
[308] Case C-200/02 *Zhu and Chen*, EU:C:2004:639, para 32. However, whether such acknowledgement sufficiently respected the choices and prerogatives of the EU legislator was called into question see eg K Hailbronner, 'Union citizenship and access to social benefits' (2005) 42 Common Market Law Review 1245; and M van den Brink, 'Justice, legitimacy and the authority of legislation within the European Union' (2019) 82 Modern Law Review 293.
[309] AG Geelhoed in Case C-413/99 *Baumbast and R*, EU:C:2001:385, para 111 of the Opinion.
[310] AG Geelhoed in Case C-209/03 *Bidar*, EU:C:2004:715, para 64 of the Opinion.
[311] Case C-378/12 *Onuekwere*, EU:C:2014:13, para 25. See further, Chapters 8 and 10.
[312] eg Case C-75/11 *Commission v Austria*, EU:C:2012:605, para 54; Case C-46/12 *LN*, EU:C:2013:97, para 33.
[313] Case C-333/13 *Dano*, EU:C:2014:2358, paras 60–62; and Case C-709/20 *CG*, EU:C:2021:602, para 66. See further, Chapter 7; and see generally, E Muir, 'EU citizenship, access to "social benefits" and third-country national family members: reflecting on the relationship between primary and secondary rights in times of Brexit' (2018) 3 European Papers 1353.
[314] See eg Case C-247/20 *Commissioners for Her Majesty's Revenue and Customs (Assurance maladie complète)*, EU:C:2022:177, paras 58–59, where a right of permanent residence in the host State was extended to a third-country national parent of a Union citizen on the basis of Article 21 TFEU directly in circumstances where the Directive did not apply. See further, Chapter 8.

limits respectively—as well as how the chosen emphasis is presented[315]—is therefore crucial in EU citizenship law and analysis of it recurs throughout the chapters that follow.

5. Legal Framework III: Significant Themes in EU Citizenship Law

Providing a frame of analysis for book overall, five cross-cutting themes are introduced in this part of the chapter: establishing a *connecting factor* to EU law (Section 5.1), ensuring the *effectiveness* of Union citizenship rights (Section 5.2), the dual role of *integration requirements* (Section 5.3), complying with the *Charter of Fundamental Rights* (Section 5.4), and the intersection of Union citizenship and *Member State competence* (Section 5.5).

5.1 Establishing a Connection with EU Law

In most situations that engage Union citizenship rights, the necessary *connecting factor* to EU law is established by the fact that 'situations falling within the scope *ratione materiae* of [Union] law include those involving the exercise of the fundamental freedoms guaranteed by the Treaty, in particular those involving the freedom to move and reside within the territory of the Member States, as conferred by Article [21(1) TFEU]'.[316] In such circumstances, the Union citizen is normally present in and seeking to establish a claim against a host State. Additionally, the exercise of free movement in the past enables claims against the home State where the citizen would otherwise be 'penalised' for having exercised the rights conferred on them by the Treaty.[317] However, the extent to which a *causal* connection must be established between the rights exercised and the restriction of rights experienced is not always clear (Section 5.1.1). Moreover, the absence of a cross-border element does not necessarily remove purely internal situations from the scope of EU citizenship law either (Section 5.1.2).

5.1.1 Causal connection between rights exercised and impact of restrictions

In some cases, hesitation about applying EU citizenship law stems from uncertainty about whether there is a (sufficient) causal link between the rights exercised and the impact of the alleged restriction of rights on the citizen concerned. In reality, most causal connections are straightforward and so there is little discussion of them in the case law. For example, where a Union citizen has been refused a benefit in a host State because a residence requirement in the applicable eligibility rules is not satisfied, there is a clear link between the citizen's exercise of the right to move and reside, on the one hand, and the benefit denied to them in the

---

[315] Exploring the significance of how judgments are framed and expressed, see esp P Phoa, 'EU citizens' access to social benefits: reality or fiction? Outlining a law and literature approach to EU citizenship' in F Pennings and M Seeleib-Kaiser (eds), *EU Citizenship and Social Rights: Entitlements and Impediments to Accessing Welfare* (Edward Elgar 2018) 199.

[316] Case C-148/02 *Garcia Avello*, EU:C:2003:539, para 24. See similarly eg Joined Cases C-11/06 and C-12/06 *Morgan and Bucher*, EU:C:2007:626, para 23; Case C-391/09 *Runevič-Vardyn and Wardyn* EU:C:2011:291, para 62; Case C-275/12 *Elrick*, EU:C:2013:684, para 20; Case C-679/16 *A (Aide pour une personne handicapée)*, EU:C:2018:601, para 57; and Case C-709/20 *CG*, EU:C:2021:602, para 84. In some cases, especially where the claims concern host State public finances, the Court adds *lawful* residence in another State to that statement, eg Case C-138/02 *Collins*, EU:C:2004:172, para 61; see further, Chapter 7.

[317] eg Case C-224/02 *Pusa*, EU:C:2004:273, para 19; and Case C-224/98 *D'Hoop*, EU:C:2002:432. See further, Chapter 9.

host State, on the other. Hypothetical cases sit at the other end of the spectrum, where there has been no exercise of Article 21 TFEU rights at all and where the threshold for Article 20 TFEU's exceptional protection of a Union citizen's *capacity* to move, returned to in Section 5.1.2, is not reached. In such circumstances, the Court considers that 'a purely hypothetical prospect of exercising that right does not establish a *sufficient* connection with [Union] law to justify the application of [Union] provisions'.[318] But what does establishing a 'sufficient' connection to EU citizenship law actually entail?

It was already seen that a direct link between the personal and material scope dimensions of a situation is not necessarily required. For example, in Section 2.2, *Martínez Sala* demonstrated that the fact that the benefit claimed being defined by the Court with reference to EU legislation on the free movement of workers did not rule out an equal treatment claim based on the appellant's personal status as a lawfully resident Union citizen. It was also seen that it is not difficult to establish a restriction of free movement rights in principle (Section 3.3.1). For example, 'national legislation which places certain nationals of the Member State concerned at a disadvantage simply because they have exercised their freedom to move and to reside in another Member State constitutes a restriction on the freedoms conferred by Article [21 TFEU]'.[319] Case law on the registration of names further demonstrates that the requirement of being 'at a disadvantage' is not a demanding threshold. In *Garcia Avello*, a Spanish mother and Belgian father resided in Belgium with their two children, who had dual Belgian and Spanish nationality. Under Belgian law, the children's surname was registered as 'Garcia Avello' (their father's surname) and a request to register them in accordance with Spanish law and practice (as 'Garcia Weber') was refused. A link with EU law was attributed to the fact that the children were 'nationals of one Member State lawfully resident in the territory of another'.[320] Explaining why the refused request resulted in the dual national children being treated differently from Belgian nationals, the Court stated that 'a discrepancy in surnames is *liable to cause serious inconvenience* for those concerned at both professional and private levels'.[321] Notably, the Court based its decision on Articles 18 and 20 TFEU—presaging the *Ruiz Zambrano* case law in protecting the children's *capacity* to move at some indeterminate point in the future (returned to in Section 5.1.2) rather than focusing on the actual exercise of freedom of movement by the children's parents under Article 21 TFEU. In later case law—both within[322] and beyond[323] the context of registering names—the 'serious inconvenience' test was also applied to restrictions of rights conferred by Article 21 TFEU.

When it is recalled that even measures *liable* to produce serious inconvenience fall within the scope of EU citizenship law, the requirement of a 'sufficient' connection seems minimal as well as difficult to pin down at the fuzzy border between potential and hypothetical restrictions. For example, in *WS*, for the purposes of confirming the admissibility of a preliminary reference under Article 267 TFEU, the Court recognised a sufficient connection to Article 21 TFEU where freedom of movement had not yet been exercised but the applicant brought the action before the referring court 'specifically in order to create the conditions necessary

---

[318] Case C-299/95 *Kremzow*, EU:C:1997:254, para 16 (emphasis added).
[319] Joined Cases C-11/06 and 12/06 *Morgan and Bucher*, EU:C:2007:626, para 25.
[320] Case C-148/02 *Garcia Avello*, EU:C:2003:539, para 27. The implications—and limits—of dual nationality are examined in Chapter 5. On the intersection of Union citizenship and 'matters coming within the competence of the Member States' (ibid para 25), see Section 5.2.4.
[321] ibid para 36 (emphasis added).
[322] Case C-353/06 *Grunkin and Paul*, EU:C:2008:559, paras 22–24; Case C-208/09 *Sayn-Wittgenstein*, EU:C:2010:806, paras 55–56, 66, and 69–70; Case C-391/09 *Runevič-Vardyn and Wardyn*, EU:C:2011:291, paras 76–77 and 81; and Case C-438/14 *Bogendorff von Wolffersdorff*, EU:C:2016:401, para 38.
[323] Case C-434/09 *McCarthy*, EU:C:2011:277, paras 48–55.

to enable him to exercise his right to freedom of movement'.³²⁴ Nevertheless, there are (relatively few) cases where the sufficiency of the causal relationship between the exercise of free movement and the obstacle claimed was indeed called into question. In free movement law generally, the concept of remoteness is engaged in such circumstances and the Court has used different expressions to capture it, including restrictions that are 'too tenuous'³²⁵ or 'too random and indirect'.³²⁶ Similar language is very rare in EU citizenship case law, though in *Morgan and Bucher*, the Court found that the 'restrictive effects' produced by the contested national rule '*cannot* be regarded as too uncertain or too insignificant ... to constitute a restriction on the freedom to move and reside within the territory of the Member States, as conferred by Article [21 TFEU].³²⁷

However, the limited extent to which connecting factors are discussed explicitly does not mean that cause and effect logic is absent from EU citizenship law. For example, in *Schempp*, while the Court was satisfied that the exercise of free movement by the applicant's former spouse established the necessary link to EU law, Advocate General Geelhoed observed that the relationship between the contested national rules and the freedoms conferred by Article 21 TFEU was 'rather tenuous' since it was 'difficult to imagine how they could restrain Mr Schempp from exercising these rights', adding that '[d]espite Mr Schempp's contention, they did not in fact prevent his former spouse from moving to a Member State which, as a matter of principle, does not subject maintenance allowances paid to divorced spouses to income tax, thus creating a tax disadvantage for him'.³²⁸ In *Iida*, that logic was applied by the Court. The applicant was a Japanese national residing in Germany, seeking a residence permit there as the family member of a Union citizen even though he was separated from his (German) spouse who had meanwhile moved to Austria with the couple's (German and US dual national) daughter. The Court confirmed that the rights derived from Union citizens by third-country national family members connect to 'the fact that a refusal to allow them would be such as to interfere with the Union citizen's freedom of movement by discouraging him from exercising his rights of entry into and residence in the host Member State'.³²⁹ In this case, however, the applicant was neither seeking a right to reside with his daughter or spouse in the host State (Austria) nor had the absence of a residence right in Germany 'discouraged his daughter or his spouse from exercising their right of freedom of movement by moving to Austria'.³³⁰ The Court therefore concluded that the contested national decision could not be said to have 'impede[d] the exercise of [the] right to move and reside freely within the

---

³²⁴ Case C-505/19 *WS*, EU:C:2021:376, para 54; for the Court, the fact that freedom of movement had not been exercised 'does not mean that the problem referred to in that request is hypothetical'. WS was the subject of an Interpol 'red notice', issued by the competent authorities in the United States, and argued, *inter alia*, that its existence precluded his exercise of free movement rights under Article 21 TFEU. The Court concluded that neither Article 54 of the Convention Implementing the Schengen Agreement nor Article 21(1) TFEU ruled out the provisional arrest of a person who is the subject of an Interpol red notice at the request of a third state 'unless it is established, in a final judicial decision taken in a Contracting State or in a Member State, that the trial of that person in respect of the same acts as those on which that red notice is based has already been finally disposed of by a Contracting State or by a Member State respectively' (para 106). Convention implementing the Schengen Agreement ('CISA') of 14 June 1985 between the Governments of the States of the Benelux Economic Union, the Federal Republic of Germany and the French Republic on the gradual abolition of checks at their common borders, signed in Schengen on 19 June 1990 and which entered into force on 26 March 1995, 2000 OJ L239/19. On the intersection of free movement and the principle of *ne bis in idem*, see eg Case C-467/04 *Gasparini and Others*, EU:C:2006:610, para 27.
³²⁵ Case C-159/90 *Grogan*, EU:C:1991:378, para 24 (Article 56 TFEU).
³²⁶ Case C-254/98 *TK-Heimdienst*, EU:C:2000:12, para 30 (Article 34 TFEU).
³²⁷ Joined Cases C-11/06 and C-12/06 *Morgan and Bucher*, EU:C:2007:626, para 32 (emphasis added).
³²⁸ AG Geelhoed in Case C-403/03 *Schempp*, EU:C:2005:62, para 39 of the Opinion.
³²⁹ Case C-40/11 *Iida*, EU:C:2012:691, para 68.
³³⁰ ibid para 74.

territory of the Member States' on the part of the applicant's daughter or spouse.³³¹ Citing *Kremzow*, it also confirmed that 'the purely hypothetical prospect of exercising the right of freedom of movement does not establish a sufficient connection with European Union law to justify the application of that law's provisions' and that '[t]he same applies to purely hypothetical prospects of that right being obstructed'.³³²

Similar reasoning can be seen in *S and G*, though derived residence rights for third-country national family members were grounded in Article 45 TFEU in that case since the Union citizens in question resided in the Netherlands but travelled to Belgium for work. However, reflecting the reasoning in *Iida*, the Court ruled that 'the grant of a derived right of residence to the third-country national in question who is a family member of a Union citizen is necessary to guarantee the citizen's *effective* exercise of the fundamental freedom guaranteed by Article 45 TFEU'.³³³ Moreover, attributing particular significance to the relationship between Union citizens and their spouses for the purpose of residence rights derived from Article 45 TFEU, the Court also held that '[t]he mere fact that it might appear desirable that the child be cared for by the third-country national who is the direct relative in the ascending line of the Union citizen's spouse is not ... sufficient in itself to constitute such a dissuasive effect'.³³⁴ Case law that requires assessment of the extent to which family life 'has been created or strengthened with a family member who is a third-country national in the host Member State' for the purpose of establishing residence rights on the return of the Union citizen to their home State, addressed in Chapter 9, provides another example of the act of movement per se not automatically engaging the protection of Article 21 TFEU.³³⁵

5.1.2 Connecting factors and internal situations

It is a basic principle of EU free movement law that, as the Court expressed it in *Saunders*, 'the provisions of the Treaty on freedom of movement ... cannot ... be applied to situations which are wholly internal to a Member State, in other words, where there is no factor connecting them to any of the situations envisaged by [Union] law'.³³⁶ In EU citizenship law, however, there is an important and material difference between two types of internal situations. First, internal situations 'which have no factor linking them with any of the situations governed by European Union law and which are confined in all relevant respects within a single Member State' are outside the scope of the Treaty.³³⁷ But second, the situation of 'a Union citizen who ... has not made use of the right to freedom of movement *cannot, for that reason alone*, be assimilated to a purely internal situation'.³³⁸ In other words, by splitting the *Saunders* formula in two, we can establish that situations that are wholly internal to one Member State do not necessarily have no (other) connection to EU law.

---

³³¹ ibid para 76. Moreover, since the Court found that the applicant was entitled to reside in Germany under Directive 2003/109, a right of residence could not be grounded in Article 20 TFEU either since 'the genuine enjoyment of the substance of the rights associated with their status of Union citizen' was not being denied (ibid paras 75–76; see further, Section 5.1.2). Directive 2003/109 concerning the status of third-country nationals who are long-term residents, 2003 OJ L16/44.
³³² *Iida*, para 77.
³³³ Case C-457/12 *S and G*, EU:C:2014:36, para 42 (emphasis added)
³³⁴ ibid para 43; citing Case C-60/00 *Carpenter*, EU:C:2002:434. Referring to the 'causal connection' that the Court draws from *Carpenter* in this respect, see AG Sharpston (EU:C:2013:837, para 117 of the Opinion). See also, para 121 of the Opinion, where a link is made to the effective exercise of EU rights (returned to in Section 5.2). The apparent hierarchy among family members suggested by the Court in *S and G* is considered further in Chapters 4 and 9.
³³⁵ eg Case C-230/17 *Deha Altiner and Ravn*, EU:C:2018:497, paras 31–34.
³³⁶ Case 175/78 *Saunders*, EU:C:1979:88, para 11.
³³⁷ Case C-256/11 *Dereci*, EU:C:2011:734, para 60.
³³⁸ ibid para 61 (emphasis added).

At a general level, the approach to internal situations taken for the economic freedoms was translated across to EU citizenship law. In *Uecker and Jacquet*, the Court confirmed that 'citizenship of the Union, established by Article [20 TFEU], is not intended to extend the scope *ratione materiae* of the Treaty also to internal situations which have no link with [Union] law' and that '[a]ny discrimination which nationals of a Member State may suffer under the law of that State falls within the scope of that law and must therefore be dealt with within the framework of the internal legal system of that State'.[339] However, the fact that 'the situation of a Union citizen who ... has not made use of the right to freedom of movement cannot, for that reason alone, be assimilated to a purely internal situation'[340] also took root. For example, in *Zhu and Chen*, discussed further in Chapter 3, no movement within the Union beyond the territory of the United Kingdom had taken place, but the necessary link to EU law was drawn from the Union citizen in question holding an Irish passport.[341] In other words, presence in one Member State while holding the nationality of another State established a sufficient connection to EU law and thus converted the situation from a purely internal one that falls outside the scope of the Treaty to one that fell within it. Similarly, in *Schempp*, the applicant was a German national residing in Germany, but his former spouse had moved to Austria, thereby constituting the necessary connecting factor to EU law in a dispute about deductibility from the applicant's taxable income in Germany of maintenance payments to his former spouse in Austria.[342]

In these kinds of cases, 'it is for the referring court to indicate to the Court [of Justice], in accordance with the requirements of Article 94 of the Court's Rules of Procedure, in what way the dispute pending before it, despite its purely domestic character, has a connecting factor with the provisions of EU law on the fundamental freedoms that makes the preliminary ruling on interpretation necessary for it to give judgment in that dispute'.[343] However, in both *Zhu and Chen* and *Schempp*, the facts *did* involve cross-border elements—reflecting the fact that 'Member States must increasingly take account of *cross-border circumstances* in their legislation as a result of citizens exercising their rights to move freely within the European Union'.[344] Perhaps straining that interpretation to some extent, it was seen in Section 5.1.1 that preparedness for exercising freedom of movement was therefore accepted by the Court in *WS* as a sufficient connecting factor to EU law. As expressed by Advocate General Bobek, '[t]he fact that a Union citizen may not (yet) have made use of his rights does not mean that the situation is purely internal. Article 21 TFEU can, to my mind, be relied on by an individual who is actually and genuinely *seeking to make use of* that freedom'.[345]

The plantation of these ideas also into Article 20 TFEU progressed Union citizenship even more forcefully into new constitutional terrain. *Ruiz Zambrano* is examined in detail in Chapter 5 but, in summary, the Court recalled, first, that the status of Union citizen is conferred on Member State nationals—there, on Mr Ruiz Zambrano's children—by Article 20 TFEU and that it is 'intended to be the fundamental status of nationals of the Member

---

[339] Joined Cases C-64/96 and C-65/96 *Uecker and Jacquet*, EU:C:1997:285, para 23.
[340] Case C-434/09 *McCarthy*, EU:C:2011:277, para 46.
[341] Case C-200/02 *Zhu and Chen*, EU:C:2004:639, para 19.
[342] Case C-403/03 *Schempp*, EU:C:2005:446, paras 23–25.
[343] Case C-343/17 *Fremoluc*, EU:C:2018:754, para 22; see generally, paras 20–29, where the Court provides detailed guidance for referring courts on the shaping of requests for a preliminary ruling when the dispute is 'confined in all respects within a single Member State' (para 20), including requirements on evidence (para 29).
[344] AG Geelhoed in Case C-403/03 *Schempp*, EU:C:2005:62, para 15 of the Opinion (emphasis added). See also, AG Sharpston in Case C-34/09 *Ruiz Zambrano*, EU:C:2010:560, esp paras 77 and 99–100 of the Opinion.
[345] AG Bobek in Case C-505/19 *WS*, EU:C:2020:939, para 32 of the Opinion (emphasis added).

States'.³⁴⁶ Second, 'Article 20 TFEU precludes national measures which have the effect of *depriving citizens of the Union of the genuine enjoyment of the substance of the rights* conferred by virtue of their status as citizens of the Union'.³⁴⁷ Third, '[a] refusal to grant a right of residence to a third-country national with *dependent* minor children in the Member State where those children are nationals and reside, and also a refusal to grant such a person a work permit, has such an effect'³⁴⁸ because '[i]t must be assumed that such a refusal would lead to a situation where those children, citizens of the Union, *would have to leave the territory of the Union* in order to accompany their parents'; relatedly, 'if a work permit were not granted to such a person, he would risk not having sufficient resources to provide for himself and his family, which would also result in the children, citizens of the Union, having to leave the territory of the Union. In those circumstances, those citizens of the Union *would, in fact, be unable to exercise the substance of the rights conferred on them* by virtue of their status as citizens of the Union'.³⁴⁹

Advocate General Sharpston had already questioned the compatibility of Union citizenship with the conventional approach on purely internal situations in free movement law even before her Opinion in *Ruiz Zambrano*. In *Government of the French Community and Walloon Government*, she observed:

> True, the Court has held that citizenship of the Union, as established by Article [20 TFEU], is not intended to extend the material scope of the Treaty to internal situations which have no link with [Union] law. However, that statement requires one to solve the logically prior question of which situations, internal or not, are deemed to have no link with [Union] law. The answer cannot be that all so-called 'internal situations' *are automatically deprived of any link to [Union] law* ... The question whether the situation is internal is therefore conceptually distinct from the question whether there is a link with [Union] law.³⁵⁰

In essence, she argued that 'the provisions on citizenship ... challenge the sustainability in its present form of the doctrine on purely internal situations'.³⁵¹ She progressed that analysis in *Ruiz Zambrano*. In her view, reverse discrimination should be addressed by EU law when three cumulative conditions are met: the situation of the static citizen should be comparable to citizens of other Member States protected by EU law in similar circumstances, violation of a fundamental right protected under EU law should be established, and EU law—specifically, Article 18 TFEU—should be triggered only as a subsidiary remedy when the violation could not be resolved by national law.³⁵²

The Court did not invoke (or change its position on) reverse discrimination in its judgment in *Ruiz Zambrano*, but it did underline that purely internal situations could nevertheless exhibit a connecting factor to EU law.³⁵³ Soon afterwards, however, it also emphasised

---

³⁴⁶ Case C-34/09 *Ruiz Zambrano*, EU:C:2011:124, paras 40–41; referring to eg Case C-184/99 *Grzelczyk*, EU:C:2001:458, para 31.
³⁴⁷ *Ruiz Zambrano*, para 42 (emphasis added); referring 'to that effect' to Case C-135/08 *Rottmann*, EU:C:2010:104, para 42.
³⁴⁸ *Ruiz Zambrano*, para 43 (emphasis added).
³⁴⁹ ibid para 44 (emphasis added).
³⁵⁰ Opinion of AG Sharpston in Case C-212/06 *Government of the French Community and Walloon Government*, EU:C:2007:398, paras 134–136 of the Opinion (emphasis added).
³⁵¹ ibid para 140 of the Opinion.
³⁵² AG Sharpston in Case C-34/09 *Ruiz Zambrano*, EU:C:2010:560, paras 144–148 of the Opinion.
³⁵³ Lenaerts and Gutiérrez-Fons thus suggested that *Ruiz Zambrano* 'served to emancipate EU citizenship from the constraints inherent in its free movement origins' (K Lenaerts and J Gutiérrez-Fons, 'Epilogue on EU

that residence rights extended to the family members of Union citizens under Article 20 TFEU have 'an *intrinsic connection* with the freedom of movement of a Union citizen'.[354] Thus, as seen in Section 5.1.1 for the Garcia Avello children yet here without the element of dual nationality, the *capacity* of the Ruiz Zambrano children to move in the future is protected by Article 20 TFEU and that provides the necessary connecting factor to EU citizenship law even where the facts are, for now, confined to a single Member State. Such circumstances cannot therefore be 'assimilated' to purely internal situations.[355] However, Article 20 TFEU can be invoked in this way in exceptional circumstances only, as explained further in Chapter 5.

5.2 Ensuring the Effectiveness of Union Citizenship Rights

It is consistently underlined by the Court of Justice that the effectiveness of rights conferred by EU citizenship law must be ensured when Member States exercise their powers, especially (but, as seen in Section 5.1.1, not only) when they are responsible for giving effect to or determining compliance with conditions and limits established in EU legislation.[356] That obligation applies even when Member States enjoy wide discretion.[357] The principle of effectiveness also underpins the idea that provisions of secondary legislation giving effect to primary rights should not be interpreted restrictively,[358] reflecting 'the importance which primary law accords to citizenship of the Union'.[359] However, while provisions of secondary law constituting a derogation *should* be interpreted restrictively, that does not require that they are themselves deprived of effectiveness,[360] since 'an interpretation of a provision of European Union law cannot have the result of depriving the clear and precise wording of that provision of all effectiveness'.[361]

How these principles relate to the EU legislator's power to set conditions and limits on the exercise of the rights conferred by Articles 20 and 21 TFEU was introduced in Sections 3.3.2 and 4.3. Looking across the span of the case law, appeals to the effectiveness of Union citizenship rights are particularly evident in two areas: first, not being penalised for exercising freedom of movement, and second, deriving rights of residence for third-country national family members. On the first point, 'opportunities offered by the Treaty in relation

---

citizenship: hopes and fears' in D Kochenov (ed), *EU Citizenship and Federalism: The Role of Rights* (CUP 2017) 751 at 761).

[354] Case C-40/11 *Iida*, EU:C:2012:691, para 72 (emphasis added); confirmed in eg Case C-165/14 *Rendón Marín*, EU:C:2016:675, para 75.
[355] eg Case C-434/09 *McCarthy*, EU:C:2011:277, para 47; Joined Cases C-356/11 and C-357/11 *O and S*, EU:C:2012:776, para 43; and *Rendón Marín*, para 42.
[356] eg In the context of the 1990s Directives, Case C-424/98 *Commission v Italy*, EU:C:2000:287, paras 34–35; on the 'margin of manoeuvre which the Member States are recognised as having under Directive 2004/38, Case C-140/12 *Brey*, EU:C:2013:237, para 71; on the obligation not to 'impair the effectiveness of EU law' in the exercise of the procedural autonomy retained by Member States under Directive 2004/38, Case C-246/17 *Diallo*, EU:C:2018:499, paras 45–46.
[357] eg Case C-83/11 *Rahman*, EU:C:2012:519, paras 24 and 39; Case C-89/17 *Banger*, EU:C:2018:570, para 40.
[358] eg Case C-50/06 *Commission v Netherlands*, EU:C:2007:325, para 35; Case C-127/08 *Metock and Others*, EU:C:2008:449, paras 82–84 and 93; Case C-162/09 *Lassal*, EU:C:2010:592, paras 31, 35–36, and 51; Case C-244/13 *Ogieriakhi*, EU:C:2014:2068, paras 39–40; Case C-673/16 *Coman*, EU:C:2018:385, para 39.
[359] Case C-249/11 *Byankov*, EU:C:2012:608, para 81. See similarly eg Case C-118/20 *Wiener Landesregierung (Révocation d'une assurance de naturalisation)*, EU:C:2022:34, para 58.
[360] Case C-300/11 *ZZ*, EU:C:2013:363, para 49. Such provisions must also be interpreted in compliance with the Charter of Fundamental Rights (para 50).
[361] Joined Cases C-147/11 and C-148/11 *Czop and Punakova*, EU:C:2012:538, para 32.

to freedom of movement' would not be 'fully effective if a national of a Member State could be deterred from availing himself of them by obstacles raised on his return to his country of origin by legislation penalising the fact that he has used them'.[362] Thus, in such circumstances, the possibility of relying on EU law can sustain even where 'considerable time has elapsed'.[363]

On the second point, the Court has linked the requirement that Union citizens should not be forced to leave the territory of the Union (Section 5.1.2) to the fact that 'a right of residence may not, exceptionally, be refused to a third country national, who is a family member of a Member State national, as the effectiveness of Union citizenship enjoyed by that national would otherwise be undermined'.[364] A relationship of dependency between the Union citizen and the family member(s) concerned is necessary in this context.[365] While the burden of proof must be discharged by the third-country national family member—that is, to 'provide evidence to prove that he or she has a right of residence under Article 20 TFEU, in particular evidence that, if residence were to be refused, the child would be obliged to leave the territory of the European Union'—the Court has also held that 'the competent national authorities must ensure that the application of national legislation on the burden of proof such as that at issue in the disputes in the main proceedings does not undermine the effectiveness of Article 20 TFEU'.[366] In the chapters that follow, the Court's emphasis on ensuring the effectiveness of rights conferred by Union citizenship will be highlighted and assessed through several different examples.

5.3 Union Citizenship and the EU Charter of Fundamental Rights

Article 6(1) TEU establishes that the Charter of Fundamental Rights 'shall have the same legal value as the Treaties' but also that 'the Charter shall not extend in any way the competences of the Union as defined in the Treaties'. Article 6(3) references fundamental rights 'as guaranteed by the European Convention for the Protection of Human Rights and Fundamental Freedoms [ECHR] and as they result from the constitutional traditions common to the Member States', stating that rights drawn from both sources 'shall constitute general principles of the Union's law'. As explained in more detail in subsequent chapters, Article 6 TEU opens up rather than closes down questions about different sources of EU fundamental rights, their interaction with each other,[367] and their interaction with, for present

---

[362] Case C-224/98 *D'Hoop*, EU:C:2002:432, paras 30 and 31. See similarly eg Case C-224/02 *Pusa*, EU:C:2004:273, para 19; Case C-499/06 *Nerkowska*, EU:C:2008:300, para 31; Case C-503/09 *Stewart*, EU:C:2011:500, para 84; and Case C-679/16 *A (Aide pour une personne handicapée)*, EU:C:2018:601, para 61. Claims against a Union citizen's home State where free movement was exercised in the past are resolved outside of (directly, at least) the framework of Directive 2004/38; see further, Chapter 9.

[363] Case C-359/13 *Martens*, EU:C:2015:118, para 32.

[364] Case C-256/11 *Dereci and Others*, EU:C:2011:734, para 67. Confirmed in eg Case C-40/11 *Iida*, EU:C:2012:691, para 71; Joined Cases C-356/11 and C-357/11 *O and S*, EU:C:2012:776, para 48; Case C-165/14 *Rendón Marín*, EU:C:2016:675, para 36; Case C-304/14 *CS*, EU:C:2016:674, para 29; Case C-115/15 *NA*, EU:C:2016:487, para 72; and Case C-165/16 *Lounes*, EU:C:2017:862, para 48. See further, Chapter 5.

[365] eg *O and S*, para 56; *Rendón Marín*, paras 74 and 78; Case C-133/15 *Chavez-Vilchez*, EU:C:2017:354, para 69; and Case C-82/16 *KA and Others*, EU:C:2018:308, paras 52 and 79. See further, Chapter 5.

[366] *Chavez-Vilchez*, para 76. The specific questions that should be examined in this context are outlined in para 77; see further, Chapter 5.

[367] eg On the interaction of EU fundamental rights and the ECHR, see Case C-218/15 *Paoletti*, EU:C:2016:748, para 21: 'Article 52(3) [CFR] provides ... that the rights contained in the Charter which correspond to rights guaranteed by the ECHR are to have the same meaning and scope as those laid down by the ECHR. The latter does not, nonetheless, constitute, as long as the European Union has not acceded to it, a legal instrument which has been formally incorporated into EU law'.

purposes, Union citizenship rights—recalling also that binding legal effect was conferred on the Charter by the Lisbon Treaty.[368] These questions are picked up across several parts of the book but a preliminary distinction is introduced briefly here: Union citizenship rights *as* fundamental rights (Section 5.3.1), and Union citizenship rights *and* fundamental rights (Section 5.3.2).[369]

5.3.1 Citizenship rights as fundamental rights

Article 45(1) CFR protects the right to move and reside freely for Member State nationals, that is, for Union citizens. This provision is just one element of Title V of the Charter, entitled 'Citizens' Rights', where other provisions similarly reflect rights also provided for in the Treaty. For example, Article 39 CFR guarantees the right to vote and to stand as a candidate at elections to the European Parliament, reflecting Article 22(2) TFEU. As discussed further in Chapter 5, some of these rights are in fact conferred on 'every person' (such as Article 41 CFR on the right to good administration) or on 'any natural or legal person having its registered office in a Member State' (such as Article 44 CFR on the right to petition the European Parliament).

Following the lead of its Advocates General,[370] the Court of Justice has amplified references to the right to move and reside freely, in particular, as a fundamental right in recent case law. It typically expresses freedom of movement and residence as a 'primary and individual right' that is 'conferred directly on Union citizens by the Treaty'.[371] But it has also referred to 'the fundamental right of residence of Union citizens in a Member State other than that of which they are a national'.[372] Similarly, the preamble to Directive 2004/38 refers to the 'fundamental and personal right of residence in another Member State [as] conferred directly on Union citizens by the Treaty' (recital 11), and theCourt has referred to the Directive with respect to its objective of 'strengthening the *fundamental* and individual right of all Union citizens'.[373] Another formulation that is sometimes used is also interesting: 'citizenship of the Union confers on each citizen a primary and individual right to move and reside freely within the territory of the Member States, subject to the limitations and restrictions laid down by the Treaty ... and the measures adopted for their implementation, freedom of movement for persons being, moreover, one of the fundamental freedoms of the internal

---

[368] Note also on this point, *Paoletti*, paras 25–26: 'it should be noted that that principle, as enshrined in Article 49(1) of the Charter, is part of primary EU law. Even before the entry into force of the Treaty of Lisbon, which conferred on the Charter the same legal value as the treaties, the Court held that that principle followed from the constitutional traditions common to the Member States and, therefore, had to be regarded as forming part of the general principles of EU law, which national courts must respect when applying national law ... The mere fact that the acts in the main proceedings took place during 2004 and 2005, that is to say before the entry into force of the Treaty of Lisbon on 1 December 2009, therefore does not preclude the application, in the present case, of Article 49(1) of the Charter'.

[369] See generally, C Hilson, 'What's in a right? The relationship between Community, fundamental and citizenship rights in EU law' (2004) 29 European Law Review 636; S Iglesias Sánchez 'Fundamental rights and citizenship of the Union at a crossroads: a promising alliance or a dangerous liaison?' (2014) 20 European Law Journal 464; S O'Leary, 'The relationship between Community citizenship and the protection of fundamental rights in Community law'(1995) 32 Common Market Law Review 519; C Raucea, 'Fundamental rights: the missing pieces of European citizenship?' (2013) 14 German Law Journal 2021; M van den Brink, 'EU citizenship and (fundamental) rights: empirical, normative, and conceptual problems' (2019) 25 European Law Journal 21; and A Yong, *The Rise and Decline of Fundamental Rights in EU Citizenship* (Hart Publishing 2019).

[370] eg AG Cosmas in Case C-378/97 *Wijsenbeek*, EU:C:1999:144, para 95 of the Opinion; and AG Tizzano in Case C-200/02 *Zhu and Chen*, EU:C:2004:307, para 73 of the Opinion.

[371] Case C-127/08 *Metock and Others*, EU:C:2008:449, para 82; confirmed in eg Case C-165/16 *Lounes*, EU:C:2017:862, para 31. The same expression is used in recital 1 of Directive 2004/38.

[372] *Metock and Others*, para 89.

[373] Case C-442/16 *Gusa*, EU:C:2017:1004, para 40 (emphasis added), referring to recitals 3 and 4 of Directive 2004/38.

market, which was also reaffirmed in Article 45 [CFR]'.[374] Here, we see the full amalgam of Treaty rights, primary and secondary law limits, fundamental rights, and fundamental freedoms that need to be mediated in the application of EU citizenship law; rooted to but now progressed significantly beyond its internal market birthplace.

As regards conditions and limits, it might be asked whether restrictions on free movement as a Charter right and on freedom of movement as a Treaty right must be assessed differently. As explained in Section 3, restrictions on the right to move and reside conferred by Article 21 TFEU are generally assessed for compliance with EU law following the approach established for the economic freedoms: is there a Treaty-based derogation (for directly discriminatory restrictions) and/or a public interest argument (for other restrictions) that justifies the restriction of free movement in principle, and is the restriction proportionate to achieving that objective?[375] Rights conferred by Article 21(1) TFEU are also expressly 'subject to the limitations and conditions laid down in the Treaties and by the measures adopted to give them effect'—a phrase that is not replicated in any of the Treaty provisions concerning the free movement of persons for purposes of economic activity.

For rights protected by the Charter, Article 52(1) CFR establishes that '[a]ny limitation on the exercise of the rights and freedoms recognised by this Charter must be provided for by law and respect the essence of those rights and freedoms. Subject to the principle of proportionality, limitations may be made only if they are necessary and genuinely meet objectives of general interest recognised by the Union or the need to protect the rights and freedoms of others'. Article 52(1) might therefore suggest a more intensive evaluation of restrictions of Charter rights compared to restrictions of Treaty rights. However, Article 52(2) CFR must also be considered. It establishes that '[r]ights recognised by this Charter for which provision is made in the Treaties shall be exercised under the conditions and within the limits defined by those Treaties'. The Explanations relating to the Charter[376]—which, according to Article 6(1) TEU, must be given 'due regard' for its interpretation and application—underline the significance of the Treaty for rights conferred by Union citizenship. In particular, the Explanation for Article 45 CFR suggests that the right to move and reside protected by the Charter 'is' the right 'guaranteed by' Articles 20(2)(a) TFEU and 21 TFEU.[377] It thus confirms that '[i]n accordance with Article 52(2) of the Charter', rights protected by Article 45 CFR are 'to be applied under the conditions and within the limits defined by the Treaties'.[378] According to the Explanations, Article 52(2) therefore 'clarifies' that rights to move and resided protected by the Charter remain 'subject to the conditions and limits applicable to the Union law on which they are based, and for which provision is made in the Treaties'. Thus, '[t]he Charter does not alter the system of rights conferred by the EC Treaty and taken over by the [TEU and TFEU]'. In that light, Article 52(2) CFR places some constraint on the idea that protecting citizenship rights *as* fundamental rights in the Charter would, in and of itself, expand the legal reach of the parent Treaty rights. As will now be seen, however, that does not mean that fundamental rights have not expanded the reach of EU citizenship law.

---

[374] Case C-162/09 *Lassal*, EU:C:2010:592, para 29; Case C-434/09 *McCarthy*, EU:C:2011:277, para 27.
[375] eg Case C-55/94 *Gebhard*, EU:C:1995:411, para 37.
[376] 2007 OJ C303/02.
[377] See similarly, on Article 45 TFEU and Article 15(2) CFR, Case C-233/12 *Gardella*, EU:C:2013:449, para 39, with the Court finding that '[c]onsequently... an analysis of Articles 45 TFEU and 48 TFEU is sufficient'.
[378] Strikingly, the Explanation for Article 52(2) CFR concerning rights 'which were already expressly guaranteed in the Treaty establishing the European Community and have been recognised in the Charter' refers 'notably' to 'the rights derived from Union citizenship' as a specific example.

5.3.2 Union citizenship and fundamental rights

Respect for fundamental rights has long been imprinted on EU free movement law and has progressed the substance of the underpinning Treaty rights in significant ways. The rights conferred by Articles 20 and 21 TFEU are therefore infused with an expectation of fundamental rights compliance and 'in particular [with] the right to respect for private and family life as set forth in Article 7 of the Charter ... and Article 8 [ECHR]'.[379] As a general rule, when Member States make or implement decisions that restrict (or potentially restrict) the rights of Union citizens, such measures can be justified only where they are 'consistent with the fundamental rights guaranteed by the Charter'.[380]

Again, though, the general provisions of the Charter must be considered to calibrate expectations about the extent to which fundamental rights can shape or progress the development of EU citizenship law. For present purposes, the key provisions are Article 51(1), which states that while the Charter is addressed to the institutions, bodies, offices, and agencies of the Union, it is addressed to the Member States—where most decisions affecting the rights of Union citizens are actually taken—only when they are 'implementing' EU law, and Article 51(2), which establishes that the Charter 'does not extend the field of application of Union law beyond the powers of the Union or establish any new power or task for the Union, or modify powers and tasks as defined in the Treaties'. Establishing when Member States are 'implementing' EU law connects to determining the scope of EU law,[381] which is not always easy to resolve.[382] For example, in situations that involve clear cross-border movement, the applicability of the Charter is fairly straightforward,[383] as will be seen especially in Chapters 4 and 9 for the rights of family members of Union citizens, and in Chapter 10 with respect to limiting free movement rights in the context of expulsion from a Member State. As discussed in Chapter 7, other factors, such as the nature and purpose of relevant EU legislation, can remove a dispute from the scope of the Charter even where cross-border movement was exercised.[384] At the same time, where freedom of movement has not (yet) been exercised, there has been a remarkable evolution in the Court's approach to the scope of the Charter vis-à-vis Article 20 TFEU.[385]

In a general sense, the Court of Justice has engaged both more widely and more deeply with the Charter since the Lisbon Treaty, and the range of Charter rights being considered in the citizenship case law has also expanded over time. Particular emphasis remains on respect for private and family life and especially for the rights of the child, protected by Articles 7 and 24 CFR. In case law on financial assistance for Union citizens who reside in the host State on the basis of national rather than EU law, the Court has also invoked Article 1 CFR, obliging such States 'to ensure that a Union citizen who has made use of his or her freedom to move and to reside within the territory of the Member States, who has a right of residence on the basis of national law, and who is in a vulnerable situation, may nevertheless live in dignified conditions'.[386] However, the Charter's role in EU citizenship law has not been linear and it

---

[379] Case C-145/09 *Tsakouridis*, EU:C:2010:708, para 52.
[380] Case C-673/16 *Coman*, EU:C:2018:385, para 47.
[381] Case C-617/10 *Åkerberg Fransson*, EU:C:2013:105, paras 17–23.
[382] See generally, M Dougan, 'Judicial review of Member State action under the general principles and the Charter: defining the "scope of Union law"' (2015) 52 Common Market Law Review 1201.
[383] eg Case C-182/15 *Petruhhin*, EU:C:2016:630, paras 31 and 52.
[384] eg Case C-333/13 *Dano*, EU:C:2014:2358, paras 85–91; see further, Chapter 7.
[385] Compare Case C-256/11 *Dereci and Others*, EU:C:2011:734, paras 70–73; Case C-87/12 *Ymeraga*, EU:C:2013:291, paras 40–44; Case C-304/14 *CS*, EU:C:2016:674, paras 34–36; and Case C-133/15 *Chavez-Vilchez*, EU:C:2017:354, paras 68–71. This case law, which is analysed in Chapter 5, also provides an interesting case study on how Advocate General Opinions can influence the findings of the Court over time.
[386] Case C-709/20 *CG*, EU:C:2021:602, para 89.

has not necessarily been comprehensive, especially when the range of rights that *might* be relevant is considered next to the range of rights that the Court has actually invoked. Uneven engagement with ECtHR case law can also be observed.[387] Nevertheless, it will be seen across the chapters that follow that the direction of travel is positive overall: progressive and, ultimately, protective. And even where the Court determines that a situation falls *outside* the scope of EU law, it has signalled the significance of fundamental rights protection generally by reminding the Member States of their commitments under the ECHR.[388]

5.4 The Dual Function of Integration Requirements

If invoking the effectiveness of EU rights tends, generally, to push in the direction of expanding the scope of Union citizenship, setting conditions or requirements relating to integration introduces a counterbalance in some respects. The concept of integration can play two different functions in EU citizenship law. At one level, free movement embodies facilitation of personal choice through the promotion of liberty and the extending of flexibility. In that light, '[t]he concept of moving and residing freely in the territory of the Member States is not based on the hypothesis of a single move from one Member State to another, to be followed by integration into the latter. The intention is rather to allow free, and possibly repeated or even continuous, movement within a single area of freedom, security and justice, in which both cultural diversity and freedom from discrimination are ensured'.[389] In terms of facilitating or promoting movement in that understanding, integration might be conceived more as something to transcend or overcome, claiming protection without any depth of connection. More positively, fostering mobility and equal treatment within a defined space entails a pluralistic version of integration: the requisite connection is not just to any one of the Member States, but to the enabling infrastructure of the Union itself. That idea also builds on the legal significance of the territory of the Union—introduced through the *Ruiz Zambrano* case law in Section 5.1.2 and, through its intersection with the Area of Freedom, Security and Justice, discussed further in Section 6.

However, if a Union citizen does choose to deepen ties with a particular (host) State, the rights conferred by the Treaty aim then to facilitate their integration there in a less transient and more stable understanding: in a way, transferring from the movement limb to the residence limb of the rights protected by Union citizenship and enabling the citizen both to 'create' and 'consolidate' bonds with the society of that State.[390] Thus, in *Lounes*, the Court held that 'the rights conferred on a Union citizen by Article 21(1) TFEU, including the derived rights enjoyed by his family members, are intended, amongst other things, *to promote*

---

[387] eg In the context of restrictions on prisoner voting rights, see H van Eijken and JW van Rossem, 'Prisoner disenfranchisement and the right to vote in elections to the European Parliament: universal suffrage key to unlocking political citizenship?' (2016) 12 European Constitutional Law Review 114 at 128–130; see further, Chapter 5. Finding more alignment in ECtHR and Court of Justice case law on fundamental rights standards in the area of deprivation of nationality, see S O'Leary, 'Nationality and citizenship: integration and rights-based perspectives' in K Lenaerts, J Bonichot, H Kanninen, C Naômé, and P Pohjankosi (eds), *An Ever-Changing Union? Perspectives on the Future of EU Law in Honour of Allan Rosas* (Hart Publishing, 2019) 51 at 59–60; see further, Chapter 3. On citation gaps with respect to ECtHR case law in EU law more generally, see G de Búrca, 'After the EU Charter of Fundamental Rights: the Court of Justice as a human rights adjudicator?' (2013) 20 Maastricht Journal of European and Comparative Law 173.
[388] eg Case C-256/11 *Dereci and Others*, EU:C:2011:734, para 73. See earlier, on the free movement of workers, Case C-109/01 *Akrich*, EU:C:2003:491, para 58.
[389] AG Jacobs in Case C-148/02 *Garcia Avello*, EU:C:2003:311, para 72 of the Opinion.
[390] Case C-22/18 *TopFit and Biffi*, EU:C:2019:497, para 34.

the gradual integration of the Union citizen concerned in the society of the host Member State,³⁹¹ perhaps eventually 'taking 'integration [there] to its logical conclusion' through naturalisation.³⁹²

It is reasonable that citizens must bear some responsibility for the choices that they make. For example, 'the Treaty offers no guarantee to a worker that extending [their] activities into more than one Member State or transferring them to another Member State will be neutral as regards social security' and that 'may be to the worker's advantage in terms of social security or not, according to circumstance'.³⁹³ Moreover, failing to integrate into the society of the host State can have consequences for the right of permanent residence (Chapter 8) and for the level of protection that EU law extends in situations of expulsion (Chapter 10).³⁹⁴ Additionally, as seen in Section 3.4.2, the protection of host State public finances can provide a legitimate defence for restricting equal treatment in certain circumstances.

Integration requirements in both EU law and national law—expressed through conditions (introduced in Section 3.4.1) such as residence requirements, economic activity, economic autonomy, or family relationships—are thus a particular way of articulating and implementing public interest arguments and there has been an interesting shift in terms of the function of integration in EU free movement law. In broad terms, integration was initially mobilised to serve an *inclusionary* purpose—recalling in particular the legislative rights created for family members in host States in the 1960s and 1970s, outlined in Section 2. But it has evolved over time to serve both an inclusionary and also *exclusionary* purpose: in the latter sense, to circumscribe what is preserved only for those who can demonstrate certain kinds of connections to the relevant State.³⁹⁵ Ultimately, integration aims to determine where and the extent to which Union citizens have 'constructed their citizenship'.³⁹⁶ Integration requirements concern, more concretely, the (proportionate) links to a State that a Union citizen can be required to demonstrate before certain protections are granted. As noted in Section 2, integration requirements could thus be argued to capture in a very general sense the fact that Union citizens not only enjoy rights but are also 'subject to the duties provided for in the Treaties' (Article 20 TFEU). Additionally, while integration is normally thought about in EU citizenship law in the context of validating *new(er)* connections and therefore host States, it can also be relevant when a Union citizen has left their home State but seeks later to (re-)establish connections with it through the framework of EU law, whether they actually return there physically or not.³⁹⁷

Specifically for the right to move and reside, integration is constitutive of the legal infrastructure established by Directive 2004/38. To recap from Section 4.3:

---

³⁹¹ Case C-165/16 *Lounes*, EU:C:2017:862, para 56 (emphasis added).
³⁹² AG Bot in Case C-165/16 *Lounes*, EU:C:2017:407, para 85 of the Opinion.
³⁹³ Joined Cases C-393/99 and C-394/99 *Hervein and Hervillie*, EU:C:2002:182, para 51.
³⁹⁴ The system of protection against expulsion established by Directive 2004/28 'is based on the degree of integration of those persons in the host Member State, so that the greater the degree of integration of Union citizens and their family members in the host Member State, the greater the degree of protection against expulsion should be' (Case C-145/09 *Tsakouridis*, EU:C:2010:708, para 25).
³⁹⁵ See generally, S Coutts, 'The absence of integration and the responsibilisation of Union citizenship' (2018) 3 European Papers 771; C O'Brien, 'Real links, abstract rights and false alarms: the relationship between the ECJ's "real link" case law and national solidarity' (2008) 33 European Law Review 643.
³⁹⁶ AG Wathelet in Case C-115/15 *NA*, EU:C:2016:259, para 115 of the Opinion.
³⁹⁷ See generally, Chapter 9. On links retained with the home State after residence has transferred to another State, see eg Case C-503/09 *Stewart*, EU:C:2011:500. On home State processes necessary to facilitate continuing exercise of Union citizenship rights, see eg Case C-490/20 *VMA v Stolichna obshtina, rayon 'Pancharevo'*, EU:C:2021:1008, discussed in Chapter 6.

Directive 2004/38 introduced *a gradual system as regards the right of residence in the host Member State*, which reproduces, in essence, the stages and conditions set out in the various instruments of European Union law and case-law preceding that directive and culminates in the right of permanent residence ... First, for periods of residence of up to three months, Article 6 of Directive 2004/38 limits the conditions and formalities of the right of residence to the requirement to hold a valid identity card or passport and, under Article 14(1) of the directive, that right is retained as long as the Union citizen and his family members do not become an unreasonable burden on the social assistance system of the host Member State ... Secondly, for periods of residence longer than three months, the right of residence is subject to the conditions set out in Article 7(1) of Directive 2004/38 and, under Article 14(2) thereof, that right is retained only if the Union citizen and his family members satisfy those conditions. It is apparent from recital 10 in the preamble to the directive in particular that those conditions are intended, inter alia, to prevent such persons from becoming an unreasonable burden on the social assistance system of the host Member State ... Thirdly, it follows from Article 16(1) of Directive 2004/38 that Union citizens acquire the right of permanent residence after residing legally for a continuous period of five years in the host Member State and that that right is not subject to the conditions referred to in the preceding paragraph. As stated in recital 18 in the preamble to the directive, once obtained, the right of permanent residence should not be subject to any further conditions, with the aim of it being a genuine vehicle for integration into the society of that State[.][398]

However, many integration requirements applied in EU citizenship law come not from the Treaties or from secondary legislation but from the case law of the Court. An example was noted in Section 3.4.2—as expressed in *Collins*, 'it is legitimate for the national legislature to wish to ensure that there is a *genuine link* between an applicant for [a jobseeker's allowance] and the geographic employment market in question'.[399] The Court considered that '[t]he existence of such a link may be determined, in particular, by establishing that the person concerned has, for a reasonable period, in fact genuinely sought work in the Member State in question'.[400] A residence requirement would therefore be, 'in principle, appropriate for the purpose of ensuring such a connection' so long as it is proportionate—more specifically, 'its application by the national authorities must rest on clear criteria known in advance and provision must be made for the possibility of a means of redress of a judicial nature', and the required period of residence 'must not exceed what is necessary in order for the national authorities to be able to satisfy themselves that the person concerned is genuinely seeking work in the employment market of the host Member State'.[401] The Court considers that participating in a host State labour market 'establishes, *in principle*, a sufficient link of integration with the society of that Member State, allowing [workers] to benefit from the principle of equal treatment, as compared with national workers, as regards social advantages'.[402] However, that economic activity might *not* provide a sufficient connection to the host State is further considered in Chapters 6, 7, and 9.

---

[398] Joined Cases C-316/16 and C-424/16 *B and Vomero*, EU:C:2018:256, paras 51–54 (emphasis added).
[399] Case C-138/02 *Collins*, EU:C:2004:172, para 67 (emphasis added).
[400] ibid para 70. Confirmed in eg Joined Cases C-22/08 and C-23/08 *Vatsouras and Koupatantze*, EU:C:2009:344, paras 38–39. See further, Chapter 6.
[401] *Collins*, para 71. However, jobseekers now have limited protection because of Article 24(2) of Directive 2004/38: see further, Chapter 6 and Chapter 7.
[402] Case C-542/09 *Commission v Netherlands*, EU:C:2012:346, para 65 (emphasis added).

In *Bidar*, the logic underpinning the genuine link requirement for jobseekers was transposed to eligibility for student maintenance grants. In line with the principle that Union citizens should not become an *unreasonable* burden in host States,[403] the Court ruled that 'it is thus legitimate for a Member State to grant such assistance only to students who have demonstrated *a certain degree of integration into the society* of that State'.[404] Moreover, a residence condition could evidence the required 'guarantee of *sufficient* integration into the society of the host Member State'.[405] Residence conditions thus constitute 'an expression of the extent to which' Union citizens are connected to the society of the relevant Member State, reflecting an 'aim of solidarity [that] may constitute an objective consideration of public interest'.[406] In *Prete*, the Court effectively merged its link to host State society and link to host State labour market criteria, finding, in the context of a national decision refusing a tideover allowance, that '[t]he existence of close ties, in particular of a personal nature, with the host Member State where the claimant has, following her marriage with a national of that Member State, settled and now habitually resides are such as to contribute to the appearance of *a lasting connection between the claimant and the Member State in which she has newly established herself, including with the labour market of the latter*'.[407]

The Court has also determined that integration has qualitative elements. This dimension of integration was first developed in case law on the right of permanent residence. In *Dias*, the Court confirmed that 'the integration objective which lies behind the acquisition of the right of permanent residence laid down in Article 16(1) of Directive 2004/38 is based not only on territorial and time factors but also on qualitative elements, relating to the level of integration in the host Member State'.[408] In *MG*, that analysis was transposed to the interpretation of Article 28(3) of the Directive, which provides for enhanced protection against expulsion in certain circumstances. The Court confirmed that 'the degree of integration of the persons concerned is *a vital consideration* underpinning both the right of permanent residence and the system of protection against expulsion measures established by Directive 2004/38'.[409] The overall assessment to be undertaken by national authorities must consider 'whether the integrating links previously forged with the host Member State *have been broken*, and thus [determine] whether the enhanced protection provided for in that provision will be granted'.[410] Integration is not, therefore, unidirectional: it can be undone as well as achieved. Conversely, where integration links have been broken, *re*-integration is possible.[411]

Finally, as introduced above, conditions imposing integration requirements will always be subject to proportionality review. In particular, recalling Section 3.4.1, they must not be too general and exclusive.[412] For example, residence conditions linked to the place of application for a benefit or grant have been defeated by the fact that the applicant is a national of

---

[403] See Section 3.4.2.
[404] Case C-209/03 *Bidar*, EU:C:2005:169, para 57 (emphasis added). This case predated the limits placed on eligibility for student maintenance grants by Article 24(2) of Directive 2004/38; see further, Chapter 7.
[405] *Bidar*, para 60 (emphasis added).
[406] Case C-192/05 *Tas-Hagen and Tas*, EU:C:2006:676, paras 34 and 35.
[407] Case C-367/11 *Prete*, EU:C:2012:668, para 50 (emphasis added).
[408] Case C-325/09 *Dias*, EU:C:2011:498, para 64; applied in eg Case C-378/12 *Onuekwere*, EU:C:2014:13, paras 24–26. See further, Chapter 8.
[409] Case C-400/12 *MG*, EU:C:2014:9, para 32 (emphasis added). See further, Chapter 10.
[410] ibid para 36 (emphasis added).
[411] Joined Cases C-316/16 and C-424/16 *B and Vomero*, EU:C:2018:256, esp paras 70–75; see further, AG Bot in Case C-247/17 *Raugevicius*, EU:C:2018:616, esp paras 62–72 of the Opinion.
[412] eg Joined Cases C-11/06 and C-12/06 *Morgan and Bucher*, EU:C:2007:626, para 46; and Case C-75/11 *Commission v Austria*, EU:C:2012:605, para 62. For an example of a Member State successfully demonstrating that the applicable conditions 'are interpreted widely, so that other connecting factors allow a sufficiently close connection to [Member State] society to be established', see Case C-103/08 *Gottwald*, EU:C:2009:597, paras 38–39.

the competent State.⁴¹³ National authorities are arguably required to take nationality into account only as part of an overall assessment: in other words, nationality will not necessarily be a determinative criterion in isolation and establishing the *sufficiency* of the claimant's integration with the competent State remains the central objective.⁴¹⁴ However, Advocate General Sharpston has suggested that 'nationality is, as the Court put it in *Rottman*, a "special relationship of solidarity and good faith" which together with "the reciprocity of rights and duties ... form[s] the bedrock of the bond of nationality"' and that it is therefore 'difficult to conceive that that is a connection that can be entirely disregarded when assessing the proportionality of the measures that a Member State adopts to achieve the integration objective'.⁴¹⁵ Acquiring the nationality of the host State is thus deemed to represent a Union citizen's intention 'to become permanently integrated in that State'.⁴¹⁶

5.5 Union Citizenship and Matters Reserved to Member State Competence

In his joint Opinion for *Rendón Marín* and *CS*, Advocate General Szpunar observed that 'it is precisely when they are exercising their powers that the Member States must take care to ensure that EU law is not deprived of its effectiveness'.⁴¹⁷ Thus while significant powers remain within national competence, EU citizenship law constricts the regulatory freedom that Member States retain when actually exercising them.⁴¹⁸ Put another way, 'if the situation comes within the scope of [Union] law, the exercise by the Member States of their retained powers *cannot be discretionary*. It is subject to the obligation to comply with [Union] rules'.⁴¹⁹ Only if the situation has no factor connecting it to EU law, as explained in Section 4.1, will review of a Member State's compliance with EU rules not be relevant.⁴²⁰

This approach is traceable, once again, to case law on the economic freedoms, where it was recognised that while the Member States retain power to establish rules in fields such as direct taxation⁴²¹ or the determination of nationality,⁴²² they must still respect the requirements of EU law in the exercise of their powers. For example, *Garcia Avello* was discussed in Section 5.1.1 in connection with the threshold of 'serious inconvenience' for restrictions of free movement rights, but it also illustrates the relevance of EU citizenship law in a policy

---

⁴¹³ eg Case C-499/06 *Nerkowska*, EU:C:2008:300, paras 41–43.
⁴¹⁴ eg Joined Cases C-523/11 and C-585/11 *Prinz and Seeberger*, EU:C:2013:524, para 38: 'a sole condition of residence ... risks ... excluding from funding students who, despite not having resided for an uninterrupted period of three years in Germany immediately prior to studying abroad, are nevertheless sufficiently connected to German society. That may be the case where the student is a national of the State concerned *and* was educated there for a significant period or on account of other factors such as, in particular, his family, employment, language skills or the existence of other social and economic factors' (emphasis added).
⁴¹⁵ AG Sharpston in Joined Cases C-523/11 and C-585/11 *Prinz and Seeberger*, EU:C:2013:90, para 98 of the Opinion, citing Case C-135/08 *Rottmann*, EU:C:2010:104, para 51.
⁴¹⁶ Case C-165/16 *Lounes*, EU:C:2017:862, para 57. See further, Chapter 5.
⁴¹⁷ AG Szpunar in Case C-165/14 *Rendón Marín* and Case C-304/14 *CS*, EU:C:2016:75, para 113 of the joint Opinion.
⁴¹⁸ See generally, B de Witte, 'Exclusive Member State competences – is there such a thing?' in S Garben and I Govaere (eds), *The Division of Competences between the EU and the Member States: Reflections on the Past, the Present and the Future* (Hart Publishing 2017) 59.
⁴¹⁹ AG Poiares Maduro in Case C-135/08 *Rottmann*, EU:C:2009:588, para 20 of the Opinion (emphasis added).
⁴²⁰ eg Case C-353/06 *Grunkin and Paul*, EU:C:2008:559, para 16 ('unless what is involved is an internal situation which has no link with [Union] law').
⁴²¹ eg Case C-279/93 *Schumacker*, EU:C:1995:31, para 21.
⁴²² eg Case C-369/90 *Micheletti*, EU:C:1992:295, para 10.

area reserved to the Member States. The Court underlined that '[a]lthough, as Union law stands at present, the rules governing a person's surname are matters coming within the competence of the Member States, the latter must none the less, when exercising that competence, comply with [Union] law … in particular the Treaty provisions on the freedom of every citizen of the Union to move and reside in the territory of the Member States'.[423] This obligation both ensures equal treatment and extends beyond non-discrimination. It has been applied at the intersection of Union citizenship and national powers across an extensive span of policy areas, including enforcement for the recovery of debts,[424] direct taxation,[425] benefits compensating civilian war victims,[426] prohibitions on the use of titles of nobility,[427] the organisation of social security schemes,[428] and rules establishing the definition of marriage.[429] Having regard to the longstanding emphasis placed on free movement for the purposes of education,[430] the delimiting of national discretion by EU citizenship law is particularly evident in case law on the exercise and supervision of Member State competence in this field.[431] Perhaps most fundamentally, though, it epitomises the Court's case law on the determination of Member State nationality.[432] Many of these examples surface briefly again in different chapters of the book, but the role of EU citizenship law in assessing Member State processes that determine the acquisition and loss of nationality is assessed in detail in Chapter 5.

6. The Territory of the Union: Integrating Law, Place, and Values

EU rights are normally invoked to protect a Union citizen or, indirectly, their family members: that is, to protect *someone*. But EU citizenship law also protects *something*. The integration requirements introduced in Section 5.4 configure a significant relationship between place—understood as a Member State—and citizen through both temporal and qualitative factors. In this part of the chapter, manyquestions and themes already examined come together through the fact that Union citizenship also generates legal connections between the citizen and another place: the territory of the Union.[433]

A protected Union citizenship place manifests most directly in the *Ruiz Zambrano* case law (returned to in Chapter 5), where protection against forced departure from the territory

---

[423] Case C-148/02 *Garcia Avello*, EU:C:2003:539, para 25.
[424] eg Case C-224/02 *Pusa*, EU:C:2004:273, para 22.
[425] eg Case C-403/03 *Schempp*, EU:C:2005:446, para 11.
[426] eg Case C-192/05 *Tas-Hagen and Tas*, EU:C:2006:676, paras 21–22.
[427] eg Case C-208/09 *Sayn-Wittgenstein*, EU:C:2010:806, para 38.
[428] eg Case C-75/11 *Commission v Austria*, EU:C:2012:605, paras 76–77.
[429] eg Case C-673/16 *Coman*, EU:C:2018:385, paras 37–38. The same approach can be seen in *Delvigne* on the definition of beneficiaries of the right to vote in European Parliament elections, though that case was resolved on the basis of Article 14(3) TEU (Case C-650/13 *Delvigne*, EU:C:2015:648, paras 30–33; see further, Chapter 5).
[430] eg Case C-224/98 *D'Hoop*, EU:C:2002:432, para 32; Case C-359/13 *Martens*, EU:C:2015:118, para 27; Case C-679/16 *A (Aide pour une personne handicapée)*, EU:C:2018:601, para 62. Students are also distinguished as regards the conditions for lawful residence in Article 7 of Directive 2004/38; see further, Chapter 7.
[431] eg '[A]s regards the content of teaching and the organisation of their respective education systems', see Joined Cases C-11/06 and C-12/06 *Morgan and Bucher*, EU:C:2007:626, para 24; Joined Cases C-523/11 and C-585/11 *Prinz and Seeberger*, EU:C:2013:524, para 26; Case C-220/12 *Thiele Meneses*, EU:C:2013:683, para 21; Case C-275/12 *Elrick*, EU:C:2013:684, para 21; Case C-359/13 *Martens*, EU:C:2015:118, para 23; and Case C-679/16 *A (Aide pour une personne handicapée)*, EU:C:2018:601, para 58.
[432] See esp Case C-135/08 *Rottmann*, EU:C:2010:104.
[433] See generally, L Azoulai, 'Transfiguring European citizenship: from Member State territory to Union territory' in D Kochenov (ed), *EU Citizenship and Federalism: The Role of Rights* (CUP 2017) 178.

of the Union brings into focus not only the capacity of the Union citizen to move and reside freely but also the territory of the Union itself. In this understanding, EU citizenship law constructs a protective shield around the place in which the rights that it confers can be realised. This conception of Union citizenship is also evident in case law on the extradition of Union citizens to third states. In that context, it connects to Article 3(2) TEU, which requires the Union to 'offer its citizens an area of freedom, security and justice [AFSJ] without internal frontiers, in which the free movement of persons is ensured in conjunction with appropriate measures with respect to external border controls, asylum, immigration and the prevention and combating of crime'. Advocate General Bobek has suggested that 'the noble dream of an area without internal frontiers can hardly be construed in a one-sided manner, whereby openness mandated from above is not accompanied by a correlating degree of responsibility and liability', since '[i]t cannot be overlooked that an increase in the free movement of persons inevitably produces certain negative externalities or, to put it differently, has a social cost'.[434] However, even in such circumstances and as explained further below, Union citizenship contributes mechanisms of protection for Member State nationals, especially when the alternative would require their extradition to third states.

The territory of the European Union essentially consists of the territories of its Member States. Article 52(1) TEU provides that the Treaties 'shall apply' to these States,[435] and the Court considers that 'EU territory corresponds to the geographical space referred to in Article 52 TEU and Article 355 TFEU which define the territorial scope of the Treaties'.[436] However, the Union's *physical* and *legal* territories do not always overlap. For example, Article 63(2) TFEU establishes that 'all restrictions on payments between Member States *and between Member States and third countries* shall be prohibited'. Additionally, the regulatory reach of the AFSJ extends beyond the physical territory of the Union in some respects, on the one hand, but can also apply in fewer than the 27 Member States, on the other. The complex geography of the Schengen Area provides a good example of both of these points: Iceland, Liechtenstein, Norway, and Switzerland are associate members; Ireland has opt-outs; Bulgaria, Croatia, Cyprus, and Romania have not yet joined.[437] Thus, while the AFSJ is a proxy for Union territory at one level, its objectives with respect to both internal and external borders[438] suggest a more composite understanding of Union territory too: something (legally) tangible beyond 27 Member State territorial units.[439] The *Boukhalfa* case provides an early intimation of what that might entail. It concerned the free movement of workers, but Advocate General Léger also reflected on the then recently created status of

---

[434] AG Bobek in Case C-129/19 *BV*, EU:C:2020:375, para 113 of the Opinion.

[435] Article 52(2) indicates that the 'territorial scope of the Treaties is specified in Article 355 [TFEU]', which concerns the extent to which the Treaties do (and do not) apply to the overseas countries and territories of the Member States.

[436] Case C-17/16 *El Dakkak and Intercontinental*, EU:C:2017:341, para 22.

[437] See further, Protocol No 19 on the integration of the Schengen *acquis*. With respect to the AFSJ more generally, see Protocol No 21 on the position of the UK and Ireland and Protocol No 22 on the position of Denmark. The intersection of Union citizenship and Schengen is also relevant in Chapter 10.

[438] See esp Article 67(2) TFEU, which establishes that the Union 'shall ensure the absence of internal border controls for persons and shall frame a common policy on asylum, immigration and external border control, based on solidarity between Member States, which is fair towards third-country nationals. For the purpose of this Title, stateless persons shall be treated as third-country nationals'. More thematic objectives—including respect for fundamental rights (Article 67(1)) and 'ensur[ing] a high level of security through measures to prevent and combat crime, racism and xenophobia' (Article 67(3))—cut across the internal and external strands of the AFSJ.

[439] Economic and social cohesion provides another example; see eg AG Sharpston in Case C-436/15 *Alytaus regiono atliekų tvarkymo centras*, EU:C:2017:33, fn 3 of the Opinion: 'EU policy on economic and social cohesion aims in particular to reduce disparities between the levels of development across the territory of the European Union and to address "the backwardness of the least favoured regions" [Article 174 TFEU]'.

Union citizenship. In particular, he considered that through the obligation 'to treat the nationals of all the Member States in the same way as those of the State concerned', the Treaty's free movement provisions 'meet the more general aim of promoting *a feeling of belonging to a common entity* enshrined in the frequently used phrase "people's Europe"', asking, conversely, what 'the effects of such a feeling of belonging or such citizenship [would be] if they disappeared once the geographical borders of the Union were crossed'.[440]

Advocate General Léger's reflection captures the impulse both to secure protection of Union citizens within the territory of the Union and to insinuate a role for EU law where situations affecting them materialise beyond it. In the Treaty provisions establishing Union citizenship, explicit references to 'territory' mainly concern the right to move and reside freely within the territory *of the Member States* (Articles 20(2) and 21(1) TFEU). There is also an *extraterritorial* dimension in the guarantee of diplomatic or consular protection in a third state (Article 23 TFEU).[441] Additionally, establish[ing] 'the procedures and conditions required for a citizens' initiative within the meaning of Article 11 [TEU]'[442] in accordance with Article 24 TFEU reflects not a national or supranational but a *transnational* understanding of Union territory through required validity thresholds.[443]

The extraterritorial and transnational aspects of Union citizenship thus began to suggest legal significance for the Union's territory although it did not feature often in the citizenship case law, with the significant exception of *Ruiz Zambrano* as noted above and examined further in Chapter 5. However, examples are also provided by *McCarthy II* and *Coman*. In the former case, the Court held that 'pursuant to Article 5 of Directive 2004/38, a person who is a family member of a Union citizen ... is not subject to the requirement to obtain a visa or an equivalent requirement in order to be able to enter the territory of that Union citizen's Member State of origin'.[444] Instead, 'the Member States are, in principle, required to recognise a residence card issued under Article 10 of Directive 2004/38, for the purposes of entry into their territory without a visa'.[445] That decision transforms entry to the territory of a Member State into entry to the territory of the Union.[446] Reflecting the vision of a 'right to enjoy *the community of values anywhere within the European Union*, regardless of territory [and allowing] people to live, at least partially, in material, social and moral conditions which reflect

---

[440] AG Léger in Case C-214/94 *Boukhalfa*, EU:C:1995:381, para 31 of the Opinion (emphasis added).

[441] See Directive 2015/637/EU on the coordination and cooperation measures to facilitate consular protection for unrepresented citizens of the Union in third countries, 2015 OJ L106/1. See further, Chapter 5.

[442] Article 11(4) TEU provides: '[n]ot less than one million citizens who are nationals of a significant number of Member States may take the initiative of inviting the European Commission, within the framework of its powers, to submit any appropriate proposal on matters where citizens consider that a legal act of the Union is required for the purpose of implementing the Treaties. The procedures and conditions required for such a citizens' initiative shall be determined in accordance with the first paragraph of Article 24 [TFEU]'.

[443] Regulation 2019/788/EU on the European citizens' initiative, 2019 OJ L 130/55; see esp Article 3 on the minimum number of signatories per Member State, explained in recital 9 on the premise of 'ensur[ing] that an initiative is representative of a Union interest'. See further, Chapter 5; and see generally, Coutts, 'The shifting geometry of Union citizenship' (n 94).

[444] Case C-202/13 *McCarthy II*, EU:C:2014:2450, paras 41–42. In *Akrich*, the Court had ruled that 'the national of a non-Member State, who is the spouse of a citizen of the Union, must be lawfully resident in a Member State when he moves to another Member State to which the citizen of the Union is migrating or has migrated' (Case C-109/01, EU:C:2003:491, para 50). It 'reconsidered' that approach in Case C-127/08 *Metock and Others*, EU:C:2008:449, on the basis that no such requirement was added to Directive 2004/38, which had been adopted in the period between *Akrich* and *Metock*. See further, Chapters 3 (family members) and 6 (the right to reside).

[445] *McCarthy II*, para 62.

[446] Underlined by the Court's observation in *Akrich* that Regulation 1612/68 was 'silent as to the rights of a national of a non-Member State, who is the spouse of a citizen of the Union, in regard to access to the territory of the [Union]' (Case C-109/01 *Akrich*, EU:C:2003:491, para 49).

a wide-reaching European society',[447] the Court in *Coman* attributed Union-wide meaning to the concept of 'spouse' for the purposes of Directive 2004/38 and determined that 'Article 21(1) TFEU must be interpreted as precluding the competent authorities of the Member State of which the Union citizen is a national from refusing to grant that third-country national a right of residence in the territory of that Member State on the ground that the law of that Member State does not recognise marriage between persons of the same sex'.[448] The facts concerned a right to reside in one Member State but the idea of the Union as a legal territory had to be engaged to achieve it, as explained further in Chapters 3 and 9: in essence, a spousal relationship created during the exercise of free movement rights had to be protected in the Union citizen's home State when he returned there, overriding the narrower scope of that State's regulation of marriage.

However, as indicated above and alongside *Ruiz Zambrano*, the most significant development of Union territory as a protective legal space is seen in case law on the extradition of Union citizens to third states. The Court had previously considered the applicability of Article 18 TFEU in the context of refusing surrender for the purposes of executing European arrest warrants, which in the Netherlands, for the nationals of other Member States, was subject to a condition of lawful residence for a continuous period of five years (found ultimately to be a proportionate integration condition).[449] The fundamental difference between surrender based on extradition and surrender based on a European arrest warrant (EAW) is that the underpinning systems are external and internal to the Union respectively.[450] In particular, the EAW system 'has as its basis the high level of trust which must exist between the Member States'.[451] The existence of mutual trust is 'based on the fundamental premiss that each Member State shares with all the other Member States, and recognises that they share with it, a set of common values on which the European Union is founded, as stated in Article 2 TEU'.[452]

In one line of EAW case law, Union citizenship was engaged to enable the refusal of extradition requests issued by third states in certain circumstances and thereby the protection of Union citizens within the territory of the Union where possible. *Petruhhin* concerned an extradition request from Russia received by Latvian authorities shortly after Mr Petruhhin—an Estonian national—was arrested in Latvia. The request indicated that he was accused of attempted drug-trafficking. His extradition to Russia was authorised by the Latvian Public Prosecutor's Office but he appealed, arguing that he should be entitled to the same protection against extradition to Russia that Latvian nationals enjoy under national law as well as under a bilateral agreement with the Russian Federation. On the basis that, under national law, only Latvian nationals who committed a criminal offence in a third country could be prosecuted for that offence in Latvia, Advocate General Bot argued that the applicant was not in a comparable situation with Latvian nationals for the purposes of Article 18

---

[447] Azoulai, 'Transfiguring European citizenship' (n433) 180 (emphasis added). See similarly, C Raucea, 'European citizenship and the right to reside: "no one on the outside has a right to be inside?" ' (2016) 22 European Law Journal 470. For a different view, G Davies, 'European Union citizenship and the sorting of Europe' (2021) 43 Journal of European Integration 49.
[448] Case C-673/16 *Coman*, EU:C:2018:385, para 51.
[449] Case C-123/08 *Wolzenburg*, EU:C:2009:616, para 73. Framework Decision 2002/584/JHA on the European arrest warrant and the surrender procedures between Member States, 2002 OJ L190/1.
[450] eg Case C-216/18 PPU *LM*, EU:C:2018:586, para 39.
[451] ibid para 40.
[452] ibid para 35. On mutual trust and the EAW, as determined by the Court, see eg K Lenaerts, '*La vie apres l'avis*: exploring the principle of mutual (yet not blind) trust' (2017) 54 Common Market Law Review 805; and L Mancano, 'Judicial harmonisation through autonomous concepts of European Union law: the example of the European Arrest Warrant Framework Decision' (2018) 43 European Law Review 69.

TFEU.⁴⁵³ In its judgment, the Court took a radically different approach. It first acknowledged that 'in the absence of an international agreement between the European Union and the third country concerned, the rules on extradition fall within the competence of the Member States'.⁴⁵⁴ But it then invoked the principle considered in Section 5.1.2 : 'in situations covered by EU law, the national rules concerned must have due regard to the latter'.⁴⁵⁵

The Court recalled that since Mr Petruhhin had moved to Latvia, 'the situation at issue in the main proceedings falls within the scope of application of the Treaties, within the meaning of Article 18 TFEU'.⁴⁵⁶ However, instead of then engaging in the comparability analysis required by equal treatment law, the Court observed that 'the unequal treatment which allows the extradition of a Union citizen who is a national of another Member State, such as Mr Petruhhin, gives rise to a restriction of freedom of movement, within the meaning of Article 21 TFEU'.⁴⁵⁷ Thus, it drew from Article 21 TFEU in two different ways: first, because Mr Petruhhin 'made use' of freedom of movement thereby triggering 'the scope of application of the Treaties, within the meaning of Article 18 TFEU'; and second, because his extradition would generate unequal treatment that 'gives rise to a restriction of freedom of movement within the meaning of Article 21 TFEU'.⁴⁵⁸ As a justification for that restriction, the Court accepted in principle that '[t]he objective of preventing the risk of impunity for persons who have committed an offence ... must be considered a legitimate objective in EU law'.⁴⁵⁹ Considering proportionality, the Court observed that while 'the non-extradition of its own nationals is generally counterbalanced by the possibility for the requested Member State to prosecute such nationals for serious offences committed outside its territory, that Member State as a general rule has no jurisdiction to try cases concerning such acts when neither the perpetrator nor the victim of the alleged offence is a national of that Member State'; in that light, '[e]xtradition thus allows offences committed in the territory of a State by persons who have fled that territory not to remain unpunished'.⁴⁶⁰

National rules allowing extradition to a third State are therefore appropriate, in principle, relative to the public interest of preventing impunity. However, in then considering 'whether there is an alternative measure less prejudicial to the exercise of the rights conferred by Article 21 TFEU which would be equally effective in achieving the objective of preventing [that risk]',⁴⁶¹ the Court animated the protective qualities of the territory of the Union, underpinned by the requirement of sincere cooperation in Article 4(3) TEU and by the responsibility of the Union 'in its relations with the wider world ... to uphold and promote its values and interests *and contribute to the protection of its citizens*, in accordance with Article 3(5) TEU'.⁴⁶² More specifically, the Court held that 'it is necessary, in order to safeguard EU nationals from measures liable to deprive them of the rights of free movement and

---

⁴⁵³ AG Bot in Case C-182/15 *Petruhhin*, EU:C:2016:330, esp paras 64–69 of the Opinion. However, he did consider that '[s]ince the situation of a national of a Member State who, like Mr Petruhhin, has exercised his freedom to move and reside in the territory of another Member State, falls ... within the scope of EU law ... Article 19(2) of the Charter may apply in such a situation' (para 75 of the Opinion, referring to Joined Cases C-404/15 and C-659/15 PPU *Aranyosi and Căldăraru*, EU:C:2016:198, para 94).
⁴⁵⁴ Case C-182/15 *Petruhhin*, EU:C:2016:630, para 26.
⁴⁵⁵ ibid para 27.
⁴⁵⁶ ibid para 31.
⁴⁵⁷ ibid para 33.
⁴⁵⁸ However, the Court did not assess if Mr Petruhhin's residence in Latvia was lawful within the meaning of Directive 2004/38: see further, Chapter 7.
⁴⁵⁹ *Petruhhin*, paras 34 and 37.
⁴⁶⁰ ibid para 39.
⁴⁶¹ ibid para 41. Challenging that assessment, see M Böse, 'Mutual recognition, extradition to third countries and Union Citizenship: *Petruhhin*' (2017) 54 Common Market Law Review 1781 at 1791.
⁴⁶² *Petruhhin*, para 44 (emphasis added).

residence provided for in Article 21 TFEU, while combatting impunity in respect of criminal offences, to apply all the cooperation and mutual assistance mechanisms provided for in the criminal field under EU law'.[463] In practical terms, this requires that 'the exchange of information with the Member State of which the person concerned is a national must be given priority in order to afford the authorities of that Member State, in so far as they have jurisdiction, pursuant to their national law, to prosecute that person for offences committed outside national territory, the opportunity to issue a European arrest warrant for the purposes of prosecution'.[464] By 'cooperating accordingly with the Member State of which the person concerned is a national *and giving priority to that potential arrest warrant over the extradition request*, the host Member State acts in a manner which is less prejudicial to the exercise of the right to freedom of movement while avoiding, as far as possible, the risk that the offence prosecuted will remain unpunished'.[465]

The Court did not formally undermine the extradition framework governed by international law, but it did invent a Union-specific workaround to protect the Union citizen within the territory of the Union to the extent possible. As in *Ruiz Zambrano*, the objective of not depriving a Union citizen of free movement and residence rights was the explanation provided, though here using Article 21 TFEU rather than Article 20 TFEU since a cross-border connection was already established. By intervening in how—and where—the criminal behaviour of Union citizens should be dealt with, the Court privileged the territory of the Union as the place *of* and *for* Union citizens.[466] Crucially, the Court cannot guarantee that the Union citizen's protection can be contained there: by engaging the Member States as the enforcers of EU law, it can only impose an obligation that they *seek* that outcome. The territory of the Union is thus safeguarded by cooperative mechanisms, demonstrating that, in accordance with the principle of sincere cooperation, the Union and the Member States 'are, in full mutual respect, to assist each other in carrying out tasks which flow from the Treaties'.[467] The result exemplifies the *additional* character of Union citizenship referred to in Article 20 TFEU as well as the additional protection offered by the territory of the Union over and above the territories of its Member States.[468]

In *Pisciotti*, the Court confirmed that *Petruhhin* applies even where the EU does have an extradition agreement with the relevant third State. Mr Pisciotti, an Italian national, was arrested on a stopover at Frankfurt Airport (as he travelled to Italy from Nigeria) pursuant to a US extradition request in connection with anticompetitive practices. In this case, his extradition had already taken place, he was convicted, and he served a prison sentence in the United States. Following his release, he initiated legal proceedings against Germany to establish liability for breach of EU law in connection with allowing his extradition in the first place. The Court stated that '[t]he fact that, when [Mr Pisciotti] was arrested, he was only in transit in Germany is not capable of casting doubt' on the fact that his situation falls

---

[463] ibid para 47.
[464] ibid para 48.
[465] ibid para 49 (emphasis added).
[466] As Coutts puts it, the Court makes 'a statement concerning the "right place" for such individuals. Citizenship can be viewed as an institution that emplaces individuals within particular territories and legal orders, which designates the right place for an individual in a normative and geographic sense' (S Coutts 'From Union citizens to national subjects: *Pisciotti*' (2019) 56 Common Market Law Review 521 at 539).
[467] Case C-182/15 *Petruhhin*, EU:C:2016:630, para 42.
[468] Lenaerts and Gutiérrez-Fons express this point through the observation that 'EU citizenship is intended to promote the feeling of *belonging to a community of values that stands up for all its citizens* when they cross the external borders of the EU' (K Lenaerts and J Gutiérrez-Fons, 'Epilogue on EU citizenship: hopes and fears' in D Kochenov (ed), *EU Citizenship and Federalism: The Role of Rights* (CUP 2017) 751 at 763 (emphasis added).

within the scope of the Treaties.⁴⁶⁹ It then found that while, '[i]n principle, Article 17 of the EU–USA Agreement ... allows a Member State, on the basis either of the provisions of a bilateral treaty or rules of its constitutional law, to provide for a particular outcome for its own nationals by prohibiting their extradition ... that discretion must still be exercised in accordance with primary law and, in particular, with the rules of the TFEU on equal treatment and the freedom of movement of Union citizens'.⁴⁷⁰

Again sidestepping the comparability of German nationals and other Member State nationals under EU equal treatment law, the Court asserted that '*the only question* is whether the Federal Republic of Germany could adopt a course of action with regard to Mr Pisciotti which would be less prejudicial to the exercise of his right to free movement by considering surrendering him to the Italian Republic rather than extraditing him to the United States of America'.⁴⁷¹ Referring to *Petruhhin*, it reiterated that 'the exchange of information with the Member State of which the person concerned is a national must be given priority in order, where relevant, to afford the authorities of that Member State the opportunity to issue a European arrest warrant for the purposes of prosecution'; acknowledging that while 'that solution was adopted ... in a context characterised by the absence of an international agreement on extradition between the European Union and the third State in question, it may be applied in a situation such as that at issue ..., in which the EU–USA Agreement gives the requested Member State the option of not extraditing its own nationals'.⁴⁷² Responding to concerns from some Member States that prioritising a request for surrender on the basis of an EAW could undermine the effectiveness of the EU–USA Agreement, the Court assured that 'a European arrest warrant issued by a Member State other than the requested Member State must, at least, relate to the same offences and ... the issuing Member State must have jurisdiction, pursuant to national law, to prosecute that person for such offences, even if committed outside its territory'.⁴⁷³

Finally, the Court noted that the 'the consular authorities of the Italian Republic were kept informed of Mr Pisciotti's situation before the request for extradition ... was granted and that the Italian judicial authorities did not issue a European arrest warrant in respect of Mr Pisciotti'.⁴⁷⁴ It then softened aspects of *Petruhhin* around that point:

Articles 18 and 21 TFEU must be interpreted as *not precluding* the requested Member State from drawing a distinction, on the basis of a rule of constitutional law, between its nationals and the nationals of other Member States and from granting that extradition whilst not permitting extradition of its own nationals, *provided that the requested Member State has already put the competent authorities of the Member State of which the citizen is a national in a position to seek the surrender of that citizen* pursuant to a European arrest warrant *and the latter Member State has not taken any action in that regard.*⁴⁷⁵

It has therefore been argued that 'the precise obligation imposed on the Member State of nationality to investigate the possibility of prosecution appears minimal' and that '[w]e are left

---

⁴⁶⁹ Case C-191/16 *Pisciotti*, EU:C:2018:222, para 34.
⁴⁷⁰ ibid paras 41–42.
⁴⁷¹ ibid para 50 (emphasis added).
⁴⁷² ibid paras 51–52.
⁴⁷³ ibid para 54; referring to *Petruhhin*, para 50.
⁴⁷⁴ *Pisciotti*, para 55.
⁴⁷⁵ ibid para 56 (emphasis added).

not so much with a right of the Union citizen to remain on the territory of the Union, but a right of the Member State of nationality to assert its jurisdiction'.[476]

Clues about what may have provoked the backtracking in *Pisciotti* can be found in the Opinion of Advocate General Bot, who noted that 'several Member States which have submitted observations in these proceedings have emphasised the legal and practical difficulties associated with the approach adopted by the Court in [*Petruhhin*]'.[477] Particular concern was raised about the fact that, 'in most cases, the Member State of which the Union citizen forming the subject of an extradition request is a national is unlikely to be in possession of the information that would enable it to issue a European arrest warrant with a view to prosecution and then to prosecute the person surrendered. In that event, the objective of preventing the risk of impunity would be jeopardised'.[478] Thus the Court preserved the *Petruhhin* obligation of cooperation on the surface of *Pisciotti*, but significantly diluted its impact in practice. In that case, Mr Pisciotti's removal from the territory of the Union was absolved in retrospect, and the concerns of certain Member States about the challenges of applying *Petruhhin* in practice were taken seriously. In *BY*, these challenges were again raised by the referring (German) court,[479] which asked whether, first, 'the home Member State that has been informed of an extradition request obliged, on the basis of [*Petruhhin*], [should] request that the case files be sent to it by the requesting third State for the purpose of assessing the possibility of itself undertaking a prosecution', and second, whether a Member State requested by a third State to extradite a Union citizen is obliged, also on the basis of *Petruhhin*, to 'refuse extradition and to undertake a criminal prosecution itself, if it is possible for it to do so under its national law'.[480]

On the first question, confirming the obligation of mutual assistance that flows from the principle of sincere cooperation under Article 4(3) TEU, 'it is incumbent on the requested Member State to inform the competent authorities of the Member State of which the requested person is a national not only of the existence of an extradition request concerning that person, but also of all the matters of fact and law communicated by the third State requesting extradition in the context of that extradition request, though those authorities are bound to respect the confidentiality of such matters where confidentiality has been sought by that third State, that State being kept duly informed on that point'.[481] However, acknowledging lack of legal basis as well as potential logistical complexities and delays, 'neither the requested Member State nor the Member State of which the requested person is a national can be obliged, under EU law, to make an application to the third State that is requesting extradition for the transmission of the criminal investigation file'.[482] Moreover, balancing the requirement to cooperate with the citizen's home State with not causing undue delay for the extradition procedure, 'it is for the requested Member State, in the interests of legal certainty, to set, for the Member State of which the requested person is a national, a reasonable

---

[476] Coutts, 'From Union citizens to national subjects' (n 466) 523.
[477] AG Bot in Case C-191/16 *Pisciotti*, EU:C:2017:878, para 51 of the Opinion.
[478] ibid.
[479] And outlined in some detail by AG Hogan, who invited the Court to reconsider *Petruhhin* in terms of both the comparability dimension of EU equal treatment law and practical difficulties for Member States trying to apply it in practice (AG Hogan in Case C-398/19 *BY*, EU:C:2020:748, paras 42–66 of the Opinion).
[480] Case C-398/19 *BY*, EU:C:2020:1032, para 21.
[481] ibid para 48.
[482] ibid para 49; see also, paras 50–52, confirming that 'any decision by the Member State of which the requested person is a national to ask the third State requesting extradition to send the criminal investigation file, to permit an assessment of the appropriateness of any prosecution, is a matter that is within the discretion of that Member State, as an element of its sovereignty in criminal matters, and in accordance with the rules of its national law' (para 52).

time limit on the expiry of which, if the latter Member State has not issued a European arrest warrant, the extradition of that person will, if appropriate, be carried out', the Court also noting that '[s]uch a time limit must be set taking account of all the circumstances of the case, including whether that person may be in custody on the basis of the extradition procedure and the complexity of the case'.[483]

For the second question, the Court determined that 'the referring court seeks, in essence, to ascertain whether Articles 18 and 21 TFEU must be interpreted as meaning that the Member State which must consider an extradition request made to it by a third State for the purposes of criminal prosecution of a Union citizen, who is a national of another Member State, is obliged to refuse extradition and itself to conduct the criminal prosecution where its national law permits it to do so'.[484] Responding in the negative, the Court circumscribed the implications of *Petruhhin*, since 'if there were an obligation on the requested Member State to refuse extradition and itself to conduct a criminal prosecution, the consequence would be that that Member State would be deprived of the opportunity to decide itself on the appropriateness of conducting a prosecution of that citizen on the basis of national law'.[485] Drawing, at the same time, a limit around the reach of EU law into matters within national competence (as discussed in Section 5.5), the Court acknowledged that 'such an obligation would go beyond the limits that EU law may impose on the exercise of the discretion enjoyed by that Member State with respect to whether or not prosecution is appropriate in an area such as criminal law which falls ... within the competence of the Member States, even though they must exercise that competence with due regard for EU law'.[486]

The significance of integration in the host State (Section 5.4), is also evident in the *Petruhhin* case law. At one level, integration requirements might seem beside the point when it is recalled that the lawfulness of Mr Petruhhin's residence in the host State was not addressed and that passing through a Member State's airport established a sufficient cross-border nexus for Article 21 TFEU purposes for Mr Pisciotti. In *BY*, the applicant was a Ukrainian national who moved to Germany in 2012, successfully applying there for Romanian nationality in 2014. The Court first recalled that a Member State national, 'who thereby has Union citizenship, and who is lawfully resident in the territory of another Member State, falls within the scope of EU law', apparently accenting the relevance of lawful residence in the host State in distinction from *Petruhhin*.[487] But it then stated that '[a]ccordingly, *by virtue of having Union citizenship*, a national of a Member State residing in another Member State is entitled to rely on Article 21(1) TFEU ... and falls within the scope of the Treaties, within the meaning of Article 18 TFEU, which sets out the principle of non-discrimination on grounds of nationality'.[488] Then, recalling the aim of not undermining the effectiveness of Union citizenship rights (addressed in Section 5.2) and the fundamental nature of the status of Union citizenship, the Court concluded that '[t]he fact that that Union citizen acquired the nationality of a Member State and, therefore, Union citizenship, only at a time when he or she was already residing in a Member State other than that of which he or she subsequently became a national is not capable of invalidating that consideration'.[489] That finding connects back to the idea that acquiring nationality represents the ultimate point of connection to a Member

---

[483] ibid para 55.
[484] ibid para 57.
[485] ibid para 65.
[486] ibid.
[487] ibid para 29.
[488] ibid para 30 (emphasis added).
[489] ibid para 31.

State, as discussed in Section 5.3. It means that 'Articles 18 and 21 TFEU must be interpreted as being applicable to the situation of a Union citizen who is a national of one Member State, who is residing in the territory of another Member State and who is the subject of an extradition request sent to the latter Member State by a third State, even where that citizen moved the centre of his or her interests to that other Member State at a time when he or she did not have Union citizenship'.[490] The significance, or otherwise, of lawful residence in this case law is picked up again in Chapter 7.

In *Raugevicius*, where *Petruhhin* was applied to requests for surrender to a third State for the purpose not of prosecuting the individual concerned but enforcing a custodial sentence already imposed, integration in the host State was also materially significant. Mr Raugevicius, a Lithuanian national, resided in Finland. He was convicted of a drugs offence in Russia in 2011 and given a suspended prison sentence. Later in 2011, a Russian court revoked that suspension on grounds of breach of supervision obligations. In December 2016, Russia sent a request to the Finnish authorities seeking the arrest and extradition to Russia of Mr Raugevicius for the purpose of enforcing his custodial sentence. In challenging his extradition, Mr Raugevicius stressed 'that he had lived in Finland for a considerable length of time and that he was the father of two children residing in that Member State who are of Finnish nationality'.[491] The referring court observed that the European Convention on Extradition, which makes it possible for the requested State to prosecute its own citizens when it does not extradite them, does not require that State to enforce a sentence pronounced by a court of another State party. However, the Court of Justice indicated that 'there are mechanisms under national law and/or international law which make it possible for those persons to serve their sentences, in particular, in the State of which they are nationals and, in doing so, increase their chances of social reintegration after they have completed their sentences'.[492] It pointed in particular to the 1983 Convention on the Transfer of Sentenced Persons, to which all EU Member States and Russia are parties and Article 2 of which allows a person to be transferred to their country of origin to serve a custodial sentence with the objective of furthering their social rehabilitation.[493]

The Court then observed that Finnish law makes it possible for its own nationals and foreign nationals permanently residing there to serve a sentence pronounced elsewhere in Finland,[494] and 'it cannot [therefore] be ruled out that Mr Raugevicius may be regarded as a foreign national permanently residing in Finland' for that purpose.[495] On that basis, he could serve his sentence in Finland 'provided that both Russia and Mr Raugevicius consent to this'.[496] The Court referred to the fundamental nature of Union citizenship,[497] and reaffirmed that the situation of a Union citizen who has exercised the right to move and reside falls within the scope of Articles 18 and 21 TFEU. In the context of preventing the risk of impunity, it equated the situation of Finnish nationals and 'nationals of other Member States who reside permanently in Finland and demonstrate a certain degree of integration into that State's society'.[498] However, if the national court were to find that Mr Raugevicius is not 'residing permanently' in Finland on that basis, his extradition should be resolved on the basis

---

[490] ibid para 34.
[491] Case C-247/17 *Raugevicius*, EU:C:2018:898, para 19.
[492] ibid para 36.
[493] ibid para 37.
[494] ibid para 38.
[495] ibid para 41.
[496] ibid para 42.
[497] ibid para 43.
[498] ibid para 46; referring to Case C-123/08 *Wolzenburg*, EU:C:2009:616, para 67.

of national or international law, subject to the proviso that 'the extradition will not infringe the rights guaranteed by the Charter of Fundamental Rights of the European Union, in particular Article 19'.[499]

In his Opinion, Advocate General Bot had directly linked the underlying aim of social rehabilitation and the concept of human dignity protected by Article 1 CFR.[500] He emphasised that 'the social rehabilitation of the Union citizen in the Member State in which he has become genuinely integrated is not only in his interest, but *also in that of the European Union in general*'.[501] Mr Raugevicius' integration in the society of the host State thus triggers the possibility to protect him in the territory of the Union 'against' the extradition request from outside. Just as in *Petruhhin*, that does not mean that the Court eschews international mechanisms: on the contrary, in *Raugevicius*, it proactively engages them to protect both Union citizens and the Union's territorial values. However, similarly to the Court's silence in *Petruhhin* about the lawfulness of the citizen's residence in the host State, there are questions about its foregrounding of freedom of movement while simultaneously bypassing the specifics of EU the regulatory framework in *Raugevicius*. In particular, the Court enabled the national authorities to consider a Finnish conception of 'permanent resident' and not the Union status provided for in Article 16 of Directive 2004/38.[502] Residing legally in accordance with Article 16 depends 'not only on territorial and time factors but also on qualitative elements, relating to the level of integration in the host Member State'.[503] Bringing complications for Mr Raugevicius, the Court had also ruled that 'the imposition of a prison sentence by a national court is such as to show the non-compliance by the person concerned with the values expressed by the society of the host Member State in its criminal law, with the result that the taking into consideration of periods of imprisonment for the purposes of the acquisition ... of the right of permanent residence for the purposes of Article 16(2) of Directive 2004/38 would clearly be contrary to the aim pursued by that directive in establishing that right of residence'.[504]

A final issue concerns extending AFSJ protection *beyond* the territory of the Union. The protective Union space shielded by the Court in the extradition case law normally engages with standards of fundamental rights protection safeguarded by the Charter. However, in *RO*, an accommodation of the complexities of Brexit signalled a wider understanding in which the ECHR was critically important. Two European arrest warrants had been issued by UK courts in connection with serious alleged crimes, after which RO was arrested and remanded in custody in Ireland. On the basis that, if surrendered, he would most likely remain in prison in the UK after the latter's withdrawal from the Union, the High Court in Ireland asked 'whether Article 50 TEU must be interpreted as meaning that a consequence of the notification by a Member State of its intention to withdraw from the European Union in accordance with that article is that, in the event that that Member State issues a European arrest warrant with respect to an individual, the executing Member State must refuse to execute that European arrest warrant or postpone its execution pending clarification as to the law

---

[499] *Raugevicius*, para 49; referring to Case C-182/15 *Petruhhin*, EU:C:2016:630, para 60. Article 19 CFR provides: '1. Collective expulsions are prohibited. 2. No one may be removed, expelled or extradited to a State where there is a serious risk that he or she would be subjected to the death penalty, torture or other inhuman or degrading treatment or punishment'.
[500] AG Bot in Case C-247/17 *Raugevicius*, EU:C:2018:616, para 61 of the Opinion.
[501] ibid para 67 of the Opinion (emphasis added); referring to Joined Cases C-316/16 and C-424/16 *B and Vomero*, EU:C:2018:256, para 75.
[502] See further, Chapter 8.
[503] Case C-325/09 *Dias*, EU:C:2011:498, para 64.
[504] Case C-378/12 *Onuekwere*, EU:C:2014:13, para 31.

that will apply in the issuing Member State after its withdrawal from the European Union'.⁵⁰⁵ Recalling the 'correspondence' of rights protected by the Charter and the ECHR,⁵⁰⁶ the Court held:

> [I]n a case such as that in the main proceedings, in order to decide whether a European arrest warrant should be executed, it is essential that, when that decision is to be taken, the executing judicial authority is able to presume that, with respect to the person who is to be surrendered, the issuing Member State will apply the substantive content of the rights derived from the Framework Decision that are applicable in the period subsequent to the surrender, after the withdrawal of that Member State from the European Union. Such a presumption can be made if the national law of the issuing Member State incorporates the substantive content of those rights, *particularly because of the continuing participation of that Member State* in international conventions, such as the European Convention on Extradition of 13 December 1957 *and the ECHR*, even after the withdrawal of that Member State from the European Union. Only if there is concrete evidence to the contrary can the judicial authorities of a Member State refuse to execute the European arrest warrant.⁵⁰⁷

Since the territory of the Union, in a physical sense, would contract following Brexit, the Court expanded a more normative conception of protected territory that took into account the specific character of the UK as a special, post-membership third state. It used the ECHR to construct the necessary bridge⁵⁰⁸—in contrast to citing only the Charter in *Petruhhin*.⁵⁰⁹

Interestingly, neither RO's nationality nor claims based on Union citizenship feature anywhere in the judgment. Thus, while Union citizenship may be drawn from to construct Union territory as a protected legal place that corresponds formally to the territories of the Member States, the case law also exhibits a more flexible understanding of Union 'territory' for AFSJ purposes: one that can be detached from Union citizenship—and even from the Member States—in some respects. That perspective is exemplified by *IN*, which extended the *Petruhhin* case law to Icelandic nationals through the framework of the Agreement on surrender concluded between the EU, Iceland and Norway.⁵¹⁰ The preliminary reference—sent by a Croatian court following the arrest a dual Icelandic and Russian national, the subject of an international wanted persons notice issued by the Russian authorities, at the border between Croatia and Slovenia—asked whether the presumption in favour of utilising a European arrest warrant over extradition to a third State developed in *Petruhhin* for Union citizens was extendable to Icelandic nationals because of the Agreement on surrender. Notwithstanding Advocate General Tanchev's view that 'the principle of mutual trust, as it has come to evolve in the European Union since the Lisbon Treaty of 2007, has no application

---

⁵⁰⁵ Case C-327/18 PPU *RO*, EU:C:2018:733, para 33.
⁵⁰⁶ ibid paras 50 and 52, addressing Article 3 ECHR and Article 4 CFR.
⁵⁰⁷ ibid para 61.
⁵⁰⁸ In other departures from established case law, the Court also gave particular weight to guarantees in national (UK) law and diminished the significance of access to the preliminary ruling procedure; see further, N Nic Shuibhne, 'Did Brexit change EU law?' (2021) 74 Current Legal Problems, forthcoming.
⁵⁰⁹ Case C-182/15 *Petruhhin*, EU:C:2016:630, paras 55–57. Similarly, in Case C-247/17 *Raugevicius*, EU:C:2018:898, the Court referred to the requirements of 'the Convention on the Transfer of Sentenced Persons of 21 March 1983 to which all Member States, like the Russian Federation, are parties' (para 37), but referred only to the Charter regarding the obligation on the requested State (Finland) to 'check that the extradition will not infringe the rights guaranteed by the Charter of Fundamental Rights of the European Union, in particular Article 19' (para 49).
⁵¹⁰ Agreement between the European Union and the Republic of Iceland and the Kingdom of Norway on the surrender procedure between the Member States of the European Union and Iceland and Norway, OJ 2006 L292/2.

in EEA law',⁵¹¹ the Court referred to the criteria of proximity, longstanding common values, and European identity in the EEA Agreement's preamble to underline 'the special relationship between the European Union, its Member States and the EFTA States'.⁵¹² For the 'special relationship' between Iceland and the Union specifically, which 'goes beyond economic and commercial cooperation', the Court observed that Iceland is a party to the EEA Agreement, applies the Schengen *acquis*, participates in the common European asylum system, and is a party to the Agreement on surrender with the Union.⁵¹³

As a result, the Court determined that the position of an Icelandic national is '*objectively comparable with* that of an EU citizen'.⁵¹⁴ Moreover, since 'the provisions of the Agreement on the surrender procedure are very similar to the corresponding provisions' of the Framework Decision on the European arrest warrant, relevant Union citizenship case law must be applied to Icelandic nationals 'by analogy'.⁵¹⁵ It was therefore suggested that the Court created a new 'fundamental status' in EU law—not the fundamental status of Union citizenship, which is confined to Member State nationality,⁵¹⁶ but a fundamental status specifically conceived for EEA nationals and premised on extending the internal market 'in the most complete way possible'.⁵¹⁷ At the same time, the extent to which Schengen and/or the surrender Agreement were important in the Court's reasoning as the EEA dimension is not clear. For present purposes, the *IN* ruling raises important questions about what is *particularly* special about Union citizenship—about what should not, in other words, be extended 'by analogy' to the nationals of third states (even third states with deep connections to the Union). These factors will need to be further worked out as the case law on the intersection of Union citizenship and other Union objectives develops.

7. Concluding Remarks

According to Article 2 TEU, the Union is 'founded on the values of respect for human dignity, freedom, democracy, equality, the rule of law and respect for human rights, including the rights of persons belonging to minorities. These values are common to the Member States in a society in which pluralism, non-discrimination, tolerance, justice, solidarity and equality between women and men prevail'. Additionally, in its 'relations with the wider world', the Union must 'uphold and promote its values and interests and contribute to the protection of its citizens' (Article 3(5) TEU)) and, on the basis of Article 8(1) TEU, 'develop a special relationship with neighbouring countries, aiming to establish an area of prosperity and good neighbourliness, founded on the values of the Union and characterised by close and peaceful relations based on cooperation'.

Threats to the values that define the Union and its territory come from within as well as outside.⁵¹⁸ In its 2020 EU Citizenship Report, the Commission highlighted, *inter alia*,

---

⁵¹¹ AG Tanchev in Case C-897/19 PPU *IN*, EU:C:2020:128, para 97 of the Opinion. Agreement on the European Economic Area, OJ 1994 L1/3.
⁵¹² Case C-897/19 PPU *IN*, EU:C:2020:262, para 50.
⁵¹³ ibid para 44.
⁵¹⁴ ibid para 58 (emphasis added).
⁵¹⁵ ibid paras 74–75.
⁵¹⁶ Case C-184/99 *Grzelczyk*, EU:C:2001:458, para 31.
⁵¹⁷ HH Fredriksen and C Hillion, 'The "Special Relationship" between the EU and the EEA EFTA States – Free Movement of EEA Citizens in an Extended Area of Freedom, Security and Justice: Case C-897/19 PPU, *Ruska Federacija v. I.N.*' (2021) 58 Common Market Law Review 851 at 869–70.
⁵¹⁸ Case C-156/21 *Hungary v Parliament and Council*, EU:C:2022:97 and Case C-157/21 *Poland v Parliament and Council*, EU:C:2022:98, paras 127 and 145 respectively, finding that the values expressed in Article 2 TEU

managing the implications of COVID-19 pandemic; rule of law challenges; the crucial importance of education, information, and cross-border exchanges; equality and exclusion; and the progression of the 'social economy' including in its digital dimensions.[519] At the time of writing this book, a pandemic caused by a virus to which borders are utterly irrelevant had caused borders within the Union to rematerialize both legally and psychologically.[520] Events just beyond (and indeed, for certain Member States, just within) the Union's borders were freighted with conflict and vulnerability, also provoking reflection on the process of accession to the Union.[521]

That is the wider world in which the status and legal framework of Union citizenship outlined in this chapter must currently be realised, protected, and progressed. In the chapters that follow, the legal work that has constructed EU citizenship law to date is presented. The future requires it to be all the more resilient.

Further Reading

L Azoulai, 'Transfiguring European citizenship: from Member State territory to Union territory' in D Kochenov (ed), *EU Citizenship and Federalism: The Role of Rights* (CUP 2017) 178.

N Cambien, D Kochenov, and E Muir (eds), *European Citizenship Under Stress: Social Justice, Brexit and Other Challenges* (Brill 2020).

C Closa Montero, 'The concept of citizenship in the Treaty on European Union' (1992) 29 Common Market Law Review 1139.

Editorial comments, 'Europe is trembling. Looking for a safe place in EU law' (2020) 57 Common Market Law Review 1675.

AC Evans, 'European citizenship' (1982) 45 Modern Law Review 497.

E Guild, S Peers, and J Tomkin, *The EU Citizenship Directive: A Commentary* (2nd edn) (OUP 2019).

D Kochenov, 'The essence of EU citizenship emerging from the last ten years of academic debate: beyond the cherry blossoms and the moon?' (2013) 62 International and Comparative Law Quarterly 97.

D Kostakopoulou, 'Ideas, norms and European citizenship: explaining institutional change' (2005) 68 Modern Law Review 233.

D Kostakopoulou, 'European citizenship: writing the future' (2007) 13 European Law Journal 623.

D Kostakopoulou and D Thym (eds), *Research Handbook on European Citizenship Law and Policy* (Edward Elgar 2022).

S O'Leary, *The Evolving Concept of Community Citizenship: From the Free Movement of Persons to Union Citizenship* (Kluwer Law International 1996).

'define the very identity of the European Union as a common legal order. Thus the European Union must be able to defend those values, within the limits of its powers as laid down by the Treaties'.

[519] European Commission, EU Citizenship Report 2020: Empowering Citizens and Protecting their Rights, COM(2020) 730 final, Section 4—note 'social economy' and not, interestingly, 'social *market* economy' (Article 3(3) TEU).

[520] eg In its 2020 EU Citizenship Report, the Commission linked 'promoting EU citizenship and EU values' to the fact that 'COVID-19 has challenged certain EU values, as it has led to temporary restrictions on fundamental rights and democratic values. Questions quickly arose on how elections should be run in these circumstances, how electoral campaigns can fairly take place, how citizens can make their opinions heard and what restrictions, if any, can be put in place. Addressing these issues is particularly important, knowing that in times of crisis the protection of democratic values is of utmost importance and that the circumstances that have led to such measures may well reoccur' (European Commission, EU Citizenship Report 2020: Empowering Citizens and Protecting their Rights, COM(2020) 730 final, para 4.2).

[521] See R Petrov and C Hillion, Guest Editorial Comment, '"Accession through war"—Ukraine's road to the EU' (2022) 59 Common Market Law Review 1289.

J Shaw, 'Citizenship: contrasting dynamics at the interface of integration and constitutionalism' in P Craig and G de Búrca (eds), *The Evolution of EU Law* (3rd edn OUP 2021) 608.

E Spaventa, *Free Movement of Persons in the European Union. Barriers to Movement in their Constitutional Context* (Kluwer Law International 2007).

D Thym (ed), *Questioning EU Citizenship: Judges and the Limits of Free Movement and Solidarity in the EU* (Hart Publishing 2017).

B de Witte, 'Democratic adjudication in Europe – how can the European Court of Justice be responsive to the citizens?' in M Dougan, N Nic Shuibhne, and E Spaventa (eds), *Empowerment and disempowerment of the European Citizen* (Hart Publishing 2012) 138.

3
Who is Protected?
Part I: Union Citizenship and Member State Nationality

1. Chapter Overview

This chapter explores the personal scope of EU citizenship law. That question has direct (Union citizens themselves) and indirect (family members who derive rights from Union citizens) dimensions. Derived rights for family members are addressed in Chapter 4. In this chapter, the constitutive link between Union citizenship and Member State nationality is examined.

Article 20(1) TFEU establishes that '[e]very person holding the nationality of a Member State shall be a citizen of the Union'. It also (since the Amsterdam Treaty) characterises Union citizenship as an 'additional' status that does 'not replace national citizenship'.[1] From the perspective of EU law, Union citizenship is therefore a *conferred* status, meaning that it cannot be acquired through a direct citizen-to-Union process: to be a Union citizen, a person must either be or become a national of one of the Union's Member States. In other words, 'there is no *autonomous* way of acquiring and losing Union citizenship. The acquisition and loss of Union citizenship are dependent on the acquisition and loss of the nationality of a Member State; Union citizenship presupposes nationality of a Member State'.[2] As a result, loss of Member State nationality entails a corresponding loss of Union citizenship. As the Court of Justice has confirmed in the context of the United Kingdom's withdrawal from the European Union, '[b]y Article 9 TEU and Article 20 TFEU, the authors of the Treaties ... established *an inseparable and exclusive link* between possession of the nationality of a Member State and not only the acquisition, but also the retention, of the status of citizen of the Union'.[3]

It does not follow, though, that there is no role for EU law as regards the processes that Member States apply to both acquiring and withdrawing nationality. To understand the reasons behind and parameters of that role, the legal implications of the constitutive link between Union citizenship and Member State nationality are examined in this chapter through two key questions. First, what is the role of EU law when Member States determine who may acquire or lose their nationality (Section 2)? Second, what are the implications in EU citizenship law when a person holds more than one nationality, whether the nationalities of one Member State and a third country, or of two Member States (Section 3)?

---

[1] See similarly, Article 9 TEU: '[e]very national of a Member State shall be a citizen of the Union. Citizenship of the Union shall be additional to and not replace national citizenship'.

[2] AG Poiares Maduro in Case C-135/08 *Rottmann*, EU:C:2009:588, para 15 of the Opinion (emphasis added). See similarly, AG Collins in Case C-673/20 *Préfet du Gers*, EU:C:2022:129, para 22 of the Opinion, who observed that 'the Member States could have decided to pool their competences and to confer on the European Union the power to determine who is entitled to become a Union citizen. That explicit choice by the Member States not only renders the European Union powerless to create Union citizenship independently from nationality as conferred by the Member States, but also raises a constitutional barrier to such a power being implied under Union law'.

[3] Case C-673/20 *Préfet du Gers*, EU:C:2022:449, para 48 (emphasis added).

2. Determining Member State Nationality: The Role of EU Law

In Chapter 2, we saw that even for areas that fall within their competence, Member States must 'exercise that competence in accordance with [Union] law, in particular the provisions of the Treaty concerning the right of every citizen of the Union to move and reside freely within the territory of the Member States'.[4] In the context of Member State naturalisation procedures, and before the inception of Union citizenship, that principle was applied mainly to ensure that decisions conferring Member State nationality were respected by the other Member States for the purpose of facilitating freedom of movement. In *Micheletti*, an application for a permanent residence card submitted by a dual Argentinian/Italian national intending to establish himself as a dentist in Spain was refused on the basis that the Spanish Civil Code precluded recognition of his Italian nationality. The applicable national provision gave precedence to the nationality linked with the habitual residence of the person concerned before their arrival in Spain (in this case, his Argentinian nationality). The Court of Justice stated that '[u]nder international law, it is for each Member State, *having due regard to [Union] law*, to lay down the conditions for the acquisition and loss of nationality'.[5] It then held that 'it is not permissible for the legislation of a Member State to restrict the effects of the grant of the nationality of another Member State by imposing an additional condition for recognition of that nationality with a view to the exercise of the fundamental freedoms provided for in the Treaty'.[6] The Court's approach in *Micheletti* was premised on ensuring mutual recognition of the nationality decisions of other Member States. It did not concern the rules and practices adopted by a Member State to confer or withdraw its own nationality, to which we now turn.

2.1 EU Law and Member State Decisions to Withdraw Nationality: *Rottmann*

Recognition of Member State nationality brings the person concerned within the personal scope of EU law, as demonstrated by *Micheletti*. But the decision of a Member State to withdraw its nationality raises a different order of concern since loss of Member State nationality could entail corresponding loss of Union citizenship if the person affected does not (also) hold the nationality of another Member State. These were the circumstances of the groundbreaking *Rottmann* case. Mr Rottmann, an Austrian national, moved to Germany and applied for German nationality in February 1998. His naturalisation document was issued in Germany in February 1999 and, in accordance with Austrian law, he then lost his Austrian nationality. However, he did not disclose in the course of the naturalisation procedure that he had been questioned as an accused in a fraud investigation in Austria in 1995, proceedings that led to the issuing of a warrant for his arrest in 1997. The German authorities

---

[4] Case C-403/03 *Schempp*, EU:C:2005:446, para 19.
[5] Case C-369/90 *Micheletti*, EU:C:1992:295, para 10 (emphasis added); confirmed post-Maastricht in eg Case C-192/99 *Kaur*, EU:C:2001:106, para 19, where the Court recognised the authority of the United Kingdom to determine whether a person is a national 'for the purposes of [Union] law' (paras 22 and 24) with respect to the status of British Overseas Citizen. However, differences in treatment with respect to Member State nationals who reside in an overseas country or territory may be objectively justifiable eg on the right to vote and to stand as a candidate in European Parliament elections, Case C-300/04 *Eman and Sevinger*, EU:C:2006:545 (see further, Chapter 5).
[6] *Micheletti*, para 10.

were informed about the arrest warrant in August 1999 and the applicant's naturalisation was withdrawn with retroactive effect on the grounds that he had 'obtained German nationality by deception'.[7] Mr Rottmann sought annulment of that decision.

The referring court noted that Mr Rottmann did not, at the material time, meet the conditions for 'immediate recovery of Austrian nationality'.[8] In the first instance judgment at national level, it was therefore acknowledged that he would lose Union citizenship as a consequence of the German decision withdrawing his naturalisation and assumed that the national authorities were obliged, in accordance with *Micheletti*, to have 'due regard' to EU law in the exercise of their discretion. However, that court also suggested that 'an obligation to refrain from withdrawing naturalisation obtained by deception would be to strike at the heart of the sovereign power of the Member States, recognised by Article [20(1) TFEU], to define the detailed rules for the application of their nationality law'.[9] In its judgment, the Court of Justice first recalled the starting point in *Micheletti*—that a Member State retain competence to set conditions for the acquisition and loss of its nationality. However, it also confirmed that this competence must be exercised 'having due regard to [Union] law'.[10] The Court acknowledged Declaration No 2 on nationality of a Member State, annexed by the Member States to the TEU,[11] which provided that 'wherever in the Treaty establishing the European Community reference is made to nationals of the Member States, the question whether an individual possesses the nationality of a Member State shall be settled solely by reference to the national law of the Member State concerned'.[12] However, it then asserted, without further analysis, that 'the fact that a matter falls within the competence of the Member States does not alter the fact that, in situations covered by European Union law, the national rules concerned must have due regard to the latter'.[13]

The Court dismissed the argument, submitted by the German and Austrian Governments, that the circumstances of the case amounted to a purely internal situation. Advocate General Poiares Maduro had suggested that Mr Rottmann's (pre-naturalisation) exercise of the right to move and reside 'had an impact on the change in his civil status' and therefore sufficed to establish the necessary connecting factor to EU law.[14] That analysis reflected the prevailing approach to free movement outlined in Chapter 2—that establishing a link to EU law through even tangential free movement grounds was not usually difficult to do. However, more radically, the Court in *Rottmann* established the necessary connecting factor independently of free movement. Instead, it ruled that the applicant's situation—resulting from the decision withdrawing his German nationality 'after he has lost the nationality of another Member State that he originally possessed'—placed him 'in a position capable of causing him to lose the status conferred by Article [20 TFEU] and the rights attaching thereto' and therefore fell

---

[7] Case C-135/08 *Rottmann*, EU:C:2010:104, para 28.
[8] ibid para 31.
[9] ibid para 32; moreover, '[a]ll the governments that submitted observations to the Court, the Freistaat Bayern and the Commission of the European Communities argue that the rules on the acquisition and loss of nationality fall within the competence of the Member States' (para 37). Eight Member States—Germany, Belgium, the Czech Republic, Estonia, Greece, Latvia, Austria, and Poland—submitted observations.
[10] *Rottmann*, para 39.
[11] Though no longer attached to the Treaties since the Lisbon Treaty.
[12] OJ 1992 C 191/98.
[13] *Rottmann*, para 41.
[14] AG Poiares Maduro in *Rottmann*, para 13 of the Opinion: 'it was because he transferred his residence to Germany that he had been able to satisfy the conditions for acquiring German nationality, namely, lawful habitual residence within that country's territory. The existence of such a link is sufficient for acceptance of a link with [Union] law'.

'*by reason of its nature and its consequences*, within the ambit of European Union law'.[15] The Court invoked the fact that Union citizenship is 'intended to be the fundamental status of nationals of the Member States' to support its reasoning.[16]

If a decision to withdraw Member State nationality falls 'within the ambit' of EU law, what does the obligation to have 'due regard' to it in such circumstances require in practice? In effect, the idea (introduced in Chapter 2) that EU law constructs outer parameters around the exercise of Member State discretion was reinforced in *Rottmann*. As the Court explained:

> The proviso that due regard must be had to European Union law does not compromise the principle of international law previously recognised by the Court ... that the Member States have the power to lay down the conditions for the acquisition and loss of nationality, but rather enshrines the principle that, in respect of citizens of the Union, the exercise of that power, in so far as it affects the rights conferred and protected by the legal order of the Union ... is *amenable to judicial review* carried out in the light of European Union law.[17]

Acknowledging the reservations submitted by 'several' Member State governments, the Court indicated that where a decision withdrawing naturalisation is based on 'the deception practised by the person concerned in connection with the procedure for acquisition of the nationality in question, such a decision could be compatible with European Union law'.[18] In other words, a decision withdrawing naturalisation in the circumstances of *Rottmann* is potentially justifiable on public interest grounds—even where that might result in the person's statelessness—since 'it is legitimate for a Member State to wish to protect the special relationship of solidarity and good faith between it and its nationals and also the reciprocity of rights and duties, which form the bedrock of the bond of nationality'.[19]

Crucially, though, the standard applied to any assessment of public interest grounds under EU law applies here too: decisions to withdraw naturalisation that lead to the loss of Union citizenship must be proportionate.[20] That assessment should be undertaken by the national court, but the Court of Justice outlined the criteria that should be taken into account. At a general level, the national court must consider 'the consequences that the decision entails for the person concerned and, if relevant, for the members of his family with regard to the loss of the rights enjoyed by every citizen of the Union' against the backdrop of the 'importance

---

[15] *Rottmann*, para 42 (emphasis added). In Case C-34/09 *Ruiz Zambrano*, EU:C:2011:124, this paragraph of *Rottmann* was invoked to establish residence rights for third-country national family members in a Union citizen's home State in certain exceptional situations; see further, Chapter 5.

[16] *Rottmann*, para 43; citing eg Case C-184/99 *Grzelczyk*, EU:C:2001:458, para 31.

[17] *Rottmann*, para 48 (emphasis added). For van Eijken, proportionality thus constructs 'one of the fences surrounding the competences of the member states in the field of nationality' (H van Eijken, 'Tjebbes in wonderland: on European citizenship, nationality and fundamental rights' (2019) 15 European Constitutional Law Review 714 at 721).

[18] *Rottmann*, para 50.

[19] ibid para 51. As regards the outcome of statelessness that is therefore accepted in certain circumstances, the Court referred to relevant instruments of international law—Articles 7(1), 7(3), and 8(2) of the Convention on the reduction of statelessness (para 52), Article 15(2) of the Universal Declaration of Human Rights (para 53), and Article 4(c) of the European Convention on nationality (para 53)—all of which make provision for deprivation of nationality in circumstances of fraud or deception. O'Leary finds common ground in comparing Court of Justice and ECtHR case law on this point, observing a similar methodology that entails 'an evaluation of consequences and a consideration of whether there has been any arbitrariness. Possible statelessness is a relevant, even weighty, consideration but it does not appear, in all cases, to be a decisive one' (S O'Leary, 'Nationality and citizenship: integration and rights-based perspectives' in K Lenaerts, J Bonichot, H Kanninen, C Naômé, and P Pohjankosi (eds), *An Ever-Changing Union? Perspectives on the Future of EU Law in Honour of Allan Rosas* (Hart Publishing 2019) 51 at 59–60).

[20] *Rottmann*, para 55.

which primary law attaches to the status of citizen of the Union'.[21] More specifically, it should consider whether the consequential loss of Union citizenship rights 'is justified in relation to the gravity of the offence committed by that person, to the lapse of time between the naturalisation decision and the withdrawal decision and to whether it is possible for that person to recover his original nationality'.[22]

The fact that the person concerned has not recovered the nationality of their Member State of origin does not create an absolute obligation on the State withdrawing naturalisation to refrain from doing so.[23] However, the national court must determine 'whether, before such a decision withdrawing naturalisation takes effect, having regard to all the relevant circumstances, observance of the principle of proportionality requires the person concerned to be afforded a reasonable period of time in order to try to recover the nationality of his Member State of origin'.[24] The Court also stated that the principles it had established 'apply both to the Member State of naturalisation and to the Member State of the original nationality'.[25]

2.2 Applying *Rottmann*

The ruling in *Rottmann* effected a significant constitutional shift, in two main ways: first, piercing the domain of Member State decision-making (and discretion) on the determination of nationality; and second, kindling rights based on Article 20 TFEU that are decoupled from the past or present exercise of free movement. Taken together, these points both draw from and add to the importance of citizenship as a *Union* status: the Court hovered at the boundaries of conferral by finding a role for EU law in situations factually internal to a Member State and in an area profoundly associated not just with national competence but also with national sovereignty. As discussed further in Chapter 5, the Court later rationalised this case law on the basis that securing the status of citizenship *now* enables the exercise of associated rights into the future.[26] For the purposes of this chapter, the implications of *Rottmann*— which 'opened the door to the possibility of subjecting to detailed examination, in the light of EU law, certain aspects of the Member States' laws on nationality'[27]—will be considered in three respects: Member State decisions withdrawing nationality (Section 2.2.1), acquiring

---

[21] ibid para 56.
[22] ibid para 56.
[23] AG Poiares Maduro considered that such an obligation would 'contravene the duty, imposed on the Union by Article 6(3) [T]EU, to respect the national identities of the Member States, of which the composition of the national body politic is clearly an essential element' (AG Poiares Maduro in *Rottmann*, para 25 of the Opinion).
[24] *Rottmann*, paras 57–58.
[25] ibid para 62. From that perspective, considering the obligations placed by EU law on Austria in circumstances of the case, the Court added that it could not assess a decision not yet adopted for compliance with EU law. But it did note that 'the Austrian authorities will possibly have to adopt a decision on the question whether the applicant in the main proceedings is to recover his nationality of origin and when that decision has been adopted the Austrian courts will, if necessary, have to determine whether it is valid in the light of the principles referred to in this judgment' (para 63) See further, Section 2.2.1.
[26] eg Explaining why residence rights for a Union citizen's family members in the citizen's home State can, in exceptional situations, be based on Article 20 TFEU, the Court acknowledges that while such situations are 'governed by legislation which falls, a priori, within the competence of the Member States, namely legislation on the right of entry and residence of third-country nationals', they 'nonetheless have an intrinsic connection with the freedom of movement and residence of a Union citizen, which prevents the right of entry and residence being refused to those nationals in the Member State of residence of that citizen, in order not to interfere with that freedom' (Case C-165/14 *Rendón Marín*, EU:C:2016:675, para 75; see further, Chapter 5).
[27] AG Szpunar in Case C-118/20 *Wiener Landesregierung (Révocation d'une assurance de naturalisation)*, EU:C:2021:530, para 49 of the Opinion.

Member State nationality (Section 2.2.2), and Member State withdrawal from the Union (Section 2.2.3).

2.2.1 Member State decisions withdrawing nationality

Two key rulings—*Tjebbes* and *Wiener Landesregierung*—have significantly progressed the principles established in *Rottmann*. In *Tjebbes*, the Court provided more guidance on the obligations that EU law places on national authorities when they are assessing the proportionality of procedures for withdrawing nationality, including compliance with the Charter of Fundamental Rights. The case concerned applications for a Netherlands passport submitted by four individuals who resided in and held the nationality of third countries. The contested national rules (the 'Law on Nationality') provided that '[a]n adult shall lose his Netherlands nationality: ... if he also holds a foreign nationality and if, after attaining his majority and while holding both nationalities, he has his principal residence for an uninterrupted period of 10 years outside the Netherlands ... and outside the territories to which the [EU Treaty] applies' (Article 15(1)(c)). According to Article 16(1)(d), a minor Netherlands national would also lose Netherlands nationality if their father or mother lost it on the basis of Article 15(1).[28]

Seeking further guidance on the application of *Rottmann*, the referring court suggested that Article 15(1)(c) was 'consistent with the principle of proportionality and compatible with Articles 20 and 21 TFEU'—as well as with Article 7 CFR (respect for private and family life)—since it 'lays down a significant period of 10 years of residence abroad before Netherlands nationality is lost, which would give grounds for assuming that the persons concerned have no, or only a very weak, link with the Kingdom of the Netherlands and, accordingly, with the European Union' and because 'it is relatively simple to retain Netherlands nationality'—on the latter point, the ten-year period is 'interrupted if, during the course of that period and for no less than one year without interruption, the person concerned resides in the Netherlands or the European Union, or obtains a declaration regarding the possession of Netherlands nationality or a travel document or a Netherlands identity card within the meaning of the Law on Passports'.[29] However, the referring court questioned 'whether or not a general statutory scheme such as that prescribed by the Law on Nationality is consistent with Articles 20 and 21 TFEU' since 'it cannot be ruled out that examining the proportionality of the consequences of the loss of Netherlands nationality for the situation of the persons concerned may require each individual case to be examined'.[30] Additionally, while acknowledging 'the importance that the national legislature has attached to unity of nationality within the family' through enacting Article 16(1)(d), the referring court did question the compatibility of that provision with both the principle of proportionality and Article 24(2) CFR.[31] In particular, it highlighted that 'a child who is a minor has little influence on the retention of his or her Netherlands nationality, and that the possibilities for interrupting

---

[28] As AG Mengozzi explained, 'Article 16(1)(d) of the Law on Netherlands nationality draws on Article 7(2) of the European Convention on Nationality, which states that a State Party to that convention may provide for the loss of its nationality by children, one of whose parents loses that nationality. In addition, the Second Protocol amending the (European) Convention on the Reduction of Cases of Multiple Nationality and Military Obligations in Cases of Multiple Nationality, signed at Strasbourg on 2 February 1993, mentions, in its third recital, encouragement of unity of nationality within the same family' (AG Mengozzi in Case C-221/17 *Tjebbes and Others*, EU:C:2018:572, para 122 of the Opinion).

[29] Case C-221/17 *Tjebbes*, EU:C:2019:189, para 22.

[30] ibid para 24.

[31] Article 24(2) CFR requires that '[i]n all actions relating to children, whether taken by public authorities or private institutions, the child's best interests must be a primary consideration'.

certain periods of time or obtaining, for instance, a declaration regarding the possession of Netherlands nationality are not grounds for exception in the case of minors'.[32]

The Court of Justice first affirmed the basic premises of *Rottmann* regarding the fundamental status of Union citizenship,[33] the competence of the Member States to determine conditions for loss and acquisition of nationality,[34] the requirement, at the same time, for Member States to have 'due regard' to EU law when exercising that competence,[35] and the fact that 'it is legitimate for a Member State to wish to protect the special relationship of solidarity and good faith between it and its nationals and also the reciprocity of rights and duties, which form the bedrock of the bond of nationality'.[36] On the latter point, the Court agreed that it was also 'legitimate for a Member State to take the view that nationality is the expression of *a genuine link between it and its nationals*, and therefore to prescribe that the absence, or the loss, of any such genuine link entails the loss of nationality' as well as 'to wish to protect the unity of nationality within the same family'.[37] In that light, national law resulting in the loss of Netherlands nationality following an uninterrupted period of residence of ten years outside the Netherlands/Union was justifiable in principle since it could be regarded as an 'indication' that there was no genuine link between the person concerned and the Netherlands,[38] bearing in mind also the fact that Netherlands nationality would only be lost in cases where the person held the nationality of another state—thus ruling out the possibility of statelessness—and where no effort to sustain Netherlands nationality had been made (such as by, for example, requesting 'a declaration regarding the possession of Netherlands nationality, a travel document or a Netherlands identity card within the meaning of the Law on Passports'[39]).

However, the Court did find that '[t]he loss of the nationality of a Member State *by operation of law* would be inconsistent with the principle of proportionality if the relevant national rules did not permit at any time an individual examination of the consequences of that loss for the persons concerned from the point of view of EU law'.[40] It then set out in more detail the requirements under EU law for national authorities and/or national courts undertaking the necessary individual examination. First, it 'requires an individual assessment of the situation of the person concerned and that of his or her family in order to determine whether the consequences of losing the nationality of the Member State concerned, *when it entails the loss of his or her citizenship of the Union*, might, with regard to the objective pursued by the national legislature, disproportionately affect *the normal development of his or her family and professional life* from the point of view of EU law. Those consequences *cannot be hypothetical or merely a possibility*'.[41] The fact that loss of Union citizenship must be at stake

---

[32] *Tjebbes*, para 25.
[33] ibid para 31.
[34] ibid para 30.
[35] ibid paras 30 and 32.
[36] ibid para 33.
[37] ibid para 35 (emphasis added).
[38] ibid para 36.
[39] ibid para 38. AG Mengozzi similarly emphasised that 'Article 15(4) of the Law on Netherlands nationality provides several possibilities for interrupting the 10-year period of uninterrupted residence in a third country, by means of simple steps' (paras 94–95 of the Opinion).
[40] *Tjebbes*, para 41 (emphasis added). Differently, arguing that nothing in the case at hand 'preclude[d], following a review of proportionality in the light of EU law, a provision of a law of a Member State of a general nature proving to be consistent with the principle of proportionality', see AG Mengozzi, para 63 of the Opinion (see generally, paras 60ff and esp paras 81–91). The emphasis on individual assessment in *Tjebbes* can also be contrasted with its displacement in case law on eligibility for social assistance in a host State where residence is not based on Directive 2004/38: see further, Chapters 2 and 7.
[41] *Tjebbes*, para 44 (emphasis added).

suggests greater Member State discretion where the nationality of another Member State is unaffected, a point returned to in Section 3. Second, to be proportionate, the loss of nationality must also comply with Articles 7 and 24(2) CFR, which protect respect for family life and the obligation to take account of the best interests of the child respectively.[42]

It is striking that the Court considered the 'normal development' of the person's 'family and professional life *from the point of view of EU law*', which addresses 'the private nature of [Union] citizenship and its internal market origins'[43]—in essence, the capacity to move freely. The Court highlighted 'in particular' the prospect of limiting freedom of movement and residence within the territory of the Member States, including 'particular difficulties in continuing to travel to the Netherlands or to another Member State in order to retain genuine and regular links with members of his or her family, to pursue his or her professional activity or to undertake the necessary steps to pursue that activity'.[44] The latter point aligns with the fact that purely internal situations can come within the scope of Article 20 TFEU: while they are 'governed by legislation which falls *a priori* within the competence of the Member States', they might 'none the less have *an intrinsic connection* with the freedom of movement of a Union citizen'.[45] The Court also pointed to the fact that the person concerned 'might not have been able to renounce the nationality of a third country and that person thus falls within the scope of Article 15(1)(c) of the Law on Nationality';[46] to 'the serious risk, to which the person concerned would be exposed, that his or her safety or freedom to come and go would substantially deteriorate because of the impossibility for that person to enjoy consular protection under Article 20(2)(c) TFEU in the territory of the third country in which that person resides';[47] and, for children, to 'possible circumstances from which it is apparent that the loss of Netherlands nationality by the minor concerned, which the national legislature has attached to the loss of Netherlands nationality by one of his or her parents in order to preserve unity of nationality within the family, fails to meet the child's best interests as enshrined in Article 24 of the Charter because of the consequences of that loss for the minor from the point of view of EU law'.[48]

On the latter point, the Court did not offer detailed guidance on the particular assessment required for minor Union citizens. However, it did indicate that conditions that might be appropriate and necessary for preserving a genuine link between a Member State and its nationals in situations of loss of nationality for adults might not be proportionate when applied to situations involving children. For the latter, *Rottmann* accommodates the fact that the 'nature and consequences'[49] of the decisions of national authorities in such cases might be

---

[42] ibid para 45.
[43] S Coutts, 'Bold and Thoughtful: The Court of Justice intervenes in nationality law Case C-221/17 Tjebbes', (2019) European Law Blog, <https://europeanlawblog.eu/2019/03/25/bold-and-thoughtful-the-court-of-justice-intervenes-in-nationality-law-case-c-221-17-tjebbes/> (accessed 29 May 2023). Coutts also emphasises the 'clear link between the status of Union citizenship referred to in Article 20 TFEU and at stake in the judgment and the rights of free movement and residence [in Article 21 TFEU]. But those rights are to be understood in their totality in the sense of offering a set of life opportunities to individual citizens across the Union as a whole'. On the relationship between Articles 20 and 21 TFEU, see further, Chapters 2 and 5.
[44] *Tjebbes*, para 46. AG Mengozzi had suggested that 'it could be envisaged that the loss of citizenship of the Union might lead to interruption or loss of payment of social benefits to the person concerned. Similarly, loss of citizenship of the Union might mean that the person concerned could no longer claim the right to reside in the territory of the Member State concerned, or even, in some situations, in the territory of the European Union' (para 76 of the Opinion).
[45] Case C-40/11 *Iida*, EU:C:2012:691, para 72 (emphasis added); confirmed in eg Case C-133/15 *Chavez-Vilchez*, EU:C:2017:354, para 64. See further, Chapter 5.
[46] *Tjebbes*, para 44.
[47] ibid.
[48] ibid para 47.
[49] Case C-135/08 *Rottmann*, EU:C:2010:104, para 42.

assessed more intensively. In that light, a thread of connection to the lack of agency of children can be drawn to the discussion in Chapter 5 as regards rights conferred by Article 20 TFEU. In essence, minor Union citizens are autonomous with respect to *holding* rights,[50] but not with respect to *exercising* them.[51]

Overall, the factors highlighted in *Tjebbes* that national authorities and national courts should take into account for the purposes of proportionality review concern the implications of loss of Member State nationality for the rights conferred by Union citizenship and not, more directly, how a Member State *should* determine who its nationals are.[52] Differently, the questions referred in *Wiener Landesregierung* involved compelling someone to give up the nationality of one Member State in order to acquire the nationality of another. The case was described by Advocate General Szpunar as 'open[ing] the third phase of a relatively delicate chapter concerning the obligations of the Member States in the sphere of the acquisition and the loss of nationality in the light of EU law'.[53] The Court focused mainly on the proportionality of the host State's naturalisation procedures in its ruling, and it is therefore discussed in more detail in Section 2.2.2. However, the Court also evolved the responsibilities of Member States taking decisions about the withdrawal of their nationality in such circumstances. In particular, when a Member State national applies to their State of origin to relinquish their nationality so that they can acquire the nationality of another Member State, 'the Member State of origin should not adopt, on the basis of an assurance given by that other Member State that the person concerned will be granted the nationality of that State, a final decision concerning the deprivation of nationality without ensuring that that decision enters into force only once the new nationality has actually been acquired'.[54] Moreover, 'the revocation of the assurance as to the naturalisation of a person who is stateless on the date of such revocation must not be considered in isolation but take into account the fact that that person was a national of another Member State and therefore held citizenship of the Union'.[55]

It may not always be possible for a Member State to refuse a request for an application to relinquish citizenship.[56] Where such a decision *is* taken and results in the temporary loss of Union citizenship for the person affected, the 'obligation to ensure the effectiveness of Article 20 TFEU falls primarily' on the host Member State.[57] But the idea of an obligation to try, at least, to coordinate relevant decisions across the relevant Member States recalls the *Petruhhin* objective of seeking to supersede the extradition of Union citizens to third countries by issuing a European arrest warrant, as discussed in Chapter 2. It provides another

---

[50] '[A] young child can take advantage of the rights of free movement and residence guaranteed by [Union]law. The capacity of a national of a Member State to be the holder of rights guaranteed by the Treaty and by secondary law on the free movement of persons cannot be made conditional upon the attainment by the person concerned of the age prescribed for the acquisition of legal capacity to exercise those rights personally' (Case C-200/02 *Zhu and Chen*, EU:C:2004:639, para 20).

[51] '[I]t is the relationship of dependency between the Union citizen who is a minor and the third-country national who is refused a right of residence that is liable to jeopardise the effectiveness of Union citizenship, since it is that dependency that would lead to the Union citizen being obliged, in fact, to leave not only the territory of the Member State of which he is a national but also that of the European Union as a whole, as a consequence of such a refusal' (Joined Cases C-356/11 and C-357/11 *O and S*, EU:C:2012:776, para 56).

[52] A line of argument that would, for AG Mengozzi, have 'particularly dangerous consequences, inter alia as regards the allocation of competences between the Member States and the European Union' (para 105 of the Opinion).

[53] AG Szpunar in Case C-118/20 *Wiener Landesregierung (Révocation d'une assurance de naturalisation)*, EU:C:2021:530, para 2 of the Opinion.

[54] Case C-118/20 *Wiener Landesregierung (Révocation d'une assurance de naturalisation)*, EU:C:2022:34, para 50.

[55] AG Szpunar in *Wiener Landesregierung*, para 56 of the Opinion.

[56] As explained in more detail by AG Szpunar (ibid paras 78–83 of the Opinion).

[57] *Wiener Landesregierung*, para 51.

reminder that Union citizenship has transnational as well as supranational and national dimensions.[58]

2.2.2 Acquiring Member State nationality

While *Micheletti* established the relevance of EU law to competence for 'lay[ing] down the conditions for the *acquisition and loss*' of Member State nationality',[59] the case itself, as explained in Section 2.1, concerned recognition of the conditions set by other Member States. It was only later, in *Rottmann*, that the Court addressed the proportionality of naturalisation procedures per se; and later still that it applied those principles at the point of acquiring as well as losing Member State nationality.

In *Wiener Landesregierung*, JY, an Estonian national at the time, applied for Austrian nationality in December 2008. In March 2014, the competent Austrian authority decided that she would be granted Austrian nationality on the condition that she could prove, within two years, that she had given up her citizenship of Estonia. This conditional assurance was provided under the applicable Austrian Law on citizenship. JY moved her primary residence to Austria and later submitted confirmation, within the requested two-year period, that her citizenship of Estonia was relinquished in August 2015. At that point, JY became a stateless person. However, in July 2017, the Wiener Landesregierung revoked the 2014 decision and rejected JY's application on the grounds that, since she had received the earlier assurance that she would be granted Austrian nationality, she had committed 'two serious administrative offences (failing to display a vehicle inspection disc and driving a motor vehicle while under the influence of alcohol)' and therefore no longer fulfilled the conditions for grant of Austrian nationality under the applicable rules.[60] In the national proceedings in which JY appealed against that decision, the referring court first suggested that the obligations established in *Rottmann* and *Tjebbes* did not apply in this case because JY was not a Union citizen at the material time, having given up her Estonian nationality and, as a result of the revocation of the assurance previously received, not become an Austrian national.[61] In the alternative, the referring court asked whether the fact that JY had 'renounced her citizenship of the Union by putting an end *herself* to the special relationship of solidarity and good faith which united her to Estonia' was 'decisive' in ruling out an obligation of proportionality assessment.[62]

For the Court of Justice, the fact that JY had 'dissolved the bond of nationality' with Estonia in the context of (and following an assurance given within) a procedure to obtain Austrian nationality meant that she 'could not be considered to have renounced *voluntarily* the status of citizen of the Union'.[63] As a consequence of seeking to comply with the requirements of the Austrian naturalisation procedure, JY was now 'in a situation in which it is impossible for [her] to continue to assert the rights arising from the status of citizen of the Union'.[64] The Court therefore concluded that her situation fell, 'by reason of its nature and

---

[58] See generally, S Coutts, 'The shifting geometry of Union citizenship: a supranational status from transnational rights' (2019) 21 Cambridge Yearbook of European Legal Studies 318.
[59] Case C-369/90 *Micheletti*, EU:C:1992:295, para 10 (emphasis added).
[60] Case C-118/20 *Wiener Landesregierung (Révocation d'une assurance de naturalisation)*, EU:C:2022:34, para 17. It was also noted that JY had committed eight other administrative offences between 2007 and 2013, ie before the 2014 assurance had been given. Thus, account could not be taken of the latter since 'they were known at the time the assurance was given to her and did not preclude that assurance being given' (para 65).
[61] ibid paras 25–26.
[62] ibid para 27 (emphasis added).
[63] ibid paras 35–36 (emphasis added).
[64] ibid para 39.

its consequences, within the scope of EU law' since the assurance provided was revoked 'with the effect of preventing that person from recovering the status of citizen of the Union'.[65] Advocate General Szpunar supported his reasoning on this point by referring to the test developed, on the basis of *Rottmann*, in the *Ruiz Zambrano* case law (discussed in Chapter 5). For him, since the contested decision in the present case meant that a Member State national 'was faced with the permanent loss of her citizenship of the Union and, therefore, not the loss of *the substance of the rights* conferred by Article 20 TFEU but that of *all of those rights*', her situation had to fall within the scope of EU law.[66]

The Court went on to consider the proportionality assessment required in such circumstances. First, it held that where, in the context of a naturalisation procedure, a Member State 'requires a citizen of the Union to renounce the nationality of his or her Member State of origin, the exercise and effectiveness of the rights which that citizen of the Union derives from Article 20 TFEU require that that person should not at any time be liable to lose the fundamental status of citizen of the Union by the mere fact of the implementation of that procedure'.[67] Second, as mentioned in Section 2.2.1, the Court confirmed paragraph 62 of *Rottmann*, which established that 'the principles stemming from EU law with regard to the powers of the Member States in the sphere of nationality, and also their duty to exercise those powers having due regard to EU law, apply both to the host Member State and to the Member State of the original nationality'.[68] However, as also noted in Section 2.2.1, while the decision of the Member State of origin to withdraw its nationality should ideally '[enter] into force only once the new nationality has actually been acquired ... the obligation to ensure the effectiveness of Article 20 TFEU falls primarily' on the host Member State.[69]

In that context, the Court affirmed once again the legitimacy of protecting the special relationship signified by Member State nationality and therefore also of 'tak[ing] the view that the undesirable consequences of one person having multiple nationalities should be avoided'.[70] Additionally, revoking an assurance about the grant of nationality 'on the ground that the person concerned does not have a positive attitude towards the Member State of which he or she wishes to acquire the nationality and that his or her conduct is liable to represent a danger to public order and security of that Member State' constitutes a legitimate public interest.[71] Nevertheless, given the importance attached to the status of citizenship by EU primary law, the Court confirmed the importance of assessing the proportionality of the decision through an individual assessment of the situation of the person concerned in

---

[65] ibid para 44. The Court also noted that JY had exercised free movement rights under Article 21(1) TFEU and considered that 'the underlying logic of gradual integration that informs that provision of the FEU Treaty requires that the situation of citizens of the Union, who acquired rights under that provision as a result of having exercised their right to free movement within the European Union and are liable to lose not only entitlement to those rights but also the very status of citizen of the Union, even though they have sought, by becoming naturalised in the host Member State, to become more deeply integrated in the society of that Member State, falls within the scope of the Treaty provisions relating to citizenship of the Union' (para 43; referring to Case C-165/16 *Lounes*, EU:C:2017:862). See further, Section 3.

[66] AG Szpunar in Case C-118/20 *Wiener Landesregierung*, EU:C:2021:530, para 69 of the Opinion (emphasis in original).

[67] *Wiener Landesregierung*, EU:C:2022:34, para 47.

[68] ibid para 49.

[69] ibid paras 50–51.

[70] ibid para 54. O'Leary asks important questions on this point, however, remarking that the Court 'accepts the objective pursued by the Dutch legislation (a system to avoid the undesirable consequences of one person having multiple nationalities) without probing further. It is slightly odd that a judgement on EU citizenship does not recognise that one of the products of the free movement of Union citizens in an area of freedom, security and justice may be precisely a generation of Union citizens with multiple nationalities, allegiances and genuine links. While such EU citizens are not the norm, they are a reality' (O'Leary 'Nationality and citizenship' (n 19) 78).

[71] *Wiener Landesregierung*, para 57; referring to para 51 of *Rottmann* 'by analogy'.

line with the criteria articulated in *Tjebbes*, which includes compatibility with the Charter of Fundamental Rights. In the course of that assessment, it should also be 'establish[ed], in particular, whether th[e] decision is justified in relation to the gravity of the offence committed by that person and to whether it is possible for that person to recover his or her original nationality'.[72] Nevertheless, a Member State seeking to revoke an assurance about the grant of nationality is not precluded from doing so solely on the ground that the person concerned 'will find it difficult to recover the nationality of his or her Member State of origin'.[73]

To assess the gravity of the offences committed by JY specifically, the Court drew from principles established more generally with respect to restricting Union citizenship rights. Thus, 'as a justification for a decision entailing the loss of the status of citizen of the Union conferred on nationals of Member States by Article 20 TFEU, the concepts of "public policy" and "public security" must be interpreted strictly, so that their scope cannot be determined unilaterally by the Member States without being subject to control by the EU institutions'.[74] Reflecting its case law on Article 21 TFEU, the Court also distinguished between the concepts of public policy and public security, recalling that, for the former, 'a genuine, present and sufficiently serious threat affecting one of the fundamental interests of society' must be established.[75] In the Court's view, these criteria were not fulfilled with respect to the offences committed by JY: '[t]raffic offences, punishable by mere administrative fines [which] resulted in minor administrative fines and did not deprive JY of the right to continue to drive a motor vehicle on the public highway'.[76] Having regard, in other words, to the 'significant consequences' produced by loss of Union citizenship, the decision to revoke the earlier assurance given to her was not proportionate.

That outcome was rather uncannily predicted by Advocate General Mengozzi in *Tjebbes*,[77] and in many respects, the ruling in *Wiener Landesregierung* consolidated the principles already established in both *Rottmann* and *Tjebbes* as to how national authorities should undertake a proportionality assessment when loss of Union citizenship is at stake. How public interest concerns should be addressed within such an assessment also joins up with the framework developed for restrictions of citizenship rights more generally, whether these connect to the exercise of free movement rights or not, and the Charter brings added concern for the affected person's family life. Overall, then, the role of EU law in the context of Member State decisions determining nationality is undeniably far-reaching. Advocate General Poiares Maduro sought to reconcile the constitutional tensions produced by *Rottmann* on the basis that 'it is not that the acquisition and loss of nationality (and, consequently, of Union citizenship) are in themselves governed by [Union] law, but [that] the conditions for the acquisition and loss of nationality must be compatible with [Union] rules and respect the rights of the European citizen'.[78]

---

[72] *Wiener Landesregierung*, para 60; referring to para 56 of *Rottmann*.
[73] *Wiener Landesregierung*, para 63.
[74] ibid para 68; referring to Case C-165/14 *Rendón Marín*, EU:C:2016:675, para 82. See further, Chapter 10.
[75] *Wiener Landesregierung*, para 69. See further, Chapter 10.
[76] ibid para 71.
[77] AG Mengozzi in Case C-221/17 *Tjebbes and Others*, EU:C:2018:572, para 88 of the Opinion: 'in an extreme — and I hope purely hypothetical — case, where the legislation of a Member State provides for withdrawal of an individual's naturalisation entailing loss of citizenship of the Union as a result of a road traffic offence, the disproportionate nature of that measure would be clear because of the disparity between the low degree of gravity of the offence and the dramatic consequence of losing citizenship of the Union'.
[78] AG Poiares Maduro in Case C-135/08 *Rottmann*, EU:C:2009:588, para 23 of the Opinion. See similarly, para 32 of the Opinion: 'State rules on nationality cannot restrict the enjoyment and exercise of the rights and freedoms constituting the status of Union citizenship without justification.'

The challenge for the Court of Justice is to ensure that, in its future case law, the Member States can continue to tell the difference. The issue of investor citizenship is likely soon to prompt further guidance on these questions and perhaps also on the limits of EU law with respect to nationality determination. The Commission defines investor citizenship schemes as those 'where citizenship is granted under less stringent conditions than under ordinary naturalisation regimes, in particular without effective prior residence in the country concerned'[79]—in effect, schemes that enable the grant of nationality on the basis of payment or investment, supplanting processes that seek to establish a genuine link to the relevant State.[80] The Commission also highlights that '[i]t is precisely the benefits of Union citizenship, notably free movement rights, that are often advertised as the main attractive features of such schemes'.[81] In October 2020, the Commission opened infringement proceedings against Cyprus and Malta on the basis that 'the granting by these Member States of their nationality—and thereby EU citizenship—in exchange for a pre-determined payment or investment and without a genuine link with the Member States concerned, is not compatible with the principle of sincere cooperation enshrined in Article 4(3) of the Treaty on European Union' and 'undermines the integrity of the status of EU citizenship provided for in Article 20 [TFEU]'.[82] In April 2022, while indicating that it was 'carefully assessing the situation in Cyprus before deciding on the next steps' in light of actions taken following a reasoned opinion sent in June 2021, the Commission sent a reasoned opinion to Malta on the basis that its investor citizenship scheme was suspended only with respect to Russian and Belarusian nationals following Russia's invasion of Ukraine.[83] In September 2022, it referred the alleged infringement to the Court of Justice.[84] The European Parliament has also asserted that investor citizenship schemes are 'objectionable from an ethical, legal and economic point of view and pose several serious security risks for Union citizens, such as those stemming from money-laundering and corruption'.[85]

Nevertheless, applying the *Rottmann* case law to review of investor citizenship schemes would require significant progression of the case law as developed to date. A basic starting point can be drawn from *Micheletti*—Member States must be mindful of their obligations under EU law when they 'lay down the conditions for the acquisition and loss' of Member State nationality.[86] Two further steps would, however, need to be taken. First, while the circumstances in all three cases differed, *Rottmann*, *Tjebbes*, and *Wiener Landesregierung* each affirmed an obligation to undertake an *individual* examination-based proportionality review

---

[79] European Commission, Investor Citizenship and Residence Schemes in the European Union, COM(2019) 12 final, 1, highlighting associated risks to, *inter alia*, security, money laundering, and tax evasion, and highlighting schemes in Bulgaria, Cyprus, and Malta. Note also, the distinction between investor citizenship ('golden passport') and investor residence ('golden visa') schemes (ibid).

[80] See eg Commission Recommendation of 28 March 2022 on immediate steps in the context of the Russian invasion of Ukraine in relation to investor citizenship schemes and investor residence schemes, C(2022) 2028 final, para 1.

[81] ibid 5.

[82] European Commission Press Release, 20 October 2020, IP/20/1925, <https://ec.europa.eu/commission/prescorner/detail/en/ip_20_1925> (accessed 29 May 2023). The Commission noted that it was also, at that time, in correspondence with Bulgaria to obtain further information about an investor citizenship scheme in operation there; in March 2022, the Bulgarian Parliament agreed to amend the Bulgarian Citizenship Act to end the investor citizenship scheme.

[83] European Commission Press Release, 6 April 2022, IP/22/2068, <https://ec.europa.eu/commission/presscorner/detail/en/IP_22_2068> (accessed 29 May 2023).

[84] European Commission Press Release, 29 September 2022, IP/22/5422, <https://ec.europa.eu/commission/presscorner/detail/en/IP_22_5422> (accessed 29 May 2023).

[85] European Parliament resolution of 9 March 2022 with proposals to the Commission on citizenship and residence by investment schemes, 2021/2026(INL), para 1.

[86] Case C-369/90 *Micheletti*, EU:C:1992:295, para 10.

where decisions taken by national authorities have implications for the loss of Union citizenship.[87] Would the Court approach review of a national *system* for acquiring Member State nationality in the same way? In *Préfet du Gers*, discussed further in Section 2.2.3, the Court emphasised that its previous case law concerned 'specific situations falling within the scope of EU law, where a Member State had withdrawn its nationality *from individual persons*, pursuant to a legislative measure of that Member State [as in *Tjebbes*] or an *individual decision* taken by the competent authorities of that Member State [as in *Rottmann* and *Wiener Landesregierung*]'.[88] That case law could not, the Court held, be applied 'to a situation such as that in the main proceedings'.[89] However, that point most likely links back to the first part of the same paragraph, where the Court had stated that 'the loss of [the status of Union citizenship] and of the right to vote and to stand as a candidate in elections held in the Member State of residence of the person concerned is the automatic result of a sovereign decision made by a former Member State, under Article 50(1) TEU, to withdraw from the European Union'.[90] It was not, in other words, about the collective or systemic nature of the claim more generally, recalling too that the 'individual decision' at issue in *Tjebbes* was taken 'pursuant to a legislative measure'.

Second, and more problematically, reviews based on the principle that national rules must have due regard to EU law concern only 'situations covered by European Union law'.[91] The factor connecting *Rottmann*, *Tjebbes*, and *Wiener Landesregierung* to EU law was either the prospect of losing or the actual loss already of Union citizenship. In other words, all individuals involved were 'faced with losing the status conferred by Article 20 TFEU and the rights attaching thereto' and that is why each situation fell 'by reason of its nature and its consequences, within the ambit of EU law. *Thus*, the Member States must, when exercising their powers in the sphere of nationality, have due regard to EU law'.[92] For investor citizenship, the Commission has made two claims to demonstrate the required connecting factor to EU law.[93] First, '[h]aving due regard to EU law means taking into account all rules forming part of the Union legal order and includes having due regard to norms and customs under international law as such norms and customs form part of EU law'.[94] Second, '[s]ince under Article 20 TFEU, citizenship of the Union is an automatic consequence of holding nationality of a Member State and a host Member State cannot limit the rights of naturalised Union citizens on grounds that they acquired the nationality of another Member State without any link with that awarding Member State, each Member State needs to ensure that nationality is not awarded absent any genuine link to the country or its citizens'.[95]

---

[87] Case C-135/08 *Rottmann*, EU:C:2010:104, para 56; Case C-221/17 *Tjebbes*, EU:C:2019:189, para 44; Case C-118/20 *Wiener Landesregierung (Révocation d'une assurance de naturalisation)*, EU:C:2022:34, para 59.
[88] Case C-673/20 *Préfet du Gers*, EU:C:2022:449, para 62 (emphasis added).
[89] ibid.
[90] ibid. See similarly, AG Collins in Case C-673/20 *Préfet du Gers*, EU:C:2022:129, para 42 of the Opinion.
[91] *Rottmann*, para 41.
[92] *Tjebbes*, para 32 (emphasis added). See similarly, *Wiener Landesregierung*, para 44. Note earlier, the ruling in *Kaur*, raising similarly 'the effect of depriving any person who did not satisfy the definition of a national of [a Member State] of rights to which that person might be entitled under Community law' (Case C-192/99 *Kaur*, EU:C:2001:106, para 25).
[93] European Commission, 'Investor Citizenship and Residence Schemes' (n 79) 5–6.
[94] Here, the Commission references AG Poiares Maduro in Case C-135/08 *Rottmann*, EU:C:2009:588, paras 28–29 of the Opinion, and the finding of the International Court of Justice in the *Nottebohm* case that 'for nationality acquired through naturalisation to be recognised in the international arena, it should be granted on the basis of a genuine connection between the individual and the State in question' (Judgment of the International Court of Justice of 6 April 1955, *Nottebohm*, ICJ Reports 1955, p 4).
[95] Here, the Commission refers to Case C-369/90 *Micheletti*, EU:C:1992:295, para 10; Case C-165/16 *Lounes*, EU:C:2017:862, para 55; and the principle of sincere cooperation with other Member States and with the Union in Article 4(3) TEU. See similarly, European Parliament resolution of 9 March 2022 with proposals to the

At the time of writing, no further details on these arguments were yet available. However, even though the Commission's approach has already produced change at national level, its assertions with respect to the reach of EU citizenship law have been resisted by legal scholars.[96] The Commission's stance also seems to depart from the general tenor of case law on the discretion that the Member States retain in order to establish how their nationality is acquired, even where it is acknowledged that that space is not an entirely EU law-free zone.[97] Both the monetisation of nationality and the genuineness of links come in many forms in all of the Member States, and it remains unclear how judicial review of investor citizenship schemes could be triggered at Union level. The Commission (and European Parliament) are seeking, in effect, to defend something that Evans suggested in 1991: that 'the free movement of persons implies that Member States should not be left entirely free unilaterally to define their nationality for [Union] law purposes'.[98]

A successful case would mean a shift from the necessary connection to EU law being located in the *loss* of something to its being located in the *gain* of something; from the ultimate restriction of Union citizenship rights to the unlocking of them in the first place. It would entail going beyond acknowledging that Member States have a legitimate interest in 'protect[ing] the special relationship of solidarity and good faith between it and its nationals and also the reciprocity of rights and duties, which form the bedrock of the bond of nationality'[99] towards significantly deeper and more intrusive assessment of *how* they do it.[100] What the Commission proposes suggests a quantum advance beyond how the Court has, to date, merely acknowledged the legitimacy of Member State processes that evaluate genuine links.[101] It would require the Court to articulate what, both precisely and persuasively, the

---

Commission on citizenship and residence by investment schemes, 2021/2026(INL), para 5. In para 6, an additional point is raised: that 'the advantageous conditions and fast-track procedures set for investors under CBI/RBI schemes, when compared to the conditions and procedures for other third-country nationals wishing to obtain international protection, residence or citizenship, are discriminatory, lack fairness and risk undermining the consistency of the Union asylum and migration *acquis*', calling in that connection for the Commission to develop legislative proposals that could be based, inter alia, on Title V TFEU.

[96] eg Calling the Commission's interpretation and application of *Nottebohm* into question, especially by distinguishing between the recognition and acquisition of citizenship, see M van den Brink, 'Revising citizenship within the European Union: is a genuine link requirement the way forward?' (2022) 23 German Law Journal 79. Van den Brink reflects too on addressing the effects of investor citizenship schemes rather than hinging citizenship acquisition on a genuine link reviewable under EU law. See also, HU Jessurun d'Oliveira 'Union citizenship and beyond', Law 2018/15, EUI Working Papers, <http://hdl.handle.net/1814/58164> (accessed 29 May 2023).

[97] See eg AG Sharpston in Case C-34/09 *Ruiz Zambrano*, EU:C:2010:560: 'I have already dealt in essence with the Irish Government's "floodgates" argument. As that Member State itself demonstrated after the Court's ruling in *Zhu and Chen*, if particular rules on the acquisition of its nationality are—or appear to be—liable to lead to "unmanageable" results, it is open to the Member State concerned to amend them so as to address the problem. In so saying, I am not encouraging the Member States to be xenophobic or to batten down the hatches and turn the European Union into "Fortress Europe". That would indeed be a retrograde and reprehensible step—and one, moreover, that would be in clear contradiction to stated policy objectives. I am merely recalling that the rules on acquisition of nationality are the Member States' exclusive province. However, the Member States—having themselves created the concept of 'citizenship of the Union'—cannot exercise the same unfettered power in respect of the *consequences*, under EU law, of the Union citizenship that comes with the grant of the nationality of a Member State' (paras 114–115 of the Opinion, emphasis added; referring to Case C-200/02 *Zhu and Chen*, EU:C:2004:639).

[98] A Evans, 'Nationality law and European integration' (1991) 16 European Law Review 190 at 190.

[99] Case C-135/08 *Rottmann*, EU:C:2010:104, para 51.

[100] A possible argument is that the principle of sincere cooperation 'could be affected if a Member State were to carry out, without consulting the Commission or its partners, an unjustified mass naturalisation of nationals of non-member States' (AG Poiares Maduro in Case C-135/08 *Rottmann*, EU:C:2009:588, para 30 of the Opinion). Another avenue to consider is the ECtHR's concern for both proportionality *and* arbitrariness when assessing conditions for acquisition of nationality; for an overview of relevant case law, see O'Leary, 'Nationality and citizenship' (n 19) 53–58.

[101] Case C-221/17 *Tjebbes*, EU:C:2019:189, paras 35–38. Note also, the caution expressed by AG Mengozzi with respect the *Union* potentially breaching its responsibilities under Article 4(2) TEU, which include an

objective of reviewing the *possibility*—and not as to date the *impossibility*—of enjoying the rights conferred by Union citizenship actually is so that, 'by reason of its nature and its consequences', the necessary connecting factor to EU law could be established. Does the 'intrinsic connection with the freedom of movement and residence of a Union citizen'[102] that Member State nationality ordains do enough work in that respect?

2.2.3 After nationality: citizenship and withdrawal from the European Union

Article 50 TEU outlines the procedure for a Member State's withdrawal from the Union. Article 50(3) establishes more specifically that '[t]he Treaties shall cease to apply to the State in question' either from the date of entry into force of the withdrawal agreement concluded with the EU or otherwise two years after the withdrawing State submits the notification of its intention to withdraw referred to in Article 50(2) TEU, 'unless the European Council, in agreement with the Member State concerned, unanimously decides to extend this period'. Article 20(1) TFEU establishes that '[e]very person *holding the nationality of a Member State* shall be a citizen of the Union'. A consequential loss of Union citizenship for British nationals was therefore, on one view, an inevitable outcome of Brexit. Advocate General Poiares Maduro foretold this in *Rottmann* when he argued that 'there is no autonomous way of acquiring and losing Union citizenship. The acquisition and loss of Union citizenship are dependent on the acquisition and loss of the nationality of a Member State; Union citizenship presupposes nationality of a Member State'.[103]

As indicated in Section 1, the Court of Justice confirmed that position in *Préfet du Gers*. The case concerned deprivation of voting rights because of Brexit and, more specifically, the removal of EP, a British national who had resided in France since 1984, from the electoral list of her commune in France in February 2020. The questions relating to Article 20(2)(b) TFEU are considered in Chapter 5 in the discussion on Union citizenship and voting rights. What is important here is the strength of the Court's language in the statement that '[b]y Article 9 TEU and Article 20 TFEU, the authors of the Treaties ... established an *inseparable and exclusive link* between possession of the nationality of a Member State and not only the acquisition, but also the retention, of the status of citizen of the Union'.[104] Since possessing the nationality of a Member State is 'an essential condition for a person to be able to acquire and retain the status of citizen of the Union and to benefit fully from the rights attaching to that status', losing that nationality 'therefore entails, for the person concerned, the *automatic loss of his or her status as a citizen of the Union*'.[105] For British nationals, that occurred on 1 February 2020 and it is 'irrelevant' that they might have previously exercised free movement rights.[106] Any obligation of transnational coordination across the Member States, noted in Section 2.2.1, also falls away: the withdrawing State 'is not required to take its decision in concert with the other Member States or with the EU institutions' since '[t]he decision to withdraw is for that Member State alone to take, in accordance with its constitutional

---

obligation to respect the national identities of the Member States, should it venture too deeply into assessing choices made by national legislatures (AG Mengozzi in *Tjebbes*, EU:C:2018:572, paras 104–107 of the Opinion).

[102] Case C-165/14 *Rendón Marín*, EU:C:2016:675, para 75.
[103] AG Poiares Maduro in Case C-135/08 *Rottmann*, EU:C:2009:588, para 15 of the Opinion.
[104] Case C-673/20 *Préfet du Gers*, EU:C:2022:449, para 48 (emphasis added).
[105] ibid para 57 (emphasis added).
[106] ibid para 58. AG Collins agreed that '[t]he exercise of rights conferred by Union law does not furnish any legal basis upon which an individual's *status* as a Union citizen falls to be determined', adding that 'the integration of third-country nationals into the societies of the Member States is not among the goals furthered by Union citizenship' (EU:C:2022:129, paras 61 and 34 of the Opinion, emphasis added).

requirements, and therefore depends solely on its sovereign choice'.[107] Advocate General Collins outlined rather bluntly the path that EP *could* take to retain or re-access the benefits of her Union citizenship:

> EP appears to assert that the links that she forged with France at a time when she was a Member State national prevent her from being deprived of Union citizenship. However, it appears from the order for reference that, notwithstanding her long residence in France and her marriage to a French national, EP has chosen not to acquire French nationality. According to the French Government, EP could apply to do so as she is married to a French national. EP need thus do no more than make the requisite application to the French authorities to acquire French nationality, which would automatically confer Union citizenship upon her. It is, to say the least, paradoxical that whilst EP relies exclusively upon her links with France in order to sustain her claim that she is entitled to retain Union citizenship, she simultaneously declines to take the one step that could lead to her retaining her Union citizenship, namely the submission of an application for French nationality.[108]

That assessment captures something vital about Union citizenship that only comes into clearer focus because the status is lost: that it sets aside, in large part,[109] the need to make choices about changing nationality in the first place.

The referring court in *Préfet du Gers* did raise a potential *Rottmann* dimension with reference to UK electoral law, which precludes British nationals who have resided abroad for more than 15 years from voting in elections in the UK, suggesting that its application 'constitutes a disproportionate infringement of EP's fundamental right to vote'.[110] The Court of Justice was not convinced. Since the UK rule concerns 'a choice of electoral law made by that former Member State, now a third State ... neither the competent authorities of the Member States nor their courts may be required to carry out an individual examination of the consequences of the loss of the status of citizen of the Union for the person concerned, in the light of the principle of proportionality'.[111] The Court underlined, once again, that loss of Union citizenship was the result of the UK's sovereign choice to leave the European Union; pointed to the fact that the Withdrawal Agreement does not extend voting rights even where free movement had been exercised before the end of the transition period (as explained further in Chapter 5),[112] and affirmed that Article 18 TFEU 'is not intended to apply in the case of a possible difference in treatment between nationals of Member States and nationals of third States'.[113]

---

[107] *Préfet du Gers*, para 53; referring to Case C-621/18 *Wightman*, EU:C:2018:999, para 50. AG Collins went further still: '[s]ince the United Kingdom's sovereign choice to leave the European Union amounts *to a rejection of the principles underlying the European Union*, and the Withdrawal Agreement is an agreement between the European Union and the United Kingdom to facilitate the latter's orderly withdrawal from the former, the European Union was in no position to insist that the United Kingdom fully adhere to any of the European Union's founding principles' (para 75 of the Opinion, emphasis added).

[108] AG Collins in *Préfet du Gers*, para 33 of the Opinion.

[109] One key exception concerns the right to vote in national elections, which is not extended through Union citizenship: see further, Chapter 5.

[110] *Préfet du Gers*, para 36.

[111] ibid paras 60–61.

[112] Agreement on the withdrawal of the United Kingdom of Great Britain and Northern Ireland from the European Union and the European Atomic Energy Community, OJ 2019 CI 384/01.

[113] *Préfet du Gers*, para 78.

Interestingly, as noted in Section 2.2.2, the Court also distinguished the *kinds* of situations to which *Rottmann* proportionality review[114] had previously applied, that is, 'specific situations falling within the scope of EU law, where a Member State had withdrawn its nationality from individual persons, pursuant to a legislative measure of that Member State [*Tjebbes*] or an individual decision taken by the competent authorities of that Member State [*Rottmann* and *Wiener Landesregierung*]'.[115] That case law could not be applied 'to a situation such as that in the main proceedings.'[116] However, and linking back to the discussion in Section 2.2.2, this proviso refers to 'the loss of that status and of the right to vote and to stand as a candidate in elections held in the Member State of residence of the person concerned is the automatic result of a sovereign decision made by a former Member State, under Article 50(1) TEU, to withdraw from the European Union and thus to become a third State with respect to the European Union'.[117]

The Withdrawal Agreement concluded between the EU and the UK reflects the *Préfet du Gers* position overall in providing a framework for protecting the post-Brexit rights for EU nationals residing in the UK and British nationals residing in EU27.[118] But the fact that the rights ultimately protected aim primarily to secure continuity of residence and/or family circumstances established before the end of the agreed transition period have attracted sharp criticism (as have the uneven effects of the Agreement in practice).[119] The European Council affirmed the significance of Union citizenship and of protecting Union citizens in its April 2017 guidelines for Brexit negotiations,[120] in terms of how those guidelines were framed,[121] how the negotiations were structured,[122] and how the objective of securing an 'orderly withdrawal' from the Union would be achieved.[123] However, while paragraph 8 of the guidelines acknowledged that 'safeguard[ing] the status and rights derived from EU law at the date of withdrawal of EU and UK citizens, and their families, affected by the United Kingdom's withdrawal from the Union w[ould] be the first priority for the negotiations', it also stated that this would be actually achieved on the basis of '[a]greeing *reciprocal guarantees*' with the UK (emphasis added).[124]

---

[114] ie 'the obligation to carry out an individual examination of the proportionality of the consequences of the loss of Union citizenship' (ibid para 62).
[115] ibid.
[116] ibid.
[117] ibid.
[118] See esp Part Two WA. See more specifically, Chapters 4 (rights of family members), 6 (right to reside), 8 (right of permanent residence), and 10 (expulsion of Union citizens).
[119] eg A Łazowski, 'When *cives europae* became bargaining chips: free movement of persons in the Brexit negotiations' (2018) 18 ERA Forum 469; C O'Brien, 'Between the devil and the deep blue sea: vulnerable EU citizens cast adrift in the UK post-Brexit' (2021) 58 Common Market Law Review 431; and E Spaventa, 'Brexit and the free movement of persons: what is EU citizenship really about?' in N Nic Shuibhne (ed), *Revisiting the Fundamentals of the Free Movement of Persons in EU Law* (OUP 2023), forthcoming.
[120] European Council (Art 50) guidelines for Brexit negotiations, 29 April 2017, <https://www.consilium.europa.eu/en/press/press-releases/2017/04/29/euco-brexit-guidelines/#> (accessed 29 May 2023).
[121] ibid: 'the Union's overall objective in these negotiations will be to preserve its interests, those of its citizens, its businesses and its Member States'; '[c]itizens who have built their lives on the basis of rights flowing from the British membership of the EU face the prospect of losing those rights'; and '[t]hroughout these negotiations the Union will maintain its unity and act as one with the aim of reaching a result that is fair and equitable for all Member States and in the interest of its citizens'.
[122] Confirming in para 4 (ibid) that one of two key aims of the first phase of the negotiations was to 'provide as much clarity and legal certainty as possible to citizens, businesses, stakeholders and international partners on the immediate effects of the United Kingdom's withdrawal from the Union'.
[123] Observing in para 8 (ibid) that '[t]he right for every EU citizen, and of his or her family members, to live, to work or to study in any EU Member State is a fundamental aspect of the European Union. Along with other rights provided under EU law, it has shaped the lives and choices of millions of people'.
[124] Paragraph 8 concluded by providing that '[s]uch guarantees must be effective, enforceable, non-discriminatory and comprehensive, including the right to acquire permanent residence after a continuous period of five years of legal residence. Citizens should be able to exercise their rights through smooth and simple

In many respects, the Withdrawal Agreement does ensure far-reaching protection of the rights of both British nationals residing in EU27 and Union citizens residing in the UK at the end of the transition period (ie on 31 December 2020). As will be seen in Chapter 4, for example, the Agreement extends protection to family members as well as to affected British nationals and Union citizens themselves. Fundamentally, it aims to mirror the framework provided for in Directive 2004/38, which means that criticisms about either exclusion from or the quality of protection provided by the Withdrawal Agreement relate in large part to the Directive itself. It also means that rights *not* protected by the Agreement connect more directly to EU primary law and therefore, arguably, more directly to the *status* of Union citizenship itself—in essence, residence rights for third-country national family members in a Union citizen's home State based on Article 20 TFEU (Chapter 5), electoral, consular protection and political rights based on Articles 22–24 TFEU (Chapter 5), and rights that manifest in a Union citizen's home State following the exercise of previous free movement based on Article 21 TFEU (Chapter 9) TFEU.

But even the most generous assessment of an Agreement that was conceived, after all, as part of a process to disentangle and therefore distance a Member State from the Union and its protective legal web cannot overlook the pressures brought about by the necessity of processing residence validation at the scale that Brexit inevitably required,[125] as well as, for present purposes, Agreement anomalies that diminish the degree of protection that *might* have been extended. Three examples demonstrate the latter point. First, while the protection extended to those who fall within the personal scope of the Agreement extends for their lifetime,[126] the rights protected are predominantly past-facing. To illustrate the distinction from EU citizenship law, with the exception of children yet to be born or adopted, Article 10 WA protects only the families of Union citizens that are already formed; in contrast to the protection of family members not yet known to Union citizens more generally.[127] Second, while Part Two of the Agreement attracts comparably stronger enforcement[128] and regulatory[129] mechanisms at Union level, it remains the case that the principles of EU citizenship law that will apply to any disputes yet to arise remain frozen in time at the end of the transition period.[130] A precedent for doing things differently can be found in the EEA Agreement, which enables the incorporation of Directive 2004/38 without recognition of the underlying concept of Union Citizenship.[131] Third, Article 18(1) WA provides that '[t]he host State may

---

administrative procedures'. The theme of reciprocity continues to be emphasised post-Brexit; see Case C-673/20 *Préfet du Gers*, EU:C:2022:449, paras 73–74 and AG Collins (EU:C:2022:129), paras 72–74 of the Opinion.

[125] For a comprehensive account of the rights protected (and not protected) by Part Two of the Withdrawal Agreement, see M Dougan, *The UK's Withdrawal from the EU: A Legal Analysis* (OUP 2021) Chapter 7. On the Agreement more generally, see M Dougan, 'So long, farewell, auf wiedersehen, goodbye: the UK's withdrawal package' (2020) 57 Common Market Law Review 631; and S Peers, 'The end – or a new beginning? The EU/UK withdrawal agreement' (2020) 39 Yearbook of European Law 122.

[126] Article 39 WA ('[t]he persons covered by [Part Two WA] shall enjoy the rights provided for in the relevant Titles of this Part for their lifetime, unless they cease to meet the conditions set out in those Titles'. The personal scope of Part Two of the Agreement is detailed in Article 10 WA).

[127] eg Case C-127/08 *Metock and Others*, EU:C:2008:449. See further, Chapter 4.

[128] eg A preliminary reference concerning Part Two may be sent to the Court of Justice where a case is 'commenced at first instance within 8 years from the end of the transition period before a court or tribunal in the United Kingdom' (Article 158(1) WA).

[129] eg Article 165(1) WA includes a Committee on citizens' rights as one of just six 'specialised committees' established as part of the Agreement's governance structures.

[130] Article 6 WA. Cf Article 36 WA, which ensures dynamic alignment with the future evolution of EU law in the area of social security coordination.

[131] Decision of the EEA Joint Committee No 158/2007 of 7 December 2007 amending Annex V (Free movement of workers) and Annex VIII (Right of establishment) to the EEA Agreement, 2008 OJ L124/20, recital 8 of which confirms that '[t]he concept of "Union Citizenship" is not included in the Agreement'.

require Union citizens or United Kingdom nationals, their respective family members and other persons, who reside in its territory in accordance with the conditions set out in this Title, to apply for a new residence status *which confers the rights* under this Title'. As the Commission has indicated, Article 18(1) thus 'stipulates that the host State has the choice to operate a *constitutive* residence scheme'.[132] This highly permissive concession to national input contrasts sharply with the approach in EU citizenship law generally, which underlines that national procedures and administrative formalities are declaratory rather than constitutive of EU rights.[133] Instead, Article 18(1) WA aligns with other portals to greater national discretion found elsewhere in the Agreement too.[134]

Brexit does mean Brexit. Yet more was expected from the Union nevertheless, especially in light of the Court of Justice's recognition in *Wightman* that 'since citizenship of the Union is intended to be the fundamental status of nationals of the Member States ... any withdrawal of a Member State from the European Union is liable to have a considerable impact on the rights of all Union citizens, including, inter alia, their right to free movement, as regards both nationals of the Member State concerned and nationals of other Member States'.[135] Even if the status of Union citizenship should be preserved for Member State nationals only,[136] it was argued that citizenship could nevertheless have rationalised post-membership protection of free movement rights for British nationals already residing in EU27 as 'former Union citizens', for example,[137] or that Brexit could have catalysed a deeper transformation of Union citizenship with more attention paid to substantive connections between the citizen and the Union than to the formal issue of Member State nationality.[138]

---

[132] European Commission, Guidance Note relating to the Agreement on the withdrawal of the United Kingdom of Great Britain and Northern Ireland from the European Union and the European Atomic Energy Community Part two—Citizens' rights, C(2020) 2939 final, para 2.6.1 (emphasis added).

[133] eg Case C-85/96 *Martínez Sala*, EU:C:1998:217, para 53; confirming in EU citizenship law the position established in Case 48/75 *Royer*, EU:C:1976:57. More therefore suggests that '[t]he principles of reciprocity, uniformity and indeed the declaratory nature of EU rights were therefore compromised on this point' (G More, 'From Union citizen to third-country national: Brexit, the UK Withdrawal Agreement, no-deal preparations and Britons living in the European Union' in N Cambian, D Kochenov, and E Muir (eds) *European Citizenship under Stress: Social Justice, Brexit and Other Challenges* (Brill 2020) 457 at 467.

[134] See esp Article 18(1)(p) WA on criminality checks: 'criminality and security checks may be carried out systematically on applicants, with the exclusive aim of verifying whether the restrictions set out in Article 20 of this Agreement may be applicable. For that purpose, applicants may be required to declare past criminal convictions which appear in their criminal record in accordance with the law of the State of conviction at the time of the application. The host State may, if it considers this essential, apply the procedure set out in Article 27(3) of Directive 2004/38/EC with respect to enquiries to other States regarding previous criminal records'. See further, Chapter 10.

[135] Case C-621/18 *Wightman*, EU:C:2018:999, para 64.

[136] eg. AP van der Mei, 'Member State nationality, EU citizenship and associate European citizenship' in Cambian, Kochenov and Muir (eds) (n 133) 441.

[137] E Spaventa, 'Mice or horses? British citizens in the EU 27 after Brexit as "former EU citizens"' (2019) 44 European Law Review 589. Trade and Cooperation Agreement between the European Union and the European Atomic Energy Community, of the one part, and the United Kingdom of Great Britain and Northern Ireland, of the other part, OJ 2020 L444/14. For a range of perspectives on post-Brexit rights and what Brexit reveals about the status of Union citizenship, see further, S Coutts, 'Citizens of elsewhere, everywhere and... nowhere? Rethinking Union citizenship in light of Brexit' (2018) Northern Ireland Legal Quarterly 231; O Garner 'After Brexit: protecting European citizens and citizenship from fragmentation' (2016) Working Paper, EUI LAW, 2016/22, available at <http://hdl.handle.net/1814/44004> (accessed 29 May 2023); D Kostakopoulou '*Scala civium*: citizenship templates post-Brexit and the European Union's duty to protect EU citizens' (2018) 56 Journal of Common Market Studies 854; and M van den Brink and D Kochenov, 'Against associate EU citizenship' (2019) 57 Journal of Common Market Studies 1366.

[138] A development that could also have led to significant deepening of the rights of long-term resident third-country nationals in the Union more generally; see eg A Wiesbrock, 'Free movement of third-country nationals in the European Union: the illusion of inclusion' (2010) 35 European Law Review 455.

No conception of acquired rights or legitimate expectations has yet been recognised in Brexit-relevant case law.[139] Both the Withdrawal Agreement and the Court's ruling in *Préfet du Gers* ultimately upheld the vital connection between Member State nationality and Union citizenship. Articles 9 TEU and 20 TFEU do not really allow for any other interpretation as regards the holding of the status of Union citizenship per se. It is also important to acknowledge that neither Article 50 TEU nor the Withdrawal Agreement 'contemplate[s] any exception to the rule that, upon its withdrawal from the European Union, the United Kingdom ceased to be a Member State, with all of the consequences that follow for British nationals'.[140] If lessons need to be learned from Brexit with respect to the Union's protection of its former citizens, adjustments to the Article 50 process may need to be considered into the future. Nevertheless, it is telling that the Court of Justice has elsewhere in its case law recognised that the position of Icelandic nationals is '*objectively comparable with* that of an EU citizen' in certain circumstances.[141] That idea does indeed suggest that the protection, if not the status, of Union citizenship is extendable in circumstances outwith the holding of Member State nationality. Whether the EU legislator[142] and/or the Court of Justice might yet explore that potential to manage the challenges produced by Brexit remains to be seen. It is arguable, for example, that the wider system of EU law—in light of its novel inclusion of individuals as well as States and the fact that rights extended to the former are considered to 'become part of their legal heritage'[143]—justifies further reflection on how and the extent to which former Member State nationals should be protected.[144] The protection of individuals in EU law did, after all, long predate the creation of Union citizenship.

3. The Legal Implications of Dual Nationality

As explained in Section 2, the consequences actually or potentially faced in *Rottmann*, *Tjebbes*, and *Wiener Landesregierung* related to loss of Union citizenship altogether, since giving effect to the contested national decisions ruled out the holding of any Member State nationality at all. For that reason, the Court positioned the situations, by reason of their nature and consequences, within the scope of Article 20 TFEU. The circumstances in *Micheletti* align with the underlying concern of that *Rottmann* trilogy too: if Mr Micheletti's Italian nationality was not recognised by Spain, the fact that he still held Argentine nationality was important in general terms, avoiding statelessness, but irrelevant for the purposes of connecting

---

[139] In *Préfet du Gers*, AG Collins dismissed this possibility rather abruptly: '[a]ny breach of legitimate expectations that EP may wish to ventilate concerning her status as a Union citizen is to be addressed to the United Kingdom, which has withdrawn from the European Union, and not to either the French authorities or to the European Union' (AG Collins in Case C-673/20 *Préfet du Gers*, EU:C:2022:129, para 44 of the Opinion). While not in the context of withdrawal from the Union, note more generally the remarks of AG Tanchev in *TopFit and Biffi* on the theme of 'the general principle of respect for acquired rights' (AG Tanchev in Case C-22/18 *TopFit and Biffi*, EU:C:2019:181, paras 81ff of the Opinion).
[140] AG Collins in *Préfet du Gers*, para 60 of the Opinion. See similarly, para 75 of the Opinion ('no response other than the exclusion of British nationals from the definition of Union citizens was possible whilst remaining within the scope of the Treaties').
[141] Case C-897/19 PPU *IN*, EU:C:2020:262, para 58 (emphasis added). See further, Chapter 2.
[142] Eg By distinguishing British nationals as a special category of third-country nationals for legislation on 'the definition of the rights of third-country nationals residing legally in a Member State, including the conditions governing freedom of movement and of residence in other Member States' (Article 79(2)(b) TFEU).
[143] Case 26/62 *Van Gend en Loos*, EU:C:1963:1.
[144] See further, N Nic Shuibhne, 'Protecting the legal heritage of former Union citizens: *EP v Préfet du Gers*' (2023) 60 Common Market Law Review 475. Note also, Case C-716/22 *EP v Préfet du Gers II*, pending at the time of writing.

him to EU law. It can therefore make a material difference whether a dual national holds the nationalities of two EU Member States or of one Member State and a third country. This was already suggested in Section 2.2.1 in *Tjebbes*, recalling that Article 20 TFEU only requires 'an individual assessment of the situation of the person concerned and that of his or her family in order to determine whether the consequences of losing the nationality of the Member State concerned, *when it entails the loss of his or her citizenship of the Union*, might ... disproportionately affect the normal development of his or her family and professional life from the point of view of EU law'.[145] But in circumstances short of the loss of Union citizenship, does dual nationality always constitute a sufficient connecting factor to EU citizenship law? In other words, does holding the passport of a(nother) Member State inherently fulfil the requirement of a cross-border connection for the purposes of engaging Article 21 TFEU?

For dual nationals in a *Micheletti* situation—that is, those holding the nationality of an EU Member State and a third country—the ruling in *Collins* provides the starting point. Mr Collins was born in the United States and held dual American and Irish nationality. The substantive dispute concerned eligibility for jobseeker's allowance in the United Kingdom.[146] But whether he fell within the personal scope of EU law was an implicit prior question since it was 'clear from the order for reference that the person concerned never resided in another Member State before seeking employment in the United Kingdom'.[147] The question was answered in essence by the Court's silence on the point: Mr Collins was simply a national of one Member State seeking employment in another Member State, and he therefore resided in the latter State on the basis of Article 45 TFEU.[148] Any consideration of links to be demonstrated in order to assess the extent of his integration concerned the *host* State only—an approach that fits with the fact that the power to confer nationality is reserved to the Member States under international law.[149] Moreover, '[h]olding dual nationality of a Member State and a third State cannot deprive the person concerned of the freedoms he derives from EU law as a national of a Member State'.[150]

However, holding the nationality of two Member States can make things more complicated. In economic free movement law, the *Gilly* case confirms that acquiring the nationality of a second Member State can materially alter an individual's legal situation to their benefit from the perspective of engaging the protection of EU law. Mrs Gilly, a German national who acquired French nationality by marriage, resided in France and taught in a school in Germany. In the context of a dispute in France about taxation of frontier workers, the Court of Justice was required first to determine whether Mrs Gilly fell within the scope of Article 45 TFEU. The French Government argued that she had not exercised free movement rights

---

[145] Case C-221/17 *Tjebbes*, EU:C:2019:189, para 44 (emphasis added).
[146] Residence rights and equal treatment claims for jobseekers are addressed in Chapters 6 and 7 respectively.
[147] Case C-138/02 *Collins*, EU:C:2004:172, para 52.
[148] Confirming pre-citizenship case law on the residence rights of jobseekers: see Case C-292/89 *Antonissen*, EU:C:1991:80. However, on the merging of Articles 45 and 21 TFEU in *Collins* for equal treatment claims, see Chapter 7.
[149] This point was also confirmed by AG Ruiz-Jarabo Colomer, who pointed out that 'the Social Security Commissioner takes it as proven that Mr Collins is an Irish national and that he travelled to the United Kingdom with the intention of living and working there. Other circumstances relating to him are irrelevant, according to the case-law of the Court, when deciding whether the person concerned may rely on the principle of freedom of movement for workers. It is of little matter, then, that, as a United States citizen, he also acquired Irish nationality, never having lived nor worked in Ireland' (AG Ruiz-Jarabo Colomer in Case C-138/02 *Collins*, EU:C:2003:409, para 23 of the Opinion; in fn 16 of the Opinion, it was also noted that 'in reply to a question put to him at the hearing, counsel for Mr Collins confirmed that his client had never lived in Ireland, a country which he had visited on three occasions for periods of, at most, 10 days').
[150] Case C-247/17 *Raugevicius*, EU:C:2018:898, para 29; confirming Case C-369/90 *Micheletti*, EU:C:1992:295, para 15 and Case C-200/02 *Zhu and Chen*, EU:C:2004:639, paras 37–39.

within the meaning of Article 45 TFEU since she worked 'in her State of origin, namely Germany'.[151] However, in the Court's view, '[t]he circumstance that she has retained the nationality of the State in which she is employed in no way affects the fact that, for the French authorities, she is a French national working in another Member State'.[152] In one sense, both interpretations are accurate as statements of fact: Mrs Gilly is, at the same time, a French national working in Germany and a German national working in Germany. For the purposes of connecting her situation to the rights conferred by Article 45 TFEU, the more beneficial interpretation was adopted, which is not surprising when it is remembered that ensuring the effectiveness of EU rights is a fundamental objective in free movement law.[153]

The fact that holding dual nationality can also make a positive material difference in EU citizenship law is illustrated by *Garcia Avello*. As introduced in Chapter 2, the applicant was a Spanish national, married to a Belgian national, who resided in Belgium with the couple's two children. The children had both Belgian and Spanish nationality. Under Belgian law, the children's surname was registered as 'Garcia Avello' (their father's surname) and a request to register them in accordance with Spanish law and practice (as 'Garcia Weber') was refused. The necessary link with EU law was drawn from the fact that the children were 'nationals of one Member State lawfully resident in the territory of another Member State'.[154] The fact that they 'also have the nationality of the Member State in which they have been resident since their birth and which, according to the authorities of that State, is by virtue of that fact the only nationality recognised by the latter' did not undermine that link.[155] At one level, that statement reflects the approach taken in *Gilly* in its decoupling of nationality and residence to establish 'who' the Union citizen is for the purposes of engaging EU law. But it also goes much further, given that Mrs Gilly was, additionally, exercising free movement rights as a frontier worker. That obvious cross-border connection was absent from *Garcia Avello* and the Court therefore based its ruling on Article 20, and not 21, TFEU. In *Zhu and Chen*, the reasoning became clearer through the language the Court normally now uses to distinguish purely internal situations with *no* factor connecting them to EU law: '[t]he situation of a national of a Member State who was born in the host Member State and has not made use of the right to freedom of movement *cannot, for that reason alone, be assimilated to a purely internal situation*, thereby depriving that national of the benefit in the host Member State of the provisions of Community law on freedom of movement and of residence'.[156] In other words, dual nationality *internal* to the Union can trigger the necessary connection to EU law even in the absence of exercised freedom of movement.[157]

In *Garcia Avello*, the Court went on to rule that 'a discrepancy in surnames is *liable to cause serious inconvenience* for those concerned at both professional and private levels'.[158] Thus, the children's dual nationality both enabled and informed an assessment of their situation

---

[151] Case C-336/96 *Gilly*, EU:C:1998:221, para 20.
[152] ibid para 21.
[153] On the objective of ensuring the effectiveness of EU citizenship rights, see Chapter 2.
[154] Case C-148/02 *Garcia Avello*, EU:C:2003:539, para 27; confirmed in Case C-541/15 *Freitag*, EU:C:2017:432, para 34.
[155] *Garcia Avello*, para 28; because '[i]t is not permissible for a Member State to restrict the effects of the grant of the nationality of another Member State by imposing an additional condition for recognition of that nationality with a view to the exercise of the fundamental freedoms provided for in the Treaty' (citing *Micheletti*, para 10).
[156] Case C-200/02 *Zhu and Chen*, EU:C:2004:639, para 19 (emphasis added); confirmed in Case C-434/09 *McCarthy*, EU:C:2011:277, para 46. See further, Chapters 2 and 5.
[157] The same reasoning has been applied outside the specific situation of dual nationality where a national of one Member State still resided in a different Member State since birth; see Case C-353/06 *Grunkin and Paul*, EU:C:2008:559, paras 16–18.
[158] *Garcia Avello*, para 36 (emphasis added).

under EU non-discrimination law, which 'requires that comparable situations must not be treated differently and that different situations must not be treated in the same way'.[159] In terms of how the contested rules on registration of surnames were applied by the Belgian authorities,[160] it was therefore crucial that the children in *Garcia Avello*, as dual nationals, were distinguishable from persons who held only Belgian nationality: dual nationals were being treated in the same way as Belgian nationals even though they were not comparable situations. Conversely, the holding of dual nationality constituted a different situation: the Court found that, '[i]n those circumstances, Belgian nationals who have divergent surnames by reason of the different laws to which they are attached by nationality may plead difficulties specific to their situation which distinguish them from persons holding only Belgian nationality, who are identified by one surname alone'.[161]

The test of 'serious inconvenience' is not unproblematic: it verges on protecting hypothetical situations in the future lives of the children concerned, it presumes a greater likelihood of transnational life in the case of dual nationals, and it sets a very low threshold for breach of EU rights, even if the inconvenience has to be 'serious'—one later pulled back to more exceptional situations in the *Ruiz Zambrano* case law.[162] These questions are revisited in Chapter 5. More importantly for present purposes, the limits of dual nationality as a convertor of legal status soon became more evident in *McCarthy*.

As explained further in Chapter 5, *McCarthy* demonstrates that holding the nationality of a second Member State does not override the conditions that determine the scope of application of Directive 2004/38, Article 3(1) of which expressly requires movement to *another* Member State.[163] In this case, Mrs McCarthy *qua* British national never moved to Ireland and Mrs McCarthy *qua* Irish national never moved to the UK. Dual nationality could not be used to generate a Directive-based right to reside in the UK—the State of which she was (also) a national—since she enjoyed an unconditional right to reside there under international law.[164] With respect to the right to move and reside conferred directly by the Treaty, the Court found, similarly, that holding the nationality of another Member State is not 'sufficient, *in itself*, for a finding that the situation of the person concerned is covered by Article 21 TFEU'.[165] Drawing a link back to *Garcia Avello*, Mrs McCarthy would also have to demonstrate either that her situation amounted to deprivation of enjoyment of the substance of Union citizenship rights (to be protected by Article 20 TFEU) or that serious inconvenience was liable to constitute an obstacle to her right to move and reside (to be protected Article 21 TFEU).[166]

---

[159] ibid para 31, citing Case C-354/95 *National Farmers' Union*, EU:C:1997:379, para 61.
[160] It was possible under Belgian law to agree to change of surname requests when 'serious grounds' applied; however, the relevant Belgian authorities systematically refused applications based on the holding of another nationality (see further, *Garcia Avello*, paras 33 and 38, and see AG Jacobs (EU:C:2003:311) at para 23 of the Opinion).
[161] *Garcia Avello*, para 37. The equal treatment reasoning applied by the Court has been criticised; see eg T Ackermann, annotation of Case C-148/02, *Carlos Garcia Avello*, (2007) 44 Common Market Law Review 141.
[162] Case C-34/09 *Ruiz Zambrano*, EU:C:2011:124.
[163] Case C-434/09 *McCarthy*, EU:C:2011:277, paras 39–41.
[164] ibid paras 29 and 34. However, these questions are less settled in the context of acts of terrorism; see eg E Cloots, 'The legal limits of citizenship deprivation as a counterterror Strategy' (2017) 23 European Public Law 5. See more generally, D Owen, 'On the right to have nationality rights: statelessness, citizenship and human rights' (2018) 65 Netherlands International Law Review 299.
[165] *McCarthy*, para 54 (emphasis added).
[166] On this point, the Court concluded that 'no element of the situation of Mrs McCarthy, as described by the national court, indicates that the national measure at issue in the main proceedings has the effect of depriving her of the genuine enjoyment of the substance of the rights associated with her status as a Union citizen, or of impeding the exercise of her right to move and reside freely within the territory of the Member States, in accordance with

The circumstances and judgment in *Lounes* bring several of the preceding threads together. A Spanish national, Ms Garcia Ormazábal, moved to the UK as a student in 1996 and was in full-time employment there since 2009. She acquired British nationality in 2009, retaining her Spanish nationality. In 2014, she married Mr Lounes, an Algerian national who had entered the UK on six-month visitor visa in January 2010 but overstayed illegally. Mr Lounes applied for a residence card as the family member of an EEA national. However, he was served with a 'notice as person liable to removal' in May 2014 on the basis that he had overstayed in breach of UK immigration rules. Shortly afterwards, his residence card application was refused on the grounds that Ms Garcia Ormazábal was no longer regarded as an EEA national since she had become British, her Spanish nationality making no material difference under the applicable national rules.[167]

The Court first confirmed *McCarthy* with respect to the beneficiaries of Directive 2004/38: 'since, under a principle of international law, a Member State cannot refuse its own nationals the right to enter its territory and remain there and since those nationals thus enjoy an unconditional right of residence there, Directive 2004/38 is not intended to govern the residence of a Union citizen in the Member State of which he is a national'.[168] Ms Garcia Ormazábal, unlike Mrs McCarthy, *had* moved to the UK from Spain. Nevertheless, the Court found that she ceased to fall within the scope of Directive 2004/38 after she acquired British nationality.[169] It followed that Mr Lounes, as a third-country national, could not claim derived rights as the family member of a Union citizen on the basis of the Directive either.[170] However, the Court did not confine itself to consideration of the Directive (or thus to the scope of the questions referred to it). Instead, as in *McCarthy*, it chose to 'provid[e] the referring court with all the elements of interpretation of EU law which may be of assistance in adjudicating on the case before it, whether or not that court has specifically referred to them in its question'.[171]

Analysing Ms Garcia Ormazábal's situation on the basis of Article 21 TFEU, the Court recalled that 'the situation of a national of one Member State ... who has exercised her freedom of movement by going to and residing legally in another Member State, cannot be treated in the same way as *a purely domestic situation* merely because the person concerned has, while resident in the host Member State, acquired the nationality of that State in addition to her nationality of origin'.[172] It then held that to deprive a Union citizen of her rights under Article 21 in such a situation would undermine the effectiveness of that provision.[173] Two reasons were provided. First, echoing *Garcia Avello*, denying rights under Article 21 TFEU in the circumstances of the case would constitute treating a citizen of the host State who resides

Article 21 TFEU' (ibid para 49). However, aspects of her personal circumstances were not taken into account in that assessment; see further, Chapter 5.

[167] In fact, the relevant rules had been amended to this effect in 2012 following *McCarthy*; see Case C-165/16 *Lounes*, EU:C:2017:862, paras 20–23.
[168] *Lounes*, para 37.
[169] ibid paras 38–43.
[170] However, elements of the Directive were applied to the circumstances of the case 'by analogy' (ibid para 61). The 'by analogy' method was introduced in Chapter 2 and is discussed further in Chapter 9.
[171] *Lounes*, para 28; and noting in para 29 that 'the information given in the order for reference indicates that the referring court's uncertainties in the case before it concern not only Directive 2004/38 but also Article 21(1) TFEU'.
[172] ibid para 49 (emphasis added). This is the Court's only use of 'purely domestic situation' in EU citizenship law to date; see also, AG Bot (EU:C:2017:407, para 35 of the Opinion). It is not clear if it is intended to overlap with or is in some way distinctive from the 'purely internal' concept.
[173] *Lounes*, para 53; in AG Bot's words, it would 'would annihilate the effectiveness of the rights which she derives from Article 21(1) TFEU' (para 86 of the Opinion).

there because she has exercised free movement rights and who has retained the nationality of her Member State of origin in the same way as citizens who never left the host State in the first place: in other words, it would treat different situations similarly.[174] In that light, and affirming the profound value attributed to freedom of movement in EU citizenship law, the Court held that '[a] Member State cannot restrict the effects that follow from holding the nationality of another Member State, *in particular* the rights which are attendant thereon under EU law and which are triggered by a citizen exercising his freedom of movement'.[175] On that basis alone, it was not entirely clear whether the fact that Ms Garcia Ormazábal's *retained* her Spanish nationality following the exercise of free movement was decisive in the Court's reasoning.[176] Arguably, though, the central concern was, more broadly, that the exercise of free movement rights prior to naturalisation in the host State should not be disregarded and remains legally meaningful.[177]

Second, the Court recalled that extending rights to the family members of Union citizens promotes 'the gradual integration of the Union citizen concerned in the society of the host Member State'.[178] In its view, Union citizens who acquire the nationality of the host State after several years of residing there on the basis of Directive 2004/38 'intend to become permanently integrated in that State'.[179] It would therefore be 'contrary to the underlying logic of gradual integration that informs Article 21(1) TFEU to hold that such citizens, who have acquired rights under that provision as a result of having exercised their freedom of movement, must forego those rights—in particular the right to family life in the host Member State—because they have sought, by becoming naturalised in that Member State, *to become more deeply integrated* in the society of that State'.[180] Once again, that could be read as suggesting that retaining the nationality of the Member State of origin is immaterial; and, in the next part of the judgment, while the Court does reiterate Ms Garcia Ormazábal's specific circumstances, the broader principle seems more concerned with recognising—rewarding—a citizen's integration in the host State.[181] Similarly, when the Court states that 'the rights

---

[174] *Lounes*, para 54.
[175] ibid para 55 (emphasis added).
[176] For a signal that it *was* arguably important, see AG Szpunar in *Chenchooliah*, who notes: 'it appears to me to be important to note that, in [*Lounes*], the Court took account, inter alia, of Ms Ormazabal's Spanish nationality, finding that "a Member State cannot restrict the effects that follow from holding the nationality of another Member State, in particular the rights which are attendant thereon under EU law and which are triggered by a citizen exercising his freedom of movement"' (AG Szpunar in Case C-94/18 Chenchooliah, EU:C:2019:433, fn 41 of the Opinion and referring to para 55 of *Lounes*). However, as Shaw underlines, if that was the Court's intention, 'the greatest challenge is that it threatens inconsistency, given the diverse rules applied by the Member States regarding both naturalization and recognition and acceptance of dual nationality' (J Shaw, 'Citizenship: contrasting dynamics at the interface of integration and constitutionalism' in P Craig and G de Búrca (eds), *The Evolution of EU Law*, 3rd edn (OUP 2021) 608 at 625). Note also, Reveillere's observation that the Court has already recognised 'the right not to suffer discrimination on grounds of nationality for a naturalized citizen who did not keep his previous nationality – considering him an "honorary foreigner"' (V Reveillere, 'Family rights for naturalised EU citizens: *Lounes*' (2018) 55 Common Market Law Review 1855 at 1869–1870; referring to Case C-419/92 *Scholz*, EU:C:1994:62).
[177] That interpretation also seems in line with the reasoning of AG Bot (see esp para 38 of the Opinion).
[178] *Lounes*, para 56.
[179] ibid para 57; AG Bot described the acquisition of host State nationality as taking 'integration in the host Member State to its logical conclusion' (para 85 of the Opinion).
[180] *Lounes*, para 58 (emphasis added).
[181] As Reveillere puts it, conceiving naturalisation 'as the prolongation of free movement' (n 176, 1877). However, O'Leary draws attention to the less appealing side of the Court's approach, observing that 'the family unit which the applicant was seeking to protect by relying on the more favourable rights conferred on EU citizens by EU law compared to those which would normally have applied to her as a (naturalised) British citizen had been formed long after her arrival in the host Member State and long after naturalisation. In addition, for all that *Lounes* may appear a very protective, and indeed laudable, solution in an individual case, it accentuates the reverse discrimination with which EU law has thus far failed to deal. The applicant's EU citizenship, as interpreted by the ECJ, conferred on her not rights equal to those enjoyed by her fellow UK nationals, but more favourable ones.

conferred on Union citizens in the host Member State, particularly the right to a family life with a third-country national' should not 'be reduced in line with their increasing degree of integration in the society of that Member State *and according to the number of nationalities that they hold*', it could be argued that the highlighted proviso works both ways, that is, as also meaning that depriving a citizen who did *not* retain the nationality of their State of origin of Article 21 TFEU rights thereafter would wrongly undercut appropriate recognition of their integration in the host State.[182]

Nevertheless, the ruling is ambiguous: is it the exercise of free movement rights, which in turn led to deep integration in the host State; the retention of nationality of the State of origin; or a combination of those elements that produced the solution reached in *Lounes*? In articulating the conclusion that that 'citizens in a situation such as Ms Ormazábal's must be able to continue to enjoy, in the host Member State, the rights arising under that provision, after they have acquired the nationality of that Member State in addition to their nationality of origin and, in particular, must be able to build a family life with their third-country national spouse',[183] the Court unhelpfully conflated the specific facts of *Lounes* with more general expression of the principles that should be drawn from in future cases. Alongside the examples of ambiguity already raised, it was not clear either if the fact that Ms Garcia Ormazábal acquired British nationality only *after* exercising free movement rights to the host State was material.

It will require future cases, including where a Union citizen had dual nationality before moving and/or is no longer a dual national (ie who did not—perhaps could not—retain the nationality of their State of origin), before the legal implications of dual nationality are more concretely apparent. The *Lounes* case therefore provides a strong example of the tension outlined in Chapter 1 between the immediate dispute resolution and wider constitutional guidance functions exercised simultaneously by the Court of Justice. For now, though, a final point on *Lounes* concerns the future legal position of the third-country national spouse. While Ms Garcia Ormazábal has an unconditional right to reside in the UK as a British national, thus making permanent residence rights under Article 16 of the Directive irrelevant to her personally, can her husband acquire permanent residence in the UK even though his derived residence right is based on Article 21 TFEU and not Directive 2004/38? After all, it might be argued that permanent residence rights are a 'creature' of the Directive—that they concern, to borrow from Article 24(1), only those who reside in a host State *on the basis of* the Directive.[184]

However, as discussed further in Chapter 8, the Court has now extended the protection of permanent residence rights to those who reside in the host State on the basis of Article 21 TFEU. In *VI*, it ruled that 'the right of permanent residence in the host Member State, conferred by EU law on a minor national of another Member State, must, for the

---

Furthermore, the judgment could be read as reducing EU citizenship to a mere vehicle for the protection of the rights of "free movers"' (O'Leary, 'Nationality and citizenship' (n 19) 62).

[182] *Lounes*, para 59 (emphasis added).
[183] ibid para 60.
[184] See esp Case C-529/11 *Alarape and Tijani*, EU:C:2013:290, where the Court held that 'only those periods of residence satisfying the conditions laid down in Directive 2004/38 may be taken into consideration for the purposes of acquisition by the family members of a Union citizen who are not nationals of a Member State of a right of permanent residence under that directive' so that '[t]he fact that the family member of a Union citizen who is not a national of a Member State has resided in a Member State *solely on the basis of Article 12 of Regulation No 1612/68* cannot therefore have any effect on the acquisition of a right of permanent residence under Directive 2004/38' (paras 39–40, emphasis added).

purposes of ensuring the effectiveness of that right of residence, be considered as necessarily implying, under Article 21 TFEU, a right for the parent who is the primary carer of that minor Union citizen to reside with him or her in the host Member State, regardless of the nationality of that parent' and it therefore 'follows that the inapplicability of the conditions set out, inter alia, in Article 7(1)(b) of Directive 2004/38, following the acquisition by that minor of a right of permanent residence under Article 16(1) of that directive, extends, pursuant to Article 21 TFEU, to that parent'.[185] As explained further in Chapter 5, the Court has distinguished in other case law between the position of dependent minor children and more autonomous spouses/adults with respect to residence rights drawn directly from Articles 20 and 21 TFEU.[186] Whether past exercise of free movement would make the necessary material difference to enable permanent residence rights for a spouse in the circumstances of *Lounes* remains to be determined. However, given the undeniably central role of free movement in the progression of EU citizenship law overall, chances are that it would.

4. Concluding Remarks

Three general themes emerged over the course of this chapter. First, how the Court of Justice rationalises a review under EU law of Member State conditions and processes for the acquisition and loss of nationality—confined, to date, to situations where loss of Union citizenship is either a potential or already experienced consequence—illustrates very well a broader quality of the division of competences between the Union and its Member States: that the formal division of competences does not, in and of itself, provide the full picture; that there are shadowlands shaped by EU legal obligation even where an area is vested exclusively in national competence. The fact that Member States ultimately retain competence for authorising access to Union citizenship is then precisely what produces tensions since a profoundly supranational status has profoundly national roots. As the legal trajectory edges further into review of Member State rules for acquiring nationality, where the boundaries of these shadowlands are located will become clearer.

Second, the developments discussed in this chapter also bring out the *transnational* dimension of EU citizenship law, in the sense that the Court has found ways to deal with the fallout from the absence of formal coordination mechanisms on nationality determination across the Member States and has thus, at the same time, encouraged alertness, at least, to the consequences that individual decisions can have across the Union as a whole. Finally, third, while the importance of Union citizenship as a fundamental status, the significance of integration, and ensuring compliance with the Charter of Fundamental Rights are all observable through the legal developments considered in this chapter, it is a concern for the effectiveness of EU rights and especially of freedom of movement—for ensuring that it remains a viable choice for Union citizens, in legal terms at least—that comes through most strongly overall. That will surprise few and disappoint some. In that light, Brexit forces us to continue to reflect on and confront both the nature and (different) futures of Union citizenship.

---

[185] Case C-247/20 *VI*, EU:C:2022:177, paras 58–59.
[186] eg Case C-434/09 *McCarthy*, EU:C:2011:277; Case C-82/16 *KA and Others*, EU:C:2018:308.

Further Reading

N Cambien, 'Case C- 135/08, *Janko Rottmann v. Freistaat Bayern*' (2011) 17 Columbia Journal of European Law 375.

A Evans, 'Nationality law and European integration' (1991) 16 European Law Review 190.

HU Jessurun d'Oliveira, 'Nationality and the European Union after Amsterdam' in D O'Keeffe and P Twomey (eds), *Legal issues of the Amsterdam Treaty* (Hart Publishing 1999) 395.

HU Jessurun d'Oliveira, G-R de Groot, and A Seling 'Double case note: Court of Justice of the European Union, Decision of 2 March 2010, Case C-315/08, *Janko Rottmann v Freistaat Bayern*, Case Note 1 Decoupling nationality and Union citizenship? Case Note 2 The consequences of the *Rottmann* judgment on Member State autonomy – The European Court of Justice's avant-gardisme in nationality matters' (2011) 7 European Constitutional Law Review 128.

S O'Leary, 'Nationality law and Community citizenship: a tale of two uneasy bedfellows' (1992) 12 Yearbook of European Law 353.

H Oosterom-Staples, 'The triangular relationship between nationality, EU citizenship and migration in EU law: a tale of competing competences' (2018) 65 Netherlands International Law Review 431.

L Orgad and J Lepoutre (eds), 'Should EU citizenship be disentangled from Member State nationality?', RSCAS 2019/24, EUI Working Papers, <http://hdl.handle.net/1814/62229> (accessed 29 May 2023).

D Sarmiento and M van den Brink, 'EU competence and investor migration' in D Kochenov and K Surak (eds), *Citizenship and Residence Sales: Rethinking the Boundaries of Belonging* (CUP 2023) forthcoming.

A Shachar and R Bauböck (eds), 'Should citizenship be for sale?', RSCAS 2014/10, EUI Working Papers, <http://hdl.handle.net/1814/29318> (accessed 29 May 2023).

J Shaw (ed), 'Has the European Court of Justice challenged Member State sovereignty in nationality law?', RSCAS 2011/62, EUI Working Papers, available at <http://hdl.handle.net/1814/19654>(accessed 29 May 2023).

M van den Brink, 'A qualified defence of the primacy of nationality over European Union citizenship' (2020) 69 The International and Comparative Law Quarterly 177.

4
Who is Protected?

Part II: Defining the Family Members of Union Citizens

1. Chapter Overview

This chapter examines the protection extended to certain family members of Union citizens by setting out how 'family members' are defined—in other words, it explains which family members do, and do not, come within the scope of EU citizenship law. The rights provided for are then discussed more substantively in the chapters that follow, as they relate to the right to reside (Chapters 5–7 and 9), permanent residence rights (Chapter 8), and protection against expulsion (Chapter 10).

As introduced in Chapter 2, extending protection to the family members of Member State nationals, irrespective of the nationality of the former, has a long history in EU free movement law. And one thing has not changed: the Treaty (still) does not 'confer any autonomous right on third-country nationals' and therefore any rights of which third-country nationals are the beneficiaries as family members are 'not autonomous rights of those nationals but rights derived from those enjoyed by a Union citizen'.[1] As the Court of Justice observed in *Metock*, '[e]ven before the adoption of Directive 2004/38, the Community legislature recognised the importance of ensuring the protection of the family life of nationals of the Member States in order to eliminate obstacles to the exercise of the fundamental freedoms guaranteed by the EC Treaty'.[2] Similarly, even where EU protection is extended to family members in a Union citizen's home State under Article 20 TFEU, '[t]he purpose and justification of those derived rights are based on the fact that a refusal to allow them would be such as to interfere, in particular, with a Union citizen's freedom of movement'.[3] However, in *Lounes*, the Court acknowledged that '[t]he rights which nationals of Member States enjoy under [Article 21 TFEU] *include the right to lead a normal family life*, together with their family members, in the host Member State'.[4] Thus, respect for family life, which is guaranteed by Article 7 of the Charter of Fundamental Rights (CFR),[5] is also woven into the framework of Union citizenship.

Against that background, this chapter first sets out the principles that guide the protection of the family members of Union citizens (Section 2) and then explains how 'family members' are defined (Section 3)—principally by the provisions of Directive 2004/38, which are, in many respects, also applied by analogy to situations protected directly by the Treaty.[6]

---

[1] Case C-133/15 *Chavez-Vilchez*, EU:C:2017:354, para 62.
[2] Case C-127/08 *Metock and Others*, EU:C:2008:449, para 56. Directive 2004/38/EC on the right of citizens of the Union and their family members to move and reside freely within the territory of the Member States, 2004 OJ L158/77.
[3] *Chavez-Vilchez*, para 62. See further, Chapter 5.
[4] Case C-165/16 *Lounes*, EU:C:2017:862, para 52 (emphasis added).
[5] Article 7 CFR provides that '[e]veryone has the right to respect for his or her private and family life, home and communications'.
[6] Confirming that Article 2(2) of the Directive, which defines 'family members' for 'the purposes of this Directive' applies by analogy in situations protected directly by Article 21 TFEU, see Case C-673/16 *Coman*, EU:C:2018:385, paras 33 and 36 (see further, Section 3.2.1.1 and Chapter 9).

Following an overview of the relevant provisions of the Directive (Section 3.1), the different categories of protected family members, the nature of the rights that they enjoy, and the conditions to which these rights are subject are then presented (Section 3.2). It will be seen that significantly stronger protection is extended to core family members, as defined by EU law, as compared to those in a Union citizen's wider family orbit. Thematic questions that arise include the influence of respect for family life, the relevance of a family member's status under a Member State's immigration rules, and the consequences of changing family circumstances. How the definitions and rights that apply in EU citizenship law compare to those in Part Two of the Withdrawal Agreement concluded between the European Union and the United Kingdom following the UK's withdrawal from the Union is signalled where relevant.[7] Finally, the requirement that certain family members must be 'dependent' on the Union citizen from whom they derive rights is considered (Section 4). In that discussion, the dependency of minor Union citizens on their parents[8] bridges to Chapter 5, which examines residence rights for third-country national family members in a dependent Union citizen's home State.[9]

2. Protecting Family Members in EU Citizenship Law: Guiding Principles

As introduced in Chapter 2, Directive 2004/38 was conceived to replace several legislative measures that dealt separately with the same or similar aspects of the free movement of persons. In terms of personal scope, Article 2 of the Directive mirrors Article 20 TFEU in defining a Union citizen as 'any person having the nationality of a Member State'. However, the Directive also lays down 'the conditions governing the exercise of the right of free movement and residence within the territory of the Member States by Union citizens *and their family members*' (Article 1 of the Directive). As also explained in Chapter 2, extending rights to the family members of Member State nationals, irrespective of the nationality of the former, was one of the most significant innovations in EU free movement law: after all, family members are (still) not mentioned anywhere in the Treaties.

Recital 5 of Directive 2004/38 connects the protection extended to family members to ensuring that a Union citizen's right to move and reside freely is 'exercised under objective conditions of freedom and dignity'.[10] That objective, originally expressed in similar terms in the preamble to Regulation 1612/68 on freedom of movement for workers, was noted in Chapter 2 as an important example of 'humanising' the economic freedoms. Thus, as also discussed in Chapter 2, while the concept of integration in EU citizenship law functions both to protect *and* to impose obligations on Member State nationals who exercise free movement, integration was conceived originally as a *right* in the context of protecting family members.[11] Over time, respect for family life, as a fundamental right protected by Article 8

---

[7] Agreement on the withdrawal of the United Kingdom of Great Britain and Northern Ireland from the European Union and the European Atomic Energy Community, 2019 OJ CI 384/01.
[8] Residence rights for certain carers other than parents can be established in different circumstances and on different legal bases: see further, Chapters 5 (right to reside in a home State), 6 (right to reside in a host State), and 7 (concept of lawful residence).
[9] Beginning with Case C-34/09 *Ruiz Zambrano*, EU:C:2011:124. See further, Chapter 5.
[10] Referred to in eg Case C-202/13 *McCarthy II*, EU:C:2014:2450, para 33.
[11] eg Case C-308/93 *Cabanis-Issarte*, EU:C:1996:169, para 38: 'freedom of movement for workers, guaranteed by Article [45 TFEU], entails the right of integration into the host State, especially for the worker's family, in order to avoid the adverse consequences for freedom of movement which would otherwise arise'.

EHCR,[12] became more visible in EU free movement law.[13] It is now guaranteed by Article 7 CFR while Article 24 CFR protects the rights of the child, with Article 24(2) requiring that '[i]n all actions relating to children, whether taken by public authorities or private institutions, the child's best interests must be a primary consideration'. The Court of Justice has therefore recognised that 'protection of the child is a legitimate interest which, in principle, justifies a restriction on a fundamental freedom guaranteed by the TFEU'.[14]

At the same time, the classic economic free movement idea—that respect for family life is protected to ensure unobstructed freedom of movement—persists in parallel with fundamental rights language per se. In *Ruiz Zambrano*, for example, and referring to recital 5 of Directive 2004/38, Advocate General Sharpston observed that

> when citizens move, they do so as human beings, not as robots. They fall in love, marry and have families. The family unit, depending on circumstances, may be composed solely of EU citizens, or of EU citizens and third country nationals, closely linked to one another. If family members are not treated in the same way as the EU citizen exercising rights of free movement, the concept of freedom of movement becomes devoid of any real meaning.[15]

In *Banger*, Advocate General Bobek wrote that '[p]erhaps it is not a front runner for a "humanist case-law award", but it has long been recognised by this Court that the derived right of residence of family members of Union citizens is instrumental in ensuring the free movement rights of the Union citizens themselves'.[16] These statements capture how both normative and functional interests feed into the protection of family members in EU citizenship law. They also reflect the movement-centric inflection of both EU citizenship law specifically and the Union as a polity more generally, differently from both Member States and the Council of Europe. Thus, a tension between protecting family life as either a primary or secondary objective runs through much of the law in this area as well as through the debates that assess it.

The Court has more recently characterised 'the right to lead a normal family life' in a host State as *itself* flowing from Article 21 TFEU.[17] It cited *Metock* 'by analogy' to support this idea, having previously established that 'if Union citizens were not allowed to lead a normal

---

[12] Article 8 ECHR provides: '1. Everyone has the right to respect for his private and family life, his home and his correspondence. 2. There shall be no interference by a public authority with the exercise of this right except such as is in accordance with the law and is necessary in a democratic society in the interests of national security, public safety or the economic well-being of the country, for the prevention of disorder or crime, for the protection of health or morals, or for the protection of the rights and freedoms of others.'

[13] eg Case 249/86 *Commission v Germany*, EU:C:1989:204, para 10, confirming an obligation to interpret Regulation 1612/68 on freedom of movement for workers in compliance with Article 8 ECHR, as one of the fundamental rights 'recognised' by Community law; Case C-60/00 *Carpenter*, EU:C:2002:434, para 40, in the context of reviewing a restriction on freedom to provide services for compatibility with 'the fundamental rights whose observance the Court ensures' and referring in para 41 to Article 8 ECHR. Similarly, in *Singh*, the Court sought to ensure security of residence for the spouses of Member State nationals so that the latter would not be deterred from exercising free movement in the first place (Case C-370/90 *Singh*, EU:C:1992:296, paras 21 and 23). See also eg Case C-459/99 *MRAX*, EU:C:2002:461, para 53; Case C-291/05 *Eind*, EU:C:2007:771, para 44; and Case C-127/08 *Metock and Others*, EU:C:2008:449, para 79.

[14] Case C-454/19 *ZW*, EU:C:2020:947, para 40; referring to Case C-244/06 *Dynamic Medien*, EU:C:2008:85, para 40 'by analogy'.

[15] AG Sharpston in Case C-34/09 *Ruiz Zambrano*, EU:C:2010:560, para 128 of the Opinion.

[16] AG Bobek in Case C-89/17 *Banger*, EU:C:2018:225, para 89 of the Opinion.

[17] Case C-165/16 *Lounes*, EU:C:2017:862, para 52. Confirmed in Case C-673/16 *Coman*, EU:C:2018:385, para 32, where that interpretation was applied in a Union citizen's home State following their return there after exercising free movement (see further, Chapter 9), and Case C-490/20 *Stolichna obshtina, rayon 'Pancharevo'*, EU:C:2021:1008, para 47.

family life in the host Member State, the exercise of the freedoms they are guaranteed by the Treaty would be seriously obstructed'.[18] What the idea of 'normal' family life entails either in a general sense or more specifically in EU citizenship law is not self-evident.[19] In *Metock*, examples of deprivation of the opportunity to lead a normal family life provided by the Court included deportation of third-country national family members and also the fact that where family members remained with Union citizens in the host State and were 'threatened with imminent deportation', refusal of a right to reside precluded these family members from taking up employment there and placed them 'in a situation of uncertainty as regards fundamental aspects of their family future'.[20]

However, the idea of 'normal' family life is not the only criterion applied in the Court's case law. Reflecting the three stages of residence in a host State mapped out by Directive 2004/38—up to three months (Article 6), between three months and five years (governed mainly by the conditions in Article 7(1) of the Directive), and after five years (where legal and continuous residence in the host State can lead to a right of permanent residence there in accordance with Article 16(1))—the Court characterises residence 'pursuant to and in accordance with Article 7(1)' of the Directive as 'genuine residence', which it considers to go 'hand in hand with *creating* and *strengthening* family life in that Member State'.[21] The concept of 'genuine residence' has particular relevance in situations where a Union citizen returns to their home State after exercising free movement:

> [D]uring the genuine residence of the Union citizen in the host Member State, pursuant to and in conformity with the conditions set out in Article 7(1) and (2) of Directive 2004/38, family life is created or strengthened in that Member State, the effectiveness of the rights conferred on the Union citizen by Article 21(1) TFEU requires that the citizen's family life in the host Member State may continue on returning to the Member of State of which he is a national, through the grant of a derived right of residence to the family member who is a third-country national. If no such derived right of residence were granted, that Union citizen could be discouraged from leaving the Member State of which he is a national in order to exercise his right of residence under Article 21(1) TFEU in another Member State because he is uncertain whether he will be able to continue in his Member State of origin a family life with his immediate family members which has been created or strengthened in the host Member State.[22]

Conversely, where a Union citizen resides in another Member State for less than three months, the inference is that family life is not *sufficiently* created or strengthened there and

---

[18] Case C-127/08 *Metock and Others*, EU:C:2008:449, para 62.

[19] In a different context, recital 8 of Directive 2003/86 signals that '[s]pecial attention should be paid to the situation of refugees on account of the reasons which obliged them to flee their country and prevent them from leading a normal family life there' (Council Directive 2003/86/EC on the right to family reunification, 2003 OJ L251/12); referred to in eg Case C-370/17 *K and B*, EU:C:2018:877, para 53.

[20] Order of the President of the Court in Case C-127/08 *Metock and Others*, EU:C:2008:235, para 13. That factor influenced the Court's finding of exceptional urgency, which, in accordance with Article 104a of the Court's Rules of Procedure, led to the accelerated procedure being applied. See further, S Currie, 'Accelerated justice or a step too far? Residence rights of non-EU family members and the Court's ruling in *Metock*' (2009) *European Law Review* 310 at 315–19. See similarly, Order of the President of the Court in Case C-300/11 *ZZ*, EU:C:2011:646, paras 11–12; and Order of the President of the Court in Case C-400/12 *G*, EU:C:2013:5, paras 15–16 (see further, Chapter 10).

[21] Case C-456/12 *O and B*, EU:C:2014:135, para 53 (emphasis added).

[22] ibid para 54; confirmed in eg Case C-230/17 *Deha Altiner and Ravn*, EU:C:2018:497, para 26.

residence rights for family members do not then 'return' to the home State with that citizen. These situations are returned to in Section 3.2 in the context of the rights of same-sex spouses and examined in more detail in Chapter 9.

Finally, as introduced in Section 1, rights conferred on family members by EU citizenship law are only ever *derived* from Union citizens, which has especially significant implications for family members who are not themselves Member State nationals.[23] As explained by the Court:

> As regards the right of residence in the host Member State of nationals of third countries who are family members of a Union citizen ... the rights conferred on third-country nationals by Directive 2004/38 are not autonomous rights of those nationals but rights derived from the exercise of freedom of movement by a Union citizen. The purpose and justification of those derived rights are based on the fact that a refusal to allow such rights would be liable to interfere with the Union citizen's freedom of movement by discouraging him from exercising his rights of entry into and residence in the host Member State.[24]

The same conception applies when protection is drawn directly from Articles 20 and 21 TFEU, reflecting the elemental concern in EU citizenship law for the effective exercise of free movement.[25] The relevant Union citizen is therefore always the 'reference person'.[26] However, certain provisions of the Directive—on family members retaining a right of residence if the Union citizen dies or leaves the host State (Article 12), or in the event of divorce, annulment of marriage, or termination of registered partnership (Article 13)—characterise the rights they confer as retained by family members 'exclusively on a personal basis', which edges close to if not over the line of 'autonomous' rights. Indeed, in *NA*, the Court referred to Article 13(2) of the Directive as 'a derogation from the principle that Directive 2004/38 confers rights of entry into and residence in a Member State not on all third-country nationals, but solely on those who are a "family member" within the meaning of [Article 2(2)]'.[27] The rights provided for by Articles 12 and 13 of the Directive are considered in Chapter 6.[28]

---

[23] Third-country national family members may benefit independently from residence rights under EU law where they meet the conditions set down in Directive 2003/109 concerning the status of third-country nationals who are long-term residents (2003 OJ L16/44; this measure does not apply in Denmark or Ireland).

[24] Case C-218/14 *Singh II*, EU:C:2015:476, para 50. See also, AG Mengozzi in Case C-423/12 *Reyes*, EU:C:2013:719, para 32 of the Opinion: '[t]he fact that the rights granted to family members are only derived rights highlights the fundamental objective pursued by Directive 2004/38, which is not family reunification, or respect for the private and family life of Union citizens, but rather those citizens' "primary and individual right to move and reside freely within the territory of the Member States". It is only *to serve that fundamental objective* that the rights of movement and residence are 'also granted to their family members, irrespective of nationality. The preservation of the unity of the family group was not overlooked by the European Union legislature, but it was not its principal concern' (referring to recitals 1 and 5 of the Directive respectively; emphasis added).

[25] Case C-165/14 *Rendón Marín*, EU:C:2016:675, paras 70–72.

[26] Case C-133/15 *Chavez-Vilchez*, EU:C:2017:354, para 55.

[27] Case C-115/15 *NA*, EU:C:2016:487, para 41, referring to the situations addressed by Article 13(2) of the Directive as 'exceptional cases' (para 42). See further, Chapter 6.

[28] Related case law has been controversial in some respects, especially on the extent of protection extended in situations of domestic violence: see Case C-218/14 *Singh II*, EU:C:2015:476 and Case C-930/19 *X v État belge*, EU:C:2021:657. See further, Chapter 6.

3. Scope of Protection and Key Definitions

In this section of the chapter, the scope of Directive 2004/38 is first introduced in general terms (Section 3.1) before the 'family members' protected by EU citizenship law are then defined (Section 3.2).

3.1 Directive 2004/38: Scope of Application

Article 3(1) of Directive 2004/38 establishes that the Directive applies 'to all Union citizens who move to or reside in a Member State other than that of which they are a national, and to their family members as defined in [Article 2(2)] who accompany or join them'. Concerning, first, the requirement that protected family members must 'accompany or join' a Union citizen who is exercising free movement, and noting the same language in Articles 6 and 7 of the Directive on the right to reside in a host State, the Court ruled in *Metock* that 'none of those provisions requires that the Union citizen must *already* have founded a family at the time when he moves to the host Member State in order for his family members who are nationals of non-member countries to be able to enjoy the rights established by that directive'.[29] Thus, '[b]y providing that the family members of the Union citizen can join him in the host Member State, the Community legislature ... accepted the possibility of the Union citizen not founding a family until after exercising his right of freedom of movement'.[30] The Court invoked both the facilitation of the 'fundamental right of residence' of Union citizens in a host State and the objective of not discouraging continued residence there to support its interpretation.[31] As a result, 'nationals of non-member countries who are family members of a Union citizen derive from Directive 2004/38 *the right* to join that Union citizen in the host Member State, whether he has become established there before or after founding a family'.[32]

In the interest of not depriving Union citizenship rights of their effectiveness, it therefore 'makes no difference' whether third-country national family members entered the host Member State 'before or after becoming family members of that Union citizen, since the refusal of the host Member State to grant them a right of residence is equally liable to discourage that Union citizen from continuing to reside in that Member State'.[33] In contrast, while the Withdrawal Agreement (WA) protects the children not yet born or adopted of British nationals who resided in EU27 and of EU27 nationals who resided in the UK at the end of the transition period (ie 31 December 2020), families must otherwise have been formed already in order that relevant family members fall within the scope of the Agreement. On the requirement in Article 9(c) WA that British nationals in EU27 and EU27 nationals in the UK must have resided in the host State 'before the end of the transition period and [must] continue to reside there thereafter', the Commission has advised that '[t]hese notions, [which] should be read together, incorporate a time stamp that requires that residence in accordance with Union law qualifies for the purposes of Part Two of the Agreement only when such residence is "continuous" at the end of the transition period

---

[29] Case C-127/08 *Metock and Others*, EU:C:2008:449, para 87 (emphasis added).
[30] ibid para 88.
[31] ibid para 89.
[32] ibid para 90 (emphasis added).
[33] ibid para 92; confirmed in eg Case C-94/18 *Chenchooliah*, EU:C:2019:693, para 57.

(31 December 2020)'.³⁴ Article 10 WA then establishes the conditions that apply to relevant family members.³⁵ While the qualifying family member does not have to have joined the Union citizen/British national in the host State before the end of the transition period (Article 10(e)(ii) WA), they must have been already 'directly related' to that person by then to be eligible to join them under the framework of the Agreement (as distinct from national immigration rules) at a later stage.³⁶

Second, Article 3(1) of the Directive confines its application to situations that (continue to) involve a host State.³⁷ As seen in Chapter 3, for example, Article 3(1) precluded the application of the Directive in *McCarthy* and *Lounes* since, while both claimants were dual nationals holding the nationality of two Member States (Ireland/UK and Spain/UK respectively), they resided in one of those States (the UK) and could not rely on the Directive as a basis for that residence following a 'literal, teleological and contextual interpretation' of Article 3(1), that is, considering its clear wording; recalling the unconditional right of residence that a Member State's nationals enjoy there under international law, and having regard to the 'relationship between residence and free movement' conveyed by the title of the Directive, most of its recitals, the rights of residence provided for in Articles 6, 7, and 16, and the territorial scope outlined in Article 22 ('the whole territory of the Member State').³⁸ However, while the Directive does not apply in a Union citizen's home State, protection for family members can in certain circumstances be drawn directly from Article 20 TFEU, in

---

[34] European Commission, Guidance Note relating to the Agreement on the withdrawal of the United Kingdom of Great Britain and Northern Ireland from the European Union and the European Atomic Energy Community Part two—Citizens' rights, C(2020) 2939 final, para 1.1.3.2.

[35] Outlining the personal scope of Part Two WA ('Citizens' Rights), Article 10(1) WA refers to 'family members of the persons referred to in points (a) to (d), provided that they fulfil one of the following conditions: (i) they resided in the host State in accordance with Union law before the end of the transition period and continue to reside there thereafter; (ii) they were directly related to a person referred to in points (a) to (d) and resided outside the host State before the end of the transition period, provided that they fulfil the conditions set out in point (2) of Article 2 of Directive 2004/38/EC at the time they seek residence under this Part in order to join the person referred to in points (a) to (d) of this paragraph; (iii) they were born to, or legally adopted by, persons referred to in points (a) to (d) after the end of the transition period, whether inside or outside the host State, and fulfil the conditions set out in point (2)(c) of Article 2 of Directive 2004/38/EC at the time they seek residence under this Part in order to join the person referred to in points (a) to (d) of this paragraph and fulfil one of the following conditions:—both parents are persons referred to in points (a) to (d);—one parent is a person referred to in points (a) to (d) and the other is a national of the host State; or—one parent is a person referred to in points (a) to (d) and has sole or joint rights of custody of the child, in accordance with the applicable rules of family law of a Member State or of the United Kingdom, including applicable rules of private international law under which rights of custody established under the law of a third State are recognised in the Member State or in the United Kingdom, in particular as regards the best interests of the child, and without prejudice to the normal operation of such applicable rules of private international law (7); (f) family members who resided in the host State in accordance with Articles 12 and 13, Article 16(2) and Articles 17 and 18 of Directive 2004/38/EC before the end of the transition period and continue to reside there thereafter'. On Articles 12 and 13 of the Directive, see Chapter 6; on Articles 16(2), 17 and 18, see Chapter 8. Points (a) to (d) of Article 10(1) WA refer to: '(a) Union citizens who exercised their right to reside in the United Kingdom in accordance with Union law before the end of the transition period and continue to reside there thereafter; (b) United Kingdom nationals who exercised their right to reside in a Member State in accordance with Union law before the end of the transition period and continue to reside there thereafter; (c) Union citizens who exercised their right as frontier workers in the United Kingdom in accordance with Union law before the end of the transition period and continue to do so thereafter; (d) United Kingdom nationals who exercised their right as frontier workers in one or more Member States in accordance with Union law before the end of the transition period and continue to do so thereafter'.

[36] European Commission, 'Guidance Note' (n 34) para 1.2.3.2.

[37] eg Case C-673/16 *Coman*, EU:C:2018:385, para 19. Ruling out the application of the Directive to family member residence rights in a Union citizen's home State, which are based on Article 20 TFEU, see Case C-34/09 *Ruiz Zambrano*, EU:C:2011:124, para 39.

[38] Case C-434/09 *McCarthy*, EU:C:2011:277, paras 31–38; see similarly, Case C-165/16 *Lounes*, EU:C:2017:862, paras 33–37.

exceptional situations where free movement has not been exercised (Chapter 5); or Article 21 TFEU, following the Union citizen's return to the home State (Chapter 9).

As also seen in Chapter 3, holding the nationality of a second Member State does not, in and of itself, override the scope of application of the Directive since 'the fact that a Union citizen is a national of more than one Member State does not mean that he has made use of his right of freedom of movement'.[39] Additionally, a Member State national who may have qualified as a beneficiary of the Directive loses that status following naturalisation in the host State. In such circumstances, the person concerned transitions to becoming a beneficiary of an 'inherently unconditional' right of residence in that State under international law.[40] While a right of residence cannot therefore be established on the basis of the Directive for the family members of naturalised Union citizens,[41] it was held in *Lounes* that derived residence rights could be based on Article 21 TFEU if the naturalised Union citizen had previously exercised freedom of movement.[42]

3.2 Family Members: Who is Protected and to What Extent?

Table 4.1 outlines (chronologically) the most significant legislation on the free movement of persons in force before the adoption of Directive 2004/38. While family members were always protected irrespective of their own nationality, relevant definitions and therefore the scope of legislative protection evolved over time:

Some variations in how family members were defined depended on the *type* of movement that Member State nationals undertook. For example, direct relatives in the ascending line did not feature in Directive 93/96 on the right of residence for students, and an obligation on Member States to facilitate the admission of a wider range of dependent relatives was included in some but not all measures. Unsurprisingly, then, even before the Commission committed to consolidating the legislative framework through Directive 2004/38, a sense that definitions of family members should be reviewed was also evident in an earlier proposal to amend Regulation 1612/68.[43]

What is clearly shared across the different measures, however, is the sense of a 'core' family unit and a wider 'extended' family circle.[44] These categories are delineated through formal criteria based on relationship type and, crucially, more protective rights are extended to core family members only. That basic distinction continues to shape EU citizenship law today. Beginning with core family members, Article 2(2) of Directive 2004/38 defines 'family member' for the purposes of a Union citizen's right to move and reside:

---

[39] *McCarthy*, para 41.
[40] *Lounes*, paras 38–43.
[41] ibid para 33.
[42] ibid paras 45–46.
[43] In 1998, the Commission published a proposal to amend the Regulation, draft Article 10 of which would have conferred on a worker's '(a) ... spouse or any person corresponding to a spouse under the legislation of the host Member State, and their descendants; (b) relatives in the ascending line of the worker and his spouse; [and] (c) any other member of the family of the worker or that of his spouse who is dependent on the worker or is living under his roof in the country whence he comes' the 'right to install themselves with a worker who is a national of one Member State and who is employed in the territory of another Member State' (COM(1998) 394 final). As will be seen below, these ideas later informed the approach originally proposed to defining family members for the purposes of Directive 2004/38.
[44] The Commission has noted that '[t]he "core" family members are defined by reference to Article 2(2) of Directive 2004/38/EC' ('Guidance Note' (n 34) para 1.1.1.1) and that those who fall within the scope of Article 3(2) of the Directive are 'extended' family members (para 1.2.3).

Table 4.1: Family Members and EU Legislation before Directive 2004/38

Regulation 15/61 (Free movement of workers)	Article 11	Spouse; children under 21; 'Member State[s] shall promote the admission of any family member who is wholly or mainly dependent on the worker and lives under his roof'
Directive 64/221 (Restrictions on free movement)	Article 1	Spouse; 'members of the family who come within the provisions of the regulations and directives adopted in this field'
Regulation 1612/68 (Free movement of workers)	Article 10	'Spouse and their descendants who are under the age of 21 years or are dependants'; 'dependent relatives in the ascending line of the worker and his spouse'; 'Member States shall facilitate the admission of any member of the family not coming within the provisions of paragraph 1 if dependent on the worker referred to above or living under his roof in the country whence he comes'
Directive 68/360 (Abolition of restrictions on movement and residence)	Article 1	Member State nationals; 'members of their families to whom Regulation (EEC) No 1612/68 applies'
Regulation 1251/70 (Right to remain in host State after being employed there)	Article 1	'Nationals of a Member State who have worked as employed persons in the territory of another Member State'; 'members of their families, as defined in Article 10 of Council Regulation (EEC) No 1612/68'
Directive 73/148 (Establishment/provision of services)	Article 1	Spouse; children under 21 years of age; 'relatives in the ascending and descending lines ... and of the spouse ... which relatives are dependent on them'; 'Member States shall favour the admission of any other member of the family of a national ... or of the spouse of that national, which member is dependent on that national or spouse of that national or who in the country of origin was living under the same roof'
Directive 90/364 (Right of residence: general)	Article 1	Spouse; 'descendants who are dependants'; 'dependent relatives in the ascending line of the holder of the right of residence and his or her spouse'
Directive 90/365 (Right of residence: retired persons)	Article 1	Spouse; 'descendants who are dependants'; 'dependent relatives in the ascending line of the holder of the right of residence and his or her spouse'
Directive 93/96 (Right of residence: students)	Article 1	Spouse; 'their dependent children'

Article 2(2)

'Family member' means:

(a) the spouse;
(b) the partner with whom the Union citizen has contracted a registered partnership, on the basis of the legislation of a Member State, if the legislation of the host Member State treats registered partnerships as equivalent to marriage and in accordance with the conditions laid down in the relevant legislation of the host Member State;

(c) the direct descendants who are under the age of 21 or are dependants and those of the spouse or partner as defined in point (b);
(d) the dependent direct relatives in the ascending line and those of the spouse or partner as defined in point (b)[.][45]

The different categories outlined in Article 2(2) will each be examined in more detail below. Two preliminary points can first be noted.

First, considering *who* is protected, it may seem obvious but it is nevertheless important to underline that only family members referred to in Article 2(2) derive rights from a Union citizen 'reference person'—in other words, 'it is not all third country nationals who are family members of a Union citizen who derive rights of entry into and residence in a Member State from [Directive 2004/38]'.[46] The closed list of core family members in Article 2(2) informs rights drawn directly from Article 21 TFEU,[47] though EU citizenship law and free movement law generally also extend rights to those who care for Union citizens in certain circumstances even if they are not 'family members' within the meaning of Article 2(2) of the Directive.[48] However, in most situations, qualifying as a family member under Article 2(2) is necessary. It is not necessarily sufficient, though, since further conditions may need to be met. For example, Articles 2(2)(c) and 2(2)(d) specify that direct descendants and direct relatives in the ascending line must be 'dependent' on the Union citizen exercising free movement, as explained further in Section 4.1. Providing another example, it was noted in Section 3.1 that Article 3(1) of the Directive requires that the family member of the Union citizen moving to or residing in a State other than that of which they are a national must *accompany or join* the citizen there.[49] That condition is considered to 'correspond to the purpose of the derived rights of entry and residence provided for by Directive 2004/38', that is, ensuring that Union citizens are not discouraged from exercising their free movement rights.[50] What the obligation to accompany or join the Union citizen means in practical terms is looked at in more detail in Section 3.2.1, considering, in particular, whether it compels family members to live together in the host State.

Thinking, in contrast, about who is not protected, Article 7(4), which concerns Union citizens studying in a host State, establishes—contrary to the Commission's first proposal[51]—a derogation from the right to reside extended to the family members listed in Article 2(2) more generally: 'only the spouse, the registered partner provided for in Article 2(2)(b) and dependent children' have a right to accompany or join a Union citizen who resides there on the basis of Article 7(1)(c). This more limited understanding of 'family members' mirrors Directive 93/96. However, Article 7(4) of Directive 2004/38 does now require that Article 3(2) shall apply to that citizen's 'dependent direct relatives in the ascending lines and those

---

[45] As noted in Section 3.1, Articles 9(a)(i) and 10(1)(e)(ii) WA cross-refer to Article 2(2) of the Directive.
[46] Joined Cases C-356/11 and C-357/11 *O and S*, EU:C:2012:776, para 41; confirmed in eg Case C-246/17 *Diallo*, EU:C:2018:499, para 53.
[47] See again, Case C-673/16 *Coman*, EU:C:2018:385, paras 33 and 36.
[48] See further, Section 4.1 (concept of dependency); Chapter 5 (rights based on Article 20 TFEU); and Chapter 9 (rights based on Article 21 TFEU, Article 45 TFEU, and Regulation 492/2011).
[49] In Case C-40/11 *Iida*, EU:C:2012:691, para 62, the Court noted that the same requirement appears in Articles 6(2) and 7(2) of the Directive (right of residence) as well as in Article 10(2)(c) (residence cards).
[50] ibid para 63; see similarly, para 68.
[51] Commission, Proposal for a Directive of the European Parliament and of the Council on the right of citizens of the Union and their family members to move and reside freely within the territory of the Member States, COM(2001) 257 final, 7.

of his/her spouse or registered partner'.⁵² Article 3(2) of the Directive establishes further categories of 'beneficiaries' by extending (more limited) protection to those who are not family members within the meaning Article 2(2):

Article 3(2)

Without prejudice to any right to free movement and residence the persons concerned may have in their own right, the host Member State shall, in accordance with its national legislation, facilitate entry and residence for the following persons:

(a) any other family members, irrespective of their nationality, not falling under the definition in point 2 of Article 2 who, in the country from which they have come, are dependants or members of the household of the Union citizen having the primary right of residence, or where serious health grounds strictly require the personal care of the family member by the Union citizen;
(b) the partner with whom the Union citizen has a durable relationship, duly attested.

The host Member State shall undertake an extensive examination of the personal circumstances and shall justify any denial of entry or residence to these people.

Article 3(2) thus concerns the extended family circle, in a formal, relationship *type* sense at least. These family members benefit from appreciably less protection under the Directive than Article 2(2) family members, as explained in Sections 3.2.2 and 4.2: in essence, they do not have a *right* to accompany or join a Union citizen in the host State.

Second, turning to *what* is protected when a family member does fall within the scope of Article 2(2), this concerns: rights of exit, entry and residence, including streamlined requirements for visas and residence cards as well as other administrative formalities (see Chapters 6 and 7); retention of residence rights, potentially on a personal basis in certain circumstances (Chapter 6); eligibility for the right of permanent residence, which entails an unconditional right to equal treatment with nationals of the host State (Chapter 8); and protection against expulsion, including procedural safeguards (Chapter 10). Additionally, Article 23 of the Directive establishes that '[i]rrespective of nationality, the family members of a Union citizen who have the right of residence or the right of permanent residence in a Member State shall be entitled to take up employment or self-employment there'.⁵³ And while Article 24(1) confers a right to equal treatment with host State nationals, within the scope of the Treaty, only on Union citizens residing there 'on the basis of' the Directive, it also requires that '[t]he benefit of this right shall be extended to family members who are not nationals of a Member State and who have the right of residence or permanent residence'. Extending the 'benefit of' equal treatment builds on previous case law in which, as the

---

⁵² See further, Common Position (EC) No 6/2004 of 5 December 2003, 2004 OJ C54 E/12), SEC/2003/1293 final, 30 (where the Council commented that 'the right to family unification for students has been limited to the core family, as in the existing *acquis*. Nevertheless, the entry and residence of dependent ascendants will be facilitated on the basis of Article 3').

⁵³ See previously, Article 11 of Regulation 1612/68, which extended that right to the spouse and descendants (either under 21 or dependent) of a Member State national employed or self-employed in another Member State. The Court has confirmed that this right could be relied on *only* in the Member State where the Union citizen concerned pursued his or her own activity as an employed or self-employed person (Case C-10/05 *Mattern and Cikotic*, EU:C:2006:220, paras 24–27).

holders of derived rights, third-country national family members came within the scope of EU equal treatment in a limited sense: for example, as 'indirect recipients' of the social and tax advantages granted to workers in a host State by Article 7(2) of Regulation 1612/68 (now 492/2011).[54]

Differently from core family members protected by Article 2(2), however, 'other family members' (Section 4.2) and partners of Union citizens (Section 3.2.2) who fall within the scope of Article 3(2) of the Directive do not have a right to enter or to reside or to undertake economic activity in the host State, or any claim to the 'benefit' of equal treatment with its nationals. These sharply different levels of protection raise fundamental questions about how EU law defines the family, highlighted where relevant below. The remainder of this section outlines the rights of spouses, partners, and direct descendants under 21, before the chapter turns to consider dependent family members (direct descendants over 21, direct relatives in the ascending line, and 'other family members' as defined by Article 3(2)(b) of the Directive) in Section 4.

3.2.1 Article 2(2)(a): spouses

As introduced in Chapter 2, actions taken by the spouse[55] of a Union citizen can have a material effect on the legal position of that citizen. For example, in *Schempp*, the fact that a former spouse transferred their residence to another Member State sufficed to connect the circumstances of the 'static' Union citizen to EU law in the latter's home State.[56] It was also seen that the Court has attributed particular significance to the contribution made by spouses, as distinct from other family members, in caring for the children of a frontier worker.[57] Here, the discussion turns more directly to how spouses are defined and protected as the family members of a Union citizen, irrespective of their own nationality.

On the definition of 'marriage' at a general level, the Commission considers in its guidance for better transposition and application of Directive 2004/38 that:

> Marriages validly contracted anywhere in the world must be in principle recognized for the purpose of the application of the Directive. Forced marriages, in which one or both parties is married without his or her consent or against his or her will, are not protected by international or Community law. Forced marriages must be distinguished from arranged marriages, where both parties fully and freely consent to the marriage, although a third party takes a leading role in the choice of partner, and from marriages of convenience ... Member States are not obliged to recognise polygamous marriages, contracted lawfully in a third country, which may be in conflict with their own legal order. This is without prejudice to the obligation to take due account of the best interests of children of such marriages.[58]

---

[54] eg Joined Cases C-401/15 to C-403/15 *Depesme and Kerrou*, EU:C:2016:955, para 40. On the breadth of the concept of social advantages, see Case C-85/96 *Martínez Sala*, EU:C:1998:217, para 25: 'all the advantages which, whether or not linked to a contract of employment, are generally granted to national workers primarily because of their objective status as workers or by virtue of the mere fact of their residence on the national territory and whose extension to workers who are nationals of other Member States therefore seems likely to facilitate the mobility of such workers within the [Union]'. See further, Chapter 2.
[55] On marriages of convenience and possible abuse of EU rights, see Chapter 6.
[56] Case C-403/03 *Schempp*, EU:C:2005:446, paras 23–25.
[57] Case C-457/12 *S and G*, EU:C:2014:36, para 43.
[58] Communication from the Commission to the European Parliament and the Council on guidance for better transposition and application of Directive 2004/38/EC on the right of citizens of the Union and their family members to move and reside freely within the territory of the Member States, COM(2009) 313 final, para 2.1.1. The Communication referred to Article 16(2) of the Universal Declaration of Human Rights, Article 16(1)(b) of the

Three interpretative questions that have reached the Court of Justice will now be looked at in more detail: first, whether the term 'spouse' in Article 2(2)(a) of the Directive includes spouses of the same sex; second, whether spouses (or the family more broadly) must reside *together* in the host State; and third, whether the position of a third-country national spouse under the immigration rules of the host State affects the protection extended under EU citizenship law.

3.2.1.1 Same-sex spouses
Looking, first, at the definition of 'spouse' for the purposes of Article 2(2)(a), whether it includes spouses of the same sex was left open after agreement could not be reached, at the political level, in the process of adopting the Directive. In its report on the Commission's original proposal, the European Parliament suggested an amendment to Article 2(2)(a) and 2(2)(b), making it explicit that the rights conferred on spouses and registered partners were 'irrespective of sex'.[59] However, in its amended proposal, the Commission observed that it was not possible to incorporate these amendments since 'harmonisation of the conditions of residence for Union citizens in Member States must not result in the imposition on certain Member States of amendments to family law legislation, an area which does not fall within the Community's legislative jurisdiction'.[60] It pointed out that, at the time, 'only two Member States ma[de] legislative provision for marriage between partners of the same sex' and that 'in its case law the Court of Justice has made it clear that, according to the definition generally accepted by the Member States, the term marriage means a union between two persons of the opposite sex'.[61] The common position adopted by the Council in December 2003 reflected the Commission's reasons.[62] However, the Commission did suggest that the adopted proposal, without the clarification called for by the European Parliament, 'allow[ed] for a possible change in interpretation in the light of developments in family law in the Member States'.[63] It also considered that same-sex spouses could otherwise fall within the scope of Article 3(2)(b) of the Directive.[64]

In *Coman*, the Court was finally asked to clarify the definition of spouse for the purposes of EU citizenship law.[65] In his Opinion, Advocate General Wathelet commented on the drafting history, summarised above:

Convention to Eliminate All Forms of Discrimination Against Women, and the ECtHR ruling in *Alilouch El Abasse v Netherlands*, App No 14501/89, 6 January 1992.

[59] European Parliament Report of 23 January 2003 on Commission proposal (COM(2001) 257), A5–0009/2003, Amendments 14 and 15.
[60] Amended Proposal on the right of citizens of the Union and their family members to move and reside freely within the territory of the Member States, COM(2003) 199 final, 3.
[61] ibid 10; referring to Joined Cases C-122/99 and C-125/99 *D and Sweden v Council*, EU:C:2001:304, para 34. While the legal picture has evolved in the two decades since Directive 2004/38 was first proposed, there are still significant differences on the legal recognition of same-sex relationships across Member States: for an overview of these 'deep-running divisions', see JJ Rijpma 'You gotta let love move' (2019) 15 European Constitutional Law Review 324 at 325–26.
[62] Common Position (n 52) 28.
[63] Amended Proposal (n 60) 3; see similarly, 11: '[t]he Commission ... prefers to restrict the proposal to the concept of spouse as meaning in principle spouse of a different sex, *unless there are subsequent developments*' (emphasis added). The Parliament's ultimate acceptance of the adopted provisions on family members was one of the key issues to which some Members continued to object; see eg the Minority Opinions attached to the recommendation for second reading in the Report (n 59).
[64] Communication to the European Parliament on the common position adopted by the Council on the draft directive (Common Position (EC) No 6/2004 of 5 December 2003, 2004 OJ C54 E/12), SEC/2003/1293 final, para 3.3.2.
[65] AG Wathelet acknowledged that the question was a 'a delicate matter for, although it relates to marriage as a *legal* institution, in the specific limited context of freedom of movement of citizens of the European Union,

[N]o argument in favour of one theory rather than the other can be derived from the drafting history of the directive. There can be no doubt that the Union legislature was perfectly aware of the controversy that could arise over the interpretation of the word 'spouse' not otherwise defined. However, it did not desire to clarify that concept, whether by limiting it to heterosexual marriage or, on the contrary, by referring to marriage between persons of the same sex—although the Commission expressly emphasised the possibility that the situation might develop. The Commission's reservation in that regard is crucial. It makes it impossible for the term 'spouse' to be definitively fixed and sealed off from developments in society.[66]

Mr Coman held both American and Romanian citizenship. In November 2010, he married Mr Hamilton, an American citizen. The couple married in Brussels, where Mr Coman had been employed since 2009. He ceased working in March 2012 but continued to reside in Belgium and received unemployment benefit there. In December 2012, he requested information from Romania on the procedure and conditions under which Mr Hamilton, as a third-country national family member of a Romanian citizen who had exercised free movement, could reside lawfully there for more than three months. The response received was that such a right could not be granted to Mr Hamilton on grounds of family reunion because same-sex marriage was not recognised under the Civil Code. Mr Coman commenced litigation in Romania to challenge that decision, during which questions about the meaning of 'spouse' in Article 2(2)(a) of Directive 2004/38 were referred to the Court of Justice.

Recalling *McCarthy* and *Lounes*, noted in Section 3.1, Mr Coman's situation could not fall within the scope of the Directive since it concerned residence rights not in a host State but in his State of nationality. However, as a Union citizen returning to the latter State after exercising free movement, derived residence rights for his family members could be sourced directly in Article 21 TFEU and the relevant provisions of the Directive apply by analogy.[67] The Court therefore proceeded to consider the meaning of 'spouse' with reference to Article 2(2)(a) of the Directive. It held, first, that spouse 'refers to a person joined to another person by the bonds of marriage'.[68] Second, the Court determined that the concept of 'spouse' within the meaning of the Directive 'is gender-neutral and may therefore cover the same-sex spouse of the Union citizen concerned'.[69] It recalled that Article 2(2)(b) of the Directive, which imposes certain conditions on the recognition of registered partnerships, includes a requirement that the legislation of the host State 'treats registered partnerships as equivalent to marriage'. However, Article 2(2)(a) contains no similar conditions and, in consequence, 'a Member State cannot rely on its national law as justification for refusing to recognise in its territory, for the sole purpose of granting a derived right of residence to a third-country

---

the definition of the concept of "spouse" to be given will necessarily affect not only the very identity of the men and women concerned, and therefore their dignity, but also the personal and social concept that citizens of the Union have of marriage, which may vary from one person to another and from one Member State to another' (AG Wathelet in Case C-673/16 *Coman*, EU:C:2018:2, para 2 of the Opinion, emphasis in original).

[66] ibid para 52 of the Opinion.
[67] Case C-673/16 *Coman*, EU:C:2018:385, paras 21–25. On this aspect of *Coman*, and the application of the Directive by analogy more generally, see Chapter 9.
[68] *Coman*, para 34.
[69] ibid para 35.

national, a marriage concluded by that national with a Union citizen of the same sex in another Member State in accordance with the law of that state'.[70]

In line with reviewing national processes for the acquisition and loss of nationality, examined in Chapter 3, the Court confirmed that while Member States are free to determine whether or not same-sex marriage is allowed under national law, they must 'comply with EU law, in particular the Treaty provisions on the freedom conferred on all Union citizens to move and reside in the territory of the Member States' when exercising that competence'.[71] Since the provisions of Directive 2004/38 must not be interpreted restrictively or deprived of their effectiveness, the refusal of entry and residence rights for third-country national same-sex spouses in a Union citizen's home State because of a prohibition on same-sex marriage in that State, following the citizen's exercise of free movement and the conclusion of a marriage in accordance with the law of the host State, 'would have the effect that the freedom of movement of Union citizens who have already made use of that freedom would vary from one Member State to another, depending on whether such provisions of national law exist'.[72] The Court acknowledged that Article 4(2) TEU obliges the Union to respect the national identities of the Member States when considering whether a restriction of free movement rights might be justified.[73] But it did not agree that recognition of marriages lawfully concluded in other Member States undermines national identity or poses a threat to public policy.[74] It further emphasised that national measures liable to obstruct freedom of movement may be justified only when they comply with the fundamental rights protected by the Charter, recalling here the respect for private and family life guaranteed by Article 7 CFR.[75] However, the Court did not refer to Article 21 CFR, which prohibits discrimination on grounds of sexual orientation, or Article 1 CFR, which requires that human dignity must be 'respected and protected'.[76]

Was the fact that the marriage in *Coman* was concluded in the host Member State a material factor in the Court's decision?[77] Recalling the significance of 'creating and

---

[70] ibid para 36. Confirming that Article 2(2)(a) of Directive 2004/38 'does not require the person concerned to satisfy any conditions other than that of being a spouse', see Case C-40/11 *Iida*, EU:C:2012:691, para 57. See further, the discussion on Case C-490/20 *VMA v Stolichna obshtina, rayon 'Pancharevo'*, EU:C:2021:1008 in Chapter 6.

[71] *Coman*, paras 37–38.

[72] ibid para 39.

[73] ibid para 43.

[74] ibid para 45. On this point, AG Wathelet suggested that the obligation to respect national identity under Article 4(2) TEU 'cannot be construed independently of the obligation of sincere cooperation set out in Article 4(3) TEU' (para 40 of the Opinion).

[75] *Coman*, paras 47–48. The Court also referred to relevant ECtHR case law confirming that 'the relationship of a homosexual couple may fall within the notion of "private life" and that of "family life" in the same way as the relationship of a heterosexual couple in the same situation (ECtHR, 7 November 2013, *Vallianatos and Others v Greece*, CE:ECHR:2013:1107JUD002938109, § 73, and ECtHR, 14 December 2017, *Orlandi and Others v Italy*, CE:ECHR:2017:1214JUD002643112, § 143)' (para 48).

[76] cf AG Wathelet, para 75 of the Opinion, noting 'another objective of Directive 2004/38, set out in recital 31, which states that Member States should implement Directive 2004/38 "without discrimination between the beneficiaries of [the] Directive on grounds such as ... sexual orientation". A definition of the term "spouse" that was limited to heterosexual marriage would inevitably give rise to situations involving discrimination on grounds of sexual orientation'. Rijpma takes a balanced view on this question overall, arguing that the Court 'should be applauded for the consistent and non-discriminatory application to all EU citizens, irrespective of sexual orientation, of its own case law on the fundamental freedom of movement. This has allowed the Court to arrive at an answer that is satisfactory from a fundamental rights perspective without taking a more controversial fundamental rights approach. At the same time, fundamental rights are an integral part of the EU legal order. The Court might have strengthened its argument whilst remaining within the boundaries of its jurisdiction, stating more explicitly that respect for fundamental rights would not have yielded any other outcome' (n 61, 338).

[77] Leaving that question open, see eg A Tryfonidou, 'The ECJ recognises the right of same-sex spouses to move freely between EU Member States: the *Coman* ruling' (2019) 44 European Law Review 663 at 676–77.

strengthening' family life in a host State, introduced in Section 2, the Court depicted the circumstances in *Coman* as follows: 'a situation in which a Union citizen has made use of his freedom of movement by moving to and taking up genuine residence, in accordance with the conditions laid down in Article 7(1) of Directive 2004/38, in a Member State other than that of which he is a national, and, whilst there, has created or strengthened a family life with a third-country national of the same sex to whom he is joined by a marriage *lawfully concluded in the host Member State*'.[78] The same language was used in the operative part of the ruling.[79] Would it therefore have made a material legal difference if the marriage had been concluded in a third state? On one view, that should not matter. As the Court pointed out, no conditions at all are specified in Article 2(2)(a) of the Directive; it had already distinguished Article 2(2)(b), a provision that *does* explicitly specify that a registered partnership must be contracted 'on the basis of the legislation of a Member State'. Additionally, as noted above, the Commission assumes that '[m]arriages validly contracted anywhere in the world must be in principle recognized for the purpose of the application of the Directive'[80] and, by the time of *Coman,* the Court had already ruled in *Metock* that 'neither Article 3(1) *nor any other provision* of Directive 2004/38 contains requirements as to the place where the marriage of the Union citizen and the national of a non-member country is solemnised'.[81]

However, it is conceivable that the fact that the marriage was concluded in the host State, thus feeding directly into the creating and strengthening of genuine family life there,[82] could make a difference at the justification stage. In that light, note the '*in principle*' proviso in the Commission's guidance on the definition of marriage and consider again how the Court framed the core justification passage in its judgment:

> [The] obligation for a Member State to recognise a marriage between persons of the same sex *concluded in another Member State in accordance with the law of that state*, for the sole purpose of granting a derived right of residence to a third-country national, does not undermine the institution of marriage in the first Member State, which is defined by national law and ... falls within the competence of the Member States. Such recognition does not require that Member State to provide, in its national law, for the institution of marriage between persons of the same sex. It is *confined to the obligation to recognise such marriages, concluded in another Member State in accordance with the law of that state*, for the sole purpose of enabling such persons to exercise the rights they enjoy under EU law.[83]

---

[78] *Coman*, para 28 (emphasis added).

[79] ibid para 51: 'in a situation in which a Union citizen has made use of his freedom of movement by moving to and taking up genuine residence, in accordance with the conditions laid down in Article 7(1) of Directive 2004/38, in a Member State other than that of which he is a national, and, whilst there, has created or strengthened a family life with a third-country national of the same sex to whom he is joined by a marriage *lawfully concluded in the host Member State*, Article 21(1) TFEU must be interpreted as precluding the competent authorities of the Member State of which the Union citizen is a national from refusing to grant that third-country national a right of residence in the territory of that Member State on the ground that the law of that Member State does not recognise marriage between persons of the same sex' (emphasis added).

[80] Communication on guidance for better transposition and application of Directive 2004/38/EC (n 58) para 2.1.1.

[81] Case C-127/08 *Metock and Others*, EU:C:2008:449, para 98 (emphasis added).

[82] However, Tryfonidou highlights important questions about recognition of spousal relationships in situations of temporary presence in a Member State too (eg for the purposes of consent to medical treatment) that are, either way, left open by *Coman* (n 77, 677–78).

[83] Case C-673/16 *Coman*, EU:C:2018:385, para 45 (emphasis added).

In a future case, where the marriage in question was not concluded in another Member State, this point will need to be resolved. In such a situation, alongside the Union's commitment to respecting the private and family life of its citizens, the prohibition of discrimination under Article 21 CFR should also be addressed. Ultimately, no conditions are specified in Article 2(2)(a) of the Directive and that provision should not be interpreted restrictively, on both free movement and equality grounds.

3.2.1.2 What does 'in the host State' mean?

Does EU law require spouses to reside *together* in a host State to benefit from the protection of Directive 2004/38? The answer to this question has particular relevance in two situations: first, where the relationship between spouses breaks down; and second, where the relationship continues but family life is split across different States for professional and/or personal reasons.

For the first situation, Articles 12 and 13 of Directive 2004/38 provide for the retention of family member residence rights in certain situations, which include, under Article 13, divorce or annulment of marriage and termination of registered partnership. These rights are examined in Chapter 6, but what happens prior to a formal divorce, annulment, or partnership termination? It is a long-established premise of free movement law that 'the marital relationship cannot be regarded as dissolved so long as it has not been terminated by the competent authority' and, crucially for present purposes, 'it is not dissolved merely because the spouses live separately, even where they intend to divorce at a later date'.[84] Therefore, 'the members of a migrant worker's family ... are not necessarily required to live permanently with him in order to qualify for a right of residence'.[85] In *Singh*, even the fact that a divorce process was underway did not alter the legal position of Mr Singh as the 'spouse' of a Member State national at the material time.[86]

These findings were later transposed to EU citizenship law. In *Iida*, the Court ruled that Article 2(2)(a) of Directive 2004/38 'does not require the person concerned to satisfy any conditions other than that of being a spouse'.[87] It referred to and confirmed the two key principles in *Diatta*: that the marital relationship is not dissolved until it is terminated by the competent authority; and that spouses do not have to reside with Union citizens permanently 'in order to hold a derived right of residence'.[88] In *Baumbast*, a ruling delivered before the adoption of Directive 2004/38, the Court confirmed that where the third-country national children of a migrant worker continued to live in the host State but not with the migrant worker—following the divorce of their parents in one case in the national proceedings, and the departure of the worker from the host State in the other—their rights to reside and complete their education in the host State under Regulation 1612/68 were not affected.[89] The Court also confirmed another aspect of *Diatta*:

> [that] Article 10 of [Regulation 1612/68] does not require that the member of the family in question must live permanently with the worker, but, as is clear from Article 10(3), only

---

[84] Case 267/83 *Diatta*, EU:C:1985:67, para 20, in the context of residence rights for family members under Article 10 of Regulation 1612/68.
[85] *Diatta*, para 22.
[86] Case C-370/90 *Singh*, EU:C:1992:296, esp paras 4, 7 and 12.
[87] Case C-40/11 *Iida*, EU:C:2012:691, para 57.
[88] ibid para 58.
[89] Case C-413/99 *Baumbast and R*, EU:C:2002:493, paras 52–62.

that the accommodation which the worker has available must be such as may be considered normal for the purpose of accommodating his family.[90]

In *Iida*, the Court observed that '[t]hat interpretation of a similar provision to Article 2(2)(a) of Directive 2004/38, one which moreover required the family of the Union citizen concerned to have normal housing, must apply *a fortiori* in connection with Article 2(2)(a), which does not impose that requirement'.[91] Additionally,

[t]he right conferred by Article 12 of Regulation No 1612/68 on the child of a migrant worker to pursue, under the best possible conditions, his education in the host Member State necessarily implies that that child has the right to be accompanied by the person who is his *primary carer* and, accordingly, that that person is able to reside with him in that Member State during his studies.[92]

That finding had particular significance in *Baumbast* as the primary carer in question was a third-country national, divorced from the Member State worker. Residence rights for 'primary carers' can still be connected to Article 10 of Regulation 492/2011 in such circumstances even after the adoption of Directive 2004/38, as explained further in Chapters 7 and 9; the concept of a primary carer also has relevance for residence rights in a Union citizen's home State, as discussed in Chapter 5.

However, notwithstanding the absence of any conditions in Article 2(2)(a) of the Directive, the case law outlined above rejected only a requirement for spouses to live together 'permanently', meaning that it was still not obvious whether *some* degree of obligation for spouses to live together, at some point, might nevertheless exist.[93] The judgment in *Onuekwere* appeared to confirm such expectations of conditionality. The case concerned whether periods spent in prison could qualify as periods of 'legal' residence in a host State for the purposes of acquiring a right of permanent residence under Article 16 of the Directive. That question is returned to in Chapter 8. For present purposes, the relevant part of the Court's ruling concerned the findings that, first, where a right of permanent residence is claimed by a third-country national family member, the Union citizen from whom they derive their rights must themselves satisfy the requirements of Article 16(1); second, that family member must 'have resided "with" [them] for the period in question', following the wording of Article 16(2).[94]

---

[90] ibid para 62; confirming *Diatta*, para 18. Article 10(3) of Regulation 1612/68 required that 'the worker must have available for his family housing considered as normal for national workers in the region where he is employed; this provision, however must not give rise to discrimination between national workers and workers from the other Member States'. Article 10 of the Regulation was repealed by Directive 2004/38, which contains no specific references to housing or accommodation.

[91] Case C-40/11 *Iida*, EU:C:2012:691, para 59.

[92] *Baumbast*, para 73 (emphasis added), having observed in para 72 that 'Regulation No 1612/68 must be interpreted in the light of the requirement of respect for family life laid down in Article 8 [ECHR]'.

[93] As seen in other areas of EU law eg in the context of the spouses of Turkish workers, see Case C-391/95 *Kadiman*, EU:C:1997:205, para 44, where the Court concluded that 'the first paragraph of Article 7 of Decision No 1/80 does not in principle preclude the competent authorities of a Member State from requiring that the family members of a Turkish worker, referred to by that provision, live with him for the period of three years prescribed by the first indent of that article in order to be entitled to reside in that Member State. There may however be objective reasons to justify the family member concerned living apart from the Turkish migrant worker'. In para 42, the Court indicated that such objective reasons included 'in particular if the distance between the worker's residence and the place of employment of the member of his family or a vocational training establishment attended by that person required him or her to live in separate accommodation'.

[94] Case C-378/12 *Onuekwere*, EU:C:2014:13, para 18; confirming Case C-529/11 *Alarape and Tijani*, EU:C:2013:290, para 34.

The Court observed that 'the word "with" reinforce[es] the condition that those family members must accompany or join that same citizen',[95] as required by Article 3(1) of the Directive. However, since living 'with' the Union citizen was invoked (among other reasons, returned to in Chapter 8) to explain why the periods that Mr Onuekwere spent in prison could not be taken into account for the purposes of eligibility for permanent residence, it also seemed that third-country national family members were obliged to reside with, very literally, the Union citizens from whom their residence rights derived.

Advocate General Bot had shown greater alertness to the implications of requiring spouses to reside 'with' each other in his Opinion, arguing that the phrase 'with the Union citizen' in Article 16(2) of the Directive 'must not be interpreted literally, and therefore strictly, unless it is to remove certain legitimate beneficiaries from the rights which that directive would normally confer on them or, also, infringe the right to respect for private and family life which everyone enjoys under Article 7 of the Charter'.[96] He envisaged situations in which

> by force of circumstances, the citizen of the Union and the national of a third State who is a member of his family cannot live permanently under the same roof. For example, the citizen of the Union may have to live during the week or even for a prolonged period of time in a region other than that in which his spouse who is a national of a third State lives. This is particularly true in today's world in which it is common for people to have to change jobs and to move from place to place.[97]

In support, he referred to *Baumbast* and *Iida* to illustrate the liberal approach applied previously to Articles 10 and 12 of Regulation 1612/68.

Subsequent case law exposed the risks that the Court's narrow language had created when applied to a wider range of circumstances, and it later confined the implications of *Onuekwere*. In *Ogieriakhi,* a Nigerian national who arrived in Ireland in May 1998 obtained a residence permit there in October 1999, following his marriage in May 1999 to a French national (Ms Georges) who was also residing in Ireland at that time. The couple lived together until August 2001, when Ms Georges left the family home to reside with a new partner. Mr Ogieriakhi subsequently had a child with an Irish national in December 2003. Mr Ogieriakhi and Ms Georges did not divorce until 2009, and Ms Georges was either working or receiving social security as a jobseeker from October 1999 until October 2004. She left Ireland in December 2004. The preliminary reference concerned a permanent residence application rejected in 2007, which is considered in substance in Chapter 8. For present purposes, the critical question was whether the couple's separation—'given that not only is there no residing together but especially, there is no true sharing of married life together'[98]—meant that

---

[95] *Onuekwere*, para 23.
[96] AG Bot in Case C-378/12 *Onuekwere*, EU:C:2013:640, para 38 of the Opinion.
[97] ibid para 39 of the Opinion. See similarly, AG Wathelet in Case C-673/16 *Coman*, EU:C:2018:2, para 28 of the Opinion: '[i]n a globalised world, it is not unusual for a couple one of whom works abroad not to share the same accommodation for longer or shorter periods owing to the distance between the two countries, the accessibility of means of transport, the employment of the other spouse or the children's education. The fact that the couple do not live together cannot in itself have any effect on the existence of a proven stable relationship—which is the case— and, consequently, on the existence of a family life' (citing relevant ECtHR case law on this point in fn 11: ECtHR, 7 November 2013, *Vallianatos and Others v Greece*, CE:ECHR:2013:1107JUD002938109, para 73; ECtHR, 21 July 2015, *Oliari and Others v Italy*, CE:ECHR:2015:0721JUD001876611, para 169; and ECtHR, 23 February 2016, *Pajić v Croatia*, CE:ECHR:2016:0223JUD006845313, para 65).
[98] Case C-244/13 *Ogieriakhi*, EU:C:2014:2068, para 36.

Mr Ogieriakhi could not satisfy the requirement in Article 16(2) to have resided 'with' Ms Georges.

A straightforward application of *Onuekwere* would suggest precisely that conclusion. However, in *Ogieriakhi*, the Court ruled that

> the fact that, during the period from 11 October 1999 to 11 October 2004, the spouses not only ceased to live together but also resided with other partners, is irrelevant for the purposes of the acquisition by Mr Ogieriakhi of a right of permanent residence under Article 16(2) of Directive 2004/38.[99]

The Court referred to *Diatta* and *Iida* to confirm that Mr Ogieriakhi and Ms Georges were 'spouses' until their divorce in 2009 and recalled that the provisions of the Directive should not be interpreted restrictively or deprived of their effectiveness. Recognising the wider implications of, in effect, forcing shared residence, the Court acknowledged that

> if Article 16(2) of the directive were to be interpreted literally, a third-country national could be made vulnerable because of unilateral measures taken by his spouse, and that would be contrary to the spirit of that directive, of which one of the objectives is precisely—according to recital 15 thereto—to offer legal protection to family members of citizens of the Union who reside in the host Member State, in order to enable them, in certain cases and subject to certain conditions, to retain their right of residence exclusively on a personal basis.[100]

Analogies were drawn with the interpretation of the housing requirement in Regulation 1612/68 in *Diatta*—yet *Onuekwere*, which arguably pointed to the opposite conclusion, was not mentioned at all.

Advocate General Bot also delivered the Opinion in *Ogieriakhi*, holding his original (*Onuekwere*) position and stressing that '[t]he vicissitudes that can occur in anyone's life, which may lead couples to live apart, must not deprive those persons of the rights to which they are entitled under EU legislation'—moreover, '[t]o require the persons concerned to live permanently under the same roof would ... constitute interference in private and family life which is contrary to Article 7 of the Charter of Fundamental Rights ... It is not the role of public authorities to impose a concept of life together as a couple or a certain way of life on nationals of other Member States and members of their family, especially as no such requirement exists for their own national'.[101] He did refer to the Court's approach in *Onuekwere*, but construed the obligation to accompany or join the Union citizen in Article 3(1) of the Directive less rigidly: 'once the initial condition of accompanying or joining the Union citizen in the host Member State is satisfied, it is immaterial whether or not the couple live together'.[102] It is also notable that, in both cases, Advocate General Bot engaged Article 7 CFR to insulate different experiences of family life from legal scrutiny vis-à-vis the conditions in the Directive—and equally notable that the Court did not refer to Article 7 CFR at all. However, the strict approach it took in *Onuekwere* did fit with a cluster of judgments

---

[99] ibid para 38.
[100] ibid para 40.
[101] AG Bot in Case C-244/13 *Ogieriakhi*, EU:C:2014:323, paras 41–42 of the Opinion.
[102] ibid para 46 of the Opinion.

delivered around the same time in which the consequences of periods spent in prison were generally severe, returned to in Chapters 8 and 10.

In *Singh II*, a case about retaining residence rights following the departure of the Union citizen from the host State (considered in Chapter 6), the Court confirmed—referring to *Ogieriakhi*, ignoring *Onuekwere*—that

> the condition that the third-country national must accompany or join the Union citizen must be understood as referring not to an obligation for the spouses to live together but an obligation for them both to remain in the Member State in which the spouse who is a Union citizen exercises his right of freedom of movement.[103]

It added in *Deha Altiner and Ravn*, distinguishing between 'accompanying' and 'joining' the Union citizen, that a derived right of residence under Article 7(2) of the Directive 'is not subject to the condition that [family members] be on the territory of [the host] Member State within a certain period after the entry of that Union citizen'.[104] However, at the other end of a residence cycle, if the Union citizen from whom a third-country national derives their rights no longer resides in the same State, the family member will lose the protection of EU citizenship law if the conditions in Articles 12 and 13 of the Directive are not met.[105]

3.2.1.3 The status of third-country national family members under host State immigration rules

Whether the residence status of third-country national spouses under a Member State's immigration rules affects their derived rights first arose in *Akrich* in the context of Article 10 of Regulation 1612/68 and the free movement of workers. That case concerned a British national returning to the UK after a period spent working in Ireland. Before moving to Ireland, she married a Moroccan national who had been refused leave to remain in the UK, had continued to reside there unlawfully, and was then deported to Ireland to join her. On the question of whether a derived right to reside in the UK could be established for Mr Akrich when the couple returned there, the Court ruled that 'the national of a non-Member State, who is the spouse of a citizen of the Union, must be lawfully resident in a Member State when he moves to another Member State to which the citizen of the Union is migrating or has migrated'.[106] The Court's reasoning focused on whether the move to another Member State 'result[ed] in the loss of the opportunity lawfully to live together',[107] which is considered further in Chapter 9.[108] The key point for the present discussion concerns the conception of, in effect, a requirement of prior lawful residence in the worker's home State before derived rights of residence for a third-country national spouse could be claimed there later following the exercise of free movement. However, in *Jia*, the Court clarified that *Akrich* should not be read as establishing a general precondition: in other words, prior lawful residence in another

---

[103] Case C-218/14 *Singh II*, EU:C:2015:476, para 54.
[104] Case C-230/17 *Deha Altiner and Ravn*, EU:C:2018:497, para 28. This case is returned to in Chapter 6 in the context of conditions placed on applications for family member residence permits; and in Chapter 9 as the duration of the gap between the Union citizen and their family member entering the territory can have implications when it is the former's home State and residence rights for the latter are claimed on the basis of Article 21 TFEU.
[105] eg Case C-94/18 *Chenchooliah*, EU:C:2019:693; see further, Chapter 6.
[106] Case C-109/01 *Akrich*, EU:C:2003:491, para 50.
[107] ibid para 52.
[108] On the question of potential abuse of free movement rights raised in *Akrich*, see Chapter 6. The case is also notable for the Court's reminder about the obligations of the Member States under the ECHR where a situation falls outside the scope of EU law (see esp paras 58–59).

Member State was not *required* before an application for a residence permit for a third-country national family member would be considered in the State in which the Member State national was exercising free movement.[109]

Following the adoption of Directive 2004/38, the Court held in *Metock* that *Akrich* 'must be reconsidered'.[110] All four applicants were third-country national spouses of Union citizens residing in Ireland. In three cases, applications for residence permits as the spouses of Union citizens residing lawfully in Ireland were refused because the applicants did not satisfy the condition of prior lawful residence in another Member State, as required by the applicable national rules; in the fourth case, a deportation order had been made against the applicant, who was therefore considered to be staying in Ireland illegally at the time of his marriage there to a British national. Bringing the four cases together, the questions referred by the High Court centred on, first, whether national legislation that required third-country national spouses of Union citizens to have been lawfully resident in another Member State before arriving in the host State was compatible with Directive 2004/38 and, second, whether when and where a marriage took place, or the circumstances under which the third-country national entered the host State, were relevant for the purposes of applying the Directive.[111]

As explained in Section 3.2.1.1, the Court ruled on the second point that '[i]t makes no difference whether nationals of non-member countries who are family members of a Union citizen have entered the host Member State before or after becoming family members of that Union citizen, since the refusal of the host Member State to grant them a right of residence is equally liable to discourage that Union citizen from continuing to reside in that Member State'.[112] On the first point, the Court observed that the definition of 'family members' in Article 2(2) of Directive 2004/38 'does not distinguish according to whether or not they have already resided lawfully in another Member State'.[113] Its reconsideration of *Akrich* was rationalised by recalling the importance of protecting the family life of Member State nationals who exercise free movement;[114] that permits issued by the Member States are declaratory rather than constitutive of the protection extended to family members, since 'the right of entry into the territory of a Member State granted to a third-country national who is the spouse of a national of a Member State derives from the family relationship alone';[115] that, as confirmed by recital 3, Directive 2004/38 'aims in particular to "strengthen the right of free movement and residence of all Union citizens"';[116] and that the Union legislator has the

> competence to regulate, as it did by Directive 2004/38, the entry and residence of nationals of non-member countries who are family members of a Union citizen in the Member State in which that citizen has exercised his right of freedom of movement, including where the family members were not already lawfully resident in another Member State.[117]

---

[109] Case C-1/05 *Jia*, EU:C:2007:1, paras 26–32.
[110] Case C-127/08 *Metock and Others*, EU:C:2008:449, para 58.
[111] Similar questions had been referred by an Austrian court, responded to by an Order of the President of the Court following the ruling in *Metock* (Case C-551/07 *Sahin*, EU:C:2008:75).
[112] *Metock*, para 92.
[113] *Metock*, para 50; the Court also pointed to the absence of any reference to prior lawful residence in Articles 5, 6(2), 7(2), 9(1), or 10(1) of the Directive (paras 51–53).
[114] ibid para 56, citing eg Case C-459/99 *MRAX*, EU:C:2002:461, para 53.
[115] *Metock*, para 58, citing eg Case C-157/03 *Commission v Spain*, EU:C:2005:225, para 28.
[116] *Metock*, para 59.
[117] ibid para 65.

The inference from the latter point is that since a condition of prior lawful residence was not explicitly included in the Directive, it could not now be added implicitly after the legislative process was concluded. Fundamentally,

> to allow the Member States exclusive competence to grant or refuse entry into and residence in their territory to nationals of non-member countries who are family members of Union citizens and have not already resided lawfully in another Member State would have the effect that the freedom of movement of Union citizens in a Member State whose nationality they do not possess would vary from one Member State to another, according to the provisions of national law concerning immigration. ... That would not be compatible with the Union's objective of establishing an internal market characterised by the abolition, as between Member States, of obstacles to the free movement of persons.[118]

Metock remains, at the time of writing, the citizenship-based case in which the highest number of Member States submitted observations, that is, ten States in addition to Ireland's submissions as the State directly involved in the proceedings. Two sets of arguments help to explain why, and they continue to shape debates about both the implementation and the worth of free movement. First, it was contended in *Metock* that 'in a context *typified by strong pressure of migration*, it is necessary to control immigration at the external borders of the Community, which presupposes an individual examination of all the circumstances surrounding a first entry into Community territory'—more specifically, that preventing a Member State from requiring prior lawful residence in another Member State 'would undermine the ability of the Member States to control immigration at their external frontiers'.[119] The 'serious consequences' of this approach amounted to 'bringing about a great increase in the number of persons able to benefit from a right of residence in the Community'.[120] These arguments, which project the perception that free movement rights are *unlimited*, have only intensified since the *Metock* case.[121] In that judgment, the Court responded with basic facts: that only the family members of Union citizens who fall within the scope of Article 2(2) of the Directive have *a right* to enter and reside in an EU Member State, that is, a limited category and 'not all nationals of non-member countries';[122] that justifiable refusals of entry and residence could be made on the grounds of public policy, public security, or public health, in accordance with the processes established by Chapter VI of the Directive; and that Article 35 of the Directive empowers the Member States to adopt proportionate measures to address demonstrated instances of abuse of rights or fraud.[123]

A second objection concerned the 'unjustified reverse discrimination' that a non-conditional interpretation of Directive 2004/38 would produce, 'in so far as nationals of the host Member State who have never exercised their right of freedom of movement would not derive rights of entry and residence from Community law for their family members who

---

[118] ibid paras 67 and 68.
[119] ibid para 71.
[120] ibid para 72.
[121] See further, U Šadl and S Sankari, 'Why did the citizenship jurisprudence change?' in D Thym (ed), *Questioning EU Citizenship: Judges and Limits of Free Movement and Solidarity in the EU* (Hart Publishing 2017) 89; and M Blauberger, A Heindlmaier, D Kramer, D Sindbjerg Martinsen, J Sampson Thierry, A Schenk, and B Werner, 'ECJ judges read the morning papers: explaining the turnaround of European citizenship jurisprudence' (2018) 25 Journal of European Public Policy 1422.
[122] *Metock*, para 73.
[123] On Article 35 of the Directive, see Chapter 6.

are nationals of non-member countries'.[124] The Court's response on this point restated the established principle that situations confined to a single Member State that do not entail any factors connecting them to EU law do not come within the scope of the Treaties.[125] Finally, as in *Akrich*, the Court did not resist the temptation to remind the Member States that they are parties to the ECHR, Article 8 of which establishes an obligation to respect private and family life.[126]

3.2.2 Partners other than spouses

In *Reed*, which concerned Regulation 1612/68, the unmarried partner of a migrant worker was considered to be entitled to reside with them in the host State if the latter's national law extended such rights to the partners of its own nationals.[127] As explained further in Section 3.2.2.2, that solution was premised on non-discrimination on grounds of nationality and not on the family member provisions of the Regulation, which made no reference to partners other than spouses. In the original proposal for Directive 2004/38, the non-discrimination approach was extended to unmarried partners generally with the *Reed* limitation attached, that is, 'if the legislation of the host Member State treats unmarried couples as equivalent to married couples and in accordance with the conditions laid down in any such legislation'.[128] The proposal was framed as responding to the fact that 'several Member States have introduced a special status, with a set of rights and obligations, which cohabiting unmarried couples can register for. In the context of the right of residence, Community law cannot ignore this development'.[129]

Directive 2004/38 reflects the Commission's proposal for partners other than spouses but only for those who are registered partners. Crucially, then, registered partners who meet the adopted criteria fall within the definition of 'family member' under Article 2(2)(b) and, as a result, have a right to move to and reside in a host State either accompanying or joining there the Union citizen from whom they derive that right. However, more generally—for partners with whom Union citizens have 'a durable relationship', or where the host State does not recognise the registered partnership as 'equivalent to marriage', or where it does but the partnership in question does not meet conditions laid down in the relevant host State legislation—very limited provision is made in Article 3(2)(b) of the Directive: the host State is obliged only to 'facilitate' their entry and residence. The implications for family life of this

---

[124] *Metock*, para 76.
[125] In its first proposal for what became Directive 2003/86/EC on the right to family reunification (2003 OJ L251/12), the Commission intended that Union citizens who had not exercised free movement rights would fall within the scope of the proposed measure (see COM(1999) 638 final, para 7.5 and draft Articles 1, 2(d) and 3(1)(c) and esp draft Article 4). In the amended proposal, referring to its parallel work on what became Directive 2004/38, the Commission noted that '[t]he former Article 4 provided for alignment of family reunification of Union citizens not covered by Community law on free movement of persons on that of citizens who have exercised their right to free movement. It has been deleted as work has begun on recasting Community law on free movement of persons. The Commission proposal for a Directive on the right of citizens of the Union and their family members to move and reside freely within the territory of the Member States governs, among other things, the definition of family members concerned. The alignment of the rights of all Union citizens to family reunification will be reviewed later, once that recasting is complete' (COM(2002) 225 final, para 2.4). No legislative provision was then (or has since been) progressed to enable family reunification for static Union citizens though rights in a Union citizen's home State can be based on Article 20 TFEU in limited and exceptional situations where free movement has not been exercised; see further, Chapter 5.
[126] *Metock and Others*, para 79.
[127] Case 59/85 *Reed*, EU:C:1986:157.
[128] Original Proposal (n 51) draft Article 2(2)(b).
[129] ibid 7–8.

'fundamental dichotomy'[130]—which can also have implications for a couple's children[131]—are obvious.

3.2.2.1 Article 2(2)(b): registered partners

In contrast to Article 2(2)(a) of the Directive, which attaches no conditions to the 'spouse' of a Union citizen, Article 2(2)(b) only confers rights on:

> the partner with whom the Union citizen has contracted a registered partnership, on the basis of the legislation of a Member State, if the legislation of the host Member State treats registered partnerships as equivalent to marriage and in accordance with the conditions laid down in the relevant legislation of the host Member State.

The first restriction—'on the basis of the legislation of a Member State'—concerns the place in which the registered partnership is contracted. In *Coman*, Advocate General Wathelet argued that, for spouses, the fact that 'the place where the marriage was entered into is irrelevant is confirmed, *a contrario*, by the Union legislature's decision to make express reference to the law of the host Member State in the case of a registered partnership'.[132] In his view, the difference:

> may easily be explained by the fact that the legal institution of marriage has, or at the very least is presumed to have, a certain universality in the rights it confers and the obligations it places on the spouses, whereas the laws on "partnerships" differ and vary in their personal and material scope, as do their legal consequences.[133]

That position reflects the idea that an expectation of mutual recognition across the Member States is required only for frameworks governing *marriage*. It also rules out an obligation to recognise registered partnerships concluded in a third state. The second restriction in Article 2(2)(b) concerns the conferring of rights only according to whether, and if so on what conditions, the host Member State itself recognises registered partnerships. The host Member must treat such partnerships as 'equivalent to marriage' and may extend to the recognition of registered partnerships contracted in other Member States compliance with 'the conditions laid down' in its own 'relevant legislation'. The latter proviso could have particular implications, for example, where the sex of the partners is relevant in national registered partnership frameworks.

As noted above, the essential premise of Article 2(2)(b) is equality of treatment with host State nationals, a position that builds on the *Reed* case. In that sense, a host State is not required to extend any further recognition of registered partnerships contracted by Union citizens than it provides with respect to its own nationals. Aside from a withdrawn preliminary reference,[134] there has been no direct case law on Article 2(2)(b) at the Court of Justice to

---

[130] AG Pitruzella in Case C-22/21 *SRS and AA*, EU:C:2022:183, para 29 of the Opinion.

[131] See further on this point, though in the context of same-sex spouses, the discussion in Chapter 6 on Case C-490/20 *VMA v Stolichna obshtina, rayon 'Pancharevo'*, EU:C:2021:1008.

[132] AG Wathelet in Case C-673/16 *Coman*, EU:C:2018:2, para 49 of the Opinion.

[133] ibid para 50 of the Opinion.

[134] Case C-459/14 *Cocaj*, 2015 OJ C7/12; removed from the register by Order in July 2015, EU:C:2015:546. The referring (Hungarian) court had sought to ascertain, *inter alia*, whether Article 2(2)(b) applied to both different-sex and same-sex partnerships, and whether the legislation of the host State not treating registered partnerships as equivalent to marriage meant, in all circumstances, that the person concerned was therefore not a 'family member' for the purposes of the Directive. Addressing the meaning of and differences between registered

date. However, in *Coman,* Advocate General Wathelet expressed doubts about the 'current validity' of the requirement that registered partnerships must be treated as 'equivalent to marriage' in host State legislation, especially since that condition is 'indisputably associated with the restriction of the scope of Article 2(2)(b)'.[135] He noted that the ECtHR has 'very clearly held that Article 8 [ECHR] placed on States Parties to the ECHR the obligation to afford homosexual couples the possibility to obtain legal recognition and legal protection of their union', which means, 'specifically, that a State that limits marriage to heterosexual couples without establishing a registered partnership open to homosexual couples violates Article 8 of the ECHR and, consequently, Article 7 of the Charter'.[136] He also referred to Article 52(3) CFR to underline that Charter rights corresponding to ECHR rights 'have the same meaning and scope as the latter'.[137]

3.2.2.2 Article 3(2)(b): unmarried partners

At the time of the Directive's drafting, the European Parliament raised concerns about the lack of provision for unmarried partners in the Commission's original proposal.[138] It therefore suggested an amendment to what is now recital 5, which would have read:

> The definition of family member must be widened and standardised for all persons entitled to the right of residence so that the diversity of family relationships that exist in today's society, whether in the form of marriage, registered partnerships or unmarried partnerships, is recognised and respected. On the basis of equality and fair treatment, the fundamental right to family life should not be made dependent on individuals choosing to enter into marriage.[139]

However, its proposed amendment to Article 2 of the draft Directive was not open-ended in the manner suggested above. Instead, it reflected an adapted version of the *Reed* principle, including in the definition of 'family member' the 'unmarried partner, irrespective of sex, with whom the applicant has a durable relationship, if the legislation of practice of the host and/or home Member State treats unmarried couples in a corresponding manner to married couples and in accordance with the conditions laid down in any such legislation'.[140] The

---

partnerships and non-marital partnerships within the specific context of the Staff Regulations, see Case T-58/08 P *Commission v Roodhuijzen*, EU:T:2009:385.

[135] AG Wathelet in *Coman*, fn 25 of the Opinion.
[136] ibid, referring to *Oliari and Others v Italy*, CE:ECHR:2015:0721JUD001876611.
[137] AG Wathelet in *Coman*, fn 25 of the Opinion.
[138] The Commission had not, therefore, adopted the advice of the Report of the High Level Panel on the free movement of persons chaired by Mrs Simone Veil, and presented to the Commission on 18 March 1997: '[t]he term "spouse" does not include an unmarried partner, which can give rise to problems. [The] "family group" is undergoing rapid change and … growing numbers of people, often with children, form *de facto* couples' (11). Reflecting *Reed*, the Panel recommended 'on the basis of the case law of the European Court, that if a Member State grants rights to its own unmarried nationals living together, it must grant the same rights to nationals of other Member States, and that a study should be made of practice in the Union' (ibid).
[139] European Parliament Report (n 59) Amendment 4.
[140] ibid Amendment 16. That proposal then filtered through to other relevant provisions of the Directive eg in Amendment 86, the Parliament proposed adding the 'cessation of unmarried partnership' to the provisions dealing with rights of family members after divorce or annulment (on the latter in the adopted Directive, see Chapter 6). Amendment 19 defined 'home Member State' not as the State of the Union citizen's nationality but as 'the Member State in which a Union citizen was residing prior to exercising his/her right of free movement to, and residence in, another Member State'. However, there was no explanation of how differences between home and host State legislation or practice in this context should be reconciled.

Commission rejected the amendment on the same basis invoked to reject incorporation of the phrase 'irrespective of sex' in the provisions on spouses and registered partners, that is, 'harmonisation of the conditions of residence for Union citizens in Member States must not result in the imposition on certain Member States of amendments to family law legislation, an area which does not fall within the Community's legislative jurisdiction'.[141]

In its adopted form, Article 3(2)(b) of the Directive makes limited provision for partners with whom Union citizens have a 'durable relationship, duly attested'. As noted in Section 3.2.2.1, this may include registered partners who do not fulfil the conditions in Article 2(2)(b) of the Directive. In terms of resulting obligations, Article 3(2) requires only that the host State 'shall, in accordance with its national legislation, facilitate entry and residence' for these persons.[142] In its amended proposal for the Directive, addressing the Parliament's perspective on unmarried partners, the Commission responded that '[r]ecognition for purposes of residence of non-married couples in accordance with the legislation of other Member States could pose problems for the host Member State if its family law does not recognise this possibility'.[143] The Commission still intended that a *Reed* solution should be applied, extending a non-discrimination approach when host State rules *did* provide for residence rights of unmarried partners in cases concerning its own nationals.[144] In contrast, however, notwithstanding the Commission's characterisation of the adopted text as a 'fair compromise',[145] Article 3(2)(b) of the Directive as adopted does not confer residence rights on unmarried partners in any circumstances. In its common position, the Council does not

---

[141] Amended Proposal (n 60) para 3.1.

[142] This obligation also extends to two other categories of family members under Article 3(2)(a); see further, Section 4.2. Article 10 WA addresses family members whose residence in the UK for EU27 nationals and British nationals in EU27 was 'facilitated' under Article 3(2) of the Directive before the end of the transition period. Article 10(2) WA ensures that such persons 'retain their right of residence in the host State in accordance with this Part, provided that they continue to reside in the host State thereafter'. That assurance also applies, under Article 10(3) WA, to 'persons falling under points (a) and (b) of Article 3(2) of Directive 2004/38/EC who have applied for facilitation of entry and residence before the end of the transition period, and whose residence is being facilitated by the host State in accordance with its national legislation thereafter'. Article 10(4) WA extends the Article 3(2)(b) process to 'the partner with whom the person referred to in points (a) to (d) of paragraph 1 of this Article has a durable relationship, duly attested, where that partner resided outside the host State before the end of the transition period, provided that the relationship was durable before the end of the transition period and continues at the time the partner seeks residence under this Part'. Finally, Article 10(5) requires that '[i]n the cases referred to in paragraphs 3 and 4, the host State shall undertake an extensive examination of the personal circumstances of the persons concerned and shall justify any denial of entry or residence to such persons'. The Commission considers that the category of 'partners in a durable relationship' covers all 'long-term "durable" partnerships, both opposite-sex and same-sex relationships' ('Guidance Note relating to the Agreement' (n 34) para 1.2.3.7).

[143] Amended Proposal (n 60) 11. The Commission also pointed out that conferring rights in such circumstances 'could in fact create reverse discrimination, which the Commission would prefer to avoid'. See further, Common Position (n 52) 28, where the Council commented that 'reference to the legislation of the home Member State is not acceptable for the purpose of defining spouse or partner'.

[144] In the Amended Proposal (n 60), the definition of 'family member' under Article 2(2)(b) therefore read: 'the partner to whom the Union citizen is linked by registered partnership or with whom he/she has a duly attested durable relationship, if the legislation of the host Member State recognises the situation of unmarried couples, in accordance with the conditions laid down in any such legislation'. For both registered partners and unmarried partners, then, the Commission had proposed removing the reference to treatment by national legislation that was 'equivalent to married couples'.

[145] 'The Commission has accepted the approach proposed by the Council. While it is true that the definition of Article 2(2)(b) is more limited than the text of the amended proposal, it must be considered that the content of Article 3 has been extended to include any type of durable relationship ... The Commission considers that the text of the common position represents a fair compromise which makes it possible to facilitate the right to free movement and residence of unmarried partners of Union citizens without imposing any chances in the national law of the Member States' and it also indicated that 'the Council decided to remove the reference to humanitarian grounds, arguing that it was too broad a concept, open to abuse' (Communication on the common position (n 64) paras 3.3.2 and 3.3.1.2).

address why—or indeed if, as returned to below—a *Reed*-based obligation was therefore ruled out or not.

The result of the Council's intervention is that Article 3(2)(b) 'does not oblige the Member States to grant every application for entry or residence' submitted by partners who fall within its scope,[146] notwithstanding the Commission's assertion that excluding durable relationships from Article 2(2) is 'offset' by Article 3(2)(b).[147] Partners who themselves hold the nationality of a Member State have the opportunity, at least, to fulfil the criteria that condition the right to enter and reside in their own capacity as Union citizens. The situation of third-country national partners is patently more precarious. There is therefore a disconnect between the extent of the obligation established and the aim underpinning that obligation in the first place, which recital 6 links to 'maintain[ing] the unity of the family in a broader sense'. No 'presumption of admission' can be derived from Article 3(2).[148] Instead,

> as is clear from the use of the words 'shall facilitate' in Article 3(2) ... that provision imposes an obligation on the Member States *to confer a certain advantage, compared with applications for entry and residence of other nationals of third States*, on applications submitted by on applications submitted by persons who have a relationship *of particular dependence* with a Union citizen.[149]

In that light, the obligation established by Article 3(2) is more procedural than substantive, requiring that the host State 'shall undertake an extensive examination of the personal circumstances and shall justify any denial of entry or residence to these people'. The Court expanded on what this requires in *Rahman*. Referring to recital 6 of the Directive, the Court held that

> it is incumbent upon the competent authority, when undertaking that examination of the applicant's personal circumstances, to take account of the various factors that may be relevant in the particular case, such as the extent of economic or physical dependence and the degree of relationship between the family member and the Union citizen whom he wishes to accompany or join.[150]

On the question of attesting durability, Articles 8(5)(f) and 10(2)f) of the Directive, which concern the issuing of registration certificates to the family members of Union citizens who are themselves Union citizens and residence cards for family members who are third-country nationals respectively, stipulate only that 'proof of the existence of a durable relationship with the Union citizen' should be presented. The Commission advises that while '[n]ational rules on durability of partnership can refer to a minimum amount of time as a criterion for whether a partnership can be considered as durable', such rules 'would need to

---

[146] Case C-83/11 *Rahman*, EU:C:2012:519, para 18. The case concerned dependent family members and Article 3(2)(a) of the Directive, which is examined in Section 4.2. However, the same principles can be applied to partners in durable relationships with Union citizens under Article 3(2)(b), as confirmed in Case C-89/17 *Banger*, EU:C:2018:570.

[147] Communication on the common position (n 64) para 3.1.

[148] AG Bot in *Rahman*, EU:C:2012:174, para 63 of the Opinion.

[149] *Rahman*, para 21 (emphasis added); confirmed in *Banger*, para 31. The 'particular dependence' referred to is considered further in Section 4.2.

[150] *Rahman*, para 23.

foresee that other relevant aspects (such as for example a joint mortgage to buy a home) are also taken into account.[151]

In *Rahman,* the Court sought to reconcile the discretion that Article 3(2) enables with the need to ensure the effectiveness of EU rights and appropriate judicial protection:

> In the light both of the absence of more specific rules in Directive 2004/38 and of the use of the words 'in accordance with its national legislation' in Article 3(2) of the directive, *each Member State has a wide discretion as regards the selection of the factors to be taken into account.* None the less, the host Member State must ensure that its legislation contains criteria which are consistent with the normal meaning of the term 'facilitate' and of the words relating to dependence used in Article 3(2), *and which do not deprive that provision of its effectiveness.* Finally, even though, as the governments which have submitted observations have correctly observed, the wording used in Article 3(2) of Directive 2004/38 is not sufficiently precise to enable an applicant for entry or residence to rely directly on that provision in order to invoke criteria which should in his view be applied when assessing his application, the fact remains that such an applicant is entitled to a judicial review of whether the national legislation and its application have remained within the limits of the discretion set by [the Directive].[152]

Advocate General Bot went further, arguing that EU primary law—specifically the obligation to respect family life as well as the fundamental nature of the right to move and reside—and Article 3(2) of the Directive

> preclude a Member State from refusing a national of a non-member country who comes within the scope of that provision residence in its territory, in the case where that national wishes to reside with a member of his family who is a Union citizen, where such refusal has the effect of unjustifiably impeding the exercise of the right of the Union citizen concerned to move and reside freely within the territory of the Member States or causes a disproportionate impairment of his right to respect for private and family life.[153]

That perspective provides a good example of the sometimes uneasy relationship between primary and secondary law in the determination of EU citizenship rights, introduced in Chapter 2 and examined in more detail in Chapter 7.

More generally, in light of the 'wide discretion' that Member States are acknowledged to have,[154] it is not surprising that 'a comparative analysis of the measures transposing Article 3(2) of Directive 2004/38 into the law of the Member States reveals significant disparities'.[155] In *Rahman,* Advocate General Bot referred to the 2008 Commission report on the application of Directive 2004/38. Having concluded that transposition of the definition of family members for Article 2(2) was 'satisfactory', the Commission then observed that 13 Member States had 'failed to transpose Article 3(2) correctly'.[156] Given that the margin of discretion

---

[151] Communication on guidance for better transposition and application of Directive 2004/38/EC (n 58) para 2.1.1.
[152] *Rahman,* paras 24–25 (emphasis added).
[153] AG Bot in *Rahman,* para 79 of the Opinion.
[154] But note the stronger tone now used in case law when the 'other family members' under Article 3(2)(a) of the Directive are children: see further, Section 4.2.
[155] AG Bot in *Rahman,* para 42 of the Opinion.
[156] Report from the Commission to the European Parliament and the Council on the application of Directive 2004/38/EC on the right of citizens of the Union and their family members to move and reside freely within the territory of the Member States, COM(2008) 840 final, para 3.1.

extended to the Member States under Article 3(2) 'necessarily means that [the relevant] conditions, criteria and factors may *differ* from one Member State to another, as Member States may fulfil their obligations to transpose this provision in different ways',[157] further explanation from the Commission of what amounted to 'incorrect' transposition would have been useful. However, it was also noted that ten Member States had transposed it 'in a more favourable way by extending the automatic right to reside with the EU citizen also to this category of family members'.[158]

The principles developed in *Rahman* apply by analogy in situations where residence rights for the non-married partner of a Union citizen fall outside the scope of the Directive—in particular, where a Union citizen has returned to their home State following the exercise of free movement, as examined in Chapter 9.[159] In such cases, Article 21 TFEU applies directly. On the question of procedural safeguards, the Court confirmed in *Banger* what was implied in *Rahman*: that 'the procedural safeguards provided for in Article 31(1) of Directive 2004/38 are applicable to the persons envisaged in point (b) of the first subparagraph of Article 3(2) of that directive'.[160] More concretely, 'a person envisaged in Article 3(2) ... is entitled to a review by a court of whether the national legislation and its application have remained within the limits of the discretion set by th[e] directive'.[161] It is, in turn, the responsibility of a national court to 'ascertain in particular whether the contested decision is based on a sufficiently solid factual basis', a review that must also consider 'compliance with procedural safeguards, which is of fundamental importance enabling the court to ascertain whether the factual and legal elements on which the exercise of the power of assessment depends were present'.[162] In the context of returning Union citizens, an examination of personal circumstances would, for Advocate General Bobek, 'logically also include taking into account for evidentiary purposes that by the issuing of a residence card by another Member State, a durable relationship had already been acknowledged and duly attested'.[163] It might be argued that the Court has extrapolated as much legal protection for unmarried partners as possible from the weak legislative rights extended to them. But that leaves the problem of weak legislative rights extended in the first place. In *Banger*, Advocate General Bobek referred to changing 'social perceptions', suggesting that 'with regard to who is effectively "close" to a person, formal box-based generalisations are hardly appropriate'.[164]

However, potentially providing some respite until or unless legislative reform is achieved, it is not actually clear that the *Reed* obligation not to treat the non-married partners of Union citizens who *work* in the host State differently from the non-married partners of nationals of that State is overridden by Article 3(2)(b) of the Directive. Directive 2004/38 amended only the provisions Regulation 1612/68 that addressed family members directly. It left untouched

---

[157] AG Bobek in Case C-89/17 *Banger*, EU:C:2018:225, para 55 of the Opinion (emphasis in original).
[158] Report on the application of Directive 2004/38 (n 156) para 3.1.
[159] Case C-89/17 *Banger*, EU:C:2018:570.
[160] ibid para 49. Article 31 of the Directive is examined in Chapter 10.
[161] *Banger*, para 50.
[162] ibid para 51.
[163] AG Bobek in Case C-89/17 *Banger*, EU:C:2018:225, para 66 of the Opinion; he stressed, however, that the discretion conferred on each Member State in the application of Article 3(2) 'may not however necessarily lead to the right of residence in the Union citizen's Member State of origin being granted (or, for that matter, in any other Member State to which the couple may decide to move) ... [T]he obligation to facilitate does not mean the obligation to automatically issue. The fact that, within limits, Member States are entitled to set their own specific criteria in this area logically means that there is neither a 'mutual recognition obligation' of the residence authorisations issued by other Member States, nor for that matter an obligation to provide at least the same or better treatment than in the preceding host Member State(s)' (para 67 of the Opinion).
[164] ibid para 37 of the Opinion, referring also to the evolving understanding of 'family' in the case law of the ECtHR on Article 8 ECHR.

Article 7(2) of the Regulation—now Article 7(2) of Regulation 492/2011—which establishes that workers who are nationals of other Member States 'shall enjoy the same social and tax advantages as national workers'. That was the provision on which the Court based residence rights for non-married partners in *Reed* to ensure alignment of treatment with host State nationals.[165] Moreover, the Court developed the Article 7(2) solution in *Reed* precisely because unmarried partners could not be treated in the same way as spouses on account of rights being extended to the latter only by the family member provisions of the Regulation. The Common Position on the draft Directive was ambiguous on this point, though there is the statement that '[w]ith regard to partners, whether they are registered partners, the Council is of the opinion that recognition of such situations must be based exclusively on the legislation of the host Member State', which does leave a door open to *Reed*.[166]

The reasoning in *Depesme and Kerrou* provides some guidance on (though perhaps not resolution of) the question. In that case, in the context of financial aid for university studies, the Court considered whether the definition of family members in Article 2 of Directive 2004/38 should also inform the concept of a family member for the purposes of equal treatment of workers under Article 7(2) of Regulation 492/2011. More specifically, the question was whether the child of a frontier worker's spouse was included. The Court observed that '[t]here is nothing to suggest that the EU legislature intended to establish, as regards family members, a watertight distinction between the scope of Directive 2004/38 and the scope of Regulation No 492/2011, under which family members of a Union citizen, within the meaning of Directive 2004/38, would not necessarily be the same persons as the family members of that citizen when he is considered in his capacity as a worker'.[167] It also referred to recital 1 of Directive 2014/54,

> under which the free movement of workers 'is further developed by Union law aiming to guarantee the full exercise of rights conferred on Union citizens and the members of their family' [so] that the expression 'members of their family' should be understood as having the same meaning as the term defined in [Article 2(2) of Directive 2004/38], which applies also to family members of frontier workers.[168]

The point about ensuring synergies across Directive 2004/38 and Regulation 492/2011 is an important one. However, applying it in *Depesme and Kerrou* enhanced rather than reduced the rights of the worker concerned. Since unmarried partners do not fall within the scope of Article 2 of the Directive—within its definition of 'family members'—in the first place, does Article 3(2)(b), which provides a right to a procedure rather than a right to enter and reside, override a right to reside construed as a social and tax advantage under Article 7(2) of the Regulation? The emphasis placed on the autonomy of the equal treatment guarantees protected by the Regulation in *Jobcenter Krefeld* would suggest not. There, the Court stated

---

[165] Case 59/85 *Reed*, EU:C:1986:157, paras 25–29. The Court emphasised that 'the possibility for a migrant worker of obtaining permission for his unmarried companion to reside with him where that companion is not a national of the host Member State, can assist with his integration in the host State and thus contribute to the achievement of freedom of movement for workers' (para 28).

[166] Common Position (n 52) 28.

[167] Joined Cases C-401/15 to C-403/15 *Depesme and Kerrou*, EU:C:2016:955, para 51. On different understandings of family members in the context of social security coordination under Regulation 883/2004, see Case 802/18 *Caisse pour l'avenir des enfants*, EU:C:2020:269.

[168] *Depesme and Kerrou*, para 53. Article 2 of Directive 2014/54/EU on measures facilitating the exercise of rights conferred on workers in the context of freedom of movement for workers, 2014 OJ L128/8, establishes that its scope is identical to that of Regulation 492/2011.

that 'the fact that JD had become economically inactive during that period *cannot lead to the result that the principle of equal treatment laid down in Article 7(2) of Regulation No 492/2011 becomes inapplicable*'.[169] Moreover, '[t]he same is true, in a situation where the children and the parent who is their primary carer have a right of residence based on Article 10 of Regulation No 492/2011, with respect to the right to equal treatment as regards entitlement to the social advantages laid down in Article 7(2) of that regulation'.[170]

These statements in *Jobcenter Krefeld* were concerned mainly to establish a right to reside under the Regulation, from which a guarantee of equal treatment then followed (as discussed further in Chapters 6 and 7). They are noted here to underline the 'specific expression' of the equal treatment right that Article 7(2) is deemed by the Court to represent, which is based on Article 45 and not Article 21 TFEU.[171] A qualifier might be read into the statement that

> the derogation from the principle of equal treatment, provided for in Article 24(2) [of Directive 2004/38], is applicable only in situations that fall within the scope of Article 24(1), namely situations where the right of residence is based on that directive, and not in situations where that right has an independent basis in Article 10 of Regulation No 492/2011.[172]

Could Article 3(2)(b) constitute a 'derogation' from equal treatment for workers in the same way, even by analogy? According to Advocate General Pitruzella in *Jobcenter Krefeld*, a 'legitimate objective pursued by the EU legislature ... cannot, by itself, justify transferring a rule of secondary legislation to a different legislative context'.[173] And the Court underlined that Article 7(2) of the Regulation 'is the particular expression, in the specific area of the grant of social advantages, of the principle of equal treatment and non-discrimination on the ground of nationality'.[174] It also stated that

> [w]hen Directive 2004/38 was adopted, Article [10 of Regulation 492/2011] was neither repealed nor amended. On the contrary, that directive was designed so as to be compatible with Article [10 of the Regulation] and with the case-law interpreting that provision. Consequently, that directive cannot, as such, either call into question the independence of the rights based on Article 10 of [the] Regulation or alter their scope.[175]

It could be argued that the Directive was consciously designed to absorb the residence rights of family members from the Regulation's repealed provisions. At the same time, neither residence nor procedural rights for unmarried partners were included in the repealed family member provisions of Regulation 1612/68 and the language of the key provision for *Reed*-based rights—Article 7(2)—was neither repealed nor amended by the coming into force of the Directive. In the context of retaining residence rights in a host State after economic activity has ceased, it has been argued that 'a legislative definition ... cannot water down the (more inclusive) scope of the constitutional category of a worker, which remains under the

---

[169] Case C-181/19 *Jobcenter Krefeld*, EU:C:2020:794, para 47 (emphasis added).
[170] ibid para 50.
[171] ibid para 44: 'Article 7(2) of Regulation No 492/2011 is the particular expression, in the specific area of the grant of social advantages, of the principle of equal treatment enshrined in Article 45(2) TFEU, and must be accorded the same interpretation as that provision.'
[172] ibid para 65.
[173] AG Pitruzella in Case C-181/19 *Jobcenter Krefeld*, EU:C:2020:377, para 39 of the Opinion.
[174] *Jobcenter Krefeld*, para 74.
[175] ibid para 64.

interpretative authority of the Court'.¹⁷⁶ Whether the rights vested in workers by Article 45 TFEU and Article 7(2) of Regulation 492/2011 can therefore—continue to—provide more extensive protection to their unmarried partners than Article 3(2)(b) of the Directive envisages remains very much to be seen.¹⁷⁷

3.2.3 Article 2(2)(c): 'direct descendants who are under the age of 21'

In *Chavez-Vilchez*, Advocate General Szpunar characterised '[t]he primacy of the best interests of the child' as 'one of the principles permeating the EU legal order'.¹⁷⁸ Several threads of EU citizenship law connect, in a general sense, to the rights of children *as* Union citizens if they are Member State nationals and to the rights of the children *of* Union citizens, irrespective of the children's nationality.

On the first point, it was established in *Zhu and Chen* that 'a young child can take advantage of the rights of free movement and residence guaranteed by [Union] law' since '[t]he capacity of a national of a Member State to be the holder of rights guaranteed by the Treaty and by secondary law on the free movement of persons cannot be made conditional upon the attainment by the person concerned of the age prescribed for the acquisition of legal capacity to exercise those rights personally'.¹⁷⁹ Thus, 'even a young child may make use of the rights of free movement and residence guaranteed by [Union] law'.¹⁸⁰ However, minor Union citizens are equally subject to the obligations of Union citizenship. For example, as discussed further in Chapter 6, they are required to fulfil the conditions for lawful residence in a host State set out in Directive 2004/38. There is flexibility about *how* these conditions are fulfilled—in particular, with regard to the origins of the financial resources required in order not to become a burden on the social assistance system of the host State:

> the expression 'have' sufficient resources in ... Article 7(1)(b) of Directive 2004/38 must be interpreted as meaning that it suffices that such resources are available to the Union citizens, and that that provision lays down no requirement whatsoever as to their origin, since they could be provided, *inter alia*, by a national of a non-Member State, the parent of the citizens who are minor children at issue.¹⁸¹

It is therefore presumed that minor Union citizens who reside legally and continuously in a host State will acquire rights to reside there permanently under Article 16 of the Directive, potentially from a very young age.¹⁸²

Residence rights for other family members can also be derived from minor Union citizens. For example, reflecting a *de facto* relationship of dependency, the primary carer of a minor Union citizen residing in a Member State other than that of which the child is a

---

¹⁷⁶ A Iliopoulou-Penot, 'Deconstructing the former edifice of Union citizenship? The *Alimanovic* judgment' (2016) 53 CML Rev 1007 at 1018, discussing Case C-507/12 *Saint Prix*, EU:C:2014:2007; see further, Chapter 6.

¹⁷⁷ Moreover, the principle of equal treatment captured specifically for workers by Article 7(2) of the Regulation has been extended to self-employed persons on the basis of Article 49 TFEU directly; see eg Case C-299/01 *Commission v Luxembourg*, EU:C:2002:394, para 12; and Case C-168/20 *BJ and OV*, EU:C:2021:907, para 85.

¹⁷⁸ AG Szpunar in Case C-133/15 *Chavez-Vilchez*, EU:C:2016:659, para 42 of the Opinion.

¹⁷⁹ Case C-200/02 *Zhu and Chen*, EU:C:2004:639, para 20.

¹⁸⁰ Case C-76/05 *Schwarz and Gootjes-Schwarz*, EU:C:2007:492, para 90.

¹⁸¹ Case C-86/12 *Alokpa and Moudoulou*, EU:C:2013:64, para 27. See also, Case C-93/18 *Bajratari*, EU:C:2019:809.

¹⁸² This can be implied from Case C-165/14 *Rendón Marín*, EU:C:2016:675, para 47; see further, Chapter 6. Under Article 28(3)(b) of the Directive, minor Union citizens also benefit from special protection against expulsion from a host Member State; see further, Chapter 10.

national must be granted a right of residence there too on the basis that 'a refusal to allow the parent, whether a national of a Member State or a national of a non-member country, who is the carer of a child to whom [Article 21 TFEU] and Directive [2004/38] grant a right of residence, to reside with that child in the host Member State would deprive the child's right of residence of any useful effect'.[183] Residence rights for primary carers are also extended when the Union citizen's right to reside in the host State is based not on the Directive but on Regulation 492/2011 as the child of a migrant worker who enjoys a right to reside in the host Member State in order to complete their education there,[184] and, in exceptional cases, in the Union citizen's home State under Article 20 TFEU.

However, as explained in Chapter 5, the Court has only recently used the term 'primary carer' in Article 20 TFEU cases.[185] It has also now addressed the status of the *other* parent in such situations: the parent who is *not* considered to be the primary carer of a minor Union citizen.[186] The significance of Article 24(3) CFR—which requires that '[e]very child shall have the right to maintain on a regular basis a personal relationship and direct contact with both his or her parents, unless that is contrary to his or her interests'—has increased in importance in this respect.[187] The Court further distinguishes between dependency on third-country national family members in situations involving minors ('and *a fortiori* minors who are young children') and situations involving family relationships between adults since 'an adult is, as a general rule, capable of living an independent existence apart from the members of his family'.[188] While the criterion of emotional dependency may be taken into account in cases engaging Article 20 TFEU, it is less pertinent in cases concerning adults.[189] This case law is examined in detail in Chapter 5. Member States may also be compelled by EU law to issue appropriate documentation to permit a child who is a Member State national to exercise the right to move and reside conferred on them by Article 21 TFEU.[190]

However, more directly for present purposes and irrespective of nationality, the 'direct descendants who are under the age of 21' of a Union citizen—or of their spouse, or of their partner as defined under Article 2(2)(b)—qualify as 'family members' under Article 2(2)(c) of Directive 2004/38 without needing to fulfil any other conditions.[191] The Commission

---

[183] *Zhu and Chen*, para 45; confirmed in eg Case C-115/15 *NA*, EU:C:2016:487, para 80, where the Court explains that this is because 'enjoyment by a young child of a right of residence necessarily implies that the child is entitled to be accompanied by the person who is his primary carer and accordingly that the carer must be in a position to reside with the child in the host Member State for the duration of such residence'. Article 9(1)(a)(ii) WA makes provision for carers as 'family members' in such circumstances, ie 'persons other than those defined in Article 3(2) of Directive 2004/38/EC whose presence is required by Union citizens or United Kingdom nationals in order not to deprive those Union citizens or United Kingdom nationals of a right of residence granted by this Part'.

[184] eg Case C-480/08 *Teixeira*, EU:C:2010:83; Joined Cases C-147/11 and C-148/11 *Czop and Punakova*, EU:C:2012:538. See further, Chapters 7 and 9.

[185] eg Case C-304/14 *CS*, EU:C:2016:674, paras 32 and 50.

[186] Case C-82/16 *KA and Others*, EU:C:2018:308; see further, Chapter 5.

[187] The Court first linked Articles 7 and 24 CFR in the context of Directive 2003/186 on the right to family reunification (2003 OJ L251/12) in Joined Cases C-356/11 and C-357/11 *O and S*, EU:C:2012:776, para 76; then to the expulsion framework established by Directive 2004/38 (*Rendón Marín*, para 66); and later, more generally, to cases where residence rights are based on Article 20 TFEU (Case C-133/15 *Chavez-Vilchez*, EU:C:2017:354, para 70). This case law is discussed in Chapter 5.

[188] *KA and Others*, para 65.

[189] ibid paras 69–70.

[190] Case C-490/20 *Stolichna obshtina, rayon 'Pancharevo'*, EU:C:2021:1008; see further, Chapter 6.

[191] For direct descendants over 21 as well as for direct relatives in the ascending line, a condition of dependency must be satisfied; see further, Section 4.1. Article 10(1)(e)(iii) WA extends the protection of the Agreement to children 'born to, or legally adopted by, persons referred to in points (a) to (d) after the end of the transition period, whether inside or outside the host State, and fulfil[ling] the conditions set out in point (2)(c) of Article 2 of Directive 2004/38/EC at the time they seek residence under this Part in order to join the person referred to in points (a) to (d) of this paragraph and fulfil one of the following conditions:—both parents are persons referred to in points (a) to (d);—one parent is a person referred to in points (a) to (d) and the other is a national of the host

considers that 'the notion of direct relatives in the descending and ascending lines extends to adoptive relationships or minors in custody of a permanent legal guardian'.[192] It also suggests that '[f]oster children and foster parents who have temporary custody *may have* rights under the Directive, depending upon the strength of the ties in the particular case'.[193] There has been limited case law on the meaning of 'direct descendant' for the purposes of Article 2(2)(c), but it was considered in *SM*. This case concerned the refusal by UK authorities to issue a residence permit for SM as the adopted child of an EEA national. SM was born in Algeria and abandoned by her parents at birth. In March 2011, she was placed in the guardianship of Mr and Mrs M, both French nationals, under the Algerian *kafala* system,[194] which was not recognised as adoption under UK law. At the material time, Mr M, who had a right of permanent residence in the UK, had returned there while Mrs M and SM remained in Algeria. The referring court (the UK Supreme Court) considered that

> SM must, at the very least, be regarded as one of the 'other family members' of a citizen of the Union as referred to in Article 3(2)(a) of Directive 2004/38. That concept is sufficiently broad to cover a child in respect of whom a citizen of the Union has parental responsibility under the law of the child's country of origin, even if there is no biological or adoptive link between the child and that citizen.[195]

The referring court acknowledged that the status of 'direct descendant' under Article 2(2)(c) 'could be derived' from the Commission's guidance on better transposition and application of Directive 2004/38, noted above;[196] but it raised a concern that

> an autonomous interpretation ... whereby a child placed under the Algerian *kafala* system would be regarded as a 'direct descendant' could lead to the placing of children in households which, according to the legislation of the host Member State, would not be regarded as suitable for hosting children. Such an interpretation could also give rise to a risk of exploitation, abuse and trafficking of children, which the 1993 Hague Convention seeks to prevent and deter.[197]

In the observations submitted to the Court, there was some disagreement: all six Member States (including the UK) 'emphasise[d] that the concept of a "direct descendant" referred

---

State; or—one parent is a person referred to in points (a) to (d) and has sole or joint rights of custody of the child, in accordance with the applicable rules of family law of a Member State or of the United Kingdom, including applicable rules of private international law under which rights of custody established under the law of a third State are recognised in the Member State or in the United Kingdom, in particular as regards the best interests of the child, and without prejudice to the normal operation of such applicable rules of private international law'.

[192] Communication guidance for better transposition and application of Directive 2004/38/EC (n 58) para 2.1.2, referring to ECtHR case law in support.
[193] ibid (emphasis added).
[194] '[U]nder Algerian law *kafala* is where an adult undertakes to assume responsibility for the care, education and protection of a child, in the same way a parent would for their child, and to assume legal guardianship of that child. Unlike adoption, which is prohibited by Algerian law, the placing of a child under *kafala* does not mean that the child becomes the guardian's heir. In addition, *kafala* comes to an end when the child attains the age of majority and may be revoked at the request of the biological parents or the guardian' (Case C-129/18 *SM*, EU:C:2019:248, para 45; see further, paras 32–57 of the Opinion of AG Campos Sánchez-Bordona, EU:C:2019:140).
[195] Case C-129/18 *SM*, EU:C:2019:248, para 36.
[196] ibid para 39.
[197] ibid para 41, referring to the Convention on Protection of Children and Co-operation in Respect of Intercountry Adoption, signed at The Hague on 29 May 1993.

to in Article 2(2)(c) of Directive 2004/38 requires there to be a parent–child relationship, either biological or adoptive, between the child and the citizen of the Union', which ruled out a child placed under the Algerian *kafala* system; while the Commission and two NGOs argued that direct descendant 'may include a child in respect of whom a citizen of the Union has assumed permanent legal guardianship, such as Algerian *kafala*' and that 'such an interpretation is necessary, in essence, in order to preserve, in the best interests of that child, the family life which he or she has with his or her guardian'.[198]

The Court pointed out that Article 2(2)(c) of Directive 2004/38 makes no express reference to national law and, in such circumstances, 'the need for a uniform application of EU law and the principle of equality require that the terms of that provision must normally be given an independent and uniform interpretation throughout the European Union'.[199] Bearing in mind the Directive's aim of facilitating freedom of movement, the Court determined that while 'direct descendant' does commonly entail a 'parent–child relationship', that concept must be 'construed broadly so that it covers any parent child relationship, whether biological or legal'.[200] Nevertheless, it held that the Commission's interpretation, which included 'a child placed in the legal guardianship of a citizen of the Union', could not be justified on that basis.[201] Thus,

> the placing of a child under the Algerian *kafala* system does not create a parent–child relationship between the child and its guardian, a child, such as SM, who is placed in the legal guardianship of citizens of the Union under that system cannot be regarded as a 'direct descendant' of a citizen of the Union for the purposes of Article 2(2)(c) of Directive 2004/38.[202]

However, the Court did go on to consider the obligations on the UK as a host State under Article 3(2)(a) of the Directive with respect to facilitating the admission of 'other family members' in certain circumstances, returned to in Section 4.2.

4. Dependent Relatives

Dependency is a critical concept for the determination of certain family member rights in EU citizenship law,[203] yet it is also a concept that has different meanings not only in different family relationship contexts but also having regard to the source of the applicable rights. Dependency comes, in other words, in various forms; for rights derived from Union citizens, material, emotional, or legal dependency can be relevant, or not, in different situations.

In its original proposal for Directive 2004/38, the Commission intended that direct relatives in the ascending line and direct descendants of a Union citizen (or of their spouse) should be defined as family members without any further conditions, on the basis that 'there is no good reason to deny children over 21 who are not dependent on their parents, or

---

[198] *SM*, paras 46 and 47.
[199] ibid para 50.
[200] ibid paras 53–54. AG Campos Sánchez-Bordona pointed to the express inclusion of adopted children in other legislative provisions eg in Article 4(1)(b)(c) and (d) of Directive 2003/86 EC on the right to family reunification, 2003 OJ L251/12 (EU:C:2019:248,; see para 71 of the Opinion).
[201] *SM*, para 55.
[202] ibid para 56.
[203] Beyond EU citizenship law, see similarly eg Article 4(2) of Council Directive 2003/86/EC on the right to family reunification, 2003 OJ L251/12, which concerns third-country nationals lawfully resident in a Member State.

relatives in the ascending line who are not dependent on their children, the right to join their family in another Member State'.²⁰⁴ The decision to reintroduce a condition with respect to age for direct descendants and a condition of dependency for both direct descendants over 21 and all direct relatives in the ascending line was taken by the Council, on the basis that such conditions reflected the *acquis* at the time.²⁰⁵

In this part of the chapter, dependency is examined with respect to three categories of family members in Directive 2004/38: relatives in the descending and ascending lines (Section 4.1) and other family members (Section 4.2). The legal significance of dependency beyond the Directive has developed further in situations confined to a Union citizen's home State (Chapter 5) and situations that arise there following the exercise of free movement (Chapter 9).

4.1 Article 2(2): Direct Relatives in the Descending and Ascending Lines

Article 2(2)(c) of Directive 2004/38 confirms that 'the direct descendants [of a Union citizen] who are under the age of 21 or are dependants and those of the spouse or [registered] partner' are family members for the purposes of the Directive. Thus, while direct descendants under 21 are family members without being required to meet any further conditions, direct descendants older than 21 must demonstrate dependency on the Union citizen from whom they derive their rights. Drawing from case law on legislation that preceded the Directive,²⁰⁶ being 'dependent' on a Union citizen in this context meant material dependency only. In *Zhu and Chen*, interpreting Directive 90/364, the Court confirmed that 'the status of "dependent" member of the family of a holder of a right of residence is the result of a factual situation characterised by the fact that material support for the family member is provided by the holder of the right of residence'.²⁰⁷ In the same case, Advocate General Tizzano ruled out consideration of emotional dependency in this context, observing that 'only the English language version [of Directive 90/364] uses a neutral term like "dependent" whereas, as the Commission correctly points out, in all the other language versions the term used relates unambiguously to material dependency'.²⁰⁸

Article 2(2)(d) of the Directive establishes that 'dependent direct relatives in the ascending line [of a Union citizen] and those of the spouse or [registered] partner' also fall within the definition of family member of a Union citizen. This situation may be distinguished from the rights extended to 'primary carers' outlined in Section 3.2.3. In *Zhu and Chen*, the third-country national mother of a minor Union citizen could not derive a right to reside from her daughter on the basis of Directive 90/364 since the minor Union citizen was dependent

---

²⁰⁴ Original Proposal (n 51) 8; see further, draft Article 2(2). That position reflects the Report of the High Level Panel on the free movement of persons (n 138) 50: '[i]n order to reinforce family unity, there are no valid grounds for denying non-dependent children more than 21 years old or relatives in the ascending line who are not dependent on their children, the right to join their parents or children, as the case may be, in the Member State where the said parents/children are installed'.
²⁰⁵ Common Position (n 52) section 3.3.2, which indicates that the Council 'decided unanimously' on this point.
²⁰⁶ eg on Article 10 of Regulation 1612/68, see Case 316/85 *Lebon*, EU:C:1987:302.
²⁰⁷ Case C-200/02 *Zhu and Chen*, EU:C:2004:639, para 43.
²⁰⁸ AG Tizzano in Case C-200/02 *Zhu and Chen*, EU:C:2004:307, para 85 of the Opinion. However, emotional dependency is relevant for 'other family members' under Article 3(2)(a) of the Directive (Section 4.2) and in the context of rights based on Article 20 TFEU (Chapter 5).

on her mother: not—as required by that Directive at the time and now by Article 2(2)(d) of Directive 2004/38, which replaces it—the other way around. Having confirmed that 'the status of "dependent" member of the family of a holder of a right of residence is the result of a factual situation characterised by the fact that material support for the family member is provided by the holder of the right of residence', the Court then pointed out that 'the position is exactly the opposite [where] the holder of the right of residence is dependent on the national of a non-member country who is her carer and wishes to accompany her'.[209] For that reason, Mrs Chen could not be a dependent family member in the ascending line within the meaning of Article 2(2)(d).[210] Specifically for direct relatives in the ascending line, it should also be recalled that when Union citizens reside in a host Member State for the purposes of studying there—that is, on the basis of Article 7(1)(c) of Directive 2004/38—residence rights for family members are only conferred on the Union citizen's spouse, registered partner, or dependent children. In such circumstances, Article 7(4) confirms that Article 3(2)(a)—returned to in Section 4.2—shall apply to the Union citizen's 'dependent direct relatives in the ascending lines and those of his/her spouse or registered partner'.

The qualities of dependency under Article 2(2)(c) of the Directive were addressed in *Reyes*. Ms Reyes, a citizen of the Philippines who was born in 1987, was cared for by her maternal grandmother after her mother moved to Germany to work. Ms Reyes' mother acquired German citizenship and sent money to support her family in the Philippines. She moved to Sweden in 2009. In March 2011, Ms Reyes applied for a residence permit in Sweden as her mother's dependent family member. That application was rejected in May 2011 on the ground that Ms Reyes 'had not proved that the money which was indisputably transferred to her by her mother and her partner had been used to supply her basic needs in the form of board and lodging and access to healthcare in the Philippines'.[211] The referring court's questions focused on the implications for the status of dependency of both the capacity and the intention of the dependent descendant to undertake paid work in order to provide for their own basic needs.

Advocate General Mengozzi summarised the referring court's first question as follows: '[m]ust the applicant merely demonstrate the *genuineness* of the material support provided by that citizen, or may the authorities further require him to provide proof that the support is *necessary*?'[212] The Court confirmed that 'in order for a direct descendant, who is 21 years old or older, of a Union citizen to be regarded as being a "dependant" of that citizen within the meaning of Article 2(2)(c) of Directive 2004/38, the existence of a situation of *real dependence* must be established'.[213] That results from 'a factual situation characterised by the fact that material support for that family member is provided by the Union citizen who has exercised his right of free movement'.[214] To determine whether or not such a situation exists, a host State 'must assess whether, having regard to his financial and social conditions, the direct descendant, who is 21 years old or older, of a Union citizen, is not in a position to support himself'.[215] Critically, '[t]he need for material support must exist in the State of

---

[209] *Zhu and Chen*, paras 43–44; referring to Case 316/85 *Lebon*, EU:C:1987:302, paras 20–22.
[210] See similarly eg Case C-40/11 *Iida*, EU:C:2012:691, paras 54–56; Case C-86/12 *Alokpa and Moudoulou*, EU:C:2013:645, paras 25–26; and Case C-165/14 *Rendón Marín*, EU:C:2016:675, para 50. However, rights of residence may be based directly on Articles 20 and 21 TFEU in certain circumstances; see further, Chapters 5 (Article 20) and 9 (Article 21).
[211] Case C-423/12 *Reyes*, EU:C:2014:16, para 13.
[212] AG Mengozzi in Case C-423/12 *Reyes*, EU:C:2013:719, para 1 of the Opinion (emphasis added).
[213] *Reyes*, para 20 (emphasis added); confirming Case C-1/05 *Jia*, EU:C:2007:1, para 42.
[214] *Reyes*, para 21.
[215] ibid para 22.

origin of that descendant or the State whence he came at the time when he applies to join that citizen'.[216] This requirement has its origins in Article 4(3) of Directive 68/360, which required dependent family members to produce in the host State 'a document issued by the competent authority of the State of origin or the State whence they came, testifying that they are dependent on the worker or that they live under his roof in such country'.[217] As will be seen in Section 4.2, a version of that requirement still applies for dependent family members who fall within the scope of Article 3(2)(a) of Directive 2004/38. However, for dependent family members within the meaning of Article 2(2), Articles 8(5)(2)(d) and 10(2)(d) of the Directive, which concern the issuing of registration certificates to the family members of Union citizens who themselves are Member State nationals and residence cards for family members who are not nationals of a Member State respectively, require only 'documentary evidence that the conditions laid down in [Articles 2(2)(c) and 2(2)(d)] are met'.

The Court also ruled in *Reyes* that the reasons for dependency—for the descendant's recourse to material support from the Union citizen—are not relevant, an interpretation explained on the basis that measures such as the Directive, 'establishing the free movement of Union citizens, which constitute[s] one of the foundations of the European Union, must be construed broadly'.[218] Applying these criteria in *Reyes*, the Court concluded that a factual situation of material dependence did exist since Ms Reyes' mother paid a sum of money to her regularly and for a significant period of time. There was no specific reference to producing evidence to this effect in *Reyes* but, more generally, the Court has drawn analogies with case law on procedures associated with legislation preceding the adoption of Directive 2004/38 and confirmed that 'evidence may be adduced by any appropriate means'.[219] However, in light of the factual dependency deemed to exist in *Reyes*, the applicant could not be required to show that she had 'tried without success to find work or obtain subsistence support from the authorities of [her] country of origin and/or otherwise tried to support [herself]'.[220]

The referring court's second question shifted attention from the dependent relative's circumstances in their country or origin to their (potential) circumstances in the host State. More specifically, it asked whether

> any significance attaches to the fact that a family member—due to personal circumstances such as age, education and health—is deemed to be well placed to obtain employment and in addition intends to start work in the Member State, which would mean that the conditions for him to be regarded as a relative who is a dependant under the provision are no longer met.[221]

This question exposes the innate circularity of grounding residence rights in a requirement of dependency as a *precondition*: must the relevant family member remain in the relationship of dependency to sustain their right to reside, or is dependency more like a gateway condition: necessary to enter the host State but capable of being displaced by opportunities

---

[216] ibid, confirming *Jia*, para 37.
[217] Council Directive 68/360/EEC on the abolition of restrictions on movement and residence within the Community for workers of Member States and their families, 1968 OJ L257/13.
[218] *Reyes*, para 23; confirming *Jia*, para 36.
[219] eg *Jia*, para 41; Case C-215/03 *Oulane*, EU:C:2005:95, para 53.
[220] *Reyes*, para 25. Such a requirement was ruled out because providing such evidence was likely to be 'excessively difficult' thereby depriving the Directive of its 'proper effect' (para 26). This part of the judgment reflects previous case law (eg *Jia*, para 36), which was also drawn from in the Communication on guidance for better transposition and application of Directive 2004/38/EC (n 58) para 2.1.4.
[221] *Reyes*, para 29.

that might then arise there? In *Reyes*, the Court opted for the latter approach. Since the factual situation of material dependency must be shown to exist in the country from which the family member comes and at the time when they seek to join the Union citizen on whom they depend,

> [i]t follows that ... any prospects of obtaining work in the host Member State which would enable, if necessary, a direct descendant, who is 21 years old or older, of a Union citizen no longer to be dependent on that citizen once he has the right of residence are not such as to affect the interpretation of the condition of being a 'dependant' referred to in Article 2(2)(c).[222]

Thus, where the initially required relationship of dependency ceases, the right of residence that was built upon it is not erased in consequence. That finding was underpinned with reference to Article 23 of the Directive, which confirms the entitlement of family members of a Union citizen to become economically active in a Member State in which they have a right to reside.[223] For Advocate General Mengozzi, that provision meant that there was

> no systemic inconsistency in granting a right of residence to a member of the family of a Union citizen because he is a dependant within the meaning of Directive 2004/38, even though the national authorities sense—or infer from the applicant's declared intentions, as seems to be the case in this instance—that the applicant appears to be in a position to integrate into employment in the society of the host Member State.[224]

A final point on *Reyes* observed by Advocate General Mengozzi: the circumstances of the case highlight the limited utility—or even credibility—of construing the rights of family members in purely instrumental terms around 'the existence or possibility of an obstacle to the freedom of movement of the citizen concerned': Ms Reyes' mother had already moved to Sweden and had no intention of leaving that State (she resided there with her retired Norwegian husband, that relationship being the reason she moved to Sweden from Germany in the first place).[225] In other words, whether her adult daughter lived with her in Sweden or not had no bearing on her own right to move and reside.[226] This insight underlines a theme that surfaces at various points across this chapter: that the question of rights for family members is *primarily* a human one and yet is typically characterised in EU citizenship law as a *secondary* offshoot of freedom of movement. The latter is, though, what normally enables

---

[222] ibid para 31.
[223] ibid para 32. Article 23 of the Directive establishes that '[i]rrespective of nationality, the family members of a Union citizen who have the right of residence or the right of permanent residence in a Member State shall be entitled to take up employment or self-employment there'.
[224] AG Mengozzi in *Reyes*, para 63 of the Opinion. The Advocate General also sought to address the referring court's depiction of 'the granting of a residence permit to a family member who is a "dependant" of a Union citizen but is nevertheless able to work in the host Member State as the affirmation of a sort of strategy for circumventing national laws on access to employment for third-State nationals, in particular when it is their first entry into the territory of the Union', also pointing out that 'the circle of beneficiaries of the rights indirectly conferred by Directive 2004/38 is rather narrowly defined and, more specifically as regards Article 2(2)(c) of the directive, the direct descendants who are over the age of 21 must, in any event, be recognised as dependants by the authorities of the host Member State' (paras 66–67 of the Opinion). Questions about the intersection of dependency (for relatives in the ascending line) and access to social assistance have also been referred to the Court (Case C-488/21 *GV v Chief Appeals Officer and Others*, pending at the time of writing).
[225] AG Mengozzi in *Reyes*, fn 13 of the Opinion.
[226] In *Banger*, AG Bobek raised similar questions about the continuing yet dubious emphasis placed on deterrence (AG Bobek in Case C-89/17 *Banger*, EU:C:2018:225, paras 39–44 of the Opinion); see further, Chapter 9.

the triggering of EU legal protection in the first place, providing the necessary connecting factor to EU law that must be established. As already seen in Chapter 3 and discussed further in Chapter 5, connecting situations to Union citizenship outwith the exercise of free movement has thus far been justified in very exceptional situations only, connected to deprivation of either the status of Union citizenship altogether or enjoyment of the rights that it confers. The Court is obliged by the Treaties and the Charter to respect and protect the fundamental rights of Union citizens. But it is not a court *of* human rights and must have regard to the Union 'ecosystem' across its case law,[227] including the constitutional parameters intended by the principle of conferral. Nevertheless, requiring a connecting factor to EU law beyond the 'fact' of Union citizenship per se diminishes for some its potential as a more boldly transformative status in EU law.[228]

4.2 Article 3(2)(a): 'Other Family Members'

In Section 3.2.2.2, we saw that Article 3(2)(b) of the Directive requires host States to 'facilitate' the entry and residence of partners within whom a Union citizen has a durable relationship. Under Article 3(2)(a), the same obligation is extended to:

> any other family members, irrespective of their nationality, not falling under the definition of [Article 2(2)] who, in the country from which they have come, are dependants or members of the household of the Union citizen having the primary right of residence, or where serious health grounds strictly require the personal care of the family member by the Union citizen.[229]

It was noted in Section 4.1 that this provision also applies to relatives in the ascending line of Union citizens who reside in a host State for the purposes of studying there.

The principles outlined in Section 3.2.2.2 for unmarried partners—essentially, that Article 3(2) does not confer rights, or presumptions of rights, with respect to applications for entry and residence, and that the principal obligations placed on the host State are to undertake

---

[227] Internal EU27 preparatory discussions on the framework for the future relationship: 'Regulatory issues', TF50 (2018) 32—Commission to EU 27, 21 February 2018, <https://ec.europa.eu/info/sites/default/files/slides_regulatory_issues.pdf> (accessed 29 May 2023).

[228] Reflecting on the different constitutional angles that require aligning in this context, see AG Sharpston in Case C-34/09 *Ruiz Zambrano*, EU:C:2010:560, paras 151–177 of the Opinion. For a range of perspectives on the relationship, both actual and potential, between Union citizenship and fundamental rights, see eg A Yong, *The Rise and Decline of Fundamental Rights in EU Citizenship* (Hart Publishing 2019); M van den Brink, 'EU citizenship and (fundamental) rights: empirical, normative, and conceptual problems' (2019) 25 European Law Journal 21; D Düsterhaus, 'EU citizenship and fundamental rights: contradictory, converging or complementary?' in D Kochenov (ed) *EU Citizenship and Federalism: The Role of Rights* (CUP 2017) 642; S Iglesias Sańchez, 'Fundamental rights and citizenship of the Union at a crossroads: a promising alliance or a dangerous liaison?' (2014) 20 European Law Journal 464; C Raucea, 'Fundamental rights: the missing pieces of European citizenship?' (2013) 14 German Law Journal 2021; and C Hilson, 'What's in a right? The relationship between Community, fundamental and citizenship rights in EU law' (2004) 29 European Law Review 636.

[229] Article 3(2)(a) of Directive 2004/38 builds on Article 10(2) of Regulation 1612/68 and Article 1(2) of Directive 73/148/EEC. Adopting an amendment proposed by the European Parliament in its Report on the Commission's original proposal (n 59), the text had referred to 'serious health *or humanitarian* grounds' (Amended Proposal, n 60). In its common position, the Council explained deletion of the reference to humanitarian grounds on the basis that 'they already constitute part of the commitments undertaken by the Member States in the field of fundamental rights' (n 52, 26). In its Communication on the common position, the Commission further indicated that 'the Council decided to remove the reference to humanitarian grounds, arguing that it was too broad a concept, open to abuse' (n 64, para 3.2.1.2).

an examination of relevant personal circumstances and to issue reasoned decisions where applications are refused—apply in Article 3(2)(a) situations too. However, in *Rahman,* the Court provided further guidance on the application and interpretation of Article 3(2)(a) specifically. Mr Rahman was a Bangladeshi national, married to an Irish national who was working in the UK. His brother, half-brother, and nephew applied (while still in Bangladesh) for EEA family permits to reside in the UK as the couple's dependants; the applications were refused on the grounds that the respondents were unable to demonstrate that they were dependent on Mr and Mrs Rahman. On appeal, an immigration judge found that the respondents were entitled to benefit from Article 3(2)(a) of the Directive and that their entry into the UK had to be 'facilitated'. The respondents then joined Mr and Mrs Rahman on that basis, but their applications for residence cards to confirm the right to reside were subsequently refused on grounds that the respondents 'had not proved that they had resided with Mrs Rahman, the relevant Union citizen, in the same EEA Member State before she came to the United Kingdom, or that they continued to be dependent on her or were members of her household in the United Kingdom'.[230]

Article 10(2)(e) of Directive 2004/38, which concerns the issuing of residence cards for family members who are not nationals of a Member State, requires 'a document issued by the relevant authority in the country of origin or country from which they are arriving certifying that they are dependants or members of the household of the Union citizens, or proof of the existence of serious health grounds which strictly require the personal care of the family member by the Union citizen' in the context of applications submitted under Article 3(2)(a).[231] The Court observed that

> there is nothing to indicate that the term 'country from which they have come' [in Article 3(2)(a)] or 'country from which they are arriving' [in Article 10(2)(e)] must be understood as referring to the country in which the Union citizen resided before settling in the host Member State. On the contrary, it is clear, on reading those provisions together, that the country referred to is, in the case of a national of a third State who declares that he is a 'dependant' of a Union citizen, the State in which he was resident on the date when he applied to accompany or join the Union citizen.[232]

The Court then referred to recital 6 of the Directive, which confirms that

> the objective of [Article 3(2)] is to 'maintain the unity of the family in a broader sense' by facilitating entry and residence for persons who are not included in the definition of family member of a Union citizen contained in Article 2(2) of Directive 2004/38 but who nevertheless maintain close and stable family ties with a Union citizen on account of specific factual circumstances, such as economic dependence, being a member of the household or serious health grounds.[233]

It considered that 'such ties may exist without the family member of the Union citizen having resided in the same State as that citizen or having been a dependant of that citizen shortly

---

[230] Case C-83/11 *Rahman*, EU:C:2012:519, para 14.
[231] Articles 8(5)(2) establishes the same requirement for the issuing of registration certificates to the family members of Union citizens who themselves are Union citizens. These provisions are outlined in Chapter 6.
[232] *Rahman*, para 31.
[233] ibid para 32.

before or at the time when the latter settled in the host State'.[234] Fundamentally, the Court applied the same rationale (seen in Section 4.1) as for dependent family members who fall within the scope of Article 2(2) of the Directive: the situation of dependence must exist in the country from which the family member comes at the time when they apply to join the Union citizen on whom they are dependent. To have their applications considered under Article 3(2)(a), the respondents in *Rahman* therefore had to prove, to the satisfaction of the referring court, that they were dependent on Mrs Rahman (the relevant Union citizen) when they still resided in Bangladesh at the time that they applied to join her in the UK.

The referring court also asked 'whether a Member State may impose particular requirements as to the nature or duration' of the dependence referred to in Article 3(2) of the Directive, in order 'to satisfy itself that such dependence is genuine and stable and has not been brought about with the sole objective of obtaining entry into and residence in its territory'.[235] As already underlined for Article 3(2)(b) in Section 3.2.4.1, the Court confirmed that Member States have wide discretion in determining the factors to be taken into account in decisions that fall within the scope of Article 3(2)(a). The exercise of that discretion entails that the host State may

> lay down in [its] legislation particular requirements as to the nature and duration of dependence, in order in particular to satisfy [itself] that the situation of dependence is genuine and stable and has not been brought about with the sole objective of obtaining entry into and residence in the host Member State.[236]

However, the Court also recalled the balance that must be struck in this context, requiring that 'those requirements be consistent with the normal meaning of the words relating to the dependence referred to in Article 3(2)(a) of Directive 2004/38 and do not deprive that provision of its effectiveness'.[237]

To respond to the questions referred in *Rahman,* the Court did not have to disaggregate the three categories provided for in Article 3(2)(a) of the Directive ('dependants *or* members of the household of the Union citizen having the primary right of residence, *or* where serious health grounds strictly require the personal care of the family member by the Union citizen'). Based on the wording alone, 'members of the household' in the country or origin do not have to be *dependants*. In *SRS and AA*, Advocate General Pitruzella suggested that their relationship to the relevant Union citizen does have to exhibit traits of *dependence—in* his view, '[s]haring the same accommodation is, admittedly, a necessary condition, but it is not enough'.[238] He first defined a member of the household

---

[234] ibid para 33.
[235] ibid para 36.
[236] ibid para 38.
[237] ibid para 39. In contrast to its determination in *Reyes* that a relationship of dependence is not required to persist to underpin family member residence rights linked to Article 2(2)(c) of the Directive, a final question from the referring tribunal in *Rahman* as to 'whether issue of the residence card referred to in Article 10 of Directive 2004/38 may be conditional on the requirement that the situation of dependence for the purposes of Article 3(2)(a) of that directive has endured in the host Member State' was considered, without any further explanation, 'not [to] fall within the scope of the directive' (para 45).
[238] AG Pitruzella in Case C-22/21 *SRS and AA*, EU:C:2022:183, para 37 of the Opinion. The judgment of the Court, delivered soon after the time of writing, largely follows the approach taken by the Advocate General (EU:C:2022:68).

in negative terms: he or she is clearly not a family member within the Union citizen's inner circle for the purposes of Article 2(2) of Directive 2004/38; in addition, nor is he or she a dependant in merely material terms (a condition linked to material and financial dependence), suffering from a serious health condition or the long-term, non-registered partner of the citizen.[239]

Referring to *Rahman*, he argued that

> [a] literal analysis also demonstrates that the common thread in the three situations referred to in Article 3(2)(a) of Directive 2004/38 is *the existence of a form of dependence*, whether it be material ('a dependant') or physical ('on serious health grounds'). A family member who 'is a member of the household' of the Union citizen is therefore in a situation of 'particular dependence' vis-à-vis the Union citizen, as is confirmed by an analysis of the case-law of the Court, but a form of dependence that is therefore neither purely material nor simply human and which remains to be defined.[240]

As a result, Advocate General Pitruzella suggested that to be considered as a 'member of the household' of a Union citizen for the purposes of Article 3(2)(a), 'there must, by definition, be a family relationship between the other family member and that citizen with whom the family member lives' as well as a 'strong emotional bond between the two over the course of a non-negligible period of cohabitation arranged for reasons other than simple convenience', and that the required emotional bond must 'be of such strength that if the family member concerned were no longer to be a member of the household of the Union citizen, that citizen would be personally affected, such that the situation may be described as one of reciprocal dependence on an emotional level'.[241] He recommended that national authorities should assess

> in particular but not exclusively, the length of time spent living together, as well as the strength of the sense of family as expressed in joint living arrangements which exhibit the characteristics of family life. An overall assessment must be made of the entire lifestyle of the purported extended family structure on a case-by-case basis, taking into account the circumstances specific to each situation based on all the relevant facts.[242]

At a general level, Advocate General Pitruzella compared the 'much more open-ended—not to say imprecise' wording of Article 3(2)(a) to that of Article 2(2) of the Directive, on the one hand, and 'the fact that the family members covered by Article 3(2)... are a residual category of family members whose entry and residence has only to be facilitated by the Member States', on the other, the latter entailing 'less weighty' obligations from the perspective of the host State.[243] He considered that the resulting 'ambiguity' around the family members to whom Article 3(2) applies 'may be a virtue, since it allows for some flexibility in its definition' and '[a]ny attempt to provide a universal definition of as fluid a concept—both sociologically and culturally—as that of "family members [who are] members of the household of the

---

[239] ibid para 36 of the Opinion.
[240] ibid (emphasis added); referring to paras 21 ('a relationship of particular dependence'), 36, 38, and 39 of Case C-83/11 *Rahman*, EU:C:2012:519.
[241] AG Pitruzella in *SRS and AA*, para 40 of the Opinion.
[242] ibid para 41 of the Opinion.
[243] ibid para 20 of the Opinion.

Union citizen" could not only prove risky but also ... run counter to the objective pursued by Directive 2004/38 given the inability to capture the entire multidimensional and multifaceted reality of the various forms which family life, in the broad sense, may take'.[244] Related questions to be determined in the future include whether 'family members' who are dependants or members of the household of a Union citizen or who require the personal care of the Union citizen for serious health grounds must be blood relatives.[245] It is also not clear what requiring the 'personal' care of the Union citizen means in the context of serious health grounds: should it be interpreted very literally so that Article 3(2)(a) could not, for example, apply in a situation where the Union citizen hoped to have a family member living near them in a full-time facility, so that they could visit them regularly and retain close oversight of their care?

These questions raise once again the nature of dependency beyond basic material needs and also how we conceive of 'family' as social norms evolve. Resolving them will bring more openly into discussion the predominance in EU citizenship law of formal criteria based on relationship *type* rather than substantive criteria based on relationship *quality*. However, as the Court's case law develops, it is arguably already possible to accord some recognition to relationship quality under Article 3(2)(a). The *SM* case was introduced in Section 3.2.3 as regards the scope of 'direct descendant' under Article 2(2)(c) of the Directive. The Court found that a child placed under the Algerian *kafala* system was not a direct descendant of a Union citizen within the meaning of that provision but did fall within the 'other family members' category protected to some degree by Article 3(2)(a). It then recalled the principles established in *Rahman* and confirmed in *Banger* on the application of Article 3(2) of the Directive, including the understanding that the provision 'imposes an obligation on the Member States to confer a certain advantage on applications submitted by the third-country nationals referred to in that article, compared with applications for entry and residence of other third-country nationals'.[246] Moreover, it confirmed the 'wide discretion' that Member States enjoy 'as regards the selection of the factors to be taken into account' when undertaking the extensive examination of personal circumstances that the provision requires, so long as the applicable national legislation 'contains criteria which are consistent with the normal meaning of the term "facilitate" used in Article 3(2) of Directive 2004/38 and which do not deprive that provision of its effectiveness'.[247]

However, as introduced in Section 3.2.2.2, the Court had also referred in *Rahman* to 'persons who have *a relationship of particular dependence* with a Union citizen' in connection with the obligations placed on Member States by Article 3(2) of the Directive.[248] It had thus established that national authorities should 'take account of the various factors that may be relevant in the particular case, such as *the extent of* economic or physical dependence and *the degree of relationship* between the family member and the Union citizen whom he wishes to accompany or join',[249] which could be read as suggesting that the corollary obligations on a host State intensify in relation to greater dependence and/or deeper degree of relationship. In *SM*, the Court went further, adding that the discretion that a Member State may exercise

---

[244] ibid.
[245] This is not required in the context of dependency as a basis for rights based on Article 20 TFEU: see eg Joined Cases C-356/11 and C-357/11 *O and S*, EU:C:2012:776, para 55; see further, Chapter 5.
[246] Case C-129/18 *SM*, EU:C:2019:248, para 61; referring to Case C-83/11 *Rahman*, EU:C:2012:519, para 21 and Case C-89/17 *Banger*, EU:C:2018:570, para 31.
[247] *SM*, para 63; referring to *Rahman*, para 24 and *Banger*, para 40.
[248] *Rahman*, para 21 (emphasis added); confirmed in *Banger*, para 31.
[249] *Rahman*, para 23 (emphasis added).

under Article 3(2)(a) 'must, having regard to recital 31 of Directive 2004/38, be exercised in the light of and in line with the provisions of the Charter of Fundamental Rights'.[250] It referred specifically to Article 7 CFR and observed—since the rights thereby guaranteed have the same meaning and scope as those guaranteed by Article 8 ECHR (following Article 53(1) CFR)—that '[i]t is apparent from the case-law of the European Court of Human Rights that the *actual relationship* which a child placed under the *kafala* system maintains with its guardian may fall under the definition of family life, having regard to the time spent living together, the *quality of the relationship*, and the role which the adult assumes in respect of the child'.[251]

Formal criteria may also play a role with respect to hierarchy among the different categories in Article 3(2)(a). In *SM,* the Court held that, under EU law, the competent national authorities must also consider the best interests of the child with reference to Article 24(2) CFR. It outlined the criteria relevant to 'mak[ing] a balanced and reasonable assessment of all the current and relevant circumstances of the case'.[252] On that basis, where it is established that the child and its guardians

> are called to lead a genuine family life and that that child is dependent on its guardians, the requirements relating to the fundamental right to respect for family life, combined with the obligation to take account of the best interests of the child, *demand, in principle*, that that child be granted a right of entry and residence as one of the other family members of the citizens of the Union for the purposes of Article 3(2)(a) of Directive 2004/38, read in the light of Article 7 and Article 24(2) of the Charter, in order to enable the child to live with its guardians in their host Member State.[253]

For the Court,

> [t]his applies *a fortiori* where, as a result of a refusal to grant the child placed under the Algerian *kafala* system a right of entry and residence in the host Member State of its guardians, who are citizens of the Union, those guardians are in fact prevented from living together in that Member State because one of them is required to remain, with the child, in that child's third country of origin in order to care for the child.[254]

In *SM,* the Court thus reflected carefully on both the formal and substantive factors that must be taken into account by national authorities making assessments under Article 3(2)(a) of the Directive, especially where the 'other family member' in question is a child. That ruling

---

[250] *SM*, para 64.

[251] ibid para 66 (emphasis added). The Court also observed that Article 8 ECHR 'protects the individual against arbitrary action by the public authorities and requires those authorities, where the existence of a family tie has been established, to enable that tie to be developed and to establish legal safeguards that render possible the child's integration in his family' (ibid).

[252] ibid para 68, which include, '*inter alia*, the age at which the child was placed under the Algerian *kafala* system, whether the child has lived with its guardians since its placement under that system, the closeness of the personal relationship which has developed between the child and its guardians and the extent to which the child is dependent on its guardians, inasmuch as they assume parental responsibility and legal and financial responsibility for the child' (para 69).

[253] ibid para 71 (emphasis added). For AG Pitruzella, the phrase 'demand, in principle' means that 'the hand of the national authorities responsible for deciding on an application for entry or residence submitted by an "other family member" for the purposes of Article 3(2)(a) of Directive 2004/38 will be guided with a little more direction from the Court, ... in particular in cases where Article 24 [CFR] is relevant ... The Member States' discretion was narrowed significantly' (*SRS and AA*, fn 30 of the Opinion).

[254] *SM*, para 72.

built significantly on the reference to Article 47 CFR in *Banger*, which concerned ensuring an effective judicial remedy and the application of the procedural safeguards in Article 31(1) of the Directive where national authorities refuse to authorise the entry and residence of a Union citizen's third-country national partner.[255] The *SM* case thus provides an example of the degree of protection that the Court is willing to consider under EU citizenship law when the situation involves children, irrespective of whether the children concerned are themselves Union citizens or not.

5. Concluding Remarks

The protection of a Union citizen's family is one of the most important dimensions of EU citizenship law. It animates the humanity of the Union citizen and of their family members, and it makes freedom of movement meaningful. In practice, EU citizenship law deploys the latter to enable the former. That structure reflects the movement-centric bias of Union citizenship and the wider idiosyncrasies that shape the Union ecosystem, and it produces in some respects an uncomfortable impression that the free movement of persons in the abstract is privileged over the actual persons who move more concretely—as well as over those who do not move at all. The EU institutions must also navigate a difficult line between the supranational impulse of Union citizenship and the inherent locality of regulating the family, with Member States progressing national frameworks at very different paces.

Against that background, three main themes emerged across the chapter. First, Article 7 CFR has become more prominent as the law in this area develops and particular weight is also now given, where relevant, to the best interests of the child as required by Article 24 CFR. The Court of Justice now engages in more detailed discussion of relevant ECtHR case law too. At the same time, second, EU citizenship law is premised on a relatively limited and conventional understanding of 'family' overall, both with respect to defining family members as a starting point and to the interpretation of operational concepts like 'dependency'. The EU legal framework is also designed more around formal criteria that privilege relationship type than substantive criteria that also recognise relationship quality. Moreover, the progressive potential of other Charter provisions, including the wide-ranging prohibition of various forms of discrimination in Article 21 CFR and the general obligation to respect human dignity in Article 1 CFR, are as yet largely unharnessed in this area.

All of this means that, third, Directive 2004/38—the measure on which the Court's case law is necessarily based—already feels more dated than its actual age, and unnecessarily complicated with respect to the conditions attached to different family member categories and to the principles that further shape these basic definitions. Even if more comprehensive reform of the Directive is not feasible in the short-term, it is remarkable that the Commission is only now refreshing its guidance on the application of the Directive for the first time since 2009.[256]

---

[255] Case C-89/17 *Banger*, EU:C:2018:570, para 40, paras 48–49. The ruling in *Banger* is further considered in Chapter 9 (returning to a Union citizen's home State) and Article 31 of the Directive is addressed in Chapter 10.

[256] See EU Citizenship Report 2020: Empowering Citizens and Protecting their Rights, 15 December 2020, COM(2020) 730 final, para 3.1, Action 7—at the time of writing, this work was underway. See also, Communication from the Commission, Union of Equality: LGBTIQ Equality Strategy 2020–2025, COM(2020) 698 final, para 3.4.

Further Reading

C Berneri, *Family Reunification in the EU: The Movement and Residence Rights of Third Country National Family Members of EU Citizens* (Hart Publishing 2017).

C Costello, '*Metock*: free movement and "normal family life" in the Union' (2009) 46 Common Market Law Review 587.

M Klaassen and P Rodrigues, 'The best interests of the child in EU family reunification law: a plea for more guidance on the role of Article 24(2) Charter' (2017) 19 European Journal of Migration and Law 191.

S Peers, 'Free movement, immigration control and constitutional conflict' (2009) 5 European Constitutional Law Review 173.

I Solanke, 'Another type of "other" in EU law? *AB (2) MVC v Home Office* and *Rahman v Secretary of State for the Home Office*' (2013) 76 Modern Law Review 383.

A Spalding, 'Where next after *Coman*?' (2019) 21 European Journal of Migration and Law 117.

F Strumia, 'The family in EU law after the *SM* ruling: variable geometry and conditional deference' (2019) 4 European Papers 38.

A Tryfonidou, 'Family reunification rights of (migrant) Union citizens: towards a more liberal approach' (2009) 15 European Law Journal 634.

A Tryfonidou, 'EU free movement law and the children of rainbow families: children of a lesser god?' (2019) 38 Yearbook of European Law 220.

5
Union Citizenship and the Home Member State

1. Chapter Overview

This chapter presents rights that protect Union citizens in their home Member States, examining two main areas: first, rights that facilitate the political connection between the Union and its citizens, and second, residence rights for the third-country national family members of Union citizens in exceptional situations where the latter would otherwise be deprived of exercising the rights that Union citizenship confers on them. The discussion thus animates in more detail ideas introduced in Chapter 2 about the Union as a distinctive *place* where 'democratic life'[1] is intended to flourish and a connection with which EU citizenship law increasingly seeks to foster.

Most legal questions, and therefore most legal developments, have to date concerned the rights of Member State nationals who are present in another Member State—the host State—as well as the conditions and limitations that may lawfully be placed on those rights. Relatedly, when a Member State national exercises freedom of movement and then returns to their home State, the relationship between that State and the Union citizen is legally transformed because a dimension of EU legal protection persists in certain circumstances. Such situations, most (though not all) of which are linked to Article 21 TFEU, are considered in Chapter 9. But the status of Union citizenship also reaches situations where free movement has not been exercised at all: where dimensions of EU legal protection manifest within the home State in a classically 'purely internal' sense. The Withdrawal Agreement concluded by the EU and the United Kingdom following the UK's departure from the Union focuses on sustaining protection in *host* States only, and therefore excludes continuation of the rights discussed in this chapter.[2] In that light, while home State rights might, at one level, seem close to the periphery of EU citizenship law, Brexit demonstrates that they arguably constitute the rights that *define* Union citizenship.[3] It is also striking that the political rights

---

[1] Article 10(3) TEU.
[2] Article 10 of the Withdrawal Agreement (WA) determines the personal scope of Part Two ('Citizens' Rights') of the Agreement, based entirely on host State presence (before the end of the transition period, ie 31 December 2020) of British nationals in EU27 and EU27 nationals in the UK (Agreement on the withdrawal of the United Kingdom of Great Britain and Northern Ireland from the European Union and the European Atomic Energy Community, 2019 OJ CI 384/01). As the Commission has underlined, 'EU citizens and UK nationals whose rights in the host State at the end of the transition period are based on the fact that they were citizens of the Union as defined in Article 20 TFEU fall outside the scope of the Agreement. Consequently, their family members also fall outside the scope of the Agreement and will be subject to rules in force in the host State' (European Commission, Guidance Note relating to the Agreement on the withdrawal of the United Kingdom of Great Britain and Northern Ireland from the European Union and the European Atomic Energy Community Part two—Citizens' rights, C(2020) 2939 final, para 1.2.2.2). Article 127(1)(b) WA already excluded during the transition period (ie since 1 February 2020) the application to and in the UK of Article 11(4) TEU, Article 20(2)(b) TFEU, Article 22 TFEU, Article 24(1) TFEU, and Articles 39 and 40 CFR (as well as 'the acts adopted on the basis of those provisions')—'namely the provisions of primary EU law relating to the right of Union citizens to vote and to stand as a candidate in elections to the European Parliament and in municipal elections in their Member State of residence' (Case C-673/20 *Préfet du Gers*, EU:C:2022:449, para 67).
[3] Reflecting that idea in a different context, Fredrikson and Franklin consider the exclusion of citizenship-specific reasoning in the context of the EEA Agreement (H Haukeland Fredriksen and CNK Franklin, 'Of pragmatism and principles: The EEA Agreement 20 years on' (2015) 52 Common Market Law Review 629 at 638–645, and esp 641–642 on purely internal situations and the implications of Case C-34/09 *Ruiz Zambrano*, EU:C:2011:124.

discussed in Section 2 of this chapter have, at least historically, been barely Court-touched while the residence rights addressed in Section 3 are wholly Court-created.

Reflecting Article 10(3) TEU's guarantee that '[e]very citizen shall have the right to participate in the democratic life of the Union', this chapter first outlines the link between EU law and voting rights in the home State (Section 2)—which, as *Delvigne* confirms,[4] are based on Article 13(3) TEU and Article 39(2) of the Charter of Fundamental Rights (CFR), being therefore distinct from but complementing the host State voting rights provided for in Article 22 TFEU. It also considers the four procedures for citizen engagement referred to in Article 24 TFEU: the European Citizens' Initiative, building on Article 11 TEU; the right to petition the European Parliament in accordance with Article 227 TFEU; applying to the European Ombudsman under Article 228 TFEU; and procedures for writing to certain Union institutions or bodies. The entitlement under Article 23 TFEU of Union citizens who are present in the territory of a third country—in which the Member State of which they are nationals is not represented—to protection by the diplomatic or consular authorities of any Member State, on the same conditions as the nationals of the relevant State, is also examined, on the basis that another Member State acts as home State 'surrogate' for Union citizens in such circumstances.

Residence rights for family members in a Union citizen's home State are more controversial (Section 3), implanting a role for EU law in what might be perceived as situations that should fall only within the scope of national immigration competence. The key to understanding the reach of EU law in this context is the material difference between two types of 'internal' situation where the relevant facts are confined to the home State. First, there are 'situations which have no factor linking them with any of the situations governed by European Union law and which are confined in all relevant respects within a single Member State' and fall therefore outside the scope of the Treaty.[5] However, second, 'the situation of a Union citizen who ... has not made use of the right to freedom of movement cannot, for that reason alone, be assimilated to a purely internal situation' and, in contrast, may therefore fall within the scope of EU law.[6] As seen in Chapter 3 with respect to determining Member State nationality, the Court, in *Rottmann*, conceived the idea that the situation of someone who finds themselves 'in a position capable of causing [them] to lose the status conferred by Article [20 TFEU] and the rights attaching thereto falls, *by reason of its nature and its consequences*, within the ambit of European Union law'.[7] The 'nature and consequences' of such situations establish the required connecting factor to EU citizenship law, even where the facts are confined to one Member State.

Building on *Rottmann*, the Court then held in *Ruiz Zambrano* that 'Article 20 TFEU precludes national measures which have the effect of depriving citizens of the Union of the genuine enjoyment of the substance of the rights conferred by virtue of their status as citizens of the Union'.[8] As a result, in 'very specific situations' in which the 'Union citizen concerned has not made use of his freedom of movement, a right of residence exceptionally cannot, without undermining the effectiveness of the Union citizenship that citizen enjoys,

---

See also, C Burke and ÓÍ Hannesson, 'Citizenship by the back door? *Gunnarsson*' (2015) 52 Common Market Law Review 1111.

[4] Case C-650/13 *Delvigne*, EU:C:2015:648.
[5] Case C-256/11 *Dereci and Others*, EU:C:2011:734, para 60.
[6] ibid para 61.
[7] Case C-135/08 *Rottmann*, EU:C:2010:104, para 42 (emphasis added).
[8] *Ruiz Zambrano*, para 42.

be refused to a third-country national who is a family member of his if, as a consequence of refusal, that citizen would be obliged in practice to leave the territory of the European Union altogether'.[9] It will be seen that both the categories of relevant family members and critical concepts such as dependency for rights based on Article 20 TFEU do not overlap precisely with the categories and concepts that apply to host State rights under Directive 2004/38.[10] However, the Court rationalises its Article 20 TFEU-based development of EU citizenship law through the reasoning that such situations have 'an intrinsic connection with the freedom of movement of a Union citizen',[11] raising again the movement-centric bias of EU citizenship law also considered in Chapter 4.

2. Rights Facilitating a Political Connection to the Union

Advocate General Poaires Maduro suggested in *Rottmann* that Union citizenship 'forms the basis of a new political area from which rights and duties emerge, which are laid down by [Union] law and do not depend on the State'.[12] As this chapter shows, independence from the Member States in a *structural* sense is not how the arc of Union citizenship has played out. However, the Advocate General clarified his conception of an 'independent' Union citizenship in a *political* sense in positing that it '[presupposes] the existence of a political relationship between European citizens, … it is not a relationship of belonging *to a people*. On the contrary, that political relationship unites *the peoples* of Europe. It is based on their mutual commitment to open their respective bodies politic to other European citizens and to construct *a new form of civic and political allegiance on a European scale*'.[13] In that understanding, Articles 10 and 11 TEU establish the basic framework for 'the broader democratic system of the European Union' in which processes for representative democracy are 'complemented and enhanced, in primary law, by the creation of avenues for participatory and deliberative democracy':[14]

Article 10 TEU

1. The functioning of the Union shall be founded on representative democracy.[15]
2. Citizens are directly represented at Union level in the European Parliament.
   Member States are represented in the European Council by their Heads of State or Government and in the Council by their governments, themselves democratically accountable either to their national Parliaments, or to their citizens.

---

[9] Case C-40/11 *Iida*, EU:C:2012:691, para 61.
[10] Directive 2004/38/EC on the right of citizens of the Union and their family members to move and reside freely within the territory of the Member States, 2004 OJ L158/77. The definition of 'family members' for the purposes of the Directive, which applies by analogy to rights based directly on Article 21 TFEU (see Chapter 9), was examined in Chapter 4.
[11] *Iida*, para 72.
[12] AG Poiares Maduro in *Rottmann*, EU:C:2009:588, para 21 of the Opinion.
[13] ibid (emphasis added).
[14] AG Bobek in Case C-418/18 P *Puppinck*, EU:C:2019:640, paras 68–69 of the Opinion.
[15] 'Article 10(1) TEU provides that the functioning of the Union is to be founded on the principle of representative democracy, which gives concrete form to the value of democracy referred to in Article 2 TEU' (Case C-502/19 *Junqueras*, EU:C:2019:1115, para 63; referring to Case C-418/18 P *Puppinck*, EU:C:2019:1113, para 64).

3. Every citizen shall have the right to participate in the democratic life of the Union. Decisions shall be taken as openly and as closely as possible to the citizen.
4. Political parties at European level contribute to forming European political awareness and to expressing the will of citizens of the Union.

Article 11 TEU

1. The institutions shall, by appropriate means, give citizens and representative associations the opportunity to make known and publicly exchange their views in all areas of Union action.
2. The institutions shall maintain an open, transparent and regular dialogue with representative associations and civil society.
3. The European Commission shall carry out broad consultations with parties concerned in order to ensure that the Union's actions are coherent and transparent.
4. Not less than one million citizens who are nationals of a significant number of Member States may take the initiative of inviting the European Commission, within the framework of its powers, to submit any appropriate proposal on matters where citizens consider that a legal act of the Union is required for the purpose of implementing the Treaties.

The procedures and conditions required for such a citizens' initiative shall be determined in accordance with the first paragraph of Article 24 of the Treaty on the Functioning of the European Union.

In this section, the rights to vote and to stand as a candidate in European Parliament and municipal elections are examined from the perspective of Union citizens who reside in their home States and also with respect to home State influence on host State voting rights (Section 2.1). The four procedures that facilitate citizens' participation in the democratic life of the Union referred to in Article 24 TFEU—the citizens' initiative, petitioning the European Parliament, applying to the European Ombudsman, and writing to the Union's institutions and bodies—are then considered (Section 2.2). Finally, Article 23 TFEU's guarantee of protection for unrepresented citizens in third countries by the diplomatic or consular authorities of any Member State is examined, detailing the processes established by Directive 2015/637 (Section 2.3).[16]

2.1 Voting Rights from the Home Member State Perspective

The right to vote and to stand as a candidate in both European Parliament and municipal elections is framed in a general way by the statement in Article 10(3) TEU that '[e]very citizen shall have the right to participate in the democratic life of the Union'. Article 14(3) TEU requires that '[t]he members of the European Parliament shall be elected for a term of five years by direct universal suffrage in a free and secret ballot'. Article 20(2)(b) TFEU establishes that Union citizens have 'the right to vote and to stand as candidates in elections to the

---

[16] Council Directive 2015/637/EU on the coordination and cooperation measures to facilitate consular protection for unrepresented citizens of the Union in third countries and repealing Decision 95/553/EC, 2015 OJ L106/1.

European Parliament and in municipal elections in their Member State of residence, under the same conditions as nationals of that State'. Article 22 TFEU then provides the necessary legal basis:

Article 22 TFEU

1. Every citizen of the Union residing in a Member State of which he is not a national shall have the right to vote and to stand as a candidate at municipal elections in the Member State in which he resides, under the same conditions as nationals of that State. This right shall be exercised subject to detailed arrangements adopted by the Council, acting unanimously in accordance with a special legislative procedure and after consulting the European Parliament; these arrangements may provide for derogations where warranted by problems specific to a Member State.
2. Without prejudice to Article 223(1) and to the provisions adopted for its implementation, every citizen of the Union residing in a Member State of which he is not a national shall have the right to vote and to stand as a candidate in elections to the European Parliament in the Member State in which he resides, under the same conditions as nationals of that State. This right shall be exercised subject to detailed arrangements adopted by the Council, acting unanimously in accordance with a special legislative procedure and after consulting the European Parliament; these arrangements may provide for derogations where warranted by problems specific to a Member State.

Article 40 CFR repeats Article 20(2)(b) TFEU for municipal elections and Article 39 CFR reinforces both TEU and TFEU guarantees for European Parliament elections:

1. Every citizen of the Union has the right to vote and to stand as a candidate at elections to the European Parliament in the Member State in which he or she resides, under the same conditions as nationals of that State.
2. Members of the European Parliament shall be elected by direct universal suffrage in a free and secret ballot.[17]

Under Articles 20(2)(b) and 22 TFEU as well as Articles 39(1) and 40 CFR, the voting rights protected apply only to Union citizens residing in a Member State of which they are not nationals i.e. in a host State.[18] However, for European Parliament elections specifically, Article 39(2) CFR is expressed in more general terms and it is here that we can root, without a cross-border requirement, a right to vote.[19]

---

[17] Assessing Articles 39 and 40 CFR from historical and legal perspectives, and in relation to their corresponding ECHR contexts, see the commentaries on Article 39 (L Khadar and J Shaw) and 40 (K Groenendijk) in S Peers, T Hervey, J Kenner, and A Ward (eds) *The EU Charter of Fundamental Rights: A Commentary* (2nd edn Hart Publishing 2021) 1085 and 1113 respectively.

[18] See esp Council Directive 93/109/EC laying down detailed arrangements for the exercise of the right to vote and stand as a candidate in elections to the European Parliament for citizens of the Union residing in a Member State of which they are not nationals, 1993 OJ L329/34; and Council Directive 94/80/EC laying down detailed arrangements for the exercise of the right to vote and to stand as a candidate in municipal elections by citizens of the Union residing in a Member State of which they are not nationals, 1994 OJ L368/38. In November 2021, the Commission published proposals to recast both measures; see further, Section 2.1.3.

[19] Confirmed in Case C-650/13 *Delvigne*, EU:C:2015:648, para 44; this judgment is returned to below. For AG Tizzano, 'citizens of the Union are, as it were, "necessary" vestees of the right to vote in the European Parliament, in the sense that, at least in principle, they can all claim that right. That is without prejudice to any limitations usually

Taking all of this together, the amendments to EU primary law effected by the Lisbon Treaty, noting not only Articles 10 and 14 TEU but also the binding effect accorded since then to Article 39 CFR, significantly progressed the more limited, host State-focused voting rights conferred by the TFEU. As Advocate General Cruz Villalón has observed, 'abandoning the previous wording contained in Article 189 EC, Article 14(2) TEU and, in keeping with that provision, Article 39(1) of the Charter, no longer refer to members of the European Parliament as "representatives of the peoples of the States brought together in the Community" but, much more directly, as "representatives of the Union's citizens"'.[20] And in *Junqueras*, the Court stated that 'in accordance with the principle of representative democracy referred to in [Article 10(1) TEU] and with Article 14 TEU, [the] composition [of the European Parliament] must reflect faithfully and completely the free expression of choices made by the citizens of the European Union, by direct universal suffrage, as regards the persons by whom they wish to be represented during a given term, but also that the European Parliament must be protected, in the exercise of its tasks, against hindrances or risks to its proper operation'.[21]

Principles that frame the procedures required for European Parliament elections—while, at the same time, allowing for significant national discretion—were established in a 1976 Act concerning the election of the members of the European Parliament by direct universal suffrage.[22] Article 1 determined that MEPs 'shall be elected on the basis of proportional representation, using the list system or the single transferable vote' in each Member State; Article 2 provided that 'each Member State may establish constituencies for elections to the European Parliament or subdivide its electoral area in a different manner, without generally affecting the proportional nature of the voting system'; and Article 3 enabled Member States to 'set a minimum threshold for the allocation of seats'. Article 8 confirmed that, '[s]ubject to the provisions of this Act, the electoral procedure shall be governed in each Member State by its national provisions', which 'may if appropriate take account of the specific situation in the Member States, shall not affect the essentially proportional nature of the voting system'.[23] Directives 93/109 and 94/80 (on European Parliament and municipal elections respectively) make further provision for voting in a host State in the context of free movement.

However, case law on the restriction of voting rights has thus far focused only on home States, addressing, first, how the national electorate is defined (Section 2.1.1), which connects back to the discussion on determination of nationality in Chapter 3, and second, limits on EU voting rights in the context of imprisonment (Section 2.1.2). Even for voting in a host State, however, the influence of the home State, especially in terms of restrictions placed on national voters who reside in other States, is evident (Section 2.1.3). All of these questions raise the intersection of the EU and ECHR frameworks that protect fundamental rights. For the ECtHR, while proportionate restrictions on voting rights can be accepted in certain circumstances, '[t]he right to vote is not a privilege. In the twenty-first century, the presumption in a democratic State must be in favour of inclusion' and '[a]ny general, automatic and

---

and lawfully imposed' (AG Tizzano in Case C-145/04 *Spain v United Kingdom* and Case C-300/04 *Eman and Sevinger*, EU:C:2006:231, para 71 of the joint Opinion).

[20] AG Cruz Villalón in *Delvigne*, EU:C:2015:363, para 100 of the Opinion.
[21] Case C-502/19 *Junqueras*, EU:C:2019:1115, para 83.
[22] 1976 OJ L 278/5, as amended (see esp Council Decision 2002/772/EC, Euratom, 2002 OJ L283/1).
[23] Relatedly, Regulation 1141/2014 establishes procedures for European political parties, which, according to Article 10(4) TEU, 'contribute to forming European political awareness and to expressing the will of citizens of the Union' (Regulation 1141/2014 on the statute and funding of European political parties, 2014 OJ L371/1).

indiscriminate departure from the principle of universal suffrage risks undermining the democratic validity of the legislature thus elected and the laws it promulgates'.[24]

2.1.1 Defining the national electorate

Two judgments delivered by the Court of Justice on the same day in September 2006—*Spain v United Kingdom* and *Eman and Sevinger*—established a role for EU law in reviewing processes for defining and empowering national electorates. In *Spain v UK*, providing an example of the relatively rare instance of infringement proceedings by one Member State against another under Article 259 TFEU, Spain challenged the extension of voting rights for European Parliament elections by the UK to residents of Gibraltar. The UK adopted the European Parliament (Representation) Act 2003—enabling 'qualifying Commonwealth citizens' residing in Gibraltar to vote and to be elected in European Parliament elections—to comply with the ECtHR judgment in *Matthews v United Kingdom*, proceedings in which a British national residing in Gibraltar successfully argued that, by failing to organise European Parliament elections in Gibraltar, the UK had violated its obligations under Article 3 of Protocol No 1 to the ECHR.[25] Spain argued that the Treaty 'establish[es] a link between citizenship of the Union and the right to vote and to stand as a candidate for the European Parliament, the consequence of that link being that only citizens of the Union can have that right'.[26] It disputed 'the argument that the rights flowing from citizenship of the Union can have different fields of application, because that would mean *dismembering that citizenship*. In its submission, *unity is one of the characteristics that define citizenship*, in the sense that all those entitled to that status should enjoy its rights and be subject to its obligations in their entirety'.[27] However, for the Commission, 'the fact that a Member State, in view of its history and constitutional traditions, extends the right to vote in elections to the European Parliament, under certain conditions, to nationals of third countries with which it has special historical links does not impair the right to vote of citizens of the Union'.[28]

These contrasting perspectives frame the key question of EU citizenship law produced by the dispute: while voting rights *must* be facilitated for Member State nationals who hold the status of Union citizen, *can* they be extended to others who are not Member State nationals and therefore not Union citizens? Spain premised its arguments on Union citizenship as a status, while the Commission focused on whether a right associated with that status was breached. The Court confirmed that neither Article 223(1) TFEU[29] nor the 1976 Act based on it 'defines expressly and precisely who are to be entitled to the right to vote and to stand as a candidate in elections to the European Parliament', thus requiring consideration of 'whether there is, as the Kingdom of Spain submits, a clear link between citizenship of the Union and the right to vote and stand for election which requires that that right be always

---

[24] *Shindler v United Kingdom* (2013) 58 EHHR 9, para 103.
[25] *Matthews v United Kingdom* (1999) 28 EHRR 361; see further, Case C-145/04 *Spain v United Kingdom*, EU:C:2006:543, paras 12–13, 60–63, and 85–96. Article 3 of Protocol 1 to the ECHR provides that '[t]he High Contracting Parties undertake to hold free elections at reasonable intervals by secret ballot, under conditions which will ensure the free expression of the opinion of the people in the choice of the legislature'.
[26] *Spain v United Kingdom*, para 59.
[27] ibid para 44 (emphasis added).
[28] ibid para 55.
[29] Article 223(1) TFEU provides that '[t]he European Parliament shall draw up a proposal to lay down the provisions necessary for the election of its Members by direct universal suffrage in accordance with a uniform procedure in all Member States or in accordance with principles common to all Member States'. However, '[t]he fact that the stipulation now included in that provision has never become reality in the sense indicated above makes it necessary for the Union to continue relying upon the assistance of the national electoral procedures, as provided for in the 1976 Act' (AG Cruz Villalón in Case C-650/13 *Delvigne*, EU:C:2015:363, para 102 of the Opinion).

limited to citizens of the Union'.[30] The Court acknowledged that 'while Article [20(2) TFEU] provides that citizens of the Union are to enjoy the rights conferred by the Treaty and be subject to the duties imposed by it, the Treaty recognises rights which are linked neither to citizenship of the Union nor even to nationality of a Member State'[31]—namely, the rights to petition the European Parliament and make a complaint to the European Ombudsman, returned to in Section 2.2. It then expressed a paradox of Union citizenship: it is 'destined to be the fundamental status of nationals of the Member States' yet 'that statement does not necessarily mean that the rights recognised by the Treaty are limited to citizens of the Union'.[32] The Court also recalled its ruling in *Kaur* to underline that '[w]hen it acceded to the European Communities, the United Kingdom notified the other Contracting Parties, by means of its 1972 Declaration, of the categories of citizens to be regarded as its nationals for the purposes of Community law by designating, in substance, those entitled to the right of residence in the territory of the United Kingdom within the meaning of the Immigration Act 1971 *and citizens having a specified connection with Gibraltar*'.[33]

Referring to the principle of equal treatment in Article 22(2) TFEU—which affirms that 'every citizen of the Union residing in a Member State of which he is not a national shall have the right to vote and to stand as a candidate in elections to the European Parliament in the Member State in which he resides, under the same conditions as nationals of that State'—the Court did not extrapolate from these words 'that a Member State in a position such as that of the United Kingdom is prevented from granting the right to vote and to stand for election to certain persons who have a close link with it without however being nationals of that State or another Member State'.[34] Instead, the Court underlined 'the absence in the Community treaties of provisions stating expressly and precisely which persons have the right to vote and to stand as a candidate in elections to the European Parliament'.[35] Thus it did *not* articulate a right to vote per se—unlike Advocate General Tizzano, who considered:

> [T]he right to vote in European elections is enjoyed by citizens of the Union primarily by virtue of the principles of democracy on which the Union is based, and in particular, to use the words of the Strasbourg Court, the principle of universal suffrage which 'has become the basic principle' in modern democratic States and is also codified within the Community legal order in Article 190(1) EC and Article 1 of the 1976 Act, which specifically provide that the members of the European Parliament are to be elected by 'direct universal suffrage'. That rule militates in favour of recognition of a right to vote attaching to the largest possible number of people and therefore, at least in principle, to all citizens of a State'.[36]

---

[30] *Spain v United Kingdom*, para 70.
[31] ibid para 73.
[32] ibid para 74.
[33] Case C-192/99 *Kaur*, EU:C:2001:106, para 22 (emphasis added); see also, *Spain v United Kingdom*, para 75.
[34] *Spain v United Kingdom*, para 76. Somewhat confusingly, the Court did note here that 'that provision, like Article [20(1) TFEU] relating to the right of Union citizens to vote and to stand as a candidate at municipal elections, implies that nationals of a Member State have the right to vote and to stand as a candidate *in their own country* and requires the Member States to accord those rights to citizens of the Union residing in their territory' (ibid, emphasis added). AG Tizzano had explained it in this way: 'Article [20(2) TFEU], by allowing the citizens of a Member State to vote in European elections in another Member State in which they reside on the same basis as citizens of that State, *in any event takes it for granted that the right in question is available to citizens of the Union*' (AG Tizzano in Case C-145/04 *Spain v United Kingdom* and Case C-300/04 *Eman and Sevinger*, EU:C:2006:231, para 68 of the Opinion).
[35] *Spain v United Kingdom*, para 79.
[36] AG Tizzano in *Spain v United Kingdom* and *Eman and Sevinger*, EU:C:2006:231, para 69 of the Opinion.

For the Court, articulation of a right to vote came later, in *Delvigne*, which is returned to in Section 2.1.2.

If *Spain v UK* underlines the discretion that Member States retain with respect to EU electoral procedures, *Eman and Sevinger* highlights, instead, the parameters that EU law sets at the outer limits of that discretion.[37] The proceedings concerned entitlement to compensation related to the Netherlands' refusal to include the applicants on its register of electors for the European Parliament because they resided in Aruba—which, for the purposes of EU law, appears in the list of 'overseas countries and territories' (OCTs) annexed to the TFEU. The Court first confirmed that to benefit from the status of Union citizenship, in accordance with the wording of Article 20(1) TFEU, '[i]t is irrelevant, in that regard, that the national of a Member State resides or lives in a territory which is one of the OCTs'.[38] At the same time, though, 'the OCTs are subject to the special association arrangements set out in Part Four of the Treaty (Articles [198-204 TFEU]) with the result that, failing express reference, the general provisions of the Treaty do not apply to them'.[39] For that reason, Member States 'are not required to hold elections to the European Parliament there' and neither Article 22(2) TFEU nor the measures adopted to implement it 'apply to a citizen of the Union residing in an OCT who wishes to exercise his right to vote in the Member State of which he is a national'.[40] The Court also confirmed that 'no argument can be based on the fact that other Member States hold elections to the European Parliament in the OCTs with which they maintain particular relations. In the absence of specific provisions in that regard in the Treaty, it is for the Member States to adopt the rules which are best adapted to their constitutional structure'.[41]

In that light, since the Treaty 'do[es] not confer on citizens of the Union an unconditional right to vote and to stand as a candidate in elections to the European Parliament', a residence criterion 'does not appear, in principle, to be inappropriate to determine who has [that] right'.[42] However, such conditions must be assessed in light of 'the principle of equal treatment or non-discrimination, which is one of the general principles of [Union] law, requir[ing] that comparable situations must not be treated differently and that different situations must not be treated in the same way unless such treatment is objectively justified'.[43] In this case, the 'relevant comparison' was between a Netherlands national who resides in Aruba and a Netherlands national 'residing in a non-member country. They have in common that they are Netherlands nationals who do not reside in the Netherlands. Yet there is a difference in treatment between the two, the latter having the right to vote and to stand as a candidate in elections to the European Parliament held in the Netherlands whereas the former has no such right', meaning that '[s]uch a difference in treatment must be objectively justified'.[44] As a result, in the context of giving effect to EU voting rights at national level, EU

---

[37] Also discussing the ECtHR dimension of this case, see L Besselink, '*Spain v UK, Eman and Sevinger, Sevinger and Eman v Netherlands*' (case comment) (2008) 45 Common Market Law Review 787.

[38] Case C-300/04 *Eman and Sevinger*, EU:C:2006:545, para 27.

[39] ibid para 46.

[40] ibid paras 47 and 53.

[41] ibid para 50; the Court also ruled out the relevance of Article 3 of Protocol No 1 to the ECHR on the basis that the European Parliament is not the 'legislature' of the OCTs (para 48).

[42] *Eman and Sevinger*, paras 52 and 55.

[43] ibid para 57. See further, applying the principles of equivalence and effectiveness, para 67: 'it is for the domestic legal system of each Member State to designate the courts having jurisdiction and to determine the detailed procedural rules governing actions at law intended to safeguard the rights which individuals derive from Community law, provided, first, that those rules are not less favourable than those governing rights which originate in domestic law (principle of equivalence) and, second, that they do not render impossible or excessively difficult in practice the exercise of rights conferred by the Community legal order (principle of effectiveness)'; confirmed in Case C-541/15 *Freitag*, EU:C:2017:432, para 42.

[44] *Eman and Sevinger*, para 58.

equal treatment applies to a difference in treatment not between Member State nationals and non-Member State nationals, but between two different cohorts of one Member State's own nationals. Since it emerged at the hearing that 'a Netherlands national who transfers his residence from Aruba to a non-member country has the right to vote in the same way as a Netherlands national transferring his residence from the Netherlands to a non-member country, while a Netherlands national resident in Aruba does not have that right', the contested rules did not constitute an unjustified 'infringement' of equal treatment.[45]

The ruling in *Eman and Sevinger* is remarkable in several respects. First, it provides a strong example of how EU legal obligations reach into matters formally within national competence, as introduced in Chapter 2 and discussed in more detail in Chapter 3 with respect to determining Member State nationality.[46] Second, it entails application of the comparator dimension of EU equal treatment law to different groups of the nationals of one Member State only—similarly to the equal treatment analysis applied to the static but dual national children in *Garcia Avello*[47]—as distinct from the more typical connecting factor of exercising free movement. In that sense, *Eman and Sevinger* foreshadows the *Rottmann* and *Ruiz Zambrano* case law too, returned to in Section 3. At the same time, it highlights that non-discrimination only goes so far. In common with the discussion in Chapter 3 on determination of nationality, both *Eman and Sevinger* and *Spain v UK* illustrate how significant differences are actively tolerated *across* Member States within EU citizenship law.[48] Third, *Eman and Sevinger* also presaged the less ambiguous articulation of a *right* to vote that followed later in *Delvigne*, returned to in Section 2.1.2.

A final dimension to consider as regards how the electorate is determined for European Parliament elections concerns the withdrawal of the UK from the Union. As noted in Section 1, and provided for in Article 127(1)(b) WA, the voting rights enjoyed by Union citizens ceased for British nationals not after the end of the transition period (ie after 31 December 2020) but at the earlier point of the UK's formal withdrawal on 1 February 2020. In *Préfet du Gers*, considered in Chapter 3 as regards the 'inseparable and exclusive link between possession of the nationality of a Member State and not only the acquisition, but also the retention, of the status of citizen of the Union',[49] EP, a British national, was removed from the electoral list of her municipality of residence in France. The case did therefore involve the exercise of free movement on the part of EP, who initiated the proceedings following Brexit. However, the Court emphasised that 'United Kingdom nationals no longer hold the nationality of a Member State, but that of a third State',[50] whereas 'the right to vote and to stand as a candidate in elections to the European Parliament and also in municipal elections ... is reserved

---

[45] ibid paras 59–60.
[46] For AG La Pergola, 'the special provisions on the prohibition of discrimination which the Treaty has laid down in relation to the right of Union citizens to vote and stand for election in elections to the European Parliament and municipal elections explicitly derogate from provisions which are clearly a matter for the legal systems and, presumably, the Constitutions of the individual Member States' (AG La Pergola in Case C-85/96 *Marténez Sala*, EU:C:1997:335, para 21 of the Opinion).
[47] Case C-148/02 *Garcia Avello*, EU:C:2003:539, discussed in Chapter 3. Downplaying the dual nationality dimension of that case, Besselink characterises *Garcia Avello* as establishing 'the right *not* to be treated the same as citizens of the Member State of residence, but rather the same as citizens of the Member State of origin' (n 37, 803). See similarly, Case C-353/06 *Grunkin and Paul*, EU:C:2008:559.
[48] eg As Besselink underlines, 'the question of who is considered a citizen enjoying the democratic political right to vote is answered differently from one Member State to another' (n 37, 801).
[49] Case C-673/20 *Préfet du Gers*, EU:C:2022:449, para 48.
[50] ibid para 56.

to every citizen of the Union,'[51] with reference, *inter alia*, to Article 39 CFR, returned to in Section 2.1.2 in the context of *Delvigne*.

Addressing the question of discrimination on grounds of nationality, the Court confirmed that Article 18 TFEU 'is not intended to apply in the case of a possible difference in treatment between nationals of Member States and nationals of third States,'[52] thus distinguishing the circumstances in *Préfet du Gers* from those in *Eman and Sevinger*. However, aligning with *Spain v United Kingdom*, the Court also recalled 'the right of Member States to grant, under conditions which they lay down in their national law, a right to vote and to stand as a candidate to nationals of a third State residing in their territory'.[53] *Préfet du Gers* thus evolves the paradox in EU citizenship law that was seeded in *Spain v United Kingdom*—there is an 'inseparable and exclusive link' between Member State nationality and Union citizenship, yet the Member States are free to extend a core Union citizenship right to third-country nationals in certain circumstances.[54]

Préfet du Gers concerned EP's inability to vote in municipal elections only.[55] But *Spain v United Kingdom* addressed European Parliament elections. The circumstances of that case—in terms of the UK's relationship to Gibraltar and the ECtHR judgment in *Matthews v UK* requiring the UK to expand its electorate—were undoubtedly special and specific. Nevertheless, the openness of the Court of Justice to voters other than Union citizens participating in European Parliament elections is striking: in its understanding, 'while citizenship of the Union is destined to be the fundamental status of nationals of the Member States ... that statement does not necessarily mean that the rights recognised by the Treaty are limited to citizens of the Union'.[56] The decoupling of the *status* and the *rights* of Union citizenship in this way arguably enables the latter to be sustained even where the former is lost—at least in some respects, which could yet be clarified as the implications of Brexit (for both former and continuing Union citizens) inevitably unfold further in the future.[57]

2.1.2 Voting rights (and the right to vote) in the context of imprisonment
Article 3 of Protocol No 1 to the ECHR provides that '[t]he High Contracting Parties undertake to hold free elections at reasonable intervals by secret ballot, under conditions which will ensure the free expression of the opinion of the people in the choice of the legislature'. In *Hirst v United Kingdom (No 2)*, the ECtHR found that that the contested UK legislation 'imposes a blanket restriction on all convicted prisoners in prison. It applies automatically to such prisoners, irrespective of the length of their sentence and irrespective of the nature or gravity of their offence and their individual circumstances. Such a *general, automatic and*

---

[51] ibid para 70. In his Opinion, AG Collins discussed the ideas expressed by AG Poiares Maduro in *Rottmann*, suggesting that they '[describe] the rationale for Union citizenship being contingent upon holding the nationality of a Member State as the Member States' mutual commitment to construct a new form of civic and political allegiance on a European scale. By its sovereign decision to leave the European Union, the United Kingdom signalled its clear determination to repudiate that commitment. In the context of that act by a sovereign State, an individual cannot seek to rely upon his or her British nationality to assert a claim either to Union citizenship or to its benefits' (AG Collins in *Préfet du Gers*, para 37 of the Opinion; referring to AG Poiares Maduro in Case C-135/08 *Rottmann*, EU:C:2009:588, para 23 of the Opinion).
[52] *Préfet du Gers*, para 78.
[53] ibid para 82.
[54] ie '[C]ertain persons who have a close link with [the Member State in question] without however being nationals of that State or another Member State' (Case C-145/04 *Spain v United Kingdom*, EU:C:2006:543, para 76).
[55] Compare eg paras 26 and 35 of *Préfet du Gers*; see also, paras 81–82.
[56] *Spain v United Kingdom*, para 74; thus, for Besselink, 'the Court had to qualify its eschatological doctrinal formula of EU citizenship as "destined to be the fundamental status of nationals of the Member States"' (n 37, 804).
[57] See further, N Nic Shuibhne, 'The legal heritage of former Union citizens: *Préfet du Gers*' (2023) 60 Common Market Law Review 475.

indiscriminate restriction on a vitally important Convention right must be seen as falling outside any acceptable margin of appreciation, however wide that margin might be'.[58] It was not obvious that similar questions would connect to EU law in the absence of a cross-border situation. That is why the ruling in *Delvigne* is so significant, enriching the political element of Union citizenship as the Lisbon Treaty required.

Mr Delvigne was a French national who was convicted of a serious crime in 1988 in France and sentenced to 12 years in prison. As a result, he was automatically and permanently deprived of the right to vote and the right to stand for election under the Criminal Code applicable at the time. That rule was subsequently replaced by a provision requiring that 'total or partial deprivation of civic rights must be the subject of a court ruling and may not exceed 10 years in the case of a conviction for a serious offence'.[59] However, Mr Delvigne continued to be deprived of civic rights on the basis that his conviction became final before the new Criminal Code entered into force. He therefore challenged a 2012 decision to remove him from the electoral role for the municipality where he resided.

Reflecting *Spain v United Kingdom* and *Eman and Sevinger*, the Court of Justice first recalled that, 'as EU law currently stands, the definition of the persons entitled to exercise [the right to vote] falls within the competence of each Member State'.[60] However, that competence must be exercised 'in compliance with EU law'.[61] In that light, Article 1(3) of the 1976 Act 'read in conjunction with Article 14(3) TEU' entails an obligation to ensure that European Parliament elections are by direct universal suffrage, free and secret.[62] Thus, where a Member State, in the course of implementing that obligation, 'mak[es] provision in national legislation for the exclusion of certain Union citizens from entitlement to vote', it is 'implementing Union law' within the meaning of Article 51(1) CFR.[63] The Court ruled out the relevance of Article 39(1) CFR, which 'corresponds to the right guaranteed in Article 20(2)(b) TFEU' and does not concern 'a Union citizen's right to vote in the Member State of which he is a national'.[64] However, since Article 39(2) CFR 'corresponds to' Article 14(3) TEU, it 'constitutes the expression in the Charter of *the right of Union citizens* to vote in elections to the European Parliament in accordance with Article 14(3) TEU and Article 1(3) of the 1976 Act'.[65] The Court also referred to the explanations relating to the Charter, which suggest that Article 39(2) CFR 'takes over the basic principles of the electoral system in a democratic State'.[66]

---

[58] *Hirst v United Kingdom (No 2)* (2006) 42 EHRR 41, para 82 (emphasis added).

[59] Case C-650/13 *Delvigne*, EU:C:2015:648, para 16.

[60] ibid para 30.

[61] ibid. In other words, it 'involves a sphere to which EU law must necessarily be applied' (AG Cruz Villalón in *Delvigne*, EU:C:2015:363, para 103 of the Opinion).

[62] *Delvigne*, para 32.

[63] ibid para 33. For van Eijken and van Rossem, 'the presence of a set of general principles is deemed sufficient to activate the scope of EU law' (H van Eijken and JW van Rossem 'Prisoner disenfranchisement and the right to vote in elections to the European Parliament: universal suffrage key to unlocking political citizenship?' (2016) 12 European Constitutional Law Review 114 at 122), producing a 'remarkable broad interpretation of Article 51(1)' CFR (ibid 122). In one sense, an analogy could be drawn with how a Member State's organisation of its judiciary was later deemed to fall within the scope of EU law (beginning with Case C-64/16 *Associação Sindical dos Juízes Portugueses*, EU:C:2018:117). However, that case law is based on Article 19(1) TEU 'interpreted in the light of' Article 47 CFR rather than more directly on Article 47 CFR (see further, Case C-896/19 *Repubblika v Il-Prim Ministru*, EU:C:2021:311, paras 40–46; Case C-157/21 *Poland v Parliament and Council*, EU:C:2021:978, paras 197–198).

[64] *Delvigne*, paras 41 and 43.

[65] ibid paras 41 and 44 (emphasis added).

[66] ibid para 41, referring to the Explanations relating to the Charter of Fundamental Rights, 2007 OJ C303/17. Article 6(1) TEU provides that '[t]he rights, freedoms and principles in the Charter shall be interpreted in accordance with the general provisions in Title VII of the Charter governing its interpretation and application *and with due regard to the explanations referred to in the Charter*, that set out the sources of those provisions'. The preamble

While the Court did not refer to *Rottmann*, there is a synergy between *Delvigne* and the Article 20 TFEU case law in the sense that disenfranchisement makes exercising the right to vote impossible and a national rule producing that outcome therefore falls, 'by reason of its nature and consequences', within the scope of EU law.[67] However, since the right to vote was sourced in Article 39(2) CFR and not in Article 20 TFEU, the restriction placed on Mr Delvigne's right to vote had to be assessed under Article 52(1) CFR and not only, as in *Rottmann*, under a proportionality test. In other words, it had to be determined whether 'the limitations are provided for by law, respect the essence of those rights and freedoms and, subject to the principle of proportionality, are necessary and genuinely meet objectives of general interest recognised by the European Union or the need to protect the rights and freedoms of others'.[68] In the Court's assessment, the limitation imposed by the Criminal Code satisfied these criteria and it was proportionate 'in so far as it takes into account the nature and gravity of the criminal offence committed and the duration of the penalty'.[69] Moreover, Article 49(1) CFR 'does not preclude national legislation … limited to maintaining the deprivation of the right to vote resulting, by operation of law, from a criminal conviction only in respect of final convictions by judgment delivered at last instance under the old Criminal Code', especially since the legislation 'expressly provides for the possibility of persons subject to such a ban applying for, and obtaining, the lifting of that ban'.[70] That option is 'available to anyone deprived of the right to vote whether as a result, by operation of law, of a criminal conviction under the old Criminal Code, or as a result of a court having imposed an additional penalty under the provisions of the new Criminal Code … pav[ing] the way for that person's individual situation to be reassessed, including with regard to the duration of that ban'.[71]

The Court's assessment of the proportionality of the national rules contested in *Delvigne* accords with both its resistance to conditions 'too exclusive and general' and its emphasis on accessible procedures for judicial review.[72] As suggested above, it also fits, in a conceptual

---

to the Charter reflects that requirement and Article 52(7) further provides that '[t]he explanations drawn up as a way of providing guidance in the interpretation of this Charter shall be given due regard by the courts of the Union and of the Member States'. Considering the implications of *Delvigne* for the structuring of the European Parliament more specifically, see J Shaw, 'Citizenship: contrasting dynamics at the interface of integration and constitutionalism' in P Craig and G de Búrca (eds) *The Evolution of EU Law* (3rd edn, OUP 2021) 608 at 634–635.

[67] Case C-135/08 *Rottmann*, EU:C:2010:104, para 42; as distinct from, in a more open sense, fundamental rights applying 'on a "free-standing" basis, ie regardless of whether the national measure at issue adversely affects the rights attaching to that status' (K Lenaerts, 'EU citizenship and democracy' (2016) 7 New Journal of European Criminal Law 164 at 169, highlighting (at 171) the problems for conferral that such arguments raise).

[68] *Delvigne*, para 46.

[69] ibid para 49.

[70] ibid para 56.

[71] ibid para 57. Article 49(1) CFR provides that '[n]o one shall be held guilty of any criminal offence on account of any act or omission which did not constitute a criminal offence under national law or international law at the time when it was committed. Nor shall a heavier penalty be imposed than the one that was applicable at the time the criminal offence was committed. If, subsequent to the commission of a criminal offence, the law provides for a lighter penalty, that penalty shall be applicable'.

[72] However, van Eijken and van Rossem question the Court's silence on ECtHR case law (esp *Hirst v United Kingdom* (2006) 42 EHRR 41and *Scoppola v Italy* (2013) 56 EHRR 19), which might have entailed more stringent proportionality review (n 62, 128–130; concluding that 'the Court of Justice follows a classical strategy for landmark decisions. It shows restraint with regard to the outcome of the case, but scores an important point as a matter of legal principle. France gets what it wants – it may continue to apply its former restrictive prisoner voting regime to old criminal convictions – yet at the same time the constitution of the EU is enriched: voting in elections to the European Parliament is now a subjective fundamental right for *all* Union citizens' (130, emphasis in original). On citation gaps with respect to ECtHR case law more generally, see G de Búrca 'After the EU Charter of Fundamental Rights: the Court of Justice as a human rights adjudicator?' (2013) 20 Maastricht Journal of European and Comparative Law 173.

sense, with the Article 20 TFEU case law considered in Section 3, even though no reference was made to Article 20 or to the status of Union citizenship per se. The Court drew instead from Article 14(3) TEU to cross the 'implementing Union law' threshold set by Article 51(1) CFR.[73] Once again, though, given the fundamental nature of the right to vote sourced in Article 39(2) CFR and the vital systemic link to the Union as a polity connected *to its citizens* through Articles 10 and 14 TEU, *Delvigne* further highlights the *Spain v United Kingdom* anomaly, that is, a Member State's capacity to confer voting rights for European Parliament elections on those who are *not* its nationals, and thus not Union citizens at all.

2.1.3 Voting rights in the context of free movement

The right to vote and to stand as a candidate in European Parliament and municipal elections in a host State—provided for by Articles 20(2)(b) and 22(1) TFEU and underpinned by Articles 39(1) CFR,[74] 40 CFR,[75] and 14(3) TEU[76]—exemplifies the importance of the guarantee in Article 10(3) TEU that '[e]*very citizen* shall have the right to participate in the democratic life of the Union'. In that light, beyond the contribution of these rights to the functioning of freedom of movement, they exemplify the additionality and distinctiveness of Union citizenship.[77] As explained in Section 2.1.1, the Court did not consider in *Préfet du Gers*, where a British national lost her *right* to vote in municipal and European Parliament elections in France, that any other conclusion was logical on account of the 'inseparable and exclusive link between possession of the nationality of a Member State and not only the acquisition, but also the retention, of the status of citizen of the Union'.[78]

It is perhaps surprising, then, that most of the case law on voting rights to date has concerned questions connected to the home and not the host State.[79] How does the role of the home State connect to voting rights in a host State in the context of free movement? Two points can be highlighted. First, the right to vote in national elections is not provided for as a Union citizenship right. That gap might be completely understandable for political reasons but it is nevertheless an obstacle to or interference with the free movement rights conferred by Article 21 TFEU—and, for present purposes, not only with respect to host State exclusion but also *home* State restrictions that curtail or negate electoral rights as a consequence of the exercise of free movement by own nationals.[80] Such rules have never been challenged directly

---

[73] *Delvigne* thus demonstrates that 'the political dimension of EU citizenship is not limited to Articles 20 to 25 TFEU, but also involves other provisions of EU law' (Lenaerts (n 67) 169).

[74] ie 'Every citizen of the Union has the right to vote and to stand as a candidate at elections to the European Parliament in the Member State in which he or she resides, under the same conditions as nationals of that State'.

[75] ie 'Every citizen of the Union has the right to vote and to stand as a candidate at municipal elections in the Member State in which he or she resides under the same conditions as nationals of that State'.

[76] ie 'The members of the European Parliament shall be elected for a term of five years by direct universal suffrage in a free and secret ballot' (repeated in Article 39(2) CFR).

[77] See generally, J Shaw, *The Transformation of Citizenship in the European Union: Electoral Rights and the Restructuring of Political Space* (CUP 2007).

[78] Case C-673/20 *Préfet du Gers*, EU:C:2022:449, para 48.

[79] However, at the time of writing, the Commission had proceeded to the judicial stage in infringement proceedings against the Czech Republic and Poland: 'having regard to the fact that citizens of the Union who are not nationals of the Czech Republic [or of Poland] but who are resident in the Czech Republic [or in Poland] do not have the right to become members of political parties or political movements, those citizens of the Union cannot exercise the political rights conferred on them [by Article 22 TFEU] under the same conditions as nationals of [those States]' (Case C-808/21 *Commission v Czech Republic*, pending; Case C-814/21 *Commission v Poland*, pending. See further, Commission Press Release IP/21/1829 of 9 June 2021, <https://ec.europa.eu/commission/presscorner/detail/en/ip_21_1829> (accessed 29 May 2023)). Note also, the developing case law on the European Parliament and the 1976 Act more generally; see eg Case C-9/08 *Donnici*, EU:C:2009:44 and Case C-502/19 *Junqueras*, EU:C:2019:1115.

[80] As Shaw underlines, '[a]cross the world, very few countries give the right to vote in national elections to resident non-nationals. Within the EU (post-Brexit), there are no longer any examples in place for voting by nationals

on that basis.[81] If they were, the most likely outcome would be confirmation that exclusion from voting of non-resident own nationals is a justifiable restriction of the rights conferred by Article 21 TFEU, constituting a legitimate, residence-based,[82] and (almost certainly) proportionate public interest exception. The challenge would be admissible: 'as EU law currently stands, the definition of the persons entitled to exercise [the right to vote] falls within the competence of each Member State' but that competence must be exercised 'in compliance with EU law'.[83] However, Article 4(2) TEU—which requires that '[t]he Union shall respect the equality of Member States before the Treaties as well as their national identities, inherent in their fundamental structures, political and constitutional, inclusive of regional and local self-government'—would most likely play a stronger role at justification stage than it has in citizenship case law to date.[84] A similarly precautionary approach was seen in Section 2.1.2 with the Court's finding in *Delvigne* that the contested restrictions on voting rights did fall within the scope of EU citizenship law yet were proportionate. In that sense, perhaps that ruling was a 'test balloon' for further review of home State voting restrictions. But to stretch the reach of EU law into, in effect, compelling fundamental redesign of national electoral processes and fundamental adjustment of national electoral cultures would be a momentous further step, without the linchpins in either the TFEU or the Charter that enabled the Court to assess restrictions of the *Union*-conferred right to vote in European Parliament elections in the home State at issue in *Delvigne*.

Nevertheless, the assertion that an Article 21 TFEU-based challenge to home State voting restrictions would not succeed does not discount the diminished participation of mobile citizens in the democratic life of the Union that such restrictions inevitably entail.[85] As the Commission has observed, '[t]he possibility for citizens to express their political will by exercising their right to vote, one of the fundamental political rights of citizenship, is part of the very fabric of democracy'.[86] In principle, since Article 25 TFEU empowers 'the Council,

---

of other Member States in the host state. There are also gaps in the coverage of *external* voting rights, which is another mechanism covering the interests of non-resident citizens via the right to vote in the home state' (n 66, 629, emphasis in original). See also, Communication from the Commission addressing the consequences of disenfranchisement of Union citizens exercising their right to free movement, COM(2014) 33 final, para 1: 'national policies which lead to disenfranchising citizens may be considered as limiting the enjoyment of rights attached to EU citizenship, such as the right to move and reside freely within the EU, a fundamental right of every EU citizen. This is at odds with the founding premise of EU citizenship, namely that it is additional to national citizenship and is designed to give additional rights to EU citizens, whereas in this case the exercise of the right of free movement may lead to losing a right of political participation'. See further, F Fabbrini, 'The political side of EU citizenship in the context of EU federalism' in D Kochenov (ed), *EU Citizenship and Federalism: The Role of Rights* (CUP 2017) 271; and D Kochenov, 'Free movement and participation in the parliamentary elections in the Member State of nationality: an Ignored link?' (2009) 16 Maastricht Journal of European and Comparative Law 197.

[81] A European Citizen's Initiative entitled 'Let me vote', which sought '[t]o strengthen the rights listed in article 20§2 TFEU by granting EU citizens residing in another Member State the right to vote in all political elections in their country of residence, on the same conditions as the nationals of that State', did not succeed in collecting the required number of signatures; see <https://europa.eu/citizens-initiative/initiatives/details/2013/000003_en> (accessed 29 May 2023).
[82] By analogy with Case C-300/04 *Eman and Sevinger*, EU:C:2006:54, para 55: 'the criterion linked to residence does not appear, in principle, to be inappropriate to determine who has the right to vote and to stand as a candidate in elections to the European Parliament'.
[83] ibid, para 31.
[84] See eg Case C-490/20 *VMA v Stolichna obshtina, rayon 'Pancharevo'*, EU:C:2021:100, discussed in Chapter 5; and see esp the Opinion of AG Kokott (EU:C:2021:296, paras 70 ff).
[85] An ambition that the Lisbon Treaty 'enhances' (Commission Recommendation addressing the consequences of disenfranchisement of Union citizens exercising their rights to free movement, 2014 OJ L32/34, recital 1). See further, the wide range of perspectives collected in Part I of R Bauböck (ed.), *Debating European Citizenship* (SpringerOpen, 2019; <https://link.springer.com/book/10.1007/978-3-319-89905-3#toc>) (accessed 29 May 2023)).
[86] Communication addressing the consequences of disenfranchisement (n 80) para 1.

acting unanimously in accordance with a special legislative procedure and after obtaining the consent of the European Parliament, [to] adopt provisions *to strengthen or to add to* the rights listed in Article 20(2)', a legal basis exists for legislative action to mitigate the impact of (both host and home State) voting exclusion rules: perhaps as a starting point, aiming at least for better coordination across diverse national electoral systems. But Article 25 TFEU requires that legislation adopted on that basis enters into force only 'after [its] approval by the Member States in accordance with their respective constitutional requirements'—instituting a significant barrier to fundamental change even if the necessary political will could be marshalled.

Thus, another paradox emerges. As argued in Chapter 3, a key objective of Union citizenship is to displace the need for naturalisation in a host State to be appropriately integrated and protected there. Yet to participate in national elections, naturalisation in a host State is often the only real option that a mobile Union citizen has. The Commission has strongly resisted this association on the grounds that 'promoting naturalisation in the host country as a means of increasing political rights would be at odds with the role of EU citizenship as the primary vehicle for promoting respect for national identity and diversity, and ensuring equality of treatment irrespective of nationality'.[87] It also 'disregards the complexity of intra-EU mobility. Individuals may reside in several countries for longer or shorter periods—eventually even returning to their home country. They could not be expected to acquire multiple or successive nationalities solely to maintain political rights'.[88] Perhaps a different tone is suggested by *Lounes*, though, as also considered in Chapter 3. There, the Court conceived host State naturalisation as more the pinnacle of freedom of movement through the understanding that Union citizens who acquire the nationality of a host State 'intend to become permanently integrated' there.[89] In any event, short of legislation at EU level and/or a '*Delvigne II*' from the Court of Justice, both of which are unlikely, Union nudging of Member State change remains the more viable pathway for now, with a template for further progress already sketched by the Commission.[90]

Second, notwithstanding the 'additional' character of the right to vote and stand as a candidate in European Parliament and municipal elections in a host State—which is profoundly free movement-driven and free movement-enabling—the procedures for these elections are still linked principally to national rules. A basic framework exists at Union level—comprising Directives 93/109[91] and 94/80,[92] which lay down 'detailed arrangements' for elections to

---

[87] Communication addressing the consequences of disenfranchisement (n 80) para 5.1.
[88] ibid.
[89] Case C-165/16 *Lounes*, EU:C:2017:862, para 57.
[90] Recommendation addressing the consequences of disenfranchisement (n 85): '1. Where Member States' policies limit the rights of nationals to vote in national elections based exclusively on a residence condition, Member States should enable their nationals who make use of their right to free movement and residence in the Union to demonstrate a continuing interest in the political life in the Member State of which they are nationals, including through an application to remain registered on the electoral roll, and by doing so, to retain their right to vote. 2. Where Member States allow their nationals residing in another Member State to retain their right to vote in national elections through an application to remain registered on the electoral roll, this should be without prejudice to the possibility for those Member States to put in place proportionate accompanying arrangements, such as reapplication at appropriate intervals. 3. Member States that allow their nationals residing in another Member State to retain their right to vote in national elections through an application or a reapplication to remain registered on the electoral roll should ensure that all relevant applications may be submitted electronically. 4. Member States providing for the loss of the right to vote in national elections by their nationals residing in another Member State should inform them by appropriate means and in a timely manner about the conditions and the practical arrangements for retaining their right to vote in national elections'.
[91] 1993 OJ L329/34. Articles 6 and 10 of Directive 93/109 were amended by Council Directive 2013/1/EU, 2013 OJ, L26/27, which addressed requirements with respect to evidencing deprivation of voting rights.
[92] 1994 OJ L368/38. The Commission took successful infringement proceedings against Belgium for failure to implement this Directive within the prescribed period (Case C-323/97 *Commission v Belgium*, EU:C:1998:347).

the European Parliament and municipal elections respectively—but it leaves considerable scope for national procedures and national discretion.[93] On the latter point, for example, Article 2(1)(b) of Directive 94/80 defines municipal elections as 'elections by direct universal suffrage to appoint the members of the representative council and, where appropriate, under the laws of each Member State, the head and members of the executive of a basic local government unit', which means, in reality, that 'what' elections a Union citizen can vote in can differ significantly depending on the Member State (or indeed *part* of a Member State) in which they reside, as elaborated in an annex to the Directive.

The right to vote and to stand as a candidate in a host State is based on equal treatment.[94] For municipal elections, it is extended through integration-based, degree of connection logic and determined by residence conditions.[95] Nevertheless, the significance of the territory of the Union, introduced in Chapter 2 and returned to in Section 3, is also evident with respect to recognizing periods of residence in other Member States.[96] Some distinctions reflecting the local and pan-European nature of municipal and European Parliament elections respectively can be noted. For example, Article 5(1) of Directive 94/80 establishes that 'Member States of residence *may* provide that any citizen of the Union who, through an individual decision under civil law or a criminal law decision, has been deprived of his right to stand as a candidate under the law of his home Member State, shall be precluded from exercising that right in municipal elections', whereas Article 6(1) of Directive 93/109 (as amended) requires that '[a]ny citizen of the Union who resides in a Member State of which he is not a national and who, through an individual judicial decision or an administrative decision provided that the latter can be subject to judicial remedies, has been deprived of his right to stand as a candidate under either the law of the Member State of residence or the law of his home Member State, *shall be precluded* from exercising that right in the Member State of residence in elections to the European Parliament'.

In its Report on the 2019 European Parliament elections, the Commission observed that '[a] relatively low number of mobile EU citizens exercised their electoral rights, and usually in their countries of origin. Ahead of the elections citizens indicated that they would prefer

---

[93] See esp the definitions in Article 2(1) of Directive 94/80; Article 5(3) of the same Directive, permitting Member States to reserve certain office-bearer roles for own nationals; and Articles 12 and 14 of Directives 94/80 and 93/109 respectively, enabling derogation options where 'the proportion of citizens of the Union of voting age who reside in it but are not nationals of it exceeds 20% of the total number of citizens of the Union residing there who are of voting age' (invoked to date only by Luxembourg, initially for both European Parliament and municipal elections, now for the latter only: see the Commission's Report on the implementation of Directive 94/80, COM(2012) 99 final). See generally, M Finck, 'Towards an ever closer union between residents and citizens? On the possible extension of voting rights to foreign residents in Luxembourg' (2015) 11 European Constitutional Law Review 78. Note also, the capacity of Member States under Article 1(2) of both Directives 'concerning the right to vote or to stand as a candidate either of its nationals who reside outside its territory or of third country nationals who reside in that State'.

[94] Including for compulsory voting where applicable: see Article 7 of Directive 94/80 and Article 8(2) of Directive 93/109. For Coutts, '[e]ven the explicitly political rights introduced alongside Union citizenship in the Treaty of Maastricht and implemented through Directive 93/109 and Directive 94/80 are in fact transnational rights and a specific manifestation of the general right to non-discrimination rather than stand-alone political rights as such' (S Coutts, '*Delvigne*: a multi-levelled political citizenship' (2017) 42 European Law Review 867 at 872).

[95] See Article 4 of Directive 94/80.

[96] See Articles 3 ('Where, in order to stand as a candidate, nationals of the Member State of residence must have been nationals for a certain minimum period, citizens of the Union shall be deemed to have met this condition when they have been nationals of a Member State for the same period') and 5 ('If, in order to vote or to stand as candidates, nationals of the Member State or residence must have spent a certain minimum period as a resident in the electoral territory of that State, Community voters and Community nationals entitled to stand as candidates shall be deemed to have fulfilled that condition where they have resided for an equivalent period in other Member States. This provision shall apply without prejudice to any specific conditions as to length of residence in a given constituency or locality') of Directive 93/109. See similarly, Article 4(1) of Directive 94/80.

to exercise their EU rights and vote in lists in their country of residence ... This suggests that choice is important to keeping participation high'.[97] In consequence, 'Member States are encouraged to ... explore options offering greater choice in how and when citizens may vote (remote and advance voting, as well as other facilitations to accommodate specific needs)'.[98] It also reinforces the significance of the home State for voting rights exercised in a context of free movement and affirms that Union citizenship comprises a complex fusion of national, supranational, and transnational elements (as developed further in Section 3).

In November 2021, building on commitments made in its 2020 EU Citizenship Report,[99] the Commission issued proposals to recast both electoral Directives.[100] Notable proposed changes include: improving the provision of electoral information for mobile Union citizens, tackling multiple voting in European Parliament elections (ie where votes are cast, illegally, in both home and host States), standardising the administrative formalities with which citizens need to comply, enhancing mechanisms for reporting and monitoring of Member State implementation, and updating electoral procedures in light of transformed technologies, including electronic voting and with express reference to voter inclusion (citing the United Nations Convention on the Rights of Persons with Disabilities as a 'source of inspiration'). Another central focus in both proposals concerns improving information exchange across the Member States. Noting that turnout for the European Parliament elections in 2019 was 'the highest in 25 years',[101] the Commission's proposals for recasting the 1990s Directives are well timed.

2.2 Mechanisms Facilitating Participation

If the political relationship between the Union and its citizens involves 'construct[ing] a new form of civic and political allegiance on a European scale',[102] mechanisms are required to ensure participation alongside representation and to facilitate active civic contributions alongside critical but more passive engagement as beneficiaries of core rights such as equal treatment. The European Citizens' Initiative—the 'agenda-setting tool'[103] introduced by the Lisbon Treaty—epitomises how Union citizens residing in their home States can engage with and invigorate the transnational dimension of Union citizenship (Section 2.2.1). Additionally, petitioning the European Parliament (Section 2.2.2) and applying to the European Ombudsman (Section 2.2.3) not only provide non-litigious routes for enforcing EU rights, but also a rich resource for better understanding of experienced Union citizenship through petitions and submissions as well as resulting actions and reports. Finally,

---

[97] Communication from the Commission, Report on the 2019 elections to the European Parliament, SWD(2020) 113 final, para 2.

[98] ibid.

[99] COM(2020) 730 final ('Empowering citizens and protecting their rights').

[100] Proposal for a Council Directive laying down detailed arrangements for the exercise of the right to vote and stand as a candidate in elections to the European Parliament for Union citizens residing in a Member State of which they are not nationals (recast) COM(2021) 732 final; and Proposal for a Council Directive laying down detailed arrangements for the exercise of the right to vote and to stand as a candidate in municipal elections by Union citizens residing in a Member State of which they are not nationals (recast), COM(2021) 733 final.

[101] Report on the 2019 elections to the European Parliament (n 97) para 1; see also, para 2: '50.66% 16 of EU citizens eligible to vote took part in the 2019 elections. This figure is a 25-year high and marks the first increase in turnout since 1979', with strong turnout among 'Europe's young and first-time voters'.

[102] AG Poiares Maduro in Case C-135/08 *Rottmann*, EU:C:2009:588, para 21 of the Opinion.

[103] European Commission, 'European Citizens' Initiative: Political agreement reached on the Commission's proposal', press release of 12 December 2018, IP/18/6792.

according to Article 24 TFEU, Union citizens may write to the European Parliament, Council or Ombudsman, or to any of the institutions and bodies further mentioned in Article 13 TEU.[104] Moreover, they may do so in any of the languages specified in Article 55(1) TEU[105] and 'have an answer in the same language'—though Article 41 CFR, which protects the right to good administration, extends the same guarantee to 'every person'.[106]

2.2.1 The European Citizens' Initiative

The European Citizens' Initiative (ECI), introduced by the Lisbon Treaty,[107] is the most prominent means through which Article 10(3) TEU's promise that '[e]very citizen shall have the right to *participate* in the democratic life of the Union' acquires an enabling infrastructure. Article 11(4) TEU provides that '[n]ot less than one million citizens who are nationals of a significant number of Member States may take the initiative of inviting the European Commission, within the framework of its powers, to submit any appropriate proposal on matters where citizens consider that a legal act of the Union is required for the purpose of implementing the Treaties', creating 'a vehicle to bring together issues of common interest between citizens across Member States' boundaries and furthe[r] strengthening ... the EU public space'.[108] Article 11(4) also indicates that '[t]he procedures and conditions required for such a citizens' initiative shall be determined in accordance with the first paragraph of Article 24 [TFEU]'. Article 24 TFEU requires, in turn, that '[t]he European Parliament and the Council, acting by means of regulations in accordance with the ordinary legislative procedure, shall adopt the provisions for the procedures and conditions required for a citizens' initiative within the meaning of Article 11 [TEU], including the minimum number of Member States from which such citizens must come'.

For the Court of Justice, 'the particular added value of the ECI mechanism resides not in certainty of outcome, but in *the possibilities and opportunities that it creates for Union citizens to initiate debate on policy within the EU institutions* without having to wait for the commencement of a legislative procedure'.[109] Advocate General Bobek has argued that the mechanism 'go[es] beyond any pre-existing channels of interaction between citizens and the EU institutions'.[110] He identified 'four distinct levels' of ECI 'added value': '(i) the promotion of public debate; (ii) enhanced visibility for certain topics or concerns; (iii) privileged access to EU institutions, enabling those concerns to be tabled in a robust way; and (iv) the entitlement to a reasoned institutional response facilitating public and political scrutiny'.[111]

---

[104] ie European Council, European Commission, Court of Justice of the European Union, European Central Bank, Court of Auditors, Economic and Social Committee, and Committee of the Regions.

[105] ie Bulgarian, Czech, Danish, Dutch, English, Estonian, Finnish, French, German, Greek, Hungarian, Irish, Italian, Latvian, Lithuanian, Maltese, Polish, Portuguese, Romanian, Slovak, Slovenian, Spanish, and Swedish.

[106] Article 41(1) CFR provides that '[e]very person has the right to have his or her affairs handled impartially, fairly and within a reasonable time by the institutions and bodies of the Union' and Article 41(4) establishes that '[e]very person may write to the institutions of the Union in one of the languages of the Treaties and must have an answer in the same language'.

[107] The introduction of the ECI at Lisbon was 'prompted by the debates on the Convention for the Future of Europe and forms part of a wider attempt to engrave the democratic principle, a founding value according to Article 2 TEU, at the heart of the EU institutional system' (AG Bobek in Case C-418/18 P *Puppinck*, EU:C:2019:640, para 67 of the Opinion).

[108] ibid para 74 of the Opinion.

[109] Case C-418/18 P *Puppinck*, EU:C:2019:1113, para 70 (emphasis added); referring to AG Bobek, para 78 of the Opinion ('the particular added value of the ECI resides, not necessarily in certainty of outcome, but in the avenues and opportunities it creates ... Therefore, the success of an ECI is measured not only by whether it is transformed into a formal proposal, but also by the democratic debate that it triggers').

[110] AG Bobek in *Puppinck*, para 73 of the Opinion.

[111] ibid.

However, Advocate General Mengozzi has pointed to more problematic aspects of the ECI from a practical perspective:

> It is a fundamental instrument for European participatory democracy which can be difficult to put into practice. Whilst the idea is to give citizens an active role in the development of EU law, it must be ensured that this right of initiative is not subject to the satisfaction of procedural or substantive conditions which are too strict or too complex — and thus ultimately difficult to understand — for non-specialists in EU law; in addition, it must be borne in mind that the EU legal order is governed by the principle of conferral of powers and participatory democracy, which Article 11(4) TEU seeks to bring to life, can thus be exercised only within these limits.[112]

Three procedural steps must be completed to produce a successful ECI: registration, collection of support, and submission. Two determinations then rest with the Commission: whether the ECI should be registered in the first place—that is whether, in effect, it reaches the required threshold of admissibility—and, for duly registered ECIs, what action (if any) will be taken as a result.

2.2.1.1 ECI procedures and conditions

Regulation 2019/788 establishes the procedures and conditions applicable to ECIs registered since 1 January 2020. It revises the original framework (Regulation 211/2011) after a reflective evaluation process undertaken to simplify ECI processes and with particular improvements on set-up, registration, collection of signatures, support, and follow-up.[113] As outlined in the Commission's proposal, the revisions sought 'to improve how the ECI functions by addressing the shortcomings identified over the past years with the main policy objectives of: (i) making the ECI more accessible, less burdensome and easier to use for organisers and supporters; and (ii) achieving the full potential of the ECI as a tool to foster debate and participation at European level, including of young people, and bring the EU closer to its citizens'.[114] Regulation 2019/788 is supplemented by Annexes (notably Annex I, which establishes the minimum number of signatories required for each Member State[115]) and by Regulation 2019/799, which establishes specific rules for online signature collection.[116]

---

[112] AG Mengozzi in Case C-589/15 P *Anagnostakis*, EU:C:2017:175, para 2 of the Opinion.

[113] European Commission, 'European Citizens' Initiative: Political agreement reached on the Commission's proposal', press release of 12 December 2018, IP/18/6792. Regulation 2019/788/EU on the European citizens' initiative, 2019 OJ L 130/55; repealing Regulation 211/2011/EU on the citizens' initiative, 2011 OJ L65/1. See further, Communication from the Commission to the European Parliament and the Council, Report on the application of Regulation (EU) No 211/2011 on the citizens' initiative, COM(2015) 145 final; and European Parliament resolution of 28 October 2015 on the European Citizens' Initiative (P8_TA(2015)0382). See also, the 2015 Decision of the European Ombudsman closing own-initiative inquiry OI/9/2013/TN concerning the European Commission ('The proper functioning of the European citizens' initiative (ECI) procedure and the Commission's role and responsibility in this regard') and offering 11 guidelines for further improving ECI procedures (<https://www.ombudsman.europa.eu/en/decision/en/59205> (accessed 29 May 2023)).

[114] Proposal for a Regulation of the European Parliament and of the Council on the European citizens' initiative, COM(2017) 482 final, 3.

[115] See also, Commission Delegated Regulation 2019/1673/EU replacing Annex I to Regulation (EU) 2019/788 of the European Parliament and of the Council on the European citizens' initiative, 2019 OJ L257/1, to take account of Brexit; updated minimums for required signatures range from 4,230 (Cyprus, Luxembourg, Malta) to 67,680 (Germany).

[116] Commission Implementing Regulation 2019/1799/EU laying down technical specifications for individual online collection systems pursuant to Regulation (EU) 2019/788 of the European Parliament and of the Council on the European citizens' initiative, 2019 OJ L274/3; updating Commission Implementing Regulation 1179/2011/EU, 2011 OJ L301/3.

From 18 July 2020 to 31 December 2022, Regulation 2020/1042 temporarily extended time-limits during the Covid-19 pandemic.[117]

Recital 6 of Regulation 2019/788 asserts that 'the procedures and conditions required for the European citizens' initiative should be effective, transparent, clear, simple, user-friendly, accessible for persons with disabilities and proportionate to the nature of this instrument' and that they 'should strike a judicious balance between rights and obligations and should ensure that valid initiatives receive an appropriate examination and response by the Commission'. Article 2(1) provides for the right to support an ECI, which is extended to every Union citizen 'who is at least of the age to be entitled to vote in elections to the European Parliament'. However, and new to the 2019 Regulation, Member States 'may set the minimum age entitling to support an initiative at 16 years, in accordance with their national laws'.[118] Article 3 then establishes that:

Article 3

1. An initiative is valid if:
   (a) it has received the support of at least one million citizens of the Union in accordance with Article 2(1) ('signatories') from at least one quarter of the Member States; and
   (b) in at least one quarter of the Member States, the number of signatories is at least equal to the minimum number set out in Annex I, corresponding to the number of the Members of the European Parliament elected in each Member State, multiplied by the total number of Members of the European Parliament, at the time of registration of the initiative.
2. For the purposes of paragraph 1, a signatory shall be counted in his or her Member State of nationality, irrespective of the place where the statement of support was signed by the signatory.

Article 3(2) provides an example of the determinative significance of nationality (rather than residence) in defining the personal scope of EU citizenship law and connects the ECI directly to the ambition of Union citizens participating in the democratic life of the Union, mirroring Article 10(3) TEU.[119] But it underlines too the interdependency of Union citizenship and national access points.

Article 4 of the Regulation sets out the means through which the Commission 'shall provide easily accessible and comprehensive information and assistance about the European citizens' initiative to citizens and groups of organisers, including by redirecting them to the relevant sources of information and assistance' (Article 3(1)). These entail online and paper guides, in all languages of the Union institutions (Article 3(1)),[120] a free of charge 'online

---

[117] Regulation 2020/1042/EU laying down temporary measures concerning the time limits for the collection, the verification and the examination stages provided for in Regulation (EU) 2019/788 on the European citizens' initiative in view of the COVID-19 outbreak, 2020 OJ L231/7.

[118] At the time of writing, three States have set the minimum age at 16—Austria, Estonia, and Malta—and Greece has set the minimum age at 17. The minimum age was reduced from 18 to 16 in Belgium as of 1 May 2023. See further, <https://europa.eu/citizens-initiative/data-requirements_en> (accessed 29 May 2023).

[119] However, Dougan points out the contradiction of excluding third-country nationals from participating in an ECI while, as discussed in Section 2.1, allowing them to vote in European Parliament elections—'the "higher" democratic right'—in certain circumstances (M Dougan, 'What are we to make of the citizens' initiative?' (2011) 48 Common Market Law Review 1807 at 1821–1822).

[120] <https://op.europa.eu/en/publication-detail/-/publication/8abe3729-640f-11ea-b735-01aa75ed71a1/language-en/format-PDF> (accessed 29 May 2023).

collaborative platform' to 'provide practical and legal advice, and a discussion forum about the European citizens' initiative for the exchange of information and best practices among citizens, groups of organisers, stakeholders, non-governmental organisations, experts and other institutions and bodies of the Union wishing to participate' (Article 3(2)),[121] an on-line register, comprising 'a public website that provides information on the European citizens' initiative in general as well as on specific initiatives and their respective status' (Article 3(3)),[122] and a file exchange service (Article 3(5)). Additionally, each Member State must establish 'one or more contact points to provide, free of charge, information and assistance to groups of organisers, in accordance with applicable Union and national law' (Article 3(6)). According to Article 3(4), responsibility lies with the Commission to provide 'translation of the content of [a registered ECI] including its annex, into all the official languages of the institutions of the Union, within the limits set out in Annex II,[123] for its publication in the register and its use for the collection of statements of support in accordance with this Regulation'. ECI organisers have the option of themselves providing 'translations into all the official languages of the institutions of the Union of the additional information on the initiative and, if any, a draft legal act referred to in Annex II'.

Article 5 details the procedures and conditions relevant to the group of organisers for an ECI, the main requirement being that each ECI must be 'prepared and managed by a group of at least seven natural persons' (Article 5(1), though Article 5(7) indicates that a legal entity may be created in accordance with the national law of a Member State specifically for the purpose of managing an ECI). These persons must 'be citizens of the Union of the age to be entitled to vote in elections to the European Parliament' and reside in at least seven different Member States (Article 5(2)). Article 6 outlines the procedures and conditions for registration of an ECI by the Commission, only after which statements of support may be collected (Article 6(1)).[124] Article 6(3) addresses when registration can be refused: for example, where all parts of the ECI 'manifestly [fall] outside the framework of the Commission's powers to submit a proposal for a legal act of the Union for the purpose of implementing the Treaties', or the ECI is 'manifestly abusive, frivolous or vexatious' or 'manifestly contrary to the values of the Union as set out in Article 2 TEU and rights enshrined in the Charter'. Article 6(7) imposes an obligation on the Commission to provide reasons when it refuses to register an ECI.[125] Article 6(4) outlines opportunities for partial registration where aspects of the ECI do *not* manifestly fall outside the scope of the Commission's powers to propose a legal act;

---

[121] <https://europa.eu/citizens-initiative-forum/> (accessed 29 May 2023).

[122] The public website can be accessed at https://europa.eu/citizens-initiative/home_en (accessed 29 May 2023); the steps required for registering an initiative are outlined at <https://europa.eu/citizens-initiative/how-it-works_en> (accessed 29 May 2023).

[123] Annex II lists the 'required information for registering an initiative' ie title, objectives, provisions of the Treaties considered relevant by the organisers for the proposed action, required information about and contact details for seven members of the group of organisers residing in seven different Member States (with relevant supporting documentary evidence), names of the other members of the group of organisers, documents pertaining to Article 5(7) of the Regulation where relevant, and all sources of funding and support at the time of the registration. Additionally, it is optional to provide an annex addressing: the subject, objectives, and background to the initiative; additional information on the subject, objectives, and background to the initiative; and a draft legal act.

[124] In *One of Us and Others*, the General Court noted that 'the objective of the registration procedure is to prevent organisers from wasting time on an ECI that, from the outset, cannot lead to the desired outcome' (Case T-561/14 *One of Us and Others*, EU:T:2018:210, para 117).

[125] For an example of the Commission failing to do so (by confining its discussion of legal basis to just one Treaty provision), see Case T-789/19 *Moerenhout v Commission*, EU:T:2021:260, esp para 34 ('even though it is implicit in the wording of the contested decision that the Commission considered that the other provisions relied on by the applicants in their proposed ECI ... could not constitute an appropriate legal basis for the measure envisaged by the proposed ECI, the Commission did not further explain its reasoning in that regard'). See further, Section 2.2.1.2.

and for an iterative process permitting amendment of the ECI by the group of organisers in situations where the Commission refuses to register the original initiative.[126]

Articles 8–14 of the Regulation establish the procedure for collecting statements of support.[127] Article 8 provides the signature collection timeframe: this must be done 'within a period not exceeding 12 months from a date chosen by the group of organisers', a date that must itself be no later than six months from the registration of the ECI (Article 8(1)). Article 9 outlines the procedure for collecting signatures, which may be signed online or in paper form. Someone may only sign a statement of support for an ECI once (Article 9(6)). According to Article 9(3), they will be required to provide only the personal data outlined in Annex III, which also includes a template statement of support. Article 10 requires the Commission to set up a (free of charge at point of use) central online collection system, to which statements collected in paper form can also be uploaded.[128] Article 12 articulates an authentication process for the verification and certification of statements, assigning responsibility to each Member State for statements signed by its nationals (Article 12(1)).

Article 13 confirms the mechanism for submission of the ECI to the Commission and Article 14 stipulates a process for notification of valid ECIs received. Article 14(2) ensures that '[w]ithin three months of the submission of the initiative, the group of organisers shall be given the opportunity to present the initiative at a public hearing held by the European Parliament'. Article 15 then establishes the procedure for examination of an ECI submitted to the Commission, including relevant time limits:

Article 15

1. Within one month of the submission of the initiative in accordance with Article 13, the Commission shall receive the group of organisers at an appropriate level to allow it to explain in detail the objectives of the initiative.

2. Within six months of the publication of the initiative in accordance with Article 14(1), and after the public hearing referred to in Article 14(2), the Commission shall set out in a communication its legal and political conclusions on the initiative, the action it intends to take, if any, and its reasons for taking or not taking action.[129]

   Where the Commission intends to take action in response to the initiative, including, where appropriate, the adoption of one or more proposals for a legal act of the Union, the communication shall also set out the envisaged timeline for these actions.

   The communication shall be notified to the group of organisers as well as to the European Parliament, the Council, the European Economic and Social Committee and the Committee of the Regions and shall be made public.

---

[126] These mechanisms, new to the 2019 Regulation, connect to Case T-646/13 *Minority SafePack*, EU:T:2017:59, returned to in Section 2.2.1.2.

[127] Investigating the 'drivers' of ECI engagement, see A Kandyla and S Gherghina, 'What triggers the intention to use the European Citizens' Initiative: the role of benefits, values and efficacy' (2018) 56 Journal of Common Market Studies 1223.

[128] Article 11 ensures that an ECI group of organisers may still opt to use an individual online collection system and establishes various requirements and safeguards for such systems including 'adequate security and technical features' (Article 11(4)).

[129] In *One of Us and Others*, addressing the same commitment expressed previously in Article 10(1)(c) of Regulation 211/2011, the General Court confirmed that 'neither the wording of Article 11(4) TEU nor the Treaty system ... supports the ... argument that the Commission is required to take the specific action proposed by the ECI' (Case T-561/14 *One of Us and Others*, EU:T:2018:210, para 122).

3. The Commission and the group of organisers shall inform the signatories on the response to the initiative in accordance with Article 18(2) and (3).

The Commission shall provide, in the register and on the public website on the European citizens' initiative, up-to-date information on the implementation of the actions set out in the communication adopted in response to the initiative.

New to the 2019 Regulation, the European Parliament is required, under Article 16, to assess measures taken by the Commission after the communication issued in accordance with Article 15(2). Nevertheless, the Commission enjoys 'broad discretion' in the context of examining actions proposed by ECIs: as affirmed by the General Court, the objective of the ECI is 'to invite the Commission, within the framework of its powers, to submit a proposal for an act … Allowing the Commission broad discretion in exercising its powers of legislative initiative does not undermine that objective'.[130]

The 'other provisions' of the Regulation address transparency (Article 17, with respect to both sources of funding and support from organisations that is not 'economically quantifiable' (Article 17(1)); communication (Article 18, establishing, in particular, a Commission responsibility to 'raise public awareness about the existence, objectives and functioning of the European citizens' initiative through communication activities and information campaigns, thereby contributing to promoting the active participation of citizens in the political life of the Union' (Article 18(1)); protection of personal data (Article 19, to ensure compliance with relevant EU law); and designation of competent authorities (Article 20). Finally, Article 25 requires that '[t]he Commission shall periodically review the functioning of the European citizens' initiative and present a report to the European Parliament and the Council on the application of this Regulation no later than 1 January 2024, and every four years thereafter', with specific reference to reporting on the minimum age to support ECIs across the Member States.

2.2.1.2 An emerging jurisprudence

A steady stream of case law on Commission responses to ECIs has already emerged, fleshing out the procedures established by the Regulation and, unusually for EU citizenship law, evolving the wider principles more through direct actions before the General Court (since decisions refusing to register ECIs are addressed to the organisers of an ECI and therefore meet the admissibility criteria or standing requirements for judicial review under Article 263 TFEU).[131] In *One of Us*, the General Court held that the communication the Commission is obliged to issue following its examination of a registered ECI, in accordance with Article 15 of Regulation 2019/788, 'produces binding legal effects such as to affect the interests of the applicants by bringing about a distinct change in their legal position' and is therefore a legal act for the purposes of judicial review under Article 263 TFEU.[132] In that case, the subject matter of the 'Uno di Noi' ECI concerned 'the juridical protection of the dignity, the right to life and of the integrity of every human being from conception in the areas of EU competence in which such protection is of particular importance' and was premised on the idea that, in order to 'ensure consistency in areas of its competence where the life of the human

---

[130] ibid para 124; this judgment is returned to in Section 2.2.1.2.

[131] The fourth paragraph of Article 263 TFEU provides that '[a]ny natural or legal person may, under the conditions laid down in the first and second paragraphs, institute proceedings against an act addressed to that person or which is of direct and individual concern to them, and against a regulatory act which is of direct concern to them and does not entail implementing measures'.

[132] *One of Us and Others*, para 77; it is not, in other words, an 'interpretative' communication' (para 83). But see also, Case C-261/13 P *Schönberger*, EU:C:2014:2423 (returned to in Section 2.2.2).

embryo is at stake, the [European Union] should establish a ban and end the financing of activities which presuppose the destruction of human embryos, in particular in the areas of research, development aid and public health'.[133] The ECI was successfully registered but the Commission then communicated that it was not taking specific action in the areas addressed by the ECI.[134] Distinguishing the mechanism for petitioning the European Parliament, returned to in Section 2.2.2, the General Court emphasised that:

> [T]he citizens' right, derived from Article 11(4) TEU, is intended *to reinforce citizenship of the Union* and to enhance the democratic functioning of the European Union … the ultimate objective being to encourage participation by citizens in democratic life and *to make the Union more accessible* (see recital 2 of Regulation No 211/2011). The non-submission of the Commission's refusal to submit to the EU legislature a proposal for a legal act, formulated in the communication provided for in Article 10(1)(c) of Regulation No 211/2011, to judicial review would compromise the realisation of that objective, in so far as the arbitrary risk on the part of the Commission *would deter all recourse to the ECI mechanism*, regard being had also to the stringent procedures and conditions to which that mechanism is subject.[135]

However, regarding the 'depth of the judicial review' to be applied, since the Commission enjoys broad discretion in exercising its powers of legislative initiative and the communication issued under Article 15 of the Regulation 'contains the final decision of the Commission not to submit a proposal for a legal act to the EU legislature', such communications 'must undergo limited review by the Court, aimed at verifying, in addition to the adequacy of its statement of reasons, the existence, *inter alia*, of manifest errors of assessment vitiating that decision'.[136] This understanding of ECI review was upheld on appeal. The Court of Justice found that 'the ECI is intended to confer on Union citizens a right comparable to that held, pursuant to Articles 225 and 241 TFEU respectively, by the Parliament and the Council, to request the Commission to submit any appropriate proposal for the purpose of implementing the Treaties'.[137] However, 'the near-monopoly of legislative initiative conferred by the Treaties on the Commission is not affected by the right to an ECI provided for in Article 11(4) TEU'.[138] Thus, even where an ECI is valid and successful in both procedural and substantive terms, whether or not legislative proposals are progressed remains within the discretion of the Commission.[139]

Two further questions have arisen in ECI case law to date: the nature and extent of the duty to give reasons when the Commission refuses to register an ECI, and the nature and extent of the obligation placed on the Commission by Article 6(3) of the Regulation to determine

---

[133] *One of Us and Others*, paras 2–3; drawing from the description of the ECI in the online register. The proposed legal acts (and potentially relevant provisions of the Treaties) addressed in the ECI are outlined in paras 4–8.

[134] COM(2014) 355 final; for an overview of the Commission's reasoning, see the appeal proceedings ie Case C-418/18 P *Puppinck*, EU:C:2019:1113, paras 19–27.

[135] *One of Us and Others*, para 93 (emphasis added).

[136] ibid paras 168, 169–170.

[137] *Puppinck*, para 61; the Court continued that 'the Commission remains free not to submit a proposal provided that it informs the institution concerned of the reasons. Consequently, an ECI submitted on the basis of Article 11(4) TEU and Regulation [2019/788] can likewise not affect that power'. Confirming the General Court's reasoning on limited judicial review, see esp paras 89 and 95.

[138] *Puppinck*, para 63; confirming *One of Us and Others*, para 111. See further, AG Bobek in *Puppinck*, EU:C:2019:640, paras 46–51 of the Opinion.

[139] Anticipating this outcome, see Dougan (n 119) esp at 1837–1843. Accepting the absence of *legal* obligation to progress legislative proposals but offering broader reflections on why the Commission might consider doing so in principle, see N Vogiatzis, 'The Commission's "communication" on a successful European citizens'

whether a proposed ECI falls manifestly outside the framework of its powers. These questions reflect the fact that 'in accordance with well-established case-law, it is necessary to distinguish *the obligation to state reasons as an essential procedural requirement*, which may be raised in a plea that inadequate or even no reasons are stated for a decision, from *review of the merits of the reasons stated*, which falls within the review of the act's *substantive legality* and requires the court to determine whether the grounds on which the act is founded are vitiated by an error'.[140]

Considering, first, the duty to give reasons when the Commission refuses registration, the applicant in *Anagnostakis* created an ECI ('One million signatures for a Europe of solidarity') with the objective of achieving 'the establishment in EU legislation of the principle of the state of necessity, in accordance with which the refusal of a Member State to repay sovereign debt is justifiable where its financial and political existence would be threatened by the repayment of that debt' and referring to '"economic and monetary policy (Articles 119 [TFEU] to 144 TFEU)" as the legal basis of its adoption'.[141] The Commission declined to register the ECI on the grounds that it manifestly fell outside the powers of the Commission—grounds found now in Article 6(3) of Regulation 2019/788 but based, at the time, on Article 4(2) of Regulation 211/2011. The General Court reiterated the two key purposes of the obligation to state reasons under Article 296 TFEU: first, 'to provide the person concerned with sufficient information to make it possible to determine whether the decision is well founded or whether it is vitiated by an error which may make it possible for its validity to be contested', and second, to enable judicial review.[142] It then held that Article 4(3) of the Regulation, 'which provides that the Commission is to inform the organisers of the reasons for any refusal to register, gives specific expression to that duty to state reasons in so far as European citizens' initiatives are concerned'.[143] In that light, 'the refusal to register the proposed ECI is an action that may impinge upon the very effectiveness of the right of citizens to submit a citizens' initiative that is enshrined in the first paragraph of Article 24 TFEU. Consequently, such a decision must disclose clearly the grounds justifying the refusal'.[144] In this instance, the General Court considered that the Commission had explained the reasons that justified, in its view, its refusal to register the proposed ECI, and that the ECI itself 'lacked clarity and precision in so far as concerns the purported legal basis of the Commission's competence to submit a proposal for a legal act of the Union for the purpose of implementing the Treaties'.[145] Thus the General Court's reasoning established a link between the level of detail provided in the proposed ECI and expectations of the level of detail that might then be provided in the Commission's registration decision.

---

initiative before the Court of Justice' (2020) 16 European Constitutional Law Review 691 esp at 703–704 and 710–711. See also, N Vogiatzis, 'Between discretion and control: reflections on the institutional position of the Commission within the European citizens' initiative process' (2017) 23 European Law Journal 25.

[140] Case T-44/14 *Costantini*, EU:T:2016:223, para 65 (emphasis added).
[141] Case T-450/12 *Anagnostakis*, EU:T:2015:739, para 3.
[142] ibid para 21. The second paragraph of Article 296 TFEU states that '[l]egal acts shall state the reasons on which they are based and shall refer to any proposals, initiatives, recommendations, requests or opinions required by the Treaties'. The General Court also affirmed that 'the duty to state adequate reasons in decisions is an essential procedural requirement which must be distinguished from the question whether the reasoning is well founded, which is concerned with the substantive legality of the measure at issue' (para 33).
[143] *Anagnostakis*, para 23.
[144] ibid para 25.
[145] ibid paras 28–30; see further, paras 31–32. On both procedural and substantive grounds, the judgment of the General Court was subsequently upheld on appeal (Case C-589/15 P *Anagnostakis*, EU:C:2017:663; see esp paras 41–42).

The duty to provide reasons was elaborated further in *Minority SafePack*. The applicant submitted a proposed ECI to the Commission calling on the EU 'to improve the protection of persons belonging to national and linguistic minorities and strengthen cultural and linguistic diversity in the Union' and, specifically, to adopt legal measures 'to improve the protection of persons belonging to national and linguistic minorities and strengthen cultural and linguistic diversity [within its territory]', which would 'include policy actions in the areas of regional and minority languages, education and culture, regional policy, participation, equality, audiovisual and other media content, and also regional (state) support'.[146] The Commission declined to register the ECI on the grounds that it manifestly fell outside its powers. That decision was challenged on the grounds of failure to give reasons: specifically, that the applicant had proposed 11 legal acts, but the Commission decision had not specified which of the proposed acts failed to comply with the registration criteria in Regulation 211/2011 (or why). Invoking the obligation to state reasons in Article 296 TFEU, as expressed more specifically in Article 4(3) of the Regulation, the applicant argued that '[i]n the absence of reasons, the organisers cannot know which parts of the proposed ECI should demonstrate that their application is well founded and they are prevented from adapting, if need be, the proposed ECI to the position expressed by the Commission in order to submit a new proposal to it'.[147]

Referring to its judgment in *Anagnostakis*, the General Court affirmed that 'the refusal to register the proposed ECI is an action that may impinge upon the very effectiveness of the right of citizens to submit a citizens' initiative', and therefore, that 'such a decision must disclose clearly the grounds justifying the refusal'.[148] Moreover, '[a] citizen who has submitted a proposed ECI must be placed in a position to be able to understand the reasons for which it was not registered by the Commission, with the result that it is incumbent on the Commission, when it receives such a proposal, to appraise it and also to state the different reasons for any refusal to register it ... This follows from the very nature of this right which ... is *intended to reinforce citizenship of the Union and to enhance the democratic functioning of the European Union* through the participation of citizens in its democratic life'.[149] That finding reflects the objectives of Article 10(3) TEU and the Lisbon-enhanced connection between the democratic life of the Union and Union citizens, also seen in the discussion on *Delvigne* in Section 2.2.1. The General Court did not dispute the Commission's substantive conclusion as regards the proposed ECI in *Minority SafePack*, but it did find that the reasoning provided was 'manifestly inadequate'.[150] Underlining that the ECI process is an iterative one, the General Court explained that 'the contested decision manifestly does not contain sufficient elements to enable the applicant to ascertain the reasons for the refusal to

---

[146] Case T-646/13 *Minority SafePack*, EU:T:2017:59, paras 14 and 1 respectively.

[147] ibid para 10. Article 4(3) of Regulation 211/2011 provided that '[w]here it refuses to register a proposed citizens' initiative, the Commission shall inform the organisers of the reasons for such refusal and of all possible judicial and extrajudicial remedies available to them'. The possibility of partial registration—which was not provided for in Regulation 211/2011—was also raised by the applicant. This issue was not picked up by the General Court, but following the annulment of its original decision (Commission Decision 2017/652/EU on the proposed citizens' initiative entitled 'Minority SafePack — one million signatures for diversity in Europe', 2017 OJ L92/100), the Commission did enable partial registration of the ECI. As noted in Section 2.2.1.1, partial registration is now provided for in Regulation 2019/788.

[148] *Minority SafePack*, para 17; referring to *Anagnostakis*, para 25.

[149] *Minority SafePack*, para 18 (emphasis added); referring to *Anagnostakis*, para 26.

[150] *Minority SafePack*, EU:T:2017:59, para 22. In particular, 'the Commission failed to identify in any way which of the 11 proposals for legal acts manifestly did not, in its view, fall within the framework of powers under which it is entitled to submit a proposal for a legal act of the European Union and also failed to provide any reasons in support of that assessment, notwithstanding the precise suggestions provided by the organisers on the proposed type of act as well as the respective legal bases and the content of those acts' (para 27).

register the proposed ECI with regard to the various information contained in that proposal and to react accordingly, and to enable the Court to review the lawfulness of the refusal to register'.[151] The Commission decision refusing to register the ECI was therefore annulled.

The General Court has further clarified that while 'the statement of reasons for a measure is intended to disclose in a clear and unequivocal fashion the reasoning of the measure's author in order to provide its addressee with the information enabling him to determine whether it is well founded or whether it may be vitiated by a defect that justifies contesting its validity, and in order to enable the EU judicature to review its lawfulness', it is not 'necessary for the reasoning to go into all the relevant facts and points of law, but only the fundamental factors underlying the decision, since the question whether the statement of reasons for a measure meets the requirements of Article 296 TFEU depends on the nature of the measure at issue and the context in which it has been adopted'.[152] In *Moerenhout*, the General Court recalled, in a general sense, that while Union institutions 'are not obliged, in the statement of reasons for decisions they adopt, to take a position on all the arguments relied on before them in the course of an administrative procedure, it nonetheless remains the case that they are required to set out the facts and the legal considerations having *decisive importance* in the context of the decision'.[153] Another relevant consideration is that '[f]ailing any complete statement of reasons, the possible introduction of a new proposed ECI, taking into account the Commission's objections on the admissibility of the proposal, would be seriously compromised, as would also be the achievement of the objectives, referred to in recital 2 of Regulation No 211/2011, of encouraging participation by citizens in democratic life and of making the European Union more accessible'.[154] The General Court has also underlined that 'fulfilment of the obligation to state reasons and other formal and procedural constraints to which it makes the adoption of the act in question subject *is of even more fundamental importance where the institutions of the European Union have a broad discretion*. Only in this way can the EU judicature verify whether the factual and legal elements upon which the exercise of the discretion depends were present'.[155]

Turning to the second main theme in ECI case law to date, Article 6(3)(b) of the Regulation requires the Commission to register a proposed ECI where 'none of the parts of the initiative manifestly falls outside the framework of the Commission's powers to submit a proposal for a legal act of the Union for the purpose of implementing the Treaties'.[156] The substantive reasoning of the Commission on this question is subject to judicial review. In *Izsák and Dabis*, the approach taken by the General Court was not upheld on appeal. According to the Court of Justice, the General Court, in considering whether specific provisions of the TFEU could serve as a legal basis for the proposed legal act, 'treated that question ... essentially as a matter of assessing the facts and evidence, laying the burden of proof in this respect on the appellants'.[157] However, 'the question whether the measure proposed in the context of an ECI falls within the framework of the Commission's powers to submit a proposal for a legal act of the European Union ... is *prima facie* not a question of fact or of the assessment of evidence subject as such to the rules on the burden of proof, but essentially *a question of the*

---

[151] ibid para 33.
[152] Case T-44/14 *Costantini*, EU:T:2016/223, paras 75–76.
[153] Case T-789/19 *Moerenhout v Commission*, EU:T:2021:260, para 30 (emphasis added).
[154] ibid para 48.
[155] *One of Us and Others*, para 145 (emphasis added).
[156] See previously, Article 4(2)(b) of Regulation 211/2011.
[157] Case C-420/16 P *Izsák and Dabis*, EU:C:2019:177, para 57; referring to the judgment of the General Court in Case T-529/13 *Izsák and Dabis*, EU:T:2016:282, paras 81, 85, and 87.

interpretation and application of the relevant provisions of the Treaties.[158] In that light, 'where the Commission receives an application for registration of a proposed ECI, it is not for it to ascertain, at that stage, that proof has been provided of all the factual elements relied on, or that the reasoning behind the proposed ECI and the proposed measures is adequate'; rather, '[i]t must confine itself to examining, for the purpose of assessing whether the condition of registration in Article 4(2)(b) of Regulation No 211/2011 is satisfied, whether from an objective point of view such measures envisaged in the abstract could be adopted on the basis of the Treaties'.[159]

Two further points have emerged from case law considering the nature of the obligation in Article 6(3)(b). First, in Section 2.2.1.1, a distinction between information that is *required* and information that is *optional* was noted, following the guidance provided in Annex II to the Regulation. In *Izsák and Dabis*, the General Court confirmed that the right under Annex II 'to provide additional information, and even a draft legal act of the European Union, has as a corollary an obligation for the Commission to consider that information as any other information provided pursuant to that annex, in accordance with the principle of sound administration, including the duty of the competent institution to examine carefully and impartially all the relevant aspects of the individual case'.[160] In that case, the additional information provided worked *against* registration of the ECI, but the General Court underlined that the applicants 'cannot claim that the measures ... outlined in the contested decision were put forward in the additional information as mere examples of draft measures potentially capable of being proposed by the Commission'—in other words, the Commission was not just obliged but 'entitled' to examine and take the additional information into account.[161]

Second, in *Effler*, assessing the proposed ECI 'Stop TTIP', the aim of which was to cease negotiations for the EU–US Transatlantic Trade and Investment Partnership agreement and prevent the conclusion of the EU-Canada Comprehensive Economic and Trade Agreement (CETA), the Commission suggested that an ECI aimed at preventing the adoption of a legal act did not come within the scope of application of what is now Article 1 of Regulation 2019/788—that is, 'to submit any appropriate proposal on matters where citizens of the Union consider that a legal act of the Union is required for the purpose of implementing the Treaties'— and therefore fell manifestly outside its powers. Disagreeing, the General Court held that, for the purposes of registering an ECI, 'the concept of a legal act ... cannot, in the absence of any indication to the contrary, be understood ... as being limited only to definitive European Union legal acts which produce legal effects *vis-à-vis* third parties'.[162] Specifically, '[n]either the wording of the provisions at issue nor the objectives pursued by them justify in particular that a decision authorising the opening of negotiations with a view to concluding an international agreement, such as in this case the TTIP and the CETA, taken under Article 207(3) and (4) TFEU and Article 218 TFEU and which clearly constitute a decision for the purposes of the fourth subparagraph of Article 288 TFEU ... be excluded from the concept of a legal

---

[158] Case C-420/16 P *Izsák and Dabis*, para 61 (emphasis added).
[159] ibid para 62.
[160] Case T-529/13 *Izsák and Dabis*, para 49; confirmed in Case C-420/16 P *Izsák and Dabis*, para 51.
[161] Case T-529/13 *Izsák and Dabis*, paras 53–54. In para 55, the General Court confirmed expressly that that conclusion 'is not called into question by the parties' line of argumentation relating to whether or not taking into account the additional information in the contested decision was, in the present case, in the applicants' interests', observing in para 56 that it is for the organisers of an ECI to consider 'whether it is in their interest' to provide the additional information specified in Annex II.
[162] Case T-754/14 *Effler*, EU:T:2017:323, para 35.

act for the purpose of an ECI'.¹⁶³ Significantly, the 'provisions at issue' included Article 11(4) TEU—not just the applicable provisions of the Regulation.¹⁶⁴

The General Court rooted its analysis in constitutional terrain by considering that 'the principle of democracy, which ... is one of the fundamental values of the European Union, as is the objective specifically pursued by the ECI mechanism, which consists in improving the democratic functioning of the European Union by granting every citizen a general right to participate in democratic life ... requires an interpretation of the concept of legal act which covers legal acts such as a decision to open negotiations with a view to concluding an international agreement, which manifestly seeks to modify the legal order of the European Union'.¹⁶⁵ Supporting an argument put forward by the applicants, it agreed that 'a decision to withdraw authorisation to open negotiations with a view to concluding an international agreement, in so far as it brings those negotiations to a close, cannot be classified as a preparatory act, but is, instead, definitive'.¹⁶⁶ Thus, 'the objective of participation in the democratic life of the European Union pursued by the ECI mechanism manifestly includes the power to request an amendment of legal acts in force or their annulment, in whole or in part'.¹⁶⁷

Even after legislative revision and judicial clarification of ECI procedures, the mechanism will not, on its own, fundamentally transform the structures or the shortcomings of EU governance.¹⁶⁸ Can it nevertheless 'increase the democratic quality of life within a Union which faces long-term challenges of accountability and legitimacy'?¹⁶⁹ Whether the complex procedural requirements, even after review and reform, unduly inhibit *activating* political engagement with Union policymaking—in the sense that the ECI is more likely to engage already active and organised civic society—is a fair point of criticism, though sustaining and enhancing political engagement poses acute challenges at national level too. Taking its different elements and qualities together, Advocate General Bobek offered a passionate defence of the ECI, arguing that:

> [T]he ECI is much more than a mere symbolic nod toward participative democracy. It constitutes an institutional vehicle to allow for the emergence of policy issues of interest to a group of citizens. It helps crystallise those issues as matters of European interest shared between different Member States. It gives visibility to matters of concern to citizens, which may not already be on the agenda of the institutions or even on the agenda of the political groups represented in the European Parliament. It allows direct access to the institution that, in the particular *sui generis* EU institutional system, holds the power of legislative initiative. Moreover, it obliges that institution — the Commission — to seriously consider

---

¹⁶³ ibid para 36.
¹⁶⁴ ibid para 35.
¹⁶⁵ ibid para 37; referring to the preamble to the TEU, Article 2 TEU, and the preamble to the Charter of Fundamental Rights. Similarly, as noted above, the Court of Justice observed in *Puppinck* that 'as stated in Article 10(1) TEU, the functioning of the Union is to be based on representative democracy, which gives concrete expression to democracy as a value. Democracy is, under Article 2 TEU, one of the values on which the Union is founded' (Case C-418/18 P *Puppinck*, EU:C:2019:1113, para 64).
¹⁶⁶ *Effler*, para 39.
¹⁶⁷ ibid para 42. The General Court reconciled its findings with respect to ongoing legislative procedures and the principle of institutional balance (paras 45–48). For AG Bobek, '[e]nhancing or encouraging participation within the existing democratic structures is not the same as bypassing or replacing those structures' (AG Bobek in *Puppinck*, EU:C:2019:640, para 71 of the Opinion).
¹⁶⁸ Considering these questions in their wider democratic context, see eg E Longo, 'The European citizens' initiative: too much democracy for EU polity?' (2019) 20 German Law Journal 181.
¹⁶⁹ Dougan (n 119) 1847.

and engage in an assessment of the proposals of a successful ECI, and to do so publicly and subject to public scrutiny. It ensures that the content of the ECI is considered and debated publicly at the democratically elected European Parliament. All these reasons highlight that, despite the fact that the ECI system as currently conceived in primary and secondary law does not lead to an obligation on the Commission to present a proposal, it has an indubitable added value as a *sui generis* agenda-setting mechanism.[170]

In that light, the ECI as an 'agenda-setting mechanism' enables Union citizens who reside in their home States to connect with Union citizens across the territory of the Union as well as to the Union institutions and law-making processes, manifesting a transnational deliberative space. The ECI also underlines Union citizenship as *additional to* national citizenship: it is about forging a complementary connection beyond any one State, not replacing nationality—or national political community.

However, at the time of writing, only six ECIs had been successful (from 90 registered) in the sense of meeting the conditions that required them to be answered by the Commission. Legislative measures were either adopted or committed to for three of these, suggesting a decent chance of *substantive* success where undeniably challenging *procedural* requirements can be met.[171] Where we can see continuing tensions goes to the heart of something not always sufficiently appreciated about the European Union: that its competences are conferred, and circumscribed by the Treaties.[172] The Commission can only, in other words, do so much; even with the best of policy ideas.

2.2.2 Petitioning the European Parliament

The right to petition the European Parliament is conferred on '[e]very citizen of the Union' by Articles 20(2)(d) TFEU and 24 TFEU. In Article 24, the right to petition is explicitly linked to Article 227 TFEU, which opens the personal scope of the right to 'any natural or legal person residing or having its registered office in a Member State'—whether 'individually or in association with other citizens or persons'—and requires that a petition should

---

[170] AG Bobek in *Puppinck*, para 80 of the Opinion. In para 84, he notes that '[a]lthough stressing in a positive light some of its novel features, this Opinion certainly does not suggest that the ECI is a perfect mechanism that provides a miraculous solution to the alleged or real shortcomings of the European Union in terms of democratic legitimacy, including the reduction of the alleged distance between citizens and the EU institutions' and also observes that the reforms to Regulation 211/2011 now in force responded to both scholarly criticism and institutional reflections.

[171] ie 'End the Cage Age' (answered by the Commission on 30 June 2021, C(2021)4747 (legislative proposals committed to by the end of 2023); 'Minority SafePack – one million signatures for diversity in Europe' (answered by the Commission on 15 January 2021, C(2021)171); 'Ban glyphosate and protect people and the environment from toxic pesticides' (answered by Communication from the Commission on 12 December 2017, C(2017) 8414 final, Regulation 2019/1381/EU on the transparency and sustainability of the EU risk assessment in the food chain, 2019 OJ L 231/1, now adopted); 'Stop vivisection' (answered by Communication from the Commission on 3 June 2015, C(2015) 3773 final); 'One of us' (answered by Communication from the Commission on 28 May 2014, COM(2014) 355 final); and 'Right2Water' (answered by Communication from the Commission on 19 March 2014, COM(2014) 177 final, Directive 2020/2184/EU on the quality of water intended for human consumption (recast), 2020 OJ L 435/1. See generally, the overview of all ECIs (both successfully registered and unsuccessful or withdrawn) at <https://europa.eu/citizens-initiative/home_en> (accessed 29 May 2023).

[172] Reflecting on these questions in terms of expectations of the ECI and institutional responses, see A Karatzia, 'The European Citizens' Initiative and the EU institutional balance: on realism and the possibilities of affecting EU lawmaking' (2017) 54 Common Market Law Review 177 esp at 197–201. See generally, J Organ, 'Decommissioning direct democracy? A critical analysis of Commission decision-making on the legal admissibility of European Citizens' Initiative proposals' (2014) 10 European Constitutional Law Review 422; A Karatzia, 'The European Citizens' Initiative in practice: legal admissibility concerns' (2015) 40 European Law Review 509; and N Athanasiadou, 'The European Citizens' Initiative: lost in admissibility?' (2019) 26 Maastricht Journal of European and Comparative Law 251.

concern 'a matter which comes within the Union's fields of activity and which affects him, her or it directly'. Article 44 CFR provides similarly that '[a]ny citizen of the Union and any natural or legal person residing or having its registered office in a Member State has the right to petition the European Parliament'.

Thus, while the right to petition is not exclusively a 'Union citizenship right', petitions do provide a useful insight into rules and practices that affect how Union citizenship is experienced in practice. In that light, relevant petitions tend to relate mainly to either freedom of movement and residence in a general sense or specifically to the right to vote in another Member State (though protection of the environment is the main subject of petitions received overall).[173] Additionally, the European Parliament's Committee on Petitions (PETI) progresses significant work on citizenship-related questions through public hearings,[174] written reports,[175] and commissioned studies.[176] An overview of the activities of PETI over the 2014–2019 parliamentary term suggested that petitions 'allow EU institutions to detect incorrect, or lack of, transposition or implementation of EU law at Member State level, and to remedy by taking the most appropriate course of action, including by opening a dialogue with the concerned institutions or Member States, by filling in legislative or policy gaps, or by taking any other appropriate initiatives'.[177] The processes for submitting and examining petitions are governed by the Rules of Procedure of the European Parliament.[178] The basic principles are set out in Rule 226 and Rule 227 establishes the procedure for how admissible petitions are then examined, which may include a fact-finding visit in accordance with Rule 228. The PETI website provides further guidance and an online portal for the submission of petitions (which can also be submitted by post).

As noted in Section 2.2.1.2, the EU Courts have reflected on both the commonalities and differences between the ECI and petition procedures. In *Schönberger*, the Court of Justice held that 'a decision by which the Parliament considers that a petition addressed to it *does not meet the conditions laid down in Article 227 TFEU* must be amenable to judicial review, since it is liable to affect the right of petition of the person concerned' and that '[t]he same applies to a decision by which the Parliament, disregarding the very essence of the right of petition, refuses to consider, or refrains from considering, a petition addressed to it and, consequently, fails to verify whether it meets the conditions laid down in Article 227 TFEU'.[179] Nevertheless, '[a] negative decision by which the Parliament takes the view that the conditions laid down in Article 227 TFEU have not been met must provide a sufficient statement of reasons to allow the petitioner to know which of those conditions was not met in his case. [T]hat requirement is satisfied by a summary statement of reasons'.[180] For the Court, 'it is

---

[173] 'Achievements of the Committee on Petitions during the 2014–2019 parliamentary term and challenges for the future', research paper requested by PETI and commissioned, overseen and published by the Policy Department for Citizens' Rights and Constitutional Affairs, July 2019, <https://www.europarl.europa.eu/RegData/etudes/STUD/2019/621917/IPOL_STU(2019)621917_EN.pdf> (accessed 29 May 2023), 47.

[174] ibid. Public hearings convened over the term are outlined at 14–15, with topics ranging from the ECI mechanism, the scope of the Charter of Fundamental Rights, restoring citizens' confidence and trust in the European project, and protection of workers in temporary or precarious employment.

[175] ibid 32–33.

[176] eg 'Obstacles to the right of free movement and residence for EU citizens and their families: Comparative Analysis' (2016, https://www.europarl.europa.eu/RegData/etudes/STUD/2016/571375/IPOL_STU(2016)571375_EN.pdf (accessed 29 May 2023)); 'The impact of Brexit in relation to the right to petition and on the competences, responsibilities and activities of the Committee on Petitions' (2017, <https://www.europarl.europa.eu/RegData/etudes/STUD/2017/583154/IPOL_STU(2017)583154_EN.pdf> (accessed 29 May 2023)).

[177] 'Achievements of the Committee on Petitions during the 2014–2019 parliamentary term' (n 173) 5.

[178] At the time of writing ie Rules of Procedure for the 9th Parliamentary term, February 2020.

[179] Case C-261/13 P *Schönberger*, EU:C:2014:2423, para 22 (emphasis added).

[180] ibid para 23.

clear from the provisions of the TFEU and from the rules adopted by the Parliament for the organisation of the right of petition that, where the Parliament takes the view that a petition *meets the conditions laid down in Article 227 TFEU*, it has a broad discretion, of a political nature, as regards how that petition should be dealt with. It follows that a decision taken in that regard is not amenable to judicial review'.[181]

In *One of Us*, the Commission argued that the reasoning in *Schönberger* was 'transposable' to the ECI mechanism 'in so far as, like the Parliament, it had discretion as regards the action to be taken following an ECI.[182] But the General Court distinguished the ECI and petition mechanisms, underlining that 'a petition is, first, examined for the purposes of assessing its admissibility in the light of the conditions laid down in Article 227 TFEU and, next, is subject to the Parliament's discretionary power as regards the action to be taken. Between those two steps, the petition is not subject to any additional condition or procedure affecting the petitioner and his legal situation'.[183] However, a registered ECI must then meet further conditions, notably concerning the collection of statements of support, before the Commission is obliged to examine it;[184] and '[o]wing to the additional conditions incumbent on the organisers and the procedural guarantees prescribed in their favour ... it must be concluded that the Commission's refusal to submit to the EU legislature a proposal for a legal act ... has binding legal effects'.[185]

2.2.3 Applying to the European Ombudsman

Similarly to the petition mechanism outlined above, the right to apply to the European Ombudsman is both expressed as a Union citizenship right in the TFEU[186] and extended further in terms of personal scope by both the TFEU and the Charter of Fundamental Rights. Article 228(1) TFEU establishes that the European Ombudsman is 'empowered to receive complaints from any citizen of the Union or *any natural or legal person residing or having its registered office in a Member State* concerning instances of maladministration in the activities of the Union institutions, bodies, offices or agencies, with the exception of the Court of Justice of the European Union acting in its judicial role. He or she shall examine such complaints and report on them'.[187] Similarly, Article 43 CFR guarantees that '[a]ny citizen of the Union and any natural or legal person residing or having its registered office in a Member

---

[181] ibid para 24 (emphasis added).

[182] The Commission further submitted that, unlike the right of petition, the right to participate in the democratic life of the Union by way of an ECI was not a fundamental right and it would therefore be inconsistent to confer on it a degree of judicial protection 'higher' than that conferred on the right of petition' (Case T-561/14 *One of Us and Others*, EU:T:2018:210, para 91). The General Court responded that 'although the right to the ECI is not included in the Charter of Fundamental Rights, as is the case with the right of petition, which is provided for in Article 44 of that charter, the fact remains that that right is provided for under the primary law of the Union, namely in Article 11(4) TEU. It is therefore enshrined in an instrument that has the same legal value as that conferred on the Charter of Fundamental Rights' (para 99).

[183] *One of Us and Others*, para 95.

[184] ibid paras 96–97; see further, the conditions and procedural guarantees now provided for by Articles 6(4), 6(7), and 15 of Regulation 2019/788, outlined in Section 2.2.1.1.

[185] *One of Us and Others*, para 98; upheld on appeal in Case C-418/18 P *Puppinck*, EU:C:2019:1113, paras 90–92.

[186] See Articles 20(2)(d) and 24 TFEU.

[187] Article 228(1) TFEU continues: '[i]n accordance with his duties, the Ombudsman shall conduct inquiries for which he finds grounds, either on his own initiative or on the basis of complaints submitted to him direct or through a Member of the European Parliament, except where the alleged facts are or have been the subject of legal proceedings. Where the Ombudsman establishes an instance of maladministration, he shall refer the matter to the institution, body, office or agency concerned, which shall have a period of three months in which to inform him of its views. The Ombudsman shall then forward a report to the European Parliament and the institution, body, office or agency concerned. The person lodging the complaint shall be informed of the outcome of such inquiries. The Ombudsman shall submit an annual report to the European Parliament on the outcome of his inquiries'.

State has the right to refer to the Ombudsman of the Union cases of maladministration in the activities of the Community institutions or bodies, with the exception of the Court of Justice and the Court of First Instance acting in their judicial role'. The Ombudsman's work on different aspects of good administration—and notably on transparency, accountability, and ethical standards[188]—intersects in a general way with Union citizenship's concern for effective mechanisms to facilitate representative and participatory democracy. More specifically for present purposes, and as indicated in Section 2.2.1, an own-initiative inquiry into the ECI (closed in 2015) fed into the reflective process that led to reform of the original ECI framework enacted in Regulation 211/2011.

In *Lamberts*, the General Court characterised the right 'to have recourse to the Ombudsman' as 'an integral part of citizenship of the Union'.[189] It considered that 'the Treaty confers on all citizens both *the subjective right to refer* to the Ombudsman complaints concerning instances of maladministration on the part of Community institutions or bodies, apart from the Court of Justice and the Court of First Instance in the exercise of their judicial functions, and *the right to be informed of the result* of inquiries conducted in that regard by the Ombudsman under the conditions laid down by Decision 94/262 and the implementing provisions'.[190] In substance, the General Court confirmed that the Ombudsman has 'very wide discretion as regards the merits of complaints and the way in which he deals with them, and in so doing he is under no obligation as to the result to be achieved', but that 'even if review by the [Union] judicature must consequently be limited, it is possible that in very exceptional circumstances a citizen may be able to demonstrate that the Ombudsman has made a manifest error in the performance of his duties likely to cause damage to the citizen concerned' (which could, in turn, form the basis of an action for damages).[191] Again, then, we see here the recurring tension between the creation of mechanisms for citizen participation and the discretion that the EU institutions and bodies benefit from in terms of responding to that engagement.

2.3 Surrogate Home States: Diplomatic and Consular Protection in Third Countries

While rights for Union citizens in their home States based on Article 20 TFEU are premised on securing residence *within* the territory of the Union,[192] consular assistance embodies protection *beyond* it. Article 3(5) TEU asserts that, '[i]n its relations with the wider world, the Union shall uphold and promote its values and interests *and contribute to the protection*

---

[188] At the time of writing, the European Ombudsman's website outlined seven thematic areas of work; see <https://www.ombudsman.europa.eu/en/areas-of-work> (accessed 29 May 2023). See generally, CH Hofmann and J Ziller (eds), *Accountability in the EU: The Role of the European Ombudsman* (Edward Elgar Publishing 2017); and N Vogiatzis, *The European Ombudsman and Good Administration in the European Union* (Palgrave Macmillan 2018).

[189] Case T-209/00 *Lamberts*, EU:T:2002:94, para 50.

[190] ibid para 56 (emphasis added). Directive 94/262/EC on the regulations and general conditions governing the performance of the Ombudsman's duties, 1994 OJ L113/15.

[191] *Lamberts*, paras 57–58; confirmed on appeal in Case C-234/02 P *Lamberts*, EU:C:2004:174, para 52: 'not only does the Ombudsman enjoy very wide discretion as regards the merits of complaints and the way in which he deals with them, and that in so doing he is under no obligation as to the result to be achieved, but also that, even if review by the Community judicature must consequently be limited, it is possible that in very exceptional circumstances a citizen may be able to demonstrate that the Ombudsman has committed a sufficiently serious breach of Community law in the performance of his duties likely to cause damage to the citizen concerned'.

[192] See further, Section 3.

of its citizens'. But the Union needs to engage its Member States as actors to realise these objectives beyond its own borders.[193]

An EU right to consular assistance in third countries materialised through the significant evolution of the Union's foreign policy.[194] Article 20(2)(c) TFEU states that Union citizens have 'the right to enjoy, in the territory of a third country in which the Member State of which they are nationals is not represented, the protection of the diplomatic and consular authorities of any Member State on the same conditions as the nationals of that State'. Article 48 CFR affirms that '[e]very citizen of the Union shall, in the territory of a third country in which the Member State of which he or she is a national is not represented, be entitled to protection by the diplomatic or consular authorities of any Member State, on the same conditions as the nationals of that Member State'. Article 23 TFEU restates that right and—only since the Lisbon Treaty—provides a legal basis for the Commission to propose implementing legislation under the special legislative procedure:[195]

Article 23 TFEU

Every citizen of the Union shall, in the territory of a third country in which the Member State of which he is a national is not represented, be entitled to protection by the diplomatic or consular authorities of any Member State, on the same conditions as the nationals of that State. Member States shall adopt the necessary provisions and start the international negotiations required to secure this protection.

The Council, acting in accordance with a special legislative procedure and after consulting the European Parliament, may adopt directives establishing the coordination and cooperation measures necessary to facilitate such protection.

Article 23 TFEU therefore places three limitations around what can be achieved: the extent of the assistance provided is based on equal treatment with nationals of the relevant State, facilitative measures should focus on 'coordination and cooperation', and 'international negotiations' are 'required to secure this protection'.[196]

---

[193] While EU law binds only the Member States and not third countries, it has been argued that actions taken by a Member State on behalf of the nationals of another Member State should be recognised by third countries on the same premise as recognition of state assistance under international law. Vigni notes that '[i]f it can be demonstrated that third countries permit Member States to act on behalf of EU citizens who are not nationals of the State acting because these third countries consider EU citizenship to have effect in international law, the EU would be the first international organisation to be deemed accountable for representing individuals at the international level' (P Vigni, 'The right of EU citizens to diplomatic and consular protection: a step towards recognition of EU citizenship in third countries?' in Kochenov (ed), n 80, 585). However, on the challenges of aligning the EU system for consular assistance with relevant principles of international law and practice, see M Moraru, 'An analysis of the Consular Protection Directive: are EU citizens now better protected in the world?' (2019) 56 Common Market Law Review 417 at 453–57. Distinguishing the right to assistance from the diplomatic or consular authorities of a Member State from the concept of diplomatic protection as recognised under international law, compare Vigni (588–91) and Moraru (435–36).

[194] See eg A Vermeer-Künzli, 'Where the law becomes irrelevant: consular assistance and the European Union' (2011) 60 International and Comparative Law Quarterly 965.

[195] Moraru argues that the Lisbon Treaty thus 'integrated the external dimension of EU citizenship within the constitutional system of EU citizenship, subjecting it to the same provisions as the internal citizenship rights. Notably, all EU citizenship rights, both internal and external, were unitarily presented as core rights associated to the fundamental status of EU citizenship, embedded within the EU constitutional system' (Moraru (n 193), 424–25).

[196] In this context, note the ongoing role of the Council's Working Party on Consular Affairs (COCON), in coordination with the Member States and the European External Action Service (EEAS), returned to below.

Council Decision 95/553 was the first measure adopted with reference to what is now expressed in Article 20(2)(c) TFEU.[197] The Decision's preamble stated that the Council was '[r]esolved to continue building a Union ever closer to its citizens' while acknowledging that Union citizenship is 'different from, and in no way a substitute for, the concept of national citizenship'. Political throat duly cleared, the preamble then recognised that common protection arrangements would strengthen both 'the identity of the Union as perceived in third countries' and 'the idea of European solidarity as perceived by the citizens in question'. In brief, the Decision established a Union citizen's entitlement to consular protection in a third country 'if, in the place in which he is located, his own Member State or another State representing it on a permanent basis has no accessible permanent representation, or accessible Honorary Consul competent for such matters' (Article 1). Such protection is subject to proof of nationality upon production of a passport or identity card (Article 2, with other means of verification allowed in cases of the theft or loss of these documents), and at the level of comparable protection as would be offered to nationals of the Member State represented (Article 3—but noting the proviso in Article 6(1) that 'except in cases of extreme urgency, no financial advance or help may be given or expenditure incurred on behalf of a citizen of the Union without the permission of the competent authorities of the Member State of which that citizen is a national, given either by the Foreign Ministry or by the nearest diplomatic mission'). Article 5(1) made provision for assistance in five situations (death, serious accident or serious illness, arrest or detention, for victims of violent crime, and for the relief and repatriation of distressed citizens) while Article 5(2) ensured that, '[i]n addition, Member States' diplomatic representations or consular agents serving in a non-member State may, in so far as it is within their powers, also come to the assistance of any citizen of the Union who so requests in other circumstances'. Article 4 empowered diplomatic and consular representations to 'agree on practical arrangements for the effective management of applications for protection'.

Notably, Article 8 of the Decision stipulated that it would only enter into force 'when all the Member States have notified the General Secretariat of the Council that the procedures required by their legal systems for the Decision to apply have been completed'—which was not achieved until May 2002. Article 7 required a review after five years. However, it took more than two further decades for the Decision to be replaced by Directive 2015/637.[198] Preceded by a Green Paper in 2006[199] and—propelled by the Lisbon amendments—a Communication to the Parliament and the Council in 2011,[200] the Commission argued in its proposal for the

---

[197] Council Decision 95/553/EC regarding protection for citizens of the European Union by diplomatic and consular representations, 1995 OJ L314/73. The Decision was supplemented by regularly updated, non-binding 'Guidelines on consular protection of EU citizens in third countries', adopted both for general (see eg Doc. 10109/2/06) and specific (eg 'Guidelines on Consular Protection of EU Citizens in the Event of a Crisis in Third Countries', Doc. 15754/03) purposes, based on what is now Article 35 TEU ('[t]he diplomatic and consular missions of the Member States and the Union delegations in third countries and international conferences, and their representations to international organisations, shall cooperate in ensuring that decisions defining Union positions and actions adopted pursuant to this Chapter are complied with and implemented. They shall step up cooperation by exchanging information and carrying out joint assessments. They shall contribute to the implementation of the right of citizens of the Union to protection in the territory of third countries as referred to in Article 20(2)(c) [TFEU] and of the measures adopted pursuant to Article 23 of that Treaty').
[198] Council Directive 2015/637/EU on the coordination and cooperation measures to facilitate consular protection for unrepresented citizens of the Union in third countries and repealing Decision 95/553/EC, 2015 OJ L106/1. The deadline for transposition of the Directive—and therefore the date from which the Decision was replaced—was 1 May 2018.
[199] COM(2006) 712 final.
[200] 'Consular protection for EU citizens in third countries: State of play and way forward', COM(2011) 149 final; at the time, the Commission pointed out that all (then) Member States were represented in only three countries worldwide: China, Russia, and the United States.

Directive that '[t]here is no clear consensus on the content of Article 23 TFEU and about the responsibilities which this right entails. *To be effective as a right with concrete meaning, the succinct wording of the Treaty article does not suffice.* National consular laws and practices diverge as do views about the underlying concepts of consular protection for unrepresented EU citizens'.[201] Questions identified for clarification included personal scope (eg when protection is or is not 'accessible', and whether third-country national family members of Union citizens are covered or not), coordination and cooperation with the Union citizen's home State; mechanisms for local coordination, and logistical questions about assistance and financial reimbursement.[202] The Commission also acknowledged and sought to address the very different circumstances that can necessitate assistance for Union citizens in third countries, ranging from 'day-to-day situations, such as in case of serious illness or when being victim of a crime' to large-scale crises and emergencies.[203]

Directive 2015/637 now establishes the mechanisms for coordination and cooperation needed to give practical effect to Article 23 TFEU.[204] Recital 3 reflects both the polity and citizen dimensions of common protection arrangements:

> The values on which the Union is founded include solidarity, non-discrimination and respect for human rights; in its relations with the wider world the Union should uphold its values and contribute to the protection of its citizens. The fundamental right to consular protection of unrepresented citizens of the Union under the same conditions as nationals, enshrined in Article 46 of the Charter of Fundamental Rights of the European Union (the Charter), is an expression of European solidarity. It provides an external dimension to the concept of citizenship of the Union and strengthens the identity of the Union in third countries.

Recital 4 establishes that the aim of the Directive is 'to lay down the cooperation and coordination measures necessary to further facilitate consular protection for unrepresented citizens of the Union', adding that '[t]hose measures should enhance legal certainty as well as efficient cooperation and solidarity among consular authorities'. Achieving an appropriate balance between effectiveness and legal certainty for citizens, on the one hand, and respect for (and sensitivities around) national prerogatives in the provision of consular assistance, on the other, was a key challenge. Recalling the qualifications in Article 23 TFEU itself, the Commission had to consider how to design (and implement) an extra-territorial regime that intersects with—and depends on—both national law and international law, which must be structured around looser mechanisms of coordination and cooperation yet, at the same time, properly protect vulnerable Union citizens who need assistance outwith the familiar processes and practices of their home States. Consular assistance is palpably State-centric in

---

[201] Proposal for a Council Directive on consular protection for citizens of the Union abroad, COM(2011) 881 final, para 1.2 (emphasis added). Assessing the nature and extent of the right conferred by Article 23 TFEU directly, before the adoption of the Directive, see Vermeer-Künzli (n 194) 969–70.

[202] Proposal for a Council Directive (ibid) para 1.2.

[203] ibid para 1.1. On crisis situations and the 1995 Decision, see F Forni, 'The consular protection of EU citizens during emergencies in third countries' in A de Guttry et al (eds) *International Disaster Response Law* (TMC Asser Press 2012) 155.

[204] Moraru suggests that 'in spite of the final version of the Directive being watered down (as compared to the Commission and European Parliament's proposals), it is nonetheless a remarkable legal achievement' (n 193, 420; noting eg the 'clearer rules, efficiency and rule of law safeguards which could remedy the key shortcomings of the previous implementation regime').

its delivery, yet it is impossible to conceive or coordinate a framework for other-State assistance at the scale required without an underpinning Union impetus.[205]

Article 4 of the Directive establishes that an 'unrepresented citizen' means 'every citizen holding the nationality of a Member State which is not represented in a third country'. Article 6 elaborates that 'a Member State is not represented in a third country if it has no embassy or consulate established there on a permanent basis, or if it has no embassy, consulate or honorary consul there which is effectively in a position to provide consular protection in a given case'. In such circumstances, Article 2(1) requires that 'Member States' embassies or consulates shall provide consular protection to unrepresented citizens on the same conditions as to their own nationals'. Clarifying a question left open by the 1995 Decision, Article 2(2) of the Directive signals that 'Member States may decide that this Directive shall apply to the consular protection provided by honorary consuls in compliance with Article 23 TFEU' and 'shall ensure that unrepresented citizens are duly informed about such decisions and the extent to which honorary consuls are competent to provide protection in a given case'.

In another advance from the 1995 Decision, Article 5 of the Directive confirms that '[c]onsular protection shall be provided to family members, who are not themselves citizens of the Union, accompanying unrepresented citizens in a third country, to the same extent and on the same conditions as it would be provided to the family members of the citizens of the assisting Member State, who are not themselves citizens of the Union, in accordance with its national law or practice'. While the reach of this provision as a legal obligation might be limited in practice, it is essentially framed as a moral obligation: referring to Article 7 CFR, recital 9 states that the Directive 'does not preclude that during the consultations which should take place before assistance is provided, the assisting Member State and the unrepresented citizen's Member State of nationality, whenever appropriate, agree on the possibility to extend assistance to third-country family members of the unrepresented Union citizen *beyond what is required by the law of the assisting Member State or what is dictated by its practice*, taking into account as much as possible requests from the unrepresented citizen's Member State of nationality, and in so far as what is agreed does not fall short of what is required by Union law'.

While citizens and protected family members are 'entitled to seek protection from the embassy or consulate of any Member State' (Article 7(1)), Member States may conclude both representation and other practical arrangements, which must be notified to the Commission and the European External Action Service (EEAS) (Article 7(2)).[206] Such arrangements may result in the redirection of assistance requests from unrepresented citizens 'unless consular protection would thereby be compromised, in particular if the urgency of the matter requires immediate action by the requested embassy or consulate' (Article 7(3)). Articles 10–13 of the Directive make provision for coordination and cooperation among the consular and diplomatic authorities of the Member States and, where relevant, Union delegations and the EEAS. However, the key actor in assisting unrepresented citizens during crises is the

---

[205] On the challenges of communicating both 'the complexity of the consular protection rules and specific practices of local cooperation in the third states' and that 'it is actually the condition of EU citizen that gives the right to assistance and thereby it is the EU's achievement that it is provided to EU citizens throughout the world', see SB Rasmussen, 'Constructing the European demos through external action? The case of consular assistance to EU citizens' in B Pérez de las Heras (ed), *Democratic Legitimacy in the European Union and Global Governance* (Palgrave Macmillan 2017) 259 at 279.

[206] The EEAS supports coordination of consular protection for unrepresented citizens on the ground through its Consular Crisis Management Division, which is part of the EEAS Crisis Response Department; see further, <https://www.eeas.europa.eu/eeas/crisis-management-and-response_en> (accessed 29 May 2023).

'Lead State' (Articles 13(3)-(4)).²⁰⁷ According to recital 23, '[t]he term "Lead State" used in this Directive refers to one or more Member State(s) represented in a given third country, and in charge of coordinating and leading the assistance of unrepresented citizens during crises'. Article 13 expands on how the Lead State works with Union bodies in practice:

> 3. The Lead State or the Member State(s) coordinating the assistance shall be in charge of coordinating any support provided for unrepresented citizens, with the support of the other Member States concerned, the Union delegation and the EEAS headquarters. Member States shall provide the Lead State or the Member State(s) coordinating assistance with all relevant information regarding their unrepresented citizens present in a crisis situation.
> 4. The Lead State or the Member State(s) coordinating assistance for unrepresented citizens may seek, if appropriate, support from instruments such as the crisis management structures of the EEAS and the Union Civil Protection Mechanism.

The comparably limited role of Union delegations is generally characterised as entrenching an intergovernmental rather than supranational approach to realising Article 23 TFEU.²⁰⁸

At one level, Article 8 of the Directive sustains the identification mechanisms provided for in the 1995 Decision while adding, in Article 8(3), that 'the identity and existence of the family relationship may be proven by any means' for the purposes of protection under Article 5. However, recital 13 of the Directive brings an added dimension in asserting that '[t]he fundamental status of citizenship of the Union is conferred directly by Union law and identity documents are of merely declaratory value'. Article 9 provides a non-exhaustive ('*inter alia*'²⁰⁹) list of types of assistance, offering as specific examples the five categories originally included in the 1995 Decision. Article 9 of the Directive also adds a sixth example: 'a need for emergency travel documents as provided for in Decision 96/409/CFSP'.²¹⁰ Decision 96/409 was repealed by Directive 2019/997 in order 'to establish a modernised and more secure format for the EU Emergency Travel Document ('EU ETD')'.²¹¹ It 'lays down rules on the conditions and procedure for unrepresented citizens in third countries to obtain an EU Emergency Travel Document ('EU ETD') and establishes a uniform format for such document' (Article 1). An EU ETD is issued to unrepresented Union citizens in a third country in situations where their 'passports or travel documents have been lost, stolen or destroyed, or can otherwise not be obtained within a reasonable time' (Article 3). It covers 'a single journey to the citizen's Member State of nationality or residence, as requested by the citizen, or exceptionally, to another destination' (Article 3).²¹² Finally, Articles 14–15 of Directive 2015/637 establish financial procedures for reimbursement of costs. These are based on

---

²⁰⁷ On the origins of the Lead State concept, see Vermeer-Künzli (n 194) 977–81; on the Lead State concept and Directive 2015/637, see Moraru (n 193) 444–46.
²⁰⁸ For an account of more ambitious proposals on Union delegations, see Vigni (n 193) 604–10. Notwithstanding their 'reduced formally established role', Rasmussen argues that 'the way forward for the Delegations is to take advantage of their presence to gain a real centrality in day-to-day consular practice. For this, the Delegations must be able to provide a real added value to the Member State representations, be it monetary resources, logistical capabilities, analytical capabilities or something different that international and EU law does not expressly prohibit' (n 205, 275).
²⁰⁹ Note also, recital 14: '[s]ince the protection needed always depends on the factual situation, consular protection should not be limited to the situations specifically mentioned in this Directive'.
²¹⁰ Council Decision 96/409/CFSP on the establishment of an emergency travel document, 1996 OJ L168/4.
²¹¹ Directive 2019/997/EU establishing an EU Emergency Travel Document and repealing Decision 96/409/CFSP, 2019 OJ L163/1, recital 3.
²¹² Directive 2019/997 also establishes the procedure for issuing an EU ETD (Article 4); relevant financial provisions (Article 5); the validity of an EU ETD (Article 6); circumstances in which an EU ETD may be issued on an optional basis (Article 7); a uniform format for EU ETDs (Articles 8–13); and provisions on more favourable

comparable treatment with own State nationals,[213] but with special provision in Article 14(3) for 'unusually high but essential and justified costs' pertaining to situations of arrest or detention and in Article 15 for crisis situations) and supported by template forms provided in Annexes I and II.

It is still not clear how the nature and extent of the right to consular assistance might be progressed through judicial interpretation since it has not (yet) been considered by the Court of Justice. However, in *Tjebbes*, the Court did highlight consular assistance in the context of national decisions withdrawing Member State nationality. When examining the proportionality of such decisions, one of the factors that national courts should take into account is 'the serious risk, to which the person concerned would be exposed, that his or her safety or freedom to come and go would substantially deteriorate because of the impossibility for that person to enjoy consular protection under Article 20(2)(c) TFEU in the territory of the third country in which that person resides'.[214]

3. Residence Rights for Family Members in the Union Citizen's Home State: Article 20 TEU

As introduced in Chapter 4, 'any rights conferred on third-country nationals by the Treaty provisions on Union citizenship are not autonomous rights of those nationals but rights derived from the exercise of freedom of movement by a Union citizen'.[215] Such rights are therefore typically based on Article 21 TFEU and defined more specifically, whether directly or by analogy, by the limits and conditions enacted in Directive 2004/38. They concern, in other words, a right to accompany or join a Union citizen in a host State or in the home State only after a Union citizen has exercised free movement, because 'EU law does not, *in principle*, apply to an application for family reunification of a third-country national with a member of his or her family who is a national of a Member State and has never exercised the freedom of movement'.[216]

In economic free movement law, decisions about family member residence rights where the facts concerned *only* the Member State national's home State were assigned solely to national immigration competence, beyond the reach of EU law. Two key principles underpinned that approach. The ruling in *Morson and Jhanjan* exemplifies the first principle: that situations must exhibit factors connecting them to EU law for the Treaty to apply. Having confirmed that Article 10 of Regulation 1612/68 did 'not cover the position of dependent relatives of a worker who is a national of the Member State within whose territory he is employed', the Court then examined 'whether it may be inferred from the context of the provisions and the place which they occupy in the Community legal system as a whole that they have a right of entry and residence'.[217] It held, however, that Articles 18 and 45 TFEU could be invoked 'only where the case in question comes within the area to which Community

---

treatment (Article 14), protection of personal data (Article 15), monitoring (Article 16), and evaluation (Article 17). A timetable for implementing the Directive was spread across 36 months from the date of its adoption.

[213] Outlining the differences in Member State practices that might prove problematic under this non-harmonised approach, see Moraru (n 193) 440.
[214] Case C-221/17 *Tjebbes*, EU:C:2019:189, para 46; see further, Chapter 3.
[215] Case C-40/11 *Iida*, EU:C:2012:691, para 67.
[216] Case C-836/18 *Subdelegación del Gobierno en Ciudad Real (Conjoint d'un citoyen de l'Union)*, EU:C:2020:119, para 33 (emphasis added).
[217] Joined Cases 35/82 and 36/82 *Morson and Jhanjan*, EU:C:1982:368, para 13.

law applies, which in this case is that concerned with freedom of movement of workers within the Community'.[218] On that basis, 'the Treaty provisions on freedom of movement for workers and the rules adopted to implement them cannot be applied to cases which have *no factor linking them* with any of the situations governed by Community law', which was 'undoubtedly the case with workers who have never exercise the right to freedom of movement within the Community'.[219]

The second principle reflects the idea that some circumstances proposed as connecting factors do not produce a *sufficient* connection to free movement law: that they fail to establish the necessary 'point of contact' with EU law.[220] In particular, the Court has determined that '[a] purely hypothetical prospect of employment in another Member State does not establish a sufficient connection with Community law to justify the application of Article [45 TFEU]'.[221] But locating the line between sufficient and insufficient connecting factors is not straightforward, especially under a free movement law framework where *potential* as well as *actual* restrictions can come within the scope of the Treaty. This distinction was introduced in Chapter 2. In *Gouvernement de la Communauté française and gouvernement wallon*, addressing Article 45 TFEU, Advocate General Sharpston differentiated hypothetical effects, on the one hand, and potential even if uncertain effects, on the other, arguing that 'for a measure to constitute an obstacle, it is sufficient that it should be *reasonably likely* to have that effect on migrant workers'.[222]

Initially, the creation of Union citizenship did not displace the approach taken for the economic freedoms. In *Uecker and Jacquet*, the Court affirmed that 'the Treaty rules governing freedom of movement and regulations adopted to implement them cannot be applied to cases which have no factor linking them with any of the situations governed by Community law and all elements of which are purely internal to a single Member State'.[223] For that reason, 'a member of the family of a worker who is a national of a Member State cannot rely on Community law to challenge the validity of a limitation on the duration of his or her contract of employment within that same State when the worker in question has never exercised the right to freedom of movement within the Community'.[224] Fundamentally, Union citizenship was '*not intended to extend the* scope ratione *materiae of the Treaty also to internal situations which have no link with Community law* ... Any discrimination which nationals of a Member State may suffer under the law of that State fall within the scope of that law and must therefore be dealt with within the framework of the internal legal system of that State'.[225] It was also confirmed in *Kremzow* that Union citizenship did not reverse case law excluding 'a purely hypothetical prospect' of exercising free movement from the scope of the Treaty: if the circumstances of a case were not connected in any way with any of the situations contemplated by the Treaty provisions

---

[218] ibid para 15. That conclusion was drawn not only from the wording of Articles 18 and 45 TFEU but also from their purpose, 'which is to assist in the abolition of all obstacles to the establishment of a common market in which the nationals of the Member States may move freely within the territory of those States in order to pursue their economic activities' (ibid).
[219] ibid paras 16 and 17 (emphasis added).
[220] AG La Pergola in Case C-299/95 *Kremzow*, EU:C:1997:58, para 6 of the Opinion.
[221] Case 180/83 *Moser*, EU:C:1984:233, para 18 (emphasis added).
[222] AG Sharpston in Case C-212/06 *Gouvernement de la Communauté française et gouvernement wallon*, EU:C:2007:398, para 65 of the Opinion (emphasis added).
[223] Joined Cases C-64/96 and C-65/96 *Uecker and Jacquet*, EU:C:1997:285, para 16.
[224] ibid para 18.
[225] ibid para 23 (emphasis added); confirmed in eg Case C-192/05 *Tas-Hagen and Tas*, EU:C:2006:676, para 23.

on freedom of movement for persons', then it fell outside the scope of EU citizenship law.[226]

At first, then, the classic statement in cases like *Saunders* was largely taken as meaning that two expressions within it meant the same thing: that the fact that '[t]he provisions of the Treaty on freedom of movement for workers cannot ... be applied to situations which are *wholly internal to a Member State*' was another way of saying that '*in other words ... there is no factor* connecting them to any of the situations envisaged by Community law'.[227] However, propelled by the 'additional impetus' of Union citizenship,[228] the correlation between situations wholly internal to a Member State, on the one hand, and those having no factor connecting them to situations envisaged by EU law, on the other, came to be interrogated more deeply. In *Gouvernement de la Communauté française and gouvernement*, Advocate General Sharpston devoted a significant part of her Opinion to unpacking different elements of the Court's case law:

> True, the Court has held that citizenship of the Union, as established by Article [20 TFEU], is not intended to extend the material scope of the Treaty to internal situations which have no link with [Union] law. However, that statement requires one to solve the logically prior question of which situations, internal or not, are deemed to have no link with [Union] law. The answer cannot be that all so-called 'internal situations' are automatically deprived of any link to Community law. Article [157 TFEU] on equal pay for men and women provides a clear example of a provision applicable to situations that are normally wholly internal to a Member State. The question whether the situation is internal is therefore conceptually distinct from the question whether there is a link with [Union] law. Both questions must be answered in the light of the goals of the relevant Treaty provisions.[229]

In her view, Union citizenship therefore 'challenge[d] the *sustainability in its present form* of the doctrine on purely internal situations',[230] and especially whether the 'reverse discrimination' experienced by citizens who did not exercise free movement was credible in an understanding of Union citizenship as the 'fundamental status of nationals of the Member State'.[231] Building on her analysis in *Gouvernement de la Communauté française and gouvernement wallon*, she examined these issues again in a case that, on the surface at least, was as close to a classic wholly internal situation as one could get: the preliminary reference in *Ruiz Zambrano*. In what follows, the *Ruiz Zambrano* Opinion and ruling (Section 3.1), the early case law's next steps (Section 3.2), and the gradual clarification and development over time

---

[226] Case C-299/95 *Kremzow*, EU:C:1997:254, para 16; confirmed in eg Case C-40/11 *Iida*, EU:C:2012:691, para 77.
[227] Case 175/78 *Saunders*, EU:C:1979:88, para 11 (emphasis added).
[228] AG Sharpston in *Gouvernement de la Communauté française and gouvernement wallon*, para 133 of the Opinion.
[229] AG Sharpston in *Gouvernement de la Communauté française and gouvernement wallon*, paras 134–136 of the Opinion.
[230] ibid para 140 of the Opinion (emphasis added).
[231] Case C-184/99 *Grzelczyk*, EU:C:2001:458, para 31. The question of the reverse discrimination produced by EU free movement law has been extensively considered in the literature: see eg N Nic Shuibhne, 'Free movement of persons and the wholly internal rule: time to move on?' (2002) 39 Common Market Law Review 731; RCA White, 'Free movement, equal treatment and citizenship of the Union' (2005) 54 International and Comparative Law Quarterly 885; A Tryfonidou, *Reverse Discrimination in EU Law* (Kluwer Law International 2009); S O'Leary, 'The past, present and future of the purely internal rule in EU law' in M Dougan, N Nic Shuibhne, and E Spaventa (eds), *Empowerment and Disempowerment of the European Citizen* (Hart Publishing 2012) 37; and S Iglesias Sanchez, 'Purely internal situations and the limits of EU law: a consolidated case law or a notion to be abandoned?' (2018) 14 European Constitutional Law Review 7.

of relevant residence rights for third-country national family members in a Union citizen's home State (Section 3.3) will be considered.

3.1 The Game-Changer: *Ruiz Zambrano*

Why was a case involving the refusal of a residence permit in Belgium for the Colombian father of Belgian minor children, who had never moved anywhere within the Union, assigned to the Grand Chamber of the Court of Justice: to agree that the established approach to internal situations was no longer tenable, or to extinguish that speculation definitively, once and for all? Whatever the motivation, Advocate General Sharpston's Opinion openly confronted both the logic and the viability of the 'purely internal' case law, framing the central question in this way:

> What precisely does Union citizenship entail? Do the circumstances giving rise to the national proceedings constitute a situation that is 'purely internal' to the Member State concerned, in which European Union ('EU') law has no role to play? Or does full recognition of the rights (including the future rights) that necessarily flow from Union citizenship mean that an infant EU citizen has a right, based on EU law rather than national law, to reside anywhere within the territory of the Union (including in the Member State of his nationality)?[232]

She then worked through three possible responses: first, exploiting the (essentially fictional[233]) reach of potential restrictions of free movement (paras 75–122 of the Opinion); second, deploying Union citizenship more directly to confront reverse discrimination (paras 123–150); and third, progressing Union protection of fundamental rights (paras 151–177). However, in its remarkably brief judgment, the Court articulated a new 'genuine enjoyment of the substance' of citizenship rights test, which it based on Article 20 TFEU.

Mr Ruiz Zambrano, his wife and their eldest child, all Colombian nationals, arrived in Belgium in 1999. Applications for refugee status submitted by Mr Ruiz Zambrano and his wife were refused in 2000 and they were ordered to leave Belgium, but the order included a *non-refoulement* clause that they should not be sent back to Colombia because of the civil war there. Mr Ruiz Zambrano and his wife remained in Belgium and sought to regularise their situation. They also had two more children, both of whom were Belgian nationals under the rules applicable in Belgium at the time. Mr Ruiz Zambrano worked and provided sufficient resources to support his family, though without a work permit. The national proceedings producing the preliminary reference concerned both his residence status in Belgium and a refusal of unemployment benefits following the loss of his job.

The Court of Justice reshaped the questions referred to consider 'whether the provisions of the TFEU on European Union citizenship are to be interpreted as meaning that they confer on a relative in the ascending line who is a third-country national, upon whom his minor children, who are European Union citizens, are dependent, a right of residence in

---

[232] AG Sharpston in Case C-34/09 *Ruiz Zambrano*, EU:C:2010:560, para 2 of the Opinion.
[233] ibid para 77 of the Opinion: 'I do not think that exercise of the rights derived from citizenship of the Union is always inextricably and necessarily bound up with physical movement. There are also already citizenship cases in which the element of true movement is either barely discernible or frankly non-existent' (citing as examples, Case C-148/02 *Garcia Avello*, EU:C:2003:53; Case C-200/02 *Zhu and Chen*, EU:C:2004:639; and Case C-135/08 *Rottmann*, EU:C:2010:104).

the Member State of which they are nationals and in which they reside, and also exempt him from having to obtain a work permit in that Member State'.[234] All eight governments that submitted observations and also the Commission argued that the situation of the Union citizen children in this case was not one of 'the situations envisaged by the freedoms of movement and residence guaranteed under European Union law' because the children 'reside in the Member State of which they are nationals and have never left the territory of that Member State'.[235]

The Court first confirmed that Directive 2004/38 did not apply in this case since, under Article 3(1) as regards its 'beneficiaries', the Directive applies to Union citizens—and by extension to their family members—only when the former move to or reside in another State.[236] The Court then articulated a new basis for derived residence rights in EU citizenship law. It first stated that the 'status of citizen of the Union' is conferred on Member State nationals—here, on Mr Ruiz Zambrano's younger children—by Article 20 TFEU.[237] It then recalled that Union citizenship is 'intended to be the fundamental status of nationals of the Member States'.[238] Therefore, '[i]n those circumstances, *Article 20 TFEU* precludes national measures which have the effect of *depriving citizens of the Union of the genuine enjoyment of the substance of the rights* conferred by virtue of their status as citizens of the Union'.[239] As a result, '[a] refusal to grant a right of residence to a third-country national with dependent minor children in the Member State where those children are nationals and reside, and also a refusal to grant such a person a work permit, has such an effect'.[240] This is because '[i]t must be assumed that such a refusal would lead to a situation where those children, citizens of the Union, *would have to leave the territory of the Union* in order to accompany their parents'.[241] Relatedly, 'if a work permit were not granted to such a person, he would risk not having sufficient resources to provide for himself and his family, which would also result in the children, citizens of the Union, having to leave the territory of the Union. In those circumstances, those citizens of the Union *would, in fact, be unable to exercise the substance of the rights conferred on them* by virtue of their status as citizens of the Union'.[242]

---

[234] Case C-34/09 *Ruiz Zambrano*, EU:C:2011:124, para 36. Focusing on whether Mr Ruiz Zambrano could derive a residence right in Belgium from his Belgian national (ie Union citizen) children, the referring court had asked if Articles 18, 20, and 21 TFEU 'confer a right of residence upon a citizen of the Union in the territory of the Member State of which that citizen is a national, irrespective of whether he has previously exercised his right to move within the territory of the Member States', as well as whether, by reading those provisions in conjunction with Articles 21, 24, and 34 CFR, such a right, first, would require that 'where that citizen is an infant dependent on a relative in the ascending line who is a national of a non-member State, the infant's enjoyment of the right of residence in the Member State in which he resides and of which he is a national must be safeguarded, irrespective of whether the right to move freely has been previously exercised by the child ... and granting the relative in the ascending line who is a national of a non-member State, upon whom the child is dependent and who has sufficient resources and sickness insurance, the secondary right of residence'; and second, 'entail[s] the grant of an exemption from the requirement to hold a work permit to the relative in the ascending line who is a national of a non-member State, upon whom the child is dependent' (ibid para 35). The relevant provisions of the Charter address non-discrimination (Article 21), the rights of the child (Article 24), and social security and social assistance (Article 34).
[235] *Ruiz Zambrano*, para 37.
[236] ibid para 39.
[237] ibid para 40.
[238] ibid para 41.
[239] ibid para 42 (emphasis added); citing, 'to that effect', *Rottmann*, para 42. This link is returned to below.
[240] *Ruiz Zambrano*, para 43.
[241] ibid para 44 (emphasis added).
[242] ibid (emphasis added). It was later confirmed that the fact that the third-country national parent was residing illegally in the dependent Union citizen's home State was 'immaterial' for residence rights based on Article 20 TFEU (reflecting the same approach to Article 21 TFEU rights in Case C-127/08 *Metock and Others*, EU:C:2008:449, discussed in Chapter 4): see Case C-82/16 *KA and Others*, EU:C:2018:308, paras 78–81 and 89. Also in *KA and Others*, AG Sharpston dismissed the idea of a '*general* presumption of abuse when a family link

The Court's ruling in *Ruiz Zambrano* provoked a storm of response,[243] not only because of the novel constitutional piercing of home State immigration competence but also because the terse ruling was so thinly reasoned, leaving several open questions. For example, how did the 'genuine enjoyment of rights' test relate to established case law on purely internal situations? What other national measures might deprive a Union citizen of the genuine enjoyment of the substance of their rights?[244] And what limits might (legitimately) be placed on rights based on Article 20 TFEU? We now know that the 'genuine enjoyment' test has not yet been applied in other contexts and, as detailed in Section 3.3.3, subsequent case law has also clarified its outer limits.

It was not clear either if the fact that *Ruiz Zambrano* involved 'dependent minor children' was legally decisive: could other family members derive residence rights based on Article 20 TFEU? Would 'family members' be defined differently from or by analogy with the provisions of Directive 2004/38? And how did the concept of 'a third-country national with dependent minor children' relate to that of the 'primary carer' of Union citizen children, which was already established in the case law?[245] Did Article 20 TFEU generate derived rights for *both* parents? (The legal position of Mrs Ruiz Zambrano, the children's mother, was not addressed in the ruling.) What was the significance of the fact that a Union citizen 'would have to leave the territory of the Union'? How could that be demonstrated? In terms of the significance of sufficient resources in EU citizenship law generally (explained further in Chapters 6 and 7), did *Ruiz Zambrano* have implications only for the granting of work permits or was it also relevant to a refusal of social assistance? Finally, what role, if any, would the Charter of Fundamental Rights play in determining the answers to these questions? After all, while neither the Charter nor respect for fundamental rights generally was mentioned in the Court's judgment, the dispute essentially concerned the implications of a decision for the family life of a State's own nationals.[246]

---

arises at the point when a third-country national finds himself to be an irregular stayer' (EU:C:2017:821, para 65 of the Opinion; see further, Chapter 10).

[243] eg S Adam and P Van Elsuwege, 'Citizenship rights and the federal balance between the European Union and its Member States' (2012) 37 European Law Review 176; K Hailbronner and D Thym, 'Case C-34/09, *Gerardo Ruiz Zambrano v. Office national de l'emploi* (ONEm)' (case comment) (2011) 48 Common Market Law Review 1253; D Kochenov, 'The right to have *what* rights? EU citizenship in need of clarification' (2013) 19 European Law Journal 502; A Lansbergen and N Miller, 'European citizenship rights in internal situations: an ambiguous revolution? Decision of 8 March 2011, Case C-34/09 *Gerardo Ruiz Zambrano v Office National De L'emploi (ONEM)*' (2011) 7 European Constitutional Law Review 287; R Morris, 'European citizenship and the right to move freely: internal situations, reverse discrimination and fundamental rights' (2011) 18 Maastricht Journal of European and Comparative Law 179; N Nic Shuibhne, 'Seven questions for seven paragraphs' (2011) 36 European Law Review 161; I Solanke, 'Using the citizen to bring the refugee in' (2012) 75 Modern Law Review 101; H van Eijken and SA de Vries, 'A new route into the promised land? Being a European citizen after *Ruiz Zambrano*' (2011) 36 European Law Review 704; and P van Elsuwege, 'Shifting the boundaries? European Union citizenship and the scope of application of EU law – Case No. C-34/09, *Gerardo Ruiz Zambrano v. Office national de l'emploi*' (2011) 28 Legal Issues of Economic Integration 263.

[244] Exploring the application of the test in a new context, see K Kalaitzaki, 'The application of EU fundamental rights during the financial crisis: EU citizenship to the rescue?' (2021) 27 European Public Law 331.

[245] eg Case C-413/99 *Baumbast and R*, EU:C:2002:493; Case C-200/02 *Zhu and Chen*, EU:C:2004:639.

[246] See further, AG Sharpston in *Ruiz Zambrano*, para 62 of the Opinion: 'the Belgian authorities' decision to order Mr Ruiz Zambrano to leave Belgium, followed by their continued refusal to grant him a residence permit, constitutes a potential breach of his children's fundamental right to family life and to protection of their rights as children; and thus ... of Mr Ruiz Zambrano's equivalent right to family life as their father. I say "potential" because Mr Ruiz Zambrano is still on Belgian territory. It is however evident that activating the deportation order would trigger the breach of those rights'. See similarly, AG Szpunar in Case C-133/15 *Chavez-Vilchez*, EU:C:2016:659, paras 95–96 of the Opinion.

These questions are examined across Sections 3.2 and 3.3, which distinguish between early (more confusing) and later (more considered) case law responses to *Ruiz Zambrano*. However, a preliminary question is first considered here: where did the Court's test actually come from, in a legal sense? As noted above, the Court invoked paragraph 42 of *Rottmann* 'to that effect' to support the finding that 'Article 20 TFEU precludes national measures which have the effect of depriving citizens of the Union of the genuine enjoyment of the substance of the rights conferred by virtue of their status as citizens of the Union'.[247] *Rottmann* was considered in Chapter 3 in terms of its implications for Member State decision-making 'in the sphere of nationality'.[248] It was observed in that discussion that while Advocate General Poiares Maduro took Mr Rottmann's previous exercise of free movement as the starting point for his analysis,[249] thereby engaging Article 21 TFEU, the Court based its ruling on Article 20 TFEU. In paragraph 42, it found that 'the situation of a citizen of the Union who, like the applicant in the main proceedings, is faced with a decision withdrawing his naturalisation, adopted by the authorities of one Member State, and placing him, after he has lost the nationality of another Member State that he originally possessed, in a position capable of causing him to lose the status conferred by Article [20 TFEU] and the rights attaching thereto *falls, by reason of its nature and its consequences, within the ambit of European Union law*'.[250]

The cross-reference to *Rottmann* in *Ruiz Zambrano*, less self-evident at the time than the Court perhaps took for granted, highlights an essential quality of Article 20 TFEU-based rights: that they manifest in *exceptional* circumstances only, approaching a point of making it impossible either to be a Union citizen or to exercise associated rights. Retaining Member State nationality—the precondition for Union citizenship and the context of the dispute in *Rottmann*—is an obvious exemplar of those qualities, but it was not clear which aspect or aspects of the situation in *Ruiz Zambrano* pushed the case across that same threshold. Further light can be found in Advocate General Sharpston's Opinion. Following her reference to paragraph 42 of *Rottmann*, she continued:

> It seems to me that the Court's reasoning in *Rottmann*, read in conjunction with its earlier ruling in *Zhu and Chen*, may readily be transposed to the present case. Here, the grant of Belgian nationality to Mr Ruiz Zambrano's children … was a matter that fell within the competence of that Member State. Once that nationality was granted, however, the children became citizens of the Union and entitled to exercise the rights conferred on them as such citizens, concurrently with their rights as Belgian nationals. They have not yet moved outside their own Member State. Nor, following his naturalisation, had Dr Rottmann. If the parents do not have a derivative right of residence and are required to leave Belgium, the children will, in all probability, have to leave with them. That would, in practical terms, place Diego and Jessica in a 'position *capable of causing them to lose the status* conferred [by their citizenship of the Union] and the rights attaching thereto'. It follows – as it did for Dr Rottmann – that the *children's situation* [emphasis in original] 'falls, by reason of its nature and its consequences, within the ambit of EU law'. Moreover, like Catherine Zhu, [the Ruiz Zambrano children] *cannot exercise their rights as Union citizens (specifically, their rights to move and to reside in any Member State) fully and effectively without the presence and support of their parents*. Through operation of the same link that the Court accepted in *Zhu*

---

[247] *Ruiz Zambrano*, para 42.
[248] *Rottmann*, para 62.
[249] AG Poiares Maduro in *Rottmann*, paras 9–13 of the Opinion.
[250] *Rottmann*, para 42 (emphasis added).

and Chen (enabling a young child to exercise its citizenship rights effectively) it follows that *Mr Ruiz Zambrano's situation* [emphasis in original] is likewise not one that is 'purely internal' to the Member State. It too falls within the ambit of EU law.[251]

Thus, the impossibility of exercising Union citizenship rights rationalised extending the reach of EU law to situations that *were* purely internal to a Union citizen's home State yet *not* devoid of a factor connecting them sufficiently to EU law by analogy with—and extension of—the *Rottmann* case's concern with losing the status of Union citizenship altogether.[252]

Advocate General Sharpston also considered a dimension of *Ruiz Zambrano* that the Court did not address: that '[i]t is of course *theoretically possible* that another Member State might be prepared to take the family'.[253] Initially, the fact that a Union citizen could leave their home State and move to another State to secure residence rights for third-country national family members was essentially presumed.[254] But the Court now considers the *practical* and not just *theoretical* prospects of relocating to another State, acknowledging that 'the option available to a third country national and his/her Union citizen children of moving to the Member State of which those children are nationals cannot exist only in the abstract'.[255] This case law is returned to in Section 3.3, following an overview of the case law that followed *Ruiz Zambrano* more immediately.

3.2 First Responses: Explaining—and Containing—*Ruiz Zambrano*

The *McCarthy* case provided an early opportunity (just two months later) for the Court to begin to unpack its cryptic reasoning in *Ruiz Zambrano*. Mrs McCarthy was a dual British/Irish national who had always lived in the UK, where she received state benefits. She married a Jamaican national who did not have leave to remain in the UK under the applicable national immigration rules. Mrs McCarthy applied for an Irish passport (for the first time) after her marriage.[256] She and her husband then applied—unsuccessfully—for residence permits in the UK as a Union citizen and the spouse of a Union citizen respectively.

For the referring court, the key question (significantly 'reformulated' by the Court of Justice[257]) was whether Mrs McCarthy's British/Irish dual nationality brought the couple

---

[251] AG Sharpston in *Ruiz Zambrano*, paras 95–96 of the Opinion (emphasis added).

[252] Further illustrating the connection between these lines of case law via the Court's subsequent emphasis on the Charter of Fundamental Rights in both Case C-221/17 *Tjebbes*, EU:C:2019:189 (Section 2) and Case C-133/15 *Chavez-Vilchez*, EU:C:2017:354 (Section 3.3), see H van Eijken, 'Connecting the dots backwards, what did *Ruiz Zambrano* mean for EU citizenship and fundamental rights in EU law?' (2021) 48 European Journal of Migration and Law 48 at 54–56. Reflecting generally on free movement, citizenship, and political inclusion, see S Raucea, 'European citizenship and the right to reside: "no one on the outside has a right to be inside?"' (2016) 22 European Law Journal 470; and connecting free movement, citizenship and 'demo(i)cracy', K Lenaerts and JA Gutiérrez-Fons, 'Epilogue on EU citizenship: hopes and fears' in Kochenov (ed) (n 80) 765.

[253] AG Sharpston in *Ruiz Zambrano*, footnote 76 of the Opinion (emphasis added).

[254] See esp Case C-86/12 *Alokpa and Moudoulou*, EU:C:2013:645, paras 32–35. The obligation to leave the home State to produce EU legal protection for family members was deeply criticised; see eg D Kochenov, 'EU citizenship: from an incipient form to an incipient substance? The discovery of the Treaty text' (2012) 37 European Law Review 369 at 393: '[s]ince the Treaties do not connect the enjoyment of the substance of EU citizenship rights with movement or limit EU citizenship rights to the right not to leave the territory of the Union, the rights paradigm should not be artificially connected to movement … It is quite sensible to expect that rights be sufficiently protected without taking a bus'. See generally, S Iglesias Sanchez, 'A citizenship right to stay? The right not to move in a Union based on free movement' in Kochenov (ed) (n 80) 371.

[255] AG Wathelet in Case C-115/15 *NA*, ECLI:EU:C:2016:259, para 114 of the Opinion.

[256] See further, AG Kokott in Case C-434/09 *McCarthy*, EU:C:2010:718, para 11 of the Opinion. Mrs McCarthy was eligible for an Irish passport because her mother was born in Ireland.

[257] Case C-434/09 *McCarthy*, EU:C:2011:277, paras 30 and 44.

within the scope of Directive 2004/38 as 'beneficiaries' within the meaning of Article 3(1). However, the Court of Justice dismissed that possibility, affirming the host State focus of the Directive and observing that 'the fact that a Union citizen is a national of more than one Member State does not mean that he has made use of his right of freedom of movement'.[258] As discussed in Chapter 3, the Court also emphasised that, as a principle of international law, a Member State is precluded 'from refusing its own nationals the right to enter its territory and remain there for any reason [and] from expelling its own nationals from its territory or refusing their right to reside in that territory or making such right conditional'.[259] Directive 2004/38 could not, in other words, extend residence rights to a Union citizen in their home State, but neither, as a matter of international law, was that necessary.

Advocate General Kokott had not considered in any depth the possibility that rights might be based on the Treaty.[260] However, by redirecting the referring court's question from the Directive to the Treaty, the Court directly addressed 'whether Article 21 TFEU is applicable to a Union citizen who has never exercised his right of free movement, who has always resided in a Member State of which he is a national and who is also a national of another Member State'.[261] In response, it extended the language applied up to that point in case law on Article 21 TFEU to situations that might fall within the scope of Article 20 TFEU: while 'the Treaty rules governing freedom of movement for persons and the measures adopted to implement them cannot be applied to situations which have no factor linking them with any of the situations governed by European Union law and which are confined in all relevant respects within a single Member State', on the one hand, 'the situation of a Union citizen who, like Mrs McCarthy, has not made use of the right to freedom of movement cannot, for that reason alone, be assimilated to a purely internal situation', on the other.[262] Referring to *Ruiz Zambrano* and its substance of rights test, the Court then held:

> [N]o element of the situation of Mrs McCarthy, *as described by the national court*, indicates that the national measure at issue in the main proceedings has the effect of depriving her of the genuine enjoyment of the substance of the rights associated with her status as a Union citizen, *or of impeding the exercise of her right to move and reside freely* within the territory of the Member States, in accordance with Article 21 TFEU. Indeed, the failure by the authorities of the United Kingdom to take into account the Irish nationality of Mrs McCarthy for the purposes of granting her a right of residence in the United Kingdom in no way affects her in her right to move and reside freely within the territory of the Member States, or any other right conferred on her by virtue of her status as a Union citizen.[263]

This paragraph is important for two reasons. First, it seeds the (now well established) perspective that Articles 20 and 21 TFEU are *alternative* sources for residence rights that can be

---

[258] ibid para 41.
[259] ibid para 29. However, note also the qualifier mentioned in Chapter 3 in this context, as states increasingly seek to rescind nationality as part of counterterrorism responses.
[260] She did note briefly that she was 'not of the view that Union citizens can derive from Article 21(1) TFEU a right of residence vis-á-vis the Member State of which they are a national even where – as in the case of Mrs McCarthy – there is no cross-border element' (AG Kokott in *McCarthy*, para 11 of the Opinion; referring (in fn 26) explicitly (and in contrast) to AG Sharpston in *Ruiz Zambrano*).
[261] *McCarthy*, para 44.
[262] ibid paras 45–46; referring to Case C-403/03 *Schempp*, EU:C:2005:446, para 22.
[263] *McCarthy*, para 49 (emphasis added).

derived from a Union citizen. Moreover, Article 21 TFEU must be considered *first*, meaning that Article 20 TFEU rights are residual or subsidiary in nature.[264]

Second, the Court framed its ruling around the circumstances 'as described by the national court' and concluded on that basis that no impediment to the exercise of free movement rights—to the prospect of residing somewhere else within the territory of the Union—therefore existed: if Mrs McCarthy wished to reside with her husband, exercising free movement rights under Article 21 TFEU and Directive 2004/38 offered her a way to do it—just in, at the time, any of the 27 (other) Member States rather than in the UK, her home State. This option emphasised that the Court never intended to manifest EU law-based residence rights for Union citizens in their home States in a general sense, but articulated, instead, a residence right in the territory of the Union per se.[265] For the Court, 'by contrast with the case of *Ruiz Zambrano*, the national measure at issue … in the present case does not have the effect of obliging Mrs McCarthy to leave the territory of the European Union. Indeed … Mrs McCarthy enjoys, under a principle of international law, an unconditional right of residence in the United Kingdom since she is a national of the United Kingdom.'[266]

However, there are two problems with that analysis in terms of what 'obliging' a Union citizen to leave the territory of the Union actually entails and how it might be demonstrated. The first is that, as indicated in Section 3.1, the Court never addressed relocation as an option in *Ruiz Zambrano*. In theory, had the family relocated to any other Member State (with sufficient resources), the Union citizen children would have fallen within the scope of Directive 2004/38. Their parents—or at least, considering the case law up to that point, their 'primary carer' per *Baumbast* and *Zhu and Chen*—could have resided there with them through rights based directly on Article 21 TFEU. In that sense, EU law offered rights in (any) host State to the Ruiz Zambrano family as much as to the McCarthys. The second problem was that the facts 'as described by the national court' did not highlight the fact that Mrs McCarthy was the full-time carer of her disabled son.[267] The implications for her capacity to move elsewhere were thus, even if inadvertently, overlooked in considering possible impediments to exercising free movement under Article 21 TFEU, with the Court suggesting that there was no 'serious inconvenience' comparable to that produced by having different surnames under two different Member State systems.[268] It also meant that the opportunity for further reflection on the beneficiaries of Article 20 TFEU rights beyond 'dependent minor children' (if any) or the role of the Charter was missed.

---

[264] eg Case C-40/11 *Iida*, EU:C:2012:691, para 72; Case C-86/12 *Alokpa and Moudoulou*, EU:C:2013:645, para 32; Case C-115/15 *NA*, EU:C:2016:487, paras 72–74; and Case C-836/18 *Subdelegación del Gobierno en Ciudad Real (Conjoint d'un citoyen de l'Union)*, EU:C:2020:119, para 42. These cases are returned to below.

[265] Confirmed in Case C-256/11 *Dereci and Others*, EU:C:2011:734, para 66: 'the criterion relating to the denial of the genuine enjoyment of the substance of the rights conferred by virtue of European Union citizen status refers to situations in which the Union citizen has, in fact, to leave not only the territory of the Member State of which he is a national but also the territory of the Union as a whole'. Compare, for rights conferred by Article 21 TFEU, AG Bot in Case C-165/16 *Lounes*, EU:C:2017:407, paras 89–90 of the Opinion: '[t]o continue the family life which she has started, she would then be forced to leave that State to move to another Member State in order to be able to claim once again the rights conferred by Directive 2004/38 and, in particular, the possibility of residing with her spouse. Consequently, in these circumstances, I think that the effectiveness of the rights conferred by Article 21(1) TFEU demands that Union citizens … who have acquired the nationality of the host Member State following and by reason of residence under and in conformity with the conditions set out in Article 16 of the directive, should be able to continue the family life they have until then led in that State with their spouse, a third-country national'.

[266] *McCarthy*, para 50.

[267] *Shirley McCarthy v Secretary of State for the Home Department* [2008] EWCA Civ 641, para 8.

[268] *McCarthy*, paras 51–54; referring to Case C-148/02 *Garcia Avello*, EU:C:2003:539 and Case C-353/06 *Grunkin and Paul*, EU:C:2008:559. See further, Chapter 3.

In the next cluster of rulings after *McCarthy*, however, more guidance emerged on the nature of Article 20 TFEU rights, the kinds of relationships that they protect, the possibility of relocating elsewhere within the territory of the Union, and the intersection of Article 20 TFEU and the Charter. These issues are separated out below for the purposes of organising the discussion, but it will become clear that they are also deeply connected.

3.2.1 The nature of *Ruiz Zambrano* rights

Rights based on Article 20 TFEU can be traced across incremental steps in three lines of family reunification case law: from residence rights in a host State for third-country national primary carers of minor Union citizens, based on Article 21 TFEU (*Zhu and Chen*); to residence rights in a Union citizen's home state following previous exercise of free movement and residence (ie 'returner' case law, discussed in Chapter 9), also based on Article 21 TFEU; to, finally, residence rights the consequence of a refusal of which would oblige a Union citizen to leave the territory of the Union, based on Article 20 TFEU (*Ruiz Zambrano*). For the Court, '[t]he common element in the above situations is that, although they are governed by legislation which falls *a priori* within the competence of the Member States, namely legislation on the right of entry and stay of third-country nationals *outside the scope of* Directives 2003/109 and 2004/38, they none the less have *an intrinsic connection with the freedom of movement of a Union citizen* which prevents the right of entry and residence from being refused to those nationals in the Member State of residence of that citizen, in order not to interfere with that freedom'.[269]

Thus, whether the Court is rationalising residence rights under Article 21 TFEU or Article 20 TFEU, the 'common element' concerns the impact on the effectiveness of a Union citizen's capacity to exercise free movement. In a sense, this reasoning blurs the extent to which *Ruiz Zambrano* constituted rights that apply in purely internal situations: free movement has not been exercised in these cases, but the 'intrinsic connection' idea fashions Article 20 rights as catalysts for the (future) exercise of Article 21 TFEU rights. Thus in *Iida*, where a Union citizen daughter had already relocated to another Member State, her third-country national father could not invoke Article 20 TFEU as a basis for derived residence rights in his daughter's home State (where he continued to reside) since the facts of the case illustrated that the Union citizen had obviously *not* been discouraged from exercising freedom of movement.[270]

3.2.2 Being 'obliged' to leave the territory of the Union

The fact that relocating to another Member State would sustain a Union citizen's right to reside *somewhere* in the territory of the Union brings the meaning of being 'obliged' to leave that territory into sharper focus. In *Dereci*, several applications for residence rights based on Article 20 TFEU[271] exhibited significant differences from the facts in *Ruiz*

---

[269] Case C-40/11 *Iida*, EU:C:2012:691, para 72 (emphasis added); confirmed in eg Case C-165/14 *Rendón Marín*, EU:C:2016:675, para 73 and Case C-133/15 *Chavez-Vilchez*, EU:C:2017:354, para 64. In *Ymeraga*, the 'intrinsic connection' idea was confirmed and the references to Directives 2003/109 and 2004/38 generalised to national legislation on the right of entry and stay of third-country nationals 'outside the scope of provisions of secondary [EU] legislation' (Case C-87/12 *Ymeraga*, EU:C:2013:291, para 37; Directive 2003/109 concerning the status of third-country nationals who are long-term residents, 2003 OJ L16/44). In *Rendón Marín*, the Court also recalled that '[c]itizenship of the Union confers on each Union citizen *a primary and individual right to move and reside freely* within the territory of the Member States' (para 70, emphasis added).

[270] Case C-40/11 *Iida*, EU:C:2012:691, esp para 74. See similarly, AG Trstenjak in *Iida*, EU:C:2012:296, paras 64–65 of the Opinion.

[271] '[T]he applicants in the main proceedings are all third-country nationals who wish to live with their family members, who are European Union citizens resident in Austria and who are nationals of that Member State.

Zambrano—notably for present purposes, where minor Union citizens were involved, one parent was *also* a national of the home State (Austria).[272] If residence rights were not conferred on the second (third-country national) parent in such circumstances, would the minor Union citizens be *obliged* to leave the territory of the Union? The Commission and seven of the eight Member States that submitted observations argued that Article 20 TFEU-based residence rights should be granted only in 'very exceptional situations' and that 'the events which gave rise to the disputes in the main proceedings differ substantially from those which gave rise to [the *Ruiz Zambrano*] judgment in so far as the Union citizens concerned were not at risk of having to leave the territory of the Union and thus of being denied the genuine enjoyment of the substance of the rights conferred by virtue of their status as citizens of the Union'.[273]

The Court agreed, affirming that the purpose of family member residence rights based on Article 20 TFEU is that 'the effectiveness of the Union citizenship enjoyed by that national would otherwise be undermined'.[274] However, it also held that 'the *mere fact that it might appear desirable* to a national of a Member State, *for economic reasons or in order to keep his family together in the territory of the Union*, for the members of his family who do not have the nationality of a Member State to be able to reside with him in the territory of the Union, is not sufficient in itself to support the view that the Union citizen will be forced to leave Union territory if such a right is not granted'.[275]

The Court went on to consider the implications of that statement vis-à-vis respect for family life, which is returned to below. However, for the threshold of being 'obliged' to leave the territory of the Union, and looking across the situations of all the families involved in the national proceedings, Advocate General Mengozzi outlined in more detail why Article 20 TFEU rights would not be triggered in the present case: 'there is no likelihood that the

---

It should also be noted that the Union citizens concerned have never exercised their right to free movement and that they are not maintained by the applicants in the main proceedings. By contrast, it must be observed that the facts giving rise to the dispute differ as regards, inter alia, whether the entry into Austria of the applicants in the main proceedings was lawful or unlawful, their current place of residence as well as the nature of their family relationship with the Union citizen concerned and whether they are maintained by that Union citizen' (Case C-256/11 *Dereci and Others*, EU:C:2011:734, paras 22–23).

[272] The other cases involved relationships between spouses or between parents and adult children (ibid paras 25–26).

[273] ibid para 40.

[274] ibid para 67; confirmed in eg *Rendón Marín*, para 74. The *KA* case, in the context of implementing Directive 2008/115 on common standards and procedures in Member States for returning illegally staying third-country nationals, 2008 OJ L348/98, provides another example of how the effectiveness of Union citizenship rights might be undermined: 'while it is true that a refusal by a third-country national to comply with the obligation to return and to cooperate in the context of a removal procedure cannot enable him to avoid, in whole or in part, the legal effects of an entry ban ... the fact remains that, when the competent national authority receives, from a third-country national, an application for a right of residence for the purposes of family reunification with a Union citizen who is a national of the Member State concerned, that authority cannot refuse to examine that application solely on the ground that the third-country national is the subject of a ban on entering that Member State. It is the duty of that authority, on the contrary, to examine that application and to assess whether there exists, between the third-country national and Union citizen concerned, a relationship of dependency of such a nature that a derived right of residence must, as a general rule, be accorded to that third-country national, under Article 20 TFEU' (Case C-82/16 *KA and Others*, EU:C:2018:308, para 57). Illustrating the fact that Article 20 TFEU rights are conferred on Union citizens and not third-country nationals, the Court further confirmed that 'in order to ensure that Article 20 TFEU has practical effect, it is necessary to withdraw or suspend such an entry ban, even when that ban has become final, if there exists, between that third-country national and a Union citizen who is a member of his family, such a relationship of dependency as to justify according to that third-country national a derived right of residence, under Article 20, in the territory of the Member State concerned' (para 83; it being 'immaterial that the entry ban has become final at the time when he submits his application for residence for the purposes of family reunification', para. 84).

[275] *Dereci and Others*, para 68 (emphasis added).

refusal by the Austrian authorities to grant Mr Dereci a residence permit could lead Mr Dereci's wife and three young children, who are all four Union citizens, to be deprived of the enjoyment of one of the rights set out in Article 20(2) TFEU ... Mrs Dereci, as an Austrian national, may continue to enjoy the right of residence in Austria and may legitimately exercise her right of free movement between the Member States. The same holds for her children who, on account of their age, however, will not be able to exercise that right independently of their mother'.[276]

Thus, Advocate General Mengozzi distinguished the *Dereci* situation from the *Ruiz Zambrano* situation because 'none of the four Union citizens is *dependent* on Mr Dereci, who is a national of a non-member country. Consequently, if Mr Dereci were not to obtain a residence permit and/or were to be expelled to Turkey, neither his wife nor his children, unlike the children of Mr Ruiz Zambrano, risk having to leave the territory of the Union'.[277] This point—which bridges to the question of Article 20 TFEU's beneficiaries, discussed in more detail in Section 3.2.3—fits with the ruling in *McCarthy* in that it seems to suggest that the option of either staying in the home State or moving to another Member State is a *fact* with reference to adult Union citizenship. It is, in other words, 'a simple application of the criteria' in *Ruiz Zambrano* and *McCarthy*.[278] In that light, a Union citizen's agency or autonomy prevails over personal preference or desirable outcome, underscoring the exceptional nature of Article 20 TFEU rights. However, Advocate General Mengozzi also acknowledged the 'paradoxes' then produced: family member residence rights could be secured in host States by the Union citizen exercising free movement; that Union citizen could then 'subsequently return to their Member State of origin, accompanied by their close relatives, irrespective of whether they are going to engage in economic activity in that Member State, since a situation of this kind cannot be regarded as a purely internal matter'.[279] Thus, 'the citizenship of the Union held by Mrs Dereci could, paradoxically, be seen as a factor which checks and/or defers family reunification. Whereas, following the judgment in *Ruiz Zambrano*, the children, who are Union citizens, of the Zambrano couple, who are both nationals of non-member countries, may immediately continue to maintain relations with their two parents in the Member State of which they are nationals and within whose territory they reside, in contrast the family life of the three young children of the Dereci couple is, in practice, subject to their mother exercising one of the freedoms of movement laid down in the TFEU'.[280]

In *O and S,* the understanding that Member State nationals always enjoy a right to reside in their home State was extended to Union citizens whose mothers held permanent residence permits there.[281] However, the Court also introduced an important new distinction—missing from *Ruiz Zambrano*, *McCarthy*, or *Dereci*—between being obliged to leave the territory of the Union 'in law' and being obliged to do so 'in fact'.[282] A first test of that distinction did not suggest that it would be meaningful. In *Alokpa and Moudoulou*, Mrs Alokpa, a citizen of Togo who had discretionary leave to remain in Luxembourg until December 2008, gave birth to twins (French nationals) in Luxembourg in August 2008. In 2010, she applied for a residence permit there on the basis of EU law, noting that she was 'unable to settle with her children in France, or reside with their father [Mr Moudoulou, a French national] on the

---

[276] AG Mengozzi in *Dereci*, EU:C:2011:626, para 34 of the Opinion.
[277] ibid para 34 of the Opinion (emphasis added).
[278] ibid para 37 of the Opinion.
[279] ibid para 44 of the Opinion.
[280] ibid para 45 of the Opinion.
[281] Joined Cases C-356/11 and C-357/11 *O and S*, EU:C:2012:776, para 50.
[282] ibid paras 50 and 51.

ground that she had no relations with the latter and that [her] children required follow-up medical treatment in Luxembourg as a result of their premature birth'.[283] That application was rejected on the grounds that Mrs Alokpa was not 'dependent' on her Union citizen children (as required by Article 2(2) of Directive 2004/38 for ascending line relatives).

The Court first confirmed that if Mrs Alokpa's Union citizen children had sickness insurance and sufficient resources within the meaning of Article 7(1) of Directive 2004/38, then resided lawfully in Luxembourg for the purposes of Article 21 TFEU and Mrs Alokpa would have a right to reside with them as their primary carer per *Baumbast* and *Zhu and Chen*.[284] However, should that not be the case, the referring court must then examine whether Article 20 TFEU conferred, exceptionally, a *Ruiz Zambrano* residence right. While acknowledging that this determination should be made by the referring court, the Court did, in one brief paragraph, observe that 'the refusal by the Luxembourg authorities to grant Mrs Alokpa a right of residence *cannot result* in her children being obliged to leave the territory of the European Union altogether' because 'as sole carer of those children since their birth, [she] could have the benefit of a derived right to reside *in France*'.[285] The Court did not cite *O and S* or trigger any assessment of the family's capacity to relocate *in fact*. However, later case law did animate that analysis more meaningfully, as shown in Section 3.3.1.

Union citizens—and the third-country national family members on whom they are dependent—may obviously *choose* to leave the territory of the Union: for example, as in *O and S*, 'to follow their respective spouses to their countries of origin in order to preserve the unity of their family life. The fact that their children have Union citizenship cannot amount to putting them "under house arrest" in the territory of the European Union'.[286] Article 20 TFEU is not concerned, therefore, with 'departure from the territory of the Union [that is] freely decided ... for a reason linked to the preservation of family life'—only with departures 'imposed under the implementation of national legislation'.[287]

3.2.3 Beneficiaries of *Ruiz Zambrano* rights: the requirement of dependency

As noted in Section 3.2.2, the *Dereci* case grouped together several sets of proceedings in which applications for residence permits in Austria were rejected.[288] The family relationships

---

[283] Case C-86/12 *Alokpa and Moudoulou*, EU:C:2013:645, para 15.
[284] ibid paras 27–30. However, AG Mengozzi (EU:C:2013:197, para 21 of the Opinion) noted that 'it is clear from the order for reference that, unlike the situation underlying *Zhu and Chen*, Ms Alokpa's children do not have any means of subsistence, a matter which led to the Grand Duchy of Luxembourg on the territory of which the three applicants in the main proceedings are residing in a hostel taking full responsibility for them and for their mother'. Nevertheless, he also pointed out (at para 23 of the Opinion) that 'Ms Alokpa never intended to become a burden on the Luxembourg State and that she has been offered a job for an indefinite period in Luxembourg, subject to the sole condition that she obtain a residence permit and a work permit in Luxembourg. It should be noted in this connection that Ms Alokpa produced a copy of that job offer in the course of proceedings before the referring court'.
[285] *Alokpa and Moudoulou*, paras 35 and 34 (emphasis added). Here, the Court referred to AG Mengozzi: 'the decision of the Luxembourg authorities requiring Ms Alokpa and (de facto) her children to leave the territory of the Grand Duchy of Luxembourg cannot require those children to leave the territory of the Union as a whole. As the mother and primary carer of the children since their birth, Ms Alokpa can herself therefore have the benefit of a derived right to reside in France. In those circumstances, it is inconceivable that the French authorities might refuse to allow Ms Alokpa to accompany her children to the Member State of which they are nationals and to reside there with them, a fortiori because she is the only person with whom they have had a family life since their birth' (paras 57–58 of the Opinion). He added that the 'geographical proximity' of France and Luxembourg would, moreover, not preclude Mrs Alokpa from accepting her job offer in Luxembourg (para 57 of the Opinion).
[286] AG Bot in Joined Cases C-356/11 and C-357/11 *O and S*, EU:C:2012:595, para 41 of the Opinion.
[287] ibid para 42 of the Opinion.
[288] Case C-256/11 *Dereci and Others*, EU:C:2011:734, para 28: 'on one or more of the following grounds: the existence of procedural defects in the application; failure to comply with the obligation to remain abroad whilst awaiting the decision on the application on account of either irregular entry into Austria or regular entry followed

involved were different, spanning third-country nationals who were spouses, parents of minor children, and parents of adult children. After *Ruiz Zambrano* and *McCarthy*, it was not clear if the nature of the family relationship was *formally* determinative: in other words, could Article 20 TFEU rights be invoked in situations that did not involve Union citizens who were minor children and their parents? Tthe significance of dependency as the necessary *substantive* requirement only became clearer in subsequent case law. It did not feature explicitly in *Dereci*, which focused more abstractly on being obliged to leave the territory of the Union. However, in *O and S*, the Court affirmed that 'it is the *relationship of dependency* between the Union citizen who is a minor and the third-country national who is refused a right of residence that is liable to jeopardise the effectiveness of Union citizenship, *since it is that dependency that would lead to the Union citizen being obliged, in fact*, to leave not only the territory of the Member State of which he is a national but also that of the European Union as a whole, as a consequence of such a refusal'.[289] What does the requirement of dependency actually entail, and what kinds of relationships might produce it?

We saw in Chapter 4 that for residence rights under Article 2(2)(c) (direct descendants over the age of 21) and Article 2(2)(d) (direct relatives in the ascending line) of Directive 2004/38, dependency concerns financial or material dependency only.[290] For Article 3(2)(a), under which entry and residence might be facilitated for 'other family members' under certain conditions, recital 6 considers 'financial or physical dependence on the Union citizen'. Under Article 20 TFEU, dependency has a distinctive meaning, but it aligns more with how the concept is applied under Article 3(2)(a) than under Article 2(2) of the Directive. In *Dereci*, Advocate General Mengozzi opened a door to the idea of a Union citizen being 'economically and/or legally, administratively and emotionally dependent' on a third-country national.[291] The Court then walked through it in *O and S*, finding that 'the third-country nationals for whom a right of residence is sought' must be 'persons on whom those citizens are legally, financially or emotionally dependent'.[292] Two further clarifications also came in *O and S*. First, it is not 'decisive' in the overall assessment that national authorities must undertake whether the family member for whom a right of residence is sought lives with the Union citizen.[293] Second, there is no requirement for a 'a blood relationship between the third-country national for whom a right of residence is sought and the Union citizen who is a minor from whom that right of residence might be derived'.[294] As expressed by Advocate General Bot, Article 20 TFEU's reach therefore extends to situations where a Union citizen 'has no other choice but to follow the person concerned, whose right of residence has been refused, because he is in that person's care and thus entirely dependent on that person to ensure his maintenance and provide for his own needs'.[295] Thus, the concept of

by an extended stay beyond that which was originally permitted; lack of sufficient resources; or a breach of public policy'.

[289] Joined Cases C-356/11 and C-357/11 *O and S*, EU:C:2012:776, para 56 (emphasis added).
[290] eg Case C-40/11 *Iida*, EU:C:2012:691, para 55: 'the status of "dependent" family member of a Union citizen holding a right of residence is the result of a factual situation characterised by the fact that material support for the family member is provided by the holder of the right of residence, so that, when the converse situation occurs and the holder of the right of residence is dependant on a third-country national, the third-country national cannot rely on being a 'dependent' relative in the ascending line of that right-holder, within the meaning of Directive 2004/38'.
[291] AG Mengozzi in Case C-256/11 *Dereci*, EU:C:2011:626, para 48 of the Opinion.
[292] *O and S*, para 56.
[293] ibid para 54.
[294] ibid para 55. As noted in Chapter 4, this point has only recently been determined for 'other family members' within the meaning of Article 3(2)(a) of the Directive (Case C-22/21 *SRS and AA*, EU:C:2022:683).
[295] AG Bot in *O and S*, EU:C:2012:595, para 44 of the Opinion.

a 'family member' under Article 20 TFEU is based more on substantive relationship quality than formal relationship type, in contrast to how 'family members' are defined in Article 2(2) of Directive 2004/38.

At this point in the case law, however, there were still several open questions regarding the beneficiaries of Article 20 TFEU residence rights. For example, what was the position of second parents—for example, for Mrs Ruiz Zambrano? In *O and S*, the *Ruiz Zambrano* case was conveyed as one in which a residence right was extended to '*a person* [Mr Ruiz Zambrano] who is a third-country national in the Member State of residence of his minor children, nationals of that Member State, who are dependent on him *and of whom he and his spouse have joint custody*'.[296] Could a Union citizen be dependent on *both* parents or only on their primary carer? How did the idea of 'emotional' dependence, acknowledged in *O and S*, relate to the previous outcome in *McCarthy*—why, in other words, did the emotional dependence shared by spouses not suffice? And what about situations of intersectional dependence: for example, even if caring obligations were not personally undertaken by the person concerned, would dimensions of emotional dependence still suffice 'in fact' in such cases? The more recent resolution of some of these questions is returned to in Section 3.3.1 .

3.2.4 The Charter of Fundamental Rights

While the Court in *Dereci* ruled out residence rights for the third-country national family members of Union citizens where the latter considered it 'merely desirable ... to keep [their] family together in the territory of the Union', it did acknowledge that '[t]hat finding is, admittedly, without prejudice to the question whether, on the basis of other criteria, inter alia, by virtue of the right to the protection of family life, a right of residence cannot be refused'— while insisting, at the same time, that this question 'must be tackled in the framework of the provisions on the protection of fundamental rights which are applicable in each case'.[297] Aligning the guarantees in Articles 7 CFR and 8 ECHR respectively,[298] the Court recalled the limits to the scope of the Charter set out Article 51(1) CFR and, in particular, that the Charter is addressed to the Member States only when they are 'implementing' EU law.[299] Rather unhelpfully, the Court then stated that the referring court should consider whether refusing a right of residence to any of the applicants in the proceedings 'undermines the right to respect for private and family life' in Article 7 CFR if any of the relevant family situations was covered by EU law, though, if they were not, then the relevant assessment should take place on the basis of Article 8 ECHR.[300] But what did that mean? In other words, at what stage of the analysis does a national court's assessment of family circumstances vis-à-vis Article 20 TFEU become one *of EU law*?[301]

Advocate General Mengozzi had considered these questions in *Dereci*, suggesting that focusing on whether or not Union citizens are obliged to leave the territory of the Union is 'based on the premiss that "the substance of the rights attaching to the status of European Union citizen" within the meaning of ... *Ruiz Zambrano* does not include the right to respect for family life enshrined in Article 7 [CFR] and in Article 8(1) of the ECHR'.[302] In other

---

[296] *O and S*, para 46 (emphasis added).
[297] Case C-256/11 *Dereci and Others*, EU:C:2011:734, paras 68 and 69.
[298] ibid para 70.
[299] ibid para 71.
[300] ibid para 72.
[301] Offering an argument that engaged Articles 7 and 24(3) CFR but as a restriction of free movement under Article 21 TFEU, see AG Trstenjak in Case C-40/11 *Iida*, EU:C:2012:296, paras 75–87 of the Opinion.
[302] AG Mengozzi in *Dereci and Others*, EU:C:2011:626, para 37 of the Opinion.

words, 'the right to respect for family life appears to be *insufficient, in itself, to bring within the scope of Union law* the situation of a Union citizen who has not exercised his right of free movement and/or, as the case may be, has not been deprived of the genuine enjoyment of one of the other rights set out in Article 20(2)(b) to (d) TFEU'.[303] He explained this position by referring to 'the concern that the Union's powers and those of its institutions should not encroach on those of the Member States in the field of immigration or on those of the European Court of Human Rights in the field of protection of fundamental rights, in accordance with Article 6(1) TEU and Article 51(2) [CFR]', so that 'the protection afforded ... by these three legal orders – national, Union and treaty law – proves to be complementary'.[304]

The Court's hesitancy about the role of the Charter in Article 20 TFEU cases was also evident in *Ymeraga*, where it held that to determine whether a decision taken by national authorities to refuse to grant residence rights to the family members of a Union citizen amounts to 'implementing Union law' as required by Article 51(1) CFR, it should be ascertained 'whether the national legislation at issue is intended to implement a provision of European Union law, what the character of that legislation is, and whether it pursues objectives other than those covered by European Union law, even if it is capable of indirectly affecting that law, and also whether there are specific rules of European Union law on the matter or capable of affecting it'.[305] In the circumstances of the case, the Court acknowledged that while the contested national rules were 'indeed intended to implement European Union law, it is none the less the case that the situation of the applicants in the main proceedings is not governed by European Union law': the facts did not come within the scope of either Directive 2004/38 or Directive 2003/86,[306] and 'the refusal to confer a right of residence on [the Union citizen]'s family members does not have the effect of denying him the genuine enjoyment of the substance of the rights conferred by virtue of his status as citizen of the Union'.[307] Once again, the Court also observed that its findings did not 'prejudge the question whether, on the basis of an examination in the light of the provisions of the [ECHR], to which all Member States are parties, to the third-country nationals in the main proceedings may not be refused a right of residence'.[308]

The Court's reasoning seems logical at one level—if a residence right cannot be based on Article 20 TFEU, the residual nature of which having already have ruled out a residence right based on any other provision of EU law, then the situation falls within national immigration competence only. It also reflects Advocate General Mengozzi's depiction of the multilevel system of protection of fundamental rights in the European legal space, which is founded on and must respect conferral of competence.[309] The problem occurs when the question of whether a residence right can be sourced in Article 20 TFEU is inevitably joined to considering *why* that is or is not the case. In other words, determining whether, and if so, why a Union citizen is obliged to leave the territory of the Union in the first place requires assessment of the relevant relationship(s) of dependency—something that would not necessarily be required under national rules alone. In *O and S*, albeit in the context of decisions taken by national authorities under Directive 2003/86 in a more straightforward sense of

---

[303] ibid para 38 of the Opinion (emphasis added).
[304] ibid paras 39–40 of the Opinion. See similarly, as discussed in Section 2, Lenaerts (n 67).
[305] Case C-87/12 *Ymeraga*, EU:C:2013:291, para 41.
[306] Council Directive 2003/86/EC on the right to family reunification, 2003 OJ L251/12.
[307] *Ymeraga*, para 42.
[308] ibid para 44.
[309] See eg S Adam and P van Elsuwege 'Citizenship rights and the federal balance between the European Union and its Member States: comment on *Dereci*' (2012) 37 European Law Review 176 esp at 182.

'implementing Union law', the Court held that Article 7 CFR *'must also be read in conjunction with the obligation to have regard to the child's best interests*, recognised in Article 24(2) of the Charter, and with account being taken of the need, expressed in Article 24(3), for a child *to maintain on a regular basis a personal relationship with both parents'*.[310] That statement would later be applied in the Article 20 TFEU context too, as returned to in Section 3.3.2.

3.3 Progressing Residence Rights Based on Article 20 TFEU

In one sense, it was fortunate that further preliminary references arrived at the Court of Justice within months of the ruling in *Ruiz Zambrano*, providing opportunities for fast and reflexive shaping of the new Article 20 TFEU rights. Less positively, though, that case law was perhaps then too rushed and arguably too sensitive to early criticism of *Ruiz Zambrano*.[311] Over time, the evolution of the case law has become more measured and more coherent. Further judgments have clarified how eligibility for residence rights based on Article 20 TFEU should be assessed (Section 3.3.1), established the role of the Charter in such situations (Section 3.3.2), and addressed Article 20 TFEU's outer limits (Section 3.3.3).

3.3.1 Refining the assessment of eligibility for Article 20 TFEU residence rights

In terms of the assessment that must be undertaken by national authorities, introducing an 'in fact' dimension in *O and S*—which considers a Union citizen's *actual* capacity to remain in the territory of the Union in the absence of residence rights for the third-country family member(s) on whom they depend being granted in the home State—signalled the possibility of significant change compared to earlier case law. It began in *Rendón Marín*. In that case, a Colombian national had sole responsibility for his two children: a Spanish national son and a Polish national daughter, both of whom had always resided in Spain. No contact was sustained with the children's mother, also a Polish national. Following *Alokpa and Moudoulou*, the Court of Justice first advised the referring court that a right to reside in Spain for Mr Rendón Marín might be derived from his Polish daughter under Article 21 TFEU (in line with *Zhu and Chen*), provided that his daughter satisfied the conditions for lawful residence in a host State in Directive 2004/38.[312] Only if those conditions were not met, the referring court should, alternatively, consider the residence rights conferred in exceptional circumstances by Article 20 TFEU.

Starting with the fact that Mr Rendón Marín was a third-country national 'to whose sole care those children have been entrusted', it therefore had to be determined if refusal to grant him a residence right based on Article 20 TFEU would mean that he would have to leave the territory of the Union, which would in turn undermine the rights of his Union citizen children because they 'could be compelled to go with him'.[313] The Court noted that '[s]everal Member States which have submitted observations have contended that Mr Rendón Marín and his children could move to Poland, the Member State of which his daughter is a national',

---

[310] Joined Cases C-356/11 and C-357/11 *O and S*, EU:C:2012:776, para 76 (emphasis added). See generally, M Klaassen and P Rodrigues, 'The best interests of the child in EU family reunification law: a plea for more guidance on the role of Art. 24(2) Charter' (2017) 19 European Journal of Migration and Law 191.
[311] See eg M Blauberger, A Heindlmaier, D Kramer, D Sindbjerg Martinsen, J Sampson Thierry, A Schenk, and B Werner, 'ECJ judges read the morning papers: explaining the turnaround of European citizenship jurisprudence' (2018) 25 Journal of European Public Policy 1422.
[312] Case C-165/14 *Rendón Marín*, EU:C:2016:675, paras 38–52. However, account could also be taken of Mr Rendón Marín's criminal record in the decision-making process; see further, Section 3.3.3.
[313] ibid para 78.

which was an entirely credible argument following *Alokpa and Moudoulou*.³¹⁴ But Mr Rendón Marín had 'stated at the hearing that he maintains no ties with the family of his daughter's mother, who, according to him, does not reside in Poland, and that neither he nor his children know the Polish language'.³¹⁵ The Court observed that the final determination of the facts was a matter for the referring court, but it strongly suggested that 'the situation at issue in the main proceedings is capable of resulting, for Mr Marín's children, in their being deprived of the genuine enjoyment of the substance of the rights which the status of Union citizen confers upon them, and that it therefore falls within the scope of EU law'.³¹⁶ There was no explicit reference to the *O and S* 'in fact' test but there was a clear engagement with its logic: in contrast to *Alokpa and Moudoulou*, the capacity to remain within the territory of the Union by relocating a family to another Member State was *probed—not presumed*.

The Court further developed its guidance in *Chavez-Vilchez*. This complex case joined eight different proceedings in the Netherlands,³¹⁷ all of which concerned applications for social assistance and child benefits submitted by third-country national mothers of one or more children of Netherlands nationality whose fathers were also of Netherlands nationality. All of the children—only one of whom had previously exercised free movement rights³¹⁸— lived primarily with their mothers and all of the applications were refused on the basis that none of the mothers held residence permits in the Netherlands (at the time of the preliminary reference³¹⁹). Addressing the relevance of derived residence rights under Article 20 TFEU, the questions referred focused on the meaning of being obliged to leave the territory of the Union, on the one hand, in light of the options for providing care for minor Union citizens that (might) exist, on the other. In particular, the referring court sought to ascertain 'what importance is to be given, in the light of the Court's case-law, to the fact that the father, a Union citizen, is staying in the Netherlands or in the European Union, as a whole'.³²⁰ Differences between various decisions at national level were highlighted:

> [I]n practice, various administrative bodies interpret the judgments [in *Ruiz Zambrano* and *Dereci*] restrictively and hold that the case-law enshrined in those judgments is applicable only in situations where the father is not, on the basis of objective criteria, in a position to care for the child because he is, for example, in prison, confined to an institution or hospitalised, or even dead. Other than in such situations, it is for the third-country national parent to establish a plausible case that the father is incapable of caring for the child, even with the possible assistance of third parties. According to the referring court, such rules stem from the guidelines in the Circular on Foreign Nationals.³²¹

---

³¹⁴ ibid para 79.
³¹⁵ ibid para79.
³¹⁶ ibid para 80.
³¹⁷ For an overview of the facts in each set of proceedings, see Case C-133/15 *Chavez-Vilchez*, EU:C:2017:354, paras 21–28.
³¹⁸ Leading to an examination of her situation under Article 21 TFEU in the first instance: ibid paras 49–57.
³¹⁹ Residence permits had been granted in the interim to two of the applicants (ibid paras 44–45).
³²⁰ ibid para 34.
³²¹ ibid para 36. The country report submitted for the 2014 FIDE Congress had illustrated the practical difficulties that national courts and tribunals in the Netherlands faced when trying to apply both national administrative guidance and the Court's early Article 20 TFEU case law (see further, N Nic Shuibhne and J Shaw, 'Union citizenship: development, impact and challenges' in U Neergaard, C Jacqueson, and N Holst-Christensen (eds), *Union Citizenship: Development, Impact and Challenges*, XXVI FIDE Congress (2014), Vol. 2, <http://fide2014.eu/pdf/FINAL-Topic-2-on-Union-Citizenship.pdf> (accessed 29 May 2023), esp 145–47; in the same volume, see also the report on the Netherlands, prepared by J Langer and A Schrauwen, 695 at 705–708).

The Court of Justice observed that 'as regards the relationships between the parents and the children, it is apparent from the order for reference that contact between the children and their fathers was, variously, frequent, seldom or even non-existent'.[322] It then summarised the question at the heart of the reference: 'whether Article 20 TFEU must be interpreted as precluding a Member State from refusing a right of residence in its territory to a parent, a third-country national, who is responsible for the primary day-to-day care of a child who is a national of that Member State, *when it cannot be excluded that the other parent, who is also a national of that Member State, might be able to take charge* of the primary day-to-day care of the child. The referring court seeks to ascertain whether the fact that the child is *not entirely dependent*, legally, financially or emotionally, on the third-country national is relevant to that issue'.[323]

The position taken by the Netherlands Government in this respect was stunningly narrow. It submitted that, 'in certain circumstances, the competent national authorities assume that the parent who is a Union citizen is unfit or unable to care for the child'—but then, that this would apply 'where that parent is dead or cannot be traced; where that parent has been imprisoned, confined to an institution or admitted to hospital for long-term treatment; where, according to objective sources, such as a statement from the police or youth assistance services, that parent is shown to be incapable of caring for the child, and, last, where an application by that parent to obtain custody, even jointly, has been dismissed by the courts'.[324]

That interpretation advances a literal and very narrow understanding of being 'obliged' to leave the territory of the Union because alternative arrangements could be made, however sub-optimal. However, it would be difficult to counter it based on *McCarthy*, *Dereci*, and *Alokpa and Moudoulou*. Thus, in *Chavez-Vilchez*, the Court finally invoked and augmented the ruling in *O and S* and developed a more rounded framework of assessment for national authorities.[325] Bridging to the significance of the Charter, returned to separately in Section 3.3.2, and in the context of the vital relationship of dependency that must underpin derived residence rights under Article 20 TFEU, the Court stated:

> [I]t is important to determine ... which parent is the primary carer of the child and *whether there is in fact a relationship of dependency* between the child and the third-country national parent. As part of that assessment, the competent authorities must take account of the right to respect for family life, as stated in Article 7 of the Charter of Fundamental Rights of the European Union, that article requiring to be read in conjunction with the obligation to take into consideration the best interests of the child, recognised in Article 24(2) of that charter. For the purposes of such an assessment, the fact that the other parent, a Union citizen, is actually able and willing to assume sole responsibility for the primary day-to-day care of the child is *a relevant factor, but it is not in itself a sufficient ground for a conclusion that there is not, between the third-country national parent and the child, such a relationship of dependency* that the child would be compelled to leave the territory of the European Union if a right of residence were refused to that third-country national.

---

[322] *Chavez-Vilchez*, para 43, continuing that 'in one case, the father could not be traced, and in another the father was in a supported accommodation scheme. In three cases, the father was contributing to maintenance costs for the child, while, in five other cases, no contribution was made. Whereas in two out of the eight cases the parents shared custody, in the six other cases the primary day-to-day care of the child was the responsibility of the mother alone. Last, in half of the cases, the child was living with the mother in an emergency refuge'.
[323] ibid para 59 (emphasis added).
[324] ibid para 67.
[325] ibid paras 68–69.

In reaching such a conclusion, *account must be taken, in the best interests of the child concerned, of all the specific circumstances*, including the age of the child, the child's physical and emotional development, the extent of his emotional ties both to the Union citizen parent and to the third-country national parent, *and the risks which separation from the latter might entail for that child's equilibrium*.[326]

The Court also provided guidance on the burden of proof, which the Netherlands Government had argued that rested with the applicants in suggested that '[i]t is for them to demonstrate that, because of objective impediments that prevent the Union citizen parent from actually caring for the child, the child is dependent on the third-country national parent to such an extent that the consequence of refusing to grant that third-country national a right of residence would be that the child would be obliged, in practice, to leave the territory of the European Union'.[327] The Court was more nuanced. It confirmed that it was indeed for the third-country national parent 'to provide evidence on the basis of which it can be assessed whether the conditions governing the application of [Article 20 TFEU] are satisfied'.[328] Nevertheless, 'when undertaking the assessment of the conditions required in order for the third-country national to be able to qualify for such a right of residence, the competent national authorities must ensure that the application of national legislation on the burden of proof ... does not undermine the effectiveness of Article 20 TFEU'.[329] In particular:

> [T]he application of such national legislation on the burden of proof does not relieve the authorities of the Member State concerned of *the obligation to undertake*, on the basis of the evidence provided by the third-country national, *the necessary inquiries* to determine where the parent who is a national of that Member State resides and to examine, first, whether that parent *is, or is not, actually able and willing to assume sole responsibility* for the primary day-to-day care of the child, and, second, whether there is, or is not, such a relationship of dependency between the child and the third-country national parent that a decision to refuse the right of residence to the latter would deprive the child of the genuine enjoyment of the substance of the rights attached to his or her status as a Union citizen by obliging the child to leave the territory of the European Union, as a whole.[330]

National rules that automatically bar an assessment of family reunification under EU law for applications submitted by third-country nationals are thus precluded.[331] While EU law 'does not, in principle, preclude legislation of a Member State under which ... family reunification [of a third-country national with a member of his or her family who is a national of a Member State and has never exercised the freedom of movement] is subject to a condition of

---

[326] ibid paras 70–71 (emphasis added).
[327] ibid para 74.
[328] ibid para 75; referring to this as the 'general rule' in para 76.
[329] ibid para 76.
[330] ibid para 77 (emphasis added). See, more generously to the applicants, AG Szpunar in *Chavez-Vilchez*, EU:C:2016:659, paras 112–113 of the Opinion.
[331] eg In *KA and Others*, the successfully contested national administrative practice meant that '[w]here a third-country national subject to a valid entry ban of at least three years which has become final subsequently makes an application from within Belgium for residence for the purposes of family reunification with an EU citizen, his application is not examined by the competent authorities. There is no leeway in specific cases to take account of family life, the best interests of the child where relevant or the fact that the Belgian family member has EU citizenship' (AG Sharpston in Case C-82/16 *KA and Others*, EU:C:2017:821, para 47 of the Opinion; see similarly, para 53 of the Opinion remarking on the 'automaticity of the national practice').

sufficient resources, ... the *systematic imposition, without any exception*, of such a condition is liable to fail to have regard to the derived right of residence which must be recognised, in very specific situations, under Article 20 TFEU'.[332]

The ruling in *Chavez-Vilchez* meant that the threshold of being obliged to leave the territory of the Union acquired meaningful substance within the *Ruiz Zambrano* framework.[333] In the comprehensive assessment required for situations involving minor children, relevant factors include who has custody; who the primary carer is; who the child lives with; and the extent of legal, financial or emotional dependence on the third-country national parent.[334] However, while the protective scope of Article 20 TFEU is not confined to minor Union citizens in principle, it will be much more difficult to satisfy the required threshold of dependency for other relationships in reality. In *KA*, the Court confirmed that, 'unlike minors and *a fortiori* minors who are young children, ... an adult is, *as a general rule*, capable of living an independent existence apart from the members of his family', with the result that 'the identification of a relationship between two adult members of the same family as a relationship of dependency, capable of giving rise to a derived right of residence under Article 20 TFEU, is *conceivable only in exceptional cases*, where, having regard to all the relevant circumstances, *there could be no form of separation* of the individual concerned from the member of his family on whom he is dependent'.[335]

Dependency that is 'purely financial' would not meet that threshold.[336] Emotional dependency is also insufficient in the context of adult relationships: for example, a relationship as the 'lawful cohabitant' of a Union citizen is not enough in and of itself.[337] This is how the *Dereci* language about the 'mere fact that it might be desirable to a national of a Member State, for economic reasons or in order to keep his family together in the territory of the Union' has acquired both nuance and clearer meaning over time.[338] It still leaves Mr McCarthy without redress under Article 20 TFEU because 'the existence of a family link, whether natural or legal ... cannot be sufficient'—dependency that compromises the continued residence of the Union citizen within the territory of the Union must be demonstrated above and beyond that link.[339] *Chavez-Vilchez* and subsequent rulings ensure that the required assessment takes account of the reality of family circumstances. But they do not rule out consequences that are profoundly 'humanly painful',[340] which bridges to the next question: when the Charter might—and does not—make a material difference.

---

[332] Case C-836/18 *Subdelegación del Gobierno en Ciudad Real (Conjoint d'un citoyen de l'Union)*, EU:C:2020:119, paras 33–34 (emphasis added). Reflecting on the central idea of 'very specific situations' through the lens of effectiveness as well as questioning 'what value the status of EU citizenship has in itself – without any reference to movement, whether free or forced' (1220), see PJ Neuvonen, 'EU citizenship and its "very specific" essence: *Rendón Marín* and *CS*' (2017) 54 Common Market Law Review 1201.

[333] For AG Wathelet, a 'factual examination of the "deprivation of the substance of rights" test is consistent with the logic that must inform our understanding of the concept of citizenship of the Union' (Case C-115/15 *NA*, EU:C:2016:259, para 110 of the Opinion).

[334] Case C-82/16 *KA and Others*, EU:C:2018:308, paras 70 and 73.

[335] *KA and Others*, para 65 (emphasis added); confirmed in *Subdelegación del Gobierno en Ciudad Real*, para 56. AG Sharpston's example of 'where an elderly or infirm [Union citizen] parent relies on the presence of his third-country national adult child and would be obliged to leave the European Union if that child is expelled from the Member State concerned' was arguably less stringent than the position established by the Court (*KA and Others*, para 79 of the Opinion).

[336] Case C-82/16 *KA and Others*, EU:C:2018:308, para 68.

[337] ibid para 69.

[338] ibid para 74; confirming *Dereci* para 68.

[339] *KA and Others*, para 75; confirmed in eg Joined Cases C-451/19 and C-532/19 *Subdelegación del Gobierno en Toledo (Séjour d'un membre de la famille—Ressources insuffisantes)*, EU:C:2022:354, para 58.

[340] G Davies, 'The right to stay at home: a basis for expanding European family rights' in Kochenov (ed) (n 80), 468 at 487, discussing the idea of 'reverse dependency'.

3.3.2 Embedding the Charter of Fundamental Rights

Alongside the Court's more nuanced approach to assessing situations of dependency, why and how it changed its position on the relevance of the Charter is also highly significant.

3.3.2.1 *From* Dereci *to* Chavez-Vilchez

It was noted in Section 3.2.4 that the Court of Justice has consistently encouraged national courts to reflect on the lawfulness of refused residence rights for family members under Article 8 ECHR when the Charter does not apply. In *Dereci*, it offered rather vague guidance on this distinction: the referring court should consider whether refusing a right of residence 'undermines the right to respect for private and family life' provided for in Article 7 CFR if it considered that the situation before it fell within the scope EU law; otherwise, the relevant assessment should take place on the basis of Article 8 ECHR.[341] A crucial difference between the family reunification inquiry undertaken by the ECtHR and the Court of Justice respectively is that the former necessarily focuses on family reunification as a prospect per se, while the Court of Justice adds the dimension of family reunification within the territory of the Union since *Ruiz Zambrano*.[342] To consider whether a situation fell within the scope of EU law in the first place, the dependency that unlocks Article 20 TFEU rights had to be considered *first* and only such dependency, within the meaning of relevant EU case law, was established would the situation *then* be considered as falling within the scope of EU law. But how was it logical to sever determination of dependency using criteria *drawn from EU law* from the obligation to respect family life *required by EU law*?[343] The paradoxical position in which national judges might then find themselves was that factual circumstances acknowledged to breach Article 8 ECHR[344] could remain detached from the scope of EU law (and thus Article 7 CFR) even though the national judge was determining the existence of rights under Article 20 TFEU: an assessment only required by *Ruiz Zambrano*—by EU law—in the first place.

National administrative authorities and national courts inevitably took diverging approaches in Article 20 TFEU cases as a result.[345] Disconnecting a determination of dependency from a fundamental rights analysis was also difficult to reconcile with ECtHR case law on Article 8 ECHR. In particular, in *Jeunesse v The Netherlands*, the ECtHR had reflected on a family situation involving a Surinamese mother and Dutch father as follows:

> Noting that the applicant takes care of the children on a daily basis, it is obvious that their interests are best served by not disrupting their present circumstances by a forced relocation of their mother from the Netherlands to Suriname or by a rupturing of their

---

[341] Case C-256/11 *Dereci and Others*, EU:C:2011:734, para 72.

[342] Article 8 ECHR 'does not guarantee foreign nationals "a right to choose the most suitable place to develop family life" and does not impose on a State "a general obligation to respect immigrants' choice of the country of their matrimonial residence and to authorise family reunion in its territory"' (AG Bot in Case C-83/11 *Rahman*, EU:C:2012:174, para 72 of the Opinion, referring to *Ahmut v The Netherlands* (1996) 24 EHRR 62 and *Gül v Switzerland* (1996) 22 EHRR 93).

[343] See eg Case C-304/14 *CS*, EU:C:2016:674, paras 33 and 36, where the scope of EU law was unlocked only *after* it was determined that the Union citizen was likely to be compelled to leave the territory of the Union with the third-country national primary carer on whom they were dependent.

[344] See eg AG Wathelet in Case C-115/15 *NA*, EU:C:2016:259, paras 116–117 of the Opinion.

[345] In the High Court (England and Wales), Purle J remarked that '[t]he precise impact of *[Ruiz] Zambrano* has a number of us scratching our heads at regular intervals' (*R (on the application of Sanneh) v Secretary of State for Work and Pensions*, [2013] EWHC 793 (Admin), para 5). See further, N Nic Shuibhne, 'Integrating Union citizenship and the Charter of Fundamental Rights' in D Thym (ed), *Questioning EU Citizenship: Judges and the Limits of Free Movement and Solidarity in the EU* (Hart Publishing 2017) 209 at 232–33.

relationship with her as a result of future separation. In this connection, the Court observes that the applicant's husband provides for the family by working full-time in a job that includes shift work. He is, consequently, absent from the home on some evenings. The applicant – being the mother and homemaker – is the primary and constant carer of the children who are deeply rooted in the Netherlands of which country – like their father – they are nationals. The materials in the case file do not disclose a direct link between the applicant's children and Suriname, a country where they have never been.[346]

However, following *Dereci* and *Alokpa and Moudoulu*, it would have been difficult to demonstrate forced departure from the territory of the Union in such circumstances on account of the father's Dutch nationality, in tension with the ECtHR's more inclusive way of conceiving family relationships.

These anomalies in the Court of Justice's case law thus began to be highlighted by its Advocates General. In particular, in her joint Opinion for *O and B* and *S and G*, Advocate General Sharpston argued that 'the Court has yet to resolve whether one applies the same test in order to determine both whether EU law (and thus also the Charter) applies and whether a measure denying residence is contrary to Article 20 or 21 TFEU'.[347] She acknowledged that 'it is necessary to look at a legal situation through the prism of the Charter if, but only if, a provision of EU law imposes a positive or negative obligation on the Member State (whether that obligation arises through the Treaties or EU secondary legislation)'.[348] But how is the obligation to assess whether or not a *Ruiz Zambrano* residence right might exist *not* one imposed on national authorities by EU law since it flows from Article 20 TFEU? In the same Opinion, the Advocate General thus argued:

> [A] provision such as Article 20 or 21 TFEU is not simply a basis for residence status separate from Article 7 of the Charter. Rather, considerations regarding the exercise of the right to a family life permeate the substance of EU citizenship rights. Citizenship rights under Article 20 or 21 TFEU must thus be interpreted in a way that ensures that their substantive content is 'Charter-compliant'. That process is separate from the question of whether a justification advanced for a restriction of EU citizenship rights ... is consistent with the Charter. Such an approach does not 'extend' the scope of EU law and thus violate the separation of competences between the Union and its constituent Member States. It merely respects the overarching principle that, in a Union founded on the rule of law, all the relevant law (including, naturally, relevant primary law in the shape of the Charter) is taken into account when interpreting a provision of that legal order. When viewed in that light, taking due account of the Charter is no more 'intrusive', or 'disrespectful of Member State competence', than interpreting free movement of goods correctly.[349]

Advocate General Wathelet developed similar arguments in *NA*, pointing out that '[i]f a Treaty provision does not preclude a Member State from refusing a right of residence subject

---

[346] *Jeunesse v The Netherlands* (2015) 60 EHRR 17, para 119. Assessing *Jeunesse* in its wider ECHR context, see E Nissen, 'A children's rights perspective to *Ruiz Zambrano* and *Chavez-Vilchez*: an Examination in light of theory, practice and child development research' (2021) 23 European Journal of Migration and Law 68 at 77–80; and C Costello, *The Human Rights of Migrants and Refugees in European Law* (OUP 2015) 103ff.

[347] AG Sharpston in Case C-456/12 *O and B* and Case C-457/12 *S and G*, EU:C:2013:837, para 58 of the Opinion.

[348] ibid para 61 of the Opinion.

[349] ibid paras 62–63 of the Opinion.

to compliance with certain conditions, *it follows by definition that the situation in question falls within the scope of that provision. If that were not the case, the Court would have to decline jurisdiction to answer the question referred*.[350] Expressly endorsing Advocate General Sharpston's remarks, he considered that 'the inclusion of Article 7 of the Charter in the national court's reflection on the application of Article 20 TFEU is not such as to have the effect of extending the scope of EU law in a manner that would be contrary to Article 51(2) of the Charter. After all, *it is European citizenship as provided for in Article 20 TFEU that triggers the protection afforded by the fundamental rights ... not the other way round*'.[351]

That reasoning integrates Article 20 TFEU and the requirements of the Charter, in contrast to the approach that had been taken by the Court. It is also legally sound.[352] Article 20 TFEU requires national authorities to consider derived residence rights in a Union citizen's home State where the denial of such rights might deprive the Union citizen of the genuine enjoyment of the substance of their Union citizenship rights. That requirement thus itself imposes an obligation on national authorities, which accords with the *Åkerberg Fransson* understanding of 'implementing' EU law in accordance with Article 51(1) CFR.[353] The instinct to limit the reach of EU law in situations that are factually confined to one Member State is understandable. But pursuing a fragmented approach to what does or does not fall within the scope of EU law to delimit the guarantees and obligations agreed to in the Charter is not a defensible solution to a more general scope of EU law problem. Where the Article 20 TFEU door is opened—and the Court of Justice itself opened it—the Charter applies in consequence.

In *Chavez-Vilchez*, the Court adjusted its earlier position by requiring that assessments of dependency involving Union citizen children should take account of Articles 7 and 24 CFR:

> [I]n order to assess the risk that a particular child, who is a Union citizen, *might be compelled to leave the territory of the European Union* and thereby be deprived of the genuine enjoyment of the substance of the rights conferred on him by Article 20 TFEU if the child's third-country national parent were to be refused a right of residence in the Member State concerned, it is important to determine ... which parent is the primary carer of the child and whether there is in fact a relationship of dependency between the child and the third-country national parent. *As part of that assessment, the competent authorities must take account of the right to respect for family life, as stated in Article 7 of the Charter* of Fundamental Rights of the European Union, that article requiring to be read in conjunction with the obligation to take into consideration the best interests of the child, recognised in Article 24(2) of that charter.[354]

---

[350] AG Wathelet in Case C-115/15 *NA*, EU:C:2016:259, para 122 of the Opinion (emphasis added). See also, AG Szpunar in Case C-165/14 *Rendón Marín* and Case C-304/14 *CS*, EU:C:2016:75, paras 119–122 of the Opinion.

[351] AG Wathelet in *NA*, para 125 of the Opinion (emphasis added).

[352] However, considering relevant complexities through an illuminating 'chicken and egg' analysis, see H van Eijken and P Phoa, 'The scope of Article 20 TFEU clarified in *Chavez-Vilchez*: are the fundamental rights of minor EU citizens coming of age? (Case Comment)' (2018) 43 European Law Review 949 at 956–59.

[353] Case C-617/10 *Åkerberg Fransson*, EU:C:2013:105; see further, Chapter 2. For a different view, see J Snell, 'Do fundamental rights determine the scope of EU law' (2018) 43 European Law Review 475.

[354] Case C-133/15 *Chavez-Vilchez*, EU:C:2017:354, para 70 (emphasis added); confirmed in eg Case C-82/16 *KA and Others*, EU:C:2018:308, para 71. Comparing the approaches to proportionality in the judgment of the Court and Opinion of AG Szpunar respectively, see F Staiano, 'Derivative residence rights for parents of Union citizen children under Art. 20 TFEU: *Chavez-Vilchez*' (2018) 55 Common Market Law Review 225 at 236–38. Highlighting the absence of reflection on State interests in *Chavez-Vilchez*, see van Eijken and Phoa (n 352) 963–64.

In *Subdelegación del Gobierno en Toledo*, the Court went even further in finding that 'where the Union citizen minor lives with both parents on a stable basis and where, therefore, the care of that child and the legal, emotional and financial responsibility in relation to that child are shared on a daily basis by those two parents, there is *a rebuttable presumption that there is a relationship of dependency* between that Union citizen minor and his or her parent who is a third-country national, irrespective of the fact that ... the other parent of that child has, as a national of the Member State in which that family is established, an unconditional right to remain in the territory of that Member State'.[355] As a result, the Court has not only recalibrated its Article 20 TFEU case law in line with its more general approach to Article 51 CFR, it has also better aligned the thinking that national judges need to do under the interlinked national, EU, and ECHR systems for protecting fundamental rights.

3.3.2.2 And beyond?
A final point to consider regarding the scope of the Charter: what next? For example, beyond Articles 7 and 24 CFR, what other Charter provisions are relevant for Article 20 TFEU assessments of dependency? For example, in Section 3.2.3, the potential for considering relationships of dependency in the context of disability was raised, which could be linked to Articles 21(1) (non-discrimination[356]) and 26 (integration of persons with disabilities) CFR.[357] Additionally, Article 7 CFR has to date been considered only in situations involving the rights of the child, in conjunction with Article 24. For Advocate General Szpunar, '[t]he primacy of the best interests of the child is one of the principles permeating the EU legal order'.[358] Conversely, we saw in Section 3.2.3 that 'identification of a relationship between two adult members of the same family as a relationship of dependency, capable of giving rise to a derived right of residence under Article 20 TFEU, is *conceivable only in exceptional cases*'.[359] In that light, consider how the Court summarised its response to the referring court's question in *KA*:

Article 20 TFEU must be interpreted as meaning that:
– where the Union citizen is an adult, a relationship of dependency, capable of justifying the grant to the third-country national concerned of a derived right of residence under Article 20 TFEU, is conceivable only in exceptional cases, where, in the light of all the relevant circumstances, any form of separation of the individual concerned from the member of his family on whom he is dependent is not possible;
– where the Union citizen is a minor, the assessment of the existence of such a relationship of dependency must be based on consideration, in the best interests of the child, of all the specific circumstances, including the age of the child, the child's physical and emotional

---

[355] Joined Cases C-451/19 and C-532/19 *Subdelegación del Gobierno en Toledo (Séjour d'un membre de la famille—Ressources insuffisantes)*, EU:C:2022:354, para 69 (emphasis added).
[356] Still in the context of Article 21(1) CFR but reflecting on *Chavez-Vilchez* from the perspective of gender, see Staiano (n 354) 238–40.
[357] Article 26 CFR provides that '[t]he Union recognises and respects the right of persons with disabilities to benefit from measures designed to ensure their independence, social and occupational integration and participation in the life of the community'. See generally, C O'Brien, 'Union citizenship and disability: restricted access to equality rights and the attitudinal model of disability' in Kochenov (ed) (n 80), 509.
[358] AG Szpunar in *Chavez-Vilchez*, EU:C:2016:659, para 42 of the Opinion; see further, paras 43–46.
[359] Case C-82/16 *KA and Others*, EU:C:2018:308, para 65 (emphasis added). In that light, Nissen discusses how the case law's emphasis on the particular dependency that characterises relationships involving children is 'rooted in the particular nature of childhood rather than in the child's citizenship status' (n 346, 85).

development, the extent of his emotional ties to each of his parents, and the risks which separation from the third-country national parent might entail for that child's equilibrium. The existence of a family link with that third-country national, whether natural or legal, is not sufficient, and cohabitation with that third-country national is not necessary, in order to establish such a relationship of dependency.[360]

Notably, Article 7 CFR is not mentioned at all in the context of relationships where the Union citizen is an adult.

Advocate General Sharpston had adopted a more expansive view than that taken by the Court and, importantly, she referred to obligations under both the Charter and the ECHR:

> Article 7 of the Charter must be construed in the light of Article 8 of the ECHR. The European Court of Human Rights ('the Strasbourg Court') has ruled that the essential object of Article 8 is to protect the individual concerned against arbitrary action by the public authorities, although that provision does not impose on a State a general obligation to authorise family reunification. The assessment for the purposes of Article 8 of the ECHR involves balancing the competing interests of the individual concerned and the State. It is necessary to consider *the consequences of the rupture of the family unit that would ensue if the third-country national family member is expelled*. In so doing, account is taken of *the length of time that the State concerned has tolerated the presence of that person on its territory*: whether spouses (or cohabitees) have a common background, whether the third-country national is responsible for the day-to-day care of any children and the financial responsibilities and emotional ties within the family.[361]

Considering Article 7 CFR in the context of adult relationships might not change the outcome of an Article 20 TFEU case, and applying greater Convention weight in family reunification cases involving children is also standard within ECtHR case law. Nevertheless, there is still quite some grey space between the dependency that defines the relationship between minor children and their carers, on the one hand, and a 'mere desire' to live together as a family in a particular place, on the other. Reflecting on the parameters of Article 7 CFR irrespective of the family relationship at issue would embed the idea that decisions of public authorities should be taken in the register of compliance with fundamental rights. Legitimate restrictions on such rights would then have to be rationalised against the criteria in Article 52(1) CFR.[362] In *Subdelegación del Gobierno en Ciudad Real*, returned to in Section 3.3.3, there are signs of the beginnings of such an approach (though, for now, in the context of assessing exceptions from rather than conferring Article 20 TFEU rights).

3.3.3 The limits of residence rights based on Article 20 TFEU

In line with rights conferred by Article 21 TFEU, 'the derived right of residence under Article 20 TFEU is not absolute, since Member States may refuse to grant it in certain specific circumstances'.[363] Two situations in which it might be justifiable not to grant Article 20

---

[360] *KA and Others*, para 76.

[361] AG Sharpston in Case C-82/16 *KA and Others*, EU:C:2017:821, para 61 of the Opinion (emphasis added); referring to ECtHR, 3 October 2014, *Jeunesse v the Netherlands* (2015) 60 EHRR 17, paras 106–109 and 115–121.

[362] Article 52(1) CFR requires that '[a]ny limitation on the exercise of the rights and freedoms recognised by this Charter must be provided for by law and respect the essence of those rights and freedoms. Subject to the principle of proportionality, limitations may be made only if they are necessary and genuinely meet objectives of general interest recognised by the Union or the need to protect the rights and freedoms of others'.

[363] Case C-836/18 *Subdelegación del Gobierno en Ciudad Real (Conjoint d'un citoyen de l'Union)*, EU:C:2020:119, para 43.

residence rights are considered here. First, 'Article 20 TFEU does not affect the possibility of Member States relying on an exception linked, in particular, to upholding the requirements of public policy and safeguarding public security.'[364] Second, can Article 20 rights be refused to protect a Member State's public finances; or conversely, where a residence right is granted under Article 20 TFEU, does it also raise obligations regarding entitlement to social assistance?

On the first question, a residence right may be refused to a third-country national family member in a Union citizen's home State for reasons of public policy or public security—even where the Union citizen who is dependent on that third-country national will be compelled to leave the territory of the Union as a result.[365] However, principles of EU law govern the taking of that decision and relevant assessments must therefore take account of the respect for private and family life guaranteed by Article 7 CFR, read in conjunction with the child's best interests protected in Article 24(2).[366] Such assessments must also take account, 'more generally, of the principle of proportionality as a general principle of EU law'.[367] The concepts of public policy and public security are defined[368] and applied in essentially the same way as for rights under Article 21 TFEU and Directive 2004/38: they must be interpreted strictly, since they are derogations from residence rights conferred by Union citizenship,[369] and their scope cannot be determined unilaterally by the Member States without oversight by the EU institutions.[370] The principles applied to determining the threat posed by the individual concerned as well as the implications that can be drawn from a criminal conviction are also broadly the same as the considerations that apply for freedom of movement, and in particular:

> [W]here refusal of the right of residence is founded on the existence of a genuine, present and sufficiently serious threat to the requirements of public policy or of public security, in view of the criminal offences committed by a third-country national who is the sole carer of children who are Union citizens, such refusal would be consistent with EU law. On the other hand, that conclusion cannot be drawn automatically on the basis solely of the criminal record of the person concerned. It can result, where appropriate, only from a specific assessment by the referring court of all the current and relevant circumstances of the case, in the light of the principle of proportionality, of the child's best interests and of the fundamental rights whose observance the Court ensures. That assessment must therefore take

---

[364] ibid para 44. Even a host State has very narrow scope to restrict entry and residence rights both for Union citizens and their family members on grounds of public health under Article 29 of Directive 2004/38 and only within the first three months after entry to that State (see further, Chapter 10): in that light, it is understandable that public health was not addressed by the Court for derived residence rights in a Union citizen's home State under Article 20 TFEU.

[365] Case C-82/16 *KA and Others*, EU:C:2018:308, para 92: 'where the refusal of a right of residence is founded on the existence of a genuine, present and sufficiently serious threat to the requirements of public policy or of public security, in view of, inter alia, criminal offences committed by a third-country national, is accordingly compatible with EU law even if its effect is that the Union citizen who is a family member of that third-country national is compelled to leave the territory of the European Union'. Confirmed in *Subdelegación del Gobierno en Ciudad Real*, para 45. As Coutts underlines, '[t]he right of the Union citizen is therefore contingent not on his or her own (in)actions but rather on those of his or her parent over which he or she has no control and therefore cannot be held responsible' (S Coutts, 'Expulsion and Article 20 TFEU: some practical and conceptual issues' (2021) 23 European Journal of Migration and Law 29 at 42).

[366] *KA and Others*, para 81.

[367] *Subdelegación del Gobierno en Ciudad Real*, para 47.

[368] Case C-165/14 *Rendón Marín*, EU:C:2016:675, para 83.

[369] ibid para 82.

[370] ibid.

account, in particular, of the personal conduct of the individual concerned, the length and legality of his residence on the territory of the Member State concerned, the nature and gravity of the offence committed, the extent to which the person concerned is currently a danger to society, the age of the children at issue and their state of health, as well as their economic and family situation.[371]

In contrast, limitations of residence rights yielded in a 'systematic and automatic'[372] way by national rules that link criminal convictions with expulsion are problematic. In other words, 'where the expulsion decision is founded on the existence of a genuine, present and sufficiently serious threat to the requirements of public policy or of public security, in view of the criminal offences committed by a third-country national who is the sole carer of children who are Union citizens, that decision *could* be consistent with EU law', but such a conclusion 'cannot be drawn automatically on the basis solely of the criminal record of the person concerned. It can result, where appropriate, only from a specific assessment by the national court of all the current and relevant circumstances of the case, in the light of the principle of proportionality, of the child's best interests and of the fundamental rights whose observance the Court ensures'.[373] Thus, while the Court has not quite gone so far as to say in the Article 20 TFEU case law that the requirements of Directive 2004/38 are applicable by analogy,[374] that is what results in substance. Moreover, it has not applied specific qualifiers to recognise that the consequences of expulsion from the territory of the Union might be significantly more severe than expulsion from a host State (since the latter still enables residence in another EU Member State).[375]

Beyond concerns for public policy and public security, there are two related but distinct questions about limitations of Article 20 TFEU rights on grounds of protecting national public finances. First, can concerns about sufficient resources defeat residence rights that might otherwise legitimately be based on Article 20? Second, where residence rights are extended on that basis, what are the implications for entitlement to social assistance? In *Ruiz Zambrano*, the Court held that a work permit should be granted to Mr Ruiz Zambrano since, otherwise, 'he would risk not having sufficient resources to provide for himself and his family, which would also result in the children, citizens of the Union, having to leave the territory of the Union'.[376] Could it be inferred from that statement that *not* having sufficient resources to provide for dependent Union citizen(s) might defeat an Article 20-based residence claim?

As discussed in Chapters 6 and 7, having sufficient financial resources,[377] within the meaning of Article 7(1) of Directive 2004/38, is usually critical to establishing *lawful* residence in a host State after an initial unconditional three-month residence period based on Article 6 of the Directive. Several rights then flow from lawful residence—most notably, for present purposes, the right to equal treatment with nationals of the host State (Article 24(1)

---

[371] ibid paras 84–86; confirmed in eg Joined Cases C-451/19 and C-532/19 *Subdelegación del Gobierno en Toledo (Séjour d'un membre de la famille—Ressources insuffisantes)*, EU:C:2022:354, para 53. See generally, Chapter 10.
[372] Case C-304/14 *CS*, EU:C:2016:674, para 44; in other words, in circumstances where 'there is a presumption that the person concerned must be expelled' (ibid).
[373] ibid paras 40–41 (emphasis added).
[374] On the application of the Directive by analogy to rights conferred by Articles 21, 45, or 49 TFEU, see Chapter 9.
[375] See generally on this point, Coutts (n 365).
[376] Case C-34/09 *Ruiz Zambrano*, EU:C:2011:124, para 44.
[377] And also: comprehensive sickness insurance cover in the host State.

of the Directive). Where the Union citizen in question is a child, resources can be provided on their behalf (normally though not necessarily from a parent).[378] But residence rights based on Article 20 TFEU concern the Union citizen's home State and, as the Court has repeatedly stated, Union citizens enjoy an unconditional right to reside in their own Member States under international law.[379] Nevertheless, a relationship of dependency with a third-country national family member could jeopardise, in practical terms, the ability of the Union citizen to remain there. In such cases, should precarious financial circumstances be overlooked by the home State when deciding either to refuse or withdraw residence rights for the third-country national, or would this constitute one of the 'specific circumstances'[380] where a home State's decision not to grant such rights is justified under EU law?

Across the discussion in this part of the chapter, several aspects of Article 20 TFEU rights suggest an alignment, in general, with the principles that apply for rights based on Article 21 TFEU and Directive 2004/38: notably, the 'intrinsic connection' to freedom of movement shared by rights conferred by both Article 20 and Article 21 TFEU, and the parallel approach taken to exceptions based on public policy and public security. At the same time, explicit references to Directive 2004/38 are conspicuous by their absence in the relevant passages of *Rendón Marín*, *CS*, and *KA and Others*—even where the referring court's questions invoked its provisions.[381] Additionally, the definition of 'family members' under the Directive, which is applied by analogy when a Union citizen returns to their home State following the exercise of free movement,[382] is not used to delimit relationships of dependency for the purposes of Article 20 TFEU. The concept of dependency that applies in that context is qualitatively different too.

Advocate General Sharpston captured the complexity of both the overlaps and the distinctions between rights based on Articles 20 and 21 TFEU respectively in *KA and Others*, with specific reference to Article 7 of the Directive:

> In response to the referring court's question as to whether the Court's case-law on Directive 2004/38 should apply, it seems to me that, as situations within the scope of that directive are also within the ambit of EU law, *it may be possible to extrapolate certain principles*, particularly those concerning the application of the Charter, which might apply by analogy.

---

[378] Case C-200/02 *Zhu and Chen*, EU:C:2004:639, paras 28–33; confirmed in eg Case C-86/12 *Alokpa and Moudoulou*, EU:C:2013:645, para 27 and Case C-93/18 *Bajratari*, EU:C:2019:809, para 30. In *Ruiz Zambrano*, raising the issue of tolerated presence, AG Sharpston observed that 'the Belgian authorities were willing to accept Mr Ruiz Zambrano's social security contributions to the coffers of the Belgian State for five years while he worked at Plastoria—a willingness that contrasts curiously with a different Belgian ministry's reluctance to grant him a residence permit' (para 65 of the Opinion). Considering the implications of tolerated presence in a host State, see Addressing residence in a host State, see eg AG Szpunar in *Bajratari*, EU:C:2019:512, para 67 of the Opinion: 'despite the loss of his work and residence permit following the expiry of his residence card on 12 May 2014, not only was the presence of the husband of Ms Bajratari tolerated by the host Member State for 5 years, during which he, I reiterate, continued to pay tax and social security contributions, but, as was also confirmed at the hearing, his second child was during that period, on 26 July 2016, granted a certificate of Irish nationality' (emphasis in original). See further, Chapter 7.

[379] Case C-434/09 *McCarthy*, EU:C:2011:277, para 29; confirmed in eg Case C-165/16 *Lounes*, EU:C:2017:862, para 37.

[380] Case C-836/18 *Subdelegación del Gobierno en Ciudad Real (Conjoint d'un citoyen de l'Union)*, EU:C:2020:119, para 43.

[381] For example, in *KA and Others*, the referring court asked, *inter alia*, if 'Articles 27 and 28 of Directive 2004/38/EC... and the associated case-law of the Court of Justice on public policy, [can] be applied by analogy to family members of static Union citizens' (Case C-82/16 *KA and Others*, EU:C:2018:308, para 32). As Coutts remarks, however, 'while not explicitly making a link with Directive 2004/38/EC and Article 21 TFEU case law, the Court of Justice effectively imports the body of law in that area and applies it to... Article 20 TFEU situations' (n 365, 37).

[382] eg Case C-673/16 *Coman*, EU:C:2018:385; see further, Chapter 9.

However, *the specific criteria that are considered under that directive cannot be transposed to an assessment under Article 20 TFEU*. The conditions that apply where an EU citizen wishes to obtain a right of residence in another Member State for a period longer than three months, pursuant to Article 7(1) of Directive 2004/38, and the derived right of residence which may extend to third-country national family members of that EU citizen by virtue of Article 7(2) of that directive are not directly relevant in any assessment for the purposes of Article 20 TFEU.[383]

It is important to underline that entitlement to *reside* in a Union citizen's home State does not necessarily equate to or generate a right to be *supported* to reside there. A negative answer as regards the second situation that came (before Brexit) from proceedings in the UK Supreme Court on the basis that it was *acte clair* was profoundly misplaced because the Court of Justice had, at that time, not considered it.[384] Similarly, each case within the complex national proceedings behind the preliminary reference in *Chavez-Vilchez* concerned, in substance, applications for social assistance: refused, at national level, on the assumption that the claimants did not have a right to reside in the Netherlands in the first place. But the Court of Justice addressed only the latter point (and that is what the questions referred to it asked).[385] Additionally, national practices trying to give effect to the protection extended by Article 20 TFEU had tended, more generally, to differ significantly.[386]

In *Subdelegación del Gobierno en Ciudad Real*, the Court finally addressed the substantive dimension of Article 20 TFEU residence rights more directly, examining not just *when* they apply but also *what* they entail. RH was a Moroccan national married to a Spanish national who had never exercised free movement. Since their marriage, the couple lived in Spain with RH's father-in-law. RH's application for a residence card as the family member of Union citizen was rejected on grounds that his wife had not demonstrated that she had sufficient resources to support her husband, a condition in the applicable national rules. Having confirmed that neither Article 21 TFEU nor Directive 2004/38 applied on the facts of the case, the Court continued:

> [W]hether Article 20 TFEU must be interpreted as precluding a Member State from rejecting an application for family reunification submitted by the spouse, who is a national of a non-member country, of a Union citizen who is a national of that Member State and who has never exercised the freedom of movement, on the sole ground that that Union citizen does not have, for him or herself and his or her spouse, sufficient resources not to become a burden on the national social assistance system, without it having been examined whether there is a relationship of dependency between that Union citizen and his or her spouse of such a kind that, if the spouse is refused a derived right of residence, that Union citizen would be obliged to leave the territory of the European Union as a whole and would thus be deprived of the effective enjoyment of the substance of the rights conferred by virtue of his or her status.[387]

---

[383] AG Sharpston in Case C-82/16 *KA and Others*, EU:C:2017:821, para 64 of the Opinion (emphasis added).
[384] *HC v SSWP* [2017] UKSC 73. See further, C O'Brien, '*Acte cryptique*? Zambrano, welfare rights, and underclass citizenship in the tale of the missing preliminary reference' (2019) 56 Common Market Law Review 1697. In the national proceedings, the Supreme Court concluded that *Ruiz Zambrano* 'only requires whatever is sufficient to prevent a *de facto* expulsion, and that the possibility of applying for some basic, last resort, discretionary provision was sufficient for that' (ibid 1699).
[385] See similarly, the discussion on Case C-507/12 *Saint Prix*, EU:C:2014:2007 in Chapter 7.
[386] See generally, Nic Shuibhne and Shaw (n 321); and O'Brien (n 384) 1721–1722.
[387] Case C-836/18 *Subdelegación del Gobierno en Ciudad Real (Conjoint d'un citoyen de l'Union)*, EU:C:2020:119, para 32.

The Court began by diplomatically, as befits the sensitivity of EU citizenship law applying in a Union citizen's home state, restating that 'EU law does not, in principle, apply to an application for family reunification of a third-country national with a member of his or her family who is a national of a Member State and has never exercised the freedom of movement and that, accordingly, it does not, in principle, preclude legislation of a Member State under which such family reunification is subject to a condition of sufficient resources'.[388] Confirming that a derived right of residence based on Article 20 TFEU 'is not absolute, since Member States may refuse to grant it in certain specific circumstances'[389]—and recalling the case law discussed above regarding exceptions based on public policy and public security—the Court next 'examined whether Article 20 TFEU *similarly allows* Member States to introduce an exception to the derived right of residence enshrined in that article which is linked to a requirement that the Union citizen have sufficient resources'.[390]

What followed is remarkable, for two reasons: first, because the case involved spouses and a father-in-law, where it is likely that a qualifying relationship of dependency did not exist anyway, as a question of fact, since that was 'conceivable only in exceptional circumstances',[391] and second, for the very different tone of the ruling compared to how protection of *host* State public finances are addressed under Article 21 TFEU and Directive 2004/38, as discussed in Chapter 7. For exceptions to Article 20 TFEU-based residence rights, the Court framed the required assessment around Article 7 CFR and the principle of proportionality,[392] since:

> to refuse a third-country national who is a family member of a Union citizen a derived right of residence in the territory of the Member State of which that citizen is a national *on the sole ground* that the latter does not have sufficient resources, even though there is, between that citizen and that third-country national, a relationship of dependency ... would constitute an impairment of the effective enjoyment of the essential rights deriving from the status of Union citizen which would be disproportionate in relation to the objective pursued by such a means test, namely to preserve the public finances of the Member State concerned. Such a purely economic objective is *fundamentally different* from that of maintaining public order and safeguarding public security and does not justify such serious interference with the effective enjoyment of the substance of the rights deriving from Union citizenship.[393]

This impression of prioritising different public interest arguments is not something that translates across to the universe of Directive 2004/38.

The consequence of the Court's reasoning in the present case is that 'where there is a relationship of dependency ... between a Union citizen and a third-country national who is a member of his or her family, Article 20 TFEU precludes a Member State from providing for an exception to the derived right of residence which that third-country national has under that article, on the sole ground that that Union citizen does not have sufficient resources'.[394]

---

[388] ibid para 33.
[389] ibid para 43.
[390] ibid para 46 (emphasis added).
[391] ibid para 56; confirming Case C-82/16 *KA and Others*, EU:C:2018:308, para 65.
[392] *Subdelegación del Gobierno en Ciudad Real*, para 47.
[393] ibid para 48 (emphasis added).
[394] ibid para 49; confirmed in Joined Cases C-451/19 and C-532/19 *Subdelegación del Gobierno en Toledo (Séjour d'un membre de la famille—Ressources insuffisantes)*, EU:C:2022:354, para 50.

And perhaps even more significantly: '*the obligation imposed on a Union citizen to have sufficient resources* for him or herself and his or her family member who is a third-country national, is such as to undermine the effectiveness of Article 20 TFEU if it results in that citizen having to leave the territory of the European Union as a whole and, by reason of the existence of a relationship of dependency between that national and the Union citizen, the latter is, in fact, obliged to accompany him or her and, consequently, also to leave the territory of the European Union'.[395] Thus, the Court does not directly articulate a *right* to be supported in a Union citizen's home State. But it is difficult to see how such a conclusion could now be avoided in substance.

How a right to be supported *would* be articulated is not straightforward. Article 20 TFEU confers residence rights directly on a Union citizen and derived rights then protect the third-country national family member on whom the Union citizen is dependent. Given that Union citizens in such circumstances are already the beneficiaries of Article 20 TFEU in their home States, a right to be supported there based on EU equal treatment law would extend even more controversially into national competence: how, specifically for the purposes of EU law, would the relevant comparator be identified? Careful language is used in Article 24(1) of Directive 2004/38, which extends in a host State not a *right* to equal treatment per se but the '*benefit* of this right' to third-country national family members.

At the same time, though, the conventional expression of EU equal treatment obligations refers quite neutrally to 'comparable *situations*'. Moreover, as seen in Section 2, such obligations have already been established in EU citizenship law with respect to differences in treatment between groups of one Member State's own nationals.[396] It is also notable that the Court invoked Article 7 CFR alongside proportionality in *Subdelegación del Gobierno en Ciudad Real*. An analogy can be drawn with the reference to Article 1 CFR in the *CG* case 'to ensure that a Union citizen who has made use of his or her freedom to move and to reside within the territory of the Member States, who has a right of residence on the basis of national law, and who is in a vulnerable situation, may nevertheless live in dignified conditions'.[397] However, while *CG* does compel national authorities to enable Union citizens to 'live in dignified conditions', it leaves some discretion with respect to the *extent* of social assistance that should then be provided, as discussed further in Chapter 7.[398]

A final reflection on the *Ruiz Zambrano* case law is that it is not yet clear if a derived residence right based on Article 20 TFEU—as distinct from rights acquired autonomously under Directive 2003/109 through lawful and continuous long-term residence, the clock for which it is assumed starts ticking once a *Ruiz Zambrano* right is granted—sustains after the dependency at the heart of the family relationship ends. For example, would a right to permanent residence in a *home* State be produced over time by analogy with such rights now being sourced in Article 21 directly as regards host States?[399] Relatedly, when does dependency actually end: is it when the minor Union citizen reaches the age of majority or,

---

[395] *Subdelegación del Gobierno en Ciudad Real*, para 50 (emphasis added).
[396] See eg Case C-300/04 *Eman and Sevinger*, EU:C:2006:545, para 57. See further, O'Brien (n 384) 1704–1705.
[397] Case C-709/20 *CG*, EU:C:2021:602, para 89.
[398] In other words, while 'protection of a child's unconditional right to reside in the territory of the state of his nationality would be nullified if an income requirement for residence of his parents were imposed' (H Kroeze, 'The Substance of Rights: New Pieces of the *Ruiz Zambrano* Puzzle' (2019) 44 European Law Review 238 at 248), the Court of Justice would still need to determine for Article 20 TFEU case law whether its guidance would to national authorities stop there, or whether it might, for example, apply the nationality-internal approach to equal treatment analysis seen in *Eman and Sevinger* and Case C-148/02 *Garcia Avello*, EU:C:2003:539 to establish more detailed welfare entitlement.
[399] See Case C-247/20 *VI*, EU:C:2022:177, paras 58–59; see further, Chapter 8.

once again by analogy residence rights based on other provisions of EU law, will a more qualitative assessment of dependency (extending beyond the age of majority in certain circumstances[400]) be required? The Article 20 TFEU story that began in *Ruiz Zambrano* is not finished yet.

4. Concluding Remarks

In this chapter, examining how Union citizens are protected by EU law in their home States in the absence of any relevant exercise of free movement rights produces a paradox. In one sense, the examples considered—with respect both to rights and mechanisms that facilitate a political connection between Member State nationals and the Union, and to residence rights for third-country national family members based on Article 20 TFEU—exemplify the supranational qualities of Union citizenship. The development of this part of EU citizenship law has exposed and fostered the aspects of Union citizenship that transcend freedom of movement and residence (the 'intrinsic connection' to movement reasoning discussed in Section 3 notwithstanding) and it has, in consequence, reconfigured the boundaries of national competence. And yet, the same developments simultaneously underscore the role of the Member States: not just in their conditioning of access to Union citizenship through the determination of nationality, as discussed in Chapter 3, but also, in their shaping of the exercise—the 'genuine enjoyment'—of Union citizenship rights. Thus, the complex transnational and supranational dimensions of Union citizenship are mutually reinforced rather than displaced or dissolved by the functioning of Union citizenship in the home State.[401]

A second thematic observation is that the legal environment of Union citizenship is broadly coherent irrespective of the source of the applicable rights. It is true that while many of the principles and conditions applicable under the scheme of Directive 2004/38 also apply to rights based on Article 20 TFEU (even if only implicitly, through the Court of Justice's 'by analogy' method), there are also points of difference: on the definition of family members, for example, or with respect to the significance of sufficient financial resources. However, where there are differences in approach, articulation of *why* that is the case is healthier than treating different situations in the same way in pursuit of more formal coherence.

Finally, the considerable heft of the Charter of Fundamental Rights has gradually become more evident in case law on the role and effects of Union citizenship in home States. In many respects, the Court has drawn from—and upheld—the baseline of protection compelled by the ECtHR, especially anent the best interests of the child. However, in other respects—both

---

[400] See eg Case C-529/11 *Alarape and Tijani*, EU:C:2013:290, para 28, confirming that a child who reaches the age of majority 'is in principle assumed to be capable of meeting his or her own needs' but that 'the right of residence of that parent [based on Regulation 492/2011] may nevertheless extend beyond that age, if the child continues to need the presence and the care of that parent in order to be able to pursue and complete his or her education'.

[401] As Shaw puts it, '[f]or those who live in complex polities like the EU, which exhibit shifting and evolving vertical and horizontal relationships between different levels and spheres of political authority, citizenship itself is best understood multi-perspectively and relationally' (n 66, 614). See also, S Coutts, 'The shifting geometry of Union citizenship: a supranational status from transnational rights' (2019) 21 Cambridge Yearbook of European Legal Studies 318 esp at 341 on the idea that '[r]ecent developments in Union citizenship taken together point to a European community based on the territory of the Union certainly, but one that emerges from relationships based on mutual responsibility between individuals and the communities of the Member States, creating a space of transnational exchanges and opportunities'. Framing the inquiry around home State responsibilities, see F Strumia, 'Supranational citizenship enablers: free movement from the perspective of home Member States' (2020) 45 European Law Review 507.

substantively, as regards the level of protection extended; and in more structural terms, as regards the significance of territory and place in EU citizenship law—the Court of Justice goes further. For questions still unanswered, there is the sense that the full potential of the Charter has yet to be unleashed.[402] Thinking about why that might be the case brings us back full circle to the inescapable and perhaps inescapably unstable positioning of Union citizenship at the intersection of national, supranational, and transnational influences; of colliding systems—and colliding interests.

Further Reading

L Azoulai, 'Transfiguring European citizenship: from Member State territory to Union territory' in D Kochenov (ed), *EU Citizenship and Federalism: The Role of Rights* (CUP 2017) 178.

S Coutts, 'The shifting geometry of Union citizenship: a supranational status from transnational rights' (2019) 21 Cambridge Yearbook of European Legal Studies 318.

H Kroeze and P Van Elsuwege (eds), Special Issue – Revisiting *Ruiz Zambrano*: A Never Ending Story? (2021) 23 European Journal of Migration and Law.

K Lenaerts, 'EU citizenship and the European Court of Justice's "stone-by-stone" approach' (2015) 1 International Comparative Jurisprudence 1.

P Magnette, 'How can one be European? Reflections on the pillars of European civic identity' (2007) 13 European Law Journal 664.

J Shaw, *The Transformation of Citizenship in the European Union: Electoral Rights and the Restructuring of Political Space* (CUP 2007).

N Nic Shuibhne, '(Some of) the kids are all right: comment on *McCarthy* and *Dereci*' (2012) 49 Common Market Law Review 349.

N Nic Shuibhne, 'The "territory of the Union" in EU citizenship law: charting a route from parallel to integrated narratives' (2019) 38 Yearbook of European Law 267.

S Reynolds, 'Exploring the "intrinsic connection" between free movement and the genuine enjoyment test: reflections on EU citizenship after *Iida*' (2013) 38 European Law Review 376.

---

[402] An impression not confined to EU citizenship law: see eg D Sarmiento and E Sharpston, 'European citizenship and its new Union: time to move on?' in Kochenov (ed) (n 80) 226 at 231–35.

6
Union Citizenship and the Host State
Part I: Rights to Enter, Reside, and Remain—Directive 2004/38

1. Chapter Overview

This chapter examines the framework established by Directive 2004/38 for the rights of Union citizens to enter, reside in, and remain in a host State, that is, a State other than that of which they are nationals.[1] The preamble to the Directive reflects both the origins of the free movement of persons as 'one of the fundamental freedoms of the internal market' (recital 2) and the fact that Union citizenship now confers on every Member State national 'a primary and individual right to move and reside freely within the territory of the Member States' (recital 1). As detailed in Chapter 4, certain family members have the right to 'accompany or join' them (Article 3(1) of the Directive), irrespective of their own nationality, to ensure that the Union citizen's freedom of movement is 'exercised under objective conditions of freedom and dignity' (recital 5). Alongside reference to the Charter of Fundamental Rights, Member States are also asked to 'implement th[e] Directive without discrimination between [its] beneficiaries on grounds such as sex, race, colour, ethnic or social origin, genetic characteristics, language, religion or beliefs, political or other opinion, membership of an ethnic minority, property, birth, disability, age or sexual orientation' (recital 31).

However, reflecting Articles 20(2) and 21(1) TFEU, the right to move and reside is not unconditional, but conferred 'subject to the limitations and conditions laid down in the Treaty and to the measures adopted to give it effect' (recital 1).[2] Additionally, while 'all Union citizens and their family members residing in a Member State on the basis of this Directive should enjoy, in that Member State, equal treatment with nationals in areas covered by the Treaty', that entitlement is similarly 'subject to such specific provisions as are expressly provided for in the Treaty and secondary law' (recital 20). The Court of Justice has further established that conditions and limits 'must be applied in compliance with the limits imposed by [Union] law and in accordance with the general principles of that law—in particular the principle of proportionality',[3] from which it follows that their application is subject to judicial review.[4]

Overall, Directive 2004/38 puts in place a 'gradual system as regards the right of residence in the host Member State, which reproduces, in essence, the stages and conditions set out in the various instruments of European Union law and case-law preceding that directive and

---

[1] Directive 2004/38/EC on the right of citizens of the Union and their family members to move and reside freely within the territory of the Member States, 2004 OJ L158/77.

[2] Article 20(1) TFEU establishes that Union citizenship rights 'shall be exercised in accordance with the conditions and limits defined by the Treaties and by the measures adopted thereunder'. Article 21(1) TFEU states that '[e]very citizen of the Union shall have the right to move and reside freely within the territory of the Member States, subject to the limitations and conditions laid down in the Treaties and by the measures adopted to give them effect'.

[3] Case C-413/99 *Baumbast and R*, EU:C:2002:493, para 91.

[4] ibid para 86.

culminates in the right of permanent residence'.[5] This 'gradual system' is punctuated by moments in time that have determinative legal significance. It also sustains some significant differences based on the purpose of movement and residence: in essence, economic activity still matters notwithstanding the 'fundamental status' of Union citizenship affirmed in recital,[6] or the Directive's objective of 'remedying [of the] sector-by-sector, piecemeal approach to the right of free movement and residence' (recital 4).

The structure of this chapter follows that of the Directive, mapping the lifecycle of presence in a host State from entering it to residing there to remaining there. Articles 4 and 5 address the right to exit the territory of a Member State to travel to (Article 4) and enter (Article 5) the territory of another Member State (Section 2). Article 6 concerns the right to reside in a host State for up to three months 'without any conditions or any formalities other than the right to hold a valid identity card or passport' (Section 3). For residence rights of more than three months (Section 4), Article 7 establishes four categories of beneficiaries: Union citizens who are economically active as workers or self-employed persons (Article 7(1)(a)), or economically autonomous (Article 7(1)(b)), or studying in the host State (Article 7(1)(c)); and certain family members accompanying or joining them (Article 7(1)(d)).[7] Article 7 also sets out the conditions that must be fulfilled to ensure that residence in the host State in any of these situations is lawful and the guiding objective is that '[p]ersons exercising their right of residence should not ... become an unreasonable burden on the social assistance system of the host Member State' (recital 10).

Directive 2004/38 also stipulates the administrative formalities that a host State can implement so that a right to reside can be evidenced, for both Union citizens and any family members who are not Member State nationals (Section 5). Compliance with these formalities is not constitutive of rights per se since '[t]he fundamental and personal right of residence in another Member State is conferred directly on Union citizens by the Treaty and is not dependent upon their having fulfilled administrative procedures' (recital 11).[8] But some of these provisions have more bite than the language of 'formalities' might suggest: for example, Article 14, which grounds substantive residence rights for jobseeking citizens, or Article 15, which concerns expulsion on grounds other than public policy or public security.

The conditions that govern retaining the right to reside are scattered across different provisions of the Directive (Section 6). Importantly, they include rights that family members can retain 'exclusively on a personal basis' when the connection to the Union citizen

---

[5] Joined Cases C-316/16 and C-424/16 *B and Vomero*, EU:C:2018:256, para 51. On the right of permanent residence, see Chapter 8.

[6] First articulated by the Court in Case C-184/99 *Grzelczyk*, EU:C:2001:458, para 31; see previously, AG La Pergola in Case C-85/96 *Martínez Sala*, EU:C:1997:335, paras 18–19 of the Opinion.

[7] For residence rights within the scope of the Withdrawal Agreement, see Article 13 WA: '1. Union citizens and United Kingdom nationals shall have the right to reside in the host State under the limitations and conditions as set out in Articles 21, 45 or 49 TFEU and in Article 6(1), points (a), (b) or (c) of Article 7(1), Article 7(3), Article 14, Article 16(1) or Article 17(1) of Directive 2004/38/EC. 2. Family members who are either Union citizens or United Kingdom nationals shall have the right to reside in the host State as set out in Article 21 TFEU and in Article 6(1), point (d) of Article 7(1), Article 12(1) or (3), Article 13(1), Article 14, Article 16(1) or Article 17(3) and (4) of Directive 2004/38/EC, subject to the limitations and conditions set out in those provisions. 3. Family members who are neither Union citizens nor United Kingdom nationals shall have the right to reside in the host State under Article 21 TFEU and as set out in Article 6(2), Article 7(2), Article 12(2) or (3), Article 13(2), Article 14, Article 16(2), Article 17(3) or (4) or Article 18 of Directive 2004/38/EC, subject to the limitations and conditions set out in those provisions. 4. The host State may not impose any limitations or conditions for obtaining, retaining or losing residence rights on the persons referred to in paragraphs 1, 2 and 3, other than those provided for in this Title. There shall be no discretion in applying the limitations and conditions provided for in this Title, other than in favour of the person concerned'. Agreement on the withdrawal of the United Kingdom of Great Britain and Northern Ireland from the European Union and the European Atomic Energy Community, OJ 2019 CI 384/01.

[8] See previously eg Case 48/75 *Royer*, EU:C:1976:57, paras 24–28.

from whom they derive their rights changes or ends.[9] However, it is also recognised that, '[t]o guard against abuse of rights or fraud, notably marriages of convenience or any other form of relationships contracted for the sole purpose of enjoying the right of free movement and residence, Member States should have the possibility to adopt the necessary measures' (recital 28) and Article 35 of the Directive (Section 7) concerns the parameters of Member State discretion in that respect. Later chapters consider equal treatment in a host State (Chapter 7), the right of permanent residence (Chapter 8), the right to move and reside beyond the Directive, based either directly on primary EU law or on other measures of secondary EU law (Chapter 9), and the procedures and principles that govern expulsion from a host State (Chapter 10). Finally, how the definitions and rights provided for in the Directive compare to Part Two of the Withdrawal Agreement concluded between the EU and the United Kingdom following the UK's withdrawal from the Union is noted where relevant.

2. Articles 4 and 5: Rights of Exit and Entry

In *Jipa*, the Court of Justice underlined that 'freedom of movement includes both the right for citizens of the European Union to enter a Member State other than the one of origin and the right to leave the State of origin' on the basis that 'the fundamental freedoms guaranteed by the ... Treaty would be rendered meaningless if the Member State of origin could, without valid justification, prohibit its own nationals from leaving its territory in order to enter the territory of another Member State'.[10] That statement reflects the logically complementary rights of exit and entry, now codified in Chapter II (ie Articles 4 and 5) of Directive 2004/38,[11] which generalises and updates procedures developed originally for the free movement of workers and freedom of establishment and services:[12]

Article 4

Right of exit

1. Without prejudice to the provisions on travel documents applicable to national border controls, all Union citizens with a valid identity card or passport and their family members who are not nationals of a Member State and who hold a valid passport shall have the right to leave the territory of a Member State to travel to another Member State.

---

[9] Recital 15 of the Directive states that '[f]amily members should be legally safeguarded in the event of the death of the Union citizen, divorce, annulment of marriage or termination of a registered partnership. With due regard for family life and human dignity, and in certain conditions to guard against abuse, measures should therefore be taken to ensure that in such circumstances family members already residing within the territory of the host Member State retain their right of residence exclusively on a personal basis'.

[10] Case C-33/07 *Jipa*, EU:C:2008:396, para 18.

[11] In the original proposal for the Directive (COM(2001) 257 final), the right of entry was included in what is now Article 6 (right of residence for up to three months); the Council's common position made the right of entry a standalone provision 'for clarity reasons' (Common Position (EC) No 6/2004, 2004 OJ C54 E/12, 30).

[12] Council Directive 68/360/EEC on the abolition of restrictions on movement and residence within the Community for workers of Member States and their families, 1968 OJ L257/13, Articles 2 and 3; Directive 73/148/EC, 1973 OJ L172/14, Articles 2 and 3. Outlining the history and the details of these measures, see E Guild, S Peers, and J Tomkin, *The EU Citizenship Directive: A Commentary*, (2nd edn OUP 2019) 89–92.

2. No exit visa or equivalent formality may be imposed on the persons to whom paragraph 1 applies.
3. Member States shall, acting in accordance with their laws, issue to their own nationals, and renew, an identity card or passport stating their nationality.
4. The passport shall be valid at least for all Member States and for countries through which the holder must pass when travelling between Member States. Where the law of a Member State does not provide for identity cards to be issued, the period of validity of any passport on being issued or renewed shall be not less than five years.

Article 5

Right of entry

1. Without prejudice to the provisions on travel documents applicable to national border controls, Member States shall grant Union citizens leave to enter their territory with a valid identity card or passport and shall grant family members who are not nationals of a Member State leave to enter their territory with a valid passport.
   No entry visa or equivalent formality may be imposed on Union citizens.
2. Family members who are not nationals of a Member State shall only be required to have an entry visa in accordance with Regulation (EC) No 539/2001[13] or, where appropriate, with national law. For the purposes of this Directive, possession of the valid residence card referred to in Article 10 shall exempt such family members from the visa requirement.
   Member States shall grant such persons every facility to obtain the necessary visas. Such visas shall be issued free of charge as soon as possible and on the basis of an accelerated procedure.
3. The host Member State shall not place an entry or exit stamp in the passport of family members who are not nationals of a Member State provided that they present the residence card provided for in Article 10.
4. Where a Union citizen, or a family member who is not a national of a Member State, does not have the necessary travel documents or, if required, the necessary visas, the Member State concerned shall, before turning them back, give such persons every reasonable opportunity to obtain the necessary documents or have them brought to them within a reasonable period of time or to corroborate or prove by other means that they are covered by the right of free movement and residence.
5. The Member State may require the person concerned to report his/her presence within its territory within a reasonable and non-discriminatory period of time. Failure to comply with this requirement may make the person concerned liable to proportionate and non-discriminatory sanctions.[14]

---

[13] See now, Regulation 2018/1806/EU listing the third countries whose nationals must be in possession of visas when crossing the external borders and those whose nationals are exempt from that requirement, 2018 OJ L303/39, which replaced Regulation 539/2001, 2001 OJ L81/1. This Regulation does not apply to Ireland.

[14] Rights of exit and entry protected by the Withdrawal Agreement—which protect those who fall within the scope of the Agreement under Article 10 WA and did not continue freedom of movement for British nationals beyond UK membership of the Union—are set out in Article 14 WA: '1. Union citizens and United Kingdom nationals, their respective family members, and other persons, who reside in the territory of the host State in accordance with the conditions set out in this Title shall have the right to leave the host State and the right to

The Court has confirmed that 'a situation in which a Union citizen crosses the border of the Member State of which he or she is a national on arriving *from* another Member State is not governed by Directive 2004/38' since Article 5 of the Directive 'governs only the conditions of entry and residence of a Union citizen in Member States *other than* that of which he or she is a national'.[15] However, that situation, premised on the previous exercise of free movement, does fall within the scope of Article 21 TFEU.[16]

For Union citizens,[17] the only condition concerning the right to *leave* a Member State to travel to another Member State—and, in turn, to be granted leave to enter the territory of the second State—is the holding of a valid identity card or passport.[18] Articles 4 and 5 therefore entail obligations on both home and host States;[19] and 'there are no stipulations regarding the purpose of the journey or stay'.[20] However, Article 5(5) of the Directive does recognise that a host State may require reporting of presence within its territory 'within a reasonable and non-discriminatory period of time' as well as potential liability to proportionate and non-discriminatory sanctions in the event of failure to comply.[21] When Member States seek to restrict the right of exit or the right of entry—which includes decisions taken by a Union citizen's home State as regards the right to leave that territory—'those limitations

enter it, as set out in Article 4(1) and the first subparagraph of Article 5(1) of Directive 2004/38/EC, with a valid passport or national identity card in the case of Union citizens and United Kingdom nationals, and with a valid passport in the case of their respective family members and other persons who are not Union citizens or United Kingdom nationals. Five years after the end of the transition period, the host State may decide no longer to accept national identity cards for the purposes of entry to or exit from its territory if such cards do not include a chip that complies with the applicable International Civil Aviation Organisation standards related to biometric identification. 2. No exit visa, entry visa or equivalent formality shall be required of holders of a valid document issued in accordance with Article 18 or 26. 3. Where the host State requires family members who join the Union citizen or United Kingdom national after the end of the transition period to have an entry visa, the host State shall grant such persons every facility to obtain the necessary visas. Such visas shall be issued free of charge as soon as possible, and on the basis of an accelerated procedure'. The Commission has noted that '[a]s is the case of Directive 2004/38/EC, Article 14(1) of the Agreement requires a valid passport or national identity card for the purpose of exercising entry and exit rights. No other conditions can be attached under domestic law (such as that the travel document must have a certain future validity). Where the right to enter or to leave can be attested by different travel documents, the choice lies with the beneficiary of the Agreement' (European Commission, Guidance Note relating to the Agreement on the withdrawal of the United Kingdom of Great Britain and Northern Ireland from the European Union and the European Atomic Energy Community Part two—Citizens' rights, C(2020) 2939 final, para 2.2.1). The Commission also considers that '[t]he right of beneficiaries of the Agreement to be absent as set out in Article 15 [WA] and the right to continue working as a frontier worker as set out in Articles 24 and 25 [WA] imply the right to leave the host State or, respectively, the State of work and to return there' (ibid).

---

[15] Case C-35/20 *A (Franchissement de frontières en navire de plaisance)*, EU:C:2021:813, paras 67–68 (emphasis added).

[16] ibid para 70; see further, Chapter 9.

[17] For family members who are not Member State nationals, the requirements outlined in Articles 5(2)–5(5) of the Directive are returned to in Section 6.3.

[18] Confirmed in eg Case C-434/10 *Aladzhov*, EU:C:2011:750, para 26. EU legislation establishes certain requirements for both identity cards (Regulation 2019/1157/EU on strengthening the security of identity cards of Union citizens and of residence documents issued to Union citizens and their family members exercising their right of free movement, 2019 OJ L188/67) and passports (Council Regulation 2252/2004/EC on standards for security features and biometrics in passports and travel documents issued by the Member States, 2004 OJ L141/1) issued by the Member States (with the exception of Ireland; see further, Council Decision 2002/192/EC concerning Ireland's request to take part in some of the provisions of the Schengen *acquis*, 2002 OJ L64/20).

[19] On the nature of that obligation under Directive 68/360, before Union citizenship, see eg Case C-376/89 *Giagounidis*, EU:C:1991:99.

[20] Opinion of the Committee of the Regions on the original Commission proposal, 2002 OJ C192/17, para 1.6.

[21] See previously, in the context of Article 8(2) of Directive 68/360 and Article 4(2) of Directive 73/148, Case 118/75 *Watson and Belmann*, EU:C:1976:106, esp paras 17–19. However, the Court also held in that case that deportation was not an appropriate response to failure to comply with reporting requirements; see further, Chapter 10. In the Commission's original proposal for Directive 2004/38, the reporting requirement was attached only to the right to reside in (and not to the right to enter) a host State (n 11, 32 and draft Article 6(5)). The European Parliament

and conditions stem, in particular, from Article 27(1) of Directive 2004/38', which 'does not allow Member States to restrict the freedom of movement of Union citizens or their family members on grounds other than public policy, public security or public health'.[22] The extent to which Article 27 curtails Member State discretion is examined in Chapter 10, but the essential point for present purposes is that 'limitations justified on grounds of public policy must be construed *not as a condition precedent* to the acquisition of the right of entry and residence, but as affording the possibility of placing restrictions, in specific cases and where the circumstances justify it, on the exercise of a right directly conferred by the Treaty'.[23]

While the reference to 'hold[ing] a valid passport' in Article 4(1) of the Directive 'aims to facilitate the exercise of the right to free movement by ensuring that any person benefiting from that right is easily identified as such in the context of a possible verification', it is also characterised by the Court as a *condition* to which the right to travel to another Member State is subject.[24] As a result, 'a Member State which requires its nationals to carry their identity card or passport when they cross a national border to travel to another Member State contributes, in so doing, to compliance with a formality which, under Directive 2004/38, is required for the exercise of the right to free movement', which means that '[s]uch a rule of national law therefore falls within the scope of the implementation' of the Directive.[25] Moreover, the abolition of border checks in accordance with the Schengen Borders Code 'does not affect the possibility, set out in Article 21 of Regulation No 562/2006, for Member States to carry out identity checks *within the territory* and to provide for the obligation to hold and carry papers and documents for that purpose'.[26]

Article 36 of the Directive permits Member States to 'lay down provisions on the sanctions applicable to breaches of national rules adopted for the implementation of this Directive' and 'to take the measures required for their application'. However, such sanctions must be effective and proportionate and, more generally, since this issue is not harmonised by EU law, the competence of the Member States to choose appropriate sanctions must be exercised 'in accordance with EU law and its general principles'.[27] Such obligations include the requirement that sanctions provided for in national criminal law should respect the right to equal treatment under EU law, not restrict 'the fundamental freedoms guaranteed by EU law', and

---

had recommended deleting it altogether as being 'out of step with the aims of the text' (European Parliament Report of 23 January 2003 on the Commission's original proposal, A5–0009/2003, Amendment 26).

[22] Case C-430/10 *Gaydarov*, EU:C:2011:749, para 30.

[23] Case C-363/89 *Roux*, EU:C:1991:41, para 30 (emphasis added). Member States may restrict the movement of Union citizens within their territories after leave to enter has been granted in connection with the implementation of their domestic criminal law (see eg on Article 45 TFEU, Case 175/78 *Saunders*, EU:C:1979:88, paras 9–11). However, in line with the prohibition on nationality discrimination in EU free movement law, Article 22 of Directive 2004/38 now requires that 'Member States may impose territorial restrictions on the right of residence and the right of permanent residence only where the same restrictions apply to their own nationals'.

[24] Case C-35/20 *A (Franchissement de frontières en navire de plaisance)*, EU:C:2021:813, paras 53 and 52; referring 'to that effect' to Case C-378/97 *Wijsenbeek*, EU:C:1999:439, para 43 and Case C-215/03 *Oulane*, EU:C:2005:95, paras 21–22.

[25] *A (Franchissement de frontières en navire de plaisance)*, para 55. The facts of the case were summarised by AG Szpunar as concerning '[a] Union citizen cross[ing] a national sea border on board a pleasure boat in the course of a round trip between two Member States, namely Finland and Estonia, without carrying travel documents' (EU:C:2021:456, para 1 of the Opinion).

[26] *A (Franchissement de frontières en navire de plaisance)*, para 62 (emphasis added). Regulation 562/2006 establishing a Community Code on the rules governing the movement of persons across borders (Schengen Borders Code), 2006 OJL105/1.

[27] *A (Franchissement de frontières en navire de plaisance)*, para 57.

comply with the Charter of Fundamental Rights, notably Article 49(3) CFR, 'according to which the severity of penalties must not be disproportionate to the offence'.[28]

In *VMA*, the Court held that Article 4(3) of the Directive compels the Member States, 'acting in accordance with their laws, to issue to their own nationals an identity card or passport stating their nationality' in order to enable their nationals to exercise the right to move and reside freely conferred by Article 21(1) TFEU.[29] The case involved a refusal by the competent Bulgarian authorities to issue a birth certificate, which was required for the issuing in turn of a Bulgarian identity document, to SDKA—a Bulgarian national who was born and resided with her parents (VMA, a Bulgarian national, and KDK, a British national) in Spain and who had been issued with a Spanish birth certificate referring to VMA as 'Mother A' and KDK as 'Mother'. The grounds for refusing to issue a birth certificate in Bulgaria (applied for by VMA) related to 'lack of information concerning the identity of the child's biological mother and the fact that a reference to two female parents on a birth certificate was contrary to the public policy of the Republic of Bulgaria, which does not permit marriage between two persons of the same sex'.[30] However, under Article 25(1) of the Bulgarian Constitution, the refusal to issue a birth certificate 'does not mean that she has been denied Bulgarian nationality' and the Court of Justice proceeded on the basis that SDKA was a Union citizen, based on the findings of the referring court.[31] Moreover, the fact that SDKA had not exercised free movement did not preclude her situation from failing within the scope of Article 21(1) TFEU: she resided in a State other than that of which she was a national and 'may rely on the rights pertaining to Union citizenship, in particular the rights provided for in Article 21(1) TFEU, including, where appropriate, against … her Member State of origin'.[32]

The Court held that the Bulgarian authorities were obliged by EU law to issue to SDKA 'an identity card or a passport stating her nationality and her surname as it appears on the birth certificate drawn up by the Spanish authorities' on the basis that Article 21 TFEU 'precludes the authorities of a Member State, in applying their national law, from refusing to recognise a child's surname as determined and registered in a second Member State in which the child was born and has been resident since birth'.[33] Moreover, Article 4(3) of the Directive required the Bulgarian authorities to issue the identity document 'regardless of whether a new birth certificate is drawn up for that child'.[34] That conclusion was underpinned by the fact that Article 21(1) TFEU includes 'the right to lead a normal family life, together with their family members, both in their host Member State and in the Member State of which they are nationals when they return to the territory of that Member State'.[35] In this case, the

---

[28] ibid paras 59 and 58; see further, paras 80–92, taking account of Article 21(1) TFEU, Articles 4(1) and 36 of Directive 2004/38 and Article 49(3) CFR, and finding that 'rules on criminal sanctions by which a Member State makes the crossing of its national border without a valid identity card or passport punishable by a fine which may, by way of illustration, amount to 20% of the offender's net monthly income, where such a fine is not proportionate to the seriousness of the offence, which is of a minor nature' (para 92).

[29] Case C-490/20 *VMA v Stolichna obshtina, rayon 'Pancharevo'*, EU:C:2021:100, para 43.

[30] ibid para 23.

[31] ibid paras 25 and 39–40. The Court added that 'if checks should reveal that S.D.K.A. did not have Bulgarian nationality, it must be noted that, irrespective of their nationality and whether or not they themselves are Union citizens, K.D.K. and S.D.K.A. must be regarded by all Member States as being, respectively, the spouse and the direct descendant within the meaning of Article 2(2)(a) and (c) of Directive 2004/38, and, therefore, as being V.M.A.'s family members' (ibid para 67).

[32] ibid para 42. See previously eg Case C-200/02 *Zhu and Chen*, EU:C:2004:639; Case C-673/16 *Coman*, EU:C:2018:385; and Case C-93/18 *Bajratari*, EU:C:2019:809. See further, Chapter 9.

[33] *VMA*, para 44; referring to Case C-353/06 *Grunkin and Paul*, EU:C:2008:559, para 39.

[34] *VMA*, para 45.

[35] ibid para 47; see further, Chapter 4. Expanding on the protection guaranteed by Articles 7 and 24(2) CFR, see also, paras 58–65, where the Court draws from ECtHR case law to confirm that 'it would be contrary to the

Spanish authorities had 'lawfully established that there was a parent-child relationship, biological or legal, between S.D.K.A. and her two parents, V.M.A. and K.D.K., and attested this in the birth certificate issued in respect of the child of those two parents'; as a result, VMA and KDK, as Union citizens themselves, 'must, therefore, pursuant to Article 21 TFEU and Directive 2004/38, as parents of a Union citizen who is a minor and of whom they are the primary carers, be recognised by all Member States as having the right to accompany that child when her right to move and reside freely within the territory of the Member States is being exercised'.[36] That right entails an obligation on the national authorities of '*any other Member State*, to recognise that parent-child relationship' in the context of permitting SDKA to exercise 'without impediment, with each of her two parents, her right to move and reside freely within the territory of the Member States as guaranteed in Article 21(1) TFEU', and thus, to recognise the birth certificate issued by the Spanish authorities, which attests to VMA and KDK 'being persons entitled to travel with' SDKA.[37]

The Court acknowledged the terms of Article 9 CFR, which stipulate that '[t]he right to marry and the right to found a family shall be guaranteed in accordance with the national laws governing the exercise of these rights' and, more generally, that 'as EU law currently stands, a person's status, which is relevant to the rules on marriage and parentage, is a matter that falls within the competence of the Member States and EU law does not detract from that competence'.[38] Nevertheless, confirming *Coman*, Member States must comply with EU law when they exercise that competence, which includes an obligation to comply with the free movement rights conferred by the TFEU 'by recognising, for that purpose, the civil status of persons that has been established in another Member State in accordance with the law of that other Member State'.[39] Also in line with *Coman*, the Court did not consider that the obligation on the Bulgarian authorities to issue an identity document in this case 'undermine[d] national identity [in breach of Article 4(2) TEU] or pose[d] a threat to the public policy of that Member State'.[40] The ruling in *VMA* therefore affirms and further develops the principles discussed in Chapter 4 with respect to *enabling* family life. It also confirms that obligations of mutual recognition are produced by free movement; the giving effect to which, in turn, galvanises the territory of the Union as a place of 'additional' (to borrow from Article 20 TFEU) legal significance for Member State nationals.[41] However, the extent to which EU citizenship law impacts on national rules (and national cultures) that determine civil status

---

fundamental rights which are guaranteed to the child under Articles 7 and 24 of the Charter for her to be deprived of the relationship with one of her parents when exercising her right to move and reside freely within the territory of the Member States or for her exercise of that right to be made impossible or excessively difficult in practice on the ground that her parents are of the same sex' (ibid para 65).

[36] ibid para 48; see further, Chapters 4 and 9.
[37] ibid paras 49–50 (emphasis added).
[38] ibid para 52 (meaning that Member States 'are thus free to decide whether or not to allow marriage and parenthood for persons of the same sex under their national law').
[39] ibid, referring to Case C-673/16 *Coman*, EU:C:2018:385, paras 36–38. See further, Chapter 4.
[40] *VMA* para 56. The referring court repeatedly invoked Article 4(2) TEU in its questions (ibid para 32). In contrast to the Court's very brief references, AG Kokott devoted significant space in her Opinion to the national identity dimension of the case by considering in detail, and differently from the judgment of the Court, whether there was an obligation on the Bulgarian authorities under EU law to issue a birth certificate to SDKA should it be found that she did not have Bulgarian nationality (AG Kokott in *VMA*, EU:C:2021:296, paras 70–100 of the Opinion; also discussing national identity in light of the values expressed in Article 2 TEU at paras 116–132 of the Opinion). Confirming the principles established in the ruling, see further the Order of the Court in Case C-2/21 *Rzecznik Praw Obywatelskich*, EU:C:2022:502, responding to a preliminary reference from a Polish court 'rais[ing] almost identical questions' (AG Kokott in *VMA*, para 4 of the Opinion).
[41] See further, Chapter 2. See generally, L Azoulai, 'Transfiguring European citizenship: from Member State territory to Union territory' in D Kochenov (ed), *EU Citizenship and Federalism: The Role of Rights* (CUP 2017) 178;

should also be acknowledged, underlining once again that the exercise of even exclusive national competence occurs within the shadowland of EU legal obligation, as introduced in Chapter 2 and discussed in Chapter 3 in connection with Member State competence to determine nationality. More generally, the intersection of the right of exit provided for in Article 4(1) of the Directive and processes of expulsion from a host State is returned to in Chapter 10.[42]

3. Article 6: The Right to Reside for up to Three Months

Chapter III of Directive 2004/38 ('Right of residence') addresses the right to reside and retaining the right to reside in a host State as well as relevant administrative formalities and procedural safeguards. Article 6 is the first provision:

Article 6

Right of residence for up to three months

1. Union citizens shall have the right of residence on the territory of another Member State for a period of up to three months without any conditions or any formalities other than the requirement to hold a valid identity card or passport.
2. The provisions of paragraph 1 shall also apply to family members in possession of a valid passport who are not nationals of a Member State, accompanying or joining the Union citizen.

Article 6(1) establishes that the right to reside in a host State for up to three months is not subject to any conditions or formalities other than the requirement to hold a valid identity card or passport, mirroring the requirement for the rights of entry and exit outlined in Section 2.[43] Article 6(2) extends the same unconditional right of residence, on the same terms, to family members who are not nationals of a Member State when they accompany or join a Union citizen.

The idea that Member State nationals could reside in another State for up to three months without a residence permit was established for workers by Article 8 of Directive 68/360 and for self-employed persons as well as the providers and recipients of services by Article 4 of Directive 73/148. As introduced in Chapter 2, a general right to move and reside was provided for in the 1990s Residence Directives,[44] but these measures—and their more stringent conditions—made no reference to duration of residence in the host State and therefore

---

S Coutts, 'The shifting geometry of Union citizenship: a supranational status from transnational rights' (2019) 21 Cambridge Yearbook of European Legal Studies 318; and N Nic Shuibhne, 'The "territory of the Union" in EU citizenship law: charting a route from parallel to integrated narratives' (2019) 38 Yearbook of European Law 267.

[42] See esp Case C-718/19 *Ordre des barreaux francophones and germanophone and Others (Mesures préventives en vue d'éloignement)*, EU:C:2021:505.
[43] Conditions and limits not set down in the Treaty or in EU legislation may not, therefore, be added in national legislation: see Case C-719/19 *FS*, EU:C:2021:506, para 89.
[44] Directive 90/364/EEC on the right of residence, 1990 OJ L180/26; Directive 90/365/EEC on the right of residence for employees and self-employed persons who have ceased their occupational activity, 1990 OJ L180/28; and Directive 93/96/EEC on the right of residence for students, 1993 OJ L317/59.

aligned more with the situations now addressed by Article 7 of Directive 2004/38 (ie a right of residence for more than three months, returned to in Section 4). In its original proposal for Directive 2004/38, the Commission recommended a generalised application of the three-month period previously extended to economically active Member State nationals as well as an increase to six months for such unconditional rights 'to cater for the modern, high mobility lifestyles, we are witnessing in Member States'.[45] That proposal received strong endorsement in the initial phase of the Directive's adoption,[46] but it was subsequently reversed by the Council.[47] In its common position, the Council communicated that, '[a]fter careful consideration', it had agreed 'to set the period at three months, as in the existing *acquis*'.[48] Importantly, however, the Council pointed out that 'a more favourable treatment is applicable to job-seekers as recognised by the case-law of the Court of Justice'.[49] What that 'more favourable treatment' entails intersects with the conditions in Article 7 of the Directive on residence rights for more than three months, the specific references to jobseekers in Article 14, and rights based directly on Article 45 TFEU, as explained further in Section 4. More generally, an opportunity to revisit the three-month period in Article 6 was built into Article 39 of the adopted Directive:

> No later than [four years from the date of entry into force of this Directive] the Commission shall submit a report on the application of this Directive to the European Parliament and the Council, together with any necessary proposals, *notably on the opportunity to extend the period of time during which Union citizens and their family members may reside in the territory of the host Member State without any conditions*. The Member States shall provide the Commission with the information needed to produce the report.

However, in its subsequent report, the Commission did not address the commitment made in respect of Article 6 at all, noting only that, '[a]t this stage, it is not necessary to propose

---

[45] Original Proposal (n 11) para 2.3. This was underlined by the text of draft recital 8: '[i]n keeping with new developments in mobility, working arrangements and lifestyles less tied to a single place, stays not exceeding six months by Union citizens should not be subject to any formalities other than the requirement to hold a valid identity card or passport'. That wording was modified by the European Parliament to refer to 'new developments in geographical mobility and working arrangements ... should not be subject to any conditions or any formalities other than' (European Parliament Report on Commission proposal (n 21), Amendment 7); accepted by the Commission in its amended proposal for the Directive (COM(2003) 199 final, 14).

[46] eg the Committee of the Regions 'unconditionally' endorsed it (n 20, para 1.7). The European Parliament's Committee on Culture, Youth, Education, the Media and Sport called, even more radically, for an extension of unconditional residence rights for 'stays not exceeding two years', making particular reference to facilitating 'mobility without excessive administrative restrictions' in the context of student mobility (n 21, 72).

[47] The Council's common position on this point was agreed at its meeting of 22 September 2003: 'the Council will not alter the period of residence (three months) during which an EU citizen does not have to fulfil any conditions for residing in another Member State, but will ask the Commission to examine this aspect in its report on the application of the directive' (Bulletin EU 9–2003, 1.4.2).

[48] Common Position (n 11) 26. In its Communication on the common position, the Commission added that the Council's decision also reflected 'the difficulties of extending [the six-month] period to family members who are not nationals of a Member State' (SEC/2003/1293 final, para 3.1; see further, para 3.3.2: '[t]he Member States emphasised the difficulty, for reasons relating to visas, of extending to six months the period which is not subject to any formality for family members who are nationals of third countries').

[49] Common Position (n 11) 26. That commitment was captured in recital 9 of the adopted Directive: 'Union citizens should have the right of residence in the host Member State for a period not exceeding three months without being subject to any conditions or any formalities other than the requirement to hold a valid identity card or passport, without prejudice to a more favourable treatment applicable to job-seekers as recognised by the case-law of the Court of Justice'.

amendments to the Directive' and emphasising more generally its concern that '[t]he Directive must be implemented by Member States more effectively'.[50]

For residence rights now based on Article 6 of the Directive, and reflecting the discussion in Section 2 on Article 5, a Member State may require the nationals of other Member States 'to provide evidence of their identity and nationality', a prerogative 'aimed, first, at simplifying the resolution of problems relating to evidence of the right of residence not only for citizens but also for national authorities and, second, at establishing the maximum that Member States may require of the persons concerned with a view to recognising their right of residence'.[51] Three further questions addressed in more detail in other parts of the book can be noted briefly here. First, while any restrictions of the right to reside on grounds of public health, public policy, or public security must conform to the requirements set out in Chapter VI of the Directive (which is examined in Chapter 10), the Court has also ruled on the conditions under which a right to reside can be (re-)established under Article 6 of the Directive following a decision to expel a citizen from the host State on grounds *other than* public health, public policy, or public security. In *FS*, a decision was taken to expel a Polish national from the Netherlands on the grounds that he was residing there illegally because he no longer satisfied the conditions in Article 7 of the Directive. Since the expulsion decision was not therefore based on public policy or public security, it concerned Article 15 rather than Article 27 of the Directive,[52] and that dimension of the case is returned to in Section 5. For present purposes, the central question was whether a Union citizen can enjoy a new right of residence in a host State under Article 6(1) of the Directive 'in the event of an immediate return to the same territory . . . or whether, on the other hand, the host Member State may adopt a new expulsion decision to prevent the repeated entry of that Union citizen to its territory for a short period of time'.[53]

A proposal submitted by the Netherlands Government—which would permit, in effect, imposing a requirement to remain outside the territory of the host State for at least three months after expulsion[54]—was defeated by the requirement in Articles 20(1) and 21(1) TFEU that conditions and limits placed on the right to move and reside must be 'laid down'.[55] As Advocate General Rantos argued, 'stating that the legal effects of an expulsion

---

[50] Report from the Commission to the European Parliament and the Council on the application of Directive 2004/38/EC on the right of citizens of the Union and their family members to move and reside freely within the territory of the Member States, COM(2008) 840 final, 11. The Commission was especially concerned by the 'rather disappointing' transposition of the Directive: '[n]ot one Member State has transposed the Directive effectively and correctly in its entirety. Not one Article of the Directive has been transposed effectively and correctly by all Member States' (ibid 3). That conclusion in turn led to the Communication from the Commission to the European Parliament and the Council on guidance for better transposition and application of Directive 2004/38/EC on the right of citizens of the Union and their family members to move and reside freely within the territory of the Member States, COM(2009) 313 final.
[51] Case C-215/03 *Oulane*, EU:C:2005:95, paras 21–22. The Court also established that '[i]f the person concerned is able to provide unequivocal proof of his nationality by means other than a valid identity card or passport, the host Member State may not refuse to recognise his right of residence on the sole ground that he has not presented one of those documents' (para 25; see further, Section 5).
[52] Article 15 of Directive 2004/38 provides: '1. The procedures provided for by Articles 30 and 31 shall apply by analogy to all decisions restricting free movement of Union citizens and their family members on grounds other than public policy, public security or public health. 2. Expiry of the identity card or passport on the basis of which the person concerned entered the host Member State and was issued with a registration certificate or residence card shall not constitute a ground for expulsion from the host Member State. 3. The host Member State may not impose a ban on entry in the context of an expulsion decision to which paragraph 1 applies'. Article 15 should be read in conjunction with Articles 7 (residence beyond three months), 8(4) (sufficient resources), and 14 (retention of the right of residence) of the Directive, addressed in Sections 4, 5, and 6.
[53] Case C-719/19 *FS*, EU:C:2021:506, para 57.
[54] ibid para 83.
[55] ibid para 89; see generally, paras 84–89, which are returned to below.

decision must *always* last for a three-month period would, in reality, require the Union citizen to prove three months' residence outside the host Member State before being able to rely on a new right of residence under Article 6 of the Residence Directive. Such an approach would ... be at odds not only with the letter but also with the spirit of that directive'.[56] However, for the Court, if 'mere physical departure' from the host State was accepted as sufficient to comply with an expulsion decision taken on the basis of Article 15 of the Directive, a Union citizen 'would only have to cross the border of the host Member State in order to be able to return immediately to the territory of that Member State and to rely on a new right of residence under Article 6' and by '[a]cting repeatedly in that way', they 'could be granted numerous rights of residence successively in the territory of a single Member State' under Article 6, 'even though, in reality, those various rights would be granted for the purposes of the same single actual residence'.[57] That scenario 'would be tantamount to rendering redundant the possibility for the host Member State to terminate the residence of a Union citizen, pursuant to Article 6 of Directive 2004/38, where that citizen reaches the end of his or her three-month residence on the territory of that Member State, by allowing him or her, in practice, to reside on that territory for more than three months despite the fact that an expulsion decision has been adopted against him or her and that the conditions laid down in Article 7 of that directive are not fulfilled'—thus ignoring the 'actual temporal limit' of periods up to three months around which Article 6 is designed.[58] The Court therefore established criteria that permit a host State to determine if a Union citizen has 'genuinely and effectively terminate[d]' their residence in the host State,[59] which are outlined in Section 5. In essence, to claim a new right of residence in a host State under Article 6(1) of the Directive, a Union citizen who has already been expelled from it on the basis of Article 15 'must not only physically leave that territory, but also have genuinely and effectively terminated his or her residence on that territory, with the result that, upon his or her return to the territory of the host Member State, his or her residence cannot be regarded as constituting in fact a continuation of his or her preceding residence on that territory'.[60]

Second, beyond the right to reside per se, what *other* rights does Union citizenship confer on the beneficiaries of Article 6 when they reside in a host State for up to three months? Member State nationals have the right to take up economic activity—as workers, self-employed persons, or the providers of services—at any point following their arrival in the host State on the basis of Articles 45, 49, or 56 TFEU respectively. Additionally, Article 23 of the Directive establishes that '[i]rrespective of nationality, the family members of a Union citizen who have the right of residence or the right of permanent residence in a Member State shall be entitled to take up employment or self-employment there'.[61] The relationship

---

[56] AG Rantos in *FS*, EU:C:2021:104, para 89 of the Opinion (emphasis in original). He considered that the 'proposal by the Netherlands Government would also run counter to the exercise of the right to move freely, as guaranteed by Article 5 of the Residence Directive, in that it would automatically impose an additional condition on the exercise of the right of entry – the "specific and concrete" justification of the citizen's visit to the host Member State. However, exercise of the right of entry, which is an expression of the freedom to move freely within the Union, is difficult to reconcile with such an obligation to provide a justification, in particular because, given its subjective and potentially arbitrary nature, it would risk deterring the persons concerned from actually exercising that right' (ibid para 92 of the Opinion).
[57] *FS*, para 73.
[58] ibid para 74.
[59] ibid para 75.
[60] ibid para 81.
[61] See similarly, Article 22 WA: '[i]n accordance with Article 23 of Directive 2004/38/EC, irrespective of nationality, the family members of a Union citizen or United Kingdom national who have the right of residence or the right of permanent residence in the host State or the State of work shall be entitled to take up employment or self-employment there'.

between the rights conferred by Article 6 and the derogation from equal treatment for the same period in Article 24(2)—which, more specifically, rules out entitlement to social assistance—is examined in Chapter 7.[62] That discussion highlights distinctions that persist between *categories* of Union citizens, notwithstanding the consolidation aims of the Directive, as the entitlement of economically active Member State nationals to social assistance within their first three months of residence in a host State is not affected by Article 24(2)'s derogation.[63] However, where benefits 'are granted independently of the individual needs of the beneficiary and are not intended to cover his or her means of subsistence', they do not constitute 'social assistance' within the meaning of Directive 2004/38.[64] In such circumstances, the derogation in Article 24(2) does not apply.[65]

Third, as discussed in Chapter 4, the Court considers that 'a Union citizen who exercises [their] rights under Article 6(1) of Directive 2004/38 does not intend to settle in the host Member State in a way which would be such as *to create or strengthen family life* in that Member State'.[66] This threshold has implications for the rights of their third-country national family members, in particular, if they return to the Union citizen's home State after residing for less than three months in another State. That question is picked up again in Chapter 9, but the resonance of a requirement to 'create or strengthen family life' with the requirement in *FS* of 'genuinely and effectively' terminating residence in a host State is notable.[67] In *FS*, the Court's resistance to instituting very specific conditions was evident;[68] and in that part of the ruling, the rights-enriching impulses of free movement were harnessed: the right to move and reside conferred on Union citizens is a 'primary and individual right', recalling recital 1 of the Directive; it is also a fundamental right, referring to recital 2 and Article 45 CFR; Directive 2004/38 aims to facilitate and 'in particular, to strengthen that right', as reflected in recital 3; and 'since freedom of movement for persons forms one of the foundations of the European Union, the provisions laying down that freedom must be given a broad interpretation, whereas exceptions and derogations from it must, on the contrary, be interpreted strictly'.[69]

Earlier in the *FS* judgment, though, where the concept of 'genuine and effective' termination of residence rights was surfacing, the Court referred only to recital 10 of the Directive

---

[62] Article 24(2) of the Directive establishes inter alia that, '[b]y way of derogation from paragraph 1, the host Member State shall not be obliged to confer entitlement to social assistance during the first three months of residence'. See eg Case C-299/14 *García-Nieto*, EU:C:2016:114, paras 42–43. For unemployed persons, the three-month period of responsibility of the home State in Article 64 of Regulation 883/2004—which enables the exporting of benefits if the Union citizen aims to seek employment in another Member State—also maps onto the exclusion of entitlement to social assistance in the host State; however, under certain conditions, that period may be extended to six months. Regulation 883/2004 on the coordination of social security systems, 2011 OJ L166/1.

[63] For workers, these rights connect to Article 45 TFEU and Regulation 492/2011 on freedom of movement for workers within the Union, 2011 OJ L141/1 (see eg Case C-181/19 *Jobcenter Krefeld*, EU:C:2020:794); for self-employed persons, they connect to Article 49 TFEU (see eg Case C-168/20 *BJ and OV*, EU:C:2021:907). See further, Chapter 7.

[64] Case C-411/20 *Familienkasse Niedersachsen-Bremen*, EU:C:2022:602, paras 47–48.

[65] ibid para 55. See further, Chapter 7.

[66] Case C-456/12 *O and B*, EU:C:2014:135, para 52 (emphasis added).

[67] AG Rantos referred expressly to that case law (AG Rantos in Case C-719/19 *FS*, EU:C:2021:104, para 100 of the Opinion), but the Court did not.

[68] Case C-719/19 *FS*, EU:C:2021:506, para 89: 'to interpret Article 15(1) of Directive 2004/38 as meaning that a Union citizen who has been the subject of an expulsion decision taken under that provision would be obliged, in all cases, to leave the host Member State for a minimum period, for example three months, in order to be able to rely on a new right of residence on the territory of that Member State, under Article 6(1) … would be to render the exercise of that *fundamental right* subject to *a limitation not provided for either by the Treaties or by Directive 2004/38*' (emphasis added).

[69] ibid paras 86–88.

and the 'specific objective' captured there: 'to prevent Union citizens and their family members exercising a right of residence under that directive from becoming an unreasonable burden on the social assistance system of the host Member State during their temporary residence'.[70] While the Court did, as noted above, reject the proposal of the Netherlands Government that a minimum period of residence outside the host State might be read 'systematically'[71] into expulsion decisions taken on the basis of Article 15(1) of the Directive, it agreed that time spent away from the host State 'may be of some importance in the context of the overall assessment' of genuinely and effectively terminating residence, as returned to in Section 5. Thus, while the Court *formally* acknowledged the requirement that conditions and limits on the right to move and reside must be 'laid down' or 'expressly provided for' in the Treaties or in EU legislation,[72] conditions and limits were nevertheless added, more subtly, through interpreting the Directive and especially through articulating criteria that national authorities are permitted to apply on a case-by-case basis. It is difficult to characterise such criteria as *not* implanting further conditions and limits on the right to move and reside, as introduced in Chapter 2 and considered further in Chapter 9.[73]

4. The Right to Reside for More than Three Months

Article 7 is the pivotal provision of Directive 2004/38. In setting the conditions that must be fulfilled for a valid right to reside in a host State for more than three months, it establishes the responsibilities of both Union citizens and host States in these circumstances,[74] cements distinctions between different categories of Union citizens (mainly between the economically active and the economically autonomous), constructs a bridge to the right of permanent residence, examined in Chapter 8, and articulates conditions that determine whether a Union citizen is residing *lawfully* in the host State, the significance and repercussions of which are considered further in Chapter 7.

Article 7(1)(a) addresses workers and self-employed persons (Section 4.1). Article 7(1)(b) guarantees a general right to reside so long as conditions concerning financial resources and sickness insurance are fulfilled (Section 4.2). Residence rights for students are provided for in Article 7(1)(c) (Section 4.3). Articles 7(1)(d) and 7(2) establish residence rights for certain family members—for those who are themselves Union citizens and for those who are not Member State nationals respectively[75]—who accompany or join Union citizens residing in another Member State, provided that the Union citizen satisfies the conditions in Article 7(1)(a), (b), or (c).[76] Finally, falling between the categories fixed by Articles 6 and 7 of the

---

[70] ibid para 72.
[71] AG Rantos in *FS*, para 93 of the Opinion.
[72] eg Case C-184/99 *Grzelczyk*, EU:C:2001:458, para 31; Case C-200/02 *Zhu and Chen*, EU:C:2004:639, paras 30–31.
[73] See further, N Nic Shuibhne, 'The "constitutional weight" of adjectives' (2014) 39 European Law Review 153.
[74] On the less developed responsibilities of home States, see F Strumia, 'Supranational citizenship enablers: free movement from the perspective of home Member States' (2020) 45 European Law Review 507.
[75] Article 7(1)(d) provides that '[a]ll Union citizens shall have the right of residence on the territory of another Member State for a period of longer than three months if they: ... are family members accompanying or joining a Union citizen who satisfies the conditions referred to in points (a), (b) or (c)'. Article 7(2) establishes that '[t]he right of residence provided for in paragraph 1 shall extend to family members who are not nationals of a Member State, accompanying or joining the Union citizen in the host Member State, provided that such Union citizen satisfies the conditions referred to in paragraph l(a), (b) or (c)'. On the definition of 'family members' of a Union citizen for the purposes of Directive, see Article 2(2); see further, Chapter 4.
[76] Confirmed in eg Case C-218/14 *Singh II*, EU:C:2015:476, para 54. On rights that family members can acquire 'exclusively on a personal basis, see Section 6.3. The dependency on the Union citizen 'reference person' (Case

Directive in some respects, the residence rights of jobseekers (ie Union citizens seeking employment in another Member State) are considered separately in Section 4.4.

4.1 Article 7(1)(a): Workers and Self-Employed Persons

Article 7(1)(a) confirms that '[a]ll Union citizens shall have the right of residence on the territory of another Member State for a period of longer than three months if they ... are workers or self-employed persons in the host Member State'. As concepts on which the enjoyment of rights under EU law depends, work and self-employment are defined by EU, not national, law.[77]

As introduced in Chapter 1, rights conferred by Articles 45 and 49 TFEU are characterised as 'specific expressions' of the right to move and reside conferred by Article 21 TFEU.[78] For workers, the right to reside in another Member State for the purposes of employment there is conferred directly by Article 45(3) TFEU,[79] with more detailed rights then provided for in Regulation 492/2011—the main legislative measure on the free movement of persons not

---

C-133/15 *Chavez-Vilchez*, EU:C:2017:354, para 55) that Article 7(1)(d) sustains was highlighted by the European Parliament's Committee on Women's Rights and Equal Opportunities in its assessment of the draft directive, noting 'negative effects on women' and criticising the 'lack of individual rights' that in turn renders the position of dependent spouses 'very unstable and vulnerable' (Opinion attached to the European Parliament Report on the Commission proposal (n 21, at 85 and 88). The Committee thus proposed adding to Article 7(1)(d): '[s]pouses are entitled to an independent legal status and work permit' (Amendment 6), explaining that '[a]s it is still most often the case that women depend on men [Article 7(1)(d)] will not work out gender neutral'. These questions are returned to in Section 6, which outlines the conditions under which family members retain the right to reside when their connection to the Union citizen ends or changes.

[77] In EU free movement law, 'work' is defined as 'the pursuit of effective and genuine activities, to the exclusion of activities on such a small scale as to be regarded as purely marginal and ancillary' (Case 53/81 *Levin*, EU:C:1982:105, para 17). Since the 'essential feature of an employment relationship ... is that for a certain period of time a person performs services for and under the direction of another person in return for which he receives remuneration' (Case 66/85 *Lawrie-Blum*, EU:C:1986:284, para 17), activity 'not carried out in the context of a relationship of subordination' means that the individual is instead 'pursuing an activity as a self-employed person within the meaning of Article [49 TFEU]' (Case C-107/94 *Asscher*, EU:C:1996:251, para 26).

[78] It is rare for the Court not to take a position on the status of the applicant (ie not to determine whether the activity in question constitutes work or self-employment for the purposes of EU law), but see eg Joined Cases C-502/01 and C-31/02 *Gaumain-Cerri and Barth*, EU:C:2004:413, esp paras 32–35, and Case C-152/03 *Ritter-Coulais*, EU:C:2006:123, in respect of which it has been argued that '[t]he consequence of the approach followed ... is that the distinction between the free movement of workers and the freedom to move on the basis of European citizenship has become blurred' (AG Geelhoed in Case C-212/05 *Hartmann*, EU:C:2006:615, para 38 of the Opinion).

[79] The Withdrawal Agreement details the protection that continues to apply to those who come within the personal scope of the Agreement (Articles 9 and 10 WA) and either work (Article 24 WA) or are self-employed (Article 25 WA) in the state in which they reside following Brexit. It makes particular provision for frontier workers: see additionally, Articles 9(d), 10(1)(c) and (d), and 26 WA. Article 17 WA further provides: '1. The right of Union citizens and United Kingdom nationals, and their respective family members, to rely directly on this Part shall not be affected when they change status, for example between student, worker, self-employed person and economically inactive person. Persons who, at the end of the transition period, enjoy a right of residence in their capacity as family members of Union citizens or United Kingdom nationals, cannot become persons referred to in points (a) to (d) of Article 10(1). 2. The rights provided for in this Title for the family members who are dependants of Union citizens or United Kingdom nationals before the end of the transition period, shall be maintained even after they cease to be dependants'. As the Commission therefore confirms, while '[f]amily members who have the right of residence in the host State in accordance with Article 13(2) or (3) of the Agreement can also change their status and remain beneficiaries of the Agreement ... the second sentence of Article 17(1) expressly prevents them from becoming right holders (ie persons referred to in Article 10(1)(a) to (d) of the Agreement). In practice, this means that they have no autonomous right under the Agreement to be joined by their own family members. This limitation applies only with regard to those persons whose residence status under the Agreement is *exclusively* derived from their being family members of right holders' (Guidance Note relating to the Agreement (n 14) para 2.5.1.1, emphasis in original). The Commission also notes that, under Article 24 WA, '[w]orkers enjoy the full panoply of rights stemming from Article 45 TFEU and Regulation (EU) No 492/2011. The rights set out in paragraph 1 of

fully repealed and replaced by the adoption of Directive 2004/38 since only Articles 10 and 11 of its ancestor measure (Regulation 1612/68) were repealed.[80] Of particular note is Article 7(2) of Regulation 492/2011, which continues to establish that a worker who is a national of another Member State 'shall enjoy the same social and tax advantages as national workers' and is returned to below. The extent to which frontier workers come within the scope of Directive 2004/38—especially as regards family reunification—depends on their nationality. Article 3(1) extends the protection of the Directive to its 'beneficiaries' only when they 'move to or reside in a Member State *other than* that of which they are a national'.[81] However, for frontier workers residing in their States of nationality, family reunification rights can be based directly on Article 45 TFEU in certain circumstances.[82]

For self-employed persons, Article 49 TFEU establishes that '[f]reedom of establishment shall include the right to take up and pursue activities as self-employed persons', which 'may be construed as prohibiting Member States from setting up restrictions or obstacles to the entry into their territory of nationals of other Member States'.[83] The rights conferred directly by Article 49 TFEU were originally 'given closer articulation'[84] by Directive 73/148, Article 4 of which provided that '[e]ach Member State shall grant the right of permanent residence to nationals of other Member States who establish themselves within its territory in order to pursue activities as self-employed persons'. Moreover, the principles of equal treatment enshrined in both Article 45 TFEU and Article 7(2) of Regulation 492/2011 'do not apply solely to employed migrant workers but also apply, *mutatis mutandis*, in respect of Article 49 TFEU, to self-employed migrant workers'.[85] Article 7(1)(a) of Directive 2004/38 thus continues a long-established approach of comparability for workers and self-employed persons. As the Court indicated in *Gusa*, Article 7(1) distinguishes, more particularly, 'the situation of economically active citizens from that of inactive citizens and students. That provision does not, however, draw a distinction, within the first category, between citizens working as employed persons and those working as self-employed persons in the host Member State'.[86]

Article 24 of the Agreement have the same scope and meaning as defined in Article 45 TFEU and Regulation (EU) No 492/2011. The rights of workers enumerated in paragraph 1 of Article 24 of the Agreement are not exhaustive and any development of those rights by future [Court of Justice] interpretations of Article 45 TFEU would, therefore, be covered (in the case of the United Kingdom, their judicial and administrative authorities would have "due regard" to the relevant case law of the [Court] handed down after the end of the transition period)' (ibid para 2.12.1.2).

[80] Regulation 1612/68/EEC on freedom of movement for workers within the Community, 1968 OJ L257/13. The repealed provisions concerned the definition and rights of family members. See also, however, the discussion in Chapter 4 on whether more extensive protection for the family members of workers continues on the basis of Article 7(2) of Regulation 492/2011, which ensures equal treatment with host State workers as regards social and tax advantages and was the basis on which residence rights for unmarried partners were developed in Case 59/85 *Reed*, EU:C:1986:157.

[81] The Court has addressed the extent to which the meaning of family members under different measures of EU law can be aligned for the protection of frontier workers: see Case C-410/18 *Aubriet*, EU:C:2019:582; and Case 802/18 *Caisse pour l'avenir des enfants*, EU:C:2020:269.

[82] See esp Case C-457/12 *S and G*, EU:C:2014:36, discussed in Chapter 9. More generally, disputes about the entitlement of frontier workers to study finance in Luxembourg have produced significant case law at the Court of Justice: see further, C Jacqueson, 'Any news from Luxembourg? On student aid, frontier workers and stepchildren: *Bragança Linares Verruga* and *Depesme*' (2018) 54 Common Market Law Review 901; and J Silga, 'Luxembourg financial aid for higher studies and children of frontier workers: evolution and challenges in light of the case-law of the Court of Justice' (2019) 19 European Public Law 13.

[83] Case 118/75 *Watson and Belmann*, EU:C:1976:106, para 12.

[84] ibid.

[85] Case C-168/20 *BJ and OV*, EU:C:2021:907, para 85.

[86] Case C-442/16 *Gusa*, EU:C:2017:1004, para 36. See further, Section 6.2.

Article 7(1)(a) of the Directive confirms a right of residence for workers and self-employed persons as economically *active* Union citizens, without any further conditions: once a Member State national meets the EU-set definition of work or self-employment, they have a right to reside in another Member State for that purpose and, in contrast to Union citizens claiming a right to reside under either Article 7(1)(b) or 7(1)(c), they do not have to demonstrate that they have sufficient resources for themselves and their family members not to become a burden on the social assistance system of, or comprehensive sickness insurance cover in, the host State.[87] Moreover, Article 24(2) of the Directive does not establish any derogations from equal treatment with host State nationals for workers or self-employed persons. Relatedly, Article 7(2) of Regulation 492/2011 continues to ensure equality of access to host State social security and social assistance.[88] In *Kempf*, the Court held that receiving income from public funds did not undermine 'worker' status under EU law: in other words, 'where a national of a Member State pursues within the territory of another Member State by way of employment activities which may in themselves be regarded as effective and genuine work, the fact that he claims financial assistance payable out of the public funds of the latter Member State in order to supplement the income he receives from those activities does not exclude him from the provisions of [Union] law relating to freedom of movement for workers'.[89] And, as noted above, while Regulation 492/2011 does not apply directly to self-employed persons, the Court has based comparable equal treatment for social and tax advantages on Article 49 TFEU directly.[90]

The asymmetry between economic *activity* and economic *autonomy*—which premises unconditional residence rights in a host State under Article 7(1)(a) for the former on the *fact* of economic activity rather than on the extent to which it ensures a Union citizen's economic autonomy—reflects an intention that 'the contribution of the European worker, that is to say, of the European citizen, to the construction of the economy and the social security system of the Member States through his work would be acknowledged'.[91] In other words, 'migrant workers contribute to the financing of the social policies of the host Member State through the tax and social security contributions which they pay in that State by virtue of their employment there. They must therefore be able to profit from them under the same conditions as national workers'.[92] These principles were fundamentally challenged by the Decision adopted in February 2016 as part of the UK's (pre-Brexit) renegotiation of its membership of the Union,[93] which established a binding commitment to amend EU legislation

---

[87] In *Grzelczyk*, AG Alber commented that 'residence by reason of paid employment and the attached rights and obligations involve a special set of rules as distinct from the general right of residence for citizens of the Union under [Article 21 TFEU]' (AG Alber in Case C-184/99 *Grzelczyk*, EU:C:2000:518, para 64 of the Opinion).

[88] The Court defines 'social and tax advantages' for the purposes of Article 7(2) as 'all social and tax advantages, whether or not linked to the contract of employment' (Case 32/75 *Cristini*, EU:C:1972:56, para 2). In *Hoeckx*, the Court ruled that 'a benefit guaranteeing a minimum means of subsistence constitutes a social advantage, within the meaning of Regulation [492/2011], which may not be denied to a migrant worker who is a national of another Member State and is resident within the territory of the State paying the benefit, nor to his family' (Case 249/83 *Hoeckx*, EU:C:1985:139, para 22). For social security benefits also falling within the scope of Regulation 883/2004, see eg Case C-111/91 *Commission v Luxembourg*, EU:C:1993:92, para 21.

[89] Case 139/85 *Kempf*, EU:C:1986:223, para 16.

[90] eg Case 63/86 *Commission v Italy*, EU:C:1988:9; Case C-299/01 *Commission v Luxembourg*, EU:C:2002:394; Case C-168/20 *BJ and OV*, EU:C:2021:907.

[91] AG Cosmas in Case C-160/96 *Molenaar*, EU:C:1997:599, para 93 of the Opinion.

[92] Case C-328/20 *Commission v Austria*, EU:C:2022:468, para 109.

[93] Section D, Decision of the Heads of State or Government, meeting within the European Council, concerning a new settlement for the United Kingdom within the European Union, 2016 OJ C691/1. See further, N Nic Shuibhne, 'Reconnecting the free movement of workers and equal treatment in an unequal Europe' (2018) 43 European Law Review 477.

and thereby to restrict equal treatment as regards 'in-work benefits' and exported family benefits in certain circumstances. It did not take effect because of the outcome of the UK referendum in June 2016.[94] Residing on the basis of Article 7(1)(a) of the Directive therefore continues to ensure comprehensive equal treatment on the grounds of nationality for economically active citizens residing in a host State—at least for the time being, as explained further in Chapter 7. It also enables additional protection from expulsion under Article 14 of the Directive (Section 6.1) and fast-tracked entitlement to permanent residence rights in certain circumstances (Chapter 8).

Finally, while the Court confirmed in *Royer* that comparing the Treaty provisions on workers, establishment, and services 'shows that they are based on the same principles both in so far as they concern the entry into and residence in the territory of Member States of persons covered by [Union] law and the prohibition of all discrimination between them on grounds of nationality',[95] and while the providers—and recipients—of services do engage in economic activity, it is not the kind of economic activity that qualifies them for the privileged residence status conferred by Article 7(1)(a) of the Directive. In the Commission's original proposal,[96] draft Article 7(1)(a) referred to residence rights for citizens '*engaged in gainful activity* in an employed or self-employed capacity', which arguably included the providers (at least) of services. That interpretation is supported by the fact that the European Parliament proposed adding *recipients* of services to that text:

> Recipients of services are not explicitly covered by the new directive and hence it is not clear to what category they below. One might therefore consider them to be covered by Article 7[1](b), but this would constitute an additional condition which is not envisaged in the law at present. The amendment is therefore in line with the current acquis.[97]

The Commission accepted the suggestion, commenting in its amended proposal that a direct reference to service recipients in Article 7(1)(a) would 'avoid confusion and a gap in the Directive, as the original text did not make it clear which provision covered this category of person'.[98] However, in its common position, the Council rejected the amendment on the basis that 'recipients of services cannot be treated on the same footing as workers or self-employed persons'[99]—'quite rightly' according to the Commission's related Communication,[100] despite its earlier acceptance of the Parliament's proposal.

As a result, both the providers and recipients of services must demonstrate economic *autonomy* for residence rights under Article 7(1)(b) of the Directive, notwithstanding the economic *activity* in which they participate. Thus, while Article 7(1)(a) *reflects* the residence rights conferred directly by Articles 45 and 49 TFEU, Article 7(1)(b) *conditions* the rights conferred directly by Article 56 TFEU where residence lasts for more than three months (Article 6 of the Directive ensuring an unconditional residence right for all Union citizens in

---

[94] One of the proposals in the Decision—that exported family benefits should be indexed to the State of the child's residence rather than the State of work—has now been found in breach EU free movement law following Austria's decision to impose such measures unilaterally: referring expressly to the 2016 Decision, the Court stated that 'if such an amendment had been adopted by the EU legislature, it would have been invalid under Article 45 TFEU' (Case C-328/20 *Commission v Austria*, EU:C:2022:468, para 57).
[95] Case 48/75 *Royer*, EU:C:1976:57, para 12.
[96] (n 11).
[97] European Parliament Report on Commission proposal (n 21) Amendment 27.
[98] Amended proposal (n 45) 5.
[99] Common Position (n 11) 29.
[100] Communication on the common position (n 48) para 3.3.2.

a host State for up to that point, including for those who provide or receive services there). That position does reflect the fact that the right to reside can be decoupled from corollary rights enjoyed during a period of residence: host State entitlement to social and tax advantages, for example, was never extended to the providers or recipients of services.[101] At the same time, while simplifying the sectoral patchwork that characterised EU free movement law was a fundamental objective in adopting Directive 2004/38, it is not the case that the categories previously legislated for became irrelevant in consequence. In other words, the Directive is a 'single reference text',[102] but it does not establish a single status framework. However, while the rights of those who provide and receive services have indeed been absorbed into the general residence scheme of Articles 6 and 7 of the Directive, the rights of jobseekers have not, as returned to in Section 4.4.

4.2 Article 7(1)(b): General Right to Reside

Article 7(1)(b) of the Directive establishes that economically inactive[103] Union citizens 'shall have the right to reside on the territory of another Member State for a period of longer than three months if they: ... have sufficient resources for themselves and their family members not to become a burden on the social assistance system of the host Member State during their period of residence and have comprehensive sickness insurance cover in the host Member State'.[104] These conditions are underpinned by recital 10, which exhorts that '[p]ersons exercising their right of residence should not ... become an unreasonable burden on the social assistance system of the host Member State during an initial period of residence. Therefore, the right of residence for Union citizens and their family members for periods in excess of three months should be subject to conditions'.

---

[101] Similarly, restrictions placed on the temporary posting of workers fall within the scope of freedom to provide services under Article 56 TFEU. As a result, Member State nationals who are posted as workers to another Member State are not workers within the meaning of Article 45 TFEU; see eg Case C-113/89 *Rush Portuguesa*, EU:C:1990:142. Standards of protection for working and social conditions in the host State are addressed by Directive 2018/957/EU, amending Directive 96/71/EC, concerning the posting of workers in the framework of the provision of services, 2018 OJ L173/16. To date, no potential intersection with Union citizenship rights under Articles 20 and 21 TFEU has arisen in the case law—there has been no direct challenge yet, in other words, to the presumption that Member State nationals who are posted workers 'move from one Member State to another in a way that is detached from EU citizenship owing to the direct connection to Article 56 TFEU and the primary nature of the posting being an exercise of the particular business's rights' (S Currie, 'Scapegoats and guinea pigs: free movement as a pathway to confined labour market citizenship for European Union accession migrants in the UK' (2022) 51 Industrial Journal 277).

[102] Opinion of the Committee of the Regions (n 20) para 2.1.

[103] The language of 'economically inactive' citizens is used in this chapter to reflect the language used in the case law, in full awareness that this terminology is problematically narrow and under-inclusive—considering, for example, how economic activity within the meaning of EU law excludes the work of caring. See further, S Currie, *Migration, Work and Citizenship in the Enlarged European Union* (Ashgate 2008); C O'Brien, 'Social blind spots and monocular policy making: the ECJ's migrant worker model' (2009) 46 Common Market Law Review 1120; D Carter, 'Inclusion and exclusion of migrant workers in the EU' in J Moritz (ed), *European Societies, Migration and the Law* (CUP 2020) 301; and A Welsh, *Vanishing Safety Nets, the Citizenship Illusion, and the Worker that Isn't: A Case Study of EU Migrant Atypical Workers' Rights in the UK* (2020, PhD thesis, University of York, <https://etheses.whiterose.ac.uk/28325/> (accessed 30 May 2023)).

[104] The adopted German version of Article 7(1)(b) provides that Union citizens should have sufficient resources 'without recourse to welfare funds in the host Member State during their stay'. In *Brey*, AG Wahl considered why the stricter understanding conveyed by the German text does not fit with the broader scheme of the Directive, pointing to Articles 8(4), 14(2), and 14(3) as well as recitals 10 and 16 (AG Wahl in Case C-140/12 *Brey*, EU:C:2013:337, paras 74–77 of the Opinion). However, the German text does reflect the original text proposed for Article 24 of the Directive, as explained further in Chapter 7.

4.2.1 'Sufficient resources'

Article 7(1)(b) requires Union citizens who are not economically active in a host State to have sufficient resources for themselves and their family members in order that they do not become a burden on its social assistance system during their period of residence there. For the purposes of the Directive, social assistance is defined as 'all assistance introduced by the public authorities, whether at national, regional or local level, that can be claimed by an individual who does not have resources sufficient to meet his own basic needs and the needs of his family and who, by reason of that fact, may become a burden on the public finances of the host Member State during his period of residence which could have consequences for the overall level of assistance which may be granted by that State'.[105]

The right of residence provided for in Article 7(1)(b) replaces the pre-citizenship rights created by Directives 90/364 and 90/365 and carries over to the post-citizenship framework the conditions on sufficient resources and sickness insurance conceived for those earlier measures. Similarly, Directive 2004/38's concern with unreasonable burdens on the social assistance systems of host States (recital 10) reflects the reference to not becoming 'an unreasonable burden on the public finances of the host Member State' in the preambles to the 1990 Directives. In early citizenship rulings such as *Grzelczyk*, *Baumbast*, and *Trojani*, the Court attributed material significance to the reference to unreasonable burdens in the sense of, conversely, accepting *reasonable* (ie proportionate) burdens are premised on a 'certain degree of a certain degree of financial solidarity between nationals of a host Member State and nationals of other Member States, particularly if the difficulties which a beneficiary of the right of residence encounters are temporary'.[106] This distinction is returned to in Chapter 7 in the discussion on lawful residence and equal treatment.

The drafting history of Directive 2004/38 reflects the aim of pursuing a balance between a meaningful and citizenship-oriented right of residence detached from economic activity, on the one hand, and the risk of (over-)burdening host State public finances, on the other—though framed, at the time, more in economic and practical terms than in the intensively politicised narratives that have come to dominate this aspect of freedom of movement since then. For example, in its original proposal for the Directive, the Commission considered that '[w]hile the exercise of [the right of residence] is to be facilitated, the fact that, at the present stage, social assistance provision is not covered by Community law and is not, as a rule, "exportable", entails that a completely equal treatment as regards social benefits is not possible without running the risk of certain categories of people entitled to the right of residence, in particular those not engaged in gainful activity, becoming an unreasonable [burden] on the public finances of the host Member State'.[107] Only the European Parliament's Committee on Legal Affairs and the Internal Market suggested that the conditions conceived for the 1990s Directives had no place in the new legislative arrangements:

---

[105] *Brey*, para 61. This definition of 'social assistance' and its relationship to social security are examined in Chapter 7. Note also the overlap between social security and social assistance in Article 8(4) of Directive 2004/38 (Section 5.1). On recourse to social assistance in the context of Directive 2003/86/EC on the right to family reunification, 2003 OJ L251/12, see eg Case C-578/08 *Chakroun*, EU:C:2009:776; and Case C-558/14 *Khachab*, EU:C:2016:285.

[106] Case C-184/99 *Grzelczyk*, EU:C:2001:458, para 44. See similarly, Case C-209/03 *Bidar*, EU:C:2005:169, para 56; and *Brey*, para 72. Expressing these principles in the language of proportionality, see Case C-413/99 *Baumbast and R*, EU:C:2002:493, para 91; and Case C-456/02 *Trojani*, EU:C:2004:488, para 34. See further, Chapter 7.

[107] Original proposal (n 11) 10–11.

Account should be taken of the way in which the Community legal system has evolved towards the establishment of a single market, European citizenship and, later, an area of freedom, security and justice. We must act consistently with this evolution and thus take the view that the principles of free movement and non-discrimination are no longer purely economic, but now apply to all EU citizens, whether they are in work or not. Thus, citizens who change their place of residence for exclusively personal (rather than work-related) reasons should be able to derive full benefit from the application of these Community principles. The requirements concerning the possession of sufficient resources *are laid down only in secondary Community legislation*. As this constitutes treatment which differentiates between nationals of a Member State and other Community nationals, which is not compatible with the principle of non-discrimination on grounds of nationality, they must be expunged from the Commission proposal.[108]

However, that radical vision of a wholly unconditional right to reside was not shared by any of the other institutions.[109]

The origin or source of a Union citizen's financial resources is not material. The ruling in *Zhu and Chen* was discussed in Chapter 4, since it confirmed that minor Union citizens have full legal capacity to exercise the right to move and reside conferred by Article 21 TFEU. However, while they are also fully expected to fulfil the conditions in EU law for lawful residence in the host State, there is flexibility about *how* these conditions are fulfilled and especially with regard to how children possess the necessary financial resources not to become a burden on the host State's social assistance system.[110] Applying that approach to Directive 2004/38, the Court has confirmed that 'the expression "have" sufficient resources in ... Article 7(1)(b) of [the Directive] must be interpreted as meaning that it suffices that such resources are available to the Union citizens, and that that provision lays down no requirement whatsoever as to their origin, since they could be provided, *inter alia*, by a national of a non-Member State, the parent of the citizens who are minor children at issue'.[111] This reasoning reflects the requirement that conditions and limits placed on the right to move and reside must be laid down or expressly provided for (Articles 20(1) and 21(1) TFEU).

The openness of the Directive to the origins of sufficient resources was particularly striking in *Bajratari*. Confirming that Article 7(1)(b) 'merely requires that the Union citizens concerned have sufficient resources at their disposal ... without establishing any other

---

[108] Opinion of the Committee on Legal Affairs and the Internal Market, attached to the European Parliament Report on the Commission proposal (n 21, 57–58). Its version of Article 7(1) of the Directive would therefore have read: '[a]ll Union citizens holding a valid passport or identity card shall have the right to reside on the territory of another Member State for a period of longer than six months' (Amendment 4).

[109] It was broadly reflected in the submissions of the Portuguese Government in Case C-184/99 *Grzelczyk*, EU:C:2001:458, para 23: '[t]he Portuguese Government points out that, since the entry into force of the Treaty on European Union, nationals of the Member States are no longer regarded in Community law as being primarily economic factors in an essentially economic community. One consequence of the introduction of Union citizenship is that the limits and conditions which Community law imposes on the exercise of the right to freedom of movement and residence within the territory of the Member States should no longer be construed as envisaging a purely economic right arising from the EC Treaty but as being concerned only with those exceptions that are based on reasons of public policy, public security or public health. Furthermore, if from the time when the Treaty on European Union entered into force, nationals of the Member States acquired the status of citizen of the Union and ceased to be regarded as purely economic agents, it follows that the application of Regulation No 1612/68 ought also to be extended to all citizens of the Union, whether or not they are workers within the meaning of that regulation'. Balancing the rights conferred by primary law with the conditions set by legislation was introduced in Chapter 2 and is returned to in Chapter 7.

[110] Case C-200/02 *Zhu and Chen*, EU:C:2004:639, para 30.

[111] Case C-86/12 *Alokpa and Moudoulou*, EU:C:2013:64, para 27. See similarly eg Case C-165/14 *Rendón Marín*, EU:C:2016:675, para 48.

conditions, in particular as regards the origin of those resources', a national measure that excluded from consideration 'income obtained from employment in the host Member State occupied by a parent, who is a third-country national without a residence and work permit'—that is, from unlawful employment—was found to restrict the Union citizen children's right to move and reside in principle, and its proportionality was therefore assessed against the objective of protecting host State public finances.[112] In determining that the contested national measure 'goes manifestly beyond what is necessary' to protect the public finances of the host State, the Court referred to 'the fact that those resources have allowed that Union citizen to support himself and his family members for the past 10 years without needing to rely on the social assistance system of that Member State'[113]—illustrating the repercussions that can follow when a Member State tolerates either the presence or the behaviour of Union citizens (or their family members). This question was introduced in Chapter 5 and is considered further in Chapter 7.

The approach taken to the origins of sufficient resources in the case law outlined above is generally applicable: in other words, it applies beyond the specific example of minor Union citizens. In *Commission v Belgium*, infringement proceedings taken in the context of Directive 90/364, one of the national practices challenged by the Commission was that 'only the *personal* resources of the citizen of the Union who is seeking a right of residence or those of the spouse or of a child of that citizen to the exclusion of resources of a third person, such as a partner with whom he has no legal link'.[114] First, the Court confirmed the finding in *Zhu and Chen* that a Union citizen may rely on the resources provided by a family member since 'a requirement as to the origin of the resources which, not being necessary for the attainment of the objective pursued, namely the protection of the public finances of the Member States, would constitute a disproportionate interference with the exercise of the fundamental right of freedom of movement and of residence'.[115] Second, that principle also applied to income provided by a Union citizen's partner residing in the host State.[116] In *Commission v Belgium*, the Court relied in part on elements of Directive 90/364—in particular, provisions addressing the monitoring of circumstances and the revalidating of residence permits—that were not carried over by Directive 2004/38, changes that are returned to in Section 5.1.

---

[112] Case C-93/18 *Bajratari*, EU:C:2019:809, paras 34 and 42. However, the Court has held that 'in view of the definitive nature of the acquisition of long-term resident status and of the objective of Article 5(1)(a) of Directive 2003/109, which is to preserve the social assistance system of the Member State concerned, the conditions of "resources" within the meaning of that directive have a scope different from that provided for in Directive 2004/38'—also noting that 'Article 5(1)(a) of Directive 2003/109 requires that the resources referred to therein be not only "sufficient" but also "stable" and "regular"' (Case C-302/18 *X v Belgische Staat*, EU:C:2019:830, paras 35–36. Nevertheless, taking account of the 'comparable provisions of Directives 2004/38 and 2003/86', the Court also found that '[r]esources from a third party or a member of the applicant's family are therefore not excluded by Article 5(1)(a) of Directive 2003/109, provided that they are stable, regular and sufficient. In that regard, ... the legally binding nature of a commitment of cost bearing by a third party or a member of the applicant's family may be an important factor to be taken into account. It is also permissible for the competent authorities of the Member States to take into account, *inter alia*, the family relationship between the applicant for long-term residence and the member or members of the family prepared to bear his costs. Similarly, the nature and permanence of the resources of the member or members of the applicant's family may be relevant factors to that effect' (ibid paras 41 and 43).

[113] *Bajratari*, para 46. AG Szpunar further explained that 'following the expiry of his residence card in 2014, Ms Bajratari's husband lost his work and residence permit, but nevertheless continued to work in the restaurant where he had been employed since 2009. Accordingly, it was only because his residence card expired that the employment of Ms Bajratari's husband became unlawful. In spite of the expiry of that card, he remained liable to pay taxes and contributions to the social security system and, as confirmed at the hearing, amounts were periodically deducted at source by his employer' (EU:C:2019:512, para 53 of the Opinion).

[114] Case C-408/03 *Commission v Belgium*, EU:C:2006:192, para 38 (emphasis added).

[115] ibid para 41.

[116] ibid para 51.

However, the essence of the judgment has been confirmed for income provided by spouses with reference to Directive 2004/38, with the Court finding in *Singh II* that 'the fact that some part of the resources available to the Union citizen derives from resources obtained by the spouse who is a third-country national from his activity in the host Member State does not preclude the condition concerning the sufficiency of resources in Article 7(1)(b) of Directive 2004/38 from being regarded as satisfied'.[117] The Court focused, as in *Bajratari*, on what was necessary 'for the attainment of the objective pursued, namely the protection of the public finances of the Member States'.[118]

The 1990s Directives and Directive 2004/38 respectively take different approaches to determining what actually constitutes 'sufficient resources', as explained further in Section 5.1 in connection with Article 8 of Directive 2004/38. More generally, the discussion in Chapter 7 considers how and in what circumstances (both of) the conditions in Article 7(1)(b) can be softened through the application of a proportionality test, as introduced first through the discussion on 'comprehensive sickness insurance' in the *Baumbast* case in Section 4.2.2. The basic starting point is that 'since the right to freedom of movement is – as a fundamental principle of EU law – the general rule, the conditions laid down in Article 7(1)(b) of Directive 2004/38 must be construed narrowly ... and in compliance with the limits imposed by EU law and the principle of proportionality'.[119] However, case law on social assistance and economically inactive citizens has modified the extent of the expected proportionality analysis in some respects.[120]

4.2.2 'Comprehensive sickness insurance'

By analogy with *Zhu and Chen* as to the origins of sufficient resources, the Court has also determined that for 'a Union citizen, who resides in the host State with a parent who is his or her primary carer, th[e] requirement [in Article 7(1)(b)] is satisfied both where this child has comprehensive sickness insurance which covers his or her parent, and in the inverse case where this parent has such insurance covering the child'.[121] But what does 'comprehensive sickness insurance' actually mean?

In *Baumbast*, addressing Directive 90/364, the Court did not expressly confirm, one way or the other, whether sickness insurance that did not cover emergency treatment in the host State constituted 'comprehensive sickness insurance cover' there. It might be inferred that it did not, since it *was* expressly noted that 'both Mr Baumbast and his family have comprehensive sickness insurance in another Member State of the Union'.[122] Nevertheless, taking account of the facts—not only that the family had comprehensive sickness insurance cover in another State but also, *inter alia*, that 'Mr Baumbast has sufficient resources within the meaning of Directive 90/364 [and] that he worked and therefore lawfully resided in the host Member State for several years, initially as an employed person and subsequently as a self-employed person'—the Court ruled that '[u]nder those circumstances, to refuse to allow Mr Baumbast to exercise the right of residence which is conferred on him by Article [21(1) TFEU] by virtue of the application of the provisions of Directive 90/364 on the ground that

---

[117] Case C-218/14 *Singh II*, EU:C:2015:476, para 76.
[118] ibid para 75.
[119] Case C-140/12 *Brey*, EU:C:2013:565, para 70.
[120] See esp Case C-67/14 *Alimanovic*, EU:C:2015:597; see further, Chapter 7.
[121] Case C-247/20 *Commissioners for Her Majesty's Revenue and Customs (Assurance maladie complète)*, EU:C:2022:177, para 67.
[122] Case C-413/99 *Baumbast and R*, EU:C:2002:493, para 92.

his sickness insurance does not cover the emergency treatment given in the host Member State would amount to a disproportionate interference with the exercise of that right.'[123]

It was not clear, therefore, whether the condition of 'comprehensive sickness insurance' was complied with (and was different from something like *complete* sickness insurance), or whether a Union citizen might in certain circumstances be eligible to reside in a host State on the basis of (now) Article 7(1)(b) of Directive 2004/38 even if they did not possess *comprehensive* sickness insurance. The Commission's guidance for better transposition and application of Directive 2004/38 reflects the *Baumbast* obfuscation of this point:

> Any insurance cover, private or public, contracted in the host Member State or elsewhere, is acceptable in principle, as long as it provides comprehensive coverage and does not create a burden on the public finances of the host Member State. In protecting their public finances while assessing the comprehensiveness of sickness insurance cover, Member States must act in compliance with the limits imposed by Community law and in accordance with the principle of proportionality. Pensioners fulfil the condition of comprehensive sickness insurance cover if they are entitled to health treatment on behalf of the Member State which pays their pension.[124]

That broad understanding was not recognised consistently by the Member States,[125] yet the meaning of comprehensive sickness insurance was not again addressed by the Court of Justice until two rulings in 2021: *A (Soins de santé publics)* and *Commissioners for Her Majesty's Revenue and Customs (Assurance maladie complète)*, which clarified critical questions about affiliation to host State public health insurance systems and the comprehensive sickness insurance requirement in Article 7(1)(b) of the Directive. It is perhaps not surprising that the Court took the opportunity to develop its guidance on these questions considering the implications for EU citizens who resided in the UK and whose continuing residence security there might have been called into question because of Brexit.[126] In any

---

[123] ibid para 93. As Advocate General Geelhoed later observed, 'the Court considered that the limitation on the right of residence amounted to a disproportionate interference with the right of residence, essentially because ... Mr Baumbast, although not fulfilling to the letter all the requirements of Article 1 of Directive 90/364, was *not likely to become* a burden on the public finances of the host Member State' (AG Geelhoed in Case C-456/02 *Trojani*, EU:C:2004:112, para 68 of the Opinion (emphasis added)).

[124] Communication from the Commission on guidance for better transposition and application of Directive 2004/38/EC (n 50) para 2.3.2.

[125] For example, Valcke noted in 2019 that 'Member States including France, Italy, the UK and Sweden refuse to accept that reliance upon the public healthcare system meets the requirement for holding "comprehensive sickness insurance" despite the Commission having indicated that this should be the case' (A Valcke, 'EU citizens' rights in practice: exploring the implementation gap in free movement law' (2019) 21 European Journal of Migration and Law 289 at 304). See generally, S De Mars, 'Managing misconceptions about EU citizens' access to domestic public healthcare: an EU-level response?' (2019) 25 European Public Law 709.

[126] The preliminary reference in this case was sent before the end of the transition period; as a result, it has 'binding force in [its] entirety on and in the United Kingdom' (Article 89(1) WA). Addressing how the ruling could have implications in practice following Brexit, see S De Mars, 'A last-minute postscript: the CJEU finally dares to find that the NHS is a provider of "comprehensive sickness insurance"' (EU Law Analysis, 16 March 2022, <http://eulawanalysis.blogspot.com/2022/03/a-possibly-pointless-postscript-cjeu.html> (accessed 30 May 2023)). See generally, C O'Brien, 'Between the devil and the deep blue sea: vulnerable EU citizens cast adrift in the UK post-Brexit' (2021) 58 Common Market Law Review 531. The Commission instituted (though did not proceed to litigate) infringement proceedings against the UK on its narrow approach to 'comprehensive sickness insurance' on more than one occasion, sending (most recently at the time of writing) in October 2020 'a complementary letter of formal notice to the United Kingdom for failing to transpose [Directive 2004/38] as regards the requirement for economically inactive EU citizens to have comprehensive sickness insurance when on UK territory. Under [that] Directive, EU citizens who settle in another EU country but do not work in that country are required to have sufficient resources and sickness insurance. However, in the United Kingdom, EU citizens who are affiliated with the UK public healthcare scheme (NHS) and are entitled to get medical treatment provided by the NHS are

event, two important principles have now been confirmed.¹²⁷ First, the requirement to have comprehensive sickness insurance 'would be rendered redundant if it were to be considered that the host Member State *is required* to grant, to an economically inactive Union citizen residing in its territory on the basis of Article 7(1)(b) of Directive 2004/38, affiliation free of charge to its public sickness insurance system'.¹²⁸ Thus, in circumstances where affiliation to such a system is required independently by Regulation 883/2004, the host State 'may provide that access to that system is not free of charge in order to prevent that citizen from becoming an unreasonable burden on that Member State'.¹²⁹ For that purpose, the host State is permitted to make affiliation of economically inactive Union citizens subject to conditions, which 'may include the conclusion or maintaining by that citizen of comprehensive private sickness insurance, enabling the reimbursement to that Member State of the health expenses it has incurred for that citizen's benefit, or the payment, by that citizen, of a contribution to that Member State's public sickness insurance system', so long as it 'ensure[s] that the principle of proportionality is observed and, therefore, that it is not excessively difficult for that citizen to comply with such conditions'.¹³⁰

Advocate General Saugmandsgaard Øe drew an interesting distinction as regards the level of 'burden' that a host State might be expected to tolerate on the basis of the wording of Article 7(1)(b):

> [U]nlike the wording of Article 7(1)(b) of Directive 2004//38 which requires the Union citizen to have sufficient resources "not to become a *burden* on the social assistance system of the host Member State during their period of residence", the EU legislature did not establish such a link between the condition requiring comprehensive sickness insurance and the existence of such a burden. Thus, the legislature considered that the lack of sufficient resources may constitute a *burden* that might justify a refusal to grant social benefits on equal terms as nationals. As regards comprehensive sickness insurance, on the other hand, the legislature's intention was to ensure that a Union citizen residing in a host Member State would not become, not simply a burden, but an *unreasonable burden*, for that Member State.¹³¹

---

not considered as having sufficient sickness insurance. The Commission considers that the UK's relevant rules are in breach of EU law', while also observing that 'the rights of EU citizens residing in the UK after the end of the transition period, as set out in the Withdrawal Agreement, are built on the rights that they currently enjoy in the United Kingdom under EU rules. The United Kingdom's shortcomings in implementing and transposing the EU free movement law also risks affecting the implementation of the citizens' rights under the Withdrawal Agreement after the end of the transition period' (<https://ec.europa.eu/commission/presscorner/detail/en/inf_20_1687> (accessed 30 May 2023)). See further, S De Mars, 'Economically inactive EU migrants and the NHS: unreasonable burdens without real links?' (2014) 39 European Law Review 770.

¹²⁷ The Court also confirmed that 'medical care, financed by the State, which is granted, without any individual and discretionary assessment of personal needs, to persons falling within the categories of recipients defined by national legislation, constitutes "sickness benefits" within the meaning of [Article 3(1)(a) of Regulation No 883/2004], thus falling within the scope of that regulation' (Case C-535/19 *A (Soins de santé publics)*, EU:C:2021:595, para 38).

¹²⁸ *A (Soins de santé publics)*, para 56 (emphasis added).

¹²⁹ ibid para 58; in the circumstances of the case, affiliation to the host State's public insurance system fell within the scope of Article 11(3)(e) of Regulation 883/2004.

¹³⁰ *A (Soins de santé publics)*, para 59.

¹³¹ AG Saugmandsgaard Øe in *A (Soins de santé publics)*, EU:C:2021:114, para 85 of the Opinion (emphasis in original).

The Court did not draw the same distinction so explicitly in its judgment, but it did use only the language of 'unreasonable burden' in its reasoning.[132] In *Commissioners for Her Majesty's Revenue and Customs (Assurance maladie complète)*, Advocate General Hogan observed similarly that, in crafting Directive 2004/38, 'the EU legislature was attentive to the fear of Member States that their public finances might be affected by the exercise of freedom of movement, but … it did not go so far as to require that the requirement of "comprehensive sickness insurance cover" be provided by a private operator and … it preferred the term "*comprehensive* sickness insurance cover", whereas Article 1(1) of Directive 90/365 previously required sickness insurance covering "*all the risks* in the host Member State"'.[133] More generally, however, the Court confirmed in *A (Soins de santé publics)* that a citizen's entitlement to equal treatment in the host State under Article 24 of the Directive does not defeat the requirement to have comprehensive sickness insurance in Article 7(1)(b).[134]

Second, in proceedings addressing the requirement to have comprehensive sickness insurance in Article 7(1)(b) of the Directive as well as eligibility for permanent residence rights under Article 16,[135] the Court held in *Commissioners for Her Majesty's Revenue and Customs (Assurance maladie complète)* that, notwithstanding a host State's capacity to impose conditions for affiliation, as noted above, 'once a Union citizen is affiliated to such a public sickness insurance system in the host Member State, *he or she has comprehensive sickness insurance* within the meaning of Article 7(1)(b)'.[136] Following that statement, the Court found, on the facts of the case, that where 'the economically inactive Union citizen at issue is a child, one of whose parents, a third-country national, has worked and was subject to tax in the host State during the period at issue, it would be disproportionate to deny that child and the parent who is his or her primary carer a right of residence, under Article 7(1)(b) of Directive 2004/38, on the sole ground that, during that period, they were affiliated free of charge to the public sickness insurance system of that State' since '[i]t cannot be considered that that affiliation free of charge constitutes, in such circumstances, an unreasonable burden on the public finances of that State'.[137] That clarification aside, the kernel of the ruling is unambiguous: where a Member State affiliates an economically inactive Union citizen to its public sickness insurance system free of charge, that decision cannot subsequently be used to undermine the citizen's claim to having 'comprehensive sickness insurance' within the meaning of Article 7(1)(b). Again, the repercussions of tolerated presence of Union citizens by the host State seem just beneath the surface of this ruling.

---

[132] Cf references to 'a burden' for the requirement to possess sufficient resources in para 53 of the judgment and also in eg Case C-333/13 *Dano*, EU:C:2014:2358, paras 63 and 77. See further, Chapter 7.

[133] AG Hogan in Case C-247/20 *Commissioners for Her Majesty's Revenue and Customs (Assurance maladie complète)*, EU:C:2021:778, para 61 of the Opinion (emphasis in original).

[134] Case C-535/19 *A (Soins de santé publics)*, EU:C:2021:595, paras 61–62; see further, Chapter 7.

[135] The relevance of the meaning of 'comprehensive sickness' insurance was not clear from the facts of the dispute; note that the Court reformulated the questions referred to it (paras 47–52) and that AG Hogan had only addressed the issue as a 'last remark', observing at para 56 of the Opinion that '[o]ne cannot, I think, ignore the fact that another fundamental question underlying the dispute between the parties to the main proceedings is probably whether the entitlement to use health care provided by a public healthcare scheme (namely the National Health Service, "NHS") is a "comprehensive sickness insurance cover" within the meaning of Article 7(1)(b) of Directive 2004/38'; and lamenting that it 'would be particularly inopportune to address this issue, notwithstanding the fact that the referring court will no longer have the opportunity to question the Court on this matter in view of the fact that the United Kingdom has chosen to leave the European Union' (para 60 of the Opinion).

[136] Case C-247/20 Commissioners for Her Majesty's Revenue and Customs (*Assurance maladie complète*), EU:C:2022:177, para 69 (emphasis added).

[137] ibid para 70.

4.3 Article 7(1)(c): Students

In Chapter 2, we saw that Member State nationals who moved to another State for the purposes of study were protected through combining what is now Article 166 TFEU on vocational training and Article 18 TFEU on nationality discrimination, especially as regards conditions of access to education (eg differential fees).[138] University studies were brought within the scope of vocational training.[139] Moreover, to ensure 'access' to education, equal treatment meant that a right to reside in the host State for the duration of the relevant course of studies was implied.[140] That case law therefore instituted a Treaty-based right to reside—before the creation of Union citizenship—that was decoupled from any requirement to pursue economic activity, especially when it is also recalled that publicly funded education fell outside the scope of the Treaty provisions on services.[141] However, associated equal treatment rights did not extend to host State obligations for the payment of maintenance grants.[142]

The principle of not being penalised for exercising free movement is regarded as 'particularly important in the field of education, in view of the aims pursued by Article 6(e) TFEU and the second indent of Article 165(2) TFEU, namely, amongst other things, encouraging mobility of students and teachers'.[143] The special position of students was also reflected in Directive 93/96.[144] In particular, and in contrast to the requirement to 'have' sufficient resources in Article 1 of Directives 90/364 and 90/365, a student just had to '[assure] the relevant national authority, *by means of a declaration or by such alternative means as the student may choose that are at least equivalent*, that he has sufficient resources to avoid becoming a burden on the social assistance system of the host Member State during their period of residence, provided that the student is enrolled in a recognized educational establishment for the principal purpose of following a vocational training course there *and that he* is covered by sickness insurance in respect of all risks in the host Member State'.[145] However, Directive 93/96 also imposed limits on residence rights for students not found in the other two Directives. Article 2 stated that '[t]he right of residence shall be restricted to the duration of the course of studies in question'. Additionally, residence rights for family members were extended only to 'the student's spouse and their dependent children' (Article 1), and not also to relatives in the ascending line. Article 3 further affirmed that '[t]his Directive shall not establish any entitlement to the payment of maintenance grants by the host Member State on the part of students benefiting from the right of residence'. Finally, Article 4 established that '[t]he right of residence shall remain for as long as beneficiaries of that right fulfil the conditions laid down in Article'.

Ambiguities flowing from the distinctive provisions of Directive 93/96 were addressed in *Grzelczyk*. While Article 3 of that measure did establish 'any entitlement to the payment of maintenance grants by the host Member State', the Court pointed out that 'there are no provisions in the directive *that preclude* those to whom it applies from receiving social

---

[138] Case 293/83 *Gravier*, EU:C:1985:69.
[139] Case 24/86 *Blaizot*, EU:C:1988:43; Case C-47/93 *Commission v Belgium*, EU:C:1994:181.
[140] Case C-357/89 *Raulin*, EU:C:1992:87, para 34.
[141] Case 263/86 *Humbel and Edel*, EU:C:1988:451, para 18.
[142] Case 39/86 *Lair*, EU:C:1988:322.
[143] Case C-679/16 *A (Aide pour une personne handicapée)*, EU:C:2018:601, para 62.
[144] Directive 93/96/EEC on the right of residence for students, 1993 OJ L317/59.
[145] Directive 93/96, Article 1. As noted in Section 4.2.2, the requirement to be 'covered by sickness insurance *in respect of all risks* in the host Member State' was common to all three Directives; but that condition further specified 'and the members of their families' for Directives 90/364 and 90/365.

security benefits' on a basis of equal treatment with host State nationals.[146] It then considered *Martínez Sala*, which had established that only 'a citizen of the European Union, *lawfully resident* in the territory of a host Member State, can rely on Article [18 TFEU] in *all situations which fall within the scope* ratione materiae *of [Union] law*'.[147] That statement presented two challenges in *Grzelczyk*. First, maintenance grants had previously been excluded from the material scope of Union law. However, the Court invoked the creation of Union citizenship to underline the intensified importance of equal treatment on grounds of nationality.[148] The benefit applied for by the applicant in *Grzelczyk* was a minimum income (ie social assistance) benefit, not a student maintenance grant per se. It was only later, in *Bidar*, that the Court held more specifically that 'the situation of a citizen of the Union who is lawfully resident in another Member State falls within the scope of application of the Treaty within the meaning of the first paragraph of Article [18 TFEU] for the purposes of obtaining assistance for students, whether in the form of a subsidised loan or a grant, intended to cover his maintenance costs'.[149] However, as discussed in Chapter 2, the Court also found that it was 'legitimate for a Member State to grant such assistance only to students who have demonstrated a certain degree of integration into the society of that State'.[150]

Second, was a student who applied for income support in the host State 'lawfully resident' there? This question is examined in more detail in Chapter 7. But for present purposes, the relationship between Articles 1 and 4 of Directive 93/96 becomes critical, remembering that Article 1 requires only that the student 'assures' the host State authorities that they 'have' sufficient resources. In *Grzelczyk*, the Court considered the nature of Article 1, which 'does not require resources of any specific amount, nor that they be evidenced by specific documents' but 'refers merely to a declaration, or such alternative means as are at least equivalent, which enables the student to satisfy the national authority concerned that he has ... sufficient resources to avoid becoming a burden on the social assistance system of the host Member State during [their] stay'.[151] In contrast, as explained further in Section 5.1, Directives 90/364 and 90/365 *did* 'indicate the minimum level of income that persons wishing to avail themselves of those directives must have'—a difference 'explained by the special characteristics of student residence in comparison with that of persons to whom Directives 90/364 and 90/365 apply'.[152] The Court then addressed Directive 93/96:

> Whilst Article 4 ... does indeed provide that the right of residence is to exist for as long as beneficiaries of that right fulfil the conditions laid down in Article 1, the sixth recital in the directive's preamble envisages that beneficiaries of the right of residence must not become an 'unreasonable' burden on the public finances of the host Member State. Directive 93/96, like Directives 90/364 and 90/365, thus accepts a certain degree of financial solidarity between nationals of a host Member State and nationals of other Member States, particularly if the difficulties which a beneficiary of the right of residence encounters are temporary. Furthermore, a student's financial position may change with the passage of time

---

[146] Case C-184/99 *Grzelczyk*, EU:C:2001:458, para 39 (emphasis added). In para 36, the Court stated that '[t]he fact that a Union citizen pursues university studies in a Member State other than the State of which he is a national cannot, of itself, deprive him of the possibility of relying on the prohibition of all discrimination on grounds of nationality laid down in Article [18] of the Treaty'.
[147] ibid para 32 (emphasis added), referring to Case C-85/96 *Martínez Sala*, EU:C:1998:217, para 63.
[148] *Grzelczyk*, paras 34–36.
[149] Case C-209/03 *Bidar*, EU:C:2005:169, para 42.
[150] ibid para 57.
[151] *Grzelczyk*, para 40.
[152] ibid para 41.

for reasons beyond his control. The truthfulness of a student's declaration is therefore to be assessed only as at the time when it is made.[153]

In *Grzelczyk*, the student's residence in the host State seemed therefore to turn on the fact that the latter had not '[taken] measures, within the limits imposed by [Union] law, either to withdraw his residence permit or not to renew it'.[154] In such circumstances, Articles 18 and 21 TFEU 'preclude[d] entitlement to a non-contributory social benefit, such as the minimex, from being made conditional, in the case of nationals of Member States other than the host State where they are legally resident, on their falling within the scope of Regulation No 1612/68 when no such condition applies to nationals of the host Member State'.[155] Whether the underlying conception of lawful residence would apply in the same way to similar facts today is considered in Chapter 7. Entitlement to student maintenance grants specifically is now governed by Article 24(2) of Directive 2004/38, which is also discussed in Chapter 7.

More generally, Article 7(1)(c) of Directive 2004/38 now provides that Union citizens have a right of residence in another Member State for a period of more than three months if they:

- are enrolled at a private of public establishment accredited or financed by the host Member State on the basis of its legislation or administrative practice, for the principal purpose of following a course of study, including vocational training;[156] and
- have comprehensive sickness insurance cover in the host Member State[157] and assure the relevant national authority, by means of a declaration or by such equivalent means as they may choose, that they have sufficient resources for themselves and their family members not to become a burden on the social assistance system of the host Member State during their period of residence.[158]

As noted above, only the spouse, registered partner, and dependent children of citizens residing in a host State on the basis of Article 7(1)(c) qualify as family members for the purposes of derived residence rights. Article 7(4) clarifies that 'Article 3(2) shall apply to his/her dependent direct relatives in the ascending lines and those of his/her spouse or registered partner'.[159] However, the special position of students evident in Directive 93/96 was

---

[153] ibid paras 44–45.
[154] ibid para 42.
[155] ibid para 46.
[156] The original proposal (n 11) referred more briefly to 'students admitted to a course of vocational training'. However, in its Opinion on the proposal, the Economic and Social Committee argued that 'restricting sub-paragraph (c) to students undergoing vocational training excludes in practice all other students and places a semantic restriction on the right of movement and residence' (2002 OJ C149/46, para 4.1.2). In its amended proposal, the Commission acknowledged that Opinion and commented that the revised wording of Article 7(1)(c) 'is clearer and in line with the text of Directive 93/96 on the right of residence for students; it [also] avoids the concept of student, which can be restrictive' (n 45, 5).
[157] Recalling the discussion in Section 4.2.2, it is presumed that recent case law on the meaning of 'comprehensive sickness insurance cover' for the purposes of Article 7(1)(b) also applies for Article 7(1)(c) with respect to the conditions that can determine and implications that then flow from affiliation to the host State public health insurance system.
[158] In its original proposal for the Directive, the Commission did not articulate these requirements as conditions on the right to reside in the draft text of what is now Article 7(1)(c) but located them instead in draft Article 8(4) as 'administrative formalities' (n 11, 11). The European Parliament proposed moving only the condition about sickness insurance back to Article 7(1)(c) (n 21, Amendment 28). The Council's common position conveys the text as finally adopted, but without particular comment in that document itself (n 11, 28) or in the Commission's subsequent Communication (n 48).
[159] On the more limited rights provided for in Article 3(2) of Directive 2004/38, see Chapter 4.

sustained regarding the adequacy of a declaration to assure host State authorities about sufficient resources compared to the requirement to 'have' them in Article 7(1)(b). The practicalities of this requirement are returned to in Section 5.1.

In *Commission v Netherlands*, Advocate General Sharpston considered that 'Article 7(1)(c) of Directive 2004/38 does not require the student to be enrolled there for the purposes of obtaining a diploma or academic qualification from that establishment, though typically that will be the case'.[160] In her view, '[w]hat matters is that the enrolment in the host Member State is "for the principal purpose of following a course of study" and thus enables a citizen of the Union to access the course of study'; in that light, '[t]he fact that Erasmus students remain registered with an establishment in another Member State does not preclude the possibility that they may also be 'enrolled' elsewhere for the purposes of Article 7(1)(c).[161] The Court has also found that '[a]lthough Article 7(1)(c) of Directive 2004/38 does provide that a Union citizen is to have the right of residence on the territory of another Member State for a period of longer than three months if he is enrolled at a 'private or public establishment' within the meaning of that provision 'for the principal purpose of following a course of study', it does not follow that 'a citizen of the Union who fulfils those conditions is thereby automatically precluded from having the status of "worker" within the meaning of Article 45 TFEU'.[162] In other words, circumstances—and thus, legal status—in a host State can change,[163] and different activities can also be undertaken there in parallel. The fact that a Union citizen who is studying in another State may therefore fall within the scope of Article 45 TFEU by also working there[164] has particular relevance for equal treatment as regards social and tax advantages and for entitlement to student maintenance grants since, as explained in Chapter 1, the provisions of the TFEU on citizenship only apply when one of the economic freedoms does not.[165] That question, which again concerns Article 24(2) of the Directive, is examined in Chapter 7.

4.4 Jobseekers

Recital 9 of Directive 2004/38 states that 'Union citizens should have the right of residence in the host Member State for a period not exceeding three months without being subject to any conditions or any formalities other than the requirement to hold a valid identity card or passport, *without prejudice to a more favourable treatment applicable to job-seekers as recognised by the case-law of the Court of Justice*'. Connecting back to the drafting history of Article 6 of the Directive, discussed in Section 3, the Council added this point to the text of recital 9 as a compromise, having ruled out the originally proposed right to reside without any conditions for up to six months.[166] Additionally, recital 16 addresses the circumstances in which Union citizens who have 'become an unreasonable burden on the social assistance system of the host Member State' may be expelled and it includes the qualifier that '[i]n no case should an

---

[160] AG Sharpston in Case C-233/14 *Commission v Netherlands*, EU:C:2016:50, para 87 of the Opinion.
[161] ibid. This question was not addressed in the judgment, with the Court focusing overall on Article 24 of the Directive; see further, Chapter 7.
[162] Case C-46/12 *LN*, EU:C:2013:97, para 36.
[163] As noted in Section 4.1, protection on change of status is also provided for in Article 17 WA.
[164] So long as they are engaged in 'effective and genuine employment' within the meaning of EU law (*LN*, para 43).
[165] A student who retains the status of worker or self-employed person under Article 7(3) of the Directive (Section 6.2) is also protected by Article 24(2) of the Directive (Chapter 7).
[166] Common Position (n 48) 26.

expulsion measure be adopted against workers, self-employed persons *or job-seekers* as defined by the Court of Justice save on grounds of public policy or public security'. Article 14(4)(b) of the Directive confirms that expulsion measures may not be adopted against Union citizens or their family members if the former 'entered the territory of the host Member State in order to seek employment. In such situations, the Union citizens and their family members may not be expelled *for as long as the Union citizens can provide evidence that they are continuing to seek employment and that they have a genuine chance of being engaged'*. But how does this protection against expulsion relate to the jobseeker's right to reside in the host State the first place?

Article 45(1) TFEU requires that '[f]reedom of movement for workers shall be secured within the Union'. Article 45(2) states that '[s]uch freedom of movement shall entail the abolition of any discrimination based on nationality between workers of the Member States as regards employment, remuneration and other conditions of work and employment'.[167] Some elements of the *search* for employment are addressed in secondary legislation. In particular, Articles 1–6 of Regulation 492/2011 outline the scope of equal treatment regarding processes and conditions of recruitment. Additionally, Article 64(1) of Regulation 883/2004 provides that '[a] wholly unemployed person who satisfies the conditions of the legislation of the competent Member State for entitlement to benefits, and who goes to another Member State in order to seek work there, shall retain his entitlement to unemployment benefits' subject to specified conditions and limits. Article 64(1)(c) states that 'entitlement to benefits shall be retained for a period of three months from the date when the unemployed person ceased to be available to the employment services of the Member State which he left, provided that the total duration for which the benefits are provided does not exceed the total duration of the period of his entitlement to benefits under the legislation of that Member State' and further provides that 'the competent services or institutions may extend the period of three months up to a maximum of six months'.[168]

However, no provisions of Regulation 883/2004 or Regulation 492/2011—or the measures they replaced[169]—explicitly address fundamental prior questions: do jobseekers have a right to reside in a host State for the purposes of seeking employment there; on what provision(s) of EU law is that right based; and what conditions apply to or delimit it? The Court of Justice first considered these questions in *Antonissen*. The case concerned a Belgian national who arrived in the UK in 1984 and was the subject of a deportation order in 1987. He argued that, as a Member State national, he could only be deported from the UK on the basis of Directive 64/221 through a decision justified by reasons of public policy, public security, or public health. Article 1 of that Directive established that it applied 'to any national of a Member State who resides in or travels to another Member State of the Community, either in order to pursue an activity as an employed or self-employed person, or as a recipient of services'. Mr Antonissen had not found work in the UK, but his situation was described throughout the judgment in terms of having entered the UK to *seek* employment there. However, the applicable national rules provided that a national of another Member State who entered the UK

---

[167] Reflecting the significance of these objectives, protection against discrimination on the grounds of nationality reaches into the regulation of private employment relationships: see Case C-281/98 *Angonese*, EU:C:2000:296; and Case C-94/07 *Raccanelli*, EU:C:2008:425.

[168] Proposals for the revision of Regulation 883/2004 include extending the minimum period that unemployed jobseekers seeking employment in another Member State may request the export of unemployment benefits from three to six months (COM(2016) 815 final).

[169] For Regulation 883/2004, see Regulation 1408/71/EC on the application of social security schemes to employed persons and their families moving within the Community, 1971 OJ L149/1; for Regulation 492/2011, see Regulation 1612/68.

to look for work could be required to leave the territory (subject to appeal) if they had not found employment after six months.

Assessing the compatibility of that condition with EU law, the Court held that 'freedom of movement for workers forms one of the foundations of the [Union] and, consequently, the provisions laying down that freedom must be given a broad interpretation'.[170] Therefore, since a strict interpretation of Article 45 TFEU would 'jeopardize the actual chances that a national of a Member State who is seeking employment will find it in another Member State, and would, as a result, make that provision ineffective', freedom of movement for workers 'also entails the right for nationals of Member States to move freely within the territory of the other Member States *and to stay there* for the purposes of seeking employment'.[171] For the Court, the effectiveness of Article 45 TFEU is 'secured in so far as [Union] legislation *or, in its absence, the legislation of a Member State* gives persons concerned *a reasonable time* in which to apprise themselves, in the territory of the Member State concerned, of offers of employment corresponding to their occupational qualifications and to take, where appropriate, the necessary steps in order to be engaged'.[172] It then established a two-part test:

> In the absence of a [Union] provision prescribing the period during which [Union] nationals seeking employment in a Member State may stay there, a period of six months, such as that laid down in the national legislation at issue in the main proceedings, *does not appear in principle* to be insufficient to enable the persons concerned to apprise themselves, in the host Member State, of offers of employment corresponding to their occupational qualifications and to take, where appropriate, the necessary steps in order to be engaged and, therefore, does not jeopardize the effectiveness of the principle of free movement. However, if after the expiry of that period the person concerned *provides evidence that he is continuing to seek employment* and that he *has genuine chances of being engaged*, he cannot be required to leave the territory of the host Member State.[173]

The Court declined to attach legal significance to a declaration recorded in Council minutes marking the adoption of both Regulation 1612/68 and Directive 68/360/EEC, which stated that '[n]ationals of a Member State ... who move to another Member State in order to seek work there shall be allowed a minimum period of three months for the purpose; in the event of their not having found employment by the end of that period, their residence on the territory of this second State may be brought to an end. However, if the abovementioned persons should be taken charge of by national assistance (social welfare) in the second State during the aforesaid period they may be invited to leave the territory of this second State'.[174] The two-part *Antonissen* test did not fix temporal limits, which fits with the Court's standard preference in EU citizenship law for case-by-case assessments of individual situations that

---

[170] Case C-292/89 *Antonissen*, EU:C:1991:80, para 11.
[171] ibid paras 12–13 (emphasis added). In para 14, the Court observed that the protection (now) outlined in Articles 1–6 of Regulation 492/2011 'presuppose[s] that Community nationals are entitled to move in order to look for employment, and hence to stay, in another Member State'. AG Darmon considered that to apply a different interpretation 'would in fact have given rise to a quite narrow, quite unrealistic conception of the circumstances in which a person obtains employment' (EU:C:1990:387, para 5 of the Opinion). Article 15(2) CFR now protects the right to 'to seek employment, to work, to exercise the right of establishment and to provide services in any Member State'.
[172] *Antonissen*, para 16 (emphasis added).
[173] ibid para 21 (emphasis added).
[174] Referred to para 17 (ibid). We can see in the declaration the seeds of becoming a burden on host State social assistance systems, which was more explicitly folded into later case law and legislation.

reflect the essential premises of proportionality analysis. However, while the requirement of evidence that a jobseeker is continuing to seek employment is unlikely to be problematic in practice, proving that someone has a 'genuine chance of being engaged' is much more difficult to demonstrate.[175] Commission guidance, which advises that jobseekers can demonstrate compliance with the *Antonissen* criteria by providing 'copies of job applications, invitations to interviews or positive reactions to ... applications', is light-touch in this respect.[176]

How does Directive 2004/38, which attaches material significance to specific periods of time for the right to reside in Articles 6 and 7, intersect with the open-ended expression of the residence rights articulated for jobseekers in *Antonissen*? Jobseekers do not fall within the scope of Article 7(1)(a) of the Directive as they are not yet economically active. Pre-Directive case law on social and tax advantages, returned to in Chapter 7, similarly reflected the comparatively weaker legal protection extended to jobseekers by Article 45 TFEU, excluding them from entitlement to social and tax advantages within the meaning of Article 7(2) of Regulation 492/2011.[177] Similarly, in *Commission v Belgium*, the Court held that rules on access to special employment and re-employment programmes were linked to unemployment and therefore fell outside the scope of Article 45 TFEU and in particular of Article 3(1) of Regulation 1612/68.[178] It considered that '[t]he application of [Union] law on freedom of movement for workers in relation to national rules concerning unemployment insurance requires that a person invoking that freedom *must have already participated in the employment market* by exercising an effective and genuine occupational activity, which has conferred on him the status of a worker within the Community meaning of that term ... By definition, that is not the case where young people are seeking their first employment'.[179] That finding also reflects a distinction between those who are seeking work for the first time in a host State and those who are doing so having already participated in the host State employment market, returned to with respect to retaining the status of worker in Section 6.2 and examined further in Chapter 7 as regards lawful residence.

At the same time, reading recitals 9 and 16 and Article 14(4)(b) of Directive 2004/38 together, neither is the jobseeker's right to reside in the host State contingent upon compliance with the conditions in Article 7(1)(b), attributing some significance to the *intention* of becoming economically active. Jobseekers seemed therefore to fall between the specific categories in Article 7(1) of the Directive.[180] Drawing very literally from the national rule

---

[175] AG Darmon had focused his analysis more on the first part of the Court's test ie being 'actively, persistently and seriously engaged' in seeking employment (AG Darmon in Case C-292/89 *Antonissen*, EU:C:1990:387, para 36 of the Opinion).

[176] European Commission, 'Frequently Asked Questions and Answers on citizens' EU rights', <http://europa.eu/youreurope/advice/docs/faq_en.pdf> (accessed 30 May 2023). However, how these conditions are applied in practice is crucial to the recognition, and often to the denial, of EU rights at national level; see eg C O'Brien, 'The pillory, the precipice and the slippery slope: the profound effects of the UK's legal reform programme targeting EU migrants' (2015) Journal of Social Welfare and Family Law 111 esp at 118–19.

[177] See esp Case 316/85 *Lebon*, EU:C:1987:302, para 26.

[178] Case C-278/94 *Commission v Belgium*, EU:C:1996:321, paras 38–39. Article 3(1) provided: '[u]nder this Regulation, provisions laid down by law, regulation or administrative action or administrative practices of a Member State shall not apply: ... where, though applicable irrespective of nationality, their exclusive or principal aim or effect is to keep nationals of other Member States away from the employment offered'. See now, Article 3(1) of Regulation 492/2011.

[179] *Commission v Belgium*, para 40 (emphasis added).

[180] AG Darmon argued in *Antonissen* that 'it would not be possible *for the Court* to lay down a requirement that a person seeking employment should have sufficient resources to avoid becoming a burden on the social assistance system of the host State without raising a number of problems of compatibility with the Court's statement in the judgment in *Kempf* ... to the effect that the Community scope of the concepts determining the extent of the field of application of the free movement of workers would be jeopardized if the enjoyment of rights conferred under the principle of freedom of movement for workers were "precluded by the fact that the person concerned

challenged in *Antonissen*, the Commission has always insisted that jobseekers have a right to reside in a host State for up to six months without any conditions, and that to retain a right of residence for longer, they must then (and only then) demonstrate compliance with both parts of the *Antonissen* test.[181] In effect, that interpretation generalised to EU-wide level one specific national rule.

Initially, the Court did not calcify the six-month period in *Antonissen* to the same extent, confirming only that Member States are entitled to 'lay down *a reasonable period* during which nationals of other Member States could stay in their territory for the purposes of seeking employment' and recognising that 'if after expiry of that period, the person concerned provides evidence that he is continuing to seek employment and that he has genuine chances of being engaged, he cannot be required to leave the territory of the host Member State'.[182] It was therefore arguable that jobseekers were exempt only from the requirements of Article 7(1)(b) of the Directive: that they enjoyed an unconditional right to reside in other Member States for up to three months on the basis of Article 6, and that they retained their residence rights for more than three months subject only to fulfilling the *Antonissen* test. More generally, where the Court had ventured beyond the system of Articles 6 and 7 of the Directive for residence rights based on Article 45 TFEU, the circumstances concerned either residence rights expressly provided for in Regulation 492/2011,[183] or residence rights connected to the retention of worker status between periods of employment.[184] Moreover, the Court did not lay down fixed time periods in either of these situations. Instead, it developed qualitative tests that required assessment of individual cases by the relevant national authorities. That case law is an important reminder that while 'Directive 2004/38 codified existing [Union] instruments which, until then, had determined the legal position of certain categories of person [and it] undeniably applies to all Union citizens and their family members ... it does not contain comprehensive and definitive rules to govern every conceivable right of residence of those Union citizens and their family members'.[185] Neither did it necessarily mean that Articles 6 and 7 of the Directive lost force as the time-keepers of conditional host State residence rights. However, in *GMA*, the Court turned the *example* of the six-month period in the national regulation challenged in *Antonissen* into a period with legal implications much more generally, notwithstanding the clear three months/more than three months distinction set by Articles 6 and 7 of the Directive.[186]

---

has had recourse to benefits chargeable to public funds and created by the domestic legislation of the host State"' (para 36 of the Opinion, emphasis added; referring to Case 139/85 *Kempf*, EU:C:1986:223, para 15).

[181] eg *Right of Union citizens and their family members to move and reside freely within the Union: Guide on how to get the best out of Directive 2004/38/EC*, Chapter 5, <https://publications.europa.eu/en/publication-detail/-/publication/480ebafc-52dc-4777-8283-9cef96ee1d15> (accessed 30 May 2023): 'Union citizens benefit from the right to reside without any conditions and formalities for a period of six months and even longer, if they continue to seek employment in the host Member State and have a genuine chance of being engaged, as the European Court of Justice confirmed'. See similarly, <https://europa.eu/youreurope/citizens/residence/residence-rights/jobseekers/index_en.htm> (accessed 30 May 2023).

[182] Case C-344/95 *Commission v Belgium*, EU:C:1997:81, para 17 (emphasis added).

[183] eg Residence rights for the children of migrant workers in host State education based on Article 10 of Regulation 492/2011; see eg Case C-310/08 *Ibrahim*, EU:C:2010:80. See further, Chapters 7 and 9.

[184] eg Retained residence rights in circumstances of childbirth and maternity leave; see eg Case C-507/12 *Saint Prix*, EU:C:2014:2007. See further, Chapters 7 and 9.

[185] AG Kokott in Case C-480/08 *Teixeira*, EU:C:2009:642, para 48 of the Opinion. The right to move and reside beyond the Directive is addressed in Chapter 9.

[186] Thereby overriding the entirely logical view that the approach in *Antonissen* 'was taken over in Directive 2004/38' (H Verschueren, 'Being economically active: how it still matters' in H Verschueren (ed) *Residence, Employment and Social Rights of Mobile Persons: On How EU Law Defines Where They Belong* (Intersentia 2016) 187 at 205).

Recalling that the free movement of workers 'forms one of the foundations of the European Union and, therefore, the provisions establishing that freedom must be interpreted broadly', the Court held in *GMA* that when a jobseeker enters a host State, their right to reside 'falls, from the time of his or her registration as a jobseeker, within the scope of Article 14(4)(b) of Directive 2004/38'.[187] It acknowledged that Article 6 of the Directive 'applies without distinction to all Union citizens, irrespective of the intention with which those citizens enter the territory of the host Member State'; thus, 'even where a Union citizen enters the territory of a host Member State with the intention of seeking employment there, his or her right of residence is also covered, during the first three months, by Article 6'.[188] However, citing *Antonissen* 'to that effect', the Court underlined that 'the effectiveness of Article 45 TFEU is secured in so far as EU legislation or, in its absence, the legislation of a Member State gives persons concerned *a reasonable time* in which to apprise themselves, in the territory of the host Member State, of offers of employment corresponding to their occupational qualifications and to take, where appropriate, the necessary steps in order to be engaged'.[189]

Crucially, this period of reasonable time 'starts to run from the time when the Union citizen concerned has decided to register as a jobseeker in the host Member State': it is disconnected from the (parallel) right to reside for up to three months under Article 6. In other words, the reasonable period of time clock starts to tick once the jobseeker registers as such in the host State, even if that decision is taken within the first three months of residence.[190] As a result, after the first three months of residence (to respect Article 6's guarantee of a right to reside 'without any conditions or any formalities other than the requirement to hold a valid identity card or passport') and during the 'reasonable time' (in respect of which six months seems 'reasonable'), jobseekers may be required to demonstrate that they are seeking employment but not (yet) that they have a genuine chance of being engaged.[191] While conceding that the ruling in *Antonissen* had not 'fix[ed] a minimum duration of the "reasonable period of time"', the Court found, nevertheless, that *Antonissen* did establish 'that a period of six months from entry into the territory of the host Member State, such as that at issue in the case which gave rise to that judgment, did not appear capable of calling that effectiveness into question'.[192]

Thus, as discussed similarly for *FS* in Section 3, while the Court did not quantify a six-month test definitively in *GMA*, it is hard to see how Member States will not do so in their national regulations and practices. Contrary to the intention of providing *more* support for

---

[187] Case C-710/19 *GMA (Demandeur d'emploi)*, EU:C:2020:1037, paras 25 and 34; building on Case C-67/14 *Alimanovic*, EU:C:2015:597, para 52. For examples of different Member State practices and conditions with respect to residence rights for jobseekers, see A Welsh, 'A genuine chance of free movement? Clarifying the "reasonable period of time" and residence conditions for jobseekers in G.M.A' (2021) 58 Common Market Law Review 1591.

[188] *GMA*, para 35. Accordingly, no further conditions can be imposed on jobseekers during the first three months of residence (ibid para 36).

[189] ibid para 26 (emphasis added).

[190] ibid para 37.

[191] The latter requirement may be imposed only after the reasonable period has elapsed, and it entails, on the basis of 'the evidence adduced to that effect by the jobseeker in question', carrying out 'an overall assessment of all relevant factors such as, for example ... the fact that the jobseeker has registered with the national body responsible for jobseekers, that he or she regularly approaches potential employers with letters of application or that he or she goes to employment interviews'; the 'situation of the national labour market in the sector corresponding to the occupational qualifications of the jobseeker in question' must also be considered, whereas, '[b]y contrast, the fact that that jobseeker refused offers of employment which did not correspond to his or her professional qualifications cannot be taken into account for the purpose of considering that that person does not satisfy the conditions laid down in Article 14(4)(b) of Directive 2004/38' (ibid para 47).

[192] ibid para 40.

jobseekers, the strong temporal signal in *GMA* might work against certain jobseekers who need more time to realise their employment goals.[193]

Article 14 of the Directive—returned to in more detail in Section 6.1—is a flawed text. Articles 14(1) and 14(2) speak of *having* a right to reside, and Article 14(4) provides a 'derogation' from those provisions, not in terms of a (different) right to reside but protection from expulsion.[194] Yet the Court reads the notion of 'derogation' extremely broadly and shapes an autonomous residence space for jobseekers that is not properly connected to the timeframes of Articles 6 and 7, which are valued profoundly in the case law generally.[195] The Court did refer to Article 21 TFEU in its ruling, but it is the jobseeker's character as an economic actor of the future, and thus Article 45 TFEU, that enabled reading more into the Directive than is arguably there. For the Court, 'a person who is genuinely seeking work *must also be classified as a worker*'—reengaging the right to reside in Article 45(3) TFEU, the basis for *Antonissen* in the first place.[196] The ruling in *GMA* therefore shows that the worker element of the jobseeker's legal profile carries sufficient primary law weight to modulate limitations and conditions expressly provided for in Directive 2004/38. Trying to reconcile the interplay of all relevant legal sources proves even more challenging on the fraught question of a jobseeker's eligibility for social assistance, which is examined in Chapter 7.

5. Administrative Formalities

Article 8 of Directive 2004/38 sets out the administrative formalities relevant to Union citizens for periods of residence in a host State of more than three months, that is, for the exercise of rights under Article 7 of the Directive. For family members who are not Member State nationals, Article 5 addresses visa requirements at the point of entry to a Member State and Articles 9–11 deal with the 'residence card' that Member States are required to issue when the planned period of residence is for more than three months and family members accompany or join Union citizens residing in a Member State on the basis of Article 7 of the Directive. This part of the Directive also provides guidance on vital concepts such as 'sufficient resources' and on how family relationships can be evidenced.

Describing the relevant provisions in the language of 'formalities' fits, on the one hand, with the nature of—and implications of (non-)compliance with—the requirements that applied previously under economic free movement law: free movement and residence rights are conferred on Member State nationals by the Treaty;[197] these rights may be evidenced

---

[193] See further, Welsh (n 187) 1607–10, discussing 'groups who face systemic barriers that can make the process of seeking employment more complex and time-consuming' (1607).

[194] Cf AG Wathelet in Case C-442/16 *Gusa*, EU:C:2017:607, paras 69–70 of the Opinion: 'contrary to what is suggested by paragraph 58 of [*Alimanovic*], the structure of Article 14 of Directive 2004/38 and the wording of Article 14(4)(b) of that directive *do not support a view of that provision as providing the basis for a right of residence*. Article 14 of Directive 2004/38 is entitled "Retention of the right of residence". That situation is provided for in the first two paragraphs of that article, which are directed at circumstances in which Union citizens and their family members "have the right of residence", which Article 14(4) of that directive is not. Moreover, Article 14(4)(b) of Directive 2004/38 expressly provides for a situation obtaining "by way of derogation" from the first two paragraphs, that is to say, therefore, one in which the right of residence no longer exists. In that situation, Union citizens who have entered the territory of the host Member State in order to seek employment there are nonetheless protected from expulsion as long as they can provide evidence that they are continuing to seek employment and they have a genuine chance of being engaged' (emphasis added).

[195] eg Joined Cases C-316/16 and C-424/16 *B and Vomero*, EU:C:2018:256, paras 51–54.

[196] Case C-85/96 *Martínez Sala*, EU:C:1998:217, para 32; confirmed in eg Case C-507/12 *Saint Prix*, EU:C:2014:2007, para 35. See also, Case C-292/89 *Antonissen*, EU:C:1991:80, para 13.

[197] In contrast, 'the Treaty provisions on citizenship of the Union do not confer any autonomous right on third-country nationals ... Any rights conferred on third-country nationals by the Treaty provisions on Union

but are not constituted by administrative formalities; and therefore, while lack of compliance may attract (proportionate) sanctions in the host State, it does not justify negation of the rights and does not, more specifically, amount in itself to conduct that breaches public policy or public security (in other words, conduct that justifies expulsion).[198] The Court has consistently emphasised that what EU law requires of Member States in the context of free movement is likely to differ from national immigration law and procedures, which must then be adapted.[199]

The declaratory rather than constitutive nature of administrative formalities has been confirmed in the case law on Union citizenship.[200] It is further reflected in the statement in recital 11 of Directive 2004/38 that '[t]he fundamental and personal right of residence in another Member State is conferred directly on Union citizens by the Treaty and is not dependent upon their having fulfilled administrative procedures'. Streamlining the procedures applicable to the third-country national family members of Union citizens specifically reflects the fact that the 'legislature has recognised the importance of ensuring protection for the family life of nationals of the Member States in order to eliminate obstacles to the exercise of the fundamental freedoms guaranteed by the Treaty'.[201] Nevertheless, the importance of complying with the requirements of Directive 2004/38 should not be dismissed and *trying to comply with them can prove difficult in practice and produce significant obstacles to the exercise of free movement*.[202]

The procedural safeguards in Article 15 of the Directive—which are considered in more detail in Chapter 10 for restrictions based on public policy, public security, and public health—should also be noted. Article 15(1) establishes that '[t]he procedures provided for by Articles 30 and 31 shall apply by analogy to all decisions restricting free movement of Union citizens and their family members *on grounds other than* public policy, public security or public health'. These guarantees—which concern notification of, the reasons given in, and judicial or administrative redress procedures to review the decisions of host State authorities—are particularly relevant, first, for decisions refusing *entry* to a Member State on grounds of non-compliance with administrative formalities; and second, where an *expulsion* decision is issued on the grounds that the person concerned (whether a Union citizen or their family

---

citizenship are not autonomous rights of those nationals but rights derived from the exercise of freedom of movement by a Union citizen. The purpose and justification of those derived rights are based on the fact that a refusal to allow them would be such as to interfere with the Union citizen's freedom of movement by discouraging him from exercising his rights of entry into and residence in the host Member State' (Case C-87/12 *Ymeraga*, EU:C:2013:291, paras 34–35).

[198] See eg Case 48/75 *Royer*, EU:C:1976:57; Case 157/79 *Pieck*, EU:C:1980:179. On national rules that automatically compel deportation for non-compliance with administrative formalities, see Case C-408/03 *Commission v Belgium*, EU:C:2006:192, esp paras 67–71. As emphasised in Chapter 3, the fact that national rules *can* constitute the rights addressed by the Withdrawal Agreement is one of its most significant departures from EU citizenship law: see Article 18(1) WA and the Commission's Guidance Note relating to the Agreement (n 14) para 2.6.1.

[199] For an example of national rules and practices constituting an infringement of EU law, see Case C-68/89 *Commission v Netherlands*, EU:C:1991:226, para 14: 'by maintaining in force and by applying legislation by virtue of which citizens of a Member State may be required to answer questions put by border officials regarding the purpose and duration of their journey and the financial means at their disposal for it before they are permitted to enter Netherlands territory, the Kingdom of the Netherlands has failed to fulfil the obligations imposed on it by Directives 68/360 and 73/148'.

[200] eg Case C-85/96 *Martínez Sala*, EU:C:1998:217, para 53. On the implications of the declaratory effect of residence permits in the context of Framework Decision 2002/584 on the European arrest warrant (2002 OJ L190/1), see Case C-123/08 *Wolzenburg*, EU:C:2009:616, paras 48–53.

[201] Case C-459/99 *MRAX*, EU:C:2002:461, para 53; referring to Case C-60/00 *Carpenter*, EU:C:2002:434, para 38.

[202] See eg Valcke (n 125); J Shaw and N Miller, 'When legal worlds collide: an exploration of what happens when EU free movement law meets UK immigration law' (2013) 38 European Law Review 137.

member) no longer resides in the host State in compliance with the provisions in Chapter III of the Directive, that is, with the conditions for the right of residence in a host State.[203]

Article 15(1) shares some conceptual similarity with Article 14(4)(b), which was discussed in Section 4.4 for the residence rights of jobseekers. For Article 15(1), a power to expel Union citizens from the host State beyond the grounds of public policy, public security, or public health has been read into a guarantee of procedural safeguards for decisions taken 'on grounds other than' such reasons. In both instances, the relevant right (Article 14) or power (Article 15) is inferred rather than conferred. Thus, the Court established in *FS* that Article 15(1) 'is intended, in particular, *to enable* the host Member State to ensure that the residence in its territory of Union citizens who do not enjoy a right of permanent residence in that territory is carried out in compliance with the scope of the temporary rights of residence provided for' in Directive 2004/38.[204] It confirmed in *Chenchooliah* that 'the scope of Article 15 must extend to an expulsion decision made … on grounds wholly unrelated to any danger to public policy, public safety or public health but which are connected to the fact that a family member of a Union citizen who, in the past, enjoyed a temporary right of residence under Directive 2004/38 deriving from the exercise by the Union citizen of his right to freedom of movement, now no longer has such a right of residence following the departure of that citizen from the host Member State and his return to the Member State of which he is a national'.[205] However, since Article 15(1) stipulates that decisions taken on that basis must comply with the requirements of Articles 30 and 31 of the Directive, then conversely, Article 30(2),[206] the third indent of Article 31(2),[207] and Article 31(4)[208] of the Directive do *not* apply in such cases 'since their application must be strictly confined to expulsion decisions made on grounds of public policy, public security or public health'.[209] Likewise, 'other provisions of Chapter VI [of the Directive], … including Articles 27 and 28 thereof, are not applicable where a decision is adopted under Article 15'.[210]

As explained in Chapter 10, Articles 27 and 28 of the Directive provide detailed guidance on the individual assessment that must be undertaken before any decision restricting the right of entry or residence on grounds of public policy, public security, or public health is taken. That guidance includes, most notably for present purposes, the requirement in Article 28(1) that 'the host Member State shall take account of considerations such as how long the individual concerned has resided on its territory, his/her age, state of health, family and economic situation, social and cultural integration into the host Member State and the extent of his/her links with the country of origin'. It was not previously clear what the Court's position

---

[203] Case C-94/18 *Chenchooliah*, EU:C:2019:693, para 74. On the requirement of residing on the basis of Directive2004/38, and the implications of not doing so, see Chapter 7.

[204] Case C-719/19 *FS*, EU:C:2021:506, para 71 (emphasis added).

[205] *Chenchooliah*, para 73. The Court had already established that Ms Chenchooliah's situation did not fall within Article 12(2) or 13(2) of the Directive (ibid para 66); see further, Section 6.3.

[206] ie 'The persons concerned shall be informed, precisely and in full, of the public policy, public security or public health grounds on which the decision taken in their case is based, unless this is contrary to the interests of State security'.

[207] ie 'Where the application for appeal against or judicial review of the expulsion decision is accompanied by an application for an interim order to suspend enforcement of that decision, actual removal from the territory may not take place until such time as the decision on the interim order has been taken, except: … where the expulsion decision is based on imperative grounds of public security under Article 28(3)'.

[208] ie 'Member States may exclude the individual concerned from their territory pending the redress procedure, but they may not prevent the individual from submitting his/her defence in person, except when his/her appearance may cause serious troubles to public policy or public security or when the appeal or judicial review concerns a denial of entry to the territory'.

[209] *Chenchooliah*, para 83.

[210] ibid para 86.

on Articles 27 and 28 might be as regards expulsion decisions taken for non-compliance with the residence conditions established by the Directive. For example, in *Rendón Marín*, it had indicated that 'in order to determine whether an expulsion measure is proportionate to the legitimate aim pursued, *in the present instance protection of the requirements of public policy or public security*, account should be taken of the criteria set out in Article 28(1) of Directive 2004/38'.[211] However, the Court did establish some backstop guarantees in *Chenchooliah*, pointing out, in particular, that procedures on the right of access to judicial redress guaranteed by Article 31(1) of the Directive constitute 'implementing Union law' for the purposes of Article 51(1) CFR and must therefore comply with the requirements of the right to an effective remedy in Article 47 CFR,[212] that under Article 31(3) of the Directive, 'the redress procedures must not only allow for an examination of the legality of the decision concerned, as well as of the facts and circumstances on which it is based, but also ensure that the decision in question is not disproportionate',[213] and that, in accordance with Article 15(3), 'the expulsion decision that may be made [under Article 15(1)] cannot, under any circumstances, impose a ban on entry into the territory'.[214]

With respect to Article 15(3) and the preclusion of bans on (re-)entry to the host State, the Court's ruling in *FS* was introduced in Section 3. In that case, the Court determined that the national authorities of the host State may consider whether someone who was expelled from that territory on the basis of Article 15(1) of the Directive 'genuinely and effectively' terminated their residence before being eligible to re-establish an unconditional right to reside there (again) on the basis of Article 6. Article 30(3)—one of the provisions that *does* apply by analogy according to the wording of Article 15(1)—specifies that when an expulsion decision is taken against a Union citizen (or their family members), 'the time allowed to leave the territory shall be not less than one month from the date of notification'. For the Court, that guarantee, 'in so far as it enables the person concerned, *inter alia*, to prepare his or her departure, supports the interpretation that an expulsion decision is not complied with solely by the physical departure of the person concerned from the host Member State, but by the fact that that person has terminated genuinely and effectively his or her residence in that Member State'.[215] However, a similarly fixed time-limit (three months, as proposed by the Netherlands Government) for remaining outside the territory of the host State before returning there on the basis of Article 6 was rejected since it is not provided for expressly in the Directive, as is required by Articles 20(1) and 21(1) TFEU.[216]

The assessment of 'genuine and effective' termination of residence developed by the Court has both host State and home/other State dimensions. First, for the host State, 'even if the length of the period spent by the Union citizen outside the territory of [that] State following the adoption of an expulsion decision taken against him or her under Article 15(1) of Directive 2004/38 is not, in itself, decisive for the purposes of assessing whether the person concerned has genuinely and effectively terminated his or her residence in that territory, that period may be of some importance in the context of th[at] overall assessment'.[217] Additionally, account must be taken of 'all the factors evidencing a break in the links' between

---

[211] Case C-165/14 *Rendón Marín*, EU:C:2016:675, para 62 (emphasis added).
[212] *Chenchooliah*, para 84.
[213] ibid para 85.
[214] ibid para 88. Article 15(3) of the Directive provides that '[t]he host Member State may not impose a ban on entry in the context of an expulsion decision to which paragraph 1 applies'.
[215] Case C-719/19 *FS*, EU:C:2021:506, para 80.
[216] ibid paras 83–89.
[217] ibid para 90.

the Union citizen and the host State.[218] The 'relevance' of such factors 'must be assessed by the competent national authority in the light of all the specific circumstances characterising the particular situation of the Union citizen concerned'.[219] Second, with respect to the home/other State dimension, 'with a view to shedding light on the question whether that Union citizen may be regarded as having actually resided outside [host State] territory' during the relevant period, 'it is necessary to take into consideration, in any event where the residence of that Union citizen in the host Member State was based on Article 7(1) of Directive 2004/38, the evidence suggesting that he or she moved the centre of his or her personal, occupational or family interests to another State during that period'.[220]

In situations where host State residence has not been 'genuinely and effectively' terminated (meaning that the expulsion decision 'has not been complied with'), the Union citizen 'therefore is still illegally resident on that territory, even when, after having temporarily left it, he or she returns to it again' and the relevant host State does not, in consequence, have to issue a fresh expulsion decision on the basis of Article 15(1) of the Directive in such circumstances, being entitled instead to rely on the original decision to 'oblige' the Union citizen to leave its territory.[221] The Court also distinguished between a right to *reside* in the host State under Article 6 and a right to *enter* it based on Article 5: for the latter, a right of entry may be exercised 'autonomously where that Union citizen, who does not have a right of residence on that territory under [the Directive], nevertheless wishes to travel to that territory on an *ad hoc* basis for purposes other than to reside there' and an expulsion decision taken on the basis of Article 15(1) 'cannot be enforced against him or her [in such circumstances] as long as his or her *presence* in the host Member State is justified under Article 5'.[222]

Moreover, should a change in circumstances mean that residence in the host State would now in fact comply with the conditions for the right to reside in Article 7 of the Directive, the citizen's residence must then 'be regarded as legal'.[223] In any event, 'where the Union citizen comes into contact with the authorities of the host Member State shortly after the expiry of the period laid down for his or her voluntary departure from that territory, that Member State may check whether the presence of that Union citizen in its territory is justified under [Directive 2004/38]'.[224] Finally, Article 15(2) of the Directive confirms that '[e]xpiry of the identity card or passport on the basis of which the person concerned entered the host Member State and was issued with a registration certificate or residence card shall not constitute a ground for expulsion from the host Member State'.[225] Article 15(2) therefore connects to the administrative formalities relevant to Union citizens and to third-country national family members respectively, which are examined in Sections 5.1 and 5.2.

---

[218] ibid para 91, continuing that '[a] request for removal from a population register, the termination of a lease contract or a contract for the provision of public services, such as water or electricity, moving house or flat, de-registration from a job placement service or the termination of other relationships which presuppose some integration of that Union citizen in that Member State may, *inter alia*, be of some relevance in that regard'.

[219] ibid para 92, continuing that '[e]specially, account should be taken of the extent to which he or she is integrated in the host Member State, the length of his or her residence in the territory of that State immediately before the expulsion decision taken against him or her, and his or her family and economic situation'.

[220] ibid para 93.

[221] ibid para 94.

[222] ibid paras 102–103 (emphasis added).

[223] ibid para 94. The Court referred expressly to 'satisfy[ing] the conditions laid down in Article 7, since that 'would deprive the expulsion decision of which he or she is the subject of any effect'. It did not consider residence based other provisions of EU law, such as the right to reside as a jobseeker under Article 45 TFEU, which was both connected to and separated from Article 6 of the Directive in *GMA* (Section 4.4).

[224] ibid para 100.

[225] See previously eg Case C-459/99 *MRAX*, EU:C:2002:461.

In its original proposal, the Commission framed the principles codified in Article 15 of the Directive as concerning the protection of Union citizens 'against arbitrary decisions by public authorities' by 'establish[ing] procedural guarantees available to a person enjoying the right of residence where a Member State takes an expulsion decision against him on grounds other than those set out in Chapter VI (public policy): the aim here is to ensure that the citizen is *no less well protected* against expulsion decisions based on administrative grounds than where there are public policy grounds'.[226] There is, nevertheless, a striking discrepancy between the system of protection designed for Union citizens and family members excluded on grounds of public policy, public security, and public health grounds, on the one hand, as examined in Chapter 10, and the curiously peripheral treatment of the same persons when excluded on different grounds, on the other. The former is detailed and strongly citizen-focused; the latter is murkier and more strongly State-privileged. At the end of the day, expulsion is expulsion, and expulsion based on protection of host State public finances can also 'seriously harm' (recital 23) the citizen concerned. Revisiting the disconnect between various forms of expulsion would therefore be welcome.

5.1 Article 8: Union Citizens

As discussed in Section 2, Union citizens have the right to enter a Member State with a valid identity card or passport and, according to Article 5(1) of the Directive, '[n]o entry visa or equivalent formality may be imposed' on them.[227] Article 5(4) underpins that right with an assurance of procedural proportionality:

> Where a Union citizen ... does not have the necessary travel documents ... the Member State concerned shall, before turning them back, give such persons every reasonable opportunity to obtain the necessary travel documents or have them brought to them within a reasonable period of time or to corroborate or prove by other means that they are covered by the right of free movement and residence.[228]

However, Article 5(5) establishes that '[t]he Member State may require the person concerned to report his/her presence within its territory within a reasonable and non-discriminatory period of time. Failure to comply with this requirement may make the person concerned liable to proportionate and non-discriminatory sanctions'.[229]

---

[226] Original proposal (n 11) 19 (emphasis added). The Commission continued that '[a]n expulsion decision taken on such grounds may not involve a ban on entry in the territory of the Member State taking the decision; this distinguishes it from a public policy decision'.

[227] Article 5(1) is framed by the statement that the right of entry is '[w]ithout prejudice to the provisions on travel documents applicable to national border controls'.

[228] This provision also applies to family members who are not Member State nationals, including in that situation having 'the necessary visas'; see Section 5.2.

[229] This possibility reflects pre-citizenship case law; see eg Case 8/77 *Sagulo and Others*, EU:C:1977:131: 'Community law has not deprived Member States of the power to adopt measures to enable the national authorities to have precise information of movements of population in its territory' (para 4). However, EU law sets limits around Member State action; see esp paras 11–12 (ibid) on the requirements of non-discrimination and proportionality. Further on non-discrimination, see eg Case 321/87 *Commission v Belgium*, EU:C:1989:176, para 12: '[t]he controls at issue are not a condition for the exercise of the right of entry into Belgian territory and it is undisputed that Community law does not prevent Belgium from checking, within its territory, compliance with the obligation imposed on persons enjoying a right of residence under Community law to carry their residence or establishment permit at all times, where an identical obligation is imposed upon Belgian nationals as regards their identity card'. On proportionate sanctions, see eg Case C-378/97 *Wijsenbeek*, EU:C:1999:439, para 44.

Similarly, we saw in Section 4 that the right to reside in a host State for up to three months is conferred 'without any conditions or any formalities other than the requirement to hold a valid identity card or passport' (Article 6(1)). For periods of residence of more than three months, Article 8 establishes administrative formalities around three main issues: registration in the host State (Section 5.1.1), specific registration requirements for family members who are themselves Union citizens (Section 5.1.2), and the meaning of 'sufficient resources' for rights based on Articles 7(1)(b) and 7(1)(c) of the Directive (Section 5.1.3).

5.1.1 Registration requirements: Union citizens

Article 8(1) establishes that '[w]ithout prejudice to Article 5(5), for periods of residence longer than three months, the host Member State may require Union citizens to register with the relevant authorities'.[230] Article 8(2) requires that '[t]he deadline for registration may not be less than three months from the date of arrival' and that a registration certificate shall then be issued 'immediately, stating the name and address of the person registering and the date of the registration'. Mirroring Article 5(5), Article 8(2) also provides that '[f]ailure to comply with the registration requirement may render the person concerned liable to proportionate and non-discriminatory sanctions'.[231]

The option to issue a registration 'certificate' was conceived as a 'new approach to the right of residence arrangements, in particular by restricting the residence card requirements to cases where it is justified'.[232] It replaced sector-by-sector requirements on residence permits that predated Union citizenship.[233] Article 8(3) of Directive 2004/38 provides that for a registration certificate to be issued, Member States may 'only' require that:

- Union citizens to whom point (a) of Article 7(1) applies present a valid identity card or passport, a confirmation of engagement from the employer or a certificate of employment, or proof that they are self-employed persons;
- Union citizens to whom point (b) of Article 7(1) applies present a valid identity card or passport, and provide proof that they satisfy the conditions laid down therein;
- Union citizens to whom point (c) of Article 7(1) applies present a valid identity card or passport, provide proof of enrolment at an accredited establishment and of comprehensive sickness insurance cover and the declaration or equivalent means referred to in

---

[230] The European Parliament's Committee on Legal Affairs and the Internal Market proposed adding an amendment permitting a registration requirement for Union citizens 'as long as [the host State] also requires its own nationals to do so', on the grounds that the amendment 'institutes treatment that does not discriminate between nationals of the host Member State and [Union] nationals' (n 21, Opinion of the Committee on Legal Affairs and the Internal Market, Amendment 6). This suggestion was rejected by the Commission as it did 'not think that it is possible to compare the administrative formalities provided for by a Member State for its own nationals with those for nationals from other Member States' (n 45, 6).

[231] The European Parliament's proposal that the Commission's original wording (n 11, 'penalties') should be amended to 'administrative penalties' (n 21, Amendment 33) was accepted by the Commission in its amended proposal (n 45). However, the reference to 'administrative' was 'not retained' in the Council's common position on the basis that the Council 'preferr[ed] to leave to Member States to decide on the nature of applicable sanctions, in conformity with their national legislation' (n 11, 26).

[232] Original proposal (n 11) para 2.3.

[233] See Directive 68/360 for workers and Directive 73/148 for services and establishment; residence permits also applied to residence rights conferred by Directives 90/364, 90/365 and 93/96. The European Parliament's Committee on Culture, Youth, Education, the Media and Sport observed in a critical tone that '[a] State does not issue residence permits to a citizen who moves from one region to another within its own territory. Neither an Andalusian who moves to Galicia nor an Alsatian who lives partly in Paris and partly in Strasbourg has any need of a residence permit. All that they need to do on national territory relates to the administrative aspects of residence formalities. The same approach should apply for citizens of another Member State ... Residence permits are a leftover from a Europe marked by frontier posts' (n 21, 71).

point (c) of Article 7(1). Member States may not require this declaration to refer to any specific amount of resources.[234]

Not all Member States have introduced a registration system for Union citizens, though it may prove useful for Union citizens to record the date on which residence rights under Article 7 of the Directive commenced: according to the Commission, the registration certificate is 'a kind of receipt for the citizen and proof for the authorities that the formality has been carried out'.[235] In that light, the Commission suggested in its amended proposal for the Directive that 'Union citizens should be able to apply to register if they so wish, even in States where this is not compulsory'.[236] It therefore accepted an amendment proposed by the European Parliament,[237] adding to draft Article 8(1) the statement that '[i]n all cases the Member States shall allow any Union citizens applying to do so to register'. However, the amendment was rejected by the Council on the basis that 'Member States should not be obliged to issue a registration certificate if they have not opted for a registration system'.[238] The Commission softened the amendment's rejection by observing that 'the fact that such a certificate can be obtained could have the effect in practice of obliging all citizens to apply for one'.[239]

However, a note of caution needs to be added by considering the sharper edge of the principle that administrative documents have *declaratory* effect only. A registration certificate noting the date on which a Union citizen registered with host State authorities, based on relevant documents submitted in accordance with Article 8(3) of the Directive, provides evidence of nothing more than the circumstances at that time. It does not communicate anything about the extent to which the citizen *sustained* compliance with the conditions for lawful residence in Article 7, for example, or about whether their residence was legal and continuous for the purposes of permanent residence rights under Article 16.[240] In *Commission v UK*, Advocate General Cruz Villalón therefore overstated the significance—or at least the temporal significance—of registration certificates:

> Directive 2004/38 provides for mechanisms (specifically in Article 8 thereof) enabling a Union citizen who is not a national of the host Member State to prove that he is lawfully

---

[234] The Commission had originally proposed a system of self-certification by declaration for residence rights under Article 7(1)(b), as explained further in Section 5.1.3. In Case C-424/98 *Commission v Italy*, EU:C:2000:28, before the adoption of Directive 2004/38, the Court held that 'by requiring students who are nationals of other Member States and who are seeking recognition of their and their families' right of residence in Italy pursuant to Directive 93/96 to guarantee to the Italian authorities that they have resources of a specific amount; secondly, as regards the means to be used for that purpose, by not clearly leaving the student the choice between a declaration and such alternative means as are at least equivalent; and, finally, by not allowing the use of a declaration where a student is accompanied by members of his family, the Italian Republic has ... exceeded the limits imposed upon it by Community law' (para 46). See similarly, censuring burdensome administrative procedures for workers, Case C-344/95 *Commission v Belgium*, EU:C:1997:81. Article 8(3) of the Directive is now referred to in Article 18(1) k) WA.
[235] Original proposal (n 11) para 2.3.
[236] Amended proposal (n 45) 6.
[237] European Parliament Report (n 21) Amendment 32.
[238] Common Position (n 11) 29.
[239] Communication on the common position (n 48) para 3.2.2.2.
[240] eg Case C-325/09 *Dias*, EU:C:2011:498, para 54: 'the declaratory character of residence permits [issued pursuant to Directive 68/360] means that those permits merely certify that a right already exists. Consequently, just as such a declaratory character means that a citizen's residence may not be regarded as illegal, within the meaning of European Union law, solely on the ground that he does not hold a residence permit, it precludes a Union citizen's residence from being regarded as legal, within the meaning of European Union law, solely on the ground that such a permit was validly issued to him'. The right of permanent residence is examined in Chapter 8.

resident by means of a certificate which the competent authorities will issue once they have checked that he satisfies, in particular, the requirements of Article 7 of that directive. When a claimant has that certificate, any inconvenience that he might suffer during the processing of a claim for a social benefit will be minimal or even non-existent: if so requested, the claimant will simply have to produce the document attesting that the Member State considers his residence in its territory to be lawful.[241]

Subsequently, in *Petrea*, the Court explicitly addressed the declaratory character of registration certificates. The specific question concerned whether Articles 27 and 32 of the Directive precluded the withdrawal of a registration certificate issued in error, a question returned to in Chapter 10. For present purposes, the Court commented more generally that:

> the right of nationals of a Member State to enter the territory of another Member State and to reside there for the purposes intended by the EC Treaty is a right conferred directly by the Treaty, or, as the case may be, by the provisions adopted for its implementation. Therefore, the grant of a residence permit to a national of a Member State is to be regarded, not as a measure giving rise to rights, but as a measure by a Member State serving to prove the individual position of a national of another Member State with regard to provisions of European Union law … Consequently, just as such a declaratory character means that a citizen's residence may not be regarded as illegal, within the meaning of European Union law, solely on the ground that he does not hold a residence permit, it precludes a Union citizen's residence from being regarded as legal, within the meaning of European Union law, solely on the ground that such a permit was validly issued to him … [T]he same is true *a fortiori* in the context of the FEU Treaty, as is moreover stated in recital 11 of Directive 2004/38. Such a declaratory character attaches, therefore, also to the registration certificate provided for in Article 8(2) of Directive 2004/38, with the result that the issue of that document cannot, in itself, give rise to a legitimate expectation on the part of the person concerned in his right to stay on the territory of the Member State concerned.[242]

Specific questions about the amount or level of sufficient resources necessary to assure such residence rights under Articles 7(1)(b) and 7(1)(c) are returned to in Section 5.1.3.

5.1.2 Registration requirements: Union citizens who are family members

Article 8(5) of the Directive outlines that, for registration certificates issued to the family members of Union citizens who are also Union citizens themselves, Member States may require presentation of:

(a) a valid identity card or passport;
(b) a document attesting to the existence of a family relationship or of a registered partnership;
(c) where appropriate, the registration certificate of the Union citizen whom they are accompanying or joining;
(d) in cases falling under points (c) and (d) of Article 2(2) [ie for direct descendants who are under the age of 21 or are dependents, and dependent direct relatives in the

---

[241] AG Cruz Villalón in Case C-308/14 *Commission v UK*, EU:C:2015:666, para 80 of the Opinion.
[242] Case C-184/16 *Petrea*, EU:C:2017:684, paras 32–35.

ascending line], documentary evidence that the conditions laid down therein are met;[243]

(e) in cases falling under Article 3(2)(a), a document issued by the relevant authority in the country of origin or country from which they are arriving certifying that they are dependents or members of the household of the Union citizen, or proof of the existence of serious health grounds which strictly require the personal care of the family member by the Union citizen;[244]

(f) in cases falling under Article 3(2)(b), proof of the existence of a durable relationship with the Union citizen.[245]

These requirements—which constitute an exhaustive list[246]—seek to institute a balance between imposing minimal administrative requirements on the exercise of free movement for Union citizens, on the one hand, and providing sufficient assurances for Member States that rights-creating relationships and circumstances can be verified, on the other.

However, there are limits on how Member States may use the information provided to them for the purposes of registration, especially having regard to data protection. In *Huber*, an Austrian national residing in Germany requested the deletion of data relating to him[247] held in the Central Register of Foreign Nationals ('the AZR'). More specifically, he argued that he 'was discriminated against by reason of the processing of the data concerning him contained in the AZR, in particular because such a database does not exist in respect of German nationals'.[248] The Court held that the data 'required for the application of the legislation relating to the right of residence would be of no practical benefit if those data were not to be stored', it was also the case that, 'since a change in the personal situation of a party entitled to a right of residence may have an impact on his status in relation to that right, it is incumbent on the authority responsible for a register ... to ensure that the data which are stored are, where appropriate, brought up to date so that, first, they reflect the actual situation of the data subjects and, secondly, irrelevant data are removed from that register'.[249]

---

[243] On dependent relatives in descending and ascending lines, see Case C-423/12 *Reyes*, EU:C:2014:16. See further, Chapter 4

[244] On Article 3(2)(a), see Case C-83/11 *Rahman*, EU:C:2012:519. See further, Chapter 4.

[245] On Article 3(2)(b), see Chapter 4; including reference to Commission guidance that '[n]ational rules on durability of partnership can refer to a minimum amount of time as a criterion for whether a partnership can be considered as durable. However, in this case national rules would need to foresee that other relevant aspects (such as for example a joint mortgage to buy a home) are also taken into account' (Communication on guidance for better transposition and application of Directive 2004/38/EC (n 50) para 2.1.1).

[246] ibid para 2.3. That conclusion is also reflected in recital 14 of the Directive, which provides that '[t]he supporting documents required by the competent authorities for the issuing of a registration certificate or of a residence card [for family members] should be comprehensively specified in order to avoid divergent administrative practices or interpretations constituting an undue obstacle to the exercise of the right of residence by Union citizens and their family members'. In its original proposal, the Commission commented that '[b]y giving a complete list of the documents to be submitted to the competent authorities in the host Member State ... this proposal ... drastically simplifies the formalities for Union citizens and their family members to exercise the right of residence, cutting them back to the bare essentials' (n 11, para 2.3).

[247] Case C-524/06 *Huber*, EU:C:2008:724, para 31 ie 'his name, given name, date and place of birth, nationality, marital status, sex; a record of his entries into and exits from Germany, and his residence status; particulars of passports issued to him; a record of his previous statements as to domicile; and reference numbers issued by the Bundesamt, particulars of the authorities which supplied the data and the reference numbers used by those authorities'.

[248] ibid para 32.

[249] ibid para 60. The EU data protection legislation in force at the time was Directive 95/46/EC of the European Parliament and of the Council on the protection of individuals with regard to the processing of personal data and on the free movement of such data, 1995 OJ L281/31; now replaced by the General Data Protection Regulation ('GDPR', Regulation 2016/679/EU, 2016 OJ L119/1).

However, 'only the grant of access to authorities having powers [relating to the right of residence] could be considered to be necessary' under EU data protection legislation.[250] Creating centralised registers would be justified only if they contribute 'to the more effective application of [legislation relating to the right of residence] as regards the right of residence of Union citizens who wish to reside in a Member State of which they are not nationals'.[251] Where registration data are collected and stored for statistical purposes, 'only anonymous information ... requires to be processed in order for such an objective to be attained'.[252] Finally, the processing of data on Union citizens who are not nationals of the relevant Member State for the purposes of 'fighting crime' (the public order argument submitted by the German Government), was roundly condemned. While the objective of fighting crime is legitimate, 'it cannot be relied on in order to justify the systematic processing of personal data when that processing is restricted to the data of Union citizens who are not nationals of the Member State concerned'.[253] After all, 'the fight against crime ... necessarily involves the prosecution of crimes and offences committed, irrespective of the nationality of their perpetrators'.[254]

5.1.3 Article 8(4): 'sufficient resources'

Article 8(4) of the Directive[255] establishes that 'Member States may not lay down a fixed amount which they regard as "sufficient resources" but they must take into account the personal situation of the person concerned'. The provision sets a 'ceiling' but not a 'floor' in continuing that: '[i]n all cases this amount shall not be higher than the threshold below which nationals of the host Member State become eligible for social assistance, or, where this criterion is not applicable, higher than the minimum social security pension paid by the host Member State'. Article 1 of Directives 90/364 and 90/365 seemed to require more definitively that:

> The resources referred to in the first subparagraph shall be deemed sufficient where they are higher than the level of resources below which the host Member State may grant social assistance to its nationals, taking into account the personal circumstances of the applicant and, where appropriate, the personal circumstances of persons admitted pursuant to paragraph 2.
>
> Where the second subparagraph cannot be applied in a Member State, the resources of the applicant shall be deemed sufficient if they are higher than the level of the minimum social security pension paid by the host Member State.

---

[250] *Huber*, para 61.
[251] ibid para 62.
[252] ibid para 65.
[253] ibid para 77. In para 80, the Court confirmed that '[t]he difference in treatment between those nationals and those Union citizens which arises by virtue of the systematic processing of personal data relating only to Union citizens who are not nationals of the Member State concerned for the purposes of fighting crime constitutes discrimination which is prohibited by Article [18 TFEU]'. AG Poiares Maduro made particularly strong statements (throughout his Opinion) on the prohibition of discrimination being 'at the heart of the concept of European citizenship' (EU:C:2008:194, para 18 of the Opinion).
[254] *Huber*, para 78; referring to para 21 of the Opinion of AG Poiares Maduro, where he also argued that '[i]f a central register is so important for effective general policing, it should obviously include everyone living within a particular country regardless of his nationality. It is not open to national authorities to say that fighting crime requires the systematic processing of personal data of EU citizens but not of that relating to nationals. This would be tantamount to saying that EU nationals pose a greater security threat and are more likely to commit crimes than citizens, which, as the Commission points out, is completely unacceptable').
[255] Now referred to in Article 18(1)(k) and (l) WA.

However, the reference to the personal circumstances of the applicant (and, where relevant, family members) left some space for host State discretion. Reflecting its specific method of self-certification by declaration, Directive 93/96 did not address what constituted sufficient resources in the same way, aside from guidance that students had to declare that they had sufficient resources to 'avoid becoming a burden on the social assistance system of the host Member State during their period of residence'.

In its original proposal for Directive 2004/38, the Commission envisaged self-certification of sufficient resources by declaration applying more generally:

> For people not in work, the right of residence will, for the first four years of residence in the host Member State, continue to be subject to their having sufficient resources and sickness insurance, so that they do not have recourse to public funds in the host Member State. However, the requirements have been relaxed in that the amount of resources considered sufficient is no longer defined in the proposal and cannot be fixed by the Member States, and evidence that the two conditions are met is replaced by a simple *bona fide* declaration, which may be checked out only if the individual concerned seeks recourse to social security or the sickness insurance scheme for persons without health insurance. Students must prove that they are enrolled in an educational establishment and assure the relevant authority, by means of a declaration, that they have sufficient resources and sickness insurance cover.[256]

The Commission suggested that '[a] false declaration could be penalised on the basis of the principle of equal treatment with nationals in compliance with the proportionality principle'.[257] However, the self-certification proposal was rejected by the Council:

> [A]s far as administrative formalities for Union citizens are concerned and in order to prevent abuses, the common position has introduced a system whereby Member States may require that Union citizens provide proof that they satisfy the conditions laid down in Article 7. Nevertheless, the system remains flexible since the registration certificate is issued on the spot and the fulfilment of conditions is verified only in specific cases where there is a reasonable doubt, as foreseen by Article 14(2) [see section 6.2 below]. In [Article 8(4)], the possibility for Member States to provide for an amount of sufficient resources has been foreseen, but allowing to take into account the personal situation of the person concerned.[258]

---

[256] Original proposal (n 11) para 2.1. That position reflects the recommendation in 1997 from the High Level Panel on the Free Movement of Persons: '[w]ithout losing sight of the major economic aspects of this issue, the requirement to provide proof of sufficient resources should be made more flexible. The system whereby the person concerned simply states that he/she has sufficient resources, as in the case of students, could be made more widespread' (Report of the High Level Panel on the free movement of persons chaired by Mrs Simone Veil, and presented to the Commission on 18 March 1997, 25). In its Opinion on the Commission's proposal, the Committee of the Regions 'strongly advocate[d] self-certification on the part of EU citizens to provide evidence of certain personal circumstances. This practice, adopted in many EU Member States, speeds up administrative procedures significantly' (n 20, para 2.6; see also, para 2.7). The European Parliament agreed that '[t]he principle of self-certification should be applied as a general rule' (n 21, 54).

[257] Original proposal (n 11) para 3.

[258] Common Position (n 11) 31. The Commission accepted the Council's approach 'because it represents a fair balance between the legitimate concern of the Member States to prevent abuse and the introduction of a more flexible system for citizens than the current acquis, as the Commission wanted' (Communication on the common position (n 48) para 3.3.2).

As a result, the premise set by Article 8(4) of the Directive for residence rights based on Article 7(1)(b) or 7(1)(c) is that a host State may not determine sufficiency of resources by setting a fixed amount, either directly or indirectly, below which a right of residence can be automatically refused.

Article 8(4) might not, therefore, seem all that different from Article 1 of Directives 90/364 and 90/365. However, with reference to Directive 2004/38, the Court has characterised the taking into account of personal situations as an obligation rather than a possibility,[259] which is also reflected in the Commission's guidance that the Member State authorities '*must take into account* the personal situation of the individual concerned'.[260] Moreover, while Article 8(4) affirms that 'EU citizens *have* sufficient resources where the level of their resources is higher than the threshold under which a minimum subsistence benefit is granted in the host Member State',[261] the opposite is not true: in other words, it does not follow that citizens *not* possessing that level of resources are deemed to have 'insufficient' resources. As the Court expressed it in *Brey*, 'although Member States may indicate a certain sum as a reference amount, they may not impose a minimum income level below which it will be *presumed* that the person concerned does not have sufficient resources, irrespective of a specific examination of the situation of each person concerned'.[262]

In its Opinion on the original Commission proposal for the Directive, the Economic and Social Committee commented that '[t]he abolition of Member States' right to fix the minimum amount of economic resources persons not working and retired persons must possess in order to reside in their territory is another improvement which should be highlighted ... Establishing minimum resources in each state affects freedom of movement and puts areas of the Union off limits to certain citizens because they lack the means'.[263] The Commission advises that '[n]ational authorities can, when necessary, undertake checks as to the existence of the resources, their lawfulness, amount and availability. The resources do not have to be periodic and can be in the form of accumulated capital. The evidence of sufficient resources cannot be limited'.[264] Where resources are considered *not* to be sufficient, the actions that the host State may take in consequence intersect with retaining residence rights under Article 14 of the Directive, examined in Section 6.2 (and building further on the discussion of expulsion decisions under Article 15(1) at the beginning of Section 5). More generally, a right to reside in a host State on limited resources, coupled with an exclusion from recourse to its social assistance system, raises complex questions about responsibility

---

[259] eg Case C-140/12 *Brey*, EU:C:2013:565. See further, Chapter 7.

[260] Communication on guidance for better transposition and application of Directive 2004/38/EC (n 50) para 2.3.1 (emphasis added). See similarly, Communication on the common position (n 48) para 3.3.2: 'it has become necessary to specify, in [Article 8(4)], the level of resources considered sufficient, while introducing a certain flexibility in order *to oblige* the Member States to take into account the personal situation of the individual concerned' (emphasis added).

[261] In situations '[w]here this criterion is not applicable, the minimum social security pension should be taken into account' (Communication on guidance for better transposition and application of Directive 2004/38/EC (n 50) para 2.3.1). In *Brey*, AG Wahl noted that because Article 8(4) allows that the minimum social security pension may be 'used instead of social assistance as a yardstick and, consequently, to determine whether the Union citizen has sufficient resources', the result is that 'for the purposes of establishing whether a particular Union citizen has a right to reside in another Member State, the concepts of "social assistance" and "social security" overlap to a certain degree' (AG Wahl in *Brey*, EU:C:2013:337, para 37 of the Opinion).

[262] *Brey*, para 68 (emphasis added).

[263] ECOSOC Opinion (n 156) para 3.9.

[264] Communication on guidance for better transposition and application of Directive 2004/38/EC (n 50) para 2.3.1, referring to Case C-424/98 *Commission v Italy*, EU:C:2000:287, para 37 (addressing Directives 90/364 and 90/365).

5.2 Articles 5–6 and 9–11: Family Members who are not Union Citizens

Articles 5 (right of entry), 6 (periods of residence up to three months), 9, 10, and 11 (periods of residence for more than three months) of Directive 2004/38 outline relevant administrative formalities for family members who accompany or join Union citizens in a host State and who are not themselves Member State nationals. These provisions will now be looked at as regards the right of entry (Section 5.2.1) and the right of residence (Section 5.2.2) respectively.[265]

5.2.1 Right of entry

Article 5(2) of the Directive requires family members—defined under Article 2(2)—who are not Member State nationals to have an entry visa in accordance with Regulation 2018/1806,[266] or national law,[267] as appropriate. Article 5(2) also requires that Member States 'shall grant such persons every facility to obtain the necessary visas', which must be 'issued free of charge as soon as possible and on the basis of an accelerated procedure'. The Commission emphasises that 'family members have not only the right to enter the territory of the Member State, but also the right to obtain an entry visa. This distinguishes them from other third country nationals, who have no such right'.[268] Illustrating the extent of the obligation on host States, the Court ruled in *Commission v Spain* that refusing an entry visa to the third-country national spouses of Union citizens 'on the sole ground that they were persons for whom alerts were entered in the [Schengen Information System] without first verifying whether the presence of those persons constituted a genuine, present and sufficiently serious threat to one of the fundamental interests of society' amounted to a failure to fulfil the obligations established by EU law on the free movement of persons (at that time, by Directive 64/221).[269]

The Commission has developed practical guidance for Member States on the application of Article 5(2). First, it considers that:

> By analogy with Article 23 of the Visa Code the Commission considers that delays of more than four weeks are not reasonable. The authorities of the Member States should guide the family members as to the type of visa they should apply for, and they cannot require them to apply for long-term, residence or family reunification visas. Member States must grant such family members every facility to obtain the necessary visas. Member States may use

---

[265] See further, Article 18(1)(l) and (m) WA.

[266] Regulation 2018/1806/EU listing the third countries whose nationals must be in possession of visas when crossing the external borders and those whose nationals are exempt from that requirement, 2018 OJ L303/39, which replaced Regulation 539/2001, 2001 OJ L81/1.

[267] This distinction reflects the fact that the Regulation 'constitutes a development of the provisions of the Schengen *acquis*' in which neither Ireland nor the UK takes part and is not therefore 'bound by it or subject to its application' (recitals 38 and 39).

[268] Communication on guidance for better transposition and application of Directive 2004/38/EC (n 50) para 2.2.1, referring to Case C-503/03 *Commission v Spain*, EU:C:2006:74, para 42.

[269] Case C-503/03 *Commission v Spain*, EU:C:2006:74, para 59. On the Schengen Information System, see Title IV of the Convention implementing the Schengen Agreement, 2000 OJ L239/19.

premium call lines or services of an external company to set up an appointment but must offer the possibility of direct access to the consulate to third country family members.[270]

Second, '[n]o additional documents, such as a proof of accommodation, sufficient resources, an invitation letter or return ticket, can be required'.[271] Third, 'Member States may encourage integration of EU citizens and their third country family members by offering language and other targeted courses on a voluntary basis', but '[n]o consequence can be attached to the refusal to attend them'.[272] This contrasts with the competence retained by the Member States to set prescriptive integration conditions for third-country nationals more generally.[273]

According to Article 5(2), where family members possess a valid residence card, they are exempt from the entry visa requirement.[274] In such circumstances, '[t]he host Member State shall not place an entry or exit stamp' in their passports (Article 5(3)). The implications of Article 5(2) are returned to below in connection with Articles 9 and 11 of the Directive. Finally, as outlined in Section 5.1, Articles 5(4) and 5(5) apply to both Union citizens and family members who are not nationals of a Member State. Article 5(4) provides:

> Where a Union citizen, or a family member who is not a national of a Member State, does not have the necessary travel documents or, if required, the necessary visas, the Member State concerned shall, before turning them back, give such persons every reasonable opportunity to obtain the necessary documents or have them brought to them within a reasonable period of time or to corroborate or prove by other means that they are covered by the right of free movement and residence.

Article 5(5) establishes that the Member State 'may require the person concerned to report his/her presence within its territory within a reasonable and non-discriminatory period of time'.[275] It also establishes that '[f]ailure to comply with this requirement may make the person concerned liable to proportionate and non-discriminatory sanctions'.

---

[270] Communication on guidance for better transposition and application of Directive 2004/38/EC (n 50) para 2.2.1, referring to COM(2006) 403 final/2. Article 23 of Regulation 810/2009/EC establishing a Community Code on Visas (Visa Code), 2009 OJ L243/1, require that: '1. Applications shall be decided on within 15 calendar days of the date of the lodging of an application which is admissible in accordance with Article 19. 2. That period may be extended up to a maximum of 30 calendar days in individual cases, notably when further scrutiny of the application is needed or in cases of representation where the authorities of the represented Member State are consulted. 3. Exceptionally, when additional documentation is needed in specific cases, the period may be extended up to a maximum of 60 calendar days'.

[271] Communication on guidance for better transposition and application of Directive 2004/38/EC (n 50) para 2.2.1.

[272] ibid para 2.2.1; referring to its Communication to the European Parliament, the Council, the European Economic and Social Committee and the Committee of the Regions on multilingualism: an asset for Europe and a shared commitment, COM(2008) 566.

[273] See esp Article 7(2) of Directive 2003/86/EC on the right to family reunification, 2003 OJ L251/12; and Article 5(2) of Directive 2003/109 concerning the status of third-country nationals who are long-term residents, 2003 OJ L16/44. Both provisions affirm that 'Member States may require third country nationals to comply with integration measures, in accordance with national law'.

[274] In its original proposal, the Commission referred to this aspect of Article 5(2) as 'a great innovation in providing for the equivalence of visas and residence documents issued by one of the Member States' (n 11, 9).

[275] In its original proposal, the Commission commented that '[t]his is compatible with [the Member States'] powers as regards measures to provide public authorities with detailed knowledge of population movements in their territory' (ibid, referring to Case 118/75 *Watson and Belmann*, EU:C:1976:106, paras 17–18).

5.2.2 Right of residence

For periods of residence up to three months, Article 6(2) of the Directive confirms that family members as defined by Article 2(2) who are not Member State nationals have a right of residence in a host State when they accompany or join a Union citizen on the same Article 6(1) basis as for Union citizens, that is 'without any conditions or any formalities other than the requirement to hold a valid identity card or passport'. For situations 'where the planned period of residence is for more than three months', Article 9(1) requires that 'Member States shall issue a residence card to family members of a Union citizen who are not nationals of a Member State'.[276] As seen in Section 5.1, retaining a residence card requirement for family members who are not Member State nationals was highlighted as a significant point of contrast with the removal of it for Union citizens. Article 9(2) establishes that '[t]he deadline for submitting the residence card application may not be less than three months from the date of arrival'. Aligning with Article 5(4), Article 9(3) assures that '[f]ailure to comply with the requirement to apply for a residence card may make the person concerned liable to proportionate and non-discriminatory sanctions'. The European Parliament had proposed incorporating the *MRAX* judgment into the text of the Directive, which had established that '[f]amily members shall not be denied a residence card solely on the grounds that their visas have expired prior to the application for a residence card'.[277] In its amended proposal, the Commission accepted Parliament's amendment, altered to 'solely on the grounds that they have no visa or that their visa has expired' to bring the amendment 'completely into line' with *MRAX*.[278] In its Common Position, the Council rejected the proposed amendment on the grounds that it would be 'contradictory to Article 10, where there is an exhaustive list of all documents required for obtaining a residence card and the visa does not appear to be one of them'.[279] More generally, *MRAX* also established that 'a Member State is not permitted to refuse issue of a residence permit and to issue an expulsion order against a third country national who is able to furnish proof of his identity and of his marriage to a national of a Member State on the sole ground that he has entered the territory of the Member State concerned unlawfully'.[280]

Article 10(1) confirms that '[t]he right of residence of family members of a Union citizen who are not nationals of a Member State shall be evidenced by the issuing of a document called "Residence card of a family member of a Union citizen"'. The Commission emphasises that '[t]he denomination of this residence card must not deviate from the wording prescribed by the Directive as different titles would make it materially impossible for the residence card to be recognised in other Member States as exempting its holder from the visa requirement under Article 5(2)'.[281] It acknowledges that '[t]he format of the residence card is not fixed, so Member States are free to lay it down as they see fit. However, the residence card

---

[276] Article 10(1) establishes that the document shall be called '[r]esidence card of a family member of a Union citizen'.

[277] European Parliament Report (n 21) Amendment 38. See also, Case C-459/99 *MRAX*, EU:C:2002:461, paras 86–91 (addressing Directive 64/221).

[278] Amended proposal (n 45) 6 and draft Article 9(2)(a).

[279] Common Position (n 11) 9. In its Communication on the Common Position (n 48), the Commission agreed that '[i]t would therefore be something of a contradiction to state that a residence card may not be refused on the grounds that the persons concerned do not have a visa' (para 3.2.2.2).

[280] *MRAX*, para 80.

[281] Communication on guidance for better transposition and application of Directive 2004/38/EC (n 50) para 2.2.2.

must be issued as a self-standing document and not in form of a sticker in a passport, as this could limit the validity of the card in violation of Article 11(1)'.[282]

Article 10(1) reflects the principle that relevant documentation does not constitute residence rights for family members by requiring that the residence card 'evidenc[ing]' shall be issued 'no later than six months from the date on which they submit the application'. It also requires that '[a] certificate of application for the residence card shall be issued immediately'. In *Diallo*, the Court confirmed the 'mandatory' nature of the six-month period in Article 10(1), clarifying that it 'implies the adoption and notification of a decision to the person concerned before that period expires'.[283] It held that '[t]he concept of "issuing", referred to in Article 10(1) of Directive 2004/38, implies ... that, within the period of six months laid down in that provision, the competent national authorities must examine the application, adopt a decision and, in the case where the applicant qualifies for the right of residence on the basis of Directive 2004/38, issue that residence card to that applicant'.[284] The Court also found that 'the notification of the decision on the application for a residence card of a family member of a Union citizen cannot be notified to the applicant within different time periods depending on whether the decision adopted by the competent national authority is in the positive or the negative'.[285]

In the Commission's view, the six-month deadline 'must be interpreted in light of Article [4(3) TEU] and the maximum period of six months is justified only in cases where examination of the application involves public policy considerations'.[286] Relatedly, the Court held in *Diallo* that 'the principle of effectiveness and the objective of rapid processing of applications inherent to Directive 2004/38 preclude national authorities automatically being allowed a new period of six months following the judicial annulment of an initial decision refusing to issue a residence card. They are required to adopt a new decision within a reasonable period of time, which cannot, in any case, exceed the period referred to in Article 10(1)'.[287] The Directive 'does not contain any provisions concerning the effects of the judicial annulment of decisions adopted by competent national authorities refusing to issue a residence card of a family member of a Union citizen, and in particular the issue of what time period those authorities have for the purposes of adopting a new decision following such an annulment',[288] which means that, in accordance with the principle of national procedural autonomy, each Member State can establish relevant conditions. However, in line with the principle of effectiveness, such rules may 'not make it excessively difficult or impossible in practice to exercise the rights conferred by EU law'.[289] In the circumstances of the *Diallo* case, the Court therefore concluded that 'the automatic opening of a new period of six months following

---

[282] ibid. In this context, the Commission refers to Article 5 of Council Regulation 1030/2002/EC laying down a uniform format for residence permits for third-country nationals, 2002 OJ L157/1, which specifies the third country nationals to whom the Regulation does not apply (including 'members of the families of citizens of the Union exercising their right to free movement'). It also refers to Article 21 of the Convention implementing the Schengen Agreement, 2000 OJ L239/19.
[283] Case C-246/17 *Diallo*, EU:C:2018:499, para 38.
[284] ibid para 36.
[285] ibid para 41.
[286] Communication on guidance for better transposition and application of Directive 2004/38/EC (n 50) para 2.2.2. The Commission also referred to its Communication to the Council and the European Parliament on the special measures concerning the movement and residence of citizens of the Union which are justified on grounds of public policy, public security or public health (COM(1999) 372), para 3.2. Reflecting Article 10 EC, Article 4(3) TEU requires that '[t]he Member States shall take any appropriate measure, general or particular, to ensure fulfilment of the obligations arising out of the Treaties or resulting from the acts of the institutions of the Unions'.
[287] *Diallo*, para 69.
[288] ibid para 59.
[289] ibid para 59.

the judicial annulment of the competent national authority's initial decision appears to be of such a nature as to render excessively difficult the exercise of the right of the family member of a Union citizen to obtain a decision on his application for a residence card on the basis of Article 10(1) of Directive 2004/38'.[290]

However, as seen in Section 5.1 for Union citizens, the fact that residence permits have declaratory effect only can also have sharper edges. In *O and B*, the Court held that EU law 'does not require the authorities of the Member State of which the Union citizen in question is a national to grant a derived right of residence to a third-country national who is a member of that citizen's family because of the mere fact that, in the host Member State, that third-country national held a valid residence permit' since '[a] residence card issued on the basis of Article 10 of Directive 2004/38 has a declaratory, as opposed to a constitutive, character'.[291] The declaratory nature of residence cards is also relevant to the outcome of national decisions on applications. In *Diallo*, national legislation required the relevant authorities 'to issue automatically a residence card of a family member of a Union citizen to the person concerned, when the period of six months, referred to in Article 10(1) of Directive 2004/38, is exceeded, without finding beforehand that the person concerned actually meets the conditions for residing in the host Member State in accordance with EU law'.[292] However, invoking the declaratory and not constitutive character of residence cards, the Court found that:

> Article 10(1) of Directive 2004/38 precludes the residence card of a family member of a Union citizen being issued to a third-country national who does not meet the requirements set out by that article for its allocation. In those circumstances, while there is nothing to prevent national legislation from providing that silence on the part of the competent administration for a period of six months from the lodging of the application constitutes a refusal, the very terms of Directive 2004/38 preclude that silence from constituting an acceptance.[293]

Article 10(2) of the Directive lists the documents that Member States may require to be presented for a residence card to be issued:

(a) a valid passport;[294]
(b) a document attesting to the existence of a family relationship or of a registered partnership;

---

[290] ibid para 62. This finding of disproportionality was because, first, 'national competent authorities must only verify, within that period, whether the third-country national is in a position to prove, through the submission of the documents stated in Article 10(2) of that directive, that he comes within the scope of the concept of 'family member' of a Union citizen, within the meaning of Directive 2004/38, in order to benefit from the residence card' (para 63); and second, since 'the purpose of Directive 2004/38 is to facilitate the exercise of the primary and individual right to move and reside freely within the territory of the Member States which is conferred directly on citizens of the Union by Article 21(1) TFEU' (para 64), '[t]hat purpose requires that a third-country national who submits proof that he comes within the scope of the concept of "family member" of a Union citizen, within the meaning of Directive 2004/38, be issued with a residence card certifying that status at the earliest opportunity' (para 65). The latter point was underlined by the fact that 'in accordance with Article 5(2) of Directive 2004/38, only the possession of a valid residence card is to exempt the family members of a Union citizen, who are not nationals of a Member State, from the obligation to obtain a visa to enter the territory of the Member States' (para 67).
[291] Case C-456/12 *O and B*, EU:C:2014:135, 60; citing Case C-291/05 *Eind*, EU:C:2007:771, para 26.
[292] *Diallo*, para 44.
[293] ibid paras 50–51.
[294] For Union citizens, Article 8(5) also allows for a valid identity card.

(c) the registration certificate or, in the absence of a registration system, any other proof of residence in the host Member State of the Union citizen whom they are accompanying or joining;[295]

(d) in cases falling under points (c) and (d) of Article 2(2) [ie for direct descendants who are under the age of 21 or are dependents, and dependent direct relatives in the ascending line], documentary evidence that the conditions laid down therein are met;[296]

(e) in cases falling under Article 3(2)(a), a document issued by the relevant authority in the country of origin or country from which they are arriving certifying that they are dependents or members of the household of the Union citizen, or proof of the existence of serious health grounds which strictly require the personal care of the family member by the Union citizen;[297]

(f) in cases falling under Article 3(2)(b), proof of the existence of a durable relationship with the Union citizen.[298]

Reflecting the view of the Council in its Common Position, noted above, recital 14 indicates that this list is exhaustive ('[t]he supporting documents required by the competent authorities for the issuing ... of a residence card should be *comprehensively specified* in order to avoid divergent administrative practices or interpretations constituting an undue obstacle to the exercise of the right of residence by Union citizens and their family members').[299] However, according to the Commission, 'Member States may require that documents be translated, notarised or legalised where the national authority concerned cannot understand the language in which the particular document is written, or have a suspicion about the authenticity of the issuing authority'.[300]

In *Rahman*, the Court was asked whether 'issue of the residence card referred to in Article 10 of Directive 2004/38 may be conditional on the requirement that the situation of dependence for the purposes of Article 3(2)(a) of that directive has endured in the host Member State',[301] noting that Article 10(2) requires presentation of a document 'issued by the relevant authority in the country of origin or country from which they are arriving certifying that they are dependents ... of the Union citizen'. According to the Court:

> The legislature did not settle, either in that provision or in other provisions of Directive 2004/38, the question whether family members of a Union citizen who do not fall under the definition in Article 2(2) of the directive and who apply for issue of a residence card by presenting a document, issued in the country from which they have arrived, certifying their dependence on that Union citizen can be refused a residence card on the ground that,

---

[295] Cf the slightly different language in Article 8(5) for Union citizens ie 'where appropriate, the registration certificate of the Union citizen whom they are accompanying or joining'.
[296] On dependent relatives in the descending and ascending lines, see Case C-423/12 *Reyes*, EU:C:2014:16; see further, Chapter 4.
[297] On Article 3(2)(a), see Case C-83/11 *Rahman*, EU:C:2012:519; see further, Chapter 4.
[298] On Article 3(2)(b), see Chapter 4; including reference to Commission guidance that '[n]ational rules on durability of partnership can refer to a minimum amount of time as a criterion for whether a partnership can be considered as durable. However, in this case national rules would need to foresee that other relevant aspects (such as for example a joint mortgage to buy a home) are also taken into account' (Communication on guidance for better transposition and application of Directive 2004/38/EC (n 50) para 2.1.1).
[299] The Commission therefore advises that '[n]o additional documents can be requested' (ibid para 2.2.2).
[300] ibid.
[301] *Rahman*, para 41.

after their entry into the host Member State, they have ceased to be dependants of that citizen.[302]

The Court therefore concluded that 'the question whether issue of the residence card referred to in Article 10 of Directive 2004/38 may be conditional on the requirement that the situation of dependence for the purposes of Article 3(2)(a) of that directive has endured in the host Member State does not fall within the scope of the directive'.[303]

Article 11 of the Directive concerns the validity of the residence card. Article 11(1) establishes that it 'shall be valid for five years from the date of issue or for the envisaged period of residence of the Union citizen, if this period is less than five years'.[304] Article 11(2) provides that the validity of the residence card 'shall not be affected by temporary absences not exceeding six months a year, or by absences of a longer duration for compulsory military service or by one absence of a maximum of twelve consecutive months for important reasons such as pregnancy or childbirth, serious illness, study or vocational training, or a posting in another Member State or a third country'.[305] These conditions are also specified in Article 16(3) of the Directive, which addresses temporary absences from the host State that do not affect continuity of residence for the purposes of acquiring a right of permanent residence there (Chapter 8).

The relationship between entry visas and residence cards in the context of preventing abuse of EU rights[306] was examined in *McCarthy II*. Mr McCarthy, who had both British and Irish nationality, was married to a Colombian national, Ms McCarthy Rodriguez. The couple resided in Spain with their daughter (also a British and Irish national). A residence card was issued by the Spanish authorities to Ms McCarthy Rodriguez in 2010. However, relevant UK legislation required her to apply for an EEA family permit before entering the UK. These permits were valid for six months and could be renewed only if the applicants travelled in person to a UK diplomatic mission—requiring travel from Marbella to Madrid in this case—and completed a form that included questions about their employment and finances. It was also shown that certain airlines had denied Ms McCarthy Rodriguez permission to board flights to the UK 'when she has presented only her residence card and not the EEA family permit required by the United Kingdom legislation', following guidance issued by the Secretary of State for the Home Department 'intended to encourage carriers not to transport passengers where they are third-country nationals who do not hold a residence card issued by the United Kingdom authorities or a valid travel document, such as the EEA family permit'.[307] The McCarthy family therefore brought an action against the Secretary of State, asserting that the UK had failed properly to transpose Article 5(2) of Directive 2004/38 into national law.

---

[302] ibid para 44.
[303] ibid para 45.
[304] In its original proposal, the Commission recommended that the residence card should be valid for at least five years from the date of issue even though a right of permanent residence would be acquired, under that proposal, after *four* years of continuous residence. In those circumstances, '[t]he fact that the initial card is valid for five years will make sure that the person concerned is not left without any documentation, should it take time to obtain the new card (to complete the administrative formalities)' (n 11, 13)—a period of overlap dissolved by the subsequent setting of a five-year period of residence for permanent residence rights (see further, Chapter 8).
[305] The extent of the time limits now specified in Article 11(2) emerged from both the European Parliament's Report (n 21) and the Council's Common Position (n 12). In its Communication on the Common Position, the Commission emphasised, however, that 'this provision does not call into question the right of residence, but simply requires those concerned to apply for a new residence card' (n 48, para 3.2.1.2).
[306] See generally, Section 7.
[307] Case C-202/13 *McCarthy II*, EU:C:2014:2450, para 23.

Before the referring court, the Secretary of State argued that there was 'a "systemic problem" of abuse of rights and fraud by third-country nationals', and more specifically, that '[t]he residence cards referred to in Article 10 of Directive 2004/38 are susceptible to forgery. In particular, there is no uniform format for those cards'.[308] On the basis of the evidence presented, the referring court concluded that 'residence cards are ripe for exploitation in the context of illegal immigration into the United Kingdom. There is a palpable risk that a significant proportion of those engaged in the "business of sham marriages" will use fake residence cards for the purpose of gaining illegal access to the United Kingdom. Thus, the refusal of that Member State to exempt holders of residence cards from the obligation to obtain an entry visa is sensible, necessary and objectively justified'.[309] Against that background, the first issue addressed by the Court of Justice was 'whether Article 35 of Directive 2004/38 and Article 1 of Protocol No 20 must be interpreted as permitting a Member State to require, *in pursuit of an objective of general prevention*, family members of a Union citizen who are not nationals of a Member State and who hold a valid residence card issued under Article 10 of Directive 2004/38 by the authorities of another Member State to be in possession, pursuant to national law, of an entry permit, such as the EEA family permit, in order to be able to enter its territory'.[310]

The Court established, first, that '[a]s regards ... any rights of family members of a Union citizen who are not nationals of a Member State, recital 5 in the preamble to Directive 2004/38 points out that the right of all Union citizens to move and reside freely within the territory of the Member States should, if it is to be exercised under objective conditions of dignity, be also granted to their family members, irrespective of nationality'.[311] It confirmed, second, that Mr McCarthy and Ms McCarthy Rodriguez were 'beneficiaries' of the Directive, within the meaning of Article 3(1), since the family resided in Spain and Ms McCarthy Rodriguez held 'a valid residence card issued by the Spanish authorities under Article 10 of Directive 2004/38 that permits her to reside lawfully in Spanish territory'.[312] Third, as regards the fact that Mr McCarthy was a British national, the Court stated:

> Article 5 of Directive 2004/38 refers to 'Member States' and does not draw a distinction on the basis of the Member State of entry, in particular in so far as it provides that possession

---

[308] ibid para 26.
[309] ibid para 27.
[310] ibid para 29 (emphasis added). Article 35 of the Directive, examined in Section 7, provides that 'Member States may adopt the necessary measures to refuse, terminate or withdraw any right conferred by this Directive in the case of abuse of rights or fraud, such as marriages of convenience. Any such measure shall be proportionate and subject to the procedural safeguards provided for in Articles 30 and 31'. Article 1 of the Protocol (No 20) on the application of certain aspects of Article 26 of the Treaty on the Functioning of the European Union to the United Kingdom and to Ireland provides: 'The United Kingdom shall be entitled, notwithstanding Articles 26 and 77 of the Treaty on the Functioning of the European Union, any other provision of that Treaty or of the Treaty on European Union, any measure adopted under those Treaties, or any international agreement concluded by the Union or by the Union and its Member States with one or more third States, to exercise at its frontiers with other Member States such controls on persons seeking to enter the United Kingdom as it may consider necessary for the purpose: (a) of verifying the right to enter the United Kingdom of citizens of Member States and of their dependants exercising rights conferred by Union law, as well as citizens of other States on whom such rights have been conferred by an agreement by which the United Kingdom is bound; and (b) of determining whether or not to grant other persons permission to enter the United Kingdom. Nothing in Articles 26 and 77 of the Treaty on the Functioning of the European Union or in any other provision of that Treaty or of the Treaty on European Union or in any measure adopted under them shall prejudice the right of the United Kingdom to adopt or exercise any such controls. References to the United Kingdom in this Article shall include territories for whose external relations the United Kingdom is responsible'.
[311] *McCarthy II*, para 33; referring to Case C-127/08 *Metock and Others*, EU:C:2008:449, para 83.
[312] *McCarthy II*, para 37.

of a valid residence card as referred to in Article 10 of the directive is to exempt family members of a Union citizen who are not nationals of a Member State from the requirement to obtain an entry visa. Thus, there is nothing at all in Article 5 indicating that the right of entry of family members of the Union citizen who are not nationals of a Member State is limited to Member States other than the Member State of origin of the Union citizen. Accordingly, it must be held that, pursuant to Article 5 of Directive 2004/38, a person who is a family member of a Union citizen and is in a situation such as that of Ms McCarthy Rodriguez is not subject to the requirement to obtain a visa or an equivalent requirement in order to be able to enter the territory of that Union citizen's Member State of origin.[313]

Rejecting the justification submitted by the Secretary of State, the Court found that 'the adoption of measures pursuing an objective of general prevention in respect of widespread cases of abuse of rights or fraud would mean, as in the case in point, that the mere fact of belonging to a particular group of persons would allow the Member States to refuse to recognise a right expressly conferred by Directive 2004/38 on family members of a Union citizen who are not nationals of a Member State, although they in fact fulfil the conditions laid down by that directive'.[314]

In essence, 'the Member States are, in principle, required to recognise a residence card issued under Article 10 of Directive 2004/38, for the purposes of entry into their territory without a visa'.[315] For Advocate General Szpunar, 'authorising a Member State not to take account of the residence card issued by another Member State would be contrary to the principle of mutual recognition'.[316] He also considered that accepting that the UK could 'implement measures of general application would be tantamount to allowing a Member State to circumvent the right of freedom of movement and would have the consequence that other Member States could also adopt such measures and unilaterally suspend the application of the directive'.[317]

6. Retaining the Right to Reside

As regards retaining a residence right in the host State, Directive 2004/38 addresses three situations: Article 14 provides generally for retention of the right to reside (Section 6.1), Article 7(3) deals with retention of worker status specifically (Section 6.2), and Articles 12 and 13 establish the circumstances in which family members retain residence rights in the event of the death or departure from the host State of the Union citizen from whom their rights derive as well as in situations of divorce, annulment of marriage, or termination of registered partnership (Section 6.3). Continuing to reside under the conditions set out in the Directive connects to being lawfully resident, which has significant consequences for

---

[313] ibid paras 41–42.
[314] ibid para 56; this dimension of the case is returned to in more detail in Section 7. The Court also ruled that 'Article 1 of Protocol No 20 authorises the United Kingdom to verify whether a person seeking to enter its territory in fact fulfils the conditions for entry, including those provided for by EU law. On the other hand, it does not permit the United Kingdom to determine the conditions for entry of persons who have a right of entry under EU law and, in particular, to impose upon them extra conditions for entry or conditions other than those provided for by EU law' (para 64).
[315] ibid para 62.
[316] AG Szpunar in *McCarthy II*, EU:C:2014:345, para 138 of the Opinion.
[317] ibid para 139 of the Opinion.

equal treatment with nationals of (Chapter 7), acquiring the right of permanent residence in (Chapter 8), and enhanced protection against expulsion from (Chapter 10) the host State.

6.1 Article 14: Retaining the Right to Reside

Article 14 of the Directive[318] addresses three situations. First, for the right to reside for up to three months, Article 14(1) confirms that 'Union citizens and their family members shall have the right of residence provided for in Article 6, as long as they do not become an unreasonable burden on the social assistance system of the host Member State'.[319] That statement also connects to Article 24(2) of the Directive, examined in Chapter 7, which provides that 'the host Member State shall not be obliged to confer entitlement to social assistance during the first three months of residence'.[320]

Second, for the right to reside for more three months, Article 14(2) establishes that 'Union citizens and their family members shall have the right of residence provided for in Articles 7, 12 and 13 as long as they meet the conditions set out therein'.[321] The conditions in Articles 12 and 13 concern family members and are considered in Section 6.3. Union citizens residing on the basis of Article 7 of the Directive must be workers or self-employed persons (Article 7(1)(a)), or retain that status in accordance with Article 7(3) (discussed in Section 6.2), or continue to meet the conditions on sufficient resources and comprehensive sickness cover (Article 7(1)(b)), or continue to be enrolled for a course of study if residing on the basis of Article 7(1)(c). Article 14(2) further provides that Member States may 'verify if these conditions are fulfilled' but only '[i]n specific cases where there is a reasonable doubt as to whether a Union citizen or his/her family members satisfies the conditions set out in Articles 7, 12 and 13'.[322] To underline that point, Article 14(2) establishes that '[t]his verification shall not be carried out systematically', suggesting a presumption that Union citizens *do* fulfil the conditions to reside in a host State and that this should be probed only where there is good reason to suggest otherwise.[323]

---

[318] Article 14 did not feature in the Commission's original proposal (n 11). The European Parliament proposed adding the following provision: '1. The right of residence shall be retained until such time as the persons entitled to that right satisfy the conditions set out in Articles 7, 12 and 13. 2. The procedures provided for by [Articles 30 and 31] shall apply by analogy to all expulsion decisions taken by the host Member State against Union citizens and their family members on grounds other than public policy, public security or public health. 3. The host Member State may not impose a ban on entry in the context of an expulsion decision to which paragraph 2 applies' (n 21, Amendment 54). That suggestion was accepted by the Commission in its amended proposal (n 45, 7), with paragraphs (2) and (3) adopted as Articles 15(1) and 15(3) of the Directive respectively.

[319] eg Case C-333/13 *Dano*, EU:C:2014:2358, para 70.

[320] eg Case C-299/14 *García-Nieto*, EU:C:2016:114, paras 42–43.

[321] eg *Dano*, para 71; referring to recital 10 of the Directive, which affirms that '[p]ersons exercising their right of residence should not … become an unreasonable burden on the social assistance system of the host Member State during an initial period of residence. Therefore, the right of residence for Union citizens and their family members for periods in excess of three months should be subject to conditions'.

[322] According to AG Cruz Villalón, 'the verification process in question, in so far as it may affect the freedom of movement and residence conferred by Union citizenship, must be interpreted in conformity with that fundamental right and be conducted as unintrusively as possible' (AG Cruz Villalón in Case C-308/14 *Commission v UK*, EU:C:2015:666, para 87 of the Opinion).

[323] On this point, see AG Cruz Villalón argued that 'European citizenship and, in particular, the affirmation of the principle that a Union citizen is entitled to establish his place of residence in any Member State on the conditions laid down by EU law, precludes national legislation from adopting any approach that might be tantamount to presuming that, after the first three months of residence and before he has acquired a permanent right of residence, such citizen is unlawfully present in that territory, so that it would systematically be for the person in question to prove that this is not the case. As a matter of principle, the opposite presumption should, in fact, be made' (ibid para 94 of the Opinion).

In *Commission v UK*, the Commission challenged a requirement in national rules that a claimant for child benefit and child tax credit (ie social benefits and not social assistance within meaning of Article 7(1)(b) of Directive 2004/38) must have a right to reside in the UK in order to be treated as 'habitually resident' there for the purposes of Regulation 883/2004. The substance of the case, including the interplay between Directive 2004/38 and Regulation 883/2004, is returned to in Chapter 7. However, the Court also reflected on the proportionality of processes for verification of the right to reside. It found that 'verification by the national authorities, in connection with the grant of the social benefits at issue, that the claimant is not unlawfully present in their territory must be regarded as a situation involving checks on the lawfulness of the residence of Union citizens, under the second subparagraph of Article 14(2) of Directive 2004/38, and must therefore comply with the requirements set out in the directive'.[324] It then confirmed that Article 14(2) excludes systematic verification of the conditions provided for in Articles 7, 12, and 13 of the Directive.

In this case, the UK clarified at the hearing that 'for each of the social benefits at issue, the claimant must provide, on the claim form, a set of data which reveal whether or not there is a right to reside in the United Kingdom, those data being checked subsequently by the authorities responsible for granting the benefit concerned' and that it was 'only in specific cases that claimants are required to prove that they in fact enjoy a right to reside lawfully in United Kingdom territory, as declared by them in the claim form'.[325] On that basis, the Court was satisfied that 'the checking of compliance with the conditions laid down by Directive 2004/38 for existence of a right of residence is not carried out systematically and consequently is not contrary to the requirements of Article 14(2) of the directive'.[326]

Third, Article 14(3) prohibits the issuing of an expulsion decision where this is 'the *automatic* consequence of a Union citizen's or his or her family member's recourse to the social assistance system of the host Member State'. In its Common Position, which added Article 14(3) (and also Article 14(4)) to the Directive, the Council stated that Article 14(3) 'integrat[es] in the text the case-law of the Court of Justice', referring to *Grzelczyk*.[327] However, while Article 14(3) is cast in protective language from the perspective of the Union citizen, the upshot is still that an expulsion measure *may* be issued for failure to comply with Articles 14(1) and 14(2), read in conjunction with Article 15(1) as discussed in Section 5. This is confirmed by considering the exceptions in Article 14(4):

> By way of derogation from paragraphs 1 and 2 and without prejudice to the provisions of Chapter VI, an expulsion measure may in no case be adopted against Union citizens or their family members if:
> (a) the Union citizens are workers or self-employed persons, or
> (b) the Union citizens entered the territory of the host Member State in order to seek employment. In this case, the Union citizens and their family members may not be expelled for as long as the Union citizens can provide evidence that there are continuing to seek employment and that they have a genuine chance of being engaged.

---

[324] Case C-308/14 *Commission v UK*, EU:C:2016:436, para 81.
[325] ibid para 83.
[326] ibid para 84. Unusually for proportionality analysis, however, the Court placed the burden of proof on the Commission and not the defendant State: this point is returned to in Chapter 7. See generally, C O'Brien, 'The ECJ sacrifices EU citizenship in vain: *Commission v. United Kingdom*' (2017) 54 Common Market Law Review 209, critiquing the ruling both substantively and in terms of the Court as a political actor (bearing in mind that the judgment was delivered just days before the UK referendum on withdrawal from the Union in June 2016).
[327] Common position (n 11) 31; referring to Case C-184/99 *Grzelczyk*, EU:C:2001:458, paras 41–43.

Article 14(4)(b) concerns protection against expulsion for jobseekers and creates by inference a right to reside that is both connected to and distinct from Article 6 of the Directive, as discussed in Section 4.4. The protection against expulsion for workers and self-employed persons in Article 14(4)(a) means, conversely, that Union citizens who no longer comply with the conditions in Articles 7(1)(b), 7(1)(c), 12, or 13 may be expelled from the host State on wider grounds: differently from workers or self-employed persons, no breach of public health, public policy, or public security is required to justify an expulsion decision in such cases. However, certain procedural safeguards are guaranteed by Article 15(1),[328] and only a measure based solely and automatically on recourse to the social assistance system of the host State would clearly contravene EU citizenship law.

Recital 16 of the Directive brings together and further clarifies the different stands of Article 14 and provides guidance for host States considering expulsion measures on the grounds of failure to comply with the conditions for retaining the right to reside:

> As long as the beneficiaries of the right of residence do not become an unreasonable burden on the social assistance system of the host Member State they should not be expelled. Therefore, an expulsion measure should not be the automatic consequence of recourse to the social assistance system. The host Member State should examine whether it is a case of temporary difficulties and take into account the duration of residence, the personal circumstances and the amount of aid granted in order to consider whether the beneficiary has become an unreasonable burden on its social assistance system and to proceed to his expulsion. In no case should an expulsion measure be adopted against workers, self-employed persons or job-seekers as defined by the Court of Justice save on grounds of public policy or public security.

Recital 16 was added by the Council, which considered that the text 'states the elements and criteria, which should be taken into consideration in order to establish if a person concerned has become an unreasonable burden and the host Member State can proceed to his expulsion'.[329] In its 2009 guidance on implementing the Directive, the Commission characterised the obligations placed on national authorities as a proportionality test, expanding on the 'three sets of criteria' in recital 16 to advise that 'Member States may develop for example a points-based scheme as an indicator' and suggesting a template for such cases:

(1) duration
    For how long is the benefit being granted?
    Outlook: is it likely that the EU citizen will get out of the safety net soon? How long has the residence lasted in the host Member State?
(2) personal situation
    What is the level of connection of the EU citizen and his/her family members with the society of the host Member State?
    Are there any considerations pertaining to age, state of health, family and economic situation that need to be taken into account?

---

[328] In *Dano*, AG Wathelet considered the fact that 'Article 14 of Directive 2004/38 strictly limits the possibilities of removing a citizen' who does not satisfy the conditions specified there as 'evidence of the fundamental nature of the freedom of movement and right of residence arising from it' (AG Wathelet in Case C-333/13 *Dano*, EU:C:2014:341, para 125 of the Opinion).

[329] Common Position (n 11) 30. The Council continued that the recital 'would provide useful indication for the criteria to follow in order to establish if a person has become an unreasonable burden'.

(3) amount
Total amount of aid granted?
Does the EU citizen have a history of relying heavily on social assistance?
Does the EU citizen have a history of contributing to the financing of social assistance in the host Member State?[330]

It should again be remembered that, according to Article 15(1) of the Directive, '[t]he procedures provided for by Articles 30 and 31 shall apply by analogy to all decisions restricting free movement of Union citizens and their family members on grounds *other than* public policy, public security or public health'.[331] In *Commission v UK*, Advocate General Cruz Villalón considered that:

> in such circumstances, the competent authorities may not confine themselves simply to refusing to grant the benefit claimed, but must, in addition, under Article 30 of Directive 2004/38, specifically when they find that there is no right of residence under Directive 2004/38, inform the persons concerned 'precisely and in full' and 'in such a way that they are able to comprehend its content and the implications for them' of the reasons on which that finding is based, also specifying the court or administrative authority with which the person concerned may lodge an appeal and the time-limit for that appeal. At the same time, the procedural safeguards under Article 31 of Directive 2004/38 are activated, enabling the person concerned to seek an administrative or judicial review of the lawfulness of the authorities' assessment.[332]

In reality, Member States rarely expel Union citizens who do not, or no longer, meet the criteria in Articles 14(1) and 14(2) of the Directive, leading to situations where these citizens can be passively tolerated but not actively supported in host States. In certain circumstances, the intensity of the required proportionality assessment is also reduced. These issues are examined in more detail in Chapter 7 in the discussion on lawful residence and equal treatment with host State nationals.

6.2 Article 7(3): Retaining the Status of Worker or Self-Employed Person

Complementing the right to reside in another Member State conferred on workers by Article 45(3)(c) TFEU, Article 45(3)(d) establishes the right 'to remain in the territory of a Member State after having been employed in that State, subject to conditions which shall be embodied in regulations to be drawn up by the Commission'. Two measures were previously relevant on that point: Directive 68/360 and Regulation 1251/70.[333] Article 7 was the key provision of Directive 68/360, entailing that:

---

[330] Communication on guidance for better transposition and application of Directive 2004/38/EC (n 50) section 2.3.1.

[331] See eg AG Wahl in Case C-140/12 *Brey*, EU:C:2013:337, para 93 of the Opinion. Additionally, as discussed in Section 5, Article 15(3) excludes imposition of a ban on entry 'in the context of an expulsion decision to which paragraph 1 applies'.

[332] AG Cruz Villalón in Case C-308/14 *Commission v UK*, EU:C:2015:666, para 95 of the Opinion. Articles 30 and 31 of the Directive are examined in Chapter 10.

[333] Council Directive 68/360/EEC of 15 October 1968 on the abolition of restrictions on movement and residence within the Community for workers of Member States and their families, 1968 OJ L257/13; Commission

1. A valid residence permit may not be withdrawn from a worker solely on the grounds that he is no longer in employment, either because he is temporarily incapable of work as a result of illness or accident, or because he is involuntarily unemployed, this being duly confirmed by the competent employment office.
2. When the residence permit is renewed for the first time, the period of residence may be restricted, but not to less than twelve months, where the worker has been involuntarily unemployed in the Member State for more than twelve consecutive months.

Regulation 1251/70 expanded on those principles, noting in its preamble that its purpose was 'to determine the conditions under which the right to remain arises'. The preamble also stated that 'account should be taken of the reasons which have led to the termination of employment in the territory of the Member State concerned and, in particular, of the difference between retirement, the normal and foreseeable end of working life, and incapacity to work which leads to a premature and unforeseeable termination of activity'. Additionally, it explained that 'special conditions must be laid down where termination of activity is the result of an accident at work or occupational disease, or where the worker's spouse is or was a national of the Member State concerned'.

The right to remain following employment can be construed in both human and instrumental terms, as an aspect of not dissuading a worker from moving to another State in the first place by managing the risks of uprooting a life.[334] The *Givane* case provides a good example of both perspectives. It concerned Article 3(2) of Regulation 1251/70, the first indent of which established that in circumstances where a worker died 'during his working life and before having acquired the right to remain in the territory of the State concerned, members of his family shall be entitled to remain there permanently' on condition that, *inter alia*, 'the worker, on the date of his decease, had resided continuously in the territory of that Member State for at least 2 years'. The question in *Givane* was whether that provision should be interpreted as meaning that the required period of two 'must immediately precede the worker's date of death or whether it is sufficient that he has completed such a period of residence at some time in the more remote past'.[335] The deceased worker's family members would be able to remain in the host State under the latter interpretation but not if the two-year residence period must 'immediately precede' the worker's death.[336]

Acknowledging that a literal interpretation of the provision did not resolve things, the Court examined Article 3(2) in relation to its 'spirit and purpose'[337] and ruled that the residence period must immediately precede the worker's death. Interestingly, the Court applied concepts from EU citizenship law in reaching that determination. For example, the language of the judgment mirrored Article 21 TFEU in stating that '[t]he exercise of the right of residence is ... subject to the limitations and conditions laid down by the EC Treaty and by the measures adopted for its application'—even though no such qualifier can be found in Article

---

Regulation 1251/70/EEC on the right of workers to remain in the territory of a Member State after having been employed in that State, 1970 OJ L142/24.

[334] Illustrating the instrumental dimension, see eg AG Darmon in Case C-171/91 *Tsiotras*, EU:C:1992:486, para 47 of the Opinion: 'I see in [the right to remain] an application of the principle of the effectiveness of the provisions of Article [45 TFEU]: a worker might be reluctant to accept work in another Member State unless he were certain of being able to remain there subsequently if he so desired. Such a right is merely the corollary of the right of residence attached to the occupational activity'.
[335] Case C-257/99 *Givane and Others*, EU:C:2003:8, para 17.
[336] The continuity of residence required by Article 3(2) of the Regulation was further explained in Article 4(1) as 'not be[ing] affected by temporary absences not exceeding a total of three months per year'.
[337] *Givane*, para 38.

45 TFEU.³³⁸ Also reflecting ideas applied in citizenship case law, the Court considered that the two-year residence period was 'intended to establish a significant connection between, on the one hand, that Member State, and on the other hand, that worker and his family, and to ensure a certain level of their integration in the society of that State'.³³⁹ The Court also noted that, in this case, the deceased worker's family members had not resided with him during his first period of employment in the host State, when he resided there for almost three years.³⁴⁰

The provisions of Directive 2004/38 that now apply to family members in situations of the death of the Union citizen are returned to in Section 6.3. For present purposes, it is the contrasting position taken by Advocate General Alber in *Givane* that should be noted in light of this remark that 'the opposing viewpoints of the parties to the proceedings are *both* based on a literal, systematic and teleological interpretation' of Regulation 1251/70.³⁴¹ Developing an outcome in favour of the claimants, he argued that '[t]he subsequent arrival of family members generally entails considerable changes for that family, such as, for example, leaving their homeland and social environment, giving up the home to which they have become accustomed, a possible transfer of school-age children to another school, establishment of a reasonable standard of accommodation and living in the host State'.³⁴² He therefore considered that denial of a right of residence in such circumstances, 'particularly where the worker dies since this is most often an unforeseeable stroke of fate for the family',³⁴³ would generate a period of legal uncertainty—the principle used for precisely the opposite conclusion by the Court, which favoured the clarity provided by adhering to the logic of the rule provided for in the Regulation.³⁴⁴

Regulation 1251/70 was not repealed by Directive 2004/38 but separately by Commission Regulation 635/2006/EC, the preamble of which acknowledged that Directive 2004/38 had 'consolidated in a single text the legislation on the free movement of citizens of the Union' and that Article 17 of the Directive 'includes the main elements of Commission Regulation (EEC) No 1251/70 ... and amends them by granting beneficiaries of the right to remain a more privileged status, namely that of the right of permanent residence'. This reference to permanent residence touches on what had always been the more complicated aspect of the right to remain—not necessarily residence rights per se, but the extent to which equal treatment continued to apply in the host State after employment there had ceased.³⁴⁵ Article 7 of Regulation 1251/70 provided that '[t]he right to equality of treatment, established by [Regulation 1612/68], shall apply also to persons coming under the provisions of this Regulation'. However, the right was limited in scope: the person was 'protected by Article [45 TFEU] and Regulation No 1612/68 against any discrimination affecting rights acquired

---

³³⁸ ibid para 46.
³³⁹ ibid para 46. The Court therefore concluded that '[t]he existence of a significant connection between the host Member State and the worker concerned could not be ensured if the right of residence in the territory of a Member State provided for by the first indent of Article 3(2) of Regulation No 1251/70 were to be acquired as soon as a worker had resided for at least two years in that State at some stage of his life, even in the distant past' (para 47).
³⁴⁰ ibid para 49.
³⁴¹ AG Alber in *Givane*, EU:C:2002:297, para 31 of the Opinion (emphasis added).
³⁴² ibid para 64 of the Opinion.
³⁴³ ibid para 64 of the Opinion.
³⁴⁴ *Givane*, para 48.
³⁴⁵ As observed by the Court in *Martínez Sala*, '[o]nce the employment relationship has ended, the person concerned as a rule loses his status of worker, although that status may produce certain effects after the relationship has ended' (Case C-85/96 *Martínez Sala*, EU:C:1998:217, para 32). A classic pre-citizenship example concerns whether continuing entitlement to study finance was retained eg Case 39/86 *Lair*, EU:C:1988:322, para 37; and Case 197/86 *Brown*, EU:C:1988:323, para 27.

during the former employment relationship but since he is not currently engaged in an employment relationship, cannot thereby claim to acquire new rights having no links with his former occupation'.[346]

Did Directive 2004/38 alter that position? Article 7(3) does not confer a right to remain per se but establishes the conditions under which a worker or self-employed person retains *that status* for the purposes of continuing to reside in the host State on the basis of Article 7(1)(a). In the Commission's original proposal—and perhaps indicative of the fact that Regulation 1251/70 was not listed as one of the measures to be repealed and replaced—the conditions for retaining the right to reside were grouped with the administrative formalities on residence in a host State for longer than (as proposed at that time) six months.[347] The Commission observed that its proposed provisions 'broadly take over certain provisions of Directive 68/360, with clarifications, and incorporate Court of Justice case-law regarding the retention of worker status where the worker is no longer engaged in any employed *or self-employed* activity'.[348] As adopted, Article 7(3) of the Directive now provides:

> For the purposes of paragraph 1(a), a Union citizen who is no longer a worker or self-employed person shall retain the status of worker or self-employed person in the following circumstances:
> (a) he/she is temporarily unable to work as the result of an illness or accident;[349]
> (b) he/she is in duly recorded involuntary unemployment after having been employed for more than one year and has registered as a job-seeker with the relevant employment office;
> (c) he/she is in duly recorded involuntary unemployment after completing a fixed-term employment contract of less than a year or after having become involuntarily unemployed during the first twelve months and has registered as a job-seeker with the relevant employment office. In this case, the status of worker shall be retained for no less than six months;
> (d) he/she embarks on vocational training. Unless he/she is involuntarily unemployed, the retention of the status of worker shall require the training to be related to the previous employment.

---

[346] Case C-43/99 *Leclere and Deaconescu*, EU:C:2001:303, para 59.

[347] It was the European Parliament that proposed placing these conditions within Article 7 of the Directive, reasoning that 'conditions relating to worker status should not come under administrative formalities' (European Parliament Report (n 21) Amendment 30). This was accepted by the Commission in its amended proposal (n 45, 6).

[348] Original proposal (n 11) 13 (emphasis added). Draft Article 8(7) of the proposed directive provided: '[t]he certificate of registration may not be refused to a worker who is no longer engaged in an employed or self-employed activity, in the following circumstances: (a) he/she is temporarily unable to work as the result of an illness or accident; (b) he/she is in duly recorded involuntary unemployment and has registered as a jobseeker with the relevant employment office; (c) he/she is in involuntary unemployment after completing a fixed-term employment contract of less than a year and have registered as a jobseeker with the relevant employment office. In such cases, he/she shall retain worker status for a period which may not be less than six months; were the person concerned has acquired entitlement to unemployment benefits, worker status shall be retained for as long as such entitlement runs; (d) he/she embarks on vocational training. Unless the person concerned is involuntarily unemployed, retaining worker status shall require the training to be related to their previous occupation'.

[349] In *Prefeta*, Advocate General Wathelet observed that 'Article 7(3)(a) of Directive 2004/38 does not impose any specific requirement as to the duration of the period of employment or self-employment which EU citizens must complete in order to retain the status of worker. It is sufficient that citizens pursue activities which are real and genuine, to the exclusion of activities on such a small scale as to be regarded as purely marginal and ancillary' (AG Wathelet in Case C-618/16 *Prefeta*, EU:C:2018:125, para 64 of the Opinion).

The reference to both employed and self-employed persons reflects the principle that 'Articles [45 and 49 TFEU] afford the same legal protection and that therefore the classification of an economic activity is without significance'.[350] As a result, 'no distinction may be drawn ... according to the basis on which the Union citizen pursued the economic activity in question (as an employed person or a self-employed person), since "the provisions of the [FEU] Treaty on freedom of movement for persons are intended to facilitate the pursuit by [Union citizens] of occupational activities of all kinds throughout the [European Union], and preclude measures which might place [EU] nationals at a disadvantage when they wish to pursue an economic activity in the territory of another Member State"'.[351]

However, the disconnect between the opening lines of Article 7(3)—which are both worker and self-employed person friendly—and the conditions then specified—which are not—is notable. Thus, the extent to which self-employed persons fell within the scope of all parts of Article 7(3)—and more specifically, Article 7(3)(b) on involuntary unemployment—was unclear. In *Gusa*, the applicant was a Romanian national who was supported by his adult children in Ireland for the first year of his own residence there. He then worked as a self-employed plasterer for four years, after which he registered as a jobseeker with the relevant employment office as he could not find further work. His application for jobseeker's allowance was refused on the grounds that he had not demonstrated a right to reside in Ireland, with the referring court noting that 'Mr Gusa does not contend that he has sufficient resources to support himself or that he has comprehensive sickness insurance cover and, therefore, does not claim to have a right to reside in Ireland pursuant to Article 7(1)(b) of Directive 2004/38'.[352] Addressing the circumstances under which retaining the status of worker or self-employed person under Article 7(3) sustained a right of residence under Article 7(1)(a), the referring court had suggested that 'it could be inferred from the wording of [Article 7(3)(b)] that that provision applies only to persons who are in duly recorded involuntary unemployment after having worked as employed persons for more than one year, and excludes those who, like Mr Gusa, are in an equivalent position after having worked as self-employed persons for that period'.[353]

The Court of Justice disagreed, ruling that 'the expression "involuntary unemployment" may, depending on the context in which it is used, refer to a situation of inactivity due to the involuntary loss of employment following, for example, a dismissal, as well as, more broadly, to a situation in which the occupational activity, whether on an employed or self-employed basis, has ceased due to an absence of work for reasons beyond the control of the person concerned, such as an economic recession'.[354] The Court compared different language versions of the Directive and observed that the phrase 'after having been employed' in Article 7(3)(b) in the English and French ('*après avoir été employé*') texts was 'formulated in more neutral terms'[355] in other language versions (noting, for example, the reference to pursuing an 'occupational activity' in the Greek-language version and pursuit of 'activity' in the Italian-language version).

---

[350] Case C-363/89 *Roux*, EU:C:1991:41, para 23.
[351] AG Wathelet in Case C-442/16 *Gusa*, EU:C:2017:60, para 73 of the Opinion; referring to Case C-104/06 *Commission v Sweden*, EU:C:2007:40, para 17.
[352] Case C-442/16 *Gusa*, EU:C:2017:1004, para 21. The Court did not address whether Mr Gusa had a right of permanent residence; see further, Chapter 8.
[353] ibid para 29.
[354] ibid para 31.
[355] ibid para 33, referring to paras 48–49 of the Opinion of AG Wathelet (EU:C:2017:607).

Since the wording of the provision was not conclusive, the Court proceeded to examine the general scheme of the Directive, emphasising that while Article 7(1) 'distinguishes, in particular, the situation of economically active citizens from that of inactive citizens and students', it does not 'draw a distinction, within the first category, between citizens working as employed persons and those working as self-employed persons in the host Member State'.[356] The Court established that the objectives of the Directive further supported the finding that Article 7(3)(b) must apply to both employed and self-employed persons, pointing, first, to the objectives of strengthening 'the fundamental and individual right of all Union citizens to move and reside freely' and remedying 'the sector-by-sector, piecemeal approach which characterised the instruments of EU law which preceded that directive and which dealt separately, in particular, with workers and self-employed persons, by providing a single legislative act codifying and revising those instruments'.[357] It observed, second, that the objective of Article 7(3)(b) specifically is 'to safeguard, by the retention of the status of worker, the right of residence of persons who have ceased their occupational activity because of an absence of work due to circumstances beyond their control'.[358]

The Court aligned the 'vulnerable position' of workers who involuntarily lose their jobs and self-employed persons who find themselves 'obliged to stop working', underlining the fact that giving effect to 'a difference in treatment' in such circumstances 'would be particularly unjustified in so far as it would lead to a person who has been self-employed for more than one year in the host Member State, and who has contributed to that Member State's social security and tax system by paying taxes, rates and other charges on his income, being treated in the same way as a first-time jobseeker in that Member State who has never carried on an economic activity in that State and has never contributed to that system'.[359] That point emphasises once again the privileged position of Union citizens who are—or have been—economically active in the host State compared to first-time jobseekers. Subsequently, in *Tarola*, the alignment of workers and self-employed persons applied in *Gusa* to Article 7(3)(b) specifically was extended across Article 7(3) more generally.[360]

The European Parliament's Committee on Women's Rights and Equal Opportunities had proposed adding one further category to the Commission's list of conditions for retaining status in Article 7(3): situations where a Union citizen 'is temporarily unable to work as the result of an illness, *pregnancy*, or accident'.[361] That suggestion was overlooked in the final phase of the Directive's drafting process, and the status of a Member State national who ceased work in a host State because of pregnancy had to be resolved much later by the Court of Justice instead. In *Förster*, referring to *Givane*, the Court indicated that '[t]he conditions of entitlement to the worker's right to remain in the host Member State are set out *exhaustively* in Article 2 of Regulation No 1251/70'.[362] If the same approach was applied to retaining worker status under Article 7(3) of Directive 2004/38, then ceasing work because of pregnancy could not constitute a situation in which worker/self-employed status, and the rights that flow from it under Article 7(1)(a), could be retained.

---

[356] Case C-442/16 *Gusa*, EU:C:2017:1004, para 36.
[357] ibid para 40; referring to recitals 3 and 4 of the Directive. See further, AG Wathelet, paras 51–59 of the Opinion.
[358] Case C-442/16 *Gusa*, EU:C:2017:1004, para 42.
[359] ibid paras 43 and 44.
[360] Case C-483/17 *Tarola*, EU:C:2019:309, esp paras 45–46.
[361] Opinion of the Committee on Women's Rights and Equal Opportunities attached to the European Parliament Report (n 21), Amendment 8 (emphasis added).
[362] Case C-158/07 *Förster*, EU:C:2008:630, para 27 (emphasis added); referring to Case C-257/99 *Givane and Others*, EU:C:2003:8, para 29.

The *Saint Prix* case concerned a claim for income support for the three-month period in which a French national residing in the UK was not working following the birth of her child. The essence of the questions referred was whether 'a woman who gives up work, or seeking work, because of the physical constraints of the late stages of pregnancy and the aftermath of childbirth, retains the status of "worker" within the meaning of [Article 45 TFEU and Article 7 of Directive 2004/38]'.[363] The Court ruled out the applicability of Article 7(3)(a) of the Directive on the grounds that it had 'consistently held that pregnancy must be clearly distinguished from illness, in that pregnancy is not in any way comparable with a pathological condition'.[364] However, 'it does not follow from either Article 7 of Directive 2004/38, considered as a whole, or from the other provisions of that directive, that, in such circumstances, a citizen of the Union who does not fulfil the conditions laid down in that article is, therefore, systematically deprived of the status of "worker", within the meaning of Article 45 TFEU'.[365] Instead, the Court ruled that '[t]he codification, sought by the directive, of the instruments of EU law existing prior to that directive, which expressly seeks to facilitate the exercise of the rights of Union citizens to move and reside freely within the territory of the Member States, cannot, by itself, limit the scope of the concept of worker within the meaning of the FEU Treaty'.[366]

Drawing from the example of jobseekers, considered in Section 4.4, the Court pointed out that 'classification as a worker under Article 45 TFEU, and the rights deriving from such status, do not necessarily depend on the actual or continuing existence of an employment relationship'.[367] Crucially, in that light, 'it cannot be argued ... that Article 7(3) of Directive 2004/38 lists *exhaustively* the circumstances in which a migrant worker who is no longer in an employment relationship may nevertheless continue to benefit from that status'.[368] The Court then drew a somewhat unexpected analogy with case law on imprisoned Member State nationals to find that the fact that the applicant 'was not actually available on the employment market of the host Member State for a few months does not mean that she has

---

[363] Case C-507/12 *Saint Prix*, EU:C:2014:2007, para 24.
[364] ibid para 29; referring to Case C-32/93 *Webb*, EU:C:1994:300, para 25. This finding contrasts with the analysis of AG Wahl, who argued that '[i]n order to avoid construing Article 45 TFEU in such a way as to create, by judicial construction, a new category of worker, I consider it imperative that the treatment of a pregnant woman in Ms Saint Prix's position also be tied to Article 7 of the Citizenship Directive ... Article 7(3)(a) of that directive is of particular significance here, given that it specifically refers to temporary inability to work on grounds of illness or accident' (AG Wahl in *Saint Prix*, EU:C:2013:841, para 31 of the Opinion). He explained his reasoning as follows: '[a]dmittedly, the line of authority devolving from *Webb* makes it clear that pregnancy is not to be treated as an illness. However, this distinction was drawn in the context of protecting pregnant women against unlawful dismissal. Indeed, the Court has consistently held – undoubtedly in order to afford special protection to pregnant women and to further substantive equality – that, by contrast with illness, pregnancy alone cannot justify dismissal (or other types of differential treatment in the workplace). In the present case, by contrast, we are dealing with a situation in which not equating pregnancy with illness would result in EU law providing protection for illness, but not for pregnancy. That would clearly amount to a breach of the principle of non-discrimination on grounds of sex' (paras 32–33 of the Opinion).
[365] *Saint Prix*, para 31.
[366] ibid para 32.
[367] ibid para 37.
[368] ibid para 38 (emphasis added). Confirmation of the significance of rights conferred directly by the Treaties can also be seen in Article 52(2) CFR, which provides that '[r]ights recognised by this Charter for which provision is made in the Treaties shall be exercised under the conditions and within the limits *defined by those Treaties*'. Note also Spaventa's observation that '[o]n the one hand, the Court seems ready to accept the consequences of Directive 2004/38: an updated instrument incorporating all of the case law of the Court including the proportionality principle, moves the "battleground" of citizenship to the interpretation of these provisions ... On the other hand ... the Court rejects the possibility that Directive 2004/38 could act as a straightjacket for its interpretation of the Treaty provisions: much as it was the case before the Directive was adopted, the purposive interpretation of the Treaty rights is unaffected by codification' (E Spaventa, 'Earned citizenship – understanding Union citizenship through its scope' in Kochenov (ed) (n 41) 204 at 208).

ceased to belong to that market during that period, provided she returns to work or finds another job within a reasonable period after confinement'.[369] Providing security of residence for workers in these circumstances ensured that Union citizens would not be deterred from exercising free movement in the first place.[370] The Court also pointed to the 'special protection for women in connection with maternity' in Article 16(3) of the Directive on permanent residence rights:[371] the conditions for retaining worker status in Article 7(3) should be considered alongside the derogations from Article 16 of the Directive (outlined in Article 17), which have the effect of 'reducing the general period of five years of continuous legal residence in the host Member State for citizens of the Union and members of their family as a condition for acquiring a right of permanent residence in that State'.[372]

The implications of *Saint Prix* for equal treatment claims specifically—beyond retaining residence rights in a host State per se—are examined in Chapter 7. However, it can be noted here that the *Saint Prix* principles were extended in *Dakneviciute* to self-employed persons who cease their activity for reasons of pregnancy and childbirth, with the Court confirming that 'Articles 45 and 49 TFEU afford *the same legal protection*, the classification of the economic activity thus being without significance'.[373] Also in line with the reasoning in *Saint Prix*, the Court considered that being forced to cease self-employed activity for reasons of childbirth might deter the exercise of free movement in the first place, justifying retention of status and thus the protection of Article 49 TFEU.[374]

In *Prefeta*, the principles established in *Saint Prix* for pregnancy and childbirth specifically were expressed more generally, with the Court ruling that 'the possibility for an EU citizen who has temporarily ceased to pursue an activity as an employed or self-employed person of retaining his status of worker on the basis of Article 7(3) of Directive 2004/38, as well as the corresponding right of residence under Article 7(1) of the directive, is based on the assumption that the citizen is available and able to re-enter the labour market of the host Member State within a reasonable period'.[375] It then addressed the relationship between Article 7(3) of the Directive and Regulation 492/2011:

> Article 7(3)(a) of Directive 2004/38 concerns the situation of an EU citizen who is temporarily unable to work as the result of an illness or accident, which implies that that citizen

---

[369] *Saint Prix*, para 41: 'the fact that the person concerned was not available on the employment market during such imprisonment does not mean, as a general rule, that he did not continue to be duly registered as belonging to the labour force of the host Member State during that period, provided that he actually finds another job within a reasonable time after his release' (referring to Joined Cases C-482/01 and C-493/01 *Orfanopoulos and Oliveri*, EU:C:2004:262, para 50). To determine 'whether the period that has elapsed between childbirth and starting work again may be regarded as reasonable', the national court must consider the 'applicable national rules on the duration of maternity leave' in accordance with Article 8 of Council Directive 92/85/EEC on the introduction of measures to encourage improvements in the safety and health at work of pregnant workers and workers who have recently given birth or are breastfeeding (1992 OJ L348/1), and, more generally, 'should take account of all the specific circumstances of the case' (*Saint Prix*, para 42). In *Dias*, the Portuguese Government had submitted, with prescient resonance for approach taken in *Saint Prix*, that 'Ms Dias did not lose her status as worker ... She was admittedly voluntarily unemployed. Since however she was not working so that she could look after her six-month old child, she remained integrated in the labour market in the United Kingdom. The national residence permit merely confirmed the right resulting from her status as worker' (AG Trstenjak in Case C-325/09 *Dias*, EU:C:2011:86, para 40 of the Opinion).

[370] *Saint Prix*, para 44.

[371] ibid para 45. On the right of permanent residence, see Chapter 8.

[372] AG Campos Sánchez-Bordona in Case C-300/15 *Kohll and Kohll-Schlesser*, EU:C:2016:86, para 39 of the Opinion. See further, Chapter 8.

[373] Case C-544/18 *Dakneviciute*, EU:C:2019:761, para 31 (emphasis added); confirming *Roux*, para 23.

[374] *Dakneviciute*, paras 32–33.

[375] Case C-618/16 *Prefeta*, EU:C:2018:719, para 37.

will be able to pursue an activity as an employed or self-employed person again once that temporary inability to work has come to an end. Moreover, Article 7(3)(b) and (c) of that directive requires economically inactive EU citizens to register as jobseekers with the relevant employment office and Article 7(3)(d) of the directive requires such persons, under specific conditions, to embark on vocational training. 39 Article 7(3) of Directive 2004/38 therefore covers situations in which the EU citizen's re- entry on the labour market of the host Member State is foreseeable within a reasonable period. Consequently, the application of that provision may not be dissociated from that of the provisions of Regulation No 492/2011 governing the eligibility for employment of a Member State national in another Member State, that is, Articles 1 to 6 of that regulation.[376]

Nevertheless, and notwithstanding the qualified language in *Prefeta*, the Court confirmed in *Tarola* (just one year later) that worker status is indeed retained 'indefinitely' for situations within the scope of Articles 7(3)(a), 7(3)(b), and 7(3)(d) of the Directive.[377] The implications for equal treatment, including the less potent role of Article 45 TFEU for jobseekers, are assessed in Chapter 7.

6.3 Articles 12 and 13: Family Members

Enhanced protection for the family members of Union citizens[378]—and especially for family members who are not themselves Member State nationals—was one of the milestone achievements of Directive 2004/38. While the fundamental principle that rights are derived from a Union citizen continues to shape how family members *acquire* their rights,[379] the statement in Articles 12(2) and 13(2) that family members can *retain* their rights of residence 'exclusively on a personal basis' undercuts the significance of that conditionality for the particular circumstances and under the specified conditions detailed in both provisions, which address the death of the Union citizen or their departure from the host State (Article 12, Section 6.3.1), or situations of divorce, annulment of marriage, or termination of registered partnership (Article 13, Section 6.3.2). The interpretation of these provisions in the case law to date is presented in Section 6.3.3.

In case law that preceded the adoption of the Directive, as well as in situations where rights in question flow from other measures of EU law,[380] the residence rights of third-country national family members are essentially contingent upon being the primary carer of children who remained in the host State either in the absence of the Union citizen[381] or in situations of divorce.[382] Articles 12 and 13 of Directive 2004/38 extend more general protection, of much wider scope, in these situations, while also establishing the conditions that must be fulfilled

---

[376] ibid paras 38–39. The Court also confirmed that Member States may derogate from the requirements of Article 7(3) of the Directive In the context of specific restrictions placed on accession workers that are permitted by the relevant Act of Accession.
[377] Case C-483/17 *Tarola*, EU:C:2019:309, para 44.
[378] See further, Articles 13(2)–(4) WA.
[379] eg AG Trstenjak in Case C-40/11 *Iida*, EU:C:2012:296, para 47 of the Opinion: 'the right of residence of the third-country national depends on the right of residence of the Union citizen in so far as he must have initially accompanied the Union citizen to a host Member State, and thus to a State other than the Union citizen's Member State of origin'.
[380] In particular, the rights conferred on the children of migrant workers by Article 10 of Regulation 492/2011; see further, Chapter 9.
[381] eg Case C-310/08 *Ibrahim*, EU:C:2010:89; see further, Chapter 9.
[382] eg Case C-413/99 *Baumbast and R*, EU:C:2002:493; see further, Chapter 4.

for the rights to apply. The provisions provide, in effect, a critical bridge to the achievement of permanent residence rights on a personal basis. In its original proposal for the Directive, the Commission expressed that point in terms of 'the need to introduce measures providing equitable solutions that respect family life and human dignity, coupled with certain conditions in order to avoid abuses of the system'.[383] That balance is also reflected in recital 15 of the adopted Directive, which confirms that '[f]amily members should be legally safeguarded in the event of the death of the Union citizen, divorce, annulment of marriage or termination of a registered partnership'; in such circumstances, [w]ith due regard for family life and human dignity, and in certain conditions to guard against abuse, measures should therefore be taken to ensure that … family members already residing within the territory of the host Member State retain their right of residence exclusively on a personal basis'.

6.3.1 Article 12: death or departure of the Union citizen

Article 12 of the Directive provides:

Article 12

Retention of the right of residence by family members in the event of death or departure of the Union citizen

1. Without prejudice to the second subparagraph, the Union citizen's death or departure from the host Member State shall not affect the right of residence of his/her family members who are nationals of a Member State.

   Before acquiring the right of permanent residence, the persons concerned must meet the conditions laid down in points (a), (b), (c) or (d) of Article 7(1).

2. Without prejudice to the second subparagraph, the Union citizen's death shall not entail loss of the right of residence of his/her family members who are not nationals of a Member State and who have been residing in the host Member State as family members for at least one year before the Union citizen's death.

   Before acquiring the right of permanent residence,[384] the right of residence of the persons concerned shall remain subject to the requirement that they are able to show that they are workers or self-employed persons or that they have sufficient resources for themselves and their family members not to become a burden on the social assistance system of the host Member State during their period of residence and have comprehensive sickness insurance cover in the host Member State, or that they are members of the family, already constituted in the host Member State, of a person satisfying these requirements. 'Sufficient resources' shall be as defined in Article 8(4).

   Such family members shall retain their right of residence exclusively on a personal basis.

3. The Union citizen's departure from the host Member State or his/her death shall not entail loss of the right of residence of his/her children or of the parent who has actual custody of the children, irrespective of nationality, if the children reside in the host Member State and are enrolled at an educational establishment, for the purpose of studying there, until the completion of their studies.

---

[383] Original proposal (n 11) para 2.4.
[384] Linked to Article 18 of the Directive; see further, Chapter 8.

This provision establishes a material distinction between family members who are themselves Union citizens—who do not lose their right to reside in the host State in situations of the Union citizen's death *or departure* therefrom (Article 12(1))—and family members who are not Member State nationals—who do not lose that right if the Union citizen dies on the condition that they have either been 'residing as family members for at least one year' beforehand (Article 12(2)),[385] or if they are the Union citizen's children and 'are enrolled at an educational establishment, for the purpose of studying there, until the completion of their studies' (Article 12(3)). In situations where the Union citizen has left the host State, Article 12(3) establishes that their children who are not Member State nationals may continue to reside there if they are 'enrolled at an educational establishment, for the purpose of studying there, until the completion of their studies'. Article 12(3) also establishes a right of residence for the 'parent who has actual custody of the children, irrespective of nationality' in that situation.

For family members who are Union citizens, Article 12(1) specifies compliance with the conditions laid down in Article 7(1)(a), (b), or (c) so that the right to reside is retained. For family members who are not Union citizens and in situations where the Union citizen has died, Article 12(2) imposes, in effect, the same conditions so that they may retain a right to reside 'exclusively on a personal basis'. Thus, they must demonstrate that 'they are workers or self-employed persons or that they have sufficient resources for themselves and their family members not to become a burden on the social assistance system of the host Member State during their period of residence and have comprehensive sickness insurance cover in the host Member State, or that they are members of the family, already constituted in the host Member State, of a person satisfying these requirements'. Compliance with these conditions bridges to the right of permanent residence.[386] Article 12(2) also refers to Article 8(4) as regards the definition of 'sufficient resources', ensuring that national authorities apply the same principles to Union citizens and to third-country national family members invoking residence rights under Article 12(2).[387]

The situation is more precarious for third-country national family members where the Union citizen dies before the family has resided in the host State for at least one year beforehand or where the Union citizen leaves the host State. In such situations, Article 12(3) essentially adopts the principles developed in case law on Article 10 of Regulation 492/2011.[388] However, while the reference to the 'parent who has actual custody of the children' is clearer

---

[385] This condition was not included in the Commission's original proposal (n 11). It was introduced by the Council in the final stages of the Directive's drafting (Common Position (n 11) 31). However, that amendment also introduced, for the first time, the statement that '[s]uch family members shall retain their right of residence exclusively on a personal basis'. The Council observed that '[t]hese conditions reflect the justified concerns of delegations to prevent abuse, but in the same time establish a proportionate link with the host Member State'.

[386] Conversely, where residence rights in the host State derive from other measures of EU law, non-compliance with the conditions for lawful residence in Article 7(1) of the Directive rules out a right of permanent residence (see eg Case C-529/11 *Alarape and Tijani*, EU:C:2013:290, para 40). See further, Chapter 8.

[387] It was noted in Section 5.1.3 that the Commission had originally proposed that Union citizens would need only to declare that they had sufficient resources in order to enjoy residence rights under Article 7(1)(b) of the Directive; in contrast with that position, the Commission indicated that, for family members who are not nationals of a Member State, '[u]nlike the case of Union citizens, a simple *bona fide* declaration would not be sufficient: the persons concerned will have to prove that they satisfy the conditions' (n 11, 14). The European Parliament had also proposed adding a statement that '[i]n the event of serious sickness, accident or other humanitarian reasons coming into play, the Member States shall not apply these criteria' (European Parliament Report (n 21) Amendment 45).

[388] See eg Case C-310/08 *Ibrahim*, EU:C:2010:89. See further, Chapter 9.

than the concept of 'primary carer' applied in that case law,[389] the two terms could lead to different answers with respect to who is and who is not covered by EU law. Additionally, while Article 12(3) extends protection beyond work/Regulation 492/2011, making the purpose of the Union citizen's residence in the host State less relevant, there is no explicit reference to acquiring a right of permanent residence in the host State for either the children or their parents. There is also no specific protection for family members in 'particularly difficult situations', as the Court observed in *NA*:

> Article 12 of Directive 2004/38 ... provides that the right of residence of his family members who do not have the nationality of a Member State is to be retained only in the event of the death of the Union citizen, and not in the event of his or her departure from the host Member State'. [I]t is therefore clear that, when that directive was adopted, the EU legislature declined to make provision, in the event of the departure from the host Member State of the Union citizen, for specific safeguards that would be available, on account of, *inter alia*, particularly difficult situations, to his family members who do not have the nationality of a Member State, that would be comparable to those provided for in Article 13(2)(c) of Directive 2004/38.[390]

Ultimately, Article 12(3) is rooted in the integration of children in a host State's education system, but does not take account of the broader societal integration that deepens in consequence.[391] When it is remembered that 'educational establishment' can include post-secondary institutions,[392] there is a striking gap between the potential duration of residence in the host State and the absence of protection, under EU law, for rights beyond the completion of studies. There is also less residence security in circumstances where a Union citizen leaves the host State and only subsequently institutes divorce proceedings: this was the situation in *Singh II*, returned to in Section 6.3.3.

6.3.2 Article 13: divorce, annulment of marriage, or termination of registered partnership

Article 13 of the Directive provides:

Article 13

Retention of the right of residence by family members in the event of divorce, annulment of marriage or termination of registered partnership

1. Without prejudice to the second subparagraph, divorce, annulment of the Union citizen's marriage or termination of his/her registered partnership, as referred to in

---

[389] No reference to either category was included in the Commission's original proposal (n 12). However, the Economic and Social Committee pointed to this gap, referring to Case C-413/99 *Baumbast and R*, EU:C:2002:493 (n 156, para 4.2), as accepted by the Commission in its revised proposal (n 45, 7).
[390] Case C-115/15 *NA*, EU:C:2016:487, paras 43–44.
[391] In the Commission's original proposal for the Directive, it commented that the children of a Union citizen in this situation 'might have difficulty integrating into a new education system for reasons such as, amongst others, language and culture' (n 11, 14).
[392] eg Case C-529/11 *Alarape and Tijani*, EU:C:2013:290; see further, Chapter 8.

point 2(b) of Article 2 shall not affect the right of residence of his/her family members who are nationals of a Member State.

Before acquiring the right of permanent residence, the persons concerned must meet the conditions laid down in points (a), (b), (c) or (d) of Article 7(1).

2. Without prejudice to the second subparagraph, divorce, annulment of marriage or termination of the registered partnership referred to in point 2(b) of Article 2 shall not entail loss of the right of residence of a Union citizen's family members who are not nationals of a Member State where:

   (a) prior to initiation of the divorce or annulment proceedings or termination of the registered partnership referred to in point 2(b) of Article 2, the marriage or registered partnership has lasted at least three years,[393] including one year in the host Member State; or

   (b) by agreement between the spouses or the partners referred to in point 2(b) of Article 2 or by court order, the spouse or partner who is not a national of a Member State has custody of the Union citizen's children; or

   (c) this is warranted by particularly difficult circumstances, such as having been a victim of domestic violence while the marriage or registered partnership was subsisting; or

   (d) by agreement between the spouses or partners referred to in point 2(b) of Article 2 or by court order, the spouse or partner who is not a national of a Member State has the right of access to a minor child, provided that the court has ruled that such access must be in the host Member State, and for as long as is required.

Before acquiring the right of permanent residence,[394] the right of residence of the persons concerned shall remain subject to the requirement that they are able to show that they are workers or self-employed persons or that they have sufficient resources for themselves and their family members not to become a burden on the social assistance system of the host Member State during their period of residence and have comprehensive sickness insurance cover in the host Member State, or that they are members of the family, already constituted in the host Member State, of a person satisfying these requirements. 'Sufficient resources' shall be as defined in Article 8(4).

Such family members shall retain their right of residence exclusively on a personal basis.

Aligning with Article 12(1), Article 13(1) adopts the same approach for family members who are Union citizens, meaning that the right to reside in the host State is retained and the conditions set out in Article 7(1) of the Directive apply before acquiring a right of permanent residence. For family members who are not Member State nationals, Article 13(2) establishes specific conditions concerning: the *duration* of the marriage or registered partnership (Article 13(2)(a), 'at least three years, including one year in the host State'), or *custody* of the Union citizen's children (Article 13(2)(b), whether by agreement between the spouses or

---

[393] In the Commission's original proposal, the three-year condition was set at five years. The Commission observed that this requirement, including at least one year in the host State, was included 'in order to avoid people using marriages of convenience to get round the residence entitlement rules' (n 11, 15). The European Parliament, considering that five years was 'too long', recommended 'at least two years, including one year in the host Member State' (n 21, Amendment 50; accepted by the Commission in its revised proposal (n 45) 7). Three years, the period finally adopted, was suggested by the European Parliament's Committee on Women's Rights and Equal Opportunities (Opinion attached to European Parliament Report (n 21) 92). The Council 'consider[ed] [three years] to be a fair duration in order to limit abuses' (Common Position (n 11) 26).

[394] Linked to Article 18 of the Directive; see further Chapter 8.

registered partners, or by court order), or where warranted by *particularly difficult circumstances* (Article 13(2)(c), 'such as having been the victim of domestic violence while the marriage or registered partnership was subsisting'),[395] or where the spouse or registered partner has a *right of access to a minor child* (Article 13(2)(d), but on the condition that 'the court has ruled that such access must be in the host Member State, and for as long as is required').[396] Finally, Article 13(2) provides the same bridge, under the same conditions, to the right of permanent residence as discussed in Section 6.3.1 for Article 12(2).

6.3.3 Interpreting Articles 12 and 13

The protection extended by 'the complicated and interlocking system of Articles 12 and 13'[397] of the Directive was considered in *Singh II*. The preliminary reference concerned three cases in which the third-country national spouses of Union citizens—initially residing with them in Ireland on the basis of Article 7(2) of Directive 2004/38—were refused either permanent residence or retention of residence rights in situations where the Union citizens had left Ireland to settle in other Member States and, from there, subsequently initiated divorce proceedings.[398] In all cases, the basic condition of Article 13(2) was satisfied, in that the marriages had lasted for at least three years before the commencement of divorce proceedings, including one year in the host State. However, also in all three cases, divorce from the Union citizen was preceded by the latter's departure from the host State. The Court observed that it was 'therefore necessary to determine what conditions are required for the application of Article 13(2)(a) of Directive 2004/38, and in particular whether the spouse who is a Union citizen of a third-country national must reside in the host Member State, in accordance with Article 7(1) of the directive, until the date on which the divorce is decreed for the third-country national to be able to rely on Article 13(2)'.[399]

Referring to Article 3(1) of the Directive, the Court confirmed that 'the condition that the third-country national must accompany or join the Union citizen must be understood as referring not to an obligation for the spouses to live together but an obligation for them both to remain in the [host State]'.[400] On that basis, third-country national family members 'can claim the right of residence provided for by Directive 2004/38 only in the host Member State in which the Union citizen resides, and not in another Member State'.[401] The Court also referred to Article 14(2) of the Directive, underlining that the right of the family members of a Union citizen to reside in the host State under Article 7(2) depends on fulfilment by the Union citizen of the conditions in Article 7(1)(a), (b), or (c). The Court concluded that in situations where a Union citizen leaves the host State 'and settles in another Member State or in a third country, the spouse of that Union citizen who is a third-country national no

---

[395] This clarification was not included in the Commission's original proposal, though it did note that '[t]he wording in this article is vague and is meant to cover, in particular, situations of domestic violence' (n 11, 15). However, others in the law-making process argued that the wording should be more explicit; see eg Opinion of the Economic and Social Committee (n 156) para 4.3. See also, European Parliament Report (n 21), Amendment 52 of which suggested 'particularly difficult circumstances such as physical or mental abuse within the family, or on humanitarian grounds'; and the European Parliament's Committee on Women's Rights and Equal Opportunities (Opinion attached to n 21, 93). This point was accepted by the Commission in its amended proposal (n 45, 7), which adopted the European Parliament's proposed wording (draft Article 13). However, the reference to 'humanitarian grounds' was removed by the Council (Common Position (n 11) 27).
[396] Subparagraph (d) was added by the Council (Common Position (n 11) 31).
[397] AG Kokott in Case C-218/14 *Singh II*, EU:C:2015:306, para 41 of the Opinion.
[398] Case C-218/14 *Singh II*, EU:C:2015:476; the common features of the cases are outlined in paras 45–47.
[399] ibid para 49.
[400] ibid para 54; referring to Case C-244/13 *Ogieriakhi*, EU:C:2014:2068, para 39. See further, Chapter 4.
[401] *Singh II*, para 55; referring to Case C-40/11 *Iida*, EU:C:2012:691, paras 63–64.

longer meets the conditions for enjoying a right of residence in the host Member State under Article 7(2) of Directive 2004/38', which in turn requires examination of 'whether, and under what conditions, that spouse can claim a right of residence on the basis of Article 13(2)(a) of Directive 2004/38 where the departure of the Union citizen is followed by a divorce'.[402]

Noting the definition of 'host Member State' in Article 2(3) of the Directive,[403] and the reference to 'initiation' of divorce proceedings in Article 13(2)(a), the Court held that a third-country national spouse can retain a right to reside on the basis of Article 13(2)(a) 'only if the Member State in which that national resides is the "host Member State" within the meaning of Article 2(3) of Directive 2004/38 *on the date of commencement* of the divorce proceedings'.[404] That interpretation cannot accommodate situations in which the Union citizen leaves the host State before commencing such proceedings: '[i]n that event the third-country national's derived right of residence based on Article 7(2) of Directive 2004/38 has come to an end with the departure of the Union citizen and can therefore no longer be retained on the basis of Article 13(2)(a)'.[405] In such circumstances, the departure of the Union citizen spouse 'has already brought about the loss of the right of residence of the spouse who is a third-country national and stays behind in the host Member State. The later petition for divorce cannot have the effect of reviving that right, since Article 13 of Directive 2004/38 mentions only the "retention" of an existing right of residence'.[406] Advocate General Kokott had reasoned similarly, though she did acknowledge the 'inequities' that the approach might produce.[407] She also highlighted 'an inconsistency in the system of Directive 2004/38':

> After the Union citizen's departure, his/her third-country national spouse may lose his/her right of residence in the previous host Member State if, for example, for career-related reasons, he/she does not accompany the Union citizen nor have custody of a common child, even despite an intact marriage, whereas if the marriage breaks down and he/she is able to obtain a divorce in time, the third-country national would retain his/her right of residence in the host Member State under Article 13 of Directive 2004/38. That may constitute interference with the protection of the family in conjunction with the freedom of movement of the Union citizen involved. It is not inconceivable, particularly in border areas, for a family to organise itself in such a way that the partners live and work in different Member States. It is not, however, necessary to pursue further this doubt regarding the consistency of the system established by the provisions of Articles 12 and 13 of the

---

[402] *Singh II*, para 58.
[403] Article 2(3) provides: '"Host Member State" means the Member State to which a Union citizen moves in order to exercise his/her right of free movement and residence'.
[404] *Singh II*, para 61 (emphasis added).
[405] ibid para 62. Expressing the point conversely, 'the spouse who is a Union citizen of a third-country national must reside in the host Member State, in accordance with Article 7(1) of Directive 2004/38, up to the date of commencement of the divorce proceedings for that third-country national to be able to claim the retention of his right of residence in that Member State on the basis of Article 13(2) of the directive' (ibid para 66).
[406] ibid para 67.
[407] AG Kokott in *Singh II*, para 40 of the Opinion: '[a]lthough it cannot be denied that inequities may arise if, in one case, a petition for divorce is filed within the country but, in another case, it is filed only after departure to another country and, where both marriages have lasted an equally long time, the right of residence of the third-country national is retained in the first case, where the Union citizen does not depart, but not in the second'; then noting that '[t]his issue has, however, been taken into account in the scheme of the Directive and clearly accepted by the legislature' (para 41 of the Opinion). She also acknowledged the risk that 'by maliciously departing from the host Member State, the Union citizen may shatter his/her spouse's expectation as to the right of residence established in Article 13' though suggesting that 'the third-country national would not be completely defenceless in the face of such a move — he/she could accompany the Union citizen or, if the marriage has broken down, him/herself institute the divorce proceedings in good time in the host Member State' (para 42 of the Opinion).

Directive. From the perspective of Article 7 of the Charter it could, at most, result in retention of the right of residence by a still-married third-country national. In the present case, however, the marriages have been dissolved.[408]

Finally, the Court pointed out that third-county nationals may be authorised to continue to reside in the host State through more extensive protection under national law, and that this appeared to have been extended in the three cases in these proceedings.[409]

In *NA*, the narrow interpretation applied to Article 13(2)(a) in *Singh II* was more problematically 'transpos[ed]' to Article 13(2)(c).[410] NA, a national of Pakistan, married a German national, KA, in 2003. The couple moved to the UK in 2004 and their two daughters, both German nationals, were born there. It was established that NA 'was the victim of domestic violence on a number of occasions'.[411] KA left the UK in 2006. NA commenced divorce proceedings in 2008, which became final in 2009. NA was granted sole custody of the couple's children, both of whom attended school in the UK. However, her application for permanent residence was rejected, with the court of first instance at national level confirming, *inter alia*, that she could not rely on Article 13(2) of the Directive 'for the reason that, on the date of the divorce, KA was no longer exercising the rights he derived from the Treaties in the United Kingdom'.[412]

Confirming *Singh II*, the Court considered that Article 13(2)(c) 'is part of Article 13(2) of Directive 2004/38, and consequently that provision must not be interpreted independently but interpreted in the light of the whole first subparagraph of Article 13(2)'.[413] Taking into account the 'wording, context and objectives' of Article 13(2), the Court found, first, that divorce does not entail the loss of a right of residence for third-country national family members 'when the conditions laid down in that provision are satisfied'.[414] Second, the Court characterised Article 13(2)(c) as a 'derogation' that covers 'exceptional cases where divorce does not mean the loss of the right of residence of the third-country nationals concerned, under Directive 2004/38, when, following their divorce, those third-country nationals no longer satisfy the conditions laid down in Article 7(2) of that directive, and in particular, the condition of being a "family member" of a Union citizen, within the meaning of Article 2(2)(a)'.[415] Moreover, the Court recalled that Article 12 of the Directive establishes that retained residence rights for third-country national family members 'only in the event of the death of the Union citizen, and not in the event of his or her departure from the host Member State'.[416] Finally, regarding the aims of the provision, the Court drew from the Commission's original proposal for the Directive to confirm that the purpose of Article 13(2) 'was to offer certain legal safeguards to third-country nationals whose right of residence was dependent on a family relationship by marriage and who could therefore be open to blackmail accompanied by threats of divorce, and that safeguards were necessary only in the event of final

---

[408] ibid paras 48–49 of the Opinion.
[409] *Singh II*, paras 68–69.
[410] Case C-115/15 *NA*, EU:C:2016:487, para 37.
[411] ibid para 16.
[412] ibid para 25. The case also involved the examination of derived residence rights on the basis of Article 21 TFEU, Regulation 492/2011 (see further, Chapter 9) and Article 20 TFEU (see further, Chapter 5).
[413] *NA*, para 38.
[414] ibid paras 39–40.
[415] ibid paras 41–42.
[416] ibid para 43. The Court further observed that 'the EU legislature declined to make provision, in the event of the departure from the host Member State of the Union citizen, for specific safeguards that would be available, on account of, inter alia, particularly difficult situations, to his family members who do not have the nationality of a Member State, that would be comparable to those provided for in Article 13(2)(c)' (para 44).

divorce, since, in the event of *de facto* separation, the right of residence of a spouse who is a third-country national is not at all affected'.[417]

The Court therefore concluded that 'an interpretation of Article 13(2)(c) of Directive 2004/38 to the effect that a third-country national is entitled to rely on the right derived from that provision where her spouse, who is a Union citizen, has resided in the host Member State, in accordance with Article 7(1) of Directive 2004/38, not until the date of the commencement of divorce proceedings but, at the latest, until the date when the domestic violence occurred, is contrary to the literal, systematic and teleological interpretation of Article 13(2) of Directive 2004/38'.[418] On that basis, where a third-country national spouse 'has been the victim during her marriage of domestic violence perpetrated by a Union citizen from whom she is divorced, that Union citizen must reside in the host Member State, in accordance with Article 7(1) of Directive 2004/38, until the date of the commencement of divorce proceedings, if that third-country national is to be entitled to rely on Article 13(2)(c)'.[419]

Advocate General Wathelet had distinguished *Singh II* because of the 'context of domestic violence' in *NA*.[420] Using the same interpretative method as the Court—assessing the wording, context and aims of Article 13(2)(c)—he reached the opposite conclusion. Since the wording of the provision 'does not in itself provide the basis for giving a useful answer' for the referring court,[421] he turned to its context and argued that 'unlike the other scenarios provided for in the first subparagraph of Article 13, the factual situation triggering retention of the right of residence is defined by reference to events which have taken place wholly in the past. Thus, Article 13(2)(c) of Directive 2004/38 applies to domestic violence "while the marriage or registered partnership was subsisting". There is therefore, necessarily, a time delay between the domestic violence, the factor triggering the application of the provision, and the divorce'.[422] On the objectives of Article 13(2)(c), he referred, as the Court also later did, to the Commission's original proposal, but highlighted a different aspect of it:

> [T]he Commission's explanatory notes relating to the proposal that led to the adoption of Article 13 of Directive 2004/38 state that 'the purpose of this provision is to provide certain legal safeguards to people whose right of residence is dependent on a family relationship by marriage and who could therefore be open to blackmail with threats of divorce'. Such a risk of 'blackmail with threats of divorce' or with a refusal to grant a divorce appears to me to be particularly significant in the context of domestic violence. After all, the loss of the derived right of residence, by a spouse who is a third country national, in the event of the Union citizen's departure could be used as a means of exerting pressure to stop the divorce at a time when the circumstances are in themselves enough to wear the victim down psychologically and, in any event, to engender fear of the perpetrator of the violence.[423]

---

[417] ibid referring to (n 11).
[418] *NA*, para 48.
[419] ibid para 50.
[420] AG Wathelet in *NA*, EU:C:2016:259, para 2 of the Opinion.
[421] ibid para 64 of the Opinion.
[422] ibid paras 65–66 of the Opinion.
[423] ibid paras 69–70 of the Opinion, referring to (n 11). Noting the 'risk of criminal penalties attaching to conduct constituting domestic violence', AG Wathelet also argued that '[i]t is not inconceivable that the perpetrator of such acts will seek to leave the territory in which those acts were committed in order to escape possible conviction, thus effectively depriving the third country national of her derived right of residence' (paras 71–72 of the Opinion).

In his view, '[a]n interpretation [of Article 13(2)(c) requiring a Union citizen spouse to be present in the territory of the host Member State until the commencement of divorce proceedings would not only be restrictive but would also deprive the provision of its effectiveness, which lies in converting the derived right of residence of a family member of a Union citizen into a personal right of residence in particular circumstances warranting protection'.[424] He considered that the conditions for retaining residence rights in Article 13(2)—employment or self-employment, or sufficient resources and comprehensive medical insurance, or being members of the family (already constituted in the host Member State) of a person satisfying these requirements—'adequately mitigated' any risk of abuse as expressed in recital 15.[425]

Advocate General Wathelet observed (as the Court did) that the applicant and her children had been granted a right to reside in the UK under Article 8 ECHR, calling to mind again the Court's observation about protection under national law in *Singh II*.[426] However, he pointed to the critical, *additional* rights that necessarily flow from residence grounded in EU law specifically, since '[i]t is not inconceivable that the Court's answers to the various questions put to it will determine whether NA is eligible for certain social security benefits and special non-contributory benefits which she is currently denied because of the restriction of the rights conferred by a right of residence based on Article 8 ECHR. A right of residence based directly on EU law would at the very least be such as to afford NA an increased level of legal certainty'.[427]

The connection between lawful residence and equal treatment in the host State is examined in Chapter 7.[428] However, most importantly for present purposes, the Court has now revisited *part* of its approach in *Singh II* and *NA* in situations involving domestic violence. In *X v Belgian State*, the referring court went so far as to query the validity of Article 13(2) of the Directive with respect to Articles 20 and 21 CFR, 'observ[ing] that third-country nationals who are victims of acts of domestic violence committed by their spouses are treated differently depending on whether they have been granted family reunification with a Union citizen or with a third-country national and that difference in treatment stems from' national law transposing Articles 13(2) of Directive 2004/38 and 15(3) of Directive 2003/86.[429] As expressed by the Court of Justice, the central question thus concerned:

> the 'making, in the event of divorce, the retention of the right of residence by third-country nationals who have been the victims of acts of domestic violence committed by their spouses who are Union citizens subject to the conditions laid down in the second subparagraph of Article 13(2) of Directive 2004/38, including, in particular, the condition relating to the sufficiency of resources, whereas Article 15(3) of Directive 2003/86 does not impose such conditions for the purpose of granting, in the same circumstances, an autonomous residence permit to third-country nationals who have been the victims of acts of violence committed by their

---

[424] AG Wathelet in *NA*, para 75 of the Opinion.
[425] ibid para 81 of the Opinion.
[426] ibid para 29 of the Opinion; see also para 29 of the ruling in *NA* and paras 68–69 of the ruling in *Singh II*.
[427] AG Wathelet in *NA*, para 30 of the Opinion.
[428] See also, Chapter 5, on equal treatment and residence rights based on Article 20 TFEU; and Chapter 9, on equal treatment and residence rights based on Article 21 TFEU.
[429] Case C-930/19 *X v Belgian State*, EU:C:2021:657, para 20. Article 15(3) of Directive 2003/86 on the right to family reunification provides that '[i]n the event of widowhood, divorce, separation, or death of first-degree relatives in the direct ascending or descending line, an autonomous residence permit may be issued, upon application, if required, to persons who have entered by virtue of family reunification. Member States shall lay down provisions ensuring the granting of an autonomous residence permit in the event of particularly difficult circumstances'.

spouses who are also third-country nationals, the EU legislature has introduced a difference in treatment between those two categories of third-country nationals who have been the victims of acts of domestic violence, to the detriment of the first category, in breach of Articles 20 and 21 of the Charter.[430]

Having recalled the basic premises of *Singh II* and *NA*, the Court acknowledged that under Article 13(2)(c), the requirement that divorce proceedings should be initiated before the departure of the Union citizen from the host State 'in order for the third-country national who has been the victim of acts of domestic violence committed by his or her spouse who is a Union citizen to retain the right of residence could provide that Union citizen with a means of exerting pressure which would clearly be contrary to the objective of ensuring the protection of the victim of such acts and thereby open ... that victim to blackmail accompanied by threats of divorce or departure'.[431] In consequence, reflecting the possibility of differentiating *types* of departure in the *FS* case (as explained in Sections 3 and 5) and '*contrary to what was held* in paragraph 51 of [*NA*], it must be held that, in order to retain the right of residence on the basis of [Article 13(2)(c)], divorce proceedings may be initiated *after the departure of the EU citizen* from the host Member State'.[432] However, in the interests of legal certainty, and aligning with the 'reasonable period' test applied in *Saint Prix* discussed in Section 6.2, 'a third-country national – who has been the victim of acts of domestic violence committed by his or her spouse who is a Union citizen and in relation to whom divorce proceedings have not been initiated before the departure of that spouse from the host Member State – can rely on the retention of his or her right of residence under that provision only in so far as those proceedings are initiated *within a reasonable period* following such departure'.[433]

What was missing up to this point was any connection to the Charter of Fundamental Rights.[434] However, addressing the validity of Article 13(2)(c) of the Directive, the Court confirmed, as regards discrimination on the grounds of nationality, that Article 21(2) CFR (which 'corresponds to' Article 18 TFEU) 'is not intended to apply to cases of a possible

---

[430] *X v Belgian State*, para 28. Article 20 CFR establishes that '[e]veryone is equal before the law'. Article 21 CFR provides: '1. Any discrimination based on any ground such as sex, race, colour, ethnic or social origin, genetic features, language, religion or belief, political or any other opinion, membership of a national minority, property, birth, disability, age or sexual orientation shall be prohibited. 2. Within the scope of application of the Treaties and without prejudice to any of their specific provisions, any discrimination on grounds of nationality shall be prohibited'.

[431] *X v Belgian State* , para 42.

[432] ibid para 43 (emphasis added).

[433] ibid (emphasis added). The Court did not consider that the three-year period after the departure of the Union citizen in this case seemed 'reasonable' but did note that residence rights had been acquired on the basis of national law (ibid paras 45–47). As had been carefully argued by AG Szpunar, it was 'necessary to update the judgment in *NA*, not only on the basis of the wording, context, purpose and origin of Article 13(2)(c) of Directive 2004/38, but also taking account of recent developments in EU rules on the protection of victims of crime and in particular victims of domestic violence' (AG Szpunar in *X v Belgian State*, EU:C:2021:225, para 92 of the Opinion; continuing that 'the legal, political and social importance of recognising the seriousness of the problem of domestic violence cannot be underestimated. To adopt the position that domestic violence should not affect the application of that provision would not be consistent with the EU legal system as a whole and would be particularly difficult to defend against EU policy with regard to the protection of victims of acts of violence in close relationships as it now stands' (ibid, para 94 of the Opinion, as explained in more detail in paras 95ff). For Strumia, the ruling takes an 'equivocal approach': '[s]oftening the approach' taken in *Singh II* and *NA* with respect to the introduction of the 'reasonable time' test; at the same time, the Court's findings with respect to the Charter (outlined below) show its 'stern face' (F Strumia, 'Speaking too little, yet saying too much. The wrong signals about EU values: X. v. Belgian State' (2022) 59 Common Market Law Review 1195 at 1195). Note also the significance of domestic violence with reference to Article 1 CFR in Case C-709/20 *CG*, EU:C:2021:602, discussed in Chapter 7.

[434] Cf AG Szpunar in *X v Belgian State*, para 66 of the Opinion, referring to Article 7 CFR (respect for private and family life). See further, Strumia (ibid) 1203–1204.

difference in treatment between nationals of Member States and nationals of third countries'.[435] Second, referring to Article 20 CFR and the principle of equality before the law, it also confirmed that 'comparable situations should not be treated differently and that different situations should not be treated in the same way, unless such different treatment is objectively justified'.[436] While acknowledging that Articles 13(2) and 15(3) of Directives 2004/38 and 2003/86 respectively 'share the objective of ensuring protection for family members who are victims of domestic violence',[437] the Court then compared the fields covered by, subject matter and objectives of, and level of discretion conferred on the Member States by the two Directives and determined that 'the regimes introduced by those directives relate to different fields, the principles, subject matters and objectives of which are also different'; finding also that 'the beneficiaries of Directive 2004/38 enjoy a different status and rights of a different kind to those upon which the beneficiaries of Directive 2003/86 may rely, and the discretion which the Member States are recognised as having to apply the conditions laid down in those directives is not the same'.[438] On that basis, affected spouses were not in a comparable situation and Article 20 CFR was not therefore breached. As a result, the requirement to be either economically active or economically autonomous (through having sufficient resources) applies validly for residence rights based on Article 13(2) of the Directive.

7. Directive 2004/38 and Abuse of Rights

Article 35 of Directive 2004/38[439] establishes that 'Member States may adopt the necessary measures to refuse, terminate or withdraw any right conferred by this Directive in the case of abuse of rights or fraud, such as marriages of convenience. Any such measure shall be proportionate and subject to the procedural safeguards provided for in Articles 30 and 31'. Additionally, recital 28 highlights 'marriages of convenience or any other form of relationships contracted for the sole purpose of enjoying the right of free movement and residence'. Neither the main provision nor the recital appeared in the Commission's original or revised proposals for the Directive. Instead, Article 35 was introduced by the Council 'to clarify that Member States may refuse, terminate or withdraw any right conferred by the Directive in the case of abuse of rights or fraud'.[440] Where a finding of abuse of rights or fraud is made, the possibility of relying on EU rights is lost: as the wording of Article 35 makes clear, such a finding can result in the denial of a right to enter the territory of a Member State in the first place or of residence rights thereafter; and it can also justify exclusion orders.[441]

---

[435] *X v Belgian State*, paras 50–51.
[436] ibid para 57.
[437] ibid para 70.
[438] ibid para 89; noting that it was 'in particular, a choice made by the Belgian authorities in connection with the exercise of the broad discretion conferred on them by Article 15(4) of Directive 2003/86 which has led to the difference in treatment complained of by the applicant in the main proceedings' (ibid para 89).
[439] See also, Article 20 WA: '3. The host State or the State of work may adopt the necessary measures to refuse, terminate or withdraw any right conferred by this Title in the case of the abuse of those rights or fraud, as set out in Article 35 of Directive 2004/38/EC. Such measures shall be subject to the procedural safeguards provided for in Article 21 of this Agreement. 4. The host State or the State of work may remove applicants who submitted fraudulent or abusive applications from its territory under the conditions set out in Directive 2004/38/EC, in particular Articles 31 and 35 thereof, even before a final judgment has been handed down in the case of judicial redress sought against any rejection of such an application.'
[440] Common Position (n 11) 32. The Commission acknowledged but did not comment on the addition in its subsequent Communication (n 48, para 3.3.2).
[441] Communication on guidance for better transposition and application of Directive 2004/38/EC (n 50) para 4; referring to Case C-127/08 *Metock and Others*, EU:C:2008:449, paras 74–75. For similar principles in EU free

In *Metock*, the Court held that 'in accordance with Article 35 of Directive 2004/38, Member States may adopt the necessary measures to refuse, terminate or withdraw any right conferred by that directive in the case of abuse of rights or fraud, such as marriages of convenience, *it being understood that* any such measure must be proportionate and subject to the procedural safeguards provided for in the directive'.[442] Though the Court did not refer expressly to Article 15(1) of the Directive, we saw in Section 5 that Article 15(1) ensures the application of Articles 30 and 31 of the Directive when expulsion is ordered on grounds other than public policy, public security, or public health. Moreover, Article 15(3) precludes Member States from imposing a ban on re-entry in such cases unless the conduct of the person concerned is serious enough to cross the threshold into public policy or public security risk (the scope of which is considered in Chapter 10). In this part of the chapter, Article 35 of the Directive is first located in the general approach to abuse of rights in EU free movement law (Section 7.1), before guidance developed by the Commission on Article 35 specifically is outlined (Section 7.2). The ruling in *McCarthy II*, introduced in Section 5.2.2, is then returned to briefly (Section 7.3).

7.1 Locating Article 35: Abuse of Rights and EU Free Movement Law

It is vital—but not always straightforward—to distinguish between situations of *use* and *abuse* of EU rights. In *Emsland-Stärke*, the Court established that a finding of abuse of EU rights requires, 'first, a combination of *objective circumstances* in which, despite formal observance of the conditions laid down by the [Union] rules, the purpose of those rules has not been achieved', and 'second, a *subjective element* consisting in the intention to obtain an advantage from the [Union] rules by creating artificially the conditions laid down for obtaining it'.[443] The Court has expressly referred to that definition of abuse of rights in EU citizenship law.[444] Moreover, it has confirmed that 'a Member State is entitled to take measures designed to prevent certain of its nationals from attempting, under cover of the rights created by the Treaty, *improperly to circumvent* their national legislation or to prevent individuals from improperly or fraudulently taking advantage of provisions of EU law'.[445]

In contrast, according to the Commission, '[t]here is no abuse where EU citizens and their family members obtain a right of residence under [Union] law in a Member State other than

---

movement law generally, the Commission also referred to Case 33/74 *Van Binsbergen*, EU:C:1974:131, para 13; Case C-370/90 *Singh*, EU:C:1992:296, para 24; and Case C-212/97 *Centros*, EUC:1999:126, paras 24–25.

[442] *Metock*, para 75.
[443] Case C-110/99 *Emsland-Stärke*, EU:C:2000:695, paras 52–53 (emphasis added). See generally, R de la Feria and S Vogenauer (eds), *Prohibition of Abuse of Law: A New General Principle of EU Law?* (Hart Publishing 2011).
[444] eg Case C-456/12 *O and B*, EU:C:2014:135, para 58; Case C-202/13 *McCarthy II*, EU:C:2014:2450, para 54.
[445] Case C-438/14 *Bogendorff von Wolffersdorff*, EU:C:2016:401, para 57 (emphasis added); referring to Case C-212/97 *Centros*, EUC:1999:126. See further, paras 86–87 of the Opinion of AG Wathelet in *Bogendorff von Wolffersdorff* (EU:C:2016:11), who explained, in the context of an application by a dual German/British national to have a name acquired under UK legislation recognised in Germany, that the German authorities would need to 'demonstrate that Mr Bogendorff von Wolffersdorff moved to the United Kingdom and resided there for several years with the sole intention of artificially creating the circumstances necessary to change his forenames and his surname in order to satisfy the conditions for application of [the relevant German rules]' to establish abuse of EU rights; adding that 'the national court is inclined to consider that Mr Bogendorff von Wolffersdorff's interests were centred in London during the period from 2001 to 2005. His link to the United Kingdom, of which he is a national, was neither fictional nor abusive'.

that of the EU citizen's nationality as they are benefiting from a*n advantage inherent in the exercise of the right of free movement* protected by the Treaty, regardless of the purpose of their move to that State'.[446] In particular, 'a marriage cannot be considered as a marriage of convenience simply because it brings *an immigration advantage*, or indeed any other advantage (for example the right to a particular surname, location-related allowances, tax advantages or entitlement to social housing for married couples)'.[447] This suggests *proper* as opposed to *improper* circumvention of national legislation, yet the line between the two is not always self-evident. In *Akrich*, the Court ruled that 'the motives which may have prompted a worker of a Member State to seek employment in another Member State are of no account' but that 'there would be an abuse if the facilities afforded by [Union] law in favour of migrant workers and their spouses were invoked in the context of marriages of convenience entered into in order to circumvent the provisions relating to entry and residence of nationals of non-Member States'.[448] In *LN*, the Court confirmed:

[T]he definition of the concept of 'worker' within the meaning of Article 45 TFEU expresses the requirement, which is inherent in the very principle of the free movement of workers, that the advantages conferred by European Union law under that freedom may be relied on only by people genuinely pursuing or genuinely wishing to pursue employment activities. It does not mean, however, that the enjoyment of that freedom may be made contingent on which objectives are being pursued by a national of a Member State in applying to enter the territory of a host Member State, provided that he pursues or wishes to pursue effective and genuine employment activities. Once that condition is satisfied, the motives which may have prompted a worker of a Member State to seek employment in another Member State are of no account and must not be taken into consideration.[449]

The factual circumstances in *Zhu and Chen* provided an opportunity for the Court to address use and abuse of rights directly in the context of Union citizenship. After giving birth to her first child in China, Mrs Chen entered the UK in May 2000 when six months pregnant with her second child; she went to Belfast in July and her daughter Catherine was born there in September. Mrs Chen and her daughter subsequently moved to Cardiff. The Court confirmed that it was 'common ground that Mrs Chen took up residence in the island of Ireland in order to enable the child she was expecting to acquire Irish nationality and, consequently, to enable her to acquire the right to reside, should the occasion arise, with her child in the United Kingdom,'[450] in line with the rules on acquiring Irish nationality applicable at that time.

---

[446] Communication on guidance for better transposition and application of Directive 2004/38/EC (n 50), para 4 (emphasis added).
[447] Commission Staff Working Document, Handbook on addressing the issue of alleged marriages of convenience between EU citizens and non-EU nationals in the context of EU law on free movement of EU citizens, SWD(2014) 284 final, 9 (emphasis added).
[448] Case C-109/01 *Akrich*, EU:C:2003:491, paras 55 and 57. See further, Chapter 9.
[449] Case C-46/12 *LN*, EU:C:2013:97, para 47.
[450] Case C-200/02 *Zhu and Chen*, EU:C:2004:639, para 11. See similarly, para 36: 'Mrs Chen admits that the purpose of her stay in the United Kingdom was to create a situation in which the child she was expecting would be able to acquire the nationality of another Member State in order thereafter to secure for her child and for herself a long-term right to reside in the United Kingdom'. See further, the Opinion of AG Tizzano: '[t]he choice of the place of birth was no accident. It is noteworthy that, when certain conditions are fulfilled, anyone born within the territory of the island of Ireland, even outside the political boundaries of Ireland (Éire), acquires Irish nationality. As is apparent from the file, it was specifically because of that particular feature of Irish law, brought to their attention by the lawyers they consulted, that Mr and Mrs Chen decided to arrange for their child to be born in Belfast. They

The UK Government contended that the applicants were not entitled to rely on Article 21 TFEU or (at the time) Directive 90/364 to establish a right to reside in the UK 'because Mrs Chen's move to Northern Ireland with the aim of having her child acquire the nationality of another Member State constitutes an attempt improperly to exploit the provisions [Union] law'.[451] That argument was based on the fact that '[t]he aims pursued by those [Union] provisions are not, in its view, served where a national of a non-member country wishing to reside in a Member State, without however moving or wishing to move from one Member State to another, arranges matters in such a way as to give birth to a child in a part of the host Member State to which another Member State applies its rules governing acquisition of nationality *jure soli*' and that it was 'settled case-law that Member States are entitled to take measures to prevent individuals from improperly taking advantage of provisions of [Union] law or from attempting, under cover of the rights created by the Treaty, illegally to circumvent national legislation'.[452]

However, the Court recalled that, 'under international law, it is for each Member State, having due regard to Community law, to lay down the conditions for the acquisition and loss of nationality';[453] that no parties involved in the case had questioned 'either the legality, or the fact, of Catherine's acquisition of Irish nationality';[454] and that it is 'not permissible for a Member State to restrict the effects of the grant of the nationality of another Member State by imposing an additional condition for recognition of that nationality with a view to the exercise of the fundamental freedoms provided for in the Treaty'.[455]

For Advocate General Tizzano, 'it is only in exceptional circumstances that the exercise of a right conferred by the Treaty can constitute an abuse, because the non-application of a national provision as a result of reliance on a right conferred by [Union] law constitutes the normal consequence of the principle of the supremacy of [Union] law'.[456] He articulated the test for abuse of EU rights as 'whether or not there has been a distortion of the purposes and objectives of the [Union] provision which grants the right in question', underlining that the *Zhu and Chen* case was not one 'of people "improperly or fraudulently invoking [Union] law", failing to observe the scope and purposes of the provisions of that legal system, but rather one of people who, apprised of the nature of the freedoms provided for by [Union] law, take advantage of them by legitimate means, specifically in order to attain the objective which the [Union] provision seeks to uphold: the child's right of residence'.[457] In his view, '[t]he problem, if problem there be, lies in the criterion used by the Irish legislation for granting nationality, the *ius soli*, which lends itself to the emergence of situations like the one at issue in this case'[458]—rules subsequently changed following a constitutional referendum in Ireland.[459]

---

intended to take advantage of the child's [Union] nationality in order to ensure that she and her mother would be able to establish themselves in the United Kingdom' (EU:C:2004:307, para 13 of the Opinion).

[451] Case C-200/02 *Zhu and Chen*, EU:C:2004:639, para 11.
[452] ibid, referring to Case C-212/97 *Centros*, EUC:1999:126.
[453] *Zhu and Chen*, para 37; referring to Case C-369/90 *Micheletti*, EU:C:1992:295, para 10; and Case C-192/99 *Kaur*, EU:C:2001:106, para 19. See further, Chapter 5.
[454] *Zhu and Chen*, para 38.
[455] ibid para 39; referring to *Micheletti*, para 10; and Case C-148/02 *Garcia Avello*, EU:C:2003:539, para 28.
[456] AG Tizzano *Zhu and Chen*, para 112 of the Opinion; in para 113, he added: '[n]or does the fact that a person knowingly places himself in a situation which causes a right deriving from Community law to arise in his favour, in order to avoid the application of certain national legislation unfavourable to him, constitute, in itself, a sufficient basis for the relevant Community provisions to be rendered inapplicable' (referring to *Centros*, para 27).
[457] AG Tizzano in *Zhu and Chen*, paras 115 and 122 of the Opinion.
[458] ibid para 124 of the Opinion.
[459] The 27th Amendment of the Constitution of Ireland inserted Article 9.2.1, the text of which provides: '[n]otwithstanding any other provision of this Constitution, a person born in the island of Ireland, which

7.2 Clarifying Article 35: Commission Guidance

Despite its low-key presence in the process of adopting the Directive, Article 35 has been subject to significant elaboration since then. In its 2009 Communication on better transposition and application of the Directive, the Commission addressed four key issues: the distinction between abuse and fraud, further guidance on marriages of convenience, other forms of abuse, and measures and sanctions against fraud and abuse. *First,* the Commission defined fraud as 'deliberate deception or contrivance made to obtain the right of free movement and residence under the Directive. In the context of the Directive, fraud is likely to be limited to forgery of documents or false representation of a material fact concerning the conditions attached to the right of residence. Persons who have been issued with a residence document only as a result of fraudulent conduct in respect of which they have been convicted, may have their rights under the Directive refused, terminated or withdrawn'.[460] Additionally, 'abuse may be defined as an artificial conduct entered into solely with the purpose of obtaining the right of free movement and residence under [Union] law which, albeit formally observing of the conditions laid down by [Union] rules, does not comply with the purpose of those rules'.[461] As introduced in Section 7.1, however, it is not easy to reconcile the 'sole purpose' criterion with the case law premise that motivation for exercising free movement is not, per se, material.

Second, the Commission provided extensive guidance on marriages of convenience, clarifying the fundamentals of that concept as follows:

> Recital 28 [of Directive 2004/38] defines marriages of convenience for the purposes of the Directive as marriages contracted for the *sole* purpose of enjoying the right of free movement and residence under the Directive that someone would not have otherwise. A marriage cannot be considered as a marriage of convenience simply because it brings an immigration advantage, or indeed any other advantage. The quality of the relationship is immaterial to the application of Article 35. The definition of marriages of convenience can be extended by analogy to other forms of relationships contracted for the sole purpose of enjoying the right of free movement and residence, such as (registered) partnership of convenience, fake adoption or where an EU citizen declares to be a father of a third country child to convey nationality and a right of residence on the child and its mother, knowing that he is not its father and not willing to assume parental responsibilities.[462]

---

includes its islands and seas, who does not have, at the time of the birth of that person, at least one parent who is an Irish citizen or entitled to be an Irish citizen is not entitled to Irish citizenship or nationality, unless provided for by law'. The Irish Nationality and Citizenship Act 2004 was subsequently adopted. See further, AG Sharpston in Case C-34/09 *Ruiz Zambrano*, EU:C:2010:560, paras 104–105 and 115 of the Opinion.

[460] Communication on guidance for better transposition and application of Directive 2004/38/EC (n 50) para 4.1.1; referring to Case C-285/95 *Kol*, EU:C:1997:280, para 29; and Case C-63/99 *Gloszczuk*, EU:C:2001:488, para 75.

[461] Communication on guidance for better transposition and application of Directive 2004/38/EC (n 50) para 4.1.2; referring to *Emsland-Stärke*, paras 52ff and *Centros*, para 25. See further, Handbook on addressing the issue of alleged marriages of convenience (n 447) 10: '[a]buse should be distinguished from fraud. Fraudsters seek to break the law by presenting fraudulent documentation alleging that the formal conditions have been duly met or which is issued on the basis of a false representation of a material fact concerning the conditions attached to the right of residence. For instance, the submission of a forged marriage certificate with a view to obtaining a right of entry and residence under the Directive would be a case of fraud and not of abuse, since no marriage was actually contracted'.

[462] Communication on guidance for better transposition and application of Directive 2004/38/EC (n 50) para 4.2 (emphasis in original). On the criterion of 'sole purpose', see further, Handbook on addressing the issue of alleged marriages of convenience (n 447) 9.

The Commission underlined that an assessment of whether or EU law was abused or not must be carried out 'in the framework of [Union] law, and not with regard to national migration laws': while '[t]he Directive does not prevent Member States from investigating individual cases where there is a well-founded suspicion of abuse', it must be remembered that 'Union law prohibits systematic checks. Member States may rely on previous analyses and experience showing a clear correlation between proven cases of abuse and certain characteristics of such cases'.[463]

The Commission offered a 'set of indicative criteria' signaling where abuse was unlikely,[464] as well as 'a set of indicative criteria suggesting the possible intention to abuse the rights conferred by the Directive for the sole purpose of contravening national immigration laws'.[465] But it emphasised that the latter criteria 'should be considered possible triggers for investigation, without any automatic inferences from results or subsequent investigations. Member States may not rely on one sole attribute; due attention has to be given to all the circumstances of the individual case'.[466] It also confirmed that the burden of proof lies with the authorities of the Member State seeking to restrict the rights conferred by the Directive, and that any investigations undertaken must comply with the fundamental rights protected by EU law (referring in particular to Articles 7 (respect for private and family life) and 9 (right to marry) CFR. In essence, '[c]ouples contracting marriages of convenience go through steps which are solely designed to achieve a legal status of marriage which is unsupported by the fundamental foundations of marriage'.[467]

Third, concerning 'other forms of abuse', the Commission focused on exercising free movement and residence rights with the *sole* purpose of evading national rules on family reunification.[468] These situations tread a delicate line between use and abuse of EU rights—between proper and improper circumvention—and they are examined in more detail in Chapter 9 in the discussion on Union citizens returning to their home States following the exercise of free movement. Finally, *fourth*, the Commission addressed the measures that Article 35 permits Member States to take where abuse of rights or fraud is determined. It indicated that '[t]hese measures can be taken at any point of time and may entail: the refusal to confer rights under [Union] law on free movement (eg to issue an entry visa or a residence card)' and 'the termination or withdrawal of rights under [Union] law on free movement (eg the decision to terminate validity of

---

[463] Communication on guidance for better transposition and application of Directive 2004/38/EC (n 50) para 4.2; referred to by AG Szpunar in Case C-202/13 *McCarthy II*, EU:C:2014:345, para 127 of the Opinion.

[464] Communication on guidance for better transposition and application of Directive 2004/38/EC (n 50) para 4.2 ie 'the third country spouse would have no problem obtaining a right of residence in his/her own capacity or has already lawfully resided in the EU citizen's Member State beforehand; the couple was in a relationship for a long time; the couple had a common domicile/household for a long time [though noting here that EU law does not require spouses to live together, referring to Case 267/83 *Diatta*, EU:C:1985:67, paras 15ff]; the couple have already entered a serious long-term legal/financial commitment with shared responsibilities (mortgage to buy a home, etc); the marriage has lasted for a long time'.

[465] Communication on guidance for better transposition and application of Directive 2004/38/EC (n 50) para 4.2 ie 'the couple have never met before their marriage; the couple are inconsistent about their respective personal details, about the circumstances of their first meeting, or about other important personal information concerning them; the couple do not speak a language understood by both; evidence of a sum of money or gifts handed over in order for the marriage to be contracted (with the exception of money or gifts given in the form of a dowry in cultures where this is common practice); the past history of one or both of the spouses contains evidence of previous marriages of convenience or other forms of abuse and fraud to acquire a right of residence; development of family life only after the expulsion order was adopted; the couple divorces shortly after the third country national in question has acquired a right of residence'.

[466] ibid para 4.2.

[467] Handbook on addressing the issue of alleged marriages of convenience (n 447) 10.

[468] Communication on guidance for better transposition and application of Directive 2004/38/EC (n 50) para 4.3. See further, Chapter 10.

a residence card and to expel the person concerned who acquired rights by abuse or fraud'.[469] It added that EU law 'does not at present provide for any specific sanctions Member States may take in the framework of fight against abuse or fraud' and suggested that 'Member States may lay down sanctions under civil (eg cancelling the effects of a proven marriage of convenience on the right of residence), administrative or criminal law (fine or imprisonment), provided these sanctions are effective, non-discriminatory and proportionate'.[470]

In 2014, responding to a 'roadmap' approved by the Justice and Home Affairs Council in 2012, the Commission supplemented the guidance outlined above by issuing both a Communication[471] and a Handbook[472] on marriages of convenience between EU citizens and third-country nationals.[473] In its Communication, the Commission acknowledged that the phenomenon of such marriages 'exists but varies significantly between Member States. Despite the limited number of cases, the implication of organised criminal networks, as acknowledged in recent Europol reports, is worrying'.[474] The Handbook is organised around three key issues: definitions, legal framework, and 'operational measures within national remit'. Its purpose is 'to help national authorities effectively tackle individual cases of abuse in the form of marriages of convenience while not compromising the fundamental goal of safeguarding and facilitating free movement of EU citizens and their family members using EU law in a *bona fide* way'.[475] The Commission clarified that the Handbook is 'neither legally binding nor exhaustive. It is without prejudice to existing EU law and its future development. It is also without prejudice to the authoritative interpretation of EU law which may be given by the Court of Justice'.[476] Additionally, the Handbook sets as its 'starting point' the 'protection of fundamental individual rights', observing that '[m]easures taken by national authorities on a discriminatory or automatic basis with a view to detect and prevent possible abuse are likely to constitute an unjustified and disproportionate intrusion into the private life of all the couples concerned'.[477] It also underlined that '[t]he right of free movement is the primary rule from which there may only be exceptional derogations in individual cases when justified by proven abuse'.[478]

Advances from the 2009 guidance in the 2014 materials include a 'double-lock mechanism' in recognition of the fact that national authorities 'may be confronted with atypical but genuine couples that appear at first to exhibit a number of features of a marriage of convenience'.[479] That mechanism implies, first, 'a rigorous application of the principle that free

---

[469] ibid para 4.4.
[470] ibid.
[471] 'Helping national authorities fight abuses of the right to free movement: Handbook on addressing the issue of alleged marriages of convenience between EU citizens and non-EU nationals in the context of EU law on free movement of EU citizens', COM(2014) 604 final.
[472] Handbook on addressing the issue of alleged marriages of convenience (n 447).
[473] The Handbook expressly confirms that marriages between two Union citizens as well as marriages between two non-EU spouses fall outside of its scope (ibid 5), building on a 1997 Council Resolution on measures to be adopted on the combating of marriages of convenience, 1997 OJ C382/1. For the purposes of the Resolution, a marriage of convenience means 'a marriage concluded between an EU citizen or a non-EU national legally resident in an EU country and a non-EU national, with the sole aim of circumventing the rules on entry and residence of non-EU nationals and obtaining for the non-EU national a residence permit or authority to reside in an EU country'. On the latter point, the Commission notes that such marriages 'constitute an abuse of EU rules on family reunification' (n 447, 5; referring to Council Directive 2003/86/EC on the right to family reunification, 2003 OJ L251/12).
[474] 'Helping national authorities fight abuses' (n 471) 2; referring to COM(2013) 837 final ('Free movement of EU citizens and their families: five actions to make a difference'), para 3.1.
[475] Handbook on addressing the issue of alleged marriages of convenience (n 447) 4.
[476] ibid 5.
[477] ibid 6.
[478] ibid 7.
[479] 'Helping national authorities fight abuses' (n 471) 7.

movement is the primary rule which can be restricted only in individual cases where it is justified on the grounds of abuse' and, second, that 'national authorities investigating abuse should not, in principle, focus primarily on hints of abuse to support their initial suspicions about the marriage at stake. On the contrary, they should first consider "hints that there is no abuse" (such as being in a long-standing relationship or in a serious long-term legal or financial commitment or sharing parental responsibility) that would support the conclusion that the couple is genuine and enjoys the right to move and reside freely.

Only if the examination of "the hints that there is no abuse" has not confirmed the genuine nature of the investigated marriage, would the authorities proceed to verify the existence of "the hints of abuse".[480] That guidance chimes with Advocate General Sharpston's statement in *KA* that 'there is no place for a *general* presumption of abuse when a family link arises at the point when a third-country national finds himself to be an irregular stayer. It should not be assumed *ipso facto* that the person concerned created the family link in order to remain in EU territory'.[481] Addressing the ECHR, she also acknowledged that 'whilst it is true that the Strasbourg Court has described the circumstance of the third-country national concerned becoming a parent during the period when their immigration status was precarious as an "important consideration", that Court has assessed that particular factor in relation to other elements of the case. Becoming the parent of a child during such a period of uncertainty is not necessarily considered to be an attempt to abuse the immigration rules'.[482]

The Handbook also 'indicates how effective detection, investigation and prosecution of marriages of convenience can be facilitated through cross-border co-operation' and 'details in particular the assistance that can be provided to national authorities by Europol, where there is involvement of organised crime in trafficking in human beings, and by Eurojust, notably as regards the investigation or prosecution of specific acts, and coordination between national authorities'.[483] It considers different types of marriages of convenience in some detail,[484] and addresses the intersection with trafficking in human beings.[485] It outlines the requirements of compliance with fundamental rights, in both ECHR and EU respects,[486] and provides extensive guidance on the burden of proof and the standard of required evidence,[487] as well as on investigative checks and techniques.[488] It also provides an interesting overview of 'practices distilled from national practices across the Member States'—which is 'not intended as a blueprint for all investigational patterns and processes' but as 'a toolbox of solutions allowing Member States to set up tailored operational schemes fitting their specific needs and available resources'[489]—and of the potential for cross-border cooperation.[490]

And yet—illustrating the politically symbolic more than substantive concern that abuse of EU rights attracts—these efforts were not enough, for some Member States at least, when it is recalled that the Commission signalled its intention 'to adopt a proposal to complement

---

[480] ibid 7–8; examples of these 'hints' are provided and elaborated in the Handbook on addressing the issue of alleged marriages of convenience (n 447), Sections 4.2, 4.3, and 4.4.
[481] AG Sharpston in Case C-82/16 *KA*, EU:C:2017:821, para 65 of the Opinion.
[482] ibid; referring, *inter alia*, to *Jeunesse v the Netherlands* (2015) 60 EHRR 17, paras 106–109 and 115–121.
[483] Helping national authorities fight abuses' (n 471) 8.
[484] Handbook on addressing the issue of alleged marriages of convenience (n 447) Section 2.2.
[485] Addressing in particular Directive 2011/36/EU on preventing and combating trafficking in human beings and protecting its victims, 2011 OJ L101/1.
[486] Handbook on addressing the issue of alleged marriages of convenience (n 447) Section 3.1; emphasising, for relevant cases, the significance of the rights of the child.
[487] ibid Section 3.2.
[488] ibid Section 4.5.
[489] ibid 33.
[490] ibid Section 4.6.

Directive 2004/38/EC on free movement of Union citizens in order to exclude, from the scope of free movement rights, third country nationals who had no prior lawful residence in a Member State before marrying a Union citizen or who marry a Union citizen only after the Union citizen has established residence in the host Member State' as part of the package agreed during the (pre-Brexit) 'renegotiation' of the relationship between the EU and the UK.[491] Had that agreement taken effect, the Commission also intended to clarify in a further Communication that 'Member States can address specific cases of abuse of free movement rights by Union citizens returning to their Member State of nationality with a non-EU family member where residence in the host Member State has not been sufficiently genuine to create or strengthen family life and had the purpose of evading the application of national immigration rules';[492] and that 'the concept of marriage of convenience – which is not protected under Union law – also covers a marriage which is maintained for the purpose of enjoying a right of residence by a family member who is not a national of a Member State'.

These statements were remarkable, especially considering the extensive guidance already outlined above. In the same Declaration, skirting close to displacement of Court of Justice case law, the Commission indicated that it also intended to clarify 'that Member States may take into account past conduct of an individual in the determination of whether a Union citizen's conduct poses a "present" threat to public policy or security. They may act on grounds of public policy or public security even in the absence of a previous criminal conviction on preventative grounds but specific to the individual concerned'. It noted that it would also examine the concepts of 'serious grounds of public policy or public security' and 'imperative grounds of public security' in Article 28 of Directive 2004/38, suggesting that 'on the occasion of a future revision' of the Directive, it would 'examine the thresholds to which these notions are connected'.

The commitments agreed to in the February 2016 negotiations fell away when the UK decided to withdraw from the Union in June of that year. But what the UK had sought—and what the other 27 States had conceded—was concerning. In particular, the political settlement called into question the sustainability of a fundamental legal aspect of asserting abuse of EU rights: that claims must be properly supported by evidence.[493]

7.3 Interpreting Article 35: *McCarthy II*

Despite the high political salience of abuse of EU rights, the Court's only substantive examination of Article 35 of the Directive to date is *Mc Carthy II*, introduced in Section 5.2.2 and concerning contested entry requirements for third-country national family members with respect to the UK, then a Member State.[494] As noted in Section 5.2.2, '[a]fter examining the evidence adduced by the Secretary of State, the referring court concluded that her concerns

---

[491] Annex VII (Declaration of the European Commission on issues related to the abuse of the right of free movement of persons) attached to the Decision of the Heads of State or Government, meeting within the European Council, concerning a new settlement for the United Kingdom within the European Union, 2016 OJ C69/1.

[492] See further, Chapter 9.

[493] See generally, N Nic Shuibhne and M Maci, 'Proving public interest: the growing impact of evidence in free movement case law' (2013) 50 Common Market Law Review 965.

[494] Note also, the questions referred in Case C-169/18 *Mahmood and Others*, EU:C:2019:5, dismissed by Order of the Court. The reasoning in Case C-719/19 *FS*, EU:C:2021:506, considered in Sections 3 and 5, arguably reflects the essence of abuse of EU rights, though the Court did not mention it (but AG Rantos did: EU:C:2021:104, paras 94–97 of the Opinion, referring to the Communication on guidance for better transposition and application of Directive 2004/38/EC (n 50) para 4.3 and Case C-456/12 *O and B*, EU:C:2014:135).

as to a 'systemic' abuse of rights appeared to it to be justified, on the basis that 'residence cards are ripe for exploitation in the context of illegal immigration into the United Kingdom. There is a palpable risk that a significant proportion of those engaged in the "business of sham marriages" will use fake residence cards for the purpose of gaining illegal access to the United Kingdom. Thus, the refusal of that Member State to exempt holders of residence cards from the obligation to obtain an entry visa is sensible, necessary and objectively justified'.[495] The first set of questions referred therefore concerned whether Article 35 of the Directive and Article 1 of Protocol No 20[496] 'must be interpreted as permitting a Member State to require, in pursuit of an objective of general prevention, family members of a Union citizen who are not nationals of a Member State and who hold a valid residence card issued under Article 10 of Directive 2004/38 by the authorities of another Member State to be in possession, pursuant to national law, of an entry permit, such as the EEA family permit, in order to be able to enter its territory'.[497]

Turning to Article 35 of the Directive, the Court characterised the contested national legislation as 'founded on the existence of a general risk of abuse of rights or fraud, described by the Secretary of State as "systemic", thereby excluding any specific assessment by the competent national authorities of the conduct of the person concerned himself as regards any abuse of rights or fraud'.[498] On that basis:

> That legislation requires an entry permit to be obtained prior to entry into United Kingdom territory, even where, as in the case in point, the national authorities do not consider that the family member of a Union citizen may be involved in an abuse of rights or fraud. Thus, the legislation imposes that requirement even though the authenticity of the residence card issued under Article 10 of Directive 2004/38 and the correctness of the data appearing on it are not called into question by the United Kingdom authorities. Effectively, therefore, the legislation denies family members of a Union citizen who are not nationals of a Member State – absolutely and automatically – the right conferred on them in Article 5(2) of Directive 2004/38 to enter the territory of the Member States without a visa, although they are in possession of a valid residence card, issued on the basis of Article 10 of Directive 2004/38 by the Member State of residence.[499]

Such rules could not be justified under Article 27 of the Directive since 'justifications that are isolated from the particulars of the case in question or that rely on considerations of general prevention are not to be accepted'.[500] For measures adopted under Article 35, 'any such measure must be proportionate and subject to the procedural safeguards provided for in the directive'.[501] In particular, 'decisions or measures adopted by the competent national authorities relating to a possible right of entry or residence, on the basis of Directive 2004/38, are intended *to establish the individual position* of a national of a Member State or of his family members with regard to that directive'.[502] Any decision taken in accordance with

---

[495] Case C-202/13 *McCarthy II*, EU:C:2014:2450, para 27.
[496] ibid paras 59–66; see further, Section 5.2.2.
[497] ibid para 29.
[498] ibid para 43. See further, AG Szpunar, para 131 of the Opinion, who remarked that 'the use of the adjective "systemic" does not seem to me to be compatible with the concept of abuse of rights in the context of EU law'.
[499] *McCarthy II*, para 44.
[500] ibid para 46.
[501] ibid para 47.
[502] ibid para 49 (emphasis added). The Court also highlighted the importance of individual in the safeguards provided for in Articles 30 and 31 of the Directive, to which Article 35 explicitly refers (paras 50–51).

Article 35 must therefore 'be based on an individual examination of the particular case' and, for residence cards issued under Article 10, 'Member States are therefore required to recognise such a residence card for the purposes of entry into their territory without a visa, unless doubt is cast on the authenticity of that card and the correctness of the data appearing on it by concrete evidence that relates to the individual case in question and justifies the conclusion that there is an abuse of rights or fraud'.[503] The Court recalled the need to establish both an objective and subjective element in that regard. Otherwise, 'to accept that the United Kingdom should implement measures of general application would be tantamount to allowing a Member State to circumvent the right of freedom of movement and would have the consequence that other Member States could also adopt such measures and unilaterally suspend the application of the directive'.[504]

As picked up again in Chapter 7, the final paragraphs of the ruling in *McCarthy II* are notable with respect to how they differ from the *absence* of similar considerations in cases such as *Dano* and *Commission v UK*.[505] In *McCarthy II*, the Court held that '[i]n the absence of an express provision in Directive 2004/38, the fact that a Member State is faced, *as the United Kingdom considers itself to be*, with a high number of cases of abuse of rights or fraud committed by third-country nationals resorting to sham marriages or using falsified residence cards cannot justify the adoption of a measure, such as that at issue in the main proceedings, founded on considerations of general prevention, to the exclusion of any specific assessment of the conduct of the person concerned himself'.[506] Moreover, 'the adoption of measures *pursuing an objective of general prevention in respect of widespread cases of abuse of rights or fraud* would mean, as in the case in point, that *the mere fact of belonging to a particular group of persons* would allow the Member States to refuse to recognise a right expressly conferred by Directive 2004/38 on family members of a Union citizen who are not nationals of a Member State, although they in fact fulfil the conditions laid down by that directive'.[507] The Court concluded that '[s]uch measures, being automatic in nature, would allow Member States to leave the provisions of Directive 2004/38 unapplied and would disregard the very substance of the primary and individual right of Union citizens to move and reside freely within the territory of the Member States and of the derived rights enjoyed by those citizens' family members who are not nationals of a Member State'.[508]

The Court did emphasise 'fulfil[ment] of the conditions laid down by [Directive 2004/38]' within these remarks. However, as explained in Chapter 7, the opposite situation is more usually *presumed* when certain citizens are excluded as a class from entitlement to equal treatment under EU law. There are therefore lessons to be drawn from *McCarthy II* about the critical importance of *demonstrating* public interest arguments,[509] and about the role of proportionality assessments; all the more at a time when the worth of authentic evidence has diminished profoundly in public life.

---

[503] ibid paras 52–53; referring by analogy to Case C-336/94 *Dafeki*, EU:C:1997:579, paras 19 and 21 (which concerned documents issued by the authorities of other Member States regarding entitlement to social security benefits).
[504] AG Szpunar in *McCarthy II*, para 139 of the Opinion.
[505] Case C-333/13 *Dano*, EU:C:2014:2358; Case C-308/14 *Commission v UK*, EU:C:2016:436.
[506] *McCarthy II*, para 55.
[507] ibid para 56 (emphasis added).
[508] ibid para 57.
[509] See more positively, AG Szpunar in Case C-411/20 *Familienkasse Niedersachsen-Bremen*, EU:C:2021:1017, paras 93–99 and 103–104 of the Opinion. See further, Chapter 7.

8. Concluding Remarks

The right to reside in another Member State under the procedures and principles of EU law is one of the most distinctive and fundamental privileges of Union citizenship, contrasting with the permission-based approach of immigration rules generally. In that light, the system envisaged and realised by Directive 2004/38, building on the rights conferred directly by EU primary law, is extraordinary. From the analysis of that system in this chapter, five themes are briefly highlighted here.

First, as Articles 20(1) and 21(1) TFEU make plain, the right to move and reside 'freely' is not unconditional: it is subject to conditions and limits. These must be 'laid down', which enhances legal certainty for citizens and enables pathways for judicial review. However, examples in this chapter of how the requirement to provide expressly for conditions and limits is met in formal terms yet not always in substantive terms call attention to the interpretation and application as much as proclamation of EU rights. Second, supporting the work of interpretation and application, it must be acknowledged that the preamble to Directive 2004/38 expresses *different* interests and objectives. As seen across this chapter, it is not uncommon that isolated interests and objectives are invoked to underpin the choices made or outcomes reached in individual cases. But it is also important to admit to and reflect on how other interests and objectives fit with the outcomes reached—not necessarily to change those outcomes, but at least to reason them fully and to locate the decisions taken more openly with reference to the complex national, supranational, and transnational dimensions of Union citizenship. Union citizenship cannot resolve all difficulties experienced when residing in a host State. But the obligations that it does produce really matter, both individually and systemically.

Third, the Court of Justice treads a difficult line between what is required of a court that must normally provide the legal tools for resolving disputes yet does not actually resolve them (acting almost always for EU citizenship law in service to a national court or tribunal), on the one hand; and a court that contributes itself to citizenship's system of residence rights, on the other. That we reach some instances where the wider implications of earlier decisions must be corrected in later cases is not surprising. However, open articulation of the reasons why is critical; and so too is engaging the wider systemic features and principles of EU law as relevant. Building on that point, fourth, and reflecting the discussion in Chapter 5, the place of the Charter of Fundamental Rights in the legal development of the right to reside in a host State is mixed: increasingly drawn from, and powerful when it is; a problematic absence, then, when it is not.

Finally, fifth, it was suggested in this chapter that Directive 2004/38 provides a 'single reference text'[510] but not a single status. Differences in legal category are a continuing feature of EU citizenship law, especially where links can be made to economic activity. In such circumstances, the obligation to be economically autonomous is displaced. This point bridges to Chapter 7, which examines not the right to reside in a host State but the extent of the right to be *protected* when residing there. That discussion assesses the link between entitlement to equal treatment in a host State and the requirement first to demonstrate that residence there is *lawful*. Fundamentally, it asks what EU citizenship law does (and can be expected to) require of host States so that Union citizens from other States who reside there may do so as *securely* as possible.

---

[510] Opinion of the Committee of the Regions (n 20) para 2.1.

Further Reading

F Ristuccia, '"Cause tramps like us, baby we were born to run": untangling the effects of the expulsion of "undesired" Union citizens: *FS*' (2022) 59 Common Market Law Review 889.

D Ritleng, 'Scope and meaning of Article 15 of Directive 2004/38: Yes but no: *Chenchooliah*' (2020) 57 Common Market Law Review 1195.

J Shaw, 'Between law and political truth? Member State preferences, EU free movement rules and national immigration law' (2015) 17 Cambridge Yearbook of European Legal Studies 247.

E Spaventa, 'The rights of citizens under the Withdrawal Agreement: a critical analysis' (2020) 45 European Law Review 193.

F Strumia, 'Divorce immediately, or leave. Rights of third country nationals and family protection in the context of EU citizens' free movement: *Kuldip Singh and Others*' (2016) 53 Common Market Law Review 1373.

A Tryfonidou, 'The ECJ recognises the right of rainbow families to move freely between EU Member States: the *VMA* ruling' (2022) 47 European Law Review 534.

7
Union Citizenship and the Host State
Part II: Equal Treatment and the Concept of Lawful Residence

1. Chapter Overview

This chapter examines the intersection of two critical dimensions of EU citizenship law as it relates to the host State: the right to equal treatment with nationals of that State, on the one hand, and the relevance of residing there lawfully in order to benefit from that right, on the other.

The right to reside in another Member State under the procedures and principles of EU law was characterised in Chapter 6 as one of the paramount privileges of Union citizenship. Expanding further on what that right actually means, the right to be treated equally with host State nationals in any situation that falls within the scope of EU law is how the 'fundamental status' of Union citizenship was conceived by the Court of Justice in the first place, in paragraph 31 of its ruling in *Grzelczyk*.[1] However, in paragraph 32, it appears that it is being '*lawfully* resident' that unlocks equal treatment with host State nationals.[2] What is it that makes residence 'lawful' in a host State in the first place? What rights flow from it and, conversely, what are the consequences when a Union citizen cannot demonstrate that they are lawfully resident?

As explained in Chapter 2, restrictions of the right to move and reside do not have to entail nationality discrimination. Home State and host State rules and practices that create obstacles to free movement, diminishing the effectiveness of EU rights, will require justification and must be proportionate. Moreover, equal treatment is not confined to considerations of nationality discrimination.[3] However, equal treatment of Union citizens that impacts host State public finances is an especially charged question. As a result, the concept of lawful residence and the case law that has evolved it claim considerable space in both Union citizenship practice and academic commentary, especially in recent years as the idea of 'welfare tourism' leeched into conceptions of *free* movement.[4] There is certainly a risk that over-emphasising

---

[1] Case C-184/99 *Grzelczyk*, EU:C:2001:458, para 31: 'Union citizenship is destined to be the fundamental status of nationals of the Member States, enabling those who find themselves in the same situation to enjoy the same treatment in law irrespective of their nationality, subject to such exceptions as are expressly provided for.' The fact that the prohibition on nationality discrimination in Article 18 TFEU applies only to situations involving Member State nationals and therefore cannot be invoked to assess differences in treatment between Union citizens and third-country nationals is also affirmed in the case law: see eg Case C-673/20 *Préfet du Gers*, EU:C:2022:449 (Chapter 5); and Case C-490/20 *VMA v Stolichna obshtina, rayon 'Pancharevo'*, EU:C:2021:1008 (Chapter 6).
[2] *Grzelczyk*, para 32: 'a citizen of the European Union, *lawfully* resident in the territory of a host Member State, can rely on Article [18] of the Treaty in all situations which fall within the scope *ratione materiae* of Community law' (emphasis added; referring to Case C-85/96 *Martínez Sala*, EU:C:1998:217, para 63).
[3] eg *VMA*, para 64 ('discrimination on the basis of the sexual orientation of the child's parents').
[4] See esp *Martínez Sala*; *Grzelczyk*; Case C-413/99 *Baumbast*, EU:C:2002:493; Case C-456/02 *Trojani*, EU:C:2004:488; Joined Cases C-22/08 and C-23/08 *Vatsouras and Koupatantze*, EU:C:2009:344; Case C-140/12 *Brey*, EU:C:2013:565; Case C-333/13 *Dano*, EU:C:2014:2358; Case C-67/14 *Alimanovic* EU:C:2015: 597; Case C-299/14 *García-Nieto*, EU:C:2016:114; Case C-308/14 *Commission v UK*, EU:C:2016:436; Case C-181/19 *Jobcenter Krefeld*, EU:C:2020:794; Case C-710/19 *GMA (Demandeur d'emploi)*, EU:C:2020:1037; Case C-719/19 *FS*, EU:C:2021:506; Case C-535/19 *A (Soins de santé publics)*, EU:C:2021:595; Case C-709/20 *CG*, EU:C:2021:602; Case C-247/20 *Commissioners for Her Majesty's Revenue and Customs (Assurance maladie complète)*, EU:C:2022:177;

these questions produces a distorted and limited understanding of Union citizenship as a source of deep legal protection in host States in the round. At the same time, lawful residence is—after the holding of Member State nationality—perhaps the most important threshold concept in EU citizenship law. It shapes not just the right to reside in a host State but residing there *securely*. Its legal arc exemplifies the complicated relationship between rights conferred by the Treaties and conditions and limits established in secondary law; underlines the significance of judicial review; challenges us to question what Union citizenship really means, and what it should mean; and raises difficult questions around themes of autonomy, responsibility, and vulnerability that we have to confront.

As a legally meaningful concept of EU citizenship law, a requirement of lawful residence predates the adoption of Directive 2004/38 (Section 2).[5] Several provisions of the Directive examined in Chapter 6—Articles 6, 7, 12, 13, and 14—establish conditions for lawful residence in a host State in specific circumstances. These conditions have both substantive and temporal elements, but they did not precisely absorb what was previously developed in the case law. Article 24 of the Directive, which outlines both a general guarantee of and specific derogations from equal treatment on the grounds of nationality, adds a further set of considerations. How the complex intersection of lawful residence, equal treatment, and proportionality has changed must therefore be considered (Section 3), acknowledging that how

---

and Case C-411/20 *Familienkasse Niedersachsen-Bremen* EU:C:2022:602. From a rich literature, see eg M Blauberger, A Heindlmaier, D Kramer, D Sindbjerg Martinsen, J Sampson Thierry, A Schenk, and B Werner, 'ECJ judges read the morning papers: explaining the turnaround of European citizenship jurisprudence' (2018) 25 Journal of European Public Policy 1422; M Cousins, 'The baseless fabric of this vision: EU citizenship, the right to reside and EU law' (2016) 23 Journal of Social Security Law 89; G Davies, 'Has the Court changed or have the cases? The deservingness of litigants as an element in Court of Justice citizenship adjudication' (2018) 5 Journal of European Public Policy 1442; M Dougan, 'The constitutional dimension to the case law on Union citizenship' (2006) 31 European Law Review 613; and 'The bubble that burst: exploring the legitimacy of the case law on the free movement of Union citizens' in M Adams, H de Waele, J Meeusen, and G Straetmans (eds), *Judging Europe's Judges: The Legitimacy of the Case Law of the European Court of Justice* (Hart Publishing 2013) 127; Editorial comments 'The free movement of persons in the European Union: salvaging the dream while explaining the nightmare' (2014) 51 Common Market Law Review 729; A Heindlmaier, 'Mobile EU citizens and the "unreasonable burden": how EU Member States deal with residence rights at the street level' in S Mantu, P Minderhoud, and E Guild (eds), *EU Citizenship and Free Movement Rights: Taking Supranational Citizenship Seriously* (Brill 2020) 140; K Hailbronner, 'Union citizenship and access to social benefits' (2005) 42 Common Market Law Review 1245; A Iliopoulou-Penot, 'Deconstructing the former edifice of Union citizenship? The *Alimanovic* judgment' (2016) 53 Common Market Law Review 1007; M Jesse and DW Carter, 'The "*Dano* evolution": assessing legal integration and access to social benefits for EU citizens' (2018) 3 European Papers 1186; D Kramer, 'Earning social citizenship in the European Union: free movement and access to social assistance benefits reconstructed' (2016) 18 Cambridge Yearbook of European Legal Studies 270; S Mantu and P Minderhoud, 'Exploring the links between residence and social rights for economically inactive EU citizens' (2019) European Journal of Migration and Law 313; N Nic Shuibhne, 'Limits rising, duties ascending: the changing legal shape of Union citizenship' (2015) 52 Common Market Law Review 889; C O'Brien, '*Civis capitalist sum*: class as the new guiding principle of EU free movement rights' (2016) 53 Common Market Law Review 937 and 'The great EU citizenship illusion exposed: equal treatment rights evaporate for the vulnerable (*CG v The Department for Communities in Northern Ireland*) (Case Comment)' (2021) 46 European Law Review 801; N Rennuy, 'The trilemma of EU social benefits law: seeing the wood and the trees' (2019) 56 Common Market Law Review 1549; U Šadl and S Sankari, 'Why did the citizenship jurisprudence change?' in D Thym (ed), *Questioning EU Citizenship: Judges and Limits of Free Movement and Solidarity in the EU* (Hart Publishing 2017) 89; M Tecqmenne, 'Migrant jobseekers, right of residence and access to welfare benefits: one step forward, two steps backwards?' (2021) 46 European Law Review 765; D Thym, 'The elusive limits of solidarity: residence rights of and social benefits for economically inactive Union citizens' (2015a) 52 Common Market Law Review 17 and 'When Union citizens turn into illegal migrants: the *Dano* case' (2015b) 40 European Law Review 249; and H Verschueren, 'Preventing "benefit tourism" in the EU: a narrow or broad interpretation of the possibilities offered by the ECJ in *Dano*?' (2015a) 52 Common Market Law Review 363 and 'Free movement of EU citizens: including for the poor?' (2015b) 22 Maastricht Journal of European and Comparative Law 10.

[5] Directive 2004/38/EC on the right of citizens of the Union and their family members to move and reside freely within the territory of the Member States, 2004 OJ L158/77.

mechanisms for establishing or demonstrating lawful residence became more constricted and, notwithstanding the regulatory cohesion that Directive 2004/38 seeks, more fragmented over time. The assessment of lawful residence and equal treatment in that part of the chapter is therefore organised around sources of residence rights, addressing, in turn, residence based on different provisions of the Directive; other measures of EU secondary law; EU primary law directly; and national law.

The capacity and/or tendency of both case law and legislative reform to react to specific flashpoints—for present purposes, deepening agitation about the impact, actual or potential, on host State public finances when Union citizens are not working or self-employed; and increasingly, when they are economically active but not economically autonomous[6]—has shaped conceptions of lawful residence that disturbed established legal principles yet failed to work into the changed legal picture what happens to residence status as well as to the fundamental principle of equal treatment in such circumstances. As a result, classes of tolerated Union citizens have been exposed: Member State nationals who are not necessarily *unlawfully* present in a host State yet who are not fully recognised or protected there under EU citizenship law either. Where and to what extent responsibility should then lie will be considered. In that light, a 'stone by stone' method may well describe how EU citizenship law *has been* constructed;[7] but it may not be enough for the optimal development of EU citizenship law into the future. Above all, the Court underlines that 'Directive 2004/38 introduced *a gradual system* as regards the right of residence in the host Member State, *which reproduces, in essence,* the stages and conditions set out in the various instruments of European Union law and case-law preceding that directive and culminates in the right of permanent residence'.[8]

The discussion in Section 3 will also show that the Court has now reconsidered some of its more fragmentary rulings and, as a result, EU citizenship law on equal treatment and lawful residence better coheres. More specifically, the Court has drawn residence based on *some* aspect of EU law back into the orbit of lawful residence, reaffirming entitlement to equal treatment in the host State in a wider than feared range of situations. Nevertheless, disparities and gaps in protection remain, notably for Member State nationals who reside lawfully in a host State under national but not EU law. These situations are reflected on in this chapter from the wider perspective of residence security (Section 4), distinguishing between functional or purposive category differences in EU citizenship law, on the one hand, and more problematic category differences that gloss over responsibility for the welfare of citizens or from transitioning between different stages of residence status, on the other. The questions considered also include the consequences of unlawful residence from the perspective of when and how a host State can trigger an expulsion decision under Article 15(1) of the Directive[9]—and the emerging role of the Charter of Fundamental Rights.

---

[6] See esp the proposals to restrict 'in-work benefits' and index exported family benefits to the child's State of residence in Section D, Decision of the Heads of State or Government, meeting within the European Council, concerning a new settlement for the United Kingdom within the European Union, 2016 OJ C691/1. See generally, N Nic Shuibhne, 'Economic activity and EU citizenship law: seeding means-based logic in a status-based freedom' in N Nic Shuibhne (ed), *Revisiting the Fundamentals of EU Law on the Free Movement of Persons* (OUP 2023) forthcoming.

[7] K Lenaerts, 'EU citizenship and the European Court of Justice's "stone-by-stone" approach' (2015) 1 International Comparative Jurisprudence 1.

[8] Joined Cases C-316/16 and C-424/16 *B and Vomero*, EU:C:2018:256, para 51 (emphasis added). Permanent residence is addressed in Chapter 8.

[9] Article 15 of the Directive is examined in Chapter 6.

2. Foundations: The Concept of Lawful Residence and Its Relationship to Equal Treatment in EU Citizenship Law

In EU law on the free movement of persons generally, there were sporadic rather than systematic references to lawful residence before Union citizenship. For example, to establish protection under EU law for Member State nationals who exercised free movement rights and then returned to their home States, the Court ruled in *Knoors* that such situations were not purely internal: rather, 'the reference in [Article 49 TFEU] to "nationals of a Member State" who wish to establish themselves "in the territory of another Member State" cannot be interpreted in such a way as to exclude from the benefit of [Union] law a given Member State's own nationals when the latter, owing to the fact *that they have lawfully resided on the territory of another Member State* and have there acquired a trade qualification which is recognized by the provisions of [Union] law, are, with regard to their State of origin, in a situation which may be assimilated to that of any other persons enjoying the rights and liberties guaranteed by the Treaty'.[10] Similarly, in *Mutsch*, the Court stated that Article 45 TFEU is 'based on the principle that nationals of any Member State *lawfully established* in another Member State for the purpose of employment must be treated in the same way as nationals of that State'.[11]

That case law provides a first characteristic of the concept of lawful residence in suggesting a *legally meaningful connection between lawful residence and equal treatment*. But such references to lawful residence were rare: even in the same paragraph in *Mutsch*, the Court stated that what is now Article 18 TFEU must be applied 'in every respect and in all circumstances governed by [Union] law to *any person established* in a Member State'.[12] For case law on work, services, or establishment, the idea of 'circumstances governed by Union law' was more concerned with whether or not the claimant met the definition of the relevant *activity*. For example, if a Member State national resided in another State and worked there within the meaning of EU law, the personal scope threshold of EU law was crossed and it made residence there 'lawful' in that narrow sense at least. At the other end of the scale, the outer parameters of lawful residence were marked by the grounds of public policy, public security, and public health. There, it was considered that the procedural safeguards provided for in Directive 64/221 required a 'broad interpretation as regards the persons to whom they apply',[13] and it will be seen in Section 3 that this idea was later transposed to lawful residence in the context of restricting EU citizenship rights—or rather, to setting lawful residence aside as a material factor in such cases since '[t]o exclude from the benefit of those substantive and procedural safeguards citizens of the Union *who are not lawfully resident* on the territory of the host Member State would deprive those safeguards of their essential effectiveness'.[14]

---

[10] Case 115/78 *Knoors*, EU:C:1979:31, para 24 (emphasis added); confirmed in eg Case C-19/92 *Kraus*, EU:C:1993:125, para 15; and Case C-234/97 *Fernández de Bobadilla*, EU:C:1999:367, para 30.
[11] Case 137/84 *Mutsch*, EU:C:1985:335, para 12 (emphasis added).
[12] ibid (emphasis added).
[13] Case C-459/99 *MRAX*, EU:C:2002:461, para 101. Directive 64/221/EEC on the coordination of special measures concerning the movement and residence of foreign nationals which are justified on grounds of public policy, public security or public health, OJ 1963–1964 Sp Ed 117.
[14] Case C-50/06 *Commission v Netherlands*, EU:C:2007:325, para 35 (emphasis added); referring to *MRAX*, para 101. Note also the silence of the Court on lawful residence in case law on Union citizenship and Council Framework Decision 2002/584/JHA on the European arrest warrant and the surrender procedures between Member States—Statements made by certain Member States on the adoption of the Framework Decision, 2002 OJ L190/1; see further, Chapter 3.

That example provides a counterpoint to the deeper connection between lawful residence and equal treatment with host State nationals, seeding a second characteristic of lawful residence: Member State nationals benefit from a (limited) set of *procedural rights in a host State irrespective of their residence status* there.

The 1990s Residence Directives did not refer expressly to lawful residence but they implied its significance for situations where free movement rights are disconnected from economic activity, establishing that 'Member States shall grant the right of residence to nationals of Member States who do not enjoy this right under other provisions of Community law and to members of their families ... *provided that* they themselves and the members of their families are covered by sickness insurance in respect of all risks in the host Member State and have sufficient resources to avoid *becoming a burden* on the social assistance system of the host Member State during their period of residence'.[15] The third characteristic of lawful residence suggested by these Directives is thus that *conditional residence in the host State* comes more sharply into focus when free movement is *decoupled from the Treaty's economic freedoms*.

Before the adoption of Directive 2004/38, the embedding of lawful residence as a significant concept of EU citizenship law specifically first surfaced in the case law (Section 2.1), producing a strengthened link between lawful residence and equal treatment in a host State, on the one hand, while emphasising the mitigating effects of proportionality, on the other. The adoption of the Directive was intended to 'to simplify and strengthen the right of free movement and residence of all Union citizens' (recital 3) and to '[remedy] th[e] sector-by-sector, piecemeal approach to the right of free movement and residence and facilitate[e] the exercise of this right' (recital 4), which suggests that relevant conditions and mechanisms for determining lawful residence in a host State should now be drawn from it. In that light, the Court's perception of the Directive's 'gradual system' of host State residence rights, which '*reproduces, in essence,* the stages and conditions set out in the various instruments of European Union law *and case-law preceding that directive*' is particularly important.[16] The drafting history and principal features of Article 24 of the Directive, which constitutes both a guarantee of and legitimate derogations from the principle of equal treatment, are also considered (Section 2.2), before equal treatment in the different stages of that system is examined in detail in Section 3.

---

[15] Directive 90/364/EEC on the right of residence, 1990 OJ L180/26, Article 1. For retired persons, see Article 1 of Directive 90/365/EEC on the right of residence for employees and self-employed persons who have ceased their occupational activity, 1990 OJ L180/28. For Directive 93/96/EEC on the right of residence for students, 1993 OJ L317/59, the requirement was slightly different, as explained in Chapter 6: Article 1 made provision for 'assur[ing] the relevant national authority, by means of a declaration or by such alternative means as the student may choose that are at least equivalent, that he has sufficient resources to avoid becoming a burden on the social assistance system of the host Member State during their period of residence ... and that he is covered by sickness insurance in respect of all risks in the host Member State'. Note also the judgments in Case C-109/01 *Akrich*, EU:C:2003:491 and Case C-127/08 *Metock and Others*, EU:C:2008:449, addressing requirements of *prior* lawful residence for the spouses of EU workers and Union citizens respectively; see further, Chapter 4.

[16] Joined Cases C-316/16 and C-424/16 *B and Vomero*, EU:C:2018:256, para 51 (emphasis added). In its response to the Commission's original proposal for Directive 2004/38 (COM(2001) 257 final), the European Parliament recommended a new provision ('Article 4a'), which would have provided that '[t]his Directive shall not lead to the withdrawal of existing rights established by the legislation of the European Union *or Court of Justice decision*' (European Parliament Report of 23 January 2003, A5–0009/2003, Amendment 23; emphasis added). In the amended proposal, the Parliament's amendment was listed with several others as amendments that 'cannot be accepted as they are not consistent with the Commission proposal', without further explanation (COM(2003) 199 final, 11).

2.1 Before Directive 2004/38: Lawful Residence, Equal Treatment, and the Case Law of the Court of Justice

In this part of the chapter, the formative link between Union citizenship, lawful residence, and equal treatment forged by the Court of Justice in the early years of EU citizenship law is first outlined (Section 2.1.1). Because the residence rights and equal treatment claims of Member State nationals seeking work in a host State connect to a distinctive 'hybrid system',[17] drawing elements from both Articles 45 and 21 TFEU, case law on similar questions for jobseekers is addressed separately (Section 2.1.2).

2.1.1 Union citizenship, equal treatment, and lawful residence: case law foundations

The rulings in *Martínez Sala*, *Grzelczyk*, *Trojani*, and *Baumbast* built the foundations of EU citizenship law. Importantly for present purposes, the concept of lawful residence was rooted into the reasoning of the Court in all of them and five key points are highlighted here.

First, but only in *Martínez Sala*, residing lawfully in the host State was applied as a *precondition to coming within the personal scope of Union citizenship*. The applicant was a Spanish national residing in Germany. She did not possess a residence permit at the material time, but the referring court 'point[ed] out that the European Convention on Social and Medical Assistance of 11 December 1953 did not ... allow her to be deported'.[18] The Court therefore found that it was 'not necessary' to examine whether the applicant could rely on what is now Article 21 TFEU 'to obtain recognition of a *new* right to reside in the territory of the Member State concerned, since it is common ground that she has already been *authorised* to reside there'.[19] In consequence, '[a]s a national of a Member State *lawfully residing* in the territory of another Member State, the appellant in the main proceedings comes within the scope *ratione personae* of the provisions of the Treaty on European citizenship'.[20] Unusually for a Union citizenship case where cross-border movement had already taken place, the Court engaged the *status* conferred by Article 20 TFEU (read in conjunction with Article 18 TFEU) rather than the *rights* conferred by Article 21 TFEU.

However, as indicated above, the link that the Court drew between lawful residence and the personal scope of the Treaty was never repeated after *Martínez Sala*. Had this part of the ruling caught on, it might have embedded systematic assessment of the residence status of a Union citizen before considering relevant substantive claims mjuch earlier in the evolution of EU citizenship law. But residence status was rarely considered as an element of personal scope: instead, confirming the existence of a factor connecting a Union citizen's situation to EU law sufficed, fulfilled normally by the act of moving to a host State in the first place. Thus, a standard expression was that '*every citizen of the Union* may rely on Article 18 TFEU, which prohibits any discrimination on grounds of nationality, in all situations falling within

---

[17] AG Ruiz-Jarabo Colomer in Joined Cases C-22/08 and C-23/08 *Vatsouras and Koupatantze*, EU:C:2009:150, paras 30 and 34 of the Opinion.

[18] Case C-85/96 *Martínez Sala*, EU:C:1998:217, para 14.

[19] ibid para 60 (emphasis added); see similarly, para 65. AG La Pergola outlined submissions from the German Government to the effect that the applicant did not fulfil the conditions for residence under EU law set out in Directive 90/364 (AG La Pergola in *Martínez Sala*, EU:C:1997:335, para 15 of the Opinion).

[20] *Martínez Sala*, para 61. In terms of material scope, discussed further in Chapter 2, the benefit claimed in *Martínez Sala* was a child-raising allowance 'automatically granted to persons fulfilling certain objective criteria, without any individual and discretionary assessment of personal needs, and which is intended to meet family expenses'; it therefore fell 'within the scope *ratione materiae* of [Union] law as a family benefit within the meaning of Article 4(1)(h) of Regulation No 1408/71 and as a social advantage within the meaning of Article 7(2) of Regulation No 1612/68' (ibid para 28).

the scope *ratione materiae* of European Union law, those situations including the exercise of the freedom conferred by Article 21 TFEU to move and reside within the territory of the Member States'.²¹ The fact that a Union citizen *was* residing lawfully was sometimes mentioned in preliminary references, though that, too, seemed to focus on the act of moving from one Member State to another. However, movement per se cannot determine the lawfulness of residence in a host State thereafter. More recently, as shown in Section 3, national courts have been instructed more directly to assess the lawfulness of the Union citizen's residence in the host State: though almost exclusively in cases where the equal treatment of Union citizens residing under Article 7(1)(b) of the Directive comes into conflict with the protection of the public finances of the host State. That does make cases where equal treatment obligations are still applied without reference to lawful residence more striking.²²

A second feature of the foundational case law concerns the *possible sources of lawful residence*. The approach taken by the Court in *Martínez Sala* meant, in effect, that residence in a host State that did not comply with the conditions in the 1990s Directives might still be *lawful* residence and therefore engage Article 20 (and Article 18) TFEU. In that case, the applicant's right to reside in Germany was based on an international convention and that was accepted by the Court as a source of lawful residence for the purposes of coming within the scope of EU citizenship law. Advocate General La Pergola observed that Mrs Martínez Sala was '*authorised* to reside in Germany, outside the ambit of the conditions laid down by [Directive 90/364]. *That does not, however,* mean ... that the plaintiff's individual situation, on which she relies in order to claim the same treatment as German nationals, rests on national law and cannot therefore have any foundation in [Union] law'.²³ The Court also referred to Mrs Martínez Sala'a residence in Germany as 'authorised'.²⁴ That could be read as requiring some active step or measure on the part of the host State, but the Court did not explain this point further.²⁵ However, the issue returned to the Court soon afterwards in *Grzelczyk*.

Mr Grzelczyk, a French national, applied for social assistance in the final year of his university studies in Belgium, demonstrating through that application that he did *not* possess sufficient financial resources. Addressing that requirement as a condition in Directive 93/96, the Court held that since the Directive only required a declaration from the student as

---

²¹ Case C-73/08 *Bressol and Others*, EU:C:2010:181, para 31 (emphasis added); see similarly, Case C-75/11 *Commission v Austria*, EU:C:2012:605, para 39.

²² See esp the line of case law based on Case C-182/15 *Petruhhin*, EU:C:2016:630, discussed in Chapter 2. In Case C-75/11 *Commission v Austria*, EU:C:2012:605, the Court stated simply that 'a national of a Member State who is studying in Austria may rely on the right, enshrined in Articles 18 TFEU and 21 TFEU, to move and reside freely within the territory of the host Member State, without being subject to direct or indirect discrimination on grounds of their nationality' (para 41), with no reference to lawful residence and the conditions in Article 7(1)(c) of the Directive. See similarly, Case C-247/17 *Raugevicius*, EU:C:2018:898, para 46. In *Prete*, the Court did refer to being 'lawfully resident' for the purposes of relying on Article 18 TFEU, but it did not mention the conditions in Directive 2004/38 specifically (Case C-367/11 *Prete*, EU:C:2012:668, para 24).

²³ AG La Pergola in *Martínez Sala*, para 19 of the Opinion (emphasis added). See similarly, para 22 of the Opinion: '[e]ntitlement to the allowance ... arises from the Member State's *authorising or allowing* a Community citizen to stay or reside in its own territory and not from the issue of the residence permit required under the German legislation for its grant' (emphasis added). In *Pereira Roque*, the same Advocate General referred to his earlier Opinion in *Martínez Sala* 'in which [he] interpreted Articles [20 and 21 TFEU] as meaning that a Community citizen *however authorised or admitted to reside or stay in the territory of a Member State* is entitled to the education allowance provided for by national legislation, irrespective of whether that person holds a valid residence permit, on the same conditions as citizens of the host State' (AG La Pergola in Case C-171/96 *Pereira Roque*, EU:C:1997:425, fn 64 of the Opinion, emphasis added).

²⁴ *Martínez Sala*, paras 47, 49, 60, and 65.

²⁵ The referring court construed it more passively as protection against expulsion, which 'of necessity entails the right to reside in the host State' (AG La Pergola in *Martínez Sala*, fn 10 of the Opinion).

regards possessing sufficient resources, it 'differ[ed] from Directives 90/364 and 90/365, which do indicate the minimum level of income that persons wishing to avail themselves of those directives must have'—a difference 'explained by the special characteristics of student residence'.[26] The Court found that 'a student's financial position may change with the passage of time for reasons beyond his control' and that '[t]he truthfulness of a student's declaration is therefore to be assessed only as at the time when it is made'.[27] The host State could take the view that a student having recourse to its social assistance system no longer fulfilled the conditions for a right of residence under Directive 93/96 and could therefore withdraw or not renew the residence permit so long as such measures were not an 'automatic consequence'.[28] But the arguable converse of that finding, even if by implication only, is that a student is lawfully resident if such measures are *not* taken. In that perspective, the Court seemed to attach more significance to the inaction and thus tolerance of the host State than to whether the student claiming financial support (still) complied with the Directive's conditions for lawful residence.[29] However, the ruling is ambiguous and therefore raises an important question: if circumstances change following the initial declaration attesting to sufficient resources, is a student still residing lawfully within the meaning of EU legislation (that legislation itself accommodating the change in circumstances) or does their residence, lawful or otherwise, now escape those boundaries? That question remains open more than two decades since the ruling in *Grzelczyk*. It is returned to in Section 3.1.

To recap up to this point: in *Martínez Sala*, the right to reside was connected to protection against expulsion under an international convention to which the host State and the citizen's home State were signatories and only the *status* of Union citizenship (and therefore Article 20 TFEU) was invoked to engage Article 18 TFEU as regards the substantive benefit being claimed. In *Grzelczyk*, the Court focused on the student's free movement *rights* under Article 21 TFEU and then explained how Directive 93/96 differed in its approach to the condition of sufficient resources compared to Directives 90/364 and 90/365, alsos highlighting that the host State had neither withdrawn the residence permit nor opted not to renew it.

Thus, the particularities of the circumstances of both cases clouded a more generalised understanding of lawful residence as a concept of EU citizenship law, which came soon afterwards in *Trojani*. Mr Trojani was a French national residing in Belgium. He was not economically active and applied for income support in Belgium, ruling out the possibility that his right to reside could be based on Article 21 TFEU because of the unambiguous sufficient resources requirement in Directive 90/364 compared to Directive 93/96.[30] However, it was found that 'according to information put before the Court, Mr Trojani is lawfully resident in Belgium, as is *attested by* the residence permit which has in the meantime been issued to him by the municipal authorities of Brussels'.[31] The Court ruled that while Member States

---

[26] Case C-184/99 *Grzelczyk*, EU:C:2001:458, para 41.
[27] ibid para 45.
[28] ibid para 43.
[29] See similarly, Case C-209/03 *Bidar*, EU:C:2005:169, para 47: '[i]n a context such as that of the main proceedings *where the right of residence of the applicant for assistance is not contested*, the assertion, made by some of the governments which have submitted observations, that [Union] law allows a Member State to take the view that a national of another Member State who has recourse to social assistance no longer fulfils the conditions of his right of residence and if appropriate to take measures, within the limits imposed by [Union] law, for the removal of that national ... is moreover immaterial' (emphasis added). See also, Case C-357/98 *Yiadom*, EU:C:2000:604, paras 39–41. See, in contrast, the submissions of the Danish Government and the Commission in *Grzelczyk* to the effect that the right of residence conferred by Article 21 TFEU is more straightforwardly conditioned by the requirement of actually possessing sufficient resources (as outlined by AG Alber in *Grzelczyk*, EU:C:2000:518, paras 43–44 and 62 of the Opinion).
[30] Case C-456/02 *Trojani*, EU:C:2004:488, paras 35–36.
[31] ibid para 37 (emphasis added).

'may make residence of a citizen of the Union who is not economically active conditional on his having sufficient resources, that does not mean that such a person cannot, during his lawful residence in the host Member State, benefit from the fundamental principle of equal treatment as laid down in Article [18 TFEU]'.[32] On the contrary, 'a citizen of the Union who is not economically active may rely on Article [18 TFEU] where he has been lawfully resident in the host Member State for a certain time *or possesses a residence permit*'.[33] Moreover, and differently from *Martínez Sala*, no reference was made to Article 20 TFEU; Article 18 TFEU was discussed much more generally with reference to Mr Trojani's Member State-authorised residence status.

As explained in Chapter 6, administrative formalities such as residence permits are declaratory rather than constitutive of the rights conferred by the Treaty.[34] However, the Court's approach in *Trojani* constituted an EU right through a national residence permit, at least in terms of what amounts to *lawful* residence. In his Opinion, Advocate General Geelhoed had emphasised the nature of the residence permit rather than the fact that it was issued under national and not EU rules. Having first characterised the situation in *Grzelczyk* as one in which a Union citizen 'derive[d] his right of residence from [Union] law' (presumably because of the Court's generous interpretation of Directive 93/96), which in turn brought Mr Grzelczyk's situation within the scope of EU citizenship law for the purposes of equal treatment, he then continued:

> [E]ven if a residence permit is *issued purely on the basis of national law*, as in the case of Mr Trojani, there remains the possibility of prohibited discrimination on grounds of nationality. This might well have been the case if Mr Trojani had been granted *indefinite leave to stay*. His residence status would then have been comparable to that of a Belgian subject and the refusal to grant an allowance would have been a consequence, not of a difference in residence status, but of a difference in nationality. However, in the present case no such permit was issued. If, on the other hand – as, according to the file, happened in this particular case – a *temporary residence permit* is issued and ... the Union citizen concerned does not have an unconditional right of residence, that citizen cannot claim social assistance from the Member State even on the basis of the non-discrimination principle. His right of residence is not comparable in all respects to that enjoyed by a person who is present and settled in the Kingdom of Belgium in accordance with the legislation of that Member State.[35]

The Court did not engage this distinction in *Trojani*, though it may have influenced the more recent *Dano* judgment, discussed in Section 3.1. It did repeat in *Trojani* the other point made in *Grzelczyk*—that Union citizens who no longer fulfil the conditions of the right to reside under EU law may be expelled from the host State 'within the limits imposed by [Union] law'.[36] Conversely, not taking that action—compounded in *Trojani* by the issuing of a residence permit—generated host State responsibility in the sphere of equal treatment. In that

---

[32] ibid para 40.
[33] ibid para 43 (emphasis added) See similarly, para 46: 'once it is ascertained that a person in a situation such as that of the claimant in the main proceedings is in possession of a residence permit, he may rely on Article [18 TFEU] in order to be granted a social assistance benefit such as the minimex'. Confirmed in *Bidar*, para 37.
[34] eg *Martínez Sala*, para 53.
[35] AG Geelhoed in *Trojani*, EU:C:2004:112, paras 73–74 of the Opinion (emphasis added). Placing similar emphasis on the argument that 'once a person's legal position has been equated as a matter of national law to that of nationals resident in a Member State this entitles that person to equality of treatment in respect of matters coming within the scope of the Treaty', see AG Geelhoed in Case C-213/05 *Geven*, EU:C:2006:616, para 35 of the Opinion.
[36] *Trojani*, para 45.

light, a third quality of lawful residence from the pre-Directive 2004/38 case law is that *a Union citizen who is lawfully resident in the territory of the host Member State can rely on Article 18 TFEU in all situations falling within the scope of Union law*.[37] Such situations 'include those involving the exercise ... of the right to move and reside freely in another Member State, as conferred by Article [21 TFEU]'.[38]

Thus, at this stage of the case law, exercising free movement under Article 21 TFEU combined with *a* lawful residence status in the host State enabled protection against nationality discrimination under Article 18 TFEU, which meant that host State restrictions had to be justified and proportionate. In *Martínez Sala*, the Commission had argued that protection against discrimination under EU law should apply only to those holding residence rights based on EU law.[39] But Advocate General La Pergola envisaged a different conclusion through the first expression of Union citizenship as the 'fundamental' status of Member State nationals.[40] He directly confronted the question of disconnect between residence rights based on international law as observed by the host State, on the one hand, and protection against discrimination under EU law, on the other:

> If – as in this case – a [Union] citizen is in any event granted the right to reside in a Member State other than his Member State of origin, his right not to be discriminated against in relation to nationals of the host State continues to exist for as long as he is resident there: *even if the person concerned is unable to rely on [Directive 90/364], that right derives directly and autonomously from the primary rule of Article [20 TFEU]*, which in the application of the Treaty is relevant in conferring on the person concerned the status of Union citizen. That individual status will always and in any circumstances be retained by the nationals of any Member State: consequently, in this case, *it does not matter whether leave to reside in the host State was derived from the directive or from the domestic law of the Member State concerned*.[41]

The 1990s Residence Directives had generalised free movement and residence rights beyond the exercise of economic activity, but they did not include equal treatment guarantees concerning financial assistance in the host State: rather, the sufficient resources and sickness insurance conditions appeared to rule that out. In *Grzelczyk*, the Court acknowledged that 'Article 3 of Directive 93/96 makes clear that the directive does not establish any right to payment of maintenance grants by the host Member State for students who benefit from the right of residence'.[42] But it then held that, '[o]n the other hand, there are no provisions in the directive that *preclude* those to whom it applies from receiving social security benefits'.[43] In *Trojani*, that approach was extended beyond the specific features of Directive 93/96, through the finding that 'while the Member States may make residence of a citizen of the Union who is not economically active conditional on his having sufficient resources, that does not mean

---

[37] *Martínez Sala*, para 63; *Grzelczyk*, para 32. Confirmed in eg Case C-138/02 *Collins*, EU:C:2004:172, para 61; and *Bidar*, para 32.
[38] *Grzelczyk*, para 33. Confirmed in eg Case C-148/02 *Garcia-Avello*, EU:C:2003:539, paras 24 and 26–27; and Case C-158/07 *Förster*, EU:C:2008:630, para 37.
[39] AG La Pergola in *Martínez Sala*, para 23 of the Opinion.
[40] ibid para 18 of the Opinion.
[41] ibid para 20 of the Opinion (emphasis added). In fn 10, the Advocate General pointed to the recognition in EU law of more extensive rights granted by international agreements in the field of social security, referring to Case C-227/89 *Rönfeldt*, EU:C:1991:52 and Case C-475/93 *Thévenon*, EU:C:1995:371.
[42] *Grzelczyk*, para 39.
[43] ibid (emphasis added).

that such a person cannot, during his lawful residence in the host Member State, benefit from the fundamental principle of equal treatment as laid down in Article [18 TFEU]'.[44] The Court made no meaningful distinction at this time between social security benefits not based on an assessment of need—for example, the child-raising allowance applied for in *Martínez Sala*—and social assistance—such as the income support applied for in *Grzelczyk* and *Trojani*. Nevertheless, an important qualifier was added. In *Grzelczyk*, the statement in the preamble to Directive 93/96 (included in all three Directives) that 'beneficiaries of the right of residence must not become an unreasonable burden on the public finances of the host Member State' was invoked to determine that some burdens must therefore be *reasonable*, evidencing, for the Court, that 'Directive 93/96, like Directives 90/364 and 90/365, thus accepts a certain degree of financial solidarity between nationals of a host Member State and nationals of other Member States'.[45] Soon afterwards, the Court reversed the exclusions from equal treatment it had established in previous case law for both student-specific and jobseeker-specific assistance,[46] rejecting the view that Union citizenship did not create rights 'more extensive than those already stemming from the ... Treaty and secondary legislation'.[47] This development is examined for jobseekers in Section 2.1.2. On maintenance grants for students, the Court articulated the legal significance of citizenship for equal treatment claims in *Bidar*:

> It is true that the Court held in *Lair* and *Brown* ... that 'at the present stage of development of [Union] law assistance given to students for maintenance and for training falls in principle outside the scope of the ... Treaty for the purposes of Article [18 TFEU]'. In those judgments the Court considered that such assistance was, on the one hand, a matter of education policy, which was not as such included in the spheres entrusted to the Community institutions, and, on the other, a matter of social policy, which fell within the competence of the Member States in so far as it was not covered by specific provisions of the ... Treaty. However, since judgment was given in *Lair* and *Brown*, the Treaty on European Union has introduced citizenship of the Union ... In view of those developments ... it must be considered that the situation of a citizen of the Union who is lawfully resident in another Member State falls within the scope of application of the Treaty within the meaning of [Article 18(1) TFEU] for the purposes of obtaining assistance for students, whether in the form of a subsidised loan or a grant, intended to cover his maintenance costs.[48]

Bidar confirmed that lawful residence in a host State following the exercise of free movement rights under Article 21 TFEU triggered an equal treatment assessment with respect to Article 18 TFEU. More broadly, reflecting *Trojani*, the Court held that 'a citizen of the Union who is not economically active may rely on the first paragraph of Article [18 TFEU] where he

---

[44] *Trojani*, para 40.
[45] Case C-184/99 *Grzelczyk*, EU:C:2001:458, para 44. In later cases, the converse of this point—that protecting host State public finances was a legitimate interest—would become more prominent, as shown below.
[46] Differently from the benefits claimed in *Martínez Sala*, *Grzelczyk*, and *Trojani*, which fell within the material scope of EU legislation on the free movement of workers and social security coordination.
[47] AG Geelhoed in Case C-413/01 *Ninni-Orasche*, EU:C:2003:117, para 71 of the Opinion.
[48] *Bidar*, paras 38–39 and 41; referring to Case 39/86 *Lair*, EU:C:1988:322, para 15 and Case 197/86 *Brown*, EU:C:198:323, para 18. In his Opinion, AG Geelhoed noted that '[a]ll Member State Governments having submitted written observations and the Commission consider that financial assistance with maintenance costs provided to students continues to fall outside the scope of application of the ... Treaty' (AG Geelhoed in *Bidar*, EU:C:2004:175, para 37 of the Opinion).

has been lawfully resident in the host Member State for a certain time *or possesses a residence permit*'.[49]

However, *Bidar* also progressed the capacity of the host State to protect its public finances since 'entitlement by lawfully resident EU citizens to social benefits in these situations is not absolute and ... the Member States may subject eligibility to these benefits to certain objective, i.e. non-discriminatory, conditions in order to protect their legitimate interests'.[50] In other words, the Court applied the genuine link test discussed in Chapter 2: permitting, for equal treatment as regards student finance, proportionate conditions that evidenced a 'certain degree of integration' with host State society.[51] The legitimate interest underpinning such conditions is that they enable a host State 'to ensure that the grant of assistance to cover the maintenance costs of students from other Member States does not become an unreasonable burden which could have consequences for the overall level of assistance which may be granted'.[52]

A fourth feature of lawful residence that emerged in the foundational case law is that while the right to reside in another State is 'conferred subject to the limitations and conditions laid down by [the] Treaty and by the measures adopted to give it effect ... *the application of the limitations and conditions acknowledged in Article [21(1) TFEU] in respect of the exercise of that right of residence is subject to judicial review*'.[53] In *Martínez Sala*, Advocate General La Pergola distinguished between the *existence* of the right to move and reside, which is based on primary EU law, and the conditions that apply to its *exercise*, found in the Treaties and in EU legislation.[54] By establishing a role for judicial review, the Court established, in turn, a role for proportionality as a principle that could mediate between the conferring and the conditioning of rights.[55] Ensuring that Union citizens who resided in a host State (and were not economically active there) did not become an *unreasonable* burden on the host State's social assistance system was a legitimate public interest; at the same time, restrictive national measures had to be both appropriate and necessary for achieving that interest.[56]

Crucially, proportionality was relevant to both the public finances of the host State in a systemic sense and the application of the conditions for lawful residence in EU legislation in an individual sense. On the first point, accepting reasonable burdens was as an expectation of host States in light of ensuring the effectiveness of rights conferred by the fundamental status of Union citizenship, especially where a citizen's financial difficulties were likely to be temporary.[57] On the second point, when applying the conditions for lawful residence in EU legislation in an individual case, 'the competent authorities and, where necessary, the national courts must ensure that those limitations and conditions are applied in compliance with the general principles of [Union] law and, in particular, the principle of proportionality'.[58] In

---

[49] *Bidar*, para 37 (emphasis added); confirming *Trojani*, para 37.
[50] AG Geelhoed in *Bidar*, para 30 of the Opinion.
[51] *Bidar*, paras 57–62. See subsequently, however, the limitations on eligibility for student finance in Article 24(2) of the Directive, discussed in Section 2.2.2. A similar but more specific test for jobseekers—reflecting links to the host State employment market rather than host State society more openly—had also recently been developed in the case law: see further, Section 2.1.2.
[52] *Bidar*, para 56.
[53] Case C-413/99 *Baumbast and R*, EU:C:2002:493, paras 85–86 (emphasis added).
[54] AG La Pergola in Case C-85/96 *Martínez Sala*, EU:C:1997:335, para 18 of the Opinion.
[55] eg *Baumbast*, paras 89–91; Case C-200/02 *Zhu and Chen*, EU:C:2004:639, para 32. The legality of EU legislative conditions was not the focal point in these rulings; but see later, Joined Cases C-22/08 and C-23/08 *Vatsouras and Koupatantze*, EU:C:2009:344, discussed in Section 2.2.2.
[56] Case C-184/99 *Grzelczyk*, EU:C:2001:458, para 44.
[57] ibid.
[58] *Baumbast*, para 94.

Baumbast, for example, the Court ruled that 'to refuse to allow Mr Baumbast to exercise the right of residence which is conferred on him by Article [21(1) TFEU] by virtue of the application of the provisions of Directive 90/364 on the ground that his sickness insurance does not cover the emergency treatment given in the host Member State would amount to a disproportionate interference with the exercise of that right'.[59]

Finally, the fifth feature of lawful residence, as developed in case law before Directive 2004/38 came into force, concerns *procedural safeguards guaranteed by EU law*. The legacy of Directive 64/221 was already referred to above in this context. In *Commission v Netherlands*, the Commission argued that 'by not applying to citizens of the Union Council Directive 64/221/EEC ... but by applying to them general legislation relating to foreign nationals which makes it possible to establish a systematic and automatic connection between a criminal conviction and a measure ordering expulsion, the Kingdom of the Netherlands ha[d] failed to fulfil its obligations under that directive'.[60] More particularly for present purposes, it also argued that 'every citizen of the Union must be able to rely on the substantive and procedural safeguards provided for by Directive 64/221, irrespective of his situation with regard to the right of residence'.[61] The Court agreed. Referring to *MRAX*, it held that '[t]o exclude from the benefit of those substantive and procedural safeguards citizens of the Union who are not lawfully resident on the territory of the host Member State would deprive those safeguards of their essential effectiveness'.[62] Union citizens could therefore be expelled 'on grounds of public policy or public security only within the strict limitations laid down by the directive'.[63]

2.1.2 Union citizenship, equal treatment, and lawful residence: jobseekers

As explained in Chapter 6, Article 6 of Directive 2004/38 establishes that, for Union citizens and certain family members,[64] the right to reside in a host State for up to three months is subject only to the condition of holding a valid identity card or passport. For rights of residence of more than three months, Article 7(1) distinguishes four categories of Member State nationals: economically active citizens who are workers or self-employed as defined by EU law (Article 7(1)(a)); economically autonomous citizens (Article 7(1)(b)); students (Article 7(1)(c)); and family members (as defined by Article 2(2)) who accompany or join a Union citizens residing on the basis of any of the first three categories and who are themselves Union citizens (Article 7(1)(d)). Residence rights based on Article 7(1)(b) and Article 7(1)(c) are subject to conditions of sufficient financial resources and comprehensive sickness insurance.

Jobseekers are not mentioned in Article 7, but they are addressed in other provisions of the Directive, almost all of which concern the right to reside. These provisions reflect significant legal differences between jobseekers who have already worked in the host State and those seeking employment there for the first time. Protection for the former can be traced

---

[59] ibid para 93. The Court's ruling was ambiguous to some extent: as noted in Chapter 6, it is not entirely clear if the Baumbast family's insurance was recognised *not* to be comprehensive (with their continuing residence in the host State thus permitted on the basis of Article 21 TFEU notwithstanding the breach of Directive 90/364) or if it was *deemed* to be comprehensive (glossing over the deficiencies for the purposes of sustaining the family's residence in the host State on the basis of the Directive). The former is more likely as Directive 90/364 was not mentioned in the operative part of the judgment and considering again the language here in para 93.

[60] Case C-50/06 *Commission v Netherlands*, EU:C:2007:325, para 1.

[61] ibid para 29.

[62] ibid para 35, referring to Case C-459/99 *MRAX*, EU:C:2002:461. See further, *Commission v Netherlands*, para 37: 'an interpretation to the effect that the provisions of Directive 64/221 apply only to citizens of the Union who are lawfully resident on the territory of the host Member State is not consistent with [Union] law'.

[63] *Commission v Netherlands*, para 40. See further, Chapter 10.

[64] ie Family members as defined by Article 2(2) of the Directive; see further, Chapter 4.

back to the earliest developments in free movement law.[65] Now, it is provided for in Article 7(3) of Directive 2004/38. First, workers and self-employed persons retain that status—and thus, continue to reside in the host State on the basis of Article 7(1)(a), with no further conditions—where they are 'in duly recorded involuntary unemployment after having been employed for more than one year and ha[ve] registered as a job-seeker with the relevant employment office' (Article 7(3)(b)).[66] While Article 7(3) 'is based on the assumption that the citizen is available and able to re-enter the labour market of the host Member State within a reasonable period',[67] a Member State national who retains the status of worker or self-employed person under Article 7(3)(b) does so 'indefinitely'.[68] In other words, it is registration as a jobseeker, and not successfully securing new employment, that fulfils the requirements of that provision. Second, Member State nationals 'in duly recorded involuntary unemployment after completing a fixed-term employment contract of less than a year or after having become involuntarily unemployed during the first twelve months and ha[ve] registered as a job-seeker with the relevant employment office' also retain the status of worker or self-employed person in the host State (Article 7(3)(c))[69]—but in this case, only 'for no less than six months'.

For jobseekers seeking to become economically active in a host State for the first time, it was also explained in Chapter 6 that their right to reside connects to both Article 6 and Article 14(4)(b) of the Directive.[70] On the basis that 'freedom of movement for workers forms one of the foundations of the European Union and, therefore, the provisions establishing that freedom must be interpreted broadly', the Court held in *GMA* that 'even where a Union citizen enters the territory of a host Member State with the intention of seeking employment there, his or her right of residence is also covered, during the first three months, by Article 6 of Directive 2004/38'.[71] In parallel, however, 'that citizen's right of residence falls, from the time of his or her registration as a jobseeker, within the scope of Article 14(4)(b) of Directive 2004/38'.[72] Reflecting the fact that jobseeker residence rights were first based on freedom of movement for workers, 'the effectiveness of Article 45 TFEU is secured in so far as EU legislation or, in its absence, the legislation of a Member State gives persons concerned *a reasonable time* in which to apprise themselves, in the territory of the host Member State, of offers of employment corresponding to their occupational qualifications and to take, where appropriate, the necessary steps in order to be engaged'.[73] That period of time 'starts to run from

---

[65] See eg on social security coordination, Case 75/63 *Unger*, EU:C:1964:19, para 2: [t]he Treaty and Regulation No 3 ... did not intend to restrict protection only to the worker in employment but tend logically to protect also the worker who, having left his job, is capable of taking another'.

[66] As explained in Chapter 6, 'the expression "involuntary unemployment' [in Article 7(3)(b)] may, depending on the context in which it is used, refer to a situation of inactivity due to the involuntary loss of employment following, for example, a dismissal, as well as, more broadly, to a situation in which the occupational activity, whether on an employed or self—employed basis, has ceased due to an absence of work for reasons beyond the control of the person concerned, such as an economic recession' (Case C-442/16 *Gusa*, EU:C:2017:1004, para 31).

[67] Case C-618/16 *Prefeta*, EU:C:2018:719, para 37.

[68] Case C-483/17 *Tarola*, EU:C:2019:309, para 44. That interpretation of Article 7(3) thus extends a bridge to the next significant timepoint of host State residence, ie permanent residence rights; see Chapter 8.

[69] *Tarola*, paras 45–46.

[70] Article 14(4)(b) of Directive 2004/38 establishes that 'without prejudice to the provisions of Chapter VI, an expulsion measure may in no case be adopted against Union citizens or their family members if: ... the Union citizens entered the territory of the host Member State in order to seek employment. In this case, the Union citizens and their family members may not be expelled for as long as the Union citizens can provide evidence that they are continuing to seek employment and that they have a genuine chance of being engaged'; reflecting Case C-292/89 *Antonissen*, EU:C:1991:80.

[71] Case C-710/19 *GMA (Demandeur d'emploi)*, EU:C:2020:1037, para 35. Accordingly, no further conditions can be imposed on jobseekers during the first three months of residence (ibid para 36).

[72] *GMA*, paras 25 and 34; building on Case C-67/14 *Alimanovic*, EU:C:2015:597, para 52.

[73] *GMA*, para 26 (emphasis added).

the time when the Union citizen concerned has decided to register as a jobseeker in the host Member State'—even if the decision is taken within the first three months of residence.[74] In consequence, after the first three months of residence and during the 'reasonable time', jobseekers may be required to demonstrate that they are seeking employment but not (yet) that they have a genuine chance of being engaged.[75] While acknowledging that the ruling in *Antonissen* had not 'fix[ed] a minimum duration of the "reasonable period of time"', the Court found in *GMA* that *Antonissen* did establish 'that a period of six months from entry into the territory of the host Member State, such as that at issue in the case which gave rise to that judgment, did not appear capable of calling that effectiveness into question'.[76]

But what protection in the host State did a jobseeker enjoy beyond the right to reside there? As introduced in Chapter 2, the Court had always interpreted the concept of 'social and tax advantages' very generously for the purposes of Article 7(2) of Regulation 492/2011.[77] However, while jobseekers fell within the scope of Article 45 TFEU as a work-relevant category of Member State national, the Court had ruled in *Lebon*—just before it confirmed jobseeker *residence* rights in *Antonissen*—that 'the right to equal treatment with regard to social and tax advantages applies *only to workers*. Those *who move in search of employment* qualify for equal treatment *only as regards access* to employment'.[78] The status of jobseeker in EU free movement law was therefore a limited one: like the free movement rights for students developing in the case law around the same time,[79] protection against nationality discrimination applied to *gateway* aspects of work-seeking, and possible financial implications for host States thereafter were carefully capped. Jobseekers who had already worked in the host State were more privileged at one level. For example, in *Commission v Belgium*, the Court held that '[t]he application of [Union] law on freedom of movement for workers in relation to national rules concerning unemployment insurance requires that a person invoking that freedom must have already participated in the employment market by exercising an effective and genuine occupational activity'—which was, '[b]y definition ... not the case where young people are seeking their first employment'.[80] But limits were placed on the equal treatment of jobseekers who had previously worked in the host State too: '[a] person in such a situation is protected by Article [45 TFEU] and Regulation No 1612/68 against any discrimination affecting rights acquired during the *former* employment relationship but, since he is

---

[74] ibid para 37.
[75] The latter requirement may be imposed after the reasonable period has elapsed, and it entails, on the basis of 'the evidence adduced to that effect by the jobseeker in question ... an overall assessment of all relevant factors such as ... the fact that the jobseeker has registered with the national body responsible for jobseekers, that he or she regularly approaches potential employers with letters of application or that he or she goes to employment interviews' (ibid para 47). The 'situation of the national labour market in the sector corresponding to the occupational qualifications of the jobseeker in question' must also be considered, whereas, '[b]y contrast, the fact that that jobseeker refused offers of employment which did not correspond to his or her professional qualifications cannot be taken into account for the purpose of considering that that person does not satisfy the conditions laid down in Article 14(4)(b) of Directive 2004/38' (ibid).
[76] ibid para 40.
[77] eg Case 32/75 *Cristini*, EU:C:1975:120, para 13: 'in view of the equality of treatment which the provision seeks to achieve, the substantive area of application must be delineated so as to include all social and tax advantages, whether or not attached to the contract of employment'. Regulation 492/2011 on freedom of movement for workers within the Union, 2011 OJ L141/1; Article 7(2) of which establishes that a worker who is a national of another Member State 'shall enjoy the same social and tax advantages as national workers'.
[78] Case 316/85 *Lebon*, EU:C:1987:302, para 26 (emphasis added).
[79] Extending equal treatment in the context of enrolment and/or tuition fees (Case 293/83 *Gravier*, EU:C:1985:69) but stopping short, as noted above, of support for maintenance aid (Case 39/86 *Lair*, EU:C:1988:322; Case 197/86 *Brown*, EU:C:1988:323).
[80] Case C-278/94 *Commission v Belgium*, EU:C:1996:321, para 40.

not currently engaged in an employment relationship, cannot thereby claim to acquire new rights having no links with his former occupation'.[81]

Presaging the case law on student maintenance addressed in Section 2.1.1, and thus also before the adoption of Directive 2004/38, the exclusion of jobseekers from equal treatment was reconsidered in *Collins*. The referring court queried 'whether there is a provision or principle of [Union] law on the basis of which a national of a Member State who is genuinely seeking employment in another Member State may claim there a jobseeker's allowance'.[82] Mr Collins, a dual Irish and American national, applied for jobseeker's allowance while seeking work in the UK. His application was refused on the grounds that he was not, as required by the relevant national rules, habitually resident in the UK. For the Commission, the applicant's status in the host State was essentially indistinguishable from the situations on which the Court had recently ruled in *Grzelczyk* and *Trojani*: 'it is not disputed that Mr Collins was genuinely seeking work in the United Kingdom during the two months following his arrival in that Member State and that he was *lawfully resident there in his capacity as a person seeking work*. As a citizen of the Union lawfully residing in the United Kingdom, he was clearly entitled to the protection conferred by Article [18 TFEU] against discrimination on grounds of nationality in any situation falling within the material scope of [Union] law'.[83] But the Commission accepted that 'the right to stay in another Member State to seek work there can be limited to a reasonable period and that Mr Collins' right to rely on Articles [18 and 20 TFEU] in order to claim the allowance, on the same basis as United Kingdom nationals, is therefore similarly restricted to that period of lawful residence'.[84]

The Court first confirmed its previous case law, which excluded jobseekers from equal treatment as regards social and tax advantages on the basis of Article 45 TFEU and Regulation 1612/68 alone.[85] But then, it invoked the legal significance of Union citizenship to recalibrate its approach. Echoing the submission of the Commission, the Court confirmed that 'citizens of the Union lawfully resident in the territory of a host Member State can rely on Article [18 TFEU] in all situations which fall within the scope *ratione materiae* of [Union] law'.[86] In essence, 'in view of the establishment of citizenship of the Union and the interpretation in the case-law of the right to equal treatment *enjoyed by citizens of the Union*, it is no longer possible to exclude *from the scope of Article [45(2) TFEU]* ... a benefit of a financial nature intended *to facilitate access to employment* in the labour market of a Member State'.[87] The Court stated that 'interpretation of the scope of the principle of equal treatment in relation to access to employment must reflect this development, as compared with the interpretation followed' in previous case law.[88] Thus, the reasoning in *Collins* fused legal elements

---

[81] Case C-43/99 *Leclere and Deaconescu*, EU:C:2001:303, para 59 (emphasis added).
[82] Case C-138/02 *Collins*, EU:C:2004:172, para 51.
[83] ibid para 48 (emphasis added); arguing also that the claimed jobseeker's allowance 'should be considered to be a social advantage within the meaning of Article 7(2) of Regulation No 1612/68'.
[84] ibid para 49.
[85] ibid para 58: 'Member State nationals who move in search of employment qualify for equal treatment only as regards access to employment in accordance with Article [45] of the Treaty and Articles 2 and 5 of Regulation No 1612/68, but not with regard to social and tax advantages within the meaning of Article 7(2) of that regulation'; referring to *Lebon*, para 26 and *Commission v Belgium*, paras 39–40.
[86] *Collins*, para 61.
[87] ibid para 63 (emphasis added).
[88] ibid para 64. AG Ruiz-Jarabo Colomer was less convinced, emphasising the very specific facts in *Martínez Sala* and *Grzelczyk*, and pointing also to the fact that in the original proposal for Directive 2004/38, full equal treatment in the host State was envisaged only after a Union citizen acquired permanent residence rights (AG Ruiz-Jarabo Colomer in *Collins*, EU:C:2003:409, esp paras 63–69 of the Opinion; referring to the Commission's original proposal, n 16). Raising questions that became more significant in later case law, he also considered that 'a condition as to residence, which is intended to ascertain the degree of connection with the State and the links which the claimant has with the domestic employment market, may be justified in order to avoid what has come

of the citizen with legal elements of the worker to reconfigure boundaries previously placed around more substantive (and more costly) equal treatment claims.

However, the Court accepted, at the same time, that it was 'legitimate for a Member State to grant such an allowance only after it has been possible to establish that *a genuine link exists between the person seeking work and the employment market of that State*. The existence of such a link may be determined, in particular, by establishing that the person concerned has, for a reasonable period, in fact genuinely sought work in the Member State in question'.[89] This conception of a genuine link requirement had already been applied in *D'Hoop*. In that case, a Belgian national who completed her secondary education in France challenged Belgian rules that made the grant of a 'tideover' allowance—that is, an allowance that 'aims to facilitate for young people the transition from education to the employment market'[90]—conditional on having completed secondary education in Belgium. In *Commission v Belgium*, the Court had classified the tideover allowance as a social and tax advantage within the meaning of Regulation 1612/68.[91] The applicant in *D'Hoop* was not working in Belgium following her period of residence as a student in France and could not, therefore, fall within the personal scope of Article 45 TFEU or the Regulation in her home State even though she had exercised free movement rights. However, the Court ruled that '[b]y linking the grant of tideover allowances to the condition of having obtained the required diploma in Belgium, the national legislation ... places at a disadvantage certain of its nationals simply because they have exercised their freedom to move in order to pursue education in another Member State'.[92] The resulting 'inequality of treatment' was 'contrary to the principles which underpin the status of citizen of the Union, that is, the guarantee of the same treatment in law in the exercise of the citizen's freedom to move'.[93]

Assessing whether the Belgian rules could be justified, the Court observed that the tideover allowance 'aims to facilitate for young people the transition from education to the employment market. In such a context it is legitimate for the national legislature to wish to ensure that there is a real link between the applicant for that allowance and the geographic employment market concerned'.[94] However, the condition 'concerning the place where the diploma of completion of secondary education was obtained' was 'too general and exclusive in nature. It unduly favours an element which is not necessarily representative of the real and effective degree of connection between the applicant for the tideover allowance and the geographic employment market, to the exclusion of all other representative elements'.[95] In was, in other words, disproportionate.

In *Collins*, the Court accepted that a link to the host State employment market 'may be determined, in particular, by establishing that the person concerned has, for a reasonable

---

to be known as "benefit tourism", where persons move from State to State with the purpose of taking advantage of non-contributory benefits, and in order to prevent abuses'—but with a proviso: 'I do not believe that that condition goes beyond what is necessary to attain the objective pursued since it is applied after examination of claimants' personal circumstances in each case' (para 75 of the Opinion). On the dilution of the latter requirement in more recent case law, see Section 3.

[89] *Collins*, paras 69–70 (emphasis added). See generally, C O'Brien, 'Real links, abstract rights and false alarms: the relationship between the ECJ's "real link" case law and national solidarity' (2008) 33 European Law Review 643.
[90] Case C-224/98 *D'Hoop*, EU:C:2002:432, para 38.
[91] Case C-278/94 *Commission v Belgium*, EU:C:1996:321, para 34.
[92] *D'Hoop*, para 34.
[93] ibid para 35.
[94] ibid para 38.
[95] ibid, para 39. On conditions 'too general and exclusive in nature', see Chapter 2.

period, in fact genuinely sought work in the Member State in question'.[96] Again, any conditions placed on demonstrating that link had to be proportionate:

> [W]hile a residence requirement is, in principle, appropriate for the purpose of ensuring such a connection, if it is to be proportionate it cannot go beyond what is necessary in order to attain that objective. More specifically, its application by the national authorities must rest on clear criteria known in advance and provision must be made for the possibility of a means of redress of a judicial nature. In any event, if compliance with the requirement demands a period of residence, the period must not exceed what is necessary in order for the national authorities to be able to satisfy themselves that the person concerned is genuinely seeking work in the employment market of the host Member State.[97]

In that respect, the Commission had acknowledged that while a residence requirement 'may be justified on objective grounds necessarily intended to avoid "benefit tourism" and thus the possibility of abuse by work-seekers who are not genuine … in the case of Mr Collins the genuine nature of the search for work is not in dispute. Indeed, it appears that he has remained continuously employed in the United Kingdom ever since first finding work there shortly after his arrival'.[98]

The Court's concern in *D'Hoop* and *Collins* was to provide a method for *quantifying* the extent to which a jobseeker claiming equal treatment was connected to the relevant labour market. But the composite nature of the tideover allowance should also be noted. Advocate General Geelhoed remarked that it was 'intended for young unemployed people seeking their first job and, *together with a monetary payment*, entitles the individual to participate in various employment programmes'.[99] Whether or to what extent the different elements of the benefit might be severable from each other is returned to in Section 3, because of the subsequent judgment in *Alimanovic*.

2.2 Directive 2004/38, Equal Treatment, and the Host State: Article 24

In the shaping of lawful residence as a central concept of EU citizenship law up to this point, the Court of Justice was the key actor. Principles established in economic free movement law and by the 1990s Residence Directives had established basic foundations, but the Court was evolving the distinctive 'fundamental status' of Union citizenship, openly acknowledging in some rulings that resetting the limits of economic free movement law was what citizenship as a legal status induced. The right to reside in a host State was not unlimited and to claim equal treatment there, establishing lawful residence was, without question, a precondition: not always, but certainly in case law where equal treatment impacted host State public finances. Articulating lawful residence as a requirement in such cases was therefore a new feature of EU free movement law, advancing beyond the previous emphasis on setting the definitions of economic activities or curbing national discretion with respect to expulsion from the host State. At the same time, different *modes* of lawful residence were recognised,

---

[96] *Collins*, para 70.
[97] ibid para 72.
[98] ibid para 50.
[99] AG Geelhoed in *D'Hoop*, EU:C:2002:103, para 1 of the Opinion (emphasis added).

including residence authorised by a host State: a residence right would normally be established straightforwardly on the basis of Article 21 TFEU, read in conjunction with Directive 90/364, 90/365, or 93/96, as relevant; but the application of these legislative conditions was subject to proportionality analysis. Additionally, no distinctions were drawn with respect to the *type* of benefit being claimed as long as it fell within the scope of the Treaty—as seen in Section 2, the principles developed by the Court were applied to both social security benefits and social assistance within the meaning of Regulation 883/2004, 'social and tax advantages' within the meaning of Article 7(2) of Regulation 492/2011, student maintenance grants, and benefits that facilitated access to the employment market for jobseekers.

There is no explicit reference to 'lawful residence' in Directive 2004/38—which, as emphasised in Section 1, *'reproduces, in essence,* the stages and conditions set out in the various instruments of European Union law and case-law preceding that directive'[100]— except for the condition of 'legal residence' in Articles 16–18 in the context of permanent residence rights, addressed in Chapter 8. Nevertheless, imprints of the more generalised, case law-based lawful residence requirement are implicitly embedded across the system of the Directive as a whole. In Chapter 6, the conditions on which residence rights in a host State are based—under different provisions of the Directive and for different time periods and/or sets of circumstances—were introduced. These are returned to in Section 3 to explain the corollary extent of equal treatment that a host State must extend to Union citizens in each situation. Article 24 of the Directive ('Equal treatment') is introduced here first.[101] Framed by recitals 20 and 21, it provides:

1. Subject to such specific provisions as are expressly provided for in the Treaty and secondary law, all Union citizens residing on the basis of this Directive in the territory of the host Member State shall enjoy equal treatment with the nationals of that Member State within the scope of the Treaty. The benefit of this right shall be extended to family members who are not nationals of a Member State and who have the right of residence or permanent residence.
2. By way of derogation from paragraph 1, the host Member State shall not be obliged to confer entitlement to social assistance during the first three months of residence or, where appropriate, the longer period provided for in Article 14(4)(b), nor shall it be obliged, prior to acquisition of the right of permanent residence, to grant maintenance aid for studies, including vocational training, consisting in student grants or student

---

[100] Joined Cases C-316/16 and C-424/16 *B and Vomero*, EU:C:2018:256, para 51 (emphasis added).

[101] See also (identically, in effect), Article 23 WA: '1. In accordance with Article 24 of Directive 2004/38/EC, subject to the specific provisions provided for in this Title and Titles I and IV of this Part, all Union citizens or United Kingdom nationals residing on the basis of this Agreement in the territory of the host State shall enjoy equal treatment with the nationals of that State within the scope of this Part. The benefit of this right shall be extended to those family members of Union citizens or United Kingdom nationals who have the right of residence or permanent residence. 2. By way of derogation from paragraph 1, the host State shall not be obliged to confer entitlement to social assistance during periods of residence on the basis of Article 6 or point (b) of Article 14(4) of Directive 2004/38/EC, nor shall it be obliged, prior to a person's acquisition of the right of permanent residence in accordance with Article 15 of this Agreement, to grant maintenance aid for studies, including vocational training, consisting in student grants or student loans to persons other than workers, self-employed persons, persons who retain such status or to members of their families'. As the Commission underlines, '[t]his provision mirrors Article 24 of Directive 2004/38/EC that provides for a specific rule on equal treatment as compared to Article 11 of the Agreement. The same rule is "extended" to family members with a right of (permanent) residence in the host State. They are to be treated as nationals of the host State, not as family members of nationals of the host State' (European Commission, Guidance Note relating to the Agreement on the withdrawal of the United Kingdom of Great Britain and Northern Ireland from the European Union and the European Atomic Energy Community Part two—Citizens' rights, C(2020) 2939 final, para 2.11).

loans to persons other than workers, self-employed persons, persons who retain such status and members of their families.[102]

Three issues are discussed here in connection with Article 24 of the Directive: its drafting history (Section 2.2.1), the express derogations from equal treatment in Article 24(2) (Section 2.2.2); and the more general, yet also conditional, guarantee of equal treatment in Article 24(1) (Section 2.2.3).

2.2.1 Article 24: drafting history

We saw in Chapter 6 that there was almost unanimous support for placing conditions and limits on the right to reside in another Member State in the process of adopting Directive 2004/38.[103] In the Commission's original proposal, Article 21 (now Article 24) of the Directive was drafted as follows:

1. All EU citizens residing on the territory of the host Member State shall enjoy equal treatment with the nationals of that country within the scope of the Treaty. The benefit of this right shall be extended to family members who enjoy the right of residence or permanent residence.
2. By way of derogation from paragraph 1, until they have acquired the right of permanent residence, the host Member State shall not be obliged to confer entitlement to social assistance on persons other than those engaged in gainful activity in an employed or self-employed capacity or the members of their families, nor shall it be obliged to award maintenance grants to persons having the right of residence who have come to the country to study.[104]

According to the Commission, the proposed text 'broadly takes up the conclusions of the Court of Justice' in *Martínez Sala* and 'establishes a direct link between the principle of non-discrimination and the right of residence'.[105] The guarantee of equal treatment in the first paragraph was more open than the adopted wording of Article 24(1), as explained further in Section 2.3.3. However:

---

[102] Relatedly, recital 20 provides: '[i]n accordance with the prohibition of discrimination on grounds of nationality, all Union citizens and their family members residing in a Member State on the basis of this Directive should enjoy, in that Member State, equal treatment with nationals in areas covered by the Treaty, subject to such specific provisions as are expressly provided for in the Treaty and secondary law'. Recital 21 continues: '[h]owever, it should be left to the host Member State to decide whether it will grant social assistance during the first three months of residence, or for a longer period in the case of job-seekers, to Union citizens other than those who are workers or self-employed persons or who retain that status or their family members, or maintenance assistance for studies, including vocational training, prior to acquisition of the right of permanent residence, to these same persons'.
[103] See exceptionally, the Opinion of the Committee on Legal Affairs and the Internal Market, attached to European Parliament Report (n 16) 57–58; see further, Chapter 6.
[104] Draft Article 21 was framed by recital 19: '[i]n accordance with the principle of non-discrimination, all Union citizens and their family members should enjoy equal treatment with nationals in areas covered by the Treaty. However, prior to the acquisition of the right of permanent residence, it is a matter for the host Member State to decide whether it will extend social assistance provision or sickness insurance coverage to persons not engaged in gainful activity, or maintenance grants to Union citizens coming to study on its territory' (n 16).
[105] Original proposal (n 16) 18; referring to Case C-85/96 *Martínez Sala*, EU:C:1998:217, para 62. The draft provision also introduced the idea of extending 'the benefit of' equal treatment rights to family members who their derived residence rights from Union citizens.

In order not to entail undue financial burdens on host Member States, *this provision qualifies the general principle of equal treatment for all Union citizens*, by not according *entitlement to* social assistance to Union citizens and family members who reside in another Member State but are not engaged in gainful activity there ... In the same vein, host Member States are not required to provide maintenance grants to Union citizens coming to the country to study as their principal occupation. Maintenance grants count as welfare assistance in the broad sense of the term and, therefore, students are not eligible for it under the terms of this Directive, since they are required to assure the relevant national authorities that they have sufficient resources to avoid being a burden on public assistance funds in the host Member State ... These qualifications apply until permanent residence status is acquired [.][106]

Reflecting on the Commission's text, the European Parliament proposed a discretionary period of entitlement to social assistance in a host State during the initial, unconditional period of residence there (which was, in the original proposal, up to six months). However, it underlined that '[i]n all other cases, equality of treatment with the Member State's own citizens applies, except in connection with maintenance grants, which fall outside the scope of the Treaty'.[107]

By the time that the Commission published its amended proposal in 2003, the ruling in *Grzelczyk* had been delivered, 'affirm[ing] that economically inactive Union citizens who are legally resident in another Member State are entitled, by virtue of their status as Union citizens, to equal treatment with nationals'.[108] The draft equal treatment provision was therefore simplified: '[b]y way of derogation from paragraph 1, until they have acquired the right of permanent residence, the host Member State shall not be obliged to award maintenance grants to persons having the right of residence who have come there to study'. In its Common Position, the Council considered—at the time, still pre-*Bidar*—that 'Member States are not obliged to grant maintenance aid for studies that consist in student grants or student loans to persons other than workers or self-employed persons'.[109] It accepted an amendment specifying that the host State 'is not *obliged* to confer entitlement to social assistance during the first three months of residence', which it linked to Article 6 of the Directive,[110] and it added jobseekers to that clause in line with the 'more favourable protection' of their right to reside under Article 14(4)(b) of the evolving Directive.[111] The Council also observed that 'in paragraph 1 it was added that the equal treatment is subject to such specific provisions as are expressly provided for in the Treaty and secondary law'.[112]

Responding to the Common Position, the Commission considered that the Council had 'accepted' the *Grzelczyk*-justified removal of the qualification 'that persons not engaged in gainful activity are not entitled to social assistance until they have acquired the right of permanent residence'.[113] The Commission's only comment on the adopted version of Article

---

[106] Original proposal (n 16) 18 (emphasis added). The proposal predated Case C-209/03 *Bidar*, EU:C:2005:169, where the Court of Justice determined that maintenance grants *did* now fall with the scope of the Treaty.
[107] Report of the European Parliament (n 16) Amendment 67.
[108] Amended proposal (n 16) 8.
[109] Common Position (EC) No 6/2004 of 5 December 2003, 2004 OJ C54 E/12, 32.
[110] ibid 27 (emphasis added).
[111] ibid 26 (emphasis added); recalling too the Council's rejection of an unconditional right to reside for up to six months, as explained in Chapter 6.
[112] ibid 32.
[113] Communication to the European Parliament on the common position adopted by the Council on the draft directive, SEC/2003/1293 final, para 3.2.1.2.

24(1) of the Directive was that 'a provision has been added to the first paragraph stating that equal treatment applies, subject to other provisions of the Treaty and of the secondary legislation, in line with [Article 18 TFEU]'.[114] No reference was made to another phrase added by the Council, which would later acquire acute significance—that equal treatment was to be enjoyed by 'all Union citizens *residing on the basis of this Directive* in the territory of the host Member State'. This language is examined further in Section 2.2.3.

2.2.2 Article 24(2): express derogations from equal treatment

Reflecting the amendments outlined above, Article 24(2) of the Directive now establishes derogations from equal treatment in three specific situations:

> By way of derogation from paragraph 1, the host Member State shall not be obliged to confer entitlement to social assistance during the first three months of residence or, where appropriate, the longer period provided for in Article 14(4)(b), nor shall it be obliged, prior to acquisition of the right of permanent residence, to grant maintenance aid for studies, including vocational training, consisting in student grants or student loans to persons other than workers, self-employed persons, persons who retain such status and members of their families.

As regards, first, *entitlement to social assistance*, we saw in Section 2.2.1 that while the Commission originally proposed a general exclusion from social assistance for Union citizens not engaged in 'gainful activity', it retracted that proposal after the ruling in *Grzelczyk*. However, an exclusion from entitlement was retained for the first three months of residence, which is enjoyed unconditionally under Article 6 of the Directive. With respect to the limits placed on equal treatment during that period, Advocate General Wathelet explained in *Alimanovic* that '[s]ince the Member States cannot require Union citizens to have sufficient means of subsistence and personal medical cover for a three-month stay, it is legitimate not to require Member States to be responsible for them'.[115] He did raise the question of benefit tourism in this context, suggesting that 'granting entitlement to social assistance to Union citizens who are not required to have sufficient means of subsistence could result in relocation *en masse* liable to create an unreasonable burden on national social security systems'.[116] However, reflecting the Court's emphasis on genuine links to (and therefore integration into) the host State in case law before the adoption of the Directive, he also observed that 'the link with the host Member State is, in all likelihood, limited during that initial period'.[117] Equal treatment within the first three months of residence is returned to in Section 3.1.

Second, for *jobseekers*—excluded from entitlement to social assistance through the reference to residence during 'the longer period provided for in Article 14(4)(b)'—Article 24(2) of the Directive appeared directly to challenge the genuine link approach developed contemporaneously by the Court in *Collins*. The lawfulness of excluding jobseekers from equal treatment with respect to social assistance was thus explicitly questioned by the referring court in *Vatsouras and Koupatantze* against the requirements of Articles 18 and 45 TFEU. In its ruling, the Court of Justice first restated the citizen–worker (Article 45/21 TFEU) hybrid

---

[114] ibid para 3.3.2.
[115] AG Wathelet in Case C-67/14 *Alimanovic*, EU:C:2015:210, para 90 of the Opinion.
[116] ibid para 91 of the Opinion.
[117] ibid para 92 of the Opinion.

applied in *Collins*,[118] and confirmed that 'nationals of the Member States seeking employment in another Member State who have established real links with the labour market of that State can rely on Article [45(2) TFEU] in order to receive a benefit of a financial nature intended to facilitate access to the labour market'.[119] Resourcefully, and thereby avoiding assessment of the validity of Article 24(2) of the Directive, the Court maintained its emphasis on workers—on Article 45 TFEU and not Article 21 TFEU[120]—and held that '[b]enefits of a financial nature which, independently of their status under national law, are intended to facilitate access to the labour market *cannot be regarded as constituting "social assistance"* within the meaning of Article 24(2) of Directive 2004/38'.[121] This interpretation meant that jobseekers were eligible in principle to receive such benefits, on the same basis as host State nationals, for as long as they could provide evidence that they were continuing to seek employment and that they had a genuine chance of being engaged. Confirming *Collins*, the proportionality of conditions specified in national rules would also be assessed: thus, Member States could require jobseekers to demonstrate a real link with the host State labour market; but if the relevant conditions went beyond what is appropriate or necessary to demonstrate such links, EU law intervened to displace them.[122]

As discussed in Chapter 6 and recapped in Section 2.1.2 of this chapter, case law has also established that when jobseekers reside in a host State on the basis of Article 14(4)(b) of the Directive, they are beyond the reach of the conditions in Article 7. This point is returned to Section 3.1, in connection with the judgment in *Alimanovic*, but we can already detect that interpretation (inversely) from the Opinion of Advocate General Wathelet in *Dano*. He recalled that Article 24(2) of the Directive permits Member States not to confer entitlement to social assistance on persons other than workers, self-employed persons, persons who retain such status, and members of their families during the first three months of residence 'or during the period of seeking employment extending beyond that initial period'.[123] However, since Ms Dano had resided in the host State for more than three months, was not seeking employment there, and had not entered the country to seek employment in the first place, the Advocate General concluded that 'she does not fall within the scope *ratione personae* of that provision. *On the other hand, her situation is covered by Article 7(1)(b)* of Directive 2004/38, relating to the requirement to have sufficient resources not to become a burden on the social assistance system of the host Member State'[124]—the implication being that Article 7(1)

---

[118] Joined Cases C-22/08 and C-23/08 *Vatsouras and Koupatantze*, EU:C:2009:344, para 37: 'in view of the establishment of citizenship of the Union and the interpretation of the right to equal treatment enjoyed by citizens of the Union, it is no longer possible to exclude from the scope of Article [45(2) TFEU] a benefit of a financial nature intended to facilitate access to employment in the labour market of a Member State', referring to Case C-138/02 *Collins*, EU:C:2004:172, para 63.
[119] *Vatsouras and Koupatantze*, para 40.
[120] ibid para 44: 'the derogation provided for in Article 24(2) of Directive 2004/38 must be interpreted in accordance with Article 45(2) TFEU'.
[121] ibid para 45 (emphasis added). See generally, D Damjanovic (Case Comment) (2010) 47 Common Market Law Review 847; and E Fahey, 'Interpretive legitimacy and the distinction between "social assistance" and "work seekers allowance"' (2009) 34 European Law Review 933.
[122] eg Case C-367/11 *Prete*, EU:C:2012:668. Here, the Court ruled that a single condition—in this case, making eligibility for a 'tideover allowance for the benefit of young people looking for their first job conditional upon the person concerned having completed at least six years' studies in an educational establishment of the host Member State' (para 14)—went beyond what is necessary 'insofar as that condition prevents other representative factors liable to establish the existence of a real link between the person claiming the allowance and the geographic labour market concerned being taken into account' (para 52).
[123] AG Wathelet in Case C-333/13 *Dano*, EU:C:2014:341, para 92 of the Opinion.
[124] ibid (emphasis added).

(b) would not apply had she been able to demonstrate that she was a jobseeker within the meaning of EU law.

The rights of jobseekers as fused 'citizen–workers' generate more than the sum of their individual parts: jobseekers are neither required to have sufficient resources to support themselves in a host State nor subject to expulsion from that State while the *Antonissen/ GMA* criteria are met. However, critical questions had not yet been addressed by the time that Directive 2004/38 was adopted: what, more precisely, are 'benefit[s] of a financial nature intended to facilitate access to employment in the labour market' and how, if at all, are they different from other social security benefits and/or social assistance? In *Vatsouras and Koupatantze*, the Court found only that such benefits are not social assistance 'within the meaning of Article 24(2) of Directive 2004/38'.[125] But what does that mean in practice?

For example, housing assistance would undoubtedly, in very practical terms, 'facilitate access to employment'. Is such a broad understanding what the Court intended? It provided three points of guidance in *Vatsouras and Koupatantze*. First, '[i]t is for the competent national authorities and, where appropriate, the national courts not only to establish the existence of a real link with the labour market, but also *to assess the constituent elements of that benefit*, in particular its purposes and the conditions subject to which it is granted'.[126] Second, 'the objective of the benefit must be analysed according to its results and not according to its formal structure'.[127] Third, a condition in national rules 'under which the person concerned must be capable of earning a living, could constitute an indication that the benefit is intended to facilitate access to employment'.[128] These criteria—and especially the distinction from social assistance suggested by the third point[129]—were further developed in *Alimanovic* and are returned to in Section 3.1.

Finally, the third derogation in Article 24(2) of the Directive is that Member States are not obliged 'prior to acquisition of the right of permanent residence, to grant *maintenance aid for studies*, including vocational training, consisting in student grants or student loans to persons other than workers, self-employed persons, persons who retain such status and members of their families'. In Section 2.1.1, we saw that the Court recalibrated equal treatment entitlement for Union citizens studying—and residing lawfully—in another Member State by ruling that maintenance grants now fell within the material scope of the Treaty. However, in the parallel process of drafting Directive 2004/38, a fixed limitation of five years on any host State obligation to grant maintenance aid—exclusion from eligibility before acquiring permanent residence rights—was written into Article 24(2). Rather oddly, the Court drew in *Bidar* from draft Article 24(2) only to confirm that maintenance grants were now considered by the EU legislator to fall within the scope of EU equal treatment law: otherwise, the exception provided for would not be necessary—a clear five-year limit, yes; but one that the Court could nevertheless ignore since the facts in *Bidar* concerned Directive 93/96, which included no such limit.[130]

---

[125] *Vatsouras and Koupatantze*, para 45.
[126] ibid para 41 (emphasis added).
[127] ibid para 42.
[128] ibid para 43.
[129] But note also the suggestion, 'despite the Commission's submissions, that there may be "social assistance" measures, as contemplated in Article 24(2) of Directive 2004/38, which promote integration into the labour market' (AG Ruiz-Jarabo Colomer in *Vatsouras and Koupatantze*, EU:C:2009:150, para 57 of the Opinion); in the context of an argument that 'the objective of the assistance must be analysed *according to its results* rather than according to the formal structure of the benefit' (emphasis in original).
[130] Case C-209/03 *Bidar*, EU:C:2005:169, paras 43–47; see similarly, AG Geelhoed (EU:C:2004:175, para 50 of the Opinion).

However, the Court did acknowledge that the earlier Directive's refererred only to a *certain degree* of solidarity and it thus permitted Member States to condition access to study finance, indicating that 'the existence of a certain degree of integration may be regarded as established by a finding that the student in question has resided in the host Member State for a certain length of time'.[131] In *Bidar*, the contested national rules required Member State nationals to obtain 'settled' status in the UK before being eligible for maintenance grants, but 'preclude[d] any possibility of a national of another Member State obtaining settled status as a student' and therefore 'ma[de] it impossible for such a national, whatever his actual degree of integration into the society of the host Member State, to satisfy that condition and hence to enjoy the right to assistance to cover his maintenance costs. Such treatment cannot be regarded as justified by the legitimate objective which those rules seek to secure'.[132]

Advocate General Geelhoed did reference the permanent residence threshold in Article 24(2) of Directive 2004/38, which was also highlighted by every Member State intervening in the case and by the Commission. However, even '[l]eaving aside that this directive entered into force on 30 April 2004, i.e. after the facts in the present case arose', the Advocate General considered that 'in applying this condition, the fundamental rights conferred directly by the ... Treaty on EU citizens must be fully respected'.[133] Emphasising that 'account must be taken of all relevant factors in determining whether or not a genuine link exists with the educational system and the society of the host Member State', he suggested that such an approach would not 'undermin[e] ... the requirement adopted by the [Union] legislature. Rather it is necessary to ensure that this requirement is applied in conformity with the fundamental provisions of the ... Treaty'.[134]

Through that analysis, Advocate General Geelhoed sustained, in effect, the threads of *Grzelczyk* and *Baumbast*. However, the Court seemed to retreat from its own earlier case law soon afterwards. Like *Bidar*, the *Förster* case involved a claim for maintenance aid before Directive 2004/38 came into effect. The contested national rules on eligibility mirrored Article 24(2) of the Directive by requiring lawful residence in the Netherlands for an uninterrupted period of five years. The Court affirmed that Article 3 of Directive 93/96 did not preclude a Union citizen residing lawfully in another Member State from relying on 'the fundamental principle of equal treatment enshrined in [Article 18(1) TFEU]'.[135] But a change came in the assessment of proportionality. Here, the Court considered that 'a condition of five years' uninterrupted residence is appropriate for the purpose of guaranteeing that the applicant for the maintenance grant at issue is integrated into the society of the host Member State' and 'cannot be held to be excessive having regard, *inter alia*, to the requirements put forward with respect to the degree of integration of non-nationals in the host Member State'.[136] It then referred to Article 24(2) of Directive 2004/38 and expressed a narrower view on the proportionality of the national rules by invoking *other* general principles of EU law: 'in order to be proportionate, a residence requirement must be applied by the national authorities on the basis of clear criteria known in advance' since '[b]y enabling those concerned to know, without any ambiguity, what their rights and obligations are, the residence requirement laid down [in the contested national rules] is, by its very existence, such as to guarantee *a significant level of legal certainty and transparency* in the context of the award of maintenance

---

[131] *Bidar*, para 59.
[132] ibid para 61.
[133] AG Geelhoed in *Bidar*, para 64 of the Opinion.
[134] ibid.
[135] Case C-158/07 *Förster*, EU:C:2008:630, para 43.
[136] ibid paras 52 and 54.

grants to students'.[137] These countervailing principles informed a further retraction of proportionality requirements in *Alimanovic*, returned to in Section 3.1.

By following previous case law, Advocate General Mazák had reached the opposite view in *Förster*, which was that the five-year rule was disproportionate. He acknowledged that 'Member States may make the right to reside subject to the conditions and limitations provided for under the various residence directives' but emphasised that 'when and as long as a Union citizen is *lawfully resident* in the host Member State concerned, *be it by virtue of [Union] law or even just national law*, as in the case of Mr Trojani, that Union citizen is entitled to equal treatment. Consequently, the only way open to a Member State to avoid granting the benefit is to terminate the Union citizen's residence'.[138] In line with Advocate General Geelhoed in *Bidar*, he argued that Article 24(2) of Directive 2004/38 'cannot detract from the requirements flowing from Article [18 TFEU] and the general principle of proportionality'.[139] He therefore considered the period of five years in Article 24(2) as 'mark[ing] the outer limit within which it may still be possible to argue that a student pursuing studies in another Member State has not established a sufficient degree of integration into the society of that State to qualify for equal treatment' because 'it would seem disproportionate, even though five years may not have yet elapsed, to refuse study finance if the student can adduce reasonable evidence that he or she is already substantially integrated into the society of the host Member State'.[140]

The different perspectives taken by the Court and Advocate General Mazák in *Förster* marked an early reflection of something later expressed directly by Advocate General Wathelet in *Bragança Linares Verruga*:

> In a world in which the dominant economic model is proving to have its limits, budgetary constraint has become a daily reality. Since the beginning of the 'European project', freedom of movement has been one of the fundamental freedoms. Its importance was then further heightened with the recognition, then the development, of a European citizenship which clearly benefits students. That freedom of movement is today being called in question and put under pressure. The regulations concerning the grant of financial aid for higher education studies are a further illustration of this. Between, on the one hand, the maintenance of the recognition of a high degree of equality likely to lead to a reduction in the amounts granted to each recipient and, on the other hand, the erosion of that equality linked to the possibility of retaining substantial aid in favour of apprenticeship and training of a smaller number of citizens, what, today, are the requirements of Union law?[141]

The contrasting responses to that dilemma in *Förster* exposed the fact that the adoption of Directive 2004/38 had unsettled the relationship between lawful residence and equal treatment and, more specifically, between the rights protected by primary EU law and the conditions and limits established in secondary EU law. Before these themes are returned to in Sections 3 and 4, more general comments about Article 24(2) and maintenance aid for studies are noted here. First, explaining why workers, self-employed persons, and persons who retain such status are treated more favourably, the Court confirmed in *Commission v*

---

[137] ibid paras 56–57 (emphasis added).
[138] AG Mazák in Case C-158/07 *Förster*, EU:C:2008:399, para 117 of the Opinion (emphasis added).
[139] ibid para 131 of the Opinion.
[140] ibid paras 132–133 of the Opinion.
[141] AG Wathelet in Case C- 238/15 *Bragança Linares Verruga and Others*, EU:C:2016:389, paras 3–5 of the Opinion.

Netherlands that '[a]s regards migrant workers and frontier workers, the fact that they have participated in the employment market of a Member State *establishes, in principle, a sufficient link of integration* with the society of that Member State, allowing them to benefit from the principle of equal treatment, as compared with national workers, as regards social advantages'.[142] More specifically, '[t]he link of integration arises from, *inter alia*, the fact that, through the taxes which he pays in the host Member State by virtue of his employment, the migrant worker also contributes to the financing of the social policies of that State and should profit from them under the same conditions as national workers'.[143] This point is picked up in Section 3.1 for residence based on Article 7(1)(a) of the Directive.

Second, a Union citizen who is both studying and working in the host State is not excluded from the scope of Article 45 TFEU when their activities meet the definition of work under EU law. As noted in Chapter 6, the applicant in *LN* was refused maintenance aid for studies on the grounds that they entered the host State 'with the principal intention of following a course of study, the purpose of his residence in Denmark being, according to the competent national authorities, such as to preclude him from having the status of "worker" within the meaning of Article 45 TFEU'.[144] However, the Court ruled that it does not follow from Article 7(1)(c) of the Directive 'that a citizen of the Union who fulfils those conditions is thereby automatically precluded from having the status of "worker" within the meaning of Article 45 TFEU'.[145] Moreover, 'the motives which may have prompted a worker of a Member State to seek employment in another Member State are of no account and must not be taken into consideration'.[146] Instead, '[i]n investigating whether a specific case involves effective and genuine employment, the national court must base itself on objective criteria and make a comprehensive assessment of all the circumstances of the case that have to do with the activities and the employment relationship concerned'.[147]

Third, 'only maintenance aid for studies "consisting in student grants or student loans" come within the derogation from the principle of equal treatment provided for in Article 24(2) of Directive 2004/38' on the basis that '[a]ny other interpretation of that provision would run counter to not only its wording but also to the Court's obligation to interpret that derogation in accordance with the provisions of the Treaty, including those relating to Union citizenship'.[148] Thus, in *Commission v Austria*, reduced fares on public transport granted only to students whose parents received Austrian family allowances were considered not to fall within the scope of 'maintenance aid' in Article 24(2).[149] However, 'a national scheme requiring a student to provide proof of a genuine link with the host Member State could, in principle, reflect a legitimate objective capable of justifying restrictions on the right to move and reside freely in the territory of the Member States provided for in Article 21 TFEU'.[150] To assess proportionality, the Court held that the 'proof required to demonstrate the genuine

---

[142] Case C-542/09 *Commission v Netherlands*, EU:C:2012:346, para 65 (emphasis added).
[143] ibid para 66. Confirmed in Case C-328/20 *Commission v Austria*, EU:C:2022:468, para 109.
[144] Case C-46/12 *LN*, EU:C:2013:97, para 38.
[145] ibid para 36.
[146] ibid para 47; responding to 'the argument put forward by the Danish and Norwegian Governments to the effect that the intention the applicant in the main proceedings had when he entered Danish territory to follow a course of study precludes him from having the status of "worker" within the meaning of Article 45 TFEU' (para 46).
[147] ibid para 43. The question of abuse of EU rights is addressed in Chapter 6.
[148] Case C-75/11 *Commission v Austria*, EU:C:2012:605, paras 55–56; referring to Joined Cases C-22/08 and C-23/08 *Vatsouras and Koupatantze*, EU:C:2009:344, para 44.
[149] Cf the nature of the benefit at issue in Case C-233/14 *Commission v Netherlands*, EU:C:2016:396, discussed in Section 3.
[150] *Commission v Austria*, para 61.

link must not be too exclusive in nature or unduly favour an element which is not necessarily representative of the real and effective degree of connection between the claimant to reduced transport fares and the Member State where the claimant pursues his studies, to the exclusion of all other representative elements'.[151] Additionally, the genuine link required 'need not be fixed in a uniform manner for all benefits, but should be established according to the constitutive elements of the benefit in question, including its nature and purpose or purposes'.[152] Importantly, therefore, *Commission v Austria* confirms that when the financial assistance claimed does not fall within the scope of benefits specified in Article 24(2) of the Directive, the real link case law still applies for the assessment of restrictive national conditions.

The Court also commented, referring to Articles 18 and 21 TFEU, that '[s]ince Article 24(2) is a derogation from the principle of equal treatment provided for in Article 18 TFEU, of which Article 24(1) of Directive 2004/38 is *merely* a specific expression, it must be interpreted narrowly'.[153] However, Advocate General Kokott observed that when the conditions in Article 7(1)(c) of the Directive are fulfilled, 'students are resident in Austria *on the basis of the directive* and enjoy equal treatment with the nationals of that Member State *under Article 24(1) thereof*'.[154] The express derogations in Article 24(2) are very limited in scope. In particular, as regards entitlement to social assistance, they do not rule out equal treatment with host State nationals in the residence period between three months and five years, echoing *Grzelczyk*. Does Article 24(1) of the Directive accomplish that instead?

2.2.3 Article 24(1): an implicit derogation from equal treatment?

Article 24(1) of the Directive establishes that '[s]ubject to such specific provisions as are expressly provided for in the Treaty and secondary law, all Union citizens residing *on the basis of this Directive* in the territory of the host Member State shall enjoy equal treatment with the nationals of that Member State within the scope of the Treaty'. It is therefore clear that citizens residing 'on the basis of' Article 7, for example, enjoy equal treatment with host State nationals subject to specific conditions in the Treaty or in secondary law—the derogations expressly provided for in Article 24(2) being the most obvious example. Thus, as the Court confirmed in *García-Nieto*, a Union citizen residing lawfully in a host State on the basis of Article 6 of the Directive is not entitled to social assistance there because Article 24(2) expressly provides that 'the host Member State shall not be obliged to confer entitlement to social assistance during the first three months of residence'.[155]

However, it was less clear how Article 24(1) of the Directive would interact with *guarantees of* (rather than *exclusions from*) equal treatment in Article 18 TFEU or in other EU measures—for example, the prohibition on nationality discrimination in Article 4 of Regulation 883/2004.[156] This question was addressed in *Commission v UK*, discussed in Section 3.[157] It was also not clear whether (or on what basis) Union citizens who do *not* reside in a host State 'on the basis of' the Directive could claim equal treatment with host State nationals. As explained in Section 2, neither *Martínez Sala* nor *Grzelczyk* addressed

---

[151] ibid para 62.
[152] ibid para 63.
[153] ibid para 54 (emphasis added).
[154] AG Kokott in Case C-75/11 *Commission v Austria*, EU:C:2012:536, para 81 of the Opinion (emphasis added).
[155] Case C-299/14 *García-Nieto*, EU:C:2016:114, paras 42–44.
[156] Article 4 of Regulation 883/2004 provides: '[u]nless otherwise provided for *by this Regulation*, persons to whom this Regulation applies shall enjoy the same benefits and be subject to the same obligations under the legislation of any Member State as the nationals thereof'.
[157] Case C-308/14 *Commission v UK*, EU:C:2016:436.

whether the Union citizens in question *could* have based their rights to reside in the host State on Directive 90/364 or Directive 93/96 (though the operative parts of the judgments suggested that they resided (only) 'on the basis of' national law and Article 21 TFEU respectively). Mr Trojani was demonstrably *not* residing in the host State 'on the basis of' Directive 90/364. However, his residence was 'authorised' by national law. All three applicants were therefore permitted to have their equal treatment claims assessed under Article 18 TFEU since they were all considered to be residing *lawfully* in the host State, and it is presumed that a similar claim for equal treatment from Mr Baumbast would also have been successful.

Would all or any of these claims succeed now? This question is complicated by the wording of Article 18 TFEU, which provides that '[w]ithin the scope of application of the Treaties, and without prejudice to any special provisions contained therein, any discrimination on grounds of nationality shall be prohibited'. That language engages the 'special provision' made in Articles 20 and 21 TFEU for conditions and limits found in secondary law. In *Förster*, Advocate General Mazák argued that the judgments in *Grzelczyk* and *Trojani* '[suggest], arguably, that secondary [Union] law laying down conditions and limitations to the right of residence is to be regarded, by virtue of the reference contained in Article [21(1) TFEU], as a type of *lex specialis* in relation *to that article*, but *not in respect* of Article [18 TFEU]'.[158] In *Commission v Austria*, the Court seemed to agree, finding that '[s]ince Article 24(2) is a derogation from the principle of equal treatment provided for in Article 18 TFEU, of which Article 24(1) of Directive 2004/38 is merely a specific expression, it must be interpreted narrowly'.[159] And all of the legislative institutions appeared to accept that the judgment in *Grzelczyk* ruled out inserting into Article 24(2) of the Directive a more general exclusion from social assistance in the host State before permanent residence rights are acquired. Yet how those principles relate to Article 24(1)'s requirement that Union citizens must reside in the host State *on the basis of* Directive 2004/38 to claim equal treatment with host State nationals fell still to be determined.

3. Union Citizenship, Lawful Residence, Equal Treatment, and Directive 2004/38: The Revised Framework

Entrenching the requirement to reside 'on the basis of the Directive' in Article 24(1) as, in effect, a *Directive-based* precondition of lawful residence—in a more citizen-friendly way at first in *Brey*, then in a more State-sympathetic way in *Dano*, *Alimanovic*, *Commission v UK*, and *CG*; either way, catalysing an exclusion from equal treatment of potent scope that transcends the impression of more limited derogations expressly and specifically provided for in Article 24(2)—is one of the most significant changes in EU citizenship case law since the foundational rulings in *Martínez Sala*, *Grzelczyk*, *Trojani*, and *Baumbast* were delivered. It disrupted fundamental principles conceived in that case law on the intersection of lawful residence, equal treatment, and proportionality; and exposed the system of citizenship-based residence rights as a more fragmented and more conditional framework than Directive 2004/38 and its underlying objectives had initially suggested. At the same time, however, the Court more recently retreated—to some extent—from the some of the

---

[158] AG Mazák in Case C-158/07 *Förster*, EU:C:2008:399, para 118 of the Opinion (emphasis added).
[159] Case C-75/11 *Commission v Austria*, EU:C:2012:605, para 54. See similarly, Case C-46/12 *LN*, EU:C:2013:97, para 33 and Case C-233/14 *Commission v Netherlands*, EU:C:2016:39, para 86.

more stringent implications that might have been drawn from *Dano* and *Alimanovic* in circumstances where lawful residence can at least be linked to some basis in EU law if not to the Directive itself.

As underlined in Section 2, it is not that a precondition of lawful residence was not previously part of EU citizenship law for claims for equal treatment: on the contrary, it always was. The significant changes concern how lawful residence is determined in the first place and the intensity of proportionality review, as explained in more detail below. The extent to which the adoption of the Directive 2004 compelled the Court of Justice's change of course will be considered. The wider context is highly relevant too. In *Brey*, Advocate General Wahl observed that '[t]he idea that a Union citizen could say "*civis europeus sum*" and invoke that status against hardships encountered in other Member States was famously pioneered 20 years ago', before asking: '[can] that status be relied upon today, against the economic difficulties of modern life'?[160] The aim of this part of the chapter is therefore to outline the lawful residence and equal treatment framework that now applies. The analysis follows the residence categories in the host State, before permanent residence,[161] that were introduced in Chapter 6 and in Section 2 of this chapter: rights to reside on the basis of Directive 2004/38 (Section 3.2), other measures of secondary EU law (Section 3.3), primary EU law (Section 3.4), and national law (Section 3.5). However, before the equal treatment obligations that attach to each of these residence categories are explained, the rulings in *Dano*, *Alimanovic*, and *Commission v UK* are first considered (Section 3.1) as they rule out entitlement to equal treatment when Union citizens cannot demonstrate a right to reside in a host State on *any* of these bases.

Section 4 then reflects on the implications for Member State nationals who do not reside lawfully in the host State as well as for Member State nationals who *do* reside there lawfully but not on a basis that *also* obliges equal treatment with host State nationals under EU law. The concept of tolerated citizens is invoked in that discussion, which also considers how the evolved system of residence rights connects to wider systemic principles of EU law, and especially to the Charter of Fundamental Rights.

3.1 No Right to Reside: *Dano*, *Alimanovic*, and *Commission v UK*

Progressing the discussion in Section 2, the analysis in this part of the chapter first considers case law on lawful residence that came after Directive 2004/38 entered into force but before the ruling in *Dano* (Section 3.1.1). It then presents the main findings in *Dano* (Section 3.1.2), *Alimanovic* (Section 3.1.3), and *Commission v UK* (Section 3.1.4) as they relate to lawful residence in the host State and the repercussions for equal treatment of *not* being lawfully resident there.

---

[160] AG Wahl in Case C-140/12 *Brey*, EU:C:2013:337, para 1 of the Opinion. See similarly, AG Pitruzella in Case C-181/19 *Jobcenter Krefeld*, EU:C:2020:377, para 1 of the Opinion: '[a]s I prepare this Opinion, the European Union is going through an unprecedented public health crisis, to which the Member States have responded by demonstrating equally unprecedented solidarity as regards health-related matters. In the present case, it is the limits of social solidarity which the Court is called upon to clarify'.

[161] Article 16(1) of the Directive commits the host State to full equal treatment in such situations: 'Union citizens who have resided legally for a continuous period of five years in the host Member State shall have the right of permanent residence there. This right *shall not be subject to the conditions* provided for in Chapter III'. See further, Chapter 8.

3.1.1 Directive 2004/38 and lawful residence: early case law

In Section 2, we saw that the Court of Justice established in *Martínez Sala* a connection between residing lawfully in a host State and claiming equal treatment with host State nationals and that it confirmed that connection in subsequent rulings, certainly when the relevant claim had implications for host State public finances. That strand of equal treatment case law was distinctive, in the sense that a lawful residence requirement did (and still does) not normally feature in other cases based on Articles 18 and 21 TFEU. But it could be explained by the approach to social assistance and 'unreasonable burdens' in the 1990s Residence Directives, which continued into Directive 2004/38.[162]

Following the entry into force of Directive 2004/38, consideration of the implications of periods of residence in a host State that did *not* constitute lawful residence first emerged in the case law on permanent residence. As explained further in Chapter 8, Article 16(1) of the Directive refers to Union citizens 'who have *resided legally* for a continuous period of five years' in a host State in connection with establishing permanent residence there. However, the second sentence of recital 17 indicates more specifically that '[a] right of permanent residence should ... be laid down for all Union citizens and their family members who have resided in the host Member State *in compliance with the conditions laid down in this Directive* during a continuous period of five years without becoming subject to an expulsion measure'.[163] In *Lassal*, Advocate General Trstenjak identified two possible ways of interpreting 'legal residence' for the purposes of Article 16: '[u]nder the first approach, legal residence can be based only on compliance with [Union] law provisions, whereas the second approach links legal residence to compliance with the provisions of national law'.[164] She considered that 'there is something to be said for interpreting the second sentence of recital 17 to mean that a right of permanent residence under Article 16 of the directive can arise *only* where the continuous period of five years' residence was completed in accordance with the provisions of [Union] law'.[165] That analysis raised, in turn, the question of whether compliance with EU law meant compliance *only* with the conditions in Directive 2004/38 or could also include compliance with EU legislation that preceded the coming into force of the Directive.[166] The Court ruled that 'for the purposes of the acquisition of the right of permanent residence provided for in Article 16 of Directive 2004/38, continuous periods of five years' residence completed before the date of transposition of that directive, namely 30 April 2006, *in accordance with the earlier EU law instruments*, must be taken into account'.[167] But *Lassal* was concerned with residence periods based on EU legislation replaced by the Directive. Would a right to reside under 'earlier EU law instruments' *not* replaced by the Directive—especially, rights based on Article 10 of Regulation 492/2011[168]—or rights based

---

[162] In *Gusa*, AG Wathelet remarked that in *Dano*, *Alimanovic*, and *García-Nieto*, 'the specific question of the right to receive social benefits in the host State [was] a question which had arisen at a point in time subsequent to the exercise of freedom of movement but was nonetheless indissociable from the legality of residence' (AG Wathelet in Case C-442/16 *Gusa*, EU:C:2017:607, para 55 of the Opinion).

[163] The first sentence of recital 17 states that '[e]njoyment of permanent residence by Union citizens who have chosen to settle long term in the host Member State would strengthen the feeling of Union citizenship and is a key element in promoting social cohesion, which is one of the fundamental objectives of the Union'.

[164] AG Trstenjak in Case C-162/09 *Lassal*, EU:C:2010:266, para 88 of the Opinion. For the second approach, she also referred to Article 37 of the Directive, which establishes that Directive 2004/38 'shall not affect any laws, regulations or administrative provisions laid down by a Member State which would be more favourable to the persons covered by this Directive'.

[165] ibid para 88 of the Opinion (emphasis added).

[166] ibid paras 89–93 of the Opinion.

[167] Case C-162/09 *Lassal*, EU:C:2010:592, para 40 (emphasis added).

[168] Article 10 of Regulation 492/2011 (which replaced Article 12 of Regulation 1612/68) provides: '[t]he children of a national of a Member State who is or has been employed in the territory of another Member State shall be

directly on Treaty provisions (eg on Article 45 TFEU for jobseekers) or on national law also be taken into account?[169]

In *Dias*, Advocate General Trstenjak was more definitive, arguing that recital 17 'can hardly be understood to mean anything other than that the European Union legislature intended to create a right of permanent residence only on the basis of the rights of residence provided for in the directive'.[170] She emphasised 'the *system of levels* laid down by the directive, which provides for three successive levels of integration of a Union citizen in the host Member State' across Articles 6, 7, and 16; and which constitutes, in turn, 'the basis for the extent of the entitlements which a Union citizen may claim from the authorities of the host Member State under Article 24 of the directive'.[171] Through this 'level-based system, the European Union legislature has achieved a balance between the Union citizen's right of free movement in the Union and the objective of social cohesion, on the one hand, and the Member States' financial interests, on the other. The greater the level of integration attained by the Union citizen in the host Member State, the less important are the Member States' financial interests'.[172] Advocate General Trstenjak rejected the possibility of residence authorised by national law only—where the Union citizen concerned did not *also* comply with the conditions in Article 7 of the Directive—produced permanent residence rights under EU law, noting, with reference to Article 37 of the Directive, that '[s]ince the adoption of more favourable provisions lies in the discretion of the Member States, they should – in so far as there are no provisions of primary law – also enjoy discretion in relation to the question which legal consequences they wish to attach to a right of residence granted under national law which goes beyond the terms of the directive'.[173]

Addressing the compatibility of her position with *Martínez Sala* and *Trojani*—in which, she acknowledged, 'the Court admittedly drew legal consequences under European Union law from a period of residence which took place on the basis of a national residence permit or a leave to remain'[174]—earlier case law was distinguished from the specific question of permanent residence on three grounds. First, differently from the right to reside addressed in earlier case law, the right of permanent residence was entirely a creature of EU legislation;[175] second, discussion of Article 21 TFEU in the earlier cases 'concerned only' the scope of a discrimination claim based on Article 18 TFEU and not the right to reside per se; and third, the Court had always emphasised that 'it remains open to a Member State also in such a situation to remove a national who no longer fulfils the conditions applicable to his right of residence and has had recourse to social assistance, provided that it acts within the limits imposed by European Union law'.[176] She therefore concluded that 'there is no rule of primary law

---

admitted to that State's general educational, apprenticeship and vocational training courses under the same conditions as the nationals of that State, if such children are residing in its territory. Member States shall encourage all efforts to enable such children to attend these courses under the best possible condition'.

[169] For example, in *McCarthy*, AG Kokott remarked that the judgment in *Lassal* 'does not in any way preclude other periods of residence, completed solely under national law on foreign nationals, from also being taken into account' (AG Kokott in Case C-434/09 *McCarthy*, EU:C:2010:718, para 50 of the Opinion).
[170] Opinion of AG Trstenjak in Case C-325/09 *Dias*, EU:C:2011:86, para 76 of the Opinion.
[171] ibid paras 77–78 of the Opinion (emphasis added).
[172] ibid para 79 of the Opinion.
[173] ibid para 82 of the Opinion.
[174] ibid para 87 of the Opinion.
[175] More recently, however, the Court has recognised permanent residence rights through derived residence rights based on Article 20 TFEU, ie detached from the Directive entirely (Case C-247/20 *VI*, EU:C:2022:177, paras 58–59; see further, Chapter 8).
[176] AG Trstenjak in *Dias*, paras 84–88 of the Opinion. For a different analysis, emphasising the obligation not to interpret the provisions of the Directive restrictively having regard to its context and objectives, see AG Kokott in *McCarthy*, paras 49–53 of the Opinion.

according to which periods of residence which occurred on the basis of a national residence permit must be regarded as periods of legal residence within the meaning of Article 16(1) of Directive 2004/38'.[177] Her reasoning left intact the continuing relevance of the foundational case law beyond eligibility for permanent residence rights. However, as returned to below, the limiting principles that she suggested were generalised in subsequent case law.

In *Dias* itself, the Court agreed that 'periods of residence completed before 30 April 2006 on the basis solely of a residence permit validly issued under Directive 68/360, *without the conditions governing entitlement to any right of residence having been met*, cannot be regarded as having been completed legally for the purposes of the acquisition of a right of permanent residence under Article 16(1)' of the Directive.[178] In *Ziolkowski and Szeja*—emphasising the need for uniform interpretation of the concept of 'legal residence'; the 'gradual system as regards the right of residence in the host Member State, *which reproduces, in essence*, the stages and conditions set out in the various instruments of European Union law *and case-law preceding the directive* and culminates in the right of permanent residence'; and the clarification added by inserting recital 17 at a late stage in the drafting of Directive 2004/38—the Court stated, more specifically, that legal residence for the purposes of Article 16(1) means 'a period of residence which complies with the conditions laid down in the directive, in particular those set out in Article 7(1)' and, conversely, residence that 'complies with the law of a Member State but does not satisfy the conditions laid down in Article 7(1) of Directive 2004/38 cannot be regarded as a 'legal' period of residence within the meaning of Article 16(1)'.[179]

The reference to the conditions in Article 7(1) 'in particular' infers that residence periods complying with other provisions of the Directive contribute to permanent residence eligibility too, namely: unconditional periods of residence of up to three months under Article 6;[180] rights retained on a personal basis by the family members of Union citizens under Articles 12 and 13, which already refer to compliance with Article 7 for the purposes of permanent residence rights in some respects (Section 3.2.5); and jobseeker residence periods based on the protection from expulsion extended by Article 14(4)(b) (Section 3.2.6). Addressing Article 37 of the Directive, the Court found that '[t]he fact that national provisions concerning the right of residence of Union citizens that are more favourable than those laid down in Directive 2004/38 are not to be affected does not in any way mean that such provisions must be incorporated into the system introduced by the directive' since 'it is for each Member State to decide not only whether it will adopt such a system but also the conditions and effects of that system, in particular as regards the legal consequences of a right of residence granted on the basis of national law alone'.[181] Arguing differently, Advocate General Bot considered that 'the degree of integration of the Union citizen does not depend upon whether the *source* of his right of residence is in European Union law or national law'.[182]

The Court then ruled out periods of residence based on *EU law* that did not comply with the conditions in Directive 2004/38. In *Alarape and Tijani*, it confirmed *Dias* and *Ziolkowski*

---

[177] AG Trstenjak in *Dias*, para 89 of the Opinion.
[178] Case C-325/09 *Dias*, EU:C:2011:498, para 55 (emphasis added).
[179] Joined Cases C-424/10 and C-425/10 *Ziolkowski and Szeja*, EU:C:2011:866, paras 38 and 46–47 (emphasis added). Residence permits had been issued by the host State on humanitarian grounds; see further, Chapter 8.
[180] In *Chavez-Vilchez*, the Court referred cumulatively to 'the conditions laid down by Directive 2004/38, in particular in *Articles 5 to 7 thereof*, which govern entry into and residence in the territory of Member States' (Case C-133/15 *Chavez-Vilchez*, EU:C:2017:354, para 56), emphasis added.
[181] *Ziolkowski and Szeja*, paras 49–50. AG Bot disagreed, arguing that Article 37 would be without 'purpose' under such an interpretation (EU:C:2011:575, para 49 of the Opinion).
[182] AG Bot in *Ziolkowski and Szeja*, para 54 of the Opinion (emphasis added; referring to AG Kokott in Case C-434/09 *McCarthy*, EU:C:2010:718, para 52 of the Opinion).

and Szeja and clarified the implications of those rulings for the family members of Union citizens. It held that for third-country national family members claiming permanent residence rights under Article 16(2) of Directive 2004/38, 'only the periods of residence of those family members which satisfy the condition laid down in Article 7(2) of that directive may be taken into consideration'.[183] Since residence rights for third-country national family members derive from the Union citizen that they accompany or join in the host State, Article 7(2) requires that it is the Union citizen who must have resided there in compliance with the conditions in Article 7(1) of the Directive for the required period.[184]

Case law on the right of permanent residence had therefore established that *legal* residence as a requirement of Article 16 of the Directive specifically meant periods in a host State that complied with the residence conditions in Directive 2004/38 only and especially the conditions in Article 7. But how did that case law relate to the more general concept of *lawful* residence for the purposes of claiming equal treatment with host State nationals? From that perspective, the *Brey* case marked, with hindsight, a turning point from the foundational case law phase outlined in Section 2 to the more recent case law principles returned to below. Three key features of *Brey* are first considered here: its apparent narrowing of lawful residence within the meaning of EU law, Directive-specific definition of social assistance, and emphasis on proportionality review to determine lawful residence (and thus equal treatment claims).

Residence certificates had been issued to a retired German couple in Austria, but Mr Brey's application for income support (submitted almost immediately after he moved there) raised the question of 'whether a Member State may refuse to grant the compensatory supplement to nationals of other Member States on the grounds that – like Mr Brey – they do not, despite having been issued with a certificate of residence, meet the necessary requirements for obtaining *the legal right to reside* on the territory of that Member State for a period of longer than three months'.[185] Under the applicable Austrian rules, 'the person concerned must have sufficient resources not to apply for, *inter alia*, the compensatory supplement' in order to have a 'legal right to reside'.[186] The Court—referring to *Martínez Sala*, *Grzelczyk*, and *Trojani* 'to that effect'—affirmed that 'there is nothing to prevent, in principle, the granting of social security benefits to Union citizens who are not economically active being made conditional upon those citizens meeting the necessary requirements for obtaining a legal right of residence in the host Member State'.[187] In *Trojani*, the paragraph of the ruling addressing a 'legal right of residence' had then continued: 'where he has been lawfully resident in the host Member State for a certain time *or possesses a residence permit*'.[188] In *Brey*, the Court referred

---

[183] Case C-529/11 *Alarape and Tijani*, EU:C:2013:290, para 37.
[184] ibid para 35. Article 7(2) of the Directive provides that '[t]he right of residence provided for in paragraph 1 shall extend to family members who are not nationals of a Member State, accompanying or joining the Union citizen in the host Member State, provided that such Union citizen satisfies the conditions referred to in paragraph l(a), (b) or (c)'. For permanent residence rights acquired following residence based on Articles 12(2) and 13(2) of the Directive, family members claiming the rights must themselves have satisfied the conditions laid down in Article 7(1) of the Directive (para 38). See further, Section 3.2.5.
[185] Case C-140/12 *Brey*, EU:C:2013:565, para 30 (emphasis added).
[186] ibid. Thus, 'even though Mr Brey's right of residence is not directly at issue in the main proceedings, which concern only the grant of the compensatory supplement, the national law itself establishes a direct link between the conditions for obtaining that benefit and the conditions for obtaining the legal right to reside in Austria for periods in excess of three months; the granting of a compensatory supplement is made conditional upon the person in question meeting the requirements for obtaining that right of residence' (para 29).
[187] ibid para 44.
[188] Case C-456/02 *Trojani*, EU:C:2004:488, para 43.

to both *Bidar* (which repeats the *Trojani* phrasing in full) and *Förster* (which cites *Bidar*) but without the element of residence authorised by a Member State.[189]

The Court then held that 'it is important that the requirements for obtaining that right of residence – such as, in the case before the referring court, the need to have sufficient resources not to apply for the compensatory supplement – are themselves consistent with EU law'.[190] It recognised that the right to move and reside conferred by Article 21(1) TFEU is not unconditional and pointed, bearing in mind the (no longer economically active) situation of the couple in this case, to the conditions in Article 7(1)(b) of the Directive. Importantly, it then provided, for the first time, a definition of 'social assistance system' for the purposes of Directive 2004/38:

> [A]ll assistance introduced by the public authorities, whether at national, regional or local level, that can be claimed by an individual who does not have resources sufficient to meet his own basic needs and the needs of his family and who, by reason of that fact, may become a burden on the public finances of the host Member State during his period of residence which could have consequences for the overall level of assistance which may be granted by that State.[191]

The Court thus detached the meaning of social assistance in the application of the Directive from other conceptions of social assistance in EU law, notably in Regulation 883/2004.[192] The definition in *Brey* was linked to recital 10 of the Directive, which is 'based on the idea that the exercise of the right of residence for citizens of the Union can be subordinated to the legitimate interests of the Member States – in the present case, the protection of their public finances'.[193] Referring to Articles 3(3) and 70(4) of Regulation 883/2004, the Commission had argued:

> [T]he requirement that, in order to receive the compensatory supplement, the person concerned must have a legal right to reside in the host Member State for a period of longer than three months is not consistent with EU law. Anyone who – like Mr Brey – falls within the scope of Regulation No 883/2004 as a retired person who has ceased all employed or self-employed activity has the right, pursuant to Article 70(4) of that regulation, to be paid special non-contributory cash benefits in his Member State of residence. Under Article 1(j) of that regulation, a person's residence is the place where he 'habitually resides', an expression which refers to the Member State in which the person concerned habitually resides and where the habitual centre of his interests is to be found. It follows, according to the Commission, that the requirement laid down in [the contested national rules], for

---

[189] Case C-209/03 *Bidar*, EU:C:2005:169, para 37; Case C-158/07 *Förster*, EU:C:2008:630, para 39.
[190] *Brey*, EU:C:2013:565, para 45.
[191] ibid para 61. The Commission had argued, to the contrary, 'that the "social assistance" benefits covered by [Article 7(1)(b) of Directive 2004/38] are those which are *not* currently covered by Regulation No 883/2004' (para 48, emphasis added)).
[192] A Directive-specific definition was introduced to ensure 'uniform application of EU law and respect for the principle of equality' (ibid para 49).
[193] ibid para 55; referring 'by analogy' to Case C-413/99 *Baumbast and R*, EU:C:2002:493, para 90; Case C-200/02 *Zhu and Chen*, EU:C:2004:639, para 32; and Case C-408/03 *Commission v Belgium*, EU:C:2006:192, paras 37 and 41. Recital 10 states that '[p]ersons exercising their right of residence should not, however, become an unreasonable burden on the social assistance system of the host Member State during an initial period of residence. Therefore, the right of residence for Union citizens and their family members for periods in excess of three months should be subject to conditions'.

such residence to be lawful represents indirect discrimination contrary to Article 4 of Regulation No 883/2004, since it affects only non-Austrian citizens of the Union.[194]

However, the Court determined that Article 70(4) of the Regulation establishes a conflict rule and 'is not intended to lay down the conditions creating the right to special non-contributory cash benefits. It is for the legislation of each Member State to lay down those conditions'.[195] Advocate General Wahl had paved the way by observing that, first, '[t]he concept of 'social assistance system of the Member State' has been held to have an autonomous meaning under EU law'; and second, 'the term "social assistance"' as used in the Directive does not necessarily have to be construed in the same way as it does in the context of other EU legislation'.[196]

The Court underlined that while a Union citizen's eligibility for income support in a host State '*could be* an indication that that national does not have sufficient resources to avoid becoming an unreasonable burden on the social assistance system of the host Member State for the purposes of Article 7(1)(b) of Directive 2004/38 ... the competent national authorities cannot draw such conclusions without first carrying out an overall assessment of the specific burden which granting that benefit would place on the national social assistance system as a whole, *by reference to the personal circumstances characterising the individual situation* of the person concerned'.[197] In other words, a proportionality assessment must be undertaken. Elaborating its guidance from previous case law, the Court in *Brey* thus sought to combine the systemic and individual elements of proportionality analysis, bearing in mind: that the Directive does not preclude nationals of other Member States from receiving benefits in the host State;[198] that Article 8(4) of the Directive prevents Member States from laying down a fixed amount for 'sufficient resources' and obliges them to take the personal situation of the person concerned into account;[199] that recital 16 makes it clear that 'to determine whether a person receiving social assistance has become an unreasonable burden on its social assistance system, the host Member State should, before adopting an expulsion measure, examine whether the person concerned is experiencing temporary difficulties and take into account the duration of residence of the person concerned, his personal circumstances, and the amount of aid which has been granted to him';[200] that since the right to move freely 'is – as a fundamental principle of EU law – the general rule, the conditions laid down in Article 7(1)(b) of Directive 2004/38 must be construed narrowly ... and in compliance with the limits imposed by EU law and the principle of proportionality',[201] and that neither the objectives nor the practical effectiveness of Directive 2004/38 should be compromised.[202]

In that light, though arguably conflating lawful residence considerations and social assistance considerations to some extent, the Court could not accept national rules 'whereby nationals of other Member States who are not economically active are *automatically barred by the host Member State from receiving a particular social security benefit*, even for the period

---

[194] *Brey*, para 37.
[195] ibid, para 41.
[196] AG Wahl in *Brey*, EU:C:2013:337, paras 39–40 of the Opinion. On the first point, he referred to Case C-578/08 *Chakroun*, EU:C:2010:117, para 45, in connection with Council Directive 2003/86/EC on the right to family reunification, 2003 OJ L251/12. See further, paras 59–65 of the Opinion.
[197] *Brey*, paras 63–64 (emphasis added).
[198] ibid para 65, referring to Case C-184/99 *Grzelczyk*, EU:C:2001:458, para 39.
[199] ibid paras 67–68.
[200] ibid para 69.
[201] ibid para 70.
[202] ibid para 71.

following the first three months of residence referred to in Article 24(2) of Directive 2004/38' since such rules would not enable host State authorities, in situations 'where the resources of the person concerned fall short of the reference amount for the grant of that benefit, to carry out – in accordance with the requirements under, *inter alia*, Articles 7(1)(b) and 8(4) of that directive and the principle of proportionality – an overall assessment of the specific burden which granting that benefit would place on the social assistance system as a whole by reference to the personal circumstances characterising the individual situation of the person concerned'.[203] Instead, national authorities were required to undertake an assessment of the particular circumstances of the Union citizen applying for the benefit, taking into account: 'the amount and the regularity of the income which he receives; the fact that those factors have led those authorities to issue him with a certificate of residence; and the period during which the benefit applied for is likely to be granted to him'.[204]

Addressing the systemic dimension, the Court advised that 'it may be relevant ... to determine the proportion of the beneficiaries of that benefit who are Union citizens in receipt of a retirement pension in another Member State'.[205] Bringing the threads of the ruling together, it then concluded:

> EU law – in particular, as it results from Article 7(1)(b), Article 8(4) and Article 24(1) and (2) of Directive 2004/38 – must be interpreted as precluding national legislation ... which, even as regards the period following the first three months of residence, *automatically – whatever the circumstances* – bars the grant of a benefit ... to a national of another Member State who is not economically active, on the grounds that, despite having been issued with a certificate of residence, he does not meet the necessary requirements for obtaining the legal right to reside on the territory of the first Member State for a period of longer than three months, since obtaining that right of residence is conditional upon that national having sufficient resources not to apply for the benefit.[206]

Mr Brey was never going to succeed in his action because the couple's financial needs, requiring ongoing income support to supplement Mr Brey's German pensions, were not temporary.[207] Nevertheless, the Court's ruling managed to attribute legal significance to lawful residence within the meaning of Directive 2004/38 while sustaining, in parallel, continuity with core principles on proportionality review established in the foundational case law. However, requiring an individual assessment in every case inevitably imposes significant administrative burdens. It also creates space for considerable differences in approach as well as outcomes, both within and across different Member States. The judgment in *Brey* was therefore a highly elegant compromise from a legal perspective, but a fragile and ultimately short-lived balancing act in practice.

---

[203] ibid para 77 (emphasis added).
[204] ibid para 78.
[205] ibid para 79. On the systemic burden point, AG Wahl commented that 'it seems difficult, at first glance, to grasp how a single individual can become an unreasonable burden on the finances of a Member State. Nevertheless, the rules in the Directive would be meaningless if this were not conceivable. Then again, had the case instead concerned a one-off payment of EUR 326.82, one could not sensibly speak of an "unreasonable burden". The unreasonableness lies in the fact that payment of the compensatory supplement is an indefinitely recurring event, yet Mr Brey is unable to demonstrate any prior links to Austrian society that would justify those payments' (AG Wahl in *Brey*, para 88 of the Opinion).
[206] *Brey*, para 80 (emphasis added).
[207] 'As Mr Brey is a pensioner, it is not apparent that his situation of financial hardship will change over time, or that the benefit is requested in order to surmount an exceptional, unforeseen hardship' (AG Wahl in *Brey*, para 84 of the Opinion).

3.1.2 *Dano*

Ms Dano and her son (who was born in Germany in 2009) were both Romanian nationals who lived with and were 'provide[d] for ... materially' by Ms Dano's sister in Leipzig.[208] Ms Dano received child benefit in Germany, but subsequent applications for social assistance submitted on behalf of herself and her son were refused.[209]

The residence certificate that had been issued to Ms Dano did not constitute legal residence under German law.[210] As a result, her situation was not straightforwardly comparable to *Martínez Sala*, *Grzelczyk*, or *Trojani*, since her residence in the host State was not similarly 'authorised' by national law. The Court of Justice, with no further comment or analysis—a point returned to below—accepted the national court's view that the proceedings 'concern[ed] persons who cannot claim a right of residence in the host State by virtue of Directive 2004/38'.[211] Moreover, since 'there [was] nothing to indicate'[212] that Ms Dano had sought work in Germany, there was no need to consider benefits that facilitated access to the host State employment market under *Vatsouras and Koupatantze*. Instead, the Court determined that the referring court was asking 'whether Article 18 TFEU, Article 20(2) TFEU, Article 24(2) of Directive 2004/38, and Article 4 of Regulation No 883/2004 must be interpreted as precluding legislation of a Member State under which nationals of other Member States who are not economically active are excluded, in full or in part, from entitlement to certain "special non-contributory cash benefits" within the meaning of Regulation No 883/2004 although those benefits are granted to nationals of the Member State concerned who are in the same situation'.[213]

The Court first repeated that '[e]very Union citizen may ... rely on the prohibition of discrimination on grounds of nationality laid down in Article 18 TFEU in all situations falling within the scope *ratione materiae* of EU law' and that '[t]hese situations include those relating to the exercise of the right to move and reside within the territory of the Member States conferred by [Articles 20(2)(a) and 21(1) TFEU]'.[214] Then came the significant change from previous case law:

> Article 18(1) TFEU prohibits any discrimination on grounds of nationality '[w]ithin the scope of application of the Treaties, and without prejudice to any special provisions contained therein'. The second subparagraph of Article 20(2) TFEU expressly states that the rights conferred on Union citizens by that article are to be exercised 'in accordance with the conditions and limits defined by the Treaties and by the measures adopted thereunder'. Furthermore, under Article 21(1) TFEU too the right of Union citizens to move and reside freely within the territory of the Member States is subject to compliance with the 'limitations and conditions laid down in the Treaties and by the measures adopted to give them effect' ... Thus, the principle of non-discrimination, laid down generally in Article 18 TFEU, *is given more specific expression in Article 24 of Directive 2004/38* in relation to Union citizens who, like the applicants in the main proceedings, exercise their right to move and reside within the territory of the Member States. That principle is *also given more specific*

---

[208] Case C-333/13 *Dano*, EU:C:2014:2358, para 37.
[209] Ms Dano and her son applied for 'the grant of benefits by way of basic provision for jobseekers' (ibid para 42).
[210] *Dano*, para 36; referring to 'a residence certificate of unlimited duration'. Explaining this point, see Thym (n 4, 2015b) 257–58.
[211] ibid para 44.
[212] ibid para 39.
[213] ibid para 56.
[214] ibid para 59.

expression in Article 4 of Regulation No 883/2004 in relation to Union citizens, such as the applicants in the main proceedings, who invoke in the host Member State the benefits referred to in Article 70(2) of the regulation. *Accordingly*, the Court should interpret Article 24 of Directive 2004/38 and Article 4 of Regulation No 883/2004.[215]

This reasoning introduces a 'specific expression' chain that links: (1) Article 24 of Directive 2004/38 as an expression of 'limitations and conditions laid down in the Treaties and [in] measures adopted to give them effect' back to (2) Article 21(1) TFEU as a 'special provision' in the Treaties, to which (3) Article 18 TFEU is therefore 'without prejudice'.[216] The Court's emphasis on Article 24 of the Directive did not take into account that the prohibition of discrimination laid down in Article 18 TFEU is itself 'merely a specific enunciation of the general principle of equality which is one of the fundamental principles of [Union] law'.[217] It also fuelled an impression that *only* residence based on Directive 2004/38 could constitute lawful residence in EU citizenship law, generalising the permanent residence case law to a remarkable extent. However, it rests on inconsistent logic: if Article 24 of the Directive is the 'specific expression' of equal treatment for citizens residing in the host State *on the basis of the Directive*, why is it relevant to those who, like Ms Dano, are not residing in the host State on that basis in the first place? This peculiarity in the Court's reasoning has since had damaging impact on equal treatment even when residence *is* authorised by national law, returned to in Section 3.5.

In the next part of its ruling in *Dano*, the Court recalled the three stages of residence mapped out by the Directive—up to three months, between three months and five years, and more than five years—and ruled that '[t]o accept that persons who do not have a right of residence under Directive 2004/38 may claim entitlement to social benefits under the same conditions as those applicable to nationals of the host Member State would run counter to an objective of the directive, set out in recital 10 in its preamble, namely preventing Union citizens who are nationals of other Member States from becoming an unreasonable burden on the social assistance system of the host Member State'.[218] Thus, 'to determine whether economically inactive Union citizens, in the situation of the applicants in the main proceedings ... can claim equal treatment with nationals of that Member State so far as concerns entitlement to social benefits, it must therefore be examined whether the residence of those citizens complies with the conditions in Article 7(1)(b) of Directive 2004/38'.[219]

In blunt tones, the Court considered that Article 7(1)(b) 'seeks to prevent economically inactive Union citizens from using the host Member State's welfare system to fund their means of subsistence'.[220] It therefore concluded that, 'according to the findings of the referring court, the applicants do not have sufficient resources and thus cannot claim a right of residence in the host Member State under Directive 2004/38'.[221] The Court acknowledged that none of the express derogations from equal treatment in Article 24(2) of the Directive applied to Ms Dano's circumstances.[222] Nevertheless, the 'residing on the basis of this Directive' phrase in Article 24(1) acted as a *general derogation* from equal treatment: since 'Article 24(1) provides

---

[215] ibid paras 60–62 (emphasis added).
[216] On this point, see AG Wathelet in Case C-299/14 *García-Nieto*, EU:C:2015:366, paras 62–66 of the Opinion.
[217] Joined Cases 117/76 and 16/77 *Ruckdeschel*, EU:C:1977:160, para 7.
[218] *Dano*, para 74.
[219] ibid para 73.
[220] ibid para 76.
[221] ibid para 81.
[222] ibid para 66.

that all Union citizens residing *on the basis of the directive* in the territory of the host Member State are to enjoy equal treatment with the nationals of that Member State within the scope of the Treaty', it followed that, 'so far as concerns access to social benefits ... a Union citizen can claim equal treatment with nationals of the host Member State *only if* his residence in the territory of the host Member State complies with the conditions of Directive 2004/38'.[223]

That analysis flirts with undermining the requirement that exceptions to equal treatment must be 'expressly provided for'—wording that frames Article 24(1) of the Directive itself.[224] It is acknowledged that opening up entitlement to social assistance on a basis of equal treatment would render the requirement to have sufficient resources in the first place potentially meaningless if such resources could be claimed 'automatically, through the grant of a special non-contributory cash benefit which is intended to cover the beneficiary's subsistence costs'.[225] The same logic was seen in Chapter 6 for the requirement in Article 7(1)(b) to have comprehensive sickness insurance.[226] However, problematic assumptions made about 'benefit tourism'[227] and the fact that the Court did not even mention the word 'proportionality' illustrate the darker corners of the *Dano* ruling. The Court suggested that the requirement to have sufficient resources in Article 7(1)(b), in distinction from the unconditional residence right in Article 7(1)(a), means that 'any unequal treatment between Union citizens who have made use of their freedom of movement and residence and nationals of the host Member State with regard to the grant of social benefits is *an inevitable consequence* of Directive 2004/38'.[228] In its view, a Member State must have the possibility 'of refusing to grant social benefits to economically inactive Union citizens who exercise their right to freedom of movement *solely in order to obtain another Member State's social assistance* although they do not have sufficient resources to claim a right of residence'.[229] That statement imputes, in a surprisingly unsophisticated and sweeping way, just one intention to Union citizens who move to another State, are not economically active there, and then (for whatever reason) apply for social benefits and/or social assistance.

Similarly, in his assessment of the public interest served by the contested national rules, Advocate General Wathelet began to shift the narrative from the previous case law's concern for both individual circumstances and systemic analysis to the latter dimension only:

> [T]he Court has held, admittedly in a different context, that 'generally speaking, it cannot be insisted that a measure ... should involve an individual examination of each particular case ... since the management of the regime concerned must remain technically and economically viable'. It has also accepted that the risk of seriously undermining the financial balance of a social security system may constitute an overriding reason in the public interest capable of justifying barriers to the fundamental freedoms. This is also the idea behind the possibility afforded to the Member States of ensuring that the grant of assistance

---

[223] ibid paras 68–69 (emphasis added). See similarly, para 81.
[224] Article 24(1) of the Directive reads: '*Subject to such specific provisions as are expressly provided for in the Treaty and secondary law*, all Union citizens residing on the basis of this Directive in the territory of the host Member State shall enjoy equal treatment with the nationals of that Member State within the scope of the Treaty'.
[225] *Dano*, para 79. See similarly, AG Wathelet in *Dano*, EU:C:2014:341, para 113 of the Opinion.
[226] Case C-535/19 *A (Soins de santé publics)*, EU:C:2021:595, paras 55–56; observing in para 56 that the comprehensive sickness insurance condition in Article 7(1)(b) 'would be rendered redundant if it were to be considered that the host Member State is required to grant, to an economically inactive Union citizen residing in its territory on the basis of Article 7(1)(b) of Directive 2004/38, affiliation free of charge to its public sickness insurance system'.
[227] AG Wathelet in *Dano*, para 131 of the Opinion.
[228] *Dano*, para 77 (emphasis added).
[229] ibid para 78 (emphasis added).

to cover the maintenance costs of students from other Member States does not become an unreasonable burden which could have consequences for the overall level of assistance which may be granted by that State.[230]

The Advocate General indicated that '[a]lthough the referring court provides *no precise information about the existence of such a risk*, it none the less refers to the limits of basic provision systems financed from taxation in the light of the amounts involved, amounts *which might encourage* immigration of Union citizens whose average income is considerably lower'.[231] On the specific circumstances of *Dano*, he suggested that 'recourse to the social assistance system will not be temporary but will be prolonged indefinitely in the absence of any attempt at all to seek employment'.[232] He therefore considered that 'the criterion chosen by the legislation at issue in the main proceedings, namely entering German territory *solely in order to seek employment or benefit from social assistance*, is such as to demonstrate the absence of a genuine link with the territory of the host Member State and of integration in it. The criterion serves to ensure that the system is economically viable and that its financial balance is not undermined'.[233] Advocate General Wathelet characterised the contested national legislation as 'a *general exclusion* from entitlement to social assistance of nationals of other Member States who have entered the territory of the host Member State in order, in the words of [the applicable national rules, "to obtain social assistance or whose right of residence arises solely out of the search for employment"'.[234] Legislation based on a 'general exclusion' would thus have seemed comparable with the 'automatic' exclusion condemned in *Brey*.

In its ruling, criss-crossing from social assistance as defined with reference to Directive 2004/38 and social assistance under EU law more generally, the Court held that 'Article 24(1) of Directive 2004/38, read in conjunction with Article 7(1)(b) thereof, does not preclude national legislation ... in so far as it excludes nationals of other Member States *who do not have a right of residence under Directive 2004/38* in the host Member State from entitlement to certain "special non-contributory cash benefits" within the meaning of [Regulation 883/2004]'.[235] The Court did find that 'the financial situation of each person concerned should be examined specifically', but only, 'without taking account of the social benefits claimed, in order to determine whether he meets the condition of having sufficient resources to qualify for a right of residence under Article 7(1)(b) of Directive 2004/38'.[236] The fact that there was no reference in the judgment to proportionality—no reference, in other words, to the detailed assessment, with both individual and systemic elements, mandated so recently by *Brey*—is utterly remarkable.

Three further points of criticism can be noted. First, as addressed in Chapter 6, the motivation of Union citizens who exercise free movement rights is generally not relevant, even where situations are constructed to acquire EU rights.[237] Intention is a factor when it

---

[230] AG Wathelet in *Dano*, para 132 of the Opinion, citing Case C-546/11 *Dansk Jurist—og Økonomforbund*, EU:C:2013:603, para 70. He also referred to Case C-158/96 *Kohll*, EU:C:1998:171, para 41; Case C-209/03 *Bidar*, EU:C:2005:169, para 59; and Case C-158/07 *Förster*, EU:C:2008:630, para 48.
[231] AG Wathelet in *Dano*, para 133 of the Opinion (emphasis added).
[232] ibid para 134 of the Opinion.
[233] ibid para 135 of the Opinion (emphasis added).
[234] ibid para 97 of the Opinion (emphasis added).
[235] *Dano*, para 82 (emphasis added). The interaction of the Directive and the Regulation is returned to in Section 3.1.3.
[236] ibid para 81.
[237] eg on Article 45 TFEU, see Case C-109/01 *Akrich*, paras 55–57; and Case C-46/12 *LN*, EU:C:2013:97, para 47. On Directive 2004/38, see esp Case C-202/13 *McCarthy II*, EU:C:2014:2450, paras 45–56.

concerns the (required) subjective element of establishing an abuse of rights, that is, 'the intention to obtain an advantage from the EU rules by *artificially creating* the conditions laid down for obtaining it'.[238] In *Dano*, the Court did not actually identify any 'artificial' dimension in the circumstances of the case.[239] There was no clear statement that Ms Dano came to Germany 'solely' to obtain social assistance, and to infer this from the fact that 'she is not seeking employment and ... did not enter Germany in order to work' (para 66) is questionable, at least, in light of the gap in time between her presence in Germany (recalling that her son was born there in 2009) and her first application for basic provision (which was rejected in 2011). Ms Dano had resided in Germany for several years before making any claim for social assistance at all. Moreover, since her son, the other named applicant for the claimed social assistance, was born in Germany, he most categorically did *not* enter the territory of the host State 'to obtain social assistance' or 'search for employment' there.

Second, what about the stated fact that Ms Dano's sister provided materially for her and for her son? Was Ms Dano's inability to seek work connected to the need to care for son as a single parent? Was her situation temporary? Would recourse to benefits be of limited duration as her son became older? These *Brey*-style questions go to the heart of assessing the sufficiency of Ms Dano's resources and the extent to which any difficulties that she faced might be limited in time. Consideration of how the relevant German rules applied to her specific circumstances, as part of a proportionality assessment based on the criteria provided in *Brey*, would have required reflection on precisely these questions. But whether the referring court ever did so was never probed.[240]

On the contrary, the Court of Justice was strangely silent on proportionality in its ruling. Similarly, Advocate General Wathelet neither applied nor referred to the guidance on both systemic and individual assessment developed in *Brey*. In *Alimanovic*, the same Advocate General did refer to paragraph 77 of *Brey* but emphasised, in line with the Court's (later) judgment in *Dano*, that 'if in that paragraph ... the Court refers to provisions of Directive 2004/38 regarding the right of residence for a period of longer than three months, the requirement of an individual examination actually concerns the application for social assistance and not the lawfulness of the residence'.[241] In that understanding, 'it is important that the competent authorities of the host Member State ... take into account, *inter alia*, not only the amount and regularity of the income received by the citizen of the Union, but also the

---

[238] *McCarthy II*, para 54 (emphasis added).

[239] The requirements on appropriate evidence for claims of abuse of EU rights in *McCarthy II* provide further striking contrast with *Dano*—even though the ruling in *McCarthy II* was delivered just six months later: see in more detail, Chapter 6. See also (published shortly before *Dano*), Communication on Free movement of EU citizens and their families: five actions to make a difference, COM(2013) 837 final, esp para 1.3: '[o]n average, mobile EU citizens are more likely to be in employment than nationals of the host country. They help the host country's economy to function better because they help to tackle skills shortages and labour market bottlenecks. In most Member States, mobile EU citizens are net contributors to the host country's welfare system—they pay more in tax and social security contributions than they receive in benefits. EU mobile citizens also tend to be net contributors to the costs of public services they use in the host Member State. They are therefore unlikely to represent a burden on the welfare systems of host Member States. This is confirmed by recent independent studies. It is also corroborated by recent data that Member States have submitted to the Commission, showing that EU citizens do not use welfare benefits more intensively than the host country's nationals', supported by several references to independent ie non-EU sources.

[240] Highlighting the importance of how facts are presented in judgments of the Court, and contrasting *Dano* and *Grzelczyk* in that respect, see P Phoa, 'EU citizens' access to social benefits: reality or fiction? Outlining a law and literature approach to EU citizenship' in F Pennings and M Seeleib-Kaiser (eds), *EU Citizenship and Social Rights: Entitlements and Impediments to Accessing Welfare* (Edward Elgar 2018) 199.

[241] ibid para 105 of the Opinion.

period during which the benefit applied for is likely to be granted to them'.²⁴² Addressing the central problem in *Brey*—the automatic exclusion of Union citizens from entitlement to special non-contributory benefits—he revived the Court's 'genuine link' case law:

> [I]n the same way as the Court has developed case-law that permits the entitlement of economically inactive citizens of the Union to certain benefits to be made subject to a requirement of integration in the host Member State ... the demonstration of a real link with that State ought to prevent automatic exclusion from those benefits. In that case-law, the Court has previously held that a single condition that is too general and exclusive in nature, in that it unduly favours an element not necessarily representative of the real and effective degree of connection between the applicant for the allowance and the geographic market in question, to the exclusion of all other representative elements, went beyond what was necessary in order to attain the aim pursued. According to the Court, matters that can be inferred from family circumstances, like the existence of close ties of a personal nature, are also such as to contribute to the appearance of a lasting connection between the person concerned and the new host Member State. Accordingly, national legislation establishing a condition that 'prevents other factors which are potentially representative of the real degree of connection of the claimant with the relevant geographic labour market being taken into account ... goes beyond what is necessary to achieve its aim.²⁴³

It is not self-evident why the Advocate General, or the Court, found that there was no need to reflect on any of these questions in *Dano*.

Finally, the Court also took an extremely narrow approach to the concept of 'implementing Union law' for the purposes of Article 51(1) CFR in *Dano*, meaning that 'whether Articles 1, 20 and 51 of the Charter must be interpreted as requiring the Member States to grant Union citizens non-contributory cash benefits by way of basic provision such as to enable permanent residence or whether those States may limit their grant to the provision of funds necessary for return to the home State' did not have to be addressed.²⁴⁴ This issue is considered separately in Section 4.

3.1.3 *Alimanovic*

In *Alimanovic*, in which the judgment was delivered just under a year after *Dano*, the applicants were Swedish nationals residing in Germany who had worked in temporary jobs for a sufficient period of time to retain their status as workers more straightforwardly under Article 7(3)(c) of the Directive. On that basis, and in accordance with the wording of Article 7(3)(c), they received subsistence allowances for the long-term unemployed for six months. These benefits were withdrawn at the end of that period since neither of the applicants had regained the status of worker or self-employed person by then and the applicable national rules precluded jobseekers from claiming social assistance.

As noted in Section 2.2, the Court had ruled in *Vatsouras and Koupatantze* that jobseekers are entitled to claim benefits that facilitate access to the labour market of the host State on a basis of equal treatment with host State nationals. Crucially, such benefits did not constitute 'social assistance' for the purposes of the derogation in Article 24(2) of Directive 2004/

---

²⁴² AG Wathelet in Case C-67/14 *Alimanovic*, EU:C:2015:210, para 106 of the Opinion; citing Case C-140/12 *Brey*, EU:C:2013:565, paras 78–79.
²⁴³ AG Wathelet in Case C-67/14 *Alimanovic*, EU:C:2015:210, paras 107–109 of the Opinion.
²⁴⁴ *Dano*, para 85.

38. But neither had they been defined more precisely on their own terms. The first significant change brought about by *Alimanovic* was therefore that the Court introduced the 'predominant function' approach to characterisation of benefits in EU citizenship law:[245] if 'the predominant function of the benefits at issue ... is in fact to cover the minimum subsistence costs necessary to lead a life in keeping with human dignity', then such benefits 'cannot be characterised as benefits of a financial nature which are intended to facilitate access to the labour market of a Member State'.[246] Thus, if a benefit, irrespective of its classification under national rules, meets the *Brey* definition of social assistance, it does not matter if it *also* or *in fact* facilitates to the employment market: a jobseeker is not entitled to receive it because of the derogation in Article 24(2) of the Directive. Through this method, the Court did not overrule *Vatsouras and Kouptantze*, but it significantly narrowed the scope of that ruling: for social assistance benefits, the Court confirmed in *Alimanovic* its finding in *Dano* that 'a Union citizen can claim equal treatment with nationals of the host Member State under Article 24(1) of Directive 2004/38 only if his residence in the territory of the host Member State complies with the conditions of Directive 2004/38'.[247] It also established that determining whether social assistance could be refused on the basis of the derogation in Article 24(2) made it 'necessary to determine beforehand whether the principle of equal treatment referred to in Article 24(1) of that directive is applicable and, accordingly, whether the Union citizen concerned is lawfully resident on the territory of the host Member State'.[248]

With respect to residing 'on the basis of the Directive' under Article 24(1), the Court considered that '[o]nly two provisions of Directive 2004/38 may confer on job-seekers in the situation of [the applicants] a right of residence in the host Member State under that directive, namely Article 7(3)(c) and Article 14(4)(b) thereof'.[249] Since Article 7(3)(c) no longer applied in the circumstances of the case, the Court focused on Article 14(4)(b). It concluded that while the applicants *could* rely on that provision, in principle, '*to establish a right of residence* even after the expiry of the period referred to in Article 7(3)(c) of Directive 2004/38, for a period, covered by Article 14(4)(b) thereof, *which entitles them to equal treatment with the nationals of the host Member State so far as access to social assistance is concerned*',[250] the obstacle for the Alimanovic claimants was that the host State could then straightforwardly rely on the derogation in Article 24(2) of the Directive 'not to grant that citizen the social assistance sought'.[251]

The Court held that a host Member State may refuse to grant social assistance to a jobseeking Union citizen only where a right of residence 'is based *solely*' on Article 14(4)(b).[252] It is not clear how that statement relates, in a general sense, to the fact that jobseeker residence rights flow from Article 45 TFEU directly. However, as explained in Section 2.2,

---

[245] Determining the predominant function of a particular benefit applies in the case law on social security coordination more generally; see eg Case 1/72 *Frilli*, EU:C:1972:56, esp paras 13 and 18–19.

[246] Case C-67/14 *Alimanovic*, EU:C:2015:597, paras 45 and 46; confirmed in Case C-299/14 *García-Nieto*, EU:C:2016:114, para 37.

[247] *Alimanovic*, para 49; referring to Case C-333/13 *Dano*, EU:C:2014:2358, para 69. In para 50 of *Alimanovic*, the Court confirmed that '[t]o accept that persons who do not have a right of residence under Directive 2004/38 may claim entitlement to social assistance under the same conditions as those applicable to nationals of the host Member State would run counter to an objective of the directive, set out in recital 10 in its preamble, namely preventing Union citizens who are nationals of other Member States from becoming an unreasonable burden on the social assistance system of the host Member State' (referring to *Dano*, para 74).

[248] *Alimanovic*, para 51.

[249] ibid para 52.

[250] This element of the Court's ruling was considered in more detail in Chapter 6; and note again the criticism of AG Wathelet in Case C-442/16 *Gusa*, EU:C:2017:607, paras 69–70 of the Opinion.

[251] *Alimanovic*, para 57 (emphasis added).

[252] ibid para 58 (emphasis added).

equal treatment had not been extended to jobseekers on the basis of Article 45 TFEU before the institution of Union citizenship anyway: the Court needed to draw also from Article 21 TFEU to achieve it *Collins*. By opening the door to rights based (even in part) on Article 21 TFEU in that way, the door was also opened to the fact that such rights are extended subject to the conditions and limits provided for in EU legislation. Also touching on rights potentially—and independently—connected to Article 45 TFEU, Advocate General Wathelet had suggested that one of the applicants in *Alimanovic* might have a derived right to reside in Germany as the primary carer of her two younger children, recalling that she had been a worker in the host State and that her children therefore had a right to reside there under Article 10 of Regulation 492/2011 to complete their education.[253] Crucially, Directive 2004/38 does not 'make the right of residence of children who are in education and the parent who is their primary carer dependent on their having sufficient resources and comprehensive sickness insurance cover or, more generally, on the conditions laid down in Directive 2004/38'.[254] The Court did not address this possibility in its ruling, but it is returned to in Section 3.3.

The second significant change produced by *Alimanovic* concerns proportionality review. As noted above, the applicants—unlike Ms Dano or her young son—had previously worked in the host State. That link with economic activity was insufficient to keep them within the protection of Article 7(3) of the Directive, though it may in some sense explain the more generous approach to proportionality adopted by Advocate General Wathelet in *Alimanovic* compared to his Opinion in *Dano*.[255] However, the Court was significantly tougher, making even plainer in *Alimanovic* what was implicit in *Dano*—that no individual assessment of a Union citizen's circumstances is required in certain situations. In *Alimanovic*, the applicants resided in the host State as jobseekers on the basis of Article 14(4)(b) of the Directive. Their entitlement to equal treatment with host State nationals in the context of social assistance was ruled out by the express derogation in Article 24(2). The Court, referring to *Brey*, considered that Directive 2004/38 'requires a Member State to take account of the individual situation of the person concerned before it adopts an expulsion measure or finds that the residence of that person is placing an unreasonable burden on its social assistance system', but that '*no such individual assessment* is necessary in circumstances such as those at issue in the main proceedings'.[256] It offered three reasons. First, 'Directive 2004/38, establishing

[253] AG Wathelet in *Alimanovic*, paras 119–121 of the Opinion, referring to eg Case C-529/11 *Alarape and Tijani*, EU:C:2013:290.

[254] AG Wathelet in *Alimanovic*, para 120 of the Opinion; referring to Case C-310/08 *Ibrahim*, EU:C:2010:89, paras 56 and 59 and Case C-480/08 *Teixeira*, EU:C:2010:83, para 70. The latter rulings are returned to in Section 3.3 and considered in more detail in Chapter 9.

[255] For example, in *Alimanovic*, he described the right to move and work as 'a fundamental and absolute freedom of EU law', while acknowledging that 'the Union legislature took the view that it was necessary to provide a framework for the right of residence of nationals of Member States' (AG Wathelet in *Alimanovic*, para 123 of the Opinion). See similarly, AG Ruiz-Jarabo Colomer in Joined Cases C-22/08 and C-23/08 *Vatsouras and Koupatantze*, EU:C:2009:150, para 63 of the Opinion: '[a]nyone wishing to join the workforce has better credentials if they have carried out responsibilities with a wage-earning aspect of some kind in the past. In addition, if there has been some exchange of services for remuneration, however minimal, there is all the more reason to apply the ... Treaty. Consequently, in a case such as that of Mr Vatsouras and Mr Koupatantze, where there has been economic activity within the first few months of arrival in Germany, it is difficult to regard them as ordinary job-seekers if they subsequently become unemployed'. As Kramer has observed with respect to *Alimanovic*, 'if mother and daughter Alimanovic had only worked one month longer, Germany should have granted them *unlimited* access to social assistance' (emphasis added) because of 'the entirely open-ended wording of Article 7(3)' (D Kramer, 'Had they only worked one month longer! An analysis of the *Alimanovic* Case [2015] Case C-67/14' (2015) European Law Blog. Available at: <https://europeanlawblog.eu/2015/09/29/had-they-only-worked-one-month-longer-an-analysis-of-the-alimanovic-case-2015-c-6714/> (accessed 5 June 2023), emphasis in original).

[256] *Alimanovic*, para 59, referring to Case C-140/12 *Brey*, EU:C:2013:565, paras 64, 69, and 78; confirmed in Case C-299/14 *García-Nieto*, EU:C:2016:114, para 46.

a gradual system as regards the retention of the status of "worker" which seeks to safeguard the right of residence and access to social assistance, *itself takes into consideration various factors characterising the individual situation of each applicant for social assistance and, in particular, the duration of the exercise of any economic activity*.'[257] But it is difficult to understand how any general EU legislative measure can 'itself' take individual situations into consideration—recalling the general exclusion in *national* rules disdained in *Brey*. The rights conferred on jobseekers are conceptually messy: they had always been excluded from equal treatment on the basis of Article 45 TFEU, the Court added aspects of Article 21 TFEU in *Collins* to overcome that, and then the EU legislator overrode that approach in Article 24(2) of the Directive. Nevertheless, the Court did not need to get into proportionality constriction in *Alimanovic* to the extent that it did since it had already contained the implications of *Vatsouras and Koupatantze* by introducing the 'predominant function' test. Thus, what seemed to matter in to the Court in *Alimanovic* was that the concern for individual situations required by *Baumbast* and *Brey* should be set aside in *some* circumstances; for certain *classes* of Union citizen, as a group. In other words, the Court seemed now to consider that Directive 2004/38 was proportionate *by design*, displacing the need to consider the proportionality of the *application* of that design.

The next two reasons provided by the Court addressed two critical questions: why is the adjusted view defensible; and to which group behaviours can it be applied? With respect to *why* individual assessment could now be displaced, the Court emphasised the benefits of legal certainty. In contrast to the discretion that necessarily characterises the administrative application of proportionality analysis in individual cases, the contested national rules in *Alimanovic* fixed a specific point in time—one that respected Article 7(3)(c) of Directive 2004/38 and after which a right to social assistance would cease unless the status of the claimant changed through the resuming of economic activity. That approach 'is consequently such as to guarantee a significant level of legal certainty and transparency in the context of the award of social assistance by way of basic provision, while complying with the principle of proportionality' by 'enabling those concerned to know, without any ambiguity, what their rights and obligations are'.[258] As to *when* individual assessment can be displaced, *Alimanovic* was premised expressly on jobseekers who reside in the host State on the basis of Article 14(4)(b) and, to date at least, its exclusion by group approach has subsequently been confirmed only for Member State nationals who are not economically active and apply for social assistance during their first three months of residence in the host State, which is also clearly ruled out by Article 24(2) of the Directive.[259]

Of more concern, however, were the broader statements in *Alimanovic* that also displaced the Court's usual emphasis on proof and evidence, requiring Member States to *substantiate* their public interest arguments, as discussed in Chapter 2. In *Alimanovic*, the Court shifted

---

[257] *Alimanovic*, para 60 (emphasis added). Confirmed in *García-Nieto*, para 47; adding that 'if such an assessment is not necessary in the case of a citizen seeking employment who no longer has the status of "worker" [as in *Alimanovic*], the same applies *a fortiori* to persons' residing in the host State on the basis of Article 6(1) of the Directive and who were not workers (ibid para 48).

[258] *Alimanovic*, para 61; confirmed in *García-Nieto*, para 49. A concern for legal certainty was evident in Opinions delivered before *Alimanovic*; see eg AG Bot in Case C-529/11 *Alarape and Tijani*, EU:C:2013:9, para 94 of the Opinion ('the setting of rigorous but clear conditions of eligibility for [the] status [of permanent resident] meets beyond doubt the requirement of legal certainty'). AG Sharpston had also reflected on how 'to reconcile a careful assessment of individual circumstances with the need to ensure legal certainty, transparency and administrative efficiency' (Joined Cases C-523/11 and C-585/11 *Prinz and Seeberger*, EU:C:2013:90, para 107 of the Opinion; see generally, paras 103–107).

[259] *García-Nieto*, para 46.

its previous focus on actual burden to projected burden on the host State social assistance system in suggesting while 'the assistance awarded to a single applicant can scarcely be described as an "unreasonable burden" for a Member State, within the meaning of Article 14(1) of Directive 2004/38 ... the accumulation of all the individual claims *which would be submitted to it* would be *bound to do so*'.[260] Even more bluntly, and even more speculatively, Advocate General Wathelet later remarked in *García-Nieto* that 'granting entitlement to social assistance to Union citizens who are not required to have sufficient means of subsistence *could result in relocation* en masse *liable* to create an unreasonable burden on national social security systems'.[261]

3.1.4 *Commission v UK*

In this action, taken in response to 'numerous complaints' from nationals of other Member States,[262] the Commission challenged a requirement in UK rules that claimants for child benefit and child tax credit (ie social benefits that were not social assistance within meaning of Art 7(1)(b) of Directive 2004/38[263]) must have a right to reside in the UK to be treated as habitually resident there under Article 1(j) of Regulation 883/1004. Article 11(3)(e) of the Regulation further provides that a person who is not economically active is subject, in principle, to the legislation of the Member State of residence. For the Commission, the place of someone's 'habitual residence' is determined through 'factual circumstances and the situation of the persons concerned regardless of their legal status in the host Member State and of whether they have a right to reside in its territory on the basis, for example, of Directive 2004/38'—in other words, it argued that Regulation 883/2004 'confers on the concept of "residence" a specific meaning which is independent of the meaning attributed to it in other measures of EU law or in national law *and is not subject to any legal pre-conditions*'.[264]

In the alternative, the Commission argued that the right to reside test was discriminatory, since it was more easily satisfied by UK nationals, and that the UK had 'not put forward any argument to show that the unequal treatment in question is appropriate and proportionate to the aim pursued by the national legislation concerned of ensuring that there is a genuine link between the benefit claimant and the host Member State'.[265] The Commission accepted that a host State 'may wish to ensure that the link between the benefit claimant and that State exists' but submitted that, 'in the case of social security benefits, it is the EU legislature itself, through Regulation No 883/2004, which has established the means of testing

---

[260] *Alimanovic*, para 62 (emphasis added); confirmed in *García-Nieto*, para 50.
[261] AG Wathelet in *García-Nieto*, para 71 of the Opinion (emphasis added).
[262] Case C-308/14 *Commission v UK*, EU:C:2016:436, para 21.
[263] The child benefit and child tax credit benefits in question were confirmed as 'benefits which are granted automatically to families that meet certain objective criteria relating in particular to their size, income and capital resources, without any individual and discretionary assessment of personal needs, and which are intended to meet family expenses' (*Commission v UK*, para 60; referring to eg Joined Cases C-245/94 and C-312/94 *Hoever and Zachow*, EU:C:1996:379, para 27).
[264] *Commission v UK*, para 31 (emphasis added). Referring to previous case law, the Commission argued that habitual residence 'designates the place where the habitual centre of interests of the person concerned is to be found. In order to determine that centre of interests, account should be taken in particular of the worker's family situation, the reasons which have led him to move, the length and continuity of his residence, whether he is in stable employment and his intention as it appears from all the relevant circumstances' (para 30, referring to Case C-90/97 *Swaddling*, EU:C:1999:96, para 29; see further, Case C-289/20 *IB (Habitual residence of a spouse—Divorce)*, EU:C:2021:955).
[265] *Commission v UK*, para 36. The Commission had originally framed its submissions around direct discrimination, as the UK rules 'impos[ed] a condition for entitlement to certain social security benefits which its own nationals *automatically* meet' (para 33, emphasis added; referring to the Opinion of AG Sharpston in Case C-73/08 *Bressol and Others*, EU:C:2009:396).

whether that link exists — ... in this instance, by means of the habitual residence criterion — and the Member States may make no changes to the provisions of that regulation or couple them with additional requirements'.[266] Moreover, Article 4 of the Regulation establishes that '[u]nless otherwise provided for *by this Regulation*, persons to whom this Regulation applies shall enjoy the same benefits and be subject to the same obligations under the legislation of any Member State as the nationals thereof'. In contrast, the UK argued that the Court had by now ruled 'on numerous occasions that it is lawful to require economically inactive EU nationals to demonstrate that they have a right of residence as a condition for qualifying for social security benefits' and that, through Directive 2004/38, 'the EU legislature expressly authorises host Member States to make their intervention subject to such a condition, in order that those nationals do not become an unreasonable burden on the social assistance system of those States. The principle of equal treatment referred to in Article 4 of Regulation No 883/2004 must be read in the light of that requirement'.[267]

The judgment of the Court was delivered just nine days before the UK's referendum on membership of the European Union in June 2016. In essence, it repeated what had already been held in *Brey* and *Dano*: that Article 11(3)(e) of Regulation 883/2004 establishes a conflict rule for determining the national legislation applicable to the payment of social security benefits within the scope of the Regulation but is 'not intended to lay down the conditions creating the right to social security benefits', which is a matter for the national legislation of each Member State; and so it cannot therefore be inferred that EU law 'precludes a national provision under which entitlement to social benefits, such as the social benefits at issue, is conditional upon the claimant having a right to reside lawfully in the Member State concerned'.[268] Advocate General Cruz Villalón had recalled the significance explicitly attached to limits and conditions laid down in secondary law by Articles 20 and 21 TFEU, and asserted that 'the provisions of Directive 2004/38 governing Union citizens' freedom of movement and residence also remain fully effective within the framework of [Regulation 883/2004], intended to give practical effect to the right of free movement and residence within the Union'—in other words, he could not 'agree with the Commission's assertion that "the concept of residence in Regulation No 883/2004 ... is not subject to any legal preconditions" '.[269] Rather, '[i]f ... EU law subjects the exercise of freedom of movement and residence to certain limitations and conditions, embodied in particular in Directive 2004/38, it seems clear that the provisions of Regulation No 883/2004 cannot be interpreted in such a way as to neutralise the conditions and limitations accompanying the grant and proclamation of that freedom'.[270]

The Court held that 'there is nothing to prevent, in principle, the grant of social benefits to Union citizens who are not economically active being made subject to the requirement that those citizens fulfil the conditions for possessing a right to reside lawfully in the host Member State'.[271] It accepted in this context the UK's submission that it had not linked the right to reside test to the determination of habitual residence: instead, the 'legality of the claimant's residence in its territory is a substantive condition which economically inactive persons must meet in order to be eligible for the social benefits at issue'.[272] However, as noted

---

[266] *Commission v UK*, para 37.
[267] ibid para 41.
[268] ibid paras 63–66.
[269] AG Cruz Villalón in *Commission v UK*, EU:C:2015:666, para 72 of the Opinion.
[270] ibid para 73 of the Opinion.
[271] *Commission v UK*, para 68; referring to Case C-140/12 *Brey*, EU:C:2013:565, para 44 and Case C-333/13 *Dano*, EU:C:2014:2358, para 83 'to this effect'.
[272] *Commission v UK*, para 72.

above, the benefits in question were social security benefits and *not* social assistance within the meaning of Directive 2004/38.[273] At one level, by accepting that the UK could legitimately seek to determine lawful residence in compliance with the Directive in order, as a corollary, to determine eligibility for equal treatment, the Court arguably does nothing new—after all, the benefit at issue in *Martínez Sala* was also a non-contributory (child-raising) benefit, not social assistance. The Court did not refer to that case in *Commission v UK*, but it did refer to *Brey* and *Dano* 'to this effect' to confirm that '[i]t is clear from the Court's case-law that there is nothing to prevent, in principle, the grant of social benefits to Union citizens who are not economically active being made subject to the requirement that those citizens fulfil the conditions for possessing a right to reside lawfully in the host Member State'.[274] Paragraph 44 of *Brey* did reference the Court's foundational case law.[275] However, also referring to paragraph 83 of *Dano* for the same proposition is more problematic, since the reasoning there concerned 'special non-contributory benefits' within the meaning of Article 70(2) of Regulation 883/2004—social assistance within the meaning of the Directive—whereas, in *Commission v UK*, 'it [was] not in dispute between the parties that they are *not* special non-contributory cash benefits within the meaning of Article 70'.[276] The judgment in *Commission v UK* therefore illustrated the distinctive spheres of influence of Article 24(1) and Article 24(2) of the Directive most strikingly: express derogations in Article 24(2) concern social assistance and study finance only; but residing 'on the basis of' the Directive is required by Article 24(1) to ensure equal treatment with host State nationals for *any* financial support within the scope of EU law.

It was recognised in *Commision v UK* that right to reside tests are more easily satisfied by host State nationals and are therefore indirectly discriminatory.[277] But it was also accepted that 'the need to protect the finances of the host Member State justifies *in principle* the possibility of checking whether residence is lawful when a social benefit is granted in particular

---

[273] ibid paras 60–61: '[a]ccording to the Court's case-law, benefits which are granted automatically to families that meet certain objective criteria relating in particular to their size, income and capital resources, without any individual and discretionary assessment of personal needs, and which are intended to meet family expenses must be regarded as social security benefits ... The result of applying the[se] ... to the social benefits at issue is that the latter must be classified as "social security benefits", as referred to in Article 3(1)(j) of Regulation No 883/2004, read in conjunction with Article 1(z) thereof'. However, as underlined by AG Cruz Villalón, '[n]owhere does the judgment in *Brey* state that the Court's findings in that judgment are confined exclusively to special non-contributory cash benefits. The same is true of the judgment in *Dano*' (AG Cruz Villalón in *Commission v UK*, para 33 of the Opinion).

[274] *Commission v UK*, EU:C:2016:436, para 68; referring to *Brey*, para 44 and *Dano*, para 83.

[275] ie 'The Court has consistently held that there is nothing to prevent, in principle, the granting of social security benefits to Union citizens who are not economically active being made conditional upon those citizens meeting the necessary requirements for obtaining a legal right of residence in the host Member State (see, to that effect, Case C-85/96 *Martínez Sala* [paras 61–63]; Case C-184/99 *Grzelczyk* [paras 32–33]; Case C-456/02 *Trojani* [paras 42–43]; Case C-209/03 *Bidar* [para 37]; and Case C-158/07 *Förster*, [para 39]'.

[276] *Commission v UK*, para 56 (emphasis added). Cf *Dano*, para 83: '[t]he benefits at issue in the main proceedings, which constitute "special non-contributory cash benefits" within the meaning of Article 70(2) of the regulation, are, under Article 70(4), to be provided exclusively in the Member State in which the persons concerned reside, in accordance with its legislation. It follows that there is nothing to prevent the grant of such benefits to Union citizens who are not economically active from being made subject to the requirement that those citizens fulfil the conditions for obtaining a right of residence under Directive 2004/38 in the host Member State' (with the Court also referring to *Brey*, para 44).

[277] *Commission v UK*, para 78. For Advocate General Cruz Villalón, the circumstances of *Commission v UK* raised two distinct questions: 'on the one hand, *the question of principle* as to whether or not the application of [Regulation 883/2004] should place "in abeyance" the provisions of Directive 2004/38 that set out the framework for determining the lawfulness of a Union citizen's residence in a Member State other than his own; on the other hand, *the intrinsically different question of the circumstances and conditions* in which any *checking of the situation of lawful residence* is compatible with the prohibition of discrimination laid down in Article 4 of Regulation No 883/2004' (para 3 of the Opinion, emphasis added).

to persons from other Member States who are not economically active, as such grant could have consequences for the overall level of assistance which may be accorded by that State'.[278] Examining how right to reside tests applied in the UK in practice, the Court characterised them as 'checks on the lawfulness of the residence of Union citizens, under the second subparagraph of Article 14(2) of Directive 2004/38', which must 'therefore comply with the requirements set out in the directive'.[279] Article 14(2) establishes that 'Union citizens and their family members shall have the right of residence provided for in Articles 7, 12 and 13 as long as they meet the conditions set out therein'. It further permits Member States to verify if these conditions are fulfilled, but only '[i]n specific cases where there is a reasonable doubt as to whether a Union citizen or his/her family members satisfies the conditions': in other words, '[t]his verification shall not be carried out systematically'.

In *Commission v UK*, it appeared from 'the observations made by the United Kingdom at the hearing before the Court that, for each of the social benefits at issue, the claimant must provide, on the claim form, a set of data which reveal whether or not there is a right to reside in the United Kingdom, those data being checked subsequently by the authorities responsible for granting the benefit concerned'.[280] Importantly, however, '[i]t is only in specific cases that claimants are required *to prove that they in fact enjoy a right to reside lawfully* in United Kingdom territory, as declared by them in the claim form'.[281] On that basis, the Court accepted that, 'contrary to the Commission's submissions, the checking of compliance with the conditions laid down by Directive 2004/38 for existence of a right of residence is not carried out systematically and consequently is not contrary to the requirements of Article 14(2) of the directive' since '[i]t is only in the event of doubt that the United Kingdom authorities effect the verification necessary to determine whether the claimant satisfies the conditions laid down by Directive 2004/38, in particular those set out in Article 7, and, therefore, whether he has a right to reside lawfully in United Kingdom territory, for the purposes of the directive'.[282]

Surprisingly, and reversing its usual approach to burden of proof, the Court then held that 'the Commission, which has the task of proving the existence of the alleged infringement and of providing the Court with the evidence necessary for it to determine whether the infringement is made out ... has not provided evidence or arguments showing that such checking does not satisfy the conditions of proportionality, that it is not appropriate for securing the attainment of the objective of protecting public finances or that it goes beyond what is necessary to attain that objective'.[283] In support of that view, the Court referred to

---

[278] *Commission v UK*, para 80 (emphasis added). See differently, the directly discriminatory residence permit requirement in Case C-85/96 *Martínez Sala*, EU:C:1998:217, para 64: '[s]ince the unequal treatment in question thus comes within the scope of the Treaty, it cannot be considered to be justified: it is discrimination directly based on the appellant's nationality and, in any event, nothing to justify such unequal treatment has been put before the Court'.

[279] *Commission v UK*, para 81.

[280] ibid para 83

[281] ibid (emphasis added). Though the Court did not address Article 14(4)(b) of the Directive in its judgment, the UK rules appeared to extend payment of the relevant benefits to jobseekers, underlining, therefore, that they were not social assistance; see AG Cruz Villalón, para 36 of the Opinion: '[t]he department responsible for administering those two benefits, Her Majesty's Revenue and Customs, takes account of, *inter alia*, the information provided by the Department for Work and Pensions to check whether a person has claimed social assistance. This enables it to ascertain whether that person has a right of residence in the United Kingdom and is therefore entitled to the two benefits at issue. In cases in which there is doubt as to whether the claimant has a right of residence, an individual assessment of the claimant's personal circumstances is carried out. This includes an examination of his contribution history, whether he is actively seeking employment and whether he has a genuine chance of being engaged'.

[282] *Commission v UK*, para 84.

[283] ibid para 85.

Commission v Greece, where it found that 'in proceedings for failure to fulfil obligations, it is for the Commission *to establish the existence of the alleged infringement* and to provide the Court with the information necessary for its verification of the existence of that breach'.[284] But it was completely at odds with established case law to read that obligation into the *justification* stage of infringement proceedings. In doing so, the Court further diluted the implications of proportionality review, in reducing what is expected of Member States when demonstrating the appropriateness and necessity of their national rules. The Commission had stated that the UK 'has not put forward *any argument* to show that the unequal treatment in question is appropriate and proportionate to the aim pursued by the national legislation concerned of ensuring that there is a genuine link between the benefit claimant and the host Member State'.[285] Such failure on the part of a defendant State usually serves to *establish* the infringement—not to defend it.

Finally, another judgment concerning infringement proceedings and also delivered in June 2016 should be noted. *Commission v Netherlands* concerned a scheme extended to students with Netherlands nationality only that provided reduced transport fares for students. In her Opinion, Advocate General Sharpston argued that a Member State 'may only rely on Article 24(2) of Directive 2004/38 *if Article 24(1) applies*—meaning, in the present case, if the residence of the students at issue satisfies the conditions of Directive 2004/38.[286] On the basis that 'there is nothing in the Commission's case as presented that suggests *that it also concerns (vocational) students whose residence in the Netherlands is not based on, or in conformity with, Directive 2004/38*',[287] she did 'not therefore explore the consequences of the requirement of lawful residence for (vocational) students whose residence in another Member State is *based on national law or some rule of EU law other than Directive 2004/38*'.[288]

Reflecting the 'specific expression' approach in *Dano*, the Court recalled that 'the principle of non-discrimination on grounds of nationality, enshrined as a general principle in Article 18 TFEU *and laid down specifically in respect of Union citizens coming within the scope of Directive 2004/38 in Article 24 thereof*, prohibits, *inter alia*, direct discrimination on grounds of nationality'.[289] However, that language arguably leaves the door open to recourse to Article 18 TFEU when Union citizens *do not* reside in the host State on the basis of Directive 2004/38, and it is thus of particular importance for three groups after *Dano* and *Alimanovic*—citizens who reside on the basis of Article 10 of Regulation 492/2011 (Section 3.3), citizens who reside on the basis of primary EU law yet not in conformity with the Directive (Section 3.4), and citizens who reside on the basis of national law/authorisation (Section 3.5).

It is difficult to overlook the fact that the shift to generalised exclusion from equal treatment with host State nationals by 'category' of citizen—emerging in *Förster*, and more developed from *Dano* onwards—is at odds with principles established in previous case law, yet without the Court or confronting and explaining the resulting disjointedness. The adoption

---

[284] Case C-180/14 *Commission v Greece*, EU:C:2015:840, para 60 (author's translation from French; emphasis added).
[285] Case C-308/14 *Commission v UK*, EU:C:2016:436, para 36 (emphasis added).
[286] AG Sharpston in Case C-233/14 *Commission v Netherlands*, EU:C:2016:50, para 85 of the Opinion (emphasis added).
[287] Case C-233/14 *Commission v Netherlands*, EU:C:2016:396, para 83: 'the Commission confirmed, in answer to a question raised by the Court at the hearing, that its action related to discrimination against students who have a right of residence under Article 7(1)(c) of Directive 2004/38. The Kingdom of the Netherlands also maintained that non-Netherlands students covered by the present action have a right of residence in the Netherlands under that provision'. See similarly, AG Sharpston, para 83 of the Opinion.
[288] AG Sharpston in *Commission v Netherlands*, para 88 of the Opinion (emphasis added).
[289] *Commission v Netherlands*, para 80 (emphasis added).

of the Directive per se is not enough to explain the shift, noting the (post-entry into force) timing of *Brey*. It also sits oddly with the focus on the individual that emits more pervasively across the scheme of the Directive itself—including from Articles 8(4) and 14(4)(b), both of which were addressed in such detail by the Court in *Brey*.

To illustrate the extent of the case law's fragmentation after *Dano*, *Alimanovic*, and *Commission v UK*, it was not clear if Mrs Martínez Sala or Mr Trojani would now be successful in their claims: would the more recent emphasis on lawful residence as residence that complies with Article 7 of the Directive accommodate residence in compliance with or authorised by national law that did not conform to the Directive's right to reside conditions? Did *Commission v UK* extinguish any sense that Mrs Martínez Sala might fare better, since her claim did not relate to social assistance? Mr Grzelczyk sat in the middle: would the special position of students with respect to sufficient resources in Directive 93/96, reproduced in Article 7(1)(c) of Directive 2004/38, suggest that he might still benefit from either being confirmed as lawfully resident under the Directive or having special recognition of his host State authorised residence, either way benefitting from review of his individual circumstances for the purposes of his equal treatment claim? And would Mr Baumbast have secured his residence in the host State, since he simply did not comply with the condition in Article 7(1)(b) on comprehensive sickness insurance? In other words, had the Court's openness to proportionality review of the application of that condition, to his individual situation, in Directive 90/364 been extinguished by the adoption of Directive 2004/38?

It will be seen in the next section that the Court has now responded to most though not all these questions. A framework of decision-making that requires case-by-case assessments to determine the repercussions of general legislative rules in individual cases is vulnerable to criticism from the perspectives of legal certainty, workability and efficiency in practice, and equity of treatment both within and across the Member States.[290] However, the Directive expressly rules out eligibility for financial support only in the very few and specific situations provided for in Article 24(2). Recital 21 does underline that 'it *should be left to the host Member State to decide* whether it will grant social assistance' to Union citizens from other Member States in all other situations (prior to permanent residence). But there is no reference to social security more generally and, for any benefit, almost all of the pre-*Dano* case law intimated an obligation on national authorities at least to *hear* a Union citizen's claim; and to do so not within the permission-based culture of immigration,[291] but recognising the rights-based singularity of a transnational order with in its own—additional—citizenship. Advocate General Sharpston's hope that it might be possible 'to reconcile a careful assessment of individual circumstances with the need to ensure legal certainty, transparency and administrative efficiency' expresses the balance that should continue to guide both EU and national institutions overall.[292]

---

[290] See eg S O'Leary, 'The curious case of frontier workers and study finance: *Giersch*' (2014) 51 Common Market Law 601 at 621–22.

[291] See eg J Shaw and N Miller, 'When legal worlds collide: an exploration of what happens when EU free movement law meets UK immigration law' (2013) 38 European Law Review 137.

[292] AG Sharpston in Joined Cases C-523/11 and C-585/11 *Prinz and Seeberger*, EU:C:2013:90, para 107 of the Opinion.

3.2 Residing on the Basis of Directive 2004/38

In situations where the rights conferred by Article 21 TFEU have been exercised, different provisions of Directive 2004/38 are potentially relevant to determining whether residence in the host State is lawful and determining, in turn, the extent of equal treatment that can be claimed with host State nationals under Article 24 of the Directive: Article 6 (Section 3.2.1), Article 7(1)(a) (Section 3.2.2), Article 7(1)(b) (Section 3.2.3), Article 7(1)(c) (Section 3.2.4), Articles 12 and 13 (Section 3.2.5), and Article 14(4)(b) (Section 3.2.6).

3.2.1 Article 6: lawful residence within the first three months

Article 6 of Directive 2004/38 establishes that Member State nationals 'shall have the right of residence on the territory of another Member State for a period of up to three months without any conditions or any formalities other than the requirement to hold a valid identity card or passport'. Along with certain family members who accompany or join them, they 'have' that right 'as long as they do not become an unreasonable burden on the social assistance system of the host Member State' (Article 14(1)). If these conditions are fulfilled, residence in the host State is lawful.

Article 24(2) of the Directive further establishes that the host State 'shall not be obliged to confer entitlement to social assistance during the first three months of residence'—a limit expressly provided for in secondary legislation, and thus in conformity with Articles 20(2) and 21(1) TFEU. Reading Articles 6, 14(1), and 24(2) of the Directive together, the reach of EU citizenship law to the first three months of residence represents a trade-off: '[s]ince the Member States *cannot require* Union citizens to have sufficient means of subsistence and personal medical cover for a period of residence of a maximum of three months in their respective territories, it is legitimate *not to require* those Member States to be responsible for those citizens during that period'.[293]

National rules may exclude economically inactive Union citizens who reside in a host State on the basis of Article 6(1) of the Directive from entitlement to social assistance without any requirement of an individual assessment of their circumstances.[294] In *García-Nieto*, the Court also held that 'it follows *from the express wording* of [Article 24(2)] that the host Member State may refuse to grant persons *other than* workers, self-employed persons or those who retain that status any social assistance during the first three months of residence'.[295] The same principle was expressed in *Vatsouras and Koupatantze* and *Brey*.[296] However, the wording of Article 24(2) is arguably not so 'express' on this point. Rather, the Court's reference to 'express wording' would require that the final phrase of that provision— 'to persons other than workers, self-employed persons, persons who retain such status and members of their families'—frames the entire provision rather than referring only to the third restriction ('maintenance aid for studies').[297] That is an interpretative choice rather

---

[293] Case C-299/14 *García-Nieto*, EU:C:2016:114, para 45 (emphasis added).
[294] ibid para 46.
[295] ibid.
[296] Joined Cases C-22/08 and C-23/08 *Vatsouras and Koupatantze*, EU:C:2009:344, para 34; Case C-140/12 *Brey*, EU:C:2013:565, para 56.
[297] Article 24(2) reads in full: '[b]y way of derogation from paragraph 1, the host Member State shall not be obliged to confer entitlement to social assistance during the first three months of residence or, where appropriate, the longer period provided for in Article 14(4)(b), nor shall it be obliged, prior to acquisition of the right of permanent residence, to grant maintenance aid for studies, including vocational training, consisting in student grants or student loans to persons other than workers, self-employed persons, persons who retain such status and members of their families'.

than something communicated by 'express wording'. However, it does reflect the fact that social and tax advantages are guaranteed—independently—to workers by Article 45 TFEU and Regulation 492/1011,[298] returned to in Section 3.2.2, and it also aligns with recital 21 of the Directive, noted in Section 3.1.

The Court addressed the reach of equal treatment within the first three months of residence in *Familienkasse Niedersachsen-Bremen*. The national proceedings concerned a claim by S, an economically inactive Bulgarian national, for a family allowance during the first three months of residence in Germany.[299] The referring court clarified that '[f]amily benefits are funded not by the beneficiaries' contributions, but by tax' and 'are granted to beneficiaries on the basis of a legally defined situation, regardless of any income requirement, and without any individual and discretionary assessment of the beneficiaries' personal needs'.[300] However, under the applicable national rules, 'nationals of another Member State, such as S, are refused entitlement to family benefits during the first three months of their residence where they do not provide proof that they were in gainful employment in Germany' while, '[i]n contrast, German nationals are entitled to such benefits as from those first three months even where they are not in gainful employment',[301] including 'during the first three months following [their] return to the same Member State after having made use, under EU law, of [the] right to move and reside in another Member State'.[302] Reflecting *Dano* and *Alimanovic*, the referring court indicated that 'the German legislature considered that that difference in treatment was compatible with EU law, as it would avoid an influx of nationals from other Member States that would place an unreasonable burden on the German social security system'.[303]

In its ruling, the Court of Justice first confirmed that 'during the first three months of her residence in Germany, S was legally resident under Article 6(1) of Directive 2004/38, read in conjunction with Article 14(1) thereof';[304] that the benefit claimed fell within the scope of EU law (more specifically, it was a 'family benefit' within the meaning of Article 3(1)(j) of Regulation 883/2004);[305] and that S was habitually resident in Germany, thus coming within the scope of both the Regulation and the relevant German legislation with respect to the grant of family benefits.[306] It confirmed that the principle of equal treatment 'benefits any Union citizen whose residence in the territory of the host Member State complies with the conditions laid down in [Directive 2004/38]'.[307] However, the derogation in Article 24(2) concerning the first three months of residence refers to social assistance only. Thus, where benefits 'are granted independently of the individual needs of the beneficiary and are not

---

[298] As explained in Chapter 6, Regulation 492/2011 does not apply to self-employment, but the Court has drawn equal treatment rights directly from Article 49 TFEU: eg on equal treatment, guaranteed minimum income benefits, and freedom of establishment, Case C-299/01 *Commission v Luxembourg*, EU:C:2002:394, para 12. See further, Section 3.2.2.

[299] For the full factual background, which included previous periods of residence in Germany, see AG Szpunar in Case C-411/20 *Familienkasse Niedersachsen-Bremen*, EU:C:2021:1017, paras 7–16 of the Opinion.

[300] Case C-411/20 *Familienkasse Niedersachsen-Bremen*, EU:C:2022:602, para 21.

[301] ibid, para 22.

[302] ibid para 27.

[303] ibid para 23. See similarly, AG Szpunar, para 84 of the Opinion ('as regards the ability of the national provision at issue to achieve the objective of protecting public finances, the German Government asserts that excluding economically inactive nationals of other Member States from family benefits during the first three months of residence reduces the incentive for those nationals to settle in Germany. In addition, the requirement for gainful employment leads to a decrease in the number of such benefit claims').

[304] *Familienkasse Niedersachsen-Bremen*, para 33.

[305] ibid para 34.

[306] ibid paras 36–37.

[307] ibid para 42.

intended to cover his or her means of subsistence', they are not 'social assistance' within the meaning of Directive 2004/38.[308] In such circumstances, the derogation in Article 24(2) of the Directive does not apply.[309]

The Court reinforced that conclusion with reference to both the wording and 'regulatory context'[310] of Article 24(2), referring on the latter to Article 14(1)'s threshold of 'unreasonable burden on the social assistance system of the host Member State'. Without expressly recalling the *Grzelczyk*-based 'certain degree of solidarity' implication from that language, the Court nevertheless found that 'Article 14 thus supports the interpretation that the possibility of derogating from the principle of equal treatment, on the basis of Article 24(2) of Directive 2004/38, is limited to social assistance and that it cannot extend to social security benefits'.[311] The Court also referred to recital 10 of the Directive to underline that Article 24(2) aims to maintain the financial balance *not of the social security system* of the Member States but of their "social assistance system".[312] Thus, the ruling reflects the judgment in *Commission v Austria* considered in Section 3.1.4 in the sense that the wording of the express derogations in Article 24(2) of the Directive will be not be stretched beyond plain meaning. As emphasised in the discussion on *Commission v UK* in Section 3.1 and returned to in Section 3.2.3, checks on residence status may intensify, even for benefits that are not social assistance, after the first three months of residence have passed and the Union citizen departs the scope of Article 6 of the Directive. Nevertheless, the cooler tone of *Familienkasse Niedersachsen-Bremen* is entirely welcome: it offered no sustenance to the submissions about prospective influxes of Union citizens; and AG Szpunar, in particular, reinstated emphasis on 'the existence of *proven* risks to public finances' to this area of EU citizenship law.[313]

Thus, in summary: Union citizens who reside lawfully within a host State on the basis of Article 6 of the Directive should be treated equally with host State nationals as regards entitlement to social security benefits that come within the scope of EU law, because the derogation in Article 24(2) of the Directive rules out entitlement to social assistance only.

3.2.2 Article 7(1)(a): lawful residence and the economically active

Article 7(1)(a) of the Directive 'guarantees'[314] an unconditional right to reside in a host State for more than three months to workers and self-employed persons[315]: as the Court expressed it in *Dano*, they 'have the right of residence without having to fulfil any other

---

[308] ibid paras 47–48.
[309] ibid, para 55.
[310] ibid para 53.
[311] ibid.
[312] ibid para 54 (emphasis added). The Court confirmed the same outcome with respect to Regulation 883/2004 (ibid paras 56ff).
[313] AG Szpunar in *Familienkasse Niedersachsen-Bremen*, para 88 of the Opinion (emphasis added); see generally, paras 88ff, which provide clear contrast with the tone and burden of proof approach in Opinions and judgments in the *Dano* line of case law (eg para 91: 'there is no evidence that the increased expenditure on the family benefits in question is caused by nationals of other Member States (or their children). In my view, the fact both that an item of expenditure such as family benefits is increasing cannot in itself be a negative indicator of the economic situation of a Member State. I think it is important to recall that, in general, social expenditure can contribute to social cohesion and economic activity, by enabling beneficiaries to be more active and to contribute more on the labour market. Furthermore, the effects on budget revenues and on the dynamism of the economy in the long term should be assessed in a context of labour market integration at EU level. Thus, the fact of receiving nationals from other Member States, with an increase in social expenditure, particularly at the outset, and, where appropriate, expenditure on training, can also meet a need within the Member State's economy by providing an adequate workforce for certain sectors that are lacking in that respect and, thus, can contribute to improving its competitiveness').
[314] Case C-483/17 *Tarola*, EU:C:2019:309, para 42.
[315] Thus excluding providers and recipients of services, who therefore reside under Article 7(1)(b); see further, Chapter 6.

conditions'[316] other than meeting the definitions of work or establishment under EU law.[317] Additionally, workers and self-employed persons who retain that status under Article 7(3) of the Directive,[318] or on the basis of Articles 45[319] or 49[320] TFEU directly—all of which secure the protection of EU law after economic activity has ceased for various reasons—continue to reside in the host State under Article 7(1)(a).[321] In other words, they continue to reside there lawfully.

No express derogations from equal treatment are provided for in Article 24(2) of the Directive. Conversely, citizens residing on the basis of Article 7(1)(a) 'enjoy equal treatment with the nationals of that Member State within the scope of the Treaty' (Article 24(1)). Moreover, as explained in Section 3.2.1, the express derogation in Article 24(2) of the Directive as regards residence based on Article 6 of the Directive—exclusion from entitlement to social assistance during the first three months of residence—does not apply to Union citizens residing in the host State on the basis of Article 7(1)(a). As a result, Member State nationals who work, are self-employed, or retain either status[322] in the host State are entitled, in principle, to equal treatment with host State nationals for all claims falling with the material scope of EU law.[323] However, as explained in Chapter 6, while the status of worker or self-employed person sustains 'indefinitely'[324] for situations falling within the scope of Articles 7(3)(a), 7(3)(b), and 7(3)(d) of the Directive, Article 7(3)(c) offers time-limited protection,[325] 'establishing a gradation with regard to the conditions for retaining [worker or self-employed] status'.[326] As a result, should economic activity within the meaning of EU law not be resumed, persons previously protected by Article 7(3)(c) lose entitlement to equal treatment after six months if they are unable to demonstrate that they fall, once again, within the scope of Article 7(1)(a). If they transition to residence based on Article 7(1)(b) or 7(1)(c), they remain lawfully resident if they fulfil the conditions on sufficient resources, comprehensive sickness insurance and, if relevant, following a course of study. Equal treatment in such circumstances is returned to in Section 3.2.3. A derived right to reside may also ensue

---

[316] Case C-333/13 *Dano*, EU:C:2014:2358, para 75.

[317] See eg Case C-46/12 *LN*, EU:C:2013:97, paras 39–40: 'the concept of "worker" within the meaning of Article 45 TFEU has an autonomous meaning specific to European Union law and must not be interpreted narrowly ... Moreover, that concept must be defined in accordance with objective criteria which distinguish the employment relationship by reference to the rights and duties of the persons concerned. The essential feature of an employment relationship is that, for a certain period of time, a person performs services for and under the direction of another person, in return for which he receives remuneration'. Conversely, if the activity is not performed 'under the direction of another person', the right of establishment and Article 49 TFEU are engaged. See further, Case 53/81 *Levin*, EU:C:1982:105, para 17; requiring 'the pursuit of effective and genuine activities, to the exclusion of activities on such a small scale as to be regarded as purely marginal and ancillary'.

[318] *Tarola*, para 39.

[319] Case C-507/12 *Saint Prix*, EU:C:2014:2007.

[320] Case C-544/18 *Dakneviciute*, EU:C:2019:761.

[321] *Dakneviciute*, para 28; Case C-618/16 *Prefeta*, EU:C:2018:719, para 37.

[322] Article 24(2) of the Directive refers expressly and inclusively to workers, self-employed persons, and 'persons who retain such status'.

[323] Underlining the equal treatment basis of that guarantee, see *Tarola*, para 56: 'where national law excludes persons who have worked in an employed or self-employed capacity only for a short period of time from the entitlement to social benefits, that exclusion applies in the same way to workers from other Member States who have exercised their right of free movement'. See further, Chapter 6, as regards the breadth of the concept of 'social and tax advantages' for workers under Article 7(2) of Regulation 492/2011 and the extension of the same principles to self-employed persons through the case law (eg Case C-168/20 *BJ and OV*, EU:C:2021:907).

[324] *Tarola*, para 44.

[325] ie Situations where a Union citizen 'is in duly recorded involuntary unemployment after completing a fixed-term employment contract of less than a year or after having become involuntarily unemployed during the first twelve months and has registered as a job-seeker with the relevant employment office. In this case, the status of worker shall be retained for no less than six months'.

[326] *Tarola*, para 43.

if they are family members of another Union citizen within the meaning of Article 7(1)(d), returned to in Section 3.2.5. If, alternatively, they continue to seek employment after six months, their right to reside would connect to Article 14(4)(b) of the Directive—relieving them of the requirement to satisfy the conditions in Article 7, but then, as in *Alimanovic*, excluding them from equal treatment with respect to social assistance on account of the express derogation in Article 24(2). Outwith claims for social assistance specifically, equal treatment for jobseekers is addressed more generally in Section 3.2.4.

Similarly, for persons residing in a host State on the basis of status retained under Articles 45 and 49 TFEU directly—which, to date, concerns only 'the physical constraints of the late stages of pregnancy and the immediate aftermath of childbirth require a woman to give up work during the period needed for recovery'[327]—the status of worker or self-employed person is not retained indefinitely but is subject to a requirement that the Union citizen concerned 'returns to work or finds another job within a reasonable period after confinement'.[328] In *Saint Prix*, the Court advised that 'to determine whether the period that has elapsed between childbirth and starting work again may be regarded as reasonable, the national court concerned should take account of all the specific circumstances of the case in the main proceedings and the applicable national rules on the duration of maternity leave'.[329] Article 8(1) of Directive 92/95 refers to 'a continuous period of maternity leave of a least 14 weeks', but does not provide guidance for situations that might involve more difficult circumstances (such as illness of the mother or of the baby).

National authorities making decisions about claims for equal treatment also face a question of timing in these cases: on what basis can a Member State national in a *Saint Prix* situation make a successful claim for retained status, and thus for equal treatment as regards income support, *before* they can demonstrate that they have returned to work or found another position 'within a reasonable period after confinement'?[330] The claimant in *Saint Prix* was working once again by the time that her case was considered by the Court of Justice, her claim for income support then facilitated for the national authorities since, by then, she had already fulfilled the Court's test. But it is logically impossible for the pregnant citizen or new mother to have already returned to work or found another position until they actually have. In other words, the approach taken by the Court constructs an *ex post* framework for demonstration of retained status, whereas income support claims will normally need to be determined prior to that. Further case law is needed to shed light on these questions. More generally, it is presumed that the same principles apply as outlined above for Article 7(3)(c) of the Directive where it is considered that the 'reasonable period' condition has not been fulfilled.

In summary: economically active Union citizens—whether working or self-employed, or retaining that status on the basis of conditions in the Directive or the case law—are the most privileged category of Member State nationals in a host State as regards lawful residence and corollary equal treatment.[331] In *Commission v Netherlands*, Advocate General Sharpston

---

[327] *Dakneviciute*, para 29.
[328] ibid.
[329] *Saint Prix*, para 41; referring to Council Directive 92/85/EEC on the introduction of measures to encourage improvements in the safety and health at work of pregnant workers and workers who have recently given birth or are breastfeeding, 1992 OJ L348/1.
[330] *Saint Prix*, para 41.
[331] As the Court points out, 'Article 7(1) of the directive distinguishes, in particular, the situation of economically active citizens from that of inactive citizens and students' (Case C-442/16 *Gusa*, EU:C:2017:1004, para 36). See further, Article 14(4)(a) of the Directive, which provides that 'without prejudice to the provisions of Chapter VI [of the Directive], an expulsion measure may *in no case* be adopted against Union citizens or their family members if... the Union citizens are workers or self-employed persons'.

considered the limits of Union citizenship, remarking that 'Directive 2004/38 ... maintains the distinction between EU citizens who have exercised an economic right of free movement and other EU citizens and expressly *preserves the right of Member States to discriminate* for a certain time against the latter'.[332] In other words, a degree of inequality between categories of citizen is a constituent feature of the rights conferred by Union citizenship. However, as emphasised in Chapter 6, the unconditional right to reside provided for in Article 7(1)(a) of the Directive privileges economic *activity* over economic *autonomy* and attention has increasingly been drawn to the sustainability of that distinction from the perspective of host State public finances, not least because of the political process undertaken prior to Brexit.[333]

3.2.3 Article 7(1)(b): lawful residence and the economically autonomous

In *A (Soins de santé publics)*, Advocate General Saugmandsgaard Øe observed that 'EU law is based on values of solidarity which have been further reinforced since the creation of citizenship of the Union'.[334] Does the case law on lawful residence and equal treatment for economically inactive Union citizens bear that out?

Article 7(1)(b) of the Directive, read in conjunction with Article 14(1)(2), establishes that economically inactive Union citizens who reside in a host State for more than three months must (continue to) demonstrate that they have sufficient resources to avoid becoming a burden on the host State's social assistance system as well as comprehensive sickness insurance. Article 8(4) of the Directive rules out specifying a 'fixed amount' of sufficient resources in national rules and establishes that such resources 'shall not be higher than the threshold below which nationals of the host Member State become eligible for social assistance, or, where this criterion is not applicable, higher than the minimum social security pension paid by the host Member State'. It also requires that Member States must 'take into account the personal situation of the person concerned' when determining whether resources are sufficient for the purposes of Article 7(1)(b). For comprehensive sickness insurance, we saw in Chapter 6 that a host State 'may provide that access to [its public health insurance] system is not free of charge in order to prevent that citizen from becoming an unreasonable burden on that Member State'.[335] However, if a host State does affiliate an economically inactive Union citizen to its public sickness insurance system free of charge, that fact cannot subsequently be used to undermine a claim to having 'comprehensive sickness insurance' within the meaning of Article 7(1)(b).[336]

When determining whether residence based on Article 7(1)(b) is lawful, a host State may take the view, as introduced in Section 2 and returned to in Section 4, that a citizen having recourse to its social assistance system no longer fulfils the conditions for a right of residence under Article 7(1)(b). Article 14(2) provides that '[i]n specific cases where there is a reasonable doubt as to whether a Union citizen or his/her family members satisfies the conditions

---

[332] AG Sharpston in Case C-542/09 *Commission v Netherlands*, EU:C:2012:79, para 95 of the Opinion (emphasis added).

[333] For now, the Court has confirmed that workers contribute to the financing of the social policies of the host Member State through the tax and social security contributions which they pay in that State by virtue of their employment there. They must therefore be able to profit from them under the same conditions as national workers' (Case C-328/20 *Commission v Austria*, EU:C:2022:468, para 109). See further, Chapter 6.

[334] AG Saugmandsgaard Øe Case C-535/19 *A (Soins de santé publics)*, EU:C:2021:114, para 153 of the Opinion; referred to by AG Szpunar in Case C-411/20 *Familienkasse Niedersachsen-Bremen*, EU:C:2021:1017, para 59 of the Opinion.

[335] Case C-535/19 *A (Soins de santé publics)*, EU:C:2021:595, para 58; in that case, affiliation to the host State's public insurance system fell within the scope of Article 11(3)(e) of Regulation 883/2004.

[336] Case C-247/20 *Commissioners for Her Majesty's Revenue and Customs (Assurance maladie complète)*, EU:C:2022:177, paras 69–70.

set out in Articles 7, 12, and 13, Member States may verify if these conditions are fulfilled. This verification shall not be carried out systematically'—though *Commission v UK* applied a generous (from the perspective of the Member States) interpretation to 'systematic verification', permitting right to reside tests to confirm lawful residence.[337] Nevertheless, Article 14(3) of the Directive affirms that '[a]n expulsion measure shall not be the *automatic* consequence of a Union citizen's or his or her family member's recourse to the social assistance system' of the host State.

As regards equal treatment when residence complies with the conditions in Article 7(1)(b), only maintenance aid for studies is expressly ruled out by Article 24(2) of the Directive. For all other sets of circumstances, principles developed in the case law will apply. First, as a general point, a host State is entitled to impose proportionate integration requirements before equal treatment is extended in situations that are not expressly determined by Directive 2004/38.[338]

Second, if the claim concerns *social security*, the principles developed in *Familienkasse Niedersachsen-Bremen*, outlined in Section 3.2.1, also apply her. The principle of equal treatment 'benefits any Union citizen whose residence in the territory of the host Member State complies with the conditions laid down in [Directive 2004/38]'.[339] Thus, where benefits 'are granted independently of the individual needs of the beneficiary and are not intended to cover his or her means of subsistence', they do not constitute 'social assistance' within the meaning of Directive 2004/38'.[340] According to recital 10 of the Directive, 'Article 24(2) aims to maintain the financial balance *not of the social security system* of the Member States but of their "social assistance system"'.[341] By analogy, the same logic applies to interpretation of Article 7(1)(b), which also refers only to a host State's social *assistance* system: citizens who are lawfully resident under Article 7(1)(b), because they do possess sufficient resources not to draw on host State social *assistance*, should therefore benefit from equal treatment as regards social *security* where the relevant benefits are granted to economically inactive host State nationals in similar situations.[342] However, as the Court established in *Commission v UK*, the grant of social benefits to Union citizens who are not economically active can be 'made subject to the requirement that those citizens fulfil the conditions for possessing a right to reside lawfully in the host Member State' so long as such requirements comply with Articles 8(4) and 14(2) of the Directive.[343]

Third, if the claim concerns *social assistance*, within the meaning of the Directive as defined by the Court in *Brey*, Member State nationals residing on the basis of Article 7(1)(b) can, in principle, submit a claim for equal treatment with host State nationals. However, that

---

[337] See further, Section 3.1.4.
[338] eg Joined Cases C-523/11 and C-585/11 *Prinz and Seeberger*, EU:C:2013:90, para 36; Case C-247/17 *Raugevicius*, EU:C:2018:898, para 46.
[339] Case C-411/20 *Familienkasse Niedersachsen-Bremen*, EU:C:2022:602 para 42.
[340] ibid paras 47–48.
[341] ibid para 54 (emphasis added). The Court confirmed the same outcome with respect to Regulation 883/2004 (ibid paras 56ff).
[342] The Court's criss-crossing from the language of 'social benefits' to 'social assistance' in *Dano* did not assist clarity; as the Advocate General observed in *CG*, '[i]n the judgment in *Dano*, the Court, after observing that the situation at issue fell outside the scope of Article 24(2) of Directive 2004/38 (45) and that that provision constitutes a derogation from the principle of non-discrimination laid down in Article 18 TFEU, nonetheless sought to ascertain, on the basis of Article 24(1) of that directive, the circumstances in which a citizen in possession of a residence permit may be refused the grant of social benefits, although the only exclusions from the principle of equal treatment are listed in paragraph 2 of that article' (AG Richard de la Tour in Case C-709/20 *CG*, EU:C:2021:515, para 58 of the Opinion).
[343] Case C-308/14 *Commission v UK*, EU:C:2016:436, para 68; referring to Case C-140/12 *Brey*, EU:C:2013:565, para 44 and Case C-333/13 *Dano*, EU:C:2014:2358, para 83 'to this effect'.

would almost certainly then raise consideration of the continuing lawfulness of their residence, and the case law provides options for what might play out in practice. Host State authorities might consider—but are not, since *Dano* and *Alimanovic*, required to undertake an assessment to consider—that the person concerned should receive the claimed assistance when the situation is placed in perspective after an examination of their individual circumstances, especially if shortfalls are likely to be temporary. However, if the host State has reasonable grounds to suspect that a Union citizen does not have sufficient resources, it may require verification of compliance with Article 7(1)'s conditions, per *Commission v UK*; and potentially take an expulsion decision under Article 15(1), per *FS*. It is just as likely, though, that a host State would do nothing—in other words, refuse the application for assistance but not progress to expulsion measures. That situation is returned to in Section 4.

Relatedly, the Court considered in *Dano* that Article 7(1)(b) 'seeks to prevent economically inactive Union citizens from using the host Member State's welfare system to fund their means of subsistence'.[344] Thus, Member States 'must ... have the possibility, pursuant to Article 7 of Directive 2004/38, of refusing to grant social benefits to economically inactive Union citizens who exercise their right to freedom of movement *solely in order to obtain another Member State's social assistance* although they do not have sufficient resources to claim a right of residence'.[345] To establish this, 'the financial situation of each person concerned should be examined specifically, without taking account of the social benefits claimed, in order to determine whether he meets the condition of having sufficient resources to qualify for a right of residence under Article 7(1)(b) of Directive 2004/38'.[346] That guidance seemed to suggest conformity with *Brey*. However, the Court also ruled in *Dano* that 'Article 24(1) of Directive 2004/38, read in conjunction with Article 7(1)(b) thereof, does not *preclude national legislation* ... in so far as it excludes nationals of other Member States who do not have a right of residence under Directive 2004/38 in the host Member State from entitlement' to social assistance.[347] Reading that statement alongside *Alimanovic*, nationals of other Member States can therefore be excluded from entitlement by legislation generally without, as noted above, any assessment of their individual circumstances.

In summary, and to illustrate the implications of the changing case law: national authorities now faced with Mrs Martínez Sala's application for a child-raising benefit (ie not social assistance)—and leaving aside for the moment whether residence authorised by national law would suffice, which is returned to in Section 3.5—could legitimately require not the possession of a residence permit per se (as in that case itself) but that she nevertheless demonstrate (since *Commission v UK*) that she is lawfully resident in compliance with Article 7(1)(b) if they had any 'reasonable doubt' that that might not be the case, following Article 14(2). Any claim for social security or social assistance from Mr Baumbast would be subject to the same principles, unless lawful residence solely linked to Article 21 TFEU could suffice (considered in Section 3.4). Mr Grzelczyk's claim for social assistance is returned to in Section 3.2.4 on Article 7(1)(c). However, and again leaving aside for now the prior question about residence authorised by national law, Mr Trojani's claim would almost certainly fail unless a *Brey*-based examination of his individual circumstances—assumed voluntarily by rather than constituting an obligation on the host State, following *Alimanovic*—determined that the burden his claim placed on host State public finances was proportionate and reasonable

---

[344] Case C-333/13 *Dano*, EU:C:2014:2358, para 76.
[345] ibid para 78 (emphasis added).
[346] ibid para 80.
[347] ibid para 82 (emphasis added).

(eg demonstrably temporary). Whether some relief might be found for him via the Charter of Fundamental Rights is returned to in Section 4.

3.2.4 Article 7(1)(c): students

Students reside in the host State on the basis of Article 7(1)(c) so long as, first, the course of study that they follow complies with the conditions noted there;[348] second, they have comprehensive sickness insurance cover; and third, they '*assure* the relevant national authority, by means of a declaration or by such equivalent means as they may choose, that they have sufficient resources for themselves and their family members not to become a burden on the social assistance system of the host Member State during their period of residence'. However, recalling *Grzelczyk*, the looser wording of that requirement (repeated from Directive 93/96) compared to Article 7(1)(b) does not 'prevent a Member State from taking the view that a student who has recourse to social assistance no longer fulfils the conditions of his right of residence or from taking measures, within the limits imposed by Community law, either to withdraw his residence permit or not to renew it'.[349] Thus, under Directive 2004/38, students are not expressly excluded from the understanding of sufficient resources in Article 8(4); or the obligation in Article 14(2) to continue to fulfil the conditions in Article 7(1)(c) to retain their right of residence; or the prospect of an expulsion decision being taken against them under Article 15(1) in situations of non-compliance with those conditions.

As regards equal treatment with host State nationals, the most significant change since the adoption of Directive 2004/38 is that, according to the derogation in Article 24(2), students who reside on the basis of Article 7(1)(c)—that is, who are not also 'workers, self-employed persons, persons who retain such status and members of their families'—are not entitled to maintenance aid for their studies from the host State. In that light, the *Bidar* window was brief indeed. As noted in Section 3.1.4, since the proceedings in *Commission v Netherlands* were confined to students conceded to be residing lawfully in the Netherlands on the basis of Article 7(1)(c), Article 24(1)'s equal treatment condition of residing on the basis of the directive was fulfilled. The central question was therefore whether financial support for travel costs fell within the scope of the derogation in Article 24(2). The Court concluded that the national scheme for reduced transport fares did have 'the characteristics of and is akin to a student grant or loan': the relevant national rules required that the assistance must be repaid if the student failed to complete his or her studies within a ten-year period and, 'unlike the case which gave rise to the judgment ... in *Commission v Austria* ... in which the Member State concerned, as a rule, granted reduced fares on public transport only to students whose parents received family allowances in that State, in the present case ... the award of financial support for travel costs to Netherlands students ... depends specifically on whether those students are studying in the Netherlands and whether they are entitled to funding for their studies under Netherlands legislation'.[350] In consequence, 'financial support for travel costs, such as that at issue in the present case, must be regarded as "consisting in student grants or student loans" within the meaning of Article 24(2) of Directive 2004/38'.[351]

---

[348] ie 'enrolled at a private or public establishment, accredited or financed by the host Member State on the basis of its legislation or administrative practice, for the principal purpose of following a course of study, including vocational training'.

[349] Case C-184/99 *Grzelczyk*, EU:C:2001:458, para 42.

[350] Case C-233/14 *Commission v Netherlands*, EU:C:2016:396, para 88; referring to Case C-75/11 *Commission v Austria*, EU:C:2012:605.

[351] *Commission v Netherlands*, para 90. See further, AG Sharpston, EU:C:2016:50, esp paras 95–100 of the Opinion.

Beyond the specific exclusion of maintenance aid, it is presumed that the same principles as regards applications for social benefits and social assistance respectively that were discussed in Section 3.2.3 for economically inactive citizens residing on the basis of Article 7(1)(b) of the Directive apply here too. However, the lingering doubt for students concerns the basis of the right to reside in *Grzelczyk*, which was never clearly articulated by the Court. One possibility is that changed financial circumstances following a sincere initial declaration attesting to sufficient resources does not undermine residence (continuing to be) based on Article 7(1)(c) of Directive 2004/38, even more so when the change in circumstances comes later in the citizen's programme of studies, thereby strongly signalling the temporary nature of any bridging support asked of the host State. This point needs to be clarified by the Court of Justice following *Dano* since if, in the alternative, the right to reside is no longer based on Article 7(1)(c) in such circumstances, lawful residence in the host State ceases to be based on the Directive, thereby also ending claims to equal treatment for financial support of any kind because of Article 24(1). Noting the parallel focus on residence authorised by a Member State in *Grzelczyk*, a student might in such circumstances claim that they reside on the basis of national law only; equal treatment in such circumstances considered in Section 3.5.

3.2.5 Articles 7(1)(d), 12, and 13: family members

Member State nationals who are 'are family members accompanying or joining a Union citizen who satisfies the conditions referred to in points (a), (b) or (c) [of Article 7(1) of Directive 2004/38]' have a right to reside in the host State under Article 7(1)d of the Directive. In consequence, they reside there lawfully within the meaning of Article 24(1). Whether they are then *independently* entitled to equal treatment with host State nationals for social benefits or social assistance in situations where the Union citizen from whom they derive their rights continues to comply with the right to reside on the basis of Article 7(1)(a), (b), or (c) has not yet arisen in the case law.

In Section 3.1, the repercussions of not being economically autonomous were noted as regards acquiring permanent residence rights. However, the case law principles developed in that context thus far simply establish that 'the concept of legal residence implied by the terms "have resided legally" in Article 16(1) of Directive 2004/38 should be construed as meaning a period of residence which complies *with the conditions laid down in the directive, in particular those set out in Article 7(1)*'.[352] That finding did not specify points (a)–(c) of Article 7(1) to the exclusion of Article 7(1)(d). Arguably, then, only access to study finance is expressly ruled out by Article 24(2) since, on the plain wording of Article 7(1)(d), the sole condition placed on Union citizen family members is to reside in the host State with the Union citizen 'reference person' they have accompanied or joined.[353] Such Member State national family members seem to benefit from the lawful residence of their Union citizen 'reference person', the burden of complying with the conditions in Article 7(1)(a)–(c) falling on the latter and not the former.

For family members who are third-country nationals, Article 7(2) of the Directive establishes a right of residence for more than three months 'provided that such Union citizen satisfies the conditions referred to in paragraph 1 (a), (b) or (c)' of Article 7 of the Directive. The 'benefit' of equal treatment in the host State is then 'extended' to the family members by Article 24(1), subject to the express exclusion of study finance in Article 24(2). Therefore,

---

[352] Joined Cases C-424/10 and C-425/10 *Ziolkowski and Szeja*, EU:C:2011:866, para 46 (emphasis added).
[353] Case C-133/15 *Chavez-Vilchez*, EU:C:2017:354, para 55. On the meaning of 'accompany or join', see Chapter 4.

the same open question about *independent* entitlement to social benefits or social assistance applies in this situation too—in other words, what is the extent of the 'benefit' of equal treatment that might apply so long as the Union citizen from whom they derive their right to reside *does* continue to comply with the conditions in Article 7(1)(a), (b), or (c)?

Additionally, Articles 12 and 13 of the Directive sustain a right to reside for family members 'exclusively on a personal basis' when the Union citizen 'reference person' either dies or leaves the host State (Article 12) or in situations where the marriage or registered partnership breaks down (Article 13), with some differences specified with respect to family members who are Member State nationals and third-country nationals respectively, as detailed in Chapter 6. In terms of the requirement to reside *lawfully*, for family members who are Member State nationals, Articles 12 and 13 state that '[b]efore acquiring the right of permanent residence, the persons concerned must meet the conditions laid down in points (a), (b), (c) or (d) of Article 7(1)'. For family members who are third-country nationals, the language is different,[354] but the same conditions are applied in effect. The principles outlined in Sections 3.2.2, 3.3.3, and 3.3.4 can therefore be mapped by analogy onto equal treatment claims for social benefits or social assistance submitted by those who reside on the basis of Article 12 or 13 of the Directive.

Additionally, for family members of any nationality, Article 12(3) specifies that a Union citizen's 'departure from the host Member State or his/her death shall not entail loss of the right of residence of his/her children or of the parent who has actual custody of the children, irrespective of nationality, if the children reside in the host Member State and are enrolled at an educational establishment, for the purpose of studying there, until the completion of their studies', with no reference to complying with Article 7(1) either expressly or in effect. Article 12(3) therefore suggests lawful residence and corollary equal treatment having regard to Article 24(1) of the Directive. However, it should be borne in mind that eligibility for permanent residence rights would be affected where, as a result of support received from the host State, residence does not then, in fact, comply with the conditions in Article 7(1)(a)–(c), as indicated in Section 3.1.1 and returned to in Chapter 8.[355]

3.2.6 Article 14(4)(b): jobseekers

Finally, while residence rights for jobseekers[356] are based on Article 45 rather than Article 21 TFEU, the Court has confirmed (in *Alimanovic* and *GMA*) that they reside in a host State under the conditions in Article 14(4)(b) of the Directive.[357] Article 24(2) of the Directive expressly rules out equal treatment for claims to social assistance, and no assessment of individual circumstances is required in such situations. However, *Alimanovic* left intact equal treatment as regards benefits that facilitate access to the host State employment, the

---

[354] ie 'Before acquiring the right of permanent residence, the right of residence of the persons concerned shall remain subject to the requirement that they are able to show that they are workers or self-employed persons or that they have sufficient resources for themselves and their family members not to become a burden on the social assistance system of the host Member State during their period of residence and have comprehensive sickness insurance cover in the host Member State, or that they are members of the family, already constituted in the host Member State, of a person satisfying these requirements.'

[355] For Article 12(3) of the Directive specifically, there is resonance with rights based on Article 10 of Regulation 492/2011, as discussed in Section 3.3.

[356] ie Jobseekers who do not meet the conditions for retaining the status of worker or self-employed person within the meaning of Article 7(3) of the Directive, which was considered in Section 3.2.2.

[357] In *Alimanovic*, the Court also considered that the applicants could rely on Article 14(4)(b) to establish a right of residence after the expiry of the period referred to in Article 7(3)(c) ie after the six-month period provided for in Article 7(3)(c) during which the status of worker is retained (Case C-67/14 *Alimanovic*, EU:C:2015:597, para 57).

predominant function of which is not social assistance. In such situations, the host State may require a jobseeker to demonstrate a real link to the host State's geographic employment market through the application of proportionate integration requirements such as residence conditions.[358]

Additionally, it is presumed that since residence based on Article 14(4)(b) is lawful residence within the meaning of Article 24(1) and the derogation in Article 24(2) references social assistance and study finance only, equal treatment with respect to social security benefits more generally applies by analogy with the discussion in Section 3.2.1 on residence in the host State based on Article 6(1) of the Directive. Finally, Article 14(4(b) underlines that jobseekers can only be expelled from the host State on grounds of public policy, public security, or public health. However, while a period of residence based on Article 14(4)(b) of the Directive does constitute lawful residence, it is difficult to conceive of a situation in which someone could meet the *GMA* tests (detailed in Chapter 6) for up to five years, thereby excluding eventual permanent residence rights on that basis alone.

3.3 Residence Based on (Other) EU Legislation: Article 10 of Regulation 492/2011

In *Alimanovic*, Advocate General Wathelet drew the referring court's attention to the possible relevance of Article 10 of Regulation 492/2011 as a basis for residence rights.[359] The Court of Justice did not pick this up—too soon, perhaps, to go there after *Dano*. The residence rights conferred by Article 10 of the Regulation are examined in more detail in Chapter 9. For present purposes, two key points are important. First, even after the adoption of Directive 2004/38, 'the children of a national of a Member State who works or has worked in the host Member State and the parent who is their primary carer can claim a right of residence in the latter State on the sole basis of Article [10] of Regulation [492/2011], without being required to satisfy the conditions laid down in' the Directive.[360] However, second, for permanent residence rights, 'the concept of legal residence implied by the terms "have resided legally" in Article 16(1) of Directive 2004/38 should be construed as meaning a period of residence which complies with the conditions laid down in the directive, in particular those set out in Article 7(1)'.[361] That meant, in turn, that periods of residence that were perfectly 'lawful' in the wider sense of being based on rights conferred by EU law would not necessarily produce lawful residence within the meaning of the Directive.

The Court had initially confined itself to not requiring the conditions in Article 7 of the Directive to be complied with by children or their primary carers residing in a host Stateon the basis of the Regulation. In other words, it did not clearly articulate an ancillary host

---

[358] Case C-224/98 *D'Hoop*, EU:C:2002:432, para 38.
[359] AG Wathelet in *Alimanovic*, EU:C:2015:210, paras 117–122 of the Opinion.
[360] Case C-310/08 *Ibrahim*, EU:C:2010:89, para 50.
[361] Joined Cases C-424/10 and C-425/10 *Ziolkowski and Szeja*, EU:C:2011:866, para 46. AG Bot was critical of this approach, observing that residence rights under Article 10 of Regulation 492/2011 had 'been freed' from the requirements of sufficient recourses and sickness insurance, making the reintroduction of these conditions 'paradoxical' for acquiring permanent residence rights; something he considered to be 'all the more striking because the principle of the autonomy of the right of residence, conceived to benefit the child by relieving him of any requirement of financial autonomy, finally rebounds against its beneficiary by depriving him of access to the status of permanent resident' (AG Bot in Case C-529/11 *Alarape and Tijani*, EU:C:2013:9, para 74 of the Opinion).

State obligation to extend equal treatment with host State nationals in such situations.[362] Subsequently, as discussed in Section 3.1.1 and separately from any consideration of residence rights not based on the Directive, *Dano* established that 'the principle of non-discrimination, laid down generally in Article 18 TFEU, is given more specific expression in Article 24 of Directive 2004/38 in relation to Union citizens who ... exercise their right to move and reside within the territory of the Member States'.[363] In consequence, the Court held in *Alimanovic* that 'a Union citizen can claim equal treatment with nationals of the host Member State under Article 24(1) of Directive 2004/38 only if his residence in the territory of the host Member State complies with the conditions of Directive 2004/38'.[364] What remained to be determined was whether this restriction would also preclude entitlement to equal treatment where residence rights were based (only) on Article 10 of the Regulation.

In *Jobcenter Krefeld*, the Court confirmed that a former worker who is no longer economically active yet continues to reside lawfully in the host State as the primary carer of children completing their education there—on the basis of Article 10 of Regulation 492/2011—may claim equal treatment with host State nationals as regards entitlement to social assistance.[365] Such claimants share with Article 21 TFEU-claimants that they do not currently exercise economic activity in the host State, yet EU law distinguishes their situations: for those residing in the host State on the basis of the Regulation, the 'particular expression' of their right to equal treatment is not Article 24 of Directive 2004/38 but Article 7(2) of the Regulation.[366] Moreover, as seen in Section 2, 'a benefit guaranteeing a minimum means of subsistence constitutes a social advantage, within the meaning of [Article 7(2) of] Regulation [492/2011], which may not be denied to a migrant worker who is a national of another Member State and is resident within the territory of the State paying the benefit, nor to his family'.[367] Reflecting on the personal scope of Article 7(2) of the Regulation, the Court referred back to Article 7(1)'s guarantee that '[a] worker who is a national of a Member State may not, in the territory of another Member State, be treated differently from national workers by reason of his nationality in respect of any conditions of employment and work, in particular as regards remuneration, dismissal, *and, should he become unemployed*, reinstatement or re-employment'. The equal treatment extended here to workers who 'become unemployed' is seems connected to their 'reinstatement or re-employment'. Yet the Court extracted equal treatment guarantees from Article 7(1) in a much more generalised way, conceiving 'a protection that extends *beyond just the period of employment* of those workers'.[368]

Since, as noted above, the Court had already established that Article 7(2) of the Regulation is the 'particular expression' of the principle of equal treatment in Article 45(2) TFEU, it then found that 'the fact that JD had become economically inactive ... cannot lead to the result that the principle of equal treatment laid down in Article 7(2) of [the] Regulation ... becomes inapplicable. Moreover ... the rights enjoyed *by the worker who is a Union citizen* and his or her family members under Regulation No 492/2011 may, in certain circumstances, persist even after the termination of the employment relationship.[369] One such set of 'certain

---

[362] In *Ibrahim*, for example, equal treatment followed under the applicable national rules if a right to reside on the basis of EU law could be established; see AG Mazák, EU:C:2009:641, para 19 of the Opinion. See also, AG Kokott in Case C-480/08 *Teixeira*, EU:C:2009:642, paras 81–85 and 122 of the Opinion.
[363] Case C-333/13 *Dano*, EU:C:2014:2358, para 61.
[364] *Alimanovic*, para 49.
[365] Case C-181/19 *Jobcenter Krefeld*, EU:C:2020:794, paras 72–78.
[366] ibid paras 77 and 78.
[367] Case 249/83 *Hoeckx*, EU:C:1985:139, para 22.
[368] *Jobcenter Krefeld*, para 43 (emphasis added).
[369] ibid paras 47–48 (emphasis added).

circumstances' concerns residence based on Article 10 of the Regulation. In these situations, 'the right of residence of the parent who cares for those children becomes, once acquired, *independent of the original right of residence that is based on the status of the parent concerned as a worker, and may continue to exist beyond the loss of that status*, in order to provide enhanced legal protection to those children, thereby ensuring that their right to equal treatment as regards access to education is not deprived of any practical effect'.[370] Moreover, the fact that the claimants '*also* fall within the scope of Article 24 of Directive 2004/38, including the derogation provided for in Article 24(2) thereof, on the ground that they have a right of residence based on Article 14(4)(b) of that directive, the fact remains that, *since they can also rely on an independent right of residence* based on Article 10 of Regulation No 492/2011, that derogation cannot be used against them'.[371]

Though the Court did not address the point expressly in *Jobcenter Krefeld*, it is presumed that permanent residence rights would not, in due course, be acquired.[372] Additionally, 'the situation of a national of another Member State who has previously entered the employment market of the host Member State and who also has a right of residence based on Article 10 of Regulation No 492/2011 must be distinguished from the situation where there are indications that the former worker concerned has abused his or her rights in a way not covered by the rules of EU law, in that he or she has *artificially created* the conditions for obtaining the social advantages at issue under Article 7(2) of [the] Regulation'.[373] However, as also noted by the Commission, the documents available to the Court contained nothing to suggest that there had been abuse of rights or fraud in this case. While the Court did not refer to *Dano* or *Alimanovic* in this part of its ruling, that case law was present in spirit. The extent of the protective shield spun from Article 10 of the Regulation, compared to the exclusionary impulse of *Dano* and *Alimanovic*, is even more striking when account is taken of JD's very limited employment history in the host State.[374]

3.4 Residence Based on EU Primary Law

3.4.1 Articles 45 and 49 TFEU

It can be recalled briefly here that the possibility of retaining the status of worker or self-employed person in circumstances of pregnancy and childbirth has been drawn from Articles 45 and 49 TFEU for workers and self-employed persons respectively.[375] In such situations, Member State nationals continue to reside in the host State as beneficiaries of Article 7(1)(a) of the Directive, requiring no further 'input' from the Treaty so long as they return

---

[370] ibid para 49 (emphasis added). It is not clear whether a primary carer of children who resides on the basis of Article 10 yet who has never been an EU worker can claim equal treatment in the same way; see further, F Ristiuccia, 'The right to social assistance of children in education and their primary carers: *Jobcenter Krefeld*' (2021) 58 Common Market Law Review 877 at 889–90.

[371] ibid para 69 (emphasis added).

[372] This is also implied by the finding that a right to reside based on Article 10 of the Regulation 'is, moreover, limited since it comes to an end, at the latest, when the child completes his or her studies' (ibid para 75).

[373] ibid para 76 (emphasis added); referring 'by analogy' to Joined Cases C-58/13 and C-59/13 *Torresi*, EU:C:2014:2088, paras 42 and 46 (which concerned abuse of EU rights and mutual recognition of professional qualifications).

[374] *Jobcenter Krefeld*, paras 20–22.

[375] Case C-507/12 *Saint Prix*, EU:C:2014:2007; Case C-544/18 *Dakneviciute* EU:C:2019:761.

to economic activity within a reasonable period. Equal treatment with host State nationals is sustained for that period as a result.[376]

3.4.2 Article 21 TFEU

Is a Member State national in a situation such as that of Mr Baumbast (but following the adoption of Directive 2004/38) residing in the host State on the basis of Article 21 TFEU directly when that their residence there patently does not comply with one of the conditions in Article 7(1)(b) of the Directive? A similar question might be raised for a student in a similar position to Mr Grzelczyk: does a student who runs out of financial resources continue to reside on the proportionality-toned basis of Article 7(1)(c) of the Directive or now directly on the basis of Article 21 TFEU only?

On one view, the Union citizen's residence in either case would be lawful within the meaning of EU law by analogy with *Jobcenter Krefeld* and Article 24(1) of Directive 2004/38 should be then sidelined as the 'specific expression' of the equal treatment on grounds of nationality guaranteed by Article 18 TFEU. However, it is unlikely that the Court would now be willing to extend that analogy to a *Baumbast* or even *Grzelczyk* situation if no residence basis in another EU *legislative* measure exists, noting its approach to the exercise of free movement under Article 21 TFEU but not in compliance with Article 7 of the Directive in *CG*, as explained in the next section, and the importance attached to economic activity and the independent framework of Regulation 492/2011 in *Jobcenter Krefeld* itself.

3.5 Residence Based on or Authorised by National Law

The final coordinate of the lawful residence matrix takes us right back to the foundational rulings in *Martínez Sala*, *Grzelczyk*, and *Trojani*—in so far as they concern a right to reside based on or authorised by national law only. Does such residence still constitute lawful residence for the purposes of equal treatment with host State nationals?

In *Teixeira*, before *Dano* and *Alimanovic*, Advocate General Kokott commented that '[i]n so far as Ms Teixeira is residing legally in the United Kingdom, *irrespective of whether her right of residence arises under Community law or only under national law*, as a Union citizen she has a right to equal treatment under Article [21 TFEU] in conjunction with [Article 18 TFEU]. As the Court stated in *Trojani* ... Union citizens can, in reliance on this right, claim social assistance in the host Member State for a limited period'.[377] In *CG*, after *Dano* and *Alimanovic*, and reflecting the caution suggested in Section 3.4.2, Advocate General Richard de la Tour commented that 'as the Court's case-law stands following the judgment in *Jobcenter Krefeld*, the benefit of equal treatment in the context of Directive 2004/38 is no longer restricted to the situations referred to in that directive but also applies to those in which the right of residence is *based on another provision of secondary law*'.[378]

Whether that benefit would still apply where residence was not based on EU law of any description was 'the novel question before the Court' in *CG*. The circumstances of the case concerned CG, a national of both Croatia and the Netherlands, who moved to Northern

---

[376] For jobseekers, see Section 3.2.6 in connection with residence based on Article 14(4)(b) of the Directive.
[377] AG Kokott in Case C-480/08 *Teixeira*, EU:C:2009:642, para 122 of the Opinion. In fn 101, she added that '[i]n so far as Ms Teixeira's right of residence arises under [Union] law, she can *also* base a claim to equal treatment on Article 24 of Directive 2004/38' (emphasis added). See similarly, AG Kokott in Case C-75/11 *Commission v Austria*, EU:C:2012:536, para 44 of the Opinion.
[378] AG Richard de la Tour in Case C-709/20 *CG*, EU:C:2021:515, para 65 of the Opinion.

Ireland with her two young children in November 2018. CG had 'never carried out an economic activity in the United Kingdom and lived there with her partner [Union citizen, of Netherlands nationality and the father of her children] until she moved to a women's refuge'.[379] Additionally, she had 'no resources at all to support herself and her two children'.[380] In June 2020, she was granted 'pre-settled status' in the UK, the status conceived by the UK for the purposes of implementing the Withdrawal Agreement and, crucially for present purposes, 'granted by the United Kingdom Home Office to Union citizens who have been resident in the United Kingdom for a period of less than five years, *without being subject to a condition that they have sufficient resources*'.[381] Shortly after CG's pre-settled status was granted, she applied for but was refused social assistance.[382]

The Court first confirmed that '[s]ince CG is a Union citizen who has made use of her right to move and to reside, in order to settle in the United Kingdom, her situation falls within the scope *ratione materiae* of EU law, with the result that she may, in principle, rely on the prohibition of discrimination on grounds of nationality contained in Article 18 TFEU'.[383] However, recalling that Articles 20(2) and 21(1) TFEU enable the placing of conditions and limits on the exercise of free movement rights, the Court stated that 'Article 18 TFEU is intended to apply independently only to situations governed by EU law with respect to which the FEU Treaty does not lay down specific rules on non-discrimination'.[384] It underlined that 'the principle of non-discrimination is given specific expression in Article 24 of Directive 2004/38 in relation to Union citizens who exercise their right to move and reside within the territory of the Member State'.[385] And it then held:

> [I]n accordance with Article 3(1) of Directive 2004/38, Union citizens who move to or reside in a Member State other than that of which they are a national, and their family members, as defined in Article 2(2) of that directive, who accompany or join them, fall within the scope of the directive and are beneficiaries of the rights conferred by it ... That is the case for a person such as CG, a dual Croatian and Netherlands national, who has made use of the right to move and reside in the territory of the United Kingdom before the end of the transition period laid down in Article 126 of the Agreement on the withdrawal of the United Kingdom. It follows that a person in CG's situation *falls within the scope of that directive, with the result that it is in the light of Article 24 of Directive 2004/38, and not of the first paragraph of Article 18 TFEU*, that it is necessary to assess whether that person faces discrimination on the grounds of nationality.[386]

---

[379] Case C-709/20 *CG*, EU:C:2021:602, para 30; CG moved to the refuge following allegations of domestic violence (See AG Richard de la Tour para 28 of the Opinion)

[380] *CG*, para 30.

[381] AG Richard de la Tour, para 29 of the Opinion (emphasis added). As noted in Chapters 4 and 6, departing from EU citizenship law and EU free movement law generally, a national status conceived to implement Part Two of the Withdrawal Agreement becomes constitutive of the rights provided for in the Agreement. Thus, it was within the UK's discretion not to require sufficient resources; see further, Article 18(1) WA (Agreement on the withdrawal of the United Kingdom of Great Britain and Northern Ireland from the European Union and the European Atomic Energy Community, OJ 2019 CI 384/01).

[382] The Court confirmed that the benefits applied for constituted social assistance within the meaning of Directive 2004/31 (*CG*, paras 68–71).

[383] ibid para 64.

[384] ibid para 65.

[385] ibid para 66.

[386] ibid para 67 (emphasis added).

Following *Dano*, 'the financial situation of each person concerned should be examined specifically, without taking account of the social benefits claimed, in order to determine whether he or she meets the condition of having sufficient resources laid down in Article 7(1)(b) of Directive 2004/38 and whether he or she can accordingly invoke, in the host Member State, the principle of non-discrimination laid down in Article 24(1) of that directive in order to enjoy equal treatment with the nationals of that Member State'.[387] However, on the basis of the information provided by the referring court, the Court of Justice had no difficulty in finding that 'CG does not have sufficient resources. Accordingly, such a person is likely to become an unreasonable burden on the social assistance system of the United Kingdom and cannot therefore rely on the principle of non-discrimination laid down in Article 24(1) of Directive 2004/38'.[388]

There was then a notable advance from *Dano* with respect to the role of the Charter of Fundamental Rights as a basic provision safety net in such situations, returned to in Section 4. But the *CG* ruling is very difficult to comprehend in terms of legal logic. First, and most basically, there was no engagement with *Martínez Sala* and, even more so, *Trojani*, which had unambiguously established that 'a citizen of the Union who is not economically active may rely on Article [18 TFEU] where he has been lawfully resident in the host Member State for a certain time or possesses a residence permit'.[389] Second, *CG* expands the range of Article 24(1) of the Directive as an equal treatment precondition very problematically: merely exercising the right to move and residing in a host State triggers Article 3(1) of the Directive and that suffices to bring all aspects of a citizen's residence within the Directive's framework—even if they demonstrably do *not* reside there 'on the basis of the Directive' at all. Article 3(1) of the Directive refers to its 'beneficiaries'. But how can someone who does not reside 'on the basis of' Directive 2004/38 be, at the same time, one of its 'beneficiaries'? In *CG*, the Court thus translated a provision intended to communicate the scope of a measure of secondary law on its own terms into a provision that defines the scope of Articles 18 and 21 TFEU much more fundamentally.

The ruling in *CG* therefore transgressed the *Baumbast* distinction between the existence and the exercise of rights conferred by primary law explained in Section 2. The Court of Justice has been criticised for extending both the idea and the legal implications of Union citizenship too far,[390] and in some of the citizenship case law, it cannot be overlooked that seeking person-specific outcomes did not always take sufficient account of relevant systemic implications. But it must also be acknowledged that the Treaties created Union citizenship as a rights-bearing status and, on that basis, the Court, rightly or wrongly, created legally meaningful rights at the level of primary EU law. In *CG*, the concept of the 'beneficiary' of a legislative measure becomes a primary law straitjacket: it no longer (only) opens access to the Directive—it (also) closes off guarantees of protection beyond the Directive and notably the elemental guarantee against nationality discrimination in Article 18 TFEU.

---

[387] ibid para 79.
[388] ibid para 80
[389] Case C-456/02 *Trojani*, EU:C:2004:488, para 43 (emphasis added) See similarly, para 46: 'once it is ascertained that a person in a situation such as that of the claimant in the main proceedings is in possession of a residence permit, he may rely on Article [18 TFEU] in order to be granted a social assistance benefit such as the minimex'. Confirmed in Case C-209/03 *Bidar*, EU:C:2005:169, para 37. Noting that *Trojani* was applied at an earlier stage of the national proceedings, O'Brien observes that '[i]t is remarkable that the CJEU *and the EU Commission* have less appetite than the Court of Appeal of England and Wales for protecting the rights of EU nationals cast adrift in the UK' (n 4 (2021) 816, emphasis in original).
[390] eg Hailbronner (n 4).

Providing a point of contrast with the public finance case law, the *Petruhhin* case was discussed in Chapter 2. In the context of a request to extradite a Union citizen to a third country, the Court invoked the Treaty provisions on citizenship of the Union and confirmed that '[t]he situations falling within their scope of application include ... those involving the exercise of the freedom to move and reside within the territory of the Member States, as conferred by Article 21 TFEU'.[391] It then observed that 'Mr Petruhhin, an Estonian national, made use, in his capacity as a Union citizen, of his right to move freely within the European Union by moving to Latvia, so that the situation at issue in the main proceedings falls within the scope of application of the Treaties, within the meaning of Article 18 TFEU, which sets out the principle of non-discrimination on grounds of nationality'.[392] There was no reference to Mr Petruhhin's *residence* in Latvia or to whether he complied with the provisions of the Directive during that period. There was no information about when he moved to Latvia and no instruction to the referring court to clarify or establish that point.

In *Petruhhin*, the Court therefore 'assumes that there is a situation "which fall[s] within the scope *ratione materiae* of [Union] law" where a Union citizen has exercised his right to freedom of movement under Article [21(1) TFEU]'.[393] In other words, in *Petruhhin*, the Court never determined—or sought to determine—whether the Union citizen in question was a 'beneficiary' of the Directive for the purposes of its equal treatment analysis. In *CG*, the Court compels lawful residence within the meaning of Directive 2004/38 on all Member State nationals who move to and reside in a host State so that they may benefit from equal treatment with host State nationals. The point of distinction for not starting with a Directive-based lawful residence check in every case entailing Article 21 TFEU, then, is context-driven and not law-driven. In *Wolzenburg*, before the Court's rulings in *Dano* and *CG*, Advocate General Bot had stated:

> [I]t is clear from the case-law that persons who have exercised a freedom of movement guaranteed by the [TFEU] are entitled to rely on Article [18 TFEU]. The *exercise of a freedom of movement constitutes the connecting factor* to [Union] law required for application of that article. It is therefore possible *to examine whether a Member State's legislation is compatible* with that article where the legislation in question applies to a person who has exercised a freedom of movement, even if that legislation concerns a reserved area of competence.[394]

Only if the situation has no factor connecting it to Union law should a review of the Member State's compliance with EU rules—which entails examination, at least, of Article 18 TFEU—not be required.[395]

Differently from *Dano*, CG resided lawfully in the host State through the grant of pre-settled status. But differently from *Jobcenter Krefeld*, the source of the right to reside in *CG* was not one of EU law given that the UK had constituted its own status under national law to implement its obligations under the Withdrawal Agreement. Moreover, in *Jobcenter*

---

[391] Case C-182/15 *Petruhhin*, EU:C:2016:630, para 30.
[392] ibid para 31. See similarly, Case C-247/17 *Raugevicius*, EU:C:2018:898, para 27.
[393] AG Kokott in Case C-192/05 *Tas-Hagen and Tas*, EU:C:2006:150, para 31 of the Opinion. She added that '[t]he Court does so even in cases in which the exercise of the right to free movement or the status of the person concerned as a Union citizen are the only links with [Union] law' (para 32 of the Opinion).
[394] AG Bot in Case C-123/08 *Wolzenburg*, EU:C:2009:183, para 111 of the Opinion (emphasis added).
[395] eg Case C-353/06 *Grunkin and Paul*, EU:C:2008:559, para 16 ('unless what is involved is an internal situation which has no link with [Union] law').

Krefeld, the right to reside was not only independent of Directive 2004/38 *but also* of Article 21 TFEU: the claimant's factual connection to economic activity was thin, but the legal connection to Article 45 TFEU did the necessary work of overriding the system of the Directive. Even though the claimant was in fact considered to be a beneficiary of the Directive, falling within the scope of the right to reside conferred on jobseekers by Article 14(4)(b), the express derogation in Article 24 of the Directive 'cannot be used against them' because 'the fact that jobseekers have specific rights under that directive cannot, having regard to the independence of the bodies of rules established by that directive and by Regulation No 492/2011 respectively, entail a diminution in the rights that such persons can derive from that regulation'.[396]

Contra *Martínez Sala* and *Trojani*, the implications of decisions taken under national law were set aside in *CG*, and the scope of Article 21 TFEU—of rights based previously on EU primary law—was significantly narrowed. Fundamentally, the Court held in *Trojani* that 'while the Member States may make residence of a citizen of the Union who is not economically active conditional on his having sufficient resources, that does not mean that such a person cannot, during his lawful residence in the host Member State, benefit from the fundamental principle of equal treatment as laid down in [Article 18 TFEU]'.[397] The Court may wish to revisit that finding. But it is legally and methodologically problematic just to ignore it—as occurred in *CG*. Agreeing with Advocate General Cosmas, 'it would be unfortunate to make citizens bear the consequences of inaction by the [Union] institutions or of the negative attitude of the Member States with regard to the progress of European integration in the field of freedom of movement of persons'.[398]

We are still left to consider, then: how can Article 24(1) even be a 'specific expression' of Article 18 TFEU for Union citizens with a right to reside authorised only by national law?[399] The Court explained in this way:

> CG does not have sufficient resources. Accordingly, such a person is likely to become an unreasonable burden on the social assistance system of the United Kingdom and cannot therefore rely on the principle of non-discrimination laid down in Article 24(1) of Directive 2004/38. That assessment cannot be called into question by the fact that CG has a right of temporary residence, under national law, which was granted without conditions as to resources. If an economically inactive Union citizen who does not have sufficient resources and resides in the host Member State without satisfying the requirements laid down in Directive 2004/38 could rely on the principle of non-discrimination set out in Article 24(1) of that directive, he or she would enjoy broader protection than he or she would have enjoyed under the provisions of that directive, under which that citizen would be refused a right of residence.[400]

---

[396] Case C-181/19 *Jobcenter Krefeld*, EU:C:2020:794, paras 69–70.
[397] Case C-456/02 *Trojani*, EU:C:2004:488, para 40.
[398] AG Cosmas in Case C-378/97 *Wijsenbeek*, EU:C:1999:144, para 111 of the Opinion.
[399] As O'Brien asks, '[h]ow on earth is an equal treatment right specifically articulated for people residing on the basis of the Directive, the appropriate "specific expression" of art.18 TFEU, for people with a right to reside *which is in no way based on the Directive*? Rather, it is an expression, as the Court itself notes, of art.21 TFEU—the primary law right to move and reside conferred upon Union citizens. It is hard to imagine a scenario better suited to an explicit analysis of art.18 TFEU rights' (n 4 (2021) 807, emphasis in original).
[400] Case C-709/20 *CG*, EU:C:2021:602, paras 80–81. The Advocate General proposed a different position somewhere between *Trojani* and *Dano*: 'in the case of a right of residence granted in more favourable conditions than those laid down in Directive 2004/38, that directive must be interpreted as allowing the host Member State to impose lawful restrictions on the grant of social benefits, in order to ensure that "persons exercising their right of residence should not ... become an unreasonable burden on the social assistance system of the host Member

That the points raised by the Court above may be true and/or reasonable still does not reconcile them with its own (non-referenced) case law—in which it had previously held precisely the opposite. The Court never confronts the plain wording of Article 24(1) either: 'all Union citizens residing *on the basis of this Directive* in the territory of the host Member State shall enjoy equal treatment with the nationals of that Member State within the scope of the Treaty'. CG did not reside on the basis of the Directive, so whether or not she complied with the residence conditions in Article 7 in order to benefit from the 'specific expression' of equal treatment in Article 24 is logically irrelevant.

More generally, the equal treatment guarantee in Article 18 TFEU is extended '[w]ithin the scope of application of the Treaties, and without prejudice to any special provisions contained therein'. The Court was clear that CG's situation fell 'within the scope of application of the Treaties'. As explained in Section 2, 'any special provisions contained therein' opens the primary law door to the conditions and limits in Directive 2004/38 via Article 21 TFEU. The difficulty remains, though, that CG's right to reside was not within the scope of the Directive. The contrast with *Jobcenter Krefeld* is again striking, where the Court stated that '[i]t is clear, first, from the very wording of Article 24(2) of Directive 2004/38 that the Member States may, "by way of derogation from paragraph 1" of Article 24, refuse, under certain conditions, to grant the right to social assistance to certain categories of persons' but then clarified that 'that derogation is applicable only to the persons who fall within the scope of Article 24(1), namely Union citizens who are residing in the territory of the host Member State "on the basis of [that] directive"'.[401] If the derogation only applies to citizens who reside in the host State on the basis of the Directive, then the expression of the guarantee has to apply only in the same circumstances too.

Third, with respect to periods of residence authorised by national law and Article 37 of the Directive, the Court found that:

> [N]ational provisions which, like the provisions at issue in the dispute in the main proceedings, grant a right of residence to a Union citizen, even where all the requirements laid down by Directive 2004/38 for that purpose have not been met, fall within the scenario referred to in Article 37 of that directive, to the effect that that directive does not preclude the law of the Member States from establishing more favourable rules than those laid down by the provisions of that directive. Such a right of residence cannot however be regarded in any way as being granted 'on the basis of' Directive 2004/38 within the meaning of Article 24(1) of that directive. The Court has held that the fact that national provisions concerning the right of residence of Union citizens, that are more favourable than those laid down in Directive 2004/38, are not to be affected does not in any way mean that such provisions must be incorporated into the system introduced by that directive and it has concluded, in particular, that it is for each Member State that has decided to adopt a system that is more

---

State", within the meaning of recital 10 of that directive' (AG Richard de la Tour in *CG*, EU:C:2021:515, para 89 of the Opinion). At the same time, he accommodated *Commission v UK* in the sense that the indirect discrimination produced by such restrictions required them to be proportionate and emphasising a review of individual circumstances linked not only to the principle of proportionality but also the Charter of Fundamental Rights: thus, 'by not providing that the competent authorities must carry out an assessment of all of the individual circumstances that characterise the situation of extreme poverty of the person concerned and of the consequences of a refusal of his or her application in consideration, according to his or her situation, of the right to respect for family life and of the best interests of the child, the national legislation goes beyond what is necessary to maintain the equilibrium of the social assistance scheme of the host Member State' (para 110 of the Opinion).

[401] Case C-181/19 *Jobcenter Krefeld*, EU:C:2020:794, para 62 (emphasis added)

favourable than that established by that directive to specify the consequences of a right of residence granted on the basis of national law alone.[402]

The Court drew here from *Ziolkowski and Szeja*, where, as explained in Section 3.1.1, it had discounted periods of residence authorised by national law when determining 'legal' residence under Article 16 of the Directive for the purposes of permanent residence rights. However, agreeing with Advocate General Richard de la Tour in *CG*, 'unlike Article 16 of Directive 2004/38, which *created* a permanent right of residence, Article 24 of that directive merely constitutes the *implementation*, in relation to the right of residence of Union citizens, of the principle of non-discrimination between Union citizens laid down in Article 18 TFEU'.[403] In Section 4, it will be seen that, confusingly, the actions of the national authorities in *CG* did nevertheless constitute 'implementing Union law' for the purposes of Article 51(1) CFR and the scope of the Charter.[404] For now, it can again be underlined that the Court ignored a clear contrary statement—'national legislation such as that at issue in the main proceedings, in so far as it does not grant the social assistance benefit to citizens of the European Union, non-nationals of the Member State, who reside there lawfully even though they satisfy the conditions required of nationals of that Member State, constitutes discrimination on grounds of nationality prohibited by Article [18 TFEU]'—in *Trojani*, where residence was similarly, and categorically, beyond the scope of Directive 90/364 yet authorised by the host State.[405]

In summary: following *CG*, residence authorised by the host State in accordance with its national law no longer, on its own terms, constitutes lawful residence for the purposes of an equal treatment claim premised on Article 18 TFEU—whether in connection with the status of Union citizenship and Article 20 TFEU (*Martínez Sala*) or the exercise of the right to move and reside under Article 21 TFEU (*Trojani*). The side-lining of rights conferred by primary EU law in *CG* not only gives effect to conditions and limits in secondary law; it amplifies them to an extraordinary degree. The Court has reversed principles established in the foundational citizenship case law, even if that has not been openly admitted.

4. Lawful Residence and Equal Treatment: Implications

The origins and the evolution of the vital link between lawful residence and equal treatment in EU citizenship law were mapped in Sections 2 and 3 of this chapter. Here, the implications of that case law are considered. Two points are addressed: first, the consequences, under EU law, of *unlawful* or *unsupported* residence in a host State (Section 4.1), and second, the developing role of the Charter of Fundamental Rights (Section 4.2). These questions highlight, overall, the situation of citizens 'tolerated' in host States,[406] whether unlawfully resident

---

[402] Case C-709/20 *CG*, EU:C:2021:602, para 82.
[403] AG Richard de la Tour in *CG*, para 72 of the Opinion (emphasis added).
[404] *CG*, esp paras 87–88; see further, Section 4.2.
[405] Case C-456/02 *Trojani*, EU:C:2004:488, para 44.
[406] The concept of the 'tolerated' citizen is not formally established in the case law of the Court per se but see AG Saugmandsgaard Øe in Case C-331/16 *K and HF*, EU:C:2017:973, para 125 of the Opinion: 'the decision refusing residence to Mr H. F. was not accompanied by an order to leave the territory. The presence of the person concerned in Belgium was, as it were, "tolerated", even though he did not have a right of residence or any particular status there'. *K and HF* is considered further in Chapter 10, in connection with Article 28 of the Directive. See also, on the concept of 'complicity', J Scott, 'The global reach of EU law' in M Cremona and J Scott (eds), *EU Law Beyond EU Borders* (OUP 2019) 21 at 54. Scott draws from C Lepora and RE Goodin, *On Complicity and Compromise* (OUP 2013).

there or lawfully resident but excluded from equal treatment. The discussion therefore animates an immediate question about residence security for Union citizens who have exercised the right to move and reside under Article 21 TFEU, therefore fall within the personal scope of EU law, and yet do not benefit from the guarantees of equal treatment in Article 18 TFEU or Article 24 of the Directive. It also raises a wider question about responsibility for the functioning of the Union's novel free movement system.

4.1 The Consequences of Unlawful and/or Unsupported Residence in a Host State

The fact that a Member State national is residing unlawfully in a host State will often come to light only in the circumstances of most of the case law discussed in this chapter, that is, when they seek to test their entitlement to equal treatment by applying for financial support in the host State, and even more so when that application concerns social assistance.[407] What are the implications of the fact that there is now a greater chance that Union citizens could be found to be unlawfully resident, or lawfully resident but unsupported, in a host State, given that the sources of lawful residence recognised in EU citizenship law have narrowed over time, the exclusion of certain groups of Union citizens from eligibility for social assistance, and the capacity of host States to apply right to reside tests so long as this is done proportionately and not systematically?

In *Grzelczyk*, the Court had acknowledged that a host State was free to withdraw or not renew residence permits in situations where Union citizen students no longer fulfilled the conditions of their right of residence. That point was generalised in *Trojani*, with the Court finding that 'it remains open to the host Member State to take the view that a national of another Member State who has recourse to social assistance no longer fulfils the conditions of his right of residence' and that, in such circumstances, the host State 'may, within the limits imposed by [Union] law, take a measure to remove him'.[408] As detailed in Chapter 6, Directive 2004/38 now articulates the 'limits imposed by Union law' in such circumstances, with Article 14(3) ensuring that 'recourse to the social assistance system by a citizen of the Union may not automatically entail such a measure'.[409] Article 15(1) of the Directive establishes (by inference[410]) a host State's competence to expel Member State nationals who are demonstrably unlawfully resident within the meaning of EU law (ie those who, prior to permanent residence rights, do not comply with the conditions in Articles 6, 7, 12, 13, or 14(4)(b) of the Directive or who do not, in the alternative, reside on the basis of Article 10 of Regulation 492/2011). As the Court held in *FS*, Article 15(1) 'is intended, in particular, to enable the host Member State to ensure that the residence in its territory of Union citizens who do not enjoy a right of permanent residence in that territory is carried out in compliance with the scope of the *temporary* rights of residence provided for in that directive'.[411]

---

[407] eg The fact that Ms Dano already received family benefits in the host State illustrates this point.
[408] Case C-456/02 *Trojani*, EU:C:2004:488, para 45.
[409] ibid.
[410] Having first considered Article 27 of the Directive, AG Rantos commented in *FS* that Article 15(1) 'pursues a less obvious but equally important objective. That article is in fact the only provision of the Residence Directive on which the Member States may rely in order to ensure, on the basis of EU law, that persons who no longer satisfy the conditions of temporary residence and who represent an unreasonable burden on their social assistance system can be removed from their territory. That provision is therefore intended to guarantee the practical effect of the provisions on the right of residence, whilst protecting a Member State's public financial resources' (AG Rantos in Case C-719/19 *FS*, EU:C:2021:104, para 72 of the Opinion).
[411] Case C-719/19 *FS*, EU:C:2021:506, para 72 (emphasis added).

When expulsion decisions are being considered under Article 15(1), a host State should first, in accordance with recital 16 of the Directive, 'examine whether it is a case of temporary difficulties and take into account the duration of residence, the personal circumstances and the amount of aid granted in order to consider whether the beneficiary has become an unreasonable burden on its social assistance system and to proceed to his expulsion'.[412] Thus, even if an individual assessment of circumstances is not required since *Alimanovic* for social assistance claims per se when Union citizens are economically inactive, the Directive does provide an individual assessment safety net at the point of their possible expulsion. If that decision is in fact progressed, Article 15(1) requires the host State to comply with the procedural safeguards in Articles 30 and 31 of the Directive.[413]

In *FS*, Advocate General Rantos considered 'how a Member State can in fact expel from its territory (on grounds other than public policy, public security, or public health) a Union citizen who, after a period of legal residence, continues to reside there without however satisfying the conditions laid down in the Residence Directive, at the risk of becoming an unreasonable burden on the social assistance system of that Member State' and suggested that Union citizens in such situations 'should not be the subject of expulsion measures *as long as* [they do] *not become* an unreasonable burden on the social assistance system of the host Member State'.[414] The Court did not consider this point in its ruling, but there are similar signals about tolerated citizens in other cases: for example, on the legal consequences that must be brooked by a host State when its authorities did not confront a citizen's situation sooner.[415] However, it could also be argued that in cases such as *Dano*, the fate of the unlawfully resident citizen was not of particular concern for EU citizenship law once the claim for social assistance was extinguished.[416] A related question concerns obligations under EU law to support Union citizens to transition between statuses in the host State: for example, a responsibility to guide an economically inactive citizen who is refused social assistance through the process of changing their status in the host State—providing jobseeker support, for example, which would also most likely reduce further potential drains on host State resources over time.

As indicated at the beginning of this chapter, the post-Directive case law on lawful residence and equal treatment has provoked an intensive debate in the field of EU citizenship law. The academic literature is extensive, raising and engaging with conceptual, constitutional, ethical, institutional, methodological, and normative questions that ask us ultimately to confront what Union citizenship means and what it should mean. These questions must be taken seriously. Ultimately, the collective vision of the EU's institutions and its Member States[417] as to how freedom of movement and residence should (and should not) be supported is set by Directive 2004/38, which institutes a 'gradual system' as regards the right to reside, the implication being that citizens integrate more deeply into a host State over

---

[412] Confirmed in eg Case C-67/14 *Alimanovic*, EU:C:2015:597, para 59; referring to Case C-140/12 *Brey*, EU:C:2013:565, paras 64, 69, and 78.

[413] Except for the guarantees in those provisions specifically addressing restrictions based on public policy, public security, or public health (Case C-94/18 *Chenchooliah*, EU:C:2019:693; see further, Chapters 6 and 10).

[414] AG Rantos in *FS*, paras 34 and 75 of the Opinion (emphasis added); see similarly, para 101 of the Opinion ('the beneficiaries of the right of residence should not be the subject of expulsion measures as long as they do not become an unreasonable burden on the social assistance system of the host Member State').

[415] See eg on the sufficient resources condition, Case C-93/18 *Bajratari*, EU:C:2019:809; and on comprehensive sickness insurance, Case C-535/19 *A (Soins de santé publics)*, EU:C:2021:595. See further, Chapter 6.

[416] But cf the role of the Charter developed more recently in *CG* (Section 4.2).

[417] As illustrated in this chapter as well as in Chapters 4, 6, and 10, the Council had significant influence on the final shape of the Directive and notably with respect to its more limiting provisions.

time, acquiring stronger protection from expulsion and greater access to equal treatment as a result.[418] Implementing that 'gradual system' connects to ensuring the effectiveness of the rights conferred—to ensuring that they are situationally apt. For citizens whose claims are ruled out by the express derogations in Article 24(2) of the Directive, there is legislatively approved less favourable treatment; recalling, for example, the comparative advantage with respect to eligibility for maintenance aid that a student who is also economically active (or the family member of such a citizen) enjoys over a student who is not. Articles 20 and 21 TFEU mandate such legislative conditioning of the right to move and reside. In contrast, Articles 45 and 49 TFEU do not. Article 24(2) of the Directive therefore aligns with the longstanding recognition of economic activity as an exemplar of sufficient integration.[419]

The economic bias that EU citizenship law thus sustains can be criticised from a normative perspective, the contrasting reasoning and outcomes in *Jobcenter Krefeld* and *CG* providing a strong example. But Article 24(2) of the Directive '*authorises* differences in treatment between Union citizens and the nationals of the host Member State' in circumstances more removed from economic activity.[420] Citizens in the latter situation are often tolerated without being supported when they move to, reside in, and stay in another Member State. The legislatively agreed limits are at least spelled out in the Article 24(2) derogations. However, more generally, the trajectory of lawful residence suggested across different provisions of the Directive and substantiated through case law produces gaps in protection that are much more difficult to rationalise. Here, citizens can get 'stuck' in sub-optimal residence situations, becoming 'liminal citizens' who are neither here nor there in terms of residence status with reference to the optimal system mapped out by the Directive.[421] Liminal citizens are then passively allowed to remain in a host State, but not proactively supported there. *CG* demonstrates that such liminality can even come about where residence is fully authorised by national law: CG's indisputable right to be in the UK sustains,[422] but her experience of residence is not bettered by EU equal treatment guarantees. At a basic level, tolerated citizens are protected by the procedural safeguards in Articles 8, 14, 15, 30, and 31 of the Directive should the host State reach the point of *intolerance* of their presence. But what happens until or unless that point is reached?

As seen in the case law discussed in Section 3, where an equal treatment claim is refuted on the grounds that the precondition of lawful residence in the host State is not met, the Court remains essentially silent about any further responsibility for the affected citizen thereafter.[423] In *Alimanovic*, Advocate General Wathelet acknowledged that '[t]he problem is sensitive in human and legal terms. It will necessarily lead to the Court ruling both on the protection offered by EU law to its citizens, as regards their financial situation and their dignity too, and on the current scope of the fundamental right to free movement, a founding principle on which the European Union is built'.[424] As a starting point, case law that prevents

---

[418] eg Case C-411/20 *Familienkasse Niedersachsen-Bremen*, EU:C:2022:602, para 78.
[419] eg Case C-542/09 *Commission v Netherlands*, EU:C:2012:346, para 65.
[420] AG Wathelet in Case C-299/14 *García-Nieto*, EU:C:2015:366, para 65 of the Opinion (emphasis added).
[421] N Nic Shuibhne, 'Limits rising, duties ascending: the changing legal shape of Union citizenship' (2015) 52 Common Market Law Review 889 at 934. See further, F de Witte, 'The liminal European: subject to the EU legal order' (2021) 40 Yearbook of European Law 56.
[422] In *Singh II*, Advocate General Kokott cited ECtHR case law to the effect that 'in so far as a family has ... *lawfully* established its residence in a particular State, withdrawal of the right of residence may amount to an infringement' (AG Kokott in Case C-218/14 *Singh II*, EU:C:2015:306, para 47 of the Opinion.
[423] However, case law does suggest that even unlawfully resident Union citizens might enjoy some protection from extradition outside the territory of the Union in certain circumstances: see Case C-182/15 *Petruhhin*, EU:C:2016:630 and Case C-191/16 *Pisciotti*, EU:C:2018:222. These judgments are discussed in Chapter 2.
[424] AG Wathelet in Case C-67/14 *Alimanovic*, EU:C:2015:210, paras 1-2 of the Opinion; also remarking that '[t]he unusual stir that [the] judgment [in *Dano*] has caused in the European media and all the political

Union citizens from acquiring permanent residence rights when their lawful residence is not the 'right' form of lawful residence could be re-considered: someone who might reside in a host State for several years yet cannot become permanently resident there remains stuck in a limited residence status rather than having the opportunity to transition to deeper residence security under EU law, no matter how deeply they have become integrated there.

Residence authorised by national law provides an obvious example. Another concerns exclusion from permanent residence rights even where residence authorised by EU law: especially for rights connected to Article 10 of Regulation 492/2011; and also since Article 12(3) of Directive 2004/38 confers residence rights in the event of a Union citizen's death or departure so that their children can complete their education in the host State, but makes no reference to conditions for retaining the right to reside or acquiring permanent residence rights in such circumstances, linking duration of residence and duration of education only.[425] As explained in Section 3.2.5, both Member State nationals and third-country nationals are eligible in principle for equal treatment with host State nationals (or for 'the benefit of' that right for third-country nationals) in such circumstances as regards social benefits other than study finance and social assistance because they reside there 'on the basis of' the Directive (Article 24(1)) and there is no specific derogation from social assistance in Article 24(2) other than that concerning the first three months of residence or assistance for jobseekers. Claiming social assistance would, however, compromise compliance with the conditions in Article 7(1), which would, in turn, preclude permanent residence rights. Just as for families residing on the basis Article 10 of Regulation 492/2011, the family-protective ethos of Article 12(3) of the Directive is out of sync with exclusion from permanent residence in due course. Member State nationals who do not enjoy a right of permanent residence in the host State can also be excluded from enhanced protection against expulsion, as explained further in Chapter 10.[426]

Overall, the case law presented in Sections 2 and 3 of this chapter shows that thinking about lawful residence and unlawful residence in a binary way misrepresents the reality. There are legitimate residence pathways even when lawful residence is decoupled from the conditions in Directive yet not all of them generate equal treatment or lead to permanent residence, that is, the most secure residence status. In *Commission v UK*, Advocate General Villalón did suggest that host States 'may not confine themselves simply to refusing to grant the benefit claimed' but should inform citizens found not to have a right to reside in the host State of that fact, observing the procedural safeguards provided for in Articles 30 and 31 of the Directive.[427] In reality, Member States tend not to progress economic expulsions and Union citizens will often continue to reside unlawfully in the host State. Where they can either commence economic activity within the meaning of EU law or otherwise acquire sufficient resources—for example, from a family member—their status is profoundly transformed: as *Jobcenter Krefeld* demonstrates, even limited levels of work can generate full entitlement to equal treatment with host State nationals for social and tax advantages. For economically active citizens, that includes equal treatment as regards social assistance

---

interpretations that have accompanied it confirm the importance and sensitivity of the subject' (para 4 of the Opinion).

[425] Article 18 of the Directive confirms only that 'the family members of a Union citizen to whom Articles 12(2) and 13(2) apply, who satisfy the conditions laid down therein, shall acquire the right of permanent residence after residing legally for a period of five consecutive years in the host Member State'.
[426] Joined Cases C-316/16 and C-424/16 *B and Vomero*, EU:C:2018:256, paras 56–60.
[427] AG Cruz Villalón in Case C-308/14 *Commission v UK*, EU:C:2015:666, para 96 of the Opinion.

and claiming it has no implications for permanent residence;[428] other than, as explained in Chapter 8, potentially to *speed up* that process in some circumstances.

The autonomy—and responsibilities—of Union citizens must be acknowledged. But it is too simplistic to assume that it is easy or even possible for all citizens to effect the necessary change of status that provides better host State security or at least to effect it *by themselves*. The case law setting out host State obligations in situations of temporary difficulty (exemplified by *Brey*) better reflects a system of shared responsibility: for citizens themselves to transition towards self-sufficiency, and for host States to *facilitate* that transition, within reason; to support the citizen to move 'inwards' towards greater protection under EU law where possible. It is important, in other words, that EU citizenship law identifies a more rounded understanding of where responsibility lies to ensure that Union citizens can transition effectively between the Directive's three main stages of residence where that is the desired objective,[429] leaving the Directive's framework of staggered conditionality intact. In *Dano*, as remarked in Section 3.1.2, the situation of the applicant was presented unfavourably. The ruling recounted her lack of schooling or professional training, her poor knowledge of German, and the fact that she had not yet worked in Germany—even the fact that the identity of the father of her son was unknown.[430] She was degraded as a person—not to mention as a citizen—before the substantive dispute was even addressed.[431] Her claim for income support failed because she did not reside in Germany on the basis of Directive 2004/38. But if Germany chooses not to deport her, is there really no corollary responsibility to support her transition to a different status beyond benefits that facilitate access to the labour market (that are not social assistance benefits) if she begins a search for work?

Advocate General Cruz Villalón framed his proposal in *Commission v UK* as one not of punishment but of responsibility: 'the competent authorities may not confine themselves *simply to refusing to grant the benefit claimed, but must, in addition*, under Article 30 of Directive 2004/38, *specifically when they find that there is no right of residence under Directive 2004/38*', also in order that the Directive's procedural guarantees would then be invoked.[432] His steering of relevant cases towards expulsion from the host State seems severe. But it does put the taking of a narrow approach to lawful residence in the first place into perspective and it would prevent tolerated Union citizens from becoming stuck in diminished circumstances irrespective of the duration for which they are otherwise left alone in a host State.

The free movement dimension of Union citizenship is unique to Union citizenship, both in terms of experience and therefore also of systemic responsibility for its consequences.[433]

---

[428] Though, again, not if social assistance is claimed in the context of residence based on Article 10 of the Regulation specifically: see further, Chapter 9.

[429] On the responsibilities of *home States* in supporting free movement, see F Strumia, 'Supranational citizenship enablers: free movement from the perspective of home Member States' (2020) 45 European Law Review 507; and in regional perspective, I Goldner Lang and M Lang, 'The dark side of free movement: when individual and social interests clash' in Mantu, Minderhoud, and Guild (eds) (n 4) 382.

[430] Case C-333/13 *Dano*, EU:C:2014:2358, paras 38–39.

[431] Reflecting conceptions of 'good' and 'bad' citizens, returned to in Chapter 10; see esp L Azoulai, 'The (mis) construction of the European individual—two essays on Union citizenship law', EUI working papers, LAW 2014/14, <https://cadmus.eui.eu/handle/1814/33293> (accessed 5 June 2023); and L Azoulai and S Coutts, 'Restricting Union citizen's residence rights on grounds of public security—where Union citizenship and the AFSJ meet: *P.I.*' (2013) 50 Common Market Law Review 553.

[432] AG Cruz Villalón in Case C-308/14 *Commission v UK*, EU:C:2015:666, para 96 of the Opinion (emphasis added).

[433] For a similar argument with respect to economic free movement, see N Nic Shuibhne, 'The "social freedom"? The free movement of persons in EU27' in S Garben and I Govaere (eds), *The Internal Market 2.0* (Hart Publishing 2020) 111. On Union citizenship more specifically, Ristuccia puts it perfectly: '[i]t is probably not free movement's task to tackle poverty by transferring the solidaristic burden between the Member States. But what is the role of fundamental rights and free movement if, in the exercise of the very core right of Union citizenship, one

That responsibility must be shared by the Union and its Member States. Free movement rights are not unlimited and realising them is not cost-free. Neither should freedom of movement, as just one objective of an ever more complex Union, always prevail over other objectives or public interests. Conditions and limits have a legitimate place in EU citizenship law. But the wording of Articles 20 and 21 TFEU, which allows for conditions and limits to be determined in secondary law, is not a *carte blanche* that exempts either Union institutions or national authorities from complying with the obligations, principles, and ethical standards inherent in the wider EU legal order. In particular, a restriction of rights must be subject to the requirements of primary EU law. In that light, the extent to which the Charter offers protection in situations of tolerated residence in a host State will now be considered.

4.2 The Charter of Fundamental Rights

In *Rottmann*, Advocate General Poiares Maduro underlined that 'if the situation comes within the scope of [Union] law, the exercise by the Member States of their retained powers cannot be discretionary. It is subject to the obligation to comply with [Union] rules'.[434] In *Commission v Austria*, before *Dano*, the Court expressed that point in the specific context of national responsibilities when setting conditions relevant to social security:

> Although Member States retain the power to organise their social security schemes, with the result that, in the absence of harmonisation at EU level, *it is for them to determine the conditions* concerning the right or duty to be insured with a social security scheme as well as the conditions for entitlement to benefits, *in exercising those powers, they must none the less comply with the law of the European Union and, in particular*, with the provisions of the FEU Treaty giving every citizen of the Union the right to move and reside within the territory of the Member States.[435]

How, then, was the relevance of the Charter ruled out in *Dano*?

As seen in previous chapters, there has been appreciable progress in applying and interpreting Union citizens' rights within the frame of the standards set and protection required by the Charter. For example, case law examined in Chapter 5 evidenced gradual recognition of respect for private and family life (Article 7 CFR) and the best interests of the child (Article 24 CFR) in situations where residence rights in a Union citizen's home State are based on Article 20 TFEU.[436] EU fundamental rights as expressed in the Charter have also been significant in case law on extradition to third countries, discussed in Chapter 2.[437] For questions on lawful residence and equal treatment, and especially where entitlement to social assistance is ruled out, several Charter rights might be relevant: notably, alongside

---

is not protected from the most serious forms of destitution? Of course, poverty does not only affect mobile citizens. But when it hits the latter, it risks pushing them into a legal no man's land, Union citizenship notwithstanding' (F Ristuccia, '"Cause tramps like us, baby we were born to run": untangling the effects of the expulsion of "undesired" Union citizens: *FS*' (2022) 59 Common Market Law Review 889 at 914).

[434] AG Poiares Maduro in Case C-135/08 *Rottmann*, EU:C:2009:588, para 20 of the Opinion.
[435] Case C-75/11 *Commission v Austria*, EU:C:2012:605, para 47 (emphasis added); referring to Case C-503/09 *Stewart*, EU:C:2011:500, paras 75–77.
[436] Builing on Case C-34/09 *Ruiz Zambrano*, EU:C:2011:124, see esp Case C-133/15 *Chavez-Vilchez*, EU:C:2017:354.
[437] Esp Case C-182/15 *Petruhhin*, EU:C:2016:630, paras 52–59.

Articles 7 and 24 CFR, Articles 1 (human dignity), 14 (right to education), 20 (equality before the law), 21 (non-discrimination), 25 (rights of the elderly), 26 (integration of persons with disabilities), 33 (family and professional life), 34 (social security and social assistance), 35 (health care), and 47 (right to an effective remedy) CFR.[438]

As introduced in Chapter 2, that Member States must 'comply with the law of the European Union' (as the Court put it in *Commission v Austria*) must also be considered with reference to the intended scope of the Charter. Article 51(1) CFR establishes that '[t]he provisions of this Charter are addressed to the institutions, bodies, offices and agencies of the Union with due regard for the principle of subsidiarity and to the Member States *only when they are implementing* Union law'. The Explanations relating to the Charter—to which the Court is required by Article 6(1) TEU to have 'due regard'—suggested that it 'follows unambiguously from the case-law of the Court of Justice that the requirement to respect fundamental rights defined in the context of the Union is only binding on the Member States when they act *in the scope of* Union law' (emphasis added).[439] In *Åkerberg Fransson*, that understanding was confirmed:

[The Court] has no power to examine the compatibility with the Charter of national legislation lying outside the scope of European Union law. On the other hand, *if such legislation falls within the scope of European Union law*, the Court, when requested to give a preliminary ruling, must provide all the guidance as to interpretation needed in order for the national court to determine whether that legislation is compatible with the fundamental rights the observance of which the Court ensure.[440]

Neither the requirement of Member States acting 'within the scope' of EU law nor the limits of that test is self-evident.[441] For example, the Court considers that the Charter applies to 'all situations governed by European Union law'[442] but not when national legislation 'falls outside the framework of EU law'.[443] But how are these situations distinguished? In *Julian Hernández*, the Court found that 'the concept of "implementing Union law" ... presupposes *a degree of connection* between the measure of EU law and the national measure at issue which goes beyond the matters covered being closely related or one of those matters having an indirect impact on the other'.[444] It is therefore necessary to determine 'whether the national legislation is intended to implement a provision of EU law; the nature of the legislation at issue and whether it pursues objectives other than those covered by EU law, even if it is capable of indirectly affecting EU law; and also whether there are specific rules of EU law on the matter or rules which are capable of affecting it'.[445] Expressed conversely, the Court held in *Siragusa* that 'fundamental EU rights could not be applied in relation to national legislation because the provisions of EU law in the subject area concerned did not impose any obligation on Member States with regard to the situation at issue in the main proceedings'.[446]

---

[438] See further, Verschueren (n 4, 2015a) 384 and 389–90.
[439] The Explanations (2007 OJ C303/2) refer to Case 5/88 *Wachauf*, EU:C:1989:321, Case C-260/89 *ERT*, EU:C:1991:254 and Case C-309/96 *Annibaldi*, EU:C:1997:631 on this point, suggesting an intention of continuity with the approach adopted in case law before the Charter acquired binding legal effect.
[440] Case C-617/10 *Åkerberg Fransson*, EU:C:2013:105, para 19 (emphasis added).
[441] See generally, M Dougan, 'Judicial review of Member State action under the general principles and the Charter: defining the "scope of Union law"' (2015) 52 Common Market Law Review 1201.
[442] Case C-45/12 *Hadj Ahmed*, EU:C:2013:390, para 56.
[443] Case C-418/11 *Texdata Software*, EU:C:2013:588, para 72.
[444] Case C-198/13 *Julian Hernández*, EU:C:2014:2055, para 34 (emphasis added).
[445] ibid para 37.
[446] Case C-206/13 *Siragusa*, EU:C:2014:126, para 26.

In *Dano*, the referring court had asked 'whether Articles 1 [human dignity], 20 [equality before the law] and 51 of the Charter [require] the Member States to grant Union citizens non-contributory cash benefits by way of basic provision such as to enable permanent residence or whether those States may limit their grant to the provision of funds necessary for return to the home State'.[447] The Court responded as follows:

> [Regulation 883/2004] is not intended to lay down the conditions creating the right to those benefits. It is thus for the legislature of each Member State to lay down those conditions. Accordingly, since those conditions result neither from Regulation No 883/2004 nor from Directive 2004/38 or other secondary EU legislation, and the Member States thus have competence to determine the conditions for the grant of such benefits, they also have competence ... to define the extent of the social cover provided by that type of benefit. Consequently, when the Member States lay down the conditions for the grant of special non-contributory cash benefits and the extent of such benefits, they are not implementing EU law.[448]

The Court recalled that 'the Charter, pursuant to Article 51(2) thereof, does not extend the field of application of EU law beyond the powers of the European Union or establish any new power or task for [it] or modify powers and tasks as defined in the Treaties',[449] and acknowledged that 'Article 51(1) ... states that the provisions of the Charter are addressed "to the Member States only when they are implementing Union law"'.[450] But the reasoning extracted above is based on an extremely literal conception of 'implementing' Union law in connection with national rules on special non-contributory benefits and the Court did not consider the more typical understanding applied in *Åkerberg Fransson*, that is, national legislation that 'falls within the scope of European Union law'.[451] In essence, how can national legislation that excludes certain nationals of other Member States from eligibility for social assistance *not* fall within the scope of Union law?[452]

In one of the earliest cases on social security coordination, the Commission already recognised the risk that later materialised in *Dano* through the argument that 'any legislative provision of domestic law concerning the matters dealt with by the [Social Security] Regulation automatically comes within its scope as from its entry into force' because '[t]he contrary view would be tantamount to giving Member States the power of deciding how far the Regulation should apply'.[453] In *Stewart*, before *Dano*, the Court had already confirmed that '[s]ituations falling within the material scope of EU law include those involving the *exercise* of the fundamental freedoms guaranteed by the Treaties, in particular those involving

---

[447] Case C-333/13 *Dano*, EU:C:2014:2358, para 85.
[448] ibid paras 89–91.
[449] ibid para 88; referring to *Åkerberg Fransson*, paras 17 and 23.
[450] *Dano*, para 87.
[451] *Åkerberg Fransson*, para 19. Notably, that Directive did not lay down the penalties that must be applied by Member States (Council Directive 2006/112/EC on the common system of value added tax, 2006 OJ L347/1). See also, Case C-40/11 *Iida*, EU:C:2012:691, paras 78–79; Case C-571/10 *Kamberaj*, EU:C:2012:233, paras 79–80; and *Julian Hernández*, paras 32–37.
[452] On this point, Dougan highlights the contrast between the *Dano* understanding of Regulation 883/2004 and the approach taken in *Kücükdeveci*, 'the logic of which should have led the Court to affirm the applicability of the Charter in *Dano*: regardless of whether or not the detailed conditions for extent of special non-contributory cash benefits are defined by Union law, such benefits are nevertheless certainly defined and regulated by Regulation 883/2004' (Dougan (n 441) 1225, referring to Case C-555/07 *Kücükdeveci*, EU:C:2010:21).
[453] Case 100/63 *van der Veen*, EU:C:1964:65, p 568.

the freedom to move and reside ... as conferred by Article 21 TFEU'.[454] Thus, in *Petruhhin*, after *Dano* and in circumstances where a Union citizen had exercised free movement rights, the '*decision of a Member State* to extradite [that] citizen ... comes within the scope of Article 18 TFEU and Article 21 TFEU and, therefore, of EU law for the purposes of Article 51(1) of the Charter'.[455] All of this case law highlights the oddity of the Court's reasoning in *Dano* as regards Regulation 883/2004.

Alternatively, the restriction placed on free movement rights in *Dano* could have been assessed with respect to the legislative choices expressed in Directive 2004/38 itself—assessing the conditions and limits established in the Directive against the rights protected by the Charter[456]—since the authority conferred on the EU legislator by Articles 20 and 21 TFEU to *set* conditions and limits is not the same thing as reviewing the substantive content of enacted conditions and limits for compliance with the wider system of EU law. As Advocate General Sharpston remarked in *Ruiz Zambrano*, '[i]t would be paradoxical (to say the least) if a citizen of the Union could rely on fundamental rights under EU law when exercising an economic right to free movement as a worker, or when national law comes within the scope of the Treaty (for example, the provisions on equal pay) or when invoking EU secondary legislation (such as the services directive), but could not do so when merely "residing" in that Member State'.[457] That paradox was realised in *Dano*, and the emphasis on lawful residence that *Dano* intensified was also reflected in later case law in a more general sense. For example, in *Lounes*, it was confirmed that 'there is *a link with EU law* with regard to nationals of one Member State *who are lawfully resident* in the territory of another Member State of which they are also nationals'.[458]

It is possible that engaging the Charter would not have changed the outcome in *Dano* in any significant way. For example, in other areas of EU law, the Court has ruled that the threshold for coming within the scope of Article 4 CFR, which prohibits inter alia inhuman or degrading treatment, requires a 'high level of severity ... where the indifference of the authorities of a Member State would result in a person wholly dependent on State support finding himself, irrespective of his wishes and personal choices, in a situation of extreme material poverty that does not allow him to meet his most basic needs, such as, *inter alia*, food, personal hygiene and a place to live, and that undermines his physical or mental health or puts him in a state of degradation incompatible with human dignity'.[459] As a result, '[t]hat

---

[454] Case C-503/09 *Stewart*, EU:C:2011:500, para 81 (emphasis added); citing Case C-184/99 *Grzelczyk*, EU:C:2001:458, para 33; Case C-224/98 *D'Hoop*, EU:C:2002:432, para 29; and Case C-544/07 *Rüffler*, EU:C:2009:258, para 63.

[455] Case C-182/15 *Petruhhin*, EU:C:2016:630, para 52 (emphasis added); see similarly, Case C-473/15 *Schotthöfer and Steiner*, EU:C:2017:633.

[456] Compare the Court's approach in eg Case C-300/11 *ZZ*, EU:C:2013:363, paras 49–52; this case is discussed in Chapter 10. In *Alokpa and Moudoulou*, Advocate General Mengozzi had considered 'the possibility that the provisions of the Charter ... might result in [the] conditions [in Article 7(1)(b) of Directive 2004/38] being relaxed or even disregarded, in particular with a view to ensuring that account is taken of the child's best interests (Article 24 of the Charter) and respect for family life (Articles 7 and 33 of the Charter)' (AG Mengozzi in Case C-86/12 *Alokpa and Moudoulou*, EU:C:2013:197, para 34 of the Opinion). He suggested that it was 'difficult to envisage such a possibility, since this would mean disregarding the limits laid down by Article 21 TFEU on the right of citizens of the Union to move and reside freely ... and would therefore ... result in the modification of the powers and tasks defined in the Treaties, in breach of Article 51(2) of the Charter' (ibid para 35 of the Opinion; though that position does not recognise that the Charter sets parameters for EU legislation; not the other way around).

[457] AG Sharpston in Case C-34/09 *Ruiz Zambrano*, EU:C:2010:560, para 84 of the Opinion.

[458] Case C-165/16 *Lounes*, EU:C:2017:862, paras 50–51 (emphasis added); referring to Case C-541/15 *Freitag*, EU:C:2017:432, para 34 ('a link with EU law exists in regard to nationals of one Member State lawfully resident in the territory of another').

[459] Case C-163/17 *Jawo*, EU:C:2019:218, para 92; referring to ECtHR, 21 January 2011, *MSS v Belgium and Greece*, CE:ECHR:2011:0121JUD003069609, paras 252–263. *Jawo* concerned Regulation 604/2013/EU

threshold cannot therefore cover situations characterised *even by a high degree of insecurity or a significant degradation of the living conditions* of the person concerned, where they do not entail extreme material poverty placing that person in a situation of such gravity that it may be equated with inhuman or degrading treatment'.[460] But other provisions of the Charter could have had an impact. For example, in *Kamberaj*, in the context of Directive 2003/109 on third-country nationals who are long-term residents, Article 34(3) CFR was invoked.[461] With particular resonance for *Dano*, the Court affirmed that, as required by that provision, 'the Union recognises and respects the right to social and housing assistance so as to ensure a decent existence for all those who lack sufficient resources'.[462]

It was therefore significant that the Court revisited its *Dano* position on the Charter in *CG*—without, however, referring to *Dano* itself and, overall, in a way that contains the potential impact of the Charter on responsible national authorities. In Section 3.3.5, the circumstances of CG and her children were outlined as was the fact that CG's entitlement to equal treatment with host State nationals as regards social assistance was ruled out by the Court since she did not reside in the host State under the conditions for lawful residence set out in Directive 2004/38. However, her residence was authorised in the host State under the UK's pre-settled status framework, which was developed to implement the Withdrawal Agreement. Albeit with jarring incoherence for its position on the non-application of Article 18 TFEU, discussed in Section 3.5, the Court followed its conclusions on lawful residence within the meaning of Directive 2004/38 with a critical qualifier absent from *Dano*: '[t]hat said, ... a Union citizen who, like CG, has moved to another Member State, has made use of his or her fundamental freedom to move and to reside within the territory of the Member States, conferred by Article 21(1) TFEU, with the result that his or her situation falls within the scope of EU law, *including where his or her right of residence derives from national law*'.[463] Furthermore, 'according to settled case-law, the fundamental rights guaranteed in the legal order of the European Union are applicable *in all situations governed by EU law*'.[464] The Court emphasised that authorising a right to reside under national law where the conditions in Directive 2004/38 were not met did *not* constitute implementation of that Directive.[465] Nevertheless, through the granting of that right, the national authorities of the host State '*implement the provisions of the FEU Treaty on Union citizenship*, which ... is destined to be

---

establishing the criteria and mechanisms for determining the Member State responsible for examining an application for international protection lodged in one of the Member States by a third-country national or a stateless person, 2013 OJ L180/31 ('Dublin III Regulation').

[460] *Jawo*, para 93 (emphasis added). But see further, fn 37 of the Opinion of AG Wathelet (EU:C:2018:613), where it is clearer that the threshold for breach of Article 3 ECHR was crossed in *MSS v Belgium* (ibid), considering, inter alia, 'prolonged uncertainty' and the inaction of the competent national authorities.

[461] Case C-571/10 *Kamberaj*, EU:C:2012:233, esp para 80: 'when determining the social security, social assistance and social protection measures defined by their national law and subject to the principle of equal treatment enshrined in Article 11(1)(d) of Directive 2003/109, the Member States must comply with the rights and observe the principles provided for under the Charter, including those laid down in Article 34 thereof. Under Article 34(3) of the Charter, in order to combat social exclusion and poverty, the Union (and thus the Member States when they are implementing European Union law) "recognises and respects the right to social and housing assistance so as to ensure a decent existence for all those who lack sufficient resources, in accordance with the rules laid down by European Union law and national laws and practices"'.

[462] ibid para 92. In full, Article 34(3) CFR provides that '[i]n order to combat social exclusion and poverty, the Union recognises and respects the right to social and housing assistance so as to ensure a decent existence for all those who lack sufficient resources, in accordance with the rules laid down by Union law and national laws and practices'.

[463] Case C-709/20 *CG*, EU:C:2021:602, para 84 (emphasis added).

[464] ibid para 86 (emphasis added).

[465] ibid para 87.

the fundamental status of nationals of the Member States, and [they] are accordingly obliged to comply with the provisions of the Charter'.[466]

Leaving to the side the difficulty of reconciling that reasoning with both the findings in *Dano* vis-à-vis the Charter and the findings on Article 18 TFEU in *CG* itself,[467] recognition that the Charter can apply in circumstances where a citizen's residence in the host State is unlawful per EU law but lawful per national law is a significant and positive step. With respect to substantive protection, the Court focused on Article 1 CFR, obliging the host State, in that light, 'to ensure that a Union citizen who has made use of his or her freedom to move and to reside within the territory of the Member States, who has a right of residence on the basis of national law, *and who is in a vulnerable situation*, may nevertheless live *in dignified conditions*'.[468] The fact that CG had children also engaged Articles 7 and 24(2) CFR, entailing that the host State 'is required to permit children, who are particularly vulnerable, to stay in dignified conditions with the parent or parents responsible for them'.[469] The final part of the guidance issued to the referring court was largely directed at the specific facts of *CG* itself:

> In the present case, it is apparent from the order for reference that CG is a mother of two young children, with no resources to provide for her own and her children's needs, who is isolated on account of having fled a violent partner. In such a situation, the competent national authorities may refuse an application for social assistance, such as Universal Credit, only after ascertaining that that refusal does not expose the citizen concerned and the children for which he or she is responsible to an actual and current risk of violation of their fundamental rights, as enshrined in Articles 1, 7 and 24 of the Charter. In the context of that examination, those authorities may take into account all means of assistance provided for by national law, from which the citizen concerned and his or her children may actually and currently benefit. In the dispute in the main proceedings, it will be for the referring court, in particular, to ascertain whether CG and her children may benefit actually and currently from the assistance, other than Universal Credit, referred to by the representatives of the United Kingdom Government and the Department for Communities in Northern Ireland in their observations submitted to the Court.[470]

The reference to domestic violence mirrors the recalibration of case law on Article 13(2) of the Directive in *X v Belgian State*.[471] What must still be determined in future cases is how far the Charter's protection extends, first, in a substantive sense: both on the facts of *CG* and because of the Court's focus on Article 1 CFR rather than on some of the more general social protections in other provisions of the Charter, there are strong signals that the impact of the ruling is intended to be relatively limited. The reference to 'tak[ing] into account all means of assistance provided for by national law' could, for example, suggest that support

---

[466] ibid para 88 (emphasis added).
[467] Constituting, for Haag, 'a striking discrepancy in the logic of the Court regarding the right to equal treatment and the applicability of the Charter. It reads almost as if two separate courts had written the two contradictory sections' (M Haag, 'The *coup de grâce* to the Union citizen's right to equal treatment: *CG v The Department for Communities in Northern Ireland*' (2022) 59 Common Market Law Review 1081 at 1101).
[468] *CG*, para 89 (emphasis added).
[469] ibid para 91.
[470] ibid para 92. Thus O'Brien asks: [c]an national authorities refuse benefits to EU nationals, even those with a right to reside, without considering fundamental rights, if there is no evidence of domestic abuse? Or if they are not similarly isolated? Or do not have young children? Or have some meagre resources? Should other vulnerabilities be taken into account—long term illnesses, or being disabled, for instance?' (n 4 (2021) 812).
[471] Case C-930/19 *X v Belgian State*, EU:C:2021:657. See further, Chapter 6.

more limited than the general social assistance scheme of the host State would suffice to meet Charter obligations under Article 1 CFR.[472] Second, a more structural limitation concerns the triggering of the Charter in *CG* through the granting of pre-settled status—that is, residence authorised by national law—in the first place. Other Member State nationals who are refused social assistance in the host State could be equally vulnerable; but unless the Court revisits its conspicuously narrow approach to Regulation 883/2004 in *Dano* or extends the logic of Article 20 TFEU case law to Article 21 TFEU case law, bringing a national decision establishing *unlawful* residence within the scope of EU law per se,[473] it is a sphere of vulnerability that EU citizenship law accepts.[474]

5. Concluding Remarks

Advocate General Poiares Maduro wrote in *Huber* that '[w]hen the Court describes Union citizenship as the "fundamental status" of nationals it is not making a political statement; it refers to Union citizenship as a *legal* concept which goes hand in hand with specific rights for Union citizens'.[475] In Chapter 2, it was suggested that there is a risk of over-investing in the potential of this 'fundamental status' as a legal concept. However, let us go back to its roots in EU citizenship law—which established that 'Union citizenship is destined to be the fundamental status of nationals of the Member States, enabling those who find themselves in the same situation to enjoy the same treatment in law irrespective of their nationality, subject to such exceptions as are expressly provided for'.[476] In this chapter, the commitment of the EU

---

[472] As Haag observed, '[t]he Court omitted Article 21(2) CFREU which also provides for the right to non-discrimination on the basis of nationality. It also did not refer to Article 34(2) CFREU on the entitlement to social security benefits and social advantages. This suggests that the protection of fundamental rights in this context is not about equal access to social assistance as compared to the nationals of the State, but rather it is about ensuring that the Union citizen is granted basic subsistence to uphold their human dignity' (n 467, 1102). The Court's ruling thus has resonance with the very limited assistance approved in a UK Supreme Court case concerning rights based on Article 20 TFEU that was never referred to the Court of Justice: discussing *HC v SSWP* [2017] UKSC 73, see C O'Brien, '*Acte cryptique?* Zambrano, welfare rights, and underclass citizenship in the tale of the missing preliminary reference' (2019) 56 Common Market Law Review 1697. In the national proceedings, it was concluded that *Ruiz Zambrano* 'only requires whatever is sufficient to prevent a *de facto* expulsion, and that the possibility of applying for some basic, last resort, discretionary provision was sufficient for that' (ibid 1699). Albeit though a different portal to the Charter (see Section 3.5), Advocate General Richard de la Tour nevertheless signalled more substantively that 'CG's situation calls for an analysis of the question of the restriction of access to social allowances in the light of the Court's decisions relating to fundamental rights other than the right to equal treatment, which goes beyond a general observation that subsistence benefits are intended to ensure that their recipients have the minimum means of subsistence necessary to lead a life in keeping with human dignity' (AG Richard de la Tour in *CG*, EU:C:2021:515, para 103 of the Opinion).

[473] See esp Case C-133/15 *Chavez-Vilchez*, EU:C:2017:354, discussed in Chapter 5. Although he enabled review through different reasoning (see Section 3.5), AG Richard de la Tour referred to *Chavez-Vilchez* and argued that 'the application of those principles seems to me to be capable of being transposed a fortiori, in matters relating to social assistance, especially where they serve to ensure a normal family life for Union citizens. It is then a matter of allowing the isolated and impoverished parent to meet his or her obligations towards his or her minor children, both for their health and security and in their relationship with their other parent, a Union citizen. As I see it, those principles provide ample justification for an individual examination of the situation of the Union citizen, an applicant for social assistance, who is lawfully resident in the host Member State' (AG Richard de la Tour in *CG*, para 10 of the Opinion).

[474] A situation that recalls the discussion on responsibility and even 'complicity' in Section 4.1, as captured by O'Brien in one critical question: '[w]hy are Member States that permit EU migrants to reside in their territories without sufficient resources, without granting access to social assistance, not also in effect recognising those migrants' art.21 TFEU rights?' (n 4 (2021) 812).

[475] AG Poiares Maduro in Case C-524/06 *Huber*, EU:C:2008:194, para 19 of the Opinion (emphasis in original).

[476] Case C-184/99 *Grzelczyk*, EU:C:2001:458, para 31.

legislator and Court of Justice to that understanding of the fundamental status of Union citizenship has been mapped; and also tested.

As emphasised throughout the chapter, lawful residence has always been a precondition for equal treatment in EU citizenship law. Tracing the evolution of the case law both before and after the adoption of Directive 2004/38, a *coherent* framework has now, for the most part, acquired shape over time. But not without cost, as the Directive has also instituted a more *bounded* framework. First, how lawful residence is determined has changed over time, most significantly for residence that is authorised by a host State but does not comply with the conditions in the Directive (and especially with Article 7 of the Directive).

Second, the role of proportionality has changed too: it remains relevant with respect to determining lawful residence in the first place and with respect to whether, if lawful residence is established, the benefit applied for should be granted. But the purpose, intensity, and scope of proportionality review have changed. On the first point, it is no longer clear that proportionality would be invoked to override the fulfilment of sufficient resources or comprehensive sickness insurance conditions, as seen most clearly in *Baumbast*. On the second point, compare the one-line references to assessment of individual circumstances in *Dano*[477] and *CG*[478] with the extensive guidance in *Brey*.[479] On the third point, note the legitimacy of exclusion by group from an assessment of individual circumstances for derogations prescribed in EU legislation (*Alimanovic*; *García-Nieto*). A conclusion reached in Chapter 6 was therefore affirmed: that the Directive is a single text, but it does not institute a single status; even though that conclusion might grate against the 'fundamental status' idea in some respects.[480]

A more logically *presented* residence system would already help. The complicated cross-referencing across multiple provisions of the Directive that is needed to comprehend fully the legislative understanding of (un)lawful residence is not helpful, cutting across parts of, *inter alia*, Articles 6, 7, 8, 14, 15, 30, and 31. There is also work to be done to capture legislatively the significant jurisprudence that has followed the adoption of the Directive. And all of us need to reflect on what *freedom* of movement really means, in both functional and wider senses.[481] At the same time, opening the Directive to a process of recasting entails significant risk because it could aggravate rather than relieve some of the residence insecurity concerns flagged at various points across the chapter.

The Court of Justice's judicial methodology has come under particular scrutiny in this area of EU citizenship law.[482] Case law necessarily evolves, but it is better to confront different positions taken previously than to disregard them. In EU free movement law generally, the Court has expressly departed from its own previous case law in two ways. First, as seen in *Collins* and *Bidar* in Section 2,[483] the institution of Union citizenship itself required rethinking of certain restrictions on freedom of movement and equal treatment. Second,

---

[477] Case C-333/13 *Dano*, EU:C:2014:2358, para 80.
[478] Case C-709/20 *CG*, EU:C:2021:602, para 79
[479] Case C-140/12 *Brey*, EU:C:2013:565, esp paras 64ff.
[480] See eg Thym's discussion on fundamental status as 'an overarching idea supporting *status convergence* by way of interpretative or legislative approximation of the diverse legal rules for the different categories of Union citizens' (n 4 (2015a) 18, emphasis added).
[481] See generally, S Barbou des Places, 'Is free movement (law) fully emancipated from migration (law)?' in N Nic Shuibhne (ed), *Revisiting the Fundamentals of EU Law on the Free Movement of Persons* (OUP 2023) forthcoming.
[482] The key issues are thoughtfully summarised in E Spaventa, 'Family rights for circular migrants and frontier workers: *O and B*, and *S and G*' (2015) 52 Common Market Law Review 753 at 777.
[483] And eg Case C-127/08 *Metock and Others*, EU:C:2008:449 in Chapter 4.

and better reflecting the case law changes traced in this chapter, the Court has only rarely admitted to policy-driven more than law-driven reassessments: as happened in *Keck and Mithouard*, for example, in narrowing the scope of measures having equivalent effect to quantitative restrictions on the free movement of goods under Article 34 TFEU because of 'the increasing tendency of traders to invoke Article [34] of the Treaty as a means of challenging any rules whose effect it is to limit their commercial freedom'.[484]

Explaining the adjusted trajectory of EU citizenship case law 'in light of the increasing tendency of citizens to move' is not going to happen but, as a statement, it exemplifies the contradiction of conferring *freedom* of movement on a *conditional* basis. Lawful residence as a starting point for equal treatment claims makes sense overall. It does not follow, though, that responsibility for supporting citizens in situations produced by free movement can be set aside when residence is unlawful or not the 'right kind' of lawful. Working through those consequences involves balancing the responsibility of home States, host States, the Union's institutions, and Union citizens themselves: as Advocate General Geelhoed so well expressed it, there is 'an inter-State dimension to the problem to which [Union] law has attached certain consequences'.[485] At a minimum, the equal treatment, permanent residence, and enhanced protection from expulsion consequences of residence that is lawful under EU law even if not under Directive 2004/38 should be reconsidered. The authorisation of lawful residence by Member States should also be better recognised, reflecting their role as the co-creators of free movement, fostering a shared sense of responsibility for it, and, as Article 4(3) TEU requires, 'facilitat[ing] the achievement of the Union's tasks and refrain from any measure which could jeopardise the attainment of the Union's objectives'.

Further Reading

C Jacqueson and F Pennings, 'Equal treatment of mobile persons in the context of a social market economy' (2019) 15 Utrecht Law Review 64.

P Neuvonen, *Equal Citizenship and its Limits in EU Law: We the Burden?* (Hart Publishing, 2016).

C O'Brien, 'Real links, abstract rights and false alarms: the relationship between the ECJ's "real link" case law and national solidarity' (2008) 33 European Law Review 643.

C O'Brien, *Unity in Adversity: EU Citizenship, Social Justice and the Cautionary Tale of the UK* (Hart Publishing, 2017).

S Seubert, 'Shifting boundaries of membership? The politicisation of free movement as a challenge for EU citizenship' (2019) 26 European Law Journal 48.

M van den Brink, 'Justice, legitimacy, and the authority of legislation in the European Union' 83 Modern Law Review 293.

AP Van der Mei, 'Residence and the evolving notion of European Union citizenship: comments on *Baumbast and R v. Secretary of State for Home Department*, 17 September 2002 (Case C-413/99)' (2003) 5 European Journal of Migration and Law 419.

H Verschueren (ed), *Residence, Employment and Social Rights of Mobile Persons: On How EU Law Defines Where They Belong* (Intersentia, 2016).

F de Witte, *Justice in the EU: The Emergence of Transnational Solidarity* (OUP, 2015).

---

[484] Joined Cases C-267/91 and C-268/91 *Keck and Mithouard*, EU:C:1993:905, para 13.
[485] AG Geelhoed in Case C-224/98 *D'Hoop*, EU:C:2002:103, para 38 of the Opinion.

8
Union Citizenship and the Host State
Part III: The Right of Permanent Residence

1. Chapter Overview

This chapter addresses eligibility for and the implications of the right of permanent residence in the host State, as provided for in Directive 2004/38 and extended in certain circumstances on the basis of the Treaty directly.[1]

In its original proposal for the Directive, the Commission characterised permanent residence as 'a new right introduced as a corollary of the fundamental personal right conferred by the Treaty on every citizen of the Union'.[2] As emphasised in Chapters 6 and 7, Directive 2004/38 'introduced a gradual system as regards the right of residence in the host Member State, which reproduces, in essence, the stages and conditions set out in the various instruments of European Union law and case-law preceding that directive and *culminates in* the right of permanent residence'.[3] Recital 17 of the Directive expresses both the purpose and objectives of permanent residence: '[e]njoyment of permanent residence by Union citizens who have chosen to settle long term in the host Member State would strengthen the feeling of Union citizenship and is a key element in promoting social cohesion, which is one of the fundamental objectives of the Union'.[4]

Permanent residence rights are thus, at one level, exemplary of Union citizenship generally and of the significance of the Directive in determining the implications of that status more specifically. However, permanent residence rights are also conferred on EEA nationals since Directive 2004/38 is a text with EEA relevance. The Directive was incorporated into EEA law by Decision 158/2007 of the EEA Joint Committee, with recital 8 of which underlining that '[t]he concept of "Union Citizenship" is not included in the Agreement'.[5] A Joint Declaration attached to that Decision established an express exclusion in that light by stating that the EEA Agreement 'does not provide a legal basis for political rights of EEA nationals'. Yet no reservations were made with respect to substantive provisions of the Directive. In *Clauder*, the EFTA Court therefore confirmed that 'Directive 2004/38 provides for three levels of residence rights *for EEA nationals*: first, in Article 6, the right of residence for up to three months; second, in Article 7, the right of residence for more than three months, which applies to workers, economically self-supporting persons or other persons to be assimilated to them; third, in Article 16(1), the right of permanent residence'.[6] Thus, while permanent

---

[1] Case C-247/20 *VI*, EU:C:2022:177, paras 58–59; see further, Section 3.1. Directive 2004/38/EC on the right of citizens of the Union and their family members to move and reside freely within the territory of the Member States, 2004 OJ L158/77.

[2] Proposal for a Directive of the European Parliament and of the Council on the right of citizens of the Union and their family members to move and reside freely within the territory of the Member States, COM(2001) 257 final, para 2.2.

[3] Joined Cases C-316/16 and C-424/16 *B and Vomero*, EU:C:2018:256, para 51 (emphasis added).

[4] Referred to in eg Case C-162/09 *Lassal*, EU:C:2010:592, para 32.

[5] Decision of the EEA Joint Committee No 158/2007 of 7 December 2007 amending Annex V (Free movement of workers) and Annex VIII (Right of establishment) to the EEA Agreement, 2008 OJ L124/20.

[6] Case E-4/11 *Clauder*, [2011] EFTA Ct. Rep. 216, para 40 (emphasis added).

residence is archetypal of Union citizenship as a *status*, on the one hand, its essential purpose is to effect a deeper level or degree of residence security in the wider free movement universe, on the other. The fact that the Withdrawal Agreement between the EU and the United Kingdom facilitates permanent residence based partly on periods of residence completed *after* Brexit underscores this point.[7]

In this chapter, the conception of permanent residence rights that emerged through the process of adopting Directive 2004/38 is first outlined (Section 2). The legal framework that governs their application is then presented (Section 3). The main features of permanent residence are outlined in Articles 16 and 17 of the Directive. It is achieved, according to recital 17, by 'all Union citizens and their family members who have resided in the host Member State *in compliance with the conditions laid down in this Directive* during a *continuous period of five years* without becoming subject to an expulsion measure'. Alongside 'continuous' residence for a period of five years, the other key condition in the Directive is that such residence must be 'legal'. Recital 18 confirms that 'the right of permanent residence, once obtained, should not be subject to any conditions' so that it might constitute 'a genuine vehicle for integration into the society of the host Member State'. Thus, acquiring permanent residence under EU law transforms the right to reside in a host State into an unconditional right, preservable over extended absences and entailing only limited administrative formalities. Additionally, it will be seen in Chapter 10 that permanent residence also enables enhanced protection against expulsion from the host State.

The right of permanent residence therefore 'confers an incomparable advantage' on Union citizens 'by ensuring that their presence is of indefinite duration, with immunity from expulsion except on serious grounds of public policy or public security, and abolishing the existing restrictions on the principle of equal treatment with nationals of the host Member State'.[8] Nevertheless, while permanent residence was conceived to progress the rights conferred by Union citizenship, relevant case law has also determined its limits. In Chapter 7, the emphasis on complying with the conditions of Directive 2004/38 to demonstrate 'legal' residence in a host State that was first developed in permanent residence case law was shown to have spread outwards to lawful residence questions more generally. In this chapter, the nature and extent of integration in the host State to which the permanent residence narrative contributes more widely are further considered.

---

[7] See further, Article 15(1) WA: 'Union citizens and United Kingdom nationals, and their respective family members, who have resided legally in the host State in accordance with Union law for a continuous period of 5 years or for the period specified in Article 17 of Directive 2004/38/EC, shall have the right to reside permanently in the host State under the conditions set out in Articles 16, 17 and 18 of Directive 2004/38/EC. Periods of legal residence or work in accordance with Union law before and after the end of the transition period shall be included in the calculation of the qualifying period necessary for acquisition of the right of permanent residence' (Agreement on the withdrawal of the United Kingdom of Great Britain and Northern Ireland from the European Union and the European Atomic Energy Community, OJ 2019 CI 384/01). In that light, however, Article 18(1)(h) sharply transgresses residence security: 'persons who, before the end of the transition period, hold a valid permanent residence document issued under Article 19 or 20 of Directive 2004/38/EC or hold a valid domestic immigration document conferring a permanent right to reside in the host State, shall have the right to exchange that document within the period referred to in point (b) of this paragraph for a new residence document upon application after a verification of their identity, *a criminality and security check* in accordance with point (p) of this paragraph and confirmation of their ongoing residence; such new residence documents shall be issued free of charge'. Article 18(1)(p) outlines the process for carrying out criminality and security checks, with the Commission conceding that 'systematic checks have been accepted in the Agreement, given its unique context' (European Commission, Guidance Note relating to the Agreement on the withdrawal of the United Kingdom of Great Britain and Northern Ireland from the European Union and the European Atomic Energy Community Part two—Citizens' rights, C(2020) 2939 final, para 2.6.12).

[8] AG Bot in Case C-529/11 *Alarape and Tijani*, EU:C:2013:9, para 4 of the Opinion.

2. Conceiving a Right of Permanent Residence: Directive 2004/38

Chapter IV of Directive 2004/38 addresses the right of permanent residence. Article 16 outlines the conditions for acquiring and retaining a right of permanent residence in a host State. It provides:

Article 16

Right of permanent residence

1. Union citizens who have resided legally for a continuous period of five years in the host Member State shall have the right of permanent residence there. This right shall not be subject to the conditions provided for in Chapter III.
2. Paragraph 1 shall apply also to family members who are not nationals of a Member State and have legally resided with the Union citizen in the host Member State for a continuous period of five years.
3. Continuity of residence shall not be affected by temporary absences not exceeding a total of six months a year, or by absences of a longer duration for compulsory military service, or by one absence of a maximum of twelve consecutive months for important reasons such as pregnancy and childbirth, serious illness, study or vocational training, or a posting in another Member State or a third country.

Article 17 then establishes a series of exemptions '[b]y way of derogation from Article 16' under which a right of permanent residence can be acquired '*before* completion of a continuous period of five years of residence'—these specific situations are returned to in Section 3.1.

A right to reside of permanent character had not been provided for in the 1990s Residence Directives,[9] but it was included in the Commission's original proposal for Directive 2004/38. Even though the proposed right of permanent residence had far-reaching implications for equal treatment with host State nationals, it attracted relatively little comment in the drafting process for Directive 2004/38 beyond being broadly 'welcomed'.[10] As indicated in Section 1 of this chapter, the Commission considered that the right of permanent residence was 'a new right introduced as a corollary of the fundamental personal right conferred by the Treaty on every citizen of the Union'.[11] But the *idea* of permanent residence was not new. As noted in Chapter 2, a right of 'permanent' residence had already formed the basis of a 1979 proposal for general free movement rights.[12] However, in contrast to the earlier conception of

---

[9] Directive 90/364/EEC on the right of residence, 1990 OJ L180/26; Directive 90/365/EEC on the right of residence for employees and self-employed persons who have ceased their occupational activity, 1990 OJ L180/28; and Directive 93/96/EEC on the right of residence for students, 1993 OJ L317/59.

[10] eg The European Parliament's Committee on Petitions 'welcomes this proposal, in particular regarding greater freedom of movement through the introduction of permanent right of residence after four years of continuous residence in the host Member State. This measure will help to overcome numerous difficulties now being encountered by Union citizens and their family members in this respect as evidenced by petitions to Parliament' (A5–0009/2003, 98).

[11] Original proposal (n 2) para 2.2.

[12] Proposal for a Council Directive on a right of residence for nationals of Member States in the territory of another Member State, 1979 OJ C207/14. One of the draft recitals characterised the free movement of persons as 'one

conditional permanent residence rights for 'citizens of another Member State ... who reside *or wish to reside* in their territory' (draft Article 4(1) of the 1979 proposal), the reworked idea of a right of permanent residence conferred by Union citizenship was that it would be acquired over time and was therefore conceptually as well as functionally linked to the extent of the Union citizen's integration in a host State.

Reflecting the importance of residence security, the Commission linked the proposed right of permanent residence to the fact that '[t]he scope of the right to remain is extremely narrow in current [Union] law and subject to restrictive conditions' and drew support for a deeper right to remain under EU law from the fact that '[i]n several Member States the law already provides for indefinite leave to remain after a certain period of residence regardless of nationality'.[13] It therefore envisaged that Union citizens with a right of permanent residence would 'no longer be subject to any conditions on the exercise of or restrictions on their right of residence, with virtually complete equality of treatment with nationals'.[14] In a controversial extension of that idea, however, the Commission further intended that Union citizens with permanent residence rights should enjoy absolute protection—in effect, immunity—from expulsion from the host State.[15] Perhaps unsurprisingly, it later conceded that while the Member States were 'almost unanimously opposed to absolute protection against expulsion', they did at least agree to 'increased protection' for citizens with a right of permanent residence, as considered further in Chapter 10.[16]

The Commission originally proposed that permanent residence rights would be acquired in the host State after four years of legal residence there. In its view, '[a]fter a sufficiently long period of residence, it may be assumed that the Union citizen has *developed close links* with the host Member State and *become an integral part of its society*, which justifies granting what may be termed an *upgraded right of residence*. Furthermore, the integration of Union citizens settled long-term in a Member State is a key element in promoting social cohesion, a fundamental objective of the Union'.[17] However, the Council changed the required period from four to five years. In its common position, it suggested that '[t]his change has made possible the inclusion of students within the beneficiaries of the right of permanent residence'.[18] The Commission's subsequent Communication makes it clearer that the choice was political rather than legal through the observation that it accepted the change 'because the addition of

---

of the foundations of the Community', which 'can be fully attained only if a right of permanent residence is granted to those Community nationals in whom such right does not already vest under the Community law in force, and to the members of their family'. Draft Article 4 proposed a right of permanent residence for 'citizens of another Member State ... who reside or wish to reside in their territory' and for their family members, subject to the fact that 'the Member States may require those citizens to provide proof of sufficient resources to provide for their own needs and the dependent members of their family' (Article 4(2)).

[13] Original proposal (n 2) 15; the Commission referred to Regulation 1251/70/EEC on the right of workers to remain in the territory of a Member State after having been employed in that State, 1970 OJ L142/24 and Directive 75/34/EEC concerning the right of nationals of a Member State to remain in the territory of another Member State after having pursued therein an activity in a self-employed capacity, 1975 OJ L14/10. See further, Section 3.1.
[14] Original proposal (n 2) para 2.2.
[15] ibid draft Article 26(2): '[a] host Member State may not take an expulsion decision on grounds of public policy or public security against EU citizens or their family members, irrespective of nationality, who have the right of permanent residence on its territory or against family members who are minors'.
[16] Communication to the European Parliament on the common position adopted by the Council on the draft directive, SEC/2003/1293 final, para 3.3.2.
[17] Original proposal (n 2) 16 (emphasis added).
[18] Common Position (EC) No 6/2004 of 5 December 2003, 2004 OJ C54 E/12, 31.

this extra year has overcome the reluctance of some Member States as regards the inclusion of students among those entitled to a right of permanent residence'.[19]

As returned to in Section 3.1, Article 16(4) of the Directive provides that '[o]nce acquired, the right of permanent residence shall be lost only through absence from the host Member State for a period exceeding two consecutive years'. The Commission had proposed a period of four years since '[t]he right of permanent residence acknowledges the integration of the Union citizen and his family members into the host Member State. Absences of more than four years would suggest a kind of "disintegration" '.[20] The European Parliament's Committee on Culture, Youth, Education, the Media and Sport proposed the deletion of this limit completely, on the basis that 'apart from the difficulty of policing it, it does not encourage mobility, and fails to take account of the tendency of citizens who are already accustomed to mobility to organise their own lives freely within Europe'.[21] Once again, however, the longer period—more advantageous to Union citizens—was reduced by the Council on the basis that 'after a two-year absence the link with the host Member State could be considered as *loosened*',[22] language explicitly referred to in due course by the Court.[23] The Commission accepted this change 'because, after two years of absence, it may be considered that the strong link with the host Member State, which justifies the entitlement to the right of permanent residence has been *broken*'.[24]

The language used in these statements is highlighted here as it reveals the fundamental concern at the heart of these conditions: an effort somehow to measure or quantify how integrated a Union citizen has become in the host State so that the additional protections and privileges of permanent residence are appropriately 'earned'.[25] In that sense, the conditions for permanent residence rights might be seen to represent a *presumed* as distinct from a *demonstrable* link in EU free movement law. To explain the distinction, the fact that economic activity constitutes, in principle, a sufficient link with a host State to be treated equally with host State nationals for the purposes of social and tax advantages is an example of the former,[26] while permitting national authorities to assess a jobseeker's degree of connection to the host State employment market before confirming eligibility for financial benefits intended to facilitate access to that employment market is an example of the latter.[27] Permanent residence rights actually entail both: completing a five-year period of residence in the host State would seem to suggest that a sufficient degree of integration there has been realised, representing a presumed link. However, more qualitative measures of integration are applied in order to demonstrate continuous and legal residence in a host State in practice, as returned to in Section 3.2.

---

[19] Communication on the common position (n 16) para 3.3.2. Moreover, the Commission's proposed wording for what is now Article 24(2) of the Directive had always referred to 'acquir[ing] the right of permanent residence' rather than to a specific period of time for the granting of maintenance aid for studies.
[20] Original proposal (n 2) 16.
[21] European Parliament Report (n 10) Amendment 12. See similarly, Amendment 15, proposing the removal of conditions on interruption of residence in what is now Article 20; and Amendment 16, proposing the removal of time-limits on absences for specific purposes in what is now Article 16(3) on the same rationale.
[22] Common Position (n 18) 31 (emphasis added). See similarly, the change from one year to two years in Article 17(4) of the Directive (discussed in Section 3.1) on the basis that '[t]his change again guarantees a strong link with the host Member State' (ibid 31).
[23] Case C-162/09 *Lassal*, EU:C:2010:592, para 55; confirmed in Case C-325/09 *Dias*, EU:C:2011:498, para 59.
[24] Communication to the European Parliament on the common position adopted by the Council on the draft directive, SEC/2003/1293 final, para 3.3.2 (emphasis added).
[25] E Spaventa, 'Earned citizenship – understanding Union citizenship through its scope' in D Kochenov (ed), *EU Citizenship and Federalism: The Role of Rights* (CUP 2017) 204.
[26] Case C-542/09 *Commission v Netherlands*, EU:C:2012:346, para 65; see further, Chapter 7.
[27] Case C-138/02 *Collins*, EU:C:2004:172 para 70; see further, Chapter 7.

3. Permanent Residence: The Legal Framework

The legal framework that governs the right of permanent residence has three main parts: conditions of eligibility (Section 3.1), the requirements of legal and continuous residence in a host State (Section 3.2), and administrative formalities (Section 3.3).

3.1 Who is Eligible and in What Circumstances?

The right of permanent residence is acquired by 'Union citizens who have resided *legally* for a *continuous* period of five years in the host State' (Article 16(1) of Directive 2004/38). Union citizens who acquire that right are no longer 'subject to the conditions provided for in Chapter III' of the Directive (Article 16(1)).[28] In *Lassal*, Advocate General Trstenjak explained the right of permanent residence in this way:

> [A]fter five years the integration goal takes precedence over the financial reservations of the Member States and therefore the right of residence is no longer subject to the conditions provided for in Chapter III of the directive. Following [that] period of residence ... in the host Member State, a Union citizen is settled there to such an extent that he should be allowed to integrate in the society of that Member State in the sense of a burden-sharing community.[29]

In *Wolzenburg*, the Court accepted the proportionality of national legislation 'under which the competent judicial authority of that State is to refuse to execute a European arrest warrant issued against one of its nationals with a view to the enforcement of a custodial sentence, whilst such a refusal is, in the case of a national of another Member State having a right of residence on the basis of Article [21 TFEU], subject to the condition that that person has lawfully resided for a continuous period of five years in that Member State of execution'— illustrating the sense of *equal-ness* beyond equality of treatment with host State nationals that permanent residence seeks to reflect.[30]

---

[28] Chapter III of the Directive includes: Article 6 (right of residence for up to three months); Article 7 (right of residence for more than three months); Article 8 (administrative formalities for Union citizens); Article 9 (administrative formalities for family members who are not nationals of a Member State); Article 10 (issue of residence cards); Article 11 (validity of the residence card); Article 12 (retention of the right of residence by family members in the event of death or departure of the Union citizen); Article 13 (retention of the right of residence by family members in the event of divorce, annulment of marriage or termination of registered partnership); Article 14 (retention of the right of residence); and Article 15 (procedural safeguards). See similarly, Article 15(1) WA; and see generally, Chapter 6.

[29] AG Trstenjak in Case C-162/09 *Lassal*, EU:C:2010:266, fn33 of the Opinion; referring to A Iliopoulou, 'Le nouveau droit de séjour des citoyens de l'Union et des membres de leur famille: la directive 2004/38/CE' (2004) *Revue du Droit de l'Union Européenne* 523 at 540.

[30] Case C-123/08 *Wolzenburg*, EU:C:2009:616, para 80. However, AG Bot highlighted responsibility as an element of freedom of movement more generally: '[c]reation of the single market and Union citizenship have ... progressively required the Member States to treat the nationals of the other Member States in the same way as their own nationals in an increasingly wider sphere of economic, social and political life. They also enable every citizen to go to live or work in the Member State of his choosing within the Union, like any other national of that State. It therefore seemed an opportune moment to supplement that legal creation with equal treatment before the courts. In other words, since a Union citizen now has, in every Member State, largely the same rights as those of that State's nationals, it is fair that he should also be subject to the same obligations in criminal matters. That means that, if he commits an offence in the host Member State, he should be prosecuted and tried there before the courts of that State, in the same way as nationals of the State in question, and that he should serve his sentence there, unless its execution in his own State is likely to increase his chances of reintegration' (AG Bot in *Wolzenburg*, EU:C:2009:183, paras 141–142 of the Opinion). See similarly AG Mengozzi in Case C-42/11 *Lopes Da Silva Jorge*,

In line with the objective of integrating Union citizens in their host States, family members who are not Member State nationals may also acquire the right of permanent residence if they have 'legally resided with the Union citizen in the host Member State for a continuous period of five years' (Article 16(2)). Additionally, Article 18 of the Directive confirms that 'the family members to whom Articles 12(2) and 13(2) apply, who satisfy the conditions laid down therein, shall acquire the right of permanent residence after residing legally for a period of five consecutive years in the host Member State'. Article 16's critical conditions of *legal* and *continuous* residence are returned to Section 3.2. Here, three issues are first considered: specific requirements for family members (Section 3.1.1), the impact of absences from the host State (Section 3.1.2), and exemptions provided for in Article 17 of the Directive, which determine the conditions under which the right of permanent residence may be acquired *before* the five-year period of residence in Article 16(1) has been completed (Section 3.1.3).

3.1.1 Family members

Article 3(1) of Directive 2004/38 establishes that it 'shall apply to all Union citizens who move to or reside in a Member State other than that of which they are a national, and to their family members as defined in point 2 of Article 2 who accompany or join them'. As seen in Chapter 6, Article 7(1)(d) provides residence rights for Union citizens who are 'family members accompanying *or joining* a Union citizen who satisfies the conditions referred to in points (a), (b) or (c)'. Article 7(2) then establishes that '[t]he right of residence provided for in paragraph 1 shall extend to family members who are not nationals of a Member State, accompanying or joining the Union citizen in the host Member State, provided that such Union citizen satisfies the conditions referred to in paragraph 1(a), (b) or (c)' However, there are no comparable provisions in Chapter IV of the Directive. In other words, Directive 2004/38 deals expressly with the conferral of a right of permanent residence on family members but it does not address whether a Union citizen who *already* has that right in a host State may generate residence rights for family members who only join them there afterwards.

The question of residence rights for 'new' family members of a Union citizen who is a permanent resident has not yet arisen before the Court of Justice but a comparable question was considered by the EFTA Court in *Clauder*, a case in which the Commission and the Netherlands Government submitted written observations while the Commission and the Danish Government submitted arguments at the oral hearing. Mr Clauder was a German national who received a permanent residence permit in Liechtenstein in 2002. He and his wife divorced in 2009, and he remarried in 2010. His application for a family reunification permit for his second wife, also a German national, was rejected on the grounds that he could not demonstrate that he had sufficient financial resources for himself and his wife without having recourse to the host State social welfare system: Mr Clauder received old-age pensions from both Germany and Liechtenstein, but also received supplementary benefits in Liechtenstein. The order for reference indicated that 'if Mrs Clauder were allowed to reside with her husband in Liechtenstein, the amount of the supplementary benefits received by Mr Clauder would increase, even if Mrs Clauder were to take up employment'.[31] The key question before the EFTA Court was thus whether 'Directive 2004/38/EC, in particular Article

---

EU:C:2012:151, paras 50–51 of the Opinion; and AG Bot in Case C-247/17 *Raugevicius*, EU:C:2018:616, paras 62–72 of the Opinion.

[31] Case E-4/11 *Clauder*, [2011] EFTA Ct. Rep. 216, para 15.

16(1) in conjunction with Article 7(1), [is] to be interpreted such that a Union citizen with a right of permanent residence, who is a pensioner and in receipt of social welfare benefits in the host Member State, may claim the right to family reunification even if the family member will also be claiming social welfare benefits'.[32]

The complainant, the EFTA Surveillance Authority, and the Commission acknowledged that 'Article 16 of the Directive does not contain any express provision regarding the acquisition of a right of residence for a family member seeking to join an EEA national who has already acquired a right of permanent residence when the family member himself does not fulfil the requirements for permanent residence'.[33] However, they argued that since the right of permanent residence 'represents the highest level of integration in the host State, it is inconceivable that the legislature did not intend to confer derived rights on family members'.[34] In essence, the EFTA Court agreed, recalling that, '[h]aving regard to the context and objectives of Directive 2004/38 – promoting the right of nationals of [EU] Member States and EFTA States and their family members to move and reside freely within the territory of the EEA States – the provisions of that directive cannot be interpreted restrictively, and must not in any event be deprived of their effectiveness'.[35] The EFTA Court also noted that 'in contrast to Article 1 of Directives 90/364/EEC and Directive 90/365/EEC, Directive 2004/38 *does not contain a general requirement of sufficient resources*. Such a requirement exists neither with regard to workers and self-employed persons nor with regard to persons who have acquired a permanent right of residence pursuant to the Directive. Moreover, in comparison to the position under earlier legislation, the Directive has expanded the rights of family members also on several other points'.[36]

The EFTA Court held, first, that 'although not explicitly stated in the wording of the provision, the right to permanent residence under Article 16(1) ... must confer a derived right of residence in the host State on the holder's family members' since '[i]t follows from the scheme and purpose of the Directive that the right to permanent residence, which represents the highest level of integration under the Directive, cannot be read as not including the right to live with one's family, or be limited such as to confer on family members a right of residence derived from a different, lower status'.[37] Second, if an EEA national holding the right of permanent residence in an EEA State other than that of which they are a national 'were precluded from founding a family in that State, this would impair the right of EEA nationals to move and reside freely within the EEA, and thus be contrary to the purpose of the Directive and deprive it of its full effectiveness ... This conclusion cannot be different even if the family member becomes a burden on the social assistance system of the host EEA State'.[38] The EFTA Court therefore considered that '[s]ince the retention of a right to permanent residence under Article 16 of the Directive is not subject to the conditions in Chapter III and it is apparent that the right must be understood to confer a derived right on the beneficiary's family members, it must be presumed *prima facie* that also the derived right is not subject to

---

[32] ibid para 18.
[33] ibid para 20.
[34] ibid para 21; see further, paras 22–27. In contrast, the Governments of Liechtenstein, the Netherlands, and Denmark argued that 'Article 16 of the Directive must be interpreted to the effect that a holder of a permanent residence right who is a pensioner may claim the right to family reunification only on the fulfilment of the conditions laid down in Article 7(1)(d) in conjunction with Article 7(1)(b) of the Directive' (*Clauder*, para 28; see also, the arguments outlined in paras 29–32).
[35] ibid para 34; referring to Case C-127/08 *Metock and Others*, EU:C:2008:449, para 84.
[36] *Clauder*, para 38 (emphasis added).
[37] ibid para 43.
[38] ibid para 46; referring to *Metock*, paras 89 and 93.

a condition to have sufficient resources'.³⁹ It added that '[t]his interpretation is underpinned by the *discontinuation of a general requirement to have sufficient resources* in [Directive 2004/38]'.⁴⁰

That analysis provides a counterpoint to questions discussed in Chapter 7 to some extent, where economic activity was shown still to attract greater protection in EU citizenship law in general. However, it fits with the general thesis that equal treatment follows lawful residence, with the right of permanent residence representing in a sense the 'most lawful' residence that EU law can confer. It also aligns with the tone of the Court of Justice's ruling in *Commissioners for Her Majesty's Revenue and Customs (Assurance maladie complète)*.⁴¹ This case was introduced in Chapter 6, in the context of the residence conditions in Article 7(1)(b) of the Directive and, more specifically, the requirement of comprehensive sickness insurance cover in the host State. The main significance of the ruling concerned the obligation on host States that affiliate Union citizens to their public sickness insurance systems free of charge to recognise that affiliation for the purposes of lawful residence within the meaning of Article 7(1)(b) of the Directive. But it also established important principles for the right of permanent residence of third-country national family members. First, where a child who is a Union citizen acquires the right of permanent residence in a host State through legal and continuous residence there in accordance with Article 16 of the Directive, their right to reside is no longer subject to any conditions. A third-country national parent of that child who resides there with them and is their primary carer is not a 'family member' within the meaning of Article 2(2) of the Directive because that provision's condition of dependency is the 'wrong way around' in such cases, as discussed in Chapter 4. In consequence, Article 16(2) of the Directive cannot extend a right of permanent residence to that parent.⁴²

However, second, '[t]*hat said*, it is settled case-law that the right of permanent residence in the host Member State, conferred by EU law on a minor national of another Member State, must, for the purposes of ensuring the effectiveness of that right of residence, be considered as necessarily implying, *under Article 21 TFEU*, a right for the parent who is the primary carer of that minor Union citizen to reside with him or her in the host Member State, regardless of the nationality of that parent'.⁴³ The Court cited previous case law 'to that effect', but the cases it referred to only addressed corollary residence in a more general sense as being for the 'duration' of the child's residence in the host State.⁴⁴ They made no reference to the right of permanent residence (and *Zhu and Chen* predated Directive 2004/38 anyway)—and certainly not to what came next: '[i]t follows that the inapplicability of the conditions set out, *inter alia*, in Article 7(1)(b) of Directive 2004/38, following the acquisition by that minor of a right of permanent residence under Article 16(1) of that directive, *extends, pursuant to Article 21 TFEU, to that parent*'.⁴⁵ The Court

---

³⁹ *Clauder*, para 47.
⁴⁰ ibid para 48 (emphasis added); continuing that, 'in the Court's view, whereas under the previous directives to have sufficient resources was a general condition for residence rights, under Directive 2004/38 it is only a legitimate condition for residence rights in the cases specifically mentioned in the Directive'. In para 49, the EFTA Court referred to the right to respect for private and family life in Article 8(1) ECHR and, for the EU legal order, Article 7 CFR.
⁴¹ Case C-247/20 *Commissioners for Her Majesty's Revenue and Customs (Assurance maladie complète)*, EU:C:2022:177.
⁴² ibid paras 56–57.
⁴³ ibid para 58 (emphasis added).
⁴⁴ ie Case C-200/02 *Zhu and Chen*, EU:C:2004:639, paras 45–46; and Case C-165/14 *Rendón Marín*, EU:C:2016:675, paras 51–52.
⁴⁵ *Commissioners for Her Majesty's Revenue and Customs*, para 59 (emphasis added).

explained that this extension is 'to ensure the effectiveness of th[e Union citizen's] right of residence'.[46]

This was an extraordinary conclusion.[47] At one level, it does fit with the generally intensifying emphasis on respect for private and family life protected by Article 7 CFR, though there is no explicit reference to the Charter in the Court's ruling. More strikingly, however, it migrates a status emblematic of the Directive itself beyond that measure, imputing it back to Article 21 TFEU and thereby grounding a conception of permanent residence directly in primary EU law for the first time. To implement that extension of the right of permanent residence in practice, the Court found that 'to determine whether that parent, a national of a third State, benefits from such a right of residence due to the situation of his or her child, a Union citizen, it is necessary to examine whether that child fulfils the conditions set out in Article 7(1)(b) of Directive 2004/38' and that, '[f]or the purposes of that examination, those conditions must be deemed to apply *mutatis mutandis* to that parent'.[48] Drawing from *Zhu and Chen*, the Court recalled that the *source* of sufficient resources and/ or comprehensive sickness insurance is irrelevant so long as the conditions in Article 7(1)(b) of the Directive are substantively met; thus, '[w]ith regard to the situation of a child, a Union citizen, who resides in the host State with a parent who is his or her primary carer, this requirement is satisfied both where this child has comprehensive sickness insurance which covers his or her parent, and in the inverse case where this parent has such insurance covering the child'.[49] On that basis, 'as regards periods before a child, a Union citizen, has acquired a right of permanent residence in the host Member State, both that child, where a right of residence is claimed for him or her on the basis of that Article 7(1)(b), and the parent who is the primary carer of that child must have comprehensive sickness insurance cover within the meaning of that directive'—fulfilled in this instance through affiliation to the host State's public sickness insurance system.[50]

As discussed in Chapter 4, the Court of Justice has also considered another aspect of family member rights in its case law, that is, the requirement in Article 16(2) of the Directive that family members who are not Member State nationals must reside 'with' the Union citizen for the relevant period. In *Onuekwere*, the Court had to consider whether periods spent in prison could qualify as periods of 'legal' residence in a host State for the purposes of acquiring permanent residence rights. In its judgment, returned to in Section 3.2, the Court held that where a right of permanent residence is claimed by a third-country national family member, first, the Union citizen from whom their right of residence derives must themselves satisfy the requirements of Article 16(1). Second, the relevant family member must 'have resided *"with"* [them] for the period in question', following the wording of Article 16(2).[51]

The Court considered that 'the word "with" reinforce[es] the condition that those family members must accompany or join that same citizen', as required by Article 3(1) of the

---

[46] ibid para 64.
[47] In his Opinion, AG Hogan considered residence rights for the primary carer/parent only with reference to Article 10 of Regulation 492/2011 (AG Hogan in *Commissioners for Her Majesty's Revenue and Customs (Assurance maladie complète)*, EU:C:2021:778, paras 51–54 of the Opinion). The Court dismissed the relevance of that provision in its ruling, since Article 10 'confers rights only on the children of the family of a national of a Member State who is or has been employed in the territory of the host Member State. VI's husband and the father of the child concerned is a third-country national' (para 71).
[48] *Commissioners for Her Majesty's Revenue and Customs*, para 65.
[49] ibid para 67, referring to *Zhu and Chen*, paras 29–33.
[50] *Commissioners for Her Majesty's Revenue and Customs*, para 72.
[51] Case C-378/12 *Onuekwere*, EU:C:2014:13, para 18 (emphasis added); confirming Case C-529/11 *Alarape and Tijani*, EU:C:2013:290, para 34.

Directive.⁵² But the narrowness of the language used arguably suggested that shared residence, in a literal sense, was necessary in order to acquire the right of permanent residence. Advocate General Bot had considered the implications of requiring family members—and spouses in particular—to reside 'with' each other, arguing that the phrase 'with the Union citizen' in Article 16(2) 'must not be interpreted literally, and therefore strictly, unless it is to remove certain legitimate beneficiaries from the rights which that directive would normally confer on them or, also, infringe the right to respect for private and family life which everyone enjoys under Article 7 of the Charter of Fundamental Rights'.⁵³ He envisaged situations in which 'by force of circumstances, the citizen of the Union and the national of a third State who is a member of his family cannot live permanently under the same roof'; where, for example, the Union citizen 'may have to live during the week or even for a prolonged period of time in a region other than that in which his spouse who is a national of a third State lives', adding that this 'is particularly true in today's world in which it is common for people to have to change jobs and to move from place to place'.⁵⁴

Subsequently, the circumstances in the *Ogieriakhi* case led the Court to revisit and clarify the position it had taken in *Onuekwere*. Mr Ogieriakhi was a Nigerian national who arrived in Ireland in May 1998 and obtained a residence permit there in October 1999, following his marriage in May 1999 to a French national (Ms Georges) who also resided in Ireland at that time. The couple lived together until August 2001, when Ms Georges left the family home to reside with a new partner. Mr Ogieriakhi subsequently had a child with an Irish national in December 2003. Mr Ogieriakhi and Ms Georges did not divorce until 2009, and Ms Georges was either working or receiving social security as a jobseeker from October 1999 until October 2004. She left Ireland in December 2004. In the context of Mr Ogieriakhi's rejected application for permanent residence, the referring court questioned whether the couple's separation—'given that not only is there no residing together but especially, there is no true sharing of married life together'⁵⁵—meant that he could not satisfy the requirement in Article 16(2) of residing 'with' Ms Georges.

A very literal application of *Onuekwere* would entail that conclusion. However, in *Ogieriakhi*, the Court found that 'the fact that, during the period from 11 October 1999 to 11 October 2004, the spouses not only ceased to live together but also resided with other partners, is irrelevant for the purposes of the acquisition by Mr Ogieriakhi of a right of permanent residence under Article 16(2) of Directive 2004/38'.⁵⁶ It referred to its earlier rulings in *Diatta* and *Iida* to underline that Mr Ogieriakhi and Ms Georges were 'spouses' until their divorce was finalised in 2009,⁵⁷ and recalled that the provisions of Directive 2004/38 should not be interpreted restrictively and deprived of their effectiveness. Recognising the wider implications of forcing actual shared residence, the Court acknowledged that 'if Article 16(2) of the directive were to be interpreted literally, a third-country national could be made

---

⁵² *Onuekwere*, para 23.
⁵³ AG Bot in *Onuekwere*, EU:C:2013:640, para 38 of the Opinion.
⁵⁴ ibid para 39 of the Opinion. See similarly, AG Wathelet in Case C-673/16 *Coman*, EU:C:2018:2, para 28 of the Opinion: '[i]n a globalised world, it is not unusual for a couple one of whom works abroad not to share the same accommodation for longer or shorter periods owing to the distance between the two countries, the accessibility of means of transport, the employment of the other spouse or the children's education. The fact that the couple do not live together cannot in itself have any effect on the existence of a proven stable relationship—which is the case—and, consequently, on the existence of a family life'.
⁵⁵ Case C-244/13 *Ogieriakhi*, EU:C:2014:2068, para 36.
⁵⁶ ibid para 38.
⁵⁷ ibid para 37, referring to Case 267/83 *Diatta*, EU:C:1985:67, paras 20 and 22, and Case C-40/11 *Iida*, EU:C:2012:691, para 58.

vulnerable because of unilateral measures taken by his spouse, and that would be contrary to the spirit of that directive, of which one of the objectives is precisely — according to recital 15 thereto — to offer legal protection to family members of citizens of the Union who reside in the host Member State, in order to enable them, in certain cases and subject to certain conditions, to retain their right of residence exclusively on a personal basis'.[58] *Onuekwere*, which pointed to the opposite conclusion reached here, was not considered at all.

Advocate General Bot also delivered the Opinion in *Ogieriakhi*, holding to his earlier view that '[t]he vicissitudes that can occur in anyone's life, which may lead couples to live apart, must not deprive those persons of the rights to which they are entitled under EU legislation'.[59] Moreover, '[t]o require the persons concerned to live permanently under the same roof would ... constitute interference in private and family life which is contrary to Article 7 [CFR]. It is not the role of public authorities to impose a concept of life together as a couple or a certain way of life on nationals of other Member States and members of their family, especially as no such requirement exists for their own national'.[60] He did refer to the judgment in *Onuekwere*, but submitted as regards the requirement to accompany or join the Union citizen in Article 3(1) of the Directive that, 'once the initial condition of accompanying or joining the Union citizen in the host Member State is satisfied, it is immaterial whether or not the couple live together'.[61] In both cases, Advocate General Bot engaged Article 7 CFR to insulate diverse experiences of family life from an overly literal interpretation of the conditions in the Directive. However, the Court's approach in *Onuekwere* did fit more generally with other judgments delivered around this time in which the consequences for Union citizenship rights of periods spent in prison were considerable, returned to in Section 3.2.

3.1.2 Absence from the host State

As indicated in Section 2, the right of permanent residence is not actually *permanent*, because Articles 16(3) and 16(4) of the Directive limit permitted absences from the host State. First, Article 16(3) addresses temporary absences with reference to the continuity of residence necessary for *acquiring* permanent residence rights. As noted in Section 2, when conceiving the right of permanent residence, the Commission aimed to sustain but also strengthen rights to remain in a host State that had already been provided for in secondary legislation, with recital 19 of the Directive confirming that '[c]ertain advantages specific to Union citizens who are workers or self-employed persons and to their family members, which may allow these persons to acquire a right of permanent residence before they have resided five years in the host Member State, should be maintained, *as these constitute acquired rights*, conferred by [Regulation 1251/70] and [Directive 75/34]'.[62] Article 4(1) of Regulation 1251/70 had established that continuity of residence was not affected by 'temporary absences not exceeding a total of three months per year, nor by longer absences due to compliance with the obligations of military service' while Article 4(2) ensured, *inter alia*, that 'absences due to illness or accident shall be considered as periods of employment'.[63]

---

[58] *Ogieriakhi*, para 40.
[59] AG Bot in *Ogieriakhi*, para 41 of the Opinion.
[60] ibid para 42 of the Opinion.
[61] ibid para 46 of the Opinion.
[62] Commission Regulation 1251/70/EEC on the right of workers to remain in the territory of a Member State after having been employed in that State, 1970 OJ L142/24. See similarly, for self-employed persons, Article 4 of Directive 75/34/EEC concerning the right of nationals of a Member State to remain in the territory of another Member State after having pursued therein an activity in a self-employed capacity, 1975 OJ L14/10.
[63] See similarly, for self-employed persons, Article 4 of Directive 75/34.

Article 16(3) of Directive 2004/38[64] thus provides for both cumulative and singular absences from the host State by establishing that '[c]ontinuity of residence shall not be affected by temporary absences not exceeding a total of six months a year, or by absences of a longer duration for compulsory military service, or by one absence of a maximum of twelve consecutive months for important reasons such as pregnancy and childbirth, serious illness, study or vocational training, or a posting in another Member State or a third country'.[65] In Chapter 6, it was noted that the Court referred to Article 16(3) in *Saint Prix* to evidence the 'special protection for women in connection with maternity' guaranteed by EU law: '[i]f by virtue of that protection, an absence for an important event such as pregnancy or childbirth does not affect the continuity of the five years of residence in the host Member State required for the granting of that right of residence, the physical constraints of the late stages of pregnancy and the immediate aftermath of childbirth, which require a woman to give up work temporarily, cannot, *a fortiori*, result in that woman losing her status as a worker'.[66]

Second, Article 16(4) provides that the right of permanent residence is lost 'through absence from the host Member State for a period exceeding two consecutive years'.[67] As noted in Section 2, the Commission originally proposed that the right would be lost after four years of absence from the host State on the basis that such absences 'would suggest a kind of "disintegration"'.[68] In *Lassal*, addressing residence periods completed before the Directive came into force, the Court confirmed that 'in so far as the right of permanent residence provided for in Article 16 of Directive 2004/38 may only be acquired from 30 April 2006, the taking into account of periods of residence completed before that date does not give retroactive effect to Article 16 of Directive 2004/38, but simply gives present effect to situations which arose before the date of transposition of that directive'.[69] Thus, 'Article 16(4) of Directive 2004/38 falls to be applied independently of whether periods of residence completed before or after 30 April 2006 are concerned'.[70] The Court underlined that 'an interpretation to the effect that only continuous periods of five years' legal residence commencing after 30 April 2006 should be taken into account for the purposes of the acquisition of a right of permanent residence would mean that such a right could be granted only from 30 April 2011', which would, importantly, 'amount to depriving the residence completed by citizens of the Union *in accordance with EU law instruments pre-dating 30 April 2006* of any effect for the purposes of the acquisition of that right of permanent residence'.[71] In other words, the residence periods being considered in this case were themselves within the bounds of EU law.

---

[64] See similarly, Article 15(2) WA.
[65] Somewhat surprisingly, the Commission is virtually silent on the conditions for the right of permanent residence in its Communication on guidance for better transposition and application of Directive 2004/38/EC on the right of citizens of the Union and their family members to move and reside freely within the territory of the Member States (COM(2009) 313 final), including with respect to guidance for national authorities making decisions on authorised absences.
[66] Case C-507/12 *Saint Prix*, EU:C:2014:2007, para 46.
[67] See differently, Article 15(3) WA: as the Commission explains, '[t]o reflect the specific context of the Agreement (under which it is not possible to simply re-exercise the right to move and reside freely even after the loss of previous right of permanent residence), Article 11 of the Agreement goes beyond the rule on the allowed two-year absence for loss of right of permanent residence under Directive 2004/38/EC (Article 16(4) of Directive 2004/38/EC) by providing for a maximum absence of five consecutive years. This extension of absence periods from two to five years (as compared to the rules under Directive 2004/38/EC) allows the persons concerned to keep their right of permanent residence under the Agreement when returning to the host State after a period of absence of up to five consecutive years' (Guidance Note relating to the Agreement (n 7) para 2.3.3).
[68] Original proposal (n 2) final, 16.
[69] Case C-162/09 *Lassal*, EU:C:2010:592, para 38.
[70] ibid para 56.
[71] ibid para 35 (emphasis added).

However, and again with resonance for the questions considered in Chapter 7, the fact that lawful residence is connected to residence based on EU law *only* was confirmed in *Dias*. For the purposes of calculating the applicant's overall period of residence in the host State with reference to Article 16(1) of the Directive, a residence permit issued on the basis of Directive 68/360 was ruled out on account of its 'declaratory, as opposed to a constitutive, character',[72] meaning that permits issued pursuant to Directive 68/360 were *not* 'capable of establishing rights for their holders'.[73] The Court then applied Article 16(4) of Directive 2004/38 by analogy in connection with periods of residence completed in a host State before 30 April 2006 'without the conditions governing entitlement to any right of residence having been satisfied'—in this case, a period of voluntary unemployment following maternity leave—and found that '[e]ven though Article 16(4) of Directive 2004/38 refers only to absences from the host Member State, the integration link between the person concerned and that Member State is also called into question in the case of a citizen who, while having resided legally for a continuous period of five years, then decides to remain in that Member State *without having a right of residence*'.[74]

Therefore, with reference to the period specified in Article 16(4), '*periods of less than two consecutive years*, completed on the basis solely of a residence permit validly issued pursuant to Directive 68/360, without the conditions governing entitlement to any right of residence having been satisfied, which occurred before 30 April 2006 and after a continuous period of five years' legal residence completed prior to that date, *are not such as to affect* the acquisition of the right of permanent residence under Article 16(1) of Directive 2004/38'.[75] Interestingly, the Commission had focused on Article 16(3) in its submissions, but its proposed approach would have separated out the need to reside *both* continuously *and* legally cemented by the judgment of the Court.[76] The condition of legal residence and related case law are picked up in more detail in Section 3.2.

3.1.3 Exemptions from Article 16

Again reflecting the objective of ensuring continuity with protection that had already been conferred by secondary legislation in connection with economic activity, Article 17 of Directive 2004/38 details a series of exemptions 'by way of derogation from Article 16' under

---

[72] Case C-325/09 *Dias*, EU:C:2011:498, para 49.
[73] ibid para 40 (emphasis added). In contrast, as discussed further in Chapter 6, 'Article 3 of Directive 90/364 referred, not to the permit issued to prove the right of residence, but to the right of residence as such and to the conditions laid down for the grant of that right' (ibid para 51).
[74] ibid paras 62–63 (emphasis added).
[75] ibid para 66 (emphasis added).
[76] The arguments of the Commission were outlined by AG Trstenjak in *Dias*, EU:C:2011:86, paras 45–46 of the Opinion: '[t]he Commission adds that while a period of residence such as that in period 3 [ie of voluntary unemployment] admittedly does not constitute legal residence within the meaning of Article 16(1) of Directive 2004/38, it does not interrupt the continuity of residence within the meaning of that provision. The directive is silent in relation to a case such as the present, in which a Union citizen resides continuously in the host Member State but did not during a certain period fulfil the conditions for legal residence within the meaning of Article 16(1) of the directive. By contrast, Article 16(3) of the directive makes special provision whereby continuity of residence is not affected by absences of a certain duration, which serve merely to "stop the clock". It would strike a fair balance between the competing interests at stake to adopt that approach for periods of residence such as period 3 too. Such periods, unlike periods of absence of the Union citizen from the host State, do not in fact diminish the level of integration attained. That is also compatible with the legislature's intention. It decided either that it was obvious that periods of voluntary unemployment did not interrupt residence and therefore failed to adopt any rules, or it simply overlooked the point. In that case, the directive should be interpreted, in the light of Article [21 TFEU], in conformity with primary law. An interpretation according to which periods of involuntary employment interrupted residence would be disproportionate'.

which a right of permanent residence is acquired 'before completion of a continuous period of five years of residence':

Article 17

Exemptions for persons no longer working in the host Member State and their family members

1. By way of derogation from Article 16, the right of permanent residence in the host Member State shall be enjoyed before completion of a continuous period of five years of residence by:
   (a) workers or self-employed persons who, at the time they stop working, have reached the age laid down by the law of that Member State for entitlement to an old age pension or workers who cease paid employment to take early retirement, provided that they have been working in that Member State for at least the preceding twelve months and have resided there continuously for more than three years.

   If the law of the host Member State does not grant the right to an old age pension to certain categories of self-employed persons, the age condition shall be deemed to have been met once the person concerned has reached the age of 60;
   (b) workers or self-employed persons who have resided continuously in the host Member State for more than two years and stop working there as a result of permanent incapacity to work.

   If such incapacity is the result of an accident at work or an occupational disease entitling the person concerned to a benefit payable in full or in part by an institution in the host Member State, no condition shall be imposed as to length of residence;
   (c) workers or self-employed persons who, after three years of continuous employment and residence in the host Member State, work in an employed or self-employed capacity in another Member State, while retaining their place of residence in the host Member State, to which they return, as a rule, each day or at least once a week.

   For the purposes of entitlement to the rights referred to in points (a) and (b), periods of employment spent in the Member State in which the person concerned is working shall be regarded as having been spent in the host Member State.

   Periods of involuntary unemployment duly recorded by the relevant employment office, periods not worked for reasons not of the person's own making and absences from work or cessation of work due to illness or accident shall be regarded as periods of employment.
2. The conditions as to length of residence and employment laid down in point (a) of paragraph 1 and the condition as to length of residence laid down in point (b) of paragraph 1 shall not apply if the worker's or the self-employed person's spouse or partner as referred to in point 2(b) of Article 2 is a national of the host Member State or has lost the nationality of that Member State by marriage to that worker or self-employed person.
3. Irrespective of nationality, the family members of a worker or a self-employed person who are residing with him in the territory of the host Member State shall have the right of permanent residence in that Member State, if the worker or self-employed person has acquired himself the right of permanent residence in that Member State on the basis of paragraph 1.

4. If, however, the worker or self-employed person dies while still working but before acquiring permanent residence status in the host Member State on the basis of paragraph 1, his family members who are residing with him in the host Member State shall acquire the right of permanent residence there, on condition that:
   (a) the worker or self-employed person had, at the time of death, resided continuously on the territory of that Member State for two years;[77] or
   (b) the death resulted from an accident at work or an occupational disease; or
   (c) the surviving spouse lost the nationality of that Member State following marriage to the worker or self-employed person.

In effect, the conditions in Article 17 'reduc[e] the general period of five years of continuous legal residence in the host Member State for citizens of the Union and members of their family as a condition for acquiring a right of permanent residence in that State'.[78]

The longer-term protection guaranteed by Article 17 complements the provision made for shorter-term incapacity to sustain economic activity in Article 7(3) of the Directive. Article 17 also provides deeper protection for family members of Union citizens who had been engaged in economic activity than the more general provision made for family members in Articles 12 and 13, discussed in Chapter 6. In particular, and recalling the *Clauder* case considered in Section 3.1.1, Article 17(3) constitutes a 'derogation from the need to have legally resided with the Union citizen for a continuous period of five years'.[79] The privileges attached to economic activity reflect at a general level the idea of 'acquired rights' acknowledged in recital 19 of Directive 2004/38. For example, in *Lassal*, the Court observed that 'prior to the adoption of [the Directive] EU law already provided in certain specific cases for a right of permanent residence, which was included in Article 17 thereof'.[80] Since the Directive 'aims to facilitate the exercise of the primary and individual right to move and reside freely within the territory of the Member States that is conferred directly on Union citizens by the Treaty and ... it aims in particular to strengthen that right ... Union citizens cannot derive less rights from that directive than from the instruments of secondary legislation which it amends or repeals'.[81] However, rights already conferred by EU law on economically active citizens were not extended to citizens more generally: rather, the legal significance of economic activity was continued through the shaping of Article 17's specific exceptions to the general permanent resident rules. Reflecting similar examples and themes examined in Chapters 6 and 7, Article 17 thus entrenches the value attributed in EU free movement law (and continued in EU citizenship law) to integration achieved through the exercise of economic activity, confirming it as a shortcut to residence security in another Member State.

To date, the main questions on the exemptions from Article 16 that have reached the Court of Justice concern Article 17(1)(a) and, more specifically, whether 'the conditions that the person must have been working in that Member State for at least the preceding 12 months and must have resided in that Member State continuously for more than 3 years apply to workers who, at the time they stop working, have reached the age laid down by the law of that Member State for entitlement to an old age pension'.[82] The referring court had essentially

---

[77] The Commission had originally proposed a period of one year in this respect (n 2, draft Article 15(4)).
[78] AG Campos Sánchez-Bordona in Case C-300/15 *Kohll and Kohll-Schlesser*, EU:C:2016:86, para 39 of the Opinion.
[79] AG Bot in Case C-529/11 *Alarape and Tijani*, EU:C:2013:9, para 46 of the Opinion.
[80] Case C-162/09 *Lassal*, EU:C:2010:592, para 35.
[81] ibid para 30.
[82] Case C-32/19 *Pensionsversicherungsanstalt (Cessation d'activité après l'âge du départ à la retraite)*, EU:C:2020:25, para 26.

queried whether a distinction should be drawn between the situations of 'the age laid down by the relevant national legislation for entitlement to an old age pension' and 'where that person stops working to take early retirement' respectively.[83] The Court found 'nothing in the terms of' Article 17(1)(a) to suggest such a distinction,[84] meaning that the conditions in that provision had to be satisfied by former workers in both situations.[85] Having regard to the 'gradual system' of residence instituted by the Directive, the Court also found that if Article 17(1)(a) 'were to be interpreted in such a way that the mere fact that a worker, at the time he or she stops working, has reached the age laid down by the law of the host Member State for entitlement to an old age pension is sufficient to be entitled to a right of permanent residence in that Member State, regardless of any period of residence in that Member State before that person stops working, the gradual system provided for by that directive would be misconstrued'.[86] The need to evidence sufficient integration in the host State that infuses the right of permanent residence was also underlined.[87]

3.2 The Requirements of Legal and Continuous Residence

The requirements to reside 'legally' in the host State (Section 3.2.2) for a 'continuous' period of five years (Section 3.2.1) constitute the critical conditions for successfully acquiring the right of permanent residence.[88] At one level, they are applied very formally. A good illustration of this point concerns children who are either Union citizens themselves or the children of a Union citizen (irrespective of their own nationality) residing—perhaps since birth—in a host State. If they reside there continuously for five years in fulfilment of the conditions in Article 7(1)(b) of the Directive, in respect of which sufficient resources and sickness insurance can be provided by their parents,[89] then they become permanent residents there and acquire lifelong protection unless they leave for a period exceeding two consecutive years (Article 16(4)).[90] However, minors will often leave a host State because of choices made by others, this lack of agency again showing that permanent residence can be more short-lived in reality than the idea of 'permanence' conveys.

---

[83] ibid para 27.
[84] ibid.
[85] Referring to recital 19 and the principle of acquired rights, the Court also pointed to continuity with the protection previously granted by Article 2(1)(a) of Regulation No 1251/70 (ibid paras 30–31).
[86] ibid para 39.
[87] ibid paras 40–43.
[88] As noted above, however, the Communication on guidance for better transposition and application of Directive 2004/38/EC (n 65) does not address these conditions at all.
[89] Case C-200/02 *Zhu and Chen*, EU:C:2004:639, paras 28–33. Sufficient resources can also be provided for parents by their children: see eg AG Wathelet in Case C-442/16 *Gusa*, EU:C:2017:607, paras 32–34 of the Opinion, pointing out that '[t]he fact that Mr Gusa considers that the support he received was limited and insufficient for the purposes of Directive 2004/38 does not seem to me to be relevant to the assessment of the applicability of Article 16(1) of that directive' (para 33) and emphasising instead that, 'from the point at which Mr Gusa stopped relying on the Irish social assistance system for financial support during his first year of residence, the resources that were available to him must be presumed to have been sufficient. They cannot be retrospectively regarded as having been insufficient for the purposes of Directive 2004/38, given that the Union citizen in question was not, to use the wording of that directive, a "burden on the social assistance system of the host Member State"' (para 34). See further, Chapter 6.
[90] eg AG Wathelet in Case C-115/15 *NA*, EU:C:2016:259, para 47 of the Opinion.

3.2.1 Continuous residence

The *continuous* residence condition is the relatively less controversial (and less examined to date) element of Article 16 of the Directive. We saw in Section 3.1.2 that Article 16(3) addresses continuity of residence by specifying the limits of both cumulative and singular absences from the host State. Additionally, Article 21 of the Directive provides that '[f]or the purposes of this Directive, continuity of residence may be attested by any means of proof for use in the host Member State'. In its proposal for the Directive, the Commission had suggested that continuity of residence 'may be proved by various means, such as evidence of being gainfully employed or self-employed or rent receipts. Member States must show flexibility regarding proof of residence duration and continuity'.[91]

Article 21 of the Directive further confirms that continuity is 'broken by any expulsion decision duly enforced against the person concerned'. In Chapter 6, the *FS* case was examined with respect to how the Court accepted the legitimacy of and developed guidance to determine 'genuine and effective' termination of residence in a host State after an expulsion decision is issued under Article 15(1) of the Directive. In summary, only where residence is demonstrably terminated in a 'genuine and effective' way can a Union citizen re-establish a right to reside in the same State under Article 6(1) of the Directive. As part of its justification for that approach, the Court referred to Article 21 of the Directive, considering that 'to regard the mere physical departure of a Union citizen from the host Member State as being sufficient for the purpose of the enforcement of an expulsion decision taken against the person concerned would also partly render redundant the distinction clearly established by Directive 2004/38 between temporary residence and permanent residence'.[92] This is because, for the Court, 'that view would allow such a Union citizen to rely on multiple successive temporary periods of residence in that Member State in order, *in fact, to reside there permanently*, even though he or she did not satisfy the conditions for a right of permanent residence laid down in that directive'.[93] The ruling in *FS* thus underlines the distinction between continuous residence as a fact and continuous residence within the meaning of Article 16 of the Directive, with only the latter—verification of which is returned to in Section 3.3—capable of substantiating the right of permanent residence.

3.2.2 Legal residence

The condition of 'legal' residence in Article 16 of the Directive folds into the more general requirement of lawful residence in EU citizenship law before equal treatment with host State nationals is guaranteed. Article 16(1) should therefore be read alongside recital 17 of the Directive, the second sentence of which indicates that '[a] right of permanent residence should ... be laid down for all Union citizens and their family members who have resided in the host Member State *in compliance with the conditions laid down in this Directive* during a continuous period of five years without becoming subject to an expulsion measure'. As noted in Section 3.1, the Court stated in *Lassal* that 'it would be incompatible with the integration-based reasoning behind Article 16 of that directive to consider that the required degree of integration in the host Member State depended on whether the continuous period of five years' residence ended before or after 30 April 2006'.[94] But it also held that for residence periods

---

[91] Original proposal (n 2), 17. The implications for continuous residence of periods spent in prison in the host State are returned to in Section 3.2.2.
[92] Case C-719/19 *FS*, EU:C:2021:506, para 77.
[93] ibid (emphasis added).
[94] Case C-162/09 *Lassal*, EU:C:2010:592, para 37.

completed prior to that date, only residence 'in accordance with the earlier EU law instruments' would be taken into account[95]—mirroring the discussion of *CG* in Chapter 7.[96]

Similarly, in *Dias*, the Court established that 'periods of residence completed before 30 April 2006 on the basis solely of a residence permit validly issued under Directive 68/360, *without the conditions governing entitlement to any right of residence having been met*, cannot be regarded as having been completed legally for the purposes of the acquisition of a right of permanent residence under Article 16(1) of Directive 2004/38'.[97] Emphasising the declaratory rather than constitutive character of residence permits in EU free movement law,[98] the Court ruled that '[t]he grant of a residence permit to a national of a Member State is to be regarded, not as a measure giving rise to rights, but as a measure by a Member State serving to prove the individual position of a national of another Member State with regard to provisions of European Union law'.[99] On that basis, 'just as such a declaratory character means that a citizen's residence may not be regarded as illegal, within the meaning of European Union law, solely on the ground that he does not hold a residence permit, it precludes a Union citizen's residence from being regarded as legal, within the meaning of European Union law, solely on the ground that such a permit was validly issued to him'.[100] The Court also observed that 'the integration objective which lies behind the acquisition of the right of permanent residence laid down in Article 16(1) of Directive 2004/38 is based not only on territorial and time factors *but also on qualitative elements*, relating to the *level* of integration in the host Member State'.[101] That idea had significant repercussions in subsequent cases concerning periods of time spent in prison in the host State, returned to below.[102]

In *Ziolkowski and Szeja*, the Court found that periods of residence completed in a host State by a national of another Member State before the accession of the latter State to the Union could be taken into account for the purposes of Article 16(1). It acknowledged that such periods 'fell not within the scope of European Union law but solely within the law of the host Member State. However, *provided the person concerned can demonstrate that such periods were completed in compliance with the conditions laid down in Article 7(1) of Directive 2004/38*, the taking into account of such periods from the date of accession of the Member State concerned to the European Union does not give retroactive effect to Article 16 of Directive 2004/38, but simply gives present effect to situations which arose before the date of transposition of that directive'.[103] The Court emphasised the need for uniform interpretation of the concept of legal residence, the 'gradual system as regards the right of residence in the

---

[95] ibid para 40 (emphasis added).
[96] Case C-709/20 *CG*, EU:C:2021:602.
[97] Case C-325/09 *Dias*, EU:C:2011:498, para 55 (emphasis added).
[98] ibid para 49; referring to Case C-408/03 *Commission v Belgium*, EU:C:2006:192, paras 62–63. However, cf. AG Trstenjak (EU:C:2011:86), para 114 of the Opinion: '[t]he Court has admittedly decided on many occasions that such a residence permit is of only declaratory effect. In my opinion it did not thereby mean to say that such a residence permit can have no effect at all of its own. That conclusion of the Court must be seen in the context of the cases concerned ... The Court has merely pointed out in those cases that rights of residence granted under European Union law do not depend on compliance with national administrative procedures but are conferred on European Union citizens directly by the provisions of European Union law. The Court was silent in those cases on the question whether a residence permit can also have an effect where the conditions for a right of residence enshrined in European Union law are not met'.
[99] *Dias*, para 48; referring to *Commission v Belgium*, para 65.
[100] *Dias*, para 54.
[101] ibid para 64 (emphasis added).
[102] AG Trstenjak already suggested that it seemed 'quite possible that unlawful conduct of a Union citizen may diminish his integration in the host State from a qualitative point of view' (*Dias*, para 106 of the Opinion).
[103] Joined Cases C-424/10 and C-425/10 *Ziolkowski and Szeja*, EU:C:2011:866, paras 61–62; confirmed in Joined Cases C-147/11 and C-148/11 *Czop and Punakova*, EU:C:2012:538, para 35.

host Member State, which reproduces, in essence, the stages and conditions set out in the various instruments of European Union law and case-law preceding the directive and culminates in the right of permanent residence',[104] and the significance of the insertion of recital 17 by the Council in the final stages of the drafting of Directive 2004/38.[105]

Thus, the Court clarified that legal residence for the purposes of Article 16(1) implies compliance 'in particular' with the conditions in Article 7(1):

> [T]he concept of legal residence implied by the terms 'have resided legally' in Article 16(1) of Directive 2004/38 should be construed as meaning a period of residence which complies with the conditions laid down in the directive, in particular those set out in Article 7(1). Consequently, a period of residence which complies with the law of a Member State but does not satisfy the conditions laid down in Article 7(1) of Directive 2004/38 cannot be regarded as a 'legal' period of residence within the meaning of Article 16(1).[106]

As explained in Chapter 7, the reference to the conditions in Article 7(1) 'in particular' accommodates situations of lawful residence based on other provisions of the Directive: initial periods of residence for less than three months under Article 6,[107] residence rights for jobseekers based on the protection from expulsion conferred by Article 14(4)(b),[108] and rights retained exclusively on a personal basis by the family members of Union citizens in the circumstances provided for in Articles 12 and 13.

In *Ziolkowski and Szeja*, residence permits had been issued on humanitarian grounds to Polish nationals residing in Germany. Several years later, their applications to extend those permits were rejected on the grounds that they were 'unable to support themselves economically. Nor was it possible to recognise their entitlement to a right of permanent residence under European Union law, since they were not in employment or able to prove that they could support themselves economically'.[109] The applicants argued, contrary to all of the Member States that submitted observations and to the Commission,[110] that '[i]n order to claim entitlement to the right of permanent residence under Article 16(1), it is sufficient to demonstrate that the period of residence was lawful, even under the law of the host Member State, and the fact that the applicant has had recourse to social assistance or that, during that period of residence, the office responsible for foreign nationals was entitled to find that the applicant no longer had the right of freedom of movement is irrelevant in that regard'.[111] However, addressing Article 37 of the Directive,[112] the Court considered that '[t]he fact that national provisions concerning the right of residence of Union citizens that are more favourable than those laid down in Directive 2004/38 are not to be affected does not in any way

---

[104] *Ziolkowski and Szeja*, para 38.
[105] ibid paras 42–43; see further on this point, AG Trstenjak in *Dias*, para 76 of the Opinion.
[106] *Ziolkowski and Szeja*, paras 46–47; confirmed in eg Joined Cases C-316/16 and C-424/16 *B and Vomero*, EU:C:2018:256, para 59; and Joined Cases C-331/16 and C-366/16 *K and HF*, EU:C:2018:296, para 74.
[107] eg In *Chavez-Vilchez*, the Court referred cumulatively to 'the conditions laid down by Directive 2004/38, in particular in Articles 5 to 7 thereof, which govern entry into and residence in the territory of Member States' (Case C-133/15 *Chavez-Vilchez*, EU:C:2017:354, para 56).
[108] Though as discussed in Chapter 7, it would be difficult to sustain residence on that basis alone for the required five-year period, given the tests for continued lawful residence within the meaning of Article 14(4)(b) in Case C-710/19 *GMA (Demandeur d'emploi)*, EU:C:2020:1037, explained further in Chapter 6.
[109] *Ziolkowski and Szeja*, para 21.
[110] ibid para 30.
[111] ibid para 29.
[112] Article 37 of the Directive provides: '[t]he provisions of this Directive shall not affect any laws, regulations or administrative provisions laid down by a Member State which would be more favourable to the persons covered by this Directive'.

mean that such provisions must be *incorporated into the system* introduced by the directive' since 'it is for each Member State to decide not only whether it will adopt such a system *but also the conditions and effects of that system*, in particular as regards the legal consequences of a right of residence granted on the basis of national law alone'.[113]

Arguing against that outcome, Advocate General Bot drew from the 'qualitative elements' of integration advanced by the Court in *Dias* to argue that 'the degree of integration of the Union citizen does not depend upon whether the *source* of his right of residence is in European Union law or national law'.[114] He also invoked the role of the host State in the circumstances of this case, echoing the theme of responsibility for choices made when authorising residence and for facilitating the transition of citizens between different stages of residence considered in Chapter 7. In his view, a citizen's degree of integration in the host State 'does not depend on the material circumstances of that citizen, that is whether they are secure or insecure, as *those circumstances have been taken into account and managed by the host Member State for a period of time*, the duration of which, being greater than the minimum duration required by Directive 2004/38, has constituted a specific demonstration of social cohesion'.[115]

We saw in Chapter 7 that the Court referred to *Ziolkowski and Szeja* in *CG* to rule out the relevance of equal treatment under Article 18 TFEU where the lawfulness of a Union citizen's residence in a host State is authorised by national law alone—contra Advocate General Richard de la Tour who had distinguished between Article 16 of the Directive, which *creates* the right of permanent residence, and Article 24 of the Directive, which *implements* the guarantee of equal treatment in Article 18 TFEU.[116] In *Jobcenter Krefeld*, the Court was willing to accept entitlement to equal treatment where the residence rights of Union citizens (and their family members) were based not on Directive 2004/38 but on Article 10 of Regulation 492/2011.[117] Reading that judgment alongside the ruling in *CG* entrenches the legal significance of economic activity in EU citizenship law. In that light, however, the discounting in certain circumstances of periods of residence based on Article 10 the Regulation as 'legal' residence for acquiring the right of permanent residence is notable. In *Alarape and Tijani*, the Court confirmed its rulings in *Dias* and *Ziolkowski and Szeja* and clarified the implications of that case law for the family members of Union citizens. It first established that for third-country national family members of a Union citizen, 'only the periods of residence of those family members which satisfy the condition laid down in Article 7(2) of that directive may be taken into consideration'.[118] Since residence rights for third-country national family members under EU law derive from the Union citizen that they accompany or join in the host State, it is thus the Union citizen who must have resided in compliance with the conditions in Article 7(1) of the Directive.[119] For family members who are not Member State nationals themselves, the Union citizen 'with' (widely construed, as explained in Section 3.1.1)

---

[113] *Ziolkowski and Szeja*, paras 49–50 (emphasis added). AG Bot had reasoned to the contrary that Article 37 would be without 'purpose' if this solution were adopted (EU:C:2011:575, para 49 of the Opinion).

[114] AG Bot in *Ziolkowski and Szeja*, para 54 of the Opinion (emphasis added; referring to AG Kokott in Case C-434/09 *McCarthy*, EU:C:2010:718, para 52 of the Opinion). He also considered that '[i]t cannot be disputed, from my point of view, that that is the situation which arises where the links between the individual and the host Member State are established in the context of humanitarian solidarity' (para 52 of the Opinion).

[115] AG Bot in *Ziolkowski and Szeja*, para 55 of the Opinion (emphasis added).

[116] AG Richard de la Tour in Case C-709/20 *CG*, EU:C:2021:515, para 72 of the Opinion.

[117] Case C-181/19 *Jobcenter Krefeld*, EU:C:2020:794.

[118] Case C-529/11 *Alarape and Tijani*, EU:C:2013:290, para 37.

[119] ibid para 35. For permanent residence rights based on Articles 12(2) and 13(2) of the Directive, the family members in question must themselves have satisfied the conditions laid down in Article 7(1) of the Directive (para 38). See further, Chapters 6 and 7.

whom they reside, within the meaning of Article 16(2) of the Directive, 'implies that those family members *necessarily and concurrently* have a right of residence under Article 7(2) of Directive 2004/38, as family members accompanying or joining that citizen'.[120]

However, the critical exception then followed: '[t]he fact that the family member of a Union citizen who is not a national of a Member State has resided in a Member State solely on the basis of Article [10] of Regulation [492/2011] cannot therefore have any effect on the acquisition of a right of permanent residence under Directive 2004/38'.[121] The Court confronted the potential for conflict with *Lassal* in this context, observing that, in the earlier case, 'the question whether the person concerned was a "worker" within the meaning of European Union law and, consequently, whether she satisfied the condition laid down in Article 7(1)(a) of Directive 2004/38 was not a matter on which there was any argument'.[122] It continued:

> It is admittedly true that, since the periods of residence of the person concerned in the Member State in question [in *Lassal*] largely preceded Directive 2004/38, those periods could not have been completed other than 'in accordance with earlier European Union law instruments'. However, that wording ... must be understood in the context of the questions put by the referring court, which concerned not the substantive conditions for legal residence within the meaning of Article 16(1) of Directive 2004/38, but the treatment of periods of residence satisfying those conditions completed before the date of transposition of that directive in that Member State. On the other hand, the concept of legal residence implied by the words 'have resided legally' in Article 16(1) of Directive 2004/38 was analysed for the first time only in *Ziolkowski and Szeja*. Further, it must be recalled that, on the one hand, the aim of Directive 2004/38 is to leave behind a sector-by-sector piecemeal approach to the right of freedom of movement and residence in order to facilitate the exercise of that right by providing a single legislative act which codifies and revises the instruments of European Union law which preceded that directive and that, on the other hand, that directive introduced a gradual system as regards the right of residence in the host Member State which, while reproducing, in essence, the stages and conditions set out in the various instruments of European Union law and case-law preceding that directive, culminates in the right of permanent residence.[123]

The Court therefore clarified that 'the phrase "earlier [than Directive 2004/38] European Union law instruments", used in paragraph 40 of *Lassal*, must be understood as referring to the instruments which that directive codified, revised and repealed and not those which, like Article [10] of Regulation [492/2011], were unaffected by that directive'.[124] While Advocate General Bot was critical of this approach in his Opinion, he did concede that periods of residence under the Regulation that did not satisfy the conditions in Article 7(1) of the Directive could not logically be taken into account for the purposes of permanent residence rights following *Ziolkowski and Szeja*.[125] That judgment reflected, in his view, 'the need to preserve the balance, desired by the Union legislature, between, on the one hand, requirements

---

[120] *Alarape and Tijani*, para 36 (emphasis added).
[121] ibid para 40.
[122] ibid para 43.
[123] ibid paras 44–46.
[124] ibid para 47.
[125] AG Bot in *Alarape and Tijani*, EU:C:2013:9, para 77 of the Opinion.

of freedom of movement and integration and, on the other, the financial interests of the Member States'.[126]

Advocate General Bot acknowledged that 'the importance of the rights conferred by the status of permanent resident, which, once acquired, confers an entitlement to social assistance which is unconditional, must have as its counterpart the rigour of the conditions laid down for its acquisition. Furthermore, the setting of rigorous but clear conditions of eligibility for that status meets beyond doubt the requirement of legal certainty'.[127] There is, nevertheless, a dissonance between recognising that being financially supported because of equal treatment guarantees that flow from Article 45 TFEU and Regulation 492/2011 is entirely *lawful* as a matter of EU law, on the one hand, while discounting such periods as *legal* residence for the purposes of permanent residence, on the other. The ruling in *Alarape and Tijani* thus provides an example of 'the fact that [the citizens in question] have participated in the employment market of a Member State establishes, *in principle, a sufficient link of integration* with the society of that Member State'[128]—that it does so only *in principle*, in other words.

That point bridges to a final issue relating to legal residence: the significance as well as the nature of 'integration' for the purposes of confirming the right of permanent residence, which was particularly evident—and controversial—in a set of judgments concerning periods spent in prison in the host State. The central concern here connects to the Court's statement in *Dias* that 'the integration objective which lies behind the acquisition of the right of permanent residence laid down in Article 16(1) of Directive 2004/38 is based not only on territorial and time factors *but also on qualitative elements*'.[129] In her Opinion, Advocate General Trstenjak had suggested that 'unlawful conduct of a Union citizen may diminish his integration in the host State from a qualitative point of view'.[130] In *Onuekwere*, in connection with the rights conferred on third-country national family members of Union citizens by Article 16(2) of the Directive, the referring court asked, first, whether a period of imprisonment in the host State could constitute 'legal' residence for the purposes of Article 16; and second, if not, whether a person who had served a term of imprisonment was permitted to aggregate periods of residence before and after that imprisonment when calculating the period of five years required for permanent residence.

On the first question, the applicant in *Onuekwere* was a Nigerian national residing in the UK who was married to an Irish national. He argued that when his wife acquired a right of permanent residence in the UK, he fell within the scope of Article 7(2) of the Directive for the same period, which should 'be taken into consideration for the purposes of his acquisition of the right of permanent residence within the meaning of Article 16(2) ... notwithstanding the fact that he was imprisoned for part of that period'.[131] However, in the Court's view, it was 'clear from the very terms and the purpose of Article 16(2) of Directive 2004/38 [that] periods of imprisonment cannot be taken into consideration for the purposes of the acquisition of a right of permanent residence'.[132] As discussed in Section 3.1.1, the Court placed considerable emphasis in this case on the requirement in Article 16(2) that family members

---

[126] ibid para 80 of the Opinion.
[127] ibid para 94 of the Opinion.
[128] Case C-542/09 *Commission v Netherlands*, EU:C:2012:346, para 65 (emphasis added).
[129] Case C-325/09 *Dias*, EU:C:2011:498, para 64 (emphasis added).
[130] AG Trstenjak in *Dias*, EU:C:2011:86, para 106 of the Opinion.
[131] Case C-378/12 *Onuekwere*, EU:C:2014:13, para 20.
[132] ibid para 22.

must reside 'with' the Union citizen for the five-year period.[133] But it also recalled the objective of promoting social cohesion in recital 17 of the Directive and the qualitative as well as territorial and temporal factors of the integration to which 'the EU legislature accordingly made the acquisition of the right of permanent residence pursuant to Article 16(1) of Directive 2004/38 subject'.[134]

However, the Court also held that 'the undermining of the link of integration between the person concerned and the host Member State justifies the loss of the right of permanent residence *even outside the circumstances* mentioned in Article 16(4) of Directive 2004/38'.[135] This is a defiant finding given that, in EU citizenship law generally, first, the Court consistently asserts that the provisions of the Directive 'may not be interpreted restrictively and, at all events, must not be deprived of their effectiveness'.[136] Second, the wording of both Articles 20(2) and 21(1) TFEU requires that conditions and limits must be articulated either in the Treaties or in secondary legislation.[137] And third, the Court has expressly connected that requirement to its understanding of Union citizenship as the fundamental status of Member State nationals, so that 'those who find themselves in the same situation ... enjoy the same treatment in law irrespective of their nationality, *subject to such exceptions as are expressly provided for*'.[138] Nevertheless, in *Onuekwere*, the Court considered that '[t]he imposition of a prison sentence by the national court is such as to show *the non-compliance by the person concerned with the values expressed by the society of the host Member State in its criminal law*, with the result that the taking into consideration of periods of imprisonment for the purposes of the acquisition by family members of a Union citizen who are not nationals of a Member State of the right of permanent residence for the purposes of Article 16(2) of Directive 2004/38 would clearly be contrary to the aim pursued by that directive in establishing that right of residence'.[139]

On the second question, characterising continuity of legal residence as a condition that 'satisfies the integration requirement which is a precondition of the acquisition of the right of permanent residence',[140] the Court confirmed similarly that 'the imposition of a prison sentence by a national court is such as to show *the non-compliance by the person concerned with the values expressed by the society of the host Member State in its criminal law*, with the result that the taking into consideration of periods of imprisonment for the purposes of the acquisition by family members of a Union citizen who are not nationals of a Member State of the

---

[133] ibid para 23; cf AG Bot (EU:C:2013:640), paras 38–41 of the Opinion.
[134] *Onuekwere*, para 24, referring in para 25 to Case C-325/09 *Dias*, EU:C:2011:498, para 64. Confirmed in Joined Cases C-316/16 and C-424/16 *B and Vomero*, EU:C:2018:256, paras 57–58.
[135] *Onuekwere*, para 25 (emphasis added).
[136] eg Case C-127/08 *Metock and Others*, EU:C:2008:449, para 84; Case C-162/09 *Lassal*, EU:C:2010:592, para 31; Case C-202/13 *McCarthy II*, EU:C:2014:2450, para 34; and Case C-673/16 *Coman*, EU:C:2018:385, para 39. But see also, AG Bot in *Onuekwere*, EU:C:2013:640, para 64 of the Opinion: 'if periods of legal residence before and after imprisonment could be taken into account in calculating the required period of five years, that would in my opinion amount, in reality, to denying that the person concerned was not integrated and would greatly diminish the effectiveness sought by Article 16(2) of Directive 2004/38'.
[137] ie '[I]n accordance with the conditions and limits defined by the Treaties and by the measures adopted thereunder' (Article 20(2) TFEU); 'subject to the limitations and conditions laid down in the Treaties and by the measures adopted to give them effect' (Article 21(1) TFEU).
[138] Case C-184/99 *Grzelczyk*, EU:C:2001:458, para 31 (emphasis added). Confirmed in eg Case C-148/02 *Garcia-Avello*, EU:C:2003:539, para 23; Case C-524/06 *Huber*, EU:C:2008:724, para 69; Case C-391/09 *Runevič-Vardyn and Wardyn*, EU:C:2011:291, para 61; Case C-220/12 *Thiele Meneses*, EU:C:2013:683, para 19; Case C-438/14 *Bogendorff von Wolffersdorff*, EU:C:2016:401, para 30; Case C-679/16 *A (Aide pour une personne handicapée)*, EU:C:2018:601, para 56; and Case C-411/20 *Familienkasse Niedersachsen-Bremen*, EU:C:2022:602, para 28.
[139] *Onuekwere*, para 26 (emphasis added).
[140] ibid para 30.

right of permanent residence for the purposes of Article 16(2) of Directive 2004/38 would clearly be contrary to the aim pursued by that directive in establishing that right of residence'.[141] Advocate General Bot had supported that position in his remark that '[t]he system set up by Directive 2004/38 and more specifically the creation of a right of permanent residence is therefore based on the idea that *genuine integration* must, in a sense, *be rewarded*, or at least that it must have an effect of strengthening the feeling of belonging to the society of the host Member State'.[142] He was even blunter on the impact of imprisonment on a person's capacity to integrate in the host State:

> [H]ow can a person who has been imprisoned on one or more occasions possibly be allowed to enjoy a right of permanent residence? Does integration within the society of the host Member State not first require the person who seeks to profit from it to respect the laws and values of that society? ... Periods of residence in prison of course make clear that the person concerned is integrated to only a limited extent. That is even more true where, as in the case in the main proceedings, that person is a multiple recidivist. Criminal conduct in my opinion clearly shows that the person concerned has no desire to integrate in the society of the host Member State.[143]

And he expressed a similarly narrow perspective on the rehabilitation objective of criminal sanctions:

> It is clear that every sentence must, in accordance with the fundamental principles of the law on sanctions, comprise a rehabilitative element to be achieved by appropriate means of implementation. Nevertheless, if a sentence has been imposed, it is precisely because societal values as expressed in the criminal law have been disregarded by the offender. And while rehabilitation must take its proper place, that is exactly because either there was no integration in society, thus explaining the commission of the offence, or because such integration was expunged by commission of the offence. Besides rehabilitation, the sentence also serves the essential purpose of retribution, which aims to make the offender pay for his crime and is proportionate to the gravity of the offence, expressed here by the penalty of imprisonment. These functions cannot operate to negate each other. The rehabilitative function cannot result in a situation where a period spent atoning for the crime committed confers on the convicted person a right the acquisition of which requires recognition and acceptance of social values which he specifically disregarded by committing his criminal act.[144]

Furthermore, '[t]hat is the reason for which, in addition, [he was] of the opinion that, even in the context of reduced sentencing which may find expression, for example, in house arrest or in a part-release scheme obliging the prisoner to return to prison in the evening, it is not possible to consider that the person concerned is residing legally within the meaning of Article 16(2) of Directive 2004/38'.[145]

---

[141] ibid para 31 (emphasis added).
[142] AG Bot in *Onuekwere*, para 47 of the Opinion (emphasis added).
[143] ibid paras 48–50 of the Opinion.
[144] ibid paras 54–55 of the Opinion.
[145] ibid para 56 of the Opinion. He suggested that 'only a period of residence in prison in the context of pre-trial detention followed by a decision not to proceed to judgment or by an acquittal could be taken into account in calculating the period of five years required for the purposes of the acquisition of the right of permanent residence' (para 73 of the Opinion).

The reasoning of the Court in *Onuekwere* was criticised on several fronts, but most especially for the outdated conception of rehabilitation projected by the reasoning of both the Court and the Advocate General. Discussion around the Court's views on 'good' and 'bad' Union citizens intensified.[146] In *Onuekwere*, the German Government had outlined a softer approach, better reflecting a sense of proportionality by suggesting that Article 16(3) rather than Article 16(4) of the Directive should be applied by analogy: on that view, 'a number of periods of imprisonment exceeding in total six months per year or a single period of imprisonment of more than twelve months would interrupt the continuity of legal residence required for the purposes of the acquisition of the right of permanent residence. Equally, periods of imprisonment of lesser duration would also interrupt the continuity of that residence where the transgression which earned imprisonment manifestly demonstrated unwillingness on the part of the person concerned to integrate in the society of the host Member State or to respect its values'.[147] Similarly, the Commission, explicitly invoking proportionality assessment, considered that 'the taking into account of certain periods spent in prison depends, inter alia, on the level of integration of the person before imprisonment, the duration of the detention, the gravity of the offence of which he was convicted and whether or not there has been recidivism'.[148] Advocate General Bot criticised that submission on the grounds that it would engender legal uncertainty, asking how it would 'be possible to reconcile it with the fact that, in a Union of 28 countries, criminal law and therefore the classification of offences diverge ... Furthermore, precise criteria would be needed to ensure that the offender knew exactly what to expect. The uncertainty which would be generated by the application of the principle of proportionality as proposed by the Commission would call into question the principle of legality'.[149]

The opposing views of the Commission and the Advocate General exemplify the tension between case-by-case assessments, which better respect proportionality requirements by taking individual circumstances into account (and specifically in this context, would also allow for differences in the criminal law environments of the Member States to be meaningful); and systemic responses, which flatten both individual circumstances and regulatory differences but offer greater predictability and deepen the prospects of equality of implementation across all of the Member States. These questions were considered in Chapter 7 in the context of assessing lawful residence. Here, the same dilemma also reflects broader questions about what integration into *a Member State* in the context of a *Union of Member States* really entails.[150] While arguments advocating a less severe outcome did not influence the decision of the Court in *Onuekwere*, they have resurfaced in more recent case law. In Chapter 10, it will be seen that fulfilling the conditions of continuous and legal residence

---

[146] See eg L Azoulai, 'The (mis)construction of the European individual—two essays on Union citizenship law", EUI working papers, LAW 2014/14, <https://cadmus.eui.eu/handle/1814/33293> (accessed 6 June 2023); S Coutts, 'Union citizenship as probationary citizenship: *Onuekwere*' (2015) 52 Common Market Law Review 531; and N Nic Shuibhne and J Shaw, 'General Report – Union citizenship: development, impact and challenges' in U Neergaard, C Jacqueson, and N Holst-Christensen (eds), *The XXVI FIDE Congress in Copenhagen 2014: Congress Publications Vol. 2* (DJOEF Publishing 2014) 65 esp at 137 and 223–24.
[147] AG Bot in *Onuekwere*, para 60 of the Opinion.
[148] ibid para 61 of the Opinion.
[149] ibid para 71 of the Opinion.
[150] For example, Azoulai has argued that 'by stating that [the] objective [of promoting social cohesion] is perfectly consistent with the fact that the EU legislature made the acquisition of the right of permanent residence "*subject to integration of the citizen of the Union in the host MS*", the Court changes the meaning of their concept of social cohesion. In this sense social cohesion is not about extending the possibility of creating bonds and promoting news forms of solidarity in Europe. It is mainly about respecting the particular value system of the host Member State' (Azoulai (n 146) 16, emphasis in original).

for permanent residence rights is, in turn, linked to enhanced protection against expulsion under Article 28 of the Directive. The implications of periods of imprisonment for integration in the host State drawn in *Onuekwere* are also evident in case law on Article 28.[151] In the latter context, however, the case law has exhibited a more balanced and progressive approach to the intersection of integration and rehabilitation, underlining that 'the social rehabilitation of the Union citizen in the State in which he has become genuinely integrated is not only in his interest but also in that of the European Union in general'.[152]

In *B and Vomero*, the Court thus moved on from the perspective that periods spent in prison *automatically* entail 'discontinuity' of residence,[153] and suggested that the condition of having resided in the host State for the previous ten years laid down in Article 28(3) of the Directive 'may be satisfied where *an overall assessment of the person's situation*, taking into account all the relevant aspects, leads to the conclusion that, *notwithstanding that detention*, the integrative links between the person concerned and the host Member State *have not been broken*'.[154] This case is discussed further in Chapter 10 in the context of expulsion from a host State. It remains to be seen whether that reasoning will be transposed back to the case law on permanent residence rights, but that would certainly address much of the concern directed at the *Onuekwere*-based conception of integration, which unsettled the very idea of 'permanence' that the Directive seeks to produce.

3.3 Administrative Formalities

Articles 19 and 20 of Directive 2004/38 establish the administrative formalities attached to the right of permanent residence for Union citizens and for family members who are not nationals of a Member State respectively. First, for Union citizens, Article 19(1) provides that '[u]pon application Member States shall issue Union citizens entitled to permanent residence after having verified duration of residence, with a document certifying permanent residence'—wording which makes it clear that applying for a permanent residence certificate is optional for Union citizens. In *Wolzenburg*, the Court acknowledged that '[w]ith regard to Union citizens who have been lawfully resident in another Member State for a continuous period of five years, [Article 19] provided merely for the issue, upon application, of a document attesting to the permanence of their residence, without requiring that formality. Such a document has only declaratory and probative force but does not give rise to any right'.[155] Second, Article 19(2) establishes that when applied for, '[t]he document certifying permanent residence shall be issued as soon as possible'. While Article 19 refers to verification of the *duration* of residence only, the case law examined in Section 3.2 demonstrates that the host State may also verify that the applicant Union citizen resided *legally* for the required

---

[151] See esp Case C-400/12 *MG*, EU:C:2014:9, paras 29–33 and 36. Analogous concerns about the paradox of a legal order grounded in Union citizenship that has nevertheless revitalised a punishment-plus-banishment approach to criminal sanctions are thus discussed in the same light: see eg L Azoulai and S Coutts, 'Restricting Union citizen's residence rights on grounds of public security: where Union citizenship and the AFSJ meet: *P.I.*' (2013) 50 Common Market Law Review 553; and D Kostakopoulou and N Ferreira, 'Testing liberal norms: the public policy and public security derogations and the cracks in European Union citizenship' Warwick School of Law, Legal Studies Paper No 2013/18, <https://papers.ssrn.com/sol3/papers.cfm?abstract_id=2271722> (accessed 6 June 2023).
[152] Joined Cases C-316/16 and C-424/16 *B and Vomero*, EU:C:2018:256, para 75.
[153] ibid para 80.
[154] ibid para 83 (emphasis added).
[155] Case C-123/08 *Wolzenburg*, EU:C:2009:616, para 51; referring 'to that effect' to Case C-85/96 *Martínez Sala*, EU:C:1998:217, para 53.

period. Article 21 of the Directive further establishes that 'continuity of residence may be attested by any means of proof in use in the host Member State'.

In contrast to the optional system in place for Union citizens—reflecting similar relative degrees of administrative burden for the right to reside more generally (Chapter 6)—Article 20 of the Directive requires family members who are not nationals of a Member State to obtain a 'permanent residence card' subject to the following conditions:

Article 20

Permanent residence card for family members who are not nationals of a Member State

1. Member States shall issue family members who are not nationals of a Member State entitled to permanent residence with a permanent residence card within six months of the submission of the application. The permanent residence card shall be renewable automatically every ten years.
2. The application for a permanent residence card shall be submitted before the residence card expires. Failure to comply with the requirement to apply for a permanent residence card may render the person concerned liable to proportionate and non-discriminatory sanctions.
3. Interruption in residence not exceeding two consecutive years shall not affect the validity of the permanent residence card.

In its original proposal for the Directive, the Commission had intended that Union citizens should also apply for a permanent residence card. In its view, '[a]cquisition of the right of permanent residence entails a series of important additional rights, such as access to social welfare in the host Member State for all categories of persons benefitting from the Directive and immunity from expulsion from the territory of the Member State of residence. That is why permanent residence should be confirmed by the issuance of a residence card'.[156] It also indicated that '[w]hile obtaining this card necessarily involves administrative formalities, once done, they are done once and for all, since the card will be valid indefinitely'.[157] But it then suggested, paradoxically, that the permanent residence card would be both valid indefinitely and automatically renewable every ten years.[158]

Almost every institution and body responding to the Commission's proposal commented on the illogical drafting on that point.[159] The European Parliament opted for indefinite validity,[160] but the issue became moot after the Council later decided to change what is now Article 19 by instituting an option rather than a requirement for Union citizens on the basis that '[t]his approach meets the objective of reducing administrative formalities for Union citizens'.[161] The Commission subsequently accepted that Union citizens could obtain 'if they

---

[156] Original proposal (n 2) 17.
[157] ibid.
[158] ibid 39.
[159] See eg in the European Parliament Report (n10) Amendment 62; Opinion of the Committee on Culture, Youth, Education, the Media and Sport (ibid) Amendment 17; and Opinion of the Committee on Petitions (ibid) Amendment 3. See also, the Council's Common Position (n 18) 29.
[160] Accepted by the Commission in its amended proposal (COM(2003) 199 final, 7).
[161] Common Position (n 18) 31.

consider it necessary or useful, a document certifying that they have acquired the right of permanent residence. This document will be issued to them as soon as possible after the request and after verification of the length of their residence. The Commission has endorsed this approach because it considers that this amendment meets the directive's objective of reducing to a minimum the administrative formalities to which Union citizens are subject'.[162] For family members who are not Member State nationals, however, the Council opted for automatic renewability every ten years rather than indefinite validity.[163] It also increased the time limit in Article 20(1) from three to six months to allow for 'the updating of data'.[164]

Finally, Articles 25 and 26 of the Directive apply to residence documents issued for both the right to reside (discussed in Chapter 6) and the right of permanent residence. Reflecting again the declaratory rather than constitutive nature of such documents under EU law, Article 25(1) establishes that '[p]ossession of a registration certificate as referred to in Article 8, of a document certifying permanent residence, of a certificate attesting submission of an application for a family member residence card, of a residence card or of a permanent residence card, may under no circumstances be made a precondition for the exercise of a right or the completion of an administrative formality, as entitlement to rights may be attested by any other means of proof'. Article 25(2) requires that '[a]ll documents mentioned in [Article 25(1)] shall be issued free of charge or for a charge not exceeding that imposed on nationals for the issuing of similar documents'. Finally, Article 26 permits Member States to 'carry out checks on compliance with any requirement deriving from their national legislation for non-nationals always to carry their registration certificate or residence card, provided that the same requirement applies to their own nationals as regards their identity card'; also establishing that '[i]n the event of failure to comply with this requirement, Member States may impose the same sanctions as those imposed on their own nationals for failure to carry their identity card'.

4. Concluding Remarks

The right of permanent residence added something new and vitally important to the legislative framework that had regulated freedom of movement for Member State nationals and their family members before the adoption of Directive 2004/38. From the discussion of that right in this chapter, three themes can be highlighted. First, permanent residence entails internal contradictions. It is emblematic of Union citizenship yet extended to EEA nationals. It is not actually permanent and can be lost by extended absences, singular or cumulative. It is both decidedly *of* the Directive yet extendable by analogy on the basis of Article 21 TFEU. Second, considering how the conditions for the right of permanent residence have been applied and interpreted by the Court of Justice, there is strong resonance with the evolution of the right to reside in EU citizenship law generally, especially as regards the interpretation of 'legal' residence for the purposes of Article 16 of the Directive and 'lawful' residence as a precondition for equal treatment with host State nationals more generally. It might not seem surprising, therefore, that the exclusion from permanent residence eligibility of periods of residence in a host State authorised by either national law or by Article 10 of Regulation 492/

---

[162] Communication on the common position (n 16) para 3.3.2.
[163] Common Position (n 18) 29.
[164] ibid 32.

2011 but not in compliance with the conditions of Directive 2004/38 was exported to the case law on lawful residence more generally. Nevertheless, as seen in Chapter 7, this cross-fertilisation came at some cost to both the protection of Union citizens and legal coherence.

Finally, the right of permanent residence is both constituted by and exemplifies the significance of integration in the host State in EU citizenship law. The case law on this aspect of permanent residence has perhaps also illustrated that both defining and measuring integration can be problematic in practice, representing choices and values that risk being more subjectively than objectively conceived. That theme is picked up again in Chapter 10, which examines exclusion from the host State on grounds of public policy, public security, and public health.

Further Reading

CNK Franklin and HH Fredriksen, 'Differentiated citizenship in the European Economic Area' in D Kostakopoulou and D Thym (eds), *Research Handbook on European Union Citizenship Law and Policy* (Edward Elgar 2022) 297.

A Łazowski, 'Children of the lesser law: comment on *Ziolkowski and Szeja* (Case Comment)' (2013) 38 European Law Review 404.

L Mancano, 'Criminal conduct and lack of integration into society under EU citizenship: this marriage is not to be performed' (2015) 6 New Journal of European Criminal Law 53.

G More, 'Comprehensive sickness insurance, EU citizenship rights and residence rights of *Chen* carers: and all this after the UK has left the EU ...: *VI*' (2022) 59 Common Market Law Review 1915.

9
The Right to Move and Reside
Beyond the Directive

1. Chapter Overview

This chapter considers the provisions of EU law that confer a right to move and reside on Member State nationals in circumstances that fall outside the scope of Directive 2004/38.[1] It therefore examines freedom of movement and residence in two main contexts—first, situations of ongoing multi-State life; and second, protection in a Member State national's home State following previous exercise of freedom of movement. These rights can be based on Articles 21, 45, or 49 TFEU, or on Article 10 of Regulation 492/2011.[2]

One of the main objectives of Directive 2004/38 was to 'codify and review the existing Community instruments dealing separately with workers, self-employed persons, as well as students and other inactive persons' (recital 3) and thereby '[remedy] the sector-by-sector, piecemeal approach to the right of free movement and residence' (recital 4) applied since the inception of free movement rights. Even so, the Directive does not capture every instance of freedom of movement and residence protected by EU law. We saw in Chapter 6, for example, that Article 7(3) of the Directive does not list '*exhaustively* the circumstances in which a migrant worker who is no longer in an employment relationship may nevertheless continue to benefit from that status'.[3] In the *Saint Prix* case, the Court therefore found that 'a woman who gives up work, or seeking work, because of the physical constraints of the late stages of pregnancy and the aftermath of childbirth retains the status of "worker", within the meaning of [Article 45 TFEU], provided she returns to work or finds another job within a reasonable period after the birth of her child'.[4]

However, the most obvious barrier to invoking Directive 2004/38 stems from its own definition of 'beneficiaries' in Article 3(1): 'all Union citizens *who move to or reside in* a Member State other than that of which they are a national'—in other words, (continuing) residence in a host State is a necessary precondition for the Directive's application and neither can its provisions be invoked directly against a Union citizen's home State.[5] Instances of movement

---

[1] Directive 2004/38/EC on the right of citizens of the Union and their family members to move and reside freely within the territory of the Member States, 2004 OJ L158/77.
[2] Regulation 492/2011 on freedom of movement for workers within the Union, 2011 OJ L141/1.
[3] Case C-507/12 *Saint Prix*, EU:C:2014:2007, para 38 (emphasis added).
[4] ibid para 47; extended to self-employed persons by Case C-544/18 *Dakneviciute* EU:C:2019:761.
[5] Relatedly, in light of its defining focus on 'the host State' both for British nationals who reside in EU27 and EU citizens who reside in the UK, the Withdrawal Agreement does not sustain protection based on return to the home State (Agreement on the withdrawal of the United Kingdom of Great Britain and Northern Ireland from the European Union and the European Atomic Energy Community, OJ 2019 CI 384/01, see esp Article 9(c) WA). As the Commission explains, '[f]or UK nationals, the host State is the EU Member State as defined in Article 2 (b) of the Agreement in which they are exercising their right of residence under Union free movement rules. The UK cannot become the host State under the Agreement for UK nationals – this means that UK nationals who have resided in the UK before the end of the transition period in accordance with rights under Union law (as beneficiaries of the case law based on judgments of the CJEU in Cases C-34/09, *Ruiz Zambrano* or C-370/90, *Singh*) do not become beneficiaries of the Agreement in their personal capacity. For EU citizens, the host State is the UK as defined in Article 3(1) of the Agreement. EU citizens do not become beneficiaries of the Agreement in their

and residence that do not meet the Article 3(1) threshold are explored in two main contexts in this chapter: where EU citizens either have current multi-State lives (Section 2) or where their past cross-borderness remains legally meaningful after they return to their home States (Section 3). Examples of these situations were already introduced in other chapters yet fuller discussion of them did not fit properly there in structural terms—in common with Chapter 5, they can involve claims against home States, but differently, free movement continues to be or has already been exercised; in common with Chapters 6 and 7, freedom of movement and host States can be involved, but differently, the Union citizen either does not reside or is no longer in the host State, as required by Article 3(1) of the Directive, or they are in the host State but do not reside there on the basis of the Directive even if still lawfully resident within the meaning of EU law more broadly.

Ongoing multi-State and return to home State situations evoke a degree of flexibility and fluidity increasingly expected of freedom of movement since, as expressed by Advocate General Jacobs, '[t]he concept of moving and residing freely in the territory of the Member States is not based on the hypothesis of a single move from one Member State to another, to be followed by integration into the latter. The intention is rather to allow free, and possibly repeated or even continuous, movement within a single area of freedom, security and justice, in which both cultural diversity and freedom from discrimination are ensured'.[6] The fact that Directive 2004/38 addresses only more rigid 'move there and stay there' situations raises questions about the appropriateness and adaptability of its free movement framework to economic and social as much as legal developments.[7]

Reflecting the scope of the book as outlined in Chapter 1, the discussion in this chapter does not aim to provide a complete or even comprehensive account of EU law in all cross-border situations. It does not, for example, examine in detail the rights of frontier workers under Article 45 TFEU and/or Regulation 492/2011; or the rights of Member State nationals who provide or receive services within the meaning of Article 56 TFEU. Instead, it focuses on situations where the relevant rights are either drawn solely from Article 21 TFEU or require blended consideration of Article 21 TFEU and the economic freedoms.[8] On the latter point, the relationship between economic free movement law and EU citizenship law is a complicated relationship overall, exhibiting both rights-enhancing and rights-curbing qualities, in both directions.

Finally, as introduced in Chapter 2, it also will be seen that even in situations that are formally outside the scope of Directive 2004/38, its provisions are increasingly applied 'by analogy'. At one level, this methodology renders rights based directly on the Treaty more functional in concrete cases and it contributes positively to the coherence of EU citizenship

---

personal capacity in any EU Member State, regardless of whether it is the Member State of their nationality or not' (European Commission, Guidance Note relating to the Agreement on the withdrawal of the United Kingdom of Great Britain and Northern Ireland from the European Union and the European Atomic Energy Community Part two—Citizens' rights, C(2020) 2939 final, para 1.1.3). With respect to multi-State life, frontier workers/self-employed persons receive specific protection under the Agreement, which continues beyond the end of the transition period: see esp Articles 9(b), 24(3), 25(1), 25(3), and 26 WA.

[6] AG Jacobs in Case C-148/02 *Garcia-Avello*, EU:C:2003:311, para 72 of the Opinion.
[7] Addressing this question for Regulation 1612/68 but with broader resonance, see AG Geelhoed in Case C-413/99 *Baumbast and R*, EU:C:2001:385, esp paras 22–27 and 87–88 of the Opinion. Regulation 1612/68/EEC on freedom of movement for workers within the Community, 1968 OJ L257/13.
[8] For an earlier example of that blending, see the discussion on jobseekers as regards the right to reside (Chapter 6) and eligibility for equal treatment (Chapter 7) in a host State, not considered in this chapter because these rights do fall within the scope of Directive 2004/38.

law overall. But it can also constrain the scope of rights protected by primary EU law more strictly than is arguably required by the Treaty itself.

2. EU Citizenship Law and Multi-State Life: Living Across Different Places

For most Union citizens who 'split' their lives across more than one Member State—whether connected to a frontier location in a geographical sense or not—relevant legal challenges tend to concern situations involving residence in one Member State and the exercise of economic activity in another. In EU free movement law generally, in consequence, key questions have concerned the allocation and coordination of rights and responsibilities for social security (Section 2.1). However, the intersection of economic free movement law and Union citizenship has not been straightforward in the multi-State context (Section 2.2). Residence rights for the family members of Union citizens who reside in one Member State and exercise economic activity in another provide an example of both the frictions and the synergies produced as a result (Section 2.3).

2.1 Coordinating Social Security for Multi-State Life: Basic Principles

Importantly, 'Article [48 TFEU] provides for the coordination, not the harmonization, of the legislation of the Member States. As a result, Article [48] leaves in being differences between the Member States' social security systems and, consequently, in the rights of persons working in the Member States'.[9] To navigate substantive, procedural, and systemic differences effectively, Regulation 883/2004 establishes a system of conflict rules.[10] Its provisions work to identify the State of responsibility for payment of social security benefits and to facilitate aggregation of entitlement across two or more systems while avoiding undue overlap of benefits. An important consequence of choosing a system of coordination is that 'the Treaty offers no guarantee to a worker that extending his activities into more than one Member State or transferring them to another Member State will be neutral as regards social security', which 'may be to the worker's advantage in terms of social security or not, according to circumstance'.[11]

Article 7 of Regulation 883/2004 establishes that '[u]nless otherwise provided for by this Regulation, cash benefits payable under the legislation of one or more Member States or under this Regulation shall not be subject to any reduction, amendment, suspension, withdrawal or confiscation on account of the fact that the beneficiary or the members of his family reside in a Member State other than that in which the institution responsible for providing benefits is situated'. Reflecting the citizenship-specific discussion of integration requirements in Chapter 2, the Court of Justice recognises that 'compulsory membership

---

[9] Case 41/84 *Pinna*, EU:C:1986:1, para 20.
[10] Regulation 883/2004 on the coordination of social security systems, 2011 OJ L166/1. Both Article 48 TFEU and Regulation 883/2004 refer to self-employed workers also. Continuing coordination of social security claims is one of the few areas of the Withdrawal Agreement that commits (the UK) to dynamic alignment with evolving EU rules (see Title III, Part Two WA; the personal scope of Title III is detailed in Article 30 WA while Article 36 WA outlines how EU regulations amended or replaced after the end of the transition period will be accommodated).
[11] Joined Cases C-393/99 and C-394/99 *Hervein and Hervillie*, EU:C:2002:182, para 51.

of the [host State] social security system, which ensures that workers pay social contributions to that system, constitutes a sufficiently close connection with [host State] society to enable cross-border workers to benefit from the social advantage in question'.[12] Recital 8 of the Regulation affirms that '[t]he general principle of equal treatment is of particular importance for workers who do not reside in the Member State of their employment, including frontier workers'. Providing a specific example, Article 67 establishes that '[a] person shall be entitled to family benefits in accordance with the legislation of the competent Member State, including for his family members residing in another Member State, as if they were residing in the former Member State'. The Court has underlined that the purpose of this provision is 'to prevent Member States from making entitlement to and the amount of family benefits dependent on residence of the members of the worker's family in the Member State providing the benefits, so that [Union] workers are not deterred from exercising their right to freedom of movement'.[13]

Separately, but creating in some respects a parallel legal route for both social security and social assistance claims, Regulation 492/2011 establishes, in Article 7(2), that a worker who is a national of another Member State 'shall enjoy the same social and tax advantages as national workers'. Regulation 492/2011 is not addressed to self-employed workers, but comparable equal treatment in this respect is conferred directly by Articles 18 and 49 TFEU.[14] The Court has established a broad understanding of 'social and tax advantages' as including 'all those which, whether or not linked to a contract of employment, are generally granted to national workers primarily because of their objective status as workers or by virtue of the mere fact of their residence on the national territory'.[15] Article 7(2) of Regulation 492/2011 thus covers benefits that are characterised as social assistance[16] as well as benefits that might also fall within the scope of Regulation 883/2004.[17] Entitlement to the social and tax advantages offered by a host State on a basis of equal treatment with workers who are nationals of that State is rooted in the EU worker's participation in the host State employment market, which 'establishes, in principle, a sufficient link of integration with the society of that Member State, allowing [workers] to benefit from the principle of equal treatment, as compared with national workers, as regards social advantages'.[18] More specifically, '[t]he link of integration arises from, *inter alia*, the fact that, through the taxes which he pays in the host Member State by virtue of his employment, the migrant worker also contributes to the financing of the social policies of that State and should profit from them under the same conditions as national workers'.[19]

The tools engaged for resolving multi-State social security questions are therefore mainly located in Articles 45, 48, and 49 TFEU and in the legislation adopted to provide in more detail for their application. At the level of framing, Union citizenship is sometimes invoked in relevant case law but only in a very general way. For example, in *Elsen*, the Court stated that Regulation 884/2004 'contains a number of provisions designed to ensure that social security benefits are payable by the competent State, even where the insured, who has worked

---

[12] Case C-269/07 *Commission v Germany*, EU:C:2009:527, para 60.
[13] Joined Cases C-245/94 and C-312/94 *Hoever and Zachow*, EU:C:1996:379, para 34.
[14] eg Case C-299/01 *Commission v Luxembourg*, EU:C:2002:394; Case C-168/20 *BJ and OV*, EU:C:2021:907. Equating work and self-employment for the purposes of the right to remain under Directive 2004/38, see Case C-442/16 *Gusa*, EU:C:2017:1004 and Case C-483/17 *Tarola*, EU:C:2019:309; see further, Chapter 6.
[15] Case 65/81 *Reina*, EU:C:1982:6, para 12; building on Case 32/75 *Cristini*, EU:C:1975:120.
[16] eg Case 249/83 *Hoeckx*, EU:C:1985:139, para 22.
[17] eg Case C-111/91 *Commission v Luxembourg*, EU:C:1993:92, para 21.
[18] Case C-542/09 *Commission v Netherlands*, EU:C:2012:346, para 65.
[19] ibid para 66.

exclusively in his State of origin, resides in or transfers his residence to another Member State', provisions which 'undoubtedly help to ensure freedom of movement not only for workers, under Article [45 TFEU], but also for citizens of the Union ... under Article [21 TFEU]'.[20] In case law on social security and frontier workers, however, transposing the ethos of EU citizenship law to the framework applied in the economic freedoms has produced both conceptual and legal disturbance, which will now be looked at in more detail.

2.2 The Intersection of the Economic Freedoms and Union Citizenship: Reinforcing or Undermining Legal Constructs of Integration?

Regulation 883/2004 establishes specific exportability rules for frontier workers where responsibility is assigned to the State of residence rather than to the State of employment. But it does not determine, as noted above, the beginning and end of eligibility questions. In *Hartmann*, a residence condition had been attached to payment of a child-raising allowance in Germany on the basis that it was 'an instrument of national family policy intended to encourage the birth-rate' and was granted 'to benefit persons who, by their choice of residence, have established a real link with German society'.[21] The applicant did not come within the personal scope of Regulation 883/2004, but the Court examined the benefit as a social advantage under Regulation 492/2011 and observed that 'under the German legislation in force at the material time, residence was not regarded as the only connecting link with the Member State concerned, and *a substantial contribution to the national labour market also constituted a valid factor of integration into the society of that Member State*. In those circumstances, the allowance at issue ... could not be refused to a couple ... who do not live in Germany, but one of whom works full-time in that State'.[22]

The Court's integration-based reasoning in *Hartmann* was amplified further in *Giersch* through the statement that 'the frontier worker is *not always integrated* in the Member State of employment *in the same way* as a worker who is resident in that State'.[23] It suggested that 'to ensure that the frontier worker who is a taxpayer and who makes social security contributions in [the host State] has a *sufficient* link with [that] society, the financial aid could be made conditional on the frontier worker ... having worked in that Member State *for a certain minimum period of time*'.[24] And it noted, in 'another context', the five-year continuous residence condition in Article 16 of Directive 2004/38 as regards acquiring the right of permanent residence.[25] However, post-*Giersch* national legislation taking that reference too literally—codifying precisely a five-year continuous employment before financial aid would be granted to frontier workers—was then rejected by the Court in *Bragança Linares Verruga* having regard to the 'significant period of time' that the applicants had worked in the host State.[26] More specifically, the fact that the grant of financial aid for higher education to a

---

[20] Case C-135/99 *Elsen*, EU:C:2000:647, para 35.
[21] Case C-212/05 *Hartmann*, EU:C:2007:437, paras 32–33.
[22] ibid paras 36–37 (emphasis added).
[23] Case C-20/12 *Giersch*, EU:C:2013:411, para 65 (emphasis added).
[24] ibid para 80 (emphasis added). See similarly, Case C-213/05 *Geven*, EU:C:2007:438, where the Court ruled that a 'sufficiently substantial occupation' requirement applicable only to workers not residing in Germany could be imposed on the granting of a child-raising allowance.
[25] *Giersch*, para 80.
[26] Case C-238/15 *Bragança Linares Verruga and Others*, EU:C:2016:949, paras 63–69. See further, C Jacqueson, 'Any news from Luxembourg? On student aid, frontier workers and stepchildren: *Bragança Linares Verruga* and *Depesme*' (2018) 54 Common Market Law Review 901; and J Silga, 'Luxembourg financial aid for higher studies

non-resident student was made conditional on at least one of that student's parents having worked in that Member State for a minimum and *continuous* period of five years at the time the application for financial aid is made was considered to be a disproportionate interference with the rights conferred by Article 7(2) of Regulation 492/2011.

In *Aubriet*, the Court summarised the consequences of this line of case law in saying that it 'accepted that indirectly discriminatory national legislation restricting the grant to frontier workers of social advantages within the meaning of Article 7(2) of Regulation No 492/2011 where there is not a sufficient connection to the society in which they are pursuing their activities without residing there may be objectively justified'.[27] However, Advocate General Wathelet was critical of these developments, contrasting them with the clearer equal treatment reasoning in previous rulings on frontier workers and questioning the relevance of 'sufficient integration or genuine link with the host Member State' to the free movement of workers.[28] Up to that point, case law 'acknowledg[ing] that States may require a certain level of integration into the host Member State to be demonstrated before granting the person in question social advantages' was 'specific to the nationals of the Member States who exercise their freedom of movement without being economically active', which had developed 'in parallel'.[29] The Advocate General acknowledged that 'the Court has accepted certain reasons as justifying legislation establishing a distinction between residents and non-residents pursuing a professional activity in the Member State concerned, according to their level of integration into the society of that State or their connection to it' but admitted that he remained 'reticent about that development'.[30] He therefore framed it as an 'exception' to the general rule that 'as regards migrant workers and frontier workers, the fact that they have participated in the employment market of a Member State establishes, in principle, a sufficient link of integration with the society of that Member State, allowing them to benefit from the principle of equal treatment, as compared with national workers, as regards social advantages'.[31]

The *Hartmann/Giersch* case law signals, above all, that different groups of workers are not necessarily equal under EU law.[32] In particular, *Aubriet* confirms that the significance and measuring of integration developed for EU citizenship law can also now apply to the economic freedoms. For frontier workers, factors that 'establish membership of a community of solidarity' can be investigated in certain circumstances—to determined whether residence alone is enough, for example, or whether, '[i]nstead, it might be considered whether it is appropriate in such cases on a supplementary basis to have recourse to additional criteria which characterise the degree of integration in an economic and social environment, for example, place of employment, distance to the frontier from the place of residence, place of

---

and children of frontier workers: evolution and challenges in light of the case-law of the Court of Justice' (2019) 19 European Public Law 13.

[27] Case C-410/18 *Aubriet*, EU:C:2019:582, para 34.
[28] AG Wathelet in *Bragança Linares Verruga*, para 36 of the Opinion.
[29] ibid para 34 of the Opinion; citing Case C-224/98 *D'Hoop*, EU:C:2002:432 and Case C-209/03 *Bidar*, EU:C:2005:169 as examples.
[30] AG Wathelet in *Bragança Linares Verruga*, paras 67–68 of the Opinion; a similarly conflicted tone can also be observed in paras 75–76 of the Opinion.
[31] ibid para 68 of the Opinion.
[32] In contrast to the previously standard view that '[w]hen interpreting Article 7(2) of Regulation [492/2011], the Court has made no distinction between the concepts of migrant worker and frontier worker precisely because [the] Regulation ... does not treat those two categories of worker differently' (AG Mengozzi in Case C-20/12 *Giersch*, EU:C:2013:70, para 30 of the Opinion).

consumption expenditure or primary location for social contacts'.[33] When, in contrast, will economic activity per se be accepted as establishing the necessary link to host State society?

When the case law on integration requirements and the free movement of workers is taken into account, the privileged position of economically active Union citizens, as outlined in Chapters 6 and 7, can be more vulnerable than is often appreciated. In particular, the concern for protecting host State public finances that features so strongly when Union citizens are not economically active within the meaning of EU law has also now reached case law concerning Union citizens who are economically active. In *Commission v Netherlands*, Court found that 'the Member States' power ... to require nationals of other Member States to show a certain degree of integration in their societies in order to receive social advantages, such as financial assistance for education, *is not limited to situations in which the applicants for assistance are economically inactive citizens*', but also that a residence requirement 'to prove the required degree of integration is, *in principle, inappropriate* when the persons concerned are migrant workers or frontier workers'.[34] Thus, for 'migrant workers and frontier workers, the fact that they have participated in the employment market of a Member State establishes, *in principle*, a sufficient link of integration with the society of that Member State, allowing them to benefit from the principle of equal treatment, as compared with national workers, as regards social advantages'.[35] This is because the required 'link of integration arises from, inter alia, the fact that, through the taxes which he pays in the host Member State by virtue of his employment, the migrant worker also contributes to the financing of the social policies of that State and should profit from them under the same conditions as national workers'.[36]

However, the 'in principle' qualification underlines that this is a presumption and not a rule. In *Tarola*, which concerned the right to remain in a host State by retaining the status of worker under EU law (discussed in Chapter 6), the Court stated, for the first time, that 'striking a fair balance between safeguarding the free movement of workers, on the one hand, and ensuring that the social security systems of the host Member State are not placed under an unreasonable burden, on the other' is one of the objectives pursued by Directive 2004/38.[37] That statement reflects the emphasis on recalibrating economic free movement rights in the EU's pre-Brexit negotiations with the UK.[38] In particular, citizenship-based public finance reasoning influenced the EU/UK February 2016 Decision's defence of proposed restrictions on the free movement of workers (with EU legislative amendments committed to in the event of a 'remain' vote in the UK referendum in June 2016).[39]

While the reforms agreed to in that Decision did not have to be implemented in light of the UK's decision to withdraw from the Union, it was rather ironic that the Commission subsequently initiated infringement proceedings against Austria for unilaterally introducing one of the restrictions proposed in 2016 (indexing exported family benefits to the family's State of residence rather than to the worker's State of employment). In his Opinion, Advocate

---

[33] AG Kokott in Case C-287/05 *Hendrix*, EU:C:2007:196, para 68 of the Opinion.
[34] Case C-542/09 *Commission v Netherlands*, EU:C:2012:346, para 63 (emphasis added).
[35] ibid para 65 (emphasis added).
[36] ibid para 66.
[37] Case C-483/17 *Tarola*, EU:C:2019:309, para 50.
[38] See esp the justification arguments accompanying the proposals to restrict 'in-work benefits' and index exported family benefits to the child's State of residence in Section D, Decision of the Heads of State or Government, meeting within the European Council, concerning a new settlement for the United Kingdom within the European Union, 2016 OJ C691/1.
[39] The proposals did not distinguish between directly and indirectly discriminatory restrictions, invoking general public interest grounds also to restrictions framed as direct discrimination: see Section D, Decision of the Heads of State or Government (ibid).

General Richard de la Tour underlined the 'fundamental importance' of the fact that 'migrant workers contribute to the financing of the social policies of the host Member State through the taxes and social contributions which they pay by virtue of their employment there, which justifies the equality of the benefits or advantages granted'.[40] The same point was made by the Court to explain why Austria's indirectly discriminatory restriction of the free movement of workers could not be saved on public interest grounds, since migrant workers 'must ... be able to profit from [their tax and social security contributions] under the same conditions as national workers'.[41] Even more remarkably, the Court also stated that '[a]s regards the conformity with EU law of the indexation mechanism which had been envisaged by the new settlement for the United Kingdom within the European Union, two factors should be noted. First, that settlement never entered into force ... Secondly, and in any event, as the judgment [in *Pinna*[42]] illustrates, if such an amendment had been adopted by the EU legislature, *it would have been invalid under Article 45 TFEU*'.[43] That statement illustrates just how disconnected the political and legal spheres of EU free movement can sometimes become.

However, recalling that economic activity only 'establishes, *in principle*, a sufficient link of integration with the society of that Member State, allowing [workers] to benefit from the principle of equal treatment, as compared with national workers, as regards social advantages',[44] the Court also held in *Commission v Austria*, in the context of justifying the restriction, that 'the risk of jeopardising the financial balance of the social security system does not result from the payment of benefits to workers whose children reside outside Austria, *since those payments are estimated to represent only around 6% of expenditure* in respect of family benefits'.[45] The emphasis on specific evidence is welcome here, noting the discussion on this point in Chapter 7. But it does leave a door open to reconsidering the implications of indexation under different empirical conditions. Similarly, the Court also considered that 'the family benefits and social advantages at issue *are not subject to the adjustment mechanism where the children reside in Austria*, even though it is common ground that there are, between the regions of that Member State, differences in price levels comparable in scale to those which may exist between the Republic of Austria and other Member States. That lack of consistency in the application of the mechanism confirms that the justification put forward by the Republic of Austria cannot be accepted'.[46] In that light, the statement in *Tarola* suggesting that economically active Union citizens *can* become an 'unreasonable burden' on host State social security systems should not be forgotten—even though the *Lawrie Blum* definition of work is met and notwithstanding the fact that 'migrant workers contribute to the financing of the social policies of the host Member State through the taxes and social contributions which they pay by virtue of their employment there'.[47]

At the same time, the discussion on *Jobcenter Krefeld* in Chapter 7, especially when placed in contrast with the ruling in *CG*, illustrates that even circumstances tangentially linked to previous economic activity can institute deep legal privilege for Member State nationals in a host State.[48] This point is picked up again in Section 3 with respect to Article 10 of Regulation

---

[40] AG Richard de la Tour in Case C-328/20 *Commission v Austria*, EU:C:2022:45, para 143 of the Opinion.
[41] Case C-328/20 *Commission v Austria*, EU:C:2022:468, para 109.
[42] Case 41/84 *Pinna*, EU:C:1986:1.
[43] *Commission v Austria*, EU:C:2022:468, para 57 (emphasis added).
[44] Case C-542/09 *Commission v Netherlands*, EU:C:2012:346, para 65 (emphasis added).
[45] *Commission v Austria*, para 107 (emphasis added).
[46] ibid, para 105 (emphasis added).
[47] AG Richard de la Tour in *Commission v Austria*, para 143 of the Opinion. Case 66/85 *Lawrie-Blum*, EU:C:1986:284.
[48] Case C-181/19 *Jobcenter Krefeld*, EU:C:2020:794; Case C-709/20 *CG*, EU:C:2021:602. See further, Chapter 7.

492/2011. For now, the key point is that the case law highlights the unpredictability of how (and when) integration requirements apply to equal treatment in the domain of economic activity. In that light, the tendency of the Court to use phrases like 'in principle' is noteworthy. Such qualifications are often overcome in individual cases, enabling genuine assessment and consideration of individual circumstances, yet using them in the first place can serve a political purpose.[49] As the discussion here and also in Chapters 6 and 7 has shown, there are contradictions within EU citizenship law in terms of the basic distinction it makes between economic activity and economic autonomy. However, case law at the intersection of the economic freedoms and Union citizenship emits a sense of instability that it is important both to observe and seek to resettle.

2.3 Multi-State Life and Family Member Residence Rights

The intersection of economic free movement law and EU citizenship law is also strongly evident in the context of facilitating the realities of multi-State life through derived residence rights for family members.[50] In particular, legal uncertainties can arise when a Union citizen resides in their home State but is economically active, within the meaning of EU law, in another Member State. Union citizenship is not necessarily invoked in such situations—in *Carpenter*, for example, the Court established a residence right in a Union citizen's home State for their third-country national spouse on the basis of the former's occasional provision of services in other Member States.[51] For present purposes, the legal significance that the Court did (or did not) attach to the fact that Mrs Carpenter provided childcare for Mr Carpenter's children when he travelled to other States to provide services is important. That angle was highlighted by the referring tribunal, which asked whether the fact that 'the non-national spouse indirectly assists the national of a Member State in carrying on the provision of services in other Member States by carrying out childcare' made a material difference to whether Mr Carpenter could rely on Article 56 TFEU and/or Directive 73/148 to establish a right of residence for his spouse in his Member State of origin.[52]

Advocate General Stix-Hackl addressed the referring tribunal's question directly but her reasoning on this point was concerned mainly with Directive 73/148: she ruled out the relevance of Article 56 TFEU on the premise that a third-country national could not derive any

---

[49] As Ristuccia argues: 'to somewhat soothe Member States' concerns of opening up their welfare systems too much' (F Ristuccia, 'The right to social assistance of children in education and their primary carers: *Jobcenter Krefeld*' (2021) 58 Common Market Law Review 877 at 893).

[50] Which can also raise issues with respect to the scope of Directive 2004/38: see eg AG Szpunar in Case C-202/13 *McCarthy II*, EU:C:2014:345, paras 74–76 of the Opinion; having observed at para 62 that '[i]n today's European Union, a citizen's origins may lie in a Member State of which he is not a national or he may be a national of one (or of several) Member State(s) in which he has never lived. He may also have several nationalities, or indeed live in two or more Member States, while retaining genuine links, both occupational and personal, with all those States'. For a multi-State life case concerning neither social security claims nor family member residence rights, see eg Case C-420/15 *U*, EU:C:2017:408, where the Court ruled that Article 45 TFEU precluded Belgian legislation that obliged a worker resident there to register in Belgium, in order to be able to drive there, even if only occasionally, a vehicle belonging to that worker that was registered in another Member State. See also, in the context of integration and the acquisition of host State nationality, the discussion on Case C-165/16 *Lounes*, EU:C:2017:862 in Chapter 3.

[51] Case C-60/00 *Carpenter*, EU:C:2002:434. See further, Chapters 2 and 4.

[52] ibid para 20. Directive 73/148/EEC on the abolition of restrictions on movement and residence within the Community for nationals of Member States with regard to establishment and the provision of services (1973 OJ L172/14) established a right to reside for family members in the State in which a Member State national provided or received services but did not address residence rights in the latter's home State.

rights from that provision.⁵³ She argued that Article 1(1) of Directive 73/148 established its scope by referring to 'a series of circumstances such as the degree of relationship, age, dependency and living together as a household. The care of children is not included in this – exhaustive – list. It may be concluded that the Community legislature manifestly attached no importance in this connection to caring for children'.⁵⁴ More generally, she considered that the Court's case law on the rights of third-country national spouses 'does not refer expressly to the circumstance that the national of a non-member country contributes to the professional activity of the citizen of the Union'.⁵⁵ In other words, also reflecting the submissions of the Commission, the fact that 'Mrs Carpenter cares for Mr Carpenter's children and thus indirectly assists him to exercise the rights deriving from the freedom to provide services *has nothing to do* with the question whether Mr Carpenter has exercised his rights in such a way that his spouse comes within Community law'.⁵⁶

In contrast, and referring to 'the importance of ensuring the protection of the family life of nationals of the Member States in order to eliminate obstacles to the exercise of the fundamental freedoms guaranteed by the Treaty', the Court drew the relevant residence right directly from Article 56 TFEU, though on the relatively ambiguous basis that 'the separation of Mr and Mrs Carpenter would be detrimental to their family life and, therefore, *to the conditions under which Mr Carpenter exercises a fundamental freedom*' since '[t]hat freedom could not be fully effective if Mr Carpenter were to be deterred from exercising it by obstacles raised in his country of origin to the entry and residence of his spouse'.⁵⁷ The Court referred expressly to Mrs Carpenter's provision of childcare only in the context of assessing the public interest justification of maintaining public order and public safety.⁵⁸

More recently, however, the Court has re-engaged the legal significance of providing childcare—and of who provides it—in its case law on family member residence rights in multi-State situations. In *S and G*, two sets of facts raised residence rights that might be derived from EU law: for a Ukrainian national seeking a right of residence with her Dutch son-in-law (sponsor S, who resided and worked in the Netherlands but travelled to Belgium for work at least once per week), on basis that she took care of her grandson (the son of sponsor S), and for a Peruvian national married to a Dutch national (sponsor G, who lived in the Netherlands but travelled daily to Belgium for work) with whom she had a daughter. Having established that both S and G fell within the scope of Article 45 TFEU, the Court confirmed that its 'interpretation of Article 56 TFEU in *Carpenter* is transposable to Article 45 TFEU' since '[t]he effectiveness of the right to freedom of movement of workers may require that a derived right of residence be granted to a third-country national who is a family member of the worker – a Union citizen – in the Member State of which the latter is a national'.⁵⁹

The Court then wove together case law on Union citizenship and Article 21 TFEU— referring to *Iida*, *Ymeraga*, and *Alokpa and Moudoulou* to affirm that 'the purpose and

---

⁵³ AG Stix-Hackl in *Carpenter*, EU:C:2001:447, paras 33–39 of the Opinion.
⁵⁴ ibid para 104 of the Opinion.
⁵⁵ ibid para 105 of the Opinion.
⁵⁶ ibid para 103 of the Opinion (emphasis added).
⁵⁷ *Carpenter*, paras 38–39 (emphasis added).
⁵⁸ ibid para 44: '[a]lthough, in the main proceedings, Mr Carpenter's spouse has infringed the immigration laws of the United Kingdom by not leaving the country prior to the expiry of her leave to remain as a visitor, her conduct, since her arrival in the United Kingdom in September 1994, has not been the subject of any other complaint that could give cause to fear that she might in the future constitute a danger to public order or public safety. Moreover, it is clear that Mr and Mrs Carpenter's marriage, which was celebrated in the United Kingdom in 1996, is genuine and that Mrs Carpenter continues to lead a true family life there, in particular by looking after her husband's children from a previous marriage'.
⁵⁹ Case C-457/12 *S and G*, EU:C:2014:36, para 40.

justification of such a derived right of residence is based on the fact that a refusal to allow it would be such as to interfere with the exercise of fundamental freedoms guaranteed by the FEU Treaty'[60]—with case law on the free movement of workers and Article 45 TFEU. Most strikingly, the very general reference to the effectiveness of freedom of movement in *Carpenter* was deployed more substantively: the referring court was instructed to determine in each individual situation whether 'the grant of a derived right of residence to the third-country national in question who is a family member of a Union citizen *is necessary* to guarantee the citizen's effective exercise of the fundamental freedom guaranteed by Article 45 TFEU'.[61] On that basis:

> [T]he fact ... that the third-country national in question takes care of the Union citizens' child *may*, as is apparent from the judgment in *Carpenter*, be a relevant factor to be taken into account by the referring court when examining whether the refusal to grant a right of residence to that third-country national may discourage the Union citizen from effectively exercising his rights under Article 45 TFEU. However, it must be noted that, although in the judgment in *Carpenter* the fact that the child in question was being taken care of by the third-country national who is a family member of a Union citizen was considered to be decisive, that child was, in that case, *taken care of by the Union citizen's spouse*. The mere fact that it might appear desirable that the child be cared for by the third-country national who is the direct relative in the ascending line of the Union citizen's spouse *is not therefore sufficient in itself to constitute such a dissuasive effect*.[62]

Emphasising that the actual impact on the exercise of the Union citizen's freedom of movement of the childcare provided should be taken into account represents already a narrowing of scope in comparison to *Carpenter*—or, at least, more explicit rendering of a conditionality that was not so clearly expressed in the earlier ruling.[63] But emphasising also that childcare provided by spouses is particularly privileged narrows the implications of *Carpenter* even further: and arguably, in ways that raise questions about Article 7 CFR and respect for private and family life.[64]

---

[60] ibid para 41; referring to Case C-40/11 *Iida*, EU:C:2012:691, Case C-87/12 *Ymeraga*, EU:C:2013:291 and Case C-86/12 *Alokpa and Moudoulou*, EU:C:2013:645.
[61] *S and G*, para 42 (emphasis added).
[62] ibid para 43 (emphasis added).
[63] In that direction, see AG Sharpston in *S and G*, EU:C:2013:837, para 117 of the Opinion: '[t]he Court's reasoning is *necessarily based* on the premiss that there was a causal connection between Mr Carpenter's exercise of economic free movement and his Filipino wife's residence in Mr Carpenter's Member State of nationality and residence. The economic activity provided support for his third country national wife. Conversely, Mr Carpenter *was dependent on his wife* in so far as she looked after his children, did the homemaking, and thereby indirectly contributed to his success. The conditions under which the right to a family life was exercised *were therefore liable* to affect the exercise of rights of free movement' (emphasis added).
[64] See eg Spaventa's criticism that 'child-caring becomes (regrettably) relevant, leaving open the question about the rights of childless couples, and couples where both parents work. It is only where the spouse "enables" the Union citizen that the denial of residency rights might be construed as a barrier. In this way, the derived rights of the family members (and consequently the primary rights of the Union citizen to be accompanied by her family) become purely instrumental to the achievement of the internal market – in a way they are demoted from rights of the person (family life) to instruments of integration' (E Spaventa, 'Family rights for circular migrants and frontier workers: *O and B*, and *S and G*' (2015) 52 Common Market Law Review 753 at 768). To date, the implications of Article 7 CFR for decisions about the organisation of family life have mainly been considered by Advocates General, in the context of spouses not (continuously) living together: see eg in the context of the meaning of family members who 'accompany or join' Union citizens in a host State for the purposes of Article 3(1) of the Directive, AG Bot in Case C-244/13 *Ogieriakhi*, EU:C:2014:323, para 42 of the Opinion; reflecting on Articles 12 and 13 of the Directive, AG Kokott in Case C-218/14 *Singh II*, EU:C:2015:306, para 49 of the Opinion; and with reference to ECtHR case law, AG Wathelet in Case C-673/16 *Coman*, EU:C:2018:2, para 28 of the Opinion.

Moreover, while it will be seen in Section 3 that the Court increasingly engages the conditions provided for in Directive 2004/38 'by analogy' in cases where the Directive does not apply directly, the approach applied in *S and G* contradicts what the Directive would require. In *O and B*, in the context of residence rights for the family members of Union citizens returning to their home States, the Court ruled that the applicable national conditions:

> should not, in principle, be more strict than those provided for by Directive 2004/38 for the grant of such a right of residence to a third-country national who is a family member of a Union citizen in a case where that citizen has exercised his right of freedom of movement by becoming established in a Member State other than the Member State of which he is a national. Even though Directive 2004/38 does not cover such a return, it should be applied by analogy to the conditions for the residence of a Union citizen in a Member State other than that of which he is a national, given that in both cases it is the Union citizen who is the sponsor for the grant of a derived right of residence to a third-country national who is a member of his family.[65]

Considering that logic in *S and G*, Advocate General Sharpston had remarked that '[u]nder Directive 2004/38, the existence of a derived right of residence no longer depends on showing the possible effect on the EU citizen of denying family members residence' and further observed that in terms of different categories of family member, the Directive's only distinction concerns that between 'the nuclear family and other family members'.[66] She acknowledged that the 'closeness of the family connection' could be a relevant factor but underlined that 'the relevance of that connection and dependency to the EU citizen's choice as to whether or not to exercise the right of free movement can ... vary greatly. A restriction of that choice exists if it is shown that denying the third country national family member residence may plausibly cause the EU citizen to move, to cease to move or to abandon the real prospect of moving'.[67] The substantive outcomes determined through that lens may end up in the same place as those achieved through the Court's ruling. However, the Advocate General's more qualitative than formalistic expression of the relevant test is preferred.

3. EU Citizenship Law and Multi-State Past Life: Protecting Leavers and Returners

The protection extended to citizens who return to their home States following the exercise of free movement rights represents, in essence, the person legally transformed by movement. In return or 'circular migration'[68] situations, there is 'an inter-State dimension to the problem to which [Union] law has attached certain consequences'.[69] The same logic also ensures continuing dimensions of protection in the *host* State after the Union citizen has

---

[65] Case C-456/12 *O and B*, EU:C:2014:135, para 50.
[66] AG Sharpston in *S and G*, para 48 of the Opinion. However, she did note the condition of dependency in Article 2(2)(d) of the Directive for direct relatives in the ascending line (see further, Chapter 4).
[67] ibid para 123 of the Opinion.
[68] Spaventa (n 64).
[69] AG Geelhoed in Case C-224/98 *D'Hoop*, EU:C:2002:103, para 38 of the Opinion. See differently, the rights of naturalised Union citizens in their 'new' home States following the exercise of free movement in Case C-165/16 *Lounes*, EU:C:2017:862, discussed in Chapter 3. On the procedural dimension of a Member State national returning to their home State, see eg Case C-35/20 *A (Franchissement de frontières en navire de plaisance)*, EU:C:2021:813, discussed in Chapter 6.

actually left it—more specifically, it explains protection that sustains in the host State for that citizen's family members—separately from the situations provided for in Articles 12 and 13 of Directive 2004/38, which are examined in Chapter 6.

Themes that emerged across Section 2 of this chapter are again reflected here in considering case law that has established and refined the scope of EU legal protection for Union citizens. We can identify a protective legal shield that was conceived for the economic freedoms, with the objective of ensuring the full effectiveness of the rights conferred by EU law and invoked mainly in the context of either financial assistance conditionality or derived residence rights for family members (Section 3.1). That starting point was later progressed through consideration also of the right to move and reside conferred on Union citizens by Article 21 TFEU (Section 3.2). However, as a result, the blending of these sources of rights has made the protection that EU law provides more conditional in some respects—especially through harnessing the provisions of Directive 2004/28 'by analogy' (Section 3.3).

3.1 The Origins of EU Legal Protection for the Leaver/Returner: Articles 45 and 49 TFEU

Foundational legislation on the free movement of workers contemplated one particular situation in which EU law would continue to apply following the departure of a Member State national from the host State: Article 12 of Regulation 1612/68 provided that '[t]he children of a national of a Member State who is *or has been* employed in the territory of another Member State shall be admitted to that State's general educational, apprenticeship and vocational training courses under the same conditions as the nationals of that State, if such children are residing in its territory. Member States shall encourage all efforts to enable such children to attend these courses under the best possible conditions'.[70] Article 12 was confirmed not to cover an *ongoing* multi-State situation. In *Humbel and Edel*, in the context of a fee charged to a French national residing in Luxembourg (where his father worked) for enrolling in secondary school in Belgium, the Court observed that Article 12 of the Regulation 'lays obligations only on the Member State in which the migrant worker resides'.[71]

However, the legally distinct position of Member State nationals returning to their home States soon came into focus. In *Echternach and Moritz*, both claimants were German national students who had been refused study grants in the Netherlands: Mr Echternach on the grounds that he was not the child of a Community worker because his father worked in the Netherlands for an international organisation, removing him from the scope of the free movement for workers (a position rejected by the Court),[72] and Mr Moritz on the grounds that his father had returned to Germany after having been employed in the Netherlands. For the Commission and the Portuguese Government, the situation of the child of a returned worker should be read through a lens of integration:

> They point out first of all that Article 12 of Regulation No 1612/68 provides that the children of a national of a Member State who 'is or has been employed' in the territory of another Member State are to enjoy certain rights with regard to education if they are residing in that territory. They also argue that the principle of equal treatment enshrined in

---
[70] Article 12 of Regulation 1612/68 was replaced by (the identically worded) Article 10 of Regulation 492/2011.
[71] Case 263/86 *Humbel and Edel*, EU:C:1988:451, para 24.
[72] Case 389/87 *Echternach and Moritz*, EU:C:1989:130, paras 10–14.

Community law must ensure as complete an integration as possible of workers and members of their families in the host country and that therefore an interruption in a family member's residence in that country must not prevent him from continuing his studies there.[73]

The Court agreed, confirming that '[w]hen, after his father's return to the Member State of origin, the child of such a worker cannot continue his studies there because there is no co-ordination of school diplomas and *has no choice but to return* to the country where he attended school in order to continue studying, he retains the right to rely on the provisions of Community law as a child "of a national of a Member State who is or has been employed in the territory of another Member State" within the meaning of Article 12'.[74] Moreover, 'such children must be eligible for study assistance from the State in order to make it possible for them to achieve integration in the society of the host country'.[75] The principle of equal treatment expressed through Article 12 of the Regulation thus facilitated the completion of education in the host State notwithstanding changed family circumstances.[76] It covered all forms and levels of education;[77] as well as 'financial assistance for those students who are already at an advanced stage in their education, even if they are already 21 years of age or older and are no longer dependants of their parents. Accordingly, to make the application of Article 12 subject to an age-limit or to the status of dependent child would conflict not only with the letter of that provision, but also with its spirit'.[78]

For Advocate General Darmon, the 'status of child of a migrant worker also entails, as far as the grant of State study assistance is concerned, a right to a more favourable treatment under Community law than that enjoyed by "ordinary" nationals – a reinforcement, as it were, of Community protection'.[79] In the particular Moritz family circumstances, he highlighted three key factors to explain the protection that should be extended under EU law. First, 'at a time when families are less stable than before, to make the maintenance of rights derived from a parent's status of migrant worker in a host State conditional upon that parent's continuing residence in the State would place the family in a highly precarious situation'.[80] Second, 'Mr Moritz's case provides a perfect illustration of what the integration of a family, and in particular of a child, in the host State ordinarily means. Mr Moritz completed most of his education in the Netherlands because his father was working there and the possibility of his satisfactorily continuing his education there cannot, in my view, depend solely on the place where his father happens to pursue his occupation'.[81] In *Baumbast*, the Court built on that insight, acknowledging that in situations where migrant workers no longer reside in the host State but children remained there under Article 12 of the Regulation for the purposes of

---

[73] ibid para 19.
[74] ibid para 21 (emphasis added). This point is now expressed in a more general way; see eg Case C-413/99 *Baumbast and R*, EU:C:2002:49, para 70: 'just like the status of migrant worker itself, the rights enjoyed by members of a Community worker's family under Regulation No 1612/68 can, in certain circumstances, continue to exist even after the employment relationship has ended'.
[75] *Echternach and Moritz*, para 35.
[76] *Baumbast*, para 69: 'Article 12 of Regulation No 1612/68 seeks in particular to ensure that children of a Community worker can, even if he has ceased to pursue the activity of an employed person in the host Member State, undertake and, where appropriate, complete their education in that Member State'.
[77] It 'extends, for the children of Community workers, to all forms of education, whether vocational or general' (*Echternach and Moritz*, para 29) ie 'any form of education, including university courses' (para 30).
[78] Case C-7/94 *Gaal*, EU:C:1995:118, para 25.
[79] AG Darmon in *Echternach and Moritz*, EU:C:1989:35, para 27 of the Opinion.
[80] ibid para 47 of the Opinion. The provision that Directive 2004/38 makes for the family members of a Union citizen following the latter's departure from the host State also reflects this reasoning; see further, Chapter 4.
[81] ibid para 48 of the Opinion.

continuing and/or completing their education, 'the parents who are their carers are at risk of losing their rights of residence as a result ... [I]t is clear that if those parents were refused the right to remain in the host Member State during the period of their children's education that might deprive those children of a right which is granted to them by the Community legislature'.[82] For that reason, and recalling too that Regulation 1612/68 'must be interpreted in the light of the requirement of respect for family life laid down in Article 8 [ECHR]', the Court held that '[t]he right conferred by Article 12 of [the Regulation] on the child of a migrant worker to pursue, under the best possible conditions, his education in the host Member State necessarily implies that that child has the right to be accompanied by the person who is his primary carer and, accordingly, that that person is able to reside with him in that Member State during his studies'.[83]

Third, Advocate General Darmon was also concerned with the effectiveness of EU rights since 'an interpretation of the [R]egulation making the derivative rights of members of migrant workers' families in a host Member State strictly conditional on those workers' maintaining their residence in the host State would be likely to affect the freedom of movement of workers within the Community, given the loss of rights which their departure would entail'.[84] The connection between leaver/returner protection and the effectiveness of free movement rights manifested even more clearly in the Court's subsequent ruling in *Singh*. In that case, an Indian national married to a British national was the subject of a deportation order in the UK. The couple had lived in Germany following their marriage (both had worked there) and established a business following their return to UK.[85] For the Court:

> A national of a Member State might be deterred from leaving his country of origin in order to pursue an activity as an employed or self-employed person as envisaged by the Treaty in the territory of another Member State if, on returning to the Member State of which he is a national in order to pursue an activity there as an employed or self-employed person, the conditions of his entry and residence were not at least equivalent to those which he would enjoy under the Treaty or secondary law in the territory of another Member State. He would in particular be deterred from so doing if his spouse and children were not also permitted to enter and reside in the territory of his Member State of origin under conditions at least equivalent to those granted them by Community law in the territory of another Member State.[86]

On that basis, 'a national of a Member State who has gone to another Member State in order to work there as an employed person pursuant to Article [45 TFEU] and returns to establish himself in order to pursue an activity as a self-employed person in the territory of the Member State of which he is a national has the right, under Article [49 TFEU], to be accompanied in the territory of the latter State by his spouse, a national of a non-member country, under the same conditions as are laid down by [the applicable EU legislation]'.[87]

---

[82] *Baumbast*, para 71.
[83] ibid paras 72–73.
[84] AG Darmon in *Echternach and Moritz*, para 49 of the Opinion.
[85] A *decree nisi* was granted in the couple's divorce proceedings in July 1987, resulting in a decision of the competent UK authorities to refuse indefinite leave to remain as the spouse of a British national to Mr Singh (the decree absolute followed in February 1989). The couple had separated but remained legally married at the time of these proceedings; see further, Chapter 4.
[86] Case C-370/90 *Singh*, EU:C:1992:296, paras 19–20.
[87] ibid para 21.

The Court acknowledged that 'a national of a Member State enters and resides in the territory of that State by virtue of the rights attendant upon his nationality and not by virtue of those conferred on him by Community law'.[88] Nevertheless, it found that 'this case is concerned not with a right under national law but with the rights of movement and establishment granted to a Community national by Articles [45 and 49 TFEU]. These rights *cannot be fully effective* if such a person may be deterred from exercising them by obstacles raised in his or her country of origin to the entry and residence of his or her spouse'.[89] Thus, when a Member State national 'who has availed himself or herself of those rights returns to his or her country of origin, his or her spouse must enjoy at least the same rights of entry and residence as would be granted to him or her under Community law if his or her spouse chose to enter and reside in another Member State'.[90] Thus, the protective shield of EU law that applies in the host State is sustained in the home State *after* the exercise of freedom of movement, *after* the leaver's return, because a Member State national should not be 'penalised' for having made the decision to move to another Member State in the first place.[91] In other words, there should be no 'migration discrimination'[92] in a (legal) space that exists precisely to facilitate 'the greatest possible freedom of movement'.[93]

At the time of the *Singh* case, the Treaty provisions on the free movement of persons were '*intended to facilitate the pursuit by Community citizens of occupational activities of all kinds throughout the Community*, and preclude measures which might place Community citizens at a disadvantage when they wish to pursue an economic activity in the territory of another Member State'.[94] *Eind* illustrates the full extent of that protection and bridges to the generalisation of leaver/returner protection under Union citizenship. Mr Eind, a national of the Netherlands working in the UK, was joined in the UK by his daughter, a third-country national. When he returned to the Netherlands, where he received social assistance because of ill health, his daughter accompanied him but her application for a residence permit was rejected on the basis that Mr Eind was not economically active since his return. The Court first confirmed that since '[t]he right to family reunification under Article 10 of Regulation No 1612/68[95] does not entail for members of the families of migrant workers any autonomous right to free movement EU law',[96] EU law did not then 'require the authorities of [the home] State to grant a right of entry and residence to a third-country national who is a member of that worker's family because of the mere fact that, in the host Member State where that worker was gainfully employed, that third-country national held a valid residence permit issued on the basis of Article 10 of Regulation No 1612/68'.[97] However, building on *Singh*,

---

[88] ibid para 22.
[89] ibid para 23 (emphasis added).
[90] ibid para 24.
[91] AG Tesauro in *Singh*, EU:C:1992:229, para 8 of the Opinion: 'it is in theory necessary to take into account the possibility that Mr Singh might have obtained an unlimited right of residence or become naturalized under United Kingdom legislation if his wife had not exercised her right of free movement. That is to say, if, after examining the relevant provisions of United Kingdom legislation, the national court were to hold ... that the fact that he resided in Germany deprived Mrs Singh's spouse of the possibility of obtaining, by a period of residence, a residence permit of unlimited duration in the United Kingdom, a permit which he would have obtained if the couple had remained in the United Kingdom, it is clear that the question would arise of the compatibility with Community law of national legislation which in substance penalizes the exercise of the right of free movement'.
[92] A Iliopoulou and H Toner, 'A new approach to discrimination against free movers?' (2003) 28 European Law Review 389 at 395.
[93] Case C-287/05 *Hendrix*, EU:C:2007:494, para 52 (in the context of workers and Article 48 TFEU).
[94] *Singh*, para 16 (emphasis added).
[95] The provisions of the Regulation that defined family members were repealed and replaced by Directive 2004/38 and esp Article 2(2) of the Directive. See further, Chapter 4.
[96] Case C-291/05 *Eind*, EU:C:2007:771, para 23.
[97] ibid para 26.

the Court found that '[a] national of a Member State could be deterred from leaving that Member State in order to pursue gainful employment in the territory of another Member State if he does not have the certainty of being able to return to his Member State of origin, *irrespective of whether he is going to engage in economic activity in the latter State*'.[98]

Moreover, '[t]hat deterrent effect would also derive simply from the prospect, for that same national, of not being able, on returning to his Member State of origin, to continue living together with close relatives, *a way of life which may have come into being in the host Member State* as a result of marriage or family reunification'.[99] The reach of returner protection is demonstrated in the statement that Ms Eind's right to reside in the Netherlands in the circumstances of the case was 'not affected by the fact that, before residing in the host Member State where her father was gainfully employed, Miss Eind did not have a right of residence, under national law, in the Member State of which Mr Eind is a national'.[100] However, presaging the discussion in Section 3.3, the Court did qualify the right extended to Miss Eind to reside in the Netherlands as being subject to the conditions laid down in Article 10(1)(a) of Regulation No 1612/68, *which apply by analogy*. Thus, a person in the situation of Miss Eind may enjoy that right so long as she has not reached the age of 21 years or remains a dependant of her father'.[101]

The relative significance of conditions in secondary legislation and rights conferred by Article 45 TFEU, as well as of freedom of movement for workers and freedom of movement for Union citizens in a more general sense, is quite difficult to unpick across the judgment in *Eind*. Perhaps this statement captures the blended nature of the Court's approach at that stage of its case law: 'the right of the migrant worker to return and reside in the Member State of which he is a national, after being gainfully employed in another Member State, is conferred by Community law, to the extent necessary to ensure the useful effect of the right to free movement for workers under Article [45 TFEU] and the provisions adopted to give effect to that right, such as those laid down in Regulation No 1612/68. *That interpretation is substantiated by the introduction of the status of citizen of the Union*, which is intended to be the fundamental status of nationals of the Member States'.[102] However, in the case law to which we now turn, it became clearer that Article 21 TFEU could generate protection for the returner on its own.

3.2 Progressing Protection for the Leaver/Returner: Article 21 TFEU

As introduced in Chapter 2, Union citizens can rely on Articles 20 and 21 TFEU as a legal 'shield' against their home States in certain circumstances,[103] but two key points can be noted

---

[98] ibid para 35 (emphasis added); see further, para 38.
[99] ibid para 36 (emphasis added).
[100] ibid para 41.
[101] ibid paras 39–40 (emphasis added)
[102] ibid para 32 (emphasis added). The Court continues to refer to the 'Community worker' when summarising its reply to the referring court on these questions (ibid para 45).
[103] See eg on Article 21 TFEU, Case C-520/04 *Turpeinen*, EU:C:2006:703, paras 20–21: 'it would be incompatible with the right to freedom of movement were a citizen to receive in the Member State of which he is a national treatment less favourable than he would enjoy if he had not availed himself of the opportunities offered by the Treaty in relation to freedom of movement ... Those opportunities could not be fully effective if a national of a Member State could be deterred from availing himself of them by *obstacles placed in the way of his stay in the host Member State by legislation in his State of origin* penalising the fact that he has used them' (emphasis added). For other examples of nationals rules examined through the lens of penalising the exercise of free movement and/or placing Union citizens at a disadvantage for that reason, see eg Case C-406/04 *De Cuyper*, EU:C:2006:491; Case C-192/05

with respect to invoking returner protection under Article 21 TFEU more specifically. First, the basic objective of not disadvantaging or deterring Union citizens from exercising free movement rights expressed in *Singh* for economic free movement law was generalised: in other words, the logic developed for situations within Articles 45 and 49 TFEU was applied to situations that fell only within the scope of Article 21 TFEU. However, second, where the situation in question falls within the scope of the economic freedoms, the protection of the latter continues to apply notwithstanding the introduction of Union citizenship (or, more specifically, the conditions put in place by Directive 2004/38).

The ruling in *D'Hoop* exemplifies the first point. In that case, a Belgian national who had completed her secondary education in France was refused a tideover allowance in Belgium shortly after she began studying at university there, on the grounds that she did not fulfil a condition in the applicable national rules: she had not completed full-time secondary education at an educational establishment run, subsidised, or approved by a community in Belgium. The referring court had framed its question around Articles 45 TFEU and 7(2) of Regulation 1612/68, and the Court of Justice confirmed that 'the tideover allowance provided for young people seeking their first employment constitutes a social advantage' within the meaning of Article 7(2) of [the Regulation].[104] However, the Court found that the applicant did not fall within the personal scope of either Article 45 TFEU or Regulation 1612/68, since it was confirmed at the oral hearing that her parents continued to reside in Belgium while she attended school in France.[105] Nevertheless, citing and extending the ruling in *Singh*, the Court held that 'it would be incompatible with the right of freedom of movement were *a citizen, in the Member State of which he is a national*, to receive treatment less favourable than he would enjoy if he had not availed himself of the opportunities offered by the Treaty in relation to freedom of movement' since '[t]hose opportunities could not be fully effective if a national of a Member State could be deterred from availing himself of them by obstacles raised on his return to his country of origin by legislation penalising the fact that he has used them'.[106]

National rules that linked the grant of a tideover allowance to obtaining the necessary secondary school diploma in Belgium were therefore considered to '[place] at a disadvantage' Belgian nationals who had exercised free movement rights and '[s]uch inequality of treatment is contrary to the principles which underpin the status of citizen of the Union, that is, the guarantee of the same treatment in law in the exercise of the citizen's freedom to move'.[107] No justification arguments were submitted to the Court, but it did observe that since the tideover allowance in question 'aims to facilitate for young people the transition from education to the employment market', it was 'legitimate for the national legislature to wish to ensure that there is a real link between the applicant for that allowance and the geographic employment market concerned'.[108] However, reflecting the discussion on conditions 'too general and exclusive in nature' in Chapter 2, the Court considered that the contested

---

Tas-Hagen and Tas, EU:C:2006:676; Joined Cases C-11/06 and 12/06 *Morgan and Bucher*, EU:C:2007:626; Case C-221/07 *Zablocka-Weyhermüller*, EU:C:2008:681; Case C-503/09 *Stewart*, EU:C:2011:500; Case C-359/13 *Martens*, EU:C:2015:118; and Case C-679/16 *A (Aide pour une personne handicapée)*, EU:C:2018:601. On Article 20 TFEU, see Chapters 3 and 5.

[104] Case C-224/98 *D'Hoop*, EU:C:2002:432, para 17.
[105] ibid paras 19–20.
[106] ibid paras 30–31 (emphasis added).
[107] ibid para 35. Moreover, '[t]hat consideration is particularly important in the field of education' (para 38); see further, Chapter 7.
[108] ibid para 38; see further, Chapter 7.

national rule 'unduly favours an element which is not necessarily representative of the real and effective degree of connection between the applicant for the tideover allowance and the geographic employment market, to the exclusion of all other representative elements. It therefore goes beyond what is necessary to attain the objective pursued'.[109]

For the second point—continuing protection under Article 45 TFEU in leaver/returner situations—there is a mixed picture. Relevant case law connects back to principles developed to protect family members in the host State, normally though not necessarily[110] after the EU worker's departure from it. In addressing such cases, the Court has both blended and differentiated the economic activity/citizenship legal frameworks. For example, in the rulings in *Ibrahim* and *Teixeira*, it held that the rights conferred by Article 12 of Regulation 1612/68 must 'be applied independently of the provisions of European Union law which govern the conditions of exercise of the right to reside in another Member State'.[111] For the Court, '[a] contrary conclusion would be liable to compromise the aim of integrating the migrant worker's family into the host Member State'.[112] Both cases concerned whether or not derived residence rights could be extended in a Member State to the primary carers (a third-country national in *Ibrahim* and a Member State national in *Teixeira*) of the children of a Member State national who had previously worked there. Also in both cases, the children remained in education in the second State (ie the host State) following the departure of the worker to the first (ie the worker's home) State, but their primary carers could not benefit from derived rights under Directive 2004/38 either because they were third-country nationals whose situations were not covered by Article 12 of the Directive (*Ibrahim*) or they were Member State nationals who did not meet the Directive's conditions for lawful residence; additionally, both cases concerned applications for housing assistance rejected by the host State, demonstrating the absence of sufficient resources.

In both rulings, the fact that the EU legislature had chosen to replace Articles 10 and 11 but not Article 12 of Regulation 1612/68 was decisive: '[s]uch a choice necessarily reveals the intention ... not to introduce restrictions of the scope of that article, as interpreted by the Court'.[113] Additionally, recalling that one of the objectives of the Directive is 'to simplify and strengthen the right of free movement and residence of all Union citizens' (recital 3), applying the conditions in Article 7 of the Directive to the children of migrant workers who resided in the host State on the basis of Article 12 of the Regulation 'would have the effect that the right of residence of those children in the host Member State in order to commence or continue their education would be subject to stricter conditions than those which applied to them before the entry into force of Directive 2004/38'.[114] For these reasons, 'the children of a national of a Member State who works or has worked in the host Member State and the parent who is their primary carer can claim a right of residence in the latter State on the sole basis of Article 12 of Regulation No 1612/68, without being required to satisfy the conditions laid down in Directive 2004/38'.[115]

---

[109] ibid para 39. The implications of *D'Hoop* for equal treatment for jobseekers are considered in Chapter 7.
[110] As noted in Section 1, see eg Case C-181/19 *Jobcenter Krefeld*, EU:C:2020:794, where the former worker continued to reside in the host State on the basis of a right of residence derived from his children who were continuing their education in the same State. See further, Chapter 7.
[111] Case C-310/08 *Ibrahim*, EU:C:2010:89, para 42; see also, Case C-480/08 *Teixeira*, EU:C:2010:83, para 53.
[112] ibid paras 43 and 66 respectively.
[113] ibid paras 46 and 67 respectively.
[114] ibid paras 49 and 60 respectively.
[115] ibid paras 50 and 61 respectively. The implications for equal treatment in claims for social assistance are discussed in Chapter 7.

In terms of the extent of the protection conferred, the fact that Article 12 of the Regulation was 'reproduced not in Directive 2004/38 but in Regulation No 492/2011' works both ways, In particular, it applies only to the children of 'employed persons' and does not protect the children of self-employed workers.[116] Beyond that limit, however, the Court has been generous. It has confirmed that 'Article 12 of Regulation No 1612/68 ... grants the children of a migrant worker an autonomous right to education. That right is not dependent on possessing the status of dependent child ... nor is it dependent on the right of residence of the children's parents in the host Member State ... Nor yet is it limited to the children of migrant workers, since it applies also to the children of former migrant workers'.[117] Moreover, 'a child of a former migrant worker, who has resided since birth in the host Member State, qualifies for the right, first, to commence or to continue his or her education in that Member State, under Article 12 of Regulation No 1612/68 and, second, as a consequence, a right of residence based on that same provision. Whether the parent, the former migrant worker, does or does not reside in that Member State on the date when that child began to attend school, is of no relevance on that point'.[118] It is also irrelevant if the primary carer and the former migrant worker are now divorced.[119] Furthermore, all levels of education are covered by (what is now) Article 10 of Regulation 492/2011:[120] even if the child in question has reached the age of majority, 'although that child is in principle assumed to be capable of meeting his or her own needs, the right of residence of that parent may nevertheless extend beyond that age, if the child continues to need the presence and the care of that parent in order to be able to pursue and complete his or her education'.[121]

However, in its case law on eligibility for permanent residence, considered in detail in Chapters 7 and 8, the Court re-joined the relevance of the conditions for lawful residence under Directive 2004/38 and the conditions under which residence rights based on Regulation 492/2011 were exercised, ruling out a right of permanent residence where residence based on the Regulation did not also comply with the conditions for lawful residence determined by the Directive.[122] Thus, even for situations where the Directive does not formally apply, the conditions that it places on the exercise of freedom of movement and residence are never too far away.

3.3 Refining the Scope of Protection

Building on the discussion above, the most significant change in the scope of leaver/returner protection under EU citizenship law concerns derived residence rights for family members through the method of applying conditions laid down in Directive 2004/38 'by analogy' even where the situation in question lies beyond the scope of the Directive more directly. The ruling in *O and B* was critical in this respect: extending the logic of *Singh* and *Eind* to the

---

[116] Joined Cases C-147/11 and C-148/11 *Czop and Punakova*, EU:C:2012:538, paras 31 and 30.
[117] Case C-542/09 *Commission v Netherlands*, EU:C:2012:346, para 49.
[118] Case C-115/15 *NA*, EU:C:2016:487, para 63.
[119] Case C-529/11 *Alarape and Tijani*, EU:C:2013:290, para 27.
[120] *Teixeira*, para 80.
[121] *Alarape and Tijani*, para 28. It was also seen in Chapter 7 that a former worker who continues to reside in the host State under Article 10 of Regulation 492/2011, on the grounds that their children are completing their education there, may benefit from equal treatment with host State nationals under Article 18 TFEU, such protection not being ruled out by the conditional equal treatment provided by Article 24 of the Directive.
[122] As well as and *Alarape and Tijani*, see esp Joined Cases C-424/10 and C-425/10 *Ziolkowski and Szeja*, EU:C:2011:866.

general right to move and reside conferred by Article 21 TFEU, on the one hand, while placing conditions on the residence rights that can be claimed on that basis, on the other. The facts concerned applications for residence permits in the Netherlands for third-country nationals who were married to Netherlands nationals following periods of time spent residing together in other Member States. First, the Court confirmed that 'the purpose and justification of that derived right of residence is based on the fact that a refusal to allow such a right would be such as to interfere with the Union citizen's freedom of movement by discouraging him from exercising his rights of entry into and residence in the host Member State'.[123]

Second, it acknowledged that it was necessary in this case 'to determine whether the case-law resulting from *Singh* and *Eind* is capable of being applied generally to family members of Union citizens who, having availed themselves of the rights conferred on them by Article 21(1) TFEU, resided in a Member State other than that of which they are nationals, before returning to the Member State of origin'[124]—confirming that this was 'indeed the case'.[125] Facilitating the continuation of the family life led by a Union citizen in the host State following return to the home State was linked to ensuring the effectiveness of the free movement rights conferred by Article 21 TFEU—'*a fortiori*' in citizenship-based circumstances.[126] As a result, 'in certain cases ... third-country nationals, family members of a Union citizen, who were not eligible, on the basis of Directive 2004/38, for a derived right of residence in the Member State of which that citizen is a national, could, nevertheless, be accorded such a right on the basis of Article 21(1) TFEU'.[127]

However, third, the Court then focused in *O and B* on the conditions applicable in such circumstances. Two clear limits can be drawn from the statement that '[t]he grant, when a Union citizen returns to the Member State of which he is a national, of a derived right of residence to a third-country national who is a family member of that Union citizen and with whom that citizen has resided, solely by virtue of his being a Union citizen, *pursuant to and in conformity with Union law in the host Member State*, seeks to remove the same type of obstacle on leaving the Member State of origin as that referred to in [*Singh* and *Eind*], by guaranteeing that that citizen will be able, in his Member State of origin, *to continue the family life which he created or strengthened in the host Member State*'.[128] The first limit signals that the Union citizen's residence *in the host State* must constitute lawful residence within the meaning of EU law: a condition that was perhaps implicit in *Singh* and *Eind* given that both Member State nationals were workers in their respective host States. However, the Court clarified in *O and B* that movement and residence exercised under Article 21 TFEU requires compliance with the conditions in Article 7 of Directive 2004/38 so that EU legal protection can then be sustained in the home State afterwards.[129]

The second limit concerns 'creating or strengthening' family life in the host State. Here, the Court reiterated that the applicable conditions 'should not, in principle, be more strict than those provided for by Directive 2004/38 for the grant of such a right of residence to a third-country national who is a family member of a Union citizen in a case where that citizen has exercised his right of freedom of movement by becoming established in a Member State other than the Member State of which he is a national' on the basis that '[e]ven though

---

[123] Case C-456/12 *O and B*, EU:C:2014:135, para 45.
[124] ibid para 48.
[125] ibid para 49.
[126] ibid para 55.
[127] Case C-673/16 *Coman*, EU:C:2018:385, para 23.
[128] *O and B*, para 49 (emphasis added)
[129] ibid para 54.

Directive 2004/38 does not cover such a return, *it should be applied by analogy* ... given that in both cases it is the Union citizen who is the sponsor for the grant of a derived right of residence to a third-country national who is a member of his family'.[130] Crucially, 'Article 21(1) TFEU does not therefore require that *every residence* in the host Member State by a Union citizen accompanied by a family member who is a third-country national necessarily confers a derived right of residence on that family member in the Member State of which that citizen is a national upon the citizen's return to that Member State'.[131]

There is, however, a strained correlation between what the Court considers to be 'genuine' residence in the host State and the concept of creating or strengthening family life there. In effect, the latter requirement is another portal to the conditions in Article 7 of the Directive, which concern economic autonomy and not the quality of family life. For the Court, 'a Union citizen who exercises his rights under Article 6(1) of Directive 2004/38 does not intend to settle in the host Member State *in a way which would be such as to create or strengthen family life in that Member State*' so that, in consequence, 'the refusal to confer, when that citizen returns to his Member State of origin, a derived right of residence on members of his family who are third-country nationals will not deter such a citizen from exercising his rights under Article 6'.[132] That interpretation does align with the finding in *Zhu and Chen* that for host State residence rights, 'the right of residence of persons receiving services by virtue of the freedom to provide services is co-terminous with the duration of the period for which they are provided. Consequently, [Directive 73/148] cannot ... serve as a basis for a right of residence of indefinite duration of the kind with which the main proceedings are concerned'.[133] At the same time, though, it applies a quantitative rather than qualitative measure of family life and thereby limits the protective EU legal shield that returners bring back to their home States, something that Advocate Sharpston had cautioned against:

> I am not persuaded by the argument that an EU citizen (whether he is, or is not, a migrant worker or a self-employed person) must have resided in another Member State for a continuous period of at least three months or some other 'substantial' period of time before his third country national family members can derive rights of residence from EU law in the home Member State ... That argument presupposes that enforced separation from a family member, such as a spouse, will not deter an EU citizen who wishes to move to settle temporarily in another Member State from exercising his rights of free movement and residence. I see no basis for saying that, in such circumstances, the EU citizen should be required temporarily to sacrifice his right to a family life (or, put slightly differently, that he should be prepared to pay that price in order subsequently to be able to rely on EU law as against his own Member State of nationality). Indeed, under Directive 2004/38, family members are entitled to accompany the EU citizen immediately to the host Member State. Directive 2004/38 does not make their entitlement to that derived right conditional on a minimum residence requirement for the EU citizen. Rather, the conditions applicable to the dependents vary with length of residence in the territory. The length of an EU citizen's

---

[130] ibid para 50 (emphasis added); confirmed in eg Case C-230/17 *Deha Altiner and Ravn*, EU:C:2018:497, para 27. In *Lounes*, AG Bot characterised the Court's ruling in *O and B* as establishing 'the principle of a right to return to the Member State of origin, in respect of which the conditions for granting in that State a derived right of residence to the third-country national who is a member of his family may not be stricter than those provided for by Directive 2004/38' (AG Bot in Case C-165/16 *Lounes*, EU:C:2017:407, para 78 of the Opinion).
[131] *O and B*, para 51 (emphasis added).
[132] ibid para 52 (emphasis added).
[133] Case C-200/02 *Zhu and Chen*, EU:C:2004:639, para 23.

stay in another Member State is *(obviously) a relevant quantitative criterion.* However, I consider that it *cannot be applied as an absolute threshold for deciding who has, or has not, exercised rights of residence* and can therefore be joined or accompanied by their family members. It is one criterion amongst those which must be taken into account.[134]

In contrast, though at least expressed as a presumption rather than a rule, the Court considered that '[r]esidence in the host Member State pursuant to and in conformity with the conditions set out in Article 7(1) of that directive is, *in principle,* evidence of settling there and therefore of the Union citizen's genuine residence in the host Member State and *goes hand in hand with creating and strengthening family life* in that Member State'.[135]

Responding to the referring court's question about 'whether the cumulative effect of various short periods of residence in the host Member State may create a derived right of residence for a family member of a Union citizen who is a third-country national on the citizen's return to the Member State of which he is a national', the Court again underlined that 'only a period of residence satisfying the conditions set out in Article 7(1) and (2) and Article 16(1) and (2) of Directive 2004/38 will give rise to such a right of residence. In that regard, short periods of residence such as weekends or holidays spent in a Member State other than that of which the citizen in question is a national, even when considered together, fall within the scope of Article 6 of Directive 2004/38 and do not satisfy those conditions'.[136] But *how* a citizen moves, including for how long, is not necessarily choice-based: or indeed, shorter periods of residence in another State can be chosen precisely to create or strengthen family life that—often, because family life is itself spread across different States, entailing parallel and sometimes competing obligations.

A concern for lawful residence in the host State is palpable in *O and B*; only such citizens 'earn'[137] the right to bring EU legal protection back with them to the home State and a Union citizen who remains in a host State for significantly longer than three months but not in compliance with the conditions in Articles 7(1) or 16(1) of the Directive will not then be able to claim protection for their family members following their return to the home State. It is not entirely clear if other instances of lawful residence should be recognised: for example, Union citizens who move to and exercise economic activity in the host State but for less than three months. On the one hand, the ruling in *O and B* was framed around Article 21 TFEU, whereas citizens exercise economic activity in the host State reside there on the basis of either Article 45 or 49 TFEU. On the other hand, the temporal threshold in *O and B* is drawn from Articles 6 and 7 of the Directive, which also address citizens residing for up to and for more than three months respectively as workers or self-employed persons. If the 'in principle' discretion in the Court's test were to be overcome by the exercise of economic activity in the host State for a period of residence of less than three months, it would underscore that the test is more about certain understandings of lawful residence—lawful *market* residence—than creating or strengthening family life, recalling similar themes evident in *S and G*.

---

[134] AG Sharpston in *O and B*, EU:C:2013:837, paras 110–111 of the Opinion (emphasis added); adding in fn91 that 'if the EU citizen had to reside continuously for *x* months before he was entitled to have his family with him, he could only be "accompanied" by them by leaving the territory after satisfying the magic period and then re-entering bringing his family with him, which would scarcely facilitate the exercise of his free movement rights'.
[135] *O and B*, para 53 (emphasis added).
[136] ibid para 59.
[137] See generally, E Spaventa, 'Earned citizenship – understanding Union citizenship through its scope' in D Kochenov (ed), *EU Citizenship and Federalism: The Role of Rights* (CUP 2017) 204.

The Court clarified the scope of the *O and B* residence right to some extent in later case law. Since that right is based on enabling the *continuation* of family life created or strengthened by the Union citizen in the host State, it was confirmed in *Deha Altiner and Ravn* that 'the competent authorities of the Member State of which the Union citizen has the nationality are entitled to verify, before granting such a right of residence, that such a family life between the Union citizen and the third-country national who is a member of his family had not been interrupted before the entry of the third country national into th[at] Member State'.[138] In that light:

> [T]he Member State concerned may take into account, as an indication, that the third-country national, who is a family member of one of its own citizens, entered its territory a significant period of time after that citizen's return to that territory. However, it cannot be ruled out that a family life, created or strengthened between a Union citizen and a member of his or her family who is a third-country national, during their stay, pursuant to and in conformity with Union law, in the host Member State, might continue despite the fact that that citizen has returned to the Member State of which he is a national without being accompanied by the family member in question, who may have been obliged, for reasons relating to his personal situation, profession or education, to delay his arrival in the Member State of origin of the Union citizen in question. Accordingly, the fact that the submission of the application for a residence permit was not 'a natural consequence' of the return of the Union citizen is a relevant factor which, although not decisive in itself, may, in the context of an overall assessment, lead the Member State of origin of the Union citizen in question to conclude that there is no link between the application and the exercise by that citizen of his freedom of movement and, consequently, to refuse to issue such a residence permit.[139]

The 'overall assessment' approach developed above is more nuanced compared to the ruling in *O and B*. It progresses things more clearly beyond the rule-based starting-point of distinguishing periods of residence based on Articles 6 and 7/16 of the Directive, reflecting some of the concerns that Advocate General Sharpston had identified in her Opinion for the earlier case. However, it leaves intact the starting-point connection between Article 7(1)-based residence in a host State, which is based on temporal (and economic) factors, and creating or strengthening family life, which is based on essentially human factors. It is also not clear why the Court continues to rule out, by the implication of specifying again only Articles 7 and 16 of the Directive, periods of (lawful) residence in a host State for more than three months for jobseekers, based on Article 14(4)(b), or for family members who resided in the host State under Articles 12 and 13, which concern Union citizen family members as well as third-country national family members. Better understanding emerges, perhaps, when the 'create or strengthen family life' test is connected to concerns about abuse of EU rights, discussed in Chapter 6 and returned to below.[140]

Applying the Directive by analogy has also had both progressive and constraining implications for how the family per se is defined. In *Coman*, the protective shield retained by returning citizens was confirmed to include same-sex spouses on the basis that 'the term

---

[138] Case C-230/17 *Deha Altiner and Ravn*, EU:C:2018:497<.IBT>, para 31.
[139] ibid paras 32–34.
[140] As Kroeze writes, '[t]here is a difference between marriages of convenience and the Europe-route. When national law is circumvented, it depends on the circumstances of the case whether it can be classified as abuse or not' (H Kroeze, 'Distinguishing between use and abuse of EU free movement law: evaluating use of the "Europe-route" for family reunification to overcome reverse discrimination' (2018) 3 European Papers 1209 at 1239).

"spouse" within the meaning of Directive 2004/38 is gender-neutral and may therefore cover the same-sex spouse of the Union citizen concerned'.[141] Thus, 'the refusal by the authorities of a Member State to recognise, for the sole purpose of granting a derived right of residence to a third-country national, the marriage of that national to a Union citizen of the same sex, concluded, during the period of their genuine residence in another Member State, in accordance with the law of that State, may interfere with the exercise of the right conferred on that citizen by Article 21(1) TFEU to move and reside freely in the territory of the Member States' since 'the effect of such a refusal is that such a Union citizen may be denied the possibility of returning to the Member State of which he is a national together with his spouse'.[142]

However, more constraining implications of the 'by analogy' method can be seen in *Banger*, where the Court declined to extend returner protection under Article 21 TFEU to the third-country national partner of a Union citizen: since the former 'may come within the concept of "partner with whom the Union citizen has a durable relationship, duly attested", in point (b) of the first subparagraph of Article 3(2) of Directive 2004/38', that provision marks the comparable basis on which any obligations on the home State are extended 'by analogy'.[143] Advocate General Bobek had taken a broader view, highlighting the human dimension of family life, in whatever State it is experienced:

> The logic of dissuasion or deterrence was built on the premiss that the Union citizen will be discouraged from moving, as those personally close to him will be barred from joining him. It ought to be acknowledged that social perceptions are changing and that there is a range of forms of cohabitation today. Thus, the potential to deter might in reality be stronger with regard to a partner under Article 3(2)(b) of Directive 2004/38 than it is perhaps with regard to some of the categories listed in Article 2(2) thereof. I am certainly not suggesting that that will always be the case. I am simply suggesting that with regard to who is effectively 'close' to a person, formal box-based generalisations are hardly appropriate. It might be added that recital 6 of Directive 2004/38 confirms that 'the unity of the family in a broader sense' is the objective which is pursued by Article 3(2) of the directive. Thus, in this sense it is equally suitable to strengthen or create 'broader' family ties in the host Member State during the genuine residence of the Union citizen, and may indeed give rise to the same type of considerations based on dissuasion.[144]

In the same Opinion, he also questioned 'dissuasion/deterrence logic' at a more general level, arguing that, '[i]n a nutshell, deterrence implies knowledge. It is rather difficult to be deterred from a certain course of action by something that I do not know exists at the time

---

[141] Case C-673/16 *Coman*, EU:C:2018:385, para 35; see further, Chapter 4. The Court underlined that 'the provisions of Directive 2004/38, applicable by analogy to the present case, may not be interpreted restrictively and, at all events, must not be deprived of their effectiveness' (ibid para 39).

[142] ibid para 40. The Court also held that '[a]s regards the term "spouse" in Article 2(2)(a) of Directive 2004/38, the right to respect for private and family life guaranteed by the Charter is a fundamental right' (para 48), citing relevant ECtHR case law to the effect that 'the relationship of a homosexual couple may fall within the notion of "private life" and that of "family life" in the same way as the relationship of a heterosexual couple in the same situation' (para 50).

[143] Case C-89/17 *Banger*, EU:C:2018:570, para 26. In such circumstances, however, 'the procedural safeguards provided for in Article 31(1) of Directive 2004/38 are applicable' (ibid para 49). See further, Chapter 4, including discussion of whether the protection extended to unmarried partners on a basis of equal treatment with host State nationals in Case 59/85 *Reed*, EU:C:1986:157, survived the adoption of Directive 2004/38.

[144] AG Bobek in *Banger*, paras 37–38 of the Opinion; referring in fn18 to ECtHR case law on the evolving concept of 'family life'.

when the decision is taken or the future existence of which is at best rather uncertain'.[145] Another angle of criticism comes from Advocate General Szpunar in *McCarthy II*. After a brief overview of the *Singh, Eind*, and *O and B* rulings, he stated that he agreed 'with the result at which the Court arrived' but was 'sceptical about the reasoning which it followed' in light of 'the principle of the hierarchy of primary law and secondary legislation. To my mind, it is secondary legislation that ought to be interpreted in the light of the Treaties, and not vice versa'.[146]

Why has the Court developed such extensive protection for Union citizens that transcends the reach of Directive 2004/38, on the one hand, yet cleaved so closely to the conditions and limits that the Directive establishes for different circumstances— obligations on a host and not a home State—on the other? As noted above and expressed in the Commission's 2009 Communication on better transposition and application of the Directive, one answer lies in the difficulty of locating the line between *use* and *abuse* of free movement rights:

> Abuse could occur when EU citizens, unable to be joined by their third country family members in their Member State of origin because of the application of national immigration rules preventing it, move to another Member State with the *sole* purpose to evade, upon returning to their home Member State, the national law that frustrated their family reunification efforts, invoking their rights under Community law. The defining characteristics of the line between genuine and abusive use of Community law should be based on the assessment of whether the exercise of Community rights in a Member State from which the EU citizens and their family members return was *genuine and effective*. In such case, EU citizens and their families are protected by Community law on free movement of persons. This assessment can only be made on a case-by-case basis. If, in a concrete case of return, the use of Community rights was genuine and effective, the Member State of origin should not inquire into the personal motives that triggered the previous move.[147]

In Chapter 6, we saw that moving to and residing lawfully in another Member State in order to activate EU rights on family reunification is not in itself an abuse of free movement rights.[148] In *Akrich*, for example, the Court held that 'the motives which may have prompted a worker of a Member State to seek employment in another Member State are of no account as regards his right to enter and reside in the territory of the latter State provided that he there pursues or wishes to pursue an effective and genuine activity'.[149] Even more importantly for present purposes, the Court also found that '[n]or are such motives relevant in assessing the legal situation of the couple at the time of their return to the Member State of which the worker is a national. Such conduct cannot constitute an abuse within the meaning of paragraph 24 of the *Singh* judgment even if the spouse did not, at the time when the couple

---

[145] ibid para 39 of the Opinion; suggesting in para 43 that 'that the Court place greater emphasis on an alternative justification for an application by analogy of the conditions of Directive 2004/38 to 'returning' Union citizens and members of their (extended) family: not necessarily that one is likely to be *ex ante* discouraged from moving, but rather that one cannot be ex post effectively penalised for doing so'.
[146] AG Szpunar in Case C-202/13 *McCarthy II*, EU:C:2014:345, para 82 of the Opinion.
[147] Communication from the Commission to the European Parliament and the Council on guidance for better transposition and application of Directive 2004/38/EC on the right of citizens of the Union and their family members to move and reside freely within the territory of the Member States, COM(2009) 313 final, para 4.3 (emphasis in original).
[148] Case C-109/01 *Akrich*, EU:C:2003:491; Case C-200/02 *Zhu and Chen*, EU:C:2004:639.
[149] *Akrich*, para 55.

installed itself in another Member State, have a right to remain in the Member State of which the worker is a national'.[150]

As discussed further in Chapter 10, however, the case law tends to be clearer about what does *not* constitute abuse of rights than on what *might* do so. In that light, and specifically in the context of leavers and returners, the 'genuine and effective' residence concept in the 2009 Communication—conceiving the idea if not the precise form of the test later developed by the Court in *O and B*—outlined factors that national authorities may 'in particular' take into account:

- the circumstances under which the EU citizen concerned moved to the host Member State (*previous unsuccessful attempts to acquire residence for a third country spouse under national law, job offer in the host Member State, capacity in which the EU citizen resides in the host Member State*);
- degree of effectiveness and genuineness of residence in the host Member State (*envisaged and actual residence in the host Member State, efforts made to establish in the host Member State, including national registration formalities and securing accommodation, enrolling children at an educational establishment*);
- circumstances under which the EU citizen concerned moved back home (*return immediately after marrying a third country national in another Member State*).[151]

Importantly, the Commission further clarified that such factors 'should be considered *possible triggers for investigation, without any automatic inferences* from results or subsequent investigations' and that '[i]In assessing whether the exercise of the right to move and reside freely in another Member State of the EU was genuine and effective, national authorities may not rely on a sole attribute but must pay due attention to all the circumstances of the individual case. They must assess the conduct of persons concerned in the light of the objectives pursued by Community law and act on the basis of objective evidence'.[152] It also confirmed the ethos of rulings such as *Akrich*, in the sense that '[t]he mere fact that a person *consciously places* himself in a situation conferring a right does not in itself constitute a sufficient basis for assuming that there is abuse'.[153]

The Court's temporal presumption in *O and B,* setting a starting point as regards the nature and quality of family life, challenges the more qualitative guidance provided by the Commission—and, indeed, by the Court's own previous case law. On a more pragmatic view, it does at least answer a question for Union citizens who have wondered since *Singh*: how long should I stay away before EU rights return with me to my home State?[154]

---

[150] ibid para 56. In *Singh*, the Court held: '[a]s regards the risk of fraud referred to by the United Kingdom, it is sufficient to note that, as the Court has consistently held ... the facilities created by the Treaty cannot have the effect of allowing the persons who benefit from them to evade the application of national legislation and of prohibiting Member States from taking the measures necessary to prevent such abuse' (Case C-370/90 *Singh*, EU:C:1992:296, para 24; referring, *inter alia*, to Case 115/78 *Knoors*, EU:C:1979:31, para 25).

[151] Communication on guidance for better transposition and application of Directive 2004/38/EC (n 147) para 4.3 (emphasis added).

[152] ibid para 4.3; referring to Case C-206/94 *Paletta*, EU:C:1996:182, para 25.

[153] Communication on guidance for better transposition and application of Directive 2004/38/EC (n147) para 4.3 (emphasis added); referring to Case C-212/97 *Centros*, EUC:1999:126, para 27.

[154] As Spaventa notes, '[i]t is no mystery, even to the most distracted reader, that these cases were really about the right to family life of own citizens in their own Member State: it is because they failed to gain the protection they wanted in national law that they turned to EU law' (Spaventa (n 64) 773).

4. Concluding Remarks

Directive 2004/38 suggests a space in which free movement is exercised either for such a brief period that the host State is minimally engaged, or for a longer period so that the right to reside in a host State becomes both more complex and more protected. The situations discussed in this chapter show that free movement is less binary than that.

In broad terms, where situations have clear cross-border effects yet do not come within the system of the Directive, EU citizenship law in combination with economic free movement law copes well, emphasising the importance of effectiveness, proportionality, and protection of the citizen's fundamental rights. Nevertheless, two main themes emerge for further reflection.

First, while coherence across different parts of free movement law is important, it is also important not to transgress the basic philosophy that different situations should not be treated in the same way in law. EU citizenship law and economic free movement law are deeply connected, and not just in terms of the latter having conceived the basic framework of the former. The interdependence continues. A connection to economic activity (including a historic connection) can promote the level of protection that EU law extends to Union citizens. However, principles that have shaped EU citizenship law do not always translate 'back' well to economic free movement law. In both citizenship and economic free movement dimensions, a fragmented understanding of the purpose of integration requirements and of how different sources of EU law interrelate is risked. It is also important to remember the legally different Treaty framing of the right to move and reside in Articles 20 and 21 TFEU compared to Articles 45 and 49 TFEU, especially with respect to the setting of conditions and limits, as well as their different legislative contexts and case law histories.

Second, the imprint of Directive 2004/38 is evident beyond its formal sphere of application through the influence of its provisions 'by analogy'. In a positive sense, this interpretative method supports coherence. It also serves, usually, to ensure that rights in ongoing multi-State or leaver/returner situations are protected at the same level as the Directive would protect them in more straightforward movement and residence situations. A caution comes with respect to how rights conferred directly by primary EU law retain that character, that particular legal quality. Similarly to previous chapters, whether applying the Directive directly or by analogy, advancing very specific tests through interpretation alone is difficult to reconcile with the requirement in Articles 20 and 21 TFEU that conditions and limits must be expressly provided for either in legislation or in the Treaties.

Further Reading

J Bierbach, 'European citizens' third-country family members and Community law' (2008) 4 European Constitutional Law Review 344.

K Hyltén-Cavallius, 'Who cares? Caregivers' derived residence rights from children in EU free movement law' (2020) 57 Common Market Law Review 399.

E Guild, 'EU citizens, foreign family members and European Union law' (2019) 21 European Journal of Migration and Law 358.

S Schoenmaekers and A Hoogenboom, '*Singh* and *Carpenter* revisited: some progress but no final clarity' (2014) 21 Maastricht Journal of European and Comparative Law 494.

P Watson, 'Free movement of workers – a one way ticket? Case C-370/90 *The Queen v. Immigration Appeal Tribunal and Surinder Singh*' (1993) 22 Industrial Law Journal 68.

10
Excluding Union Citizens
Public Policy, Public Security, and Public Health

1. Chapter Overview

This chapter examines the legal framework that determines the lawfulness of restrictions on freedom of movement and residence that are based on public policy, public security, or public health, which normally entail a decision to expel a Union citizen from the territory of a host State. It considers how the concepts of public policy, public security, and public health are defined and applied in EU citizenship law, both substantively and procedurally. It therefore complements and builds on the discussion of restricting rights in the home State in Chapter 5 and of expulsion decisions based on the protection of host State public finances in Chapters 6 and 7.[1]

It has always been recognised that EU free movement law is not unlimited, and that Member States may restrict freedom of movement and residence for good reasons of public policy, public security, or public health. However, when doing so, they must act within the framework of EU law. In several respects, the discretion that Member States retained within that framework was further narrowed down by the introduction of Union citizenship. In *Orfanopoulos and Oliveri*, the Court recalled that it had 'consistently held that the principle of freedom of movement for workers must be given a broad interpretation ... whereas derogations from that principle must be interpreted strictly'.[2] It then stated, drawing from the idea of Union citizenship as the fundamental status of Member State nationals, that 'a *particularly restrictive* interpretation of the derogations from that freedom is required by virtue of a person's status as a citizen of the Union'.[3] In that light, '[i]n accordance with the principle of sincere cooperation, the Member States are obliged to exercise their competence in the sphere of the maintenance of public order and public security in such a way as not to compromise the full effectiveness of the provisions of the Treaties'.[4] The Court has therefore held

---

[1] Article 27(1) of Directive 2004/38 affirms that 'Member States may restrict the freedom of movement and residence of Union citizens and their family members, irrespective of nationality, on grounds of public policy, public security or public health', but also that '[t]hese grounds shall not be invoked to serve economic ends'. Decisions to expel a Union citizen on the grounds of protection of host State public finances are therefore both conceptually and legally distinct and they are taken on the basis of Article 15 of the Directive. As the Court confirmed in *B and Vomero*, 'unlike a Union citizen with a right of permanent residence, who may only be expelled from the territory of the host Member State on the grounds stated in Article 28(2) of Directive 2004/38, a citizen who has not acquired that right may, where appropriate, be expelled from that territory if he becomes an unreasonable burden on the social assistance system of that Member State, as is apparent from Chapter III of that directive' (Joined Cases C-316/16 and C-424/16 *B and Vomero*, EU:C:2018:256, para 55). In consequence, 'a Union citizen who, because he does not have a right of permanent residence, may be expelled if he becomes such an unreasonable burden, cannot, at the same time, enjoy the considerably enhanced protection provided for in Article 28(3)(a) of that directive' (ibid, para 56). On Article 28(3) of the Directive, see Section 3.2. On expulsion based on unreasonable burden on host State public finances, see Chapters 6 and 7. Directive 2004/38/EC on the right of citizens of the Union and their family members to move and reside freely within the territory of the Member States, 2004 OJ L158/77.

[2] Joined Cases C-482/01 and C-493/01 *Orfanopoulos and Oliveri*, EU:C:2004:262, para 64; referring to eg Case 67/74 *Bonsignore*, EU:C:1975:34, para 6 and Case C-357/98 *Yiadom*, EU:C:2000:604, para 24.

[3] *Orfanopoulos and Oliveri*, para 65 (emphasis added).

[4] AG Szpunar in Case C-165/14 *Rendón Marín* and Case C-304/14 *CS*, EU:C:2016:75, para 143 of the Opinion.

that 'an appraisal as to whether measures designed to safeguard public policy are justified must have regard to all rules of [Union] law which are designed to limit the discretion of Member States in that respect and to ensure that the rights of persons subject to restrictive measures under such legislation are protected'.[5] In contrast, 'excessive or arbitrary recourse to the public policy or public security exception in dealings with Union citizens would create a risk of rendering their rights wholly ineffective, in particular their rights of free movement and residence'.[6]

In this chapter, the principles that determined when and how the right to move and reside may be restricted, as established in foundational EU legislation and case law, are first introduced (Section 2), demonstrating overall that there is a strong thread of continuity between the measures and principles applied then and now (though with welcome progression of language from 'aliens' to 'citizens'[7]). Decisions taken on the grounds of public policy, public security, or public health can restrict the right of entry to a Member State. However, expulsion from a host State[8]—which cuts to the heart of free movement and 'can seriously harm persons who, having availed themselves of the rights and freedoms conferred on them by the Treaty, have become genuinely integrated into the host Member State' (recital 23 of Directive 2004/38)—compels the most detailed legal rules. In some respects, excluding Union citizens and their family members is still an aspect of national immigration systems. For example, '[d]etermining the competent authorities for adopting the various measures provided for by Directive 2004/38 is a matter for the procedural autonomy of the Member States, since that directive contains no provisions in that regard'.[9] Nevertheless, EU citizenship law significantly constrains national discretion, both substantively and procedurally, in several critical respects.

Directive 2004/38 thus instituted a revised framework for decisions restricting free movement and residence, conceived in reflection of a rich case law on expulsion generally and the legal implications of Union citizenship (Section 3). The key concepts of public health, public policy, and public security as well as the significant framing principles that determine their application, especially proportionality and compliance with EU fundamental rights, are examined in detail. The Directive's tiered system of protection against expulsion—connected, like the right of permanent residence, to *duration* but also *quality* of residence in a host State—is also explained. Finally, the administrative formalities and procedural safeguards mandated by EU law are also presented (Section 4). How the definitions and rights that apply with respect to the Directive compare to those in Part Two of the Withdrawal Agreement concluded between the EU and the United Kingdom following the UK's withdrawal from the Union is noted across the chapter where relevant.[10]

---

[5] Case C-100/01 *Oteiza Olazabal*, EU:C:2002:712, para 30.

[6] AG Szpunar in *Rendón Marín* and *CS*, para 143 of the Opinion

[7] That change does not overcome the 'legal otherness' that expulsion exemplifies in any context, however, which is complex and gradated not just with respect to a State's own nationals and Union citizens, but also across and within different groups of third-country nationals within the Union more generally; see further, K Hamenstädt, 'Expulsion and "legal otherness" in times of growing nationalism' (2020) 45 European Law Review 452.

[8] Described as 'basically constitut[ing] an "exportation of danger"' by AG Stix-Hackl in *Orfanopoulos and Oliveri*, EU:C:2003:455, para 40 of the Opinion.

[9] Case C-184/16 *Petrea*, EU:C:2017:684, para 53. The Court also observed that Member States may 'draw inspiration from the provisions of Directive 2008/115 to designate competent authorities and to define the procedure applicable to the adoption of a decision ordering the return of an EU citizen ... if that is not precluded by any provisions of EU law' (ibid para 52; Directive 2008/115 on common standards and procedures in Member States for returning illegally staying third-country nationals, 2008 OJ L348/98).

[10] Agreement on the withdrawal of the United Kingdom of Great Britain and Northern Ireland from the European Union and the European Atomic Energy Community, OJ 2019 CI 384/01.

2. Before Directive 2004/38: Foundational Principles

The right to move and reside is not unconditional. Articles 45(2) (workers), 52(1) (establishment), and 62 (services) TFEU, reflecting their ancestor provisions in the EEC and EC Treaties, have always permitted limitations that are justified on grounds of public policy, public security, or public health.[11] However, '[t]he [Union] legislature has nevertheless made reliance by the Member States on such grounds subject to strict limits.[12] Directive 64/221[13] established a series of principles in this respect: public policy, public security, or public health could not 'be invoked to service economic ends' (Article 2(2)); measures taken 'shall be based exclusively on the personal conduct of the individual concerned' (Article 3(1)); '[p]revious criminal convictions shall not in themselves constitute grounds for the taking of such measures' (Article 3(2)); and '[e]xpiry of the identity card or passport used by the person concerned to enter the host country and to obtain a residence permit shall not justify expulsion from the territory' (Article 3(4)).

For public health specifically, Article 4 established that '[t]he only diseases or disabilities justifying refusal of entry into a territory or refusal to issue a first residence permit shall be those listed in the Annex to this Directive' (Article 4(1))[14] and that '[d]iseases or disabilities occurring after a first residence permit has been issued shall not justify refusal to renew the residence permit or expulsion from the territory' (Article 4(2)). Member States were also prohibited from introducing 'new provisions or practices which are more restrictive than those in force at the date of notification of this Directive' (Article 4(3)). Finally, Articles 5–9 of the Directive outlined administrative formalities and procedural safeguards, underlining the critical importance of legal remedies 'in respect of any decision concerning entry, or refusing the issue or renewal of a residence permit, or ordering expulsion from the territory' (Article 8).[15]

---

[11] The Treaty also provides for more limited restrictions connected to employment in the public service (Article 45(4)) and the exercise of official authority (Articles 51 and 62). Both concepts are interpreted narrowly by the Court of Justice. The scope of 'employment in the public service' has been interpreted to mean only 'posts which involve direct or indirect participation in the exercise of powers conferred by public law and duties designed to safeguard the general interests of the State or of other public authorities and thus presume on the part of those occupying them the existence of a special relationship of allegiance to the State and reciprocity of rights and duties which form the foundation of the bond of nationality' (Case C-405/01 *Colegio de Oficiales de la Marina Mercante Española*, EU:C:2003:515, para 39), while the 'exercise of official authority' as it relates to establishment and services 'must be restricted to activities which in themselves are directly and specifically connected with the exercise of official authority' and, conversely, 'does not extend to certain activities that are auxiliary or preparatory' in that context' (Case C-61/08 *Commission v Greece*, EU:C:2011:340, paras 77 and 78).

[12] Case C-441/02 *Commission v Germany*, EU:C:2006:253, para 33.

[13] Directive 64/221/EEC on the coordination of special measures concerning the movement and residence of foreign nationals which are justified on grounds of public policy, public security, or public health, OJ 1963–1964 Sp Ed P117.

[14] The Annex to Directive 64/221 specified: 'A. Diseases which might endanger public health: 1. Diseases subject to quarantine listed in International Health Regulation No 2 of the World Health Organisation of 25 May 1951; 2. Tuberculosis of the respiratory system in an active state or showing a tendency to develop; 3. Syphilis; 4. Other infectious diseases or contagious parasitic diseases if they are the subject of provisions for the protection of nationals of the host country. B. Diseases and disabilities which might threaten public policy or public security: 1. Drug addiction; 2. Profound mental disturbance; manifest conditions of psychotic disturbance with agitation, delirium, hallucinations or confusion.'

[15] With respect to Article 8 of the Directive, 'the party concerned must at least have the opportunity of lodging an appeal and thus obtaining a stay of execution before the expulsion order is carried out' (Case 48/75 *Royer*, EU:C:1976:57, para 57). On the significance of the right of defence in this context, see eg Joined Cases 115 and 116/81 *Adoui and Cornuaille*, EU:C:1982:183, paras 15–19. Following its approach to judicial protection more generally, the Court also confirmed that '[w]hile it is for the domestic legal system of each Member State to lay down the detailed procedural rules governing actions for safeguarding rights which individuals derive from [Union] law, the fact remains that those rules must not be such as to render virtually impossible or excessively difficult the exercise of rights conferred by [Union] law' (Joined Cases C-482/01 and C-493/01 *Orfanopoulos and Oliveri*,

Case law further developed the framework instituted by Directive 64/221. *First*, the Court established that residence permits are declaratory rather than constitutive of the free movement rights conferred directly by the Treaty,[16] as examined in various contexts in Chapters 5–8. In *Royer*, the Court determined that the 'logical consequence' of that position is that 'the mere failure by a national of a Member State to complete the legal formalities concerning access, movement and residence of aliens does not justify a decision ordering expulsion'.[17] However, EU law 'does not prevent the Member States from providing, for breaches of national provisions concerning the control of aliens, any appropriate sanctions – other than measures of expulsion from the territory – necessary in order to ensure the efficacy of those provisions'.[18]

With respect to the safeguards provided for by Directive 64/221, the Court required 'a broad interpretation as regards the persons to whom they apply'.[19] In that light, 'Member States must take all steps to ensure that the safeguard of the provisions of the directive is available to any national of another Member State who is subject to a decision ordering expulsion' since '[t]o exclude from the benefit of those substantive and procedural safeguards citizens of the Union who are not lawfully resident on the territory of the host Member State would deprive those safeguards of their essential effectiveness'.[20] Therefore, as noted in Chapter 7, Member State nationals were not required to be lawfully resident in the host State in order to benefit from the safeguards guaranteed by the Directive.[21] Relatedly, 'any foreign national married to a Member State national claiming to meet the conditions necessary to qualify for the protection afforded by Directive 64/221 benefits from the minimum procedural guarantees laid down in Article 9 of the directive, even if he is not in possession of an identity document or, requiring a visa, he has entered the territory of a Member State without one or has remained there after its expiry'.[22]

Second, the Court defined the scope, and the limits, of public policy and public security. In the context of public policy, it aimed to balance uniformity of application of EU rules, on the one hand, with accommodating legitimate differences in the conception of public policy across the Member States, on the other. In that light, it held in *Van Duyn* that:

> The concept of public policy in the context of the [Union] and where, in particular, it is used as a justification for derogating from the fundamental principle of freedom of movement for workers, *must be interpreted strictly*, so that *its scope cannot be determined unilaterally* by each Member State without being subject to control by the institutions of the [Union]. Nevertheless, the particular circumstances justifying recourse to the concept of public policy *may vary from one country to another and from one period to another*, and it is therefore necessary to allow the competent national authorities an area of discretion within the limits imposed by the Treaty.[23]

EU:C:2004:262, para 80). These themes are returned to in Section 3.3, outlining the procedural safeguards currently in force under Directive 2004/38.

[16] *Royer*, paras 31–33; confirmed in eg Case C-408/03 *Commission v Belgium*, EU:C:2006:192, para 63.
[17] *Royer*, para 38. In para 39, the Court confirmed more specifically that 'such conduct cannot be regarded as constituting in itself a breach of public policy or public security'. See similarly, paras 47 and 51.
[18] ibid para 42.
[19] Case C-50/06 *Commission v Netherlands*, EU:C:2007:325, para 35.
[20] ibid para 35.
[21] ibid para 36.
[22] Case C-459/99 *MRAX*, EU:C:2002:461, para 102.
[23] Case 41/74 *Van Duyn*, EU:C:1973:133, para 18 (emphasis added). Confirmed in eg Case C-208/09 *Sayn-Wittgenstein*, EU:C:2010:806, para 86; and Case C-673/16 *Coman*, EU:C:2018:385, para 44.

In *Bouchereau*, the Court confirmed these principles but added that national authorities retain 'an area of discretion within the limits imposed by the Treaty *and the provisions adopted for its implementation*'.[24] It also held that 'recourse by a national authority to the concept of public policy presupposes ... the existence, in addition to the perturbation of the social order which any infringement of the law involves, of a *genuine and sufficiently serious threat* to the requirements of public policy affecting *one of the fundamental interests of society*'.[25]

Third, the requirement in Article 3(1) of Directive 64/221 that restrictive measures should be 'based exclusively on the personal conduct of the individual concerned'[26] and in Article 3(2) that previous criminal convictions 'shall not in themselves constitute grounds for the taking of such measures' meant that, conversely, a Member State national could not be deported from the host State 'if such deportation is ordered for the purpose of deterring other aliens, that is, if it is based ... on reasons of a "general preventive nature"'.[27] Commenting on deportation not only as a security measure but also as having effects 'at the social and human level', Advocate General Mayras suggested that '[t]he authors of the directive ... wished that, independently of any conviction, the national authorities should be able to order deportation only to the extent to which the personal conduct of the [Union] national who had committed an offence constituted or was likely to constitute in the future such a threat to national public policy that the presence of the individual concerned in the territory of the host country could no longer be tolerated'.[28]

The Commission underlined that '[t]he Member States have discretionary powers to apply public policy and public security measures to prevent violence and hooliganism at sports events', for example, but also that 'the extensive use of these grounds may lead to detentions and expulsions, which are not based on any individual grounds. The measures should be targeted at individuals – or sometimes on justified grounds to a specific group of individuals – whose personal behaviour may cause a threat to public policy or public security. The general principle is that any security measures should be applied in a non- discriminatory

---

[24] Case 30/77 *Bouchereau*, EU:C:1977:172, para 34 (emphasis added).

[25] ibid para 35 (emphasis added); the 'genuine and sufficiently serious threat' criterion comes from Case 36/75 *Rutili*, EU:C:1975:137, para 28.

[26] In *Commission v Spain*, the Court confirmed that 'the concept of public policy within the meaning of Article 2 of Directive 64/221 does not correspond to that in Article 96 of the [Convention Implementing the Schengen Agreement (CISA)]. According to the latter, an alert in the [Schengen Information System (SIS)] for the purposes of refusing entry may be based on a threat to public policy where the person concerned has been convicted of an offence carrying a penalty involving deprivation of liberty of at least one year (Article 96(2)(a)), or if he has been subject to a measure based on a failure to comply with national regulations on the entry or residence of aliens (Article 96(3)). Unlike the rules laid down by Directive 64/221, as interpreted by the Court, such circumstances justify in themselves an alert irrespective of any specific assessment of the threat represented by the person concerned' (Case C-503/03 *Commission v Spain*, EU:C:2006:74, para 48, referring to the Convention implementing the Schengen Agreement ('CISA') of 14 June 1985 between the Governments of the States of the Benelux Economic Union, the Federal Republic of Germany and the French Republic on the gradual abolition of checks at their common borders, signed in Schengen on 19 June 1990 and which entered into force on 26 March 1995, 2000 OJ L239/19). See similarly, Case C-380/18 *EP (Menace pour l'ordre public)*, EU:C:2019:1071, para 34 ('[a]s regards ... the wording of Article 6(1)(e) of the Schengen Borders Code, it is to be noted that, unlike *inter alia* Article 27(2) of Directive 2004/38, it does not expressly require the personal conduct of the individual concerned to represent a genuine, present and sufficiently serious threat affecting one of the fundamental interests of society in order for that individual to be capable of being regarded as a threat to public policy'). Regulation 2016/399/EU on a Union Code on the rules governing the movement of persons across borders (Schengen Borders Code), 2016 OJ 2016 L77/1). On the intersection of Article 21 TFEU and Schengen, see further Case C-505/19 *WS*, EU:C:2021:376. For the same distinction in the context of Directive 2003/86 on the right to family reunification, 2003 OJ L251/12, see Joined Cases C-381/18 and C-382/18 *GS and VG (Menace pour l'ordre public)*, EU:C:2019:1072, para 56.

[27] Case 67/74 *Bonsignore*, EU:C:1975:34, para 7. Confirmed in eg Case C-441/02 *Commission v Germany*, EU:C:2006:253, para 93; and Case C-165/14 *Rendón Marín*, EU:C:2016:675, para 61.

[28] AG Mayras in *Bonsignore*, EU:C:1975:22, p 311; see further, p 316.

basis to own nationals and nationals of another Member State'.[29] It further suggested that '[t]he threat caused by a person also depends upon whether a person belonging to a specific group is entering the country to attend a certain event involving security risks or whether he is entering the country at another time of the year clearly for other purposes (business, holiday with the family etc.)'.[30]

To assess whether criminal convictions could justify the restriction of free movement and residence rights, national authorities were required 'to carry out a specific appraisal from the point of view of the interests inherent in protecting the requirements of public policy, which does not necessarily coincide with the appraisals which formed the basis of the criminal conviction'.[31] A previous criminal conviction could, therefore, 'only be taken into account in so far as the circumstances which gave rise to that conviction are evidence of personal conduct constituting a *present* threat to the requirements of public policy'.[32] In the Court's view, 'a finding that such a threat exists implies the existence in the individual concerned of a propensity to act in the same way in the future' although it is also 'possible that past conduct alone may constitute such a threat to the requirements of public policy'.[33] In its 2009 Communication on better transposition and application of Directive 2004/38, the Commission referred to the case law on Directive 64/221 to confirm that '[p]ast conduct may be taken into account only where there is a likelihood of reoffending'; it emphasised that '[t]he threat must exist at the moment when the restrictive measure is adopted by the national authorities or reviewed by the courts', which requires in turn that '[s]uspension of sentence constitutes an important factor in the assessment of the threat as it suggests that the individual concerned no longer represents a real danger'.[34]

The Court considered applications for re-admission to a Member State following an expulsion decision in *Adoui and Cornuaille*, ruling that '[s]uch an application, when submitted *after a reasonable period has elapsed*, must be examined by the competent administrative authority in the host State', which 'must take into account, in particular, the arguments put forward by the person concerned purporting to establish that there has been a *material change* in the circumstances which justified the first decision ordering his expulsion'.[35] However, where an expulsion decision has been 'validly adopted ... in accordance with [Union] law and continues to be legally effective such as to exclude him from the territory of the State in question, [Union] law contains no provision conferring upon him a right of entry into that territory during the examination of his further application'.[36] The rules currently in force under Directive 2004/38 are examined in Section 3.3.

Fourth, while the Court acknowledged that Member States 'have no authority to expel [their own nationals] from the national territory or to deny them access thereto',[37] it

---

[29] Communication from the Commission to the Council and the European Parliament on the special measures concerning the movement and residence of citizens of the Union which are justified on grounds of public policy, public security or public health, COM(1999) 372 final, para 3.3.1.

[30] ibid.

[31] Case 30/77 *Bouchereau*, EU:C:1977:172, para 27.

[32] ibid para 28 (emphasis added). Confirmed in eg Case C-348/96 *Calfa*, EU:C:1999:6, para 24.

[33] *Bouchereau*, para 29.

[34] Communication from the Commission to the European Parliament and the Council on guidance for better transposition and application of Directive 2004/38/EC on the right of citizens of the Union and their family members to move and reside freely within the territory of the Member States, COM(2009) 313 final, 11; referring to *Bouchereau*, paras 25–30 and Joined Cases C-482/01 and C-493/01 *Orfanopoulos and Oliveri*, EU:C:2004:262, para 82.

[35] Joined Cases 115 and 116/81 *Adoui and Cornuaille*, EU:C:1982:183, para 12 (emphasis added).

[36] ibid.

[37] ibid para 7. See similarly, Joined Cases C-65/95 and C-111/95 *Shingara and Radiom*, EU:C:1997:300, para 28; and Case C-100/01 *Oteiza Olazabal*, EU:C:2002:712, para 40.

emphasised that measures adopted to restrict the free movement and residence rights of the nationals of other Member States must not be based 'on assessments of certain conduct which would have the effect of applying an arbitrary distinction to the detriment of nationals of other Member States'.[38] Recalling the requirement of 'a genuine and sufficiently serious threat affecting one of the fundamental interests of society' in *Bouchereau*, the Court found in *Adoui and Cornuaille* that while EU law 'does not impose upon the Member States a uniform scale of values as regards the assessment of conduct which may be considered as contrary to public policy ... conduct may not be considered as being of a sufficiently serious nature to justify restrictions on the admission to or residence within the territory of a Member State of a national of another Member State in a case where the former Member State does not adopt, with respect to the same conduct on the part of its own nationals repressive measures or other genuine or effective measures intended to combat such conduct'.[39] The Commission advises that '[p]resent membership of an organisation may be taken into account where the individual concerned participates in the activities of the organization and identifies with its aims or designs. Member States do not have to criminalize or to ban the activities of an organisation to be in a position to restrict the rights under the Directive, as long as some administrative measures to counteract the activities of that organisation are in place. Past associations cannot, in general, constitute present threat'.[40]

Additionally, in principle, 'a measure limiting the exercise of the right of free movement must ... be adopted in the light of considerations pertaining to the protection of public policy or public security *in the Member State imposing the measure*. Thus it cannot be based exclusively on reasons advanced by another Member State to justify a decision to remove a [Union] national from the territory of the latter State'.[41] However, that 'does not ... rule out the possibility of such reasons being taken into account in the context of the assessment which the competent national authorities undertake for the purpose of adopting the measure restricting freedom of movement'.[42] In *Jipa*, the Court explained this point by finding that 'the fact that a citizen of the Union has been subject to a measure repatriating him from the territory of another Member State, where he was residing illegally, may be taken into account by his Member State of origin for the purpose of restricting that citizen's right of free movement only to the extent that his personal conduct constitutes a genuine, present and sufficiently serious threat to one of the fundamental interests of society'.[43]

Fifth, the Court consistently emphasised compliance with the principles that shape the wider EU legal order, especially proportionality and respect for fundamental rights. Expressing this point with reference to Article 21 TFEU but before the adoption of Directive 2004/38, the Court considered that '[a]mong the limitations and conditions laid down or authorised by [Union] law, Directive 64/221 permits Member States to expel nationals of other Member States from their territory on grounds of public policy or public security, subject to compliance with the substantive and procedural safeguards laid down by that directive and with the general principles of [Union] law'.[44] According to the Commission, '[p]roportionality requires justified grounds for a measure [adopted for the protection of public

---

[38] *Adoui and Cornuaille*, para 7.
[39] ibid para 8.
[40] Communication on guidance for better transposition and application of Directive 2004/38/EC (n 34) 11; referring to Case 41/74 *Van Duyn*, EU:C:1973:133, para 17 et seq.
[41] Case C-33/07 *Jipa*, EU:C:2008:396, para 25 (emphasis added).
[42] ibid.
[43] ibid para 26.
[44] Case C-50/06 *Commission v Netherlands*, EU:C:2007:325, para 34.

policy, public security or public health], justified balance between the measure and the objective, and justified balance of interests of the individual and the State concerned'.[45]

The Court established in *Watson and Belmann* that while 'the competent authorities in the Member States may require nationals of the other Member States to report their presence to the authorities of the State concerned'—and that 'such an obligation could not in itself be regarded as an infringement of the rules concerning freedom of movement for persons'—an infringement 'might result from the legal formalities in question if the control procedures to which they refer were such as to restrict the freedom of movement required by the Treaty or to limit the right conferred by the Treaty on nationals of the Member States to enter and reside in the territory of any other Member State for the purposes intended by [Union] law'.[46] In particular, 'as regards the period within which the arrival of foreign nationals must be reported, the provisions of the Treaty are only infringed if the period fixed is *unreasonable*.'[47] Moreover, '[a]s regards other penalties, such as fines and detention, whilst the national authorities are entitled to impose penalties in respect of a failure to comply with the terms of provisions requiring foreign nationals to notify their presence which are comparable to those attaching to infringements of provisions of equal importance by nationals, they are not justified in imposing a penalty so *disproportionate* to the gravity of the infringement that it becomes an obstacle to the free movement of persons'.[48] Applied as a penalty for failure to comply with administrative formalities, 'deportation, in relation to persons protected by [Union] law, is certainly incompatible with the provisions if the Treaty since ... such a measure negates the very right conferred and guaranteed by the Treaty'.[49]

In general, therefore, 'a measure restricting one of the fundamental freedoms guaranteed by the Treaty may be justified only if it complies with the principle of proportionality. In that respect, such a measure must be appropriate for securing the attainment of the objective which it pursues and must not go beyond what is necessary in order to attain it'.[50] Linking back to the requirement to base any expulsion decision on the personal conduct of the person concerned, 'the competent national authorities must assess, *on a case-by-case basis*, whether the measure or the circumstances which gave rise to that expulsion order prove the existence of personal conduct constituting a present threat to the requirements of public policy'.[51] In *Calfa,* the Court held that national rules under which 'expulsion for life automatically follows a criminal conviction, without any account being taken of the personal conduct of the offender or of the danger which that person represents for the requirements of public policy' are precluded by EU law.[52] EU law precludes, more generally, national rules 'relating to foreign nationals [that make] it possible to establish a systematic and automatic connection between a criminal conviction and a measure ordering expulsion in respect of citizens of the Union'.[53]

According to the Commission, '[n]ational legislation may quite correctly provide that the national authorities or national court may make an expulsion order after taking into

---

[45] Communication on grounds of public policy, public security or public health (n 29) para2.2 (emphasis added).
[46] Case 118/75 *Watson and Belmann,* EU:C:1976:106, para 18.
[47] ibid para 19 (emphasis added).
[48] ibid para 21 (emphasis added).
[49] ibid para 20.
[50] Case C-100/01 *Oteiza Olazabal,* EU:C:2002:712, paras 40 and 43.
[51] Joined Cases C-482/01 and C-493/01 *Orfanopoulos and Oliveri,* EU:C:2004:262, para 77 (emphasis added).
[52] Case C-348/96 *Calfa,* EU:C:1999:6, para 27.
[53] Case C-50/06 *Commission v Netherlands,* EU:C:2007:325, para 46; see similarly eg Case C-165/14 *Rendón Marín,* EU:C:2016:675, para 61.

consideration all the relevant factors', but should not be 'applied automatically in individual cases with sole reference to the criminal conviction and without any individual or specified reasoning'.[54] It defined an 'automatic' system as 'any national provision the wording of which leaves the national authorities or the national court no margin for appreciation or for taking into consideration any individual circumstances'.[55] Additionally, EU law 'precludes a national practice whereby the national courts may not take into consideration, in reviewing the lawfulness of the expulsion of a national of another Member State, factual matters which occurred after the final decision of the competent authorities which may point to the cessation or the substantial diminution of the present threat which the conduct of the person concerned constitutes to the requirements of public policy'—particularly 'if a lengthy period has elapsed between the date of the expulsion order and that of the review of that decision by the competent court'.[56] The Court has determined that '[t]o assess whether the interference envisaged is proportionate to the legitimate aim pursued, in this instance the protection of public policy, account must be taken, particularly, of the nature and seriousness of the offences committed by the person concerned, the length of his residence in the host Member State, the period which has elapsed since the commission of the offence, the family circumstances of the person concerned and the seriousness of the difficulties which the spouse and any of their children risk facing in the country of origin of the person concerned'.[57]

In *MRAX*, the Court considered the requirements of proportionality alongside 'the importance which the [Union legislature has attached to the protection of family life'[58] when considering the implications that should—and should not—flow from a third-country national family member's failure to comply with certain administrative formalities.[59] It stated in *Orfanopoulos and Oliveri* that, when determining whether the personal conduct of a Member State national constitutes a present threat to a host State's public policy, 'it is necessary to take into account the fundamental rights whose observance the Court ensures. Reasons of public interest may be invoked to justify a national measure which is likely to obstruct the exercise of ... freedom of movement ... only if the measure in question takes account of such rights'.[60] The Court emphasised, in particular, 'the importance of ensuring the protection of the family life of [Union] nationals in order to eliminate obstacles to the exercise of the fundamental freedoms guaranteed by the Treaty has been ecognized under [Union] law', observing that '[i]t is clear that the removal of a person from the country where close members of his family are living may amount to an infringement of the right to respect for family life as guaranteed by Article 8 of the ECHR, which is among the fundamental rights, which, according to the Court's settled case-law, are protected in [Union] law'.[61]

As will be seen in Section 3, Directive 2004/38 both captured and deepened the already comprehensive legal framework for restricting the right to move and reside constructed over several decades through the combination of Treaty foundations, legislative development, and judicial interpretation summarised above.

---

[54] Communication on grounds of public policy, public security or public health (n 29) para 3.3.2.
[55] ibid.
[56] *Orfanopoulos and Oliveri*, para 82. See further, Section 3.
[57] ibid para 99.
[58] Case C-459/99 *MRAX*, EU:C:2002:461, para 61; see also, para 53.
[59] See further, Chapter 6.
[60] *Orfanopoulos and Oliveri*, para 97.
[61] ibid para 98.

3. Directive 2004/38: The Revised Legal Framework

In 1999, the Commission issued a Communication on Directive 64/221, recognising that '[d]evelopments in European integration, and particularly the introduction of the concept of citizenship of the Union in Article [21 TFEU], have also changed the context in which the Directive falls to be interpreted'.[62] The Commission disclosed that it had received 'an ever-increasing number of complaints concerning the application of the Directive', suggesting that 'the interpretation and implementation of some of its basic principles differ widely amongst the Member States'.[63] The principal purpose of the Communication was essentially to provide more guidance about how to resolve these difficulties in connection with Directive 64/221 rather than to reconceive the expulsion framework because of Union citizenship. Nevertheless, citizenship-specific nuances were evident.

For example, the Commission advocated that Article 21 TFEU 'should be accorded its full weight by national authorities when they contemplate the application of Directive 64/221/EEC to a Union citizen' and that '[t]his is *especially true for specific categories of Union citizens*: nationals of other Member States who were either born, or have lived since childhood, in the Member State of residence and who have virtually all their cultural, social and family ties to that Member State, as well as other long-term residents and minors'.[64] Reflecting the significance of integration in EU citizenship law, it explained that '[t]he fact that a person was born and educated in the country of residence or has resided there from an early age strengthens considerably his ties to that country. Furthermore, in such circumstances the person's behaviour reflects, *both in its good and bad aspects*, and can be evaluated against the behaviour of his peers who are nationals of the country of residence and are shaped by the same society'.[65] The Commission also considered that the public health grounds in the Annex to Directive 64/221 were 'somewhat outdated given the current level of integration of the European Union and the development of new means to handle public health problems. Therefore, restrictions of free movement can no longer be considered as necessary and effective means of solving public health problems. The situation has changed radically from what it was in 1964, even though the concept of public health still forms part of Union law'.[66]

Building on the Communication, the process of drafting and adopting Directive 2004/38 very naturally enabled comprehensive reflection on and review of Directive 64/221, both in general terms and with reference to the status of Union citizenship more specifically. In

---

[62] Communication on grounds of public policy, public security or public health, COM(1999) 372 final (n 29) para 1.2. See similarly, para 4: 'the personal, fundamental right to free movement of the citizens of the Union (Article [21 TFEU]) combined with the principle of proportionality should guide the national authorities when they take any decision concerning [any measure taken on grounds of public policy, public security or public health]'.

[63] ibid para 1.2.

[64] ibid para 3.1.1 (emphasis added). See further, para 3.4.1 on the specific level of protection that should be extended to long-term residents in a host State, including the guidance that 'a much stricter burden of proof is required of the Member State to justify the proportionality of [an expulsion] measure' and adding that the 'specific concern about long-term residents applies also to minors, whose rights, including the right to the protection of family life, should be protected following the same principles'.

[65] ibid para 3.3.1 (emphasis added).

[66] ibid para 3.1.3. For example, in fn 26, the Commission highlighted that '[i]n the documents adopted by the [Union] institutions, it has been clearly stated that the full respect of free movement of persons and equality of treatment must be guaranteed for persons affected by HIV/AIDS. The Commission rejects the use of any measures, which could lead to social exclusion, discrimination or stigmatisation of persons with HIV/AIDS', referring to several examples including Decision 647/96/EC of the European Parliament and of the Council adopting a programme of Community action on the prevention of AIDS and certain other communicable diseases within the framework for action in the field of public health (1996 to 2000), 1996 OJ L95/16.

its original proposal, the Commission indicated that the purpose of the new Directive was both to capture interpretations by the Court of Justice that clarified aspects of Directive 64/221 and also to introduce 'new provisions drawing on the concept of fundamental rights [to] provide Union citizens with greater protection and better safeguards in dealings with both administrative authorities and the courts concerning any decisions restricting their fundamental right of movement and residence'—most notably, and in the end most controversially (as returned to below), the Commission proposed that such protection should be 'absolute for minors who have family ties in the host country and people who have acquired a right of permanent residence'.[67]

Recital 22 indicates that Directive 2004/38 replaced Directive 64/221 '[i]n order to ensure a tighter definition of the circumstances and procedural safeguards subject to which Union citizens and their family members may be denied leave to enter or may be expelled'. Recital 23 then acknowledges that '[e]xpulsion of Union citizens and their family members on grounds of public policy or public security is a measure that can seriously harm persons who, having availed themselves of the rights and freedoms conferred on them by the Treaty, have become genuinely integrated into the host Member State'; in consequence, '[t]he scope for such measures should therefore be limited in accordance with the principle of proportionality to take account of the degree of integration of the persons concerned, the length of their residence in the host Member State, their age, state of health, family and economic situation and the links with their country of origin'.[68]

Article 27(1) of Directive 2004/38 reflects Article 2(2) of Directive 64/221 in stating that '[s]ubject to the provisions of this Chapter, Member States may restrict the freedom of movement and residence of Union citizens and their family members, irrespective of nationality, on grounds of public policy, public security or public health' and that '[t]hese grounds shall not be invoked to serve economic ends'. With reference to the fact that 'the right of free movement of Union citizens is not unconditional but may be subject to the limitations and conditions imposed by the Treaty and by the measures adopted to give it effect', the Court considers that 'those limitations and conditions derive in particular from Article 27(1) of Directive 2004/38'.[69] It has also confirmed the application of Article 27 to a Union citizen's family members irrespective of their nationality.[70] In *Sahin*, for example, the Court confirmed that 'compliance with Article 27 is required in particular where the Member State wishes to penalise the national of a non-member country for entering into and/or residing in its territory in breach of the national rules on immigration before becoming a family member of a Union citizen'.[71] It has also found that Article 27 has direct effect, meaning that

---

[67] Proposal for a Directive of the European Parliament and of the Council on the right of citizens of the Union and their family members to move and reside freely within the territory of the Member States, COM(2001) 257 final, para 2.5.

[68] Referred to in eg Joined Cases C-316/16 and C-424/16 B and Vomero, EU:C:2018:256, para 43.

[69] Case C-33/07 *Jipa*, EU:C:2008:396, paras 21–22. See similarly, Case C-430/10 *Gaydarov*, EU:C:2011:749, paras 29–30. These judgments also confirmed that Article 27 applies to decisions taken by national authorities that restrict the free movement of Union citizens who are nationals of the State in question. As the Court explained in *Aladzhov*, 'the right of freedom of movement includes both the right for citizens of the European Union to enter a Member State other than the one of origin and the corresponding right to leave the State of origin. As the Court has already had occasion to state, the fundamental freedoms guaranteed by the Treaty would be rendered meaningless if the Member State of origin could, without valid justification, prohibit its own nationals from leaving its territory in order to enter the territory of another Member State' (Case C-434/10 *Aladzhov*, EU:C:2011:750, para 25, referring to *Jipa*, para 18).

[70] Case C-127/08 *Metock and Others*, EU:C:2008:449, para 95: '[f]rom the time when the national of a non-member country who is a family member of a Union citizen derives rights of entry and residence in the host Member State from Directive 2004/38, that State may restrict that right only in compliance with Articles 27 and 35 of that directive'. Confirmed in eg Case C-202/13 *McCarthy II*, EU:C:2014:2450, para 45.

[71] Case C-551/07 *Sahin*, EU:C:2008:75, para 30; referring to *Metock*, para 96.

'the provisions of that article, which are unconditional and sufficiently precise, may be relied on by an individual vis-à-vis the Member state of which he is a national'.[72]

The discussion of the legal framework instituted by Chapter VI of Directive 2004/38 is organised around two key issues in this part of the chapter: first, the definitions and general principles applied in respect of measures adopted on the grounds of public policy, public security, and public health (Section 3.1), and second, the Directive's tiered system of increased protection against expulsion for certain categories of Union citizen (Section 3.2).

3.1 Public Policy, Public Security, and Public Health: General Principles

The concepts of public policy, public security, and public health retain for the purposes of Directive 2004/38 the essential features established under Directive 64/221.[73] However, Directive 2004/38 has progressed that framework in several respects. As the most limited of the three grounds, the scope of public health restrictions under Article 29 of the Directive will first be outlined (Section 3.1.1). The concepts of public policy and public security (which are not defined by Directive 2004/38) are then addressed in Section 3.1.2, exploring, in particular, differences between the two grounds. Finally, the principles that should frame assessments made by national authorities and national courts on the grounds of public policy and

---

[72] *Gaydarov*, para 31.
[73] The Withdrawal Agreement marks a significant point of departure from EU citizenship law in this respect, with Article 18(1)(p) WA establishing that 'criminality and security checks *may be carried out systematically* on applicants [for residence documents], with the exclusive aim of verifying whether the restrictions set out in Article 20 of this Agreement may be applicable. For that purpose, applicants may be required *to declare past criminal convictions* which appear in their criminal record in accordance with the law of the State of conviction at the time of the application. The host State may, if it considers this essential, apply the procedure set out in Article 27(3) of Directive 2004/38/EC with respect to enquiries to other States regarding previous criminal records'. Article 20 WA then provides, inter alia: '1. The conduct of Union citizens or United Kingdom nationals, their family members, and other persons, who exercise rights under this Title, where that conduct occurred before the end of the transition period, shall be considered in accordance with Chapter VI of Directive 2004/38/EC. 2. The conduct of Union citizens or United Kingdom nationals, their family members, and other persons, who exercise rights under this Title, where that conduct occurred after the end of the transition period, may constitute grounds for restricting the right of residence by the host State or the right of entry in the State of *work in accordance with national legislation*'. The Commission further advises: 'Article 18(1)(p) authorises the host State operating a new constitutive scheme to carry out systematic criminal record checks. Such systematic checks have been accepted in the Agreement, given its unique context. Applicants may be required to self-declare those past criminal convictions that still appear in their criminal record in accordance with the law of the State of conviction at the time of the application. Spent convictions should not be part of that self-declaration. The State of conviction can be any country in the world. Making an untruthful declaration does not, in itself, make any rights under the Agreement void and null – it can nevertheless have consequences under public policy or fraud rules. The burden of proof in such cases lies with national authorities. The host State may also lay down provisions on proportionate sanctions applicable to untruthful declarations. Paragraph 1(p) of Article 18 does not prevent the host State from checking its own criminal record databases, even systematically. Checks of criminal record databases of other States can be requested, but only if that is considered essential and in accordance with the procedure set out in Article 27(3) of Directive 2004/38/EC that requires that such enquiries are not made as a matter of routine. Criminality and security checks under paragraph 1(p) of Article 18 correspond to checks on grounds of public policy or public security carried out in accordance with Chapter VI of Directive 2004/38/EC for the purpose of restricting the rights in accordance with Article 20(1) of the Agreement. Any restrictive measures taken on the grounds of criminality and security checks under paragraph 1(p) of Article 18 must comply with the rules laid down in Article 18(1)(r), and Articles 20 and 21 of the Agreement' (Guidance Note relating to the Agreement on the withdrawal of the United Kingdom of Great Britain and Northern Ireland from the European Union and the European Atomic Energy Community Part two—Citizens' rights, C(2020) 2939 final, para 2.6.12, emphasis added; see further, para 2.8, outlining guidance on Article 20 WA and distinguishing in particular how 'conduct' is to be determined before and after the end of the transition period, in accordance with EU law and national law respectively).

public security—that is, the requirements set out in Articles 27(2), 27(3), 27(4), and 28(1) of the Directive—are presented in Section 3.1.3.

3.1.1 Defining public health

Replacing Article 4 and the annex to Directive 64/221, which had determined the 'diseases or disabilities justifying refusal of entry into a territory or refusal to issue a first residence permit', Article 29 of Directive 2004/38 now provides:

Article 29

Public health

1. The only diseases justifying measures restricting freedom of movement shall be the diseases with epidemic potential as defined by the relevant instruments of the World Health Organisation and other infectious diseases or contagious parasitic diseases if they are the subject of protection provisions applying to nationals of the host Member State.
2. Diseases occurring after a three-month period from the date of arrival shall not constitute grounds for expulsion from the territory.
3. Where there are serious indications that it is necessary, Member States may, within three months of the date of arrival, require persons entitled to the right of residence to undergo, free of charge, a medical examination to certify that they are not suffering from any of the conditions referred to in paragraph 1. Such medical examinations may not be required as a matter of routine.

Article 29 of the Directive significantly curtails the discretion of the Member States to restrict freedom of movement and residence on the grounds of public health, the outdatedness of Directive 64/221 in this respect having already been flagged by the Commission in its 1999 Communication.[74] Its central purpose is to ensure that, in effect, the right to reside in a host State cannot be contested on health grounds.

The adopted version of Article 29 is more restrictive than the text originally proposed by the Commission in some respects. For example, while the Commission had intended that the capacity to require medical examinations referred to in Article 29(3) should be 'only used in exceptional circumstances, where there are serious indications that the person concerned suffers from one of the diseases or disabilities that can justify refusal of leave to enter or reside',[75] the specific time limit of three months—linked to the unconditional right to reside in Article 6 of the Directive—was added by the European Parliament.[76] Similarly, the Council changed the reference to International Health Regulation No 2 of the World Health

---

[74] Communication on grounds of public policy, public security or public health (n 29) para 3.1.3.
[75] Original proposal (n 67) 21.
[76] European Parliament Report of 23 January 2003 on Commission proposal (COM(2001) 257), A5–0009/2003, Amendment 79. That Report also removed reference in the original draft of Article 29(2) to the registration procedure provided for in Article 8 of the Directive (Amendment 78) with the Commission recognising in its amended proposal that the simpler text as adopted 'will also encompass the situation of the Member States who do not introduce the registration requirement' (COM(2003) 199 final, 8).

Organisation (1951) to 'a more general reference to the relevant instruments of the WHO', later accepted as 'far more appropriate' by the Commission.[77]

Perhaps reflecting both the prescribed nature and time-restricted applicability of Article 29, questions concerning its interpretation have not yet been decided by the Court of Justice. However, the extent of the public health restrictions enacted during the Covid-19 pandemic necessarily raised significant free movement challenges, prompting deeper interrogation of public health as a public interest ground in both specific[78] and more general[79] senses. Case law on some of these questions, including with respect to Union citizenship, was pending before the Court at the time of writing.[80]

3.1.2 Defining public policy and public security

With respect to *public policy*, the foundational principles outlined in Section 2 have been sustained in the context of Union citizenship. Thus, in a general sense, 'the concept of public policy as justification for a derogation from a fundamental freedom must be interpreted strictly, so that its scope cannot be determined unilaterally by each Member State without any control by the EU institutions. It follows therefrom that public policy may be relied on only if there is a genuine and sufficiently serious threat to a fundamental interest of society'.[81] More specifically, the requirement of a genuine and sufficiently serious threat affecting one of the fundamental interests of society is embedded in Article 27(2) of the Directive, returned to in Section 3.1.3.

At the same time, however, 'the specific circumstances which may justify recourse to the concept of public policy may vary from one Member State to another and from one era to another. In that regard, it is therefore necessary to accord the competent national authorities a certain discretion within the limits laid down in the Treaty'.[82] The extent of that discretion can be meaningful in practice, but mainly in cases that do not concern situations of expulsion from the host State. In *Bogendorff von Wolffersdorff*, for example, the German Government submitted that 'the third subparagraph of Article 109 of the Weimar Constitution, which abolishes the privileges and titles of nobility as such and prohibits the creation of titles giving the appearance of noble origins, even in the form of part of a name, constitutes the implementation of the more general principle of equality before the law of all German citizens'.[83] The Court of Justice agreed that 'the EU legal system undeniably seeks to ensure the observance of the principle of equal treatment as a general principle of law. That principle is also enshrined in Article 20 of the Charter. There can therefore be no doubt that the objective of

---

[77] Common Position (EC) No 6/2004 of 5 December 2003, 2004 OJ C54 E/12, 27; Communication to the European Parliament on the common position adopted by the Council on the draft directive, SEC/2003/1293 final, para 3.3.2.

[78] See eg S Carrera and N Chun Luk, 'In the name of COVID: an assessment of the Schengen internal border controls and travel restrictions in the EU', study requested by the LIBE Committee of the European Parliament, September 2020, <https://www.europarl.europa.eu/RegData/etudes/STUD/2020/659506/IPOL_STU(2020)659506_EN.pdf> (accessed 6 June 2023); I Goldner Lang, '"Laws of fear" in the EU: the precautionary principle and public health restrictions to free movement of persons in the time of COVID-19' (2021) 12 European Journal of Risk Regulation 1; and D Thym and J Bornemann, 'Schengen and free movement law during the first phase of the COVID-19 pandemic: of symbolism, law and politics' (2020) 5 European Papers 1143.

[79] See eg S Coutts, 'Citizenship, territory and COVID-19' in D Kostakopoulou and D Thym (eds), *Research Handbook on European Citizenship Law and Policy* (Edward Elgar 2022) 116; and Editorial comments 'Charting deeper and wider dimensions of (free) movement in EU law' (2021) 58 Common Market Law Review 969.

[80] eg Case C-128/22 *NORDIC INFO*, pending. On free movement law generally eg on frontier workers, see Case C-411/22 *Thermalhotel Fontana*, pending.

[81] Case C-438/14 *Bogendorff von Wolffersdorff*, EU:C:2016:401, para 67.

[82] ibid para 68.

[83] ibid para 69.

observing the principle of equal treatment is compatible with EU law'.[84] In both *Bogendorff von Wolffersdorff* and *Sayn-Wittgenstein*, the Court also referred to Article 4(2) TEU, in accordance with which 'the European Union is to respect the national identities of its Member States, which include the status of the State as a Republic'.[85] These cases highlight that the exercise of national discretion can be underpinned by values or objectives also adhered to by the Union.

In general, however, the boundaries of public policy are tightly drawn in EU free movement law. As noted at the beginning of Section 3, for example, Article 27(1) of Directive 2004/38 establishes that the grounds of public policy, public security, or public health 'shall not be invoked to serve economic ends'. As discussed in Chapter 2, Article 27(1) does not rule out public interest arguments that have an economic dimension. For the justification of free movement restrictions in a general sense, the Court considers that 'while budgetary considerations may underlie a Member State's choice of social policy and influence the nature or scope of the social protection measures which it wishes to adopt, they do not in themselves constitute an aim pursued by that policy'.[86] However, '[r]easons of a *purely economic nature* cannot constitute overriding reasons in the public interest justifying a restriction of a fundamental freedom guaranteed by the Treaty'.[87] Similarly, protecting national public finances as a legitimate justification for restricting free movement was considered in Chapter 7. While Member States are permitted, under Article 15 of the Directive, to expel *individual* Union citizens who are not lawfully resident there because they are neither economically active nor economically autonomous, such decisions may not be conceived in *public policy* terms: in other words, the fact that a Union citizen does not have the right to reside in a host State under EU law is something that can only be determined following an assessment of their individual circumstances.

Similar questions about the line between public interest grounds with an economic dimension and public interest reasons 'of a purely economic nature' have been considered by the Court in its interpretation of Article 27(1) of the Directive. In *Aladzhov*, the applicant was a Bulgarian national and one of three managers of a company from which the Bulgarian authorities unsuccessfully sought to recover a tax debt, leading to the adoption of a decision that prohibited him from leaving the country until the debt owed was paid or security covering full payment was provided. To defend that restriction of the free movement rights conferred by Article 21 TFEU, the referring court noted 'the public interest involved in the responsibility of the public authorities to ensure budgetary revenue and to the objective of protection of the rights of other citizens which is pursued by the recovery of debts owed to a public authority' and suggested that 'the non-payment of the tax liability of the debtor company in the main proceedings is a threat to a higher interest of society'.[88]

---

[84] ibid paras 70–71; referring to Case C-208/09 *Sayn-Wittgenstein*, EU:C:2010:806, para 89. Cf the much more critical view of AG Wathelet in *Bogendorff von Wolffersdorff*, EU:C:2016:11, paras 97–108 of the Opinion; he considered that 'in order for a rule to be one of public policy, it must be a mandatory rule *so fundamental* to the legal order in question that *no* derogation from it would be possible in the context of the case at issue (para 100 of the Opinion, emphasis in original) and demonstrated that this was not the case with respect to the contested German rules.

[85] *Bogendorff von Wolffersdorff*, para 73; *Sayn-Wittgenstein*, para 92. See similarly, Case C-673/16 *Coman*, EU:C:2018:385, para 43: 'the European Union is required, under Article 4(2) TEU, to respect the national identity of the Member States, inherent in their fundamental structures, both political and constitutional'.

[86] Case C-220/12 *Thiele Meneses*, EU:C:2013:683, para 43.

[87] ibid (emphasis added).

[88] Case C-434/10 *Aladzhov*, EU:C:2011:750, para 36.

The Court of Justice first recalled the prohibition on invoking public policy grounds to serve economic ends in Article 27(1) of the Directive. It admitted that 'the possibility cannot be ruled out as a matter of principle, as has moreover been recognised by the European Court of Human Rights ... that non-recovery of tax liabilities may fall within the scope of the requirements of public policy' but emphasised that this could only occur 'in the light of the rules of European Union law relating to the freedom of movement of Union citizens ... in circumstances where there is a genuine, present and sufficiently serious threat affecting one of the fundamental interests of society related, for example, to the amount of the sums at stake or to what is required to combat tax fraud'.[89] It added that 'since the purpose of recovery of debts owed to a public authority, in particular the recovery of taxes, is to ensure the funding of actions of the Member State concerned on the basis of the choices which are the expression of, inter alia, its general policy in economic and social matters ... the measures adopted by the public authorities in order to ensure that recovery also *cannot be considered, as a matter of principle, to have been adopted exclusively to serve economic ends*, within the meaning of Article 27(1) of Directive 2004/38'.[90] The determination of these questions in *Aladzhov* was returned to the referring court.

Case law on the free movement of persons had not addressed the concept of *public security* before the adoption of Directive 2004/38 or, relatedly, how it differs from public policy. In its 2009 Communication on better transposition and application of the Directive, the Commission considered that public policy 'is generally interpreted along the lines of preventing disturbance of social order'.[91] Drawing from case law more widely, it suggested that public security is 'generally interpreted to cover both internal and external security along the lines of preserving the integrity of the territory of a Member State and its institutions'.[92] The Court essentially implanted that understanding of public security into EU citizenship law in *Tsakouridis*, returned to in Section 3.2 in connection with the enhanced protection against expulsion conferred by Articles 28(2) and 28(3) of the Directive. For present purposes, the Court also addressed the concept of public security in a more general sense in that ruling.

The criminal offences committed by Mr Tsakouridis included dealing in narcotics as part of an organised group. In his Opinion, Advocate General Bot had suggested that the case law did not clearly distinguish between the concepts of public policy and public security. In one sense, that point is evidenced by the fact that the Court does sometimes state that 'Member States essentially retain the freedom to determine the requirements of public policy *and public security* in accordance with their national needs, which can vary from one Member State

---

[89] ibid para 37; referring to the ECtHR judgment of 23 May 2006 in *Riener v Bulgaria* (No 46343/99), paras 114–117.
[90] *Aladzhov*, para 38 (emphasis added); referring 'to that effect' to Case C-398/09 *Lady & Kid and Others*, EU:C:2011:540, para 24.
[91] Communication on guidance for better transposition and application of Directive 2004/38/EC (n 29) 10.
[92] ibid; referring to Case C-423/98 *Albore*, EU:C:2000:401, para 18 and Case C-285/98 *Kreil*, EU:C:2000:2, para 15. The classic judgment on public security in free movement law is Case 72/83 *Campus Oil*, EU:C:1984:256, where the Court ruled for Article 36 TFEU that 'petroleum products, because of their exceptional importance as an energy source in the modern economy, are of fundamental importance for a country's existence since not only its economy but above all its institutions, its essential public services and even the survival of its inhabitants depend upon them. An interruption of supplies of petroleum products, with the resultant dangers for the country's existence, could therefore seriously affect the public security that Article 36 of the Treaty allows States to protect ... [I]n light of the seriousness of the consequences that an interruption in supplies of petroleum products may have for a country's existence, the aim of ensuring a minimum supply of petroleum products at all times is to be regarded as transcending purely economic considerations and thus as capable of constituting an objective covered by the concept of public security' (paras 34–35).

to another and from one era to another'.[93] Thus, Advocate General Bot argued that 'public security must therefore be understood to include not only the security of the Member State and its institutions, but also all the measures designed to counteract serious threats to the values essential to the protection of its citizens' and he considered, in consequence, that 'the grounds regarded by the Court as included in the concept of public policy *may equally be covered* by the concept of public security'.[94]

In contrast, at least at a formal level, the Court did distinguish between the concepts of public policy and public security in *Tsakouridis*. Drawing from its wider case law, it established that public security 'covers both a Member State's internal and its external security'[95] and that 'a threat to the functioning of the institutions and essential public services and the survival of the population, as well as the risk of a serious disturbance to foreign relations or to peaceful coexistence of nations, or a risk to military interests' may affect it.[96] The Court has subsequently applied that definition in other areas of EU law.[97] However, in *Tsakourisis* itself, the meaning of public security more substantively was less clearly distinct from public policy concerns since the Court also concluded that 'objectives such as the fight against crime in connection with dealing in narcotics as part of an organised group are [not] necessarily excluded from [public security]'.[98] It explained that finding as follows:

> Dealing in narcotics as part of an organised group is a diffuse form of crime with impressive economic and operational resources and frequently with transnational connections. In view of the devastating effects of crimes linked to drug trafficking, Council Framework Decision 2004/757/JHA of 25 October 2004 laying down minimum provisions on the constituent elements of criminal acts and penalties in the field of illicit drug trafficking ... states in recital 1 that illicit drug trafficking poses a threat to health, safety and the quality of life of citizens of the Union, and to the legal economy, stability and security of the Member States. Since drug addiction represents a serious evil for the individual and is fraught with social and economic danger to mankind ... trafficking in narcotics as part of an organised group could reach a level of intensity that might directly threaten the calm and physical security of the population as a whole or a large part of it.[99]

The Court then considered that since a Member State 'may, in the interests of public policy, consider that the use of drugs constitutes a danger for society such as to justify special measures against foreign nationals who contravene its laws on drugs ... it must follow that dealing in narcotics as part of an organised group is *a fortiori* covered by the concept of "public

---

[93] Case C-33/07 *Jipa*, EU:C:2008:396, para 23 (emphasis added). See previously, Case C-54/99 *Église de scientology*, EU:C:2000:124, para 17. See similarly eg Case C-348/09 *PI*, EU:C:2012:300, para 23; Case C-430/10 *Gaydarov*, EU:C:2011:749, para 32; and Joined Cases C-331/16 and C-366/16 *K and HF*, EU:C:2018:296, para 40.
[94] AG Bot in Case C-145/09 *Tsakouridis*, EU:C:2010:322, paras 65 and 77–78 of the Opinion (emphasis added).
[95] Case C-145/09 *Tsakouridis*, EU:C:2010:708, para 43; referring to Case C-273/97 *Sirdar*, EU:C:1999:523, para 17; Case C-285/98 *Kreil*, EU:C:2000:2, para 15; Case C-423/98 *Albore*, EU:C:2000:401, para 18; and Case C-186/01 *Dory*, EU:C:2003:146, para 32.
[96] *Tsakouridis*, para 44; referring to *Campus Oil*, paras 34–35; Case C-70/94 *Werner*, EU:C:1995:328, para 27; *Albore*, para 22; and Case C-398/98 *Commission v Greece*, EU:C:2001:565, para 29.
[97] eg In connection with Directive 2004/114/EC on the conditions of admission of third-country nationals for the purposes of studies, pupil exchange, unremunerated training or voluntary service (2004 OJ L375/12), see Case C-544/15 *Fahimian*, EU:C:2017:255, para 39. For Directive 2013/33/EU laying down standards for the reception of applicants for international protection (2013 OJ L180/96), see Case C-601/15 PPU *JN*, EU:C:2016:84, para 66.
[98] *Tsakouridis*, para 45 (emphasis added).
[99] ibid paras 46–47; referring 'to that effect' to Case 221/81 *Wolf*, EU:C:1982:363, para 9 and *Aoulmi v France*, No 50278/99, § 86, ECHR 2006-I. Council Framework Decision 2004/757/JHA laying down minimum provisions on the constituent elements of criminal acts and penalties in the field of illicit drug trafficking, 2004 OJ L335/8.

policy" for the purposes of Article 28(2) of Directive 2004/38', reflecting Advocate General Bot's contention that the distinction between the two concepts might be less meaningful in substance than it seems more formally.[100] The Court did, however, underline the importance of the procedural guarantees in Articles 27 and 28(1) of the Directive, which are addressed in Section 4. Additionally, the implications of *Tsakouridis* for the distinction between 'serious' and 'imperative' grounds of public security in Articles 28(2) and 28(3) of the Directive are returned to in Section 3.2.

3.1.3 Restricting free movement on grounds of public policy or public security: principles of assessment

What are referred to here as principles of assessment—in other words, the principles that must be applied when measures restricting free movement on the grounds of public policy or public security are adopted by Member State authorities—are set out in Articles 27 ('general principles') and 28(1) ('protection against expulsion') of the Directive:

Article 27

General principles

...

2. Measures taken on grounds of public policy or public security shall comply with the principle of proportionality and shall be based exclusively on the personal conduct of the individual concerned. Previous criminal convictions shall not in themselves constitute grounds for taking such measures.

    The personal conduct of the individual concerned must represent a genuine, present and sufficiently serious threat affecting one of the fundamental interests of society. Justifications that are isolated from the particulars of the case or that rely on considerations of general prevention shall not be accepted.

3. In order to ascertain whether the person concerned represents a danger for public policy or public security, when issuing the registration certificate or, in the absence of a registration system, not later than three months from the date of arrival of the person concerned on its territory or from the date of reporting his/her presence within the territory, as provided for in Article 5(5), or when issuing the residence card, the host Member State may, should it consider this essential, request the Member State of origin and, if need be, other Member States to provide information concerning any previous police record the person concerned may have. Such enquiries shall not be made as a matter of routine. The Member State consulted shall give its reply within two months.

4. The Member State which issued the passport or identity card shall allow the holder of the document who has been expelled on grounds of public policy, public security, or public health from another Member State to re-enter its territory without any formality even if the document is no longer valid or the nationality of the holder is in dispute.

---

[100] *Tsakouridis*, para 45; referring to Case C-348/96 *Calfa*, EU:C:1999:6, para 22 and Joined Cases C-482/01 and C-493/01 *Orfanopoulos and Oliveri*, EU:C:2004:262, para 67.

Article 28

Protection against expulsion

1. Before taking an expulsion decision on grounds of public policy or public security, the host Member State shall take account of considerations such as how long the individual concerned has resided on its territory, his/her age, state of health, family and economic situation, social and cultural integration into the host Member State and the extent of his/her links with the country of origin.

....

These provisions reflect, once again, both continuity with and advancement of Directive 64/221. In its original proposal for Directive 2004/38, the Commission indicated that Article 27(3) 'takes over the wording, slightly modified, of Article 5(2) of Directive 64/221' while Article 27(4) 'reproduces Article 3(4) of Directive 64/221'.[101] The requirements set out in Articles 27(2) and 28(1) have been considered in more detail in the case law and will now be looked at in turn.

Article 27(2) of Directive 2004/38 reflects the fundamentals of both Directive 64/221 and the case law that interpreted it, as outlined in Section 2.[102] On the requirement that '[p]revious criminal convictions shall not in themselves constitute grounds for taking' measures on the grounds of public policy or public security, the Economic and Social Committee noted in its Opinion on the Commission's original proposal for the Directive that 'previous criminal convictions do not in themselves constitute grounds for refusal of the right of entry or expulsion from the territory of the Member State of a Union citizen or a family member' but considered that 'some situations are sufficiently serious to warrant exclusion from the provisions of this paragraph. It should be qualified further, on the basis of the principle of proportionality, to provide for cases where persons are found to have previous convictions for crimes such as terrorism, trafficking in weapons or drugs and crimes against the person'.[103] Arguably, that concern is precisely what later shaped the Court's judgment in *PI*, returned to in Section 3.2.

In its 2009 Communication on better transposition and application of the Directive, the Commission provided further guidance:

> The [competent national] authorities must base their decision on an assessment of the future conduct of the individual concerned. The kind and number of previous convictions must form a significant element in this assessment and particular regard must be had to the seriousness and frequency of the crimes committed. While the danger of re-offending is of considerable importance, a remote possibility of new offences is not sufficient. In certain

---

[101] Original proposal (n 29) 20 and 21 respectively.

[102] In its original proposal for the Directive (ibid 20), the Commission confirmed that Article 27(2) reflects Articles 3(1) and 3(2) of Directive 64/221 as well as the definition of public policy established in Case 30/77 *Bouchereau*, EU:C:1977:172, para 35. The Commission had proposed an additional paragraph (draft Article 25(2) to reflect Joined Cases 115 and 116/81 *Adoui and Cornuaille*, EU:C:1982:183, para 8, which would have established that '[p]ersonal conduct shall not be considered a sufficiently serious threat unless the Member State concerned takes serious enforcement measures against the same conduct on the part of its own nationals'). However, the Council deleted this part of the text 'because its interpretation could allow for considering as a threat for public policy any behaviour punished on a domestic level' (Common Position (n 77) 32; accepted by the Commission in its Communication on the common position (n 77) para 3.3.2).

[103] 2002 OJ C149/46, paras 4.6.2–4.6.3.

circumstances, persistent petty criminality may represent a threat to public policy, despite the fact that any single crime/offence, taken individually, would be insufficient to represent a sufficiently serious threat as defined above. National authorities must show that the personal conduct of the individual concerned represents a threat to the requirements of public policy. When assessing the existence of the threat to public policy in these cases, the authorities may in particular take into account the following factors: the nature of the offences; their frequency; damage or harm caused. The existence of multiple convictions is not enough, in itself.[104]

In *E*, the Court ruled that 'the fact that a person is imprisoned at the time the expulsion decision was adopted, without the prospect of being released in the near future, does not exclude that his conduct represents, as the case may be, a present and genuine threat for a fundamental interest of the society of the host Member State'.[105] It referred to Article 33(1) of the Directive, which 'provides for the possibility, for the host Member State, to adopt, in conformity, *inter alia*, with the requirements of Article 27 of that directive, an expulsion order as a consequence of a custodial sentence' to affirm that '[t]he Union legislator therefore provided for the possibility for Member States to adopt an expulsion order concerning a person sentenced to a custodial sentence, if it is established that his conduct represents a genuine, present threat affecting one of the fundamental interests of the society of that Member State'.[106] Article 33(1) is returned to in Section 4.

The Court provided significant further guidance on the *process* of expelling Union citizens in accordance with Article 27 of the Directive in *Ordre des barreaux francophones and germanophone and Others*. The proceedings concerned Belgian legislation, the purpose of which was 'to establish an effective removal policy in respect of Union citizens and members of their families, ensuring that it is humane and fully respects their fundamental rights and dignity' while 'seek[ing] to guarantee a removal regime for Union citizens and their family members that is no less favourable than that for third-country nationals'.[107] In the context of national measures applied following expulsion decisions taken against Union citizens or their family members on the grounds of public policy, and 'aimed at avoiding the risk of those individuals absconding',[108] the Court was asked to consider, in essence, the comparable treatment of Union citizens and their family members, on the one hand, and third-country nationals, on the other, though with respect to EU rules concerning *voluntary* departure for the latter.[109]

The Court first established that the aim of the national legislation was 'to guarantee a removal regime for Union citizens and their family members that is no less favourable than that for third-country nationals' and in connection with, 'more specifically, the national

---

[104] Communication on guidance for better transposition and application of Directive 2004/38/EC (n 34) 12.
[105] Case C-193/16 *E*, EU:C:2017:542, para 27.
[106] ibid para 25.
[107] Case C-718/19 *Ordre des barreaux francophones and germanophone and Others (Mesures préventives en vue d'éloignement)*, EU:C:2021:505, para 18.
[108] ibid para 30.
[109] For third-country nationals, the contested national legislation implemented Directive 2008/115 on common standards and procedures in Member States for returning illegally staying third-country nationals, 2008 OJ L348/98. Article 7(3) of that Directive permits Member States 'to impose obligations on a third-country national in order to avoid the risk of that individual absconding during the period for voluntary departure, the obligations expressly set out to that effect being to report regularly to the authorities, to deposit an adequate financial guarantee, to submit documents or to stay at a certain place. Similarly, an entire chapter of that directive, Chapter IV, entitled "Detention for the purpose of removal", which comprises Articles 15 to 18 of the directive, provides that a third-country national may be kept in detention for the purpose of removal and establishes a detailed framework

provisions aimed at avoiding the risk of individuals absconding, these are based to a large extent on the provisions of Directive 2008/115. The national provision relating to the detention of individuals for the purpose of removal reproduces the rules laid down in national law for third-country nationals and thus establishes that Union citizens and their family members will be treated in exactly the same way as third-country nationals who are subject to a return procedure under that directive, in particular as regards the maximum period of detention for the purpose of removal of the person concerned'.[110] It also confirmed that 'while the mere existence of national rules, provided for by the host Member State, that are applicable in the context of the enforcement of a decision to expel Union citizens and their family members and that are based on the rules applicable to the return of third-country nationals whose purpose is to transpose Directive 2008/115 into national law is not, in itself, contrary to EU law, such rules must nevertheless comply with EU law'—namely, Articles 20 and 21 TFEU and Directive 2004/38.[111]

Reviewing the measures provided for in the national legislation, the Court pointed to those 'specifically designed to limit the movements of the person concerned, [which] necessarily have the effect of restricting that person's freedom of movement and residence during the period allowed for leaving the territory of the host Member State, particularly when the person has been placed under house arrest'; as well as to 'the possibility of keeping Union citizens and their family members in detention for the purpose of removal for a maximum of eight months'.[112] It found that while Union citizens who do not comply with an expulsion decision taken against them do not have a right to reside in the host State after the period specified in that decision for leaving the territory, 'the existence of such a decision does not in any way alter the restrictive nature of a detention measure, which places limitations on an individual's movements beyond those arising from the expulsion decision itself, restricting the opportunities for the individual concerned to stay and to move freely outside the territory of the host Member State throughout the period of that individual's detention', constituting a restriction of the right of exit provided for in Article 4(1) of the Directive and, in consequence, of Articles 20(2) and 21(1) TFEU.[113] The Court therefore considered whether such a restriction could be justified, observing that a national measure 'aimed at avoiding the risk of a person absconding ... necessarily contributes to the protection of public policy, in so far as it is aimed, ultimately, at ensuring that a person who is considered to represent a threat to public policy in the host Member State is expelled from the territory of that State, and thus relates to the purpose of the expulsion decision itself'.[114]

The restriction was therefore capable of being justified within the meaning of Article 27(1) of the Directive. Moreover, the contested rules were not contrary to that provision '*solely* on the ground that they, and the measures which, as regards third-country nationals, are intended to transpose Article 7(3) of Directive 2008/115 into national law, are similar' because

---

for the safeguards granted to third-country nationals as regards both the removal decision and the detention decision' (*Ordre des barreaux francophones and Germanophone*, para 36).

[110] *Ordre des barreaux francophones and germanophone*, para 38.
[111] ibid para 39.
[112] ibid paras 41–42.
[113] ibid paras 43–44. On Article 4(1) of the Directive, see Chapter 6.
[114] ibid paras 49 and 51, noting that 'there is nothing in the wording of Article 27(1) of Directive 2004/38 to exclude the possibility that measures restricting the freedom of movement and residence referred to in that provision may be applied during the period allowed for the person to leave the territory of the host Member State following the adoption of an expulsion decision taken against that person or during an extension of that period' (para 50).

'[i]n both cases, the objective of the measures is to avoid the person concerned absconding and thus, ultimately, to ensure that the expulsion or return decision taken against that person is enforced effectively'.[115] However, in considering the proportionality of the rules provided for in the national legislation, the Court distinguished Union citizens as beneficiaries of Directive 2004/38 and third-country nationals as beneficiaries of Directive 2008/115, with the former 'enjoy[ing] a status and rights entirely different' as compared to the latter.[116] In consequence, the referring court was tasked with ensuring that 'measures aimed at avoiding the risk of absconding which may be imposed in the context of the expulsion of Union citizens and their family members on grounds of public policy or public security [were no] less favourable than measures provided for under national law to avoid the risk of third-country nationals absconding, during the period for voluntary departure, where such third-country nationals are subject to a return procedure under Directive 2008/115'.[117]

Finally, the Court considered the possibility in the contested national rules of detaining Union citizens or their family members for a maximum period of eight months, emphasising again the importance of proportionality, procedural safeguards, and the fact that neither Union citizens nor their family members who fell within the scope of Directive 2004/38 were 'in a comparable situation to that of third-country nationals who are covered by Directive 2008/115'.[118] Not only because 'practical difficulties' in terms of return journeys were unlikely to be the same: the Court also highlighted that EU Member States 'have systems of cooperation and facilities in the context of the expulsion of a Union citizen or family member to another Member State that they do not necessarily have in the context of the removal of a third-country national to a third country'; emphasising too that 'relations between Member States, which are based on the duty of sincere cooperation and the principle of mutual trust, should not give rise to the same difficulties as those which may arise where there is cooperation between Member States and third countries'.[119] Also taking into account potential challenges around administrative and documentation issues with respect to third-country nationals,[120] the Court concluded that setting 'a maximum period of detention for Union citizens and their family members who, in that capacity, come within the scope of Directive 2004/38 ... goes beyond what is necessary to achieve the objective pursued'.[121]

The basic principle of distinguishing Union citizens and third-country nationals that shaped the ruling in *Ordre des barreaux francophones and germanophone* is returned to in Section 3.2 in the context of enhanced protection from expulsion and Article 28 of the Directive. Above all, Article 27(2) of the Directive emphasises the need for case-by-case decisions that are based on the personal conduct of the individual concerned and comply with the principle of proportionality. As expressed by the Court in *McCarthy II*, 'justifications that are isolated from the particulars of the case in question or that rely on considerations of general prevention are not to be accepted'.[122] As regards personal conduct, the requirements of

---

[115] ibid para 52 (emphasis added).

[116] ibid para 53. See generally, paras 54–56 on the status within EU law of freedom of movement and Union citizenship.

[117] ibid para 57. The Court also underlined the importance of proportionality for measures applied in *individual* cases (para 58).

[118] ibid para 65.

[119] ibid para 66; reflecting the *transnational* as well as national and supranational dimensions of Union citizenship discussed in Chapters 3 and 5.

[120] ibid paras 69–71.

[121] ibid para 72.

[122] Case C-202/13 *McCarthy II*, EU:C:2014:2450, para 46; referring to Case C-127/08 *Metock and Others*, EU:C:2008:449, para 74; Case C-33/07 *Jipa*, EU:C:2008:396, para 24; and Case C-434/10 *Aladzhov*, EU:C:2011:750, para 42. On 'considerations of general prevention' in the context of abuse of EU rights, see *McCarthy II*, paras 55–57 (discussed in Chapter 6).

Directive 2004/38 were indicated in *Fahimian* as a point of contrast with the 'wide discretion' enjoyed by the Member States under Directive 2004/114 when determining whether 'the admission of a third country national may be refused if the national authorities competent to process that national's application for a visa consider, on the basis of an assessment of the facts, that he is a threat, if only "potential", to public security'.[123] In contrast to Article 27(2) of Directive 2004/38, '[t]hat assessment may thus take into account not only the personal conduct of the applicant but also other elements relating, in particular, to his professional career'.[124]

As regards compliance with proportionality, Advocate General Mengozzi distinguished this stage of analysis from the prior question of whether justification of a measure restricting freedom of movement on public policy or public security grounds falls within Article 27(1) in the first place.[125] For Article 27(2), the standard free movement law criteria apply: the measure restricting freedom of movement must be 'appropriate to ensure the achievement of the objective it pursues' and 'not go beyond what is necessary to attain it'.[126] The Commission further advises that '[n]ational authorities must identify protected interests. It is in the light of these interests that they must carry out an analysis of the characteristics of the threat'.[127] It also suggests that '[t]he following factors could be taken into account: degree of social danger resulting from the presence of the person concerned on the territory of that Member State; nature of the offending activities, their frequency, cumulative danger and damage caused; time elapsed since acts committed and behaviour of the person concerned' as well as 'good behaviour in prison and possible release on parole'.[128]

The circumstances of *K and HF* required rounded consideration of the different elements of Article 27(2). The questions referred to the Court of Justice concerned family reunification with Union citizens in circumstances where residence permits had been refused by other Member States for the family members concerned on the grounds 'there were serious reasons to believe that [they] had been guilty of acts referred to in Article 1F of the Geneva Convention or in Article 12(2) of Directive 2011/95', that is, commission of a crime against peace, a war crime, or a crime against humanity.[129] In that context, the Court was asked to determine whether the competent authorities of a host State may 'consider automatically that the mere presence of that person in its territory constitutes, whether or not there

---

[123] Case C-544/15 *Fahimian*, EU:C:2017:255, paras 42 and 40. Council Directive 2004/114/EC on the conditions of admission of third-country nationals for the purposes of studies, pupil exchange, unremunerated training or voluntary service, 2004 OJ L375/12.

[124] *Fahimian*, para 40. The Court also provided guidance on the scope and limits of judicial review of the discretion enjoyed by national authorities in that respect (paras 44–46). On the extent to which the free movement law expulsion framework can be extended beyond that context more generally, see eg Case C-349/06 *Polat*, EU:C:2007:581, on the EEC-Turkey relationship.

[125] AG Mengozzi in Case C-434/10 *Aladzhov*, EU:C:2011:547, para 26 of the Opinion.

[126] eg *Jipa*, para 29. In the context of restricting the right of exit, the Court has also required that the referring court should 'determine that there were no other measures other than that of a prohibition on leaving the territory which would have been equally effective ... but would not have encroached on freedom of movement' (*Aladzhov*, para 47). In the same context, the Court referred in *Byankov* to ECtHR case law, which requires that 'measures, such as the prohibition on leaving the territory at issue in the main proceedings, which curb a person's right to leave his country, must, inter alia, be regularly reviewed if the measures are not to be regarded as 'disproportionate' within the meaning of that case-law' (Case C-249/11 *Byankov*, EU:C:2012:608, para 47; referring to the decisions of the ECtHR in *Ignatov v Bulgaria*, judgment of 2 July 2009, Application No 50/02 (§ 37) and *Gochev v Bulgaria*, judgment of 26 November 2009, Application No 34383/03 (§§ 55 to 57).

[127] Communication on guidance for better transposition and application of Directive 2004/38/EC (n 34) 13.

[128] ibid.

[129] Joined Cases C-331/16 and C-366/16 *K and HF*, EU:C:2018:296, para 38. Directive 2011/95/EU on standards for the qualification of third-country nationals or stateless persons as beneficiaries of international protection, for a uniform status for refugees or for persons eligible for subsidiary protection, and for the content of the protection granted, 2011 OJ L337/9.

is any risk of re-offending, a genuine, present and sufficiently serious threat affecting one of the fundamental interests of society, within the meaning of Article 27(2) of Directive 2004/38'.[130] If national authorities do not have that capacity, the Court was then asked to consider 'how the existence of such a threat should be assessed and, in particular, to what extent there is any need to take account of the time that has elapsed since the alleged commission of those acts' and to consider the 'effect of the principle of proportionality, referred to in Article 27(2) of Directive 2004/38, on the adoption of a decision that an individual who has been the subject of a decision excluding him from refugee status is an undesirable immigrant to the Member State concerned'.[131]

The Court first assessed whether a declaration issued by the Netherlands that applicant K was an undesirable immigrant and a refusal of residence of more than three months in Belgium for applicant HF could be justified on grounds of public policy or public security within the meaning of Article 27(1) of the Directive. The reasons underpinning these decisions were summarised as '(i) the fact that, since they had previously been excluded from refugee status on the basis of Article 1F of the Geneva Convention or Article 12(2) of Directive 2011/95, the mere presence of K. and H.F. in the territory of the Member States concerned would be detrimental to the international relations of those Member States and (ii) the necessity of ensuring that those individuals could not come into contact with citizens of those Member States who had been victims of the crimes and acts that K. and H. F. were alleged to be guilty of, and who might be in the territory of those Member States'.[132] The Governments of France and the UK further submitted that the decisions that had been taken with respect 'contribute both to ensuring the protection of the fundamental values of society in a Member State and of the international legal order and to maintaining social cohesion, public confidence in the justice and immigration systems of the Member States and the credibility of their commitment to protect the fundamental values enshrined in Articles 2 and 3 TEU'.[133] The Court agreed that these reasons could be 'considered by the Member States to constitute grounds of public policy or public security, within the meaning of Article 27(1) of Directive 2004/38, capable of justifying the adoption of measures that restrict the freedom of movement and residence, in their territory, of Union citizens or their third-country national family members'.[134]

Turning then to consider the requirements of Article 27(2) of the Directive, the Court first noted that 'the grounds for exclusion from refugee status laid down in Article 1F of the Geneva Convention and in Article 12(2) of Directive 2011/95 were established with the aim of excluding from that status individuals judged to be undeserving of the protection which refugee status entails and of ensuring that the granting of that status does not enable the perpetrators of certain serious crimes to escape criminal liability, and consequently exclusion from refugee status is not dependent on the existence of a present danger to the host Member State'.[135] For that reason, 'the fact that the person concerned has been the subject, in the past, of a decision excluding him from refugee status pursuant to one of those provisions

---

[130] *K and HF*, para 38.
[131] ibid para 38.
[132] ibid para 43.
[133] ibid para 44.
[134] ibid para 45. In para 46, the Court further 'emphasised that the crimes and acts that are the subject of Article 1F of the Geneva Convention or Article 12(2) of Directive 2011/95 seriously undermine both fundamental values such as respect for human dignity and human rights, on which, as stated in Article 2 TEU, the European Union is founded, and the peace which it is the Union's aim to promote, under Article 3 TEU'.
[135] *K and HF*, para 50; referring to Joined Cases C-57/09 and C-101/09 *B and D*, EU:C:2010:661, para 104.

cannot *automatically* permit the finding that the mere presence of that person in the territory of the host Member State constitutes a genuine, present and sufficiently serious threat affecting one of the fundamental interests of society' within the meaning of Article 27(2) of Directive 2004/38.[136] Instead, the required 'case-by-case assessment by the competent national authorities ... must take into account the findings of fact made in the decision of exclusion from refugee status taken with respect to the individual concerned and the factors on which that decision was based, in particular the nature and gravity of the crimes or acts that that individual is alleged to have committed, the degree of his individual involvement in them and the possible existence of grounds for excluding criminal liability such as duress or self-defence'.[137]

However, and in contrast to how past conduct is addressed generally, while establishing a genuine, present, and sufficiently serious threat affecting one of the fundamental interests of society, in line with Article 27(2) of Directive 2004/38, 'implies the existence in the individual concerned of a propensity to repeat the conduct constituting such a threat in the future, it is also *possible that past conduct alone* may constitute such a threat to the requirements of public policy'.[138] The Court acknowledged that the time that had elapsed since the assumed commission of the acts in question is a 'relevant factor for the purposes of assessing whether there exists a threat such as that referred to in the second subparagraph of Article 27(2) of Directive 2004/38',[139] but found that 'the possible exceptional gravity of the acts in question may be such as to require, even after a relatively long period of time, that the genuine, present and sufficiently serious threat affecting one of the fundamental interests of society be classified as persistent'.[140]

The Court then addressed the relevance for the assessment to be undertaken by the national authorities of the risk of re-offending in the host State 'where the crimes or acts referred to in Article 1F of the Geneva Convention or in Article 12(2) of Directive 2011/95 took place in the country of origin of the individual concerned, in a specific historical and social context that is not liable to recur in that Member State'.[141] In its view, 'however improbable it may appear that such crimes or acts may recur outside their specific historical and social context, conduct of the individual concerned that shows the persistence in him of a disposition hostile to the fundamental values enshrined in Articles 2 and 3 TEU, such

---

[136] *K and HF*, para 51 (emphasis added). See similarly, para 79 of the Opinion of AG Saugmandsgaard Øe, EU:C:2017:973: '[t]he requirement for an examination of the personal conduct of the individual concerned, which flows from the wording of Article 27(2) of Directive 2004/38, does not, to my mind, allow any derogation, even where the conduct of which he is accused is extremely serious'.

[137] *K and HF*, paras 52 and 54. In para 55, the Court underlined that '[s]uch an examination is all the more necessary in a situation where, as in the main proceedings, the person concerned has not been convicted of the crimes or acts that were relied on to justify the rejection, in the past, of his asylum application'.

[138] ibid para 56 (emphasis added); referring to Case 30/77 *Bouchereau*, EU:C:1977:172, para 29. Criticised by eg S Coutts, 'The expressive dimension of the Union Citizenship expulsion regime' (2018) 3 European Papers 833 at 839, who contrasts 'the striking admission that past conduct alone can constitute a threat to public security or public policy' with how 'the concept of threat is normally future (and risk) orientated and in light of the emphasis prior case-law and the Directive itself places on the need to establish some future threat or, in the case of persons convicted of crimes, the need to identify some risk of recidivism. This is possible by a focus not on any possible risk of re-occurrence – after all unlikely considering the very special historical circumstances at issue in these cases – but rather on the *presence* of the individual in the host Member State. Simply being there and sharing the same geographic and social space with the citizens of the host society is sufficient to constitute a threat to the fundamental interests of the host society ... Quite literally, it is their presence which disturbs and offends' (emphasis in original).

[139] *K and HF*, para 58; referring to Case C-554/13 *Zh and O*, EU:C:2015:377, paras 60–62.

[140] *K and HF*, para 58. See similarly, para 106 of the Opinion of AG Saugmandsgaard Øe: '[t]he risk of disturbance of the social order and international relations as a consequence of the presence in the territory of a Member State of a person suspected of crimes against peace, war crimes or crimes against humanity may continue to exist even – and sometimes all the more so – where that person has enjoyed a long period of impunity'.

[141] *K and HF*, para 59.

as human dignity and human rights, as revealed by those crimes or those acts, is, for its part, capable of constituting a genuine, present and sufficiently serious threat affecting one of the fundamental interests of society' within the meaning of Article 27(2).[142] The Court framed the required proportionality assessment as 'entail[ing] that the threat that the personal conduct of the individual concerned represents to the fundamental interests of the host society, on the one hand, must be weighed against the protection of the rights which Union citizens and their family members derive from Directive 2004/38, on the other'.[143] It emphasised the taking into account of fundamental rights in that respect, adding that the host State 'is, in particular, required to determine, in that context, whether it was possible to adopt other measures less prejudicial to the freedom of movement and residence of the person concerned which would have been equally effective to ensure the protection of the fundamental interests invoked'.[144]

Building on the general reference to proportionality in Article 27(2), Article 28(1) of the Directive proceeds to outline a non-exhaustive ('such as') list of integration-based, proportionality-oriented considerations that national authorities must take into account before taking an expulsion decision on grounds of public policy or public security: how long the individual concerned has resided on its territory, his/her age, state of health, family and economic situation, social and cultural integration into the host Member State and the extent of his/her links with the country of origin. As Recital 23 explains, expulsion of Union citizens or their family members on grounds of public policy or public security 'is a measure that can seriously harm persons who, having availed themselves of the rights and freedoms conferred on them by the Treaty, have become genuinely integrated into the host Member State', requiring that '[t]he scope for such measures should therefore be limited in accordance with the principle of proportionality to take account of the degree of integration of the persons concerned'. In its original proposal for Directive 2004/78, the Commission indicated that Article 28(1) was 'intended to provide greater safeguards against expulsion, by requiring the Member States, before ordering the expulsion of a Union citizen or family member, to take account of the person's degree of integration in the host country on the basis of certain criteria referred to by way of examples'.[145] It also pointed to the link with proportionality in outlining the legal effect of the provision, 'since any decision by a Member State that failed to take these criteria into account would be open to the charge that it was disproportionate and could, therefore, be overturned by national courts, which, as explicitly stipulated in this Directive [Article 31(3)], are required to check that these criteria have been properly taken into account'.[146]

The fact that the criteria listed in Article 28(1) derive from more general roots in the EU legal order is well demonstrated by Advocate General Saugmandsgaard Øe's analysis in *K and HF*. Mr HF had been refused a right of residence in Belgium but an order to leave the territory was not issued. Recalling the discussion in Chapter 7, the Advocate General therefore described his presence there as ' "tolerated", even though he did not have a right of residence or any particular status there'.[147] He then considered whether 'the adoption of this restrictive

---

[142] ibid para 60.
[143] ibid para 62.
[144] ibid paras 63–64.
[145] Original proposal (n 67) 21.
[146] ibid. See similarly, Case C-165/14 *Rendón Marín*, EU:C:2016:675, para 62: 'in order to determine whether an expulsion measure is proportionate to the legitimate aim pursued, in the present instance protection of the requirements of public policy or public security, account should be taken of the criteria set out in Article 28(1) of Directive 2004/38'.
[147] AG Saugmandsgaard Øe in *K and HF*, para 125 of the Opinion.

measure, even though it does not entail the removal of the person to whom it is addressed, nonetheless requires the criteria listed in Article 28(1) of Directive 2004/38 to be taken into account'.[148] In his view:

> deprivation of a right of residence is – like an expulsion decision, although to a lesser degree – liable to jeopardise the integration of the person concerned in the host Member State and harm his private and family life', and argued that '[a] number of the factors listed in Article 28(1) of Directive 2004/38, such as the person's length of residence and the strength of his ties with the host Member State, are intrinsically linked to the integration following upon residence in that Member State. With that in mind, those factors may be relevant when assessing the proportionality and compatibility with Article 7 of the Charter of a restrictive measure that does not involve the removal of the person concerned, in so far as that person has already been able to integrate and develop a private and family life in that Member State by reason of his residence there.[149]

Relatedly, but conversely, where the measure adopted by the national authorities *is* an expulsion decision but not one that falls within the scope of Directive 2004/38, the considerations set out in the Directive are, in effect, applied by analogy.[150]

In its 2009 Communication on better transposition and application of the Directive, the Commission expanded further on what is required by Article 28(1):

> The personal and family situation of the individual concerned must be assessed carefully with a view to establishing whether the envisaged measure is appropriate and does not go beyond what is strictly necessary to achieve the objective pursued, and whether there are less stringent measures to achieve that objective. The following factors, outlined in an indicative list in Article 28(1), should be taken into account: impact of expulsion on the economic, personal and family life of the individual (including on other family members who would have the right to remain in the host Member State); the seriousness of the difficulties which the spouse/partner and any of their children risk facing in the country of origin of the person concerned; strength of ties (relatives, visits, language skills) – or lack of ties – with the Member State of origin and with the host Member State (for example, the person concerned was born in the host Member State or lived there from an early age); length of residence in the host Member State (the situation of a tourist is different from the situation of someone who has lived for many years in the host Member State); age and state of health.[151]

Importantly, as indicated above by Advocate General Saugmandsgaard Øe and alongside compliance with proportionality, these requirements are underpinned by the more general obligation in EU law 'to take account of the fundamental rights whose observance the Court ensures, in particular the right to respect for private and family life, as laid down in Article 7 of the Charter of Fundamental Rights'.[152] The criteria in Article 28(1) are therefore also influential in the context of expulsion decisions that do not fall within the scope of the Directive;

---

[148] ibid para 126 of the Opinion.
[149] ibid paras 127–128 of the Opinion.
[150] See eg for expulsion decisions and residence rights based on Article 20 TFEU, *Rendón Marín*, paras 81–86; see also, AG Szpunar (EU:C:2016:75), esp para 151 of the Opinion. This case is discussed in Chapter 5.
[151] Communication on guidance for better transposition and application of Directive 2004/38/EC (n 34) 13.
[152] *Rendón Marín*, para 66.

for example, as seen in Chapter 5, where residence rights for family members are based on Article 20 TFEU in a Union citizen's home State.[153]

Two final points concerning Article 28 of the Directive can be noted here. First, the Court has considered the intersection of Article 28(1) with the enhanced protection against expulsion provided for in Articles 28(2) and 28(3), returned to in Section 3.2. Second, in the process of adopting Directive 2004/38, the European Parliament had proposed a new requirement that Member States should 'notify the Commission of all decisions to expel [Union] citizens or members of their families' on the basis that the Commission 'must have a comprehensive overview of expulsions planned by the Member States'.[154] Expulsion practice had raised concerns (highlighted, for example, in the Commission's 1999 Communication on Directive 64/221) about the extent of compliance with the requirements of EU law when measures restricting free movement and residence rights are adopted by national authorities. The Commission therefore responded positively to Parliament's idea in its amended proposal, observing that a notification requirement was 'reasonable' since 'all such decisions are exceptional'.[155] But it was rejected by the Council, which considered 'that this procedure would be too cumbersome for Member States without offering any advantages by Member States'.[156] Work undertaken to investigate national practices in this context confirms, however, that the Council was optimistic in taking that position, in light of continuing, significant, and widespread mismatch between the requirements of EU law and national expulsion practices.[157]

3.2 Articles 28(2) and 28(3): Enhanced Protection Against Expulsion

Recital 24 of Directive 2004/38 proclaims that 'the greater the degree of integration of Union citizens and their family members in the host Member State, the greater the degree of protection against expulsion should be'. In its original proposal for the Directive, the Commission had therefore included a provision that stated: '[a] host Member State may not take an expulsion decision on grounds of public policy or public security against EU citizens or their family members, irrespective of nationality, who have the right of permanent residence

---

[153] eg Case C-304/14 *CS*, EU:C:2016:674, paras 40–42: 'where refusal of the right of residence is founded on the existence of a genuine, present and sufficiently serious threat to the requirements of public policy or of public security, in view of the criminal offences committed by a third- country national who is the sole carer of children who are Union citizens, such refusal would be consistent with EU law. [T]hat conclusion cannot be drawn automatically on the basis solely of the criminal record of the person concerned. It can result, where appropriate, only from a specific assessment by the referring court of all the current and relevant circumstances of the case, in the light of the principle of proportionality, of the child's best interests and of the fundamental rights whose observance the Court ensures. That assessment must therefore take account, in particular, of the personal conduct of the individual concerned, the length and legality of his residence on the territory of the Member State concerned, the nature and gravity of the offence committed, the extent to which the person concerned is currently a danger to society, the age of the children at issue and their state of health, as well as their economic and family situation'. See further, Chapter 5.
[154] European Parliament Report (n 76) Amendment 76.
[155] Amended proposal (n 76) para 3.1.
[156] Common Position (n 77) 29.
[157] eg S Mantu, P Minderhoud, and C Grütters, 'Legal approaches to "unwanted" EU citizens in the Netherlands' (2021) 10 Central and Eastern European Migration Review 35 esp at 44–46; and N Nic Shuibhne and J Shaw, 'General Report – Union citizenship: development, impact and challenges' in U Neergaard, C Jacqueson, and N Holst-Christensen (eds), *The XXVI FIDE Congress in Copenhagen 2014: Congress Publications Vol. 2* (DJOEF Publishing 2014) 65 esp at 125–38.

on its territory or who are minors'.[158] The Commission acknowledged that its draft provision 'introduces *absolute protection* against expulsion' in such cases.[159] For minors, the Commission considered that 'this protection is dictated by humanitarian considerations'; for permanent residents, it reflected the 'very close ties integrating them into the host Member State, which would make expulsion unjustifiable' on the basis that expulsion orders 'have a very serious impact on the person concerned, destroying the emotional and family ties they have developed in the host country'.[160]

The European Parliament responded cautiously—and conditionally: it considered that the proposal 'puts an end to the historic sovereignty of the Member States in this area', making it a 'controversial provision, particularly in cases where there has been a serious breach of public security'.[161] It also linked the proposal to the Amsterdam Treaty's objective of creating 'a border-free area of freedom, security and justice, in which expulsion is a thing of the past and freedom of movement has become a reality for all' and thus concluded that, '[f]or the moment, the rapporteur has left the Commission proposal as it stands, but reserves the right to table further amendments at a later stage'.[162] However, in its common position, the Council communicated that it was 'almost unanimously against the absolute protection against expulsion, *although it has accepted an increased protection* for Union citizens who have been residing for a long period in the host Member State'.[163] The Commission accepted this compromise as 'strik[ing] a balance between the positions of the Member States' yet mark[ing] a major step forward in terms of freedom of movement and residence in relation to the existing situation'.[164]

As adopted, 'Directive 2004/38, as is apparent from recital 24 in the preamble, establishes a system of protection against expulsion measures which is based on the degree of integration of those persons in the host Member State, so that the greater the degree of integration of Union citizens and their family members in the host Member State, the greater the guarantees against expulsion they enjoy'.[165] Framed by recital 24,[166] the compromise reached in the adoption process is now codified in Articles 28(2) and 28(3) of the Directive:

Article 28

Protection against expulsion

...

2. The host Member State may not take an expulsion decision against Union citizens or their family members, irrespective of nationality, who have the right of permanent residence on its territory, except on serious grounds of public policy or public security.

---

[158] Original proposal (n 67) draft Article 26(2).
[159] Original proposal (n 67) 21.
[160] ibid.
[161] European Parliament Report (n 76) 55.
[162] ibid.
[163] Common Position (n 77) 32 (emphasis added).
[164] Communication on the common position (n 77) para 3.1.
[165] Joined Cases C-316/16 and C-424/16 *B and Vomero*, EU:C:2018:256, para 44.
[166] Recital 24 states in full: 'the greater the degree of integration of Union citizens and their family members in the host Member State, the greater the degree of protection against expulsion should be. Only in exceptional circumstances, where there are imperative grounds of public security, should an expulsion measure be taken against Union citizens who have resided for many years in the territory of the host Member State, in particular when they were born and have resided there throughout their life. In addition, such exceptional circumstances should also apply to an expulsion measure taken against minors, in order to protect their links with their family, in accordance with the United Nations Convention on the Rights of the Child, of 20 November 1989'.

3. An expulsion decision may not be taken against Union citizens, except if the decision is based on imperative grounds of public security, as defined by Member States, if they:
   (a) have resided in the host Member State for the previous ten years; or
   (b) are a minor, except if the expulsion is necessary for the best interests of the child, as provided for in the United Nations Convention on the Rights of the Child of 20 November 1989.

Three time-points—alongside certain qualitative factors—are critical within this system: first, residence periods in the host State for *up to five years* (permitting expulsion of Union citizens or their family members on grounds of public policy or public security under Article 27(1)), second, residence periods between five and ten years (permitting expulsion of Union citizens or their family members *who have permanent residence rights* only on *serious* grounds of public policy or public security under Article 28(2)), and third, residence periods for more than ten years *or for minors* (permitting expulsion of Union citizens only on *imperative* grounds of *public security* and, where relevant, demonstrating for minors that the expulsion is necessary in their best interests, under Article 28(3)). A key difference between the Commission's proposal and the system as adopted is that the deepest level of protection against expulsion, provided for by Article 28(3), is extended to Union citizens only and not to their third-country national family members.

Articles 28(2) and 28(3) of the Directive are ambiguous on certain key questions in comparison to, for example, the more detailed provisions on the implications of absence from the host State for permanent residence rights, considered in Chapter 8. For example, the Court acknowledged in *Tsakouridis* that 'Article 28(3)(a) of Directive 2004/38, while making the enjoyment of enhanced protection subject to the person's presence in the Member State concerned for 10 years preceding the expulsion measure, is silent as to the circumstances which are capable of interrupting the period of 10 years' residence for the purposes of the acquisition of the right to enhanced protection against expulsion laid down in that provision'.[167] It confirmed that the 'decisive criterion' in Article 28(3) is 'whether the Union citizen has lived in that Member State for the 10 years preceding the expulsion decision'.[168] It then considered the extent to which absences from the host State during that period prevent a Union citizen from enjoying enhanced protection under Article 28(3)(a), determining that the criteria in Article 16(4), in connection with the implications of absences for permanent residence rights, could not be applied by analogy and that instead:

> [A]n overall assessment must be made of the person's situation on each occasion at the precise time when the question of expulsion arises. The national authorities responsible for applying Article 28(3) of Directive 2004/38 are required *to take all the relevant factors into consideration in each individual case*, in particular the duration of each period of absence from the host Member State, the cumulative duration and the frequency of those absences, and the reasons why the person concerned left the host Member State. It must be ascertained whether those absences *involve the transfer to another State of the centre of the personal, family or occupational interests* of the person concerned. The fact that the person in question has been the subject of a forced return to the host Member State in order to serve a term of imprisonment there and the time spent in prison may, together with the factors listed [above], be taken into account as part of the overall assessment required for

---

[167] Case C-145/09 *Tsakouridis*, EU:C:2010:708, para 29.
[168] ibid para 31.

determining *whether the integrating links previously forged with the host Member State have been broken.*[169]

If, on the basis of that assessment, it is found that a Union citizen does not satisfy the residence condition in Article 28(3)(a), it may be possible to revert to Article 28(2), meaning if the Union citizen had acquired a right of permanent residence in the host State, then an expulsion measure 'could in an appropriate case be justified on "serious grounds of public policy or public security" as laid down in Article 28(2)'.[170] In either case, the requirements of Article 27(2) must also be satisfied.[171]

Another ambiguity concerns whether the required period of ten years of residence in the host State in Article 28(3)(a) of the Directive should be calculated backwards—from the date on which an expulsion order is made, or forwards—from the commencement of residence in the host State. The Court dealt with this question in *MG*, returned to below in the context of the intersection of permanent residence rights and enhanced protection against expulsion. Here, the meaning of—and distinction between—the concepts of *serious grounds* of public policy and public security in Article 28(2) and *imperative grounds* of public security in Article 28(3) will first be considered. In its 2009 Communication on better transposition and application of the Directive, the Commission indicated that '[t]here must be a *clear distinction* between normal, "serious" and "imperative" grounds on which the expulsion can be taken'.[172] In Section 3.1.2, we saw that the Court developed an understanding of public security for the purposes of Directive 2004/38 in *Tsakouridis*. It established that '[t]he concept of "imperative grounds of public security" presupposes not only the existence of a threat to public security, but also that such a threat is of a particularly high degree of seriousness'.[173] It also confirmed that 'by subjecting all expulsion measures in the cases referred to in Article 28(3) of that directive to the existence of "imperative grounds" of public security, a concept which is *considerably stricter* than that of "serious grounds" within the meaning of Article 28(2), the European Union legislature clearly intended to limit measures based on Article 28(3) to "exceptional circumstances", as set out in recital 24'.[174]

But the Court did not clearly or coherently disentangle the concepts of 'serious' and 'imperative' grounds of public security per se—or distinguish them from public policy—across the judgment as a whole. It defined public security in a general sense in paragraphs 43–47, also confirming in that part of the judgment that 'objectives such as the fight against crime in connection with dealing in narcotics as part of an organised group' could fall within the meaning of that concept. But later, it extrapolated that conclusion to 'imperative grounds' of public security, finding that Article 28(3) of the Directive 'must be interpreted as meaning that the fight against crime in connection with dealing in narcotics as part of an organised group is capable of being covered by the concept of "imperative grounds of public security" which may justify a measure expelling a Union citizen who has resided in the host Member State for the preceding 10 years'.[175] The Court did refer more specifically to Article 28(3)— 'imperative' grounds of public security—in paragraph 49, but here to underline that 'an

---

[169] ibid paras 32–34 (emphasis added).
[170] ibid para 37.
[171] ibid paras 48–49.
[172] Communication on guidance for better transposition and application of Directive 2004/38/EC (n 34) para 3.4.
[173] *Tsakouridis*, para 41.
[174] ibid para 40 (emphasis added).
[175] ibid para 56.

expulsion measure must be based on an individual examination of the specific case ... and can be justified on imperative grounds of public security within the meaning of Article 28(3) of Directive 2004/38 only if, having regard to the exceptional seriousness of the threat, such a measure is necessary for the protection of the interests it aims to secure, provided that that objective cannot be attained by less strict means, having regard to the length of residence of the Union citizen in the host Member State and in particular to the serious negative consequences such a measure may have for Union citizens who have become genuinely integrated into the host Member State'.

The Court then jumped to serious grounds of *public policy* in paragraph 54 ('since the Court has held that a Member State may, in the interests of public policy, consider that the use of drugs constitutes a danger for society such as to justify special measures against foreign nationals who contravene its laws on drugs ... it must follow that dealing in narcotics as part of an organised group is a fortiori covered by the concept of "public policy" for the purposes of Article 28(2) of Directive 2004/38'); before concluding that, in fact, '[i]t is for the referring court to ascertain, taking into consideration all the factors mentioned above, whether Mr Tsakouridis's conduct is covered by "serious grounds of public policy or public security" within the meaning of Article 28(2) of Directive 2004/38 or "imperative grounds of public security" within the meaning of Article 28(3) of that directive, and whether the proposed expulsion measure satisfies the conditions referred to above'.[176]

The Court's reluctance to be more definitive in *Tsakouridis* reflects the wording of Article 28(3) itself, since that provision refers to imperative grounds of public security *as defined by Member States*.[177] In that way, it seeks to tread a careful line between 'unilateral' determinations by the Member States, which could have the effect of undermining the system of protection against expulsion mandated by the Directive; and accommodating some degree of Member State discretion in such a sensitive field. But that ambition is more problematic from the perspective that what is intended to constitute the deepest form of protection against expulsion for Union citizens is tied explicitly to grounds 'defined by Member States'. In its case law, the Court uses the requirements of proportionality and compliance with fundamental rights to mediate the balance that Article 28 of the Directive suggests, emphasising in *Tsakouridis* that 'a balance must be struck more particularly between the exceptional nature of the threat to public security as a result of the personal conduct of the person concerned, assessed if necessary at the time when the expulsion decision is to be made ... by reference in particular to the possible penalties and the sentences imposed, the degree of involvement in the criminal activity, and, if appropriate, the risk of reoffending ... on the one hand, and, on the other hand, the risk of compromising the social rehabilitation of the Union citizen in the State in which he has become genuinely integrated, which ... is not only in his interest but also in that of the European Union in general'.[178] However, the circumstances in *PI* required a very difficult reflection on these aims.

The applicant was born in Italy in 1965 but had lived in Germany since 1987. In 2006, he was sentenced to seven years and six months in prison for the sexual assault, sexual coercion, and rape of a minor for acts that took place from 1990–2001. The victim was his former partner's daughter, who was eight years old when the offences commenced. In 2008,

---

[176] ibid para 54.
[177] On this point, see AG Bot in *Tsakouridis*, EU:C:2010:322, paras 71–72 of the Opinion.
[178] *Tsakouridis*, para 50; referring to Joined Cases C-482/01 and C-493/01 *Orfanopoulos and Oliveri*, EU:C:2004:262, paras 77–79 and Case 30/77 *Bouchereau*, EU:C:1977:172, para 29. See further paras 52 (proportionality) and 53 (fundamental rights) of *Tsakouridis*.

PI was ordered to leave Germany or face deportation to Italy. In proceedings challenging that decision, the referring court asked 'if the term "imperative grounds of public security" contained in Article 28(3) of Directive [2004/38] cover[s] only threats posed to the internal and external security of the State in terms of the continued existence of the State with its institutions and important public services, the survival of the population, foreign relations and the peaceful co-existence of nations'.[179] In particular, '[i]n response to a written question put by the Court following the judgment in *Tsakouridis*, the referring court stated that doubts remained ... as to whether and, if so, under what conditions, the fight against other forms of crime than drug-related crime as part of an organised group may also constitute an "imperative ground of public security" within the meaning of Article 28(3) of Directive 2004/ 38'.[180] Additionally, it asked 'whether it is possible to expel ... Union citizens who, whilst not belonging to a group or any other kind of criminal organisation, have committed extremely serious criminal offences which affect individual interests benefiting from legal protection, such as sexual autonomy, life, freedom and physical integrity, where there is a high level of risk that they will re-offend, committing other similar offences'.[181]

The Court of Justice first confirmed three central premises of the judgment in *Tsakouridis*: public security concerns 'both a Member State's internal and its external security';[182] the concept of 'imperative grounds' of public security in Article 28(3) of the Directive 'is considerably stricter than that of "serious grounds" within the meaning of Article 28(2)', demonstrating that 'the European Union legislature clearly intended to limit measures based on Article 28(3) to "exceptional circumstances", as set out in recital 24';[183] and '"imperative grounds of public security" presupposes not only the existence of a threat to public security, but also that such a threat is of a particularly high degree of seriousness'.[184] Moreover, because EU law 'does not impose on Member States a uniform scale of values as regards the assessment of conduct which may be considered to be contrary to public security',[185] Article 28(3) specifies imperative grounds of public security 'as defined by Member States', reflecting the balance sought between the authority of the Union and the discretion of the Member States, respectively, in determining the requirements of public policy and public security.[186]

Turning to the specific offences committed and whether they constituted 'imperative grounds' of public security, the Court emphasised Article 83(1) TFEU, which 'provides that the sexual exploitation of children is one of the areas of particularly serious crime with a cross-border dimension in which the European Union legislature may intervene'.[187] It concluded that 'it is open to the Member States to regard criminal offences such as those referred to in [Article 83(1) TFEU] as constituting a particularly serious threat to one of the fundamental interests of society, which might pose a direct threat to the calm and physical security

---

[179] Case C-348/09 *PI*, EU:C:2012:300, para 14.
[180] ibid para 16.
[181] ibid para 17.
[182] ibid para 18; referring to *Tsakouridis*, para 43.
[183] *PI*, para 19; referring to *Tsakouridis*, para 40.
[184] *PI*, para 20; referring to *Tsakouridis*, para 41.
[185] *PI*, para 21; referring 'by analogy' to Case C-268/99 *Jany*, EU:C:2001:616, para 60 (which concerned public policy, not public security).
[186] *PI*, paras 22–23.
[187] ibid para 25. In paras 26–27, the Court also referred to Directive 2011/93/EU on combating the sexual abuse and sexual exploitation of children and child pornography, 2011 OJ L335/1,which is underpinned by 'the rights of children to the protection and care necessary for their well-being, as provided for by the United Nations Convention on the Rights of the Child of 20 November 1989 and the Charter of Fundamental Rights of the European Union' (para 26).

of the population and thus be covered by the concept of "imperative grounds of public security", capable of justifying an expulsion measure under Article 28(3) of Directive 2004/38, as long as the manner in which such offences were committed discloses particularly serious characteristics, which is a matter for the referring court to determine on the basis of an individual examination of the specific case before it'.[188] Noting Article 27(2) of the Directive, the Court observed that expulsion is not the inevitable outcome since 'the personal conduct of the individual concerned must represent a genuine, present threat affecting one of the fundamental interests of society or of the host Member State, which implies, in general, the existence in the individual concerned of a propensity to act in the same way in the future'.[189] It also underlined the importance of the assessment required by Article 28(1).[190] Finally, as regards Article 27(2), the Court found that 'where an expulsion measure has been adopted as a penalty or legal consequence of a custodial penalty, but is enforced more than two years after it was issued', Article 33(2) of the Directive 'requires the Member State to check that the individual concerned is currently and genuinely a threat to public policy or public security and to assess whether there has been any material change in the circumstances since the expulsion order was issued'.[191]

The extremely difficult question at the heart of *PI* was more evident in Advocate General Bot's Opinion: while 'it is indisputable that sexual abuse of a 14 year old minor, sexual coercion and rape constitute a particularly serious threat to one of the fundamental interests of society, I do not think that this type of act is covered by the concept of "public security" within the meaning of Article 28(3) of Directive 2004/38'.[192] Differently from his view in *Tsakouridis*, he indicated in *PI* that 'a comparison of paragraphs 2 and 3 of Article 28 of Directive 2004/38 clearly shows that its wording establishes a clear difference between the concept of public policy and that of public security, the second having a higher degree of seriousness than the first, preventing the enhanced protection enjoyed by the Union citizen'.[193] More particularly, '[t]he reference to the concept of public security clearly seems to derive not automatically merely from the fact of having committed an offence, but from criminal conduct which is particularly serious in principle and also in its effects, which go beyond the individual harm caused to the victim or victims. The two concepts are therefore not the same and although any conduct which creates a threat to public security by definition disturbs public policy, the opposite is not true, even if, once known, the act committed may give rise in public opinion to an emotion which reflects the disturbance caused by the offence'.[194]

The Advocate General also recalled that, in *Tsakouridis*, 'the Court considered that dealing in narcotics as part of an organised group was a diffuse form of crime and could reach a level of intensity that might directly threaten the calm and physical security of the population as a whole or a large part of it', but on the question of whether the offences committed in *PI* met that definition, '[h]owever much we may wish to reply in the affirmative, such is the spontaneous disapproval and repulsion aroused from a moral point of view by the acts committed, the legal analysis seems to me to call for a negative response'.[195] In particular,

---

[188] *PI*, para 28. See similarly, Case C-193/16 *E*, EU:C:2017:542, para 20.
[189] *PI*, para 30.
[190] ibid para 32.
[191] ibid para 31.
[192] AG Bot in *PI*, EU:C:2012:123, para 28 of the Opinion.
[193] ibid para 34 of the Opinion.
[194] ibid para 38 of the Opinion.
[195] ibid paras 42–43 of the Opinion.

he distinguished between the threat posed by the applicant in PI 'in the family sphere' and 'a threat to the security of the citizens of the Union'.[196]

Advocate General Bot argued instead—drawing from the qualitative understanding of integration in *Dias*[197] and by analogy with case law establishing that fraudulent conduct may deprive the perpetrator of EU rights and does not generate any legitimate expectation on their part[198]—that the offences committed by PI removed him, on their own terms, from the scope of enhanced protection against expulsion in Articles 28(2) and 28(3) of the Directive. He considered that PI's conduct 'constitutes a serious disturbance of public policy, shows a total lack of desire to integrate into the society in which he finds himself and some of whose fundamental values he so conscientiously disregarded for years. Today he relies on the consequences of having completed a period of 10 years which was not interrupted because his conduct remained hidden owing to the physical and moral violence horribly exercised on the victim for years. An offence of that nature, just because it has lasted a long time, cannot create a right'.[199] He proposed, in effect, that the system of the Directive should be displaced, except for the safeguards in Article 28(1),[200] since '[t]o acknowledge that Mr I. may derive from his criminal conduct the right to the enhanced protection provided for in Article 28(2) and (3) of that directive would, in my view, conflict with the values on which citizenship of the Union is based'.[201]

Arguably, in stretching the definition of imperative grounds of public security to cover the situation in *PI*, the Court did the same thing in substance; illustrating that tolerance of Union citizens reaches a limit in the context of national criminal law and the values that it expresses.[202] Reading *Tsakouridis* and *PI* together,[203] both the extent of permitted alienation of Union citizens and the approach of the Court to interpreting the Directive were strongly criticised,[204] notably with respect to the good/bad and insider/outsider citizen narratives that integration-focused assessments feed.[205]

---

[196] ibid para 44 of the Opinion.
[197] Case C-325/09 *Dias*, EU:C:2011:498, para 64. See further, Chapter 8.
[198] Case C-285/95 *Kol*, EU:C:1997:280, para 28.
[199] AG Bot in *PI*, paras 60–61 of the Opinion.
[200] ibid para 63 of the Opinion.
[201] ibid para 62 of the Opinion.
[202] But see eg M Meduna, '"*Scelestus europeus sum*": what protection against expulsion does EU citizenship offer to European offenders?' in D Kochenov (ed), *EU Citizenship and Federalism: The Role of Rights* (CUP 2017) 395 at 415: '[n]ationality on its own cannot properly justify treating mobile and home-grown offenders differently. After all, expulsion of EU citizens is just a fancy synonym for shuffling the problematic offender from one corner to another corner of what is an allegedly borderless "common space for living and moving". Such an irrational out-of-sight-out-of-mind policy offers no real advantage for the security of the EU, its Member States and its citizens' (referring to AG Bot in *PI*, para 46 of the Opinion).
[203] Described by Coutts as reflecting 'the moralisation of the public policy/public security exception' and 'the growing expressive dimension to the use of criminal law in the Union legal regime' (n 138, 839 and 840).
[204] See eg G Anagnostaras, 'Enhanced protection of EU nationals against expulsion and the concept of internal public security: comment on the *PI* Case' (2012) 37 European Law Review 630; D Kochenov and B Pirker, 'Deporting the citizens within the European Union' (2013) 19 Columbia Journal of European Law 372; and D Kostakopoulou-Douchery and N Ferreira, 'Testing liberal norms: the public policy and public security derogations and the cracks in European Union citizenship' (2014) 20 Columbia Journal of European Law 167.
[205] See eg L Azoulai, 'The (mis)construction of the European individual—two essays on Union citizenship law', EUI working papers, LAW 2014/14, <https://cadmus.eui.eu/handle/1814/33293> (accessed 7 June 2023); L Azoulai and S Coutts, 'Restricting Union citizen's residence rights on grounds of public security—where Union citizenship and the AFSJ meet: P.I.' (2013) 50 Common Market Law Review 553; S Coutts, 'Supranational public wrongs: the limitations and possibilities of European criminal law and a European community' (2017) 54 Common Market Law Review 771; D Kostakopoulou, 'When EU citizens become foreigners' (2014) 20 European Law Journal 447; and L Mancano, 'Punishment and rights in European Union citizenship: persons or criminals?' (2018) 24 European Law Journal 206.

Turning to another ambiguity in the Directive, Article 28(2) requires that expulsion decisions must be based on serious grounds of public policy or public security where Union citizens or their family members 'have the right of permanent residence' in the host State. But Article 28(3)(a) refers only to residence in the host State 'for the previous ten years'. Thus, are the conditions for acquiring the right of permanent residence—legal residence in the host State for a continuous period of five years—relevant to Article 28(3)(a)? Reflecting the discussion in Chapter 8 about how the *nature* of a Union citizen's integration in the host State determines their 'legal' residence for the purposes permanent residence there, the Commission noted in its 2009 Communication on better transposition and application of the Directive that, '[a]s a rule, Member States are not obliged to take time actually spent behind bars into account when calculating the duration of residence under Article 28 where no links with the host Member State are built'.[206] However, in *B and Vomero*, Advocate General Szpunar suggested that '[i]t may be inferred, *a contrario*, that the Commission has started from the premiss that, when the question arises of the level of protection against expulsion in terms of Article 28(2) and (3) of Directive 2004/38, periods of imprisonment are not irrelevant *provided that* the Union citizen concerned is one who is firmly settled in the host Member State'.[207]

In *MG*, in which an application for a permanent residence certificate in the host State was submitted while the Union citizen was in prison there, two questions were addressed by the Court of Justice: first, 'whether the 10-year period of residence referred to in Article 28(3)(a) of Directive 2004/38 must be calculated by counting backwards (from the decision ordering the expulsion of the person concerned) or forwards (from the commencement of that person's residence)'; and second, 'whether that period must be continuous'.[208] The Court first recalled *Tsakouridis* to confirm that, according to Article 28(3)(a), the 'decisive criterion' is whether the Union citizen lived in the host State *for the ten years preceding the expulsion decision*', that is, the ten year period referred to in Article 28(3)(a) must be calculated by counting backwards from the date of the decision ordering the expulsion.[209] Recalling, second, the finding in *Tsakouridis* that absences may be taken into consideration on a case-by-case basis to determine whether or not enhanced protection should be extended under Article 28(3), 'the period of residence referred to in that provision must, in principle, be continuous'.[210]

The Court then considered whether a period of imprisonment 'is capable of interrupting' continuity of residence even where, as in this case, the applicant had resided in the host State for ten years *prior* to imprisonment.[211] It emphasised the significance of integration in the host State in the permanent residence case law—in particular, 'the fact that a national court has imposed a custodial sentence is an indication that the person concerned has not respected the values of the society of the host Member State, as reflected in its criminal law'[212]—and concluded that '[s]ince the degree of integration of the persons concerned is

---

[206] Communication on guidance for better transposition and application of Directive 2004/38/EC (n 34) para 3.4.
[207] AG Szpunar in Joined Cases C-316/16 and C-424/16 *B and Vomero*, EU:C:2017:797, para 82 of the Opinion.
[208] Case C-400/12 *MG*, EU:C:2014:9, para 22.
[209] ibid para 23, in contrast to 'the requisite period for acquiring a right of permanent residence, which begins when the person concerned commences lawful residence in the host Member State' (para 24); referring to Case C-145/09 *Tsakouridis*, EU:C:2010:708, para 31. Confirmed in Joined Cases C-316/16 and C-424/16 *B and Vomero*, EU:C:2018:256, para 64.
[210] *MG*, para 27; confirmed in *B and Vomero*, para 66.
[211] Case C-400/12 *MG*, EU:C:2014:9, para 29 (emphasis added).
[212] Ibid para 31; referring to Case C-378/12 *Onuekwere*, EU:C:2014:13, para 26.

a vital consideration underpinning both the right of permanent residence and the system of protection against expulsion measures established by Directive 2004/38, the reasons making it justifiable for periods of imprisonment not to be taken into consideration for the purposes of granting a right of permanent residence or for such periods to be regarded as interrupting the continuity of the period of residence needed to acquire that right *must also be borne in mind* when interpreting Article 28(3)(a)'.[213]

However, less stringently than in case law on permanent residence, periods of imprisonment interrupt continuity of residence for the purposes of Article 28(3)(a) only 'in principle' and therefore 'may – together with the other factors going to make up the entirety of relevant considerations in each individual case – be taken into account by the national authorities responsible for applying Article 28(3) of that directive as part of the overall assessment required for determining whether the integrating links previously forged with the host Member State *have been broken*, and thus for determining whether the enhanced protection provided for in that provision will be granted'.[214] In other words, 'imprisonment of the Union citizen *allows doubt to be cast* on his integration' in the host State, but it is not determinative per se.[215]

Addressing the specific circumstances in *MG*, the Court found that even though the residence period is counted backwards from when the expulsion order was issued, the fact that MG had already resided in the host State for ten years before being imprisoned there 'may be taken into consideration as part of th[at] overall assessment'.[216] Interestingly, there was no opinion in *MG*, notwithstanding Advocate General Bot's observation in *Onuekwere* that the concept of legal residence is 'absent from the wording of Article 28' and, therefore, 'the conditions for the grant and loss of the right of permanent residence must be distinguished from those relating to the loss of enhanced protection'.[217] For the Court, the 'vital consideration' of integration instated the connective—and overarching—link between the two parts of the Directive, a link that it deepened in *B and Vomero*. Thus, the system of lawful residence mapped out by the Directive is again invoked to do much of the significant work of integration, potentially conflating compliance with the temporal and economic activity/economic autonomy conditions for lawful residence in the Directive and presumptions of more substantive, more qualitative integration.[218]

However, as indicated in Chapter 8, the Court was notably more progressive on the implications of imprisonment in *B and Vomero*, where one of the applicants had resided in the host State for 20 years before receiving a custodial sentence, in comparison to how it addressed the repercussions of prison terms in previous (permanent residence) case law. Better reflecting how circumstances can change over a long period of residence, the Court found:

> [P]articularly in the case of a Union citizen who was already in a position to satisfy the condition of 10 years' continuous residence in the host Member State in the past, even before

---

[213] *MG*, para 32 (emphasis added).
[214] Ibid para 36 (emphasis added). Cf *Onuekwere*, para 26: '[t]he imposition of a prison sentence by the national court is such as to show the non-compliance by the person concerned with the values expressed by the society of the host Member State in its criminal law, with the result that the taking into consideration of periods of imprisonment for the purposes of the acquisition by family members of a Union citizen who are not nationals of a Member State of the right of permanent residence for the purposes of Article 16(2) of Directive 2004/38 would clearly be contrary to the aim pursued by that directive in establishing that right of residence'.
[215] AG Szpunar in *B and Vomero*, para 83 of the Opinion (emphasis added).
[216] *MG*, para 37.
[217] AG Bot in *Onuekwere*, EU:C:2013:640, para 28 of the Opinion (emphasis added).
[218] Case C-456/12 *O and B*, EU:C:2014:135; see further, Chapter 9.

he committed a criminal act that resulted in his detention, the fact that the person concerned was placed in custody by the authorities of that State *cannot be regarded as automatically breaking the integrative links that that person had previously forged with that State* and the continuity of his residence in that State for the purpose of Article 28(3)(a) of Directive 2004/38 and, therefore, depriving him of the enhanced protection against expulsion provided for in that provision. Moreover, *such an interpretation would deprive that provision of much of its practical effect*, since an expulsion measure will most often be adopted precisely because of the conduct of the person concerned that led to his conviction and detention. As part of the overall assessment ... which, in this case, is for the referring court to carry out, it is necessary to take into account, as regards the integrative links forged by B with the host Member State during the period of residence before his detention, the fact that, *the more those integrative links with that State are solid* — including from a social, cultural and family perspective, to the point where, for example, the person concerned is genuinely rooted in the society of that State, as found by the referring court in the main proceedings — *the lower the probability that a period of detention could have resulted in those links being broken* and, consequently, a discontinuity of the 10-year period of residence referred to in Article 28(3)(a) of Directive 2004/38.[219]

The Court was also more cognisant of the rehabilitative dimension of custodial sentences, outlining '[o]ther relevant factors' that should be taken into account in the national court's assessment: 'first, the nature of the offence that resulted in the period of imprisonment in question and the circumstances in which that offence was committed, and, secondly, all the relevant factors as regards the behaviour of the person concerned during the period of imprisonment'.[220] The Court acknowledged that '[w]hile the nature of the offence and the circumstances in which it was committed shed light on the extent to which the person concerned has, as the case may be, *become disconnected from the society of the host Member State*, the attitude of the person concerned during his detention may, in turn, reinforce that disconnection or, conversely, *help to maintain or restore links previously forged* with the host Member State with a view to his *future social reintegration* in that State'.[221]

The Court also considered whether 'it is a prerequisite of eligibility for the protection against expulsion provided for in that provision that the person concerned must have a right of permanent residence, within the meaning of Article 16 and Article 28(2) of [Directive 2004/38].[222] It outlined the Directive's 'system of protection against expulsion measures which is based on the degree of integration of those persons in the host Member State' and reiterated that '[i]t thus follows *from the wording and the structure* of Article 28 of Directive 2004/38 that the protection against expulsion provided for in that provision gradually increases in proportion to the degree of integration of the Union citizen concerned' in the host State.[223] It concluded that '[i]n those circumstances, *and even though it is not specified in the*

---

[219] *B and Vomero*, paras 71–72 (emphasis added). The Court thus 'develops a far more balanced and richer conception of what could be a "genuinely rooted EU citizen" in his host Member State' (M Benlolo Carabot, 'Citizenship, integration and the public policy exception: *B. and Vomero* and *K. and H.F.*' (2019) 56 Common Market Law Review 771 at 787).

[220] ibid paras 73; referring to paras 123–125 of the Opinion of AG Szpunar (EU:C:2017:797); see further, paras 108–110 of the Opinion.

[221] *B and Vomero*, para 74 (emphasis added), recalling in para 75 that 'the social rehabilitation of the Union citizen in the State in which he has become genuinely integrated is not only in his interest but also in that of the European Union in general'.

[222] ibid para 40.

[223] ibid paras 44 and 48 (emphasis added).

wording of the provisions concerned, the enhanced protection provided for in Article 28(3)(a) of Directive 2004/38 is available to a Union citizen only in so far as he first satisfies the eligibility condition for the protection referred to in Article 28(2) of that directive, namely having a right of permanent residence under Article 16'.[224]

The Court then mapped its analysis onto the 'gradual system' of residence provided for in the Directive.[225] First, a Union citizen may be expelled before acquiring the right of permanent residence if they become an unreasonable burden on the host State's social assistance system—thus, that citizen 'cannot, at the same time, enjoy the considerably enhanced protection provided for in Article 28(3)(a)'.[226] Second, reiterating the significance of integration— more specifically, conditions for legal residence in the host State and 'in particular' those in Article 7(1)[227]—for permanent residence, the Court reasoned that '[a] Union citizen who has not acquired the right to reside permanently in the host Member State because he has not satisfied those conditions and who cannot, therefore, rely on the level of protection against expulsion guaranteed by Article 28(2) of Directive 2004/38 cannot, *a fortiori*, enjoy the considerably enhanced level of protection against expulsion provided for in Article 28(3)(a) of that directive'.[228]

However, if the 'actual enforcement' of an expulsion decision 'is deferred for a certain period of time, it may be necessary to carry out a fresh, updated assessment of whether there are still "grounds of public policy or public security", "serious grounds of public policy or public security" or "imperative grounds of public security", as applicable'.[229] This finding reflects the requirement, as noted in Section 2, that national courts must consider, 'in reviewing the lawfulness of an expulsion measure taken against a national of another Member State, factual matters which occurred after the final decision of the competent authorities which may point to the cessation or the substantial diminution of the present threat which the conduct of the person concerned constitutes to the requirements of public policy or public security'; especially where 'a lengthy period has elapsed between the date of the expulsion order and that of the review of that decision by the competent court'.[230]

Finally, the ruling in *Ziebell*, which concerned the procedures for expulsion of Turkish workers under Decision 1/80, illustrates that certain principles that underpin the Directive can be transposed to the Ankara Agreement and associated measures, reflecting their history in connection with the Treaty's economic freedoms. But it also demonstrates the limits of that method because of the status of Union citizenship. Mr Ziebell was a Turkish national born in Germany who resided there on the basis of an unlimited residence permit. An expulsion order issued in connection with criminal offences committed and a risk of re-offending raised the question of whether the protection conferred on Member State nationals by Article 28(3)(a) of Directive 2004/38 applied to Turkish nationals in the context of Decision 1/80.

The Court first confirmed that 'members of a Turkish worker's family who fulfil the conditions laid down in the first paragraph of Article 7 of Decision No 1/80 can lose the rights conferred on them by that provision only in two cases, that is to say, either where the presence of the Turkish migrant in the host Member State constitutes, by reason of his personal conduct,

---

[224] ibid para 49 (emphasis added).
[225] ibid para 51, the 'stages and conditions' of which are then outlined in paras 52–54.
[226] ibid para 56.
[227] ibid para 59. See similarly, Joined Cases C-331/16 and C-366/16 *K and HF*, EU:C:2018:296, paras 73–74.
[228] *B and Vomero*, para 60.
[229] ibid para 91. See further on Article 33(2) of the Directive, Section 4.
[230] ibid para 94; referring to Joined Cases C-482/01 and C-493/01 *Orfanopoulos and Oliveri*, EU:C:2004:262, para 82 and Case C-371/08 *Ziebell*, EU:C:2011:809, para 84.

a genuine and serious threat to public policy, public security or public health, within the terms of Article 14(1) of that decision, or where the person concerned has left the territory of that State for a significant length of time without legitimate reason'.[231] It referred to its own 'consistent case-law to the effect that both the very concept of public policy within the meaning of [Article 14(1)] and the relevant criteria in that regard and the guarantees on which the person concerned may rely in that context must be interpreted by analogy with the principles recognised for Union nationals in connection with Article [45(3) TFEU] as implemented and given specific expression in Directive 64/221'.[232]

The key question for present purposes was whether the enhanced protection against expulsion conferred by Article 28 of Directive 2004/38 also applied to the protection against expulsion conferred by Article 14(1) of Decision No 1/80.[233] The Court first confirmed its general approach to interpreting Decision 1/80, which requires that EU Treaty provisions on the free movement of workers 'must be extended, as far as possible, to Turkish nationals who enjoy rights under the EEC-Turkey Association'.[234] However, notwithstanding the fact that 'Article 14(1) is formulated in almost identical terms to Article [45(3) TFEU]',[235] the Court found that the 'EEC-Turkey Association pursues a solely economic purpose'.[236] While that understanding does not necessarily disregard the fact that the Agreement 'includes *the perspective of* accession to the Union'[237] — and while it was acknowledged in Ziebell that Decision 1/80 is 'aimed at improving the social treatment accorded to Turkish workers and members of their families'[238] — it was nevertheless emphasised that the intended scope of cooperation is 'restricted to the gradual achievement of the free movement of workers'.[239]

The Court then distinguished, '[b]y contrast, *the very concept of citizenship*, as it results from the mere fact that a person holds the nationality of a Member State and not from the fact that that person has the status of a worker, and which ... is intended to be the fundamental status of nationals of the Member States'.[240] That difference in intended scope of protection justifies 'the recognition, *for Union citizens alone*, of guarantees which are considerably strengthened in respect of expulsion, such as those provided for in Article 28(3)(a) of Directive 2004/38'.[241] As a result, while the extent to which Mr Ziebell was connected to and integrated in (as well as his capacity for reintegrating into[242]) Germany society had to be taken into account when determining the lawfulness of the expulsion order, and while

---

[231] *Ziebell*, para 49.
[232] ibid para 52; referring inter alia to Case C-303/08, *Bozkurt*, EU:C:2010:800, para 55.
[233] *Ziebell*, para 53.
[234] ibid para 58.
[235] ibid para 67.
[236] ibid para 64. See similarly but less definitively, Case C-221/11 *Demirkan*, EU:C:2013:583, para 56 (emphasis added): 'under European Union law, protection of passive freedom to provide services is based on the objective of establishing an internal market, conceived as an area without internal borders, by removing all obstacles to the establishment of such a market. It is precisely that objective which distinguishes the Treaty from the Association Agreement, which pursues *an essentially* economic purpose'. In Case 12/86 *Demirel*, EU:C:1987:400, the Association Agreement had been referred to as 'creating special, privileged links with a non-member country which must, at least to a certain extent, take part in the Community system' (para 9).
[237] AG Cruz Villalón in *Demirkan*, EU:C:2013:237, para 65 of the Opinion (emphasis added).
[238] *Ziebell*, para 65.
[239] ibid para 72.
[240] ibid para 73. See similarly, AG Cruz Villalón in *Demirkan*, para 67 of the Opinion: 'a true internal market can only develop if citizens are acknowledged and protected also in spheres outside of their economic activities ... Placing the Union citizen at the heart of EU law connects the EU with its objectives going far beyond the economic dimension'.
[241] *Ziebell*, para 73 (emphasis added).
[242] ibid para 85.

that assessment engaged both proportionality and protection of fundamental rights,[243] 'the *substantial differences* to be found *not only in their wording but also in their object and purpose* between the rules relating to the EEC–Turkey Association and European Union law concerning citizenship that the two legal schemes in question cannot be considered equivalent'.[244] Instead, since Directive 64/221 was repealed by Directive 2004/38, the Court engaged Directive 2003/109, which protects third-country nationals lawfully resident in the Union, as the 'appropriate ... reference framework under [EU] law for the purposes of applying Article 14(1) of Decision No 1/80'.[245]

4. Directive 2004/38: Administrative Formalities and Procedural Safeguards

Recital 25 of Directive 2004/38 indicates that procedural safeguards should 'be specified in detail in order to ensure a high level of protection of the rights of Union citizens and their family members in the event of their being denied leave to enter or reside in another Member State, as well as to uphold the principle that any action taken by the authorities must be properly justified'.[246] Recital 26 emphasises that 'judicial redress procedures should be available to Union citizens and their family members who have been refused leave to enter or reside in another Member State'. For restrictions of free movement based on public policy, public security, or public health, these objectives are realised in Chapter VI of the Directive through Articles 30 (notification of decisions), 31 (procedural safeguards, which include appeal against or review of decisions taken on grounds of public policy, public security, or public health), 32 (duration of exclusion orders), and 34 (expulsion as a penalty

---

[243] ibid para 81; referring to *Bozkurt*, paras 57–60. The Court's previous case law had transposed to expulsion decisions taken under Decision 1/80 the principles of EU free movement law developed for Directive 64/221; see eg Case C-340/97 *Nazli*, EU:C:2000:77, paras 57–58).

[244] *Ziebell*, para 74 (emphasis added).

[245] ibid para 78. Directive 2003/109 concerning the status of third-country nationals who are long-term residents, 2003 OJ L16/44. However, Peers argues that '[i]t would have been perfectly sensible to link the rules on the expulsion of Turkish workers at least to the general rules on expulsion of EU citizens set out in art 27(1) and (2) of [Directive 2004/38], which do not differ from the previous substantive rules on expulsion of EU citizens, while reserving the application of the special rules set out in art 28(2) and (3) ... for EU citizens and their family members only'; in this view, Directive 2004/38 'is *not* confined in scope exclusively to EU citizens, but rather applies in full also to nationals of Member States of the European Economic Area (EEA) and their family members' (S Peers, 'Expulsion of Turkish citizens: a backwards step by the Court of Justice?' (2012) 26 Journal of Immigration Asylum and Nationality Law 56 at 60–61, emphasis in original).

[246] Relatedly, Article 21 WA establishes that '[t]he safeguards set out in Article 15 and Chapter VI of Directive 2004/38/EC shall apply in respect of any decision by the host State that restricts residence rights of the persons referred to in Article 10 of this Agreement'. The Commission further advises: '[t]his provision covers all situations in which residence rights under the Agreement can be restricted or denied. It ensures that the procedural safeguards of Chapter VI of Directive 2004/38/EC fully apply in all situations, i.e.: (a) abuse and fraud (Article 35 of Directive 2004/38/EC); (b) measures taken on grounds of public policy, public security or public health (Chapter VI of Directive 2004/38/EC) or in accordance with national legislation; and (c) measures taken on all other grounds (Article 15 of Directive 2004/38/EC) which include situations such as when an application for a residence document is not accepted as made, when an application is refused because the applicant does not meet the conditions attached to the right of residence or decisions taken on the ground that the person concerned does no longer meet the conditions attached to the right of residence (*such as when an economically non-active EU citizen becomes an unreasonable burden to the social assistance scheme of the host State*) (emphasis in original). It also ensures that the material safeguards of Chapter VI of Directive 2004/38/EC fully apply with regard to restriction decisions taken on the basis of conduct that occurred before the end of the transition period. In line with the CJEU's established case law on the general principles of EU law, *restriction decisions taken in accordance with national legislation must comply also with the principle of proportionality and fundamental rights, such as the right to family life*' (Guidance Note relating to the Agreement (n 73) para 2.9, emphasis added).

or legal consequence). The procedural safeguards provided for in this part of the Directive apply irrespective of the residence status of the Union citizen concerned; as the Court has determined, '[t]o exclude from the benefit of those substantive and procedural safeguards citizens of the Union who are not lawfully resident on the territory of the host Member State would deprive those safeguards of their essential effectiveness'.[247]

Articles 30–34 of the Directive connect to the requirements of Article 47 CFR, which guarantees the right to an effective remedy and to a fair trial.[248] As expressions of more general principles of judicial protection, the safeguards in Chapter VI have also been drawn from as 'inspiration' where the Directive itself does not apply.[249] Additional safeguards apply to decisions ordering expulsion from the territory of a Member State: as explained by Advocate General Léger, '[t]he limited nature of the legal remedies reserved to persons who are turned back at the frontier on grounds of public policy is explained, consequently, by the fact that their interest in entering and in residing in the Member State of destination is not, in principle, as marked as if they had already resided there'.[250]

4.1 Article 30: Notification of Decisions

Article 30(1) of Directive 2004/38 builds on elements of Article 7 of Directive 64/221:[251]

Article 30

Notification of decisions

1. The persons concerned shall be notified in writing of any decision taken under Article 27(1), in such a way that they are able to comprehend its content and the implications for them.
2. The persons concerned shall be informed, precisely and in full, of the public policy, public security or public health grounds on which the decision taken in their case is based, unless this is contrary to the interests of State security.

---

[247] Case C-50/06 *Commission v Netherlands*, EU:C:2007:325, para 35; see similarly, para 40.

[248] Article 47 CFR provides: '[e]veryone whose rights and freedoms guaranteed by the law of the Union are violated has the right to an effective remedy before a tribunal in compliance with the conditions laid down in this Article. Everyone is entitled to a fair and public hearing within a reasonable time by an independent and impartial tribunal previously established by law. Everyone shall have the possibility of being advised, defended and represented. Legal aid shall be made available to those who lack sufficient resources in so far as such aid is necessary to ensure effective access to justice'.

[249] eg Referring to the principles that underpin Articles 30(2) and 31(1), Case T-228/02 *Organisation des Modjahedines du peuple d'Iran v Council*, EU:T:2006:384, paras 149–150 and 156–157. See similarly, Case T-47/03 *Sison v Council*, EU:T:2007:207, paras 196–197 and 204.

[250] AG Léger in Case C-357/98 *Yiadom*, EU:C:2000:174, para 56 of the Opinion. The application of certain procedural safeguards in cases of expulsion on grounds *other than* public policy, public security or public health taken in accordance with Article 15(1) of the Directive is discussed in Chapters 6 and 7; see esp Case C-94/18 *Chenchooliah*, EU:C:2019:693.

[251] Article 7 of Directive 64/221 provided that '[t]he person concerned shall be officially notified of any decision to refuse the issue or renewal of a residence permit or to expel him from the territory. The period allowed for leaving the territory shall be stated in this notification. Save in cases of urgency, this period shall be not less than fifteen days if the person concerned has not yet been granted a residence permit and not less than one month in all other cases'.

3. The notification shall specify the court or administrative authority with which the person concerned may lodge an appeal, the time limit for the appeal and, where applicable, the time allowed for the person to leave the territory of the Member State. Save in duly substantiated cases of urgency, the time allowed to leave the territory shall be not less than one month from the date of notification.

In its original proposal for Directive 2004/38, the Commission indicated that the last phrase of what is now Article 30(1)—'in such a way that they are able to comprehend its content and the implications for them'—is based on the finding in *Adoui and Cornuaille* that '[i]t is sufficient ... if the notification is made in such a way as to enable the person concerned to comprehend the content and effect thereof'.[252] Thus, 'the decision does not have to be translated into the language of the person concerned, particularly where it is a lesser known language, but it does require Member States to do what they can to make sure that the person concerned understands what the decision is about and what it means for them'.[253] That interpretation has not been tested against Article 21(1) CFR, which prohibits discrimination on several grounds including language, but the extent of the obligation that Article 30(1) generates was considered in *Petrea*. The applicant argued that an exclusion order issued against him, on the basis of which he was removed from the host State territory, was not notified to him in line with the requirements of Article 30(1). In such circumstances, the principle of effectiveness should override the expiry of time limits for challenging the order.[254]

The Court observed that Mr Petrea was aware of the order, complied with it, and, before the order was adopted, received 'an information bulletin for foreigners subject to exclusion (informing him, in a language he understood, of his rights and redress available to him, and the possibility of requesting a written or oral translation of the or the main parts of the return decision'); he had also 'declared in writing that he waived all legal remedies against the order'.[255] In such circumstances, the Court indicated that he had 'sufficient evidence in order to rely in legal proceedings on the possible infringement of the notification requirements imposed by Article 30' of the Directive, though that was for the referring court to determine.[256]

The Court then considered whether Article 30(1) requires a decision adopted under Article 27(1) of the Directive to be notified to the addressee in a language that they understand even they did not bring an application to that effect. It first confirmed that neither the wording nor *travaux préparatoires* of the Directive require that a removal order 'is to be translated into the language of the person concerned, but [require] by contrast that the Member States take the necessary measures to ensure that the latter understands the content and implications of that decision, in accordance with the Court's findings in [*Adoui and Cornuaille*]'.[257] It also pointed, in contrast, to Article 12(2) of Directive 2008/115, which expressly requires that Member States must 'provide,

---

[252] Original proposal (n 67) 21; referring to Joined Cases 115 and 116/81 *Adoui and Cornuaille*, EU:C:1982:183, para 13.
[253] Original proposal (n 67) 21–22. The Economic and Social Committee had argued for an obligation of translation, considering that 'the best way of understanding a decision which curtails a right is to receive it in a language that is understood by the person concerned. [The Committee] therefore believes that Union citizens should be entitled to receive this document in the language of the State which issues it and in the language of the Member State of which they are nationals' (n 103, para 4.8.3).
[254] Case C-184/16 *Petrea*, EU:C:2017:684, para 62.
[255] ibid para 63.
[256] ibid para 64.
[257] ibid para 70; referring to *Adoui and Cornuaille*, para 13. AG Szpunar further pointed to the objection raised by the Economic and Social Committee, noted above, but therefore concluded that 'the legislature did not alter the position stated in the explanatory memorandum and did not consider the translation of every decision to be necessary' (AG Szpunar in *Petrea*, EU:C:2017:324, para 101 of the Opinion).

upon request, a written or oral translation of the main elements of decisions related to return, including information on the available legal remedies in a language the third-country national understands or may reasonably be presumed to understand'.[258] However, while supporting the Court's conclusion, Advocate General Szpunar observed that '[o]ne might wonder how the national authorities would be able to determine which language the person concerned understands if he has not submitted an express application to that effect. In that context, it should be noted that Article 30 of Directive 2004/38, read in conjunction with Article 27(1) thereof, concerns not only Union citizens but also their family members, irrespective of their nationality'.[259]

In its original proposal for Directive 2004/38, the Commission confirmed that Article 30(2) is based upon Article 6 of Directive 64/221,[260] 'with two additions based on Court of Justice case-law, requiring Member States, when notifying the individual concerned of a decision taken against them, to specify the exact reasons for the decision in full, so that the person is in a position to prepare their defence properly; and '[a] further safeguard is that decisions refusing leave to enter or reside must not only state the reasons on which they are based, but also be done in writing, so that the courts can, if necessary, carry out a proper judicial review'.[261] In its 2009 Communication on better transposition and application of the Directive, the Commission expanded on the requirements of Article 30(2), emphasising that '[d]ecisions must be fully reasoned and list all the specific factual and legal grounds on which they are taken so that the person concerned may take effective steps to ensure his or her defence and that national courts may review the case in accordance with the right to an effective remedy, which is a general principle of [Union] law reflected in Article 47 of the EU Charter'.[262] It therefore considered that forms may be used to notify the decisions but must always allow for a full justification of the grounds on which the decision was taken': in that light, 'just indicating one or more of several options by ticking a box is not acceptable'.[263]

ZZ represents one of the most detailed analyses of the Charter across any part of EU citizenship law to date.[264] In its ruling, the Court first characterised Article 30(2) of the Directive as ensuring 'that the person concerned may make effective use of the redress procedures ... established by the Member States' and underlined that '[i]t is only by way of derogation that Article 30(2) of Directive 2004/38 permits the Member States to limit the information sent to the person concerned in the interests of State security. As a derogation ... this provision must be interpreted strictly, but without depriving it of its effectiveness'.[265] For Advocate General Mengozzi, Article 30(2) 'constitutes above all an expression of "the principle that any action taken by the authorities must be properly justified", in the words used by the Union legislature in recital 25'.[266]

---

[258] *Petrea*, para 71. Directive 2008/115 on common standards and procedures in Member States for returning illegally staying third-country nationals, 2008 OJ L348/98.
[259] AG Szpunar in *Petrea*, para 102 of the Opinion.
[260] Article 6 of Directive 64/221 provided that '[t]he person concerned shall be informed of the grounds of public policy, public security, or public health upon which the decision taken in his case is based, unless this is contrary to the interests of the security of the State involved'.
[261] Original proposal (n 67) 22; referring to Case 36/75 *Rutili*, EU:C:1975:137, para 35. The Economic and Social Committee considered that the public security exception 'would leave the person concerned unable to defend themselves at law' and therefore recommended that the paragraph be deleted (n 103, para 4.9.2).
[262] Communication on guidance for better transposition and application of Directive 2004/38/EC (n 34) para 3.6.
[263] ibid.
[264] Assessing the ruling in its wider context of secret evidence, disclosure and procedural rights, see N De Boer 'Secret evidence and due process rights under EU law: *ZZ (France) v Secretary of State for the Home Department* (C-300/11)' (2014) 51 1235.
[265] Case C-300/11 ZZ, EU:C:2013:363, paras 48–49.
[266] AG Mengozzi in *ZZ*, EU:C:2012:563, para 54 of the Opinion.

The Court then examined the limits of the State security derogation—linked by the Advocate General to Articles 4(2) TEU and 346(1)(a) TFEU[267]—against the requirements of Article 47 CFR. First, it emphasised that 'interpretation in compliance with those requirements must take account of the significance, as resulting from the system applied by the Charter as a whole, of the fundamental right guaranteed by Article 47 thereof', and therefore, while Article 52(1) CFR 'admittedly allows limitations on the exercise of the rights enshrined by the Charter, it nevertheless lays down that any limitation must in particular respect the essence of the fundamental right in question and requires, in addition, that, subject to the principle of proportionality, the limitation must be necessary and genuinely meet objectives of general interest recognised by the European Union'.[268] Second, 'if the judicial review guaranteed by Article 47 of the Charter is to be effective, the person concerned must be able to ascertain the reasons upon which the decision taken in relation to him is based, either by reading the decision itself or by requesting and obtaining notification of those reasons, without prejudice to the power of the court with jurisdiction to require the authority concerned to provide that information'.[269] This is necessary 'to make it possible for him to defend his rights in the best possible conditions and to decide, with full knowledge of the relevant facts, whether there is any point in his applying to the court with jurisdiction, and in order to put the latter fully in a position in which it may carry out the review of the lawfulness of the national decision in question'.[270]

The Court acknowledged that 'it may prove necessary, both in administrative proceedings and in judicial proceedings, not to disclose certain information to the person concerned, in particular in the light of overriding considerations connected with State security'.[271] For judicial proceedings generally, 'having regard to the adversarial principle that forms part of the rights of the defence, which are referred to in Article 47 of the Charter, the parties to a case must have the right to examine all the documents or observations submitted to the court for the purpose of influencing its decision, and to comment on them'.[272] However, 'if, in exceptional cases, a national authority opposes precise and full disclosure to the person concerned of the grounds which constitute the basis of a decision taken under Article 27 of Directive 2004/38, by invoking reasons of State security, the court with jurisdiction in the Member State concerned must have at its disposal and apply techniques and rules of procedural law which accommodate, on the one hand, legitimate State security considerations regarding the nature and sources of the information taken into account in the adoption of such a decision and, on the other hand, the need to ensure sufficient compliance with the person's

---

[267] ibid paras 66–67 of the Opinion. Article 4(2) TEU provides that the Union 'shall respect their essential State functions, including ensuring the territorial integrity of the State, maintaining law and order and safeguarding national security. In particular, national security remains the sole responsibility of each Member State'. Article 346(1)(a) TFEU states that 'no Member State shall be obliged to supply information the disclosure of which it considers contrary to the essential interests of its security'.

[268] *ZZ*, para 51.

[269] ibid para 53; referring to Joined Cases C-372/09 and C-373/09 *Peñarroja Fa*, EU:C:2011:156, para 63 and Case C-430/10 *Gaydarov*, EU:C:2011:749, para 41.

[270] *ZZ*, para 53; referring 'to this effect' to Case 222/86 *Heylens and Others*, EU:C:1987:442, para 15 and Joined Cases C-402/05 P and C-415/05 P *Kadi and Al Barakaat International Foundation*, EU:C:2008:461, para 337.

[271] *ZZ*, para 54; referring 'to this effect' to *Kadi*, para 342.

[272] *ZZ*, para 55; referring to Case C-450/06 *Varec*, EU:C:2008:91, para 45; Case C-89/08 P *Commission v Ireland and Others*, EU:C:2009:742, para 52; and Case C-472/11 *Banif Plus Bank*, 2013:88, para 30. The Court also referred to the judgment of the ECtHR in *Ruiz-Mateos v Spain*, 23 June 1993, § 63, Series A no. 262, and held that '[t]he fundamental right to an effective legal remedy would be infringed if a judicial decision were founded on facts and documents which the parties themselves, or one of them, have not had an opportunity to examine and on which they have therefore been unable to state their view' (*ZZ*, para 56)

procedural rights, such as the right to be heard and the adversarial principle'.[273] The Court then established guiding principles for such situations. First, Member States must provide for effective judicial review 'both of the existence and validity of the reasons invoked by the national authority with regard to State security and of the legality of the decision taken under Article 27 of Directive 2004/38' and also 'prescribe techniques and rules relating to that review' in order to meet the objective just noted, that is, 'to ensure sufficient compliance with the person's procedural rights'.[274] Second, they must also 'lay down rules enabling the court entrusted with review of the decision's legality to examine both all the grounds and the related evidence on the basis of which the decision was taken'.[275]

Specifically for judicial review 'of the existence and validity of the reasons invoked by the competent national authority with regard to State security of the Member State concerned, it is necessary for a court to be entrusted with verifying whether those reasons stand in the way of precise and full disclosure of the grounds on which the decision in question is based and of the related evidence'.[276] In that context, 'the competent national authority has the task of proving, in accordance with the national procedural rules, that State security would in fact be compromised by precise and full disclosure to the person concerned of the grounds which constitute the basis of a decision taken under Article 27 of Directive 2004/38 and of the related evidence' and 'there is no presumption that the reasons invoked by a national authority exist and are valid'.[277] Thus, the national court must 'carry out an independent examination of all the matters of law and fact relied upon by the competent national authority and it must determine, in accordance with the national procedural rules, whether State security stands in the way of such disclosure'.[278] Where that assessment leads to the conclusion that State security does *not* preclude a 'precise and full disclosure to the person concerned of the grounds on which a decision refusing entry taken under Article 27 of Directive 2004/38 is based, it gives the competent national authority the opportunity to disclose the missing grounds and evidence to the person concerned'.[279] The legality of refusal to authorise disclosure may itself be reviewed by the national court.

However, where State security does preclude disclosure, a judicial review procedure that 'strikes an appropriate balance between the requirements flowing from State security and the requirements of the right to effective judicial protection whilst limiting any interference with the exercise of that right to that which is strictly necessary' must be carried out.[280] Compliance with Article 47 CFR would then require that the adversarial procedure is complied with 'to the greatest possible extent ... to enable the person concerned to contest the grounds on which the decision in question is based and to make submissions on the evidence relating to the decision and, therefore, to put forward an effective defence', and they must therefore be informed of the 'essence of the grounds on which a decision refusing entry' was based.[281] However, 'the weighing up of the right to effective judicial protection against the necessity to protect the security of the Member State concerned ... is not applicable in

---

[273] ZZ, para 57; referring 'by analogy' to *Kadi*, para 344.
[274] ZZ, paras 58 and 57.
[275] ibid para 59.
[276] ibid para 60.
[277] ibid para 61.
[278] ibid para 62.
[279] ibid para 63.
[280] ibid para 64.
[281] ibid para 65, highlighting that 'the necessary protection of State security cannot have the effect of denying the person concerned his right to be heard and, therefore, of rendering his right of redress as provided for in Article 31 of that directive ineffective'.

the same way to the evidence underlying the grounds that is adduced before the national court with jurisdiction', with the Court acknowledging that, '[i]n certain cases, disclosure of that evidence is liable to compromise State security in a direct and specific manner, in that it may, in particular, endanger the life, health or freedom of persons or reveal the methods of investigation specifically used by the national security authorities and thus seriously impede, or even prevent, future performance of the tasks of those authorities'.[282] In such situations, the national court should inform the person concerned of 'the essence of the grounds which constitute the basis of the decision in question in a manner which takes due account of the necessary confidentiality of the evidence'.[283]

Finally, according to the Commission's 2009 Communication on better transposition and application of the Directive, for Article 30(3), '[t]he justification of an urgent removal must be genuine and proportionate' and '[i]n assessing the need to reduce this time in cases of urgency, the authorities must take into account the impact of an immediate or urgent removal on the personal and family life of the person concerned (e.g. need to give notice at work, terminate a lease, need to arrange for personal belongings to be sent to the place of new residence, the education of children, etc.)'.[284] Importantly, '[a]dopting an expulsion measure on imperative or serious grounds does not necessarily mean that there is urgency. The assessment of urgency must be clearly and separately substantiated'.[285]

4.2 Article 31: Procedural Safeguards

In *Gaydarov*, concerning a restriction on the right to leave a Member State, the Court emphasised that 'the person to whom such a measure is applied must have an effective judicial remedy'.[286] It clarified that such a remedy 'must permit a review of the legality of the decision at issue as regards matters of both fact and law in the light of European Union law',[287] and that, '[i]n order to ensure that such review by the courts is effective, the interested party must be able to obtain the reasons for the decision taken in relation to him, either by reading the decision itself or by requesting and obtaining notification of those grounds, without prejudice to the power of the court with jurisdiction to require the authority concerned to provide that information'.[288]

Prior to the adoption of Directive 2004/38, Article 8 of Directive 64/22 had required that '[t]he person concerned shall have the same legal remedies in respect of any decision concerning entry, or refusing the issue or renewal of a residence permit, or ordering expulsion from the territory, as are available to nationals of the State concerned in respect of acts of the administration'. In its 1999 Communication on that Directive, the Commission considered that Article 8 did 'not impose on the Member States any obligation to offer legal remedies in

---

[282] ibid para 66.
[283] ibid para 68.
[284] Communication on guidance for better transposition and application of Directive 2004/38/EC (n 34) para 3.5.
[285] ibid.
[286] Case C-430/10 *Gaydarov*, EU:C:2011:749, para 41, referring to Case 222/84 *Johnston*, EU:C:1986:206, paras 18 and 19; Case 222/86 *Heylens and Others*, EU:C:1987:442, para 14; and Case C-50/00 P *Unión de Pequeños Agricultores*, EU:C:2002:462, para 39.
[287] *Gaydarov*, para 41; referring 'to that effect' to Case C-69/10 *Samba Diouf*, EU:C:2011:524, para 57.
[288] *Gaydarov*, para 41, referring 'to that effect' to *Heylens*, para 15 and Joined Cases C-372/09 and C-373/09 *Peñarroja Fa*, EU:C:2011:156, para 63.

cases where legal remedies are not available to their own nationals, but it guarantees equality of treatment'.[289] It also advised that 'legal remedies may include suspension of the measure, although according to the Court of Justice Article 8 does not contain any specific obligation to this effect'.[290] Additionally, on the ruling in *Royer* that a decision ordering expulsion should not be carried out (except in urgent cases) before the person concerned could complete the formalities necessary to avail of a remedy, the Commission suggested that '[t]his does not mean that a person is necessarily entitled to remain in the territory of the State concerned throughout the duration of the proceedings initiated by him. In the light of the principle of proportionality, a measure with suspensory effect should be more readily available to those already resident in the country rather than to persons who have recently entered the country. In the case of residents immediate implementation of an expulsion order should be exceptional and there should be particularly strong grounds for that decision'.[291] In *Yiadom*, where seven months had elapsed between the admission of the applicant to the host State and a subsequent decision refusing him entry, the Court commented that if the host State 'has accepted the physical presence of that national in its territory for a period which is manifestly longer than is required for such an investigation, it can also accept that national's presence during the time needed for him to exercise the rights of appeal'.[292] That ruling has resonance with the theme of responsibility for tolerated citizens highlighted in Chapter 7.

Article 31 of Directive 2004/38 now reflects, along with the other provisions presented in this part of the chapter, the central objective that 'judicial redress procedures are always available':[293]

Article 31

Procedural safeguards

1. The persons concerned shall have access to judicial and, where appropriate, administrative redress procedures in the host Member State to appeal against or seek review of any decision taken against them on the grounds of public policy, public security or public health.
2. Where the application for appeal against or judicial review of the expulsion decision is accompanied by an application for an interim order to suspend enforcement of that decision, actual removal from the territory may not take place until such time as the decision on the interim order has been taken, except:
    – where the expulsion decision is based on a previous judicial decision; or
    – where the persons concerned have had previous access to judicial review; or

---

[289] Communication on grounds of public policy, public security or public health (n 29) para 3.5.1; referring to referring to Joined Cases C-65/95 and C-111/95 *Shingara and Radiom*, EU:C:1997:300, para 20; Joined Cases C-297/88 and C-197/89 *Dzodzi*, EU:C:1990:360, para 60; and Case 98/79 *Pecastaing*, EU:C:1980:69, paras 10–11.

[290] Communication on grounds of public policy, public security or public health (n 29) para 3.5.1; referring to *Pecastaing*, paras 12–13 and Case C-175/94 *Gallagher*, EU:C:1995:415.

[291] Communication on grounds of public policy, public security or public health (n 29) para 3.5.1; referring to Case 48/75 *Royer*, EU:C:1976:57, para 60.

[292] Case C-357/98 *Yiadom*, EU:C:2000:604, para 41.

[293] Original proposal (n 67) 20.

- where the expulsion decision is based on imperative grounds of public security under Article 28(3).
3. The redress procedures shall allow for an examination of the legality of the decision, as well as of the facts and circumstances on which the proposed measure is based. They shall ensure that the decision is not disproportionate, particularly in view of the requirements laid down in Article 28.
4. Member States may exclude the individual concerned from their territory pending the redress procedure, but they may not prevent the individual from submitting his/her defence in person, except when his/her appearance may cause serious troubles to public policy or public security or when the appeal or judicial review concerns a denial of entry to the territory.

The Council emphasised similarly, in its common position, that 'there must always be judicial redress possibilities' and that administrative redress is '*also* possible if it is provided for by the host Member State'.[294] However, as regards interim arrangements, the exceptions in Article 31(2) were also added by the Council.[295]

In its original proposal, the Commission considered that Article 31(3) of the Directive 'mak[es] it clear that the national court's job is to review not only the legality of the contested decision (which is of limited importance in such cases), but also the facts which form the basis for it'.[296] It then linked Article 31(4) to case law of the Court of Justice,[297] but the Council introduced the 'exception to the principle of submitting one's defence in person, if the appearance may cause serious troubles to public policy or public security or when the appeal or review concerns a refusal of entry to the territory'.[298] In ZZ, the Court confirmed that Article 31 'obliges the Member States to lay down, in domestic law, the measures necessary to enable Union citizens and members of their families to have access to judicial *and, where appropriate*, administrative redress procedures to appeal against or seek review of any decision restricting their right to move and reside freely in the Member States on the grounds of public policy, public security or public health'.[299]

4.3 Article 32: Duration of Exclusion Orders

Similarly to Article 15(3),[300] considered in Chapter 6, Article 32 of Directive 2004/38 highlights by inference that Member States have the capacity not only to expel a Union citizen from their territory, but also to set conditions of *exclusion* in consequence:

---

[294] Common Position (n 77) 27 (emphasis added); see further, Commission communication (n 77) para 3.3.2, noting that for Article 31(1), 'the common position confirms the obligation on the Member States to always provide for the possibility of judicial redress'.
[295] Common Position (n 77) 28; in its subsequent Communication, the Commission accepted the exceptions, 'taking the view that the principle (sic) objective of the provision is intact: to guarantee individuals the possibility of actually appealing against a removal decision, by ensuring that they cannot be removed before they have had the opportunity to lodge an appeal' (n 77, para 3.3.2).
[296] Original proposal (n 67) 22; referring to Joined Cases 115 and 116/81 *Adoui and Cornuaille*, EU:C:1982:183, para 15.
[297] Original proposal (ibid); referring to Case 98/79 *Pecastaing*, EU:C:1980:69, para 13.
[298] Common Position (n 77) 32.
[299] Case C-300/11 ZZ, EU:C:2013:363, para 47.
[300] Article 15(3) of the Directive provides that '[t]he host Member State may not impose a ban on entry in the context of an expulsion decision to which paragraph 1 applies' (ie expulsion decisions taken on the grounds that a Member State national does not reside there lawfully, principally through becoming an unreasonable burden on the host State's social assistance system). See further, Chapters 6 and 7.

Article 32

Duration of exclusion orders

1. Persons excluded on grounds of public policy or public security may submit an application for lifting of the exclusion order after a reasonable period,[301] depending on the circumstances, and in any event after three years[302] from enforcement of the final exclusion order which has been validly adopted in accordance with Community law, by putting forward arguments to establish that there has been a material change in the circumstances which justified the decision ordering their exclusion.
   The Member State concerned shall reach a decision on this application within six months of its submission.[303]
2. The persons referred to in paragraph 1 shall have no right of entry to the territory of the Member State concerned while their application is being considered.

In the original proposal for the Directive, the draft of what is now Article 32(1) sought to establish that 'Member States may not issue orders excluding persons covered by this Directive from their territory for life', with the Commission indicating that the provision incorporated into the legislation a right already recognised by the Court of Justice, that is, 'prohibiting lifelong exclusion orders against people who have been expelled on grounds of public policy or public security'.[304] In its common position, the Council deleted that text, indicated that its contents were expressed in recital 27 already, and concluded that, '[i]n line with the case-law of the Court of Justice prohibiting Member States from issuing orders excluding for life persons covered by this Directive from their territory, the right of Union citizens and their family members who have been excluded from the territory of a Member State to submit a fresh application after a reasonable period, and in any event after a three year period from enforcement of the final exclusion order, should be confirmed'.[305] Article 32(2) was considered by the Commission to be 'needed to avoid leaving the way open for abuses of the system'.[306] However, its 1999 Communication on Directive 64/221, the Commission had indicated the 'problem in a number of cases where a Member State refuses re-entry or the reversal of the expulsion order by citing as grounds for refusal the existence of an earlier expulsion order, which had been issued a number of years previously. For example, the cases of third-country national family members of Union citizens, who at the time of the previous decision were not beneficiaries of [Union] law, deserve re-examination solely on the basis of the change of status, which is indeed a new factor to be taken into consideration in the re-evaluation'.[307]

---

[301] In circumstances where a Member State may not impose a ban on re-entry, the Court has developed a concept of 'genuine and effective termination of residence' to prevent the undermining of the expulsion decision per se; see Case C-719/19 *FS*, EU:C:2021:506, discussed in Chapter 6.

[302] The Commission originally proposed a period of two years, changed to three years by the Council and accepted as 'reasonable' by the Commission in its subsequent Communication (n 77, para 3.3.2).

[303] The Commission originally proposed a period of three months, changed to six months—as a 'more reasonable timescale'—by the European Parliament (n 76, Amendment 86); also acknowledged as 'more realistic' by the Council in its common position (n 77, 28).

[304] Original proposal (n 67) 22; referring to Joined Cases 115 and 116/81 *Adoui and Cornuaille*, EU:C:1982:183, para 12 and Case C-348/96 *Calfa*, EU:C:1999:6.

[305] Common Position (n 77) 32.

[306] Original proposal (n 67) 23; referring to *Adoui and Cornuaille*, para 12.

[307] Communication on grounds of public policy, public security or public health (n 29) para 3.5.2.

In *Byankov*, the Court confirmed that 'the safeguards imposed by the EU legislature in Article 32 of Directive 2004/38 are applicable to measures prohibiting citizens of the Union from leaving the territory of a Member State'[308]—with Advocate General Mengozzi conceding that 'Article 32 must therefore be interpreted beyond its letter'.[309] The contested measure had not been 'validly adopted in accordance with [Union] law', as is required by Article 32(1). In such cases, 'in the absence of relevant EU rules, it is, under the principle of procedural autonomy of the Member States, for the domestic legal system of each Member State to regulate the legal procedures designed to ensure the protection of the rights which individuals acquire under EU law provided, however, that they are not less favourable than those governing similar domestic situations (principle of equivalence) and that they do not render impossible in practice or excessively difficult the exercise of rights conferred by the European Union legal order (principle of effectiveness)'.[310]

The principle of equivalence 'requires that all the rules applicable to actions, including the prescribed time-limits, apply without distinction to actions based on infringement of EU law and those based on infringement of national law'; while the principle of effectiveness requires that national rules 'do not make it excessively difficult or impossible in practice to exercise the rights conferred by EU law'.[311] Assessing the contested national legislation in *Byankov* in light of the principle of effectiveness, and also the principle of sincere cooperation in Article 4(3) TEU, the Court concluded that that legislation, 'which makes no provision for regular review, maintains for an unlimited period a prohibition on leaving the territory and thereby perpetuates an infringement of the right laid down in Article 21(1) TFEU to move and reside freely within the territory of the Member States. In such circumstances, a prohibition of that kind is *the antithesis of the freedom conferred by Union citizenship to move and reside* within the territory of the Member States'.[312]

Additionally, even though Article 32 of the Directive was not directly applicable in the case, the Court underlined that because 'the EU legislature has placed an obligation on the Member States to ensure that it is possible for measures which prohibit a person from entering or leaving their territories to be reviewed, even where those measures have been validly adopted under EU law and even where they have... become final', it was 'all the more reason why that should be the case in relation to prohibitions on leaving the territory, such as that at issue before the referring court, which have not been validly adopted under EU law and are the antithesis of the freedom laid down in Article 21(1) TFEU'.[313] Neither did the Court consider, having regard to 'the importance which primary law accords to citizenship

---

[308] Case C-249/11 *Byankov*, EU:C:2012:608, para 67; on the basis that freedom of movement 'includes both the right for citizens of the Union to enter a Member State other than the one of origin and the right to leave the State of origin. As the Court has already had occasion to state, the fundamental freedoms guaranteed by the FEU Treaty would be rendered meaningless if the Member State of origin could, without due justification, prohibit its own nationals from leaving its territory in order to enter the territory of another Member State' (para 31).

[309] AG Mengozzi in *Byankov*, EU:C:2012:380, para 34 of the Opinion.

[310] *Byankov*, para 69; referring to Case C-91/08 *Wall*, EU:C:2010:182, para 63; Case C-312/93 *Peterbroeck*, EU:C:1995:437, para 12; Joined Cases C-392/04 and C-422/04 *i-21 Germany and Arcor*, EU:C:2006:586, para 57; and Case C-378/10 *VALE ÉpítÉsi*, EU:C:2012:440, para 48. AG Mengozzi also referred to the fact that 'to maintain a degree of legal stability, review as defined by Directive 2004/38 is limited to cases in which a "material change in the circumstances which justified the decision" ordering exclusion has taken place. That material change may lie in the fact that the public policy threat which the person concerned may have constituted is no longer present' (para 36 of the Opinion).

[311] *Byankov*, para 69 (emphasis added); referring to Case 63/08 *Pontin*, EU:C:2009:666, para 45; and Case C-591/10 *Littlewoods Retail and Others*, EU:C:2012:478, para 31.

[312] *Byankov*, para 79.

[313] ibid para 80.

of the Union', that the national rules could be justified by recourse to the principle of legal certainty.[314]

The Court provided further guidance on the principle of equivalence in *Bensada Benallal*—in that case, acknowledging that while Directive 2004/38 establishes 'a number of rules to be respected by Member States for the purpose of a possible limitation on the right of residence of an EU citizen ... it does not, by contrast, contain provisions concerning the detailed rules governing administrative and judicial procedures relating to a decision which results in the withdrawal of an EU citizen's residence permit'.[315] The dispute concerned the inadmissibility, under contested national rules, of pleas raised for the first time at the stage of an appeal on a point of law and which were not based on 'public policy'.

The Court clarified that the principle of equivalence 'requires that the national rule at issue be applied without distinction, whether the action is based on rights which individuals derive from EU law or whether it is based on an infringement of national law, where the purpose and cause of action are similar', emphasising that '[r]espect for that principle requires equal treatment of claims based on a breach of national law and of similar claims based on a breach of EU law'.[316] However, while 'it is for the national court to determine whether the right to be heard, as guaranteed by national law, satisfies the conditions required by national law for it to be classified as a matter of public policy',[317] the Court signalled that 'respect for the rights of the defence is, in all proceedings initiated against a person which are liable to culminate in a measure adversely affecting that person, a fundamental principle of EU law which must be guaranteed *even in the absence of any rules* governing the proceedings in question'.[318]

In *Petrea*, a registration certificate was issued by the Greek authorities to a Romanian national, but then withdrawn on the grounds that he was still subject to an exclusion order. The Court first reiterated the 'declaratory character' of a registration certificate issued under Article 8(2) of Directive 2004/38, meaning that 'the issue of that document cannot, in itself, give rise to a legitimate expectation on the part of the person concerned in his right to stay on the territory of the Member State concerned'.[319] It added that nothing in the order of reference indicated any other conduct on the part of the national authorities that could have given rise to expectations concerning the applicant's right to stay 'by providing him with precise assurances' and that the withdrawal of the registration certificate had been justified 'by legitimate reasons, in particular by the fact that it was issued in error'.[320] The Court confirmed that the requirements in Articles 27(1), 27(2), and 28(1) of Directive 2004/38, 'which cover all expulsion decisions, apply therefore in particular to exclusion decisions which are expressly referred to by Article 32'.[321]

---

[314] ibid para 81.
[315] Case C-161/15 *Bensada Benallal*, EU:C:2016:175, para 23.
[316] ibid para 29; referring to Case C-93/12 *Agrokonsulting-04*, EU:C:2013:432, para 39 and Case C-69/14 *Târşia*, EU:C:2015:662, para 34.
[317] *Bensada Benallal*, para 34.
[318] ibid para 33 (emphasis added), in the context of 'enabl[ing] the referring court to determine whether the plea alleging infringement of the right to be heard in EU law is similar to a plea alleging infringement of such a right in [national] law' and referring to Case C-287/02 *Commission v Spain*, EU:C:2005:368, para 37.
[319] Case C-184/16 *Petrea*, EU:C:2017:684, para 35. Conversely, 'the exclusion order produces its effects notwithstanding the fact that the Greek authorities issued that certificate to Mr Petrea' (AG Szpunar in *Petrea*, EU:C:2017:324, para 45 of the Opinion).
[320] *Petrea*, paras 36 and 37.
[321] ibid para 41.

However, while the Directive does not expressly address situations in which someone re-enters the territory of a Member State in infringement of an exclusion order, the 'entirety of the provisions' and especially Article 32 demonstrate that Member States 'possess the power to ensure compliance' with exclusion orders. In particular, it is 'expressly apparent from the wording of [Articles 32(1) and 32(2)] that Directive 2004/38 in no way prevents a Member State from adopting a return decision in relation to a person who applied for the lifting of the exclusion order imposed on him, in accordance with Article 32(1) of that directive, as long as the examination of that application has been concluded with a successful outcome for the applicant'.[322] In such circumstances, national authorities are not required to verify again whether the conditions in Articles 27 and 28 are satisfied, since 'it follows from the very nature of an exclusion order that it remains in force as long as it has not been lifted and that the mere finding that it has been infringed allows those authorities to adopt a new removal decision against the person concerned'.[323]

With respect to challenging a return decision—exemplifying the blending of EU rights and principles, on the one hand, and national procedures for their safeguard, on the other—the Court determined that 'EU law in no way precludes national legislation from providing that it is not possible to rely, against an individual measure, such as a return decision, on the unlawfulness of an exclusion order which has become final, either because the time limit for bringing an action against that order expired, or because the action brought against it was dismissed'.[324] On the contrary, reasonable time limits are an accepted element of legal certainty, 'which protects both the individual and the administrative authority concerned'.[325]

4.4 Article 33: Expulsion as a Penalty or Legal Consequence

Finally, Article 33 of the Directive connects back to the discussion in Section 3 on the intersection of the EU legal framework on expulsion and a Member State's criminal law powers:

Article 33

Expulsion as a penalty or legal consequence

1. Expulsion orders may not be issued by the host Member State as a penalty or legal consequence of a custodial penalty, unless they conform to the requirements of Articles 27, 28 and 29.

---

[322] ibid para 46. The Court also confirmed in para 47 that this applied in the circumstances of the case ie where 'the person concerned re-entered the Member State concerned without having applied for the lifting of the exclusion order imposed on him'. See further, AG Szpunar (EU:C:2017:324), para 38 of the Opinion: '[i]f the authorities of that Member State were required to assess again whether the individual could be removed on grounds of public policy, the situation of a person to whom an exclusion order applies would be the same as a Union citizen who had never been the subject of a measure of that kind. With a view to curbing such possible 'misuse', an exclusion order seeks to restrict the rights of entry' (referring to Joined Cases 115 and 116/81 *Adoui and Cornuaille*, EU:C:1982:183, para 12).
[323] *Petrea*, para 48.
[324] ibid para 59.
[325] ibid para 60. However, as indicated above, if the requirements of Article 30 are not met, 'the principle of effectiveness precludes the conclusion that the time limit for bringing an action against the first order had expired, and the unlawfulness of that order could still be raised in support of the action against the second order' (para 62).

2. If an expulsion order, as provided for in paragraph 1, is enforced more than two years after it was issued, the Member State shall check that the individual concerned is currently and genuinely a threat to public policy or public security and shall assess whether there has been any material change in the circumstances since the expulsion order was issued.

In its original proposal for the Directive, the Commission invoked the *Cowan* case to explain Article 33(1), pointing out that while 'in principle criminal legislation and the rules of criminal procedure, among which the national provision in issue is to be found, are matters for which the Member States are responsible, the Court has consistently held … that [Union] law sets certain limits to their power. Such legislative provisions may not discriminate against persons to whom [Union] law gives the right to equal treatment or restrict the fundamental freedoms guaranteed by [Union] law'.[326] The Commission had proposed including, in Article 31(2), a more general obligation, that is, '[b]efore enforcing an expulsion order, the Member State shall check that the individual concerned is currently and genuinely a threat to public policy and public security and shall assess whether there has been any change in the circumstances since the expulsion decision was taken'. However, the Council 'clarified' in its common position that 'the assessment of whether there has been any change of circumstances since the expulsion decision was taken shall be made only if the expulsion order is enforced more than two years after it was issued'.[327] For the Commission, this clarification was 'positive and totally in line with the objective of the provision, which is to require the Member States to examine the situation when, between the decision to expel and the actual enforcement of the decision, there is a long period during which the circumstances on which the decision was based may have changed'.[328]

Nevertheless, the Court observed the converse point in *E*—that 'Article 33(1) of Directive 2004/38 provides for the possibility, for the host Member State, to adopt, in conformity, *inter alia*, with the requirements of Article 27 of that directive, an expulsion order as a consequence of a custodial sentence'; and so the 'Union legislator therefore provided for the possibility for Member States to adopt an expulsion order concerning a person sentenced to a custodial sentence, if it is established that his conduct represents a genuine, present threat affecting one of the fundamental interests of the society of that Member State'.[329] The scope of that 'possibility' is limited by the requirements of the Directive: but it provides a conceivable course of action for the Member States, nevertheless.

5. Concluding Remarks

Union citizenship pierces national immigration powers in almost every respect, but perhaps most visibly through considering the comprehensive, rights-driven EU legal framework that curtails State discretion and State preferences about who 'belongs' on its territory. Three main themes can be drawn from the discussion in this chapter.

---

[326] Original proposal (n 67) 23 referring to Case 186/87 *Cowan*, EU:C:1989:47, para 19. See further, Chapter 2.
[327] Common Position (n 77) 32.
[328] Commission communication (n 77) para 3.3.2.
[329] Case C-193/16 *E*, EU:C:2017:542, para 25.

First, this part of EU citizenship law embodies, at one level, the 'ideal' Union citizenship story—principles established in foundational legislation and case law on the free movement of persons, enriched conceptually through the creation of Union citizenship, functionally through the adoption of Directive 2004/38, and constitutionally through growing engagement with general principles of EU law and the Charter of Fundamental Rights. However, second, the success of the system mapped by the Directive and elaborated in the case law depends on its implementation. National powers and practices have not yet adjusted to the extent that EU citizenship law requires, and there are signs that the expectations of the Union are changeable too. For example, we saw in this chapter an uncommon judicial/legislative dynamic compared to Chapter 7. In the discussion on lawful residence, the Court of Justice was usually more criticised for side-lining *restrictive* choices made by the EU legislator in order to extend greater protection for Union citizens. However, in the context of expulsion, greater protection in the Directive was sidelined in the case law in some situations. The latter are marked by deep sensitivity and either clashing or uncertain perspectives on core values. Nevertheless, case law that overlooks the enhanced protection against expulsion that the legislator did conceive for certain situationss compromises the requirement in Articles 20(2) and 21(1) TFEU that conditions and limits on the right to move and reside must be expressly provided for in the Treaties or in legislation.

Finally, the depreciating of State borders through the construction and significance of the territory of the Union was introduced in Chapter 2 and considered further in Chapter 5 with respect to Union citizenship and the home State. In this chapter, Member State borders come sharply back into view; in literal, legal, and normative senses. EU citizenship law guards the parameters, but it does not take down the fences. The very possibility of expelling and excluding Union citizens therefore highlights, above all, fundamental and unresolved questions about Union citizenship itself and about the Union as the place within which that citizenship is determined and experienced; about identity, values, integration, and responsibility—about, most fundamentally, *home*.

Further Reading

S Coutts, 'A contingent citizenship – Union citizenship and expulsion' in S Mantu, P Minderhoud, and E Guild (eds), *EU Citizenship and Free Movement Rights: Taking Supranational Citizenship Seriously* (Brill 2019).

S Coutts, 'Supranational public wrongs: the limitations and possibilities of European criminal law and a European community' (2017) 54 Common Market Law Review 771.

K Hamenstädt, 'Expulsion and "legal otherness" in times of growing nationalism' (2020) 45 European Law Review 452.

M Meduna, '*Scelestus europeus sum*': what protection against expulsion does EU citizenship offer to European offenders?' in D Kochenov (ed), *EU Citizenship and Federalism: The Role of Rights* (CUP 2017) 395.

Index

For the benefit of digital users, indexed terms that span two pages (e.g., 52–53) may, on occasion, appear on only one of those pages.

A *(Soins de santé publics)* 284–85, 286, 410
absences, extended 469
abuse of rights and/or fraud 69, 110–11, 161, 262–63, 340–50, 393–94, 533
  see also deception; marriage of convenience
accident at work or occupational disease 455
accountability 216, 219–20
acquired rights 452, 456
'additional' citizenship 40–41
administrative formalities 296–317
  family members (not Union citizens) 309–17
    entry right 309–10
    residence right 311–17
  registration requirements 302–4
    family members 304–5
  sufficient resources 306–9
  Union citizens 301–9
  see also under expulsion on grounds of public policy, public security or public health
adoptive relationships 172–73
Adoui and Cornuaille 504–5, 541–4
adversarial principle 543–45
agenda-setting mechanism 217
Agreement on surrender 105–6
aid, amount of 320, 321
Åkerberg Fransson 250, 432, 433
Akrich 159–60, 161–62, 341–42, 496–97
Aladzhov 54–55, 513
Alarape and Tijani 385–86, 461–62, 463
Algerian *kafala* system 172–74, 183–84
Alimanovic 59, 370, 374, 375–76, 403
  economically active citizens and lawful residence 408–9
  economically autonomous citizens and lawful residence 411–13
  equal treatment and lawful residence 381–82, 394–99, 403–4, 416–17, 418, 438
  jobseekers and lawful residence 415–16
  lawful residence within first three months 406
  residence based on national law 419
  unlawful residence 426, 428–29
Alokpa and Moudoulou 238–39, 243–44, 245, 249, 480
Anagnostakis 212, 213–14
Ankara Agreement 537
annulment of marriage *see* divorce, annulment of marriage or termination of registered partnership
Antonissen 28–29, 291–96, 366–68, 376

area of freedom, security and justice (AFSJ) 2, 9, 45, 89, 94–96, 104–6, 281, 472, 527
arranged marriages 150
association arrangements, special 195
asylum system 105–6
asymmetric movement 63–67
Aubriet 476–77
Austria 21–22, 82, 110–12, 118–19, 237, 380, 386–87, 477–78

B and Vomero 467, 534, 535
Bajiratari 281–83
Banger 141, 168, 183, 184–85, 494–95
Baumbast 45, 58, 155, 156, 157, 235, 239, 280, 283–85
  equal treatment and lawful residence 358, 364–65, 380–82, 397–98, 403–4, 412–13, 419, 421, 438
Baumbast and R 484–85
Belgium 21–22, 61, 65–66, 79, 131–32, 152, 360–61, 369, 480, 488–89
beneficiaries 148–49
benefits
  child 47–48, 362–63, 390, 399, 412–13, 475
  minimex (non-contributory social benefit) 289
  non-contributory cash 338, 393, 395, 400–1, 433
  unemployment 291
  see also social security and social assistance
Bickel and Franz 35
Bidar 38, 55–56, 92, 287–88, 363–64, 376–77, 378, 386–87, 413, 438–39
bilateral arrangements 67, 97–98, 99–100
blackmail and threats of divorce 336–37, 339
Bogendorff von Wolffersdorff 38, 512
Bouchereau 503, 504–5
Boukhalfa 37, 95–96
Bragança Linares Verruga 378, 475–76
Bressol 57, 61, 63, 65–66
Brey 53, 56–57, 58, 308
  equal treatment and lawful residence 381–82, 386–88, 389, 393, 394–95, 397–98, 400–1, 403–4, 405, 411–13, 430, 438
Brown 363
Bulgaria 267–69, 513
BY 101, 102–3
Byandov 549

Calfa 506
Carpenter 479–81
CG 419–23, 428, 435–37, 438, 458–59, 478–79

change in circumstances, material 504, 531–32, 548, 552
Charter of Fundamental Rights 27, 69, 71, 85–89, 103–4, 105
  citizenship rights as fundamental rights 86–87
  equal treatment and lawful residence 431–37
  family members 139
  nationality 114, 119–20, 136
  residence rights 248–52
    family members 241–43
  union citizenship and fundamental rights 88–89
Chavez-Vilchez 171, 244, 245, 247, 250, 256
Chenchooliah 298–99
child benefit 47–48, 362–63, 390, 399, 412–13, 475
child custody 333–34, 336
child exploitation, abuse and trafficking 173
childcare 479–81
children/minors
  access rights 333–34
  Charter of Fundamental Rights 436
  connecting factors 82–83
  dependent relatives 174–76
  direct descendants under 21 171
  dual nationality 131–32, 196
  expulsion and expulsion protection 506–7, 508–9, 527, 528
  family member residence rights 230–31, 235, 239–40, 246, 247, 250–52, 254
  family members 139–40, 148–49, 155
  foster children and foster parents with temporary custody 172–73
  guardianship 172–74, 183–84
  nationality 114–15, 116–17
  permanent residence 457
  residence of more than three months 281–83, 286, 289–90
  right to remain in education system 74–75, 330, 332, 428–29, 483–85
  rights 88–89
  unmarried partners 169
  see also Algerian *kafala* system
child's best interests
  Charter of Fundamental Rights 431–32
  dependent relatives 184
  direct descendants under 21 171
  expulsion and expulsion immunity 528
  family member residence rights 242–43, 245–46, 251–52, 253–54
  family members 140–41, 150, 185
  home Member State 259–60
  nationality 115–16
Circular on Foreign Nationals 244
circular migration 482–83
  see also leavers and returners
citizen choice 6
Civil Protection Mechanism 225
clarity and precision criteria 45
Clauder 441, 447–48, 456
close connection 473–74

Collins 56–57, 91, 130, 368–70, 374–75, 396–98, 438–39
Coman 49, 70, 96–97, 151–54, 163–64, 268–69, 494–95
Commission Communication and Handbook 346
Commission v Austria 61–62, 63, 64, 379–80, 381, 407, 413, 431, 432, 478
Commission v Belgium 44, 53, 282–83, 293, 367–68, 369
Commission v Greece 402–3
Commission v Netherlands 290, 365, 378–79, 403, 409–10, 413, 477
Commission v Spain 309
Commission v UK 61–62, 303, 319, 321, 350
  equal treatment and lawful residence in host State 380–82, 399–404, 410–13, 429–30
Commissioners for Her Majesty's Revenue and Customs (Assurance maladie complète) 284–85, 286, 449
Committee on Culture, Youth, Education, the Media and Sport 445
Committee of the Regions 15
Committee on Women's Rights and Equal Opportunities 326
common values 105–6
competence 27, 43–44, 93–94
  asymmetric movement 67
  entry right 268–69
  European Citizens Initiative (ECI) 210–11, 212
  family member residence rights 242–43, 258
  home Member State 259
  nationality 110, 111, 113–14, 115, 116, 118, 136
  voting rights 196, 200–1
comprehensive sickness insurance 36–37
  administrative formalities 302–3, 307
  death or departure of Union citizen 330, 331
  divorce, annulment of marriage or termination of registered partnership 333, 338
  economically active citizens and lawful residence 408–9
  economically autonomous citizens and lawful residence 410
  equal treatment and lawful residence 357, 362–63, 364–65, 438
  family member residence rights 239
  family members and permanent residence 449–50
  jobseekers, equal treatment and lawful residence 365
  no right to reside 392, 396, 403–4
  permanent residence 457
  proportionality 55, 57–58
  residence right of more than three months 274–75, 277, 279, 280, 283–86, 287, 289
  students and lawful residence 413
compulsory military service 443, 452–53
confidentiality 101–2
conflict rules 388, 473
connecting factors
  dependent relatives 178–79

INDEX 557

family member residence rights 227
   insufficient 227
   nationality 111–12, 122
   residence based on national law 422
   voting rights 196
connection
   close 473–74
   intrinsic 236, 255, 259
   sufficient 53, 78–81, 82, 129–30, 227
   see also establishing connection with EU law; political connection
continuous residence 452–53, 458
   see also residence duration
Convention on the Transfer of Sentenced Persons (1983) 103
coordination and cooperation 4, 66, 106, 136, 347
   diplomatic and consular protection 221, 222–25
   see also sincere cooperation
core family members 139–40, 146, 148
corruption 121
Costa v ENEL 17
Court of Justice (interpreting law) 8, 19–23
Covid-19 pandemic 512
Cowan 34, 552
crime against humanity 521–22
crime against peace 521–22
crime against the person 517
criminal conduct 99, 530–31, 532–33, 535–36
criminal convictions 102, 253–54, 365
   previous 501, 503–4, 516, 517–18
criminal investigation file 101–2
criminal offences 514, 515, 530–32, 537
   gravity of 119–20
criminality, petty and persistent 517–18
Croatia 105–6
CS 19, 93, 255
cultural aspects of migration 29, 62–63
cultural diversity 89, 472
custodial sentence 103
   see also imprisonment
Cyprus 121
Czech Republic 21–22

Dakneviciute 328
Dano 22, 58–59, 61–62, 350
   Charter of Fundamental Rights 431, 433–37
   economically active citizens and lawful residence 407–8
   economically autonomous citizens and lawful residence 411–12
   equal treatment derogations 375–76
   equal treatment and lawful residence 361–62, 381–82, 390–95, 397–98, 400–1, 403–4, 416–17, 418, 438
   lawful residence within first three months 406
   no right to reside (*Commission v UK*) 403–4
   residence based on national law 419, 421
   students and lawful residence 414
   unlawful residence 427, 430

Dassonville 33
data protection 305
death or departure of citizen
   divorce, annulment of marriage or termination of registered partnership 336–37
   family members 143, 329, 415
   retention of right to reside 317–18, 330–32
   retention of worker or self-employment status 322–23
   unlawful residence 428–29
debt recovery 513
deception 111, 112
   see also abuse of rights and/or fraud
declaratory character of rights 297, 303, 304, 313, 361, 454, 459, 467–68, 469, 550
degree of integration 53
Deha Altiner and Ravn 159, 494
deliberative democracy 189
Delvigne 188, 196–98, 199–201, 213–14
Delvigne II 202
democracy 216
   deliberative 189
   participatory 6, 45, 189, 205–6, 216–17, 219–20
   representative 6, 45, 189, 192, 219–20
denial of right to enter 340
Denmark 21–22, 379
dependency 85, 188–89
   of adult 251, 252
   due to disability 251
   economical, legal, administrative and emotional 172, 183–84, 240–41, 247
   family member residence rights 242–43, 245–46, 248, 254–55, 256, 257, 258–59
   genuine and stable 181
   intersectional 241
   material 175, 177–78, 182, 240–41
   nature or duration of 181
   physical 183–84, 240–41, *see also* serious health grounds requiring personal care of family member
   real 176–77
   relatives 148–49, 174–85
      direct relatives in descending and ascending lines 175–79
      'other family members' 179–85
   requirement 239–41
   see also children/minors
Depesme and Kerrou 169–70
Dereci 236–37, 238, 239–42, 244, 245, 247, 249
derived residence rights 244, 246–47, 250
   family members 251, 252–53, 255–59
   leavers and returners 490–93, 494–95
detention 225–26, 503, 506
D'Hoop 52, 369, 370, 488
Diallo 311–13
Dias 92, 384, 385–86, 454, 459, 460–62, 463, 533
Diatta 155–56, 158, 451–52
diplomatic and consular protection 3, 4, 5, 96, 116, 127, 188, 220–26

direct descendants and direct relatives in ascending line 148, 240–41, 289–90, 314
direct descendants over 21 174–75, 176–77, 240–41
direct descendants under 21 148, 171–74, 175, 314
direct effect 44–46, 76–77
Directive 2004/38 67–78
  aims and objectives 69–72
  conditions and limits, balancing rights with 75–78
  scope of application 72–75, 144–46
  see also under equal treatment and lawful residence; expulsion on grounds of public policy, public security or public health
disclosure 543–45
discrimination 82, 197, 227–28
  direct 49, 50–51, 87
  indirect 49–50, 61, 65–66, 387–88
  partial (differential) 63–66, 67
  restrictions 46–47, 48–49, 50–51
  reverse 83–84, 161–62, 228–29
  see also non-discrimination
diseases or disabilities 501, 511
dismissal 325
divorce, annulment of marriage or termination of registered partnership 155, 158, 332–34
  death or departure of Union citizen 332
  family members 143
  family members and retention of right to reside 329–30
  retention of right to reside 317– , 32–
domestic violence 333–34, 336, 337, 338–40, 436–37
double-lock mechanism 346–47
dual nationality 196
durable relationships 149, 162–63, 165–67, 168, 179
duration of residence 53, 320, 426, 428–29, 500
duress 522–23

E 518, 552
Echternach and Moritz 483, 484–85
economic free movement rights 30–33, 34
economic freedoms 28, 35–36, 87
Economic and Social Committee 4, 308–9, 517
economically active citizens
  and economic autonomy transition 36–37
  equal treatment and lawful residence 355, 365, 407–10
  exemptions and permanent residence 454–55, 456
  family member residence rights 479
  integration requirements: dual function 90
  multi-state life 477, 478
  residence right of more than three months 274, 276–79, 280
  residence right of up to three months 272–73
  rights to enter, reside and remain 261
  see also self-employed citizens; workers
economically autonomous citizens 90
  equal treatment and lawful residence 365, 409–13
  residence right of more than three months 274, 277–79
economically inactive citizens 16

administrative formalities 308–9
Directive 2004/38 69, 70, 71–72
economically autonomous citizens and lawful residence 410, 411, 412
equal treatment and lawful residence State 360–61, 362–63, 364, 373, 417–18
multi-state life 471
no right to reside 388–89
no right to reside (*Commission v UK*) 399–401
no right to reside (*Dano*) 391–92, 395
proportionality 56–57, 58–59, 61–62
residence based on national law 422–23
residence right of more than three months 276, 279–80, 283, 284–85, 286
unlawful residence 426–27, 429–30
see also jobseekers; pregnancy and childbirth; retirement and pensions; students; unemployment
education rights 35–36, 38, 54, 64, 67
EEA Agreement 72–73, 105–6, 127–28
EEA family permit 315
EEA nationals 106
EEA States 72–73, 74, 448
EEC-Turkey Association 538–39
effective remedy, right to 298–99, 540, 542
effectiveness principle 19–20, 84–85, 312–13, 541, 545, 549
Effler 215–16
EFTA Court 74
EFTA States 72–73, 106, 448
Eind 486–87, 490–91, 495–96
Elsen 474–75
Eman and Sevinger 193, 195, 196, 197, 198
Emergency Travel Document (ETD) 225–26
employment contract
  duration limitation 227–28
  fixed term 365–66
employment programmes, special 293
Emsland-Stärke 341
entry right 309–10
entry right see also under rights to enter, reside and remain
equal treatment 6, 14–15, 19–20, 32, 37, 38, 204–5
  abuse of rights and fraud 350
  administrative formalities 307
  asymmetric movement 63–64, 65, 67
  competence 93–94
  connecting factors 79
  diplomatic and consular protection 221
  direct descendants under 21 174
  Directive 2004/38 69, 74–75, 76–78
  divorce, annulment of marriage or termination of registered partnership 338, 339–40
  expulsion and expulsion immunity 512, 545–46, 550
  family member residence rights 254, 258
  family members 149–50
  family members and permanent residence 449
  incremental entitlement 76

INDEX

integration of law, place and values 98, 99–100
integration requirements: dual function 90, 91
language used in criminal proceedings 35
leavers and returners 483–84
legal residence 458–59, 461–62, 463
multi-state life 473–74, 476, 477–79
permanent residence 443–44, 446, 469
proportionality 58, 60
registered partners 163–64
residence right of more than three months 276–78, 280, 286, 287, 290, 291
residence right of up to three months 272–73
retention of right to reside 317–18, 321
retention of worker or self-employment status 323–24, 328, 329
rights to enter, reside and remain 261, 262–63, 266–67, 351
unmarried partners 169–70
voting rights 194, 195–96, 202, 203
see also equal treatment and lawful residence; non-discrimination
equal treatment and lawful residence 353–439
  case law foundations 358–65
  Directive 2004/38: Art. 24 370–81
    drafting history 372–74
    express derogations 374–80
    implicit derogations 380–81
  Directive 2004/38: revised framework 381–425
    Alimanovic 381–82, 394–99, 403–4
    Commission v UK 381–82, 399–404
    Dano 381–82, 390–95, 397–98, 400–1, 403–4
    family members 414–15
    jobseekers 415–16
    lawful residence: early case law 383–89
    lawful residence and economically active citizens 407–10
    lawful residence and economically autonomous citizens 409–13
    lawful residence within first three months 405–7
    no right to reside 382–404
    residing 405–16
    students 413–14
  implications 425–37
    Charter of Fundamental Rights 431–37
    unlawful residence: consequences 426–31
  jobseekers 365–70
  Regulation 492/2011: residence 416–18
  residence based on national law 419–25
  residence based on primary law 418–19
    Art. 21 TFEU 419
    Arts. 45 and 49 TFEU 418–19
equivalence principle 549–50
'equivalent to marriage' 163–64
establishing connection with EU law 78–84
  causal connection between rights exercised and impact of restrictions 78–81
  connecting factors and internal situations 81–84
establishment 29–30, 501
ethical standards 219–20

EU Citizenship Report (2020) 106–7, 203–4
EU legislator role (implementation of law) 16–18
EU-Canada Comprehensive Economic and Trade Agreement (CETA) 215–16
EU-Turkey Association Agreement 11–12, 73
EU-USA Agreement 99–100, 215–16
Eurojust 347
European arrest warrant (EAW) 11–12, 97–99, 100, 101, 104–6, 110–11, 117–18
European Citizens Initiative (ECI) 15, 45, 188, 190, 204–17
  Art. 3 207–9
  Art. 15 209–10
  emerging jurisprudence 210–17
  procedures and conditions 206–10
European Convention on Extradition (1957) 103, 105
European Convention for the Protection of Human Rights and Fundamental Freedoms (ECHR) 32, 85–86, 104–5, 192–93, 197–98
European Convention on Social and Medical Assistance 358
European External Action Service (EEAS) 224–25
European Ombudsman application rights 3, 4, 5, 15, 188, 190, 193–94, 204–5, 217–20
European Parliament Committee on Legal Affairs and the Internal Market 280
European Parliament Committee on Petitions (PETI) 15, 218
European Parliament, petitioning 1, 188, 190–91, 204–5, 217–19
European Parliament Rules of Procedure 218
Europol 347
exceptional circumstances 83–84, 145–46, 232, 243, 247, 257, 336–37
  abuse of rights and fraud 343, 346
  dependent relatives 178–79
  European Ombudsman 220
  expulsion and expulsion immunity 511, 529, 531, 543–44
  family member residence rights 251
  residence rights 187
exit rights 263–64
expulsion and expulsion immunity 62, 141–42, 514
  abuse of rights and fraud 341, 345–46
  administrative formalities 297–300, 301, 468, 520
  continuous residence 458
  Directive 2004/38 73
  economically autonomous citizens and lawful residence 411–12
  equal treatment and lawful residence 355, 360, 365, 439
  family members 149–50
  fundamental rights 88
  imperative grounds 529–32, 533, 537, 545
  integration requirements: dual function 90, 92
  jobseekers and lawful residence 416
  legal residence 460, 466–67
  no right to reside 385
  permanent residence 442

expulsion and expulsion immunity (*cont.*)
  procedural safeguards 520
  residence right of more than three months 277–78, 295–96
  residence right of up to three months 271–72, 273
  retention of right to reside 317–18, 319–20
  serious grounds for expulsion 529–30, 531, 537, 545
  unlawful residence 426–27, 430
  see also expulsion on grounds of public policy, public security or public health
expulsion on grounds of public policy, public security or public health 262, 499–553
  Directive 2004/38: administrative formalities and procedural safeguards 501–2, 505–6, 508–9, 539–52
  Directive 2004/38: administrative formalities and procedural safeguards
    exclusion orders: duration 547–51
    expulsion as penalty or legal consequence 551–52
    notification of decisions 540–45
    procedural safeguards 500, 545–47
  Directive 2004/38: revised legal framework 508–39
  Directive 2004/38: revised legal framework
    assessment principles 516–26
    general principles 510–26
    protection against expulsion 517–39
    public health (defined) 511–12
    public policy and public security (defined) 512–16
  foundational principles 501–7
expulsion orders 53, 160, 291–92, 340, 518, 547–51
external border controls, asylum, immigration and prevention and combating of crime 45, 94–95
extradition 27, 50–51, 94–95, 97–103, 104–6, 117–18, 431–32

Fahimian 520–21
fair treatment 164
fair trial right 540
Familienkasse Niedersachsen-Bremen 406–7, 411
family circumstances 139–40, 241, 395, 506–7
family members 8, 16, 28, 36, 41, 139–85
  abuse of rights and fraud 348–50
  administrative formalities 296, 297–98, 299, 300–1, 302, 307, 468–69
  connecting factors 80–81, 83–84
  dependent relatives 174–85
    direct relatives in descending and ascending lines 175–79
    'other family members' 179–85
  derogations and justifications 50
  diplomatic and consular protection 222–23, 224–25
  direct descendants under age of 21 171–74
  Directive 2004/38 69, 71, 72, 73, 74–75, 76, 144–46
  dual nationality 134–35

economically active citizens and lawful residence 408–9
economically autonomous citizens and lawful residence 410–11
effectiveness of rights 84–85
entry right 264, 265–66, 267–68
equal treatment and lawful residence 365, 371, 372, 373, 414–15, 417–18
exemptions and permanent residence 455, 456
exit right 263, 264
expulsion and expulsion immunity 500, 508–10, 517, 518–20, 521–22, 523–24, 526–27, 534, 539–40, 541, 548
extended family circle 146, 149
fundamental rights 88
guiding principles 140–43
integration of law, place and values 94, 96–97
integration requirements: dual function 89–90, 91
jobseekers, equal treatment and lawful residence 365
lawful residence within first three months 405
leavers and returners 482–83, 489, 490–94, 496
legal residence 460, 461–62, 463–65
move and reside rights 479–82
multi-state life 473–74
nationality 109, 112–13, 114–16
no right to reside 383–84, 385–86, 401–2
non-Union citizens
  administrative formalities of host state 309–17
  entry right 309–10
  residence right 311–17
partners other than spouses 149–50, 162–71
  registered partners 163–64
  unmarried partners 164–71
permanent residence 443, 447–52, 469
proportionality 55
registration requirements 304–5
residence permits 42
residence right of more than three months 274–75, 277, 279–80, 281–83, 287, 289–91, 294
residence right of up to three months 269, 272–73
residence rights *see under* home Member State
retention of right to reside 317–18, 319, 329–40
rights to enter, reside and remain 261–63
serious health grounds requiring personal care of 149, 179, 180, 181, 182–83
spouses 148–49, 150–62
  'in the host State' definition 155–59
  same-sex spouses 151–55
  status under host State immigration rules 159–62
students and lawful residence 413
unlawful residence 428–29
withdrawal from EU 127–28
see also children/minors; dependency; direct descendants; registered partnerships; spouses
family and professional life 115–16, 129–30
family relationships 90, 296
family reunification 8–10, 28–29, 33
  abuse of rights and fraud 345–46

divorce, annulment of marriage or termination of registered partnership 338
expulsion and expulsion immunity 521–22
family member residence rights 236, 246–47, 248, 252, 256–57
family members and permanent residence 447–48
leavers and returners 486–87, 496–97
residence right of more than three months 275–76
financial procedures for reimbursement costs 225–26
financial solidarity 55–57, 280, 288–89, 363
fines *see* sanctions
Finland 103–4
forced marriages 150
Förster 60, 326, 377–79, 381, 386–87, 403–4
foster children and foster parents with temporary custody 172–73
France 21–22, 64, 130–31, 200, 488, 522
 Criminal Code 197–98, 199
fraud *see* abuse of rights and/or fraud
Fredriksen, H.H. 106
free movement and residence rights 3, 5, 6–7, 33–38, 200–4
free riding 57
freedom from discrimination *see* non-discrimination
frontier workers
 asymmetric movement 63–64
 dual nationality 130–31
 equal treatment derogations 378–79
 family members 150
 multi-state life 472, 473–77
 residence right of more than three months 275–76
 unmarried partners 169
FS 271, 273, 295–96, 299, 339, 411–12, 426–27, 458
functional or purposive category differences 355
fundamental rights 32–33, 88–89
 Article 21 44–45
 citizenship rights as 86–87
 derogations and justifications 48, 49
 family member residence rights 229, 252, 253–54

Garcia Avello 79, 83–84, 93–94, 131–32, 133–34, 196
García-Nieto 380, 398–99, 405, 438
Gaydarov 545
genuine enjoyment of rights 229, 231, 234, 236–37, 241–42, 243–44, 246, 250, 259
genuine link requirement 52, 91–92
 equal treatment derogations 374–75, 377, 379–80
 equal treatment and lawful residence 363–64, 369
 multi-state life 476
 nationality 115, 116–17, 121, 123–24
 no right to reside 393, 399–400
genuine, present and sufficiently serious threat 504–5, 512, 513, 516, 518, 521–23, 531–32, 537, 552
genuine residence 142, 153–54
Germany 21–22, 30, 80–81, 82, 99–100, 101
 equal treatment and lawful residence 358, 359, 430
 expulsion and expulsion immunity 512, 537, 538–39
 lawful residence within first three months 406–7
 Member State nationality 110–12, 130–31

multi-state life 475
 no right to reside 390, 393–94, 395
 permanent residence 460–61, 466
 rights to enter, reside and remain 305
Gibraltar 193–94, 197
Giersch 475–77
Gilly 130–31
Givane 322, 326
GMA 294, 295–96, 366–67, 376, 415–16
good administration, right to 86
good faith 92–93, 112
Government of the French Community and Walloon Government 83, 227, 228–29
gradual system 355
Gravier 65
Greece 21–22, 550
Green Paper (2006) 222–23
Grzelczyk 55–56, 57–58, 280, 287–88, 289
 economically autonomous citizens and lawful residence 412–13
 equal treatment derogations 374, 377, 380–81
 equal treatment and lawful residence 353, 358, 359–60, 361–63, 368, 373–74, 381–82
 lawful residence within first three months 407
 no right to reside 390, 403–4
 residence based on national law 419
 residence based on primary law 419
 rights to enter, reside and remain 280, 287–88, 289
 students and lawful residence 413, 414
 unlawful residence 426
guardianship of minors 172–74, 183–84
Gusa 325, 326

habitual residence 319, 387–88, 399–401, 406–7
Hartmann 475–77
heard, right to be 543–44, 550
HF 522
High Level Panel Report (1997) 37–38, 71
Hillion, C. 106
Hirst v United Kingdom (No 2) 197–98
Hirvonen 22
home Member State 187–260
 political connection 187–88, 189–226, 259
  Art. 10 189–90
  Art. 11 190
  diplomatic and consular protection in third countries 220–26
  European Citizens Initiative (ECI) 205–17
  European Ombudsman, application to 219–20
  European Parliament, petitioning 217–19
  voting rights 190–204
 residence rights 243–59
  Charter of Fundamental Rights 248–52
  Dereci and *Chavez-Vilchez* 248–51
  eligibility assessment 243–47
  limits 252–59
  family members 226–59
  see also *Ruiz Zambrano*
homosexual couples 163–64
 see also same-sex marriage

honorary consuls 224
housing assistance 376
Huber 305, 437–38
human dignity 33, 104, 152, 153, 185, 316, 329–30, 428–29, 433, 523
human trafficking 347
'humanising' aspect 28–29, 140–41
Humbel and Edel 483
'hybrid' protection 13–14

Ibrahim 489
Iceland 105–6, 129
identity cards or passports
    administrative formalities 300, 301, 302–3, 304, 311, 313
    Directive 2004/38 76
    entry right 264, 266, 267–68
    exit right 263, 264, 265–66
    expiry 501
    expulsion and expulsion immunity 516
    integration requirements: dual function 91
    jobseekers, equal treatment and lawful residence 365
    nationality 115
    residence right of more than three months 290–91, 295
    residence right of up to three months 269, 405
Iida 80–81, 155, 156, 157, 158, 236, 451–52, 480
illegal immigration 316, 348–49
illness or accident 443, 452–53, 455
    see also injury compensation
imperative grounds for expulsion 529–32, 533, 537, 545
imprisonment 104, 518
    continuous residence 458
    expulsion and expulsion immunity 528–29, 530–31, 534–35, 536
    family members 156–57, 158–59, 450
    legal residence 463–67
    voting rights 192–93, 197–200
IN 105–6
'in fact' dimension 243
'in the host State' definition 155–59
individual circumstances 392, 404, 438
inherently unconditional right of residence 146
inhuman or degrading treatment prohibition 434–35
injury compensation 34–35
integration
    degrees of 19–20
    Directive 2004/38 77–78
    dual function 27, 89–93
    family members 140–41
    of law, place and values 94–106
    legal constructs 475–79
internal situations 228
    and connecting factors 81–84
intrinsic connection 236, 255, 259
investor citizenship schemes 121–23
Ireland 21–22, 104–5, 451
    family members 145–46, 157–58, 160, 161
    rights to enter, reside and remain 325, 334, 342–43

Italian Government v Commission 64
Italy 21–22, 37
Izsák and Dabis 214–15

Jeuness v The Netherlands 248–49
Jia 159–60
Jipa 263, 505
Jobcenter Krefeld 169–70, 461–62, 478–79
    equal treatment and lawful residence 417, 418, 419, 422–23, 424, 428, 429–30
jobseekers 28–29, 408–9
    administrative formalities 298
    Directive 2004/38 71–72
    equal treatment derogations 374–76
    equal treatment and lawful residence 365–71, 373, 415–16
    'hybrid' protection 13–14
    leavers and returners 494
    legal residence 460
    no right to reside 385, 395, 397–98
    permanent residence 445
    proportionality 59
    residence based on national law 422–23
    residence right of more than three months 274–75, 290–96
    residence right of up to three months 269–70
    retention of right to reside 319–20
    rights to enter, reside and remain 262
jobseeker's allowance 56–57, 130, 325, 363, 427, 428–29
judicial review 542–45, 546, 547
    Directive 2004/38 76–77
    equal treatment and lawful residence 353–54, 364
    European Citizens Initiative (ECI) 210–11, 212, 214–15
    European Parliament 218–19
    rights to enter, reside and remain 261, 351
Julian Hernández 432
Junqueras 192
Justice and Home Affairs 9
Justice and Home Affairs Council 346

K 522
K and HF 521–22, 524–25
KA 247, 251, 255, 346–47
Kamberaj 434–35
Kaur 193–94
Keck and Mithouard 438–39
Kempf 277
Knoors 356
Konstantinidis 32
Kremzow 80–81, 227–28

Lair 363
Lamberts 220
language 3, 4, 541
Lassal 383–84, 446, 453, 456, 462–63
Latvia 97–98, 421–22
lawful residence 43–44, 469

expulsion and expulsion immunity 535, 553
leavers and returners 490, 493
proportionality 56–57
residence right of more than three months 280
temporary absence and permanent residence 454
see also equal treatment and lawful residence
Lawrie-Blum 31–32, 478
Lead State 224–25
leavers and returners 236, 482–97
Lebon 367–68
legal certainty 53, 59–60, 75, 101–2
legal framework 2–7, 27–107
  Article 20 3, 39–44
  Article 21 3, 44–46
  Article 22 3–4
  Article 23 4
  Article 24 4–7
  asymmetric movement 63–67
  Charter of Fundamental Rights 85–89
  competence of Member States 93–94
  Directive 2004/38 67–78
  effectiveness of rights 84–85
  establishing connection with EU law 78–84
  integration of law, place and values 94–106
  integration requirements: dual function 89–93
  origins 28–38
    economic free movement rights 30–33
    general free movement rights 33–38
  restricting rights: derogation and justification 46–51
  restricting rights: proportionality 51–63
legal residence 156–57, 442, 458–67, 469, 537
liberty, promotion of 89
Liechtenstein 447–48
living and working conditions 32
LN 341–42, 379
long-term residence 10, 39–40
  see also permanent residence
Lounes 89–90, 133, 135–36, 139, 145–46, 152–53, 202, 433–34
Luisi and Carbone 34

McCarthy 20–21, 69–70, 132, 133, 145–46, 152–53, 233–36, 238, 239–40, 241, 245
McCarthy II 96–97, 315, 316–17, 341, 348–50, 495–96, 520–21
maintenance allowances to divorced spouses 80–81
maladministration 219–20
Malta 121
marriage 96–97, 487
  annulment *see* divorce, annulment of marriage or termination of registered partnership
  arranged 150
  definition 150
  dissolution 415
  forced 150
  polygamous 150
  rights 345
  same-sex 49, 96–97, 143, 267, 494–95

  sham marriages 316, 348–49, 350
  see also spouses
marriage of convenience 69, 150, 262–63, 340–42, 344, 345–48
  see also sham marriages
Martínez Sala 47–48, 79, 287–88, 358–59, 360, 362, 364, 372, 381–82
  economically autonomous citizens and lawful residence 412–13
  implicit derogation from equal treatment 380–81
  no right to reside 383, 384–85, 386–87, 390, 400–1, 403–4
  residence based on national law 419, 422–23, 425
material change in circumstances 504, 531–32, 548, 552
material scope 12–15, 34, 38, 47–48, 72, 79
material support 175–77
Matthews v United Kingdom 193, 197
medical examinations 511
medical services, access to 54, 61
Metock 22, 69–70, 139, 141–42, 144, 153–54, 160, 161, 341
MG 92, 529, 534, 535
Micheletti 110–11, 118, 121–22, 129–30
migrant workers
  equal treatment and lawful residence 378–79, 417
  leavers and returners 483, 485, 487, 489–90
  multi-state life 474, 476, 477
  residence right of more than three months 276, 277–78
minimex (non-contributory social benefit) 289
Minority SafePack 213–14
Moerenhout 214
money-laundering 121
Morgan and Bucher 79–80
Morson and Jhanjan 226–27
move and reside rights 471–98
  leavers and returners 482–97
    Art. 21 TFEU 487–90
    Arts. 45 and 49 TFEU 483–87
    refining scope of protection 490–97
  multi-state life 473–82
    family members 479–82
    legal constructs of integration 475–79
    social security: basic principles 473–75
MRAX 311, 365, 507
multilateral agreements 19
Mutsch 356
mutual assistance 101–2
mutual recognition 163, 268–69, 317
mutual trust 97, 105–6, 520
My 42

NA 143, 331–32, 336, 337, 338, 339
name registration 38, 79, 131–32
narcotics trafficking 515–16, 529–30, 532
national identity 153, 202
national procedural autonomy principle 312–13
national sovereignty 113–14

nationality 39–41, 109–36
    acquiring 118–24
    applying *Rottmann* 113–29
    citizenship and withdrawal from EU 124–29
    competence 93–94
    determination 192–93
    diplomatic and consular protection 222
    dual nationality 129–36
    equal treatment and lawful residence 354–55
    integration requirements: dual function 92–93
    involuntary loss of 39–40
    monetisation *see* investor citizenship schemes
    voluntary loss of 39–40
    voting rights 196–97
    withdrawing nationality 114–18
    withdrawing nationality, *Rottmann* 110–13
    see also nationality discrimination and non-discrimination
nationality discrimination and non-discrimination 2, 10–11, 12–13, 14–15, 28, 35–36
    asymmetric movement 65
    derogations and justifications 46–48
    divorce, annulment of marriage or termination of registered partnership 339–40
    equal treatment derogations 380–81
    equal treatment and lawful residence 353–54, 358–59, 361, 362, 367–68
    family members 162
    integration of law, place and values 102–3
    no right to reside 390–91, 403
    residence based on national law 420, 421, 425
    residence right of more than three months 278, 281, 287–88, 291
    unmarried partners 170
negative guidance 61
Netherlands 21–22, 97, 114–15, 116, 377–78, 480, 490–91, 522
    home Member State 195–96, 244, 245, 246, 248–49, 256
    rights to enter, reside and remain 271–72, 273, 299
no right to reside 382–404
non-contributory cash benefits 338, 393, 395, 400–1, 433
non-discrimination 2, 35
    asymmetric movement 64–65
    diplomatic and consular protection 223
    dual nationality 131–32
    equal treatment and lawful residence 372, 416
    family members 155, 185, 251
    integration requirements: dual function 89
    multi-state life 472
    residence based on national law 421, 423
    restrictions 46–47, 49–50
    rights to enter, reside and remain 261
    unmarried partners 165–66
    voting rights 195–96
    see also nationality discrimination and non-discrimination
non-refoulement clause 229
Northern Ireland 419
    Charter of Fundamental Rights 436

Norway 105–6
nuclear family 10

O and B 249, 313, 482, 490–91, 493–94, 495–96, 497
O and S 238–41, 242–43, 245
occupational qualifications 292, 295, 366–67
O'Flynn 65
Ogieriakhi 157–59, 451–52
One of Us 210–11, 219
Onuekwere 77–78, 156–59, 450–52, 463–67, 535
Ordre des barreaux francophones and germanophone and Others 518
Orfanopoulos and Oliveri 49–50, 499–500, 507
organised crime networks 346, 347, 515–16, 529–31, 532
overseas countries and territories (OCTs) 195

participatory democracy 6, 45, 189, 205–6, 216–17, 219–20
partners other than spouses 149–50, 162–71
    see also durable relationships; registered partnerships; unmarried partners
passports *see* identity cards or passports
past conduct 523
pensions *see* retirement and pensions
permanent incapacity to work 455
permanent residence 11–12, 36, 441–70
    administrative formalities 467–69
    after five years 76
    Charter of Fundamental Rights 433
    Directive 2004/38 75, 443–45
    eligibility 446–57
        continuous residence 458
        exemptions 454–57
        family members 447–52
        legal residence 458–67
        temporary absence from host State 452–54
    equal treatment and lawful residence 355, 371, 372, 373–74, 377, 416, 439
    exemptions 454–57
    expulsion and expulsion immunity 508–9, 527, 528, 529, 534–35, 536–37
    family members 142, 149–50, 156–57, 414, 415
    integration requirements: dual function 90, 91, 92
    leavers and returners 490
    no right to reside 383–86, 395
    residence based on national law 425
    residence right of more than three months 274, 277–78, 286
    retention of right to reside 317–18
    retention of worker or self-employment status 323–24
    rights to enter, reside and remain 261, 262–63
permanent residence cards/certificates 467–68, 534
personal circumstances 166, 168, 320, 388–89
    administrative formalities 307, 308
    dependent relatives 177, 179–80, 183
    expulsion and expulsion immunity 525
    proportionality 54
    unlawful residence 426

personal conduct 503–4, 505, 506, 507, 516, 517–18, 520–21, 523, 530, 531–32, 537
personal data protection 210
personal freedom 29
personal guarantee 44–45
personal liberty 30
personal rights 45
personal scope 8–12, 34, 38, 72, 356–57, 358–59
  connecting factors 79
  equal treatment and lawful residence 417, 425–26
  family members 140
  nationality 109
Petrea 304, 541, 550
Petruhhin 22, 97–98, 99–100, 101, 102–3, 104, 105, 117–18, 421–22, 433–34
PI 517, 530–31, 532–33
Pinna 478
Pisciotti 99–100, 101, 102–3
Poland 21–22
political connection *see under* home Member State
political rights 39, 127, 201–2
polygamous marriages 150
predominant function approach 395, 397–98
Préfet du Gers 39–40, 121–22, 124–26, 129, 196–97, 200
Prefeta 328
pregnancy and childbirth 74, 409
  multi-state life 471
  permanent residence 443
  residence based on primary law 418–19
  temporary absence and permanent residence 453, 454
  and temporary unemployment 326–28
Prete 92
primary carers 74–75, 156, 175–76
  death or departure of Union citizen 331–32
  direct descendants under 21 171–72
  dual nationality 135–36
  entry right 267–68
  equal treatment and lawful residence 416–18
  family member residence rights 231, 235, 236, 239, 241, 245–46, 247, 250
  family members and permanent residence 449–50
  family members and retention of right to reside 329–30
  leavers and returners 489–90
  no right to reside 396
  residence right of more than three months 283, 286
  unmarried partners 169–70
problematic category differences 355
procedural autonomy 500, 549
procedural differences 473
procedural guarantees 301
procedural rights 356–57
procedural safeguards 149–50, 168, 184–85, 297–98, 356–57, 365, 428, 429–30
  see also under expulsion on grounds of public policy, public security or public health
proportionality 19–20, 44–45, 46
  abuse of rights and fraud 350

administrative formalities 301, 307
asymmetric movement 65–66, 67
diplomatic and consular protection 226
Directive 2004/38 76–77
equal treatment derogations 374–75, 377–78, 379–80
equal treatment and lawful residence 354–55, 357, 364–65, 370–71, 381–82, 386, 438
expulsion and expulsion immunity 500, 505–6, 507, 508–9, 516, 517, 519–22, 523–24, 525–26, 530, 542, 545–46
family member residence rights 253–54, 257, 258
fundamental rights 87
integration of law, place and values 98
integration requirements: dual function 92–93
multi-state life 498
nationality 113, 114–16, 117, 118, 119–20
no right to reside 388–89, 394, 397–98, 402–4
residence based on primary law 419
residence right of more than three months 281–82, 283, 284–85
retention of right to reside 320, 321
rights to enter, reside and remain 261
voting rights 199–200
withdrawal from EU 125
see also restricting rights: proportionality
proximity 72–73, 105–6
public finances protection
  equal treatment and lawful residence 353–54, 358–59, 370–71
  expulsion and expulsion immunity 513
  family member residence rights 252–53, 254
  integration requirements: dual function 90
  no right to reside 384, 402–3
  proportionality 54–60
  residence right of more than three months 282–83, 284, 286
  see also sufficient financial resources not to become unreasonable burden on social assistance
public interest grounds
  abuse of rights and fraud 350
  derogations and justifications 49–50
  equal treatment and lawful residence 364
  expulsion and expulsion immunity 512, 513
  family member residence rights 257
  fundamental rights 87
  integration of law, place and values 98–99
  integration requirements: dual function 90, 92
  nationality 112–13, 119–20
  no right to reside 392–93, 398–99
  proportionality 54–55, 60
  voting rights 200–1
public policy, public security or public health 43–44
  abuse of rights and fraud 341, 347–48
  administrative formalities 297–99, 301, 305, 312–13
  derogations and justifications 49–51
  Directive 2004/38 67–68, 72, 73
  entry right 265–66, 267, 268–69
  equal treatment and lawful residence 356–57, 365

public policy, public security or public health (*cont.*)
  expulsion 262
  family member residence rights 252–54, 255, 257
  family members 153, 163
  jobseekers and lawful residence 416
  nationality 119–20
  permanent residence 442
  proportionality 54–55, 61
  residence right of more than three months 290–92
  residence of right up to three months 271
  retention of right to reside 320, 321
  see also expulsion on grounds of public policy, public security or public health
purely internal situations 229, 231, 232–33, 236

qualitative factors 94, 104, 459, 460–61, 463–64
quality of residence 500

Rahman 166, 167–68, 179–81, 182, 183–84, 314
Raugevicius 103–4
re-admission following expulsion 504
re-employment 293, 417
re-integration 92
re-offending risk 530–31, 537
reasonable doubt 318
reasonable period of time 339, 506
  administrative formalities 301
  equal treatment and lawful residence 366–67, 368, 369
  expulsion 548
  non-discriminatory 310, 312–13
  residence right of more than three months 292, 293–94, 295
reciprocal guarantees 126
redress procedures 297–99, 542, 546, 547
Reed 162, 163–66, 168–69, 170–71
'reference person' 143, 148
refugee status, refusal of 522–23
refusal, termination or withdrawal of rights 340
registered partnerships 147, 148–49, 151, 152–54, 162–66
  dependent relatives 175–76
  residence right of more than three months 289–90
  termination *see* divorce, annulment of marriage or termination of registered partnership
  termination 143, 155
registration certificates
  administrative formalities 300, 302, 303–4, 307, 314
  dependent relatives 176–77
  expulsion and expulsion immunity 516, 550
  unmarried partners 166–67
registration requirements
  family members (Union citizens) 304–5
  Union citizens 302–4
Regulation 492/2011: residence 416–18
relationship
  degree of 183–84
  quality 183–84, 185
  type 185
remoteness concept 79–80

Rendón Marín 19, 43, 93, 243, 255, 298–99
representative democracy 6, 45, 189, 192, 219–20
residence cards
  abuse of rights and fraud 345–46, 348–50
  administrative formalities 296, 300, 310, 311–13, 314–17, 469
  dependent relatives 176–77, 180
  dual nationality 133
  entry right 264
  expulsion and expulsion immunity 516
  family members 149–50
  integration of law, place and values 96–97
  nationality 110
  unmarried partners 166–67, 168
  see also permanent residence cards/certificates
residence certificates 386–87, 388–89, 390
  see also permanent residence cards/certificates
residence duration
  five years 534
    administrative formalities 467–68
    exemptions and permanent residence 456
    integration of law, place and values 97
    integration requirements: dual function 91
    legal residence 458–59
    multi-state life 475–76
    no right to reside 383–84
    permanent residence 442, 443, 444–45, 446–47, 457
    temporary absence and permanent residence 453
  five years or more (up to ten years) 18, 76, 142, 377–78, 391, 528
  ten years or more 76, 528, 529, 534, 535–36
  three months or more (up to five years) 18, 76, 391, 394–95, 528
    administrative formalities 296, 302, 311
    Directive 2004/38 76
    economically active citizens and lawful residence 407–8
    family members 142
    family members and lawful residence 414–15
    integration requirements: dual function 91
    jobseekers, equal treatment and lawful residence 365
    no right to reside 387–88
    permanent residence 442
    retention of right to reside 318
    rights to enter, reside and remain 262
    see also under rights to enter, reside and remain
  up to three months 18, 142–43, 254, 269–74
    administrative formalities 302, 311
    Directive 2004/38 76
    equal treatment derogations 374, 375–76
    equal treatment and lawful residence 405–7
    family members 142
    integration requirements: dual function 91
    jobseekers, equal treatment and lawful residence 365, 366–67
    no right to reside 385, 391
    permanent residence 442

retention of right to reside 318
  rights to enter, reside and remain 262
residence of indefinite duration 35
residence permits 9, 42, 53, 304, 313
  declaratory nature of 502
  equal treatment and lawful residence 360–62, 363–64
  leavers and returners 486–87, 490–91
  legal residence 459, 460–61
  no right to reside 385, 386–87
  refusal of issue or renewal 501
  residence right up to three months 269–70
  retention of worker or self-employment status 322
  revalidation 282–83
  temporary absence and permanent residence 454
respect for private and family life 8, 33, 49, 71, 88–89, 245–46, 248, 249, 250
  abuse of rights and fraud 345
  Charter of Fundamental Rights 431–32
  dependent relatives 184
  dual nationality 134–35
  expulsion and expulsion immunity 507, 525–26
  family members 139–42, 153, 155, 157, 158–59, 161–62, 167
    and permanent residence 450, 452
    residence rights 237, 241–42, 253, 481
    and retention of right to reside 329–30
  leavers and returners 484–85
  nationality 114–15, 120, 144
restricting rights 27
  defining restriction of rights 46–49
  derogation and justification 49–51
  on goods and services 30
  impacts 78–81
  potential 227, 229
  proportionality 51–63
    conditions 'too general and exclusive' 52–54
    evidencing proportionality 60–63
    public finances protection 54–60
retention of right to reside *see also under* rights to enter, reside and remain
retirement and pensions 284, 308–9, 322, 387–88, 389, 447–48, 455, 456–57
returners *see* leavers and returners
reverse discrimination 83–84, 161–62, 228–29
Reyes 176, 177–79
rights and duties 92–93
rights to enter, reside and remain 187–89, 259, 261–351
  abuse of rights 340–50
  entry right 264–69
  exit right 263–64
  family members 188–89
    not Union citizens 309–17, *see also under* home Member State
    retention of right to reside 317–40
      death or departure of Union citizen 330–32
      divorce, annulment of marriage or termination of registered partnership 332–34
      family members 329–40

retention of worker or self-employed person status 321–29
right to reside for more than three months 274–96
  comprehensive sickness insurance 283–86
  general right to reside 279–86
  jobseekers 290–96
  students 287–90
  sufficient resources 280–83
  workers and self-employed persons 275–79
right to reside for up to three months 269–74
see also administrative formalities
RO 104–5
Romania 152
Rottmann 42, 92–93, 129–30, 188–89, 196, 199, 232–33, 431
see also under nationality
Royer 277–78, 502, 545–46
Ruiz Zambrano 22, 42, 188–89, 433–34
  connecting factor 79, 82–84
  family members 141, 228–29, 243, 244, 247, 248, 249, 254, 258–59
  integrating law, place and values 94–95, 96–97, 99
  Member State nationality 118–19, 132
  proportionality 53
  residence rights for family members 233–43
    being 'obliged' to leave 236–39
    Charter of Fundamental Rights 241–43
    dependence requirement 239–41
    first responses: explaining and containing *Ruiz Zambrano* 233–43
    nature of *Ruiz Zambrano* rights 236
  voting rights 196
Runevič-Vardyn and Wardyn 50–51
Russia 97–98

S and G 80–81, 249, 480, 482, 493
Sahin 509–10
Saint-Prix 74, 327, 328, 339, 409, 453, 471
same-sex marriage 49, 96–97, 143, 267, 494–95
sanctions, proportionate and non-discriminatory 506
  abuse of rights and fraud 344, 345–46
  administrative formalities 296–97, 301, 302, 310–11, 468
  entry right 264, 265–67
  expulsion 502, 506
  legal residence 465
Saunders 81, 228
Sayn-Wittgenstein 512
Schempp 80–81, 82, 150
Schengen Area 95–96, 105–6
Schengen Borders Code 266
Schengen Information System 309
Schönberger 218–19
self-certification of sufficient resources 307
self-defence 523
self-employed citizens 16, 32
  death or departure 331
  Directive 2004/38 69, 71–72
  divorce, annulment of marriage or termination of registered partnership 333, 338

self-employed citizens (*cont.*)
  economically active citizens and lawful residence 407–10
  equal treatment derogations 378–79
  equal treatment and lawful residence 355, 365–66, 372, 373
  exemptions and permanent residence 455–56
  family members 149–50
  lawful residence within first three months 405
  leavers and returners 485, 493
  multi-state life 471
  residence right of more than three months 274–79
  residence right up to three months 269–70, 272–73
  retention of right to reside 318, 319
  rights to enter, reside and remain 262
  status, retention of 321–29
  temporary absence and permanent residence 452
serious grounds for expulsion 529–30, 531, 537, 545
serious health grounds requiring personal care of family member 149, 179, 180, 181, 182–83
serious illness 443, 453
serious inconvenience test 79–80, 93–94, 132
services, providers and recipients of 16, 28–30, 35, 71–72, 501
  residence right of more than three months 278–79
  residence right up to three months 269–70, 272–73
sexual offences 530–32
sexual orientation non-discrimination 153
sham marriages 316, 348–49, 350
Shingara and Radiom 37
sincere cooperation 98–99, 101–2, 121, 499–500, 520, 549
Singer 30–31
Singh 155, 485–88, 490–91, 495–97
Singh II 159, 282–83, 332, 334, 336–37, 338, 339
Siragusa 432
SM 172–73, 174, 183–85
social assistance *see* social security and social assistance
social cohesion 384, 444–45, 463–64, 522
social rehabilitation 104
social reintegration 103
social security and social assistance 3, 6–7, 13–14, 30–31, 222–23
  administrative formalities 303–4, 306, 307, 308–9, 468
  Article 21 44
  asymmetric movement 67
  Charter of Fundamental Rights 431, 433–34, 435–37
  Directive 2004/38 74–75
  divorce, annulment of marriage or termination of registered partnership 338
  economically active citizens and lawful residence 408–9
  economically autonomous citizens and lawful residence 410–13
  equal treatment derogations 374, 380
  equal treatment and lawful residence 370–71, 373, 376, 417
  family member residence rights 231, 244, 252–53, 254, 256, 258
  family members and lawful residence 414–15
  integration requirements: dual function 90, 92–93
  jobseekers and lawful residence 415–16
  lawful residence within first three months 405, 406–7
  leavers and returners 483, 486–87
  legal residence 460–61, 463
  move and reside rights 473–75
  multi-state life 473–76, 477–78
  no right to reside 386, 387, 388
  no right to reside (*Alimanovic*) 396, 398–99
  no right to reside (*Commission v UK*) 399–401, 404
  no right to reside (*Dano*) 392–95
  proportionality 54–56, 58, 59, 60, 61–62
  residence based on national law 419
  residence of more than three months 277–78, 280, 283, 292–93, 295–96
  residence up to three months 272–73
  retention of right to reside 319, 320, 321
  retention of worker or self-employment status 326
  students and lawful residence 414
  unlawful residence 426, 428–30
  see also child benefit; jobseeker's allowance; student maintenance grants; sufficient financial resources not to become unreasonable burden on social assistance; tideover allowance; welfare benefit tourism
social and tax advantages 32, 34
  derogations and justifications 47–48
  equal treatment derogations 378–79
  equal treatment and lawful residence 367–69, 370–71
  family members 149–50
  integration requirements: dual function 91
  lawful residence within first three months 405
  leavers and returners 488
  multi-state life 474, 476, 477–78
  permanent residence 445
  residence of more than three months 275–76, 277, 278–79, 290, 293
  retention of worker or self-employment status 326
  unlawful residence 429–30
  unmarried partners 168–70
solidarity 66, 92–93, 112, 115, 123–24, 223–24
  see also financial solidarity
sound administration principle 215
Spaak Report 28n.5
Spain 131, 145–46, 193–94, 256, 315, 316
  Civil Code 110
Spain v United Kingdom 193, 195, 196, 197, 198, 199–200
special conditions 322
special relationship between Member States 72–73, 105–6, 119–20
'special rights' 36
specific circumstances 245–46, 251–52, 254, 257, 299–300
specific expression method 1–2, 275–76, 391, 403

spouses 147–49, 150–62, 164–65
  dependent relatives 175–76
  expulsion and expulsion immunity 506–7
  'in the host State' definition 155–59
  residence of more than three months 289–90
  same-sex spouses 151–55
  status under host State immigration rules 159–62
statelessness 117
statement of reasons 214, 218–19
statement of support 219
Stewart 54–55, 433–34
'Stop TTIP' 215–16
student maintenance grants 38, 39
  economically autonomous citizens and lawful residence 411
  equal treatment derogations 378–80
  equal treatment and lawful residence 363–64, 368, 370–71, 373, 376–80
  integration requirements: dual function 92
  lawful residence within first three months 405
  multi-state life 475–76, 477
  no right to reside 392–93
  proportionality 55–56
  residence of more than three months 287–88, 289, 290
  unlawful residence 427–28
  unmarried partners 169
students 16, 36, 37
  administrative formalities 307
  Directive 2004/38 69, 70
  economically active citizens and lawful residence 408–9
  equal treatment and lawful residence 359–60, 362–63, 365, 367–68, 413–14
  multi-state life 471
  no right to reside 403–4
  permanent residence 443, 444–45
  proportionality 57
  residence based on primary law 419
  residence of more than three months 274–75, 276, 287–90
  rights to enter, reside and remain 262
  temporary absence and permanent residence 453
  unlawful residence 426
  see also student maintenance grants; vocational training
Subdelegación del Gobierno en Ciudad Real 252, 256, 258
Subdelegación del Gobierno en Toledo 251
subjective circumstances 341, 349–50, 393–94
subsidiarity principle 45, 65–66, 67, 432
substantive claims 368–69
substantive differences 473
substantive factors 184–85, 239–40, 354–55
substantive relationship 241
substantive rights and obligations 2
substantive safeguards 356–57, 365, 502, 505–6
sufficient connection 53, 78–81, 82, 129–30, 227
sufficient financial resources not to become unreasonable burden on social assistance 36

administrative formalities 296, 302, 304, 306–9
death or departure of Union citizen 330, 331
direct descendants under 21 68, 76, 171
Directive 2004/38 68, 69, 76
divorce, annulment of marriage or termination of registered partnership 333, 338–40
economically active citizens and lawful residence 408–9
economically autonomous citizens and lawful residence 410, 411–12
equal treatment derogations 374, 375–76, 381
equal treatment and lawful residence 357, 359–60, 362–65, 373, 438
expulsion and expulsion immunity 537
family member residence rights 231, 235, 239, 246–47, 254, 257
family members and permanent residence 447–48, 450
home Member State 259
integration requirements: dual function 91
jobseekers, equal treatment and lawful residence 365
lawful residence within first three months 405, 406, 407
leavers and returners 489
multi-state life 477–78
no right to reside 383, 386–87, 388–89
no right to reside (*Alimanovic*) 396–98
no right to reside (*Commission v UK*) 399–400, 403–4
no right to reside (*Dano*) 391, 392, 393, 394
permanent residence 457
proportionality 55, 56, 57–59
residence based on national law 421, 422–23
residence of more than three months 274–75, 277, 279–85, 286, 287, 288–91
retention of right to reside 318
self-certification 307
students 37, 413, 414
unlawful residence 426–27, 429–30
sufficient link of integration 476, 478
sufficiently serious situations 517
supremacy principle 343

Tarola 70, 326, 329, 477–78
tax advantages *see* social and tax advantages
taxation, direct 93–94
Teixeira 419, 489
temporal factors 94, 104, 354–55, 408–9
  see also reasonable period of time
temporary absences from host State 315, 443, 452–54
temporary residence 423
  permit 361
  rights 298, 426
temporary unemployment 322, 324, 328–29
termination of employment 322
termination of registered partnership *see* divorce, annulment of marriage or termination of registered partnership
termination of residence 299–300

territorial factors 104
territorial scope 72–73, 95–96
terrorism 517
Thiele Meneses 54–55
tideover allowance 52, 369, 370, 488–89
Tjebbes 114, 117, 118, 119–20, 121–22, 125, 129–30, 226
TopFit and Biffi 46
trade qualification *see* vocational training
trafficking in weapons or drugs 517
transparency 53, 59–60, 210, 219–20
travel costs financial support 413
travel document 115
Trojani 280, 358, 360–64, 381–82, 384–85, 386–87, 403–4
   economically autonomous citizens and lawful residence 412–13
   equal treatment derogations 378, 380–81
   jobseekers 368
   no right to reside 390
   residence based on national law 419, 422–23, 425
   unlawful residence 426
Tsakouridis 514–16, 528, 529, 530–31, 532–33, 534

U 42
Uecker and Jacquet 82, 227–28
unemployment 355, 417
   benefits 291
   insurance 293, 367–68
   involuntary 322, 324, 325–26, 365–66, 455
   voluntary 454
Unger 30–31
United Kingdom 21–22, 65, 376
   abuse of rights and fraud 342, 347–49, 350
   administrative formalities 315–16, 317
   Brexit 39–40, 63–64, 104–5, 109, 284–85
      Member State nationality 109, 124–25, 126, 127–29, 136
      voting rights 196–97
   Charter of Fundamental Rights 436
   divorce, annulment of marriage or termination of registered partnership 336, 338
   dual nationality 130, 132–33
   equal treatment and lawful residence 368, 370
   expulsion and expulsion immunity 522
   family members 145–46, 159–60, 172–73, 174
   home Member State 193–94, 256
   legal residence 463–64
   Member State nationality 125
   multi-state movements: right to move 485, 486–87
   residence based on national law 419, 420
   residence of more than three months 277–78, 291–92
   retention of right to reside 319
   retention of worker or self-employment status 327
   unlawful residence 428
   voting rights 197
   see also Withdrawal Agreement (EU-UK)

United Nations Convention on the Rights of Persons with Disabilities 203–4
universal suffrage 190–91, 192–93, 194, 198, 202–3
university education 61, 63, 65–66
   see also students; student maintenance grants
unlawful residence: consequences 355, 426–31
unmarried partners 164–71, 179–80
   see also durable relationships

Vaasen-Göbbels 31
Van Binsbergen 30
van Dijk 30–31
Van Duyn 502
Vatsouras and Koupatantze 22, 374–75, 376, 390, 395, 397–98, 405
very exceptional situations 236–37
VI 135–36
violence and hooliganism prevention at sports events 503
visas 9, 149–50, 264, 296, 309, 315–16, 345–46
VMA 267, 268–69
vocational training 35–36, 38, 287, 289, 324, 356, 376, 443, 453, 483
voluntary unemployment 454
voting rights and right to stand as candidates in elections 3–4, 5, 86, 121–22, 126–27, 188, 190–204
   Art. 22 191–93
   deprivation of 124–25
   free movement 200–4
   and imprisonment 197–200
   national electorate defined 193–97

war crime 521–22
Watson and Belmann 34, 506
welfare benefit tourism 56–57, 353–54, 370, 374, 392
Wiener Landesregierung 114, 117, 118, 120, 121–22, 126, 129–30
Wightman 128
Wijsenbeek 45
Withdrawal Agreement (EU-UK) 12, 125–27, 129, 139–40, 144–45, 187–88, 419, 422–23, 435–36, 442, 477, 500
Wolzenburg 422, 446, 467–68
workers 16, 32
work permits 231
worker status, retention of 317–18, 321–29
workers
   death or departure 330, 331
   Directive 2004/38 69, 70, 71–72
   divorce, annulment of marriage or termination of registered partnership 333, 338
   economically active citizens and lawful residence 407–10
   equal treatment derogations 378–79
   equal treatment and lawful residence 365–66, 372, 373
   exemptions and permanent residence 455–56
   expulsion and expulsion immunity 501
   family members 149–50

leavers and returners 485, 493
multi-state life 471, 474
residence of more than three months 274–79
residence up to three months 269–70, 272–73, 405
retention of right to reside 318, 319
rights to enter, reside and remain 262
temporary absence and permanent residence 452
see also frontier workers; migrant workers
WS 79–80, 82

X v Belgian State 338, 436–37

Yiadom 545–46
Ymeraga 242, 480

Zhu and Chen 35–36, 82, 131, 492
　family members 171, 175–76, 450
　home Member State 232–33, 235, 236, 239, 243
　rights to enter, reside and remain 281, 282–83, 342–43
Ziebell 73, 537–39
Ziolkowski and Szeja 18, 385–86, 425, 459–63
ZZ 542, 547